STRUCTURED COBOL PROGRAMMING

STRUCTURED COBOL PROGRAMMING

Fifth edition

Nancy Stern

Hofstra University

Robert A. Stern

Nassau Community College

WILEY

John Wiley & Sons

New York   Chichester   Brisbane   Toronto   Singapore

Cover: Photograph by Paul Silverman

Library of Congress Cataloging in Publication Data

Stern, Nancy B.
   Structured COBOL programming.

   Includes index.
   1. COBOL (Computer program language) 2. Structured
programming. I. Stern, Robert A. II. Title
QA76.73.C25S75 1988   005.13'3   87-28003
ISBN 0-471-63287-2

Printed in the United States of America

10 9 8 7 6 5 4 3 2

To Lori Anne and Melanie

PREFACE

TO THE INSTRUCTOR

A. Overall Market

This book is intended for readers with no previous programming or computer experience as well as for those with some background in the computing field. It has been specifically designed for use in college courses on COBOL both in two-year and four-year schools.

B. Objectives of this Book

This book has the following main objectives.

1. To teach students how to design programs so that they are easy to read, debug, modify, and maintain.
2. To provide students with the ability to write well-designed elementary, intermediate, and advanced COBOL programs in their entirety.
3. To familiarize students with information processing and systems concepts that will help them interact with users and systems analysts when designing programs.
4. To highlight key elements of the new 1985 ANS COBOL standard that will facilitate and promote the writing of well-designed structured programs.
5. To familiarize students with programming tools such as pseudocode and hierarchy charts that make program logic more structured and modular.

C. How This Book Differs From *Structured COBOL Programming*, 4th edition

1. The fifth edition of *Structured COBOL Programming* has been streamlined. The narrative has been tightened, and the illustrations and exercises pared down so that they retain their usefulness in reinforcing the material presented without being repetitive or verbose.
2. The focus of this book is on design elements and logical control constructs that form the conceptual basis for programming. Chapter 5 on The Theory of Structured Program Design is an entirely new chapter that provides the philosophic foundation for this book. Structured techniques, the top-down approach to programming, and program modularity are concepts that not only are highlighted but are fully integrated in all

programs discussed in the text. Program design tools such as pseudocode and hierarchy charts are discussed in detail and illustrated throughout as well. Stylistic guidelines such as naming conventions for data-names and paragraph-names and the use of comments for documentation are also highlighted and illustrated in *all* programs.

3. COBOL 85 has been fully integrated into the text. Key elements of COBOL 85 that make the language more suitable for structured programming are discussed in great detail. For example, the EVALUATE verb, scope terminators, the in-line PERFORM, and the methods used to avoid GO TOs entirely, even in SORT procedures, are discussed in depth here. COBOL 85 is not simply presented as an addendum or supplement as in other texts. It has been fully integrated and highlighted with a shaded background to set it apart from COBOL 74.

4. Systems analysis and design concepts such as data validation, error control procedures, file design, report design, and screen layout design are presented in detail. We believe students in programming courses should be familiar with these concepts. Knowledge of such systems concepts will provide a kind of bridge to more advanced systems courses that students are apt to take later on.

5. Several advanced topics have been expanded. These include indexed file processing, relative file processing, interactive processing, and the Report Writer Feature, as well as some additional emphasis on specific verbs.

6. Several topics have been added to this text. These include the non-standard SCREEN SECTION used in many organizations for interactive processing and an appendix on text editing concepts.

7. There has been some reorganization as well. For example, the PERFORM statement and all its options are discussed in an earlier chapter; an overview of the four divisions is more succinctly presented in just three chapters.

D. How This Book Differs From *Structured COBOL By Design*

Our new text *Structured COBOL By Design* is specifically intended for a *first course* in COBOL. It covers elementary and many intermediate concepts but does not cover advanced topics. In *Structured COBOL By Design*, subjects such as sorting and merging, table handling, and indexed file processing are briefly discussed but are not considered in their entirety while other subjects such as the Report Writer Feature, STRING and UNSTRING, COPY and CALL, and relative file processing are not discussed at all.

Both texts, however, are similar in their focus on design elements and logical control constructs as a conceptual basis for programming. Similarly, both texts use pseudocode and hierarchy charts as programming tools. Finally, they both focus on COBOL 85 and on systems concepts with which programmers should be familiar.

E. The Pedagogic Approach

This book basically follows CIS-2 and CIS-3 of the DPMA Model Curriculum and COMP.4 of the Associate-Level Model Curriculum.

In this, as in our other programming books, we have attempted to write a stand-alone text with all the instructional material, examples, self-tests, and exercises the student needs to learn the language.

We have provided students with a step-by-step introduction to the subject, one that has thorough explanations followed by programs or program excerpts that reinforce and illustrate all concepts.

Each concept is thoroughly explained and illustrated with actual examples. Self-test questions, designed to help students evaluate their understanding of the material, appear after major concepts are discussed and also at the end of each chapter.

The book is segmented into *units*, each of which has a specific focus. After completing the first unit, students will be able to write elementary COBOL programs *in their entirety*. Subsequent units focus on program design and build up to more advanced programming concepts.

F. Instructional Aids

An instructor's resource manual is available. It contains (1) solutions to all text questions and programming assignments, (2) full examinations, and (3) course outlines. It is packaged with a 5-1/4-inch disk that contains (1) test data for all programming assignments and (2) additional debugging exercises. Transparency masters will be provided on request.

The reviewers who provided many helpful suggestions throughout the development of this project are acknowledged on page xiii. We thank them for their effort. We also thank Nancy Sager, Christopher Hammel, and Gloria Fishman for their assistance in the preparation of computer printouts, and Carol L. Eisen for her invaluable assistance in the preparation of the manuscript. Our special thanks to Gene Davenport, Senior Editor at John Wiley and Sons, for his support and guidance in this project, and to the following individuals at Wiley: Ann Renzi, Design; Suzanne Ingrao, Director of Production; Ed Burke, Project Manager; and Ernie Kohlmetz, Copy Editor.

One last word of thanks to Hofstra University for giving us the opportunity to experiment with some new ideas and techniques, and to our students whose interesting and insightful questions helped us improve our pedagogic approach.

We update our programming texts every few years and welcome your comments, criticisms, and suggestions. We can be reached c/o:

Nancy Stern
Robert A. Stern
BCIS Department
Hofstra University
Hempstead, NY 11550

You can also contact us using CompuServ's EasyPlex electronic mail service. Our user id is 76505,1222. Our Bitnet address is ACSNNS@Hofstra.

PREFACE

TO THE STUDENT

Goals

The primary goal of this book is to teach you how to design COBOL programs. To accomplish this, we focus on two topics: (1) how structured programs are best designed and organized, and (2) the rules for programming in COBOL. Learning how to design programs will provide you with the basic tools for writing a program in *any* language. Learning the COBOL rules will specifically prepare you for writing programs in the COBOL language.

Features of the Text

Format

The format of this text is designed to be as helpful as possible. Each chapter begins with:

1. A detailed chapter outline.
   Before beginning a chapter, you can get an overview of its contents by looking at this outline. In addition, after you have read the chapter, you can use the outline as a summary of the overall organization.
2. A list of objectives.
   We believe it is helpful to see what the chapter is intended to teach even before you read it.

The material is presented in a step-by-step manner with numerous examples and illustrations. Within each chapter there are self-tests, with solutions, that are designed to help you evaluate your own understanding of the material presented. We encourage you to take these tests as you go along. They will help pinpoint any misunderstandings you may have.

End-of-Chapter Material

Each chapter ends with learning aids consisting of:

1. Chapter Summary.
2. Chapter Self-Test—with solutions so you can test yourself on your understanding of the chapter as a whole.
3. Practice Program—a full program is illustrated. We recommend you read the definition of the problem and try to code the program yourself. Then compare your solution to the one illustrated.

4. Key Terms. This is a list of all new terms defined in the chapter. Appendix H is a glossary that lists all key terms in the text along with their definitions.

5. Review Questions. These are general questions that may be assigned by your instructor for homework.

6. Debugging Exercises. These are program excerpts with errors in them. You are asked to correct the coding. The errors highlighted are those commonly made by students and entry-level programmers.

7. Programming Assignments. The assignments appear in increasing order of difficulty. These assignments include a full set of specifications similar to those that programmers are actually given in the "real world." You are asked to code and debug each program using test data. You will need to either create your own test data or receive it from your instructor. Appendix E includes sample test data that can be used for Programming Assignment 2 in each chapter.

Assumptions About the Reader

This book has been written on a level that is appropriate for introductory computer students. No previous programming experience is required. For those with no background, we encourage you to read the text in sequence and pay particular attention to end-of-chapter tools for reinforcing and for testing your knowledge.

If you know another language, you may be able to proceed more quickly through the text, but we do not believe you will find it simplistic or, worse, boring. Because we emphasize program design features and aim to teach you not only syntax but programming form, we hope you will find the approach more conceptual than you might have experienced with other texts. Accordingly, we recommend that you read the text in sequence and skim the end-of-chapter material.

We update our programming texts every few years and welcome your comments, criticisms, and suggestions. We can be reached c/o:

Nancy Stern
Robert A. Stern
BCIS Department
Hofstra University
Hempstead, NY 11550

Acknowledgments

We thank the following reviewers for their many helpful suggestions: Henry Austin, Oakland Community College; Dennis Benincasa, Macomb Community College; Norman D. Brammer, Colorado State University; Jack V. Breglio, Rancho Santiago Community College District; Pricilla H. Caira, Northern Essex Community College; R. J. Daigle, University of South Alabama; Dana Edberg, University of Nevada, Reno; Bernadine Kolbet Esposito, University of Baltimore; Raymond K. Fanselau, American River College; Kent Fields, Auburn University; Thomas E. Gorecki, Charles County Community College; Jan Hooper, Citrus College; Roger Knights, consultant; Clarence L. Krantz, Mansfield University; Marilyn Meyers, Fresno City College; Josephine F. Morecroft, Virginia Commonwealth University; Beverly Rosendorf, LaGuardia Community College.

The following acknowledgment has been reproduced from COBOL Edition, U.S. Department of Defense, at the request of the Conference on Data Systems Languages.

"Any organization interested in reproducing the COBOL report and specifications in whole or in part, using ideas taken from this report as the basis for an instruction manual or for any other purpose is free to do so. However, all such organizations are requested to reproduce this section as part of the introduction to the document. Those using a short passage, as in a book review, are requested to mention 'COBOL' in acknowledgment of the source, but need not quote this entire section.

"COBOL is an industry language and is not the property of any company or group of companies, or of any organization or group of organizations.

"No warranty, expressed or implied, is made by any contributor or by the COBOL Committee as to the accuracy and functioning of the programming system and language. Moreover, no responsibility is assumed by any contributor or by the committee, in connection therewith.

"Procedures have been established for the maintenance of COBOL. Inquiries concerning the procedures for proposing changes should be directed to the Executive Committee of the Conference on Data Systems Languages.

"The authors and copyright holders of the copyrighted material used herein

FLOW-MATIC (Trademark of Sperry Rand Corporation), Programming for the Univac (R) I and II, Data Automation Systems copyrighted 1958, 1959, by Sperry Rand Corporation; IBM Commercial Translator Form No. F28-8013, copyrighted 1959 by IBM; FACT, DSI 27A5260-2760, copyrighted 1960 by Minneapolis-Honeywell

have specifically authorized the use of this material in whole or in part, in the COBOL specifications. Such authorization extends to the reproduction and use of COBOL specifications in programming manuals or similar publications."

N. S.
R. A. S.

CONTENTS

UNIT I
THE BASICS

1

An Introduction to Structured Program Design in COBOL

OBJECTIVES

To familiarize you with

1. Why COBOL is such a popular business-oriented language.
2. Programming practices and techniques.
3. A history of how COBOL evolved and the use of the current ANS standard versions of COBOL.
4. An overview of the four divisions of a COBOL program.

I. Computer Programming: An Overview

A. What Is a Program?

No matter how complex a computer is, its actions are directed by individual computer instructions that operate on **input** data and convert it to meaningful **output** information. The set of instructions is called a **program,** and it is written by a computer professional called a **programmer.**

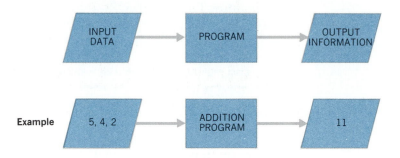

A computer, then, can process data only as efficiently and effectively as it is programmed.

B. Machine Language Programs

All instructions to be executed by the computer must be in **machine language.** It would be very tedious and cumbersome for the programmer to code instructions in this form. He or she would need to reference actual addresses or locations in memory and use complex instruction codes.

C. Symbolic Programs

Since programming in machine language is so difficult, programming languages were developed to enable the programmer to write English-like or symbolic instructions. However, before symbolic instructions can be executed or run, they must be translated or **compiled** into machine language. The computer itself uses a translator program or **compiler** to perform this conversion into machine language.

There are numerous **symbolic programming languages** that can be translated into machine language. COBOL is one such language; it is the one used most extensively for commercial applications. Other symbolic programming languages include BASIC, Pascal, and Ada.

II. The Program Development Process

A. An Overview

Most novices believe that computer programming begins with coding or writing program instructions and ends with program testing. You will find, however, that programmers who begin with the coding phase often produce poorly designed or inadequate programs.

The steps involved in programming should be developmental, where coding is undertaken only *after* the program requirements have been fully specified and the logic to be used has been clearly understood.

Moreover, there are steps required *after* a program has been coded and tested. Each program must be documented, that is, accompanied with a formal set of procedures and instructions that specify how it is to be used. This

documentation is meant for (1) those who will be working with the output and (2) computer operators who will run the program on a regularly scheduled basis.

An overview of the steps involved in the program development process follows. Each of these steps will then be discussed in detail.

PROGRAM DEVELOPMENT PROCESS

1. Obtaining Program Specifications
   a. A systems analyst is the computer professional who provides the programmer with input and output layouts and with the processing requirements.
   b. The programmer discusses the program requirements with the systems analyst who is responsible for the design of the overall set of procedures and with the user who will work with the program output.
2. Using Program Planning Tools
   Programmers use design tools such as flowcharts, pseudocode, and hierarchy charts to help map out the structure and logic of a program before the program is actually coded.
3. Coding the Program
   The programmer writes and then keys or enters the source program into the computer system using a keyboard.
4. Compiling and Testing the Program
   The programmer makes certain that the program works properly.
5. Documenting the Program
   The programmer writes procedure manuals for users and computer operators.

B. Obtaining Program Specifications

When a company decides to computerize a business application such as payroll or accounts receivable, a systems analyst is typically assigned the task of designing the entire computerized application. This systems analyst works closely with users in the specific business area to determine such factors as output needs, how many programs are required, and input requirements. A **user** is the businessperson who, when the application is computerized, will depend on or work with the output.

When a systems analyst decides what programs are required, he or she prepares **program specifications** to be given to the programmers so that they can perform their tasks.

Typically, the program specifications consist of:

1. **Record layout forms** to describe the formats of the input and output data on disk, tape, or other storage medium. Figure 1.1 illustrates a sample record layout. It indicates:
   a. The data items or fields within each record.
   b. The location of each data item within the record.
   c. The size of each data item.
   d. For numeric data items, the number of decimal positions. For example, xxx.xx is a five-digit field with three integer and two decimal places. (Two decimal places are typically used in dollars and cents fields.)
   e. In some organizations, standard names of the fields to be used in a

Figure 1.1
Sample record layout.

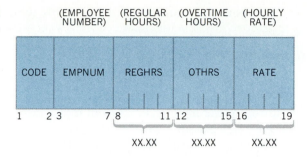

program are specified on the record layouts. In other organizations, names of fields are assigned by the programmer.

2. Printer Spacing Charts for printed output. Printed output has special requirements not typically needed for other types of output:
   a. Headings are usually printed.
   b. Data must be spaced neatly across the page, allowing for margins.
   c. Sometimes additional lines for error messages or totals are required.

A **Printer Spacing Chart,** as illustrated in Figure 1.2, is a tool used for determining the proper spacing of printed output. It specifies the print positions to be used in the output. It also includes all data items to be printed and their formats.

Thus, the analyst typically provides the programmer with record layout forms and/or a Printer Spacing Chart to indicate the precise format of the input and output. Along with these layout forms, a set of notes is provided by the systems analyst indicating the specific requirements of the program.

Illustrative programs and assignments in this text will include these same program specifications so that you will become familiar with them as you read through the book and will know what you can expect to receive from a systems analyst if you work as a programmer. In addition, the more common systems design techniques used to prepare these forms will be explained.

Figure 1.2
Sample Printer Spacing Chart.

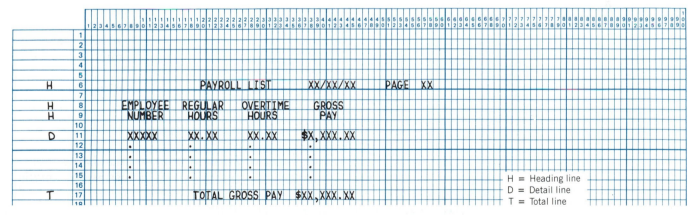

C. Using Program Planning Tools

Before a programmer begins to code, he or she should *plan the logic* to be used in the program. Just as an architect draws a blueprint before undertaking the construction of a building, a programmer should use a planning tool before a program is coded.

The three most common planning tools used by programmers are:

1. Flowcharts.
2. Pseudocode.
3. Hierarchy charts.

A **flowchart** is a conventional block diagram providing a pictorial representation of the logic to be used in a program. **Pseudocode** uses written English-like expressions rather than diagrams and is specifically suited for depicting logic in a structured program. **Hierarchy** or **structure charts** provide an excellent tool for showing the relationships among sections in a program.

In most of our illustrations beginning with Unit II, we will depict the logic flow to be used in a program with a flowchart or pseudocode. Hierarchy charts will also be included. We end this chapter with a brief overview of these tools; in Chapter 5 we provide an in-depth discussion of them.

D. Coding the Program

The programmer writes a set of instructions, called the **source program,** in a symbolic programming language. This program *cannot* be executed or run by the computer until it has been compiled or translated into machine language.

The source program is generally *keyed* into a computer using a terminal and then *stored* on disk, tape, or other storage medium. In companies with older computer systems, the source program may be punched into cards by a keypunch machine and then read by a card reader of a computer system.

E. Compiling the Source Program

After the source program has been read from a disk or tape drive or other input device, the computer must translate it into a machine language program called the **object program** before execution can occur. A program called a **compiler** translates source progams into object programs.

F. Testing the Program

1. Debugging Phases

When the computer translates a COBOL program, any errors detected by the compiler will be listed. That is, any violation of programming rules is noted as a **syntax error.** For example, if the COBOL instruction to add two numbers is spelled AD instead of ADD, the computer will print a message indicating that a syntax error has occurred. If such errors are very serious, then execution of the program cannot begin until the errors are corrected.

Note that the syntax errors detected during a compilation are just one type of programming error. A **logic error,** which is detected during program execution, is one in which the *sequence* of programming steps is not specified properly. Or it can be one in which the wrong instruction is coded; if you include an ADD instruction instead of a MULTIPLY, for example, this would result in a logic error.

Logic errors are detected by the programmer when the program is tested. A program is run or tested with *sample or test data* to see if it will process the data correctly. The test run should read the sample data as input and produce the desired output. The programmer then checks the output to be sure it is correct. If it is not correct, a logic error has occurred.

Sample data should be prepared carefully to ensure that during program testing or **debugging** all conditions provided for in a program are actually

Figure 1.3
Steps involved in coding and
testing a program.

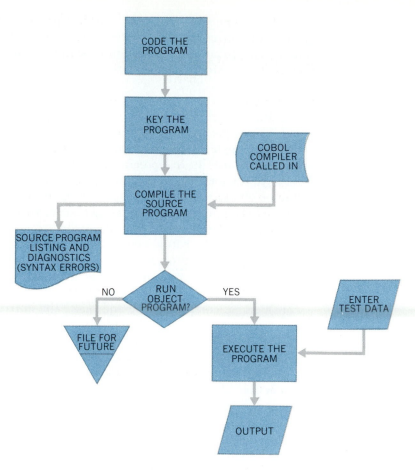

tested. If not, a program that has begun to be used on a regularly scheduled production basis may eventually produce logic errors.

If there are no errors in the source program or if only minor violations of rules occur, all instructions will be translated into machine language. The program can then be executed, or tested. If, however, execution is not necessary at this time, the object program may be stored, usually on magnetic disk or tape. In this way, an object program may be used to execute the instructions at some future time without the necessity of recompiling the source program. Figure 1.3 illustrates the steps involved in coding and testing a program.

2. Debugging Techniques

We have seen that after a program has been planned and coded, it must be compiled and executed with test data. It is not unusual for errors to occur during either compilation or execution. Eliminating these errors is called **debugging.** Several methods of debugging should be used by the programmer.

a. Desk Checking.

Programmers should carefully review their programs *before* they are keyed in and again after they have been keyed for typing errors. **Desk checking** will minimize computer time and reduce the overall time it takes to debug a program. Frequently, programmers fail to see the need for this phase, on the assumption that it is better to let the computer find errors. Note, however, that omitting the desk checking phase can result in undetected *logic* errors that could take hours or even days to debug later on. Efficient programmers carefully review their programs before and after keying them.

b. Correcting Syntax Errors.

After a program has been translated or compiled, the computer will print a source listing along with diagnostic messages that point to any rule violations or syntax errors. The programmer must then correct the errors and recompile the program before it can be run with test data.

c. Program Walkthroughs.

After a program has been listed by the computer in a source listing, programmers test the logic by executing it with test data. It is best, however, to "walk through" the program first to see if it will produce the desired results. In a program **walkthrough,** the programmer manually steps through the logic of the program using the test data to see if the correct results will be obtained. This is done *prior to* machine execution. Such walkthroughs can help the programmer find logic errors without wasting machine time.

Sometimes structured walkthroughs are performed directly from pseudocode, *prior to* the actual coding of a program. This procedure will also minimize the need for program changes later on.

Frequently, programming teams work together to test the logic in their programs using the walkthrough approach. This method of debugging can save considerable computer time and make the entire debugging phase more efficient as well.

d. Detecting Logic Errors by Executing the Program.

In many ways, detecting logic errors by executing the program is the most difficult and time-consuming method of debugging. If desk checking and program walkthroughs are performed, the number of logic errors that are likely to occur during program execution will be minimized. Chapter 13 focuses on additional techniques used for finding and correcting logic errors in COBOL programs.

As noted, the preparation of test data is an extremely critical aspect of debugging. The programmer should prepare data which will test *every possible condition* that the program is likely to encounter under normal operating conditions. It is not uncommon for a program that has been thought to be fully tested and that has been operational for some time to suddenly experience problems. Most often, these problems arise because a specific condition not previously encountered has occurred and the program does not account for that situation.

Self-Test   Self-test questions are provided throughout the text, with solutions that follow, to help you determine whether you understand the material presented.

1. A program must be in _____ language to be executed or run by a computer.
2. Programs are typically written in a _____ language rather than in machine language because _____ .
3. Programs written in a language other than machine language must be _____ before execution can occur.
4. _____ is the process of converting a source program into machine language.
5. The program written in a programming language such as COBOL is called the _____ program.
6. The object program is the _____ .
7. A _____ converts a source program into a(n) _____ program.
8. The errors that are detected during compilation denote _____ ; they are usually referred to as _____ errors.
9. Before executing a program with test data, the logic of the program can be checked by a _____ .
10. After a program has been compiled, it may be either _____ or _____ .

Solutions
1. machine
2. symbolic; machine languages are very complex (They use cumbersome instruction codes and the programmer must specify actual machine locations or addresses for storing data.)
3. translated or compiled
4. Compilation or Translation
5. source
6. set of instructions that has been converted into machine language
7. compiler or translator program; object or machine language
8. any violation of programming rules in the use of the symbolic programming language; syntax
9. program walkthrough
10. executed or run; saved in translated or object form for future processing

III. The Nature of COBOL

A. COBOL as a Business-Oriented Language

COBOL is the most widespread commercial programming language in use today. The reasons for its vast success are discussed in this section.

The name COBOL is an abbreviation for *CO*mmon *B*usiness *O*riented *L*anguage. It is a business-oriented computer language designed specifically for commercial applications. The rules governing the use of the language make it ideally suited for commercial problems. This means that COBOL is best able to handle complex input/output functions where a large volume of data needs to be processed at one time. It is less suitable, however, for handling scientific problems where complex calculations are required.

B. COBOL as a Standard Language

COBOL is a programming language that is common to most computers. This means that COBOL compilers are available for most computers, so that the same COBOL program may be compiled and run on a variety of different machines, such as an IBM 4381 and a VAX 11/780, with only minor variations.

The universality of COBOL allows computer users greater flexibility than they would have with many other languages. A company is free to acquire different brands of computers while using a single programming language. Similarly, conversion from one model computer to a more advanced or newer one presents no great problem as long as there is a COBOL compiler for each model. Because the language is so widely used, computers of a future generation will undoubtedly support COBOL. Even microcomputers use COBOL widely. (Appendix D discusses the features of some popular micro-based versions of the language.)

C. COBOL as an English-like Language

In summary, the meaning of the name COBOL suggests two of its basic advantages. It is *common* to most computers, and it is *business oriented*. There are, however, additional reasons why it is such a popular language.

COBOL is an English-like language. All instructions can be coded using English words rather than complex codes. To add two numbers together, for example, we use the word ADD. Similarly, the rules for programming in COBOL conform to many of the rules for writing in English, making it a relatively simple language to learn. It therefore becomes significantly easier to train programmers.

D. COBOL as a Self-Documenting Language

The English-like quality of COBOL makes it easy to read programs as well as to write them. Thus, businesspeople or users who rely on computer output but have no computer expertise may be able to understand the logic and instructions in a program.

Because COBOL can be read and understood by people who will rely on the program, we call it a *self-documenting language*. This means that the program is relatively self-explanatory, needing less documentation or supporting material to explain it than is required of other languages. Because users are frequently able to understand the English-like instructions of COBOL, it is considered a user-friendly language; this means that it is not overly technical like other languages.

IV. A History of COBOL and the ANS Versions

A. When It Began

COBOL was developed in 1959 by a group called the CODASYL Committee. CODASYL is an abbreviation for *CO*nference on *DA*ta *SY*stems *L*anguages. This committee included representatives from academia, user groups, and computer manufacturers. The ultimate objective of this committee was to develop a *standard* business-oriented language for which all major manufacturers would provide compilers. The Department of Defense convened this conference since it, as well as other government agencies, was particularly dissatisfied with the lack of standards in the computing field.

B. The American National Standards (ANS) Versions of COBOL

As a result of the CODASYL effort, the first COBOL compilers became available in 1960. But as years passed, users became dissatisfied with the wide variations among COBOL compilers produced by the different computer manufacturers.

The **American National Standards Institute (ANSI)** is an organization that develops standards in numerous fields. It is the current overseeing organization for COBOL standards. Like CODASYL, ANSI's COBOL committee consists of representatives from academia, user groups, and computer vendors.

In 1968, the first American National Standards (ANS) version of COBOL was developed and approved. Beginning in 1968, all major computer manufacturers and software suppliers provided compilers that adhered to the COBOL language formats specified in this ANS version of COBOL. In 1974, a second version of ANS COBOL was developed to make the language even more efficient and standardized. The 1985 version of ANS COBOL is currently being implemented; it goes beyond the previous versions in increasing the versatility and the structure of the language. Originally, this was to be the 1980 ANS standard, but it took longer than expected to actually implement it. Since it was finally approved in 1985, we refer to it as COBOL 85.

All versions of ANS COBOL are very similar, although there are some variations. This text focuses on COBOL 85 but when there are differences between COBOL 85 and COBOL 74, we indicate them. You should determine what COBOL standard your computer uses so that you will be more attuned to the slight variations among the different versions that are mentioned in this text.

Note that an individual COBOL compiler (whether it is a 68, 74, or 85 version) may include **enhancements**, which provide the programmer with additional options not required in the standard. The reference manual for each compiler indicates these enhancements as shaded entries to distinguish them from the ANS standard. We use this shading technique to highlight special features of COBOL 85.

Self-Test

1. COBOL is an abbreviation for ＿＿＿＿ .
2. COBOL is a common language in the sense that ＿＿＿＿ .
3. ANS is an abbreviation for ＿＿＿＿ ; the three major ANS versions of COBOL are ＿＿＿＿ , ＿＿＿＿ , and ＿＿＿＿ .
4. (T or F) COBOL is ideally suited for scientific as well as business problems.
5. Since a COBOL program typically needs very little supporting documentation to explain the logic, we call COBOL a ＿＿＿＿ language.

Solutions

1. Common Business Oriented Language
2. it can be used on many computers
3. American National Standards; 1968; 1974; 1985
4. F—It is ideally suited for business applications.
5. self-documenting or user-friendly

V. Techniques for Improving Program Design

A. Structured Programming

When programming became a major profession in the 1960s and 1970s, the primary goal of programmers was getting programs to work. Although this is still a programmer's main objective, writing programs so that they are easy to read, debug, and modify is also considered a very important goal. That is, as the computer field develops, more and more attention is being given to programming style and technique, as well as to making programs as efficient as possible.

The most important technique for improving the design of a program in any language is called **structured programming.** In general, structured programs are easier to read than are nonstructured programs. They are also easier to debug and modify if changes are required. Moreover, they are easier to evaluate so that programming managers are better able to assess programmers' skills.

For those of you who have had some previous programming experience, you may have encountered nonstructured techniques that include frequent use of GO TOs or branch points. These GO TOs often make it very difficult to follow the logic of a program; they can also make debugging a program more difficult.

One major purpose of structured programming is to simplify debugging by reducing the number of entry and exit or branch points in a program. For that reason, structured programming is sometimes referred to as GO-TO-less programming, where a GO TO statement is the COBOL code for a branch. Using the techniques of structured programming, the GO TO or branch statement is avoided entirely. In COBOL, this means writing programs where sequences are controlled by PERFORM statements. (In other languages, this would mean writing programs where sequences are controlled by DO or WHILE statements.)

Using this structured technique, each section of a program can be written and even debugged independently without too much concern for where it enters the logic flow.

The typical structured program is subdivided into paragraphs or **modules,** where a main module calls in other modules as needed. That is, the programmer codes one main routine, and when some other routine is required, a PERFORM statement calls for this routine which appears elsewhere in the program. The terms paragraph, routine, and module can be used interchangeably.

With a modularized concept, routines can be tested independently. Moreover, it is feasible for different programmers to code different modules or sections of a large and complex program. The main routine simply calls for the execution of the other modules or sections as needed.

Chapter 5 provides an in-depth view of the types of logical control sequences used in all structured programs.

B. The Top-Down Approach

Another common technique for making programs easier to read and more efficient is called **top-down programming.** The term implies that proper program design is best achieved by designing and coding major modules or procedures before minor ones. Thus, in a top-down program, the main routines are coded first and are followed by intermediate routines and then minor ones.

By coding modules in this top-down manner, the *organization* or flow of the program is given primary attention. Details are deferred or saved for the minor modules, which are coded last. Top-down programming is analogous to designing a term paper by developing an outline first, which gets more and more detailed only after the main organization or structure has been established. This standardized top-down technique provides an excellent complement to the structured approach for achieving efficient program design.

In this text we will use structured techniques in all our programs and avoid the use of GO TOs. In addition, we will code in a top-down format so that you will learn to program in a style that is widely accepted as a standardized and effective one. Chapter 5 discusses in depth the design features used in structured and top-down programs. In fact, all of Unit II focuses on proper program design.

VI. A Sample Program

A. An Overview of the Four Divisions

Every COBOL program consists of four separate *divisions,* each with a specific function:

THE FOUR DIVISIONS	
Name	**Purpose**
IDENTIFICATION DIVISION	Identifies the program to the computer. It also provides documentation that is useful to users who may want to read or work with the program.
ENVIRONMENT DIVISION	Describes the specific computer equipment that will be used by the program.
DATA DIVISION	Describes the input and output formats to be used by the program. It also defines any constants and work areas necessary for the processing of data.
PROCEDURE DIVISION	Contains the instructions necessary for reading input, processing it, and creating output.

The structure and organization of a COBOL program are best explained by an illustration. Note that this illustration is intended to familiarize you with a sample COBOL program; do not expect to be able to code a program yourself, in its entirety, until you have read the next few chapters.

B. Definition of the Problem

A computer center of a large company is assigned the task of calculating weekly wages or gross pay for all nonsalaried personnel. The employee name, hourly rate, and number of hours worked are supplied as input for each employee, and the weekly wages figure is to be computed as follows:

WEEKLY-WAGES = HOURS-WORKED × HOURLY-RATE

Before processing can begin, the input must be in a form that is "readable" or understandable to the computer. The input may have been keyed on a terminal and then stored on magnetic disk or tape (or their micro-equivalents—floppy disk or cassette tape). The punched card is another possible form of input, although it is considered obsolete by most organizations.

C. Input Layout

Assume that the employee data is entered on magnetic disk. As we will see, the device used for entering the input does not really affect the program's logic. The data entered as input has the format specified in the record layout form in Figure 1.4. A **record** is the collection of data for each employee.

Figure 1.4
Input disk record layout for sample program.

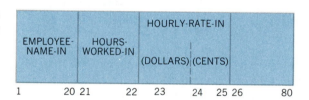

The employee record consists of three data items called **fields.** The three fields are called EMPLOYEE-NAME-IN, HOURS-WORKED-IN, and HOURLY-RATE-IN. Positions 1 through 20 of each record contain EMPLOYEE-NAME-IN. If any name contains less than 20 characters, the **low-order,** or rightmost, **positions** are left blank. Alphabetic data is always entered from left to right. HOURS-WORKED-IN will be placed in positions 21–22 and HOURLY-RATE-IN in positions 23–25. If HOURS-WORKED-IN is less than 10, then 0 will be placed in the leftmost or **high-order position** of the field. Thus, if HOURS-WORKED-IN equals 7, the data would be entered as 07. Numeric data is always zero-filled in this way.

The HOURLY-RATE-IN figure, as a dollars and cents amount, is to be interpreted as a field with two decimal positions. That is, 925 in record positions 23–25 will be interpreted by the computer as 9.25. The decimal point is *not* entered on the record, since it would waste a storage position. We will see that COBOL uses **implied decimal points** when representing numbers with decimal components that are to be used in arithmetic operations.

We use the suffix -IN with each field name of EMPLOYEE-RECORD to reinforce the fact that these are input fields. This is a recommended naming convention, *not* a required one. Because all employee records have exactly the same format, we call this a fixed-length record.

D. Output Layout and Definition

A file or collection of employee records with the above format will be read as input to the program. WEEKLY-WAGES-OUT will be calculated by the computer as HOURS-WORKED-IN multiplied by HOURLY-RATE-IN. Suppose we wanted to store this new WEEKLY-WAGES-OUT field as part of a file. A computed figure cannot be added directly to the input data. That is, we usually do not add output data directly to an input record. In general, input and output use separate devices.

If we wanted this WEEKLY-WAGES-OUT field as part of a payroll file, we would create an output file that contained all input data *in addition to* the computed wage figure. The output PAYROLL-FILE could be placed on a second magnetic disk. Or we could print the output on a file called PAYROLL-LIST-ING that would include the input fields along with the computed weekly wages. We will create printed output for this sample program. The Printer Spacing Chart in Figure 1.5 illustrates the format for each printed line.

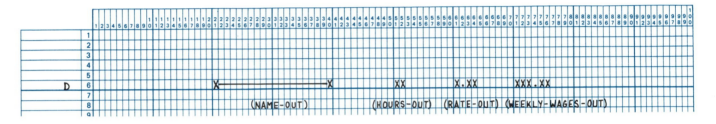

Figure 1.5
Printer Spacing Chart for sample program.

Figure 1.5 indicates the print positions we will use for the output. Print positions 1–20 are left blank, as a margin, and the name is printed in print positions 21–40. The X's in 21–40 indicate this. NAME-OUT is the field name to be assigned to this output area.

Print positions 41–50 are left blank for readability, and the hours worked are printed in 51–52. Similarly, the hourly rate is printed in print positions 61–64 and weekly wages in print positions 71–76. The entries in parentheses are the names to be used for each item.

The **file** or collection of data that serves as input to the system will be called EMPLOYEE-DATA. The computer will calculate WEEKLY-WAGES-OUT from the two input fields HOURS-WORKED-IN and HOURLY-RATE-IN. The input data along with the computed figure will be used to create the output print file called PAYROLL-LISTING. All fields within each record of the PAY-ROLL-LISTING file have the suffix -OUT to make it clear that they are output fields.

The systems specifications depicting the overall relationships among elements in this program appear in Figure 1.6. These specifications are typically supplied by the systems analyst and indicate the input and output for the program.

Figure 1.6
Systems specifications for sample program.

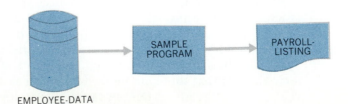

E. The Program Illustrated

1. Reviewing the Specifications

The program specifications include the input and output record formats that are illustrated in Figures 1.4 and 1.5. As noted, the input layout form and the Printer Spacing Chart would typically be given to the programmer by the systems analyst who is responsible for designing the input and output forms.

Once these specifications have been supplied, the programmer should plan the program's design. This means mapping out the logic to be used in the program. Figure 1.7 illustrates a program flowchart and a sample pseudocode that explains the logic to be used in the program. The techniques used to draw a flowchart or write in pseudocode are explained in detail in Chapter 5. We include these planning tools here because we believe you should become familiar with reading them even before you prepare your own. The basic rules for interpreting these tools are provided in the next section.

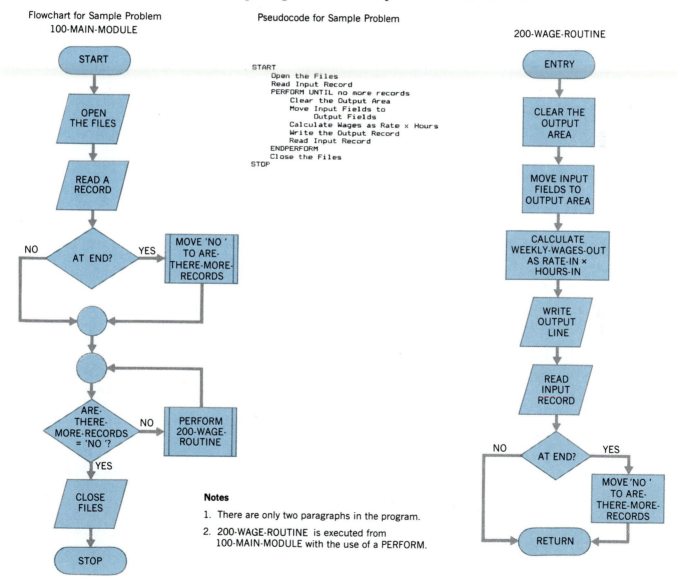

Flowchart for Sample Problem
100-MAIN-MODULE

Pseudocode for Sample Problem

200-WAGE-ROUTINE

```
START
    Open the Files
    Read Input Record
    PERFORM UNTIL no more records
        Clear the Output Area
        Move Input Fields to
            Output Fields
        Calculate Wages as Rate x Hours
        Write the Output Record
        Read Input Record
    ENDPERFORM
    Close the Files
STOP
```

Notes

1. There are only two paragraphs in the program.

2. 200-WAGE-ROUTINE is executed from 100-MAIN-MODULE with the use of a PERFORM.

Figure 1.7
Program flowchart and pseudocode for sample program.

After the program has been designed or planned, it is written. You will recall that a program is a set of instructions that operate on input to produce output. Figure 1.8 is a simplified COBOL program that will operate on employee disk records to create a printed payroll report which contains the computed wages for each employee along with the input data.

2. Coding Rules

Note that in the case of page and line numbers, the number zero is distinguished from the letter O on the coding form by slashing zeros. This convention will be used throughout this book. Note also that the program is divided into four major divisions. The IDENTIFICATION, ENVIRONMENT, DATA, and PROCEDURE DIVISIONs are coded on lines 01, 03, 07, and 26, respectively. Every COBOL program *must* contain these four divisions in this order. To avoid any misinterpretations, we use uppercase letters in all our coding.

3. The IDENTIFICATION and ENVIRONMENT DIVISIONs

In this program, the IDENTIFICATION DIVISION has, as its only entry, the PROGRAM-ID. That is, the IDENTIFICATION DIVISION of this program merely serves to identify the program. We will see that there are other entries that may be included in the IDENTIFICATION DIVISION, but PROGRAM-ID is the only *required* entry.

The ENVIRONMENT DIVISION assigns the input and output files to specific devices in the INPUT-OUTPUT SECTION. The input file, called EMPLOYEE-DATA, will be on a disk. Similarly, PAYROLL-LISTING is the output file and is assigned to the printer, called SYSLST in our program (but it may be called by a different name at your computer center).

4. The DATA DIVISION

The DATA DIVISION describes the format of the input and output files. The areas in memory where input and output records will be stored are fully described in the DATA DIVISION, in the FILE SECTION. The *File Description,* or FD, for EMPLOYEE-DATA describes the input disk file, which in this case has identifying labels (LABEL RECORDS ARE STANDARD).

The record format for the input file is called EMPLOYEE-RECORD. It has three input fields—EMPLOYEE-NAME-IN, HOURS-WORKED-IN, and HOURLY-RATE-IN. Each field has a corresponding PICTURE clause denoting the size and type of data that will appear in the field.

The EMPLOYEE-NAME-IN field is a data field containing 20 characters. PICTURE X(20) indicates that the size of the field is 20 characters. The X in the PICTURE clause means that the field can contain any character, including a space. Similarly, HOURS-WORKED-IN is a two-position numeric field. PICTURE 9(2) indicates the type and size of data: 9 denotes numeric data, and (2) denotes a two-position area. HOURLY-RATE-IN is a three-position numeric field with an implied decimal point. That is, PICTURE 9V99 indicates a *three-position* numeric field with an implied or assumed decimal point after the first position; the V means an implied decimal point. Thus 925 in this field will be interpreted by the computer as 9.25. The decimal point does *not* appear in the input disk record, but the V in the PICTURE clause ensures that the number will be treated by the computer as if a decimal point had been specified.

The output print file called PAYROLL-LISTING does not have identifying labels because print files can be checked manually. It has a record format called PRINT-REC, which is subdivided into eight fields, each with an appropriate PICTURE clause.

The fields called FILLER set aside space in the record but are not used in the PROCEDURE DIVISION. They will contain blanks. They are used in the

COBOL Program Sheet

System				Punching Instructions					Sheet	of	
Program	FIRST SAMPLE PROGRAM		Graphic					Card # Form	Identification		
Programmer	N. STERN		Punch						73	80	

Sequence (Page) (Serial)	Cont.	A	B	COBOL Statement

```
001 01    IDENTIFICATION DIVISION.
001 02    PROGRAM-ID.  SAMPLE.
001 03    ENVIRONMENT DIVISION.
001 04    INPUT-OUTPUT SECTION.
001 05    FILE-CONTROL.    SELECT EMPLOYEE-DATA    ASSIGN TO DISK.
001 06                     SELECT PAYROLL-LISTING  ASSIGN TO SYSLST.
001 07    DATA DIVISION.
001 08    FILE SECTION.
001 09    FD  EMPLOYEE-DATA    LABEL RECORDS ARE STANDARD.
001 10    01  EMPLOYEE-RECORD.
001 11        05   EMPLOYEE-NAME-IN      PICTURE X(20).
001 12        05   HOURS-WORKED-IN       PICTURE 9(2).
001 13        05   HOURLY-RATE-IN        PICTURE 9V99.
001 14    FD  PAYROLL-LISTING    LABEL RECORDS ARE OMITTED.
001 15    01  PRINT-REC.
001 16        05   FILLER                PICTURE X(21).
001 17        05   NAME-OUT              PICTURE X(20).
001 18        05   FILLER                PICTURE X(10).
001 19        05   HOURS-OUT             PICTURE 9(2).
001 20        05   FILLER                PICTURE X(8).
00121         05   RATE-OUT              PICTURE 9.99.
00122         05   FILLER                PICTURE X(6).
00123         05   WEEKLY-WAGES-OUT      PICTURE 999.99.
00124    WORKING-STORAGE SECTION.
00125    01  ARE-THERE-MORE-RECORDS    PICTURE XXX VALUE 'YES'.
00126    PROCEDURE DIVISION.
00127    100-MAIN-MODULE.
00128        OPEN INPUT EMPLOYEE-DATA
00129             OUTPUT PAYROLL-LISTING.
00130        READ EMPLOYEE-DATA
00131            AT END MOVE 'NO ' TO ARE-THERE-MORE-RECORDS.
00132        PERFORM 200-WAGE-ROUTINE
00133            UNTIL ARE-THERE-MORE-RECORDS = 'NO '.
00134        CLOSE EMPLOYEE-DATA
00135             PAYROLL-LISTING.
00136        STOP RUN.
00137    200-WAGE-ROUTINE.
00138        MOVE SPACES TO PRINT-REC.
00139        MOVE EMPLOYEE-NAME-IN TO NAME-OUT.
00140        MOVE HOURS-WORKED-IN TO HOURS-OUT.
00141        MOVE HOURLY-RATE-IN TO RATE-OUT.
00142        MULTIPLY HOURS-WORKED-IN BY HOURLY-RATE-IN
00143             GIVING WEEKLY-WAGES-OUT.
00144        WRITE PRINT-REC.
00145        READ EMPLOYEE-DATA
00146            AT END MOVE 'NO ' TO ARE-THERE-MORE-RECORDS.
```

Figure 1.8
Sample program on COBOL coding form.

print record so that the output fields will be separated from one another across each line that is printed.

The first blank or FILLER area is defined with a PICTURE of X(21), which means it has 21 characters. The leftmost or first character of this field is used for controlling whether double or triple spacing of forms (or other spacing) is required. We will always leave the first character in a print record blank in our programs.

Thus, to obtain a 20-character blank area for a left margin we say 05 FILLER PICTURE X(21). The leftmost position is for spacing, and the next 20 are for obtaining a 20-character blank area at the left margin. NAME-OUT will follow in print positions 21–40 as noted on the Printer Spacing Chart in Figure 1.5. FILLER PICTURE X(10) means that the next field is a 10-position blank area that will separate the name from HOURS-OUT, which is two numeric positions. After the next eight-position FILLER, a RATE-OUT field is denoted as PICTURE 9.99. This is a *four-position field* that actually contains a decimal point. RATE-IN has a PICTURE of 9V99. Suppose we read a value of 123, for example, into RATE-IN; it will be stored as 1$_\wedge$23 with the *decimal point implied*. All arithmetic and move operations will be decimally aligned when we move RATE-IN TO RATE-OUT. Because RATE-OUT has a PICTURE of 9.99, the MOVE will result in 1.23 at RATE-OUT *with the actual decimal point printing*. Then a six-position blank FILLER will be followed by a six-position WEEKLY-WAGES-OUT field with the decimal point printing again.

The first three data fields of PRINT-REC (NAME-OUT, HOURS-OUT, and RATE-OUT) will contain data copied directly from each input record. The last field, WEEKLY-WAGES-OUT, must be computed.

The field or data item called ARE-THERE-MORE-RECORDS is defined in the WORKING-STORAGE SECTION of the DATA DIVISION. This field is initialized with a value of 'YES'. The quote marks are always used to designate non-numeric values. The field called ARE-THERE-MORE-RECORDS will be used in the PROCEDURE DIVISION as an indicator, sometimes referred to as a "flag" or "switch." That is, it will have a value of 'YES' until the last data record has been read and processed, at which time a 'NO ' will be moved into it. When this field contains 'YES', it means there are still more records to process; when it contains 'NO ', there are no more input records.

The data-name ARE-THERE-MORE-RECORDS was chosen because the field is used to indicate when the last data record has been read and processed. This indicator field will be programmed to contain the value 'YES' when there are still records to process; we set it to 'NO ' only when there are *no* more input records. Any field name could have been used, but the name ARE-THERE-MORE-RECORDS is both descriptive and self-explanatory.

5. The PROCEDURE DIVISION

The PROCEDURE DIVISION contains the set of instructions to be executed by the computer. Each instruction is executed in the order in which it appears on the coding sheets. The PROCEDURE DIVISION is divided into two paragraphs or modules, 100-MAIN-MODULE and 200-WAGE-ROUTINE. All instructions within these paragraphs are coded in sentence form. We will consider margin rules later.

The first PROCEDURE DIVISION entry is the following:

```
OPEN INPUT EMPLOYEE-DATA
     OUTPUT PAYROLL-LISTING.
```

This instruction accesses the devices assigned to the files and indicates to the computer which file is input and which is output. It extends to two lines but is treated as a single unit. This is because the period appears on the second line.

The second instruction in the `PROCEDURE DIVISION` is:

```
READ EMPLOYEE-DATA
     AT END MOVE 'NO ' TO ARE-THERE-MORE-RECORDS.
```

This is an instruction that causes the computer to read *one* data record into an area of storage referred to as the input area. Note that data must be in storage in order to be operated on. If there are no more records to be read when this `READ` statement is executed, the value `'NO '` will be moved to the field called `ARE-THERE-MORE-RECORDS`; otherwise the field remains unchanged at its initial value of `'YES'`. Given that there are input records to process at the beginning of the run, the first attempt to read a record causes data to be transmitted from disk to storage for processing. After a record has been read, the next instruction in sequence is executed.

Suppose the first input record is as follows:

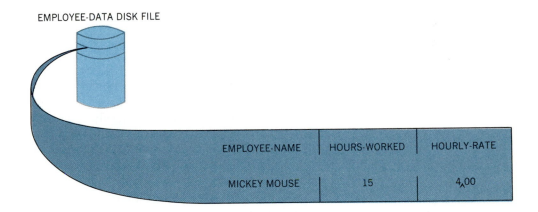

The instruction `READ EMPLOYEE-DATA AT END MOVE 'NO ' TO ARE-THERE-MORE-RECORDS` reads the preceding record into storage and transmits it to the Central Processing Unit or CPU for processing. This record is stored in symbolic storage addresses, which are data-names that are defined by the programmer in the `DATA DIVISION`. When this first record is read, the CPU will contain the following:

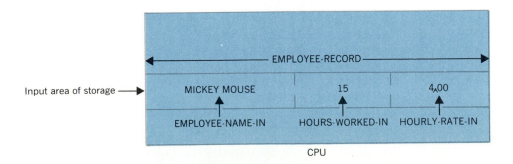

The next instruction that is executed is the following:

```
PERFORM 200-WAGE-ROUTINE
    UNTIL ARE-THERE-MORE-RECORDS = 'NO '.
```

This instruction will cause all the statements within the paragraph named 200-WAGE-ROUTINE (from line 37 through line 46) to be executed repeatedly until ARE-THERE-MORE-RECORDS is equal to 'NO '. A quick glance at the statements within 200-WAGE-ROUTINE indicates that the instructions will be executed until the value 'NO ' is moved to ARE-THERE-MORE-RECORDS by the READ ... AT END sentence. Thus ARE-THERE-MORE-RECORDS will be set equal to 'NO ' only when there are no more input records.

Once ARE-THERE-MORE-RECORDS = 'NO ', the statement to be executed next in 100-MAIN-MODULE is the one immediately following the PERFORM. That is, PERFORM 200-WAGE-ROUTINE UNTIL ARE-THERE-MORE-RECORDS = 'NO ' causes execution of 200-WAGE-ROUTINE until there are no more input records, at which time control returns to the statement following the PERFORM. The instructions on lines 34–36, CLOSE and STOP RUN, are executed only after all input records have been processed in 200-WAGE-ROUTINE.

In summary, the first instruction within 100-MAIN-MODULE in the PROCEDURE DIVISION is the OPEN statement and it activates the files. The next instruction, READ, causes a single record to be read. Then the PERFORM executes 200-WAGE-ROUTINE repeatedly until the field called ARE-THERE-MORE-RECORDS is set equal to 'NO '. In 200-WAGE-ROUTINE, the first record is processed and subsequent records are read and processed until there is no more input and ARE-THERE-MORE-RECORDS is set to 'NO '. Then control returns to the statement after the PERFORM in 100-MAIN-MODULE. This is the CLOSE statement, which deactivates the files. The STOP RUN is executed as the last instruction, and the program is terminated. The first five steps—OPEN, READ, PERFORM, CLOSE, and STOP RUN—represent the main module of the PROCEDURE DIVISION. These statements appear within the module or paragraph labeled 100-MAIN-MODULE.

Let us look more closely at the instructions to be executed in the 200-WAGE-ROUTINE paragraph. First, MOVE SPACES TO PRINT-REC clears out or initializes PRINT-REC at blanks or spaces. This ensures that even after we move data into output fields, all FILLER areas will be blank. Then, EMPLOYEE-NAME-IN of the *first* disk record, which was read with the READ statement on line 30, is moved to NAME-OUT of the output area. The fields called HOURS-WORKED-IN and HOURLY-RATE-IN of this first record are also moved to the output area. WEEKLY-WAGES-OUT, an output field, is then calculated by multiplying HOURS-WORKED-IN by HOURLY-RATE-IN.

The three MOVE and one MULTIPLY instructions executed in 200-WAGE-ROUTINE for the first record produce the following results in the CPU:

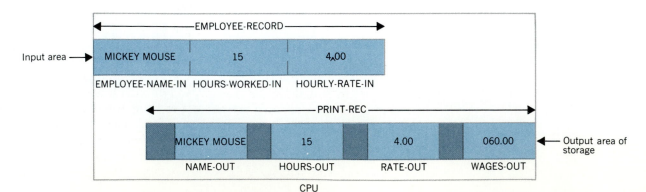

After the data has been moved to the area reserved in storage for output (called the output area), a WRITE instruction is executed. This WRITE statement takes the information in the output area and prints it.

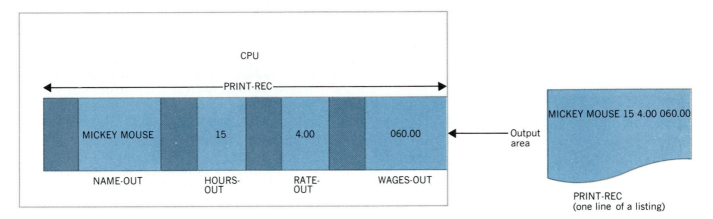

The preceding set of instructions will process the *first* disk record and create one print line or record. The READ statement is then executed on lines 45–46, and data from the next input record is transmitted to storage.

The sequence of instructions within 200-WAGE-ROUTINE is executed under the control of the PERFORM statement on lines 32–33. That is, execution of 200-WAGE-ROUTINE instructions will be repeated until the field called ARE-THERE-MORE-RECORDS is equal to 'NO ', which will only occur after all input records have been processed. Hence, after the second record has been read, 200-WAGE-ROUTINE will be executed again, the input data moved, the calculation performed, a second print line written, and a third input record read. This will continue until there are no additional disk records available for processing and 'NO ' is moved to ARE-THERE-MORE-RECORDS. Then control returns to the main module, at which point the instructions on lines 34–36, the CLOSE and STOP RUN, are executed.

Figure 1.8, then, represents an entire sample COBOL program. It will run on any computer, although minor changes may be necessary in the SELECT statements because some computers have specific requirements for the AS-SIGN clause. You may want to key in and run this program on your system just to familiarize yourself with COBOL. Figure 1.9 is the computer listing of the same program.

An examination of the program might reveal to you two of COBOL's characteristics. The English-like manner and the organization of a structured COBOL program make it comparatively easy to learn. Similarly, the relative ease with which a COBOL program may be read by users makes the language a distinct asset at most computer installations.

F. A Brief Overview of Program Planning Tools

A program such as the one shown in Figure 1.8 would first be planned using either a flowchart or pseudocode to map out the logic. These planning tools are particularly useful in helping programmers determine the best type of structure for their programs. Moreover, for complex programs, these tools are essential for ensuring that the program to be written is a well-designed one.

In Chapter 5 we discuss the techniques used for planning a program in detail. In Figure 1.7 in this chapter, we simply illustrate what these planning tools look like. The following are some basic rules for *reading* a flowchart and a pseudocode. For now, you should try to understand how to interpret these tools. Later on, you will learn how to plan your own programs using these tools.

Figure 1.9
Computer listing of sample
program.

```
00101    IDENTIFICATION DIVISION.
00102    PROGRAM-ID. SAMPLE.
00103    ENVIRONMENT DIVISION.
00104    INPUT-OUTPUT SECTION.
00105    FILE-CONTROL. SELECT EMPLOYEE-DATA    ASSIGN TO DISK.
00106                  SELECT PAYROLL-LISTING  ASSIGN TO SYSLST.
00107    DATA DIVISION.
00108    FILE SECTION.
00109    FD  EMPLOYEE-DATA      LABEL RECORDS ARE STANDARD.
00110    01  EMPLOYEE-RECORD.
00111        05   EMPLOYEE-NAME-IN    PICTURE X(20).
00112        05   HOURS-WORKED-IN     PICTURE 9(2).
00113        05   HOURLY-RATE-IN      PICTURE 9V99.
00114    FD  PAYROLL-LISTING    LABEL RECORDS ARE OMITTED.
00115    01  PRINT-REC.
00116        05   FILLER             PICTURE X(21).
00117        05   NAME-OUT           PICTURE X(20).
00118        05   FILLER             PICTURE X(10).
00119        05   HOURS-OUT          PICTURE 9(2).
00120        05   FILLER             PICTURE X(8).
00121        05   RATE-OUT           PICTURE 9.99.
00122        05   FILLER             PICTURE X(6).
00123        05   WEEKLY-WAGES-OUT   PICTURE 999.99.
00124    WORKING-STORAGE SECTION.
00125    01  ARE-THERE-MORE-RECORDS  PICTURE XXX VALUE 'YES'.
00126    PROCEDURE DIVISION.
00127    100-MAIN-MODULE.
00128        OPEN INPUT EMPLOYEE-DATA
00129             OUTPUT PAYROLL-LISTING.
00130        READ EMPLOYEE-DATA
00131             AT END MOVE 'NO ' TO ARE-THERE-MORE-RECORDS.
00132        PERFORM 200-WAGE-ROUTINE
00133             UNTIL ARE-THERE-MORE-RECORDS = 'NO '.
00134        CLOSE EMPLOYEE-DATA
00135             PAYROLL-LISTING.
00136        STOP RUN.
00137    200-WAGE-ROUTINE.
00138        MOVE SPACES TO PRINT-REC.
00139        MOVE EMPLOYEE-NAME-IN TO NAME-OUT.
00140        MOVE HOURS-WORKED-IN TO HOURS-OUT.
00141        MOVE HOURLY-RATE-IN TO RATE-OUT.
00142        MULTIPLY HOURS-WORKED-IN BY HOURLY-RATE-IN
00143             GIVING WEEKLY-WAGES-OUT.
00144        WRITE PRINT-REC.
00145        READ EMPLOYEE-DATA
00146             AT END MOVE 'NO ' TO ARE-THERE-MORE-RECORDS.
```

INTERPRETING THE FLOWCHART IN FIGURE 1.7

General Rules

1. Each flowchart symbol denotes a specific operation.

2. In each symbol is a note describing a particular function.

3. Flowcharts are read from top to bottom.

Specific Rules

4. There are two modules or paragraphs in this program, one labeled `100-MAIN-MODULE` and the other labeled `200-WAGE-ROUTINE`. Modules begin and end with a terminal symbol:

5. The main module, labeled `100-MAIN-MODULE`, performs the following:

a. Files are opened or prepared for processing using an input/output (I/O) symbol:

b. The output area is cleared; this is a processing operation.
c. A record is read.
d. A test is performed using a decision symbol:

This test determines if there are still input records to process. If an AT END condition is met, designated by the 'YES' flow, then the letters 'NO ' are moved to a field called ARE-THERE-MORE-RECORDS. This is designated in a processing symbol:

If an AT END condition is not met, this means there are still input records to process. In either case, the next operation in sequence is performed.
e. The following symbols represent a specific logical control construct:

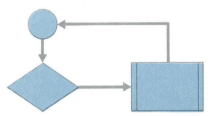

It means that a given series of operations, designated in the 200-WAGE-ROUTINE paragraph, are to be executed until the condition is met. That is, 200-WAGE-ROUTINE is executed repeatedly until ARE-THERE-MORE-RECORDS = 'NO '. As we will see in 200-WAGE-ROUTINE, this condition is only met when an AT END occurs, which means there are no more records to process. Thus 200-WAGE-ROUTINE is executed repeatedly until all input records have been processed.

The following symbol is called a predefined process, meaning that it is described in a separate module:

f. Files are then closed and the run is terminated.

6. The module called `200-WAGE-ROUTINE` is repeatedly executed from the main module until there are no more records to process. For each record, the following operations are performed:
   a. The input fields are moved to the output area.
   b. The wages are calculated.
   c. Another record is read; but if there are no more records to process, the letters `'NO '` are moved to the field called `ARE-THERE-MORE-RECORDS`.
   d. This module, as all modules, begins and ends with a terminal symbol:

Pseudocode is a separate planning tool used by many programmers instead of a flowchart for planning the logic to be used in a program. The following are basic rules for reading the pseudocode in Figure 1.7.

RULES FOR INTERPRETING PSEUDOCODE

General Rules
1. A pseudocode begins with a `START` and ends with a `STOP`.
2. All instructions are read in sequence.
3. The instructions between the `PERFORM ... ENDPERFORM` in the illustration are executed repeatedly `UNTIL` there are no more records to process.

Finally, Figure 1.10 illustrates a **hierarchy** or **structure chart,** which shows the relationships among modules in a program. This figure illustrates that there are two modules or paragraphs and that `200-WAGE-ROUTINE` is the paragraph executed from `100-MAIN-MODULE`. That is, within `100-MAIN-MODULE` there is a `PERFORM 200-WAGE-ROUTINE` statement.

Figure 1.10
Hierarchy or structure chart
for sample program.

We will see in Chapter 5 that structure charts are extremely useful for illustrating the logic flow in a program with many `PERFORM` statements.

CHAPTER SUMMARY
A. The Nature of COBOL
    1. The most widespread commercial programming language in use today.
    2. COBOL is an abbreviation for Common Business Oriented Language.
    3. It is an English-like language.
    4. It is a self-documenting language.

5. The American National Standards (ANS) versions of COBOL are 1968, 1974, and 1985. (This text focuses on COBOL 85 and indicates how it differs from COBOL 74.)

B. Program Preparation and Debugging
   1. Get program specifications from the analyst.
   2. Use planning tools—flowcharts, pseudocode, hierarchy charts—for program design.
   3. Code the program.
   4. Test the program using debugging techniques.
      a. Desk check.
      b. Correct syntax errors.
      c. Perform program walkthroughs.
      d. Check for logic errors after program execution.
   5. Document the program.

C. Techniques for Improving Program Design
   1. Structured programming.
      a. Referred to as GO-TO-less programming.
      b. Structured programs are subdivided into paragraphs or modules.
   2. Top-Down Programming.
      a. Major modules or procedures are coded before minor ones.
      b. Analogous to developing an outline before writing a report—the organization and structure are most important; details are filled in later.

D. The COBOL Divisions
   1. IDENTIFICATION DIVISION.
      a. Identifies the program to the computer system.
      b. May provide documentation information as well.
      c. PROGRAM-ID is the only required entry within the division.
   2. ENVIRONMENT DIVISION.
      a. Indicates the computer equipment to be used with the program.
      b. Assigns a file-name to each file used in the program, and specifies the device that the file will use.
   3. DATA DIVISION.
      a. Defines and describes the formats of all input, output, and work areas used for processing.
      b. FILE SECTION
         (1) Each file-name defined in the ENVIRONMENT DIVISION must be described in an FD in the DATA DIVISION.
         (2) Each record format within every file is defined as an 01 entry.
         (3) Fields within each record are described with a PICTURE clause that specifies the size and type of data.
      c. WORKING-STORAGE SECTION
         (1) Defines any work areas needed for processing.
         (2) An end-of-file indicator is coded in the WORKING-STORAGE SECTION; we will refer to this field as ARE-THERE-MORE-RECORDS. In our examples, the field called ARE-THERE-MORE-RECORDS will contain the value 'YES' when there are input records to process, and a value of 'NO ' when there is no more data.
   4. PROCEDURE DIVISION.
      a. Is subdivided into paragraphs or modules.
      b. Includes all instructions that are required to process input and produce output.
      c. All instructions are executed in sequence, but a PERFORM transfers control to another paragraph; after a paragraph is executed with a PERFORM, control returns to the next instruction, in sequence, following the PERFORM.
      d. Main module or paragraph.
         The following are typical entries in a main module.
         (1) Files are designated as INPUT or OUTPUT and activated in an OPEN statement.

> (2) An initial READ brings the first record into storage.
> (3) PERFORM paragraph-name UNTIL ARE-THERE-MORE-RECORDS = 'NO ' temporarily transfers control to some calculation or processing module that processes a record and then reads the next record; this processing routine is repeated until there is no more data.
> (4) A CLOSE statement deactivates all the files.
> (5) A STOP RUN terminates processing.
>
> e. Calculation or processing paragraphs.
> (1) Calculation or processing paragraphs are executed when a statement in the main module indicates PERFORM paragraph-name.
> (2) A calculation or processing paragraph is required to process each input record and read subsequent records.
> (3) This calculation or processing paragraph is executed until there is no more data, that is, until ARE-THERE-MORE-RECORDS = 'NO '.

CHAPTER SELF-TEST

At the end of each chapter there is a self-test that covers the material in the entire chapter. The solutions follow the test.

1. All COBOL programs are composed of ___(no.)___ divisions.
2. The names of these divisons are _____ , _____ , _____ , and _____ .
3. The function of the IDENTIFICATION DIVISION is to _____ .
4. The function of the ENVIRONMENT DIVISION is to _____ .
5. The function of the DATA DIVISION is to _____ .
6. The function of the PROCEDURE DIVISION is to _____ .
7. Another term for incoming data is _____ .
8. Another term for outgoing information is _____ .
9. _____ , _____ , and _____ are examples of computer input media.
10. Two techniques for simplifying the design of a COBOL program and facilitating debugging are called _____ and _____ .
11. (T or F) Structured programs are sometimes called GO-TO-less programs.
12. A(n) _____ statement indicates which files are input and which are output.

Consider Figure 1.9 for the following.

13. The execution of a COBOL program is terminated when a _____ statement is encountered.
14. The only entry required in the IDENTIFICATION DIVISION is _____ .
15. (T or F) A division name appears on a line by itself and ends with a period.

Solutions
1. four
2. IDENTIFICATION; ENVIRONMENT; DATA; PROCEDURE
3. identify the program
4. describe the equipment to be used in the program
5. describe the input, output, and work areas used in the program
6. define the instructions and operations necessary to convert input data into output
7. input
8. output
9. Magnetic disk; magnetic tape; punched cards; floppy disk; terminal data
10. structured programming; top-down programming
11. T
12. OPEN

13. STOP RUN
14. PROGRAM-ID
15. T

KEY TERMS

American National
   Standards Institute
   (ANSI)
Compile
Compiler
Debugging
Desk checking
Documentation
Enhancements
Field
File
Flowchart
Hierarchy chart

High-order position
Implied decimal point
Input
Logic error
Low-order position
Machine language
Module
Object program
Output
Printer Spacing Chart
Program
Program specifications

Programmer
Pseudocode
Record
Record layout form
Source program
Structure chart
Structured programming
Symbolic programming
   language
Syntax error
Top-down programming
User
Walkthrough

REVIEW QUESTIONS

T F

I. True-False Questions

1. A COBOL program that compiles without any errors will always run properly.
2. Programs written in COBOL need not be compiled.
3. COBOL programs must be converted into machine language before execution can occur.
4. Although COBOL is a commercial programming language, it contains advanced mathematical functions that can be used for highly sophisticated scientific problems.
5. COBOL may be used only on a small number of commercial computers.
6. A COBOL program typically contains four divisions.
7. The sequence in which the divisions in a COBOL program are written is IDENTIFICATION, DATA, ENVIRONMENT, PROCEDURE.
8. The division that changes depending on the computer equipment used is the DATA DIVISION.
9. The division that seems to require the least programming effort is the IDENTIFICATION DIVISION.
10. Instructions are coded in the PROCEDURE DIVISION.

II. General Questions

1. Define the following terms.
   (a) Program.
   (b) Compiler.
   (c) Source program.
   (d) Object program.
2. State the differences between a symbolic programming language and a machine language.
3. State the major reasons why COBOL is such a popular language.
4. What is the meaning of the term "structured programming"?
5. What is the meaning of the term "ANS COBOL"?

6. Indicate the purpose of each of the following.
   (a) IDENTIFICATION DIVISION   (c) DATA DIVISION
   (b) ENVIRONMENT DIVISION   (d) PROCEDURE DIVISION
7. What is the meaning of the term "syntax error"?
8. What is the purpose of the PICTURE clause?
9. What is the purpose of the SELECT statement?
10. What is the purpose of the WORKING-STORAGE SECTION?

PROGRAMMING ASSIGNMENTS

Completing the following assignments will help you learn how to enter a program on your system. If terminals are used at your computer center, enter one or more of these programs, compile, and debug them. If cards are used at your computer center, key-punch a program, compile, and debug it.

Before you begin, you will need to be provided with the following system-dependent information.

A. The method of accessing a computer at your center.
B. The job control requirements for entering a program, compiling, and executing it.
C. The ASSIGN clause requirements for SELECT statements.

To run the program, you may use test data supplied by an instructor or you may create your own input.

1. Key in and run the program in Figure 1.8 using your own sample data file.
2. Figure 1.11 is an illustration of a sample COBOL program.
   (a) Describe the input by providing a layout of the input record.
   (b) Describe the output by providing a layout of the output record.
   (c) Describe, in your own words, the processing that converts the input data into output.
   (d) Key in and run the program using your own sample data file.
3. Figure 1.12 is an illustration of a sample COBOL program.
   (a) Describe the input by providing a layout of the input record.
   (b) Describe the output by providing a layout of the output record.
   (c) Describe, in your own words, the processing that converts the input data into output.
   (d) Key in and run the program using your own sample data file.

Figure 1.11

Program for Programming
Assignment 2.

```
00101    IDENTIFICATION DIVISION.
00102    PROGRAM-ID.   PROBLEM2.
00103    ENVIRONMENT DIVISION.
00104    INPUT-OUTPUT SECTION.
00105    FILE-CONTROL.   SELECT SALES-FILE ASSIGN TO TAPE-1.
00106                    SELECT PRINT-FILE ASSIGN TO PRINTER.
00107    DATA DIVISION.
00108    FILE SECTION.
00109    FD  SALES-FILE LABEL RECORDS ARE STANDARD.
00110    01  SALES-REC.
00111        05  NAME-IN                 PICTURE X(15).
00112        05  AMOUNT-OF-SALES-IN      PICTURE 999V99.
00113    FD  PRINT-FILE LABEL RECORDS ARE OMITTED.
00114    01  PRINT-REC.
00115        05  FILLER                  PICTURE X(21).
00116        05  NAME-OUT                PICTURE X(15).
00117        05  FILLER                  PICTURE X(20).
00118        05  AMT-COMMISSION-OUT      PICTURE 99.99.
00119        05  FILLER                  PICTURE X(72).
00120    WORKING-STORAGE SECTION.
00121    01  ARE-THERE-MORE-RECORDS      PICTURE XXX VALUE 'YES'.
00122    PROCEDURE DIVISION.
00123    100-MAIN-MODULE.
00124        OPEN INPUT SALES-FILE
00125             OUTPUT PRINT-FILE.
00126        READ SALES-FILE
00127             AT END MOVE 'NO ' TO ARE-THERE-MORE-RECORDS.
00128        PERFORM 200-COMMISSION-RTN
00129             UNTIL ARE-THERE-MORE-RECORDS = 'NO '.
00130        CLOSE SALES-FILE
00131              PRINT-FILE.
00132        STOP RUN.
00133    200-COMMISSION-RTN.
00134        MOVE SPACES TO PRINT-REC.
00135        MOVE NAME-IN TO NAME-OUT.
00136        IF  AMOUNT-OF-SALES-IN IS GREATER THAN 100.00
00137            MULTIPLY .03 BY AMOUNT-OF-SALES-IN
00138                GIVING AMT-COMMISSION-OUT
00139        ELSE
00140            MULTIPLY .02 BY AMOUNT-OF-SALES-IN
00141                GIVING AMT-COMMISSION-OUT.
00142        WRITE PRINT-REC.
00143        READ SALES-FILE
00144             AT END MOVE 'NO ' TO ARE-THERE-MORE-RECORDS.
```

COBOL Program Sheet

System			Punching Instructions		Sheet	of
Program	PROBLEM #3		Graphic			Identification
Programmer	R. STERN	Date	Punch	Card Form #	73	80

```
001 01     IDENTIFICATION DIVISION.
001 02     PROGRAM-ID. PROBLEM3.
001 03     ENVIRONMENT DIVISION.
001 04     INPUT-OUTPUT SECTION.
001 05     FILE-CONTROL.    SELECT PAYROLL-IN ASSIGN TO READER.
001 06                     SELECT PAYROLL-OUT ASSIGN TO TAPE-1.
001 07     DATA DIVISION.
001 08     FILE SECTION.
001 09     FD  PAYROLL-IN  LABEL RECORDS ARE OMITTED.
001 10     01  PAYROLL-REC.
001 11         05 EMPLOYEE-NUMBER-IN    PICTURE 9(5).
001 12         05 EMPLOYEE-NAME-IN      PICTURE X(20).
001 13         05 LOCATION-CODE-IN      PICTURE 9999.
001 14         05 ANNUAL-SALARY-IN      PICTURE 9(6).
001 15     FD  PAYROLL-OUT LABEL RECORDS ARE STANDARD.
001 16     01  RECORD-OUT.
001 17         05 EMPLOYEE-NUMBER-OUT   PICTURE 9(5).
001 18         05 EMPLOYEE-NAME-OUT     PICTURE X(20).
001 19         05 ANNUAL-SALARY-OUT     PICTURE 9(6).
001 20     WORKING-STORAGE SECTION.
00121      01  ARE-THERE-MORE-RECORDS  PICTURE X(3) VALUE 'YES'.
00122      PROCEDURE DIVISION.
00123      100-MAIN-MODULE.
00124          OPEN INPUT PAYROLL-IN
00125               OUTPUT PAYROLL-OUT.
00126          READ PAYROLL-IN
00127              AT END MOVE 'NO ' TO ARE-THERE-MORE-RECORDS.
00128          PERFORM 200-WAGE-ROUTINE
00129              UNTIL ARE-THERE-MORE-RECORDS = 'NO '.
00130          CLOSE PAYROLL-IN
00131                PAYROLL-OUT.
00132          STOP RUN.
00133      200-WAGE-ROUTINE.
00134          MOVE EMPLOYEE-NUMBER-IN TO EMPLOYEE-NUMBER-OUT.
00135          MOVE EMPLOYEE-NAME-IN TO EMPLOYEE-NAME-OUT.
00136          ADD 1000, ANNUAL-SALARY-IN
00137               GIVING ANNUAL-SALARY-OUT.
00138          WRITE RECORD-OUT.
00139          READ PAYROLL-IN
00140              AT END MOVE 'NO ' TO ARE-THERE-MORE-RECORDS.
```

Figure 1.12
Program for Programming
Assignment 3.

2

COBOL Language Fundamentals: The IDENTIFICATION and ENVIRONMENT DIVISIONS

OBJECTIVES

To familiarize you with

1. The basic structure of a COBOL program.
2. General coding and format rules.
3. IDENTIFICATION and ENVIRONMENT DIVISION entries.

I. Basic Structure of a COBOL Program

A. Coding a Source Program

You will recall that *all* COBOL programs consist of *four divisions*. In the next few chapters, we discuss each division in detail. At the end of this discussion, you will be able to write elementary programs using all the divisions of a COBOL program. Before we begin, however, some basic rules for coding these programs must be understood.

COBOL programs are generally written on **coding** or **program sheets** before they are keyed into a computer. Programmers who key in programs without first writing them on coding sheets generally find that the debugging process takes more time. Figure 2.1 illustrates a coding sheet and includes some notes indicating the purpose of various parts of the sheet.

The coding sheet has space for 80 columns or positions of information. Each *line* of a program sheet will be keyed into one line on a terminal.

Most COBOL program sheets have 20 numbered lines with serial or line numbers 01–20 respectively in columns 4–6. They also have four or more additional unnumbered lines that can be used for insertions in case a programmer has accidentally omitted one or more lines. More on this later.

For every line written on the coding sheet, we will key in one line on a terminal. The entire program is referred to as the *COBOL source program*.

B. The Coding Sheet Itself

1. The Main Body of the Coding Sheet

Let us examine the COBOL coding sheet more closely. The main body of the form is subdivided into 72 positions or columns. For each coding line, the information or COBOL statement in columns 1–72 will be keyed into positions 1–72, respectively, on the terminal. Figure 2.2 illustrates how an excerpt of a COBOL program sheet is converted into two lines of code.

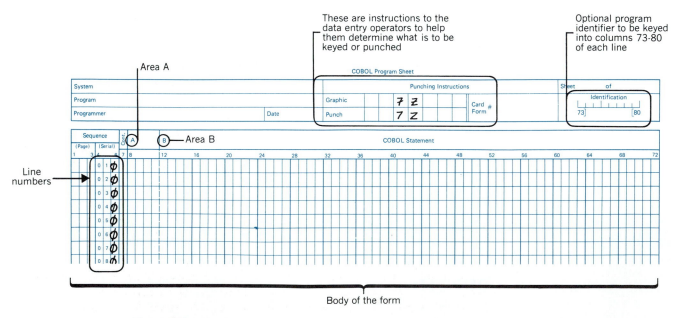

Figure 2.1
Main body of a COBOL coding sheet.

Figure 2.2
Using a terminal to enter a
COBOL program.

2. Optional Entries: Identification and Page and Serial Numbers

On the top right side of the coding sheet there is provision for a program identification, labeled positions 73–80. This identification entry may be entered into positions 73–80 of all lines keyed from this form.

The rest of the data recorded on the top of the form is *not* keyed into the source program. It is for informational purposes only.

The identification entry, positions 73–80, and the page and serial numbers, positions 1–6, are *optional* in a COBOL program. Both, however, can be extremely useful for ensuring that a program is sequenced properly and that one program is not intermixed with another. We sequence programs by line or serial numbers using multiples of 10. For example, we start with line or serial number 010, then use line 020, and so on. If you look at a coding sheet, you will see that the first two positions of this serial number (01–20) are preprinted on the form. Typically, you would add a 0 to each serial number to get line 010, 020, and so on. In this way, we have enough extra numbers so that it is an easy task to insert lines in their proper place.

When line numbers are supplied, insertions can be easily made. If a line is inadvertently omitted between lines 020 and 030, for example, we can give it a line number of 024 or 025.

Page number generally refers to the coding sheet number. The first page is usually numbered 001, the second 002, and so on. Programmers frequently omit page and line numbers because the compiler automatically assigns sequence numbers to each program line.

Like page and serial numbers, the identification field is optional and is frequently not used. It can sometimes be useful, particularly when a data entry operator, rather than the programmer, keys in the program. That is, a coded identification entry in columns 73–80 may make it easy to distinguish one keyed program from another. But when programmers key their own programs, they most frequently omit this entry.

3. Column 7: For Continuation of Nonnumeric Literals, Comments, and Starting a New Page

Column 7 of the program sheet is a **continuation position** labeled CONT. on the form. It has three primary purposes: (1) it is used for the continuation of nonnumeric literals, as we will see in Chapter 7; (2) it can be used for designating an entire line as a comment by coding an * (asterisk) in column 7; and (3) it can be used to force the printing of subsequent instructions on the next page of the source listing.

a. Comments.   Comment lines are useful for providing documentary information on how a program will process data. Comments are also used to remind the programmer about some specific aspects of the program. The following illustrates the use of a comment in a COBOL program:

```
IDENTIFICATION DIVISION.
PROGRAM-ID. SAMPLE.
*************************************************************
*   THIS PROGRAM READS TWO INPUT FILES, COMPARES THE PART   *
*   NUMBERS, AND PRINTS PART NUMBERS MISSING FROM EITHER     *
*   FILE.                                                    *
*************************************************************
```

We will use comments in our programs to clarify the logic used. Also, in many of our programs, we will insert a *blank comment line* with an * in column 7 just to separate divisions; this use of comment lines makes the program easier to read. If column 7 of any line contains an *, that entire line is not compiled, but is printed on the listing for documentation purposes only. A blank line could be used in place of a comment line to separate entries in a program.

b. Page-Eject with a Slash (/) in Column 7.   Column 7 can also be used for causing the printer to skip to the next page when the source listing is being printed. In long programs, for example, we might want each division on a separate page. To skip to a new page after each division, insert a line that is blank except for a slash (/) in column 7.

4. Areas A and B

Positions 8–72 of a standard COBOL program contain program statements. Note, however, that column 8 is labeled *A*, and column 12 is labeled *B*. These are referred to as *Areas.* Certain entries must begin in Area A and others must begin in Area B.

If an entry is to be coded in **Area A,** it may begin in position 8, 9, 10, or 11. Most often, Area A entries begin in position 8. If an entry is to be coded in **Area B,** it may begin anywhere after position 11. That is, it may begin in position 12, 13, 14, and so on. Note that margin rules specify the *beginning* point of entries. A word that must *begin* in Area A may *extend* into Area B.

Example   AUTHOR, a paragraph-name in the IDENTIFICATION DIVISION, must begin in Area A. Any entry referring to AUTHOR may then follow in Area B as in the following:

```
 A   B
 7 8    12      16      20      24      28      32      36      40      44      48      52      56      60      64      68      72
 AUTHOR. NANCY STERN.
```

The A of AUTHOR is placed in column 8, or Area A. The word itself extends into Area B. The next entry must begin in Area B or in any position after column 11. In our example, the author's name begins in position 16.

C. Types of COBOL Entries

COBOL programs are divided into **divisions.** The divisions have fixed names: IDENTIFICATION, ENVIRONMENT, DATA, and PROCEDURE. They must *always* appear in that order in a program. Some divisions are subdivided into **sections.** The DATA DIVISION, for example, which describes all storage areas for data needed in the program, is divided into two main sections: the FILE SECTION and the WORKING-STORAGE SECTION. The FILE SECTION of the DATA DI-

VISION describes the input and output areas, and the WORKING-STORAGE SEC-TION of the DATA DIVISION describes the intermediate work areas necessary for processing. Each section may be further subdivided into **paragraphs.**

All other entries in the program are considered COBOL **statements.** A state-ment or series of statements that ends with a period is referred to as a **sentence.**

TYPES OF COBOL ENTRIES

Divisions, sections, and paragraphs begin in Area A

Divisions
Examples: IDENTIFICATION DIVISION.
ENVIRONMENT DIVISION.
DATA DIVISION.
PROCEDURE DIVISION.

Sections
Examples: FILE SECTION.
WORKING-STORAGE SECTION.

Paragraphs
Examples: PROGRAM-ID.
200-CALC-RTN.

Statements and sentences begin in Area B

Statements and Sentences
Examples: MOVE NAME-IN TO NAME-OUT.
ADD AMT-IN TO TOTAL.

MARGIN RULES

1. Division, section, and paragraph-names begin in Area A.
2. All other statements, clauses, and sentences begin in Area B.

We will see that the great majority of COBOL entries, including all PROCE-DURE DIVISION instructions, begin in Area B.

Figure 2.3 provides an example of these margin rules. The ENVIRONMENT DIVISION entry begins in Area A, as does the CONFIGURATION SECTION entry. SOURCE-COMPUTER and OBJECT-COMPUTER are paragraph-names, which must also begin in Area A. SOURCE-COMPUTER and OBJECT-COMPUTER must have COBOL statements following them in Area B, either on the same line or the next line. Each entry is followed by a period.

Note that ENVIRONMENT DIVISION, CONFIGURATION SECTION, and SOURCE-COMPUTER are each followed by a period. A sentence, which consists of a statement or series of statements, must also end with a period.

Division and section names *must* always appear on a line with no other entry. Paragraph-names may appear on the same line as statements. Keep in mind that each period must be followed by at least one space. The following, then, is acceptable.

```
ENVIRONMENT DIVISION.
CONFIGURATION SECTION.
SOURCE-COMPUTER. VAX-11.
OBJECT-COMPUTER. VAX-11.
INPUT-OUTPUT SECTION.
FILE-CONTROL. SELECT SALES-FILE ASSIGN TO DISK1.
```

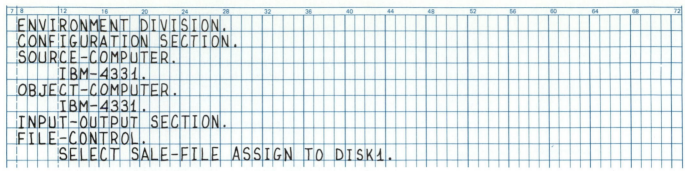

Figure 2.3
Illustration of Area rules.

In the PROCEDURE DIVISION, several sentences may appear on one line, but we will use the convention of coding one statement per line for the sake of clarity and for ease of debugging. This method of coding is also considered good style.

REVIEW OF COBOL CODING FORM		
Columns	**Use**	**Explanation**
1–6	Sequence numbers or Page and Line numbers (optional)	Used to ensure that lines are sequenced properly.
7	Continuation, comment, or starting a new page	Used to continue nonnumeric literals (see Chapter 7), to denote a line as a comment (* in column 7), or to cause the printer to skip to a new page when printing the source listing (use a / in column 7).
8–11	Area A	Specific entries such as DIVISION, SECTION, and paragraph-names must begin in Area A.
12–72	Area B	Most COBOL entries, particularly those in the PROCEDURE DIVISION, are coded in Area B.
73–80	Program identification (optional)	Used to identify the program.

REVIEW OF CODING RULES

1. Division and Section Names
   a. Begin in Area A.
   b. End with a period.
   c. Must appear on a line with no other entries.

2. Paragraph-names
   a. Begin in Area A.
   b. End with a period.
   c. May appear on a line by themselves or with other entries; must always be followed by at least one space.
3. Sentences
   a. Begin in Area B.
   b. End with a period.
   c. May appear on a line by itself or with other entries; must always be followed by at least one space.
   d. A sentence consists of a statement or series of statements.

D. Getting Started

After your program is coded, you will usually key it into the computer using a terminal. If you are using a mainfame or minicomputer, you will need to obtain the log-on and authorization codes that will enable you to access the computer. You will also need to learn the system commands for accessing the COBOL compiler and executing COBOL programs.

In most instances, you will use a *text editor* for entering the program. It will enable you to easily correct any mistakes you make. Most text editors have common features, such as commands for deleting lines, adding lines, and changing or replacing entries. The ways in which these features are implemented, however, may vary. Appendix C provides some details about system commands and text editors in general. In particular, we focus on system commands and text editors used with the IBM 4300 series and the DEC VAX computers.

In summary, then, before you enter a program on a mainframe you will need to learn (1) the appropriate log-on codes and system commands for translating and running COBOL programs and (2) how to use a text editor.

If you are using a microcomputer, you can use *any* text editor or word processing package for creating your COBOL program. Then you will need to consult a user's manual for accessing your COBOL compiler. Popular micro-based packages are highlighted in Appendix D.

Self-Test

1. COBOL programs are written on _____ .
2. Each line of the coding sheet corresponds to one _____ on a terminal.
3. The entire program keyed from the coding sheets is called the _____ .
4. The optional entries on the coding sheet are _____ and _____ .
5. If an entry must begin in Area A, it may begin in position _____ ; if an entry must begin in Area B, it may begin in position _____ .
6. In the order in which they must appear, the four divisions of a COBOL program are _____ , _____ , _____ , and _____ .
7. All _____ , _____ , and _____ names must be coded beginning in Area A.
8. Most entries such as PROCEDURE DIVISION instructions are coded in Area _____ .
9. All sentences must end with a _____ , which is followed by a _____ .
10. _____ and _____ must each appear on a separate line. All other entries may have several statements on the same line.

Solutions

1. coding or program sheets
2. line
3. COBOL source program
4. identification (positions 73–80); sequence, or page and serial numbers (positions 1–6)
5. 8, 9, 10, or 11; 12, 13, 14, and so on
6. IDENTIFICATION; ENVIRONMENT; DATA; PROCEDURE
7. division; section; paragraph-
8. B
9. period; space
10. Division names; section names

II. Coding Requirements of the IDENTIFICATION DIVISION

A. Paragraphs in the IDENTIFICATION DIVISION

The **IDENTIFICATION DIVISION** is the smallest, simplest, and least significant division of a COBOL program. As the name indicates, it supplies identifying data about the program.

The IDENTIFICATION DIVISION has *no* effect on the execution of the program but is, nevertheless, *required* as a means of identifying the program to the computer.

The IDENTIFICATION DIVISION is divided into paragraphs, not sections. The following paragraphs may be coded:

Format

```
IDENTIFICATION DIVISION.
PROGRAM-ID.   program-name.
[AUTHOR.   [comment-entry] . . .]
[INSTALLATION.   [comment-entry] . . .]
[DATE-WRITTEN.   [comment-entry] . . .]
[DATE-COMPILED.   [comment-entry] . . .]
[SECURITY.   [comment-entry] . . .]
```

The division name, IDENTIFICATION DIVISION, is coded in Area A. Paragraph-names are also coded in Area A, and each must be followed by a period. The above format is the same as the one that appears in COBOL reference manuals. The next section discusses the rules for interpreting instruction formats such as the preceding.

B. Understanding Instruction Formats as They Appear in Reference Manuals

Programming texts, such as this one, are written to help you learn the basic rules of a language. They do not, in general, attempt to be complete because that would require many more pages.

To learn *all* the rules of a language and all the options available, you would consult a *reference manual* that is available for each major language. Reference manuals are very concise and, as a result, are often difficult to read. Nonetheless, most programmers consult them for reference purposes as the need arises.

Like reference manuals, we will use the basic *instruction format* for presenting the syntax of a language. This will not only familiarize you with COBOL's syntax but will help you to read and understand a COBOL reference manual with relative ease.

The following are instruction format rules. These will assist you in interpreting the format for the IDENTIFICATION DIVISION entries just described.

RULES FOR INTERPRETING INSTRUCTION FORMATS

1. Capitalized words are COBOL reserved words with special meaning to the compiler.
2. Lowercase words represent programmer-supplied entries.
3. Underlined words are required in the paragraph.
4. If punctuation is specified in the format, it is required.
5. Brackets [ ] mean the clause or paragraph is optional.
6. The use of dots or ellipses (. . .) means that additional entries of the same type may be included if desired.

These rules appear on the inside of the front cover of this text for ease of reference.

As noted, understanding how to read instruction formats will help you decipher COBOL reference manuals when the need arises. We will use simplified formats here so as not to overwhelm you with too much detail. Thus, all our instruction formats will be correct but not necessarily complete. Appendix A includes the full instruction formats for most COBOL entries.

C. Examples

The instruction format for the IDENTIFICATION DIVISION entries indicates that the only entry *required* is the **PROGRAM-ID**. That is, COBOL programs must be identified by a program name. All other entries are enclosed in brackets, meaning that they are optional.

In summary, the first two entries of a program must be IDENTIFICATION DIVISION and PROGRAM-ID, with an appropriate program name as follows:

PROGRAM-ID is followed by a period and then at least one space. The program name itself is coded in Area B. We use names of eight characters or less, letters and digits only, because such names are accepted on *all* systems.

The two entries may also be coded as follows:

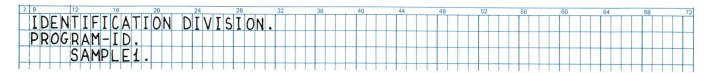

Since PROGRAM-ID is a paragraph-name, the user-defined program name SAMPLE1 may appear *on the same line* as PROGRAM-ID, or *on the next line*. In either case, PROGRAM-ID and the program name must each be followed by a period.

The other paragraph-names listed in the instruction format are bracketed [ ] and are therefore optional. They can be used to help document the program. If you include any of these, however, they must be coded in the sequence specified in the instruction format. Each paragraph-name is followed by a period and at least one space. The actual entry following the paragraph-name is treated as a comment and can contain *any* character including a period. The instruction format calls this a "comment-entry."

If used, **AUTHOR** would include the name of the programmer; **INSTALLATION** would be the name of the company or the computer organization; **DATE-WRITTEN** is the date the program was coded. For most ANS COBOL users, the **DATE-COMPILED** paragraph can be coded with an actual date entered but is more often written simply as:

When DATE-COMPILED is coded *without* a comment-entry, the compiler itself will automatically *fill in the actual date of compilation.* Thus, if the program is compiled three different times on three separate dates, it is not necessary to keep revising this entry. The compiler itself will list the actual date of compilation if the entry DATE-COMPILED appears on a line by itself. Because of this feature, DATE-COMPILED is considered one of the most useful options in this division.

SECURITY would simply indicate whether the program is classified or confidential. This coding would not, however, actually control access to the program. That would be done by passwords or other job control techniques.

In addition to PROGRAM-ID, any, or all, of the preceding paragraphs may be included in the IDENTIFICATION DIVISION. As paragraph-names, these entries are coded in Area A.

The IDENTIFICATION DIVISION, as well as the other divisions, frequently includes comments that describe the program. Recall that an * in column 7 may be used to designate any line as a comment line. Comments are extremely useful for documentation purposes and for making programs user-friendly or easy for noncomputer professionals to read.

The following is an example of IDENTIFICATION DIVISION coding:

```
IDENTIFICATION DIVISION.
PROGRAM-ID. EXHIBIT1.
AUTHOR. R. A. STERN.
INSTALLATION. COMPANY ABC
             ACCOUNTING DEPT.
DATE-WRITTEN. JAN. 1, 1989.
DATE-COMPILED.
SECURITY  CONFIDENTIAL.
*  THIS PROGRAM WILL CREATE A MASTER PAYROLL FILE, EDITING   *
*  THE INPUT DATA AND PRODUCING AN ERROR LIST.               *
```

The comment entry for INSTALLATION, as well as the other entries, may extend to several lines. Each entry *within* a *paragraph* must, however, be coded in Area B.

Self-Test

1. The first two entries of a COBOL program must always be _____ and _____ .

2. Each of these entries must be followed by a _____ , which, in turn, must be followed by a _____ .

3. The preceding entries are both coded beginning in Area _____ .

4. Code the IDENTIFICATION DIVISION for a program called EXPENSES for a corporation, Dynamic Data Devices, Inc., written July 15, 1988. This program has a security classification and is available to authorized personnel only. It produces a weekly listing by department of all operating expenses.

5. The DATE-COMPILED paragraph usually does not include an entry because _____ .

Solutions   1.

2. period; space or blank
3. A
4. The following is a *suggested* solution:

```
IDENTIFICATION DIVISION,
PROGRAM-ID, EXPENSES,
AUTHOR, N, B, STERN,
INSTALLATION, DYNAMIC DATA DEVICES, INC,
DATE-WRITTEN, 7/15/88,
SECURITY, AUTHORIZED PERSONNEL ONLY,
*    THIS PROGRAM PRODUCES A WEEKLY LIST BY DEPARTMENT    *
*    OF ALL OPERATING EXPENSES,                           *
```

Note: Only the IDENTIFICATION DIVISION and PROGRAM-ID are required.

5. the computer itself can supply the date of the compilation (The current date is stored in the CPU when processing begins for the day.)

III. The Sections of the ENVIRONMENT DIVISION

The **ENVIRONMENT DIVISION** is the only machine-dependent division of a COBOL program. It supplies information about the hardware or *computer equipment* to be used in the program. That is, the entries in this division will be dependent on (1) the computer system and (2) the specific devices used in the program.

The ENVIRONMENT DIVISION is composed of two sections:

> **SECTIONS OF THE** ENVIRONMENT DIVISION
>
> CONFIGURATION SECTION.
> INPUT-OUTPUT SECTION.

The CONFIGURATION SECTION supplies information concerning the computer on which the COBOL program will be compiled and executed. The INPUT-OUTPUT SECTION supplies information concerning the specific devices used in the program. For example, terminals, printers, disk drives, and tape drives are devices that are typically referred to in the INPUT-OUTPUT SECTION of the ENVIRONMENT DIVISION.

The ENVIRONMENT DIVISION is the only division of a COBOL program that will change significantly if the program is to be run on a different computer. Since computers have various models and equipment, each computer center or installation will require different ENVIRONMENT DIVISION specifications. The entries coded in the ENVIRONMENT DIVISION are generally supplied to the programmer by the installation. Throughout this discussion, we will use some *sample* statements, keeping in mind that such entries are dependent on the actual computer used and the devices that will be accessed by the program. You will need to ask your computer manager or instructor for the device specifications used at your computer center.

A. CONFIGURATION SECTION

The **CONFIGURATION SECTION** of the ENVIRONMENT DIVISION indicates: (1) the **SOURCE-COMPUTER**—the computer that will be used for compiling the program—and (2) the **OBJECT-COMPUTER**—the computer that will be used for executing or running the program. SOURCE-COMPUTER and OBJECT-COMPUTER provide documentation information only.

Recall that this text focuses on the two versions of standard COBOL, the 1974 standard that we call COBOL 74 and the newer 1985 standard that we call COBOL 85. Officially, the CONFIGURATION SECTION is required for COBOL 74 users and is optional with COBOL 85. In actuality, however, most COBOL 74 compilers include an *enhancement* that permits the user to omit this section if desired. We will briefly consider the CONFIGURATION SECTION, but generally we omit it from our programs.

As noted, all section names, like division names, are coded in Area A. Thus, the CONFIGURATION SECTION, if coded, will follow the ENVIRONMENT DIVISION entry in Area A. SOURCE-COMPUTER and OBJECT-COMPUTER, as paragraph-names, would also be coded in Area A.

The SOURCE- and OBJECT-COMPUTER entries specify:

ENTRIES FOR SOURCE-COMPUTER **AND**
OBJECT-COMPUTER **PARAGRAPHS**

1. The computer manufacturer.
2. The computer number.
3. The computer model number, if needed.

Consider the following sample entries:

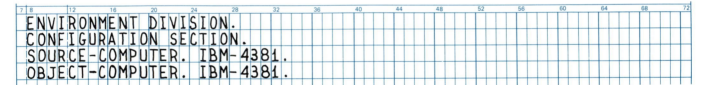

```
ENVIRONMENT DIVISION.
CONFIGURATION SECTION.
SOURCE-COMPUTER. IBM-4381.
OBJECT-COMPUTER. IBM-4381.
```

Each paragraph-name is directly followed by a period and then a space. The designated computer, IBM-4381, is also followed by a period.

In the example, the source and object computers are the same. In general, this will be the case, since compilation and execution are usually performed on the same computer. If, however, the program will be compiled on one model computer and executed, at some future time, on another model computer, these entries will differ, as in the following example.

Example

```
ENVIRONMENT DIVISION.
CONFIGURATION SECTION.
SOURCE-COMPUTER. VAX-11.
OBJECT-COMPUTER. HP-3000.
```

In this illustration, the program will be compiled on a VAX computer and executed on a Hewlett Packard 3000.

A third paragraph that is optional in the CONFIGURATION SECTION is called SPECIAL-NAMES. We discuss the SPECIAL-NAMES paragraph of the CONFIGURATION SECTION in Chapter 19, which focuses on special devices used for reading or displaying data.

B. INPUT-OUTPUT SECTION

The **INPUT-OUTPUT SECTION** of the ENVIRONMENT DIVISION follows the CONFIGURATION SECTION (if coded) and supplies information concerning the input and output devices used in the program. In the next section, we will discuss the **FILE-CONTROL** paragraph of the INPUT-OUTPUT SECTION. In this paragraph, a file-name is selected for each file to be used in the program; in addition, each file-name selected is assigned to a device.

IV. Assigning Files to Devices in the ENVIRONMENT DIVISION

A. Overall Format

Thus far, we have the following entries that may be coded in the ENVIRONMENT DIVISION:

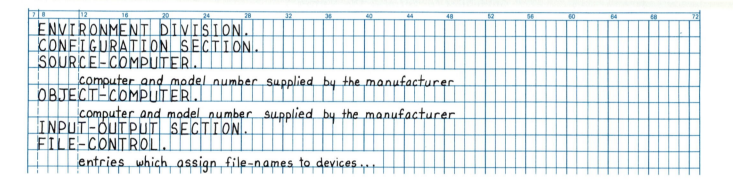

```
ENVIRONMENT DIVISION.
CONFIGURATION SECTION.
SOURCE-COMPUTER.
     computer and model number supplied by the manufacturer
OBJECT-COMPUTER.
     computer and model number supplied by the manufacturer
INPUT-OUTPUT SECTION.
FILE-CONTROL.
     entries which assign file-names to devices...
```

The FILE-CONTROL paragraph consists of **SELECT** statements, each of which is coded in Area B followed by a period. A SELECT statement defines a file-name and assigns a device to that file. A **file** is the major collection of data for a given application. Typically, we have an input file and an output file: one collection of data serves as input and a second collection of data serves as output. The instruction format for a SELECT statement is as follows:

Format

> SELECT file-name-1
>   ASSIGN TO implementor-name-1

The **implementor-name** is a machine-dependent device specification provided by the computer center.

RECAP OF INSTRUCTION FORMAT RULES

1. Uppercase words are reserved words; lowercase are programmer-supplied.
2. Underlined words are required in the statement.

Guidelines for SELECT **Statement**

We use two lines for a SELECT statement, with the second line indented for ease of reading.

1. File-Name

The file-name assigned to each device must conform to the rules for forming user-defined words. A user-defined word is a word chosen by the programmer to represent some element in a program. Here, it is used to define a file-name.

RULES FOR FORMING USER-DEFINED WORDS (Such as File-Name)

1. 1 to 30 characters.
2. Letters, digits, and hyphens (-) only.
3. No embedded blanks.
4. At least one alphabetic character.

For each device used in the program, a SELECT statement must be specified. If a program requires a disk as input and produces a printed report as output, two SELECT statements will be specified. One file-name will be assigned to the disk file, and the other to the print file.

Guidelines for Forming File-Names

We recommend that file-names assigned by the programmer be meaningful. Thus, SALES-IN would be a more appropriate file-name than S-IN. Also, avoid the use of device-specific file-names such as SALES-DISK. The medium used for storing a given file might change over time, so that the use of a device-dependent name could prove to be misleading.

2. Implementor-Names or Device Specifications

The implementor-names or device specifications vary widely among computer manufacturers. We will consider both the simplified versions and the more detailed ones. You will need to obtain the exact device specifications for your system from your computer center or your instructor.

Most systems enable the programmer to access frequently used devices by special device names. The following are common shorthand device specifications that you may be able to use with your system:

Input from a terminal	SYS$IN
Output on a terminal	SYS$OUT
Card reader	SYSIPT, SYSRDR, or SYSIN
Printer	SYSLST or SYSOUT
Disk	DISC

For many systems the following entries would be valid for a program that reads input from a terminal and prints a report as output:[*]

Example
```
FILE-CONTROL.
    SELECT TRANSACTION-FILE
        ASSIGN TO SYS$IN.
    SELECT REPORT-FILE
        ASSIGN TO SYSLST.
```

Sometimes the device specification can be any user-defined word that refers to an area on disk reserved for your data entries. Consider the following, which is valid on a DEC VAX system:

---

[*]Consult your computer's specifications manual to see if these device specifications are used.

```
SELECT SALES-FILE
    ASSIGN TO DATA1.
```

During program execution, the user will be able to access data assigned to a disk area called DATA1.

B. More Detailed Device Specifications

As noted, device specifications vary among computer manufacturers. The following expanded format of a SELECT statement is standard for some computers:

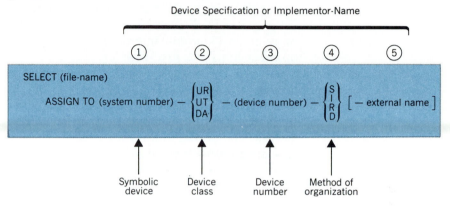

Examples

```
SELECT PAYROLL-IN
    ASSIGN TO SYS005-UR-2540R-S.
SELECT SALES-OUT
    ASSIGN TO SYS006-UT-3400-S.
```

Shorter versions that may be acceptable include:

```
SELECT SALES-IN
    ASSIGN TO SYS007-DA-S.
```

The FILE-CONTROL paragraph may seem unnecessarily complex, but the entries are standard for each installation. The only user-defined word is the file-name.

C. Interpreting the Device Specification

In this section, we briefly explain the meaning of the five entries for the device specification just described. You may skip this section if you are not required to provide specific device assignments with your programs.

DEVICE SPECIFICATIONS

1. Symbolic Device
   Supplied by the computer center that assigns a number to each device.
   SYSnnn is common, where nnn may be a number from 001 to 256.
2. Device Class {UR, UT, DA}
   The braces mean that any one of the following may be used.
   UR—unit-record (terminal, printer, cards)
   UT—utility (tape or sequential disk)
   DA—direct-access (disk)

> 3. Device Number
>   Supplied by the computer manufacturer.
> 4. Method of Organization
>   S for sequential (printer, terminal, disk, tape, or cards)
>   I, R, or D may be used for disk files to be accessed randomly
> 5. External-Name (optional on many systems)

1. Symbolic Device

The system number or symbolic device is dependent on the particular installation. The item will vary among computer centers. Each physical device in a computer facility will have a unique system number. The system number may be an external-name or may have the format SYSnnn, where nnn is a number from 001 to 256.

2. Device Class

The classifications that may be used are standard entries. There are three types of device classifications: UR for unit-record, UT for utility, and DA for direct-access. The printer and terminal are unit-record devices because each record associated with these devices is always the same *fixed length*. A line on a terminal, for example, is a unit-record, since it must consist of a fixed number of positions of data; with most terminals, this number is 80. A printed form is similarly a unit-record document since each line *always* consists of the same number of print positions. Thus terminal and print devices will have a classification of UR for unit-record.

Tape is *not* a unit-record device since tape records can be any size. Some tape files have 80-character records, for example; others have 100- or 200-character records. Tape and sequential disk can be classified as UT for utility device. Direct-access units such as disk are classified as DA.

3. Device Number

The device number is designated by the computer manufacturer. IBM, for example, most often uses the following device numbers for its input/output units:

Tape	3400
Reader	2540R or 2501
Printer	1403 or 3203
Disk	3330, 3340, 3350, 2311, 2314

4. Method of Organization

The method of file organization will always be S (sequential) for tape, terminal, and print files. S may also be specified for disks that are organized sequentially, although disk files can be organized in different ways so that records can be accessed randomly.

5. External-Name

Some operating systems require an external-name to access a file; for others, this entry is optional. The rules for forming external-names are system-dependent, so you should check your computer's manual for the requirements.

In summary, the implementor-name following ASSIGN TO contains a device specification entry separated by hyphens. Omitting these hyphens in coding will cause syntax errors. The precise coding for each device will be given to you at your computer center.

Let us consider the following illustration, using an arbitrary system number since this will depend on the installation.

Example   A disk file, consisting of transaction data, may be assigned as follows for an IBM system:

```
SELECT TRANS-FILE
       ASSIGN TO SYS004-DA-3330-S.
```

The file-name, TRANS-FILE, is supplied by the programmer. The remaining data in the statement is necessary when using a disk drive. The disk is a DA or direct-access device with number 3330 that is assigned to SYS004 for this installation. This disk will be accessed sequentially, which means that records are read or written in the order they enter the system.

Note that SELECT statements are coded in Area B.

In summary, the entry in the SELECT statement that is most important to you is the file-name assigned. This name is referenced in the DATA DIVISION to designate the input or output area to be used by the file. It is also referenced in the PROCEDURE DIVISION to access the file. The other entries in the SELECT statement are computer-dependent.

The preceding discussion should serve as a general guide for users. Consult your specifications manual or instructor for the requirements of the SELECT statements at your computer center.

CODING GUIDELINES FOR THE IDENTIFICATION AND ENVIRONMENT DIVISIONS

1. Use a blank comment line with an * in column 7, or a page eject (/ in column 7) to separate divisions.
2. For long programs, use a blank line or a comment line to separate sections as well.
3. Code a single statement per line for the sake of clarity and to make debugging easier.
4. In general, put paragraph-names on lines by themselves.
5. Be liberal in your use of comments—they can make programs easier to read and debug.
6. Box lengthy comments using asterisks:

```
******************************************
*                                        *
*            (Comments go here)          *
*                                        *
******************************************
```

7. The sequence in which files are selected in SELECT statements is not critical, but for documentation purposes, it is more logical to select and define the input file(s) first, followed by output file(s).
8. Code each SELECT on two lines. The best format is as follows:

```
SELECT  file-name
     ASSIGN TO  device.
```

9. Avoid the use of device-specific file-names such as SALES-TAPE.

CHAPTER SUMMARY

I. The IDENTIFICATION DIVISION

   A. The IDENTIFICATION DIVISION and its paragraphs do not affect the execution of the program. They are used as documentation entries.

   B. The first two items to be coded in a program are:

```
IDENTIFICATION DIVISION.
PROGRAM-ID.  program-name.
```

   C. A program name that is up to eight characters, letters and digits only, is acceptable on all computers.

   D. All other paragraphs and identifying information in this division are optional. Paragraphs that may be included are as follows: (Be sure you code these in the sequence specified.)

```
AUTHOR.
INSTALLATION.
DATE-WRITTEN.
DATE-COMPILED.
SECURITY.
```

     For many systems, if no entry follows the DATE-COMPILED paragraph, the compiler will insert the date of compilation on the source listing.

   E. Comments can be included in the IDENTIFICATION DIVISION, as well as all other divisions, by coding an * in position 7. This makes the entire line a comment. We encourage you to use comments throughout your programs for documentation.

   F. A slash (/) in column 7 will cause the subsequent lines to be printed on the next page of the source listing.

II. The ENVIRONMENT DIVISION

   A. The format for the ENVIRONMENT DIVISION is as follows:

```
ENVIRONMENT DIVISION.
[CONFIGURATION SECTION.
[SOURCE-COMPUTER.  computer-name]
[OBJECT-COMPUTER.  computer-name]]
[INPUT-OUTPUT SECTION.
 FILE-CONTROL.
      SELECT  file-name-1
          ASSIGN TO  implementor-name-1
      ⋮
                                              ]
```

     Note: The entire ENVIRONMENT DIVISION is optional for COBOL 85.

   B. The CONFIGURATION SECTION is usually optional. It supplies documentary information on the computer(s) being used.

   C. The INPUT-OUTPUT SECTION is also optional but must be included if any files are assigned to devices in a program. Since practically all programs use files, we will always include the INPUT-OUTPUT SECTION.

   D. The ENVIRONMENT DIVISION is the only division of a COBOL program that may vary depending on the computer used. You will need to obtain the exact device specifications for each file from your computer center or your instructor.

     If you look at Appendix A, you will find that the full format for the ENVIRONMENT DIVISION is far more extensive than specified in this chapter. We have extracted the most commonly used elements.

CHAPTER SELF-TEST

1. The IDENTIFICATION DIVISION entry is always followed by the _____ paragraph.
2. The entries in the ENVIRONMENT DIVISION are dependent on _____ and _____ .
3. The two sections of the ENVIRONMENT DIVISION are the _____ SECTION and the _____ SECTION.
4. The device specifications in the ENVIRONMENT DIVISION (will, will not) change significantly if the program is run on a different computer.
5. The two main paragraphs of the CONFIGURATION SECTION, if coded, are _____ and _____ .
6. Files are defined and assigned in the _____ paragraph of the INPUT-OUTPUT SECTION.
7. For every device used in the program, a _____ -name must be specified.
8. The file-name used in the SELECT statement must conform to the rules for forming _____ .
9. SELECT statements are coded in Area _____ .
10. Code the IDENTIFICATION and ENVIRONMENT DIVISION entries for a program that reads an input transaction tape, creates an error listing for all erroneous records, and creates a master disk file that is organized sequentially.

Solutions

1. PROGRAM-ID
2. the computer; the specific devices used
3. CONFIGURATION; INPUT-OUTPUT
4. will—These are the only entries in a COBOL program that are apt to change significantly.
5. SOURCE-COMPUTER; OBJECT-COMPUTER
6. FILE-CONTROL
7. file
8. user-defined words or programmer-supplied data-names
9. B
10.
```
    IDENTIFICATION DIVISION.
    PROGRAM-ID. EDIT1.
    AUTHOR. N. B. STERN.
    *    THIS PROGRAM READS INPUT TAPE RECORDS, CREATES
    *    A MASTER DISK AND ERROR LISTING.
    ENVIRONMENT DIVISION.
    CONFIGURATION SECTION.
    SOURCE-COMPUTER. IBM-4341.
    OBJECT-COMPUTER. IBM-4341.
    INPUT-OUTPUT SECTION.
    FILE-CONTROL.
        SELECT TRANSACTION-FILE
            ASSIGN TO SYS005-UT-2400-S.
        SELECT ERROR-FILE
            ASSIGN TO SYS006-UR-1403-S.
        SELECT MASTER-FILE
            ASSIGN TO SYS007-DA-8433-S.
```

Note: ASSIGN clauses depend on the computer system you are using.

PRACTICE PROGRAM

Code the IDENTIFICATION and ENVIRONMENT DIVISION entries for the following program:

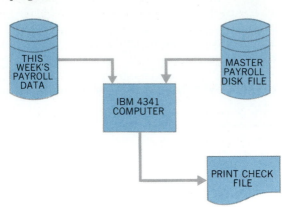

All SELECT statements are coded in Area B. The order in which the files are specified is not significant, but usually we SELECT input files before output files. The following is a suggested solution:

```
IDENTIFICATION DIVISION.
PROGRAM-ID. SAMPLE2.
AUTHOR R. A. STERN.
*** THE PROGRAM PRODUCES A PRINTED REPORT FROM      ***
*** A MASTER DISK FILE AND THE WEEK'S PAYROLL DATA ***
ENVIRONMENT DIVISION.
CONFIGURATION SECTION.
SOURCE-COMPUTER. IBM-4341.
OBJECT-COMPUTER. IBM-4341.
INPUT-OUTPUT SECTION.
FILE-CONTROL.   SELECT WEEKLY-WAGES
                    ASSIGN TO SYS005-DA-3300-S.
                SELECT PAYROLL
                    ASSIGN TO SYS008-DA-3340-S.
                SELECT PRINT-CHECKS
                    ASSIGN TO SYS006-UR-1403-S.
```

KEY TERMS

Area A	ENVIRONMENT DIVISION	PROGRAM-ID
Area B	File	Program sheet
AUTHOR	FILE-CONTROL	Section
Coding Sheet	IDENTIFICATION	SECURITY
CONFIGURATION	DIVISION	SELECT
SECTION	Implementor-name	Sentence
Continuation position	INPUT-OUTPUT SECTION	SOURCE-COMPUTER
DATE-COMPILED	INSTALLATION	Statement
DATE-WRITTEN	OBJECT-COMPUTER	
Division	Paragraph	

REVIEW QUESTIONS

I. True-False Questions

T   F

1. It is best to code only one statement on each coding line.
2. IDENTIFICATION DIVISION, PROGRAM-ID, and AUTHOR are the first three required entries of a COBOL program.
3. FILE 12 is a valid file-name.
4. A division name must appear as an independent item on a separate line.
5. The IDENTIFICATION DIVISION contains instructions that significantly affect execution of the program.
6. Information supplied in the IDENTIFICATION DIVISION makes it easier for users to understand the nature of the program.
7. COBOL programs should be designed to be self-documenting.
8. DATE-COMPILED is a paragraph-name that typically requires no additional entries.
9. Every period in a COBOL program must be followed by at least one space.
10. The INSTALLATION paragraph is restricted to one line.
11. The ENVIRONMENT DIVISION, like the other three divisions, is generally the same regardless of the computer on which the program is run.
12. The INPUT-OUTPUT SECTION of the ENVIRONMENT DIVISION assigns the file-names.
13. FILE-CONTROL is a required entry in the ENVIRONMENT DIVISION for programs that use files.
14. A file-name is an example of a user-defined word.
15. A maximum of three files may be defined in the INPUT-OUTPUT SECTION.

II. General Questions

Make necessary corrections to each of the following (1–5).

1.

```
IDENTIFICATION DIVISION
PROGRAM-ID SAMPLE1.
```

2.

```
IDENTIFICATION DIVISION.
PROGRAM-ID. SAMPLE2
```

3.

```
ENVIRONMENT DIVISION.
    CONFIGURATION SECTION.
```

4.

```
IDENTIFICATION DIVISION.
AUTHOR.MARY DOE.
PROGRAM-ID. SAMPLE4.
```

5.

```
DATA DIVISION. FILE SECTION.
```

6. State which of the following entries are coded in Area A.
   (a) IDENTIFICATION DIVISION
   (b) PROGRAM-ID
   (c) (name of author)
   (d) FILE SECTION
   (e) (COBOL statement) ADD TAX TO TOTAL
   (f) ENVIRONMENT DIVISION.
   (g) CONFIGURATION SECTION.
   (h) SOURCE-COMPUTER.
   (i) FILE-CONTROL.
   (j) SELECT statement.

Make necessary corrections to each of the following and assume that the device specification, where noted, is correct (7–10).

7.

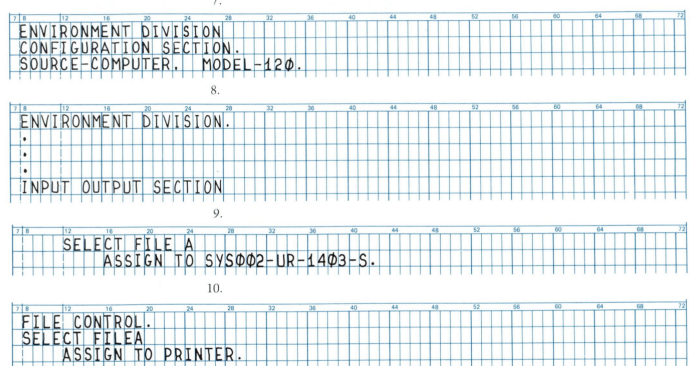

```
ENVIRONMENT DIVISION
CONFIGURATION SECTION.
SOURCE-COMPUTER.   MODEL-12Ø.
```

8.

```
ENVIRONMENT DIVISION.
 .
 .
 .
INPUT OUTPUT SECTION
```

9.

```
    SELECT FILE A
        ASSIGN TO SYSØØ2-UR-14Ø3-S.
```

10.

```
FILE CONTROL.
SELECT FILEA
    ASSIGN TO PRINTER.
```

PROGRAMMING ASSIGNMENTS

1. Code the IDENTIFICATION DIVISION for a program called UPDATE for the United Accounting Corp. The program must be written by 8/25/89 and completed by 10/25/89, and it has a top secret security classification. The program will create a new master disk each month from the previous master disk and selected transaction tape records.

2. Consider the program excerpt in Figure 2.4. Code the IDENTIFICATION DIVISION. Include numerous paragraphs for documentation purposes. Also include comments that describe the program.

For the following problems, code the SELECT statements using the implementor-names relevant for your computer center.

COBOL Program Sheet

System					Punching Instructions						Sheet	of	
Program				Graphic								Identification	
Programmer		Date		Punch					Card # Form		73		80

```
*** CODE IDENTIFICATION DIVISION HERE ***
ENVIRONMENT DIVISION.
INPUT-OUTPUT SECTION.
FILE CONTROL.
    SELECT TRANS-FILE   ASSIGN TO SYSIN.
    SELECT SALES-FILE   ASSIGN TO SYSOUT.
DATA DIVISION.
FILE SECTION.
FD  TRANS-FILE  LABEL RECORDS ARE OMITTED.
Ø1  TRANS-REC.
    Ø5  NAME-IN         PIC X(2Ø).
    Ø5  UNIT-PRICE-IN   PIC 9(3)V99.
    Ø5  QTY-SOLD-IN     PIC 999.
FD  SALES-FILE  LABEL RECORDS ARE STANDARD.
Ø1  SALES-REC.
    Ø5  NAME-OUT        PIC X(2Ø).
    Ø5  TOTAL-PRICE-OUT PIC 9(6)V99.
WORKING-STORAGE SECTION.
Ø1  ARE-THERE-MORE-RECORDS  PIC X(3) VALUE 'YES'.
PROCEDURE DIVISION.
1ØØ-MAIN-MODULE.
    OPEN INPUT TRANS-FILE
         OUTPUT SALES-FILE.
    READ TRANS-FILE
        AT END MOVE 'NO ' TO ARE-THERE-MORE-RECORDS.
    PERFORM 2ØØ-CALC-RTN
        UNTIL ARE-THERE-MORE-RECORDS = 'NO '.
    CLOSE TRANS-FILE
          SALES-FILE.
    STOP RUN.
2ØØ-CALC-RTN.
    MOVE NAME-IN TO NAME-OUT.
    MULTIPLY UNIT-PRICE-IN BY QTY-SOLD-IN GIVING TOTAL-PRICE-OUT.
    WRITE SALES-REC.
    READ TRANS-FILE
        AT END MOVE 'NO ' TO ARE-THERE-MORE-RECORDS.
```

Figure 2.4
Program for Programming
Assignment 2.

3. Write the IDENTIFICATION and ENVIRONMENT DIVISION entries for the following systems flowchart:

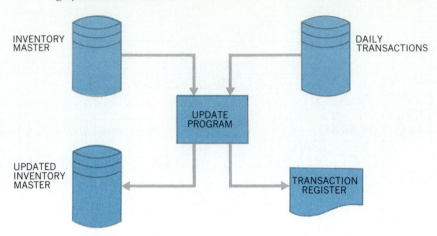

4. Code the IDENTIFICATION DIVISION and the ENVIRONMENT DIVISION for a COBOL update program that uses an input transaction file and last week's master inventory tape file to create a current master inventory tape file.

5. Code the IDENTIFICATION DIVISION and the ENVIRONMENT DIVISION for a COBOL program that will use a sequential master billing disk to print gas bills and electric bills.

6. Consider the program excerpt in Figure 2.5. Code the IDENTIFICATION and ENVIRONMENT DIVISIONs for this program. Be as complete and as specific as possible. Include comments that describe the program.

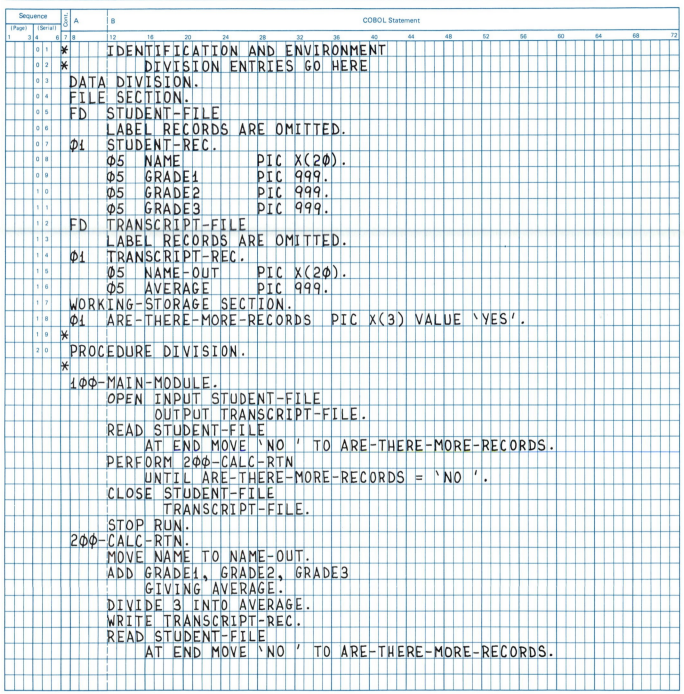

COBOL Program Sheet

```
*        IDENTIFICATION AND ENVIRONMENT
*            DIVISION ENTRIES GO HERE
DATA DIVISION.
FILE SECTION.
FD  STUDENT-FILE
    LABEL RECORDS ARE OMITTED.
Ø1  STUDENT-REC.
    Ø5  NAME        PIC X(2Ø).
    Ø5  GRADE1      PIC 999.
    Ø5  GRADE2      PIC 999.
    Ø5  GRADE3      PIC 999.
FD  TRANSCRIPT-FILE
    LABEL RECORDS ARE OMITTED.
Ø1  TRANSCRIPT-REC.
    Ø5  NAME-OUT    PIC X(2Ø).
    Ø5  AVERAGE     PIC 999.
WORKING-STORAGE SECTION.
Ø1  ARE-THERE-MORE-RECORDS  PIC X(3) VALUE 'YES'.
*
PROCEDURE DIVISION.
*
1ØØ-MAIN-MODULE.
    OPEN INPUT STUDENT-FILE
         OUTPUT TRANSCRIPT-FILE.
    READ STUDENT-FILE
        AT END MOVE 'NO ' TO ARE-THERE-MORE-RECORDS.
    PERFORM 2ØØ-CALC-RTN
        UNTIL ARE-THERE-MORE-RECORDS = 'NO '.
    CLOSE STUDENT-FILE
          TRANSCRIPT-FILE.
    STOP RUN.
2ØØ-CALC-RTN.
    MOVE NAME TO NAME-OUT.
    ADD GRADE1, GRADE2, GRADE3
        GIVING AVERAGE.
    DIVIDE 3 INTO AVERAGE.
    WRITE TRANSCRIPT-REC.
    READ STUDENT-FILE
        AT END MOVE 'NO ' TO ARE-THERE-MORE-RECORDS.
```

Figure 2.5
Program for Programming
Assignment 6.

3

Defining Files, Records, and Fields in the DATA DIVISION

OBJECTIVES

To familiarize you with

1. Systems design considerations that relate to programming.
2. The ways in which data is organized.
3. The rules for forming data-names and constants in COBOL.
4. How input and output files are defined and described in the DATA DIVISION.
5. How storage can be reserved for fields not part of input or output, such as constants and work areas.

I. Systems Design Considerations

A. The Relationship between a Business System and Its Programs

Programs are not usually written as independent entities. Rather, they are part of an overall set of procedures called a computerized **business system.** Each program, then, as written by a programmer is really only *one part* of an overall systems design.

A systems analyst is the computer professional responsible for the entire design of this computerized business system. Thus, if the sales department of a major company is not running smoothly or is too costly to operate, the company's management may call on a systems analyst to design a more efficient business system. Because such a design would typically include computerization of various aspects of the department's functions, the systems analyst should have considerable computer expertise.

The systems analyst first determines what the outputs from the entire system should be and then designs the inputs necessary to produce these outputs. The analyst also determines what programs are required to read the inputs and to produce the required outputs. Each set of program specifications would include a copy of the input and output layouts for that specific aspect of the overall system. The analyst provides the programmer with these specifications so that he or she will know precisely what the input and output will look like.

B. Designing Input for Business Applications That Process a High Volume of Data

Some business applications simply accept input data from a keyboard of a terminal or computer. This input is then immediately processed, and the output is displayed on a monitor or CRT (Cathode Ray Tube) of the same terminal. A few business programs, particularly those written in BASIC, process data in this interactive manner. Such applications, however, are only suitable if the input is *not voluminous* and a permanent copy of the output is *not required.*

Most businesses, however, need programs that process *large volumes of input* and also need permanent copies of output for future reference. For these types of applications, data is entered in the form of a **file,** which is a major collection of data for a given application.

For most commercial applications, then, each set of inputs and outputs typically consists of a *file,* which itself contains groups of **records.** A payroll file, for example, would be the major collection of payroll data for a company. It would consist of employee records, where each record contains data for a single employee:

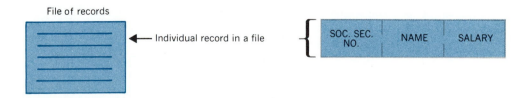

File of records   ← Individual record in a file   { SOC. SEC. NO. | NAME | SALARY }

The systems analyst who designs the files provides the programmer with a description of the input and output. A *record layout form* is used for describing each type of input or output in a program. If the output is a print file, the analyst prepares a Printer Spacing Chart instead of a record layout form. This chart describes the precise format for each print line. In Chapter 1, there are some illustrations of these record layouts and Printer Spacing Charts.

All our programs will be accompanied by record layouts and Printer Spacing Charts so that you will become very familiar with them.

In summary, the programmer should be aware of the following:

SYSTEMS DESIGN CONSIDERATIONS

1. Each program is written as part of an integrated set of procedures called a business system.
2. The files that will serve as input and output are designed by the systems analyst.
3. Record layouts and Printer Spacing Charts are designed by the analyst and are provided to the programmer as part of the program's input and output specifications. They describe the files that will be used in the program.

II. Forming Data-Names

A. Rules

As we have seen from the program illustrations in the previous chapter, areas are reserved in memory for files and records. Each record is itself divided into fields of data such as Name, Address, and Salary.

Files, records, and fields are categories of data in a COBOL program. They are each assigned a name called a **data-name** or **identifier.** Data-names are the most common type of user-defined words; we will see later that there are other types of user-defined words. In COBOL, data-names must conform to the following rules.

RULES FOR FORMING USER-DEFINED DATA-NAMES

1. 1 to 30 characters.
2. Letters, digits, and hyphens (-) only. (We use uppercase letters in all our illustrations.)
3. May not begin or end with a hyphen.
4. No embedded blanks are permitted (that is, no blanks within the data-name).
5. Must contain at least one alphabetic character.
6. May not be a COBOL **reserved word.** A reserved word, such as ADD, MOVE, or DATA, is one that has special significance to the COBOL compiler.

COBOL 74 and COBOL 85 reserved words are listed in Appendix A. If a compiler has features that go beyond the standard, it will have *additional* COBOL reserved words. The full range of COBOL reserved words for your specific compiler will be listed in the COBOL reference manual at your computer center.

The following are examples of valid data-names.

EXAMPLES OF VALID DATA-NAMES

```
DATE-IN
NAME-OUT
LAST-NAME-IN
AMOUNT1-IN
AMOUNT-OF-TRANSACTION-OUT
```

The suffixes `-IN` and `-OUT` are recommended naming conventions, but they are not required.

The following are examples of invalid data-names.

EXAMPLES OF INVALID DATA-NAMES

Data-Name	Reason It Is Invalid
EMPLOYEE NAME	There is an *embedded blank* between `EMPLOYEE` and `NAME`. Because of the blank, the compiler would interpret this as two separate names, `EMPLOYEE` and `NAME`. `EMPLOYEE-NAME` is, however, okay.
DISCOUNT-%	%, as a special character, is invalid.
INPUT	`INPUT` is a COBOL reserved word.
123	A data-name must contain at least one alphabetic character.

Although reserved words cannot be used as data-names, they can be modified to be acceptable. `INPUT-1`, for example, would be a permissible data-name.

Consider the following record layout within an output disk file:

DATE OF TRANSACTION	AMOUNT	INVOICE NUMBER	CUSTOMER NAME

The fields may be named as follows: `DATE-OF-TRANS-OUT`, `AMOUNT-OUT`, `INVOICE-NO-OUT`, `CUSTOMER-NAME-OUT`.

Hyphens are used in place of embedded blanks for data-names that incorporate more than one word. This improves readability.

Each file, record, and field of data must be assigned a name in the COBOL program. Once a name is assigned, the *same* name must be used throughout when referring to the specific unit of data. `CREDIT-AMT-IN`, defined as a data-name in the `DATA DIVISION`, may *not* be referred to as `CR-AMT-IN` in the `PROCEDURE DIVISION`. To do so, would result in a syntax error.

B. Guidelines

1. Use Meaningful Names

The data-names used should describe the type of data within the field. `DATE-OF-TRANS-IN` is a more meaningful data-name than `D1`, for example, although both names are valid. Using data-names that describe the contents of the fields makes it easier to debug a program; it also makes the coding more readable by enabling users to better understand the meaning of the overall program.

2. Use Prefixes or Suffixes Where Appropriate

Prefixes or suffixes are commonly used to indicate the type of data within a record. Thus NAME-OUT might be used as an output field to distinguish it from NAME-IN, which could be the same field on an input record.

To make our program easier to read and more standardized, we will use prefixes or suffixes such as -IN and -OUT along with meaningful names. Later on, we will describe a heading line that is to be printed, with a prefix of HL-, a total line with a prefix of TL-, and so on.

III. The DATA DIVISION

A. The FILE SECTION

The **DATA DIVISION** is that part of a COBOL program that defines and describes fields, records, and files in storage. Any area of storage that is required for the processing of data must be established in the DATA DIVISION.

We focus on the following two main sections of the DATA DIVISION in this text.

THE TWO MAIN SECTIONS OF THE DATA DIVISION

1. **FILE SECTION**—defines all data areas that are part of input or output files.
2. **WORKING-STORAGE SECTION**—reserves memory or storage for fields not part of input or output but nonetheless required for processing. These include constants, end-of-file indicators, and work areas. This section will be discussed in detail in Chapter 7.

The sections used in the DATA DIVISION must appear in the sequence shown.

Any program that (1) reads data from input files or (2) produces output files, requires a FILE SECTION to describe the input and output areas. Since almost all programs read input files, operate on them, and produce output files, the FILE SECTION will be an essential part of almost all programs.

Defining a File

As noted previously, a file is the overall collection of data pertaining to a specific application. Company ABC, for example, may have an inventory file that contains all current inventory information. The same company may also have an accounts receivable file of customer information, a payroll file of employee information, and so on.

A file enters the computer as input, is processed, and an output file is produced. Thus, files appear as either input or output in COBOL programs. Most programs use at least one input and one output file.

A typical program may read an input file from disk or tape and produce a printed output file of bills, checks, or summary totals. Other programs may be written to incorporate changes into a **master file.** A master file contains the *major collection* of data for a particular application. Thus, we may have an input file of master payroll records along with an input file of transaction records that contain changes to be made to the master. These changes may include new hires, salary increases for current employees, changes in the number of dependents, and so on. The two input files—the master payroll file and the transaction file—would be used to create a new master payroll file that incorporates all the changes. This process of using a file of transaction records along with an existing master file to produce a new master is called an **update procedure** and is a common programming application. The old master file and the transaction file of changes serve as input and a new master file with the changes incorporated would be the output file:

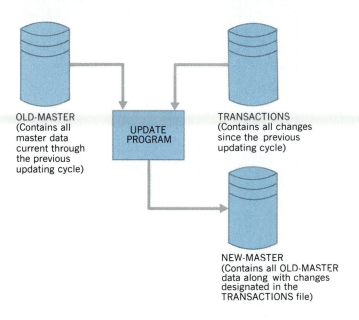

OLD-MASTER
(Contains all
master data
current through
the previous
updating cycle)

UPDATE
PROGRAM

TRANSACTIONS
(Contains all changes
since the previous
updating cycle)

NEW-MASTER
(Contains all OLD-MASTER
data along with changes
designated in the
TRANSACTIONS file)

Thus, for *each* form of input and output used in a business application, we have *one* file. That is, three files would typically be used for the preceding update procedure: an input master file, an input transaction file, and a new output master file. We discuss update procedures in detail in Chapter 15.

The FILE SECTION, as the name implies, describes all input and output files used in the program. Each file has already been defined in the ENVIRON-MENT DIVISION in a SELECT statement, where the file-name is designated and an input or output device is assigned to it. Thus, for every SELECT statement, we will have one file to describe in the FILE SECTION of the DATA DIVISION.

The FILE SECTION, then, describes the input and output areas used in the program. An *input area* is storage reserved for records from an incoming file. A READ instruction, in the PROCEDURE DIVISION, will transmit *one* record of the designated file to this input area. Similarly, an *output area* is storage reserved for a record to be produced in an output file. When a WRITE statement is executed, data stored in this output area is transmitted as *one* record to the specified output device.

1. File Description Entries

Each file is described in the FILE SECTION with an FD sentence that may consist of a series of clauses. After the clauses are specified, the FD sentence ends with a period. **FD** is an abbreviation for **File Description.** Each FD entry will describe a file defined in a SELECT statement in the ENVIRONMENT DI-VISION. Thus, as an example, we may have:

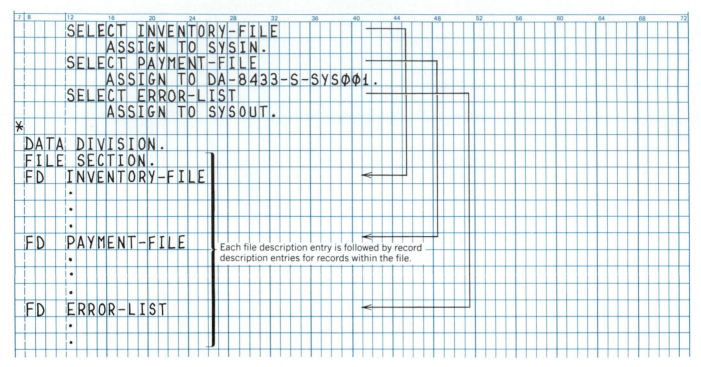

```
SELECT INVENTORY-FILE
     ASSIGN TO SYSIN.
SELECT PAYMENT-FILE
     ASSIGN TO DA-8433-S-SYS001.
SELECT ERROR-LIST
     ASSIGN TO SYSOUT.
*
DATA DIVISION.
FILE SECTION.
FD  INVENTORY-FILE
     .
     .
     .

FD  PAYMENT-FILE            Each file description entry is followed by record
     .                      description entries for records within the file.
     .
     .

FD  ERROR-LIST
     .
     .
```

Every FD entry will be followed by a file-name and certain clauses that describe the file and the format of its records. Since there are three SELECT statements in the preceding example, there will be three FD entries in the FILE SECTION.

The two entries, DATA DIVISION and FILE SECTION, are coded in Area A. FD is also coded in Area A. The file-name, however, is typically coded in Area B. If FD clauses are used, no period follows the file-name. FD ACCTS-RE-CEIVABLE, for example, signals the compiler that the ACCTS-RECEIVABLE file is about to be described.

Several clauses may be used to describe a file. These will follow the FD file-name, and no period will be written until the last clause is specified. Consider the following examples that include full FD entries:

```
FD  PAYROLL-FILE
LABEL RECORDS ARE OMITTED               File Description
RECORD CONTAINS 80 CHARACTERS           entries
DATA RECORD IS EMPLOYEE-REC.                            PAYROLL-FILE
     .                                                  descriptions
     .                                  Record Description
     .                                  entries for that
     .                                  file

FD  TRANSACTION-FILE
LABEL RECORDS ARE STANDARD
RECORD CONTAINS 50 CHARACTERS           File Description
BLOCK CONTAINS 20 RECORDS               entries
DATA RECORD IS TRANSACTION-REC.                         TRANSACTION-FILE
     .                                                  descriptions
     .                                  Record Description
     .                                  entries for that
                                        file
```

We will focus on File Description entries first and then consider Record Description entries for records within each file. Note that all these FD clauses are optional for COBOL 85.

a. LABEL RECORD(S) Clause—(Required for COBOL 74, optional for COBOL 85)

Format

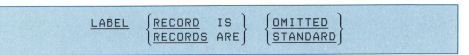

Interpreting Instruction Formats

Each set of braces { } denotes that one of the enclosed items is required when the specific clause is used. We can, for example, code LABEL RECORD IS OMITTED or LABEL RECORDS ARE OMITTED; both have the same significance.

What Is a Label Record?

Data on a disk or a tape cannot be "read" as one reads a book, a line on a terminal, or a printed report; that is, data is stored on disk or tape as magnetized bits that cannot be seen by the naked eye. **Label records,** then, are usually created as the first and last records of a disk or tape to provide identifying information about the file.

Since the data on a disk or tape is not visible, these label records will provide a check to see if the correct file is being used for a specific program. Labels are created on output files so that, when the same file is later read as input, the labels may be checked. That is, labels are *created* on output files and *checked* on input files. The COBOL compiler will supply the routine for writing labels on output files or for checking labels on input files if the following entry is included:

```
LABEL RECORDS ARE STANDARD
```

This clause will result in the following:

1. The first record on a disk or tape file will be a standard 80-position **header label** identifying the file to the system; similarly, the last record will be a **trailer label.**
2. With input files, these labels will be computer-checked; with output files, they will be computer-created.

Although no further COBOL statements are necessary to perform the label routines, the information that should appear on the labels will need to be supplied to the system. This is done with system commands or job control statements and are separate from the COBOL program.

> With COBOL 85 the LABEL RECORDS clause is optional. When the clause is not included, the computer assumes that LABEL RECORDS ARE STANDARD. *The clause must, however, appear with all* FDs *when using COBOL 74.*

The clause LABEL RECORDS ARE STANDARD is permitted for disk and tape files *only.* Unit-record devices such as printers and terminals do *not* use label records, since identifying information is unnecessary where data is visible to the human eye. The following entry, then, is used for unit-record files.

```
                    LABEL RECORDS ARE OMITTED
```

Similarly, a disk or tape file may sometimes include the entry LABEL RECORDS ARE OMITTED; this means that the checking for correct files is not needed. In that case, label records will be neither created nor checked.

If an output disk or tape file is created with standard labels, then LABEL RECORDS should be STANDARD when reading that same file as input at some later date.

Example 1   A print file called EMPLOYEE-FILE would include the following:

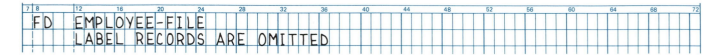

```
FD  EMPLOYEE-FILE
    LABEL RECORDS ARE OMITTED
```

Example 2   A disk or tape file called INVENTORY-FILE would include the following:

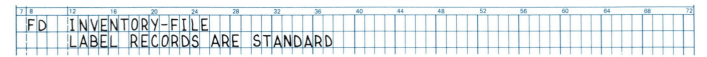

```
FD  INVENTORY-FILE
    LABEL RECORDS ARE STANDARD
```

b. RECORD CONTAINS Clause—(Optional)

Format
```
            RECORD CONTAINS integer-1 CHARACTERS
```

The **RECORD CONTAINS** clause indicates the size of each record. A print file, for example, may have the following entry:

```
            RECORD CONTAINS 133 CHARACTERS
```

Interpreting Instruction Formats

Note that in the instruction format, only the word RECORD is underlined. This means that the other words are optional. The clause RECORD 133 could be coded, then, instead of the preceding because CONTAINS and CHARACTERS are not required. The full sentence is more user-friendly. Note that the only user-defined entry in this clause is the integer specified.

Record Size for Print Files

You will recall that printers vary in the number of characters they can print per line—80, 100, 120, and 132 are common. We will typically assume 132 characters per line. The RECORD CONTAINS clause will always include one extra position that is used for *forms control*. Forms control indicates the spacing of the form (e.g., single spacing, double spacing). Thus, for 132-character printers, we establish our record size as *133* characters. Typically, the *first* or leftmost position in these 133-position print records is the forms control position; it is *not* actually printed. Thus, positions 2–133 of the record represent the actual data that will be printed; position 1 is used by the printer for spacing of the form.

Record Size for Other Files

Data entered on a terminal is typically specified with the clause RECORD CON-
TAINS 80 CHARACTERS, although the number of characters will depend on
how many characters can be stored on one line of the specific terminal.

For disk or tape files, the RECORD CONTAINS clause varies. One of the advantages of storing data on these media is that records can be any size.

Coding the RECORD CONTAINS Clause for Checking Purposes

The RECORD CONTAINS clause in the File Description entry is always *optional.*
It is, however, advisable to include it, since it provides a check on record size.
For example, if the RECORD CONTAINS clause indicates 80 CHARACTERS in
the record, but inadvertently the PICTURE clauses add up to 81 characters, a
syntax error will occur during the compilation. If the RECORD CONTAINS clause
were not included, however, the inclusion of an 81st position in the record
would *not* be detected until the program is actually run.

Example 3   An FD entry for a disk file called SALES-FILE with 150-character records may be:

```
FD   SALES-FILE
     LABEL RECORDS ARE STANDARD
     RECORD CONTAINS 150 CHARACTERS
```

C. BLOCK CONTAINS Clause—(Optional)

Format

> BLOCK CONTAINS integer-1 RECORDS

What Is Blocking?

The **BLOCK CONTAINS** clause is only included in the File Description entry
for files in which disk or tape records have been blocked. **Blocking** is a technique that increases the speed of input/output operations and makes more
effective use of storage space on disk and tape. A group of logical records is
included within one block to maximize the efficient use of a disk or tape area.
That is, reading in a block of 10 disk records, for example, is apt to be more
efficient than reading in each disk record separately.

Even though a disk or tape file may be blocked, the program processes
records in the standard way, that is, one logical record at a time.

By indicating BLOCK CONTAINS n RECORDS for an input disk or tape, the
computer is able to read the full block correctly. Similarly, by indicating the
number of records in a block for an output disk or tape, the computer is able
to create the correct block of records. Thus, the BLOCK CONTAINS clause of a
disk or tape file is the *only* entry required to read or write a block of records.
No additional COBOL statements are necessary.

The BLOCK CONTAINS clause itself is *omitted* when records are not blocked,
as with unit-record devices and some disk or tape files.

The programmer is typically given the blocking factor by the systems analyst, who determines the most efficient block size to use.

Suppose we have an input file with the following FD entries:

```
FD   TRANSACTION-FILE
     LABEL RECORDS ARE STANDARD
     RECORD CONTAINS 50 CHARACTERS
     BLOCK CONTAINS 20 RECORDS.
```

With a record size of 50 and a block of 20, 1000 characters (50 × 20) are read into the input area reserved for this file. For the initial read, the first 50 characters in main memory are processed. For the next read, the second 50 characters in memory are processed. This will continue until the entire block is accessed; *then* the next block is read and the procedure is repeated. See Appendix B for a full discussion of blocking.

> The BLOCK CONTAINS entry is optional for COBOL 85 *even when records are blocked*. This is because job control statements or system commands can be used to indicate the blocking factor.

d. DATA RECORD(S) Clause—(Optional)

Format

```
DATA   {RECORD  IS  }   record-name . . .
       {RECORDS ARE }
```

The **DATA RECORD(S)** clause identifies the record formats within the file. If there is only one record type or layout, DATA RECORD IS record-name may be used. Any record-name may be specified. The name, however, must conform to the rules for forming user-defined words or data-names. A record-name must also be unique. That is, a name that appears as a file or record-name may not be used for any other item in the program. The DATA RECORD(S) clause serves as a documentation entry, since all it does is name the record formats.

> The DATA RECORDS clause has been categorized as obsolete under COBOL 85. This means that it is still optional but will not be part of the next standard. As we will see in the next section, it is actually a redundant entry because the record description entries themselves must include each record-name.

Multiple Records per File

If more than one record format exists for a file, you may specify DATA RECORDS ARE record-name-1 record-name-2 . . . . If a payroll file, for example, has a salary record and an employee history record, then two record formats would be specified: DATA RECORDS ARE SAL-REC EMP-HISTORY-REC.

Note that while DATA RECORDS ARE . . . specifies more than one format for the file, additional storage is *not* reserved for the input or output area. Specifying several record formats for one file does *not* set up extra I/O areas; it merely redefines a *single* input or output area in several ways.

Example 4   The following is a description of a disk file containing transaction credit records and transaction debit records. Record size is 50, block size is 20.

```
FD   TRANSACTION-FILE
     LABEL RECORDS ARE STANDARD
     RECORD CONTAINS 50 CHARACTERS
     DATA RECORDS ARE TRANS-DEBIT, TRANS-CREDIT.
```

When a transaction record is read, it is placed into a 50-position input area reserved for it. Both TRANS-DEBIT and TRANS-CREDIT records use this same 50-position area, which will be described in two different ways by record description entries.

The four clauses discussed are the most commonly used entries in the FD, but they are not the only ones. For most applications in COBOL, they are quite adequate. Table 3.1 provides a summary of these clauses. After all clauses within the FD are coded, place a period at the end. Note that no other period will appear in the FD.

Clause	Entries	Optional or Required	Use
LABEL RECORD(S)	$\begin{bmatrix} \text{IS} \\ \text{ARE} \end{bmatrix} \begin{Bmatrix} \underline{\text{OMITTED}} \\ \underline{\text{STANDARD}} \end{Bmatrix}$	Required for COBOL 74; optional for COBOL 85	STANDARD is specified if header and trailer labels are used on disk or tape; OMITTED is used for unit-record files
RECORD CONTAINS	(Integer) CHARACTERS	Optional	Indicates the number of characters in the record
BLOCK CONTAINS	(Integer) RECORDS	Optional	Indicates the blocking factor for disk or tape
DATA RECORD(S)	$\begin{bmatrix} \text{IS} \\ \text{ARE} \end{bmatrix}$ (record-name(s))	Optional	Indicates the name of each record in the file

Table 3.1
Summary of FD entries

RULES FOR CODING FILE DESCRIPTION ENTRIES

1. FD is coded in Area A.
2. All other entries should be coded in Area B.
3. No period is coded until the last clause has been specified.
4. Commas are always optional in a program to separate clauses. If used, they must be followed by at least one blank.
5. It is recommended that each clause appear on a separate line for clarity and ease of debugging.
6. For COBOL 74 the only clause required in a FD is a LABEL RECORD(S) clause. The BLOCK CONTAINS clause may also be required for COBOL 74 if disk or tape records are blocked. For COBOL 85 all clauses are optional.

You will see from the instruction format that the words IS and ARE are *not underlined* in any clause, which means that they may be omitted. Thus, to say LABEL RECORDS STANDARD, for example, is entirely appropriate.

Last, the order of the preceding entries within the FD is *not* significant. Any clause may appear first in an FD entry.

Example 5 The following is a correctly coded File Description specification, even though the sequence of clauses is not the same as previously described.

```
FD   INVENTORY-IN
       LABEL RECORDS ARE OMITTED
       RECORD CONTAINS 100 CHARACTERS
       DATA RECORD IS RECORD-1
       BLOCK CONTAINS 10 RECORDS.
```

Self-Test
1. The DATA DIVISION is that part of a COBOL program that _____ .
2. The two primary sections of a DATA DIVISION are the _____ and the _____ .
3. The FILE SECTION of the DATA DIVISION defines all data areas _____ .

4. The first time a file-name appears in a COBOL program is in a _____ statement of the _____ DIVISION.

5. File-names must be from one to __(no.)__ characters in length, contain at least one _____ , and have no _____ .

6. FILE 1 is not a valid file-name because it _____ .

7. File-names (must, need not) be unique.

8. For every file defined in a SELECT statement, there will be one _____ entry in the FILE SECTION.

9. The four clauses that may be used with an FD entry are _____ , _____ , _____ , and _____ .

10. For unit-record devices, LABEL RECORDS ARE _____ .

11. When LABEL RECORDS ARE STANDARD is specified, header and trailer labels will be _____ on input files and _____ on output files.

12. The BLOCK CONTAINS clause is only used for _____ .

13. Write an FD entry for an input sales file on a tape, blocked 20 with 100-position records and standard labels; one record format exists.

14. Write an FD entry for an error report to be printed with a heading line and detail records. (Note that HEADING and DETAIL are reserved words.)

15. Make any necessary corrections to the following DATA DIVISION entries.

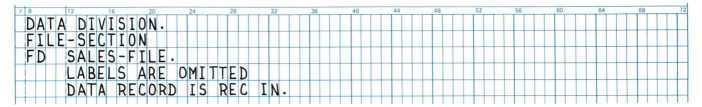

```
DATA DIVISION.
FILE-SECTION
FD  SALES-FILE.
    LABELS ARE OMITTED
    DATA RECORD IS REC IN.
```

Solutions

1. defines and describes fields, records, and files in storage

2. FILE SECTION; WORKING-STORAGE SECTION

3. that are part of input or output

4. SELECT; ENVIRONMENT

5. 30; alphabetic character; special characters (except -)

6. contains an embedded blank

7. must

8. FD

9. LABEL RECORD(S); RECORD CONTAINS; BLOCK CONTAINS; DATA RECORD(S)

10. OMITTED

11. checked; created

12. blocked disk or tape files

13.
```
FD   SALES-FILE
     LABEL RECORDS ARE STANDARD
     RECORD CONTAINS 100 CHARACTERS
     BLOCK CONTAINS 20 RECORDS
     DATA RECORD IS REC-IN.
```

14.
```
FD   ERROR-REPORT
     LABEL RECORDS ARE OMITTED
     RECORD CONTAINS 133 CHARACTERS
     DATA RECORDS ARE HEADING-LINE, DETAIL-LINE.
```

15. No hyphen between FILE and SECTION.
Periods are required after all section names.
No period after FD SALES-FILE.
The LABEL clause should read LABEL RECORDS ARE OMITTED (assuming that it does not have any labels).
REC IN must *not* have an embedded blank.
A period is required after the last clause.

Corrected Entry
```
DATA DIVISION.
FILE SECTION.
FD  SALES-FILE
    LABEL RECORDS ARE OMITTED
    DATA RECORD IS REC-IN.
```

2. Record Description Entries

a. Defining a Record.
A **record** is a unit of related data *within a file* that contains information of a specific nature. Most often, a file consists of records that all have the same format. An inventory disk file, for example, where all records have the following fields is said to contain only one record format:

A record, then, is a specific format of data within a file. We have one file for each form of input and one file for each form of output that the program processes. We have one record format for each type of data within the file.

As noted, most files have only one record format, but some consist of numerous record formats. Consider the following magnetic disk payroll file containing several different types of records:

NAME	PRESENT SALARY	PAST SALARY	DATE OF SALARY CHANGE	

SALARY HISTORY RECORD

NAME	SALARY	NO. OF DEPENDENTS	LIFE INSURANCE PREMIUMS	HEALTH INSURANCE PREMIUMS	

CURRENT PAYROLL RECORD

NAME	FEDERAL TAX	STATE TAX	CITY TAX	

TAX RECORD

Note that *three* record formats exist within this file: a salary history record, a current payroll record, and a tax record. Usually, however, most disk or tape files have a single record format.

Usually, however, most disk or tape files have a single record format.

The one file type that commonly requires numerous record formats is a print file. Consider the Printer Spacing Chart in Figure 3.1. There would be *three* record formats for the print file because there are three types of lines: (1) a heading record or line (denoted as an H line in the left margin); (2) a record or line containing detail or transaction data (denoted as a D line); (3) a record or line containing a final total (denoted as a T line).

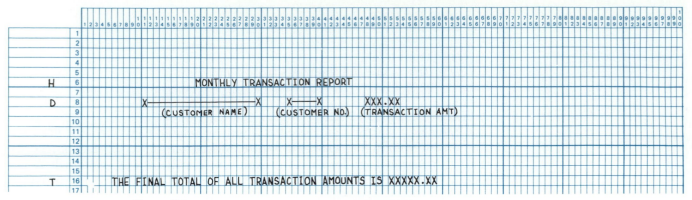

Figure 3.1
Printer Spacing Chart with
three record formats.

b. Level Numbers.   After a file is described by an FD, the record description entries for each record format within the file follow. A **record description** is required for each type of record in the FD. The record description specifies the format of a record. Record description entries indicate:

1. The items or fields to appear in the record.
2. The order in which the fields appear.
3. How these fields are related to one another.

Just as the file-name is specified on the FD level, a record-name is coded on the *01 level*.

Examine the following illustrations.

Example 1   A transaction file that has only one record format may have the following entries:

```
FD   TRANSACTION-FILE
     LABEL RECORDS ARE OMITTED
     RECORD CONTAINS 80 CHARACTERS
     DATA RECORD IS TRANSACTION-REC-IN.
01   TRANSACTION-REC-IN.
     •
     • } Entries to be discussed
     •
```

Example 2   An accounts receivable file that has two record formats may have the following entries:

```
FD   ACCTS-RECVABLE
     LABEL RECORDS ARE STANDARD,
     RECORD CONTAINS 10 CHARACTERS,
     BLOCK CONTAINS 50 RECORDS,
     DATA RECORDS ARE CR-REC-IN, DB-REC-IN.
01   CR-REC-IN.
     •
     • } Entries to be discussed
     •

01   DB-REC-IN.
     •
     • } Entries to be discussed
     •
```

In summary, each FD must be followed by record description entries for the file. We have observed that records are defined on the 01 level. We now indicate what fields are contained in each record of the file and how the fields are organized.

Data is grouped in COBOL using the concept of a *level*. Records are considered the *highest level of data* in a file, and thus are coded on the 01 level. A field of data within the record is coded on a level *subordinate to* 01, that is, 02, 03, and so on. Any **level number** between 02 and 49 may be used to describe data fields within a record.

c. Describing Fields within a Record.   A field of data is a group of consecutive storage positions reserved for an item of data.

Example 3   Let us examine the following record layout:

Employee Record (input)

The record description entries following the FD may be as follows:

```
01   EMPLOYEE-REC-IN,
     05   NAME-IN
     05   ANN-SALARY-IN
     05   JOB-DESCRIPTION-IN
```

The name of the record, EMPLOYEE-REC-IN, is coded on the 01 level, which is an Area A entry. All fields within the record are coded on any level between 02 and 49, anywhere in Area B. By specifying these fields on the 05 level, we indicate that:

1. All fields on the 05 level are *subordinate to*, or part of, the 01-level entry.
2. All fields that are coded on the same level, 05 in this example, are *independent* items; that is, they are *not* subordinate to one another.

Thus NAME-IN, ANN-SALARY-IN, and JOB-DESCRIPTION-IN are fields within EMPLOYEE-REC-IN, and each is independent of the others.

We use 05 rather than 02 to define fields within a record in case we wish to provide additional levels between 01 and the level specified. That is, if NAME-IN and ANN-SALARY-IN are later to be accessed together, they can be made subordinate to a field called MAJOR. We could easily modify our coding as follows, without changing the existing level numbers:

```
01   EMPLOYEE-REC-IN,
     03   MAJOR
          05   NAME-IN
          05   ANN-SALARY-IN
     03   JOB-DESCRIPTION-IN
```

In general, we will use 05 as the level of fields that are subdivisions of 01. We use the suffix -IN to indicate that these are input fields within an input record.

Although COBOL 85 permits the use of Area A for level numbers, we recommend you denote fields within a record by indenting, that is, using Area B for all levels except 01.

Let us redefine the preceding input.

Employee Record (input)

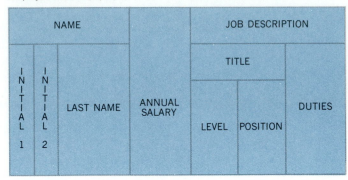

In this case, all fields are *not* independent of one another, as in the preceding input layout. Recall that a field may be subordinate to, or contained within, *another* field in a record. INITIAL1-IN, INITIAL2-IN, and LAST-NAME-IN, for example, may be fields within NAME-IN, which itself is contained within a record. INITIAL1-IN, INITIAL2-IN, and LAST-NAME-IN, then, would be coded on a level subordinate to NAME-IN. If NAME-IN were specified on level 05, INITIAL1-IN, INITIAL2-IN, and LAST-NAME-IN could each be specified on either level 06 or level 07, and so forth. To allow for possible insertions later on, we will use 10 for the level subordinate to 05.

Example 4   The record description for the preceding redefined input is as follows:

```
01   EMPLOYEE-REC-IN.
     05   NAME-IN
          10   INITIAL1-IN
          10   INITIAL2-IN
          10   LAST-NAME-IN
     05   ANN-SALARY-IN
     05   JOB-DESCRIPTION-IN
          10   JOB-TITLE-IN
               15   LEVEL-IN
               15   JOB-POSITION-IN
          10   DUTIES-IN
```

There are three major fields within the record: NAME-IN, ANN-SALARY-IN, and JOB-DESCRIPTION-IN, all coded on the 05 level. The NAME-IN field is further subdivided into INITIAL1-IN, INITIAL2-IN, and LAST-NAME-IN. These level-10 items are contained within NAME-IN. Similarly, JOB-TITLE-IN and DUTIES-IN are subdivisions of JOB-DESCRIPTION-IN. JOB-TITLE-IN is further subdivided into LEVEL-IN and JOB-POSITION-IN.

Names used to define fields, like the names of records and files, must conform to the rules for establishing user-defined data-names.

A REVIEW OF RULES FOR DEFINING DATA-NAMES

1. From 1 to 30 characters.
2. No special characters except a hyphen.
3. No embedded blanks.
4. At least one alphabetic character.
5. No COBOL reserved words.
6. The name used should be meaningful. Use suffixes or prefixes such as -IN or -OUT where appropriate.

Coding Guidelines for Record Description Entries

Note that we code all fields in Area B and code the highest level of organization, the record, in Area A. We also indent subordinate levels. Although this indentation is not required by the compiler, it does make the lines easier to read. Using this method, the fact that `INITIAL1-IN`, `INITIAL2-IN`, and `LAST-NAME-IN` are contained within `NAME-IN` is quite clear.

Level numbers may vary from `02` to `49` for fields of data. As we have seen, level numbers need not be consecutive. As a matter of style, we will use `05`, `10`, `15`, and so on as level numbers so that other level numbers can be inserted later on if the need arises. The following, however, are also valid entries:

```
01  REC-A-OUT.
    03  DATE-OF-HIRE-OUT
        07  MONTH-OUT
        07  YEAR-OUT
    03  NAME-OUT
```

`MONTH-OUT` and `YEAR-OUT` on the `07` level are contained within `DATE-OF-HIRE-OUT` on the `03` level. As such, `MONTH-OUT` and `YEAR-OUT` must have the same level number.

Although consecutive level numbers can be used, we will avoid them because they make it difficult to insert elements later on if the need arises.

Invalid Use of Level Numbers

Observe the following illustration, which is not valid:

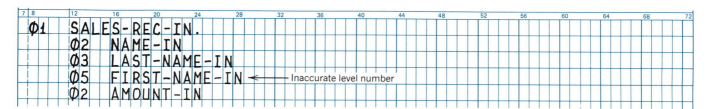

This entry is *not* correct. It implies that `FIRST-NAME-IN`, as an `05`-level item, is contained in `LAST-NAME-IN`, an `03`-level item. To indicate that `LAST-NAME-IN` and `FIRST-NAME-IN` are *independent* subdivisions of `NAME-IN`, they both must be coded on the same level. To place them both on either the `03` or `04` or `05` level would be accurate.

Specifying the Order of Fields in a Record

The order in which fields are placed within the record is crucial. If `NAME-IN` is the first item specified within `EMPLOYEE-REC-IN`, this implies that `NAME-IN` is the first data field in the record.

Relationships among Entries

The relationships among data elements in a program are described in Figure 3.2.

d. Elementary and Group Items. A field that is *not* further subdivided is called an **elementary item.** A field that is further subdivided is called a **group item.** In Example 4, `NAME-IN` is a group item that is subdivided into three elementary items, `INITIAL1-IN`, `INITIAL2-IN`, and `LAST-NAME-IN`. `ANN-SALARY-IN`, on the same level as `NAME-IN`, is an elementary item since it is not further subdivided.

Figure 3.2
The relationships among
SELECT, FD, 01, and field
entries.

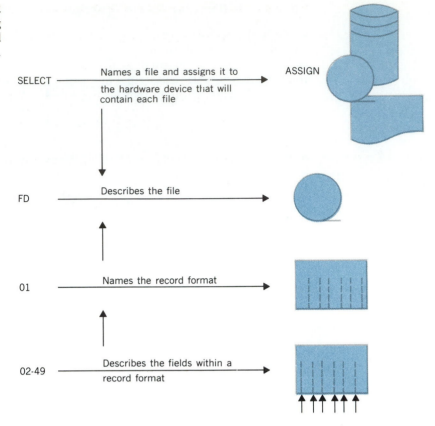

All elementary items must be additionally described with a PICTURE clause that indicates the *size* and *type* of the field. A group item, because it is subdivided, needs no further specification and ends with a period. Thus we have, for example:

```
01   ACCOUNT-REC-IN,
     05   CUSTOMER-NAME-IN,
          10   LAST-NAME-IN           (PICTURE clause)
          10   FIRST-NAME-IN          (PICTURE clause)
     05   TRANSACTION-NUMBER-IN       (PICTURE clause)
     05   DATE-OF-TRANSACTION-IN,
          10 MONTH-IN                 (PICTURE clause)
          10 YEAR-IN                  (PICTURE clause)
```

Note that there is a period at the end of each group item in this illustration. Each elementary item requires further description with a PICTURE clause. We treat the record entry, on the 01 level, as a group item, since it is, in fact, a data element that is further subdivided.

Self-Test
1. All records are coded on the _____ level.
2. Levels _____ to _____ may be used to represent fields within a record.
3. An 03-level item may be subordinate to an _____ -level item if it exists.
4. What, if anything, is wrong with the following user-defined data-names?
   (a) CUSTOMER NAME
   (b) TAX%
   (c) DATA
5. An elementary item is defined as _____ , and a group item is defined as
   _____ .

6. The level number 01 is coded in Area _____ ; level numbers 02–49 are coded in Area _____ .

7. Write record description entries for the following insofar as you are able.

TRANSACTION RECORD

INVOICE NUMBER	LOCATION			PRODUCT DESCRIPTION		
	WAREHOUSE	CITY	JOB LOT	NO. OF ITEM		ITEM NAME
				SIZE	MODEL	

Solutions

1. 01
2. 02; 49
3. 02 (or 01)
4. (a) No embedded blanks allowed (CUSTOMER-NAME would be okay).
   (b) No special characters other than the hyphen are permitted—% is not valid.
   (c) DATA is a COBOL reserved word.
5. one that is not further subdivided; one that is further subdivided
6. A; B
7.

```
Ø1  TRANSACTION-REC-IN.
    Ø5  INVOICE-NO-IN              (PICTURE required)
    Ø5  LOCATION-IN.
        1Ø  WAREHOUSE-IN          (PICTURE required)
        1Ø  CITY-IN               (PICTURE required)
        1Ø  JOB-LOT-IN            (PICTURE required)
    Ø5  PRODUCT-DESCRIPTION-IN.
        1Ø  NO-OF-ITEM-IN.
            15  SIZE-IN           (PICTURE required)
            15  MODEL-IN          (PICTURE required)
        1Ø  ITEM-NAME-IN.
```

Note: Periods follow group items only. Elementary items will contain PICTURE clauses as specified in the next section.

e. PICTURE (PIC) Clauses. Group items are defined by a level number and a name, and end with a period. Elementary items are those fields that are *not* further subdivided but must be described in detail with a **PICTURE** (or **PIC**, for short) clause.

FUNCTIONS OF THE PICTURE CLAUSE

1. To specify the *type* of data contained within an elementary item.
2. To indicate the *size* of the field.

A PICTURE clause associated with an elementary item will describe the type and size of data in that elementary item.

(1). Types of Data Fields.   There are *three* types of data fields.

TYPES OF DATA FIELDS

1. **Alphabetic**
   A field that may contain only letters or blanks is classified as alphabetic. A name field or an item description field can be considered alphabetic.
2. **Alphanumeric**
   A field that may contain *any* character is considered alphanumeric. An address field, for example, would be classified as alphanumeric (or alphameric), since it may contain letters, digits, blanks, and/or special characters.
3. **Numeric**
   Any signed or unsigned field that will contain digits only is considered numeric. We typically define as numeric those fields to be used in arithmetic operations.

To denote the type of data within an elementary field, a `PICTURE` or `PIC` clause will contain:

CHARACTERS USED IN `PICTURE` **CLAUSES**

A for alphabetic

X for alphanumeric

9 for numeric

---

(2). Size of Data Fields.   We denote the *size* of the field by the *number* of A's, X's, or 9's used in the `PICTURE`. For example, consider the following:

```
05   AMT-OUT   PICTURE IS 99999.
```

`AMT-OUT` is an elementary item consisting of *five positions of numeric data.*
  The entry

```
05   CODE-IN   PICTURE XXXX.
```

defines a four-position storage area called `CODE-IN` that will contain alphanumeric data, that is, it can contain any character. Consider the following entries:

```
01   CUST-REC-IN.
     05   CUST-ID-IN     PICTURE XXXX.
     05   AMT-IN         PICTURE 99999.
     05   CODE-IN        PICTURE XX.
```

`CUST-ID-IN` is the first data field in the record `CUST-REC-IN`. This means that the first four positions of the record represent the field called `CUST-ID-IN`. `AMT-IN`, as the second entry specified, would be describing the next field of data, or positions 5–9 of the record. That is, the five positions directly following `CUST-ID-IN` would represent the field called `AMT-IN`.

If a field is numeric, its `PICTURE` clause will contain 9's; if a field is alphabetic, its `PICTURE` clause will contain only A's; if a field may contain any character or combination of digits, letters, and special symbols, it is defined with a PICTURE of X's. Numeric fields may contain a maximum of 18 digits. Thus a PICTURE clause with 20 9's, for example, is typically invalid unless the compiler permits its use as an enhancement.

The following defines a 10-position alphanumeric field.

```
05   NAME-IN   PICTURE IS X(10).
```

Rather than coding 10 X's, we may use *parentheses* to designate the size of the field. The word IS in the PICTURE clause is optional, as in all COBOL statements, and may always be omitted. A period will follow each PICTURE clause in the FILE SECTION. Because the abbreviation **PIC** may be used in place of PICTURE, the preceding field can be defined as

```
05   NAME-IN   PIC X(10).
```

(3). A Matter of Style

(a). We recommend that you use X's rather than A's in PIC clauses because an X is applicable to any nonnumeric field. Since nonnumeric fields are all represented the same way internally in the computer, we will follow the convention of designating each such item (e.g., NAME-IN, ADDRESS-IN) with a PICTURE of X's, avoiding the use of A's entirely. We use 9's for numeric fields that will be used in arithmetic operations.

(b) X(nn) **or** 9(nn) **format.** Some organizations prefer a format whereby all PIC clauses are specified as X(nn) or 9(nn), where nn indicates the number of characters. In this way it is easier to read the record description entries because they are all properly aligned as in the following.

```
01   INVENTORY-REC-IN.
     05   ITEM-IN     PIC X(14).
     05   AMT-IN      PIC 9(05).
     05   CODE-IN     PIC X(02).
```

In this text, we will simply align PIC clauses for ease of reading.

(4). Format of PIC Clauses.

Group items are those fields that are further subdivided and are coded without PICTURE clauses. Elementary items require a PICTURE clause, which denotes the size of a field and its type, that is, the type of data it will contain.

Consider the following record layout for an output disk record:

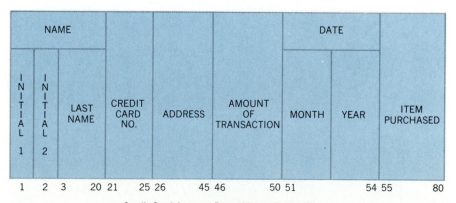

Credit Card Account Record in an Output File

Its record description entry could appear as follows:

```
01   CREDIT-CARD-ACCT-OUT.
     05   NAME-OUT.
          10   INIT1-OUT          PICTURE X.
          10   INIT2-OUT          PICTURE X.
          10   LAST-NAME-OUT      PICTURE X(18).
     05   CREDIT-CARD-NO-OUT      PICTURE 9(5).
     05   ADDRESS-OUT             PICTURE X(20).
     05   AMT-OF-TRANS-OUT        PICTURE 9(5).
     05   DATE-OF-TRANS-OUT.
          10   MONTH-OUT          PICTURE 99.
          10   YEAR-OUT           PICTURE 99.
     05   ITEM-PURCHASED-OUT      PICTURE X(26).
```

A `PICTURE` clause may appear *anywhere* on the line following the data-name. As noted, for purposes of clarity, we will place each `PICTURE` clause in the same position on each line; this is not, however, required. At least one space must follow the word `PICTURE`. All A's, X's, or 9's should appear consecutively with no spaces between these characters. Similarly, if parentheses are used to denote the size of a field, no spaces should appear within the parentheses. The following entries are typically invalid:

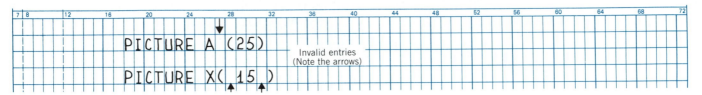

The `PICTURE` clauses in a record description entry should, in total, yield the number of characters in the record. Thus, if `CREDIT-CARD-ACCT-OUT` is a disk record consisting of 80 characters, all `PICTURE` clauses on the elementary level would total 80 positions of storage.

As indicated, the A specification is rarely used in actual practice. The X specification can encompass alphabetic data and is usually used to represent all nonnumeric data. Typically, we use X's in a `PICTURE` clause for any field *not* used in arithmetic operations.

f. Use of `FILLER`s in Record Description Entries.

Examine the following record layout:

SAMPLE RECORD LAYOUT FOR AN INPUT EMPLOYEE RECORD	
Positions in Record	**Field**
1–25	EMPLOYEE-NAME-IN
26–30	Not used
31–35	HOURS-WORKED-IN
36–80	Not used

Record positions 26–30 and 36–80 may contain data, but it is not pertinent to the processing of our program. These areas, however, must be noted as fields in the record description entry. Note that the following is *not correct coding* for this sample layout:

```
01   EMPLOYEE-REC-IN.
     05   EMPLOYEE-NAME-IN       PICTURE X(25).
     05   HOURS-WORKED-IN        PICTURE 9(5).
```

The preceding record description entries cause two major errors:

1. The computer will assume that HOURS-WORKED-IN *immediately follows* EMPLOYEE-NAME-IN, since it is the next designated field. A READ instruction, then, would place record positions 26–30, not 31–35, in the storage area called HOURS-WORKED-IN.
2. The PICTURE clauses should account for 80 positions of storage. Instead, only 30 positions have been defined.

Thus, the preceding is incorrect and could be coded correctly as:

```
01  EMPLOYEE-REC-IN.
    05  EMPLOYEE-NAME-IN      PIC X(25).
    05  UNUSED1               PIC X(5).
    05  HOURS-WORKED-IN       PIC 9(5).
    05  UNUSED2               PIC X(45).
```

The COBOL reserved word **FILLER** may be used to denote fields of data that will not be specifically referenced in the program. Instead of creating data-names such as UNUSED1 and UNUSED2 in the preceding, we may use the word FILLER. A FILLER with an appropriate PICTURE clause designates an area set aside for some part of a record that will *not* be individually referenced in the PROCEDURE DIVISION. To say: MOVE FILLER TO OUT-AREA, for example, is invalid because the word FILLER indicates that the field will not be accessed in this program. Our record description entry could be coded, then, as:

```
01  EMPLOYEE-REC-IN.
    05  EMPLOYEE-NAME-IN      PIC X(25).
    05  FILLER                PIC X(5).
    05  HOURS-WORKED-IN       PIC 9(5).
    05  FILLER                PIC X(45).
```

Using COBOL 85, the word FILLER can be omitted entirely. Thus the preceding can be coded as:

```
01  EMPLOYEE-REC-IN.
    05  EMPLOYEE-NAME-IN      PIC X(25).
    05                        PIC X(5).
    05  HOURS-WORKED-IN       PIC 9(5).
    05                        PIC X(45).
```

Except for the COBOL reserved word FILLER, we will keep all other data-names unique for now; that is, we will *not* use the same name for different fields. As we have seen, a record- or a file-name must *never* be used more than once in the DATA DIVISION, but field-names need not be unique. In general, however, we will use separate data-names. We will see in Chapter 6 that the same data-name may, in fact, be used to define several fields if it is properly qualified.

g. Summary of PIC Specifications. In general, a field is denoted as numeric, with a PICTURE of 9's, when an arithmetic operation is to be performed. When a field is so designated, the data in the field may consist of digits and a sign only. A space, for example, *is not a valid character in a numeric field*. Thus, if a field is denoted as numeric, it must contain only valid numeric characters.

An alphanumeric field may contain any data, including all numbers. Thus 123 in CODE-IN, where CODE-IN has PICTURE XXX, is entirely acceptable. CODE-IN, however, with a PIC of XXX may not be used in *arithmetic* operations. This is because only fields with *numeric* PICTURE clauses may be specified in computations. In short, then, fields that are to be used in calculations must be defined with a PICTURE of 9's; all other fields are typically coded with a PICTURE of X's.

h. The Use of the Implied Decimal Point in PIC Clauses. Suppose a five-position input amount field, with contents 10000, is to be interpreted as 100.00. We want the computer to "assume" that a decimal point exists. When any calculations are performed on the amount field, the computer is to consider the data as having three integer positions and two decimal positions. Its PICTURE clause, then, is:

```
        05   AMT-IN      PICTURE 999V99,
```

The symbol V denotes an implied decimal point, and the V does *not* occupy a storage position. Thus, the field AMT-IN is five positions. We have merely indicated that data entering the field is to have three integer and two decimal positions. If 38726 is read into the area, it will be interpreted as 387.26 when the program is executed. All arithmetic operations will function properly with decimal alignment when we specify the PIC as 999V99. A PICTURE of 9(3)V99 or 9(3)V9(2) could be used as well.

i. Summary of Record Description Entries. In summary, for *every* record format in a file, an 01-level entry and its corresponding field descriptions must be included.

All record formats within an FD are described before the next FD is defined. The DATA DIVISION in Figure 3.3 indicates the sequence in which entries are coded.

j. File Design Considerations If There Are Multiple Record Formats Within a File. The input file called ACCTS-RECEIVABLE-FILE in Figure 3.3 has two records. Assume that the debit record has a 1 in record position 80, and the credit record has a 2 in record position 80. The computer establishes only *one* input area for this file. When a record is read, the computer must be instructed as to whether it is a debit or credit record. That is, do we move AMT-OF-DEBIT-IN or AMT-OF-CREDIT-IN to the output record? We must check record position 80 to determine if the record is a credit or a debit. If, for example, CODE-1-IN (position 80 of the incoming record) is equal to 1, then we can treat this record as a debit record and move AMT-OF-DEBIT-IN to the output area. This test and MOVE operation is performed in the PROCEDURE DIVISION as follows:

```
     IF   CODE-1-IN = 1
          MOVE AMT-OF-DEBIT-IN TO AMT-OF-TRANS-OUT,
```

If CODE-1-IN (record position 80) is not equal to 1, then unless there is an error in the data, CODE-2-IN (record position 80 *of the same record*) should equal 2, and this should be a credit record.

Thus, each input record is placed in a single input area. The field designations of that input area will be determined by what type of record it is. If there is more than one record format in a file, a code is usually established to specify the type of record being processed and the record format to be used.

Characters in the COBOL Character Set

All fields consist of individual units of data called **characters.** The characters permitted in a COBOL program are collectively referred to as the **COBOL**

COBOL Program Sheet

System					Punching Instructions						Sheet	of
Program			Graphic						Card #		Identification	
Programmer		Date	Punch						Form		73	80

Sequence		Cont.	A	B	COBOL Statement
(Page)	(Serial)				

```
DATA DIVISION.
FILE SECTION.
FD  ACCTS-RECEIVABLE-FILE
    LABEL RECORDS ARE OMITTED,
    RECORD CONTAINS 80 CHARACTERS,
    DATA RECORDS ARE DEBIT-REC-IN, CREDIT-REC-IN.
01  DEBIT-REC-IN.
    05  CUSTOMER-NAME-IN      PIC X(20).
    05  ADDRESS-IN            PIC X(15).
    05  AMT-OF-DEBIT-IN       PIC 999V99.
    05  FILLER               PIC X(39).
    05  CODE-1-IN             PIC 9.
01  CREDIT-REC-IN.
    05  NAME-IN               PIC X(20).
    05  AMT-OF-CREDIT-IN      PIC 999V99.
    05  FILLER               PIC X(54).
    05  CODE-2-IN             PIC 9.
FD  OUTPUT-FILE
    LABEL RECORDS ARE STANDARD,
    RECORD CONTAINS 25 CHARACTERS,
    DATA RECORD IS REC-OUT.
01  REC-OUT.
    05  NAME-OUT              PIC X(20).
    05  AMT-OF-TRANS-OUT      PIC 999V99.
```

Figure 3.3
Sample DATA DIVISION entries.

character set. These include letters (both uppercase and lowercase), digits (0–9), and special symbols such as a dollar sign ($) or a percent sign (%). The full set of these characters appears in Appendix A.

IV. Types of Data

A. Variable and Constant Data

Thus far, we have discussed the organization of data as it appears in a COBOL program. Input and output files have records that are described by record formats. Each record has fields classified as group items or elementary items.

By defining files, records, and fields and assigning corresponding user-defined data-names in the DATA DIVISION, we reserve storage for data. The File Description entry, as illustrated in the previous section, reserves storage for the records in the input and output files. The area described by the File Description entry is said to contain **variable data.**

Variable data is the data that is entered into storage as a result of a READ instruction. The contents of the fields containing variable data are not known until the program is actually executed. We say, then, that the contents of data fields in the input area is variable because it changes with each READ instruction. The clause READ PAYROLL-FILE ... results in the reading of one input record, which is stored in the area defined by the File Description or FD for PAYROLL-FILE. After input fields are processed, the results are placed in the output area, which is defined by another FD. Thus we say that the contents of output fields are also variable.

When we define a data field with a data-name, we need not know anything about its contents. AMT-IN, for example, is the name of a data field within PAYROLL-REC-IN; the content of AMT-IN, however, is variable. It depends on the input record being processed, and thus changes with each run of the program. Any field described within an input or output file is said to contain variable data.

A **constant,** on the other hand, is a form of data required for processing that is *not* dependent on the input to the system. A constant, as opposed to variable data, is coded directly in the program. Suppose, for example, we wish to multiply each amount field of every input record by .05, a fixed tax rate. The tax rate, .05, is *not* a variable in the input record but is nevertheless required for processing. We call .05 a *constant,* since it is a form of data required for processing that is not dependent on the input to the system. It is always fixed, with the same value.

Similarly, suppose we wish to check input records and print the message 'INVALID RECORD' if the data is erroneous. The message 'INVALID RECORD' will be part of the output line, but is *not* entered as input to the system. It is a constant with a fixed value that is required for processing.

A constant may be defined directly in the PROCEDURE DIVISION of a COBOL program. AMT-IN, a field within each input record, is to be multiplied by the tax rate, .05, to produce TAX-AMT-OUT, a field within each output record. The PROCEDURE DIVISION entry to perform this operation is as follows:

```
          MULTIPLY AMT-IN BY .05
              GIVING TAX-AMT-OUT.
```

The two data fields, AMT-IN and TAX-AMT-OUT, are described in the DATA DIVISION. The constant .05 is defined directly in the preceding PROCEDURE DIVISION entry, so it need *not* be described in the DATA DIVISION. A constant may also be defined in the WORKING-STORAGE SECTION of the DATA DIVISION with a **VALUE** clause as follows:

```
WORKING-STORAGE SECTION.
01  TAX-RATE    PICTURE V99    VALUE .05.
```

Thus we may define TAX-RATE in the WORKING-STORAGE SECTION and give it a VALUE of .05. In this way, we may multiply AMT-IN by TAX-RATE in the PROCEDURE DIVISION:

```
MULTIPLY AMT-IN BY TAX-RATE
    GIVING TAX-AMT-OUT.
```

For now, we will focus on constants defined directly in the PROCEDURE DIVISION.

Three types of constants may be defined in a COBOL program: numeric literals, nonnumeric literals, and figurative constants. Each type will be discussed here in detail. (The word "literal" and the word "constant" may be used interchangeably.)

B. Types of Constants

1. Numeric Literal

A **numeric literal** is a constant used primarily for arithmetic operations. The number .05 in the preceding example is a numeric literal. The rules for forming numeric literals are as follows:

RULES FOR FORMING NUMERIC LITERALS
1. 1 to 18 digits.
2. A + or − sign may be used, but it must appear to the *left* of the number.
3. A decimal point is permitted *within* the literal. The decimal point, however, may not be the last character of the literal.

A plus or minus sign is *not* required within the literal, but it *may* be included to the left of the number. That is, +16 and -12 are valid numeric literals but 16+ and 12- are not. If no sign is used, the number is assumed positive. Since a decimal point may not appear as the last character in a numeric literal, 18.2 is a valid literal but 16. is not; however, 16.0 is valid.

The following are valid numeric literals that may be used in the PROCEDURE DIVISION of a COBOL program.

VALID NUMERIC LITERALS
+15.8
-387.58
42
.05
-.97

Suppose we wish to add 10.3 to a field, TOTAL-OUT, defined within an output record in the DATA DIVISION. The following is a valid instruction:

```
ADD 10.3 TO TOTAL-OUT.
```

The following are *not* valid numeric literals for the reasons noted.

INVALID NUMERIC LITERALS	
Literal	**Reason It Is Invalid**
1,000	Commas are *not* permitted.
15.	A decimal point is not valid as the last character.
$100.00	Dollar signs are not permitted.
17.45-	Operational signs, if used, must appear to the left of the number.

A numeric literal, then, is a constant that may be used in the PROCEDURE DIVISION of a COBOL program. Numeric literals are numeric constants that can be used for arithmetic operations. The preceding rules must be employed when defining a numeric literal.

Representing Decimal Data in Storage

Suppose we have an output field defined in a disk record as follows:

```
01  REC-OUT.
    05  AMT-OUT PIC 99V99.
```

The `AMT-OUT` field can accept a value of 2150, for example. When 2150 is transmitted to the `AMT-OUT` area it is decimally aligned as 21.50.

If, however, we wish to move a constant to `AMT-OUT` in the `PROCEDURE DIVISION`, the constant would actually include the decimal point as in the following:

```
MOVE 21.50 TO AMT-OUT.
```

Thus a decimal point is merely assumed on disk and tape input and output in order to save storage; a decimal point must, however, actually be included in a numeric constant when decimal alignment is required.

2. Nonnumeric Literal

A **nonnumeric** or **alphanumeric literal** is a constant that is used in the `PROCEDURE DIVISION` for all operations *except* arithmetic. The following rules must be employed when defining a nonnumeric or alphanumeric literal.

RULES FOR FORMING NONNUMERIC LITERALS

1. The literal must be enclosed in quotation marks.
2. From 1 to 160 characters, including spaces, may be used. (Only 120 characters are permitted for COBOL 74.)
3. Any character permitted in the COBOL character set may be used except the quotation mark.

As noted, the COBOL character set includes those characters that are permitted within a COBOL program. Appendix A lists these characters.

We have adopted the notation of a single quotation mark or apostrophe to delineate nonnumeric literals. Some compilers, however, use double quotation marks (''). Check your COBOL manual. On all systems there are commands that enable you to change the specification for a nonnumeric literal from an apostrophe (single quote) to a quotation mark (double quotes) or from double quotes to an apostrophe.

The following are valid nonnumeric literals.

VALID NONNUMERIC LITERALS

```
'CODE'
'ABC 123'
'1,000'
'INPUT'
'$100.00'
'MESSAGE'
```

Moving any of these literals to a print area and then writing the print record results in the printing of those characters *within* the quotation marks; that is CODE, ABC 123, 1,000, and so on will print if they are moved to a print area. Note that a nonnumeric literal may contain *all* numbers. '123' is a valid nonnumeric literal, but it should be distinguished from the numeric literal 123, which is the only type of literal permitted in an arithmetic operation.

Suppose we wish to move the message 'INVALID RECORD' to an output field, `MESSAGE-FIELD-OUT`, before we write an output record. The following is a valid COBOL instruction.

```
MOVE 'INVALID RECORD' TO MESSAGE-FIELD-OUT.
```

'INVALID RECORD' is a nonnumeric literal. It is a value specified in the PROCEDURE DIVISION and does *not* appear in the DATA DIVISION. MESSAGE-FIELD-OUT is not a literal but a data-name. It conforms to the rules for forming user-defined words. It could not be a nonnumeric literal, since it is not enclosed in quotation marks. All data-names, such as MESSAGE-FIELD-OUT, would be defined in the DATA DIVISION.

In summary, a nonnumeric literal is any constant defined directly in a source program that is not used for arithmetic operations. It must conform to the rules previously specified. Any character may be used to form a nonnumeric literal. That is, once the string of characters is enclosed within quotes, the computer does *not* check to determine if a reserved word is being used. Thus 'DATA' and 'MOVE' are valid nonnumeric literals.

With COBOL 85, you may use nonnumeric literals that are up to 160 characters in length. With COBOL 74, you are limited to 120 characters.

3. Figurative Constant

A **figurative constant** is a COBOL reserved word that has special significance to the compiler. In this section we discuss two figurative constants: ZEROS and SPACES.

The figurative constant ZEROS is a COBOL reserved word meaning all zeros. Consider the following instruction:

```
MOVE ZEROS TO TOTAL-OUT.
```

This operation results in the field called TOTAL-OUT being filled with all zeros. ZEROS is a figurative constant having the value of all zeros. ZERO, ZEROES, and ZEROS are equivalent figurative constants, all having the same value. They may be used interchangeably in the PROCEDURE DIVISION of a COBOL program.

SPACES is a figurative constant meaning all blanks. Consider the following instruction:

```
MOVE SPACES TO CODE-OUT.
```

This results in blanks being placed in every position of the field CODE-OUT. The word SPACES is a COBOL reserved word having the value of all blanks. It may be used interchangeably with the figurative constant SPACE.

ZEROS and SPACES are the two figurative constants most frequently used. We will discuss other figurative constants later in this book.

In summary, three types of constant data may be specified in the PROCEDURE DIVISION: a numeric literal, a nonnumeric literal, and a figurative constant. Fields that contain variable data must be described in the DATA DIVISION and may be accessed in the PROCEDURE DIVISION.

In future discussions of PROCEDURE DIVISION entries, the use of constants will become clearer. Right now, you should be able to recognize literals and to distinguish them from the names used to define data fields. The specific formats of ADD and MOVE statements, in which these literals were illustrated, are discussed more fully later.

V. The WORKING-STORAGE SECTION: An Overview

The following discussion provides a preliminary introduction to the WORKING-STORAGE SECTION of the DATA DIVISION. Chapter 7 gives more details.

Any field necessary for processing that is not part of input or output may be defined in the WORKING-STORAGE SECTION. It may also be established with a constant as its value. For example, if an end-of-job indicator field called ARE-THERE-MORE-RECORDS is to be initialized with a value of 'YES' and changed to 'NO ' only when the last record has been read, we can define that field and give it an initial value in the WORKING-STORAGE SECTION. If some intermediate total areas are necessary for processing, they, too, may be defined in this section. If we want to count given occurrences of a specific condition, we can establish a counter in WORKING-STORAGE.

RULES FOR USING THE WORKING-STORAGE SECTION

1. The WORKING-STORAGE SECTION follows the FILE SECTION.

2. WORKING-STORAGE SECTION is coded on a line by itself beginning in Area A and ending with a period.

3. A group item that will be subdivided into individual storage areas as needed may then be defined. All necessary fields can be described within this 01-level entry:

```
WORKING-STORAGE SECTION.
01   WS-STORED-AREAS.
     05   ARE-THERE-MORE-RECORDS       PIC X(3).
     05   WS-GROSS-AMT                 PIC 999V99.
```

4. Names associated with group items and with elementary items must conform to the rules for forming data-names. WS- is frequently used as a prefix to denote these fields as WORKING-STORAGE entries.

5. Each elementary item must contain a PIC clause.

6. Each elementary item may contain an initial value, if desired:

```
WORKING-STORAGE SECTION.
01   WS-STORED AREAS.
     05   ARE-THERE-MORE-RECORDS   PIC X(3)     VALUE 'YES'.
     05   WS-GROSS-AMT             PIC 999V99   VALUE 0.
```

VALUE clauses for initializing fields may *only* be used in the WORKING-STORAGE SECTION, *not* in the FILE SECTION. Either figurative constants or literals may be used in VALUE clauses.

The field called ARE-THERE-MORE-RECORDS is usually initialized at 'YES' in the WORKING-STORAGE SECTION. It remains at 'YES' until there are no more input records to be processed, at which point a 'NO ' is moved into the field in the PROCEDURE DIVISION:

```
READ FILE-IN
    AT END MOVE 'NO ' TO ARE-THERE-MORE-RECORDS.
```

WS-GROSS-AMT is an item that may be defined in WORKING-STORAGE for storing an intermediate total. WORKING-STORAGE entries may have VALUE clauses to initialize fields, but these are not required.

COBOL 85: Summary of DATA DIVISION **Changes**

1. The entire DATA DIVISION is itself optional. This means that file specifications may be copied from a library, eliminating the need for FDs in some user programs.
2. The LABEL RECORDS clause is optional. The reading or writing of label records can be left entirely to the operating system. If the clause is omitted, LABEL RECORDS are assumed to be STANDARD.
3. The BLOCK CONTAINS clause may be deleted for blocked records if blocking is handled by the operating system.
4. The DATA RECORDS clause is classified as "obsolete," meaning that it is still optional but will not be part of the *next* COBOL standard.
5. The word FILLER is now optional in record descriptions. The following is acceptable:

```
01   EMPLOYEE-OUTPUT-REC.
     05                    PIC X(6).
     05   NAME-OUT         PIC X(10).
     05                    PIC X(30).
     05   ADDRESS-OUT      PIC X(14).
```

CHAPTER SUMMARY

A. Data Organization
   1. **File**—An overall classification of data pertaining to a specific business use or application.
   2. **Record**—A unit of data within a file that contains information of a specific nature.
   3. **Field**—A group of consecutive positions reserved for an item of data.

   Note: Files, records, and fields are all defined in a COBOL program with data-names.

B. Types of Data
   1. **Variable Data**—Data that originates outside the program and will vary with each run.

   Files
   Records } Defined by data-names
   Fields

   2. **Constant or Literal**—Data that is defined within the program; it is *not* entered as input to the system.
      a. Numeric Literal—A constant that may be used in the PROCEDURE DIVISION for arithmetic operations.
      b. Nonnumeric Literal—A constant that may be used in the PROCEDURE DIVISION for all operations except arithmetic.
      c. Figurative Constant—A COBOL reserved word with special significance to the COBOL compiler such as ZERO or ZEROES or ZEROS, SPACE or SPACES.

C. The DATA DIVISION
   1. FD Entries
      a. FD is coded in Area A.
      b. The file-name, which is typically coded in Area B, must be the same name that is used in the SELECT statement.
      c. Clauses: LABEL RECORDS ARE { OMITTED / STANDARD }

      RECORD CONTAINS integer CHARACTERS
      BLOCK CONTAINS integer RECORDS
      DATA RECORD IS record-name

All clauses are optional for COBOL 85. The LABEL RECORDS clause is required for COBOL 74.

   d. After any clauses have been specified, a single period ends the FD.

2. Record Description Entries

   a. Record-names are coded on the 01 level.

   b. Field-names are coded on levels 02-49. We will use 05, 10, 15, and so on to allow for insertions if they become necessary.

   c. Level 01 is coded in Area A. All other levels are coded in Area B for COBOL 74, although Area A can be used for COBOL 85.

   d. Items with higher-level numbers are considered subordinate to, that is, contained within, items with lower-level numbers. In the following, DEPT-IN is contained within JOB-DESCRIPTION-IN:

```
02   JOB-DESCRIPTION-IN
04   DEPT-IN
```

   e. We indent subordinate items for the sake of clarity:

```
02   JOB-DESCRIPTION-IN
   04   DEPT-IN
```

   f. Group items are further subdivided; elementary items are not.

   g. Only elementary items have PICTURE or PIC clauses to describe the data:

     X—alphanumeric

     A—alphabetic

     9—numeric

     V—implied decimal position (used only with numeric fields)

   h. Fields must be defined in the DATA DIVISION in the same sequence as they appear in the record being described.

   i. FILLER is a COBOL reserved word used to define areas within a record that will not be referenced individually during processing.

   j. A period must follow a PICTURE clause in an elementary item; a period directly follows a group item name.

CHAPTER SELF-TEST

1. The contents of fields defined within input and output records is (fixed, variable).

2. A constant may be used directly in the _____ DIVISION as part of an instruction.

3. Fields whose names appear in PROCEDURE DIVISION statements must be defined in the _____ DIVISION.

4. What, if anything, is wrong with the following numeric literals?
   (a) 123.
   (b) 15.8-
   (c) 1,000,000.00
   (d) $38.90
   (e) 58

5. What, if anything, is wrong with the following nonnumeric literals?
   (a) 'THE MESSAGE 'CODE' MUST BE PRINTED'
   (b) 'INPUT'
   (c) 'ZERO'
   (d) '123'
   (e) '   '

6. The literal '   ', if printed, would result in the printing of two _____ .

7. Two examples of figurative constants are _____ and _____ .

8. Consider the following instruction: MOVE '1' TO FLD1.
   '1' is a _____ .
   FLD1 is a _____ and must be defined in the _____ DIVISION.

9. To print 'ZEROS' results in the printing of _____ . To print ZEROS results in the printing of _____ . ZEROS is called a _____ .

10. A PICTURE clause must be used in conjunction with each _____ item in a record description.

11. A PICTURE clause specifies the _____ and the _____ of a data field.

12. The characters that may be included in an alphabetic field are _____ .

13. The characters that may be included in an alphanumeric field are _____ .

14. The characters that may be included in a numeric data field are _____ .

15. An alphanumeric PICTURE clause contains _____ ; an alphabetic PICTURE clause contains _____ ; a numeric PICTURE clause contains _____ .

What, if anything, is wrong with the following entries (16–18)? Consider each separately.

16. 01   TRANSACTION-REC.
        05   DATE-OF-SALE PICTURE 9999.
            10   MONTH   PICTURE 99.
            10   YEAR   PICTURE 99.

17. 03 FIELDA PICTURE XX.

18. 04 FIELDB PICTURE X (22).

19. The sum of the X's, A's, or 9's in all the PICTURE clauses in a record description should, in total, equal _____ .

20. The COBOL reserved word _____ is used to denote an area of a record that will not be used for processing.

21. A PICTURE clause of 9V9 indicates a __(no.)__-position numeric data field.

22. If a three-position tax field is to be interpreted as .xxx, its PICTURE clause should be _____ .

23. The _____ SECTION of the DATA DIVISION usually follows the FILE SECTION.

24. WORKING-STORAGE entries may contain _____ clauses to indicate the initial contents of fields.

25. Is the use of level numbers in the following correct? Explain your answer.

```
01   INREC.
    05   NAME-IN.
        07   LAST-NAME        PIC X(10).
        07   FIRST-NAME       PIC X(10).
        07   MIDDLE-NAME      PIC X(10).
    05   ADDRESS-IN.
        10   STREET           PIC X(10).
        10   CITY             PIC X(10).
        10   STATE            PIC X(10).
```

Solutions

1. variable

2. PROCEDURE

3. DATA

4. (a) A decimal point may not be the last character.
   (b) A minus sign must be to the left of the number.
   (c) Commas are not permitted.
   (d) A dollar sign is not permitted.
   (e) Nothing is wrong.

5. (a) Quotation marks may not be used within a nonnumeric literal.
   (b) Nothing is wrong.
   (c) Nothing is wrong.

(d) Nothing is wrong.

(e) Nothing is wrong.

6. blanks or spaces

7. ZERO, ZEROES, ZEROS; SPACE, SPACES

8. nonnumeric literal (enclosed in quotes); data-name (not enclosed in quotes); DATA

9. the word ZEROS; a zero value (all 0's); figurative constant

10. elementary

11. size; type

12. letters and blanks

13. any characters in the COBOL character set (letters, digits, and special symbols)

14. digits, and a plus or minus sign

15. X's; A's; 9's

16. Group items, such as DATE-OF-SALE, should not have PICTURE clauses.

17. Okay

18. Should be: 04 FIELDB PICTURE X(22). There is no space between X and (.

19. the number of positions in the record

20. FILLER

21. two (the V does not occupy a storage position)

22. V999.

23. WORKING-STORAGE

24. VALUE

25. Yes, although it is somewhat unusual. All level 07 items are contained within NAME-IN, and all level 10 items are contained within ADDRESS-IN. Thus, the same level number need not be used throughout for elementary items. In the first case, LAST-NAME with a level of 07 is an elementary item and, in the second case, STREET with a level number of 10 is also an elementary item.

PRACTICE PROGRAM

Figure 3.4 shows the input and output layouts for a program to create a master customer disk file (CUSTOMER-MASTER) from a customer transaction disk file (CUSTOMER-TRANS).

Figure 3.4
Input and output layouts for Practice Program.

CUSTOMER-TRANS Record Layout

CUSTOMER-MASTER Record Layout

Notes

1. If sales exceed $100.00, allow 3% discount. If sales are $100.00 or less, allow 2% discount.

2. Discount Amount = Sales × Discount %.

3. New Amount = Sales − Discount Amount.

The following is the pseudocode used to plan the program. It may be helpful in evaluating the logic.

Pseudocode for Practice Problem

    START
        Open the Files
        Read a Record
        PERFORM UNTIL no more records

```
        Clear the Output Area
        Move Input to Output
        Calculate Discount Amount
        Calculate Net
        Write a Record
        Read a Record
    ENDPERFORM
    End-of-Job Operations
STOP
```

The following are the PROCEDURE DIVISION entries to produce the required results:

```
PROCEDURE DIVISION.
100-MAIN-MODULE.
    OPEN INPUT  CUSTOMER-TRANS
         OUTPUT CUSTOMER-MASTER.
    READ CUSTOMER-TRANS
        AT END MOVE 'NO ' TO ARE-THERE-MORE-RECORDS.
    PERFORM 200-PROCESS-DATA
        UNTIL ARE-THERE-MORE-RECORDS = 'NO '.
    CLOSE CUSTOMER-TRANS
          CUSTOMER-MASTER.
    STOP RUN.
200-PROCESS-DATA.
    MOVE SPACES TO MASTER-REC.
    MOVE IDENT-IN TO IDENT-OUT.
    MOVE SALES-IN TO SALES-AMT-OUT.
    IF  SALES-IN > 100.00
        MOVE .03 TO DISC-PERCENT-OUT
    ELSE
        MOVE .02 TO DISC-PERCENT-OUT.
    MULTIPLY SALES-IN BY DISC-PERCENT-OUT GIVING WS-DISC-AMT.
    SUBTRACT WS-DISC-AMT FROM SALES-IN GIVING NET-OUT.
    WRITE MASTER-REC.
    READ CUSTOMER-TRANS
        AT END MOVE 'NO ' TO ARE-THERE-MORE-RECORDS.
```

Code the first three divisions of the program and indicate what this program accomplishes.

The following is the hierarchy or structure chart that indicates the relationship between modules in this program. Here we indicate that 200-PROCESS-DATA is a paragraph performed within 100-MAIN-MODULE.

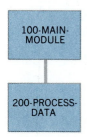

The following is a suggested solution:

```
IDENTIFICATION DIVISION.
PROGRAM-ID. SAMPLE.
AUTHOR. NANCY STERN.
DATE-COMPILED.
****************************************************************
*       THIS PROGRAM CREATES A MASTER CUSTOMER DISK FROM      *
*       TRANSACTION RECORDS                                   *
****************************************************************
ENVIRONMENT DIVISION.
INPUT-OUTPUT SECTION.
```

```
FILE-CONTROL.
    SELECT CUSTOMER-TRANS
        ASSIGN TO DATA1.
    SELECT CUSTOMER-MASTER
        ASSIGN TO DATA2.
*
 DATA DIVISION.
 FILE SECTION.
 FD  CUSTOMER-TRANS
     LABEL RECORDS ARE STANDARD
     RECORD CONTAINS 80 CHARACTERS.
 01  TRANS-REC.
     05  IDENT-IN                 PIC 9(5).
     05  SALES-IN                 PIC 9(3)V99.
     05  FILLER                   PIC X(70).
 FD  CUSTOMER-MASTER
     LABEL RECORDS ARE STANDARD
     RECORD CONTAINS 100 CHARACTERS.
 01  MASTER-REC.
     05  IDENT-OUT                PIC 9(5).
     05  SALES-AMT-OUT            PIC 9(3)V99.
     05  DISC-PERCENT-OUT         PIC V99.
     05  NET-OUT                  PIC 999V99.
     05  FILLER                   PIC X(83).
 WORKING-STORAGE SECTION.
 01  WS-STORED-AREAS.
     05  ARE-THERE-MORE-RECORDS   PIC X(3)      VALUE 'YES'.
     05  WS-DISC-AMT              PIC 9(3)V99.
```

KEY TERMS

Alphanumeric literal	Field	Numeric literal
BLOCK CONTAINS	Figurative constant	PICTURE (PIC)
Blocking	File	Record
Business system	FILE SECTION	RECORD CONTAINS
Characters	FILLER	Record description
COBOL character set	Group item	Reserved word
Constant	Header label	Trailer label
DATA DIVISION	Identifier	Update procedure
Data-name	LABEL RECORD(S)	VALUE clause
DATA RECORD(S)	Level number	Variable data
Elementary item	Master file	WORKING-STORAGE
FD (File Description)	Nonnumeric literal	SECTION

REVIEW QUESTIONS

I. True-False Questions

T   F

__ __ 1. A field is a collection of data records.

__ __ 2. Files are collections of data records.

__ __ 3. PICTURE clauses are used to describe elementary fields in record description entries.

__ __ 4. Numeric literals use quotation marks.

__ __ 5. A numeric literal may be from 1 to 30 characters long.

__ __ 6. A comma may not be used in a numeric literal.

__ __ 7. Data-names are names that may be assigned to fields and records.

__ __ 8. SPACE is a figurative constant.

___ ___ 9. The contents of a field may not exceed 30 characters.

___ ___ 10. MOVE SPACES TO FLD1 is a valid statement regardless of the size of FLD1.

___ ___ 11. There may be only one 01 level for a specific file.

___ ___ 12. The order in which fields are specified in a record description is not significant.

___ ___ 13. Group items must not have PICTURE clauses.

___ ___ 14. Elementary items may or may not have PICTURE clauses.

___ ___ 15. A FILLER is a COBOL reserved word that may be used in the DATA and PROCEDURE DIVISIONs.

___ ___ 16. A record-name is assigned in the ENVIRONMENT DIVISION.

___ ___ 17. Two files may be assigned the same name in a COBOL program.

___ ___ 18. Levels 03, 08, 75 may be subordinate to a record level.

___ ___ 19. The WORKING-STORAGE SECTION follows the FILE SECTION.

___ ___ 20. Entries not part of input or output but necessary for processing are coded in the WORKING-STORAGE SECTION.

II. General Questions

1. Make necessary corrections to the following data-names.
   - (a) CUSTOMER NAME
   - (b) AMOUNT-
   - (c) INVOICE-NO.
   - (d PROCEDURE
   - (e) TAX-%
   - (f) QUANTITY-OF-PRODUCT-ABC-ON-HAND
   - (g) AMT-OF-SALES

2. Make necessary corrections to the following literals.
   - (a) '123'
   - (b) 123
   - (c) 'ABC'
   - (d) ABC
   - (e) $100.00
   - (f) '$100.00'
   - (g) 1,000
   - (h) 100.7-
   - (i) 54

In Questions 3–6, state the contents of the data field, FIELDA, after the MOVE operation.

3. MOVE 'ABC' TO FIELDA.

4. MOVE ABC TO FIELDA.

5. MOVE 'SPACES' TO FIELDA.

6. MOVE SPACES TO FIELDA.

7. Which of the following entries should be coded in Area A?
   - (a) FD
   - (b) FILE SECTION
   - (c) 01
   - (d) 03
   - (e) LABEL RECORDS ARE OMITTED

8. What are the rules for forming data-names?

9. Correct the following DATA DIVISION.

```
DATA DIVISION.
FILE-SECTION.
FD   TAPE FILE.
     DATA RECORD IS INPUT.
01   INPUT.
     05   TRANS.NO                PICTURE 9999.
     05   TRANSACTION-NAME        PICTURE 20X.
     05   ADDRESS
          10   NUMBER             PICTURE XXXX.
          10   STREET             PICTURE A(15).
          10   CITY               PICTURE AAA.
     05   CREDIT-RATING           PICTURE XX.
          10   CREDIT-CODE        PICTURE X.
          10   LIMIT OF PURCHASE  PICTURE X.
     05   UNIT-PRICE              PICTURE 99.9.
     05   QTY-PURCHASED           PICTURE 9(5).
     05   DISCOUNT-%              PICTURE V99.
```

10. Consider the following pictorial description of a record called PURCHASE-ORDER. Code the record description entries for it.

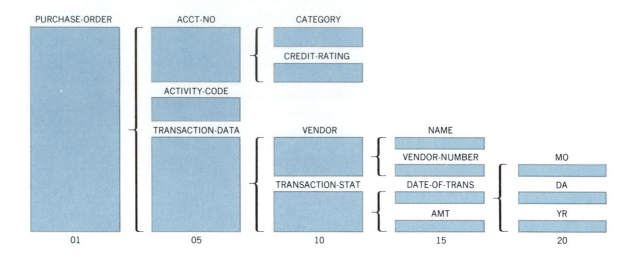

PROGRAMMING ASSIGNMENTS

1. Using Figure 1.8 in Chapter 1, indicate which elements in the program are (a) files, (b) records, (c) fields, (d) numeric literals, (e) nonnumeric literals, (f) figurative constants.

2. Using Figure 1.11 in Chapter 1, indicate which elements in the program are (a) files, (b) records, (c) fields, (d) numeric literals, (e) nonnumeric literals, (f) figurative constants.

3. Using Figure 1.12 in Chapter 1, indicate which elements in the program are (a) files, (b) records, (c) fields, (d) numeric literals, (e) nonnumeric literals, (f) figurative constants.

4. Write the FD and record description entries necessary for an inventory file with the following record format. The inventory file will be on magnetic tape with standard labels and a blocking factor of 20.

LOCATION				PART NO.	PART NAME	REORDER LEVEL	UNIT COST	TOTAL SALES	TOTAL SALES
STATE (Alphabetic)	WAREHOUSE				Alphanumeric		XXX.XX	2 MOS. AGO XXX.XX	LAST MO XXX.XX
	FLOOR	BIN	CITY (Alphabetic)						
1 3	4 5	6 7	8 11	12 16	17 25	26 29	30 34	35 39	40 44

BALANCE ON HAND	QTY. SOLD	TOTAL COST	BIN CAPACITY	DESCRIPTION OF PART
		XXXXX.XX		Alphanumeric
45 50	51 55	56 62	63 67	68 100

(Unless otherwise noted, fields are numeric)
XXX.XX denotes a PICTURE clause of 999V99

5. Write the FD and record description entries for the following purchase record.

Item Description	Field Type	Field Size	Positions to Right of Decimal Point
Name of item	Alphabetic	20	—
Date of order (month, day, year)	Numeric	6	0
Purchase order number	Numeric	5	0
Inventory group	Alphanumeric	10	—
Number of units	Numeric	5	0
Cost per unit	Numeric	4	0
Freight charge	Numeric	4	0
Tax percent	Numeric	2	2

6. Write FD and record description entries for the following disk format.

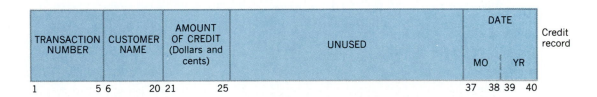

7. Write FD and record description entries for a master transaction disk file with the following two record formats. The master disk has standard labels and is blocked 10.

8. Consider the following pseudocode and PROCEDURE DIVISION for a program that reads in customer records, each with three amount fields, and calculates a total price. Write the first three divisions for the program. Both files are on disk, with standard labels and a blocking factor of 25. Each input field, and its corresponding output field, has a PICTURE of 9(5); the total field has a PICTURE of 9(6).

Pseudocode
```
START
     Open Files
     Read a Record
     PERFORM UNTIL no more records
          Move Input Customer Number to Output Customer Number
          Add Three Amount Fields and Place Sum in Output Total Area
          Write Output Record
          Read a Record
     ENDPERFORM
     End-of-Job Operations
STOP
```

PROCEDURE DIVISION
```
100-MAIN-MODULE.
     OPEN INPUT TRANSACTION-FILE
          OUTPUT TOTAL-FILE.
     READ TRANSACTION-FILE
          AT END MOVE 'NO ' TO ARE-THERE-MORE-RECORDS.
     PERFORM 200-CALC-RTN
          UNTIL ARE-THERE-MORE-RECORDS = 'NO '.
     CLOSE TRANSACTION-FILE
          TOTAL-FILE.
     STOP RUN.
200-CALC-RTN.
     MOVE CUST-NO-IN TO CUST-NO-OUT.
     ADD AMT1-IN, AMT2-IN, AMT3-IN
          GIVING TOTAL-OUT.
     WRITE TOTAL-REC-OUT.
     READ TRANSACTION-FILE
          AT END MOVE 'NO ' TO ARE-THERE-MORE-RECORDS.
```

4

Designing Complete COBOL Programs: A Closer Look at the PROCEDURE DIVISION

OBJECTIVES

To familiarize you with the methods used to

1. Access input and output files.
2. Read data from an input file.
3. Perform simple move operations.
4. Write information onto an output file.
5. Accomplish end-of-job operations.
6. Execute paragraphs from a main module and then return control to that main module.

I. A Review of the First Three Divisions

Thus far, three of the four divisions of a COBOL program have been discussed in detail. The PROCEDURE DIVISION, the last to be studied, is unquestionably the most significant. The **PROCEDURE DIVISION** contains all the instructions that the computer will execute. The logic of the program is coded with these instructions.

The IDENTIFICATION and ENVIRONMENT DIVISIONs supply information about the nature of the program and the specific equipment that will be used. The FILE SECTION of the DATA DIVISION defines, in detail, the input and output areas. The input area is storage reserved for one record from an input file. The output area is storage reserved for the data to be produced as output by the program. The WORKING-STORAGE SECTION of the DATA DIVISION is used for defining any areas not part of input and output but nonetheless required for processing; these include work areas such as counters and end-of-file indicators. The instructions in the PROCEDURE DIVISION, however, actually read and process the data and produce the output information. Since all instructions are written in the PROCEDURE DIVISION, the majority of chapters in this book will focus on these entries.

In this chapter, we will consider simple instructions that access files, read data, move fields from one area to another, produce output, and accomplish end-of-job functions. Knowledge of these types of instructions will be sufficient for writing elementary COBOL programs *in their entirety*. The PROCEDURE DIVISION coding used in the book will illustrate the structured, top-down approach to writing COBOL programs.

II. The Format of the PROCEDURE DIVISION

A. Paragraphs That Serve as Modules

1. Defining Paragraphs

The PROCEDURE DIVISION is divided into **paragraphs.** Each paragraph consists of an independent **module** or **routine** that includes a series of instructions designed to perform a specific set of operations. As noted, we use the terms paragraph, module, and routine interchangeably.

Paragraph-names, like the PROCEDURE DIVISION entry itself, are coded in Area A. All other entries in the PROCEDURE DIVISION are coded in Area B. Paragraph-names, like the PROCEDURE DIVISION entry, end with a period.

2. Rules for Forming Paragraph-Names

Rules for forming paragraph-names are the same as rules for forming data-names except that a paragraph-name can be all digits. Paragraph-names must be unique in a COBOL program. Thus, two paragraphs may *not* have the same name. Similarly, a data-name cannot also serve as a paragraph-name.

Coding Guidelines

We will use descriptive paragraph-names along with a numeric prefix such as 200-CALC-RTN to identify the type of paragraph. A paragraph with a prefix of 200- is located after paragraph 100-XXX and before paragraph 300-YYY. In very long programs, you may wish to use page and line numbers as a prefix to descriptive paragraph-names as follows:

Sequence No.	COBOL Coding
002010	PROCEDURE DIVISION.
002020	002020-MAIN-MODULE.
⋮	⋮
004050	004050-CALC-RTN.
⋮	⋮

B. Statements and Sentences within Paragraphs

Each paragraph in a COBOL program consists of **sentences.** A sentence is a statement or group of statements to be treated as a unit, where each sentence ends with a period.

A **statement** in COBOL begins with a verb such as READ, MOVE, or WRITE, or a condition such as IF A = B ....

As noted, all COBOL statements are coded in Area B whereas paragraph-names are coded in Area A.

Coding Guidelines

Although sentences and statements can be written across the coding sheet in paragraph form, it is highly recommended that each statement be coded on an individual line as in Figure 4.1. This format will make it much easier to read and debug programs.

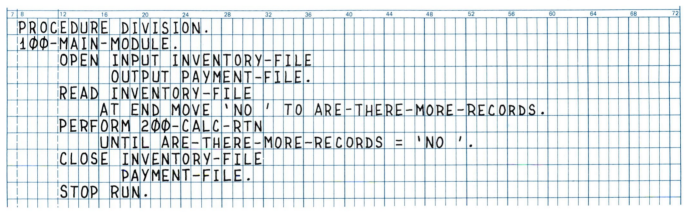

Figure 4.1
PROCEDURE DIVISION entries coded in a user-friendly way.

```
PROCEDURE DIVISION.
100-MAIN-MODULE.
    OPEN INPUT INVENTORY-FILE
        OUTPUT PAYMENT-FILE.
    READ INVENTORY-FILE
        AT END MOVE 'NO ' TO ARE-THERE-MORE-RECORDS.
    PERFORM 200-CALC-RTN
        UNTIL ARE-THERE-MORE-RECORDS = 'NO '.
    CLOSE INVENTORY-FILE
        PAYMENT-FILE.
    STOP RUN.
```

C. The Sequence of Instructions in a Program

The computer executes each statement in the order written unless a PERFORM instruction transfers control temporarily to another paragraph in the program. For example, in Figure 4.1, the OPEN statement will be executed first followed by a READ. This is referred to as executing a program in **sequence.**

Figure 4.1 illustrates a paragraph labeled 100-MAIN-MODULE. It contains instructions that are normally coded in the first or main paragraph of all programs. All processing is controlled by PERFORM statements in this main module. The actual processing of input records in Figure 4.1, for example, depends on what is coded in the paragraph labeled 200-CALC-RTN, which is executed from the main module.

Let us begin by discussing the instructions in the paragraph labeled 100-MAIN-MODULE. These instructions are usually included in most programs. The only changes that will be necessary will be in the data- and paragraph-names used; it also may be necessary to add some functions to our main module in more complex programs.

After this main module has been explained in detail, we will discuss sample entries that can be coded in `200-CALC-RTN`.

D. The Top-Down Approach for Coding Paragraphs

You may recall that well-designed programs are written using a top-down approach. This means that the **main module** is coded first and that subsequent modules are coded from the major level to the detail level. That is, you should code the more general paragraphs first and end with the most detailed ones. This will help ensure that the program is properly designed and well organized. Think of the main module as a general outline of a term paper. It is best to write the major paragraphs of a paper first (I, II, III, A, B, C, etc.) and leave minor levels for later on (1, a., etc.). This top-down approach is useful when writing programs as well.

III. Statements Typically Coded in the Main Module

A. OPEN Statement

1. The Instruction Format: A Review

Before discussing the OPEN statement in detail, let us review the instruction format that will be used to describe it. The **OPEN** statement accesses the input and output files in a program and has the following instruction format.

Format

$$\text{OPEN} \begin{Bmatrix} \underline{\text{INPUT}} & \text{file-name-1} \ldots \\ \underline{\text{OUTPUT}} & \text{file-name-2} \ldots \end{Bmatrix}$$

The following rules will help you interpret instruction formats in general.

A REVIEW OF INSTRUCTION FORMAT SPECIFICATIONS

1. Capitalized words are COBOL reserved words.
2. Underlined words are required elements in the statement or option specified.
3. Lowercase entries are user-defined words.
4. Braces { } denote that one of the enclosed items is required.
5. Brackets [ ] denote that the enclosed item is optional.
6. Punctuation, when included in the format, is required.
7. The use of three dots or ellipses (. . .) indicates that the preceding type of entry (a file-name in this case) may be repeated if desired.

These rules are repeated on the inside of the front cover of this text for ease of reference.

Standard COBOL reference manuals use the same instruction formats as specified in this book. Thus, as you become familiar with the meaning of these instruction formats, it will be easier for you to consult a reference manual for additional information.

Sometimes we simplify an instruction format by including only those options pertinent to our discussion or only those most frequently used.

The preceding specifications tell us the following about an OPEN statement:

1. The word OPEN is a COBOL reserved word because it is capitalized; it is also required in the statement because it is underlined.
2. Either the {INPUT file-name-1 ...} or {OUTPUT file-name-2 ...} clause must be used since they are in braces. Most frequently, they are both used.

   If the first clause is used, the underlined word INPUT is required. The file-name, which appears as a lowercase entry, is user-defined. The dots or ellipses mean that any number of input files may be included. Similarly, if the {OUTPUT file-name-2 ...} clause is used, the word OUTPUT is required. The output file-names are also user-defined entries. Thus, if there are both input *and* output files to process, which there usually are, we would include both an INPUT and an OUTPUT clause in the OPEN statement.

2. The Purpose of the OPEN statement

Before an input or output file can be read or written, it must first be activated or accessed with the use of an OPEN statement.

Recall that for every SELECT statement in the ENVIRONMENT DIVISION, a file-name is defined and a device is assigned.

Example

```
SELECT PAYROLL-FILE
    ASSIGN TO DISK1.
SELECT PAYCHECKS-OUT
    ASSIGN TO SYSOUT.
```

We use the SELECT statement to assign a disk drive to the file-name PAYROLL-FILE. The file-name PAYCHECKS-OUT is assigned to a device called SYSOUT, which is typically the printer or a display unit.

Files that are defined in SELECT statements must be described in FD entries. The OPEN statement, however, actually tells the computer which files will be *input* and which will be *output*. Consider the following:

This statement informs the computer that the storage positions assigned to PAYROLL-FILE will serve as an input area and the storage positions assigned to PAYCHECKS-OUT will serve as an output area. The data from PAYROLL-FILE will be read by the computer, and the data in PAYCHECKS-OUT will be written by the computer.

An OPEN statement, then, designates files as either input or output. It also accesses the specific devices. Since PAYROLL-FILE, for example, is an input disk file in the program, the OPEN statement accesses the specific disk drive to determine if it is ready to read data. If not, execution would be suspended until the operator makes the device ready.

In addition to distinguishing input files from output files and accessing specified devices, an OPEN statement performs certain checking functions. If label records for an input disk or tape file are indicated as STANDARD, an OPEN statement checks the header label to determine if the correct file has been accessed. If label records for an output disk or tape file were designated as STANDARD, the OPEN statement creates the header label. The actual header information, however, is frequently entered using a system command or job control statement that is separate from the program.

In summary, three basic functions are performed by the OPEN statement.

> ### FUNCTIONS OF THE OPEN STATEMENT
> 1. Indicates which files will be input and which will be output.
> 2. Makes the files available for processing.
> 3. Performs header label routines if label records are STANDARD.

Programs are often written using several input and output files. An update program, for example, takes an OLD-MASTER-IN file and a file of transaction or change records called TRANS-FILE and uses them to create a NEW-MASTER-OUT. In addition, a printed file of errors called ERR-LIST may also be produced. The OPEN statement for such a program can be coded as:

```
OPEN INPUT   OLD-MASTER-IN
             TRANS-FILE
      OUTPUT NEW-MASTER-OUT
             ERR-LIST.
```

In this case, there are two input files and two output files. Although the OPEN statement can be written across the coding form, it is far better to put each clause on a separate line, as shown here, for ease of reading and debugging.

All input files follow the COBOL reserved word INPUT and, similarly, all output files follow the COBOL word OUTPUT. The word INPUT need not be repeated for each incoming file. The word OUTPUT may also be omitted after the first output file is noted. The preceding OPEN statement may also be written as four distinct sentences:

```
OPEN INPUT OLD-MASTER-IN.
OPEN INPUT TRANS-FILE.
OPEN OUTPUT NEW-MASTER-OUT.
OPEN OUTPUT ERR-LIST.
```

When separate sentences are used, the word INPUT or OUTPUT must be included for each file that is opened. This method is preferable when files are to be opened at different points throughout the program; that is, if a program processes one entire file before it accesses the next, the files should be opened separately. Unless such periodic intervals are required for the opening of files, however, it is considered inefficient to code an independent OPEN sentence for each file.

The order in which files are opened is *not* significant. The only restriction is that a file must be opened before it may be read or written; a file must be *accessed* before it may be *processed*. Since the OPEN statement allows the accessing of files, it is generally one of the first instructions coded in the PROCEDURE DIVISION.

Coding Guidelines for the OPEN Statement

1. Each file to be opened should appear on a separate line. This makes it easier to read the sentence and makes debugging easier as well. When an error occurs, the computer will print the erroneous line number. If each file is opened on a separate line and an OPEN error occurs, it is easier to pinpoint the file that caused the error.
2. Indent each line within an OPEN sentence as illustrated. This makes a

program more readable. For the OPEN sentence, we typically indent so that the words INPUT and OUTPUT are aligned. For other entries we indent four spaces.

B. READ **Statement**

After an input file has been opened, it may be read. A **READ** statement transmits data from the input device, assigned in the ENVIRONMENT DIVISION, to the input storage area, defined in the FILE SECTION of the DATA DIVISION.

The following is the instruction format for a READ statement.

Format

> READ file-name-1
>   AT END statement-1 ...

The file-name specified in the READ statement appears in three previous places in the program:

1. The SELECT statement, indicating the name and the device assigned to the file. If a file is stored on a disk, for example, a READ operation transmits data from the disk to the input area.
2. The FD entry, describing the file.
3. The OPEN statement, accessing the file and activating the device.

The primary function of the READ statement is to transmit *one data record* to the input area reserved for that file. That is, each time a READ statement is executed, *one record* is read.

The READ statement has, however, several other functions. Like the OPEN statement, it performs certain checks. It checks the length of each input record to ensure that it corresponds to the length specified in a RECORD CONTAINS clause in the DATA DIVISION, if specified. If a discrepancy exists, an error message prints, and execution of the program is terminated.

The READ statement will also use the BLOCK CONTAINS clause, if specified, to perform a check on the blocking factor. Although the primary function of the READ command is the transmission of data, these checking routines are essential for proper execution of the program.

The **AT END** clause in the READ statement tests to determine if there is any more input. An AT END clause of the READ statement tells the computer what to do if there is no more data to be read. The READ instruction generally has the following form:

> READ file-name
>   AT END MOVE 'NO ' TO ARE-THERE-MORE-RECORDS.

The clause MOVE 'NO ' TO ARE-THERE-MORE-RECORDS is executed only when there are no more input records to process. The field called ARE-THERE-MORE-RECORDS is a WORKING-STORAGE item that always contains a 'YES' except when an end-of-file condition occurs, at which point a 'NO ' will be moved to the field. The AT END clause in a READ statement is ignored entirely if there are records to process. Thus, only when there are no more records to read is the AT END clause executed.

Example

> READ MASTER-INVENTORY-FILE
>   AT END MOVE 'NO ' TO ARE-THERE-MORE-RECORDS.

An input record will be read from the input device specified, and the next sequential instruction in the program will be executed unless there are no more input records. If, in fact, there are no more input records, the literal 'NO ' is moved to the field called ARE-THERE-MORE-RECORDS. For example, if 10 records constitute the input file, the eleventh attempt to read a record will cause 'NO ' to be moved to ARE-THERE-MORE-RECORDS.

An AT END is specified whenever a file is being read sequentially. It tells the computer what to do when there is no more data to process.

Examine the following DATA DIVISION entry:

```
FD    ACCOUNTS-RECEIVABLE
      LABEL RECORDS ARE OMITTED
      RECORD CONTAINS 20 CHARACTERS
      DATA RECORD IS REC-IN.
01    REC-IN.
      05   NAME-IN                    PIC X(15).
      05   AMT-OF-TRANS-IN            PIC 9(5).
```

Suppose the statement READ ACCOUNTS-RECEIVABLE AT END MOVE 'NO ' TO ARE-THERE-MORE-RECORDS is executed. The first 15 positions of data from the disk will be placed in storage in the field called NAME-IN. The next five disk positions will be placed in the field called AMT-OF-TRANS-IN. The sequence in which entries are coded in the DATA DIVISION is crucial; data is placed in the fields in the order in which the data-names are specified. If records are blocked for the sake of efficiency, the READ statement will make sure that each block has the correct number of records.

Similarly, if data is read from a terminal, the first columns would be placed in the first data field specified in the DATA DIVISION.

Coding Guideline for the READ Statement

Code the AT END clause on a separate line and indent it for readability.

The following is the instruction format for the READ for COBOL 85.

Format

```
READ file-name-1
     AT END statement-1 . . .
     [NOT AT END statement-2 . . .]
[END-READ]
```

The NOT AT END clause can be used for accomplishing specific tasks when an AT END has *not* been reached:

Example

```
READ ACCTS-PAYABLE
     AT END PERFORM 900-END-OF-JOB-RTN
     NOT AT END PERFORM 800-UPDATE-RTN.
```

Also, the END-READ clause clearly delineates the READ statement:

```
IF  AMT = ZERO
    READ IN-FILE
        AT END MOVE 'NO ' TO ARE-THERE-MORE-RECORDS
    END-READ.
```

The significance of the END-READ delimiter will become clearer as we proceed through the text.

C. PERFORM ... UNTIL **Statement: A Structured Programming Technique**

The instruction format of the **PERFORM ... UNTIL** statement is as follows:

Format

```
PERFORM procedure-name-1
    UNTIL condition-1
```

This statement is critical for implementing the *structured programming technique.* First, it transfers control to the procedure or paragraph named. This named paragraph is executed continually until the condition specified is met. When the condition is met, control returns to the statement *directly following* the PERFORM.

Example

```
PERFORM 200-CALC-RTN
    UNTIL ARE-THERE-MORE-RECORDS = 'NO '.
```

The instructions in the paragraph called 200-CALC-RTN will be executed repeatedly until ARE-THERE-MORE-RECORDS = 'NO '. Recall that ARE-THERE-MORE-RECORDS is a user-defined field. It is a WORKING-STORAGE area that serves as an end-of-file indicator. It is initialized at 'YES' and will contain the letters 'NO ' only when an AT END condition is met. Hence, the PERFORM statement is really indicating that all instructions in 200-CALC-RTN are to be executed until there are no more records to process, at which point control will return to the statement *following* the PERFORM in the main module.

The condition used to terminate the PERFORM should be one that is eventually reached within the paragraph named. To say PERFORM 200-CALC-RTN UNTIL ARE-THERE-MORE-RECORDS = 'NO ' implies that 200-CALC-RTN will have an instruction that at some point moves 'NO ' to ARE-THERE-MORE-RECORDS. The READ ... AT END MOVE 'NO ' TO ARE-THERE-MORE-RECORDS is the instruction that changes the value of ARE-THERE-MORE-RECORDS. In order for the PERFORM to be executed properly, this READ must be an instruction within 200-CALC-RTN. If it were not included, 200-CALC-RTN would be executed endlessly. We have been using the data-name ARE-THERE-MORE-RECORDS for an end-of-file indicator, but any user-defined data-name could be used.

The following sequence of instructions is typical of those that appear in most COBOL programs:

```
PROCEDURE DIVISION.
100-MAIN-MODULE.
    OPEN ...
    READ ...
        AT END MOVE 'NO ' TO ARE-THERE-MORE-RECORDS.
    PERFORM 200-CALC-RTN
        UNTIL ARE-THERE-MORE-RECORDS = 'NO '.
    CLOSE ...
    STOP RUN.
200-CALC-RTN.
    .
    .
    READ ...
        AT END MOVE 'NO ' TO ARE-THERE-MORE-RECORDS.
```

After a file is opened, an input record is read. The PERFORM statement then transfers control to 200-CALC-RTN, where the following steps are executed.

> **HOW INSTRUCTIONS ARE EXECUTED IN** `200-CALC-RTN`
>
> 1. The first input record is processed in `200-CALC-RTN`.
> 2. The next input record is read in `200-CALC-RTN`.
> 3. A test is then made by the `PERFORM` to see if `ARE-THERE-MORE-RECORDS = 'NO '`. It will only be a `'NO '` if the `AT END` condition has been met.
> 4. If there are more records to process, the field called `ARE-THERE-MORE-RECORDS` will not equal `'NO '` and `200-CALC-RTN` will be executed again. That is, the next input record will be processed.
> 5. This sequence continues until there are no more input records to process, at which point `ARE-THERE-MORE-RECORDS` will be set equal to `'NO '` when the `AT END` clause of the `READ` is executed. When `ARE-THERE-MORE-RECORDS = 'NO '`, control returns to the statement following the `PERFORM` in the main module, in this case the `CLOSE` statement.

If there are 10 input records to process, the *eleventh* attempt to read a record is the one that causes an `AT END` condition to be executed. The very last record, therefore, is processed in the usual way—it does *not* cause an `AT END` condition to be executed; it is the *next* `READ` that results in an `AT END` condition.

The use of the `PERFORM ... UNTIL` within the first paragraph labeled `100-MAIN-MODULE` enables that module to serve as an independent routine—in fact, the main routine. `200-CALC-RTN` is also a separate module that processes the input data.

The `PERFORM` statement causes all instructions within the named paragraph to be executed. Consider the following:

```
PERFORM 100-RTN1
    UNTIL ARE-THERE-MORE-RECORDS = 'NO '.
        :
        :
100-RTN1.
        :
        :
200-RTN2.
```

Those instructions that follow `100-RTN1` and precede `200-RTN2` will be executed by the `PERFORM`. The range of the `PERFORM` includes all instructions within the named paragraph until another paragraph-name is sensed or until there are no more instructions. Within `100-RTN1` there should be a statement that includes: `READ ... AT END MOVE 'NO ' TO ARE-THERE-MORE-RECORDS`.

The `PERFORM ... UNTIL` includes a conditional test. That is, a condition must be met for control to return to the statement following the `PERFORM`. Note that the test is made *initially* even before the named paragraph is executed, and then again each time the named paragraph has been executed in its entirety. Thus, if the condition is met when the `PERFORM` is first encountered, the named paragraph will be executed 0, or *no* times.

The flowchart and pseudocode for a `PERFORM ... UNTIL` are as follows:

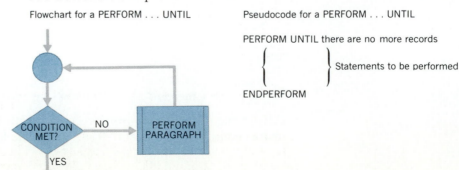

Flowchart for a PERFORM . . . UNTIL

Pseudocode for a PERFORM . . . UNTIL

PERFORM UNTIL there are no more records

Statements to be performed

ENDPERFORM

CONDITION MET?   NO   PERFORM PARAGRAPH

YES

Flowcharts and pseudocodes will be explained in their entirety in the next chapter.

Examine the following and see if you can determine why it is *not* a correct alternative for the previous example:

Incorrect Structuring of a Program

```
100-MAIN-MODULE.
    OPEN ...
    PERFORM 200-CALC-RTN
        UNTIL ARE-THERE-MORE-RECORDS = 'NO '.
    .
    .
    .
200-CALC-RTN.
    READ ...   ◀────────── READ is at the beginning of the paragraph
        AT END MOVE 'NO ' TO ARE-THERE-MORE-RECORDS.
    .          { Continue processing the record }
    .
```

In our original example, a data record was read *in the main module* and then control was transferred to the 200-CALC-RTN module, where that first record was processed, another record read, and so on. Here, the main module does *not* contain this initial READ. Instead, 200-CALC-RTN begins by reading a record and processing it.

The sequence of steps in both these procedures is exactly the same *except* for the processing of the *last* record. We have seen in our original example that when an effort is made to read a record and there is no more input, an AT END condition occurs. In a structured program with an initial READ in the main module, the READ is also typically the *last instruction* in 200-CALC-RTN. Hence, once an end-of-file condition is reached, control *immediately returns* to the main module, that is, to the statement after the PERFORM. This is not so with the preceding incorrect coding.

What happens in the preceding incorrect case when an effort is made to read a record and there is no more input? The AT END condition is executed, and the field called ARE-THERE-MORE-RECORDS is set equal to 'NO '. But the test to return control to the main module is not performed *until after the entire paragraph is executed.* This means that processing will continue in 200-CALC-RTN even though there are no more input records. Only after this processing of a nonexistent record is completed will control return to the main module. What usually results if the preceding incorrect entry is coded and an AT END condition occurs is either (1) the last data record is processed twice or (2) the computer aborts the run because there is no record to process.

In short, when using the PERFORM paragraph-name UNTIL ARE-THERE-MORE-RECORDS = 'NO ' instruction, the paragraph named should contain *as its last instruction* a READ statement. In this way, an AT END condition will always result in the *immediate transfer* of control back to the main module.

In summary, all our structured programs will have the following form:

```
paragraph-name-1.
    OPEN ...
    READ ...
    PERFORM paragraph-name-2
        UNTIL ARE-THERE-MORE-RECORDS = 'NO  .
    .
    .
    .
paragraph-name-2.
    .
    .
    .
    READ ...
        AT END MOVE 'NO ' TO ARE-THERE-MORE-RECORDS. ◀──── Last sentence
                                                            in the paragraph
```

Sometimes programmers code ARE-THERE-MORE-RECORDS in an alternative way, as a one-position numeric field called EOF that is an abbreviation for end-of-file. EOF is a field that serves as a flag or switch. It is initialized at

0 and remains at 0 until an end-of-file condition is reached and a 1 is moved
to it:

```
WORKING-STORAGE SECTION.
01   WS-STORED-AREAS.
     05  EOF               PIC 9      VALUE 0.
PROCEDURE DIVISION.
paragraph-name-1.
     OPEN ...
     READ ...
     PERFORM paragraph-name-2
         UNTIL EOF = 1.
         .
         .
         .
paragraph-name-2.
         .
         .
         .
     READ ...
         AT END MOVE 1 TO EOF.
```

Thus, EOF may be a one-position numeric field with a value of 0 until an
end-of-file condition occurs and 1 is moved to it. Or, ARE-THERE-MORE-
RECORDS, or any other data-name, may be a three-position alphanumeric field
with a value of 'NO ' until an end-of-file condition is reached and 'YES' is
moved to it. You may use either method for coding an end-of-file indicator.

Coding Guideline for the PERFORM Statement

Code the UNTIL clause on a separate line, indented for readability.

Self-Test

1. The PROCEDURE DIVISION contains all _____ to be executed.
2. The PROCEDURE DIVISION is divided into _____ .
3. A routine or module is a _____ .
4. Paragraphs are divided into _____ .
5. Statements are executed in the order _____ unless a _____ occurs.
6. The purpose of an OPEN statement is _____ .
7. Before a file may be read, it must be _____ .
8. The OPEN statement is coded in Area _____ .
9. The PERFORM paragraph-name UNTIL (condition) transfers control to the
   _____ . When the condition specified is met, control returns to the
   _____ .
10. In the statement PERFORM RTN1 UNTIL EOF = 1, EOF should be initialized at
    _____ . Provide the required WORKING-STORAGE entries for defining and ini-
    tializing EOF.
11. Sketch out the first three instructions that would normally be coded in the main
    module of a simple structured COBOL program.
12. (T or F) In Question 11, the paragraph named in the PERFORM statement will
    normally have a READ as its first instruction.
13. Consider the following statement:

    ```
    PERFORM 200-CALC-RTN
        UNTIL END-OF-FILE = 'YES'.
    ```

    Code the *last* instruction that should be included within 200-CALC-RTN.
14. Why should the last statement in the paragraph include a READ statement?
15. If there are 15 records to be read, the ___(no.)___ attempt to read a record causes
    an AT END condition to be executed.

Solutions

1. instructions
2. paragraphs or modules or routines
3. series of instructions designed to perform a specific set of operations

4. sentences, which consist of statements
5. in which they appear; PERFORM
6. to indicate which files are input and which are output; to access or activate the devices; to check or write labels
7. opened
8. B (All statements or sentences are coded in Area B.)
9. named paragraph; statement directly following the PERFORM
10. 0—Actually any other value but 1.

```
WORKING-STORAGE SECTION,
01  WS-STORED-AREAS,
    05  EOF  PIC 9  VALUE 0,
```

11.
```
OPEN ...
READ ...
PERFORM paragraph-name
    UNTIL condition
```

12. F—The first record read in the main module has not yet been processed. The named paragraph should begin with a set of instructions for processing that first record and should end with a READ.
13. READ file-name AT END MOVE 'YES' TO END-OF-FILE. (END-OF-FILE is simply a data-name.)
14. The condition in the PERFORM statement is tested initially and then again *after* the paragraph has been executed. Once the AT END is executed, when there are no more input records, we want to *immediately* transfer control back to the main module. This can only be accomplished if the READ is the last statement in the paragraph.
15. sixteenth

D. End-of-Job Processing: The CLOSE and STOP RUN Statements

Let us continue with the main module of Figure 4.1 before considering the instructions to be included in 200-CALC-RTN.

200-CALC-RTN will be performed until ARE-THERE-MORE-RECORDS = 'NO ', that is, until there are no more records to process. At that point, control will return to the instruction directly following the PERFORM statement in the main module. After all records have been processed, we will want to execute end-of-job functions. This usually includes releasing all files and terminating the processing (see Figure 4.1). It may contain other procedures as well, such as printing totals.

There are *two* statements, however, that are typically a part of every end-of-job routine. We first CLOSE all files to indicate that they are no longer needed for processing, and we instruct the computer to STOP, or terminate execution of the program.

1. CLOSE Statement

As we have seen, files must be accessed or activated by an OPEN statement before data may be read or written. Similarly, a **CLOSE** statement is coded at the end of the job after all records have been processed to release these files and deactivate the devices. The format of the CLOSE is:

Format

> CLOSE   file-name-1 . . .

All files that have been opened at the beginning of the program are closed at the end of a program. The CLOSE statement, like the OPEN, will perform additional functions. When creating disk or tape records, for example, the CLOSE will create trailer labels; it will also rewind a tape.

Note that a CLOSE statement, unlike an OPEN, does *not* specify which files are input and which are output. We say, for example, OPEN INPUT PAYROLL-FILE OUTPUT PAYCHECKS to access the files, but to release them, we simply say CLOSE PAYROLL-FILE PAYCHECKS. Distinguishing between input and output files is essential *before* processing begins, but is not meaningful when the job is being terminated.

Using Separate Lines Rather Than Commas to Set Clauses Apart

You could use commas to separate file-names, but we recommend that you use separate lines instead for ease of reading and for debugging purposes.

As noted, when an error occurs, the computer will print the line number that caused the error. If each file is closed on a separate line and a CLOSE error occurs, it is very easy to pinpoint the file that caused the error.

Using Separate CLOSE Statements

As with an OPEN statement, the following two routines are equivalent:

```
1. CLOSE PAYROLL-FILE          2. CLOSE PAYROLL-FILE.
        PAYCHECKS                    CLOSE PAYCHECKS.
        ERR-LIST.                    CLOSE ERR-LIST.
```

Unless files are closed at different points in the program, the second method, with separate CLOSE instructions, is considered inefficient.

Coding Guideline for the CLOSE Statement

Code each file-name on a separate line, indented for readability.

2. STOP RUN Statement

The **STOP RUN** instruction tells the computer to terminate the program. All programs end with a STOP RUN statement. This instruction will cause the computer to discontinue the processing of the program and automatically load in the next program.

> With COBOL 85, when a STOP RUN statement is executed, it will close any files that are still opened. Thus, with COBOL 85, a CLOSE statement is unnecessary. We recommend you use it, however, for documentation and debugging purposes.

In summary, we have discussed the following main module in detail:

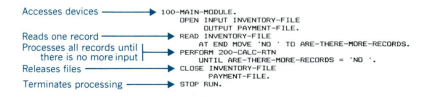

```
Accesses devices  ──────►  100-MAIN-MODULE.
                              OPEN INPUT INVENTORY-FILE
                                   OUTPUT PAYMENT-FILE.
Reads one record  ──────►     READ INVENTORY-FILE
Processes all records until        AT END MOVE 'NO ' TO ARE-THERE-MORE-RECORDS.
   there is no more input  ──►  PERFORM 200-CALC-RTN
                                   UNTIL ARE-THERE-MORE-RECORDS = 'NO '.
Releases files  ──────►       CLOSE INVENTORY-FILE
                                    PAYMENT-FILE.
Terminates processing  ──►    STOP RUN.
```

IV. Statements Typically Coded for Processing Input Records and Producing Output

The instructions specified at 200-CALC-RTN will include:

1. The processing of an input record.
2. A READ instruction to read additional records.

3. An AT END condition that instructs the computer to MOVE 'NO ' TO ARE-THERE-MORE-RECORDS when there is no more data.

Using a top-down approach, this module would be coded *after* the main module.

Example
```
200-CALC-RTN.
    ·
    ·
    READ TRANSACTION-FILE
        AT END MOVE 'NO ' TO ARE-THERE-MORE-RECORDS.
```

At 200-CALC-RTN we will want to process data in some way and then produce output records. For now, let us concentrate on the simplest processing instructions—the MOVE operation and the WRITE operation.

Now that we are able to OPEN and READ files, it will be necessary to store data in the output area so that when we use a WRITE instruction, there will be some information to be produced as output.

A. Simplified MOVE Statement

A simple **MOVE** statement has the following instruction format:

Format

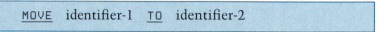

```
MOVE  identifier-1  TO  identifier-2
```

Fields in storage may be moved to other fields with the use of the MOVE instruction. The word 'identifier' is used in place of 'data-name' in this instruction format.

Sample Problem

Consider the following input and output formats for a program that is to produce output disk records from an input tape.

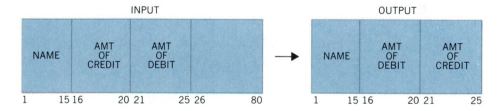

The first three divisions of the program conform to the rules of the last three chapters. Figure 4.2 illustrates the coding of these divisions. Note that ENVIRONMENT DIVISION entries are machine-dependent.

We may include the following coding in the PROCEDURE DIVISION:

```
PROCEDURE DIVISION.
100-MAIN-MODULE.
    OPEN INPUT ACCOUNT-IN-FILE
        OUTPUT ACCOUNT-OUT-FILE.
    READ ACCOUNT-IN-FILE
        AT END MOVE 'NO ' TO ARE-THERE-MORE-RECORDS.
    PERFORM 200-CALC-RTN
        UNTIL ARE-THERE-MORE-RECORDS = 'NO '.
    CLOSE ACCOUNT-IN-FILE
        ACCOUNT-OUT-FILE.
    STOP RUN.
200-CALC-RTN.
    MOVE NAME-IN TO NAME-OUT.
    MOVE AMT-OF-CREDIT-IN TO AMT-OF-CREDIT-OUT.
    MOVE AMT-OF-DEBIT-IN TO AMT-OF-DEBIT-OUT.
        ·
        ·
        ·
```

Will begin by moving the first record's data

Figure 4.2
IDENTIFICATION,
ENVIRONMENT, and DATA
DIVISIONs for Sample
Problem.

```
IDENTIFICATION DIVISION.
PROGRAM-ID. SAMPLE.
*
ENVIRONMENT DIVISION.
INPUT-OUTPUT SECTION.
FILE-CONTROL.
    SELECT ACCOUNT-IN-FILE
        ASSIGN TO UT-S-SYS008.
    SELECT ACCOUNT-OUT-FILE
        ASSIGN TO DA-S-SYS007.
*
DATA DIVISION.
FILE SECTION.
FD  ACCOUNT-IN-FILE
    LABEL RECORDS ARE STANDARD.
01  INPUT-REC.
    05  NAME-IN                 PIC X(15).
    05  AMT-OF-CREDIT-IN        PIC 9(5).
    05  AMT-OF-DEBIT-IN         PIC 9(5).
    05  FILLER                  PIC X(55).
FD  ACCOUNT-OUT-FILE
    LABEL RECORDS ARE STANDARD.
01  OUTPUT-REC.
    05  NAME-OUT                PIC X(15).
    05  AMT-OF-DEBIT-OUT        PIC 9(5).
    05  AMT-OF-CREDIT-OUT       PIC 9(5).
WORKING-STORAGE SECTION.
01  WS-STORED-AREAS.
    05  ARE-THERE-MORE-RECORDS  PIC XXX    VALUE 'YES'.
```

Assuming the PIC clause of an output field is the same as the PIC clause of the corresponding input field, a MOVE operation *duplicates* input data at the output area. That is, the input field still retains its value. Note that the technique of using the same base name for different fields while altering only the prefix or suffix is considered good programming form. That is, the distinction between AMT-OF-CREDIT-IN, as an input field, and AMT-OF-CREDIT-OUT, as the same field for the output, is clear.

Recall that 200-CALC-RTN is a *separate* module. It is executed under the control of the PERFORM statement. To complete 200-CALC-RTN, we will WRITE the record stored at the output area and then READ the next input record.

B. WRITE **Statement**

The **WRITE** instruction takes data stored in the output area of the DATA DIVISION and transmits it to the device specified in the ENVIRONMENT DIVISION.

A simple WRITE statement has the following format:

Format

> WRITE   record-name-1

Note that although *files* are *read,* we *write records.* The record-name appears on the 01 level and is generally subdivided into fields. The record description specifies the *format* of the output. With each WRITE instruction, we tell the computer to write data that is in the output area.

Thus, in our example, the appropriate instruction is WRITE OUTPUT-REC, *not* WRITE ACCOUNT-OUT-FILE. When we *write* or produce information, we use the 01 *record-name;* when we read from a file, we use the FD or file-name.

To say WRITE OUTPUT-REC transmits data to the output device according to the way in which data has been stored in the record called OUTPUT-REC. If more than one record format were specified for OUTPUT-FILE, then the record format to be created would be indicated in the WRITE statement. For example, consider the following:

```
FD  PRINT-FILE
    LABEL RECORDS ARE OMITTED
    RECORD CONTAINS 133 CHARACTERS
    DATA RECORDS ARE HEADING-REC
                    DETAIL-REC.
01  HEADING-REC.
    .
    .
01  DETAIL-REC.
    .
    .
```

Depending on the format desired, we would code *either* WRITE HEADING-REC or WRITE DETAIL-REC.

We may now code the PROCEDURE DIVISION for our sample program in its entirety, keeping in mind that after a complete record has been processed and an output record created, we want to read another input record.

```
PROCEDURE DIVISION.
100-MAIN-MODULE.
    OPEN INPUT ACCOUNT-IN-FILE
        OUTPUT ACCOUNT-OUT-FILE.
    READ ACCOUNT-IN-FILE
        AT END MOVE 'NO ' TO ARE-THERE-MORE-RECORDS.
    PERFORM 200-CALC-RTN
        UNTIL ARE-THERE-MORE-RECORDS = 'NO '.
    CLOSE ACCOUNT-IN-FILE
        ACCOUNT-OUT-FILE.
    STOP RUN.
200-CALC-RTN.
    MOVE NAME-IN TO NAME-OUT.
    MOVE AMT-OF-CREDIT-IN TO AMT-OF-CREDIT-OUT.
    MOVE AMT-OF-DEBIT-IN TO AMT-OF-DEBIT-OUT.
    WRITE OUTPUT-REC.
    READ ACCOUNT-IN-FILE
        AT END MOVE 'NO ' TO ARE-THERE-MORE-RECORDS.
```

Note that each clause is coded on a separate line for readability and ease of debugging.

V. Looking Ahead

The following is a brief introduction to two classes of verbs—arithmetic and conditional. We explain the formats, options, and rules for using these verbs in Chapters 8 and 9. We merely introduce them here so that you can begin to write meaningful programs. Once you begin using these verbs, questions may occur to you, mainly because we have not yet explained them fully. If you adhere to the instruction format rules provided here, you will be able to code simple but complete COBOL programs.

The four basic arithmetic verbs have the following simple formats.

Formats

$$\underline{\text{ADD}} \left\{ \begin{array}{l} \text{identifier-1} \\ \text{literal-1} \end{array} \right\} \cdots \underline{\text{TO}} \text{ identifier-2}$$

$$\underline{\text{SUBTRACT}} \left\{ \begin{array}{l} \text{identifier-1} \\ \text{literal-1} \end{array} \right\} \underline{\text{FROM}} \text{ identifier-2}$$

$$\underline{\text{MULTIPLY}} \left\{ \begin{array}{l} \text{identifier-1} \\ \text{literal-1} \end{array} \right\} \underline{\text{BY}} \text{ identifier-2}$$

$$\underline{\text{DIVIDE}} \left\{ \begin{array}{l} \text{identifier-1} \\ \text{literal-1} \end{array} \right\} \underline{\text{BY}} \text{ identifier-2}$$

Examples

```
ADD AMT1-IN AMT2-IN TO WS-TOTAL.
SUBTRACT 100 FROM SALARY.
MULTIPLY .0715 BY SALARY.
DIVIDE WS-TOTAL BY UNIT-PRICE.
```

There are many other options of these four arithmetic verbs that we will discuss in Chapter 8.

The basic instruction format for a conditional is as follows:

Format

> IF   (condition)
>   (statement-1) . . .
>   [ELSE
>   (statement-2) . . .]

The simple conditions that can be tested are as follows:

$$(\text{identifier-1}) \begin{Bmatrix} = (\text{or IS EQUAL TO}) \\ < (\text{or IS LESS THAN}) \\ > (\text{or IS GREATER THAN}) \end{Bmatrix} \begin{Bmatrix} \text{identifier-2} \\ \text{literal-1} \end{Bmatrix}$$

Note that the ELSE clause is optional. Numerous statements can follow each IF or ELSE clause.

Examples

Coding	Explanation
1. IF AMT-IN IS GREATER THAN ZERO ADD AMT-IN TO WS-TOTAL.	If the input field AMT-IN is greater than zero, add the AMT-IN field to a total.

2. IF   AMT1-IN > AMT2-IN
        ADD AMT1-IN TO WS-TOTAL1
    ELSE
        ADD AMT1-IN TO WS-TOTAL2.
	If AMT1-IN exceeds AMT2-IN, add AMT1-IN to a field called WS-TOTAL1; otherwise (if AMT1-IN is *not* greater than AMT2-IN), ADD AMT1-IN to WS-TOTAL2.

Conditional statements are discussed in depth in Chapter 9.

VI. Review of Comments in COBOL

You will find that as programs become more complex, comments are helpful as reminders and explanations of the processing being performed.

The following is the method that may be used for inserting comments in a COBOL program.

COMMENTS IN COBOL

An asterisk (∗) in column 7 (the continuation position) of any line makes the entire line a comment. Use comments freely to make your program user-friendly and easier to understand.

Example of a program excerpt with a comment:

```
PROCEDURE DIVISION.
****************************************************************
*          THIS PROGRAM USES THE STRUCTURED APPROACH          *
****************************************************************
100-MAIN-MODULE.
     OPEN INPUT INVENTORY-FILE
          OUTPUT PAYMENT-FILE.
     READ INVENTORY-FILE
          AT END MOVE 'NO ' TO ARE-THERE-MORE-RECORDS.
     PERFORM 200-CALC-RTN
          UNTIL ARE-THERE-MORE-RECORDS = 'NO '.
```

Sometimes programmers enter their comments in lowercase letters to even more clearly set them apart from actual instructions.

We recommend that each program contain a comment in the IDENTIFI-CATION DIVISION to describe the program and that each module in the PRO-CEDURE DIVISION contain a comment that describes it. As your programs become more complex, you may want to add comments in other places as well. For very long programs, code a line with a / in column 7 after each division to begin the next division on a new page of the source listing.

Coding Guidelines for PROCEDURE DIVISION Entries

1. Each clause should be on a separate line indented for readability. For example:

```
PERFORM ...
    UNTIL ...
```

2. Each sentence should end with a period.
3. Each paragraph-name should begin with a sequence number that helps to pinpoint the location of the paragraph; a descriptive name should follow this number (e.g., 100-MAIN-MODULE, 200-CALC-RTN).

CHAPTER SUMMARY

Most programs illustrated or assigned as homework in this text will use the following structure:

```
                          PROCEDURE DIVISION.
                          paragraph-name-1.
                              OPEN INPUT file-name-1
                                  OUTPUT file-name-2.
Main module               READ file-name-1
                              AT END MOVE 'NO ' TO ARE-THERE-MORE-RECORDS.
                          PERFORM paragraph-name-2
                              UNTIL ARE-THERE-MORE-RECORDS = 'NO '.
                          CLOSE file-name(s).
                          STOP RUN.
                          paragraph-name-2.
                              .
Processing steps          .
for each record           .
                              WRITE ...
                              READ file-name-1
                                  AT END MOVE 'NO ' TO ARE-THERE-MORE-RECORDS.
```

(Lowercase entries are user-defined names.)

A. Paragraph-names are coded in Area A and end with a period. Rules for forming paragraph-names are the same as for data-names except that a paragraph-name can have all digits. We use a prefix such as 100-, 200-, 300-, along with a descriptive name such as HEADING-RTN or MAIN-MODULE. A paragraph with a prefix of 200- is located after a paragraph with prefix 100- and before a paragraph with prefix 300-.

B. All statements are coded in Area B, either in paragraph form or one statement per line. The latter is highly recommended.

C. Instructions are executed in the order in which they appear unless a PERFORM statement transfers control.

D. When the main module's PERFORM is encountered, the paragraph specified is executed repeatedly until there are no more input records.

E. The last statement in the paragraph specified by the PERFORM is usually a READ statement:

```
200-CALC-RTN.
    .
    .
    READ file-name
        AT END MOVE 'NO ' TO ARE-THERE-MORE-RECORDS.
```

CHAPTER SELF-TEST

1. Before a file may be read it must be _____ .

2. Consider the following instruction: READ PAY-FILE AT END MOVE 'NO ' TO ARE-THERE-MORE-RECORDS. PAY-FILE appears in a _____ statement of the ENVIRONMENT DIVISION, an _____ entry of the DATA DIVISION, and _____ statements of the PROCEDURE DIVISION.

3. With every READ statement for sequential files, a(n) _____ clause is used.

4. The AT END clause tells the computer what to do if _____ .

5. In the instruction READ SALES-IN AT END MOVE 'NO ' TO ARE-THERE-MORE-RECORDS, if there are 20 input records, the __(no.)__ attempt to read a record will cause 'NO ' to be moved to the field called ARE-THERE-MORE-RECORDS.

6. Unlike READ statements in which the _____-name is specified, a WRITE statement specifies the _____-name.

7. The PROCEDURE DIVISION is divided into _____ .

8. What is wrong with the following?
   (a) WRITE REC-1
            AT END MOVE 1 TO EOF.
   (b) PRINT REC-2.

9. When using a MOVE, to obtain *exactly* the same data at the output area that appears in the input area, the _____ clause of both fields should be identical.

10. The instruction used to transfer control from the main module to some other part of the program is a _____ instruction.

11. If PERFORM 500-STEP-5 UNTIL ARE-THERE-MORE-RECORDS = 'NO ' is a statement in the program, 500-STEP-5 is a _____ that must appear somewhere in the program in Area _____ .

12. Paragraph-names (must, need not) be unique within a program.

13. The statement CLOSE INPUT ACCTS-PAYABLE (is, is not) valid.

14. The purpose of a STOP RUN instruction is to _____ .

15. If PERFORM 600-STEP-1 UNTIL END-OF-FILE = 'YES' is a coded statement in the main module, the last instruction of 600-STEP-1 should be a _____ .

Solutions

1. opened
2. SELECT; FD; OPEN and CLOSE
3. AT END
4. there is no more input data
5. twenty-first
6. file; record
7. paragraphs
8. (a) The AT END clause is only specified with a READ statement.
   (b) A WRITE instruction should be used, not PRINT.
9. PICTURE or PIC
10. PERFORM ... UNTIL
11. paragraph-name; A
12. must
13. is not (INPUT or OUTPUT is *not* specified with CLOSE statements.)
14. terminate the job (With COBOL 85, STOP RUN also closes the files.)
15. READ file-name AT END MOVE 'YES' TO END-OF-FILE

PRACTICE PROGRAM

From this point on, each chapter includes one practice program with a suggested solution provided to assist you in reviewing the material and in coding the programming assignments that follow. Make every effort to plan and code the practice program on your own. Then check your solution against the one illustrated. A problem definition is provided that includes (1) a systems flowchart, which is an overview of the input and output, (2) record layout forms, and (3) Printer Spacing Charts, if printed output is required.

Write a program to write an output salary disk from input employee tape records. The problem definition is as follows:

Systems Flowchart

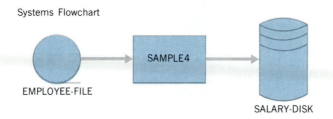

EMPLOYEE-FILE   SAMPLE4   SALARY-DISK

EMPLOYEE- FILE Record Layout

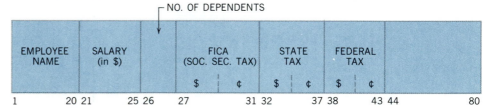

SALARY-DISK Record Layout

(***Hint:*** You should move SPACES to the output record to ensure that the FILLER in the last 55 positions is blank.)

Figure 4.3 illustrates the pseudocode and flowchart for this problem. Both these planning tools will be discussed in detail in the next chapter. Look at the planning tools first to see if you understand the logic and then try to write the program yourself. Compare your coding with the solution in Figure 4.4.

Figure 4.3
Pseudocode and flowchart for
Practice Program.

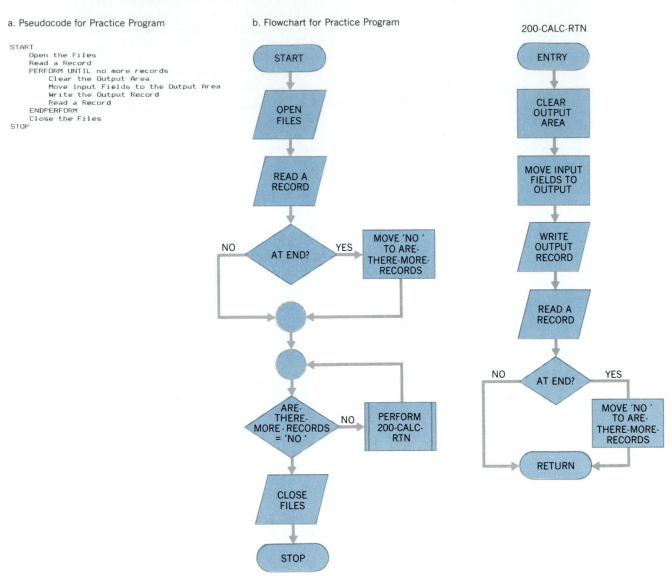

a. Pseudocode for Practice Program

```
START
    Open the Files
    Read a Record
    PERFORM UNTIL no more records
        Clear the Output Area
        Move Input Fields to the Output Area
        Write the Output Record
        Read a Record
    ENDPERFORM
    Close the Files
STOP
```

b. Flowchart for Practice Program

200-CALC-RTN

Figure 4.4
Solution to Practice Program.

(a) Program

```
 IDENTIFICATION DIVISION.
 PROGRAM-ID. SAMPLE.
*****************************************
*  SAMPLE  - UPDATES A FILE WITH EMPLOYEES *
*            NAMES AND SALARIES          *
*****************************************
 ENVIRONMENT DIVISION.
 CONFIGURATION SECTION.
 SOURCE-COMPUTER. IBM-4341.
 OBJECT-COMPUTER. IBM-4341.
 INPUT-OUTPUT SECTION.
 FILE-CONTROL.
     SELECT IN-EMPLOYEE-FILE ASSIGN TO DATA4E.
     SELECT OUT-SALARY-FILE  ASSIGN TO DATA4S.
```

Figure 4.4
(continued)

```
*
 DATA DIVISION.
 FILE SECTION.
 FD  IN-EMPLOYEE-FILE
     LABEL RECORDS ARE STANDARD.
 01  IN-EMPLOYEE-REC.
     05   IN-EMPLOYEE-NAME            PIC X(20).
     05   IN-SALARY                   PIC 9(5).
     05   IN-NO-OF-DEPENDENTS         PIC 9.
     05   IN-FICA                     PIC 9(3)V99.
     05   IN-STATE-TAX                PIC 9(4)V99.
     05   IN-FED-TAX                  PIC 9(4)V99.
     05   FILLER                      PIC X(37).
 FD  OUT-SALARY-FILE
     LABEL RECORDS ARE STANDARD.
 01  OUT-SALARY-REC.
     05   OUT-EMPLOYEE-NAME           PIC X(20).
     05   OUT-SALARY                  PIC 9(5).
     05   FILLER                      PIC X(55).
 WORKING-STORAGE SECTION.
 01  WS-WORK-AREAS.
     05  ARE-THERE-MORE-RECORDS       PIC X(3)      VALUE 'YES'.
*
 PROCEDURE DIVISION.
****************************************************************
*   100-MAIN-MODULE - CONTROLS OPENING AND CLOSING FILES    *
*                     DIRECTION OF PROGRAM LOGIC            *
*                     RETURNS CONTROL TO OPERATING SYSTEM    *
****************************************************************
 100-MAIN-MODULE.
     OPEN INPUT   IN-EMPLOYEE-FILE
          OUTPUT OUT-SALARY-FILE.
     READ IN-EMPLOYEE-FILE
         AT END MOVE 'NO ' TO ARE-THERE-MORE-RECORDS.
     PERFORM 200-CALC-RTN
         UNTIL ARE-THERE-MORE-RECORDS = 'NO '.
     CLOSE IN-EMPLOYEE-FILE
           OUT-SALARY-FILE.
     STOP RUN.
****************************************************************
*   200-CALC-RTN - PERFORMED FROM 100-MAIN-MODULE          *
*                  MOVES EMPLOYEE INFORMATION TO OUTPUT    *
*                  AREAS, WRITES THE RECORD THEN READS     *
*                  THE NEXT INPUT RECORD                   *
****************************************************************
 200-CALC-RTN.
     MOVE SPACES TO OUT-SALARY-REC.
     MOVE IN-EMPLOYEE-NAME TO OUT-EMPLOYEE-NAME.
     MOVE IN-SALARY TO OUT-SALARY.
     WRITE OUT-SALARY-REC.
     READ IN-EMPLOYEE-FILE
         AT END MOVE 'NO ' TO ARE-THERE-MORE-RECORDS.
```

(b) Sample Input Data

```
NANCY STERN          09898212300098900029900
ROBERT STERN         10923221000098890092830
CHRISTOPHER HAMMEL   08437138370067373073700
GEORGE WASHINGTON    03383239390003920039200
TOM JEFFERSON        08383832200093830039200
LORI STERN           29339163600129290029290
MELANIE STERN        02384102938338382023838
TEDDY SMITH          10293902239328339382839
JOHN DOE             00338229387493038330393
BILL FIXER           08383820028303939029383
```

(c) Sample Output

```
NANCY STERN          09898
ROBERT STERN         10923
CHRISTOPHER HAMMEL   08437
GEORGE WASHINGTON    03383
TOM JEFFERSON        08383
LORI STERN           29339
MELANIE STERN        02384
TEDDY SMITH          10293
JOHN DOE             00338
BILL FIXER           08383
```

KEY TERMS

AT END	Paragraph	Sentence
CLOSE	PERFORM ... UNTIL	Sequence
Main module	PROCEDURE DIVISION	Statement
Module	READ	STOP RUN
MOVE	Routine	WRITE
OPEN		

REVIEW QUESTIONS

T   F

I. True-False Questions

__ __ 1. Paragraph-names are coded in Area A of the PROCEDURE DIVISION.

__ __ 2. An OPEN statement must be executed before a file is read.

__ __ 3. Files must be opened in the order in which they are read or written.

__ __ 4. A structured program treats each paragraph as an independent module.

__ __ 5. A PERFORM ... UNTIL will be executed continuously until the condition specified is met.

__ __ 6. Consider the following statement: PERFORM 200-CALC-RTN UNTIL ARE-THERE-MORE-RECORDS = 'NO '. The data-name ARE-THERE-MORE-RECORDS must be defined in the FILE SECTION.

__ __ 7. Suppose EOF were initialized at 1. It would be correct to use the following as an end-of-file test: READ FILE-IN AT END MOVE 0 TO EOF.

__ __ 8. Consider the following statement.

```
PERFORM 200-CALC-RTN
    UNTIL ARE-THERE-MORE-RECORDS = 'NO '.
```

The last statement in 200-CALC-RTN would usually be a WRITE statement.

__ __ 9. The last instruction to be executed in a program should be a STOP RUN.

__ __ 10. Using COBOL 85, it is unnecessary to close files at an end of job.

II. General Questions

1. Indicate the DIVISION in which each of the following is coded and state its purpose.
   - (a) DATE-COMPILED
   - (b) WORKING-STORAGE SECTION
   - (c) paragraph-name
   - (d) CONFIGURATION SECTION
   - (e) FD
   - (f) level numbers
   - (g) LABEL RECORDS
   - (h) FILE SECTION
   - (i) SELECT
   - (j) AUTHOR
   - (k) STOP RUN
   - (l) AT END clause
   - (m) INPUT-OUTPUT SECTION
   - (n) VALUE
   - (o) PICTURE
   - (p) FILE-CONTROL
   - (q) FILLER
   - (r) OPEN

2. When the computer encounters a READ instruction in the PROCEDURE DIVISION, how does it know which of its input units to activate?

3. Give two functions of the OPEN statement.

4. When are paragraph-names assigned in the PROCEDURE DIVISION?

5. State which of the following, if any, are invalid paragraph-names.
   - (a) INPUT-RTN
   - (b) MOVE
   - (c) 123
   - (d) %-RTN

6. If a READ statement is used for a sequential file, what clause is required? Why?

Make necessary corrections to the following. Assume that spacing and margins are correct.

```
7. PROCEDURE DIVISION.
   100-MAIN MODULE.
       OPEN INPUT OLD-FILE
            OUTPUT NEW-FILE.
       PERFORM 200-UPDATE-RTN
            UNTIL ARE-THERE-MORE-RECORDS = 'NO '.
       CLOSE OLD-FILE
            NEW-FILE.
       STOP RUN.
   200-UPDATE-RTN.
       READ OLD-FILE
            AT END MOVE 'NO ' TO ARE-THERE-MORE-RECORDS.
       MOVE OLD-REC TO NEW-REC.
       WRITE NEW-REC.
```

III. Interpreting Instruction Formats

Use the instruction formats in this book or in your reference manual to determine if the following instructions have the correct syntax.

```
1. READ INFILE-1, INFILE-2
       AT END MOVE 'NO ' TO MORE-RECORDS.
2. OPEN FILE-1 FILE-2 AND FILE-3.
3. WRITE REC-A
       AT END MOVE 0 TO EOF.
4. READ FILE-1
       AT  END MOVE 1 TO EOF
               WRITE FINAL-LINE.
5. CLOSE INPUT IN-FILE
       OUTPUT OUT-FILE.
```

DEBUGGING EXERCISES

> Beginning in this chapter, we will illustrate common programming mistakes and ask you to identify and correct them.

Consider the following PROCEDURE DIVISION coding:

```
PROCEDURE DIVISION.
100-MAIN-MODULE.
    OPEN SALES-FILE
         PRINT-FILE.
    PERFORM 200-CALC-RTN
         UNTIL ARE-THERE-MORE-RECORDS = 'NO '.
    CLOSE SALES-FILE
         PRINT-FILE.
    STOP RUN.
200-CALC-RTN
    READ SALES-FILE
         AT END MOVE 'NO ' TO ARE-THERE-MORE-RECORDS.
    MOVE SALES-FILE TO PRINT-FILE.
    WRITE PRINT-FILE.
```

1. The OPEN statement will result in a syntax error. Indicate why.
2. The MOVE statement will result in a syntax error. Indicate why.
3. The WRITE statement will result in a syntax error. Indicate why.

4. This programming excerpt does not follow the appropriate structured format. In fact, it will result in a logic error when the last record has been processed. Indicate why.

5. The CLOSE statement does not have commas separating the files. Will this result in a syntax error? Explain your answer.

6. Indicate how you can determine what device SALES-FILE uses.

7. Suppose the READ statement was coded as READ SALES-FILE with no AT END clause. Would this cause an error? Explain your answer.

8. The line that contains the paragraph-name called 200-CALC-RTN will be listed as a syntax error. Why?

PROGRAMMING ASSIGNMENTS

The following notes apply to all Programming Assignments in this and subsequent chapters.

1. Each of the following assignments specifies a particular form of input, such as disk, tape, or terminal, as well as a particular form of output such as a printed report, disk, or tape. Your instructor may choose to modify these device assignments to make more effective use of the computer facilities at your school or installation.

   A program assignment that specifies 80-position disk records as input could easily be modified to indicate tape or terminal input instead. Only the SELECT statement and possibly the LABEL RECORDS and BLOCK CONTAINS clauses would need to be altered.

2. The first two or three Programming Assignments in each chapter will be specified in traditional problem definition form. Any additional assignments will be specified in narrative form to familiarize you with an alternative method for designating programming specifications.

3. A sample data set for Problem 2 of each chapter is provided in Appendix E. Your instructor may require you to use the data set provided. For all other programs you will need to create your own input data files or obtain them from your instructor. You can create data files using your computer's text editor. Or, you can write a COBOL program that creates a disk or tape file.

4. For Programming Assignments 1 through 3, if printed output is required, a Printer Spacing Chart will be included with the problem definition. For additional programming assignments where printed output is required, you should create your own Printer Spacing Chart. There are blank Printer Spacing Charts at the end of the text.

5. When output is created on disk or tape, you will need to include a command that prints the contents of the output disk or tape so you can check it during debugging. You may code DISPLAY record-name prior to each WRITE record-name to print each disk or tape record before actually creating it. Or you may use a job control command such as /PRINT to print the entire output file after it has been created. You will need to ask your instructor or a computer aide how this job control command is specified for your system.

6. The Programming Assignments are arranged in increasing order of difficulty, with the last ones considered to be the most difficult.

1. Write a program to create a sequential master disk file from input sales records on tape. The problem definition is shown in Figure 4.5.

2. Write a program to print all information from payroll records. The problem definition is shown in Figure 4.6. The words in parentheses ( ) on the Printer Spacing Chart identify the fields to be printed.

Systems Flowchart

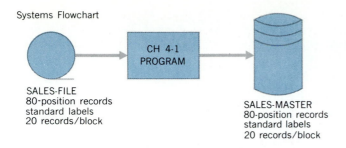

SALES-FILE
80-position records
standard labels
20 records/block

SALES-MASTER
80-position records
standard labels
20 records/block

SALES-FILE Record Layout

SALESPERSON NO.	SALESPERSON NAME	TERRITORY CODE			YEAR-TO-DATE FIGURES			CURRENT PERIOD FIGURES			
		REGION NO.	DISTRICT NO.	OFFICE NO.	QUOTA XXXX.XX	SALES XXXX.XX	COMMISSION XXXX.XX	QUOTA XXXX.XX	SALES XXXX.XX	COMMISSION XXXX.XX	
1 5	6 25	26 27	28 29	30 31	32 37	38 43	44 49	50 55	56 61	62 67	68 80

SALES-MASTER Record Layout

SALESPERSON NO.	SALESPERSON NAME	TERRITORY CODE			YEAR-TO-DATE FIGURES			CURRENT PERIOD FIGURES			
		REGION NO.	DISTRICT NO.	OFFICE NO.	QUOTA XXXX.XX	SALES XXXX.XX	COMMISSION XXXX.XX	QUOTA XXXX.XX	SALES XXXX.XX	COMMISSION XXXX.XX	
1 5	6 25	26 27	28 29	30 31	32 37	38 43	44 49	50 55	56 61	62 67	68 80

Figure 4.5
Problem definition for
Programming Assignment 1.

3. XYZ Utility Company has master tape records, each of which will be used to produce two disk records on a sequential disk file. The problem definition is shown in Figure 4.7. Note that for each input record the program will create two disk records that will later be printed as bills.

Hint: The DATA RECORDS clause for the output file includes *two* record formats. You may code, for example, DATA RECORDS ARE GAS-BILL, ELEC-BILL for the output file. The sequence of instructions at 200-CALC-RTN after a tape record has been read would be: MOVE, WRITE, MOVE, WRITE, READ. Thus, we code *two* write instructions for every read instruction.

4. Each input record consists of a person's name, street address, city, state, and zip. Write a program to produce a mailing list like the following one. Note that there are two sets of addresses for each individual.

```
----------------------------------------------------------------
PHIL COLLINS                      PHIL COLLINS
1 MAIN ST.                        1 MAIN ST.
MIAMI, FL 33431                   MIAMI, FL 33431
----------------------------------------------------------------
BILLY JOEL                        BILLY JOEL
26 FIFTH AVE.                     26 FIFTH AVE.
NEW YORK, NY 10158                NEW YORK, NY 10158
```

Systems Flowchart

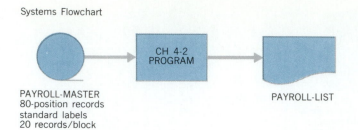

PAYROLL-MASTER
80-position records
standard labels
20 records/block

PAYROLL-LIST

PAYROLL-MASTER Record Layout

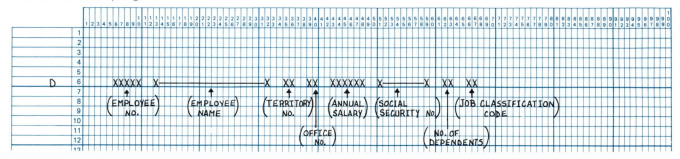

PAYROLL-LIST Printer Spacing Chart

Figure 4.6
Problem definition for
Programming Assignment 2.

5. Two input tape files are used to create one output master tape file. The format for the two input files is as follows:

File-1		File-2	
1–20	Employee name	1–20	Employee name
21–40	Address	21–40	Address
41–43	Hours worked	41–45	Salary
44–46	Wages X.XX	46	No. of dependents
47	No. of dependents	47–51	F.I.C.A. XXX.XX
48–52	F.I.C.A. XXX.XX	52–57	Fed. tax XXXX.XX
53–58	Fed. tax XXXX.XX	58–63	State tax XXXX.XX
59–64	State tax XXXX.XX	64	Unused

The format for the output file is the same as for the input files. Write a program to write on the output file all records from File-1 and *then* all records from File-2. All files have standard labels. The blocking factor is 30 for all files.

6. Modify Problem "5" to *first* write on tape a record from File-1 and then a record from File-2. Alternate writing in this way until all records from both files are processed. Assume that File-1 and File-2 have the same number of records.

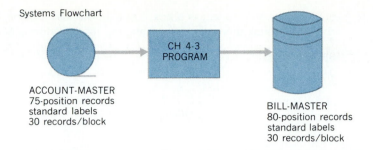

Systems Flowchart

ACCOUNT-MASTER
75-position records
standard labels
30 records/block

CH 4-3
PROGRAM

BILL-MASTER
80-position records
standard labels
30 records/block

ACCOUNT-MASTER Record Layout

ACCOUNT NO.	NAME OF CUSTOMER	ADDRESS	KILOWATT HRS. OF ELECTRICITY USED	GAS USED	ELEC. BILL XXX.XX	GAS BILL XXX.XX	

1   5 6   25 26   45 46   50 51   55 56   60 61   65 66   75

BILL-MASTER Record Layouts

ELEC-BILL

ACCOUNT NO.	CUSTOMER NAME	ADDRESS	KILOWATT HRS. OF ELECTRICITY USED	ELEC. BILL XXX.XX	

           5 6   25 26   45 46   50 51   55 56   80

GAS-BILL

ACCOUNT NO.	CUSTOMER NAME	ADDRESS	GAS USED	GAS BILL XXX.XX	

1   5 6   25 26   45 46   50 51   55 56   80

Figure 4.7
Problem definition for
Programming Assignment 3.

7. Write a program to create a sequential disk file from transaction tape records. Block size is 20 for each file.

   Notes:

   a. Total = Amount 1 + Amount 2.
   b. Amount due = Total − Amount of discount.

   Input `ACCOUNT-TRANS`

1-5	`ACCT-NO-IN`
6-25	`CUST-NAME-IN`
26-30	`AMT1-IN` xxx.xx
31-35	`AMT2-IN` xxx.xx
36-40	`DISC-AMT-IN` xxx.xx

   Output `ACCOUNT-MASTER`

1-5	`ACCT-OUT`
6-25	`CUST-NAME-OUT`
26-31	`TOTAL-OUT` xxxx.xx
32-37	`AMT-DUE-OUT` xxxx.xx
38-40	`FILLER`

8. Write a program for a college bursar to compute for each semester the tuition for

each student. If a student is taking 12 credits or less, tuition is $525 per credit. If a student is taking more than 12 credits, the total tuition is $6300.

Input: Disk File	**Output:** Print File
1–20 Student name	1–20 Student name
21–22 Number of credits	41–42 Number of credits
23–80 Not used	63–66 Tuition
(block size is 15; standard labels)	

Unit I

Coding Guidelines

1. User-defined names (data-names and paragraph-names) should be meaningful.

2. Use hyphens to separate words or abbreviations in user-defined names.

3. Use prefixes or suffixes with data-names to help identify the data (e.g., -IN and -OUT for input and output fields, WS- for WORKING-STORAGE areas, HL- for heading line fields).

4. Use numeric prefixes with paragraph-names to help pinpoint their location in a program (100-MAIN-MODULE, 200-CALC-RTN, 900-END-OF-JOB).

5. Avoid the use of commas. Instead, code each clause or statement on a separate line. Indent clauses to improve readability.

Examples
```
    a. PERFORM ...
            UNTIL ...
    b. READ ...
            AT END ...
    c. OPEN INPUT ...
            OUTPUT ...
```

6. Align statements and clauses, such as PIC clauses, for readability.

UNIT II

DESIGNING STRUCTURED PROGRAMS

5

The Theory of Structured Program Design

OBJECTIVES

To familiarize you with

1. The way structured programs should be designed.
2. Flowcharts and pseudocode as planning tools used to map out the logic in a structured program.
3. Hierarchy or structure charts as planning tools used to illustrate the relationships among modules in a top-down program.
4. The logical control structures of sequence, selection, iteration, and case.
5. Techniques used to make programs easier to code, debug, maintain, and modify.

I. What Makes a Well-Designed Program?

Many programming texts teach the instruction formats and coding rules necessary for writing programs without ever fully explaining the way programs are actually designed. In this chapter, you will learn how to construct or design a program so that you can create structures that are easy to understand, debug, maintain, and modify.

We use the term *program design* to mean the development of a program so that its elements fit together logically and effectively in an integrated way. In Chapter 1, we discussed several program design techniques. Let us review them here.

A. Program Logic Should Be Mapped Out Using a Planning Tool

If programs are systematically planned before they are coded, they will be better designed. Planning tools such as flowcharts, pseudocode, and hierarchy charts help programmers map out program logic. Just as architects prepare blueprints before buildings are constructed, so, too, should programmers use planning tools before a program is coded. The planning process minimizes logic errors by helping the programmer determine how all instructions will interrelate when the program is actually coded.

B. Programs Should Be Structured

Well-designed programs are those that have a logical structure, where the *order* in which instructions are executed *is standardized.* Structured programming is a technique that provides this logical construct. In structured programs, each set of instructions that performs a specific function is represented as a **module** or program segment. A module can also be called a routine or, in COBOL, a paragraph. It consists of a series of statements. Each module is executed in its entirety from specific places in a program. In the program in Chapter 1, for example, there were two modules or paragraphs, one labeled `100-MAIN-MODULE` and one labeled `200-WAGE-ROUTINE` (see Figure 1.8 on page 17).

In COBOL, modules are executed using a `PERFORM` statement, which allows control to pass temporarily to a different module and then return to the original one from which the `PERFORM` was executed. A simple `PERFORM` (without an `UNTIL` clause) results in the following sequence of operations:

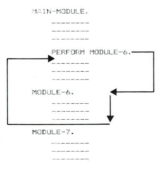

`MODULE-6` is executed from the main module and then control returns to the statement following the `PERFORM`.

An unconditional branch to different routines, called a `GO TO` in most languages, is *avoided entirely* in a structured program. Thus, `GO TO` statements should *not* be used in well-designed programs.

As you will see later on, the modular technique, combined with the use of PERFORM statements for executing modules, makes structured programs easier to code, debug, maintain, and modify.

C. Programs Should Use a Top-Down Approach

In summary, well-designed programs use structured techniques for coding and executing modules or program segments. These modules should also be coded in a *hierarchical order*, with the secondary modules initially sketched out and then *later* filled in with details. The coding of modules in a hierarchical manner is called **top-down programming.**

Top-down programming is analogous to the technique of outlining a paper before it is actually written. First, each topic in a paper is sketched out until the organization is clear; only then are the details filled in. Similarly, the main-module of a top-down program is coded first, with the details for each subordinate module left for later. Only after the organization of the program has been determined will the programmer code the specific instructions in each module. This top-down approach is sometimes called *stepwise refinement.*

D. Programs Should Be Modular

Each well-defined unit or program segment should be written as a module and executed with a PERFORM. This makes a program more structured and helps the programmer incorporate the top-down approach. The subordinate modules can be written after the main structure has been mapped out.

Consider a program that is to execute a sequence of steps if two fields are equal, and a different sequence of steps if the fields are not equal. We could code the instructions as:

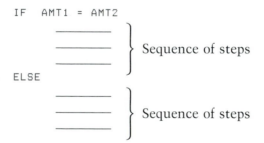

A modular approach is, however, preferred as follows:

```
IF  AMT1 = AMT2
    PERFORM 100-RTN1
ELSE
    PERFORM 200-RTN2.
```

In this way, the main module focuses on the primary issue of whether the two fields are equal. Later on, in subordinate modules 100-RTN1 and 200-RTN2, we focus on the detailed instructions to be executed depending on whether the fields are equal.

If a sequence of steps is to be executed when a specific condition exists, code the sequence in a separate module such as 100-RTN1 or 200-RTN2. In this way, each group of instructions to be executed under different conditions will be treated as a unit.

II. Designing Programs before Coding Them

A. How Programs Are Designed

Most students believe, quite understandably, that learning the rules of a programming language is all that is needed to write well-designed programs. It is, of course, true that you must learn programming rules, or *syntax*, before instructions can be coded. Unfortunately, however, knowledge of a programming language's rules will not guarantee that programs will be designed properly. That is, it is possible for elements of a program to be coded correctly and yet the entire set of procedures might not work properly or efficiently. In addition to learning syntax, then, programmers must learn how to *design a program* so that it functions effectively *as an integrated whole*. Thus, programmers must be familiar with the techniques used to structure programs as well as with the programming rules.

Learning syntax, then, is only one step in the process of developing programs. The syntax you learn is language-specific, meaning that each programming language has *its own particular rules.* Knowing COBOL's syntax, then, will be of only minimal value in learning Pascal's syntax, for example, although many other languages do share common features.

But the *techniques* for developing well-designed programs are *applicable to all languages.* That is, the logical control structures for designing a COBOL program are very similar to those in all languages. Once you know how to design programs efficiently and effectively, then, you need only learn the syntax rules of a specific language to implement these design elements.

In this chapter, we will introduce the *logical control structures* used to design a program. We will be illustrating them throughout the text, and you will use them in the COBOL programs that you will code. This discussion, then, is meant as an introduction to logical control structures and will be reinforced and reviewed in subsequent chapters.

Logical control structures refer to the different ways in which instructions may be executed. Sometimes instructions are executed in order, that is, in the sequence in which they appear in the program. Other times, different sequences of instructions are executed depending on the outcome of a test that the computer performs. Still other times, a series of instructions might be executed repeatedly from different points in a program. The way in which a set of instructions is executed is called a *logical control structure.*

We will illustrate these structures using the two most common structured program planning tools—the flowchart and pseudocode. Both of these planning tools are language independent. That is, they help plan the logic to be used in *any program* regardless of the language in which the program will be coded. Thus, they afford us the benefit of illustrating the control structures in a general or theoretical way, without being dependent on any specific language rules. Once you understand how to plan the logical control structure of a program using pseudocode and flowcharts, you need only learn the specific language's rules to implement that logic.

Later on, we will illustrate how to plan a program using a *hierarchy chart*, which is still another planning tool. This tool, however, is not intended to map out logical control structures but to illustrate the top-down approach to programming. More about hierarchy charts later on.

For now, we will focus on flowcharts and pseudocode and how they illustrate the ways in which a program can be logically structured. First, let us introduce flowchart and pseudocode concepts.

B. Flowcharts and Pseudocode: An Introduction

Two useful tools for planning the logic to be used in a program are **flowcharts** and **pseudocode.** A flowchart is a diagram or pictorial representation of the instructions and logical control structures that will be used in a program. Similarly, a pseudocode is a set of written statements that specifies the instructions and logical control structures that will be used in a program.

Flowcharts and pseudocode are planning tools that should be prepared *before* the program is coded. They map out and then verify the logic to be incorporated in the program. Usually a program is planned with *either* a flowchart or pseudocode.

1. Flowcharts

The following symbols are the ones most frequently used in program flowcharts:

Symbol	Name	Use
	Input/Output or I/O	Used for all I/O operations. For example, the reading of a disk record, the writing of a line, and the writing of a disk record are considered I/O functions.
	Processing	Used for all arithmetic and data transfer operations. For example, moving of data from an input storage area to an output storage area is an example of a processing operation. Similarly, multiplying a tax rate by total sales is another example of a processing function.
	Decision or Selection	Used to test for a condition. For example, testing whether one field is larger than another is an example of a decision function. Similarly, testing whether a given field has specific contents (e.g., zeros or blanks) is also considered a decision function.
	Terminal	Used to indicate the beginning and end of a program or routine.
	Connector	Used to indicate the point at which a transfer of control operation occurs.
	Predefined Process	Used to indicate the name of a module to be executed at a given point; the actual instructions in this module are explained elsewhere in the flowchart.

FLOWCHARTING CONVENTIONS

1. Each symbol denotes a type of operation.
2. A note is written inside each symbol to indicate the specific function to be performed.
3. The symbols are connected by flowlines.
4. Flowcharts are drawn and read from top to bottom unless a specific condition is met that alters the path.
5. A sequence of operations is performed until a terminal symbol designates the sequence's end or the end of the program.
6. Sometimes several steps or statements are combined in a single processing symbol for ease of reading.

Consider the following simple flowchart:

This sequence of instructions is called a *module.* The beginning and end of the module or sequence are designated with terminal symbols that are labeled START and STOP respectively. The first instruction or statement is READ AMT1, AMT2 meaning "read into storage a value for a field called AMT1 and a value for a field called AMT2." This is an input operation and is coded in an input/output or I/O symbol. The words used in the symbol need not be precisely as written. For example, INPUT AMT1, AMT2 would also be acceptable. Because a flowchart is a planning tool that is language-independent, you need not follow any language's specific syntax rules when drawing the flowchart.

When coded and executed, the first instruction in the sequence will read into storage a value for AMT1 and a value for AMT2, where AMT1 and AMT2 are field-names or symbolic addresses:

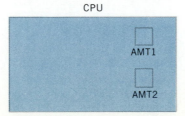

The next instruction in the illustrated flowchart module computes TOTAL as the sum of AMT1 and AMT2; it is a processing operation and is coded in a processing symbol. All arithmetic operations are considered processing operations.

In the program, this computation will add AMT1 and AMT2 and put the result in a field or symbolic storage address called TOTAL. Suppose 10 is entered as input for AMT1 and 15 is entered as input for AMT2. Then the CPU would have the following contents in the fields or symbolic storage addresses defined in this program:

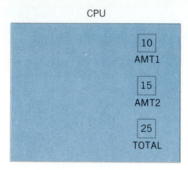

The next instruction, WRITE TOTAL, is an output operation that will print the contents of the field called TOTAL. It is also coded in an I/O symbol.

The flowchart is read from top to bottom. Since there is no need to repeat instructions or to test for any conditions, this simple flowchart indicates that two numbers will be read, added together, and the sum printed.

Specific instructions or statements are coded in each of the following flowchart symbols: input/output, processing, and decision. Terminal symbols indicate the beginning and end points of each module. A predefined process is drawn as a single step within the sequence; it indicates that another module is to be executed at that point. The steps within the named module are specified in detail in a different module or sequence.

Suppose we wish to print not only TOTAL but a series of headings and other data. We can include each of these processing steps in our module or sequence, or we can indicate a 'PRINT-MODULE' as a separate series of steps to be performed. The following illustrates how we would draw a flowchart symbol to indicate that a predefined process called PRINT-MODULE is to be executed at a specific point:

In a COBOL program we can execute such a PRINT-MODULE by coding
`PERFORM PRINT-MODULE`. PRINT-MODULE, then, would be defined in detail
in a separate sequence:

PRINT-MODULE

The term PRINT-MODULE itself can identify the entire sequence, as in the
preceding, or replace the word ENTRY in the terminal symbol.

Most programs make use of additional logical control structures, which will
be explained in the next section.

2. Pseudocode

Flowcharts have been used as planning tools for four decades. Structured programming, on the other hand, is a technique that has only been developed in
the last two to three decades. When structured programming became an established method for designing programs, flowchart symbols had to be modified to accurately depict a structured design. Many programmers and managers
have found that these modifications make flowcharts difficult to use as a
planning tool. As a result, although flowcharts are still widely used in some
organizations, other tools have been developed for more clearly depicting the
logic in a *structured program.* Pseudocode is one such tool.

Pseudocode has been designed *specifically* as a method for representing the
logic in a structured program. No symbols are used as in a flowchart; rather,
a series of logical control terms define the structure. Each processing or input/
output step is denoted by a line or group of lines of pseudocode. As with
flowcharts, the pseudocode need not indicate *all* the processing details; abbreviations are permissible. Also as with flowcharts, you need not follow any
language rules when using pseudocode; it is a language-independent tool. We
will see that logical control constructs are more easily specified using pseudocode.

Like a flowchart, pseudocode is read in sequence unless a logical control
structure is encountered. In the preceding section, we focused on a flowchart
for a program that reads in two numbers, adds them, and prints the total. The
pseudocode for this sequence is as follows:

    START
            Read Amt1, Amt2
            Compute Total = Amt1 + Amt2
            Write Total
    STOP

As with flowcharts, the START and STOP delineate the beginning and end points of the program module. The words such as "Read Amt1, Amt2" are used to convey a message and need not be written precisely as shown. Thus, "Input Amt1, Amt2" would be acceptable. Similarly, "Let Total = Amt1 + Amt2" could be used rather than "Compute Total = Amt1 + Amt2" for the second instruction.

To illustrate the performing of a PRINT-MODULE as we did with a flowchart, we would have the following in pseudocode.

```
PERFORM
    Write 'AMT1 = ', AMT1
    Write 'AMT2 = ', AMT2
    Write 'THE SUM OF AMT1 and AMT2 = ', TOTAL
ENDPERFORM
```

Thus, instructions to be executed within a PERFORM are coded *in place* with pseudocode, not as part of a separate routine.

The more advanced logical control structures that are part of most structured programs will be illustrated in the next section.

C. The Four Logical Control Structures

Structured programs use logical control structures to specify the order in which instructions are executed. These structures are the same for all languages. Thus, if you learn how to use them in COBOL, it will make learning to program in other languages much easier. These structures integrate to form the logical design in a program.

The four logical control structures are:

LOGICAL CONTROL STRUCTURES

1. Sequence.
2. Selection.
3. Iteration.
4. Case Structure.

---

1. Sequence

When instructions are to be executed in the order in which they appear, we call this a **sequence.** The first flowchart and pseudocode in the preceding section illustrated a module executed as a sequence, one instruction after the other. Thus if all data is to be processed step-by-step in some fixed way, we use a sequence to depict the logic. That is, when instructions are executed in order *regardless of any existing condition*, we code them as a sequence. As another example, the following instructions would represent a sequence. The ellipses (dots) within each symbol just mean that each statement has other components.

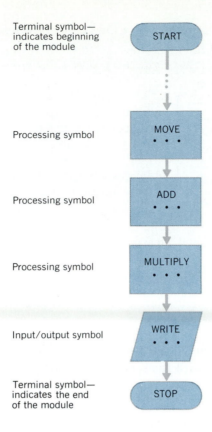

The preceding sequence or set of instructions would always be executed in the order in which it appears. These instructions are executed as they appear in the flowchart, from top to bottom. When they are coded in a program, they will also be executed in sequence.

Beginning and Ending Modules

All modules or sequences in a program flowchart and a pseudocode should be clearly delineated. To denote the beginning and end of a module or sequence in a flowchart, we use a terminal symbol. Similarly, the pseudocode could use START and STOP as code words to delineate a sequence or module, particularly the main module.

START

       ———
       ———
       ———
       ———

STOP

Each instruction in a structured program is executed in sequence unless one of the other logical control structures is specified. We now consider these other structures.

2. Selection

Selection is a logical control construct that executes instructions *depending on the existence of a condition.* It is sometimes called an **IF-THEN-ELSE**

logical control structure. In COBOL, for example, we can code an IF-THEN-ELSE structure as follows:

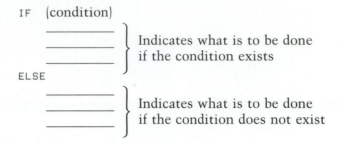

IF   (condition)

‾‾‾‾‾‾‾‾ } Indicates what is to be done
‾‾‾‾‾‾‾‾ } if the condition exists

ELSE

‾‾‾‾‾‾‾‾ } Indicates what is to be done
‾‾‾‾‾‾‾‾ } if the condition does not exist

Example   The following COBOL program excerpt illustrates the IF-THEN-ELSE logical control structure.

```
IF   AMT IS LESS THAN ZERO
     ADD 1 TO ERR-COUNTER
ELSE
     WRITE NEW-RECORD.
```

The general flowchart representation for an IF-THEN-ELSE logical control structure along with the specific flowchart excerpt for the preceding example are as follows:

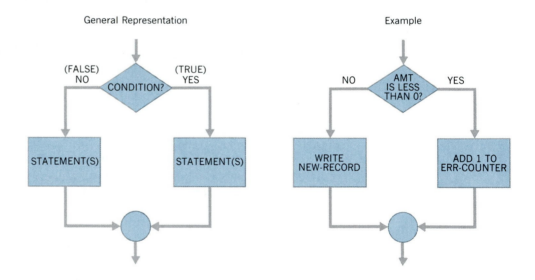

If the condition is true (or exists), we execute the statement or statements on the right. If the condition does not exist, we execute the statement or statements on the left. In either case, the flow returns to the circle or connector, where the next instruction, in sequence, is executed.

The general pseudocode format for the IF-THEN-ELSE logical control structure along with the specific pseudocode for the preceding example are as follows:

General Pseudocode for a Selection	**Example**
IF condition	IF Amt is Less Than Zero
THEN	THEN
_____	Add 1 to Error Counter
_____	ELSE
_____	Write a New Record
ELSE	ENDIF
_____	
_____	
_____	
ENDIF	

In pseudocode, the word IF is followed by the condition to be tested, the word THEN is followed by the statements to be executed if the condition exists, the word ELSE is followed by the statements to be executed if the condition does not exist, and the word ENDIF ends the selection process. All coded entries except the words IF, THEN, ELSE, and ENDIF are *indented* on a separate line so that the format of the selection structure is highlighted. We capitalize only the logical control terms IF, THEN, ELSE, and ENDIF, which also helps to highlight the structure.

We will see later that a COBOL 85 program can look *essentially just like pseudocode*. That is, the word THEN may be used to indicate which statements to execute if the condition exists. Similarly, END-IF can be used to mark the end of the IF statement itself—but only with COBOL 85. Thus the pseudocode for the preceding example with IF-THEN-ELSE-ENDIF resembles a COBOL 85 program excerpt—the only difference is that END-IF, with a hyphen, is used with COBOL 85 rather than the pseudocode delimiter ENDIF.

Here we present the general form for IF-THEN-ELSE and focus on the flowchart and pseudocode techniques that illustrate this logical control structure. The precise details for coding COBOL programs using IF-THEN-ELSE are discussed in Chapter 9.

3. Iteration

In our sample programs in Unit I, we illustrated a major logical control structure referred to as the PERFORM ... UNTIL. This instruction enables us to execute a series of steps from the main module repeatedly until a specific condition exists. The logical control structure that makes use of the PERFORM ... UNTIL is called iteration. **Iteration** is a term used in programming for indicating the repeated execution of a series of steps. One type of iteration is performed by the following logical control sequence.

```
PERFORM 200-CALC-RTN
     UNTIL ARE-THERE-MORE-RECORDS = 'NO '.
```

This means that the module that we have called 200-CALC-RTN is executed *repeatedly* until the field labeled ARE-THERE-MORE-RECORDS is equal to 'NO '. This type of iteration is flowcharted as:

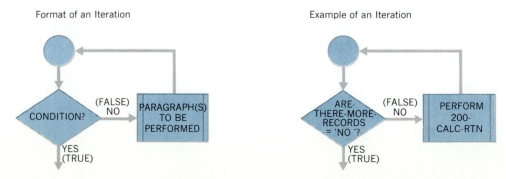

Format of an Iteration   Example of an Iteration

The flowchart symbol used to indicate a `PERFORM` is referred to as a *predefined process*. If the condition tested in the decision symbol is *not* met, we execute the named paragraph using the predefined process symbol. This means that the instructions in the paragraph named within the predefined process symbol will be defined or described in detail in a separate module. The flowchart indicates that we continue to execute that named module until the specified condition is met. In the example, the paragraph named `200-CALC-RTN` will be executed until the field called `ARE-THERE-MORE-RECORDS` has a value of `'NO '`. When the condition is finally met, we continue with the next step in sequence after the decision test. This type of iteration is frequently referred to as **looping.**

The paragraph defined in the predefined process symbol would be flowcharted as a separate sequence. The following is an example of the relationship between two modules:

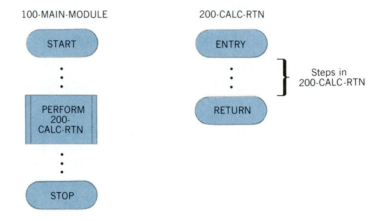

The pseudocode for a `PERFORM ... UNTIL` type of iteration is as follows:

PERFORM UNTIL   condition

     ⋮   }   Instructions to be performed

ENDPERFORM

The module or series of steps to be performed would be coded on the lines between the words PERFORM and ENDPERFORM. These instructions are indented to highlight the fact that they are part of a separate logical control structure.

`PERFORM ... UNTIL` is a type of iteration that is most commonly used for logical control structures in COBOL. The same type of structure is frequently called `DO ... WHILE` or `WHILE ... DO` in other languages. Here again, the words used to describe an iteration are not as important as the concept itself.

Note, too, that a simple `PERFORM` can also be used for iteration. That is, we can execute a module once from any point in our program with the use of a simple `PERFORM`:

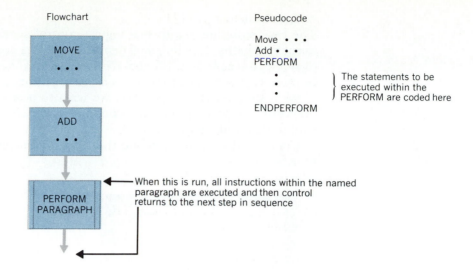

Flowchart

Pseudocode

Move • • •
Add • • •
PERFORM
•
•
•
ENDPERFORM

} The statements to be executed within the PERFORM are coded here

When this is run, all instructions within the named paragraph are executed and then control returns to the next step in sequence

We will see later that there are other formats of the PERFORM, such as PERFORM ... TIMES and PERFORM ... VARYING, that can also be used in COBOL for iteration.

The Infinite Loop: An Error to Be Avoided

Let us again consider the PERFORM ... UNTIL in which a predefined process is executed as part of an iteration. Keep in mind that the module executed is under the control of the PERFORM. The module will be executed repeatedly until a specified condition exists or is true. The condition being tested must at some point be true for the PERFORM ... UNTIL to terminate properly. PERFORM 400-PROCESS-DATA UNTIL ARE-THERE-MORE-RECORDS = 'NO ' means that the paragraph called 400-PROCESS-DATA must contain an instruction that, at some point, causes the contents of the field ARE-THERE-MORE-RECORDS to be changed to 'NO '. If the field ARE-THERE-MORE-RECORDS is never changed to 'NO ', then 400-PROCESS-DATA will be executed repeatedly without any programmed termination. This error is called an **infinite loop.** We avoid infinite loops by ensuring that the field tested in the UNTIL clause of a PERFORM is changed within the paragraph or module that is being executed.

Consider the following flowchart excerpt:

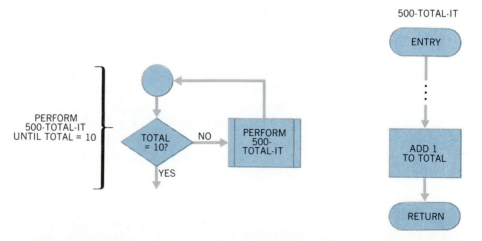

If the instruction ADD 1 TO TOTAL were omitted from the 500-TOTAL-IT module, then the sequence of instructions at 500-TOTAL-IT would result in an infinite loop.

4. Case Structure

The **case structure** is a special logical control structure used when there are numerous paths to be followed depending on the contents of a given field. For example, if a code field is equal to 1, we want to perform a print routine; if it is equal to 2, we want to perform a total routine, and so on.

With the case structure, then, we wish to perform one of several possible procedures depending on some condition. We will discuss this type of structure in detail in Chapter 13.

Consider the following menu that may be displayed to determine a course of action:

The procedure or module to be executed depends on the entry made by a user. This can best be described with a flowchart as:

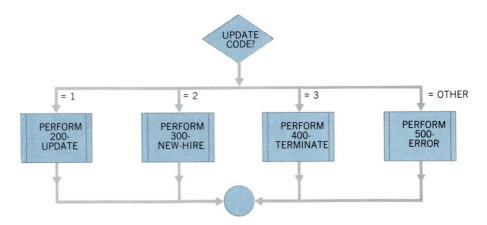

Although this may be coded with a series of simple conditions, such coding can be complex because once a valid entry such as 1, 2, or 3 has been determined, we want to skip over the other tests. As we will see in Chapter 13, the best way to accomplish the case structure is with the EVALUATE verb in COBOL:

```
EVALUATE MENU-ENTRY
    WHEN 1
        PERFORM 200-UPDATE
    WHEN 2
        PERFORM 300-NEW-HIRE
```

```
WHEN 3
    PERFORM 400-TERMINATE
WHEN OTHER
    PERFORM 500-ERROR.
```

If additional valid values need to be added, it is a simple task to add the appropriate clauses. EVALUATE is part of COBOL 85 but not part of COBOL 74; most 1974 compilers, however, include it as an enhancement.

The case structure is becoming very important in processing menus interactively and in helping to validate data so that errors are minimized.

With the use of the EVALUATE, you can perform different routines depending on the contents of a field. You can also determine if a field has valid contents with the use of the WHEN OTHER clause. In the preceding, we perform the appropriate procedure depending on the contents of the UPDATE-CODE entered; if the code is invalid with a value other than 1, 2, or 3, an error message would be printed.

The pseudocode for a case structure is as follows:

```
CASE Update-Code
        WHEN 1
             PERFORM
             ⋮                    } Salary Update Procedure
             ENDPERFORM
        WHEN 2
             PERFORM
             ⋮                    } New Hire Procedure
             ENDPERFORM
        WHEN 3
             PERFORM
             ⋮                    } Terminate Procedure
             ENDPERFORM
        WHEN OTHER
             ⋮                    } Error Procedure
             ENDPERFORM
ENDCASE
```

III. Illustrating Logical Control Structures Using Flowcharts and Pseudocode

A. Example 1

Let us review the following rules of flowcharting.

FLOWCHART RULES

1. A flowchart is drawn and read from top to bottom unless a specific condition alters the path.
2. Different symbols are used to denote different functions.
3. All symbols have explanatory notes indicating the specific operations to be performed. Since a symbol denotes a major category of operations such as input/output or processing, a note is required within the symbol to describe the *specific* operations to be performed such as read a record or add amount to total.

Similarly, the following are pseudocode rules.

PSEUDOCODE RULES

1. Pseudocode is written and read from top to bottom.
2. The logical control structure of pseudocode is defined with the use of key terms such as PERFORM . . . ENDPERFORM and IF-THEN-ELSE . . . ENDIF.
3. The operations to be executed within a PERFORM or IF-THEN-ELSE are coded in sequence.
   a. PERFORM
      :   } Write instructions to be performed here
      ENDPERFORM
   b. IF condition
      THEN
      :

      ELSE
      :

      ENDIF
4. Similarly the case structure is defined with a CASE . . . ENDCASE format.

Consider the flowchart and corresponding COBOL program excerpt in Figure 5.1. This is a basic flowchart that reads disk records and prints the data contained in them.

You will note that there are two separate sequences or modules defined in this flowchart. These two modules are labeled 100-MAIN-MODULE and 200-PROCESS-DATA. Both modules begin and end with terminal symbols. The main module, which is labeled 100-MAIN-MODULE, includes the logical control structures of selection and iteration. In this instance, selection is illustrated with the use of a READ ... AT END. The AT END clause functions like an IF (no more records) . . . statement; that is, we will treat this clause as a simple conditional test. Iteration is accomplished with a PERFORM ... UNTIL. The main module has the following operations.

INSTRUCTIONS IN THE 100-MAIN-MODULE
(Labeled 1–6 in the flowchart in Figure 5.1)

1. Files are opened, that is, prepared for processing.
2. A 'YES' is moved to a field called ARE-THERE-MORE-RECORDS. The field called ARE-THERE-MORE-RECORDS is an end-of-file indicator. It is initialized with a value of 'YES' and changed to 'NO ' only after the last input record has been read and processed. Thus, ARE-THERE-MORE-RECORDS is 'YES' throughout the entire program except when there are no more records to process. The specific field named ARE-THERE-MORE-RECORDS and the values 'YES' and 'NO ' are included here to make the program easier to understand. This technique of using meaningful terms makes programs easier to code, debug, and maintain.
3. A record is read. If a record cannot be read because there are no more records, an AT END condition will be met, and 'NO ' will be moved to ARE-THERE-MORE-RECORDS. Thus a decision symbol is

---

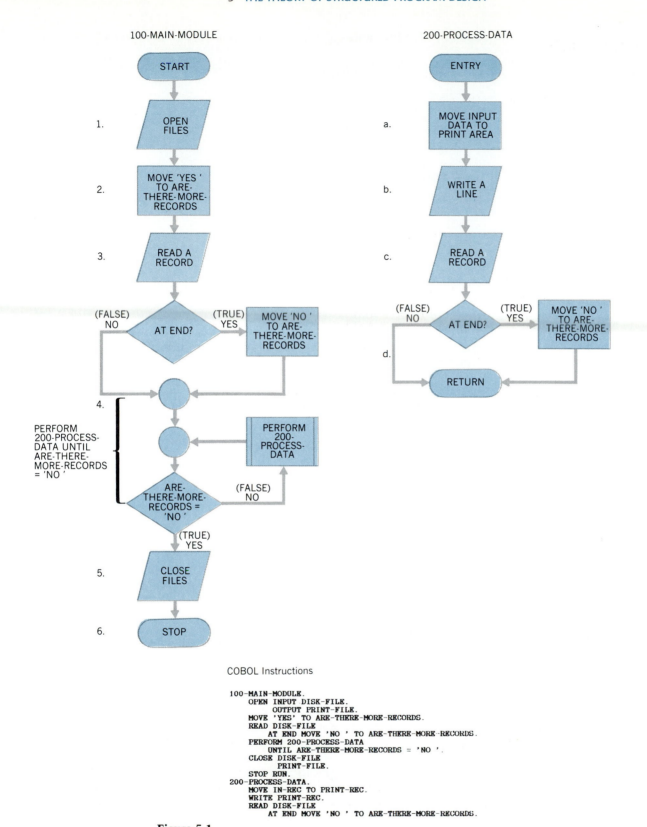

Figure 5.1
Flowchart for Example 1.

used to illustrate a READ ... AT END instruction as follows.

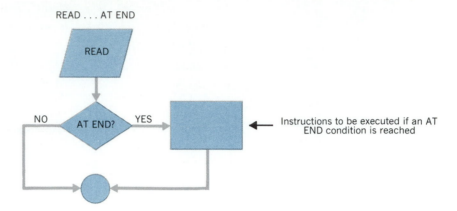

READ ... AT END

Instructions to be executed if an AT END condition is reached

4. A separate routine called 200-PROCESS-DATA is executed repeatedly until ARE-THERE-MORE-RECORDS = 'NO ', which means there are no more records to process. This procedure of repeating a series of steps until a condition is met is called iteration. Three symbols—a connector, a decision symbol, and a predefined process—are used to illustrate iteration:

Example of an Iteration

PERFORM paragraph UNTIL condition

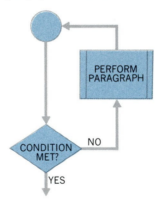

The module called 200-PROCESS-DATA will be executed until all input records have been processed; after all records have been processed, control returns to the next sequential instruction in 100-MAIN-MODULE.

5. After all records have been processed, files are closed or deactivated.
6. The job is terminated by a STOP RUN instruction.

200-PROCESS-DATA contains the sequence of steps that will be executed if there are more records to process. This module, then, performs the required operations for each input record. When 200-PROCESS-DATA is executed for the first time, a record has already been read in the routine labeled 100-MAIN-MODULE. That is, an initial READ has been performed in the 100-MAIN-MODULE routine. 200-PROCESS-DATA operates on that first record and then reads and processes each additional record until there is no more data. At 200-PROCESS-DATA, we have the following steps.

INSTRUCTIONS AT `200-PROCESS-DATA`
(Labeled a–d in the flowchart in Figure 5.1)

a. The input data is moved from the input area to the print area.

b. A line is written.

c. A new record is read.

d. The sequence of steps at `200-PROCESS-DATA` is executed under the control of `PERFORM ... UNTIL` in `100-MAIN-MODULE`. It is repeated until an `AT END` condition occurs. When an `AT END` occurs, `'NO '` is moved to the field called `ARE-THERE-MORE-RECORDS`. The sequence is then terminated and control returns to `100-MAIN-MODULE`, where files are closed and the program is terminated.

The following is the pseudocode for Example 1.

```
START
      Housekeeping Operations
      Read an Input Record
      PERFORM UNTIL no more records
            Move Input Data to the Print Area
            Write a Line
            Read an Input Record
      ENDPERFORM
      End-of-Job Operations
STOP
```

The structure of the PERFORM . . . ENDPERFORM in a pseudocode is as follows.

```
PERFORM

      ————  ⎫ Instructions to be performed
      ————  ⎬ (indented for ease of reading)
      ————  ⎭
ENDPERFORM
```

The indented statements would be those under the control of a PERFORM. We would write a PERFORM . . . UNTIL in exactly the same way. That is, statements under the control of a logical control structure are always indented.

The actual words used in a pseudocode need not follow any specific rules. We can say "Housekeeping Operations" to mean any initializing steps, or we can say "Open Files." Similarly, we can say "PERFORM UNTIL no more records" or "PERFORM UNTIL ARE-THERE-MORE-RECORDS = 'NO' ". As a rule, however, the logical control words such as PERFORM . . . ENDPERFORM are capitalized. This serves to highlight the control structures in a pseudocode.

The degree of detail used in a pseudocode can vary. Only the logical control structures such as PERFORM . . . ENDPERFORM, IF . . . THEN . . . ELSE . . . ENDIF, CASE . . . ENDCASE need to be precisely defined. The actual instructions themselves may be abbreviated. For example, the Move and Write instructions within the PERFORM . . . UNTIL structure in Figure 5.2 might be abbreviated as "Process the data". You will find that the more detailed a pseudocode becomes, the closer it is to COBOL. We will be fairly detailed in our illustrations.

The flowchart and pseudocode for Example 1 are shown here to help you understand how a full program uses the logical control structure of iteration with a PERFORM ... UNTIL and the logical control structure of selection with a READ ... AT END.

Typically, programmers plan the logic to be used in a program with *either* a flowchart *or* pseudocode. Your instructor or computer center may require that you use one or the other. If not, feel free to use the planning tool you prefer.

B. Example 2

Consider now the full program flowchart and the corresponding COBOL program excerpt in Figure 5.2.

The flowchart depicts the logic used to print salary checks for all salespeople in a company. The salary is dependent on how much sales the salesperson generated. If a salesperson has made more than $100 in sales, the commission is 10% or .10 of sales, which is added to the person's salary. If a salesperson has made $100 or less in sales, then the commission is only 5% or .05 of sales.

Here, again, there are two sequences: one labeled 100-MAIN-PARAGRAPH and the other 200-PROCESS-DATA-PARAGRAPH. Selecting paragraph-names that are meaningful will make programs easier to code, debug, and maintain. Note that 100-MAIN-PARAGRAPH, which serves as a main module, has the very same set of instructions as the previous illustration. The major difference in this flowchart is the actual operations to be performed on input records in 200-PROCESS-DATA-PARAGRAPH. This paragraph uses the logical control structure called *selection* in two different ways.

If sales are greater than $100, 10% of sales is used to determine the commission; otherwise, the commission is 5% of sales. After the percentage or commission rate has been determined, the amount is calculated, and a check is written with name and amount. Another salesperson's record is then read, and the module called 200-PROCESS-DATA-PARAGRAPH is repeated until an AT END condition exists. When AT END occurs, the value 'NO ' is moved to ARE-THERE-MORE-RECORDS and control is returned to the module called 100-MAIN-PARAGRAPH, where files are closed and the run is terminated.

The flowchart excerpt that compares sales to 100.00 is a logical control structure called a standard IF-THEN-ELSE or selection. Recall that it has the following general format:

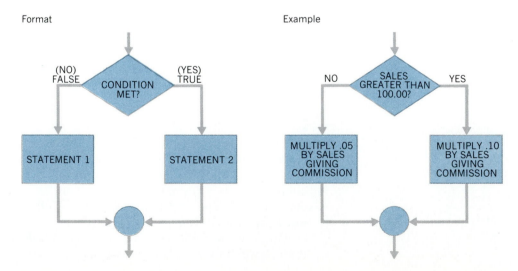

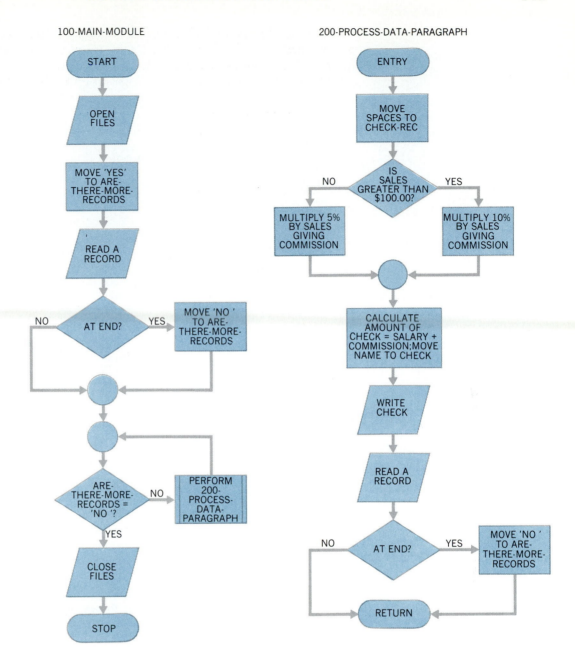

Figure 5.2
Flowchart for Example 2.

COBOL Coding

```
100-MAIN-PARAGRAPH.
    OPEN INPUT SALES-FILE
         OUTPUT CHECK-FILE.
    MOVE 'YES' TO ARE-THERE-MORE-RECORDS.
    READ SALES-FILE
        AT END MOVE 'NO ' TO ARE-THERE-MORE-RECORDS.
    PERFORM 200-PROCESS-DATA-PARAGRAPH
        UNTIL ARE-THERE-MORE-RECORDS = 'NO '.
    CLOSE SALES-FILE
          CHECK-FILE.
    STOP RUN.
200-PROCESS-DATA-PARAGRAPH.
    MOVE SPACES TO CHECK-REC.
    IF SALES-IN IS GREATER THAN 100.00
        MULTIPLY .10 BY SALES-IN GIVING WS-COMMISSION
    ELSE
        MULTIPLY .05 BY SALES-IN GIVING WS-COMMISSION.
    COMPUTE AMT-OUT = SALARY-IN + WS-COMMISSION.
    MOVE NAME-IN TO NAME-OUT.
    WRITE CHECK-REC.
    READ SALES-FILE
        AT END MOVE 'NO ' TO ARE-THERE-MORE-RECORDS.
```

We have classified the READ ... AT END sequence as a *selection*, but the preceding comparison of sales to 100.00 more closely adheres to the format for an IF-THEN-ELSE structure.

The following pseudocode is used for an IF-THEN-ELSE structure.

IF	condition
THEN	operations to be performed
ELSE	operations to be performed if condition is not met

ENDIF

The full pseudocode for Example 2 is as follows:

```
START
      Housekeeping Operations
      Read a Sales Record
      PERFORM UNTIL no more records
          IF   Sales Greater than 100.00
          THEN
                  Multiply 10% (.10) by Sales Giving Commission
          ELSE
                  Multiply 5% (.05) by Sales Giving Commission
          ENDIF
          Calculate Amount of Check = Salary + Commission
          Move Name to Check
          Write Check
          Read a Sales Record
      ENDPERFORM
      End-of-Job Operations
STOP
```

The flowchart and pseudocode for Example 2 are illustrated here to help you understand the logical control structures of sequence, iteration, and selection as used in a full program. We will be depicting the logic for the practice programs at the end of each chapter with either a flowchart or pseudocode.

IV. Hierarchy Charts for Top-Down Programming

Flowcharts and pseudocode are used to plan a program so that the structured design concept is implemented properly and efficiently. But what about the other major component of well-designed programs—the top-down approach? We need a tool that will illustrate the top-down relationships among modules in a structured program.

The planning tool best used for illustrating a *top-down approach* to a program is a **hierarchy** or **structure chart.** A hierarchy or structure chart provides a graphic method for segmenting a program into its components or modules. You will find that the hierarchy chart clearly illustrates how modules in a program relate to one another. Its main purpose is to provide a visual or graphic overview of the relationships among modules in a program. With a hierarchy chart, an entire set of procedures can be segmented into a series of manageable functions.

Thus, before writing a program you will need to plan the logic in two ways: (1) with a flowchart or pseudocode to illustrate the logical structure, that is, how instructions are actually executed, and (2) with a hierarchy chart to illustrate how the modules should relate to one another in a top-down fashion.

In COBOL, the concept of top-down or hierarchical programming is accomplished by coding main modules first, with minor ones detailed later. These modules, then, are said to be coded hierarchically.

A main module is subdivided into its components, which are considered subordinate modules. Think of a top-down design as an outline of a paper. Begin by pencilling in the main subject areas and components and focus on the minor details after the main organization has been defined.

Note the following about hierarchy charts.

HIERARCHY CHARTS

1. A hierarchy chart is a structure chart that represents program modules as rectangular boxes and illustrates the interrelationships among these modules with the use of connecting lines.

2. A module is a well-defined program segment that performs a specific function. A module may be a heading routine, an error-checking routine, a calculation routine, and so forth.

The following example illustrates the relationships of modules in a hierarchy chart. In practice, we would use meaningful names for modules. The letters A through H are used here as paragraph-names for the sake of brevity and to highlight the concepts being illustrated.

Example of a Hierarchy Chart

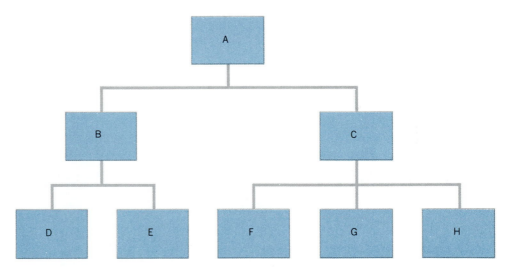

Note that letters A through H represent paragraph-names that are executed with the use of a PERFORM as follows:

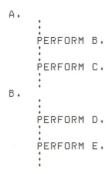

```
A.
    .
    .
    PERFORM B.
    .
    .
    PERFORM C.
    .
B.  .
    .
    PERFORM D.
    .
    PERFORM E.
    .
```

```
C.
    :
    :
  PERFORM F.
    :
    :
  PERFORM G.
    :
    :
  PERFORM H.
```

The hierarchy chart, then, only illustrates modules executed from other modules. Unlike a flowchart or pseudocode, actual instructions are *not* depicted. Each block or box in a hierarchy chart represents a module. If a module calls for another module, this is depicted in a separate box. Consider the following section of the preceding hierarchy chart:

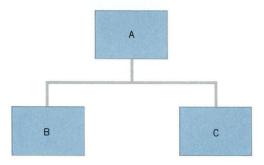

From this excerpt, we see that modules B and C are executed from module A.

Note that a module that is executed by a PERFORM can itself have a PERFORM in it. Module D, for example, is performed in Module B, which itself is executed from the main module, Module A.

Consider the following excerpt, which is different from the preceding:

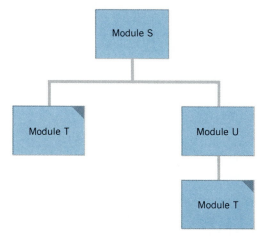

This excerpt indicates that Module T is executed from both Module S and Module U. To highlight the fact that Module T is executed from more than one point in the program, we use a corner cut in both boxes labeled Module T.

In summary, the hierarchy chart illustrates how modules relate to one another, which modules are subordinate to others, and whether or not a module is executed from more than one point in the program. This structure chart makes it easier to keep track of the logic in a program. Moreover, if a module must be modified at some later date, the hierarchy chart will tell you how the change might affect the entire program. It does not consider the actual instructions within each module, just the relationships among them. The actual

Figure 5.3
Sample payroll program.

```
100-MAIN-MODULE.
    OPEN INPUT PAYROLL
        OUTPUT PRINT-REPORT.
    PERFORM 200-INITIALIZE-RTN.
    PERFORM 300-HEADING-RTN.
    PERFORM 400-READ-PAYROLL-REC.
    PERFORM 500-COMPUTE-WAGES
        UNTIL ARE-THERE-MORE-RECORDS = 'NO '.
    CLOSE PAYROLL
        PRINT-REPORT.
    STOP RUN.
200-INITIALIZE-RTN.
    MOVE 'YES' TO ARE-THERE-MORE-RECORDS.
    MOVE 1 TO WS-PAGE-CT.
300-HEADING-RTN.
    WRITE PRINT-REC FROM HEADING1
        AFTER PAGE.
    WRITE PRINT-REC FROM HEADING2
        AFTER ADVANCING 2 LINES.
    ADD 1 TO WS-PAGE-CT.
    MOVE 0 TO WS-LINE-CT.
400-READ-PAYROLL-REC.
    READ PAYROLL
        AT END MOVE 'NO ' TO ARE-THERE-MORE-RECORDS.
500-COMPUTE-WAGES.
    IF HOURS-IN > 40
        PERFORM 600-OVERTIME-RTN
    ELSE
        COMPUTE WAGES-OUT = HOURS-IN * RATE-IN.
    PERFORM 700-WRITE-RTN.
    PERFORM 400-READ-PAYROLL-REC.
600-OVERTIME-RTN.
    COMPUTE WAGES-OUT = 40 * RATE-IN + (HOURS-IN - 40) *
        RATE-IN * 1.5.
700-WRITE-RTN.
    WRITE PRINT-REC FROM DETAIL-REC
        AFTER ADVANCING 2 LINES.
    ADD 1 TO WS-LINE-CT.
    IF WS-LINE-CT = 25
        PERFORM 300-HEADING-RTN.
```

sequence of instructions is depicted in a flowchart or pseudocode, which would accompany a hierarchy chart as a program planning tool.

A hierarchy chart is sometimes called a **Visual Table of Contents (VTOC)** because it provides a graphic overview of a program.

Consider the COBOL program in Figure 5.3, which calculates wages for each employee, where overtime is calculated as time-and-a-half. The program is designed to print 25 lines on a page, after which a new page with headings is generated.

The hierarchy chart or VTOC for this payroll program is illustrated in Figure 5.4. Even if you are not entirely familiar with all the specific instructions in Figure 5.3, you will note that the hierarchy chart provides a visual overview of the relationships among modules. Modules marked with a black corner cut are performed from more than one point in the program.

Note that when a subordinate module such as 600-OVERTIME-RTN is executed in its entirety, control then returns to the next highest module, 500-COMPUTE-WAGES in this instance. When 500-COMPUTE-WAGES has been executed in its entirety, that is, when ARE-THERE-MORE-RECORDS = 'NO ' in the program, control returns to 100-MAIN-MODULE. Because logical control is depicted in this hierarchical fashion in a hierarchy or structure chart, it is referred to as a *top-down* tool.

In summary, then, a hierarchy chart has the following advantages.

ADVANTAGES OF A HIERARCHY OR STRUCTURE CHART

1. It helps programmers, systems analysts, and users see how modules interrelate.
2. It helps programmers debug and modify programs.
3. It helps users understand the logical flow in a program.
4. It helps programming managers assess the efficiency of programs.

Figure 5.4
Hierarchy chart for sample
payroll program.

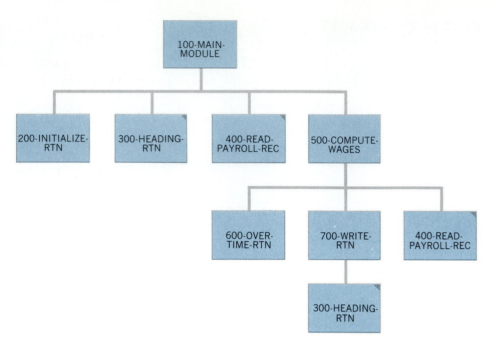

Thus the hierarchy chart, like a pseudocode and flowchart, is both a design and documentation tool.

You can see that a hierarchy chart is *not* designed to highlight individual instructions; flowcharts and pseudocode serve that purpose. Rather, a hierarchy chart provides an overview of the interrelationships, hierarchy, and structure of modules. It also serves as a kind of table of contents, helping users and programmers locate modules in a program. This is why the term "visual table of contents" (VTOC) is sometimes used.

From this point on, each chapter in the text will illustrate program logic with flowcharts, pseudocode, and hierarchy charts. Examine these charts and be sure you understand the logic and the relationships among modules before you look at the programs.

When you design your own programs, we recommend that you begin by drawing a flowchart or pseudocode and a hierarchy chart. You will find that these tools are extremely helpful in mapping out the logic to be used in your program. Although our early programs have relatively simple logical control constructs, the habitual use of program planning tools will be extremely helpful later on when you write more complex programs. When a flowchart or pseudocode is written correctly, it is a relatively easy matter to convert it to a program, assuming you know the syntax or rules of the programming language. You may also find that these planning tools will help you spot potential logic errors that, if coded in a program, may produce erroneous results.

Experienced programmers use *either* flowcharts or pseudocode as a planning tool. Writing both is really "overkill." Some computing organizations specify whether you should use pseudocode or flowcharting; others allow the programmer to choose the tool to be used. We illustrate both. We recommend that you plan your program with either tool, whichever you prefer.

V. Naming Modules or Paragraphs

In most of our programs, a module or set of related instructions is equivalent to a paragraph. We have been using module or paragraph-names such as 100-MAIN-MODULE and 200-PROCESS DATA without really reviewing why those names were selected. Recall that paragraph-names can be a combination of letters, digits, and hyphens up to 30 characters. We will, however, use one standard method for naming paragraphs in all programs. First, as previously noted, we will choose a meaningful name, one that describes the module. Names such as MAIN-MODULE, PROCESS-DATA, and ERROR-ROUTINE are descriptive in that they provide the reader with some idea of the type of instructions within the module.

In our examples, we also use 100-, 200-, and so on as prefixes to these descriptive names. Module-names are given prefixes that provide information on their location. That is, module 100- precedes module 200-, which precedes module 300-, and so forth. You will find that in very large programs that require several pages for listing, this type of numbering makes it much easier to locate a module during debugging or program modification.

This numbering system usually uses intervals of 100 for ease of reading and to allow for possible insertions later on. In complex programs, a letter may precede the number. A, for example, may be used to identify a section or a particular level of a module on a hierarchy chart. B may be used for sublevels, and so on. Consider the following hierarchy chart notation:

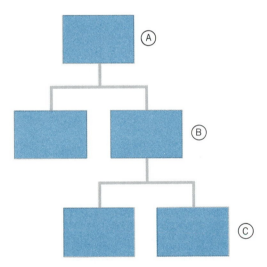

A, B, and C designate *levels* on the chart. Since levels of hierarchy could change during program development, we do not encourage you to use these letters unless your programs are segmented into sections. Later on, we will demonstrate how letters with numbers can be used to designate sections.

We will be using numeric prefixes along with meaningful names to identify paragraphs in all our programs.

VI. Modularizing Programs

We have seen that top-down programs are written with main units or modules planned and coded first, followed by more detailed ones. Structure or hierarchy charts illustrate the relationships among these modules. All statements that represent a unit or a set of instructions that together achieve a given task should be coded as a module. Consider the following:

```
100-MAIN-MODULE.
    PERFORM 200-INITIALIZE-RTN.
    PERFORM 300-PROCESS-DATA
        UNTIL ARE-THERE-MORE-RECORDS = 'NO '.
    PERFORM 400-END-OF-JOB-RTN.
    STOP RUN.
```

200-INITIALIZE-RTN would OPEN all files, READ the first record, and perform any other operations required prior to the processing of data. These instructions could have been coded directly in 100-MAIN-MODULE, but because they are really a related set of instructions we treat them as a separate unit. We encourage this type of modularity especially for complex programs or when standard initializing procedures are required by an organization.

Similarly, 400-END-OF-JOB-RTN would CLOSE all files but might also include other procedures such as the printing of final totals. Here, again, such statements represent a unit and should be modularized.

Most programmers use initializing and end-of-job procedures as modules rather than including the individual instructions in the main module. In this way, the main module provides a "bird's eye" view of the entire structure in the program. This modularization eliminates the need to get involved in detailed coding until after the structure has been fully developed.

We will use initializing and end-of-job modules extensively beginning with Chapter 10 where we discuss the PERFORM statement in full detail.

VII. A Review of Two Coding Guidelines

A. Code Each Clause on a Separate Line

In general, we code COBOL programs with *one clause per line*.

Examples

```
1. READ INVENTORY
       AT END MOVE 'NO ' TO ARE-THERE-MORE-RECORDS.
2. PERFORM 100-CALC-RTN
       UNTIL ARE-THERE-MORE-RECORDS = 'NO '.
```

Words and clauses can be separated with any number of blank spaces. Therefore, we can be as generous as we wish in our use of coding lines. Coding one clause per line makes programs easier to read, and it also helps during debugging. Consider the following example again.

```
OPEN INPUT INVENTORY
     OUTPUT PRINTOUT.
```

Suppose a program error or interrupt occurs and the OPEN statement is determined to be the one with the error. OPEN errors can occur if a file has incorrect labels or if devices are not ready. If the OPEN statement was coded on a single line, it would be difficult to determine which file or device in the example caused the error. When the OPEN statement uses two lines, debugging is easier. As we will see later, this is because we can determine not only the instruction that caused an error but the actual line. Once we identify the erroneous line, we will know the actual file or device that caused the OPEN error. That is, if the error occurred on the first line of the OPEN, then we need to check the INVENTORY file. If the error occurred on the second line, we would check the PRINTOUT file. If both files were opened on the same line, we would not know which caused the error.

B. Indent Lines within a Sentence

In addition to coding one clause per line, we *indent* clauses as well. Indentation makes programs easier to read. In general, we will indent four spaces on each line.

Examples

```
1. SELECT INVENTORY
       ASSIGN TO DISK1.
2. PERFORM 200-CALC-RTN
       UNTIL ARE-THERE-MORE-RECORDS = 'NO '.
```

Sometimes we indent more than four spaces for the sake of alignment.

Example

```
OPEN INPUT INVENTORY
     OUTPUT PRINTOUT.
```

To align the words INPUT and OUTPUT we indented more than four spaces on the second line.

In summary, we recommend that you indent clauses at least four spaces per line. Sometimes a clause has several components, and the way we indent can help make the logic clearer.

Suppose we want to add 1 to TOTAL *and* read an input record if AMT1 = 100:

```
IF  AMT1 = 100
    ADD 1 TO TOTAL
    READ INFILE
        AT END MOVE 'NO ' TO ARE-THERE-MORE-RECORDS.
```

Notice the use of indentation here. We actually indent *twice* on the fourth line to help clarify that the AT END clause is part of a READ, which itself is part of an IF statement.

As you proceed through this text, you will see how indentation is used to clarify the logic. You should use this technique in your programs as well. Note, however, that indentation does not affect the program logic at all. It is simply a tool that helps people *read* the program.

CHAPTER SUMMARY

A. Logical Control Structures
   The full range of logical control structures is as follows.
   1. Sequence

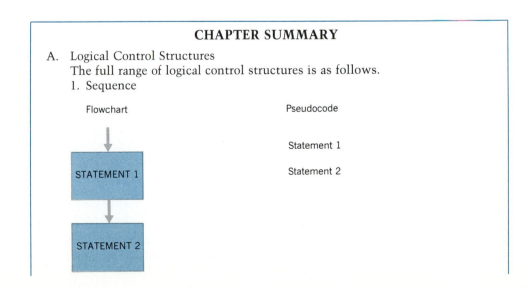

2. IF-THEN-ELSE or Selection

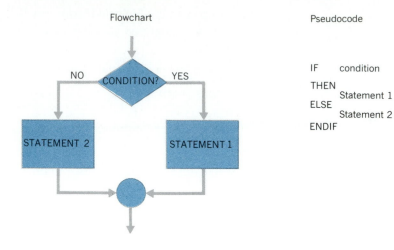

3. Iteration Using a PERFORM . . . UNTIL

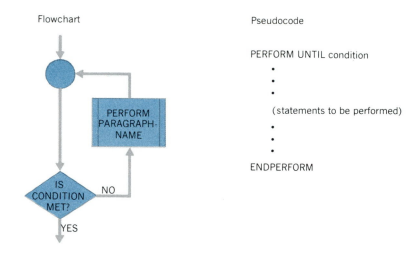

The processing symbol with two parallel bars is used to denote a predefined function, which is a module to be executed under the control of a PERFORM statement. That is, control is passed to the named module and then returns to the point directly following the PERFORM when the condition is met.

4. Case Structure

This logical control structure is used when there are numerous paths to be followed depending on the contents of a given field.

Example

```
if MARITAL-STATUS = "D" execute DIVORCE-MODULE
if MARITAL-STATUS = "S" execute SINGLE-MODULE
if MARITAL-STATUS = "M" execute MARRIED-MODULE
otherwise execute OTHER-MODULE
```

The way this structure is implemented will be considered in detail in Chapter 13.

B. Program Planning Tools

1. To structure a program, use a flowchart or pseudocode.
2. To illustrate the top-down approach showing how modules interrelate, use a hierarchy chart.

C. Naming Modules
   Use descriptive names along with numeric prefixes that help locate the paragraphs quickly (200-PRINT-HEADING, 500-PRINT-FINAL-TOTAL).
D. A Well-Designed Program Uses
   1. Structured programming techniques.
   2. A modularized organization.
   3. A top-down approach.
      Code main modules first, followed by minor ones.
   4. Meaningful names for fields and paragraphs.
   5. One clause per line and indented clauses within a sentence.

CHAPTER SELF-TEST

True-False Questions

T F

— — 1. In general, programs that are first planned with a flowchart or pseudocode take less time to code and debug.

— — 2. Programmers should draw a flowchart and write a pseudocode before coding a program.

— — 3. To ensure that flowcharts are correct, it is best to draw them after you have coded the program.

— — 4. Well-designed programs should be structured.

— — 5. The terms "top-down" and "structured" are used synonymously in this chapter.

— — 6. The terms "module" and "paragraph" may be used synonymously in COBOL.

— — 7. A flowchart for a COBOL program should generally be the same as for a Pascal program.

— — 8. The syntax for COBOL and Pascal are, in general, the same.

— — 9. A hierarchy chart can illustrate how the logical control structure of selection is used in a program.

— — 10. The four logical control structures used in well-designed programs are sequence, selection, iteration, and case structure.

Fill in the Blanks

1. The program planning tool specifically designed for depicting the logic in a structured program is _____ .

2. The program planning tool specifically designed for depicting the top-down approach used in a structured program is the _____ .

3. If instructions are executed step-by-step without any change in control, we call this a _____ .

4. Another name for selection, when used in pseudocode or in a COBOL program, is called _____ .

5. Iteration, or the repeated execution of a module, is accomplished using a _____ statement.

6. The flowchart symbol used for performing a module is called _____ .

7. Paragraph- or module-names should consist of two components: the first or prefix is used for _____ ; the second is used for _____ .

8. The pseudocode structure for a selection begins with the word _____ and ends with the word _____ .

9. We indent statements within a PERFORM . . . ENDPERFORM of a pseudocode so that _____ .

10. Another name for a hierarchy chart is _____ .

Solutions:
True-False

1. T
2. F—Usually they use one *or* the other.
3. F—A flowchart is not very useful as a planning tool if it is drawn after a program.
4. T
5. F—"Top-down" refers to the hierarchical representation of modules; "structured" refers to the fact that a program uses the modular approach.
6. T—Routine is also a synonym.
7. T—Flowcharts and pseudocode are language-independent.
8. F—Syntax is language-dependent.
9. F—A hierarchy chart illustrates the relationships among modules.
10. T

Solutions:
Fill in the Blanks

1. pseudocode (Flowcharts have been used for several decades and were not originally developed for structured programs.)
2. hierarchy or structure chart
3. sequence
4. IF-THEN-ELSE
5. PERFORM . . . UNTIL
6. a predefined process
7. numbering modules to help locate them in a large program (100-, 200-, etc.); describing the nature of the module (ERROR-ROUTINE, TOTAL-ROUTINE, etc.)
8. IF; ENDIF
9. the structure is highlighted
10. structure chart or visual table of contents (VTOC)

ILLUSTRATIVE PROGRAM

Consider a program to determine the overall effect on a university budget if faculty are given salary increases as follows:

        6.2% for full professors (Rank = FP)
        8.1% for associate professors (Rank = AS)
        8.3% for assistant professors (Rank = AP)
    10.2% for instructors (Rank = IP)

Read in a file of faculty records and print a payroll report. The input and output formats are as follows:

Input Format

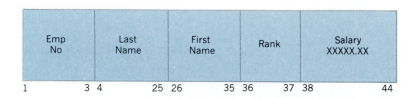

Output Format

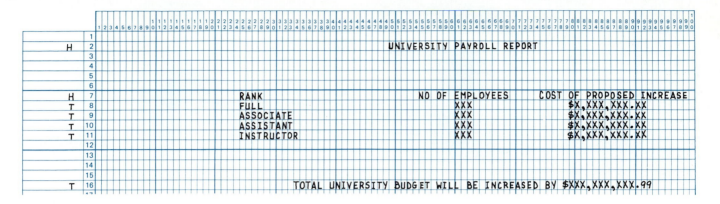

The flowchart and pseudocode are illustrated in Figure 5.5 and the program in Figure 5.6. The hierarchy chart is in Figure 5.7. Do not be overly concerned about instructions that we have not yet discussed in detail. The purpose of these illustrations is to familiarize you with the structure of a program.

Figure 5.5
Pseudocode and flowchart for
Illustrative Program.

```
START
    Housekeeping Operations
    Read a Record
    PERFORM UNTIL no more records
        IF  Rank = 'FP'
        THEN
            Calculate Increase and Add to Professor Total
            Add 1 to Professor Counter
        ENDIF
        IF  Rank = 'AS'
        THEN
            Calculate Increase and Add to Associate Professor Total
            Add 1 to Associate Professor Counter
        ENDIF
        IF  Rank = 'AP'
        THEN
            Calculate Increase and Add to Assistant Professor Total
            Add 1 to Assistant Professor Counter
        ENDIF
        IF  Rank = 'IP'
        THEN
            Calculate Increase and Add to Instructor Total
            Add 1 to Instructor Counter
        ENDIF
        Read a Record
    ENDPERFORM
    PERFORM
        Write Headings
        Move Professor Data to Total Line
        Write Output Line
        Move Associate Professor Data to Total Line
        Write Output Line
        Move Assistant Professor Data to Total Line
        Write Output Line
        Move Instructor Data to Total Line
        Write Output Line
        Add all Totals
        Write a Total Line
    ENDPERFORM
    End-of-Job Operations
STOP
```

Figure 5.5
(continued)

200-CALC-RTN

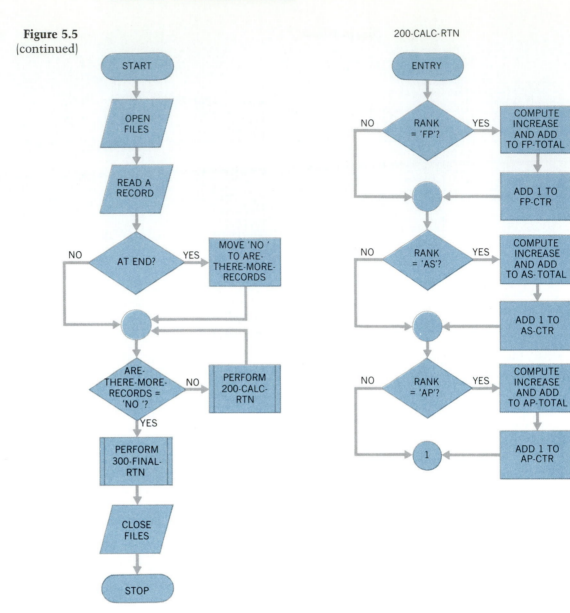

Figure 5.5
(continued)

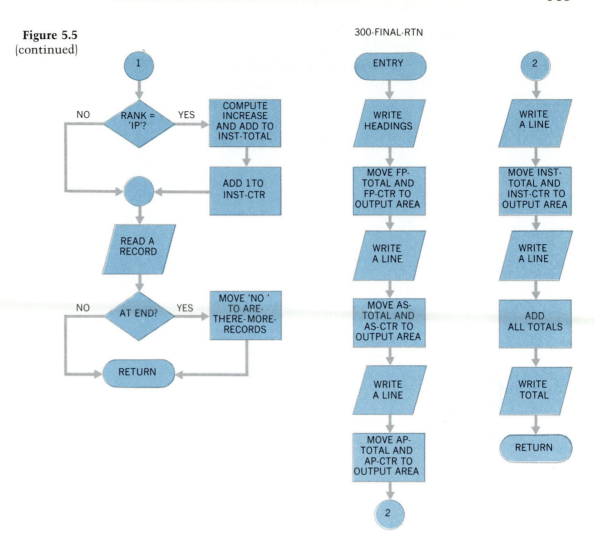

Figure 5.6
Illustrative Program.

```
IDENTIFICATION DIVISION.
PROGRAM-ID. SAMPLE.
AUTHOR. CHRISTOPHER HAMMEL.
*****************************************************************
*   SAMPLE    - DETERMINES THE EFFECT OF SALARY INCREASES FOR  *
*                 THE UNIVERSITY - THE COST FOR EACH RANK OF    *
*              EMPLOYEE WILL BE CALCULATED AND ADDED TO TOTALS  *
*****************************************************************
*
ENVIRONMENT DIVISION.
INPUT-OUTPUT SECTION.
FILE-CONTROL.
    SELECT IN-EMPLOYEE-FILE ASSIGN TO DATA5.
    SELECT OUT-REPORT-FILE  ASSIGN TO SYS$OUTPUT.
*
DATA DIVISION.
FILE SECTION.
FD  IN-EMPLOYEE-FILE
    LABEL RECORDS ARE OMITTED.
01  IN-EMPLOYEE-REC.
    05  IN-EMPLOYEE-NO          PIC 9(3).
    05  IN-EMPLOYEE-LAST-NAME   PIC X(20).
    05  IN-EMPLOYEE-FIRST-NAME  PIC X(10).
    05  IN-RANK                 PIC XX.
    05  IN-SALARY               PIC 9(5)V99.
```

Figure 5.6
(continued)

```
FD  OUT-REPORT-FILE
    LABEL RECORDS ARE OMITTED.
01  OUT-REPORT-REC               PIC X(133).
WORKING-STORAGE SECTION.
01  WS-WORK-AREAS.
    05  ARE-THERE-MORE-RECORDS PIC X(3)       VALUE 'YES'.
    05  WS-PROFESSOR-CTR        PIC 9(3)       VALUE ZEROS.
    05  WS-ASSOCIATE-CTR        PIC 9(3)       VALUE ZEROS.
    05  WS-ASSISTANT-CTR        PIC 9(3)       VALUE ZEROS.
    05  WS-INSTRUCTOR-CTR       PIC 9(3)       VALUE ZEROS.
    05  WS-PROFESSOR-COST       PIC 9(7)V99    VALUE ZEROS.
    05  WS-ASSOCIATE-COST       PIC 9(7)V99    VALUE ZEROS.
    05  WS-ASSISTANT-COST       PIC 9(7)V99    VALUE ZEROS.
    05  WS-INSTRUCTOR-COST      PIC 9(7)V99    VALUE ZEROS.
    05  WS-TOTAL-COST           PIC 9(9)V99    VALUE ZEROS.
    05  WS-WORK1                PIC 9(7)V99    VALUE ZEROS.
01  HL-HEADER-1.
    05  FILLER                  PIC X(50)      VALUE SPACES.
    05  FILLER                  PIC X(25)
        VALUE 'UNIVERSITY PAYROLL REPORT'.
    05  FILLER                  PIC X(58)      VALUE SPACES.
01  HL-HEADER-2.
    05  FILLER                  PIC X(25)      VALUE SPACES.
    05  FILLER                  PIC X(30)
        VALUE 'RANK'.
    05  FILLER                  PIC X(20)
        VALUE 'NO OF EMPLOYEES'.
    05  FILLER                  PIC X(25)
        VALUE 'COST OF PROPOSED INCREASE'.
    05  FILLER                  PIC X(33)      VALUE SPACES.
01  DL-DETAIL-LINE.
    05  FILLER                  PIC X(25)      VALUE SPACES.
    05  DL-RANK                 PIC X(10).
    05  FILLER                  PIC X(26)      VALUE SPACES.
    05  DL-NO-OF-EMPLOYEES      PIC 9(3).
    05  FILLER                  PIC X(16)      VALUE SPACES.
    05  DL-COST                 PIC $Z,ZZZ,ZZ9.99.
    05  FILLER                  PIC X(41)      VALUE SPACES.
01  DL-TOTAL-LINE.
    05  FILLER                  PIC X(34)      VALUE SPACES.
    05  FILLER                  PIC X(46)
        VALUE 'TOTAL UNIVERSITY BUDGET WILL BE INCREASED BY '.
    05  DL-TOTAL-COST           PIC $ZZZ,ZZZ,ZZ9.99.
    05  FILLER                  PIC X(39)      VALUE SPACES.
*
 PROCEDURE DIVISION.
****************************************************************
*  100-MAIN-MODULE - CONTROLS THE OPENING AND CLOSING OF *
*                    FILES, DIRECTION OF PROGRAM LOGIC & *
*                    RETURNS CONTROL TO OPERATING SYSTEM *
****************************************************************
100-MAIN-MODULE.
    OPEN INPUT  IN-EMPLOYEE-FILE
         OUTPUT OUT-REPORT-FILE.
    READ IN-EMPLOYEE-FILE
        AT END MOVE 'NO ' TO ARE-THERE-MORE-RECORDS.
    PERFORM 200-CALC-RTN
        UNTIL ARE-THERE-MORE-RECORDS = 'NO '.
    PERFORM 300-FINAL-RTN.
    CLOSE IN-EMPLOYEE-FILE
          OUT-REPORT-FILE.
    STOP RUN.
*********************************************************
*  200-CALC-RTN - PERFORMED FROM 100-MAIN-MODULE.  *
*                 DETERMINES RANK OF EMPLOYEE       *
*                 CALCULATES SALARY INCREASE        *
*********************************************************
200-CALC-RTN.
    IF  IN-RANK = 'FP'
        MULTIPLY IN-SALARY BY .062 GIVING WS-WORK1
        ADD WS-WORK1 TO WS-PROFESSOR-COST
        ADD 1 TO WS-PROFESSOR-CTR.
    IF  IN-RANK = 'AS'
        MULTIPLY  IN-SALARY BY .081 GIVING WS-WORK1
        ADD WS-WORK1 TO WS-ASSOCIATE-COST
        ADD 1 TO WS-ASSOCIATE-CTR.
    IF  IN-RANK = 'AP'
        MULTIPLY IN-SALARY BY .083 GIVING WS-WORK1
        ADD WS-WORK1 TO WS-ASSISTANT-COST
        ADD 1 TO WS-ASSISTANT-CTR.
```

Figure 5.6
(continued)

```
        IF  IN-RANK = 'IP'
            MULTIPLY IN-SALARY BY .102 GIVING WS-WORK1
            ADD WS-WORK1 TO WS-INSTRUCTOR-COST
            ADD 1 TO WS-INSTRUCTOR-CTR.
        READ IN-EMPLOYEE-FILE
            AT END MOVE 'NO ' TO ARE-THERE-MORE-RECORDS.
 ****************************************************************
 *  300-FINAL-RTN - PERFORMED FROM 100-MAIN-MODULE          *
 *                  PRINTS PAGE AND COLUMN HEADINGS         *
 *                  CALCULATES AND PRINTS TOTAL FOR RANKS *
 ****************************************************************
  300-FINAL-RTN.
      WRITE OUT-REPORT-REC FROM HL-HEADER-1
          AFTER ADVANCING PAGE.
      WRITE OUT-REPORT-REC FROM HL-HEADER-2
          AFTER ADVANCING 5 LINES.
      MOVE 'FULL' TO DL-RANK.
      MOVE WS-PROFESSOR-CTR TO DL-NO-OF-EMPLOYEES.
      MOVE WS-PROFESSOR-COST TO DL-COST.
      WRITE OUT-REPORT-REC FROM DL-DETAIL-LINE
          AFTER ADVANCING 2 LINES.
      MOVE 'ASSOCIATE' TO DL-RANK.
      MOVE WS-ASSOCIATE-CTR TO DL-NO-OF-EMPLOYEES.
      MOVE WS-ASSOCIATE-COST TO DL-COST.
      WRITE OUT-REPORT-REC FROM DL-DETAIL-LINE
          AFTER ADVANCING 2 LINES.
      MOVE 'ASSISTANT' TO DL-RANK.
      MOVE WS-ASSISTANT-CTR TO DL-NO-OF-EMPLOYEES.
      MOVE WS-ASSISTANT-COST TO DL-COST.
      WRITE OUT-REPORT-REC FROM DL-DETAIL-LINE
          AFTER ADVANCING 2 LINES.
      MOVE 'INSTRUCTOR' TO DL-RANK.
      MOVE WS-INSTRUCTOR-CTR TO DL-NO-OF-EMPLOYEES.
      MOVE WS-INSTRUCTOR-COST TO DL-COST.
      WRITE OUT-REPORT-REC FROM DL-DETAIL-LINE
          AFTER ADVANCING 2 LINES.
      ADD WS-PROFESSOR-COST, WS-ASSOCIATE-COST,
          WS-ASSISTANT-COST, WS-INSTRUCTOR-COST
             GIVING WS-TOTAL-COST.
      MOVE WS-TOTAL-COST TO DL-TOTAL-COST.
      WRITE OUT-REPORT-REC FROM DL-TOTAL-LINE
          AFTER ADVANCING 5 LINES.
```

B. Sample Input Data

```
001STERN              ROBERT     FP5000000
002STERN              NANCY      FP5000000
003SMITH              JOHN       AP2000000
004WASHINGTON         GEORGE     IP1000000
005JONES              SAM        AS1800000
006PHILLIPS           TOM        AS2500000
007JOHNSON            DAVID      IP3000000
008THOMAS             STEVE      AP1600000
009SMITH              ADAM       FP4000000
010DOE                JOHN       IP1000000
```

C. Sample Output

UNIVERSITY PAYROLL REPORT

RANK	NO OF EMPLOYEES	COST OF PROPOSED INCREASE
FULL	003	$ 8,680.00
ASSOCIATE	002	$ 3,483.00
ASSISTANT	002	$ 2,988.00
INSTRUCTOR	003	$ 5,100.00

TOTAL UNIVERSITY BUDGET WILL BE INCREASED BY $ 20,251.00

Figure 5.7
Hierarchy chart for Illustrative
Program.

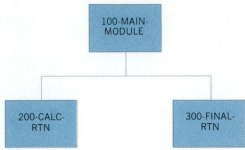

PRACTICE PROBLEM

Read in records with the following fields.

Name
Sex (M = male, F = female)
Color of eyes (1 = Blue, 2 = Brown, 3 = Other)
Color of hair (1 = Brown, 2 = Blonde, 3 = Other)

Draw a flowchart and pseudocode to print the names of all (1) blue-eyed, blonde males and (2) all brown-eyed, brown-haired (brunette) females. See Figure 5.8 for a suggested solution.

KEY TERMS

Case structure	Logical control structure	Sequence
Flowchart	Looping	Structure chart
Hierarchy chart	Module	Top-down programming
IF-THEN-ELSE	Pseudocode	Visual Table of Contents
Infinite loop	Selection	(VTOC)
Iteration		

REVIEW QUESTIONS

I. Fill in the Blanks

1. A flowchart is used for analyzing the _____ in a program.
2. A flowchart is drawn (before/after) the problem is coded.
3. A program flowchart is read from _____ to _____ .
4. Different symbols in a flowchart are used to denote different _____ .
5. The input/output symbol is coded as _____ .
6. A processing symbol is coded as _____ .
7. A READ instruction is flowcharted using a(n) _____ symbol.
8. A MOVE instruction is flowcharted using a _____ symbol.
9. After a paragraph has been performed the required number of times, the logic flow continues with _____ .
10. All flowchart symbols have notes within them indicating the specific _____ to be performed.
11. Pseudocodes have been used with increasing frequency in place of _____ for representing the logical flow to be used in a program.
12. A hierarchy chart is used for depicting the _____ in a program.
13. A decision symbol corresponds to the logical control structure of _____ .

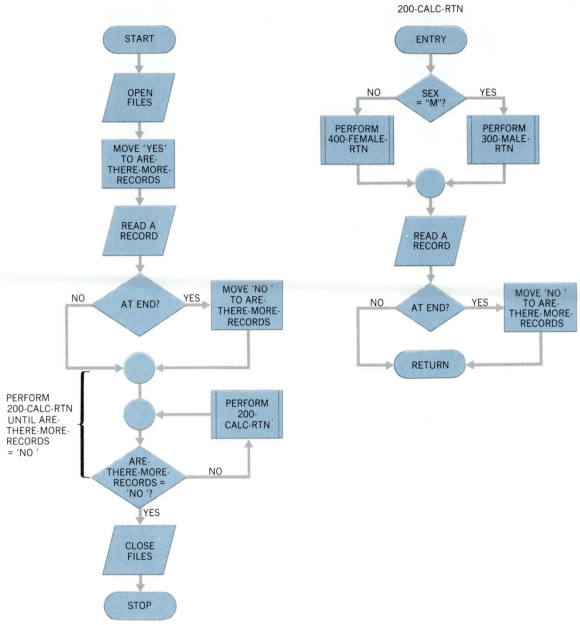

Figure 5.8
Flowchart and pseudocode for
Practice Problem.

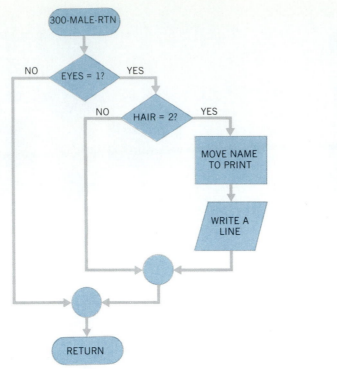

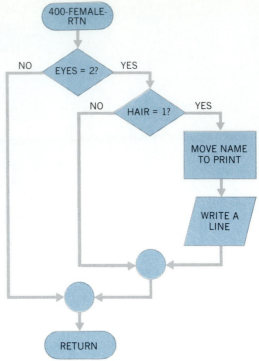

Pseudocode

```
START
    Housekeeping Operations
    Read a Record
    PERFORM UNTIL no more records
        IF  Sex = "M"
        THEN
            PERFORM
                IF  Eyes = 1
                THEN
                    IF  Hair = 2
                    THEN
                        Move Name to Print
                        Write a Line
                    ENDIF
                ENDIF
            ENDPERFORM
        ELSE
            PERFORM
                IF  Eyes = 2
                THEN
                    IF  Hair = 1
                    THEN
                        Move Name to Print
                        Write a Line
                    ENDIF
                ENDIF
            ENDPERFORM
        ENDIF
        Read a Record
    ENDPERFORM
    End-of-Job Operations
STOP
```

Figure 5.8
(continued)

14. The last word written in a PERFORM sequence in a pseudocode is _____ .

15. The last word written in an IF sequence in a pseudocode is _____ .

II. General Questions

1. Indicate in each case whether the flowchart and pseudocode accomplish the same thing:

(a)

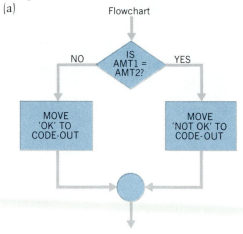

Flowchart

Pseudocode

```
IF      Amt1 = Amt2
THEN
        Move 'OK' to Code-Out
ELSE
        Move 'Not OK' to Code-Out
ENDIF
```

(b)   Flowchart

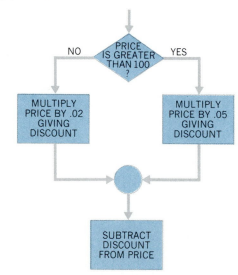

Pseudocode

```
IF    Price is Greater Than 100
THEN
        Multiply Price by .05
              Giving Discount
ELSE
        Multiply Price by .02
              Giving Discount
ENDIF
Subtract Discount from Price
```

(c)   Flowchart

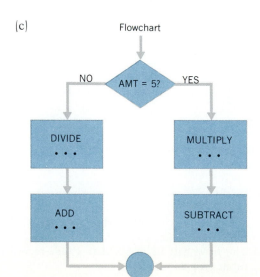

Pseudocode

```
IF      AMT = 5
THEN
        Multiply • • •
        Subtract • • •
ELSE
        Divide • • •
        Add • • •
ENDIF
```

2. Is the following selection permitted in a flowchart? Explain your answer.

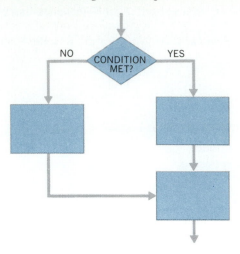

3. Draw a flowchart and write a pseudocode to accomplish each of the following:
   (a) Add 1 to MINOR if a field called AGE is 17 or less.
   (b) Add 1 to LARGE if SIZE-IN is greater than 500; add 1 to SMALL if SIZE-IN is less than or equal to 500.
   (c) If the value of a field called HOURS-WORKED is anything but 40, perform a routine called 200-ERROR-RTN.
   (d) Read in an exam grade. If the grade is 60 or greater, print the word PASS; otherwise print the word FAIL.

PROGRAMMING ASSIGNMENTS

1. Consider the flowchart in Figure 5.9.

   With the following input records, what will be the contents of TOTAL at the end of all operations?

Record No.	Contents of Record Position 18	Contents of Record Position 19
1	1	2
2	1	3
3	1	2
4	1	0
5	(blank)	(blank)
6	(blank)	1
7	1	(blank)
8	1	2
9	1	2
10	(blank)	2

2. Write a pseudocode for the program logic depicted in Question 1.
3. Use the flowchart in Figure 5.10 to answer the following questions.

   (a) In this flowchart, a record is written on disk after reading how many input records? Explain.
   (b) The flowchart indicates that a record is printed after reading how many input records? Explain.
   (c) The flowchart indicates that a tape record is written after reading how many input records? Explain.

4. Write a pseudocode equivalent to the flowchart in Figure 5.10.

5–9. Although flowcharts, pseudocode, and hierarchy charts should be drawn before a program is written, go back to Chapter 4 and draw a flowchart, pseudocode, and hierarchy chart for each of the Programming Assignments numbered 1–5.

Figure 5.9
Flowchart for Programming Assignment 1.

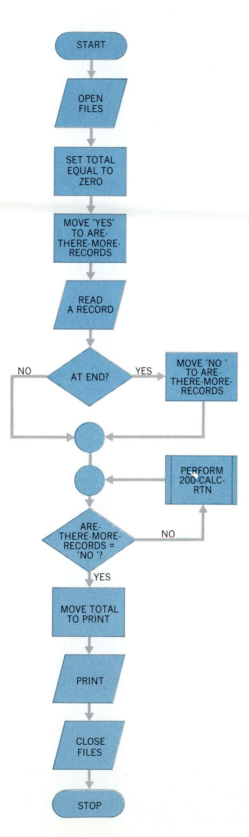

Figure 5.9
(continued)

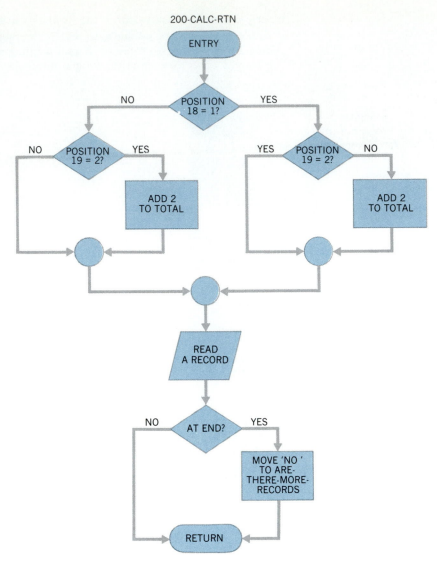

Figure 5.10
Flowchart for Programming
Assignment 3.

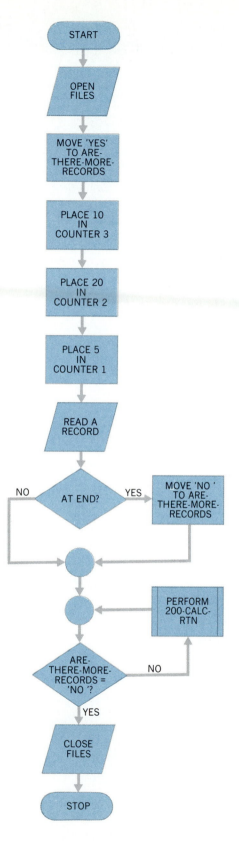

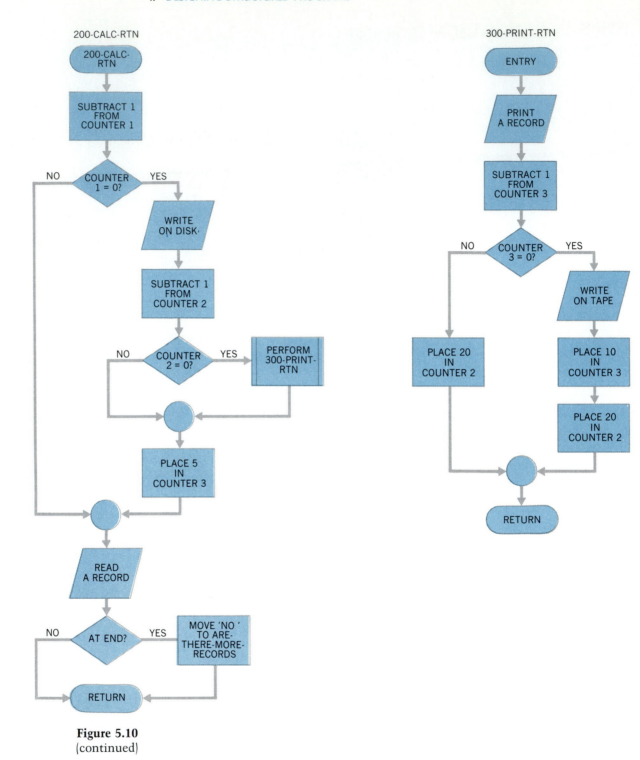

Figure 5.10
(continued)

6

Transferring Data: The MOVE Statement

OBJECTIVES

To familiarize you with

1. The various options of the MOVE statement.
2. The rules for moving fields and literals.
3. How to print decimal points and dollar signs.

I. Introduction

The **MOVE** statement has the following components:

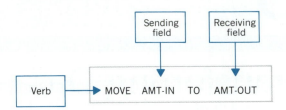

Every COBOL statement in the PROCEDURE DIVISION, like every English sentence, must contain a verb. However, unlike English, a COBOL statement usually starts with a verb. In the preceding, MOVE is the verb. The identifier or data-name AMT-IN is called the **sending field.** The contents of AMT-IN will be transmitted, that is, copied or sent, to the second field, AMT-OUT, as a result of the MOVE operation. AMT-OUT is called the **receiving field.** The contents of AMT-OUT will be replaced by the contents of AMT-IN when the MOVE operation is executed. AMT-IN will remain unchanged.

The MOVE statement, like all COBOL imperative statements, appears only in the PROCEDURE DIVISION. AMT-IN and AMT-OUT are identifiers and must be defined in the DATA DIVISION. You will recall that elementary items in the DATA DIVISION require PICTURE or PIC clauses to indicate (1) the type of data in the field (numeric, alphanumeric, or alphabetic) and (2) the size of the field. To perform a MOVE operation that replaces the contents of AMT-OUT with the *very same contents* as AMT-IN, the PICTURE clauses of both fields must be identical.

Example 1

```
                    MOVE TAX-IN TO TAX-OUT
```

TAX-IN   PICTURE   999   TAX-OUT   PICTURE   999
         Contents 123   Contents 456

If the statement MOVE TAX-IN TO TAX-OUT is executed, the contents of TAX-OUT will be replaced by 123, the contents of TAX-IN. This will occur only if TAX-IN and TAX-OUT have identical PIC clauses (in this case, 999). The original contents of the receiving field, TAX-OUT in this case, is lost during the MOVE operation.

Note also that in a MOVE operation, the contents of the sending field, TAX-IN in this case, is duplicated or copied at the receiving field, TAX-OUT. Thus, at the end of the MOVE operation, both fields will have *the same contents*. The contents of TAX-IN remains unchanged after the MOVE.

Example 2

```
                    MOVE CODE-IN TO CODE-OUT
```

CODE-IN   PICTURE   XXXX   CODE-OUT   PICTURE   XXXX
          Contents ABCD   Contents EFGH

After MOVE CODE-IN TO CODE-OUT is executed, CODE-OUT has ABCD as its contents and CODE-IN also remains with ABCD. Since the fields have the same PICTURE clauses, they will have identical contents at the end of the MOVE operation.

II. The Instruction Formats of the MOVE Statement

We have thus far discussed one instruction format of the MOVE statement.

Format 1

> MOVE identifier-1 TO identifier-2

Identifier-1 and identifier-2 are data-names that must be defined in the DATA DIVISION. To obtain in identifier-2 the same contents as in identifier-1, the PICTURE clauses of both fields must be the same.

A second form of the MOVE statement is as follows:

Format 2

> MOVE literal-1 TO identifier-2

Recall that there are two kinds of literals: numeric and nonnumeric. The rules for forming these literals are as follows:

REVIEW OF LITERALS

Numeric Literals
1. 1 to 18 digits.
2. Decimal point (optional, but it may not be the rightmost character).
3. Sign (optional, but if included it must be the first character).

Nonnumeric or Alphanumeric Literals
1. 1 to 120 characters (160 is upper limit for COBOL 85).
2. Any characters may be used (except the quote mark or apostrophe).
3. The literal is enclosed in single quotes or apostrophes (some systems use double quotes instead).

The following are examples of MOVE statements where a literal is moved to a data-name or identifier.

Example 1
```
05   DEPT-OUT                      PIC 999.
     :
     :
MOVE 123 TO DEPT-OUT.
```

Example 2
```
05   CLASSIFICATION-OUT        PIC X(5).
     :
     :
MOVE 'CODE1' TO CLASSIFICATION-OUT.
```

(Your computer system may require double quotes rather than single quotes for nonnumeric literals.)

Although identifiers must be defined in the DATA DIVISION, literals may be defined directly in the PROCEDURE DIVISION. Assuming an appropriate PICTURE clause in the receiving field, the exact contents or value of the literal will be moved to the field. Keep in mind that the receiving field of any MOVE instruction must *always* be an identifier, not a literal.

In Example 1, 123 is a numeric literal. It must be a literal and not an identifier because it contains all numbers; identifiers must have at least one alphabetic character. To move a numeric literal to a field, the field should have the same data type as the literal. Thus, in Example 1, the receiving field,

DEPT-OUT, should be numeric. To obtain exactly 123 in DEPT-OUT, DEPT-OUT should have a PIC of 999, which indicates that it is a three-position numeric field.

In Example 2, 'CODE1' is a nonnumeric literal. We know that it is not an identifier because it is enclosed in quotation marks. To move a nonnumeric literal to a field, the field must have the same format as the literal. Thus, in Example 2, CLASSIFICATION-OUT must have a PIC of X's to indicate that it is alphanumeric. To obtain exactly 'CODE1' as the contents of CLASSIFI-CATION-OUT, CLASSIFICATION-OUT must have a PIC clause of X(5), which defines a five-position alphanumeric field.

To say MOVE 123 TO ADDRESS-OUT would be poor form if ADDRESS-OUT had a PICTURE of XXX, because the literal does *not* have the same format as the receiving field. If ADDRESS-OUT has a PICTURE of X(3), the literal to be moved to it should be nonnumeric. Thus, we should code: MOVE '123' TO ADDRESS-OUT.

The MOVE statement can also move a figurative constant to an identifier. You will recall that a figurative constant is a COBOL reserved word, such as SPACE (SPACES) or ZERO (ZEROS or ZEROES), that represents a specific value.

The following examples illustrate the use of figurative constants in a MOVE statement.

Example 3

> MOVE ZEROS TO TOTAL-OUT

ZEROS is a figurative constant meaning all 0's. Since 0 is a valid numeric character and also a valid alphanumeric character, TOTAL-OUT may be numeric, with a PIC of 9's, or alphanumeric, with a PIC of X's. In either case, TOTAL-OUT will be filled with all zeros. In this case, the size of TOTAL-OUT is unimportant; a zero will be placed in every position of that field regardless of its size. Thus, when using a figurative constant as the sending field, the size of the receiving field need not be any specific length.

Example 4

> MOVE SPACES TO HEADING1

SPACES is a figurative constant meaning all blanks. Since blanks are not valid numeric characters, the PICTURE clause of HEADING1 must specify X's, indicating an alphanumeric field, or A's, indicating an alphabetic field. Again, the size of HEADING1 is unimportant since blanks will be placed in every position.

Coding Guidelines

Any nonnumeric literal may be moved to an alphanumeric field. As noted previously, we typically use X's in a PICTURE clause of nonnumeric fields and avoid the use of A's. We will see that it is always the receiving field that determines the type of move.

Self-Test   Use the following statement to answer Questions 1–5.

> MOVE NAME-IN TO NAME-OUT.

1. MOVE is called the _____ . NAME-IN is called the _____ . NAME-OUT is called the _____ .
2. Assume NAME-IN has contents of SAM and NAME-OUT has contents of MAX; assume also that the fields have the same PICTURE clauses. At the end of the MOVE operation, NAME-OUT will have _____ as its contents and NAME-IN will contain _____ .

3. In a MOVE operation, the sending field may be a(n) _____ or a(n) _____ or a(n) _____ .

4. The two kinds of literals that may serve as a sending field in a MOVE operation are _____ and _____ .

5. The receiving field in a MOVE operation is always a(n) _____ .

Use the following statement to answer Questions 6 and 7.

> MOVE A12 TO FIELD3.

6. A12 must be a(n) _____ and not a nonnumeric literal because it is not _____ .

7. If the identifier A12 has contents of 453, _____ will be moved to FIELD3 and A12 will have _____ as its contents at the end of the operation.

Use the following statement to answer Questions 8–11.

> MOVE 'AB1' TO FIELD6.

8. The sending field is a _____ .

9. The sending field cannot be an identifier because it is _____ .

10. To obtain exactly AB1 in FIELD6, the PICTURE clause of the receiving field should be _____ .

11. 'AB1' (is, is not) defined in the DATA DIVISION.

12. In the statement MOVE 12384 TO SAM, the sending field must be a numeric literal and not a data-name because it _____ .

13. In the statement MOVE SPACES TO HEADING-OUT, SPACES is a _____ , and HEADING-OUT would have a(n) _____ PICTURE clause. The contents of HEADING-OUT will be replaced with _____ at the end of the operation.

14. In the statement MOVE ZEROS TO TOTAL-OUT, TOTAL-OUT may have a(n) _____ PICTURE clause. After the MOVE, TOTAL-OUT will contain _____ .

15. In the statement MOVE 'SPACES' TO CODE-OUT, where CODE-OUT has a PICTURE OF X(6), 'SPACES' is a _____ . The contents of CODE-OUT will be _____ at the end of the operation.

Solutions

1. verb or operation; sending field; receiving field

2. SAM; SAM (*Note:* The contents of a sending field remains unchanged in a MOVE operation.)

3. literal; identifier (data-name); figurative constant

4. numeric; nonnumeric or alphanumeric

5. identifier or data-name

6. identifier; enclosed in quotation marks

7. 453; 453

8. nonnumeric literal

9. enclosed in quotation marks

10. XXX or X(3)

11. is not (Literals appearing in the PROCEDURE DIVISION need not be defined elsewhere in the program.)

12. contains no alphabetic character

13. figurative constant; alphanumeric or alphabetic; blanks or spaces

14. alphanumeric or numeric; 0's (*Note:* Zero is a valid numeric and alphanumeric character.)

15. nonnumeric literal (it is enclosed in quotes); the word SPACES

III. Numeric MOVE

We will divide our discussion of the MOVE statement into two parts: numeric MOVE operations and nonnumeric MOVE operations. We discuss numeric moves in this section.

A numeric MOVE operation is one in which a numeric field or literal is moved to a numeric receiving field.

A. When Sending and Receiving Fields Have the Same PIC Clauses

Consider the following, where both fields have numeric PIC clauses.

MOVE identifier-1 TO identifier-2

If the PIC clauses of both fields are identical, the contents of identifier-2 will be replaced with the contents of identifier-1; the sending field will be unchanged.

B. When Sending and Receiving Fields Have Different PIC Clauses

Often in a COBOL program, it will be necessary to move one numeric field to another, where the sizes of the two fields differ. You might want to move a smaller field to a larger one to perform an arithmetic operation on it; or you may want to move a work area with precision of three decimal places (V999) to an output area that requires precision of only two decimal places (V99). In both cases, the MOVE operation will *not* produce the same contents in the receiving field as in the sending field, since the sizes of the two fields differ. We will see that in no case is any data of the original receiving field retained after the MOVE. We will also see that decimal alignment is always maintained.

Two rules apply in all numeric MOVE operations—one for the movement of the integer portion of a number, and one for the movement of the decimal or fractional portion. Let us focus first on the rule for integer moves.

1. Moving Integer Portions of Numeric Fields

> **RULE 1: MOVING INTEGER PORTIONS OF NUMERIC FIELDS**
> When moving an integer sending field or an integer *portion* of a numeric sending field to a numeric receiving field, movement is from *right* to *left*. All nonfilled **high-order** (leftmost) integer positions of the receiving field are replaced with zeros.

Example 1
The Receiving Field Has More Integer Positions Than The Sending Field

Operation:	MOVE AMT-IN TO AMT-OUT

AMT-IN   PICTURE   999   AMT-OUT   PICTURE   9(4)
         Contents 123   Contents 4567

According to Rule 1, movement is from right to left:

(a) The 3 in AMT-IN replaces the 7 in AMT-OUT.
(b) The 2 in AMT-IN replaces the 6 in AMT-OUT.
(c) The 1 in AMT-IN replaces the 5 in AMT-OUT.

and all nonfilled high-order positions are filled with zeros:

(d) 0 replaces the 4 in AMT-OUT.

Thus we obtain 0123 in AMT-OUT:

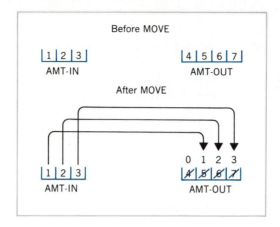

As noted, no portion of the original contents of the receiving field is retained after any MOVE is performed.

Avoiding Truncation

A good rule-of-thumb to follow in numeric MOVE operations is to be sure that the receiving field has at least as many whole number or integer positions as the sending field. If the receiving field has more integer positions than does the sending field, its high-order positions will be replaced with zeros, which do not affect the result. If, however, the receiving field has fewer integer positions than the sending field, you may inadvertently **truncate** or cut off the most significant digits.

Example 2
An Illustration of Truncation

Operation:	MOVE TAKE-HOME-PAY TO AMT-OF-CHECK

TAKE-HOME-PAY   PICTURE   9(4)   AMT-OF-CHECK   PICTURE   999
                 Contents 1000   Contents 999

In this example, the receiving field has only three positions. Since movement of integer positions is from right to left, 000 will be placed in AMT-OF-CHECK. The high-order 1 is truncated, a fact that will undoubtedly upset the check's recipient:

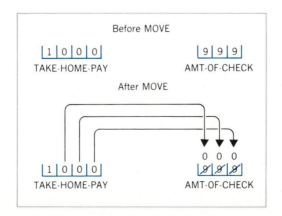

If a sending field has more integer positions than a receiving field, most compilers will print a warning-level syntax error during compilation. This will not, however, affect execution of the program, so that the program would run with this error in it. It is the programmer's job to ensure that the receiving field has at least as many integer positions as does the sending field.

2. Moving Decimal Portions of Numeric Fields

We will now consider the movement of fields that have fractional components, that is, numeric fields with decimal positions following the implied decimal point. The rule is as follows:

RULE 2: MOVING DECIMAL PORTIONS OF NUMERIC FIELDS

When moving a decimal or fractional portion of a numeric sending field to the fractional portion of a numeric receiving field, movement is from *left* to *right*, beginning at the implied decimal point. **Low-order** (rightmost) nonfilled decimal positions of the receiving field are replaced with zeros.

Example 3
The Receiving Field Has
More Decimal Positions
Than The Sending Field

Operation:	MOVE COST-IN TO COST-OUT

```
COST-IN   PICTURE   99V99          COST-OUT   PICTURE   99V999
          Contents  12ʌ34                     Contents  56ʌ789
```

The integer portion of COST-IN replaces the integer portion of COST-OUT, according to Rule 1. The decimal portion of each field initially contains the following:

According to Rule 2, movement is from the implied decimal point on and is from left to right:

(a) The 3 of COST-IN replaces the 7 of COST-OUT.
(b) The 4 of COST-IN replaces the 8 of COST-OUT.

Low-order nonfilled decimal positions of the receiving field are replaced with zeros:

(c) 0 replaces the 9 of COST-OUT.

Thus we have the following in the receiving field after the MOVE:

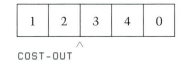

Note that decimal alignment will always be maintained in a numeric MOVE.

Example 4
The Receiving Field Has
Fewer Decimal Positions
Than The Sending Field

Operation:	MOVE DISCOUNT-IN TO DISCOUNT-OUT

```
DISCOUNT-IN   PICTURE   V99          DISCOUNT-OUT   PICTURE   V9
              Contents  ʌ12                         Contents  ʌ3
```

Movement from the implied decimal point on is from left to right. Thus the 1 of

DISCOUNT-IN replaces the 3 of DISCOUNT-OUT. The operation is terminated at this point since DISCOUNT-OUT has only one decimal position.

Example 5
The Sending Field Has
More Integer and Decimal
Positions Than the
Receiving Field

Operation: MOVE QTY-IN TO QTY-OUT

QTY-IN PICTURE 999V9	QTY-OUT PICTURE 99
Contents 123ᴧ4	Contents 00

Since integer movement is from right to left, the 3 of QTY-IN replaces the low-order or rightmost 0, and the 2 of QTY-IN replaces the high-order or leftmost zero. Since there are no more integer positions in the receiving field, the integer portion of the move is terminated. The operation itself is terminated at this point, since there are no decimal positions in QTY-OUT. Thus the contents of QTY-OUT is 23 after the MOVE:

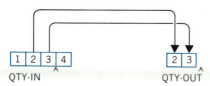

C. Moving Numeric Literals to Numeric Fields

Numeric literals are moved to fields in exactly the same manner as numeric fields are moved. The same rules for moving integer and decimal portions of one field to another apply.

Example 6

Operation: MOVE 123 TO LEVEL-NO-OUT

    05 LEVEL-NO-OUT   PICTURE 9(4).

Since we are concerned with only integers in this example, movement is from right to left and nonfilled high-order positions of the receiving field are replaced with zeros. Thus we obtain 0123 in LEVEL-NO-OUT. Treat the literal 123 as if it were LEVEL-NO-IN with a PICTURE of 999, contents 123, and proceed as previously; that is, it is as if MOVE LEVEL-NO-IN TO LEVEL-NO-OUT is performed.

Example 7

Operation: MOVE 12.34 TO PRICE-OUT

    05 PRICE-OUT   PICTURE 99V999.

Note that the numeric literal is coded with a decimal point where intended, but the decimal point is only implied in PRICE-OUT. The integers in the sending field are transmitted, so that 12 is moved to the integer positions of PRICE-OUT. Movement from the implied decimal point on is from left to right, the result being 34 in the first two decimal positions of PRICE-OUT. Nonfilled low-order decimal positions of PRICE-OUT are replaced with zeros. Thus we obtain 12ᴧ340 in PRICE-OUT. Note again that the result is the same as if we had performed the operation MOVE PRICE-IN TO PRICE-OUT, where PRICE-IN had a PICTURE of 99V99, and contents 12ᴧ34.

The numeric MOVE operation functions exactly the same whether the sending field is a literal or an identifier. Treat a numeric literal as if it were a field in storage, and proceed according to the two rules specified in this section.

Self-Test   Use the following statement to complete Questions 1–4.

MOVE TAX TO TOTAL

	TAX			**TOTAL**
	PICTURE	*Contents*	PICTURE	*Contents (after MOVE)*
1.	99V99	10ₐ35	999V999	_____
2.	9(4)	1234	999	_____
3.	99V99	02ₐ34	9V9	_____
4.	9V9	1ₐ2	_____	ₐ20

5. The specific questions from the preceding group that might give undesirable results are _____ .

6. The operation MOVE 12.487 TO WORK-AREA is performed. To obtain the *exact* digits of the literal in the field called WORK-AREA, its PICTURE clause must be _____ .

7. In a numeric MOVE operation, there (are, are not) instances when some significant portion of the data in the receiving field is retained and not replaced with something else.

Use the following statement to complete Questions 8–10.

MOVE 12.35 TO AREA-1

	PICTURE	AREA-1 *Contents (after MOVE)*
8.	999V999	_____
9.	9V9	_____
10.	_____	012ₐ3

Solutions
1. 010ₐ350
2. 234
3. 2ₐ3
4. V99
5. 2 and 4—Truncation of the high-order or most significant digit occurs.
6. 99V999
7. are *not* (*Note: All* positions of the receiving field are replaced either with positions of the sending field or with zeros.)
8. 012ₐ350
9. 2ₐ3
10. 999V9

IV. Nonnumeric or Alphanumeric MOVE

A. Basic Rules

You will recall that the MOVE operation was separated into two categories: *numeric* MOVE and *nonnumeric* or alphanumeric MOVE. The latter type is discussed in this section. By a nonnumeric MOVE operation, we mean:

NONNUMERIC MOVE

1. Moving an alphanumeric or alphabetic field, defined by a PICTURE of X's or A's, to another alphanumeric or alphabetic field.
2. Moving a nonnumeric literal to an alphanumeric or alphabetic field.
3. Moving a numeric field or numeric literal to an alphanumeric field or to any group item.

Thus, when the receiving field has a PICTURE of X's or A's, or is a group item, the move is treated as a nonnumeric move. There is only one rule for such moves.

RULE FOR NONNUMERIC MOVE

In a nonnumeric move, data is transmitted from the sending field to the receiving field from *left* to *right*. Low-order or rightmost positions of the receiving field that are not replaced with sending field characters are filled with spaces.

Example 1
The Receiving Field is Larger Than the Sending Field

Operation: MOVE NAME-IN TO NAME-OUT

NAME-IN PICTURE XXX   NAME-OUT PICTURE X(5)
         Contents ABC   Contents DEFGH

According to the rule, data is transmitted from left to right. Thus,

(a) The A of NAME-IN replaces the D of NAME-OUT.
(b) The B of NAME-IN replaces the E of NAME-OUT.
(c) The C of NAME-IN replaces the F of NAME-OUT.

Low-order positions of NAME-OUT are replaced with spaces. Thus,

(d) A blank replaces the G of NAME-OUT.
(e) A blank replaces the H of NAME-OUT.

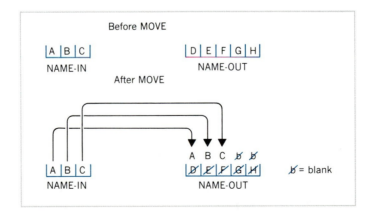

NAME-OUT will contain ABCƀƀ after the MOVE, where ƀ represents a blank. Again, no portion of the receiving field is retained after the move.

The effect of this operation would have been the same if the following were performed: MOVE 'ABC' TO NAME-OUT.

Example 2
The Receiving Field
is Smaller Than the
Sending Field

Operation: MOVE CODE-IN TO CODE-OUT

```
CODE-IN   PICTURE   X(4)              CODE-OUT   PICTURE   XXX
          Contents  NAME                         Contents  (blanks)
```

In this case

(a) The N of CODE-IN replaces the leftmost blank of CODE-OUT.

(b) The A of CODE-IN replaces the middle blank of CODE-OUT.

(c) The M of CODE-IN replaces the rightmost blank of CODE-OUT.

The operation is terminated at this point, since the entire receiving field is filled. Again, truncation occurs, but this time it is the rightmost characters that are truncated. As in the case of numeric moves, truncation will be avoided if the receiving field is at least as large as the sending field. The result would have been the same if the following were performed: MOVE 'NAME' TO CODE-OUT. As in the case with numeric moves, a warning level syntax error will alert the programmer to the fact that a sending field is larger than a receiving field, but program execution will continue.

Example 3
The Sending Field is
Numeric and the Receiving
Field is Nonnumeric

Operation: MOVE UNIT-IN TO UNIT-OUT

```
UNIT-IN   PICTURE   999              UNIT-OUT   PICTURE   XXXX
          Contents  321                         Contents  DCBA
```

Note that although UNIT-IN is numeric, this operation is considered to be an *alphanumeric* MOVE because the receiving field is alphanumeric. It is always the receiving field that determines the type of move.

(a) The 3 of UNIT-IN replaces the D of UNIT-OUT.

(b) The 2 of UNIT-IN replaces the C of UNIT-OUT.

(c) The 1 of UNIT-IN replaces the B of UNIT-OUT.

(d) A space replaces the A of UNIT-OUT.

UNIT-OUT will contain 321ƀ after the MOVE, where ƀ represents a blank.

Moving Literals or Figurative Constants to Nonnumeric Fields

Literals or figurative constants can also be moved to nonnumeric receiving fields.

Example 4

Operation: MOVE 'ABC' TO CODE-OUT

```
05  CODE-OUT   PICTURE  X(5).
```

The result will be ABCƀƀ in CODE-OUT.

Example 5

Operation:	MOVE SPACES TO NAME-OUT

```
05   NAME-OUT    PICTURE X(5).
```

Regardless of the size of NAME-OUT, it will contain all blanks after the MOVE.

You may have observed that although nonnumeric MOVE instructions include moving data from *numeric* to *alphanumeric* fields, no mention has been made of the reverse situation, moving data from alphanumeric to numeric fields. Suppose you know that CODE-IN, with a PIC of X's, has numeric data. Can CODE-IN be moved to a numeric field? Similarly, can MOVE '123' TO CODE-OUT be performed if CODE-OUT has a PICTURE of 9's?

The question can be simplified: Should you move alphanumeric fields or literals to numeric receiving fields? The answer is *no*. If you know that a field is numeric, define it with a PICTURE of 9's. *Do not move alphanumeric fields to numeric fields.* The move will be performed by the computer, but the results could cause an abnormal end or termination of the job if the receiving field is used later on in an arithmetic operation and it does not contain numeric data.

B. A Group Move Is Considered a Nonnumeric Move

We now consider how group items, or fields that are further subdivided, are treated in MOVE operations. All group items, even those with numeric subfields, *are treated as alphanumeric fields.*

Consider the following:

Example

Suppose we want to represent January 1988 as 0188 in DATE-OUT, which has been defined as a group item.

```
05   DATE-OUT.
     10   MONTH-OUT    PICTURE 99.
     10   YEAR-OUT     PICTURE 99.
```

Because MONTH-OUT and YEAR-OUT are numeric fields, MOVE 1 TO MONTH-OUT and MOVE 88 TO YEAR-OUT would result in 0188 in DATE-OUT. If, however, the programmer attempts to move data into DATE-OUT, DATE-OUT will be treated as an alphanumeric field because it is a group item. The statement MOVE '188' TO DATE-OUT would erroneously result in 188b in DATE-OUT, *not* 0188 as it would if the month and year were moved separately.

We typically initialize a record with a group MOVE. Consider the following:

```
01   REC-OUT.
     05   FILLER      PIC X(10).
     05   NAME-OUT    PIC X(20).
     05   FILLER      PIC X(8).
     05   ADDR-OUT    PIC X(20).
     05   FILLER      PIC X(75).
```

We could clear the entire output area with the following group MOVE instruction.

```
MOVE SPACES TO REC-OUT.
```

Figure 6.1 is a chart outlining the various MOVE operations. A check (√) denotes that the move is permissible; an X denotes that it is not.

Sending fields are of six types: numeric, alphabetic, alphanumeric, the figurative constant ZEROS, the figurative constant SPACES, and group item. Numeric, alphabetic, and alphanumeric sending fields can be either identifiers *or*

Figure 6.1
Permissible MOVE operations.

Sending Field	Receiving Field			
	Numeric	Alphabetic	Alphanumeric	Group item
Numeric	✓	x	✓	✓
Alphabetic	x	✓	✓	✓
Alphanumeric	x	✓	✓	✓
ZEROS ⎫ Figurative SPACES ⎬ constants	✓ x	x ✓	✓ ✓	✓ ✓
Group item	x	✓	✓	✓

literals. A numeric field is moved in the same manner as a numeric literal. The receiving fields refer only to identifiers that can be numeric, alphabetic, alphanumeric, and group fields. A literal or figurative constant cannot serve as a receiving field.

Note that when mixed data types appear, the MOVE operation, if permissible, is always performed in the format of the receiving field.

Self-Test

1. In a nonnumeric move, data is transmitted from (left, right) to (left, right).
2. In a nonnumeric move, if the receiving field is larger than the sending field, (right-, left-) most positions are replaced with _____ .

Use the following statement to complete Questions 3–5.

> MOVE CODE-IN TO CODE-OUT

	CODE-IN		**CODE-OUT**		
	PICTURE	*Contents*	PICTURE	*Contents*	*(after MOVE)*
3.	X(4)	AB12	X(6)	_____	
4.	X(4)	AB12	X(3)	_____	
5.	XXX	ABC	_____	AB	

Solutions

1. left; right
2. right-; spaces or blanks
3. AB12b̷b̷ (b̷ denotes a blank)
4. AB1
5. XX

V. Other Options of the MOVE Statement

A. Qualification of Names

We may use *qualification of names* to access individual fields that have the same name within different records or group items. If the same name is used to define fields in different records or group items, indicate which record or group item is to be accessed by qualifying the identifier with the word OF or IN. If AMT is both an input and an output field, we cannot ADD AMT TO TOTAL, since AMT is the name of two different fields and it is unclear which is to be added. We could say instead ADD AMT OF RECORD-IN TO TOTAL.

When more than one field in storage has the same name, we qualify the name in the PROCEDURE DIVISION as follows:

Format

$$\text{identifier-1} \left\{ \begin{array}{c} \underline{OF} \\ \underline{IN} \end{array} \right\} \left\{ \begin{array}{c} \text{record-name-1} \\ \text{group-item-name-1} \end{array} \right\}$$

Examples
```
ADD AMT OF IN-REC TO TOTAL.
IF  NAME OF IN-REC = SPACES
    MOVE 'MISSING' TO NAME IN OUT-REC.
```

The words OF and IN may be used interchangeably to qualify a name.

A field-name may be qualified by using OF or IN with the name of either a record or group item of which the field is a part. Consider the following:

```
01  REC-IN.
    05  CODE-IN.
        10  SEX                 PIC X.
        10  MARITAL-STATUS      PIC X.
        10  AGE                 PIC 99.
```

If the identifier SEX defines more than one field in the DATA DIVISION, the SEX field may be accessed as SEX OF REC-IN or SEX OF CODE-IN. Both REC-IN and CODE-IN serve to uniquely identify the SEX field referenced.

QUALIFICATION OF NAMES

1. File-names and record-names must always be unique.
2. Names or identifiers that define fields within records need not be unique. That is, the same name may define several fields in different records of the DATA DIVISION.
3. Each time these fields are individually accessed in the PROCEDURE DIVISION, however, they must be qualified with the use of the word OF or IN.

Coding Guidelines

Coding the same identifier to define several fields in separate records is frequently considered a useful programming tool. Many people believe that qualification of names makes PROCEDURE DIVISION entries easier to understand for someone reading the program, and easier to debug.

On the other hand, most installations prefer programmers to use unique names with descriptive prefixes or suffixes to define data. To say, for example, MOVE AMT-IN TO AMT-OUT, where AMT-IN is an input field and AMT-OUT is an output field, is frequently considered better form than saying MOVE AMT OF IN-REC TO AMT OF OUT-REC.

B. The MOVE CORRESPONDING Statement

The instruction format for the **MOVE CORRESPONDING** is as follows:

Format

```
MOVE  {CORRESPONDING}  group-item-1 TO group-item-2
      {CORR         }
```

In the MOVE CORRESPONDING statement, all elementary items within group-item-1 that have the *same names* as corresponding elementary items in group-item-2 will be moved. Recall that a group item is a field or record that is further subdivided into any number of elementary entries.

Example

```
7 8    12    16    20    24    28    32    36    40    44    48    52    56    60    64    68    72
         MOVE CORRESPONDING RECORD-IN TO RECORD-OUT.
```

With the MOVE CORRESPONDING statement, all fields in RECORD-IN that have *the same names* as fields in RECORD-OUT are moved. The same-named fields in RECORD-OUT need not be in any specific order. Any fields of the sending record, RECORD-IN, that are not matched by the same-named fields in the receiving record, RECORD-OUT, are ignored. As in all MOVE operations, sending fields remain unchanged.

Up to this point, we have been using unique names for different fields or we have qualified names when using them in the PROCEDURE DIVISION. For the MOVE CORRESPONDING statement, however, we establish fields *with the same name* within two different records or group items. Consider the following records and how they are affected by the statement MOVE CORRESPONDING RECORD-IN TO RECORD-OUT:

				Contents before MOVE	Contents after MOVE
01	RECORD-IN.				
	05	NAME	PIC X(6).	ARNOLD	ARNOLD
	05	AMT	PIC 999V99.	100ʌ00	100ʌ00
	05	CODE1	PIC X(5).	12345	12345
	05	DATEX	PIC 9(4).	0688	0688
		⋮			
01	RECORD-OUT.				
	05	NAME	PIC X(6).	PETERS	ARNOLD
	05	DATEX	PIC 9(4).	0585	0688
	05	AMT	PIC 999V99.	000ʌ00	100ʌ00
	05	DISCOUNT	PIC V99.	ʌ10	ʌ10

Thus, we see that the MOVE CORRESPONDING performs a series of simple moves. All fields in RECORD-IN with the same name as fields in RECORD-OUT are moved.

NAME, AMT, and DATEX of RECORD-OUT are *not* in the same order in which they appear in RECORD-IN. The contents of these fields in RECORD-IN are, nevertheless, transmitted to the same-named fields in RECORD-OUT, regardless of the order in which they appear.

Entries in RECORD-OUT for which there are no corresponding items in RECORD-IN are unaffected by the MOVE CORRESPONDING statement. For example, DISCOUNT, a field in RECORD-OUT, retains its original contents, since there is no corresponding DISCOUNT field in RECORD-IN.

Entries in RECORD-IN for which there are no corresponding items in RECORD-OUT are not transmitted. For example, CODE1, a field in RECORD-IN, is not moved, since there is no corresponding CODE1 field in RECORD-OUT. In all cases, sending fields remain unchanged after the MOVE.

The MOVE CORRESPONDING option is used in place of a series of simple MOVE instructions. All fields in the sending area are moved to the same-named fields in the receiving area. All rules for MOVE operations apply when using the MOVE CORRESPONDING option. Note, however, that fields to be moved *must* have the same name in the sending and receiving group items.

Coding Guidelines

We avoid the use of MOVE CORRESPONDING in this text because it is a potential source of error in programs that may be modified after they have become part of a regularly scheduled production run. Suppose the name of an identifier is changed in the DATA DIVISION during program modification, and the standard MOVE is used for transmitting data. During compilation, a syntax error will occur if the name of the identifier was not also changed in the PROCEDURE DIVISION. Thus, the programmer will be alerted to the fact that the MOVE statement is invalid because an identifier is undefined. With a MOVE COR-RESPONDING, however, a change in the name of an elementary identifier in the DATA DIVISION will simply mean that the MOVE is not performed for that identifier; no error message will occur. An error of this type may go undetected for some time before it is discovered. To avoid this problem in programs that might be modified at some later date, use a series of simple MOVEs rather than a MOVE CORRESPONDING.

C. Performing Multiple Moves with a Single Statement

The full instruction format for a MOVE statement is as follows:

Full Format for the
MOVE Instruction

$$\text{MOVE} \begin{Bmatrix} \text{identifier-1} \\ \text{literal-1} \end{Bmatrix} \text{TO identifier-2} \ldots$$

A Review of Instruction Format Rules

The braces { } indicate that *any one* of the two elements may be used as a sending field. The receiving field must always be a data-name or identifier. Capitalized words like MOVE and TO are COBOL reserved words. Because they are underlined, they are required in the statement. The ellipses or dots at the end of the statement mean that a single sending field can be moved to numerous receiving fields.

Example

```
MOVE 'ABC' TO CODE-1, CODE-2, CODE-3.
```

If CODE-1, CODE-2, and CODE-3 each has a PIC of X(3), then the literal ABC will be transmitted to all three fields. Recall that the commas in this example are for readability only; they do not affect the compilation.

One way of initializing a series of fields to zero at the beginning of a procedure is to use a multiple move:

```
MOVE ZEROS TO WS-AMT, WS-TOTAL, WS-COUNTER.
```

IV. Moving Data to Fields in a Print Record

A. Spacing Output Data for Readability

Consider the following:

				Actual Values for the First Record
01	IN-REC.			
	05	CUST-NO-IN	PIC 9(5).	00287
	05	AMT-OF-TRANS-IN	PIC 9(5)V99.	12345ᴧ67

Suppose we wish to print the contents of each IN-REC. We could code the OUT-REC descriptions as follows:

```
01   OUT-REC.
      05   FILLER                    PIC X(20).
      05   CUST-NO-OUT               PIC 9(5).
      05   FILLER                    PIC X(20).
      05   AMT-OF-TRANS-OUT          PIC 9(5)V99.
      05   FILLER                    PIC X(81).
```

The FILLERs are to contain spaces for readability. If OUT-REC is initialized with SPACES, the placement of the FILLERs ensures that there will be blanks between each field.

Suppose we code the PROCEDURE DIVISION as follows:

```
PROCEDURE DIVISION.
100-MAIN-MODULE.
    OPEN INPUT IN-FILE
         OUTPUT OUT-FILE.
    MOVE SPACES TO OUT-REC.
    READ IN-FILE
        AT END MOVE 'NO ' TO ARE-THERE-MORE-RECORDS.
    PERFORM 200-PRINT-RTN
        UNTIL ARE-THERE-MORE-RECORDS = 'NO '.
    CLOSE IN-FILE
          OUT-FILE.
    STOP RUN.
200-PRINT-RTN.
    MOVE CUST-NO-IN TO CUST-NO-OUT.
    MOVE AMT-OF-TRANS-IN TO AMT-OF-TRANS-OUT.
    WRITE OUT-REC.
    READ IN-FILE
        AT END MOVE 'NO ' TO ARE-THERE-MORE-RECORDS.
```

The first line would print as

```
00287               1234567
(CUST-NO-OUT)       (AMT-OF-TRANS-OUT)
```

Note that the decimal point does *not* print in AMT-OF-TRANS-OUT since it is only implied. Thus to someone reading the report, it would not be at all obvious that the transaction amount is actually $12345.67.

For printed output only, the PIC clause should contain punctuation or **edit symbols** that make the output readable. In the following section we show you how to move numeric fields to fields with edit symbols in them.

B. Printing a Decimal Point

For printing a decimal point in an amount field, OUT-REC may have the following specification.

```
01   OUT-REC.
      :
      :
      05   AMT-OF-TRANS-OUT    PIC 9(5).99.
```

In this instance, AMT-OF-TRANS-OUT is no longer a numeric field; it is a **report-item,** or edited field, suitable for printing. Unlike the V in a numeric field, the decimal point in a report-item actually uses a position of storage. Thus AMT-OF-TRANS-OUT is *eight* positions long, whereas AMT-OF-TRANS-IN is *seven* positions long. In the preceding, the MOVE will result in the transmission of 12345.67 to AMT-OF-TRANS-OUT, which is a better form of printed output than 1234567.

C. Printing a Dollar Sign

We can also print a dollar sign in the output record by including it in the `PIC` clause of `AMT-OF-TRANS-OUT`.

```
01   OUT-REC.
       :
       :
     05   AMT-OF-TRANS-OUT   PIC $9(5).99.
```

In this case $12345.67 would print for the first record. Note that `AMT-OF-TRANS-OUT` is now *nine* positions long. The final `FILLER` for `OUT-REC`, then, should have a `PIC` of `X(79)`, not `X(81)` as originally specified.

In summary, if a receiving field is to be *printed*, we use an *actual decimal point* rather than an implied decimal point in the `PIC` clause of the receiving field for readability. This makes the receiving field one position longer. A dollar sign may also be included, if desired. Any field with these edit symbols in its `PIC` clause is no longer numeric and may *not* be used in a calculation.

Many other types of editing can be performed for printed output. These are discussed fully in Chapter 11.

D. Referencing Segments of a Field Using COBOL 85

It is possible to reference and access a portion of an elementary item with COBOL 85. Consider the following:

```
MOVE CODE-IN (4:3) TO CODE-OUT.
```

The first digit in parentheses indicates the start of the `MOVE`. Thus, movement begins with the fourth position of `CODE-IN`. The second digit in parentheses indicates the length of the `MOVE`. Thus, positions 4–6 of `CODE-IN` are moved to `CODE-OUT`. Suppose `CODE-IN` has `PIC 9(8)` with contents 87325879 and `CODE-OUT` has `PIC 9(3)`. The preceding `MOVE` will result in 258 being moved to `CODE-OUT`.

CHAPTER SUMMARY

A. Numeric Move—Sending and receiving fields are both numeric.

Rules
1. Integer portion.
   a. Movement is from right to left.
   b. Nonfilled high-order positions are replaced with zeros.
   c. Truncation of high-order digits occurs if the receiving field is not large enough to hold the results.
2. Decimal portion.
   a. Decimal alignment is maintained.
   b. Movement is from left to right, beginning at the decimal point.
   c. Nonfilled low-order positions are replaced with zeros.
B. Nonnumeric Move—Receiving field is nonnumeric.

Rules
1. Movement is from left to right.
2. Low-order nonfilled positions are replaced with spaces.
3. Truncation of low-order characters occurs if the receiving field is not large enough to hold the results.
C. The format of the *receiving* field determines the type of `MOVE` operation that is performed—either numeric or nonnumeric.

D. A field-name may be qualified by using `OF` or `IN` with the name of a record or group item of which the field is a part.

E. Printing numeric data in edited form.
1. A numeric field is moved to a report-item, which is a field to be printed. The `PIC` clause of a report-item contains edit symbols, such as a dollar sign and a decimal point, to make the output readable.
2. Each edit symbol uses one position of storage.
3. Unlike a numeric field, a report-item may not be used as part of a calculation.

CHAPTER SELF-TEST

1. (T or F) In a nonnumeric move, high-order nonfilled positions are replaced with spaces.

2. Indicate the result in each of the following cases.

   `MOVE TAX TO TOTAL.`

	TAX		**TOTAL**	
	PIC	Contents	PIC	Contents (after MOVE)
(a)	9(3)	123	9(4)	
(b)	V99	∧67	V9(3)	
(c)	V99	∧53	9(2)	
(d)	9(2)	67	9V9	
(e)	9(3)V9(3)	123∧123	9(4)V99	

3. Indicate the result in each of the following cases.

   `MOVE CODE-1 OF IN-REC TO CODE-1 OF OUT-REC.`

	IN-REC **CODE-1**		**OUT-REC** **CODE-1**	
	PIC	Contents	PIC	Contents (after MOVE)
(a)	X(4)	ZZYY	X(5)	
(a)	X(4)	ABCD	X(3)	

4. (T or F) A `MOVE CORRESPONDING` may produce unintended results if identifiers are altered during program modification.

5. (T or F) Two files may be given the same file-names as long as the names are qualified when used in the `PROCEDURE DIVISION`.

6. Assume an input field is defined as

   `05  SOC-SEC-NO-IN    PIC 9(9).`

   Write a program excerpt to print this Social Security number as xxx-xx-xxxx. Make any changes necessary to the input field description and describe the output.

Solutions

1. F—*Low-order* nonfilled positions are replaced with spaces.
2. (a) 0123; (b) ∧670; (c) 00; (d) 7∧0; (e) 0123∧12
3. (a) ZZYYƀ; (b) ABC
4. T
5. F—File-names (as well as record-names) must be unique; only names that define fields may be qualified.
6. The input field would be revised as follows:

```
05  SOC-SEC-NO-IN.
    10   S1          PIC 9(3).
    10   S2          PIC 9(2).
    10   S3          PIC 9(4).
```

The output would be described as:

```
05  SOC-SEC-NO-OUT.
       10  S1-OUT        PIC 9(3).
       10  DASH1         PIC X.
       10  S2-OUT        PIC 9(2).
       10  DASH2         PIC X.
       10  S3-OUT        PIC 9(4).
```

The MOVE statements would be:

```
MOVE S1 TO S1-OUT.
MOVE S2 TO S2-OUT.
MOVE S3 TO S3-OUT.
MOVE '-' TO DASH1, DASH2.
```

PRACTICE PROGRAM

Using the following problem definition, print all fields for each input record on a single line. The Printer Spacing Chart indicates how each output record is to be spaced. For readability, place a period after each initial of the name, and a / between month and year of the date. Also print column headings at the top of the first page of the report. That is, print the word NAME above where the name field will be printed, and so on. Figure 6.2 presents the flowchart and pseudocode; Figure 6.3 shows the solution; and Figure 6.4 illustrates the hierarchy chart. The planning tools will become more useful as the logic in our programs becomes more complex. (*Note:* Chapter 11 will illustrate other methods for aligning and printing data.)

Systems Flowchart

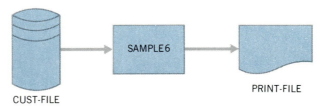

CUST-FILE   SAMPLE6   PRINT-FILE

CUST-FILE Record Layout

CUSTOMER NAME			DATE OF TRANSACTION		TRANSACTION AMOUNT (IN DOLLARS)	
INITIAL 1	INITIAL 2	LAST NAME	MONTH	YEAR		
1 2 3		12	13 14	15 16	17 22	23 80

PRINT-FILE Printer Spacing Chart

Sample Input Data

```
PQNEWMAN     0188001250
RRREDFORD    0688123453
ELTAYLOR     0488010000
NBSTERN      0988020000
CDHAMMEL     0788065450
RASTERN      1188884008
LOSTERN      0788688778
MESTERN      0288009899
HRFORD       1288684800
CRFISHER     0188086212
```

Sample Output

```
        NAME       DATE OF TRANSACTION    AMOUNT OF TRANSACTION
P.Q.NEWMAN              01/88                   001250
R.R.REDFORD            06/88                   123453
E.L.TAYLOR            04/88                   010000
N.B.STERN            09/88                   020000
C.D.HAMMEL            07/88                   065450
R.A.STERN            11/88                   884008
L.O.STERN            07/88                   688778
M.E.STERN            02/88                   009899
H.R.FORD            12/88                   684800
C.R.FISHER            01/88                   086212
```

KEY TERMS

Edit symbol	MOVE	Report-item
High-order position	MOVE CORRESPONDING	Sending field
Low-order position	Receiving field	Truncation

REVIEW QUESTIONS

T F

I. True or False

___ ___   1. Elementary numeric items within a group item are treated as nonnumeric fields.

___ ___   2. Group items, although they contain elementary numeric items, are treated as nonnumeric fields.

___ ___   3. XYZbb will be moved to a three-position alphanumeric field as Zbb.

___ ___   4. 66200 will be moved to a numeric field with PIC 9(3) as 200.

___ ___   5. 92.17 will be moved to a field with a PICTURE of 999V999 as 092ᴧ017.

___ ___   6. The statement MOVE ZEROS TO FLD1 is only valid if FLD1 is numeric.

___ ___   7. A MOVE CORRESPONDING statement requires fields in both records to have unique names.

___ ___   8. Blanks in a numeric field are valid characters.

___ ___   9. Data is always left-justified in a field.

___ ___   10. Group items are never defined with PICTURE clauses.

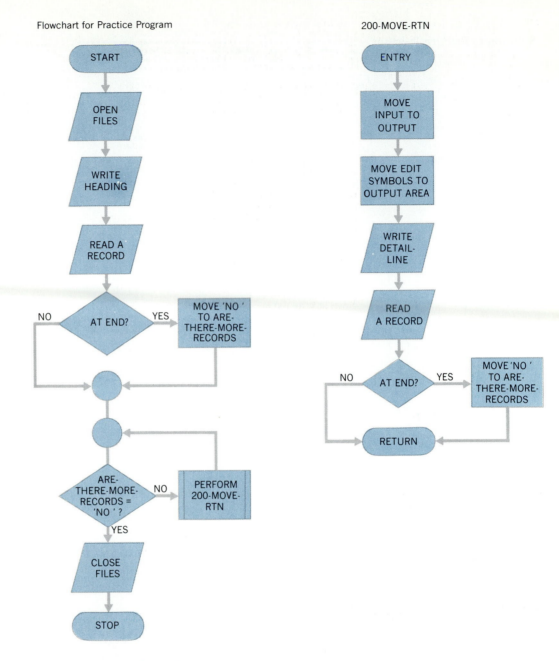

Flowchart for Practice Program

200-MOVE-RTN

Pseudocode for Practice Program

```
START
    Housekeeping Operations
    Print Headings
    Read a Record
    PERFORM UNTIL no more records
        Move Data from Input Area to Output Area
        Move Edit Symbols to Output Area
        Write Detail Record
        Read a Record
    ENDPERFORM
    End-of-Job Operations
STOP
```

Figure 6.2
Flowchart and pseudocode for
Practice Program.

Figure 6.3
Solution to Practice Program.

```
IDENTIFICATION DIVISION.
PROGRAM-ID. SAMPLE.
*****************************************************
*  SAMPLE   - WILL GENERATE A LIST CONSISTING OF  *
*            NAME AND TRANSACTION AMOUNT          *
*****************************************************
*
ENVIRONMENT DIVISION.
CONFIGURATION SECTION.
SOURCE-COMPUTER. IBM-4341.
OBJECT-COMPUTER. IBM-4341.
INPUT-OUTPUT SECTION.
FILE-CONTROL.
    SELECT IN-CUST-FILE   ASSIGN TO DATA6.
    SELECT OUT-PRINT-FILE ASSIGN TO SYS$OUTPUT.
*
DATA DIVISION.
FILE SECTION.
FD  IN-CUST-FILE
    LABEL RECORDS ARE STANDARD.
01  IN-CUST-REC.
    05   IN-CUST-NAME.
        10   IN-INITIAL-1          PIC X.
        10   IN-INITIAL-2          PIC X.
        10   IN-LAST-NAME          PIC X(10).
    05   IN-DATE-OF-TRANSACTION.
        10   IN-MONTH              PIC 99.
        10   IN-YEAR               PIC 99.
    05   IN-AMOUNT-OF-TRANSACTION  PIC 9(6).
    05   FILLER                    PIC X(58).
FD  OUT-PRINT-FILE
    LABEL RECORDS ARE OMITTED.
01  HEADING1-OUT.
    05   FILLER                    PIC X(6).
    05   LITERAL1-OUT              PIC X(4).
    05   FILLER                    PIC X(5).
    05   LITERAL2-OUT              PIC X(19).
    05   FILLER                    PIC X(3).
    05   LITERAL3-OUT              PIC X(21).
    05   FILLER                    PIC X(75).
01  DETAIL-LINE-OUT.
    05   FILLER                    PIC X.
    05   INIT1-OUT                 PIC X.
    05   POINT1-OUT                PIC X.
    05   INIT2-OUT                 PIC X.
    05   POINT2-OUT                PIC X.
    05   LAST-NAME-OUT             PIC X(10).
    05   FILLER                    PIC X(6).
    05   MONTH-OUT                 PIC 99.
    05   SLASH-OUT                 PIC X.
    05   YEAR-OUT                  PIC 99.
    05   FILLER                    PIC X(13).
    05   AMOUNT-OUT                PIC 9(6).
    05   FILLER                    PIC X(88).
WORKING-STORAGE SECTION.
01  WORK-AREAS.
    05 ARE-THERE-MORE-RECORDS      PIC X(3) VALUE 'YES'.
*
PROCEDURE DIVISION.
*************************************************************
*  100-MAIN-MODULE - CONTROLS OPENING AND CLOSING FILES   *
*                    DIRECTION OF PROGRAM LOGIC           *
*                    RETURNS CONTROL TO OPERATING SYSTEM  *
*************************************************************
100-MAIN-MODULE.
    OPEN INPUT IN-CUST-FILE
         OUTPUT OUT-PRINT-FILE.
    MOVE SPACES TO HEADING1-OUT.
    MOVE 'NAME' TO LITERAL1-OUT.
    MOVE 'DATE OF TRANSACTION'   TO LITERAL2-OUT.
    MOVE 'AMOUNT OF TRANSACTION' TO LITERAL3-OUT.
    WRITE HEADING1-OUT.
    READ IN-CUST-FILE
        AT END MOVE 'NO ' TO ARE-THERE-MORE-RECORDS.
    PERFORM 200-MOVE-RTN
        UNTIL ARE-THERE-MORE-RECORDS = 'NO '.
    CLOSE IN-CUST-FILE
          OUT-PRINT-FILE.
    STOP RUN.
*************************************************************
*  200-MOVE-RTN - PERFORMED FROM 100-MAIN-MODULE          *
*                 MOVES AND PRINTS DATA FROM OUTPUT AREAS *
*                 READS NEXT RECORD                       *
*************************************************************
200-MOVE-RTN.
    MOVE SPACES TO DETAIL-LINE-OUT.
    MOVE '.' TO POINT1-OUT POINT2-OUT.
    MOVE '/' TO SLASH-OUT.
    MOVE IN-INITIAL-1 TO INIT1-OUT.
    MOVE IN-INITIAL-2 TO INIT2-OUT.
    MOVE IN-LAST-NAME TO LAST-NAME-OUT.
    MOVE IN-MONTH TO MONTH-OUT.
    MOVE IN-YEAR TO YEAR-OUT.
    MOVE IN-AMOUNT-OF-TRANSACTION TO AMOUNT-OUT.
    WRITE DETAIL-LINE-OUT.
    READ IN-CUST-FILE
        AT END MOVE 'NO ' TO ARE-THERE-MORE-RECORDS.
```

Figure 6.4
Hierarchy chart for Practice Program.

II. General Questions

For Questions 1–8, determine the contents of the receiving field:

Sending Field			Receiving Field	
PICTURE	Contents		PICTURE	Contents (after MOVE)
1. 99V99	12ᴧ34		9(3)V9(3)	
2. 9V99	7ᴧ89		9V9	
3. 999V9	678ᴧ9		99V99	
4. 99	56		XXX	
5. XX	AB		XXX	
6. X(4)	CODE		XXX	
7. XXX	124		999	
8. XXX	ABC		X(5)	

For Questions 9 and 10, determine the contents of UNIT-PRICE if the operation performed is:

```
            MOVE 13.579 TO UNIT-PRICE.
```

	UNIT-PRICE	
	PICTURE	Contents (after MOVE)
9.	999V9(4)	
10.	99V9	

INTERPRETING INSTRUCTION FORMATS

Based on the instruction format for the MOVE statement described in this chapter, indicate what, if anything, is wrong with the following:

1. MOVE 'ABC', AMT1 TO AMT-OUT.
2. MOVE 1 TO AMT1 AND AMT2.
3. MOVE AMT2 TO 123.

DEBUGGING EXERCISES

Consider the following PROCEDURE DIVISION entries.

```
PROCEDURE DIVISION.
100-MAIN-MODULE.
    MOVE 'NO ' TO EOF-FLAG.
    READ TRANS-FILE
        AT END MOVE 'YES' TO EOF-FLAG.
    PERFORM 200-CALC-RTN
        UNTIL EOF-FLAG = 'YES'.
```

```
    CLOSE TRANS-FILE
          PRINT-FILE.
    STOP RUN.
200-CALC-RTN.
    MOVE SPACES TO PRINT-REC.
    MOVE ACCT-NO TO ACCT-NO-OUT.
    WRITE PRINT-REC.
    MOVE SPACES TO PRINT-REC.
    MOVE TRANS-AMT TO AMT-OUT.
    WRITE PRINT-REC.
    READ TRANS-FILE
        AT END MOVE 'YES' TO EOF-FLAG.
```

1. There is a major omission in the 100-MAIN-MODULE that will cause a syntax error. Indicate what this omission is and provide the correct coding for the entry.

2. Note that we move 'NO ' TO EOF-FLAG initially and then test it for 'YES' in an AT END clause. Will this work properly? Explain your answer.

3. Suppose EOF-FLAG has a PIC of X. Several syntax errors will result. Indicate why.

4. There are two MOVE SPACES TO PRINT-REC sentences. Are they necessary? What would happen if you omitted the first? What would happen if you omitted the second?

5. For each input record read, how many lines are printed?

6. From this coding can you determine how many input records have been read? Explain your answer.

7. Since the DATA DIVISION entries have not been provided, we have no way of knowing the positions on the print line where ACCT-NO-OUT and AMT-OUT will print. They may print, for example, as:

```
(ACCT-NO-OUT)

              (AMT-OUT)
```

Suppose we want AMT-OUT to print directly below ACCT-NO-OUT:

```
(ACCT-NO-OUT)
(AMT-OUT)
```

What entries in the DATA DIVISION would need to be modified to achieve this? Provide the coding that is necessary.

PROGRAMMING ASSIGNMENTS

For each assignment, plan the program first with pseudocode or a flowchart and a hierarchy chart. Remember that programs are not complete until they have been tested or debugged.

1. Write a program to print data from a magnetic disk. The problem definition is shown in Figure 6.5.

   Notes

   a. Print the heading lines shown in the Printer Spacing Chart.
   b. In addition to the disk fields, print the effective date of the run. Define effective date of the run as a literal (e.g., JANUARY 15).

2. Write a program to print data from a payroll disk file. The problem definition is shown in Figure 6.6.

3. Write a program to print a mailing list from a name and address file. The problem definition is shown in Figure 6.7.

Figure 6.5
Problem definition for
Programming Assignment 1.

Systems Flowchart

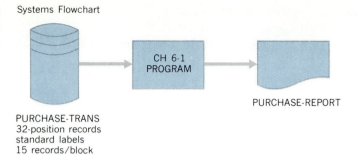

PURCHASE-TRANS
32-position records
standard labels
15 records/block

PURCHASE-REPORT

PURCHASE-TRANS Record Layout

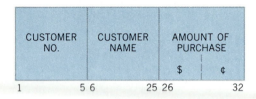

PURCHASE-REPORT Printer Spacing Chart

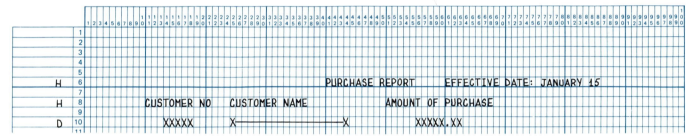

Notes

a. Each input record generates three output lines.
b. Leave one blank line after each set of three lines is printed.

4. Write a program to (a) create a sequential disk file from a tape file and (b) produce a printed listing of the records on the tape file.

Notes

a. Records in the tape and disk files have the same format.

    1–5   Salesperson number
    6–25 Salesperson name
    26–27 Region number
    28–29 District number
    30–31 Office number
    32–61 Other data
    62–67 Commission earned (xxxx.xx)
    68–80 Other data

    Both files have standard labels and a blocking factor of 20.

b. The printed report should contain all fields, except those designated "Other data", spaced across the line for each input record. Print the heading COMMISSION REPORT centered at the top of the page. In addition, print appropriate column headings to identify the fields that will be printed.

c. Print Commission earned with a dollar sign and decimal point.

Figure 6.6
Problem definition for
Programming Assignment 2.

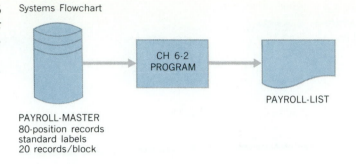

Systems Flowchart

PAYROLL-MASTER
80-position records
standard labels
20 records/block

PAYROLL-MASTER Record Layout

EMPLOYEE NO.	EMPLOYEE NAME	TERRITORY NO.	OFFICE NO.	ANNUAL SALARY (in $)	SOCIAL SECURITY NO.	

1   5 6   25 26   27 28   29 30   35 36   44 45   80

PAYROLL-LIST Printer Spacing Chart

```
                                    PAYROLL LISTING
H 6
H 8   EMPLOYEE NO.   EMPLOYEE NAME        TERR NO.  OFFICE NO.  ANNUAL SALARY  SOC SEC NO.
D 10     XXXXX       X--------------X       XX         XX        $XXXXXX      XXX-XX-XXXX
```

5. The following is a file of data records containing information on subscribers to a magazine. The record format is as follows:

Record Position	Field
1–20	Customer name
21–40	Street address
41–60	City, State, and Zip
61–62	Number of labels needed

Prepare planning tools and write a program that prints the required number of mailing labels in the following format.

Name
Street address
City, State Zip

If positions 61–62 indicate 05, you will perform a print module 5 times. *Hint:* `PERFORM 300-PRINT-RTN NO-OF-LABELS TIMES`, where `NO-OF-LABELS` is an input field.

Figure 6.7
Problem definition for
Programming Assignment 3.

Systems Flowchart

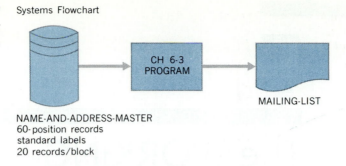

NAME-AND-ADDRESS-MASTER
60-position records
standard labels
20 records/block

NAME-AND-ADDRESS-MASTER Record Layout

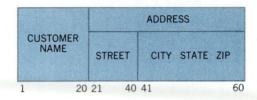

MAILING-LIST Printer Spacing Chart

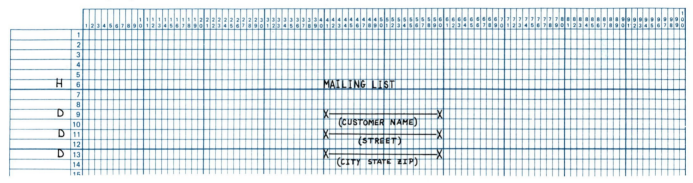

7

The WORKING-STORAGE SECTION

OBJECTIVES

To familiarize you with

1. The use of `WORKING-STORAGE` for storing work areas and for describing data to be printed.
2. How `VALUE` clauses are used in `WORKING-STORAGE` to initialize fields.

I. Storing Data in WORKING-STORAGE

A. Introduction

The DATA DIVISION contains all storage areas necessary for the processing of data. It is subdivided into two main sections: the FILE SECTION and the WORKING-STORAGE SECTION. In the FILE SECTION, input and output files are defined and their records are described. The **WORKING-STORAGE SECTION** contains all other fields and records necessary for processing data. Any constants, intermediate totals, or work areas that are not part of the input or output files but are used for processing data are defined in the WORKING-STORAGE SECTION. Thus far, we have seen how an end-of-file indicator that we called ARE-THERE-MORE-RECORDS is used as a WORKING-STORAGE entry. As we develop more sophisticated programs, our use of WORKING-STORAGE will expand considerably.

The WORKING-STORAGE SECTION contains two categories of data:

1. 01-level records and other group items that can be subdivided into elementary items.
2. Independent data items on the 77-level.

If 77-level items are used, they begin in Area A. If you are using a COBOL 74 compiler, they must be coded *first* in the WORKING-STORAGE SECTION. With COBOL 85, they may appear anywhere in the SECTION.

We will *not* emphasize the use of 77-level items in this text because it is best to group all independent entries as elementary items under one or more comprehensive 01-level entries called, for example, WS-STORED-AREAS or WS-WORK-AREAS.

```
WORKING-STORAGE SECTION.
01   WS-STORED-AREAS.
     05   ARE-THERE-MORE-RECORDS      PIC X(3).
     05   WS-SUM-TOTAL                PIC 99.
     05   WS-COUNTER                  PIC 999.
```

The prefix WS- is commonly used to identify elements as being part of WORKING-STORAGE. Thus, ARE-THERE-MORE-RECORDS could have been called WS-ARE-THERE-MORE-RECORDS.

B. Uses of WORKING-STORAGE

We will provide some examples of how the WORKING-STORAGE SECTION is used. Keep in mind that the purpose of these examples is to explain why WORKING-STORAGE is used in a program. The actual PROCEDURE DIVISION entries necessary for using WORKING-STORAGE will be explained as we proceed through the text.

**Example 1
Storing Intermediate
Results**

Consider the following input and output layouts:

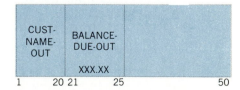

Input Record Layout: CUSTOMER-IN

Output Record Layout: BILLING-OUT

Note: BALANCE-DUE-OUT is equal to UNIT-PRICE-IN
      multiplied by QUANTITY-IN minus DISCOUNT-AMT-IN.

Using the basic arithmetic verbs that will be discussed in detail in the next chapter, we would code the following to obtain the output BALANCE-DUE field.

```
MULTIPLY UNIT-PRICE-IN BY
    QUANTITY-IN GIVING WS-GROSS-AMT.
SUBTRACT DISCOUNT-AMT-IN FROM WS-GROSS-AMT
    GIVING BALANCE-DUE-OUT.
```

UNIT-PRICE-IN, QUANTITY-IN, and DISCOUNT-AMT-IN are input fields defined for the CUSTOMER-IN disk file. BALANCE-DUE-OUT is a field in the BILLING-OUT disk file. WS-GROSS-AMT, however, is an **intermediate result field** necessary for calculating BALANCE-DUE-OUT; it is not part of either the input or the output areas. As an intermediate result, it is stored in a work area defined with an appropriate PICTURE clause in WORKING-STORAGE. It could be defined as follows:

```
WORKING-STORAGE SECTION.
01   WS-WORK-AREAS.
     05   WS-GROSS-AMT        PIC 9(5)V99.
***************************************************************
*   ANY OTHER WORK AREAS NECESSARY FOR PROCESSING WILL    *
*   BE PLACED HERE                                        *
***************************************************************
```

As noted, we could also use a 77-level item for defining fields such as WS-GROSS-AMT, but it is better to place WS-GROSS-AMT within a group item called WS-WORK-AREAS.

Example 2
Storing Counters

Suppose we wish to count the number of input records contained within a file and store that number in a **counter field.** The following program excerpt could be used.

```
100-MAIN-MODULE.
    MOVE ZERO TO WS-COUNTER.
    READ INVENTORY-FILE
        AT END MOVE 'NO ' TO ARE-THERE-MORE-RECORDS.
    PERFORM 200-COUNT-THE-RECORDS
        UNTIL ARE-THERE-MORE-RECORDS = 'NO '.
    PERFORM 300-PRINT-TOTAL.
         :
200-COUNT-THE-RECORDS.
    ADD 1 TO WS-COUNTER.
    READ INVENTORY-FILE
        AT END MOVE 'NO ' TO ARE-THERE-MORE-RECORDS.
```

WS-COUNTER could be a field defined in WORKING-STORAGE. It is incremented by one each time a record is read; hence, after all records have been read, it will contain a sum equal to the total number of records read as input. WS-COUNTER would be defined as part of WS-WORK-AREAS in WORKING-STORAGE.

```
WORKING-STORAGE SECTION.
01   WS-WORK-AREAS.
     05   WS-GROSS-AMT        PIC 9(5)V99.
     05   WS-COUNTER          PIC 9(3).
```

Example 3
Using an End-of-File
Indicator

We have been using the data-name ARE-THERE-MORE-RECORDS as an *end-of-file in-dicator.* ARE-THERE-MORE-RECORDS is initialized at 'YES'. During program execution, when an AT END condition is reached, 'NO ' is moved to ARE-THERE-MORE-RECORDS. Thus, ARE-THERE-MORE-RECORDS contains a 'YES' as long as there are still records to process. We perform a standard calculation or process routine on all records until ARE-THERE-MORE-RECORDS = 'NO ', that is, until an AT END condition occurs, at which point 'NO ' is moved to ARE-THERE-MORE-RECORDS. ARE-THERE-MORE-RECORDS would be an elementary work field in WORKING-STORAGE.

```
WORKING-STORAGE SECTION.
01  WS-WORK-AREAS.
        05  WS-GROSS-AMT              PIC 9(5)V99.
        05  WS-COUNTER                PIC 9(3).
        05  ARE-THERE-MORE-RECORDS    PIC X(3).
```

Several alternative names for ARE-THERE-MORE-RECORDS would serve just as well. EOF or WS-EOF could be used as a field name, with EOF an abbreviation for *end of file*. Note that the identifier can be any programmer-supplied data-name. We could also define EOF as follows:

```
01  WS-WORK-AREAS.
    :
    05  EOF                           PIC 9.
```

In our PROCEDURE DIVISION we could indicate an end-of-file condition when EOF = 1 as follows:

```
PROCEDURE DIVISION.
100-MAIN-MODULE.
    :
    MOVE 0 TO EOF.
    READ INFILE
        AT END MOVE 1 TO EOF.
    PERFORM 200-PROCESS-RTN
        UNTIL EOF = 1.
    :
200-PROCESS-RTN.
    :
    READ INFILE
        AT END MOVE 1 TO EOF.
```

**Example 4
Storing Input and
Output Records**

WORKING-STORAGE is also used for storing input and output records that must be retained for processing later on in the program.

Suppose, for example, that the first *input* record during each run is a control record containing three fields that indicate: (1) the number of records that will be processed, (2) the total amount for all transactions, and (3) the date of the last transaction. These fields might be used for checking purposes at the end of the run.

After we read this control record we must *store* it before we read the next record. Since each read instruction replaces the contents of an input area with the new input record's data, we would need to move the control record's contents to another storage area so that it is available for processing later on. We can establish a storage area for the control record in WORKING-STORAGE as follows:

```
WORKING-STORAGE SECTION.
01  WS-WORK-AREAS.
    :
01  CONTROL-RECORD.
        05  CR-RECORD-COUNT           PIC 9(3).
        05  CR-TRANS-TOTAL            PIC 9(6)V99.
        05  CR-DATE-IN                PIC 9(6).
```

The prefix CR- may be used as an abbreviation for *control record*.

To store this record in WORKING-STORAGE, we may code:

```
100-MAIN-MODULE.
    :
    READ IN-FILE
        AT END MOVE 'NO ' TO ARE-THERE-MORE-RECORDS.
    MOVE IN-REC TO CONTROL-RECORD.
    :
```

Thus WORKING-STORAGE can consist of group items such as WS-WORK-AREAS and records such as CONTROL-RECORD.

RULES FOR CODING WORKING-STORAGE **ITEMS**

1. The WORKING-STORAGE SECTION, like all section names, is coded in Area A.
2. The WORKING-STORAGE SECTION must follow the FILE SECTION in the DATA DIVISION.
3. Independent data items may be coded on the 01 level or as subdivisions of an 01. 77-level items could also be used. We will avoid 77-level items since they are really unnecessary; that is, elementary fields within an 01-level item in WORKING-STORAGE help to organize entries better.
4. The group item is coded on the 01 level in Area A; the independent items would then be coded on some level subordinate to 01 (i.e., 05, 10, and so on) in Area B.
5. Names given to items in this section conform to the rules for forming data-names.
6. All elementary items must have PICTURE or PIC clauses: X denotes alphanumeric; 9 denotes numeric; A denotes alphabetic.

C. VALUE **Clauses for** WORKING-STORAGE **Entries**

1. The Purpose of VALUE Clauses

Many computers do *not* automatically clear storage when reading in new programs. Thus, an area that is specified in the DATA DIVISION has an undefined value when a program begins execution. Unless the programmer moves an initial value into a field, it cannot be assumed that the field will be established with initial contents of blanks or zeros.

Elementary items in the WORKING-STORAGE SECTION can be *initialized* by the programmer. That is, they may be given initial contents by a **VALUE clause.** If these entries are given initial values, there will be no need to move literals or figurative constants into them in the PROCEDURE DIVISION.

To ensure that output records or fields specified in the FILE SECTION contain blanks when program execution begins, we MOVE SPACES to these areas in the PROCEDURE DIVISION before any processing is performed. When fields are defined in the WORKING-STORAGE SECTION, however, we have the added flexibility of being able to initialize them with VALUE clauses.

Examples

```
WORKING-STORAGE SECTION.
01   WS-WORK-AREAS.
     05   WS-TOTAL          PIC 999    VALUE ZEROS.
     05   WS-CONSTANT-1     PIC XXXX   VALUE SPACES.
```

We align VALUE clauses as well as PIC clauses, to make programs easier to read.

With some compilers, we may also use a VALUE clause on the group level if all items are to be initialized with the same value.

```
01   WS-WORK-AREAS          VALUE ZEROS.
     05   WS-COUNTER        PIC 999.
     05   WS-AMT            PIC 9(5).
```

A VALUE clause is *not required* for any item. If it is omitted, however, no assumption can be made about the initial contents of the field. Where no VALUE clause has been coded, use a MOVE instruction in the PROCEDURE DIVISION to obtain an initial value in the field.

Four entries, then, can be used to define independent or elementary items in the WORKING-STORAGE SECTION. We will always use the first three, but it is recommended that you use the fourth as well.

ITEMS IN WORKING-STORAGE

1. Level 01, coded in Area A, may be used to define a group of independent or elementary items. These independent or elementary items would be coded on a level subordinate to 01 in Area B.
2. A programmer-supplied data-name or identifier defines each field. Frequently, we use the prefix WS- to denote WORKING-STORAGE entries.
3. The size of a field and its data type are defined by the PIC clause.
4. An initial value may be stored in the field by a VALUE clause defined on the elementary level. Some systems allow VALUE clauses to be defined on the group level for initializing a series of fields.

---

2. Literals and Figurative Contents in VALUE Clauses

The VALUE clause contains a literal or figurative constant to be placed in the field. It must be the same data type as the PICTURE clause. If the PICTURE denotes a numeric field, for example, the value must be a numeric literal or the figurative constant ZERO.

Examples

```
WORKING-STORAGE SECTION.
01   WS-WORK-AREAS.
     05   WS-SOC-SEC-TAX-RATE      PIC V9999      VALUE .0715.
     05   WS-CONSTANT-1            PIC 9(5)       VALUE 07600.
     05   WS-TOTAL                 PIC 9999       VALUE ZERO.
```

Notice that to say 05 WS-TOTAL PICTURE 9999 VALUE ZERO is the same as defining the 05-level item *without* the VALUE clause and coding the following in the PROCEDURE DIVISION before processing any data: MOVE ZERO TO WS-TOTAL. Similarly, the entry 05 WS-SOC-SEC-TAX-RATE PICTURE V9999 VALUE .0715 is the same as coding MOVE .0715 TO WS-SOC-SEC-TAX-RATE before processing data, where WS-SOC-SEC-TAX-RATE has no VALUE clause.

Since the VALUE clause performs the same operation as a MOVE instruction, all rules for MOVE operations apply. Consider the following:

Example

```
 7 8      12      16      20      24      28      32      36      40      44      48      52      56      60      64      68      72
     05   WS-CODE        PICTURE 999 VALUE 12.
 *   NOTE: FIELD LENGTH IS LARGER THAN VALUE
```

This is the same as moving 12 to WS-CODE in the PROCEDURE DIVISION. According to the rules for numeric MOVE operations specified in the previous section, 012 will be placed in WS-CODE.

In general, to obtain in the receiving field the *same contents* as the literal, use a PICTURE clause with the same length and number of decimal positions. To obtain exactly 12 in WS-CODE, for example, WS-CODE should have PICTURE 99. If WS-CODE had PIC 999, give it a VALUE of 012.

The rules for alphanumeric moves also apply to independent items in WORKING-STORAGE. If a field contains an alphanumeric or alphabetic PICTURE clause, a VALUE clause, if used, must contain a nonnumeric literal.

Examples

```
*************************************************************
*   ALPHA FIELDS MUST HAVE VALUES ENCLOSED IN QUOTES   *
*************************************************************
WORKING-STORAGE SECTION.
01   WS-WORK-AREAS.
     05   WS-DATE          PIC X(5)   VALUE 'APRIL'.
     05   WS-NAME          PIC XXX    VALUE SPACES.
```

It is poor programming style to code, for example:

Poor Style

```
05 WS-CODE      PICTURE X      VALUE 3.
```

In fact, on some systems a syntax error will occur if the preceding is coded. If a field is defined with PIC X, the VALUE should contain a nonnumeric literal and *not* the value 3, which is a numeric literal. The entry, therefore, is more appropriately coded as:

Corrected Entry

```
05 WS-CODE      PICTURE X      VALUE '3'.
```

Similarly, we should *not* code:

Incorrect Coding

```
05 WS-TOTAL     PICTURE 9(5)   VALUE SPACES.
```

This will always result in a syntax error. Digits 0–9, a decimal point, and a plus or minus sign are the only characters that may be used in a numeric literal. To clear a numeric field, we fill it with zeros, not blanks. The preceding entry should read:

Corrected Entry

```
05 WS-TOTAL     PICTURE 99     VALUE ZERO.
```

VALUE clauses for initializing fields may *not* be used in the FILE SECTION of the DATA DIVISION. Only WORKING-STORAGE entries may have VALUE clauses for this purpose.

We have seen that we can initialize WS-TOTAL by (1) moving zeros to it in the PROCEDURE DIVISION before processing any data or by (2) using a VALUE of ZERO in WORKING-STORAGE. If information is then accumulated in WS-TOTAL during execution, the initial value of zero will be replaced.

```
WORKING-STORAGE SECTION.
01   WS-WORK-AREAS.
     05   WS-TOTAL        PIC 9(5)   VALUE ZERO.
       :
PROCEDURE DIVISION.
       :
     ADD AMT-IN TO WS-TOTAL.
```

After the ADD instruction is executed the first time, WS-TOTAL will contain the value of AMT-IN and *not* zero. If, however, we did not initialize WS-TOTAL at ZERO, the contents of WS-TOTAL after the ADD would be unpredictable. It may even cause an **abend**, or *ab*normal *end*, to the program. This is because we cannot assume a value of zero or blanks in a field that is not initialized.

Note: Failure to initialize a field used in an arithmetic operation is a frequent cause of abends or program interrupts.

We may use a `WORKING-STORAGE` entry defined with a `VALUE`, in place of a literal in the `PROCEDURE DIVISION`. Consider the following coding:

```
IF   CODE-IN = 0
     MOVE 'CR' TO CREDIT-AREA-OUT.
```

This is the same as

```
IF   CODE-IN = 0
     MOVE WS-CREDIT TO CREDIT-AREA-OUT.
```

where `WS-CREDIT` is an independent item defined as follows:

```
05   WS-CREDIT        PICTURE XX     VALUE 'CR'.
```

Coding Guideline

The programmer decides whether to use a `WORKING-STORAGE` data item to store a constant in a work area or to code the constant as a literal in the `PROCEDURE DIVISION`. As a general rule, however, any literal that will be used more than once in the `PROCEDURE DIVISION` should be given an assigned storage area and a data-name in `WORKING-STORAGE`. It is more efficient to use this data-name several times in the program than to redefine the same literal again and again in the `PROCEDURE DIVISION`.

3. Continuation of Nonnumeric Literals in `VALUE` Clauses from One Line to the Next

You will recall that numeric literals and numeric fields may not exceed 18 digits in length. Similarly, the `VALUE` and `PICTURE` clauses of a numeric item in the `WORKING-STORAGE SECTION` may not exceed 18 digits.

A nonnumeric literal, however, may contain up to 120 characters for COBOL 74 or 160 characters for COBOL 85. Similarly, a nonnumeric literal in a `VALUE` clause, like any other nonnumeric literal, is enclosed in quotes and contains a maximum of 120 characters (COBOL 74) or 160 characters (COBOL 85).

Since the `VALUE` clause for an alphanumeric field in the `WORKING-STORAGE SECTION` may contain as many as 120 or 160 characters, it is sometimes necessary to continue the `VALUE` from one line of the coding sheet to the next line. The continuation of nonnumeric literals to two or more lines conforms to the following rules.

**RULES FOR CONTINUATION OF LITERALS
FROM ONE LINE TO ANOTHER**

1. Begin the literal in the `VALUE` clause with a quotation mark.
2. Continue the literal until position 72, the end of the line, is reached. Do *not* end with quotation marks on this line.
3. Place a hyphen in the position marked CONTINUATION of the *next line* (position 7 of the coding sheet).
4. Continue the literal in any position beginning in Area B of the next line. Begin with a quotation mark.
5. End the literal with a quotation mark.

The same rules may be applied to the continuation of nonnumeric literals defined in the `PROCEDURE DIVISION`.

Examples   1. The following illustrates the continuation of a literal to a second line:

2. Figure 7.1 illustrates the continuation of a nonnumeric literal to three lines.

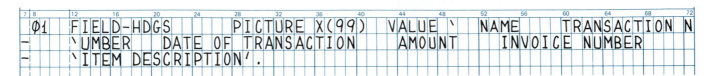

Figure 7.1
Continuation of a nonnumeric
literal to three lines in
`WORKING-STORAGE`.

A nonnumeric literal may be continued from one line to the next when defined in the `PROCEDURE DIVISION` as well. Consider the following `WORK-ING-STORAGE` entry.

```
05  MESSAGE-FIELD   PICTURE X(60).
```

Figure 7.2 illustrates how a nonnumeric literal moved to `MESSAGE-FIELD` in the `PROCEDURE DIVISION` is continued from one line to the next. Note that the continuation rules are the same as specified in Example 1.

Figure 7.2
Continuation of a nonnumeric
literal from one line to the
next in the `PROCEDURE`
`DIVISION`.

4. Clearing Fields Using the `INITIALIZE` Verb (COBOL 85)

With COBOL 85, a series of elementary items contained within a group item can all be initialized with the **INITIALIZE** verb. Numeric items will be initialized at zero, and nonnumeric items will be initialized with blanks.

```
01  WS-REC-1.
    05  FILLER      PIC X(20).
    05  NAME        PIC X(20).
    05  FILLER      PIC X(15).
    05  AMT-1       PIC 9(5)V99.
    05  FILLER      PIC X(15).
```

```
      05  AMT-2       PIC 9(5)V99.
      05  FILLER      PIC X(15).
      05  TOTAL       PIC 9(6)V99.
      05  FILLER      PIC X(13).
         :
  PROCEDURE DIVISION.
         :
      INITIALIZE WS-REC-1.
```

The preceding will set AMT-1, AMT-2, and TOTAL to zeros and will set all the other fields to spaces.

Self-Test

1. The two main sections of the DATA DIVISION are the _____ SECTION and the _____ SECTION.

2. Independent data items such as _____ , _____ , or _____ are defined in WORKING-STORAGE.

3. Elementary items in WORKING-STORAGE are usually coded as part of a(n) __(no.)__ level-item.

4. The entry WORKING-STORAGE SECTION is coded in Area _____ , that is, beginning in column _____ .

5. WORKING-STORAGE SECTION and its entries follow the _____ SECTION and precede the _____ DIVISION.

6. The VALUE specified for a field must be the same data type as the _____ clause.

Make any necessary corrections to the following statements (Questions 7–10). (Assume correct margins.)

7. 05 WS-CODE1 PICTURE X   VALUE 4.

8. 05 WS-CODE2 PICTURE X   VALUE ZERO.

9. 05 WS-AMT1 PICTURE 99   VALUE SPACES.

10. 05 WS-AMT2 PICTURE 99V99 VALUE 12.34.

Solutions

1. FILE; WORKING-STORAGE
2. constants; intermediate totals; work areas
3. 01
4. A; 8
5. FILE; PROCEDURE
6. PICTURE
7. 05 WS-CODE1 PICTURE X VALUE '4'. (The type of literal should be the same type as the PIC clause.)
8. Nothing wrong—Zero may be placed in either a numeric or a nonnumeric field.
9. Numeric fields cannot have a value of SPACES.
10. Nothing wrong.

II. Describing Print Records in WORKING-STORAGE

A. Each Record Is Established as a Separate Area in WORKING-STORAGE

Printed output typically has lines containing headings, error messages, final totals, and so on. Each type of output line would be defined as a record. To use the FILE SECTION to define multiple records in a print file is both cumbersome and inefficient.

Suppose we code the FD for a PRINT-FILE as follows:

```
FD   PRINT-FILE
     LABEL RECORDS ARE OMITTED
     RECORD CONTAINS 133 CHARACTERS
     DATA RECORDS ARE HEADING-LINE
                      DATA-LINE
                      TOTAL-LINE.
```

The computer will reserve just 133 positions of storage for the file's output area. It does *not* reserve 133 positions for *each* record described. Thus the 01s for HEADING-LINE, DATA-LINE, and TOTAL-LINE will all be specifying a single 133-position area:

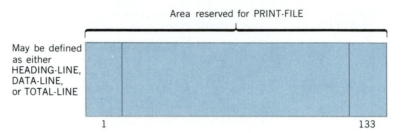

As a result, the following type of coding will *not* produce the correct results:

```
* NOTE: HEADING-LINE AND DATA-LINE USE THE SAME 133 POSITIONS *
     MOVE 'MONTHLY SALES REPORT' TO HEADING-LINE.
     MOVE SPACES TO DATA-LINE.
     WRITE HEADING-LINE.
```

          Prints a   Clears the   Moves a heading
          blank line   print area   to the print area

If this program excerpt were executed, HEADING-LINE would print *erroneously* as spaces and not as the desired 'MONTHLY SALES REPORT'. This is because HEADING-LINE and DATA-LINE actually occupy *the same 133 positions of storage*. The heading 'MONTHLY SALES REPORT' is moved into that 133-position area, but the instruction that follows it clears the same area to spaces.

To eliminate this problem of a single output area for multiple records, it is best to define each type of line to be printed as a *separate* 133-position area in WORKING-STORAGE. Then, each record can be treated independently and moved to the print area when it is to be written.

```
FD   PRINT-FILE
     LABEL RECORDS ARE OMITTED.
01   PRINT-REC            PIC X(133).
WORKING-STORAGE SECTION.
**********************************************************
*    NOTE: EACH 01 OCCUPIES SEPARATE AREAS OF STORAGE.   *
**********************************************************
01   HEADING-LINE.
       :
01   DATA-LINE.
       :
01   TOTAL-LINE.
       :
*
PROCEDURE DIVISION.
       :
     MOVE HEADING-LINE TO PRINT-REC.
     WRITE PRINT-REC.
       :
```

```
MOVE DATA-LINE TO PRINT-REC.
WRITE PRINT-REC.
  :
  :
MOVE TOTAL-LINE TO PRINT-REC.
WRITE PRINT-REC.
```

Since printed output usually involves writing not only data lines but heading and total lines as well, programmers usually define the different records to be printed in WORKING-STORAGE and move them to the print area before writing. In summary, then, one major reason for using WORKING-STORAGE areas for describing multiple output formats is that WORKING-STORAGE reserves *separate areas* for each of these formats.

B. Fields Can Be Initialized with VALUE Clauses

The second major reason for establishing print records in WORKING-STORAGE is that we can use VALUEs to initialize fields to be outputted. This eliminates the need for numerous MOVE instructions in the PROCEDURE DIVISION.

Consider the following Printer Spacing Chart:

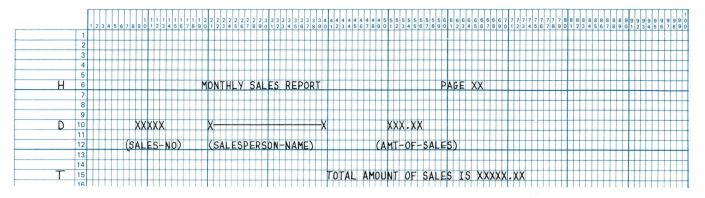

To obtain the appropriate output, we may code the following. Note that we use the prefix HL- for fields in the HEADING-LINE record. This prefix describes the fields more precisely.

```
WORKING-STORAGE SECTION.
01  HEADING-LINE.
    05  FILLER          PIC X(20).
    05  HL-LITERAL-1    PIC X(20).
    05  FILLER          PIC X(20).
    05  HL-LITERAL-2    PIC X(5).
    05  HL-PAGE-CT      PIC 99.
    05  FILLER          PIC X(66).
*
PROCEDURE DIVISION.
    :
    :
    MOVE SPACES TO HEADING-LINE.
    MOVE ZEROS TO HL-PAGE-CT.
    MOVE 'MONTHLY SALES REPORT' TO HL-LITERAL-1.
    MOVE 'PAGE' TO HL-LITERAL-2.
    PERFORM 300-HEADING-RTN.
    :
    :
300-HEADING-RTN.
    ADD 1 TO HL-PAGE-CT.
    MOVE HEADING-LINE TO PRINT-REC.
    WRITE PRINT-REC.
```

It is rather cumbersome and inefficient to use the PROCEDURE DIVISION to define literals and move them to storage areas in this manner. We may use FILLERs with VALUE clauses to define fields and to provide them with values.

```
WORKING-STORAGE SECTION.
01  HEADING-LINE.
    05  FILLER          PIC X(20)      VALUE SPACES.
    05  FILLER          PIC X(20)
                        VALUE 'MONTHLY SALES REPORT'.
    05  FILLER          PIC X(20)      VALUE SPACES.
    05  FILLER          PIC X(5)       VALUE 'PAGE '.
    05  HL-PAGE-CT      PIC 99         VALUE ZEROS.
    05  FILLER          PIC X(66)      VALUE SPACES.
```

All fields, including those defined as FILLERs, are initialized with their appropriate VALUE clauses. We do not need to move literals or constants to fields in the PROCEDURE DIVISION; thus we may substitute FILLER for the data-names HL-LITERAL-1 and HL-LITERAL-2, since we do not need to access these fields in the PROCEDURE DIVISION. Thus, using VALUE clauses in the WORKING-STORAGE SECTION simplifies the PROCEDURE DIVISION considerably.

```
    PERFORM 300-HEADING-RTN.
      .
      .
300-HEADING-RTN.
    ADD 1 TO HL-PAGE-CT.
    MOVE HEADING-LINE TO PRINT-REC.
    WRITE PRINT-REC.
```

With COBOL 85, you may omit the word FILLER entirely from each of the preceding lines.

C. Printing Data in Edited Form

1. Formatting Print Records

You will find that using WORKING-STORAGE to store data lines to be printed also reduces programming effort. Consider the Printer Spacing Chart in Figure 7.3. We wish to print the contents of each input record, which includes an amount field (AMT-IN) with PIC 999V99. As noted in the previous chapter, if AMT-IN contained $123_\wedge 45$, for example, and we printed it as is, it would print as 12345 because the decimal point is only implied. To actually print the decimal point, we code the amount field in the output record, called DL-AMT-OUT, with a PIC of 999.99.

```
WORKING-STORAGE SECTION.
01  DATA-LINE.
    05  FILLER          PIC X(19)      VALUE SPACES.
    05  DL-CUST-NO-OUT  PIC 9(5).
    05  FILLER          PIC X(20)      VALUE SPACES.
    05  DL-NAME-OUT     PIC X(20).
    05  FILLER          PIC X(10)      VALUE SPACES.
    05  DL-ADDR-OUT     PIC X(20).
    05  FILLER          PIC X(5)       VALUE SPACES.
    05  DL-AMT-OUT      PIC 999.99.
    05  FILLER          PIC X(28)      VALUE SPACES.
*************************************************************
*  NOTE: DECIMAL POINT IS ASSUMED WHEN A  V  IS USED;    *
*        TO ACTUALLY PRINT THE DECIMAL POINT CODE A       *
*        PERIOD INSTEAD OF A V.                           *
*************************************************************
```

DL- is used as a prefix to mean Data Line.

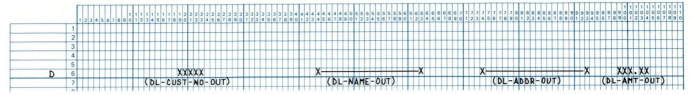

Figure 7.3
Sample Printer Spacing Chart.

In DATA-LINE, all FILLER areas that should contain blanks have been initialized with SPACES. The data for DL-CUST-NO-OUT, DL-NAME-OUT, DL-ADDR-OUT, and DL-AMT-OUT will be moved to these fields from the input areas by PROCEDURE DIVISION entries. Note that to print a decimal point in DL-AMT-OUT, we include the decimal point itself in the PIC clause as a period, *not* as a V.

A decimal point must *not* be used in a PIC clause of an arithmetic field since it is not a valid numeric character. In fact, decimal points are used only for print purposes and in numeric literals. The instruction MOVE AMT-IN TO DL-AMT-OUT will work properly only if AMT-IN has a PIC 9(3)V99. AMT-IN could be used in arithmetic operations, but DL-AMT-OUT could not. Moreover, AMT-IN is a *five*-position field but DL-AMT-OUT is a *six*-position field because it contains an actual decimal point.

Assume that an error line is to print for input amount fields in excess of 100.00. We could code this error line as follows:

```
WORKING-STORAGE SECTION.
01   ERROR-LINE.
     05   FILLER          PIC X(19)       VALUE SPACES.
     05   EL-CUST-NO-ERR  PIC 9(5).
     05   FILLER          PIC X(20)       VALUE SPACES.
     05   EL-NAME-ERR     PIC X(20).
     05   FILLER          PIC X(20)       VALUE SPACES.
     05   EL-AMT-ERR      PIC 999.99.
     05   FILLER          PIC X(13)       VALUE SPACES.
     05   FILLER          PIC X(30)
                          VALUE 'TRANSACTION AMT EXCEEDS 100.00'.
```

EL- is a prefix to denote these fields as part of the Error Message Line.

The relevant PROCEDURE DIVISION entries follow. The IF statement is used for illustrative purposes here and is meant to be self-explanatory (IF statements are explained in detail in Chapter 9).

```
PROCEDURE DIVISION.
     .
     .
     IF  AMT-IN IS GREATER THAN 100.00
         PERFORM 500-ERROR-CHECK.
     .
     .
500-ERROR-CHECK.
     MOVE CUST-NO-IN TO EL-CUST-NO-ERR.
     MOVE NAME-IN TO EL-NAME-ERR.
     MOVE AMT-IN TO EL-AMT-ERR.
     MOVE ERROR-LINE TO PRINT-REC.
     WRITE PRINT-REC.
```

An error line prints if the input amount field is in excess of 100.00.

2. The WRITE ... FROM Statement
Consider the following two instructions.

```
MOVE HEADING-LINE TO PRINT-REC.
WRITE PRINT-REC.
```

These two instructions can be replaced with the following single statement.

```
WRITE PRINT-REC FROM HEADING-LINE.
```

The **WRITE** (record-1) **FROM** (record-2) statement performs two operations: (1) it moves record-2 to record-1 and (2) it writes record-1. Record-1 is defined as a record in the FILE SECTION, and record-2 is defined in the WORKING-STORAGE SECTION.

With this introduction, you should be able to print simple reports. Remember that a Printer Spacing Chart is very helpful in vertically aligning headings over the appropriate data entries. There are several blank charts at the end of this book. Chapter 11 provides a more in-depth treatment of printed reports.

In the following chapters, we will use WORKING-STORAGE and appropriate VALUE clauses for establishing records to be printed. We will then move these records to the output area before each WRITE instruction or use a WRITE ... FROM to print the records.

III. The READ ... INTO **Statement**

In our introduction to the WORKING-STORAGE SECTION, we noted that WORKING-STORAGE is sometimes used for storing input records. Suppose the first input record contains information to be stored, such as the number of records to be processed. After it is read, such a record must be moved from the input area to WORKING-STORAGE. If it is not, the next read will replace the first record's data with that of the second record. We could READ the first record and then MOVE it to WORKING-STORAGE. Or we could combine a READ and MOVE with a single statement:

```
READ file-name
    INTO (WORKING-STORAGE-record-area)
```

Example

```
FD  IN-TRANS
        .
        .
WORKING-STORAGE SECTION.
01  CONTROL-RECORD-1.
        .
        .
PROCEDURE DIVISION.
        .
        .
    READ IN-TRANS
        INTO CONTROL-RECORD-1.
```

The **READ ... INTO** is very similar to the WRITE ... FROM. Both have uses in addition to those discussed here; we will consider these later on.

Coding Guideline

Align PIC and VALUE clauses for ease of reading.

CHAPTER SUMMARY

A. Uses of WORKING-STORAGE.
  1. For storing intermediate results, counters, and end-of-file indicators such as the data-name ARE-THERE-MORE-RECORDS; also used for storing input and output records.
B. Advantages of WORKING-STORAGE.
  1. Used for defining multiple records as in a print file, such as heading lines, detail lines, error lines, and total lines.

2. Allows the use of VALUE clauses to initialize fields.
C. Using WORKING-STORAGE for print files.
   1. The FD for a print file typically includes a standard record description as follows:

   ```
   01  PRINT-REC        PIC X(133).
   ```

   No field descriptions are necessary within the record.
   2. All print records are described with field descriptions and VALUE clauses in WORKING-STORAGE.
   3. Each print record defined in WORKING-STORAGE should allow for right and left margins and proper spacing between fields. A Printer Spacing Chart is very useful for preparing layouts of printed reports.
   4. Where appropriate, fields within print records defined in WORKING-STORAGE should have VALUE clauses unless data is to be moved into them. If a field within a heading record is *not* accessed individually, it is typically called FILLER.

   ```
   01  HEADING-LINE.
       05 FILLER        PIC _____    VALUE _____.
       05 FILLER        PIC _____    VALUE _____.
       05 FILLER        PIC _____    VALUE _____.
   ```

   With COBOL 85, the word FILLER can be omitted entirely so that fields that are not accessed in the PROCEDURE DIVISION can be coded with just a PIC clause and no data-name.
   5. Records defined in WORKING-STORAGE that are to be outputted must be moved to the record defined in the output file before they can be written. We can use a WRITE output-record-name FROM (WORKING-STORAGE-record-name) to accomplish both the MOVE and the WRITE.

CHAPTER SELF-TEST

1. (T or F) Elementary items in WORKING-STORAGE must have VALUE clauses.
2. Two examples of data that might be stored in WORKING-STORAGE are _____ and _____ .
3. Why do we use WORKING-STORAGE for storing record formats to be printed?
4. To print data that is accumulated in WORKING-STORAGE, it must first be _____ to the output area before a WRITE statement is executed.
5. (T or F) The WORKING-STORAGE SECTION may either precede or follow the FILE SECTION.
6. (T or F) A VALUE clause always contains numeric literals.
7. (T or F) The following entry can be coded in either the FILE SECTION or the WORKING-STORAGE SECTION: 05 TOTAL-AMT   PIC 9(5) VALUE ZERO.
8. (T or F) Either of the following VALUE clauses can be used to initialize TAX-RATE (PIC V9999) with a value of .0825.
   (a) VALUE '.0825'.
   (b) VALUE .0825.
9. A numeric literal may not exceed __(no.)__ digits in length; a nonnumeric literal may contain up to __(no.)__ characters.
10. (T or F) Nonnumeric literals may be continued from one line to the next in the PROCEDURE DIVISION using the same rules for continuing nonnumeric literals in VALUE clauses.

Solutions

1. F—VALUE clauses are optional (but recommended).
2. counters; totals; work areas
3. (a) Fields can contain specific VALUES.
   (b) Each record—headings, data lines, error lines, and total lines—would occupy separate storage areas.

4. moved
5. F—It must follow the FILE SECTION.
6. F—The literal in the VALUE clause must correspond to the data format specified in the PICTURE clause; if the PIC is alphanumeric, the VALUE should contain an alphanumeric literal.
7. F—VALUE clauses for initializing fields may not be used in the FILE SECTION.
8. F—Since the PICTURE clause is numeric, a numeric literal, as illustrated in (b), must be used.
9. 18; 120 for COBOL 74 or 160 for COBOL 85
10. T

PRACTICE PROGRAM

Using the problem definition that follows, print all fields in each input record on a single line. Spacing is shown on the Printer Spacing Chart. For readability, place a period between initials of the name, and a / between month and year of the date. Also print column headings at the top of the page. That is, print the word NAME above where the name field will be printed, and so on. Use WORKING-STORAGE with VALUE clauses for describing output lines. Figure 7.4 illustrates the pseudocode and the hierarchy chart for this problem, and Figure 7.5 illustrates the COBOL program. Note that this is the same practice problem that appears in Chapter 6. Here we use WORKING-STORAGE for describing output, which simplifies PROCEDURE DIVISION coding.

Systems Flowchart

CUST-FILE   SAMPLE7   PRINT-FILE

CUST-FILE Record Layout

CUSTOMER NAME			DATE OF TRANSACTION		AMOUNT OF TRANSACTION	
INIT 1	INIT 2	LAST NAME	MONTH	YEAR	(IN $)	
1	2 3	12	13 14	15 16	17 22	23 80

PRINT-FILE Printer Spacing Chart

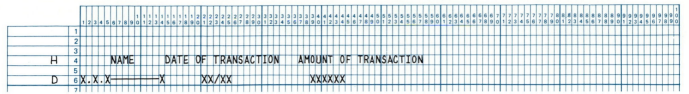

	NAME	DATE OF TRANSACTION	AMOUNT OF TRANSACTION
H	NAME	DATE OF TRANSACTION	AMOUNT OF TRANSACTION
D	X.X.X——————X	XX/XX	XXXXXX

SAMPLE OUTPUT

NAME	DATE OF TRANSACTION	AMOUNT OF TRANSACTION
P.Q.NEWMAN	01/88	001250
R.R.REDFORD	06/88	123453
E.L.TAYLOR	04/88	010000
N.B.STERN	09/88	020000
C.D.HAMMEL	07/88	065450
R.A.STERN	11/88	884008
L.O.STERN	07/88	688778
M.E.STERN	02/88	009899
H.R.FORD	12/88	684800
C.R.FISHER	01/88	086212

SAMPLE INPUT DATA

PQNEWMAN	0188001250
RRREDFORD	0688123453
ELTAYLOR	0488010000
NBSTERN	0988020000
CDHAMMEL	0788065450
RASTERN	1188884008
LOSTERN	0788688778
MESTERN	0288009899
HRFORD	1288684800
CRFISHER	0188086212

Figure 7.4
Pseudocode and hierarchy
chart for Practice Program.

Pseudocode for Practice Program

```
START
    Housekeeping Operations
    Write a Heading
    Read an Input Record
    PERFORM UNTIL no more records
        Move Input Fields to the Output Area
        Write an Output Record
        Read an Input Record
    ENDPERFORM
    End-of-Job Operations
STOP
```

Hierarchy Chart for Practice Program

Note: Advanced programs with more logical
control structures will have more
meaningful hierarchy charts.

```
        IDENTIFICATION DIVISION.
        PROGRAM-ID. SAMPLE.
        ******************************************************************
        * SAMPLE    - TRANSACTION REPORT                                 *
        *              CONTAINS CUSTOMER NAME, TRANSACTION DATE AND AMOUNT *
        ******************************************************************
        *
        ENVIRONMENT DIVISION.
        CONFIGURATION SECTION.
        SOURCE-COMPUTER. IBM-4341.
        OBJECT-COMPUTER. IBM-4341.
        INPUT-OUTPUT SECTION.
        FILE-CONTROL.
            SELECT IN-CUST-FILE    ASSIGN TO DATA6.
            SELECT OUT-PRINT-FILE ASSIGN TO SYS$OUTPUT.
        *
        DATA DIVISION.
        FILE SECTION.
        FD  IN-CUST-FILE
            LABEL RECORDS ARE STANDARD.
        01  IN-CUST-REC.
            05  IN-CUST-NAME.
                10  IN-INITIAL-1            PIC X.
                10  IN-INITIAL-2            PIC X.
                10  IN-LAST-NAME            PIC X(10).
            05  IN-DATE-OF-TRANSACTION.
                10  IN-MONTH                PIC 99.
                10  IN-YEAR                 PIC 99.
            05  IN-AMOUNT-OF-TRANSACTION    PIC 9(6).
            05  FILLER                      PIC X(58).
        FD  OUT-PRINT-FILE
            LABEL RECORDS ARE OMITTED.
        01  OUT-PRINT-REC                   PIC X(133).
        WORKING-STORAGE SECTION.
        01  WORK-AREAS.
            05 ARE-THERE-MORE-RECORDS       PIC X(3)      VALUE 'YES'.
        01  HL-HEADING1-OUT.
            05  FILLER                      PIC X(6)      VALUE SPACES.
            05  FILLER                      PIC X(4)
                VALUE 'NAME'.
            05  FILLER                      PIC X(5)      VALUE SPACES.
            05  FILLER                      PIC X(19)
                VALUE 'DATE OF TRANSACTION'.
            05  FILLER                      PIC X(3)      VALUE SPACES.
            05  FILLER                      PIC X(21)
                VALUE 'AMOUNT OF TRANSACTION'.
            05  FILLER                      PIC X(75)     VALUE SPACES.
        01  DL-DETAIL-LINE-OUT.
            05  FILLER                      PIC X         VALUE SPACE.
            05  DL-INIT1-OUT                PIC X.
            05  DL-POINT1-OUT               PIC X         VALUE '.'.
            05  DL-INIT2-OUT                PIC X.
            05  DL-POINT2-OUT               PIC X         VALUE '.'.
            05  DL-LAST-NAME-OUT            PIC X(10).
            05  FILLER                      PIC X(6)      VALUE SPACES.
            05  DL-MONTH-OUT                PIC 99.
            05  DL-SLASH-OUT                PIC X         VALUE '/'.
            05  DL-YEAR-OUT                 PIC 99.
            05  FILLER                      PIC X(13)     VALUE SPACES.
            05  DL-AMOUNT-OUT               PIC 9(6).
            05  FILLER                      PIC X(88)     VALUE SPACES.
        *
        PROCEDURE DIVISION.
        ****************************************************************
        * 100-MAIN-MODULE - CONTROLS OPENING AND CLOSING FILES  *
        *                     DIRECTION OF PROGRAM LOGIC             *
        *                     RETURNS CONTROL TO OPERATING SYSTEM *
        ****************************************************************
        100-MAIN-MODULE.
            OPEN INPUT IN-CUST-FILE
                 OUTPUT OUT-PRINT-FILE.
            WRITE OUT-PRINT-REC FROM HL-HEADING1-OUT.
            READ IN-CUST-FILE
                AT END MOVE 'NO ' TO ARE-THERE-MORE-RECORDS.
            PERFORM 200-MOVE-RTN
                UNTIL ARE-THERE-MORE-RECORDS = 'NO '.
            CLOSE IN-CUST-FILE
                  OUT-PRINT-FILE.
            STOP RUN.
        ****************************************************************
        * 200-MOVE-RTN - PERFORMED FROM 100-MAIN-MODULE          *
        *                  MOVES AND PRINTS DATA FROM OUTPUT AREAS *
        *                  READS NEXT RECORD                        *
        ****************************************************************
        200-MOVE-RTN.
            MOVE IN-INITIAL-1 TO DL-INIT1-OUT.
            MOVE IN-INITIAL-2 TO DL-INIT2-OUT.
            MOVE IN-LAST-NAME TO DL-LAST-NAME-OUT.
            MOVE IN-MONTH TO DL-MONTH-OUT.
            MOVE IN-YEAR TO DL-YEAR-OUT.
            MOVE IN-AMOUNT-OF-TRANSACTION TO DL-AMOUNT-OUT.
            WRITE OUT-PRINT-REC FROM DL-DETAIL-LINE-OUT.
            READ IN-CUST-FILE
                AT END MOVE 'NO ' TO ARE-THERE-MORE-RECORDS.
```

KEY TERMS

Abend	Intermediate result field	WORKING-STORAGE
Counter field	READ ... INTO	SECTION
INITIALIZE	VALUE clause	WRITE ... FROM

REVIEW QUESTIONS

I. True-False Questions

T F

___ ___ 1. WORKING-STORAGE entries can be elementary items or group items.

___ ___ 2. VALUE clauses may be used in the WORKING-STORAGE SECTION and the FILE SECTION to specify an initial contents for a field.

___ ___ 3. A field called END-OF-FILE may be initialized by giving it a VALUE in WORKING-STORAGE.

___ ___ 4. A VALUE clause is frequently used in an input area to specify the contents of an input field.

___ ___ 5. The WORKING-STORAGE SECTION may either precede or follow the FILE SECTION.

___ ___ 6. The literals in VALUE clauses are restricted to 132 characters.

___ ___ 7. The literal in a VALUE clause should be consistent with the data format specified in the PICTURE clause of a WORKING-STORAGE item.

___ ___ 8. Nonnumeric literals may be continued from one line to the next with the use of the continuation column (column 7).

___ ___ 9. 01-level items may or may not be subdivided.

___ ___ 10. WORKING-STORAGE entries are sometimes used for the accumulation of output data.

II. General Questions

Make necessary corrections to each of the following (1–8). Assume that margin use and spacing are correct.

```
1. 05  CONSTANTA PICTURE X VALUE 2.

2. 01 DATE-OUT.
      05  MONTH-OUT      PICTURE 99.
      05  YEAR-OUT       PICTURE 99
   77 TOTAL              PICTURE 9(5).

3. 05 CONSTANTB  PICTURE X VALUE A.

4. 05 SUM-IT  PICTURE 999 VALUE SPACES.

5. 77 HEADER.
      05 H-FLDA PICTURE X(4).
      05 H-FLDB PICTURE X(4).

6. WORKING STORAGE SECTION
   01 WS-FLD1 PICTURE X VALUE ZERO.

7. 05 WS-FLD2 VALUE 3.

8. 05 FIELDA PICTURE X (132) VALUE SPACES.
```

9. Write a WORKING-STORAGE description of a three-position alphanumeric field called BOB with an initial value of zero.

10. Which of the following are coded in Area A?
   (a) WORKING-STORAGE SECTION
   (b) 77 level
   (c) 01 level
   (d) 05 level

11. Write a WORKING-STORAGE description of a 120-position independent field with the following contents.

```
THIS  REPORT  IS RUN MONTHLY TO DETERMINE THE  NAMES  OF  ALL
EMPLOYEES WHO HAVE BEEN PROMOTED
```

DEBUGGING EXERCISES

Consider the following WORKING-STORAGE entries for Questions 1–5.

```
1    WORKING-STORAGE SECTION
2    01   STORED AREAS.
3         05   EOF        PIC 9.
4         05   COUNTER    PIC 9(4) VALUE SPACES.
5         05   DATA       PIC 9(3).
```

1. There is a syntax error on the first line. Correct it.
2. There is a syntax error on the second line. Correct it.
3. There is a syntax error on line 5. Correct it.
4. Will a syntax error occur because EOF has no VALUE clause? What PROCEDURE DIVISION entry should be coded before we READ file-name AT END MOVE 1 TO EOF?
5. The definition of COUNTER will result in a syntax error. Why? Make the necessary corrections.
6. Suppose we accumulate a FIN-TOT that contains the sum of TRANS-AMTs of all records read. We wish to print the value of FIN-TOT at the end of the run; we define its PIC clause as PIC $9(4).99. After each READ, we code: ADD TRANS-AMT TO FIN-TOT. Will this cause an error? Explain your answer. If you think an error will occur, make the necessary corrections.
7. Suppose the PIC clauses of a HEADING-REC totaled 103 instead of 133. Would a syntax error occur? Would the computer abort the run during execution? How would the heading print?

PROGRAMMING ASSIGNMENTS

For each assignment, plan the program first with pseudocode or a flowchart and a hierarchy chart. Remember that programs are not complete unless they have been fully tested and debugged.

1. Redo Programming Assignment 1 in Chapter 6 using
   (a) WORKING-STORAGE for establishing print records.
   (b) Literals and VALUE clauses for describing headings, rather than PROCEDURE DIVISION entries.
2. Redo Programming Assignment 2 in Chapter 6 using
   (a) WORKING-STORAGE for establishing print records.
   (b) Literals and VALUE clauses for describing headings, rather than PROCEDURE DIVISION entries.
3. Disk input consists of the following accounts receivable data.

1–5	Customer number
6–25	Customer name
26–30	Invoice number
31–36	Invoice date
37–42	Invoice amount xxxx.xx

Produce a report with page and column headings that has the following form.

```
          1111111111222222222233333333334444444444555555555566666666667777777777888888888899999999990
 123456789012345678901234567890123456789012345678901234567890123456789012345678901234567890123456789012345678901234567890

 1
 2
 3
 4
H  5                ACCOUNTS RECEIVABLE REGISTER
 6
H  7 CUSTOMER  CUSTOMER                    INVOICE   INVOICE      INVOICE
H  8 NUMBER    NAME                        NUMBER    DATE         AMOUNT
H  9 -----------------------------------------------------------------------
10
D 11 XXXXX     X----------------------X   XXXXX     XX XX XX    $XXXX.XX
12        .                         .               .              .
13        .                         .               .              .
14        .                         .               .              .
15        .                         .               .              .
16
T 17                                        TOTAL     $XXXXX.XX *
18
```

Use an ADD (invoice amount) TO FIN-TOT to obtain the final total. The disk has a blocking factor of 20 and standard labels.

4. To count the number of records processed, we can ADD 1 TO COUNTER after each READ. COUNTER would be defined in WORKING-STORAGE. To obtain a final total of all input amount fields, we would code ADD AMT-IN TO FIN-TOT, where FIN-TOT is defined in WORKING-STORAGE.

   Write a program to read in 80-position disk records with an AMT-IN field in positions 11–15 (XXX.XX). The disk has a blocking factor of 20 and standard labels. At the end of the job, print the following:

```
TOTAL NUMBER OF RECORDS PROCESSED - XXXX
FINAL TOTAL OF ALL AMOUNT FIELDS -  $XX,XXX.XX
```

5. To subtract an input field called AMT1-IN from a second input field called AMT2-IN and place the difference in an output field called AMT-OUT, we code:

```
SUBTRACT AMT1-IN FROM AMT2-IN
    GIVING AMT-OUT.
```

   Assume the input is as follows:

   1–4   Customer number
   6–25 Customer name
   26–30 Invoice number
   31–35 Gross amount xxx.xx
   36–40 Discount amount xxx.xx

   Print an accounts receivable register that contains (a) a heading entitled ACCOUNTS RECEIVABLE REGISTER, and (b) a line for each input record with

   Customer number
   Customer name
   Invoice number
   Balance due (Gross amount − Discount amount)

8

Computing in COBOL: The Arithmetic Verbs

OBJECTIVES

To familiarize you with

1. The ways in which arithmetic may be performed in COBOL.
2. The formats and options available with the arithmetic verbs.

226

I. The Basic Arithmetic Verbs

A. ADD Statement

A simple **ADD** statement has the following two instruction formats.

Format 1
(ADD ... TO)

$$ \underline{ADD} \begin{Bmatrix} \text{identifier-1} \\ \text{literal-1} \end{Bmatrix} \ldots \underline{TO} \text{ identifier-2} \ldots $$

Format 2
(ADD ... GIVING)

$$ \underline{ADD} \begin{Bmatrix} \text{identifier-1} \\ \text{literal-1} \end{Bmatrix} \ldots \underline{GIVING} \text{ identifier-2} \ldots $$

Examples 1–4

1. ADD DEPOSIT TO BALANCE.
2. ADD 15.80 TO TAX.
3. ADD 40, OVERTIME-HOURS
       GIVING TOTAL-HOURS.
4. ADD AMT1, AMT2
       GIVING TOTAL-AMT.

Fields Used in an ADD

The specified **operands** or fields that are added should be numeric when used in an ADD or other arithmetic statement. The computer will not perform an arithmetic operation on a nonnumeric field. Thus, in Examples 1 through 4, all literals are numeric, and it is assumed that all data-names or identifiers, when specified in the DATA DIVISION, have numeric PICTURE clauses.

The Resultant Field in an ADD

The result, or sum, of an ADD operation is always placed in the last field mentioned. The *only* field that is altered as a result of the ADD operation is this last field, which is the one directly following the word TO, when using Format 1, or GIVING, when using Format 2. Thus, in Example 1, the sum of DEPOSIT and BALANCE is placed in BALANCE. DEPOSIT remains unchanged.

In all cases, *the resultant field must be an identifier or data-name.* It cannot be a literal. The statement ADD HOURS-WORKED TO 40, for example, is incorrect. This is because 40, which immediately follows the word TO, would be the resultant field, and resultant fields may not be literals.

When using the TO format in an ADD statement, *all* the data-names and literals are added together, and the result is placed in the last field specified.

Example 5

(5)   ADD HOURS-WORKED TO WEEKLY-HOURS.

The fields HOURS-WORKED and WEEKLY-HOURS are added together. The sum is placed in WEEKLY-HOURS; HOURS-WORKED remains unchanged.

When using the GIVING format, all fields and literals *preceding* the word GIVING are added together and the sum is placed in the field *following* the word GIVING. Thus, when using the GIVING format, the last data field is *not* part of the ADD operation. Because it is not part of the arithmetic operation, it can be an edit field, that is, a report-item with edit symbols.

Example 6

The same addition is performed as in Example 5: HOURS-WORKED and WEEKLY-HOURS are summed. In this case, however, the result is placed in TOTAL-HOURS. The original contents of TOTAL-HOURS do not in any way affect the arithmetic operation. TOTAL-HOURS may contain a decimal point and a dollar sign if it is to be printed.

Keep in mind that the data-names specified in any arithmetic statement must be defined in the DATA DIVISION. They may appear in an input or output area of the FILE SECTION, or in the WORKING-STORAGE SECTION.

The COBOL words TO and GIVING may *not* be used in the same ADD operation for COBOL 74 users. To say ADD TAX TO NET GIVING TOTAL, then, is incorrect unless you are using a COBOL 85 compiler. With COBOL 74 you may code ADD TAX TO NET, in which case the result is placed in NET; or you may code ADD TAX NET GIVING TOTAL, in which case the result is placed in TOTAL.

Thus Format 2 for the ADD instruction with COBOL 85 is

$$\underline{\text{ADD}} \begin{Bmatrix} \text{identifier-1} \\ \text{literal-1} \end{Bmatrix} \ldots \text{TO} \begin{Bmatrix} \text{identifier-2} \\ \text{literal-2} \end{Bmatrix}$$
$$\underline{\text{GIVING}} \text{ identifier-3} \ldots$$

Commas may be used to separate operands, but they are optional. Thus ADD HOURS-WORKED, WEEKLY-HOURS GIVING TOTAL-HOURS is a correct statement.

Deciding Which Format to Use

A rule-of-thumb to follow when using an ADD statement is to use the GIVING format when the contents of operands are to be retained. When you will no longer need the original contents of an operand after the addition, the TO format may be used.

Let us review some rules for interpreting instruction formats that will help in evaluating Formats 1 and 2 of the ADD statement just specified.

INTERPRETING FORMATS

1. Underlined words are required.
2. Capitalized words are COBOL reserved words.
3. The word "identifier" means a field or record in storage.
4. The braces { } mean that one of the enclosed words is required.
5. The ellipses or dots (. . .) indicate that *two or more fields or literals* may be specified.

Adding More Than Two Fields

As you can see from the instruction formats, we are not restricted to two operands when using an ADD operation.

Example 7

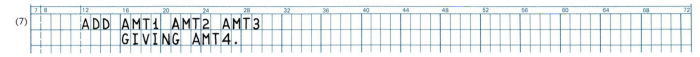

	AMT1	AMT2	AMT3	AMT4
Before the ADD:	2	4	6	15
After the ADD:	2	4	6	12

Note that the original contents of AMT4, the resultant field, are destroyed and have no effect on the ADD operation. The three operands AMT1, AMT2, and AMT3 are unchanged.

Example 8

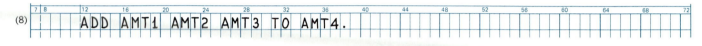

	AMT1	AMT2	AMT3	AMT4
Before operation:	2	4	6	15
After operation:	2	4	6	27

AMT1, AMT2, and AMT3 are added to the original contents of AMT4. The result is again placed in AMT4, whereas the other three fields remain the same.

Producing More Than One Sum

It is also possible to perform *several* ADD operations with a single statement, using the TO format. That is, the following is a valid statement.

```
ADD AMT1 AMT2 TO TOTAL1
                TOTAL2.
```

This results in the same series of operations as:

```
ADD AMT1 AMT2 TO TOTAL1.
ADD AMT1 AMT2 TO TOTAL2.
```

The rules specified thus far for addition are as follows:

RULES FOR ADDITION

1. All literals and fields that are part of the addition must be numeric. After the word GIVING, however, the field may be a report-item.

2. The resultant field, following the word TO or the word GIVING, must be a data-name and may not be a literal.

3. When using the TO format, the data-name following the word TO is the receiving field. This receiving field is part of the ADD; that is, its initial contents are summed along with the other fields. The receiving field must be numeric when using this format.

4. When using the GIVING format, the data-name following the word GIVING is the receiving field. It will contain the sum, but its original contents will not be part of the ADD. It may be either a numeric field or a field that contains edit symbols such as a $ or a decimal point.

5. The words TO and GIVING may be specified in the same statement, but only if you are using a COBOL 85 compiler.

Self-Test   Indicate the errors, if any, in Statements 1 and 2.

1. ADD '12' TO TOTAL.
2. ADD TAX TO TOTAL
      GIVING AMT.
3. If ADD 1, 15, 3 TO COUNTER is performed and COUNTER is initialized at 10, the sum of ___(no.)___ will be placed in _____ at the end of the operation.
4. Without using the word TO, write a statement equivalent to the one in Question 3.
5. If ADD 1, 15, 3 GIVING COUNTER is performed, ___(no.)___ will be the result in _____ .

Solutions   1. '12' is not a numeric literal.
2. For COBOL 74, the words TO and GIVING may not appear in the same ADD statement; for COBOL 85, the statement is okay.
3. 29; COUNTER
4. ADD 1, 15, 3, COUNTER GIVING WS-AREA1. In this case, the result is placed in WS-AREA1 and COUNTER remains unchanged. The arithmetic is, however, the same as in the previous problem.
5. 19; COUNTER

B. SUBTRACT **Statement**

The **SUBTRACT** operation has the following two instruction formats.

Format 1

$$\underline{\text{SUBTRACT}} \left\{ \begin{array}{l} \text{identifier-1} \\ \text{literal-1} \end{array} \right\} \ldots \underline{\text{FROM}} \text{ identifier-2} \ldots$$

Format 2

$$\underline{\text{SUBTRACT}} \left\{ \begin{array}{l} \text{identifier-1} \\ \text{literal-1} \end{array} \right\} \ldots \underline{\text{FROM}} \left\{ \begin{array}{l} \text{identifier-2} \\ \text{literal-2} \end{array} \right\}$$
$$\underline{\text{GIVING}} \text{ identifier-3} \ldots$$

Rules for Interpreting the Instruction Format
1. Notice the placement of ellipses or dots in Format 1. The first set after identifier-1 means that two or more operands may be subtracted from identifier-2. In addition, operands may be subtracted from identifier-3, identifier-4, and so on.
2. With Format 2, any number of identifiers can follow the word GIVING, but after the word FROM only one identifier or literal is permitted.

Examples 1–4
1. SUBTRACT CHECK-AMOUNT FROM BALANCE.
2. SUBTRACT CHECK-AMOUNT SERVICE-CHARGE FROM OLD-BALANCE
      GIVING NEW-BALANCE.
3. SUBTRACT TAX FROM GROSS-PAY-IN
      GIVING NET-PAY-OUT.
4. SUBTRACT TAX FICA INSUR-PREM FROM GROSS-PAY-IN
      GIVING NET-PAY-OUT.

The rules for a SUBTRACT are similar to those for an ADD.

RULES FOR SUBTRACTION

1. All literals and data-names that are part of the subtraction must be numeric; after the word GIVING, however, the field specified may be a report-item.
2. The receiving field, which is the one that will hold the result, must be a data-name and *not* a literal.
   The following statement is incorrect: SUBTRACT TAX FROM 100.00. If you want to subtract a quantity from a literal (e.g., 100.00), you *must* use the GIVING format: SUBTRACT TAX FROM 100.00 GIVING NET.
3. All fields and literals preceding the word FROM will be added together and the sum subtracted from the field following the word FROM. The result, or difference, will be placed in this same field if no GIVING option is used. All other fields will remain unchanged.
4. When using the GIVING option, the operation performed is the same as in Rule 3, but the answer, or difference, is placed in the field following the word GIVING. The initial contents of the resultant field following the word GIVING do *not* take part in the arithmetic operation.

Example 5

```
(5)    SUBTRACT 15.40 TAX TOTAL FROM AMT.
```

	TAX	TOTAL	AMT
Before the SUBTRACT:	30∧00	10∧00	100∧00
After the SUBTRACT:	30∧00	10∧00	044∧60

Example 6

```
(6)    SUBTRACT 15.40 TAX TOTAL FROM AMT
          GIVING NET.
```

	TAX	TOTAL	AMT	NET
Before the SUBTRACT:	30∧00	10∧00	100∧00	87∧00
After the SUBTRACT:	30∧00	10∧00	100∧00	44∧60

Examples 5 and 6 produce the same result but in different storage areas. In Example 6, the original contents of NET are destroyed and do *not* affect the calculation.

Deciding Which Format to Use

As a rule, when the contents of an operand are not needed after the SUBTRACT operation, Format 1 may be used. When the contents of all operands are to be retained, use Format 2.

As in ADD operations, all commas are optional and are only used for clarity. A space must, however, follow each comma.

As noted, it is possible to perform several SUBTRACT operations with a single statement using Format 1. That is, the following is a valid statement.

```
SUBTRACT AMT1 AMT2 AMT3
    FROM TOTAL1
         TOTAL2
         TOTAL3.
```

The preceding results in the same series of operations as:

```
SUBTRACT AMT1 AMT2 AMT3 FROM TOTAL1.
SUBTRACT AMT1 AMT2 AMT3 FROM TOTAL2.
SUBTRACT AMT1 AMT2 AMT3 FROM TOTAL3.
```

Self-Test

1. In the operation SUBTRACT 1500 FROM GROSS GIVING NET, the result, or difference, is placed in _____ . The original contents of GROSS _____ . If GROSS has an original value of 8500, and NET has an original value of 2000, the result in NET would be _____ .

What is wrong with Statements 2 and 3?

2. SUBTRACT $23.00 FROM AMOUNT.
3. SUBTRACT AMT FROM 900.00.
4. Change the statement in Question 3 to make it valid.
5. Use one SUBTRACT statement to subtract three fields (TAX, CREDIT, DISCOUNT) from TOTAL and place the answer in WS-AMT.

Solutions

1. NET; remains unchanged; 7000 (The original 2000 in NET does not enter into the calculation.)
2. $23.00 is an invalid numeric literal—numeric literals may not contain dollar signs.
3. The resultant field of a SUBTRACT operation may not be a literal.
4. SUBTRACT AMT FROM 900.00 GIVING TOTAL.
5. SUBTRACT TAX CREDIT DISCOUNT FROM TOTAL GIVING WS-AMT.

C. MULTIPLY and DIVIDE Statements

1. Basic Instruction Format

Because of their similarities, the MULTIPLY and DIVIDE statements are discussed together.

The **MULTIPLY** statement has the following instruction formats.

Format 1

$$\text{MULTIPLY} \begin{Bmatrix} \text{identifier-1} \\ \text{literal-1} \end{Bmatrix} \text{BY identifier-2} \ldots$$

Format 2

$$\text{MULTIPLY} \begin{Bmatrix} \text{identifier-1} \\ \text{literal-1} \end{Bmatrix} \text{BY} \begin{Bmatrix} \text{identifier-2} \\ \text{literal-2} \end{Bmatrix}$$
$$\text{GIVING identifier-3} \ldots$$

Examples

1. MULTIPLY HOURS-WORKED BY HOURLY-RATE.
2. MULTIPLY QTY BY PRICE.
3. MULTIPLY 1080 BY NO-OF-EXEMPTIONS
      GIVING EXEMPTION-AMT.
4. MULTIPLY 60 BY HOURS
      GIVING MINUTES.

The **DIVIDE** statement has the following instruction formats.

Format 1

$$\underline{\mathtt{DIVIDE}} \begin{Bmatrix} \text{identifier-1} \\ \text{literal-1} \end{Bmatrix} \underline{\mathtt{INTO}} \ \text{identifier-2} \dots$$

Format 2

$$\underline{\mathtt{DIVIDE}} \begin{Bmatrix} \text{identifier-1} \\ \text{literal-1} \end{Bmatrix} \underline{\mathtt{INTO}} \begin{Bmatrix} \text{identifier-2} \\ \text{literal-2} \end{Bmatrix}$$
$$\underline{\mathtt{GIVING}} \ \text{identifier-3} \dots$$

Format 3

$$\underline{\mathtt{DIVIDE}} \begin{Bmatrix} \text{identifier-1} \\ \text{literal-1} \end{Bmatrix} \underline{\mathtt{BY}} \begin{Bmatrix} \text{identifier-2} \\ \text{literal-2} \end{Bmatrix}$$
$$\underline{\mathtt{GIVING}} \ \text{identifier-3} \dots$$

Either the word INTO or BY may be used with a DIVIDE statement. The GIVING clause is optional with INTO but required with BY.

Examples

```
1. DIVIDE HOURS BY 60
      GIVING MINUTES.
2. DIVIDE 60 INTO HOURS
      GIVING MINUTES.
3. DIVIDE 12 INTO ANN-SAL-IN
      GIVING MONTHLY-SAL-OUT.
4. DIVIDE ANN-SAL-IN BY 12
      GIVING MONTHLY-SAL-OUT.
```

Notice that all arithmetic statements may have a GIVING clause. When the contents of the operands are to be retained during an arithmetic operation, use the GIVING option. If operands need not be retained and are large enough to store the answer, the GIVING option is not required. In either case, the resultant field must always be a data-name or identifier and *never* a literal.

All arithmetic operations can have more than one resultant field. Although ADD and SUBTRACT instructions can operate on numerous fields, the MULTI-PLY and DIVIDE instructions are limited in the number of operations performed. For example, suppose we wish to obtain the product of PRICE x QTY x DISCOUNT. *Two* operations would be used to obtain the desired product: (1) MULTIPLY PRICE BY QTY. The result, or product, is placed in QTY. Then, (2) MULTIPLY QTY BY DISCOUNT. The product of the three numbers is now in DISCOUNT. Hence, with each MULTIPLY or DIVIDE statement specified, *only two operands* can be multiplied or divided.

One operand can, however, be multiplied by numerous fields.

Example

Find PRICE x QTY1 and PRICE x QTY2

Coding MULTIPLY PRICE BY QTY1, QTY2.

This is equivalent to the following two statements.

```
MULTIPLY PRICE BY QTY1.
MULTIPLY PRICE BY QTY2.
```

The preposition used with the MULTIPLY verb is always BY. To say MULTIPLY PRICE TIMES QTY is incorrect. In the DIVIDE operation, the preposition is either BY or INTO. To say DIVIDE QTY INTO TOTAL places in the resultant field, TOTAL, the quotient of TOTAL divided by QTY. Note that the following two operations produce the same results.

   1. DIVIDE 6 BY 3
       GIVING AMT.

   2. DIVIDE 3 INTO 6
       GIVING AMT.

In both cases, the result in AMT will be 6/3 or 2.

Note that the following two statements produce the same results.

   1. DIVIDE 3 BY AMT
       GIVING AMT.

   2. DIVIDE 3 BY AMT.

2. Examples of Arithmetic Operations

Let us now use these arithmetic rules to perform some operations. Assume that all fields used in the following examples have the proper numeric PICTURE clauses. Keep in mind that the solution indicated for each example is only *one* method for solving the problem.

Example 1   Celsius temperatures are to be converted to Fahrenheit temperatures according to the following formula.

$$F = (9 / 5) C + 32$$

C is a field in the input area, and F is a field in the output area. Both have numeric PICTURE clauses in the DATA DIVISION.

One solution may be specified as follows:

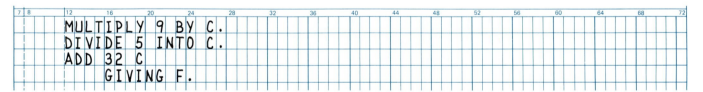

```
MULTIPLY 9 BY C.
DIVIDE 5 INTO C.
ADD 32 C
    GIVING F.
```

If C had an initial value of 20, its value at the end of the operation would be 36 [i.e., (9 * C) / 5] and F would be equal to 68 (36 + 32).

You may have realized that 9/5 C = 1.8 C. Thus, the preceding solution may be reduced to two steps:

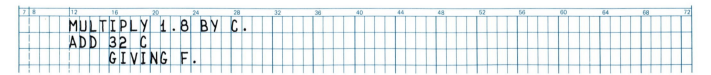

```
MULTIPLY 1.8 BY C.
ADD 32 C
    GIVING F.
```

Example 2   Compute the average of three fields: EXAM1, EXAM2, EXAM3. Place the answer in AVERAGE, and do not alter the contents of the three fields.

One solution may be specified as follows:

```
ADD EXAM1 EXAM2 EXAM3
    GIVING AVERAGE.
DIVIDE 3 INTO AVERAGE.
```

Example 3 Find C = A² + B². Again, it is assumed that A, B, and C are fields defined in the DATA DIVISION.

Solution

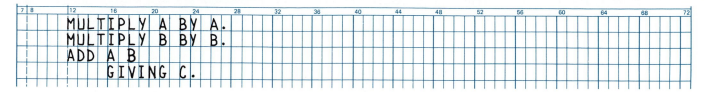

```
MULTIPLY A BY A.
MULTIPLY B BY B.
ADD A B
     GIVING C.
```

Note that to multiply A by itself places A × A or A² in the field called A.

Observe that the following is *not* a correct solution:

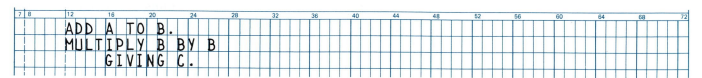

```
ADD A TO B.
MULTIPLY B BY B
     GIVING C.
```

The initial ADD operation places in B the sum of A + B. The multiplication would then result in the product of (A + B) × (A + B), which is $(A + B)^2$, *not* $A^2 + B^2$. If A = 2 and B = 3, the result in C should be $2^2 + 3^2 = 4 + 9 = 13$. You will find that the preceding coding places the value 25 in C, which is $(2 + 3)^2$.

3. Use of the REMAINDER Clause in the DIVIDE Operation

When performing a division operation, the result will be placed in the receiving field according to the specifications of that field. Consider the following:

Example 4

```
DIVIDE 130 BY 40
    GIVING WS-TOTAL.
```

WS-TOTAL has a PICTURE of 99.

Result: 03 is placed in WS-TOTAL:

```
      3
40 | 130
   -120
     10  ◄──── Remainder
```

It is sometimes useful to store the remainder of a division operation for additional processing. The DIVIDE operation can be used for this purpose by including a **REMAINDER** clause.

Additional Instruction Formats for the DIVIDE Statement

Format 4

$$\underline{DIVIDE} \begin{Bmatrix} \text{identifier-1} \\ \text{literal-1} \end{Bmatrix} \underline{INTO} \begin{Bmatrix} \text{identifier-2} \\ \text{literal-2} \end{Bmatrix} \underline{GIVING} \text{ identifier-3}$$

$$\underline{REMAINDER} \text{ identifier-4}$$

Format 5

$$\underline{DIVIDE} \begin{Bmatrix} \text{identifier-1} \\ \text{literal-1} \end{Bmatrix} \underline{BY} \begin{Bmatrix} \text{identifier-2} \\ \text{literal-2} \end{Bmatrix} \underline{GIVING} \text{ identifier-3}$$

$$\underline{REMAINDER} \text{ identifier-4}$$

To retain the remainder for future processing in the preceding example, we have:

```
WORKING-STORAGE SECTION.
01   WORK-AREAS.
        05   WS-REMAINDER        PIC 99.
        05   WS-TOTAL            PIC 99.
            .
            .
    *
    PROCEDURE DIVISION.
        .
        .
        DIVIDE 130 BY 40
            GIVING WS-TOTAL
                REMAINDER WS-REMAINDER.
```

The use of the REMAINDER clause is optional; including it does *not change*, in any way, the results of the original divide operation. We may use the RE-MAINDER clause, for example, to determine if a DIVIDE operation produces a quotient with no remainder at all. That is, we could test the REMAINDER field to see if it is zero.

Table 8.1 summarizes the arithmetic operations we have discussed.

Arithmetic Statement	Value *After* Execution of the Statement			
	A	B	C	D
1. ADD A TO B	A	A + B		
2. ADD A, B, C TO D	A	B	C	A + B + C + D
3. ADD A, B, C GIVING D	A	B	C	A + B + C
4. ADD A TO B, C	A	A + B	A + C	
5. SUBTRACT A FROM B	A	(B - A)		
6. SUBTRACT A, B FROM C	A	B	[C - (A + B)]	
7. SUBTRACT A, B FROM C GIVING D	A	B	C	C - (A + B)
8. MULTIPLY A BY B	A	(A X B)		
9. MULTIPLY A BY B GIVING C	A	B	A X B	
10. DIVIDE A INTO B	A	(B/A)		
11. DIVIDE A INTO B GIVING C	A	B	(B/A)	
12. DIVIDE A BY B GIVING C	A	B	(A/B)	
13. DIVIDE A INTO B GIVING C REMAINDER D	A	B	$\left(\begin{matrix}\text{Integer Value}\\\text{of B/A}\end{matrix}\right)$	$\left(\begin{matrix}\text{Integer}\\\text{Remainder}\end{matrix}\right)$

Table 8.1
Summary of How Arithmetic
Operations Are Performed

Self-Test   1.   DISTANCE is the distance traveled in a specific car trip, and GAS is the number of gallons of gas used. Calculate the average gas mileage and place it in a field called AVERAGE.

2.   Using MULTIPLY and DIVIDE verbs, compute: (C / B + E / F) × S.

What, if anything, is wrong with the following three statements?

3.   DIVIDE -35 INTO A.

```
4.  MULTIPLY A TIMES B
        GIVING C.
5.  MULTIPLY A BY B BY C
        GIVING D.
```

Solutions
```
1.  DIVIDE DISTANCE BY GAS
        GIVING AVERAGE.
2.  DIVIDE B INTO C.
    DIVIDE F INTO E.
    ADD C E
        GIVING WS-HOLD-AREA.
    MULTIPLY WS-HOLD-AREA BY S
        GIVING ANS.
```
3. Nothing wrong (Negative numbers may be used as literals.)
4. The preposition must be BY in the MULTIPLY operation.
5. Only two operands may be multiplied together with one MULTIPLY verb.

II. Options Available with Arithmetic Verbs

A. ROUNDED **Option**

Consider the following example:

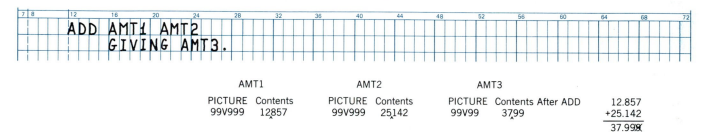

AMT1		AMT2		AMT3		
PICTURE	Contents	PICTURE	Contents	PICTURE	Contents After ADD	12.857
99V999	12857	99V999	25142	99V99	3799	+25.142
						37.999

Performing arithmetic operations on fields that have different numbers of decimal positions is not uncommon in programming. In the preceding example, two fields, each with three decimal positions, are added together, and the answer desired is only accurate to two decimal places. The computer adds the two fields AMT1 and AMT2, with the sum 37∧999 placed in an accumulator. It attempts to move this result into AMT3, a field with only two decimal positions. The effect is the same as performing the following MOVE operation: MOVE 37.999 TO AMT3. The low-order decimal position is truncated. Thus, AMT3 is replaced with 37∧99.

A more desirable result would be 38∧00 since 38 is closer to the sum of 37.999 than is 37.99. Generally, we consider results more accurate if they are **rounded** to the nearest decimal position.

To obtain rounded results, the ROUNDED option may be specified with any arithmetic statement. In all cases, it directly follows the resultant data-name. The following examples serve as illustrations.

Examples 1–6
```
1.  ADD AMT1 TO AMT2 ROUNDED.
2.  SUBTRACT DISCOUNT FROM TOTAL ROUNDED.
3.  MULTIPLY QTY BY PRICE ROUNDED.
4.  DIVIDE UNITS-OF-ITEM INTO TOTAL ROUNDED.
```

```
5. ADD AMT1 AMT2
        GIVING TOTAL1 ROUNDED.
6. ADD AMT1 AMT2
        GIVING TOTAL1 ROUNDED
            TOTAL2 ROUNDED.
```

If AMT1 and AMT2 had contents of 12.8576 and 25.142 in Examples 5 and 6, and TOTAL1 had a PIC of 99V99, the computer would round the answer to 38ₐ00.

How Rounding Is Accomplished

ROUNDED is optional with all arithmetic operations. If the ROUNDED option is not specified, truncation of decimal positions will occur if the resultant field cannot accommodate all the decimal positions in the answer. With the ROUNDED option, the computer will always round the result to the PICTURE specification of the receiving field. Consider the following example:

Example 7

	DISCOUNT			TOTAL			AMT	
	PICTURE	*Contents*		PICTURE	*Contents*		PICTURE	*Contents*
	99V99	87ₐ23		99V99	99ₐ98		99	00

In this case, 87.23 is subtracted from 99.98 and the result, 12.75, is placed in an accumulator. The computer moves this result to AMT. Since AMT has no decimal positions, truncation occurs and 12 is placed in AMT.

Now consider the following SUBTRACT operation:

In this case, 12.75 is rounded to the PICTURE specification of the receiving field; that is, rounding to the nearest integer position will occur. 12.75 rounded to the nearest integer is 13, and thus, 13 is placed in AMT. In actuality, .5 is added to 12.75 producing 13.25, which is then truncated to an integer:

$$
\begin{array}{r}
12.75 \\
+ \quad .5 \\
\hline
13.25
\end{array}
$$

If ROUNDED and REMAINDER are to be used in the same DIVIDE statement, ROUNDED must appear first.

Format

```
DIVIDE    ...
    [ROUNDED] [REMAINDER identifier]
```

B. ON SIZE ERROR **Option**

Let us suppose that the following operation was performed:

Before the operation, the fields contained the following:

AMT1		AMT2		AMT3	
PICTURE	*Contents*	PICTURE	*Contents*	PICTURE	*Contents*
999	800	999	150	999	050

The computer will add 800, 150, and 050 in an accumulator. It will attempt to place the sum, 1000, into AMT3, which is a three-position field. The effect would be the same as a MOVE operation: MOVE 1000 TO AMT3. Since numeric MOVE operations move integer data from right to left, 000 will be placed in AMT3. In this case, the resultant field is not large enough to store the accumulated sum. We say that an **overflow** or size error condition has occurred.

Note that an overflow condition can cause unpredictable results. The computer will not generally stop or abort the run because of a size error condition; instead, it will truncate high-order or leftmost positions of the field. In our example, 000 will be placed in AMT3.

Avoiding Size Errors

The best way to avoid a size error condition is to be absolutely certain that the receiving field is large enough to accommodate any possible result. Sometimes, however, the programmer forgets to account for the rare occasion when an overflow might occur. COBOL has a built-in solution. Use an **ON SIZE ERROR** clause with any arithmetic operation as follows:

Format

> arithmetic statement
> [ON SIZE ERROR imperative statement . . .]

The word ON is optional; hence it is not underlined. By an **imperative statement,** we mean any COBOL statement that gives a direct command and does not perform a test. Statements beginning with the COBOL word IF are conditional statements and are not considered imperative. This concept will become clearer in the next chapter when we discuss conditional statements.

Coding Guideline

Since ON SIZE ERROR is a separate clause, we place it on a separate line for ease of reading and debugging.

Examples 1–2

```
1. ADD AMT1 AMT2 TO TOTAL-OUT
      ON SIZE ERROR MOVE ZERO TO AMT3.
2. DIVIDE 60 INTO HOURS
      ON SIZE ERROR MOVE 'INVALID DIVIDE' TO ERROR-MESSAGE.
```

How ON SIZE ERROR **Works**

The computer performs the arithmetic and ignores the SIZE ERROR clause if there is no size error condition. If a size error occurs, the computer does *not* perform the arithmetic but instead executes the statement(s) in the SIZE ER-ROR clause. In Example 1, the computer will move zeros to AMT3 and leave TOTAL-OUT unchanged only if AMT3 does not contain enough integer positions to accommodate the sum of AMT1, AMT2, and TOTAL-OUT. If TOTAL-OUT is large enough for the result, zeros will *not* be moved to AMT3 and execution will continue with the next statement.

Dividing by Zero Causes a SIZE ERROR

A size error, then, is a condition in which the receiving field does not have enough *integer* positions to hold the result of an arithmetic operation. In a divide, the size error condition has additional significance. If an attempt is made to *divide by zero*, a size error condition will occur. This is because division by zero yields a result of infinity, which makes it impossible to define a sufficiently large receiving field.

Consider the following:

Example 3

```
DIVIDE QTY INTO TOTAL
     ON SIZE ERROR MOVE ZERO TO TOTAL.
```

Assume that the fields contain the following data before the operation.

QTY		TOTAL	
PICTURE	*Contents*	PICTURE	*Contents*
9999	0000	99	10

A size error occurs during the DIVIDE operation because QTY = 0. When the SIZE ERROR clause is executed, TOTAL is set equal to 0. If a SIZE ERROR clause were not specified, the computer would attempt to divide by zero, an impossible feat. The result of such a division would be unpredictable or may even cause an abend. When you specify ON SIZE ERROR, the computer will make certain that the divisor is *not* zero before attempting to DIVIDE. You will see in the next chapter that you may also avoid errors by coding:

```
IF  QTY IS NOT ZERO
      DIVIDE QTY INTO TOTAL
ELSE
      MOVE 0 TO TOTAL.
```

If the ON SIZE ERROR option is employed along with the ROUNDED option, the word ROUNDED always precedes ON SIZE ERROR:

Format

> arithmetic statement
> [ROUNDED] [ON SIZE ERROR imperative statement . . .]

When using a REMAINDER in a DIVIDE operation, we would have the following sequence of clauses.

Format

> DIVIDE . . . [ROUNDED] [REMAINDER identifier]
> [ON SIZE ERROR imperative statement . . .]

The ON SIZE ERROR clause functions like a selection structure. It can therefore be flowcharted as:

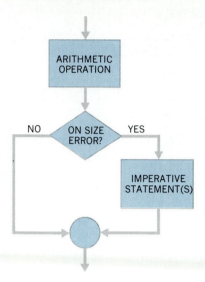

With COBOL 85, another permissible test that may be used with any arithmetic operation is NOT ON SIZE ERROR.

Example

```
ADD AMT1 AMT2
    GIVING TOTAL-AMT
    NOT ON SIZE ERROR
        PERFORM 300-WRITE-RTN.
```

300-WRITE-RTN is executed only if the ADD operation results in a valid addition, that is, only if TOTAL-AMT is large enough to hold the sum of AMT1 and AMT2.

With COBOL 85, *both* ON SIZE ERROR *and* NOT ON SIZE ERROR can be specified with any arithmetic operation.

C. Scope Terminators

Consider the following coding.

```
ADD AMT TO TOTAL
    ON SIZE ERROR PERFORM ERROR-RTN
WRITE OUT-REC.
```

Suppose we intend to perform an error routine if an overflow occurs. In the next sentence, we wish to write a record. To accomplish this, a period should have been included on the second line of the program excerpt. When ON SIZE ERROR is used and an overflow occurs, the computer will execute all statements following the words ON SIZE ERROR *until a period is reached.* Because there is no period until *after* the WRITE statement, the computer assumes that *both* the PERFORM and the WRITE are to be executed *only if an overflow occurs.* Thus, even though the WRITE is not indented, it is treated as part of the ON SIZE ERROR clause.

There are *two* ways to avoid this logic error.

1. Be very careful about the placement of periods.

```
ADD AMT TO TOTAL
    ON SIZE ERROR PERFORM ERROR-RTN.
WRITE OUT-REC.
```

2. Use a *scope terminator* to delimit the end of an arithmetic statement. In the following, END-ADD marks the end of the operation.

```
ADD AMT TO TOTAL
    ON SIZE ERROR PERFORM ERROR-RTN
END-ADD
WRITE OUT-REC.
```

Because END-ADD delimits the ADD, a period is not required after the PERFORM. All arithmetic verbs have scope terminators: END-ADD, END-SUBTRACT, END-MULTIPLY, END-DIVIDE.

Note that scope terminators are only available with COBOL 85.

D. Determining the Size of Receiving Fields

When performing arithmetic, you must make certain that the receiving field is large enough to accommodate the result. In an ADD, determine the largest quantity that can be stored in each field and manually perform an addition. Use the result to determine how large to make the receiving field. With a subtract, manually subtract the smallest possible number from the largest possible number to determine how large to make the receiving field.

As a general rule, the number of integer positions in the receiving field of a MULTIPLY operation should be equal to the *sum* of the integers of the operands being multiplied. Suppose we code MULTIPLY QTY BY PRICE GIVING TOTAL. If QTY has a PIC of 99 and PRICE has a PIC of 999, then to ensure that TOTAL is large enough to accommodate the result it should have a PIC of 9(5), which is the sum of two integers in QTY plus three integers in PRICE. The number of decimal positions in the receiving field will depend on the decimal precision desired in the result. We will discuss this sizing issue in more depth later on.

For DIVIDE operations, the PIC clause of the quotient or receiving field is dependent on the type of divide. Consider the following:

```
DIVIDE TOTAL-PRICE BY QTY
    GIVING UNIT-COST.
```

If TOTAL-PRICE and QTY have PIC 9, the receiving field may have PIC 9V99 or 9V9, to allow for fractional results (e.g., 3/6 = .5). But suppose TOTAL-PRICE has PIC 9V9 and contents of 9$_\wedge$0, and QTY has the same PIC clause with contents of .1. The result of the divide is 9/.1, which is equal to 90. Hence UNIT-COST would need a PIC of 99. As a rule, determine the range of values that the fields can have and establish the PIC clause of the receiving field accordingly.

Examples to Help Determine the Size of a Resultant Field

Arithmetic Operation	Example		A General Rule-of-Thumb
1. Addition of two operands	999 +999 1998	PIC 9(3) PIC 9(3) PIC 9(4)	Resultant field should be one position larger than the largest field being added.

2. Subtraction (assuming positive numbers)	$\begin{array}{r}999\\ -\quad 1\\ \hline 998\end{array}$	PIC 9(3) PIC 9 PIC 9(3)	Resultant field should be as large as the minuend (field being subtracted from) if a smaller number is subtracted from a larger number.
3. Multiplication	$\begin{array}{r}999\\ \times\,999\\ \hline 998001\end{array}$	PIC S9(3) PIC S9(3) PIC S9(6)	Resultant field size should equal the sum of the lengths of the operands being multiplied.

4. Division	$\begin{array}{r}9990\\ .1\,\overline{\smash{\big)}\,999}\end{array}$	Dividend:
		  PIC 9(3)
		Divisor:
		  PIC V9
		Quotient (result):
		  PIC 9(4)
			To be safe, the resultant field size should equal the sum of the number of digits in the divisor and dividend.

Self-Test   State the result in the following cases.

		A		B		C		D	
	PIC	Contents	PIC	Contents	PIC	Contents	PIC	Contents
1. SUBTRACT A B FROM C GIVING D	99V9	12∧3	99V9	45∧6	999V9	156∧8	999	—
2. DIVIDE A INTO B GIVING C	9V9	5∧1	9V9	8∧0	9	—		
3. DIVIDE A INTO B GIVING C ROUNDED	9V9	5∧1	9V9	8∧0	9	—		
4. DIVIDE A INTO B GIVING C ROUNDED REMAINDER D	99	20	99	50	99	—	99	—

5. An ON SIZE ERROR condition occurs when _____ or when _____ .
6. The word ROUNDED (precedes, follows) the ON SIZE ERROR clause in an arithmetic statement.
7. DIVIDE 0 INTO A GIVING B (will, will not) result in an ON SIZE ERROR condition.
8. DIVIDE 0 BY A GIVING B (will, will not) result in an ON SIZE ERROR condition if A = 2.
9. ADD 50, 60 TO FLDA ON SIZE ERROR MOVE 1 TO COUNT results in _____ if FLDA has a PICTURE of 99.
10. ADD 50, 60 TO FLDA ON SIZE ERROR MOVE 1 TO COUNT results in _____ if FLDA has a PICTURE of 999.

Solutions
1. 098
2. 1
3. 2
4. C = 03, D = 10 (*Note:* D is calculated as follows: 50/20 = 2 with a remainder of 10. Rounding of the quotient to 3 occurs afterward.)

5. the resultant field does not have enough integer positions to hold the entire result; an attempt is made to divide by zero

6. precedes

7. will

8. will not (0 divided by any positive number = 0)

9. COUNT = 1, because FLDA is not large enough to be incremented by 110

10. 110 added to FLDA (assuming that the result is less than 1000, i.e., assuming FLDA had contents less than 890 before the ADD operation)

III. The COMPUTE Statement

A. Basic Format

Most business applications operate on large volumes of input and output and require comparatively few numeric calculations. For this type of processing, the four arithmetic verbs just discussed may be adequate.

If complex or extensive arithmetic operations are required in a program, however, the use of the four arithmetic verbs may prove cumbersome. The **COMPUTE** verb provides a more compact method of performing arithmetic.

The COMPUTE statement uses arithmetic symbols rather than arithmetic verbs. The following symbols may be used in a COMPUTE statement:

SYMBOLS USED IN A COMPUTE	
Symbol	**Meaning**
+	ADD
−	SUBTRACT
*	MULTIPLY
/	DIVIDE
**	exponentiation (no corresponding COBOL verb exists)

The following examples illustrate the use of the COMPUTE verb.

Examples 1–3

1. COMPUTE TAX = .05 * AMT.
2. COMPUTE DAILY-SALES = QTY * UNIT-PRICE / 5.
3. COMPUTE NET = AMT - .05 * AMT.

Note that the COMPUTE statement has a data-name or identifier to the left of, or preceding, the equal sign. The value computed in the arithmetic expression to the right of the equal sign *is placed in* the field preceding the equal sign.

Thus, if AMT = 200 in Example 1, TAX will be set to .05 × 200, or 10, at the end of the operation. The original contents of TAX, before the COMPUTE is executed, are not retained. The fields specified to the right of the equal sign remain unchanged.

Example 4

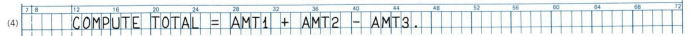

(4) COMPUTE TOTAL = AMT1 + AMT2 - AMT3.

	Contents before operation	Contents after operation
TOTAL	100	95
AMT1	80	80
AMT2	20	20
AMT3	5	5

AMT1, AMT2, and AMT3 remain unchanged after the COMPUTE. TOTAL is set equal to the result of AMT1 + AMT2 − AMT3. The previous contents of TOTAL do not affect the operation. 95 is moved to TOTAL.

The fields specified after the equal sign in a COMPUTE statement may be numeric literals or data-names. Literals need not be defined elsewhere in the program, but fields must be given specifications in the DATA DIVISION. All fields and literals operated on in a COMPUTE statement must be numeric.

The COMPUTE statement may include more than one operation. In Example 2, both multiplication and division operations are performed. The following two statements are equivalent to the single COMPUTE statement in Example 2.

```
MULTIPLY QTY BY UNIT-PRICE
     GIVING DAILY-SALES.
DIVIDE 5 INTO DAILY-SALES.
```

The COMPUTE statement has the advantage of performing more than one arithmetic operation with a single verb. For this reason, it is often less cumbersome to use COMPUTE statements to code complex arithmetic.

Thus ADD, SUBTRACT, MULTIPLY, and DIVIDE correspond to the arithmetic symbols +, −, *, and /, respectively. In addition, we may raise a number to a power with the use of the arithmetic symbol ** in a COMPUTE statement. No COBOL verb corresponds to this operation. Thus COMPUTE B = A ** 2 is identical to multiplying A by A and placing the result in B. A ** 2 is expressed mathematically as A^2. A ** 3 is the same as A^3 or $A \times A \times A$. To find B^4 and place the results in C, we could code: COMPUTE C = B ** 4.

Spacing Rules with a COMPUTE

On most systems, you must follow COBOL rules for spacing when using the COMPUTE statement. That is, arithmetic symbols must be *preceded and followed* by a space. This rule applies to the equal sign as well. Thus, to calculate $A = B + C + D^2$ and place the result in A, we use the following COMPUTE statement:

So far, we have used arithmetic expressions to the right of the equal sign. We may also have literals or data-names as the *only* entry to the right of the equal sign. To say COMPUTE AMT1 = 10.3 is the same as saying MOVE 10.3 TO AMT1. We are placing the literal 10.3 in the AMT1 field. Similarly, to say COMPUTE AMT2 = AMT3 places the contents of AMT3 in the field called AMT2.

This is the same as saying MOVE AMT3 TO AMT2. Thus, in a COMPUTE statement, we may have one of the following three entries after the equal sign.

1. An arithmetic expression. For example,

2. A literal. For example,

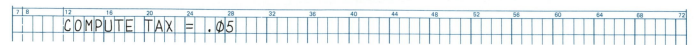

3. A data-name or identifier. For example,

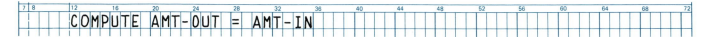

The ROUNDED and ON SIZE ERROR options may be used with the COMPUTE as well. The rules governing the use of these clauses in ADD, SUBTRACT, MULTIPLY, and DIVIDE operations apply to COMPUTE statements as well.

To round the results in a COMPUTE statement to the specifications of the receiving field, we use the ROUNDED option directly following the receiving field. The ON SIZE ERROR clause, if used, is last. The instruction format for the COMPUTE follows:

Format

$$\underline{\text{COMPUTE}} \text{ identifier-1 } [\underline{\text{ROUNDED}}] \ldots = \begin{Bmatrix} \text{arithmetic expression-1} \\ \text{literal-1} \\ \text{identifier-2} \end{Bmatrix}$$

$$[\underline{\text{ON}} \ \underline{\text{SIZE}} \ \underline{\text{ERROR}} \text{ imperative statement-1}]$$

Example 5

a. COMPUTE A = B + C + D
b. COMPUTE A ROUNDED = B + C + D

	B		**C**		**D**
PICTURE	Contents	PICTURE	Contents	PICTURE	Contents
9V99	1$_\wedge$05	9V99	2$_\wedge$10	9V99	6$_\wedge$84

Result in A

	PICTURE	Contents
Example 5(a)—without rounding	99V9	09$_\wedge$9
Example 5(b)—with rounding	99V9	10$_\wedge$0

We test for an arithmetic overflow in a COMPUTE statement with an ON SIZE ERROR clause. A size error occurs if the receiving field lacks enough integer positions for the result. As noted, the SIZE ERROR clause would be the last one in the statement.

With COBOL 85, NOT ON SIZE ERROR may also be used with a COMPUTE statement. If it is used, then it would be the last clause.

END-COMPUTE is also available as a scope terminator to mark the end of a COMPUTE statement.

Example 6

This COMPUTE statement would result in an overflow condition if AMT1 has a PICTURE of 99. The computed result should be 102. To place 102 in AMT1, a two-position numeric field, results in the truncation of the most significant digit, the hundreds position. Thus 02 will be placed in AMT1. To protect against this type of truncation of high-order integer positions, we use an ON SIZE ERROR test as follows:

In summary, the primary advantage of a COMPUTE statement is that several arithmetic operations may be performed with one instruction. The data-name preceding the equal sign is made equal to the literal, identifier, or arithmetic expression to the right of the equal sign. Thus, the following two arithmetic expressions are identical:

```
ADD 1 TO TOTAL.
COMPUTE TOTAL = TOTAL + 1.
```

A COMPUTE statement often requires less coding than if the arithmetic verbs such as ADD or SUBTRACT were used. The expression $C = A^2 + B^2$, for example, is more easily coded with only one COMPUTE statement:

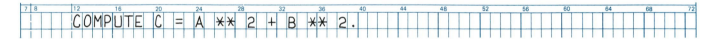

There is no COBOL arithmetic symbol to perform a square root operation. Mathematically, however, the square root of any number is that number raised to the ½ or .5 power. Thus $\sqrt{25} = 25^{.5} = 5$.

Since we cannot use square root symbols in COBOL, the square root of any number will be represented as the number raised to the .5 power.

Formula: $C = \sqrt{A}$

The COBOL equivalent is:

```
COMPUTE C = A ** .5.
```

B. Order of Evaluation

The order in which arithmetic operations are performed will affect the results in a COMPUTE statement. Consider the following example.

Example 7   `COMPUTE UNIT-PRICE = AMT1-IN + AMT2-IN / QTY-IN`

Depending on the order of evaluation of arithmetic operations, one of the following would be the mathematical equivalent of the preceding:

a. $\text{UNIT-PRICE-OUT} = \dfrac{\text{AMT1-IN} + \text{AMT2-IN}}{\text{QTY-IN}}$

b. $\text{UNIT-PRICE-OUT} = \text{AMT1-IN} + \dfrac{\text{AMT2-IN}}{\text{QTY-IN}}$

Note that (a) and (b) are *not* identical. If `AMT1-IN = 3`, `AMT2-IN = 6`, and `QTY-IN = 3`, the result of the `COMPUTE` statement evaluated according to the formula in (a) is 3 [(3 + 6) / 3] but according to the formula in (b) is 5 [3 + (6 / 3)].

The hierarchy of arithmetic operations is as follows:

THE SEQUENCE IN WHICH OPERATIONS ARE PERFORMED IN A `COMPUTE` STATEMENT

1. `**`
2. `*` or `/` (whichever appears first from left to right)
3. `+` or `−` (whichever appears first from left to right)
4. The use of parentheses overrides these rules. That is, operations within parentheses are performed first.

Without parentheses, exponentiation operations are performed first. Multiplication and division operations follow any exponentiation and precede addition or subtraction operations. If there are two or more multiplication or division operations, they are evaluated from left to right in the expression. Addition and subtraction are evaluated last, also from left to right.

Thus, in Example 7, `COMPUTE UNIT-PRICE-OUT = AMT1-IN + AMT2-IN / QTY-IN` is calculated as follows:

1. `AMT2-IN / QTY-IN`
2. `AMT1-IN + (AMT2-IN / QTY-IN)`

The result, then, is that (b) is the mathematical equivalent of the original `COMPUTE` statement.

As another example, `COMPUTE A = C + D ** 2` results in the following order of evaluation.

1. `D ** 2`   Exponentiation
2. `C + (D ** 2)`   Addition

The result, then, is $A = C + D^2$, *not* $A = (C + D)^2$.

The statement, `COMPUTE S = T * D + E / F`, results in the following order of evaluation.

1. `T * D`   Multiplication
2. `E / F`   Division
3. `(T * D) + (E / F)` Addition

The result, then, is:

$$S = T \times D + \frac{E}{F}$$

We may alter the standard order of evaluation in a `COMPUTE` statement with the use of parentheses. Parentheses supersede all hierarchy rules. That is, operations within parentheses are evaluated first.

Suppose we wish to compute `AVERAGE-SALES` by adding `DAYTIME-SALES` and `EVENING-SALES` and dividing the sum by two. The instruction `COMPUTE AVERAGE-SALES = DAYTIME-SALES + EVENING-SALES / 2` is *not* correct. The result of this operation is to compute `AVERAGE-SALES` by adding `DAYTIME-SALES` and one half of `EVENING-SALES`. To divide the sum of `DAYTIME-SALES` and `EVENING-SALES` by two, we must use parentheses to override the standard hierarchy rules.

```
COMPUTE AVERAGE-SALES = (DAYTIME-SALES + EVENING-SALES) / 2
```

All operations within parentheses are evaluated first. Thus we have:

1. (DAYTIME-SALES + EVENING-SALES)

2. (DAYTIME-SALES + EVENING-SALES) / 2

The following will provide additional examples of the hierarchy rules.

Operation	Evaluation
A / B + C	Divide A by B and add C.
A / (B + C)	Add B and C and divide A by the sum.
A + B * C	Multiply B by C and add A.
A * B / C	Multiply A by B and divide the result by C.

Example 8 We wish to obtain NET = GROSS − DISCOUNT, where DISCOUNT = GROSS X .03:

```
COMPUTE NET = GROSS - (.03 * GROSS)
```

In this example, the parentheses are not really needed, since the standard hierarchy rules produce the correct results. Including parentheses for clarity, however, is not incorrect. The following would also be correct:

```
COMPUTE NET = GROSS - .03 * GROSS
```

A simpler method of obtaining the correct result is

```
COMPUTE NET = .97 * GROSS
```

or

```
MULTIPLY GROSS BY .97 GIVING NET
```

C. Comparing the COMPUTE to the Arithmetic Verbs

As we have seen, any calculation can be performed using *either* the four arithmetic verbs or the COMPUTE. Exponentiation, which has no corresponding verb, is more easily handled with a COMPUTE but can be accomplished with a MULTIPLY statement as well.

In general, programs using the four arithmetic verbs tend to be more user-friendly because they are more familiar to users. But these verbs can make a program more cumbersome. On the other hand, the COMPUTE is viewed by some as too mathematical in nature.

A Potential Source of Errors When Using a COMPUTE

Note that the way in which a COMPUTE performs its arithmetic operations varies from compiler to compiler. Consider, for example, the following, where AMT-OUT has PIC 9(3):

```
COMPUTE AMT-OUT ROUNDED = (AMT-IN + 2.55) * 3.6
```

With some compilers, *each arithmetic operation* (in this case, the addition and multiplication) would be calculated to three integer positions (the size of AMT-OUT), whereas other compilers round to three integers only at the end. This means that two different runs of a program that use this COMPUTE could produce different results. This is another reason why some programmers use arithmetic verbs instead of the COMPUTE.

We make no formal recommendation as to which you should use. We believe programmers should make their own decisions unless the organization itself specifies a preference.

IV. Use of Signed Numbers in Arithmetic Operations

A. The Use of S in PIC Clauses for Fields That Can Be Negative

In our illustrations, we have assumed that numbers used in calculations are *positive* and that results of calculations produce positive numbers. If, however, a number may be negative or if a calculation may produce negative results, we must use an S in the PICTURE clause of the field. Thus AMT1 with a PIC of S9(3) is a field that may have positive or negative contents. The S, like an implied decimal point, does not use a storage position; thus, S9(3) represents a *three-position* signed field. If AMT1 with a PIC of S9(3) has an initial value of 010 and we subtract 15 from it, the result will be −5. But if we had defined AMT1 with a PIC of 9(3), then the result would have been incorrectly retained without the sign as 5.

In summary, if a field used in an arithmetic operation may contain a negative number, use an S in the PICTURE clause. Without an S in the PICTURE clause, the field will always be considered positive.

You will see in Chapter 11 that *printing a negative number* requires a minus sign in the PICTURE clause of the receiving field.

```
01   IN-REC.
      .
      .
     05   AMT1-IN          PIC S9(3).
      .
01   OUT-REC.
      .
      .
     05   AMT1-OUT         PIC -9(3).
```

Suppose AMT1-IN has contents of −123. To print −123 correctly when we move AMT1-IN TO AMT1-OUT, the latter should have a PICTURE of -9(3).

B. Rules for Performing Arithmetic with Signed Numbers

The following are rules for performing arithmetic using signed numbers.

I. Multiplication

$$\frac{\begin{array}{r}\text{Multiplicand}\\ \times\ \text{Multiplier}\end{array}}{\text{Product}}$$

A. Product is + if multiplicand and multiplier have the same sign.
B. Product is − if multiplicand and multiplier have different signs.

Examples

$$1.\quad \frac{\begin{array}{r}+\ 5\\ \times\ -\ 3\end{array}}{-15} \qquad 2.\quad \frac{\begin{array}{r}-\ 3\\ \times\ -\ 2\end{array}}{+\ 6}$$

II. Division

$$\text{Divisor}\ \overline{\left)\,\text{Dividend}\right.}^{\ \text{Quotient}}$$

A. Quotient is + if dividend and divisor have the same sign.
B. Quotient is − if dividend and divisor have different signs.

Examples

$$1.\quad -3\ \overline{\left)\,-6\right.}^{\ 2} \qquad 2.\quad -1\ \overline{\left)\,5\right.}^{\ -5}$$

III. Addition
   A. If signs of the fields being added are the same, add and use the sign.

Examples

1. $\begin{array}{r} +\ 15 \\ +\ 10 \\ +\ 20 \\ \hline +\ 45 \end{array}$ 2. $\begin{array}{r} -\ 15 \\ -\ 10 \\ -\ 20 \\ \hline -\ 45 \end{array}$

   B. If signs of the fields being added are different, add all + numbers, and add all − numbers separately. Then subtract smaller total from larger total and use sign of the larger.

Examples

1. $\begin{array}{r} +\ 15 \\ +\ 10 \\ -\ 15 \\ \hline -\ 5 \end{array}$ 2. $\begin{array}{r} +\ 25 \\ -\ 20 \\ \hline +\ 5 \end{array}$

IV. Subtraction

$$\begin{array}{l} \text{Minuend} \\ -\ \text{Subtrahend} \\ \hline \text{Difference} \end{array}$$

Change the sign of the subtrahend and proceed as in addition.

Examples

1. $15 - 5 = 15 + (-5) = +10$
2. $-3 - (+2) = -3 + (-2) = -5$

C. Entering Negative Numbers

Suppose we establish an input field, with one integer, as PIC S9. This is a *one-position field*. How do we enter or key −1, for example, into a one-position field?

The way in which a negative number is entered as input varies from computer to computer. One common method is as follows:

Value	How It Is Entered
−0	}
−1	J
−2	K
−3	L
−4	M
−5	N
−6	O
−7	P
−8	Q
−9	R

Thus, to enter −5 in a one-position field, we would key in the *letter N*.

If a field has two or more integers, a negative value is represented with a letter J–R that is typically entered as the *rightmost* or low-order *digit*. −12, for example, would be entered as 1K; −228 would be entered as 22Q.

To enter a sign as a *separate character*, use the clause:

$$\text{SIGN IS} \begin{Bmatrix} \text{TRAILING} \\ \text{LEADING} \end{Bmatrix} \text{SEPARATE}$$

That is, to enter −1234 in a field with PIC S9(4), code the field as 05 AMT PIC S9(4) SIGN IS LEADING SEPARATE. Similarly, to enter 1234− in a field, code it as 05 AMT PIC S9(4) SIGN IS TRAILING SEPARATE. Note, however, that these SIGN clauses make AMT five positions instead of four.

CODING GUIDELINES FOR ARITHMETIC OPERATIONS

1. Code the GIVING clause, if used, on a separate line.
2. Code the ON SIZE ERROR clause, if used, on a separate line.
3. Leave at least one space between every arithmetic operator (*, /, etc.) and the = sign in a COMPUTE statement.

CHAPTER SUMMARY

(Appendix A has the full format for each arithmetic instruction.)

A. The ADD, SUBTRACT, MULTIPLY, and DIVIDE verbs all have a GIVING format. With this GIVING format, the receiving field is *not* part of the arithmetic and can be a report-item (a field with edit symbols).
B. A COMPUTE can be used for performing multiplication, division, addition, subtraction, exponentiation, or a combination of these.
C. The COMPUTE can save coding effort if used in place of the ADD, SUBTRACT, MULTIPLY, and DIVIDE verbs.
D. The purpose of the COMPUTE is to perform several arithmetic operations with one statement.

OPERATIONS	
+	Addition
−	Subtraction
*	Multiplication
/	Division
**	Exponentiation

E. Order of evaluation: If several operations are performed with one COMPUTE statement, the sequence is as follows:
1. **
2. * or / in sequence left to right
3. + or − in sequence left to right

   Note: Parentheses ( ) override normal hierarchy rules.
F. The ROUNDED and ON SIZE ERROR options can be used with the four arithmetic verbs and with the COMPUTE.

CHAPTER SELF-TEST

Indicate what, if anything, is wrong with the following arithmetic statements (1–5).

```
1. ADD AMT1 TO AMT1-OUT, AMT2-OUT.
2. ADD AMT1 TO AMT2
      GIVING TOTAL.
3. MULTIPLY A BY B BY C.
4. DIVIDE AMT BY 5
      REMAINDER REM-1.
5. SUBTRACT AMT1 AMT2 FROM AMT3 AMT4.
```

6. The word directly following the verb COMPUTE must be a(n) _____ .
7. What, if anything, is wrong with the following COMPUTE statements?
   (a) COMPUTE TOTAL = AMT1 + AMT2 ROUNDED
   (b) COMPUTE AMT-OUT = 10.5
   (c) COMPUTE OVERTIME-PAY = (HOURS - 40.) * 1.5
   (d) COMPUTE E = A * B /* C + D
   (e) COMPUTE X + Y = A
   (f) COMPUTE 3.14 = PI
8. Do the following pairs of operations perform the same function?
   (a) COMPUTE SUM-1 = 0.
       MOVE ZEROS TO SUM-1.
   (b) COMPUTE AMT = AMT - 2.
       SUBTRACT 2 FROM AMT.
   (c) COMPUTE X = A * B - C * D.
       COMPUTE X = (A * B) - (C * D).
   (d) COMPUTE Y = A - B * C - D.
       COMPUTE Y = (A - B) * (C - D).
9. Using a COMPUTE statement, find the average of EXAM1, EXAM2, and EXAM3.
10. Using a COMPUTE statement, find total wages = rate × 40 + (1.5 × rate × overtime hours). *Two* fields are supplied: RATE and HRS-WORKED. Overtime hours are hours worked in excess of 40 hours. (Assume everyone works at least 40 hours.)

Solutions

1. Okay.
2. TO and GIVING in the same statement are only permissible using COBOL 85; ADD AMT1 AMT2 GIVING C is acceptable with all compilers.
3. Cannot have two multiply operations as specified:

```
MULTIPLY A BY B
    GIVING Q.
MULTIPLY Q BY C.
```

4. The GIVING clause must be used when a REMAINDER is specified:

```
DIVIDE AMT BY 5
    GIVING STORE-IT
    REMAINDER REM-1.
```

5. Okay.
6. identifier
7. (a) ROUNDED follows the receiving field: COMPUTE TOTAL ROUNDED = AMT1 + AMT2
   (b) Okay.
   (c) 40. is not a valid numeric literal; numeric literals may not end with a decimal point.
   (d) /* may not appear together; each symbol must be preceded by and followed by an identifier or a numeric literal.
   (e) Arithmetic expressions must follow the equal sign and not precede it: COMPUTE A = X + Y.
   (f) Identifiers, not literals, must follow the word COMPUTE: COMPUTE PI = 3.14.
8. (a) Same.
   (b) Same.
   (c) Same.
   (d) In the first statement, the order of evaluation is A − (B × C) − D; in the second statement, the order is (A − B) × (C − D); Thus, these two are not equivalent.
9. COMPUTE AVERAGE = (EXAM1 + EXAM2 + EXAM3) / 3
10. COMPUTE WAGES = RATE * 40 + 1.5 * RATE * (HRS-WORKED - 40)

PRACTICE PROGRAM

Write a program to create a salary disk file from a tape file. The problem definition is as follows. Since the salary disk file will be printed at a later date, it contains FILLERs between fields.

Systems Flowchart

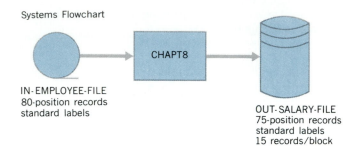

IN-EMPLOYEE-FILE
80-position records
standard labels

CHAPT8

OUT-SALARY-FILE
75-position records
standard labels
15 records/block

IN-EMPLOYEE-FILE Record Layout

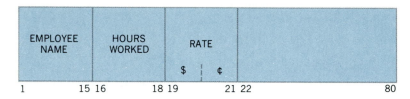

EMPLOYEE NAME	HOURS WORKED	RATE $ ¢	
1 15	16 18	19 21	22 80

OUT-SALARY-FILE Record Layout

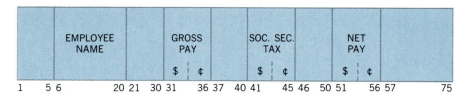

	EMPLOYEE NAME		GROSS PAY $ ¢		SOC. SEC. TAX $ ¢		NET PAY $ ¢	
1 5	6 20	21 30	31 36	37 40	41 45	46 50	51 56	57 75

SAMPLE INPUT DATA		LISTING OF DISK RECORDS CREATED FROM SAMPLE INPUT			
P NEWMAN	050525	P NEWMAN	026250	01876	024374
R REDFORD	040810	R REDFORD	032400	02316	030084
E TAYLOR	035925	E TAYLOR	032375	02314	030061
N STERN	070615	N STERN	043050	03078	039972
K ROGERS	032785	K ROGERS	025120	01796	023324
R STERN	012345	R STERN	004140	00296	003844
C HAMMEL	157577	C HAMMEL	090589	06477	084112
M STERN	070654	M STERN	045780	03273	042507
L STERN	100987	L STERN	098700	07057	091643
S SMITH	097667	S SMITH	064699	04625	060074

(a) Gross pay = Hours worked × Rate

(b) Social security tax = 7.15% of Gross pay

(c) Net pay = Gross pay − Social security tax

Figure 8.1 illustrates the flowchart, pseudocode, and hierarchy chart. Figure 8.2 shows the solution.

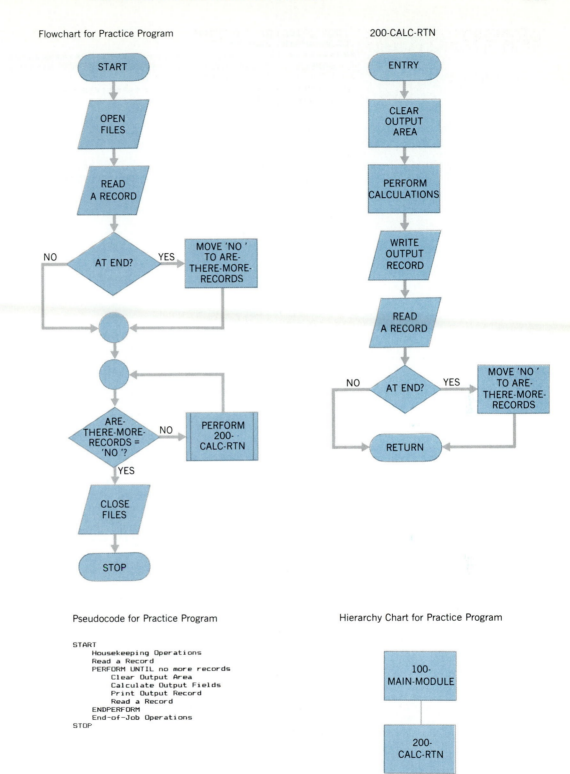

Flowchart for Practice Program

200-CALC-RTN

Pseudocode for Practice Program

```
START
    Housekeeping Operations
    Read a Record
    PERFORM UNTIL no more records
        Clear Output Area
        Calculate Output Fields
        Print Output Record
        Read a Record
    ENDPERFORM
    End-of-Job Operations
STOP
```

Hierarchy Chart for Practice Program

Figure 8.1
Flowchart, pseudocode, and hierarchy chart for Practice Program.

Figure 8.2
Solution to Practice Program.

```
IDENTIFICATION DIVISION.
PROGRAM-ID. SAMPLE.
****************************************************
*  SAMPLE     - COMPUTES AND CREATES FILE CONTAINING*
*               EMPLOYEE SALARY DATA                 *
****************************************************
ENVIRONMENT DIVISION.
CONFIGURATION SECTION.
SOURCE-COMPUTER. IBM-370.
OBJECT-COMPUTER. IBM-370.
INPUT-OUTPUT SECTION.
FILE-CONTROL.
    SELECT IN-EMPLOYEE-FILE ASSIGN TO DATA8.
    SELECT OUT-SALARY-FILE  ASSIGN TO SYS$OUTPUT.
*
DATA DIVISION.
FILE SECTION.
FD  IN-EMPLOYEE-FILE
    LABEL RECORDS ARE STANDARD.
01  IN-EMPLOYEE-REC.
    05  IN-NAME                 PIC X(15).
    05  IN-HOURS                PIC 999.
    05  IN-RATE                 PIC 9V99.
    05  FILLER                  PIC X(59).
FD  OUT-SALARY-FILE
    LABEL RECORDS ARE STANDARD.
01  SALARY-REC-OUT.
    05  FILLER                  PIC X(5).
    05  NAME-OUT                PIC X(15).
    05  FILLER                  PIC X(10).
    05  GROSS-PAY-OUT           PIC 9(4)V99.
    05  FILLER                  PIC X(4).
    05  SOC-SEC-TAX-OUT         PIC 999V99.
    05  FILLER                  PIC X(5).
    05  NET-PAY-OUT             PIC 9(4)V99.
    05  FILLER                  PIC X(19).
WORKING-STORAGE SECTION.
01  WORK-AREAS.
    05 ARE-THERE-MORE-RECORDS  PIC X(3)     VALUE 'YES'.
*
PROCEDURE DIVISION.
****************************************************
*  100-MAIN-MODULE - CONTROLS OPENING AND CLOSING FILES  *
*                    DIRECTION OF PROGRAM LOGIC          *
*                    RETURNS CONTROL TO OPERATING SYSTEM *
****************************************************
100-MAIN-MODULE.
    OPEN INPUT IN-EMPLOYEE-FILE
         OUTPUT OUT-SALARY-FILE.
    READ IN-EMPLOYEE-FILE
        AT END MOVE 'NO ' TO ARE-THERE-MORE-RECORDS.
    PERFORM 200-CALC-RTN
        UNTIL ARE-THERE-MORE-RECORDS = 'NO '.
    CLOSE IN-EMPLOYEE-FILE
          OUT-SALARY-FILE.
    STOP RUN.
****************************************************
*  200-CALC-RTN - PERFORMED FROM 100-MAIN-MODULE       *
*                 COMPUTES SOCIAL SECURITY TAX AND NET PAY  *
*                 WRITES DATA TO FILE AND READS NEXT RECORD *
****************************************************
200-CALC-RTN.
    MOVE SPACES TO SALARY-REC-OUT.
    MOVE IN-NAME TO NAME-OUT.
    MULTIPLY IN-HOURS BY IN-RATE
        GIVING GROSS-PAY-OUT.
    MULTIPLY .0715 BY GROSS-PAY-OUT
        GIVING SOC-SEC-TAX-OUT.
    SUBTRACT SOC-SEC-TAX-OUT FROM GROSS-PAY-OUT
        GIVING NET-PAY-OUT.
    WRITE SALARY-REC-OUT.
    READ IN-EMPLOYEE-FILE
        AT END MOVE 'NO ' TO ARE-THERE-MORE-RECORDS.
```

KEY TERMS

ADD	MULTIPLY	REMAINDER
COMPUTE	ON SIZE ERROR	ROUNDED
DIVIDE	Operand	SUBTRACT
Imperative statement	Overflow	

REVIEW QUESTIONS

I. True-False Questions

T F

___ ___ 1. The GIVING option may be used with all four arithmetic verbs.

___ ___ 2. One purpose of the COMPUTE is to reduce the number of arithmetic statements necessary to obtain a result.

___ ___ 3. Anything that can be coded with a COMPUTE statement can be coded with the use of the four arithmetic verbs as well.

___ ___ 4. The ON SIZE ERROR clause is executed if an overflow occurs.

___ ___ 5. The DIVIDE operation can produce a remainder as well as a quotient.

___ ___ 6. The word ROUNDED must be used with a COMPUTE statement.

___ ___ 7. It is possible to multiply three fields together with a single MULTIPLY operation.

___ ___ 8. A literal may not appear as the resultant field in an arithmetic operation.

___ ___ 9. Several fields may be added together with a single ADD operation.

___ ___ 10. If both the ROUNDED and ON SIZE ERROR options are used, the ROUNDED always appears first.

II. General Questions

Fill in the missing columns (1–3).

COBOL Statement	Result in	Result if A = 3, B = 2, X = 5 (PIC of each is 99V99)
1. ADD A B GIVING X		
2. ADD A B TO X ON SIZE ERROR MOVE ZERO TO X		
3. DIVIDE A INTO B ROUNDED		

4. Write a routine to calculate the number of miles traveled. There are two input fields, MPG, for miles per gallon, and GAS, for the number of gallons of gas used.

5. Write a routine to find Y = (A + B)² / X.

Determine what, if anything, is wrong with the following statements (6–10).

6. SUBTRACT A FROM 87.3 GIVING B.

7. ADD A, 10.98, B TO 100.3.

8. ADD AMT. TO TOTAL GIVING TAX.

9. DIVIDE A BY B AND MULTIPLY B BY C.

10. COMPUTE X = Y + Z ROUNDED.

11. Calculate the most economical quantity to be stocked for each product that a manufacturing company has in its inventory. This quantity, called the *economic order quantity*, is calculated as follows:

$$\text{Economic order quantity} = \sqrt{\frac{2RS}{I}}$$

R, S, and I are input fields.

R = total yearly production requirement
S = setup cost per order
I = inventory carrying cost per unit

Write the program excerpt to calculate the economic order quantity.

12. Use a COMPUTE statement to add one to A.

13. Read in as input the length and width of a lawn. Write a program excerpt to calculate the amount and cost of the grass seed needed. One pound of grass seed costs $2.50 and can plant 1000 square feet.

14. Using the instruction formats for the SUBTRACT statement, indicate whether the following is correct.

```
SUBTRACT AMT1 FROM AMT2, AMT3
    GIVING AMT4
```

Write a single statement to carry out the following operations (15–20):

(a) Using the COMPUTE verb
(b) Using the four arithmetic verbs

15. Add the values of OVT-HOURS and HOURS, with the sum replacing the value of HOURS.

16. Determine the number of feet in X inches, placing the quotient in FEET and the remainder in INCHES.

17. Add the values of FRI, SAT, and SUN, and place the sum in WEEK-END.

18. Add the values of AMT1, AMT2, and AMT3 to TOTAL.

19. Decrease the value of AMT-X by 47.5.

20. Divide the TOTAL-TUITION by 15 to determine TUITION-PER-CREDIT.

DEBUGGING EXERCISES

Consider the following arithmetic statements.

```
1       ADD AMT1 TO FIN-TOT.
2       ADD AMT1 TO AMT2 GIVING AMT3.
3       COMPUTE AVERAGE = AMT1 + AMT2 / 2
4       COMPUTE AMT4 = AMT1 + AMT2 ROUNDED.
5       MULTIPLY AMT1 BY AMT2.
6       DIVIDE AMT1 BY 2.
7       MULTIPLY AMT4 TIMES AMT3.
```

1. Which statements will produce syntax errors? Correct these.

2. Suppose AMT1 is an input field with PIC 99V99. FIN-TOT has the following specification in WORKING-STORAGE:

```
01   STORED-AREAS.
    05  FIN-TOT    PIC 9(4)V99.
```

Will line 1 always produce the correct results? Explain your answer.

3. On line 3, will a correct average of AMT1 and AMT2 be computed? If your answer is no, make whatever changes you think are necessary to obtain the correct results.

4. For line 5, suppose the PIC clause of AMT1, as previously noted, is 99V99. AMT2 has a PIC clause of 9(4)V99. Under what conditions will a logic error result? What can you do to prevent such an error?

5. Code COMPUTE statements to perform the operations on line 1, line 2, line 5, line 6, and line 7.

6. Assume that all the syntax and logic errors have been corrected on lines 1 through 7 and that the preceding steps are executed in sequence. What will be the results in the following fields: AMT1; AMT2; AMT3; AMT4; AVERAGE?

PROGRAMMING ASSIGNMENTS

Round all the results and stop the run on a size error condition.

1. Write a program to print out each student's average. The problem definition is shown in Figure 8.3.

   Notes

   a. STUDENT-MASTER is a sequential disk file.
   b. Each student's average should be rounded to the nearest integer (e.g., 89.5 = 90).

Figure 8.3
Problem definition for
Programming Assignment 1.

Systems Flowchart

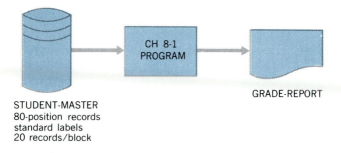

STUDENT-MASTER
80-position records
standard labels
20 records/block

GRADE-REPORT

STUDENT-MASTER Record Layout

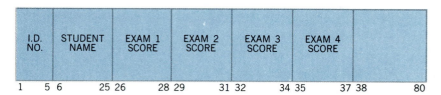

GRADE-REPORT Printer Spacing Chart

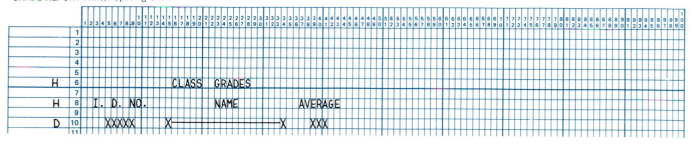

2. Write a program to print out payroll information for each employee. The problem definition is shown in Figure 8.4.

Notes

a. Each employee's salary is to be increased by 7%.
b. The union dues have increased by 4%.
c. The insurance has increased by 3%.
d. The amounts for dues and insurance are to be printed with actual decimal points.

Figure 8.4
Problem definition for
Programming Assignment 2.

Systems Flowchart

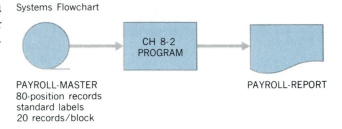

PAYROLL-MASTER
80-position records
standard labels
20 records/block

PAYROLL-REPORT

PAYROLL-MASTER Record Layout

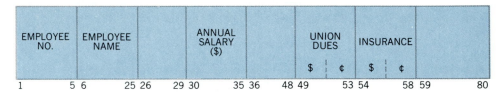

PAYROLL-REPORT Printer Spacing Chart

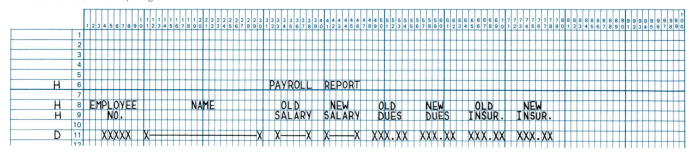

3. Write a program to create a master sales file from input sales records on tape that have the following format.

  1–5   Salesperson number
  6–11 Net price XXXX.XX (i.e., PICTURE 9999V99)
  12–80 Unused

The output file is created on magnetic tape with the following fields.

  1–5   Salesperson number
  6–11 Sales price XXXX.XX
  12–17 Commission XXXX.XX
  18–50 Unused

Notes

a. Output sales price is equal to the input net price with an added 5% sales tax.
b. Commission is 20% of the price *exclusive* of the tax.

4. Write a program to convert British pounds to dollars and cents. The disk input has the following format.

  1–25 Name of British agency
26–30 Number of pounds
31–80 Not used

A report is to be printed that lists, for each input record, the following:

1. Name of British agency.
2. Number of U.S. dollars.
3. Number of U.S. cents.

Notes

a. The input disk is blocked 20 and has standard labels.
b. 1 pound = $1.50.
c. Dollars and cents are two *separate* data fields.
d. Include appropriate headings and spacing on the output.

Extra Assignment: Redo this problem allowing for a variable conversion rate that is to be read in as input from a separate record. The first three positions of this input record will indicate the dollar amount equivalent to 1 pound.

5. Your company has a fleet of taxis and you wish to determine the energy efficiency of each taxi in the fleet as well as that of the entire fleet. Input consists of records with the following format:

  1–10 Vehicle identification
11–20 Vehicle description
21–24 Miles traveled
25–28 No. of gallons of gas used (XX.XX)

Print a report that indicates the miles per gallon for each taxi and for the fleet as a whole.

9

Selection Using the IF Statement

OBJECTIVES

To familiarize you with

1. The use of IF statements for selection.
2. The variety of formats and options available with the conditional statement.

I. Selection Using a Simple IF Statement

A. A Review of Logical Control Structures

Thus far we have learned the rules for using a number of COBOL instructions. We have coded programs that execute these instructions *in sequence*. The flowchart excerpt for a *sequence of instructions* is as follows:

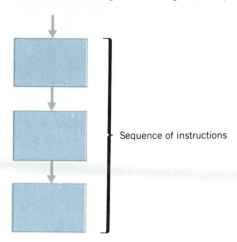

The pseudocode specification for a sequence is equally simple:

But a *sequence of instructions* is only one method for executing instructions. In this chapter we will focus on some instructions that enable the computer to make decisions that affect the order in which instructions are executed. Such instructions are referred to as *logical control structures*.

The full range of logical control structures used in any program, regardless of the language, is as follows:

LOGICAL CONTROL STRUCTURES
1. Sequence
2. Selection (IF-THEN-ELSE)
3. Iteration (PERFORM)
4. Case (EVALUATE)

In this chapter we focus on the IF-THEN-ELSE structure, which permits us to execute an instruction or series of instructions depending on the contents of fields. The IF-THEN-ELSE structure is coded in COBOL with the IF statement. In the next chapter, we will consider iteration with the PERFORM statement. The case structure is discussed in detail in Chapter 13.

B. Basic Conditional Statements

1. The Instruction Format for an IF Statement
We define a **conditional statement** as one that performs an operation depending on the existence of some condition. In COBOL, such statements generally begin with the word IF and are called IF-THEN-ELSE or selection structures.

The basic instruction format for IF statements is as follows:

Format

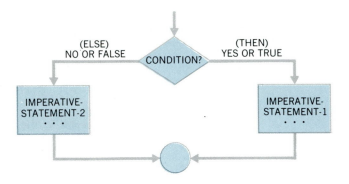

IF   condition-1
[THEN]*
            imperative statement-1 . . .
[ELSE
            imperative statement-2 . . .]

*The word THEN is an option with COBOL 85 only.

An **imperative statement,** as opposed to a conditional statement, is one that performs an operation, regardless of any existing conditions. ADD AMT-IN TO AMT-OUT, MOVE NAME-IN TO NAME-OUT, and OPEN INPUT MASTER-PAYROLL are examples of imperative statements that do not test for conditions but simply perform operations. Hence, we say that COBOL statements are divided into two broad categories: (1) **imperative,** which perform operations, and (2) **conditional,** which test for the existence of one or more conditions.

The flowchart excerpt that corresponds to an IF-THEN-ELSE selection structure is:

The pseudocode is as follows:

```
IF  condition
THEN
       ----------
       ----------  } Imperative statement(s)
       ----------
ELSE
       ----------
       ----------  } Imperative statement(s)
       ----------
ENDIF
```

A condition may test for a specific relation. A **simple condition** may be a single relational test of the following form.

SIMPLE RELATIONAL CONDITIONS
1. IF identifier-1 IS EQUAL TO identifier-2
2. IF identifier-1 IS LESS THAN identifier-2
3. IF identifier-1 IS GREATER THAN identifier-2

These three tests are considered simple relational conditions.

An illustration of a simple conditional is as follows:

PROGRAM EXCERPT

```
IF  AMT1 IS EQUAL TO AMT2
        DIVIDE QTY INTO TOTAL
ELSE
        ADD UNIT-PRICE TO FINAL-TOTAL.
```

There are two possible results of the test performed by the preceding statement:

1. AMT1 is equal to AMT2
2. AMT1 is not equal to AMT2

Explanation

1. If AMT1 is equal to AMT2, the DIVIDE operation is performed. The second part of the statement, beginning with the ELSE clause, is ignored. The program will continue executing with the next sentence, disregarding the clause that begins with the word ELSE.
2. If the two fields are not equal, then the DIVIDE operation is *not executed.* Only the ELSE portion of the statement, the ADD operation, is executed. In either case, the program continues executing with the next sentence.

Thus, by using the word IF, we test the initial condition and perform the instruction specified. By using ELSE, we can perform an operation if the initial condition is not met or is "false."

> The word THEN is permitted with COBOL 85 to make the IF statement totally consistent with structured programming terminology and pseudocode. That is, COBOL 85 conforms completely to the IF-THEN-ELSE logical control structure.

2. Interpreting Instruction Formats

a. ELSE Is Optional. The ELSE option in the instruction format is bracketed with [ ], which means that it is optional. If some operation is required *only if* a condition exists and nothing different need be done if the condition does not exist, the entire ELSE clause may be omitted.

b. Example of an IF Statement Without an ELSE Clause

```
MOVE NAME-IN TO NAME-OUT.
MOVE AMOUNT-IN TO AMOUNT-OUT.
IF  AMOUNT-IN IS EQUAL TO ZEROS
    MOVE 'NO TRANSACTIONS THIS MONTH' TO OUT-AREA.
WRITE PRINT-REC.
```

In this case, the message 'NO TRANSACTIONS THIS MONTH' is printed only if AMOUNT-IN is zero. If AMOUNT-IN is not zero, we continue with the next sentence without performing any operation. Since no operation is required if AMOUNT-IN is not zero, the ELSE clause is unnecessary in this instance.

c. More Than One Operation Can Be Performed When a Condition Exists. The instruction format also indicates that more than one operation may be executed for each condition. Thus, the following will perform two MOVE opera-

tions if AMT1 is equal to AMT2, and two ADD operations if AMT1 is not equal to AMT2.

```
IF  AMT1 IS EQUAL TO AMT2
     MOVE NAME-IN TO NAME-OUT
     MOVE DESCRIPTION-IN TO DESCRIPTION-OUT
  ELSE
     ADD AMT1 TO TOTAL1
     ADD AMT2 TO TOTAL2.
```

To ensure that the IF instruction is executed properly, remember to include a period at the end of the entire sentence. The difference between a statement and a sentence is as follows:

Statement   A combination of COBOL words and separators that begin with a COBOL verb such as ADD, READ, and IF.

Sentence   Consists of one or more statements and ends with a period.

3. Coding Guidelines

a. Indenting.   We indent statements within the IF instruction for ease of reading and to make debugging simpler as well. We use the following coding style for conditionals:

```
IF   condition
        imperative  statement
          :
  ELSE
        imperative  statement
          :
```

The entire IF sentence ends with a period.

This technique of indenting and coding each statement on a separate line makes reading the program easier, but it does not affect the compilation process. That is, coding this way is not a requirement, even though we strongly recommend you use it. Suppose you determine that an error occurred when the first line just shown was executed. It will be easier to determine the cause of error if that line contained a single statement than if it were coded as follows:

```
IF AMT1 IS EQUAL TO AMT2 ADD 5 TO TOTAL ELSE ADD 10 TO TOTAL.
```

In this sentence, the exact clause or statement that caused an error would be more difficult to determine.

b. Using Relational Operators in Place of Words.   The following symbols for the three simple relational conditions are valid within a COBOL statement.

RELATIONAL OPERATORS	
Symbol	**Meaning**
<	IS LESS THAN
>	IS GREATER THAN
=	IS EQUAL TO

A COBOL conditional, then, may have the following form:

```
IF  AMT1 IS GREATER THAN AMT2
     ADD AMT1 TO TOTAL
  ELSE
     MULTIPLY UNIT-PRICE BY QTY.
```

Or, the first line could be replaced by:

```
IF   AMT1  >  AMT2
   .
   .
   .
```

The flowchart and pseudocode for this excerpt are as follows:

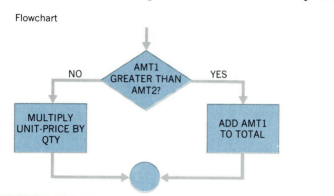

Flowchart

Pseudocode

```
IF  Amt1 greater than Amt2
THEN
    Add Amt1 to Total
ELSE
    Multiply Unit-Price by Qty
ENDIF
```

Most COBOL compilers require a blank on each side of the relational symbols <, >, =.

Some organizations encourage the use of the words (e.g., IS GREATER THAN) rather than the symbols (e.g., >) because they are easier for users to understand. We will sometimes use the words and sometimes the symbols in our illustrations. You are free to use either.

Additional relational operators permitted with COBOL 85 are:

ADDITIONAL RELATIONAL OPERATORS	
Symbols	**Meaning**
< =	Less than or equal to
> =	Greater than or equal to
< >	Not equal to

Example
```
IF   AMT1 <= ZERO
     MOVE 'NOT POSITIVE' TO CODE-OUT.
```

With COBOL 85 a conditional can also compare a field to an arithmetic expression.

Example
```
IF   AMT1 = AMT2 + 500
     PERFORM 100-A-OK.
```

c. Do Not Mix Field Types in a Comparison.   Keep in mind that conditional statements must use fields with the same data types to obtain proper results. In the statement, IF CODE-IN = '123' MOVE NAME-IN TO NAME-OUT, CODE-IN should be a nonnumeric field, since it is compared to a nonnumeric literal. As in MOVE operations, the literal should have the same format as the data item. If CODE-OUT has a PICTURE clause of 9's, the following conditional would be appropriate: IF CODE-OUT = 123 MOVE AMT-IN TO AMT-OUT.

Similarly, to ensure correct results, *fields* that are compared to one another should have the same data types, whether numeric or nonnumeric. Thus, in the statement, IF CTR1 = CTR2 ADD AMT1 TO TOTAL, *both* CTR1 and CTR2 should be either numeric or nonnumeric.

Numeric Fields Should Not Contain Blanks

If AMT-IN were a field defined as numeric, but actually contained all blanks, the following instruction would cause a **data exception error** to occur: IF AMT-IN IS EQUAL TO 10 ADD 1 TO COUNTER. This error will occur because *blanks are not valid numeric characters.* Be certain, then, that if a field is defined as numeric, that it actually contains numbers. We will discuss this again in Chapter 13 when we consider data validation techniques.

C. Planning Conditional Statements with Flowcharts and Pseudocode

Recall that ELSE clauses are optional in an IF statement. The flowchart and pseudocode that correspond to a simple condition without an ELSE clause are as follows:

General Format

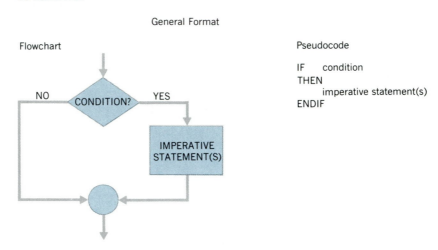

The following indicates the processing if multiple statements are to be executed when a condition is true:

Example

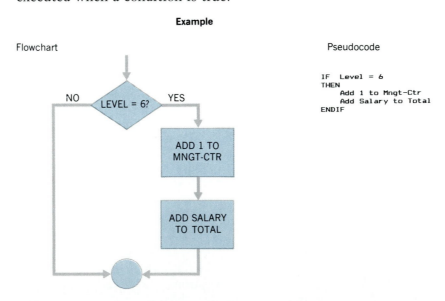

D. How Comparisons Are Performed

When comparing numeric fields, the following are all considered equal:

    012   12.00   12   +12

Numeric comparisons are performed in COBOL *algebraically*. Although 12.00 does not have the same internal configuration as 012, their numeric values are known to be equal.

Similarly, when comparing nonnumeric fields, the following are considered equivalent:

ABC   ABCb̸ (b̸ denotes a blank position)   ABCb̸b̸

Low-order or rightmost blanks will not upset the equivalence. Only significant or nonblank positions are compared, from left to right. Consequently, b̸ABC is *not* equal to ABCb̸ since A is not equal to b̸.

E. ASCII and EBCDIC Collating Sequences

When performing an alphanumeric comparison, the hierarchy of the comparison, called the **collating sequence,** depends on the computer being used.

The two types of internal codes that are most commonly used for representing data are **EBCDIC,** for IBM and IBM-compatible mainframes, and **ASCII,** used on most micros and many mainframes. The collating sequences for these differ somewhat. Characters are compared to one another in EBCDIC and ASCII as follows:

COLLATING SEQUENCES

	EBCDIC	ASCII
Low	Special characters	Special characters
	a–z	0–9
	A–Z	A–Z
High	0–9	a–z

On both ASCII and EBCDIC computers a numeric comparison or an alphabetic comparison will be performed properly. That is, 012 < 022 < 042, and so on, on both types of computers. Similarly, all computers will be able to determine if data is arranged alphabetically because A is considered less than B, which is less than C, and so on. Thus, ABCD < BBCD < XBCD, and so on.

Note, however, that on ASCII computers uppercase letters are less than lowercase letters whereas the reverse is true with EBCDIC computers. Suppose you are performing an alphabetic sequence check. SMITH is considered < Smith on ASCII computers but on EBCDIC computers Smith < SMITH. Similarly, if alphanumeric fields are being compared where there may be a *mix of letters and digits* or uppercase and lowercase letters, the results of the comparison will differ, depending on whether you are running the program on an EBCDIC or an ASCII computer. On EBCDIC machines, letters are all less than numbers; on ASCII machines, numbers are less than letters.

Consider the following comparison:

```
IF  ADDRESS-IN < '100 MAIN ST'
    ADD 1 TO TOTAL.
```

If ADDRESS-IN has a value of 'ROUTE 109', the result of the comparison will *differ* depending on whether you are using an ASCII or EBCDIC computer. On EBCDIC computers, 'ROUTE 109' is less than '100 MAIN ST' because the first character, R, compares "less than" the number 1; hence 1 *would be added to* TOTAL. On ASCII computers the reverse is true; that is, letters are "greater than" numbers so that 1 *would not be added to* TOTAL.

These differences are worth mentioning, but not worth dwelling on since alphanumeric comparisons of these types are not usually required in programs. For comparisons of fields containing *either* all numbers *or* all uppercase letters (or all lowercase letters), both ASCII and EBCDIC computers will produce exactly the same results. In addition, you can usually tell the computer which collating sequence you prefer, regardless of the internal code, by issuing a job control or system command.

F. Ending Conditional Sentences with a Period or an END-IF Scope Terminator (COBOL 85)

As indicated, several imperative statements may appear within one conditional. Indentation is used to make the entire sentence easier to read. Also, the placement of periods can affect the logic in an IF statement. Consider the following:

```
IF  PRICE1 IS LESS THAN PRICE2
    ADD PRICE1 TO TOTAL
    MOVE 2 TO ITEM1
ELSE
    ADD PRICE2 TO TOTAL.◄─────── Note the period
MOVE 0 TO ITEM2.
```

Because the statement ADD PRICE2 TO TOTAL ends with a period, the last statement MOVE 0 TO ITEM2 is *always executed* regardless of the comparison.

The preceding program excerpt may be flowcharted and written as pseudocode as follows:

Flowchart   Pseudocode

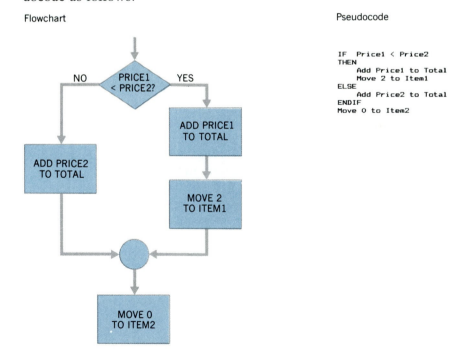

```
IF  Price1 < Price2
THEN
    Add Price1 to Total
    Move 2 to Item1
ELSE
    Add Price2 to Total
ENDIF
Move 0 to Item2
```

If a period were inadvertently omitted after ADD PRICE2 TO TOTAL, then MOVE 0 TO ITEM2 would be considered *part of the* ELSE *clause* and would *not* be executed if PRICE1 were less than PRICE2. You can see, then, that the placement of the period can significantly affect the logic.

If you are using an ELSE clause, *never* place a period before the ELSE. Include a period only at the end of the sentence following all imperative statements that apply to the ELSE.

To definitively specify the boundaries of an IF, then, you would use periods to end the sentences. With COBOL 85, you can also use END-IF as a scope terminator:

```
IF   PRICE1 < PRICE2
THEN
      ADD PRICE1 TO TOTAL
      MOVE 2 TO ITEM1
ELSE
      ADD PRICE2 TO TOTAL
END-IF
MOVE 0 TO ITEM2.
```

The END-IF clearly marks the boundary of the IF statement without the need for periods.

The END-IF also enables COBOL 85 to even more closely resemble pseudocode, which uses IF-THEN-ELSE-ENDIF for selection.

G. The NEXT SENTENCE Clause

There are times when you might want to execute a series of steps only if a certain condition does *not* exist. The COBOL expression, NEXT SENTENCE, will enable you (1) to avoid performing any operation if a condition exists and (2) to execute instructions only if the ELSE condition is met.

Example 1   Consider the following flowchart and pseudocode.

Adding to a Total If a Condition is False

Flowchart   Pseudocode

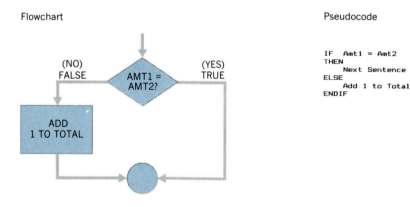

```
IF   Amt1 = Amt2
THEN
        Next Sentence
ELSE
        Add 1 to Total
ENDIF
```

The COBOL excerpt is as follows:

```
IF   AMT1 = AMT2
        NEXT SENTENCE
ELSE
        ADD 1 TO TOTAL.
```

If AMT1 is equal to AMT2, *no* operation will be performed and the computer will continue execution with the next sentence, which is the statement following the period. If AMT1 is not equal to AMT2, 1 is added to TOTAL and the next sentence will be executed.

With COBOL 85 the word THEN can precede the NEXT SENTENCE clause.

Example 2   Note that the following two statements produce identical results.

```
A. IF   TOTAL1 IS EQUAL TO TOTAL2
          ADD 1 TO COUNTER
   ELSE
          NEXT SENTENCE.
B. IF   TOTAL1 IS EQUAL TO TOTAL2
          ADD 1 TO COUNTER.
```

The phrase ELSE NEXT SENTENCE in statement A is unnecessary; if TOTAL1 is not equal to TOTAL2, the computer will proceed to the next sentence anyway. Thus, with a simple IF, the ELSE clause is used only when a specific operation is required if a condition does *not* exist.

Note that the following is invalid.

Invalid Coding

Invalid coding:

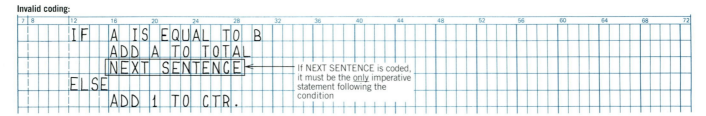

If NEXT SENTENCE is coded, it must be the <u>only</u> imperative statement following the condition

NEXT SENTENCE must be the *only* clause following a condition, since it indicates that no action is to be performed. To correct the preceding, we code:

Corrected Coding

```
IF   A IS EQUAL TO B
       ADD A TO TOTAL
ELSE
       ADD 1 TO CTR.
```

Self-Test   What is wrong with the following statements (1–6)?

```
1.  IF   A IS LESS THAN B
          GO TO NEXT SENTENCE
    ELSE
          ADD 1 TO XX.
2.  IF   A IS EQUAL TO '127'
          ADD A TO B.
3.  IF   A EQUALS B
          MOVE 1 TO A.
4.  IF   A IS LESS THEN B
          MOVE 2 TO CODE1.
5.  IF   C = D
          MOVE 0 TO COUNTER.
    ELSE
          MOVE 100 TO COUNTER.
6.  IF   C = D
          MOVE 0 TO COUNTER
    ELSE
          NEXT SENTENCE.
```

7. Will the following pair of statements cause the same instructions to be executed?

(a) ```
IF A IS EQUAL TO C
        MOVE 1 TO C
    ELSE
        NEXT SENTENCE.
```

(b) ```
IF  A IS EQUAL TO C
        MOVE 1 TO C.
```

8. Code the following routine.

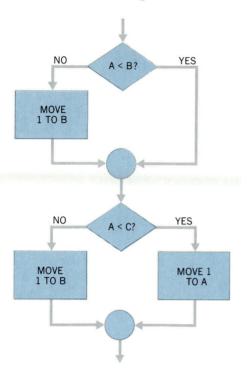

9. Write a routine to move the smallest of three numbers A, B, and C to a field called PRINT-SMALL.

10. Indicate the difference between the following two routines.

(a) ```
IF A IS EQUAL TO B
        ADD C TO D
        MOVE E TO TOTAL.
```

(b) ```
IF  A IS EQUAL TO B
        ADD C TO D.
        MOVE E TO TOTAL.
```

Solutions

1. You cannot say: GO TO NEXT SENTENCE:

```
IF  A IS LESS THAN B
        NEXT SENTENCE
ELSE
        ADD 1 TO XX.
```

2. Since A is compared to a nonnumeric literal, it should be an alphanumeric field. But A is *added* to another field, which implies that it is numeric. Hence a contradiction of data types exists. Although this may, in fact, produce the correct results (depending on the contents of A), it is an inadvisable technique to make a comparison where one field or literal is alphanumeric and the other is numeric.

3. This should be: IF A IS EQUAL TO B ....

4. When the words GREATER and LESS are used, the COBOL word that follows is THAN and not THEN.

5. There should be no period after MOVE 0 TO COUNTER.

6. ELSE NEXT SENTENCE, although not incorrect, is unnecessary.

7. Yes.

8.
```
IF   A IS LESS THAN B
       NEXT SENTENCE
   ELSE
       MOVE 1 TO B.
   IF   A IS LESS THAN C
       MOVE 1 TO A
   ELSE
       MOVE 1 TO B.
```

9.
```
MOVE A TO PRINT-SMALL.
IF   B IS LESS THAN PRINT-SMALL
       MOVE B TO PRINT-SMALL.
IF   C IS LESS THAN PRINT-SMALL
       MOVE C TO PRINT-SMALL.
```
(*Note:* This is *not* the only way to write this routine.)

10. They are different because of the periods. In (a), MOVE E TO TOTAL is performed only if A = B. In (b), however, a period follows ADD C TO D. Thus, if A is equal to B, only one imperative statement is executed. Then, regardless of whether A equals B, E is moved to TOTAL. The indenting included in both (a) and (b) does not affect the execution—the placement of the period is the critical factor.

II. Selection Using Other Options of the IF Statement

A. Nested Conditional

A **nested conditional** is a conditional in which an IF statement itself can contain additional IF clauses. Consider the following:

```
IF   condition-1
       statement-1
ELSE
       IF   condition-2
             statement-2
       ELSE
             statement-3
```

This is an example of a nested conditional. Because complex nesting of conditions can sometimes be confusing, we recommend that nested conditionals always be *balanced* by having each IF clause paired with an ELSE, as shown in the following:

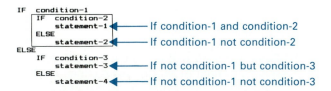

Example 1
```
IF  AMT IS EQUAL TO 6
    IF  TAX IS EQUAL TO 10
        PERFORM 200-RTN-2
    ELSE
        PERFORM 300-RTN-3
ELSE
    PERFORM 100-RTN-1.
```

This example conforms to the original format specified for an IF instruction, but statement-1 is a conditional, not an imperative statement. This makes Example 1 a *nested conditional*. The tests performed are:

1. If AMT is not equal to 6, the last ELSE, PERFORM 100-RTN-1, is executed.
2. If AMT = 6, the second condition (which corresponds to statement-1) is tested as follows:
   (a) (if AMT = 6) and TAX = 10, 200-RTN-2 is performed.
   (b) (If AMT = 6) and TAX is not equal to 10, 300-RTN-3 is performed.

This procedure may also be written in terms of a decision table:

Decision Table for Example 1		
Condition 1	**Condition 2**	**Action**
AMT = 6	TAX = 10	PERFORM 200-RTN-2
AMT = 6	TAX $\neq$ 10	PERFORM 300-RTN-3
AMT $\neq$ 6	TAX = anything	PERFORM 100-RTN-1

Decision tables list the various conditions that may occur and the actions to be performed. Decision tables are frequently prepared by systems analysts and programmers to map out or chart complex logic that requires execution of different modules depending on the results of numerous tests.

A nested conditional is really a shortcut method of writing a series of simple conditionals. Thus, any nested conditional may be written instead with simple conditionals. The nested conditional in Example 1 may also be coded as follows, but note that this coding is awkward and not well-structured.

```
500-CALC-RTN.
    IF  AMT IS NOT EQUAL TO 6
        PERFORM 100-RTN-1.
    IF  TAX IS EQUAL TO 10 AND AMT = 6
        PERFORM 200-RTN-2.
    IF  TAX NOT = 10 AND AMT = 6
        PERFORM 300-RTN-3.
```

In this procedure, we need to include all conditions in each test to ensure proper processing. Note that the preceding could also be written in a number of different ways but care must be taken that all conditions are tested properly.

Nested conditionals are used in COBOL for the following reasons:

WHY USE A NESTED CONDITIONAL

1. It minimizes coding effort where numerous conditions are to be tested.
2. It tests conditions just as they appear in a decision table.

Example 2   Consider the following decision table:

Condition	Condition	Action
A = B	C = D	PERFORM 100-RTN-A
A = B	C ≠ D	PERFORM 200-RTN-B
A ≠ B	anything	PERFORM 300-RTN-C

We could code this decision table as a nested conditional. To help clarify the sentence, parentheses may be used as follows:

```
IF   A IS EQUAL TO B
     (IF  C IS EQUAL TO D
          PERFORM 100-RTN-A
     ELSE
          PERFORM 200-RTN-B)
ELSE
     PERFORM 300-RTN-C.
```

The indenting of clauses helps to clarify the relationships between statements and should be consistently employed when coding nested conditionals. This will not only help in reading the sentence, but it will make it easier to debug your program as well. Parentheses may be included for clarification if you wish.

Thus, the general format for an IF is:

Format

$$
\begin{array}{l}
\underline{IF}\ condition\text{-}1 \\
[\underline{THEN}]^{*} \\
\qquad \left\{ \begin{array}{l} statement\text{-}1 \ldots \\ \underline{NEXT}\ \underline{SENTENCE} \end{array} \right\} \\
[\underline{ELSE} \\
\qquad \left. \left\{ \begin{array}{l} statement\text{-}2 \ldots \\ \underline{NEXT}\ \underline{SENTENCE} \end{array} \right\} \right] \\
[\underline{END\text{-}IF}]^{*}
\end{array}
$$

*These are valid for COBOL 85.

In a nested conditional, statements 1 and 2 above can themselves be conditional statements.

B. Compound Conditional

We have seen that selection and iteration structures provide programs with a great deal of logical control capability. The **compound conditional** provides even greater flexibility for selection and enables the IF statement to be used for more complex problems. With the compound conditional, the programmer can test for several conditions with one statement.

1. OR in a Compound Conditional

To perform an operation or a series of operations if *any one of several conditions exists,* the compound conditional with conditions separated by OR may be used. This means that if *any one of several conditions* exists, the imperative statement(s) specified will be executed.

Format

$$
\begin{array}{l}
\underline{\text{IF}} \quad \text{condition-1} \ \underline{\text{OR}} \ \text{condition-2} \ldots \\
[\underline{\text{THEN}}]^* \\
\qquad \left\{ \begin{array}{l} \text{statement-1} \ldots \\ \underline{\text{NEXT SENTENCE}} \end{array} \right\} \\
[\underline{\text{ELSE}} \\
\qquad \left. \left\{ \begin{array}{l} \text{statement-2} \ldots \\ \underline{\text{NEXT SENTENCE}} \end{array} \right\} \right] \\
[\underline{\text{END-IF}}]^*
\end{array}
$$

*Here, again, THEN and END-IF may be used by COBOL 85 users.

Examples

```
1. IF   AMT1 = AMT2 OR AMT2 > AMT3
         PERFORM 500-TOTAL-RTN.
2. IF   AMT1 < AMT3 OR AMT1 = AMT4
         ADD AMT1 TO TOTAL
     ELSE
         PERFORM 600-ERR-RTN.
```

By using OR in a compound conditional, *any* of the conditions specified will cause execution of the statement(s). If none of the conditions is met, the computer will execute either the ELSE option, if coded, or the next sentence. Any number of conditions separated by ORs may be specified in a single statement.

In the second example, the paragraph 600-ERR-RTN is executed only if AMT1 is greater than or equal to AMT3 *and* AMT1 is not equal to AMT4. If *either* AMT1 is less than AMT3, or AMT1 is equal to AMT4, AMT1 will be added to TOTAL and then the next sentence will be executed.

Limitations on a Compound Conditional

Using the preceding instruction format, note that the following is invalid:

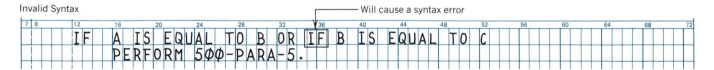

```
IF  A IS EQUAL TO B OR IF B IS EQUAL TO C
PERFORM 500-PARA-5.
```

With compound conditionals of this type, the word IF must be used only once.

Implied Operands

In compound conditionals, it is not always necessary to specify both operands for each condition. To say IF TOTAL = 7 OR 8 PERFORM 500-PRINT-RTN tests two simple conditions: (1) TOTAL = 7 and (2) TOTAL = 8. Since the identifier TOTAL is omitted from the second condition test, we say that it is an *implied operand.* For most compilers, a compound conditional statement with an implied operand is valid; that is, both operands need not be included for each condition. The preceding statement can also be coded as:

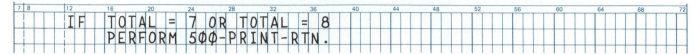

```
        IF  TOTAL = 7 OR TOTAL = 8
            PERFORM 500-PRINT-RTN.
```

The following use of an implied operand, however, is *not* valid.

Invalid Use of an Implied Operand

```
IF TOTAL-1 OR TOTAL-2 = 7
```

Following the word IF, *a full condition* must be specified. In a conditional such as IF condition-1 OR condition-2 ..., condition-1 must include a *full test*, but subsequent conditions can have implied operands, where the first operand of the next condition is the one that is implied. In the clause IF TOTAL = 7 OR 8, for example, the compiler assumes you mean to compare TOTAL to 8 as well as to 7.

Not Greater Than or Equal To Is Equivalent to Less Than

Note that the following two routines produce identical results.

```
1. IF  AMT-IN IS GREATER THAN 5 OR EQUAL TO 5
        PERFORM 100-STEP1
   ELSE
        PERFORM 200-STEP2.
2. IF  AMT-IN IS LESS THAN 5
        PERFORM 200-STEP2
   ELSE
        PERFORM 100-STEP1.
```

That is, if AMT-IN is not greater than or equal to 5 it must be less than 5.

> With 1985 compilers, the first routine above can be coded as IF AMT-IN >= 5 .... That is, >= and <= are permitted in compound conditionals when using COBOL 85 compilers.

2. AND in a Compound Conditional

If a statement or statements are to be executed only when *all* of several conditions are met, use the word AND in the compound conditional.

Format

```
IF   condition-1 AND condition-2 ...
[THEN]*
        ⎰ statement-1 ...      ⎱
        ⎱ NEXT SENTENCE ⎰
[ELSE
        ⎰ statement-2 ...      ⎱ ]
        ⎱ NEXT SENTENCE ⎰
[END-IF]*
```

*THEN and END-IF are optional with COBOL 85.

All conditions must be met when AND is used in a compound condition. The ELSE clause is executed if *any one* of the stated conditions is not met.

Example Suppose we wanted to perform `400-PRINT-RTN` if all the following conditions are met:

```
AMT1 = AMTA; AMT2 = AMTB; AMT3 = AMTC
```

otherwise we wish to perform `500-ERR-RTN`. That is, if one or more of these conditions are *not* met we wish to perform `500-ERR-RTN`. We may use a compound conditional for this:

```
IF   AMT1 IS EQUAL TO AMTA
          AND  AMT2 IS EQUAL TO AMTB
                  AND AMT3 IS EQUAL TO AMTC
        PERFORM 400-PRINT-RTN
    ELSE
        PERFORM 500-ERR-RTN.
```

If all the conditions are met, `400-PRINT-RTN` is executed. If any condition is *not* met, `500-ERR-RTN` is executed.

3. Using `AND` and `OR` in the Same Statement

a. Introduction.   There are times when *both* the `AND` and `OR` are required within the same compound conditional.

Example Write a routine to perform `700-PRINT-RTN` if `AMT` is between 10 and 20, inclusive of the end points (i.e., including 10 and 20). Assume `AMT` is an independent item in `WORKING-STORAGE`.

On first sight, we might code a compound conditional as follows:

```
IF   AMT = 10 OR AMT = 11 OR AMT = 12 ... OR AMT = 20
    PERFORM 700-PRINT-RTN.
```

This statement, however, will function properly *only if* `AMT` *is an integer.* The number 10.3, for instance, is between 10 and 20, but it will not pass the preceding tests. For a similar reason, we cannot say: IF AMT > 9 AND AMT < 21 PERFORM 700-PRINT-RTN. If AMT is 9.8, it is *not* between 10 and 20 but it passes both tests. Thus, we want to perform `700-PRINT-RTN` if:

   1. `AMT = 10`

or

   2. `AMT > 10 AND AMT < 20`

or

   3. `AMT = 20`

We could code the compound conditional as follows:

```
IF   AMT IS EQUAL TO 10
    OR   AMT IS GREATER THAN 10 AND AMT IS LESS THAN 20
    OR   AMT IS EQUAL TO 20
        PERFORM 700-PRINT-RTN.
```

b. Order of Evaluation of Compound Conditionals.   When using both `AND` and `OR` in the same compound conditional as in the preceding example, the order of evaluation of each condition is critical. For example, look at the following:

```
IF   A = B OR C = D AND E = F
        PERFORM 600-PARA-1.
```

Suppose A = 2, B = 2, C = 3, D = 4, E = 5, and F = 6. Depending on the order in which these conditions are evaluated, 600-PARA-1 may or may not be executed. Suppose the statement is evaluated as follows:

I. Order of Evaluation: Possibility 1

(a) IF A = B OR C = D and (b) E = F

If this is the order of evaluation, there are two ways that 600-PARA-1 will be executed: (1) A = B and E = F, or (2) C = D and E = F. That is, E and F must be equal *and* either A must be equal to B or C must be equal to D. Since E does not equal F, 600-PARA-1 will not be executed if this order of evaluation is correct.

Suppose, however, that the preceding instruction is evaluated as follows:

II. Order of Evaluation: Possibility 2

(a) IF A = B or (b) C = D AND E = F

If this is the order of evaluation, there are two ways that 600-PARA-1 will be executed: (1) A = B, or (2) C = D and E = F. That is, either A and B are equal *or* C must equal D and E must equal F. Because the first condition, A = B, is met, the PERFORM will occur if this order of evaluation is correct.

Hence, if the second order of evaluation is the one actually used by the computer, 600-PARA-1 is executed; but if the first is used, the paragraph is not executed. It should be clear, at this point, that only one of these evaluations will prove to be correct. Now that the importance of the order of evaluation is clear, we will consider the hierarchy rules.

HIERARCHY RULES FOR COMPOUND CONDITIONALS

1. Conditions surrounding the word AND are evaluated first.
2. Conditions surrounding the word OR are evaluated last.
3. When there are several AND or OR connectors, the AND conditions are evaluated first, as they appear in the statement, from left to right. Then the OR conditions are evaluated, also from left to right.
4. To override Rules 1–3, use parentheses around conditions you want to be evaluated first.

Using these hierarchy rules and the preceding example, the conditions will be evaluated as follows:

(a) IF C = D AND E = F or (b) A = B

With the given contents in the fields, 600-PARA-1 will be executed because A = B. To change the order so that the evaluation is performed as in Possibility 1 above, code the condition as follows:

```
IF (A = B OR C = D) AND E = F
    PERFORM 600-PARA-1.
```

In this case, if A = 2, B = 2, C = 3, D = 4, E = 5 and F = 6 as specified previously, 600-PARA-1 will *not* be executed.

c. Examples.   As in a previous example, we want to print AMT if it is between 10 and 20, inclusive. This is often written mathematically as $10 \leq AMT \leq 20$; if 10 is less than or equal to AMT and, at the same time, AMT is less than or equal to 20, then we wish to print AMT.

Let us determine if the following statement results in the proper test:

```
IF  AMT < 20 OR AMT = 20 AND AMT = 10 OR AMT > 10
        PERFORM 700-PRINT-RTN.
```

Using the hierarchy rules for evaluating compound conditionals, the first conditions tested are those surrounding the word AND. Then, from left to right, those surrounding the OR expressions are evaluated. Thus, we have:

1. IF AMT = 20 AND AMT = 10

or

2. AMT < 20

or

3. AMT > 10

The compound conditional test in (1) is always false because the value for AMT can never equal 10 and, at the same time, be equal to 20. Since the first expression tested will never be true, it can be eliminated from the statement, which then reduces to:

Obviously, this is *not* the solution to the original problem. In fact, using the preceding conditional, *all* values for AMT will cause 700-PRINT-RTN to be executed. If AMT were, in fact, more than 20, it will cause 700-PRINT-RTN to be performed since it passes the test: AMT > 10. If AMT were less than 10, it will cause 700-PRINT-RTN to be executed since it passes the test: AMT < 20.

The original statement would be correct if we could change the order of evaluation. We want the comparisons performed according to the following hierarchy:

1. IF AMT < 20 OR AMT = 20

and

2. AMT = 10 OR AMT > 10

To change the normal order of evaluation, place parentheses around the conditions you want to be evaluated first, as a unit. *Parentheses override the other hierarchy rules*—all conditions within parentheses are evaluated together. Thus, the following statement is correct:

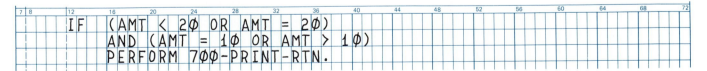

When in doubt about the normal sequence of evaluation, use parentheses. Even when they are not necessary for proper execution, as in IF (A = B AND C = D) OR (E = F) ..., they ensure that the statements are performed in the proper sequence. Moreover, they help a user better understand the logic of a program.

With COBOL 85, the preceding can be simplified as follows:

```
IF  AMT <= 20 AND AMT >= 10
    PERFORM 700-PRINT-RTN.
```

C. Sign and Class Tests

In addition to simple and compound conditionals, there are various specialized tests that can be performed with the IF statement.

1. Sign Test

a. Instruction Format.   We can test whether a field is POSITIVE, NEGATIVE, or ZERO with a **sign test.**

Format

$$
\text{IF} \quad \text{identifier-1} \quad \text{IS} \quad \left\{ \begin{array}{l} \underline{\text{POSITIVE}} \\ \underline{\text{NEGATIVE}} \\ \underline{\text{ZERO}} \end{array} \right\}
$$

[THEN]*

$$
\left\{ \begin{array}{l} \text{statement-1} \dots \\ \underline{\text{NEXT}} \; \underline{\text{SENTENCE}} \end{array} \right\}
$$

[ELSE

$$
\left. \left\{ \begin{array}{l} \text{statement-2} \dots \\ \underline{\text{NEXT}} \; \underline{\text{SENTENCE}} \end{array} \right\} \right]
$$

[END-IF]*

*THEN and END-IF are options with COBOL 85 only.

b. Designating Fields as Signed Negative or Positive.   To test a field for its sign implies that the field may have a negative value. As noted in Chapter 8, a numeric field will be considered unsigned or positive by the computer unless there is an S in its PICTURE clause. This S, like the implied decimal point V, does not occupy a storage position. Thus 05 AMT1 PIC 99 is a two-position *unsigned field* and 05 AMT2 PIC S99 is a two-position *signed field*, unless SIGN IS LEADING SEPARATE or TRAILING SEPARATE is specified.

If you move −12 to AMT1, AMT1 will contain 12 because it is unsigned; moving −12 to AMT2 will result in −12 in AMT2, since AMT2 allows for a sign. Use S in a PIC clause of a numeric field that may have negative contents.

On most computers, the phrase IF A IS EQUAL TO ZERO is the same as IF A IS ZERO. If a numeric field contains an amount less than zero, it is considered negative. If it has an amount greater than zero, then it is considered positive.

> −382 is negative
>   382 is positive
> +382 is positive

0 is neither negative nor positive in this context, unless it is indicated as −0 or +0, respectively.

Example   Suppose we want to compute the distance of AMT from zero, regardless of its sign. For instance, if AMT = 2, its distance from zero is 2. If AMT = −2, its distance from zero is also 2, since we do not consider the sign. We call this quantity the *absolute value* of AMT, denoted mathematically as |AMT|. It is formulated as follows:

If AMT is greater than or equal to 0, then,

$|AMT| = AMT$

If AMT is less than 0, then,

$|AMT| = -AMT = -1 \times AMT$

In other words, if AMT is greater than or equal to zero, the absolute value of AMT is simply the value of AMT. If AMT is less than zero, the absolute value of AMT is equal to -1 times the value of AMT, which will be a positive number. Let us find the absolute value of AMT.

```
MOVE ZERO TO ABS-A.
IF   AMT IS POSITIVE
     MOVE AMT TO ABS-A.
IF   AMT IS NEGATIVE
     MULTIPLY -1 BY AMT GIVING ABS-A.
```

The clause IF AMT IS NEGATIVE is equivalent to saying IF AMT < 0, and IF AMT IS POSITIVE is the same as IF AMT > 0. If AMT is 0, the contents of ABS-A remain unchanged; that is, it contains zero.

2. Class Test

We can test for the type of data in a field as follows:

Format

$$
\text{\underline{IF} identifier-1 IS } \left\{ \begin{array}{l} \text{\underline{NUMERIC}} \\ \text{\underline{ALPHABETIC}} \end{array} \right\}
$$

$$[\underline{THEN}]^*$$

$$\left\{ \begin{array}{l} \text{statement-1 ...} \\ \underline{\text{NEXT}} \; \underline{\text{SENTENCE}} \end{array} \right\}$$

$$[\underline{ELSE}$$

$$\left\{ \begin{array}{l} \text{statement-2 ...} \\ \underline{\text{NEXT}} \; \underline{\text{SENTENCE}} \end{array} \right\}]$$

$$[\underline{END\text{-}IF}]^*$$

*THEN and END-IF are options with COBOL 85 only.

If the ELSE option is executed with the NUMERIC **class test,** this implies that either the field contains alphabetic data (only letters and/or spaces) or it contains alphanumeric data, meaning any possible characters. Suppose we code the following:

```
IF   AMT-IN IS NUMERIC
     PERFORM 300-CALC-RTN
ELSE
     PERFORM 400-ERROR-RTN.
```

If the field contains 123AB, for example, the ELSE clause will be executed since the contents of the field are not strictly numeric.

Using Class Tests for Validating Data

A class test is a useful tool for minimizing program errors. Suppose we wish to add AMT-IN to TOTAL, where AMT-IN is an input field. Since input is always subject to data-entry errors, it is possible that the field might be entered erroneously with nonnumeric data or spaces. In such a case, an ADD AMT-IN TO TOTAL instruction can cause the computer to abort the run.

The following may be used to minimize such errors.

```
IF   AMT-IN IS NUMERIC
     ADD AMT-IN TO TOTAL
ELSE
     PERFORM 500-ERR-RTN.
```

In the preceding, we are *validating* the AMT-IN field before we perform arithmetic.

Example   A one-position field in a record contains the number of dependents an employee claims for income tax purposes. To obtain the exemption amount to be deducted, we multiply the number of dependents by 1080. If, however, the employee claims 10 dependents, an A is placed in the field; if he or she claims 11 dependents, a B is placed in the field, and so on. We can only perform the multiplication if the field does not contain a letter.

```
IF  NO-OF-DEPTS IS ALPHABETIC
    PERFORM 8ØØ-EXCEPTION-RTN
ELSE
    PERFORM 2ØØ-CALC-RTN.
```

ALPHABETIC **Class with COBOL 85**

When COBOL was originally developed, most computers were unable to represent lowercase letters. Thus, only uppercase letters were used.

When computers began to have internal codes for lowercase letters, the use of the ALPHABETIC class test became ambiguous. Some COBOL compilers considered both 'abc' and 'ABC' to be ALPHABETIC, for example, whereas others considered only 'ABC' as ALPHABETIC.

COBOL 85 has eliminated this ambiguity by specifying that any letter—either uppercase or lowercase, or any blank—must be considered ALPHABETIC. Moreover, two new *class tests* have been added: ALPHABETIC-UPPER and ALPHABETIC-LOWER. Thus the three alphabetic class tests for COBOL 85 are:

Alphabetic Class Tests

Reserved Word	Meaning
ALPHABETIC	A–Z, a–z, and blank
ALPHABETIC-UPPER	A–Z and blank
ALPHABETIC-LOWER	a–z and blank

Example

```
IF NAME-IN IS ALPHABETIC-LOWER
THEN
       PERFORM 600-LOWER-CASE-RTN.
```

D. Negating Conditionals

1. Negating Simple Conditionals

All simple relational, class, or sign tests may be coded using a **negated conditional** as follows:

Format

```
IF identifier-1 IS [NOT]   { { GREATER THAN (>)  }            }
                           { { LESS THAN (<)     } identifier-2}
                           { { EQUAL TO (=)      }            }
                           {                                  }
                           { ( ALPHABETIC )                   }
                           { { NUMERIC     }                  }
                           { { POSITIVE    }                  }
                           { { NEGATIVE    }                  }
                           { ( ZERO        )                  }

   [THEN]*
         { statement-1 ... }
         { NEXT SENTENCE   }
   [ELSE
         { statement-2 ... }
         { NEXT SENTENCE   } ]
   [END-IF]*
```

*THEN and END-IF are options with COBOL 85 only.

With COBOL 85 we may also have the following tests:

Greater than or equal to	>=
Less than or equal to	<=
Unequal (less than or greater than)	<>

Examples   The following two statements are equivalent.

```
1. IF   AMT1 IS EQUAL TO AMT2
         PERFORM 100-EQUAL-RTN
   ELSE
         PERFORM 200-EQUAL-RTN.
2. IF   AMT1 IS NOT EQUAL TO AMT2
         PERFORM 200-EQUAL-RTN
   ELSE
         PERFORM 100-EQUAL-RTN.
```

NOT NEGATIVE **Is Not Equal to** POSITIVE

To say, however, IF AMT1 IS NOT NEGATIVE, is *not* the same as saying AMT1 IS POSITIVE. If AMT1 is zero, it is *neither*. Thus, the following two statements are *not* identical.

```
1.    IF  AMT1 IS NEGATIVE
              PERFORM 100-NEG-RTN
      ELSE
              PERFORM 200-ADD-RTN.
                                        These are not equivalent
                                        if AMT1 = 0
2.    IF  AMT1 IS NOT POSITIVE
              PERFORM 100-NEG-RTN
      ELSE
              PERFORM 200-ADD-RTN.
```

Suppose AMT1 is equal to 0. In sentence (1), 200-ADD-RTN is executed; in sentence (2), 100-NEG-RTN is executed. Similarly, to say IF CODE-IN IS NOT ALPHABETIC, is *not* the same as saying IF CODE-IN IS NUMERIC. If CODE-IN is alphanumeric, containing combinations of letters, digits, and special characters, then it is neither ALPHABETIC nor NUMERIC. Thus, the following two statements are *not* equivalent:

```
1.   IF  CODE-X IS NOT ALPHABETIC
             PERFORM 100-RTN1
     ELSE
             PERFORM 200-RTN2.


2.   IF  CODE-X IS NUMERIC
             PERFORM 200-RTN2
     ELSE
             PERFORM 100-RTN1.
```

These are <u>not</u> equivalent

2. Negating Compound Conditionals

A common error may occur when you negate compound conditionals. The following will explain the error and how it can be avoided.

Example   Write a routine to perform 200-MARRIED-RTN if MARITAL-CODE is not equal to 'S' (single) or 'D' (divorced); otherwise perform 100-UNMARRIED-RTN. We can write this as follows:

```
IF  MARITAL-CODE IS EQUAL TO 'S'
        OR MARITAL-CODE IS EQUAL TO 'D'
        PERFORM 100-UNMARRIED-RTN
ELSE
        PERFORM 200-MARRIED-RTN.
```

But suppose we want to use negated conditionals. On first thought, you may decide simply to negate each simple condition:

```
IF  MARITAL-CODE IS NOT EQUAL TO 'S'
        OR MARITAL-CODE IS NOT EQUAL TO 'D'
        PERFORM 200-MARRIED-RTN
ELSE
        PERFORM 100-UNMARRIED-RTN.
```

An evaluation of this statement will show that the preceding is *not* correct. As coded, one of two conditions must exist for 200-MARRIED-RTN to be executed:

    a. MARITAL-CODE IS NOT EQUAL TO 'S'

or

    b. MARITAL-CODE IS NOT EQUAL TO 'D'

Suppose MARITAL-CODE is 'M' (for married); 200-MARRIED-RTN will be executed, which is what we want. If MARITAL-CODE is 'S', however, we wish 100-UNMARRIED-RTN to be executed. In the preceding conditional, condition (a) is *not met* since MARITAL-CODE does equal 'S'. However, condition (b) *is met* since MARITAL-CODE *is not equal to* 'D', but is equal to 'S'. Only one condition needs to be satisfied for 200-MARRIED-RTN to be executed, and since condition (b) is satisfied, 200-MARRIED-RTN will be executed *instead of* 100-UNMARRIED-RTN, which is really the procedure we should execute.

Similarly, suppose MARITAL-CODE is 'D'. We want 100-UNMARRIED-RTN to be executed, but again we will see that 200-MARRIED-RTN is executed. Condition (a) is satisfied, because MARITAL-CODE is not equal to 'S' (it is equal to 'D'). Since only one condition needs to be satisfied, 200-MARRIED-RTN is executed. In fact, you can now see that the sentence as coded will *always* cause 200-MARRIED-RTN to be executed, regardless of the contents of MARITAL-CODE.

The "moral" of this illustration is a lesson in Boolean algebra, which is: When negating conditions separated by OR: IF NOT (CONDITION1 OR CONDITION2 ...), the stated conditions become: IF NOT CONDITION1 **AND**

NOT CONDITION2 **AND** .... Hence, the IF statement could be coded as IF NOT (MARITAL-CODE = 'S' OR MARITAL-CODE = 'D') or as:

```
IF   MARITAL-CODE IS NOT EQUAL TO 'S'
      AND  MARITAL-CODE IS NOT EQUAL TO 'D'
     PERFORM 200-MARRIED-RTN
ELSE
     PERFORM 100-UNMARRIED-RTN.
```

E. Condition-Names

A **condition-name** is a user-defined word established in the DATA DIVISION that gives a name to a specific value that an identifier can assume. In the DATA DIVISION, it is coded with the level number 88. An 88-level entry is a condition-name that denotes a possible value for an identifier. Consider the following example:

Suppose that an 'S' in the field called MARITAL-STATUS denotes that the person is single. We may use a condition-name SINGLE to indicate this value:

When the field called MARITAL-STATUS is equal to 'S', we will call that condition SINGLE. The 88-level item is not the name of a *field* but the name of a *condition*. The 88-level item refers only to the elementary item *directly preceding it*. SINGLE is a condition-name applied to the field called MARITAL-STATUS, since MARITAL-STATUS directly precedes the 88-level item. The condition SINGLE exists or is "true" if MARITAL-STATUS = 'S'.

A condition-name is always coded on the 88 level and has only a VALUE clause associated with it. Since a condition-name is *not* the name of a field, it will *not* contain a PICTURE clause.

The following is the format for 88-level items.

Format

> 88 condition-name <u>VALUE</u> literal.

The condition-name, which must be unique, refers only to the elementary item preceding it. The VALUE of the condition-name must be a literal consistent with the data type of the corresponding field:

```
05  CODE-IN              PIC XX.
    88  STATUS-OK        VALUE '12'.
```

For readability, an 88-level item is indented to clarify its relationship to the data-name directly preceding it.

Condition-names refer only to *elementary* items in the DATA DIVISION. The identifier to which the condition-name refers must contain a PICTURE clause. Items on level numbers 01–49 in the FILE SECTION and WORKING-STORAGE SECTION may have condition-names associated with them; so, too, may 77-level items, if used, in the WORKING-STORAGE SECTION.

Condition-names are defined in the DATA DIVISION to simplify processing in the PROCEDURE DIVISION. A condition-name is an alternate method of expressing a simple relational test in the PROCEDURE DIVISION. Consider the following DATA DIVISION entries:

```
05   MARITAL-STATUS        PIC X.
     88   DIVORCED          VALUE 'D'.
```

We may use *either* of the following tests in the PROCEDURE DIVISION:

```
IF   MARITAL-STATUS IS EQUAL TO 'D'
     PERFORM 600-DIVORCE-RTN.
```

or

```
IF   DIVORCED
     PERFORM 600-DIVORCE-RTN.
```

The condition-name DIVORCED will test to determine if MARITAL-STATUS does, in fact, have a value of 'D'.

You may code as many 88-level items for a field as you wish:

```
05   MARITAL-STATUS        PIC X.
     88   DIVORCED          VALUE 'D'.
     88   MARRIED           VALUE 'M'.
```

Condition-names may be used in the PROCEDURE DIVISION to make programs easier to read and debug. They may refer to fields with or without VALUE clauses.

Condition-names are frequently used for indicating when an AT END condition has been reached, as in the following:

Example
```
05   ARE-THERE-MORE-RECORDS          PIC X(3)   VALUE 'YES'.
     88   THERE-ARE-MORE-RECORDS                 VALUE 'YES'.
     88   THERE-ARE-NO-MORE-RECORDS              VALUE 'NO '.
         :
         :
IF   THERE ARE-NO-MORE-RECORDS
     PERFORM 900-END-OF-JOB-RTN.
```

Using the condition-name THERE-ARE-NO-MORE-RECORDS may be more meaningful in a conditional or PERFORM ... UNTIL statement than simply comparing ARE-THERE-MORE-RECORDS to 'NO '.

SUMMARY—CONDITION-NAMES

1. 88-level items are used to represent condition-names.
2. A condition-name specifies the value that a field can contain.
3. The format for a condition-name is as follows:

    88 condition-name VALUE literal.

4. The 88-level item refers to the elementary item preceding it.

CHAPTER SUMMARY

A.   Simple Relational for Selection
    1. Relations

$$
\text{IF} \quad \text{identifier-1} \left\{ \begin{array}{l} \left\{ \begin{array}{l} \text{IS EQUAL TO} \\ = \end{array} \right\} \\ \left\{ \begin{array}{l} \text{IS LESS THAN} \\ < \end{array} \right\} \\ \left\{ \begin{array}{l} \text{IS GREATER THAN} \\ > \end{array} \right\} \end{array} \right\} \quad \text{identifier-2}
$$

(<= , >= , and <> are also available with COBOL 85.)

2. If the condition exists, all statements up to the period or to the ELSE clause are executed.
3. If the condition does not exist, the statements after the word ELSE, if coded, are executed, or (if there is no ELSE clause) processing continues with the next sentence.
4. Comparisons
   a. Are algebraic or logical
      (1) Numeric

$$12.0 = 12.00 = 12 = +12$$

      (2) Nonnumeric

$$ABC = ABC\text{b} = ABC\text{bb}$$

   b. Collating sequences (EBCDIC and ASCII) are the same with regard to A–Z, 0–9, and a–z. They differ when upper- and lowercase letters are compared or when letters and digits are compared. With ASCII, lowercase letters are greater than uppercase letters; with EBCDIC, lowercase letters are less than uppercase letters. With EBCDIC, letters are less than numbers. With ASCII, numbers are less than letters.

B. Other Types of IF Statements
   1. Compound Condition
      a. Format

```
IF condition-1 OR condition-2 . . .
IF condition-1 AND condition-2 . . .
```

      b. Hierarchy
         (1) If ORs and ANDs are used in the same sentence, ANDs are evaluated first from left to right, followed by ORs.
         (2) Parentheses can be used to supersede hierarchy rules.
   2. Other Tests
      a. Sign test

```
IF   identifier-1   IS   { POSITIVE  }  . . .
                         { NEGATIVE  }
                         { ZERO      }
```

      Identifier-1 must have an S in its PIC clause if it is to store data with a negative value.
      b. Class Test

```
IF   identifier-1   IS   { NUMERIC    }  . . .
                         { ALPHABETIC }
```

      c. Negated Conditionals
         (1) Any test can be preceded with a NOT to test the negative of a conditional.
         (2) IF NOT (A = B OR A = C) is the same as IF A NOT = B **AND** A NOT = C.
   3. Condition-Names
      a. Coded on 88-level directly following the field to which it relates. For example:

```
05  CODE-IN            PIC X.
    88  OK-CODE        VALUE '6'.
```

      b. Condition-name specifies a condition in the PROCEDURE DIVISION. For example:

```
IF  OK-CODE
    PERFORM 200-OK-RTN.
```

CHAPTER SELF-TEST

What, if anything, is wrong with the following entries (1–5)? Correct all errors.

```
1. IF   A = B OR IF A = C
       PERFORM 100-RTN-X.

2. IF   B = 3 OR 4
       PERFORM 100-RTN-X.

3. IF   C < A + B
       PERFORM 500-STEP-5.

4. IF   A < 21 OR A = 21 AND A = 5 OR A > 5
       PERFORM 100-RTN-1.

5. IF   A IS NOT EQUAL TO 3 OR A IS NOT EQUAL TO 4
       PERFORM 600-RTN-X.
```

6. The hierarchy rule for evaluating compound conditionals states that conditions surrounding the word _____ are evaluated first, followed by conditions surrounding the word _____ .

7. Indicate whether the following two statements are equivalent.
```
(a) IF   AMT < 3 OR AMT > 4
        PERFORM 700-ERR-RTN.
(b) IF   AMT IS NOT EQUAL TO 3 AND AMT IS NOT EQUAL TO 4
        PERFORM 700-ERR-RTN.
```

8. Write a single statement to `PERFORM 500-PARA-5` if A is between 3 and 13, *inclusive of the end points*.

9. Write a single statement to execute `500-PARA-5` if A is between 3 and 13, *exclusive of the end points*.

10. Write a single statement to perform `300-PARA-3` if the following conditions are all met; otherwise perform `200-PARA-2`: (a) A = B; (b) C = D; (c) E = F.

Solutions

1. The word `IF` should appear only once in the statement:
```
IF   A = B OR A = C
     PERFORM 100-RTN-X.
```

2. Nothing wrong—implied operands are permitted. The statement is the same as:
`IF B = 3 OR B = 4 PERFORM 100-RTN-X.`

3. This is okay for COBOL 85. For COBOL 74, each element in a condition must be an identifier or a literal; `A + B` as an arithmetic expression would not be permitted. For COBOL 74, the following would be valid:
```
ADD A TO B.
IF   C < B
     PERFORM 500-STEP-5.
```

4. Parentheses must be used to make the statement logical: `IF (A < 21 OR A = 21)` `AND (A = 5 OR A > 5) PERFORM 100-RTN-1.` Without the parentheses, the statement reduces to: `IF A < 21 OR A > 5 PERFORM 100-RTN-1.` This is because the clause `A = 21 AND A = 5` is a compound condition that cannot be met.

5. A branch to `600-RTN-X` will always occur. This should read:
```
IF   A IS NOT EQUAL TO 3 AND A IS NOT EQUAL TO 4
     PERFORM 600-RTN-X.
```

6. `AND`; `OR`

7. Only if `AMT` is an integer field.

8. `IF A = 13 OR A < 13 AND A > 3 OR A = 3 PERFORM 500-PARA-5.` (*Note:* This is *not* the only way to write the statement. Note, too, that there is no need for parentheses, but including them would be okay.)

```
 9. IF   A > 3 AND A < 13
          PERFORM 500-PARA-5,
10. IF   A = B AND C = D AND E = F
          PERFORM 300-PARA-3
     ELSE
          PERFORM 200-PARA-2,
```

PRACTICE PROGRAM

Write a program for a rental car company that prints the amount owed by each customer. The amount owed depends on the miles driven, the number of days the car was rented, and the type of car rented. Toyotas rent at $26 per day and 18¢ per mile. Oldsmobiles rent at $32 per day and 22¢ per mile. Cadillacs rent for $43 per day and 28¢ per mile. The first 100 miles are free regardless of the car rented.

The format of the input is as follows:

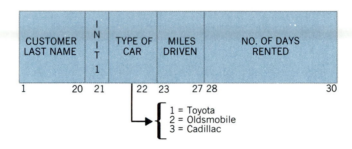

The flowchart and pseudocode that describe the logic of this program are in Figure 9.1. The solution is shown in Figure 9.2.

KEY TERMS

ASCII code	Condition-name	Negated conditional
Class test	Data exception error	Nested conditional
Collating sequence	EBCDIC code	Sign test
Compound conditional	Imperative statement	Simple condition
Conditional statement		

REVIEW QUESTIONS

T F

I. True-False Questions

__ __ 1. In a compound conditional, statements surrounding the word AND are evaluated first.

__ __ 2. The phrase ELSE NEXT SENTENCE can always be eliminated from conditional statements without changing the meaning of the IF statement.

__ __ 3. The clause IF A IS POSITIVE is the opposite of the clause IF A IS NEGATIVE.

__ __ 4. The clause IF A IS NUMERIC is the opposite of the clause IF A IS ALPHABETIC.

__ __ 5. Fields being compared in an IF statement must always be the same size.

__ __ 6. On most computers, at least one space must precede and follow every symbol such as <, >, and =.

__ __ 7. Comparing numeric fields to nonnumeric literals can cause erroneous results.

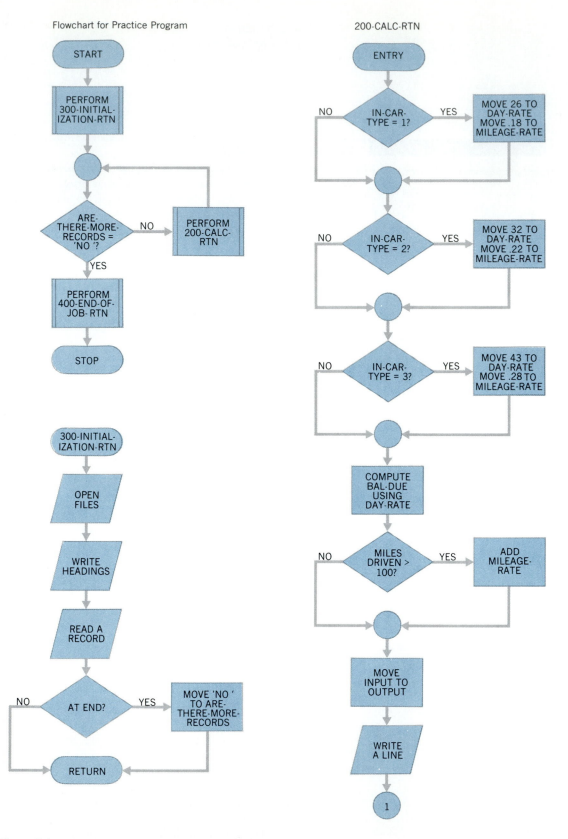

Figure 9.1
Flowchart and pseudocode for
Practice Program.

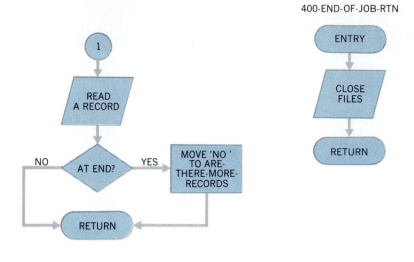

400-END-OF-JOB-RTN

Pseudocode for Practice Program

```
START
    Housekeeping Operations
    Write Headings
    Read a Record
    PERFORM UNTIL no more records
        IF  In-Car-Type = 1
        THEN
            Move 26 to Day-Rate
            Move .18 to Mileage-Rate
        ENDIF
        IF  In-Car-Type = 2
        THEN
            Move 32 to Day-Rate
            Move .22 to Mileage-Rate
        ENDIF
        IF  In-Car-Type = 3
        THEN
            Move 43 to Day-Rate
            Move .28 to Mileage-Rate
        ENDIF
        Compute Bal-Due Using Day-Rate
        IF  Miles Driven > 100
        THEN
            Add Mileage-Rate
        ENDIF
        Move Input to Output
        Write a Line
        Read a Record
    ENDPERFORM
    End-of-Job Operations
STOP
```

Figure 9.1
(continued)

Figure 9.2
Solution to Practice Program.

(a) Program

```
IDENTIFICATION DIVISION.
PROGRAM-ID. SAMPLE.
**************************************************
*   PROGRAM CREATES A REPORT LISTING RENTER   *
*   MILES DRIVEN AND BALANCE ON RENTAL.       *
**************************************************
ENVIRONMENT DIVISION.
INPUT-OUTPUT SECTION.
FILE-CONTROL.
    SELECT IN-RENTER-FILE        ASSIGN TO DATA3.
    SELECT OUT-RECEIVABLE-FILE ASSIGN TO SYS$OUTPUT.
DATA DIVISION.
FILE SECTION.
FD  IN-RENTER-FILE
    LABEL RECORDS ARE OMITTED.
01  IN-RENTER-REC.
    05  IN-RENTER-LAST-NAME      PIC X(20).
    05  IN-RENTER-FIRST-INIT     PIC X.
    05  IN-CAR-TYPE              PIC 9.
    05  IN-MILES-DRIVEN          PIC 9(5).
    05  IN-DAYS-RENTED           PIC 999.
FD  OUT-RECEIVABLE-FILE
    LABEL RECORDS ARE OMITTED.
01  OUT-RECEIVABLE-REC           PIC X(80).
WORKING-STORAGE SECTION.
01  WORK-AREAS.
    05  ARE-THERE-MORE-RECORDS  PIC X(3)     VALUE 'YES'.
    05  WS-BALANCE-DUE          PIC 9(4)V99 VALUE ZEROS.
    05  WS-DAY-RATE             PIC 99       VALUE ZEROS.
    05  WS-MILAGE-RATE          PIC V99      VALUE ZEROS.
01  HL-HEADING1.
    05  FILLER                   PIC X(23)    VALUE SPACES.
    05  FILLER                   PIC X(33)
        VALUE 'ABC RENT-A-CAR RECEIVABLES REPORT'.
    05  FILLER                   PIC X(24)    VALUE SPACES.
01  HL-HEADING2.
    05  FILLER                   PIC X(5)     VALUE SPACES.
    05  FILLER                   PIC X(20)
        VALUE 'NAME'.
    05  FILLER                   PIC X(7)     VALUE SPACES.
    05  FILLER                   PIC X(8)
        VALUE 'CAR TYPE'.
```

Figure 9.2
(continued)

```
          05  FILLER                      PIC XX       VALUE SPACES.
          05  FILLER                      PIC X(5)
            VALUE 'MILES'.
          05  FILLER                      PIC X(5)     VALUE SPACES.
          05  FILLER                      PIC X(4)
            VALUE 'DAYS'.
          05  FILLER                      PIC X(4)     VALUE SPACES.
          05  FILLER                      PIC X(11)
            VALUE 'BALANCE DUE'.
          05  FILLER                      PIC X(9)     VALUE SPACES.
      01  DL-DETAIL-LINE.
          05  FILLER                      PIC X(5)     VALUE SPACES.
          05  DL-LAST-NAME                PIC X(20).
          05  FILLER                      PIC X(5)     VALUE SPACES.
          05  DL-FIRST-NAME               PIC X.
          05  FILLER                      PIC X(5)     VALUE SPACES.
          05  DL-CAR-TYPE                 PIC 9.
          05  FILLER                      PIC X(5)     VALUE SPACES.
          05  DL-MILES-DRIVEN             PIC ZZZZ9.
          05  FILLER                      PIC X(5)     VALUE SPACES.
          05  DL-DAYS-RENTED              PIC ZZ9
          05  FILLER                      PIC X(5)     VALUE SPACES.
          05  DL-BALANCE-DUE              PIC $$,$$9.99.
          05  FILLER                      PIC X(9)     VALUE SPACES.
      *
      PROCEDURE DIVISION.
      ********************************************
      *   CONTROLS DIRECTION OF PROGRAM LOGIC   *
      ********************************************
      100-MAIN-MODULE.
          PERFORM 300-INITIALIZATION-RTN.
          PERFORM 200-CALC-RTN
              UNTIL ARE-THERE-MORE-RECORDS = 'NO '.
          PERFORM 400-END-OF-JOB-RTN.
          STOP RUN.
      ****************************************************************
      *   PERFORMED FROM 100-MAIN-MODULE. DETERMINES TYPE OF CAR,  *
      *   CALCULATES THE BALANCE DUE ON RENTAL, MOVES FIELDS TO    *
      *   THE OUTPUT AREAS AND PRINTS THE DETAIL LINE AND READS    *
      *   THE NEXT RECORD.                                         *
      ****************************************************************
      200-CALC-RTN.
          IF  IN-CAR-TYPE = 1
              MOVE  26 TO WS-DAY-RATE
              MOVE .18 TO WS-MILAGE-RATE.
          IF  IN-CAR-TYPE = 2
              MOVE  32 TO WS-DAY-RATE
              MOVE .22 TO WS-MILAGE-RATE.
          IF  IN-CAR-TYPE = 3
              MOVE  43 TO WS-DAY-RATE
              MOVE .28 TO WS-MILAGE-RATE.
          COMPUTE WS-BALANCE-DUE = IN-DAYS-RENTED * WS-DAY-RATE.
          IF  IN-MILES-DRIVEN IS GREATER THAN 100
              COMPUTE WS-BALANCE-DUE =
                  WS-BALANCE-DUE + ((IN-MILES-DRIVEN - 100) * WS-MILAGE-RATE).
          MOVE IN-RENTER-LAST-NAME   TO DL-LAST-NAME.
          MOVE IN-RENTER-FIRST-INIT TO DL-FIRST-NAME.
          MOVE IN-CAR-TYPE        TO DL-CAR-TYPE.
          MOVE IN-MILES-DRIVEN TO DL-MILES-DRIVEN.
          MOVE IN-DAYS-RENTED   TO DL-DAYS-RENTED.
          MOVE WS-BALANCE-DUE   TO DL-BALANCE-DUE.
          WRITE OUT-RECEIVABLE-REC FROM DL-DETAIL-LINE.
          READ IN-RENTER-FILE
              AT END MOVE 'NO ' TO ARE-THERE-MORE-RECORDS.
      ****************************************************************
      *   PERFORMED FROM 100-MAIN-MODULE, OPENS FILES, PRINTS OUT  *
      *   HEADINGS, AND READS INITIAL RECORD FROM IN-RENTER-FILE.  *
      ****************************************************************
      300-INITIALIZATION-RTN.
          OPEN INPUT  IN-RENTER-FILE
               OUTPUT OUT-RECEIVABLE-FILE.
          WRITE OUT-RECEIVABLE-REC FROM HL-HEADING1.
          WRITE OUT-RECEIVABLE-REC FROM HL-HEADING2.
          READ IN-RENTER-FILE
              AT END MOVE 'NO ' TO ARE-THERE-MORE-RECORDS.
```

Figure 9.2
(continued)

```
****************************************************************
*   PERFORMED FROM 100-MAIN-MODULE-RTN, CLOSES FILES,   *
*   AND RETURNS CONTROL TO OPERATING SYSTEM.            *
****************************************************************
  400-END-OF-JOB-RTN.
      CLOSE IN-RENTER-FILE
            OUT-RECEIVABLE-FILE.
```

(b) Sample Input Data

```
WASHINGTON              G100285006
ADAMS                   J300300004
JEFFERSON               T200600008
LINCOLN                 A200115002
WILSON                  W300822007
HAMMEL                  C201567020
STERN                   N300200002
STERN                   R100075003
KENNEDY                 J200289009
SMITH                   S303000025
```

(c) Sample Output

```
                    ABC RENT-A-CAR RECEIVABLES REPORT
NAME                    CAR TYPE   MILES      DAYS      BALANCE DUE
WASHINGTON               G    1     285        6         $189.30
ADAMS                    J    3     300        4         $228.00
JEFFERSON                T    2     600        8         $366.00
LINCOLN                  A    2     115        2          $67.30
WILSON                   W    3     822        7         $503.16
HAMMEL                   C    2    1567       20         $962.74
STERN                    N    3     200        2         $114.00
STERN                    R    1      75        3          $78.00
KENNEDY                  J    2     289        9         $329.58
SMITH                    S    3    3000       25       $1,887.00
```

__ __ 8. The class test is frequently used before an arithmetic operation to ensure that a field designated as numeric actually contains only numeric data.

__ __ 9. The hierarchy of operations in a compound conditional can be overridden by parentheses.

__ __ 10. The symbol < may be used in place of 'IS GREATER THAN' in a conditional.

II. General Questions   Code the following flowchart exercises with a single statement (1–3).

1.

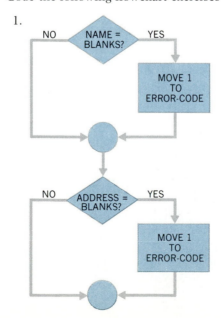

2.   3.

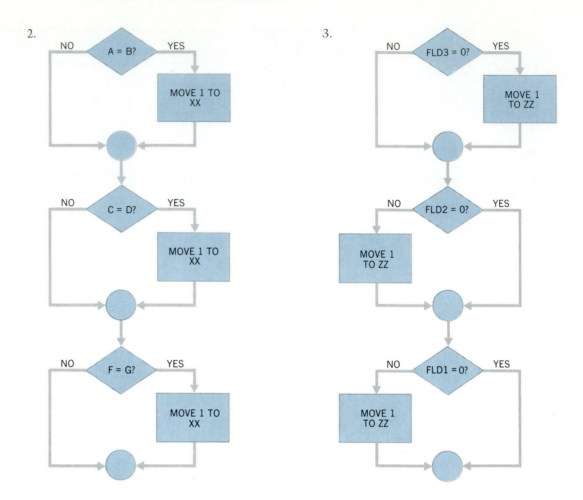

State whether AMT1 is equal to, greater than, or less than AMT2 (4–7).

	AMT1	AMT2
4.	012	12
5.	12.0	12
6.	ABC	ABCⱷ
7.	43	+43

8. Write a routine for determining FICA (Social Security tax) where a field called SALARY is read in as input. FICA is equal to 7.15% of SALARY up to $43,800. SALARY in excess of $43,800 is not taxed.

9. Find the largest of four numbers A, B, C, and D and place it in the field called HOLD-IT.

Are the following groups of statements equivalent (10–12)?

10. (a) IF   A = B
         ADD C TO D
     ELSE
         ADD E TO F.
     PERFORM 600-PRINT-RTN.
   (b) IF   A = B
         ADD C TO D
         PERFORM 600-PRINT-RTN
     ELSE
         ADD E TO F.

```
11. (a) IF   A IS POSITIVE
              PERFORM 600-RTN-X
          ELSE
              PERFORM 700-RTN-Y.
    (b) IF   A IS NOT NEGATIVE
              PERFORM 600-RTN-X
          ELSE
              PERFORM 700-RTN-Y.
12. (a) IF   DISCOUNT IS GREATER THAN TOTAL
              PERFORM 500-ERR-RTN
          ELSE
              SUBTRACT DISCOUNT FROM TOTAL.
    (b) IF   TOTAL > DISCOUNT OR TOTAL = DISCOUNT
              NEXT SENTENCE
          ELSE
              PERFORM 500-ERR-RTN.
          SUBTRACT DISCOUNT FROM TOTAL.
```

What, if anything, is wrong with the following statements (13–14)?

```
13. IF   A IS NOT EQUAL TO B OR A IS NOT EQUAL TO C
         PERFORM 400-RTN-4.
14. IF   A = 3 OR IF   A = 4
         PERFORM 200-PRINT-RTN.
```

15. Doughnuts cost 25¢ each if a customer purchases less than a dozen. The doughnuts are 18¢ if 12 or more are purchased. Write a program excerpt to read in the number of doughnuts purchased and calculate the total price.

16. Write a program excerpt to determine and print the concert ticket price for each purchase order. The ticket price depends on whether or not the request is for (1) a weekend and (2) orchestra seats. The following table shows the various prices for different combinations of requests.

Weekend	Yes	Yes	No	No
Orchestra	Yes	No	Yes	No
Price	$48	$36	$44	$24

Input is as follows:

CUST NO.	CUST NAME	REQUEST WEEKEND	REQUEST ORCHESTRA
1 5 6	25	26	27

		1 = Yes	1 = Yes
		0 = No	0 = No

17. Write a program excerpt to read in a file of exam grades and print the percent of students who received a grade of 85 or better.

18. Write a program excerpt to prepare a multiplication table.

Number	2X	3X	4X	5X	. . .	10X
1	2	3	4	5	. . .	10
2	4	6	8	10	. . .	20
.	.	.	.	.		.
.	.	.	.	.		.
.	.	.	.	.		.
10	20	30	40	50		100

19. Consider the following conditional.

```
IF  XX NOT = ZERO
    AND ZZ = 1
    AND XX NOT = 1
    OR XX NOT = 2
    PERFORM 900-FINISH.
```

Indicate whether 900-FINISH will be performed if XX and ZZ contain the following:

	XX	ZZ
(a)	0	0
(b)	0	1
(c)	0	2
(d)	0	3
(e)	1	0
(f)	1	1
(g)	1	2
(h)	1	3

20. Write a program excerpt to determine whether a field, called FLDA, with a PIC 99, contains an odd or even number.

Hint: You may use the DIVIDE ... REMAINDER for this, or some other technique.

DEBUGGING EXERCISES

1. Consider the following coding:

```
    ⋮
    ⋮
    PERFORM 200-CALC-RTN
        UNTIL NO-MORE-RECORDS.
    ⋮
    ⋮
200-CALC-RTN.
    IF  AMT1 = 5400
        ADD AMT2 TO TOTAL
    ELSE
        ADD 1 TO ERR-CT
    WRITE OUT-REC FROM DETAIL-REC
    READ TRANS-REC
        AT END MOVE 'NO ' TO ARE-THERE-MORE-RECORDS.
```

(a) Under what conditions is a record written?
    (*Hint:* The punctuation is more critical here than the indentations.)
(b) Suppose AMT1 = 5400 initially. The program will abend. Determine why.
(c) Correct this program so it will run properly.

2. The following coding will result in a syntax error. Explain why.

```
IF  AMT1 = AMT2
    ADD AMT3 TO TOTAL.
ELSE
    ADD AMT4 TO TOTAL.
```

3. Consider the following specifications:

```
01  REC-1.
    05  A       PIC X.
    05  B       PIC 9.
    05  C       PIC 9.
```

(a) The following coding will result in a syntax error. Explain why.

```
IF  A IS POSITIVE
    PERFORM 900-GO-TO-IT.
```

(b) Consider the following:

```
IF  A NOT EQUAL TO '6' OR
    B NOT EQUAL TO 7
    PERFORM 800-RTN-X.
```

Will a syntax error result? Explain your answer. Under what condition will 800-RTN-X be performed?

(c) Suppose that REC-1 was not initialized and you included the following coding in the PROCEDURE DIVISION:

```
IF  B = 6
    PERFORM 500-RTN5.
```

Under what conditions, if any, will a syntax error occur? Under what conditions, if any, would an abend condition occur?

PROGRAMMING ASSIGNMENTS

Because of the importance of conditional statements, an extended list of programming assignments has been included. We recommend that you begin by planning your logic with a flowchart or pseudocode and a hierarchy chart for each program before coding it.

1. Write a program to create a master customer file. The problem definition is shown in Figure 9.3.

   Notes

   a. If sales exceed $500.00, allow 5% discount.
      If sales are between $100.00 and $500.00, allow 2% discount.
      If sales are less than $100.00, allow 1% discount.
   b. Discount amount = Sales × Discount %.
   c. Net amount = Sales − Discount amount.

Systems Flowchart

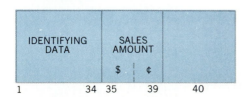

CUSTOMER-TRANS
40-position records
standard labels
10 records/block

CUSTOMER-MASTER
75-position records
standard labels
10 records/block

CUSTOMER-TRANS Record Layout   CUSTOMER-MASTER Record Layout

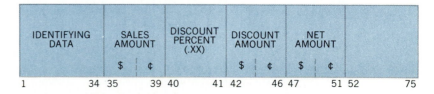

Figure 9.3
Problem definition for Programming Assignment 1.

2. Write a program to list all employees who meet all of the following conditions:
   a. Annual salary is at least $20,000.
   b. Job classification code is 02.
   c. Territory number is 01.
   The problem definition is shown in Figure 9.4.

3. Write a program for a modeling agency. The problem definition is shown in Figure 9.5. Output is a printed report with the names of all
   a. Blond hair, blue-eyed males over 6 feet tall and weighing between 185 and 200 pounds.
   b. Brown hair, brown-eyed females between 5 feet 2 inches and 5 feet 6 inches and weighing between 110 and 125 pounds.
   All other combinations should *not* be printed.

4. Write a program to create a sequential disk file from the following input tape records.

   Input: Tape file
   1–5   Employee number
   6–25   Employee name
   26–27 Hours worked
   28–31 Rate XX.XX
   32–80 Not used
   (Block size is 20; standard labels)

Figure 9.4
Problem definition for
Programming Assignment 2.

Systems Flowchart

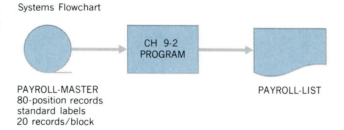

PAYROLL-MASTER
80-position records
standard labels
20 records/block

PAYROLL-LIST

PAYROLL-MASTER Record Layout

EMPLOYEE NO.	EMPLOYEE NAME	TERRITORY NO.		ANNUAL SALARY (in $)		JOB CLASSIFICATION CODE	
1 5	6 25	26 27	28 29	30 35	36 46	47 48	49 80

PAYROLL-LIST Printer Spacing Chart

Output: Sequential disk file
1–5   Employee number
6–25   Employee name
26–31 Gross pay XXXX.XX
32–37 Tax XXXX.XX
38–50 Not used
(Block size is 10; standard labels)

Notes

1. Calculating gross pay

   Gross pay = Regular hours × Rate + Overtime hours × 1.5 × Rate

   Overtime hours are those hours exceeding 40.

2. Calculating tax
   The tax is computed as follows:

Gross Pay	Tax
Less than 150.00	0
Between 150.00 and 500.00	5% of Gross pay greater than 150.00
Over 500.00	$25.00 + 10% of the Gross pay over 500.00

Figure 9.5
Problem definition for
Programming Assignment 3.

Systems Flowchart

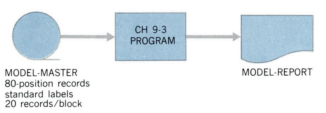

MODEL-MASTER
80-position records
standard labels
20 records/block

MODEL-REPORT

MODEL-MASTER Record Layout

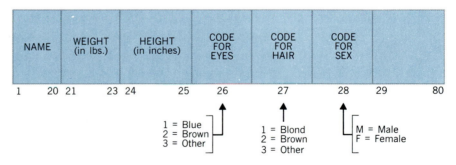

MODEL-REPORT Printer Spacing Chart

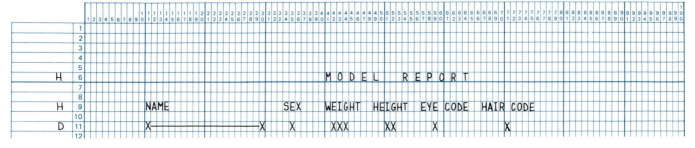

5. The terms of a revolving credit account are as follows:

Current Balance	Interest Rate Per Month
$0–$500	1.5%
$500.01–$1000	1.25%
Over $1000	1%

New Balance (Current balance and interest for first month)	Minimum Payment
$0–$10	New balance (all)
$10.01–$250	$10
Over $250	10% of new balance

Read in customer records with the following format:

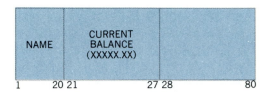

Print the new balance for each customer and the minimum payment he or she must make.

6. Write a program to summarize accident records to obtain the following information.
   a. The percentage of drivers under 25.
   b. The percentage of drivers who are female.
   c. The percentage of drivers from New York.
   There is one disk record for each driver involved in an accident in the past year:

   1–4   Driver number
   5–6   State code (01 for New York)
   7–10 Birth date (month and year)
     11 Sex (M for male, F for female)
   (Block size is 50; standard labels)

   Results should be printed with constants.

   ```
   % OF DRIVERS UNDER 25          XX.XX
   % OF DRIVERS WHO ARE FEMALE    XX.XX
   % OF DRIVERS FROM NY           XX.XX
   ```

7. Write a program to compute the number of $20, $10, $5, and $1 bills that an employee should be paid when his or her salary is provided as input. Each person should be paid with bills of the highest possible denominations.

   Input: Tape records
    1–5   Employee number
    6–25 Employee name
   26–29 Salary (in $)
   30–80 Not used
   (Block size is 20; standard labels)

   Output: A printed report with each employee's number, name, salary, and appropriate messages (i.e., NO. OF 20's, etc.).

8. Write a program to read a detail bank transaction disk with the following format.

       1–5   Account number
       6–25 Name of depositor
         26 Type: 1-Previous balance, 2-Deposit, 3-Withdrawal
      27–33 Amount XXXXX.XX
      34–50 Not used

   The disk has standard labels and a blocking factor of 50. The disk is in sequence by account number. Type 1 records exist for each account number followed by types 2 and 3, if they exist. Types 2 and 3 may be present for a given account number and may appear in any sequence.
       Print out the name of the depositor and his or her current balance (Previous Balance + Deposits − Withdrawals). Include appropriate headings.

9. Write a program to print out patient name and diagnosis for each input medical record. Figure 9.6 illustrates the input record layout.

Figure 9.6
Input record layout for
Programming Assignment 9.

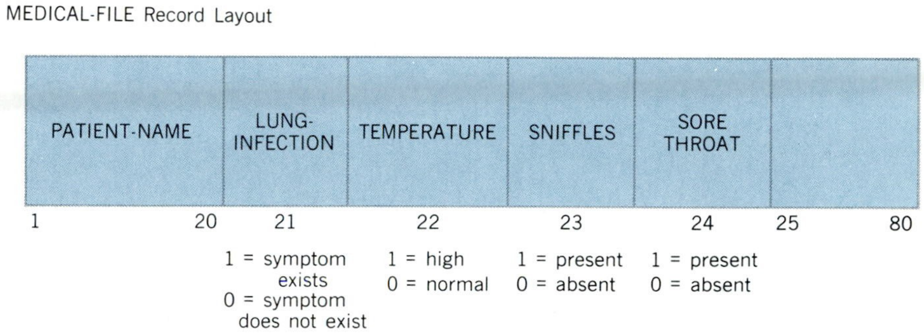

MEDICAL-FILE Record Layout

Notes

a. Output is a printed report with the heading DIAGNOSIS REPORT.
b. It is assumed that all patients have at least one symptom.
c. If a patient has lung infection and temperature, the diagnosis is PNEUMONIA.
d. If the patient has a combination of two or more symptoms (except the combination of lung infection and temperature), the diagnosis is COLD.
e. If the patient has any single symptom, the diagnosis is OK.

10

Iteration Using the PERFORM Statement

OBJECTIVES

To familiarize you with

1. The simple PERFORM.
2. How PERFORM statements are used for iteration.
3. The various options available with the PERFORM statement.

I. A Simple PERFORM

A. The Basic Format

In this section, we will consider the simple **PERFORM** statement, which is used for executing a specified routine once *from one or more points in a program.* Later on, we will consider how other options of the PERFORM are used for iteration or looping. The format of the basic PERFORM is as follows:

Basic Format

> <u>PERFORM</u> paragraph-name-1

The PERFORM statement will

1. Execute all instructions in the named paragraph.
2. Transfer control to the next instruction in sequence, after the PERFORM.

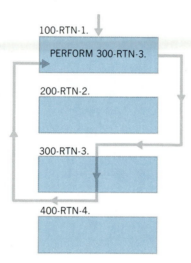

If you look at a reference manual you will find that the format for a PERFORM uses the word "procedure-name" rather than paragraph-name. Because all paragraph-names are also procedure-names, we will use the terms interchangeably for now. In Chapter 17, we will consider procedure-names in more detail.

A simple PERFORM statement is used whenever a series of instructions at a particular paragraph is to be executed from different points in the program. An example of this is the printing of a heading at the top of a new page. Most often, a printed report consists of more than a single page. Generally, we should print a heading not only on the first page at the beginning of the program but also whenever a new page is printed. Consider the following program excerpt, which uses a PERFORM to print headings on each new page from various points in the program.

Example 1

```
PROCEDURE DIVISION.
100-MAIN-MODULE.
    .
    .
    PERFORM 400-HEADING-RTN.
    .
    .
200-CALC-RTN.
    .
    .
    WRITE PRINT-REC FROM DETAIL-REC.
    ADD 1 TO LINE-CTR.
    IF  LINE-CTR = 25
        PERFORM 400-HEADING-RTN.
```

```
         :
         :
300-ERR-RTN.
         :
         :
    WRITE PRINT-REC FROM ERROR-REC.
    ADD 1 TO LINE-CTR.
    IF  LINE-CTR = 25
       PERFORM 400-HEADING-RTN.
         :
         :
400-HEADING-RTN.
         :
         :
```

Whenever a line is printed, we add one to a line counter. After 25 lines have printed on a page, we print headings on a new page. (We will see that to print a heading on a new page, we code: WRITE PRINT-REC FROM HEADING-REC AFTER ADVANCING PAGE.)

A flowchart for a simple PERFORM is as follows:

100-MAIN-MODULE

We flowchart the sequence of steps within a paragraph that is executed with a PERFORM as follows:

Paragraph-name

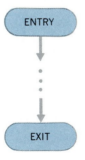

The pseudocode for this program excerpt would be:

```
PERFORM
     :      } Statements to be performed go here
     :
ENDPERFORM
```

Note that with a PERFORM . . . ENDPERFORM structure, the pseudocode omits mention of a paragraph-name entirely. The sequence of steps to be performed is indented in the pseudocode to make it easier to read.

COBOL 85 can use an **in-line PERFORM** just like pseudocode. That is, the actual paragraph-name can be omitted entirely as in the following:

```
PERFORM
    MOVE 0 TO TOTAL.
    MOVE 1 TO NUM.
    WRITE ANS-REC.
END-PERFORM
```

With COBOL 85, END-PERFORM is required to designate the end of the in-line PERFORM. END-PERFORM is called a **scope terminator.**

Suppose you code PERFORM 200-PROCESS-RTN. When this instruction is encountered, the computer will execute all statements in 200-PROCESS-RTN. The computer terminates execution of 200-PROCESS-RTN when it reaches a new paragraph-name or the end of the program, if there is no new paragraph-name found.

B. Nested PERFORM: A PERFORM **within a** PERFORM

PERFORM statements are permitted within the range of a PERFORM statement. This is called a **nested PERFORM**. To say PERFORM 200-PARA-1 is permissible even if 200-PARA-1 has a PERFORM statement as one of its instructions. The following is a valid structure:

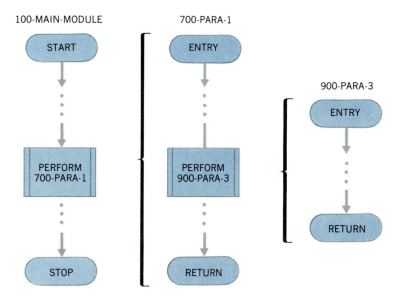

C. Modularizing Programs Using PERFORM **Statements**

As noted in Chapter 5, well-designed programs should be modular. This means that each set of related instructions should be set aside as a **module** rather than coded line-by-line. Consider the following two program excerpts. They execute the same series of instructions, but the second is better designed because it includes the modular approach.

Version 1: Nonmodular Approach

```
IF  AMT1-IN < AMT2-IN
    ADD AMT1-IN TO TOTAL-1
    ADD AMT2-IN TO TOTAL-2
    ADD 1 TO OK-REC-CTR
```

Version 2: Modular Approach

```
IF  AMT1-IN < AMT2-IN
    PERFORM 300-OK-RTN
ELSE
    PERFORM 400-ERR-RTN.
```

```
        ELSE                                    :
            ADD AMT2-IN TO TOTAL-3          300-OK-RTN.
            ADD 1 TO ERR-REC-CTR.               ADD AMT1-IN TO TOTAL-1.
                                                ADD AMT2-IN TO TOTAL-2.
                                                ADD 1 TO OK-REC-CTR.
                                            400-ERR-RTN.
                                                ADD AMT2-IN TO TOTAL-3.
                                                ADD 1 TO ERR-REC-CTR.
```

The IF sentence in version 2 uses a *top-down, modular approach*. That is, the details for processing correct and incorrect records are left for subordinate modules. This makes the program easier to design because the programmer can begin by focusing on the major elements and leave minor considerations for later. We recommend that you use this approach.

Using a top-down approach, the main module is best coded as:

```
100-MAIN-MODULE.
    PERFORM 500-INITIALIZATION-RTN.
    PERFORM 400-HEADING-RTN.
    READ ...
        AT END ...
    PERFORM 200-PROCESS-RTN
        UNTIL NO-MORE-DATA.
    PERFORM 900-END-OF-JOB-RTN.
        :
500-INITIALIZATION-RTN.
    OPEN ...
    (initialize fields)
        :
900-END-OF-JOB-RTN.
    (print any final totals)
    CLOSE ...
    STOP RUN.
```

By coding 100-MAIN-MODULE with a series of PERFORMs, the details for initializations, headings, and end-of-job procedures are left for subordinate modules.

Note that NO-MORE-DATA is a condition-name associated with the field we call ARE-THERE-MORE-RECORDS:

```
05  ARE-THERE-MORE-RECORDS    PIC X(3)    VALUE 'YES'.
    88  NO-MORE-DATA                      VALUE 'NO '.
```

D. Executing a Group of Paragraphs with a Simple PERFORM

The following is an expanded format for the PERFORM statement:

Format 1

$$\text{PERFORM} \quad \text{paragraph-name-1} \quad \left[\left\{ \begin{array}{c} \underline{\text{THROUGH}} \\ \underline{\text{THRU}} \end{array} \right\} \text{paragraph-name-2} \right]$$

The PERFORM executes all statements beginning at paragraph-name-1 until the *end* of paragraph-name-2 is reached. Control is then transferred to the statement directly following the PERFORM. The following schematic illustrates how the PERFORM ... THRU may be used:

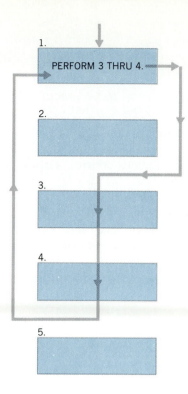

E. The Use and Misuse of GO TO Statements

The format for a GO TO is:

Format

> GO TO   paragraph-name-1

Unlike the PERFORM, which returns control to the statement following the PERFORM, the **GO TO** permanently transfers control to another paragraph. Figure 10.1 illustrates the distinction between a PERFORM and a GO TO.

Why Well-Designed Programs Avoid the Use of GO TOs

In structured, top-down programming, we use one main routine followed by a series of subordinate routines. All paragraphs are executed from the main routine or subordinate routines using PERFORM statements. In this way, the overall logical structure of the program is easy to follow. Because a GO TO permanently transfers control to another paragraph, its use makes it difficult to achieve the same level of control. Moreover, the risk of logic errors is much greater with GO TOs than with PERFORMs. We focus, then, on structured, GO-TO-less coding so that programs will be easier to read, code, and modify.

There are, however, times in which GO TO statements are permissible. If you use the THRU option of the PERFORM statement, a GO TO may appear *within the paragraphs being performed*. Consider the following:

```
      PERFORM 100-STEP1 THRU 400-STEP4.
        .
        .
 100-STEP1.
     ADD A TO B.
     IF  C = ZERO
         GO TO 300-STEP3.
```

```
200-STEP2.
    MULTIPLY C BY C.
300-STEP3.
    MOVE B TO EDIT1.
400-STEP4.
    WRITE PRINTOUT FROM DETAIL-REC
        AFTER ADVANCING 2 LINES.
```

Although a conditional branch in 100-STEP1 transfers control to another paragraph, 300-STEP3, the latter is included within the range of the PERFORM. Because the GO TO still keeps control within the range of the PERFORM, it is considered acceptable.

In summary, when using the THRU option of the PERFORM statement, branches, or GO TO statements, are permitted as long as they are *within the range of the named paragraphs.* Note, however, that to say PERFORM 100-STEP1 THRU 200-STEP2 in the preceding would *not* be valid, because the conditional branch transfers control to 300-STEP3, which is *outside* the PER-FORM range. In this case, control would not return to the statement directly following the PERFORM.

Figure 10.1
The distinction between a
PERFORM and a GO TO.

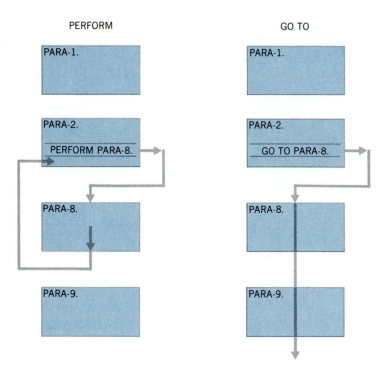

F. The EXIT Statement

Consider the following procedure, which is designed to process only those amount fields that are valid, or numeric. The accompanying program excerpt is one way to code the procedure.

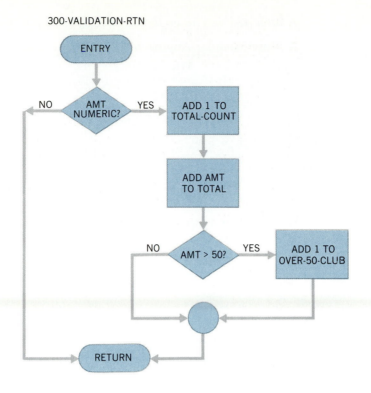

300-VALIDATION-RTN

```
300-VALIDATION-RTN.
    IF  AMT IS NOT NUMERIC
        GO TO 400-VALIDATION-RTN-EXIT.
    ADD 1 TO TOTAL-COUNT.
    ADD AMT TO TOTAL.
    IF  AMT IS GREATER THAN 50
        ADD 1 TO OVER-50-CLUB.
400-VALIDATION-RTN-EXIT.
    EXIT.
```

To execute this routine properly, the PERFORM statement should read:

```
PERFORM 300-VALIDATION-RTN
    THRU 400-VALIDATION-RTN-EXIT.
```

EXIT is a COBOL reserved word that performs *no operation*. It is used to allow execution to pass over other statements or to transfer control back to the statement following the original PERFORM. It is used, when necessary, as an end point in a paragraph being performed. In the preceding example, we used the paragraph called 400-VALIDATION-RTN-EXIT to avoid processing incorrect data the same way we process valid data.

A GO TO is permitted within 300-VALIDATION-RTN since it causes a branch to 400-VALIDATION-RTN-EXIT, which is still within the range of the paragraphs being performed.

We use the name 400-VALIDATION-RTN-EXIT for documentation purposes, but *any* paragraph-name could be used. With COBOL 74, EXIT must be the only word in the paragraph; with COBOL 85, EXIT can be used *in addition to* other statements within a paragraph.

A preferred way to code 300-VALIDATION-RTN is as follows:

A More Modular Approach

```
300-VALIDATION-RTN.
    IF  AMT IS NOT NUMERIC
        NEXT SENTENCE
    ELSE
        PERFORM 400-PROCESS-REC.
          :
400-PROCESS-REC.
    ADD 1 TO TOTAL-COUNT.
    ADD AMT TO TOTAL.
    IF  AMT IS GREATER THAN 50
        ADD 1 TO OVER-50-CLUB.
```

The preceding is not only more modular, it avoids the use of EXITs and GO TOs entirely.

II. Iteration Using Other Types of PERFORMs

A. PERFORM ... UNTIL

As noted, one type of logical control structure is a sequence where instructions are executed in the order in which they appear. A second type of logical control structure is the IF-THEN-ELSE or selection structure in which instructions are executed depending on whether a condition is true or false. We have also seen in Chapter 5 that the third type of logical structure called **iteration** means that a series of instructions in a different module can be executed repeatedly. Iteration is performed in COBOL using a **PERFORM ... UNTIL** statement.

The format of a PERFORM ... UNTIL is:

Format 2

$$\text{\underline{PERFORM}} \quad \text{paragraph-name-1} \quad \left[\left\{ \begin{array}{l} \underline{\text{THROUGH}} \\ \underline{\text{THRU}} \end{array} \right\} \text{paragraph-name-2} \right]$$

$$\underline{\text{UNTIL}} \quad \text{condition-1}$$

Any simple or compound condition can be specified.

Examples

```
1. PERFORM 600-ERROR-CHECK1
       THRU 800-ERROR-CHECK3 UNTIL X = 2.
2. PERFORM 200-VALIDITY-CHECK
       UNTIL X > 7.
3. PERFORM 800-PRINT-RTN
       UNTIL A = B OR A = C.
4. PERFORM 900-ERROR-RTN
       UNTIL A > B AND A > C.
```

The contents of the identifiers used in the UNTIL clause should be changed within the paragraph(s) being performed. To say PERFORM 600-PRINT-RTN UNTIL X = 5, for example, implies that X will change somewhere within 600-PRINT-RTN. If X remains as 3, for example, then 600-PRINT-RTN will be performed indefinitely or until an abend occurs.

A PERFORM ... UNTIL Tests for the Condition First

If the condition indicated in the UNTIL clause is met at the time of execution, then the named paragraph(s) will be executed 0, or no, times. If PERFORM 600-

PROCESS-RTN UNTIL X = 3 is executed and X equals 3 initially, then 600-PROCESS-RTN will not be performed at all. This condition does *not* imply that an error has occurred. Keep in mind, then, that the condition in a PERFORM ... UNTIL is tested *before* the named paragraph is executed even once.

B. Coding a Loop with a PERFORM

PERFORM ... UNTIL is a type of iteration used for programming a **loop,** which is a sequence of steps that is executed until a condition exists.

You have thus far been using the PERFORM ... UNTIL to transfer control to another paragraph until there are no more records to process. In this section, we will see that the PERFORM ... UNTIL is also used for other types of loops.

Suppose we want to print five mailing labels for each input record. The flowchart and pseudocode excerpt for this problem are as follows:

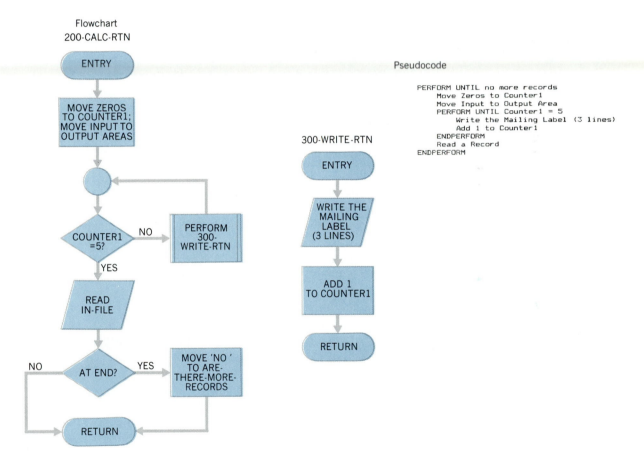

```
Flowchart
200-CALC-RTN
```

```
Pseudocode

PERFORM UNTIL no more records
    Move Zeros to Counter1
    Move Input to Output Area
    PERFORM UNTIL Counter1 = 5
        Write the Mailing Label (3 lines)
        Add 1 to Counter1
    ENDPERFORM
    Read a Record
ENDPERFORM
```

The following coding illustrates the COBOL instructions to perform the required operation:

```
PROCEDURE DIVISION.
100-MAIN-MODULE.
    OPEN INPUT IN-FILE
        OUTPUT PRINT-FILE.
    READ IN-FILE
        AT END MOVE 'NO ' TO ARE-THERE-MORE-RECORDS.
    PERFORM 200-CALC-RTN
        UNTIL NO-MORE-RECORDS.
    CLOSE IN-FILE
            PRINT-FILE.
    STOP RUN.
```

```
200-CALC-RTN.
    MOVE ZEROS TO COUNTER1.
    MOVE NAME TO WS-NAME OF MAIL-LINE-1.
    MOVE ST-ADDR TO WS-ADDR OF MAIL-LINE-2.
    MOVE CITY-STATE-ZIP TO WS-CITY OF MAIL-LINE-3.
    PERFORM 300-WRITE-RTN
        UNTIL COUNTER1 = 5.
    READ IN-FILE
        AT END MOVE 'NO ' TO ARE-THERE-MORE-RECORDS.
200-WRITE-RTN.
    WRITE PRINT-REC FROM MAIL-LINE-1.
    WRITE PRINT-REC FROM MAIL-LINE-2.
    WRITE PRINT-REC FROM MAIL-LINE-3.
    ADD 1 TO COUNTER1.
```

Note that the routine called 200-CALC-RTN, which is performed from 100-MAIN-MODULE, has its own PERFORM statement. This is an example of a nested PERFORM.

We will first discuss the 200-CALC-RTN and 300-WRITE-RTN modules.

200-CALC-RTN **and** 300-WRITE-RTN **Modules**

As in previous illustrations, the PERFORM ... UNTIL in 100-MAIN-MODULE determines if the routine called 200-CALC-RTN is to be repeated or if the job should be terminated. 200-CALC-RTN will be executed repeatedly until there are no more input records to process. NO-MORE-RECORDS is a condition-name equivalent to testing whether ARE-THERE-MORE-RECORDS is equal to 'NO '.

Each time 200-CALC-RTN is executed, COUNTER1 is set to zero. We call this *initializing* COUNTER1 at zero. Data in the input area is then moved to WORKING-STORAGE in preparation for printing. Since COUNTER1 was initialized at zero, it is not equal to 5 at this point; thus, PERFORM 300-WRITE-RTN will be executed from 200-CALC-RTN.

300-WRITE-RTN begins by printing three output lines, or one mailing label. Recall that WRITE PRINT-REC FROM MAIL-LINE-1 is the same as moving MAIL-LINE-1 to PRINT-REC and then writing PRINT-REC.

After a mailing label is written, one is added to COUNTER1. Thus, COUNTER1 is equal to 1 after three lines or the first mailing label is printed. Since COUNTER1 is not yet equal to 5, 300-WRITE-RTN is executed again. The second three-line mailing label is printed, and 1 is added to COUNTER1, giving COUNTER1 a value of 2. This process is repeated until a fifth label is printed and COUNTER1 contains a value of 5. At that point, COUNTER1 is compared to 5; since COUNTER1 now equals 5 and we have printed exactly 5 labels, control returns to the statement within 200-CALC-RTN after the PERFORM. This is a READ statement, which causes another input record to be read.

If there are more records to process, 200-CALC-RTN is executed again; COUNTER1 is initialized at zero each time.

Since COUNTER1 begins at zero, the steps at 300-WRITE-RTN will be repeated five times for each input record, that is, UNTIL COUNTER1 = 5. Each execution of this series of steps is called one *iteration*. Note that COUNTER1 would be defined in the WORKING-STORAGE SECTION.

The preceding type of iteration within 200-CALC-RTN is called a *loop*, which means that the sequence of steps at 300-WRITE-RTN is repeated until a condition exists.

The following operations are generally used for looping:

PROCEDURES USED IN LOOPING

Paragraph Containing the PERFORM **that "Loops"**
1. Initialize the field to be tested. (e.g., MOVE 0 TO COUNTER1)
2. Code a PERFORM paragraph-name UNTIL condition.

Paragraph or Loop to be Performed
1. Code the steps required in the loop.
2. Increment the field to be tested. (e.g., ADD 1 TO COUNTER1)

Thus the counter controls the number of times that the loop is performed.

Common Errors to Avoid

Consider the following program excerpt and see if you can find the logic error that results.

Problem: To add the amount fields of 10 input records to a TOTAL.

Looping: With an Error

```
        MOVE 0 TO COUNTER-A.
        PERFORM 400-ADD-RTN
            UNTIL COUNTER-A = 10.
        WRITE TOTAL-REC.
            :
            :
400-ADD-RTN.
        ADD AMT TO TOTAL.
        READ IN-FILE
            AT END MOVE 'NO ' TO ARE-THERE-MORE-RECORDS.
```

An error will occur because 400-ADD-RTN does not include an instruction that increments COUNTER-A. Thus, COUNTER-A is initialized at 0 and *will remain at zero*. Each time 400-ADD-RTN is executed, a test is performed to determine if COUNTER-A is equal to 10. Since 400-ADD-RTN does not include ADD 1 TO COUNTER-A, the PERFORM statement will cause 400-ADD-RTN to be executed over and over again. This type of error is called an **infinite loop.** What will actually happen is that the computer's built-in clock will sense that 400-ADD-RTN is being executed more times than would normally be required by any program and will then, after a fixed period of time, automatically terminate the job.

Corrected Program Excerpt

The correct coding for 400-ADD-RTN is:

```
400-ADD-RTN.
        ADD AMT TO TOTAL.
        ADD 1 TO COUNTER-A.
        READ IN-FILE
            AT END MOVE 'NO ' TO ARE-THERE-MORE-RECORDS.
```

The ADD may be placed anywhere in the paragraph because COUNTER-A is compared to 10 initially and then each time 400-ADD-RTN has been executed in its entirety.

C. PERFORM ... TIMES

We have thus far focused on the PERFORM ... UNTIL as one type of iteration that is used extensively for looping. We can also program a loop by instructing the computer to execute a sequence of steps a *fixed number of times*. The following is an alternative to the preceding coding:

```
PERFORM 400-ADD-RTN 10 TIMES.
   WRITE TOTAL-REC.
     :
     :
400-ADD-RTN.
   ADD AMT TO TOTAL.
   READ IN-FILE
      AT END MOVE 'NO ' TO ARE-THERE-MORE-RECORDS.
```

With a PERFORM ... TIMES, it is *not* necessary to establish a counter that must be incremented each time through the loop.

The format for a **PERFORM ... TIMES** is:

Format 3

$$\underline{\text{PERFORM}} \text{ (paragraph-name-1)} \left[\left\{ \begin{array}{l} \underline{\text{THROUGH}} \\ \underline{\text{THRU}} \end{array} \right\} \text{paragraph-name-2} \right]$$

$$\left\{ \begin{array}{l} \text{integer-1} \\ \text{identifier-1} \end{array} \right\} \underline{\text{TIMES}}$$

Example 1   A program creates department store credit cards. Each customer is issued two cards:

```
PERFORM 400-CREDIT-CARD-RTN 2 TIMES.
```

Example 2   Each customer indicates the number of credit cards desired. This data is entered in a field in a disk record called NO-OF-COPIES. The following program excerpt describes the disk record along with the PERFORM statement used to print the desired number of credit cards:

```
01  IN-REC.
    05  NAME              PICTURE X(20).
    05  NO-OF-COPIES      PICTURE 9.
      :
      :
    PERFORM 600-CREDIT-CARD-RTN
       NO-OF-COPIES TIMES.
```

When using the TIMES format (PERFORM paragraph-name-1 identifier-1 TIMES), several rules are applicable. The identifier must be specified in the DATA DIVISION, have a *numeric* PICTURE clause, and contain only integers or zeros. To say PERFORM 100-RTN-1 COPY-IT TIMES is valid if COPY-IT has a numeric PICTURE clause and integer or zero contents. If COPY-IT has zero as its value, then RTN-1 will be performed 0, or *no*, times.

> With all versions of COBOL, the word preceding TIMES may be either an integer or an identifier, but with COBOL 85 it can also be *an arithmetic expression*. To say PERFORM 100-PARA-1 B+1 TIMES, for example, is valid with COBOL 85.

The THRU clause is optional with any PERFORM statement. The statement PERFORM 100-RTN1 THRU 800-RTN8 5 TIMES, then, is correct.

When using the *integer* option with the PERFORM ... TIMES format, only the actual number is acceptable. We may *not* say PERFORM RTN-1 FIVE TIMES unless FIVE is a field defined in the DATA DIVISION with a VALUE of 5. Typically, the integer itself is used: PERFORM 100-RTN1 5 TIMES.

D. Examples of Loops

In this section we illustrate how loops can be executed with different options of the PERFORM.

Example 1   To further illustrate looping, let us multiply two numbers together using a series of successive additions. If four is added to itself three times, for example, the result is 12, which is the product of 3×4. We will use both a PERFORM ... UNTIL and a PERFORM ... TIMES for this type of looping. We begin with a PERFORM ... UNTIL:

```
100-PARA-1.
    MOVE ZEROS TO TOTAL.
    PERFORM 200-PARA-2
        UNTIL A = 0.
    WRITE ANS-REC.
        :
        :
200-PARA-2.
    ADD B TO TOTAL.
    SUBTRACT 1 FROM A.
```

Suppose A = 3 and B = 4; let us see how the correct value of 12 is stored in TOTAL.

No. of Times Through 200-PARA-2	Results at End of Loop		
	TOTAL	A	B
0	0	3	4
1	4	2	4
2	8	1	4
3	12	0	4

Control returns to the statement after the PERFORM. This will work properly for all positive integer values for A.

The flowchart and pseudocode for this problem are as follows:

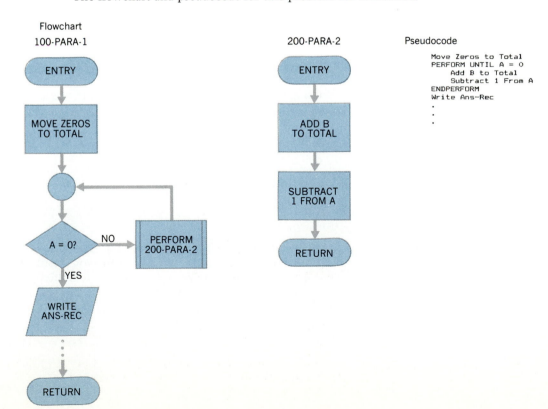

Flowchart
100-PARA-1

200-PARA-2

Pseudocode

```
Move Zeros to Total
PERFORM UNTIL A = 0
    Add B to Total
    Subtract 1 From A
ENDPERFORM
Write Ans-Rec
```

We could also code the preceding with a PERFORM ... TIMES option:

```
MOVE ZEROS TO TOTAL.
PERFORM 200-PARA-2 A TIMES.
WRITE ANS-REC.
    .
    .
200-PARA-2
    ADD B TO TOTAL.
```

The format for the PERFORM ... TIMES permits an identifier as the delimiter, which indicates the number of times the paragraph is to be performed. To PERFORM a paragraph A TIMES when A has a value of 4, for example, means that the paragraph will be executed four times. The identifier must define a numeric, integer field.

Example 2 Sum the odd numbers from 1 through 99 (TOTAL = 1 + 3 + ... 99). Draw your own flowchart or pseudocode. Then try to code the program and compare your results with the following, which uses a PERFORM ... UNTIL:

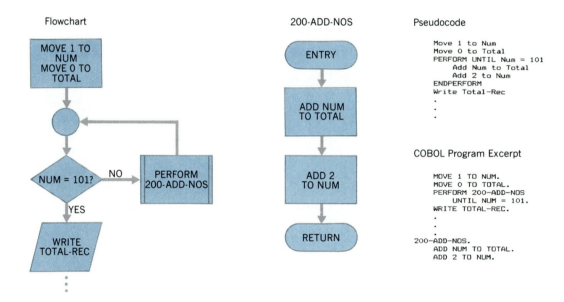

Flowchart

200-ADD-NOS

Pseudocode

```
Move 1 to Num
Move 0 to Total
PERFORM UNTIL Num = 101
    Add Num to Total
    Add 2 to Num
ENDPERFORM
Write Total-Rec
    .
    .
```

COBOL Program Excerpt

```
MOVE 1 TO NUM.
MOVE 0 TO TOTAL.
PERFORM 200-ADD-NOS
    UNTIL NUM = 101.
WRITE TOTAL-REC.
    .
    .
200-ADD-NOS.
    ADD NUM TO TOTAL.
    ADD 2 TO NUM.
```

Using a PERFORM ... TIMES option for this, we have:

```
MOVE 1 TO NUM.
MOVE 0 TO TOTAL.
PERFORM 200-ADD-NOS 50 TIMES.
WRITE TOTAL-REC.
200-ADD-NOS.
    ADD NUM TO TOTAL.
    ADD 2 TO NUM.
```

Example 3 Sum the even integers from 2 through 100 (2 + 4 + ... 100). First plan the program with a flowchart or pseudocode and compare your results to the one that follows. Then code a program and compare yours to the illustrated program. Remember that your program may differ slightly and still be correct, so test it to be sure.

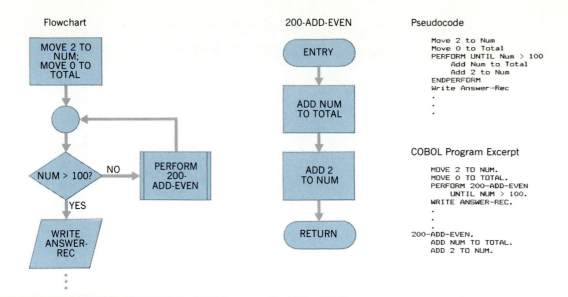

Example 4   The following, although not typically used in business applications, is useful in illustrating program logic with a PERFORM ... UNTIL statement.

Each record has a value N. Find N!, called "N factorial." N! = N × N−1 × N−2 × ... × 1. For example, 5! = 5 × 4 × 3 × 2 × 1 = 120; 3! = 3 × 2 × 1 = 6.

```
200-CALC-RTN.
    MOVE N TO M, PROD.
    PERFORM 300-FACT-RTN
        UNTIL M = 1.
    MOVE PROD TO FACTORIAL OF DETAIL-REC.
    WRITE PRINT-REC FROM DETAIL-REC.
    READ INPUT-FILE
        AT END MOVE 'NO ' TO ARE-THERE-MORE-RECORDS.
300-FACT-RTN.
    SUBTRACT 1 FROM M.
    MULTIPLY M BY PROD.
```

M and PROD are defined in WORKING-STORAGE. M has the same PICTURE as N, and PROD is defined with a PICTURE that is large enough to hold the result.

As previously noted, in a PERFORM ... UNTIL the condition specified is tested *before* the paragraph to be performed is executed. This means that if the condition is met initially, the named paragraph is simply not executed at all. Thus, in the preceding, if N had an initial value of 1, then 300-FACT-RTN would not be executed. The 1 initially moved to PROD would print as the correct answer (1! = 1).

Loops within Loops

Suppose we wish to read in 50 records as five groups of 10 records. The amount fields of each group of 10 input records are to be added and a total printed. Thus *five* totals will print. That is, we wish to execute a routine five times that adds 10 amounts and reads 10 records. The following coding is correct:

```
100-MAIN-MODULE.
    OPEN INPUT SALES-FILE
        OUTPUT PRINT-FILE.
```

```
      READ SALES-FILE
          AT END MOVE 'NO ' TO ARE-THERE-MORE-RECORDS.
      PERFORM 200-MAJOR-RTN 5 TIMES.
      CLOSE SALES-FILE
            PRINT-FILE.
      STOP RUN.
200-MAJOR-RTN.
      MOVE ZEROS TO TOTAL.
      PERFORM 300-ADD-RTN 10 TIMES.
      MOVE TOTAL TO EDIT1.
      WRITE PRINT-OUT FROM TOTAL-REC.
300-ADD-RTN.
      ADD AMT TO TOTAL.
      READ SALES-FILE
          AT END MOVE 'NO ' TO ARE-THERE-MORE-RECORDS.
```

If we are certain that we have exactly 50 records to process, then `PERFORM 200-MAJOR-RTN 5 TIMES` in `100-MAIN-MODULE` could be replaced with:

```
PERFORM 200-MAJOR-RTN
    UNTIL THERE-ARE-NO-MORE-RECORDS.
```

After `300-ADD-RTN` is executed the 50th time, an `AT END` condition will occur and `ARE-THERE-MORE-RECORDS` will be set to `'NO '`. The condition-name `THERE-ARE-NO-MORE-RECORDS` will test `ARE-THERE-MORE-RECORDS` for a `'NO '` at the end of `200-MAJOR-RTN` after the last total is printed.

E. `PERFORM ... VARYING`

The last format for a `PERFORM` statement is the most comprehensive:

Format 4

$$\text{PERFORM}\quad \text{paragraph-name-1}\quad \left[\left\{ {\text{THROUGH} \atop \text{THRU}} \right\} \text{paragraph-name-2}\right]$$

$$\underline{\text{VARYING}}\quad \text{identifier-1}\quad \underline{\text{FROM}}\quad \left\{ {\text{identifier-2} \atop \text{integer-1}} \right\}\quad \underline{\text{BY}}\quad \left\{ {\text{identifier-3} \atop \text{integer-2}} \right\}$$

$$\underline{\text{UNTIL}}\quad \text{condition-1}$$

Suppose we wish to sum all odd-numbered integers from 1 through 1001. We could use the **PERFORM ... VARYING** format as follows:

```
200-CALC-RTN.
    PERFORM 300-ADD-RTN VARYING X1 FROM 1
        BY 2 UNTIL X1 > 1001.
      :
300-ADD-RTN.
    ADD X1 TO ODD-CTR.
```

The `PERFORM ... VARYING`:

1. Initializes X1 at 1.
2. Tests to see if X1 > 1001.
3. If X1 does not exceed 1001: (a) `300-ADD-RTN` is performed; (b) 2 is added to X1; and (c) steps 2 and 3 are repeated.
4. When X1 exceeds 1001, execution continues with the instruction following the `PERFORM`.

Examples

```
(1)     PERFORM 3ØØ-READ-RTN
            VARYING CTR FROM Ø BY 1 UNTIL CTR = 2Ø.
(2)     PERFORM 3ØØ-READ-RTN
            VARYING CTR FROM 1 BY 1 UNTIL CTR IS
                GREATER THAN 2Ø.
```

These two statements perform the same functions. CTR is used to control the number of times 300-READ-RTN is performed. With a PERFORM ... VARYING, CTR should *not* be modified within the loop.

Identifier-1 (CTR in the preceding examples) must be defined in the DATA DIVISION, usually in WORKING-STORAGE, and have a PICTURE clause large enough to hold the maximum value that it can assume. Thus, for these examples, the following WORKING-STORAGE entry would be appropriate:

```
WORKING-STORAGE SECTION.
01  WORK-AREAS.
    05  CTR         PIC 99.
```

If CTR had a PIC of 9, a syntax error may not occur, but a logic error would most certainly result because CTR is not large enough to hold an upper limit of 20.

It is not necessary to use a VALUE clause to initialize CTR, since CTR will *automatically* be initialized with the PERFORM ... VARYING statement.

Other examples of the PERFORM ... VARYING option are as follows:

```
3. PERFORM 100-RTN1 THRU 500-RTN5
        VARYING DATEX FROM 1900 BY 10
            UNTIL DATEX > 1990.
4. PERFORM 200-RTN2
        VARYING COUNTER FROM 10 BY -1
            UNTIL COUNTER = 0.
```

Notice in Example 4 that the counter or loop control field can be *decreased*, rather than increased, each time through the loop.

III. Using Nested PERFORM ... VARYING **Statements**

Figure 10.2 illustrates how a PERFORM ... VARYING statement can be used to print the class average on a final exam for each of 10 classes. For simplicity, we are assuming that each class has exactly 20 students and that each student took every exam. Thus 200 records will be read; we are assuming that the first 20 records are for Class 1, the next 20 are for Class 2, and so on.

This program illustrates nested PERFORM ... VARYING loops, or a PERFORM ... VARYING within a PERFORM ... VARYING. The basic rules for the execution of a nested PERFORM ... VARYING are as follows:

> **RULES FOR USING A NESTED** PERFORM ... VARYING
>
> 1. The *innermost* PERFORM ... VARYING loop is executed *first*.
> 2. The *next outer* PERFORM ... VARYING loop in sequence is then executed.

Figure 10.2
Example of nested PERFORM
... VARYING loops.

```
WORKING-STORAGE SECTION.
01  WORK-AREAS.
    05  CLASS-TOTAL                 PIC 9(4).
    05  CLASS-CTR                   PIC 99.
    05  STUDENT-CTR                 PIC 99.
    05  ARE-THERE-MORE-RECORDS      PIC X(3)    VALUE 'YES'.
        88  NO-MORE-RECORDS                     VALUE 'NO '.
01  OUT-REC.
    05  FILLER                      PIC X(15)   VALUE SPACES.
    05  FILLER                      PIC X(22)
                                VALUE  'THE AVERAGE FOR CLASS '.
    05  CLASS-NUMBER                PIC 99.
    05  FILLER                      PIC XXX     VALUE 'IS '.
    05  CLASS-AVERAGE               PIC 999.99.
    05  FILLER                      PIC X(85)   VALUE SPACES.
PROCEDURE DIVISION.
*****************************************************************
*           THE MAIN MODULE CONTROLS ALL PROCESSING            *
*****************************************************************
100-MAIN-MODULE.
    OPEN INPUT STUDENT-FILE
         OUTPUT PRINT-FILE.
    READ STUDENT-FILE
        AT END MOVE 'NO ' TO ARE-THERE-MORE-RECORDS.
    PERFORM 200-MAJOR-RTN
        VARYING CLASS-CTR FROM 1 BY 1 UNTIL CLASS-CTR > 10.
    CLOSE STUDENT-FILE
          PRINT-FILE.
    STOP RUN.
*****************************************************************
*     THIS IS THE MAJOR OR OUTER LOOP THAT IS EXECUTED 10 TIMES *
*****************************************************************
200-MAJOR-RTN.
    MOVE ZEROS TO CLASS-TOTAL.
    PERFORM 300-CALC-RTN
        VARYING STUDENT-CTR FROM 1 BY 1 UNTIL STUDENT-CTR > 20.
    PERFORM 400-WRITE-RTN.
*****************************************************************
* THIS IS THE MINOR OR INNER LOOP THAT IS EXECUTED 20 TIMES FOR *
* EACH CLASS                                                   *
*****************************************************************
300-CALC-RTN.
    ADD GRADE TO CLASS-TOTAL.
    READ STUDENT-FILE
        AT END MOVE 'NO ' TO ARE-THERE-MORE-RECORDS.
*****************************************************************
* EACH WRITE INSTRUCTION PRINTS ONE CLASS AVERAGE. THIS ROUTINE *
* IS EXECUTED 10 TIMES, ONE FOR EACH CLASS                     *
*****************************************************************
400-WRITE-RTN.
    MOVE CLASS-CTR TO CLASS-NUMBER.
    DIVIDE CLASS-TOTAL BY 20
        GIVING CLASS-AVERAGE.
    WRITE PRINT-REC FROM OUT-REC.
```

In Figure 10.2 the *innermost* loop is controlled by:

```
PERFORM 300-CALC-RTN
    VARYING STUDENT-CTR FROM 1 BY 1 UNTIL STUDENT-CTR > 20.
```

The next loop (in this case the outer loop) is controlled by:

```
PERFORM 200-RTN-1
    VARYING CLASS-CTR FROM 1 BY 1 UNTIL CLASS-CTR > 10.
```

We thus have the following sequence of values for CLASS-CTR and STUDENT-CTR in this program:

Number of Times Through 300-CALC-RTN	CLASS-CTR	STUDENT-CTR
1	1	1
2	1	2
3	1	3
.	.	.
.	.	.
.	.	.
.	1	20

```
  .                    ┌────┐              ┌────┐
  .                    │ 2  │              │ 1  │
  .                    │ 2  │              │ 2  │
  .                    │ 2  │              │ 3  │
  .                    │ .  │              │ .  │
  .                    │ .  │              │ .  │
  .                    │ .  │              │ .  │
  .                    │ 2  │              │ 20 │
                       └────┘              └────┘

  .                    ┌────┐              ┌────┐
  .                    │ 3  │              │ 1  │
  .                    │ 3  │              │ 2  │
  .                    │ 3  │              │ 3  │
  .                    │ .  │              │ .  │
  .                    │ .  │              │ .  │
  .                    │ .  │              │ .  │
  .                    │ 3  │              │ 20 │
                       └────┘              └────┘

  .                      .                   .
  .                      .                   .
  .                      .                   .

  .                    ┌────┐              ┌────┐
  .                    │ 10 │              │ 1  │
  .                    │ 10 │              │ 2  │
  .                    │ 10 │              │ 3  │
  .                    │ .  │              │ .  │
  .                    │ .  │              │ .  │
  .                    │ .  │              │ .  │
 200                   │ 10 │              │ 20 │
                       └────┘              └────┘
```

The first time through 300-CALC-RTN, CLASS-CTR is 1 and STUDENT-CTR is 1. After 300-CALC-RTN has been executed once, the computer increments STUDENT-CTR by 1 since the innermost loop is:

```
PERFORM 300-CALC-RTN
    VARYING STUDENT-CTR FROM 1 BY 1 UNTIL STUDENT-CTR > 20.
```

Stepping through the logic of a program using sample data as we have here is an example of a *structured walkthrough*.

IV. The PERFORM WITH TEST AFTER OPTION (COBOL 85)

The type of iteration using a PERFORM (paragraph) UNTIL (condition) is similar to a DO ... WHILE in other languages. With this structure, a test for the condition is made *first*, even before the sequence of steps within the PERFORM is executed. If the condition is *not* met initially, then the named paragraph is executed at least once. If the condition is met initially, then the paragraph is *not executed at all*.

Most languages also have an iteration structure that executes the named paragraph *even before the test is made*. Pascal, for example, uses the Repeat ... Until structure. This ensures that the sequence of steps within the module to be performed is executed *at least once*. With versions of COBOL prior to COBOL 85, there was no convenient way of executing a named module once *before* testing the condition.

With COBOL 85, a PERFORM ... UNTIL can be made equivalent to a Repeat ... Until with the use of a TEST AFTER clause. This means we instruct the computer to test for the condition in the PERFORM ... UNTIL *after* the paragraph is executed. The format for this is:

Format

> PERFORM paragraph-name-1
>
> [WITH TEST {BEFORE / AFTER}] UNTIL condition-1

To execute 400-TEST-RTN at least once and then test an ERR-CTR field, we can code:

```
PERFORM 400-TEST-RTN WITH TEST AFTER
    UNTIL ERR-CTR > 0.
```

The WITH TEST AFTER clause can also be used with the UNTIL and VARYING options of the PERFORM.

V. A Review of Scope Terminators (COBOL 85)

With COBOL 85, the END-PERFORM may be used to terminate a PERFORM. This enables COBOL 85 to more closely resemble a pseudocode iteration as specified with PERFORM ... ENDPERFORM.

Why Scope Terminators Are Useful

As we have seen, all COBOL arithmetic verbs can use the END- as a scope terminator. The READ can use it as well. Consider the following pseudocode excerpt:

Pseudocode Excerpt

```
IF    Amount = 0
THEN
      Read a Record
      Move 0 to Total
ENDIF
```

To code this in COBOL is not as simple as it appears. The following is *not* correct:

Incorrect Coding

```
IF  AMT = 0
    READ IN-FILE
        AT END MOVE 'NO ' TO ARE-THERE-MORE-RECORDS
    MOVE 0 TO TOTAL.
```

Despite the indentation, the MOVE 0 to TOTAL will be considered *part of the* AT END *clause*. That is, READ ... AT END ... assumes that all clauses following AT END are to be executed only if an AT END condition occurs. Thus 0 will be moved to TOTAL only once: when AMT = 0 *and* an AT END condition has been reached. One way to correct this sentence is to use an END-READ *scope terminator* to definitively delineate the end of the READ:

```
IF  AMT = 0
    READ IN-FILE
        AT END MOVE 'NO ' TO ARE-THERE-MORE-RECORDS
```

```
END-READ
MOVE 0 TO TOTAL.
```

Thus far, we have discussed END-ADD, END-COMPUTE, END-DIVIDE, END-IF, END-MULTIPLY, END-PERFORM, END-READ, and END-SUBTRACT as scope terminators available with COBOL 85. We will specify additional ones when we discuss the respective verbs.

CHAPTER SUMMARY

A. Formats of the PERFORM Statement
   1. Simple PERFORM statement

      PERFORM paragraph-name-1 [THRU paragraph-name-2]

      a. Causes execution of the instructions at the named paragraph(s).
      b. After execution of the named paragraph(s), control is transferred to the statement directly following the PERFORM.
      c. In structured programs, GO TOs are only permitted within the range of the named paragraphs.
   2. The PERFORM ... UNTIL statement
      a. The identifier(s) used in the UNTIL clause must be altered within the paragraph(s) being performed; otherwise, the paragraphs will be performed indefinitely.
      b. If the condition in the UNTIL clause is met at the time of execution, then the named paragraph(s) will not be executed at all. (With COBOL 85, the WITH TEST AFTER clause can be used to test the condition *after* the paragraph has been executed once.)
   3. The PERFORM ... TIMES statement
      a. An identifier or an integer can precede the word TIMES; with COBOL 85, an arithmetic expression can be used as well.
      b. If an identifier is used to indicate the number of times the named paragraph(s) are to be performed, it must: (a) be specified in the DATA DIVISION; (b) have a numeric PICTURE clause; and (c) contain only integers or zeros.
   4. The PERFORM ... VARYING statement
      a. The counter or loop control field must be defined in the DATA DIVISION, typically in WORKING-STORAGE. An initial VALUE for the loop control field is not required.
      b. The PERFORM ... VARYING automatically does the following:
         (1) Initializes the counter with the value specified in the FROM clause.
         (2) Tests the counter for the condition specified in the UNTIL clause.
         (3) Continues with the statement directly following the PERFORM if the condition specified in the UNTIL clause is satisfied.
         (4) Executes the named paragraph(s) if the condition specified in the UNTIL clause is not met.
         (5) After execution of the named paragraph(s), increases (or decreases) the counter by the value of the integer or identifier specified in the VARYING clause.
B. Additional Considerations
   1. The THRU option can be included with all versions of the PERFORM.
   2. PERFORM statements within PERFORM statements are permissible. These are called nested PERFORMs.
   3. EXIT is a reserved word that can be used to indicate the end point of paragraph(s) being performed. EXIT must be the only entry in a paragraph when it is used with COBOL 74.

CHAPTER SELF-TEST

1. After a PERFORM statement is executed, control returns to _____ .
2. Suppose X = 0 when PERFORM 200-PROCESS-RTN X TIMES is executed, then 200-PROCESS-RTN will be performed _____ times.
3. PERFORM 300-PRINT-RTN ITEMX TIMES is valid only if ITEMX has contents of _____ or _____ .
4. How many times will the paragraph named 400-PROCESS-RTN be executed by the following PERFORM statements?
   (a) PERFORM   400-PROCESS-RTN
           VARYING X FROM 1 BY 1 UNTIL X = 10.
   (b) PERFORM   400-PROCESS-RTN
           VARYING X FROM 1 BY 1 UNTIL X > 10.
   (c) PERFORM   400-PROCESS-RTN
           VARYING X FROM 0 BY 1 UNTIL X = 10.
5. Write a PERFORM routine to add A to B five times using (a) the TIMES option, (b) the UNTIL option, (c) the VARYING option.

What, if anything, is wrong with the following routines (Questions 6–8)?

6.   PERFORM 300-ADD-RTN
           VARYING A FROM 1 BY 1 UNTIL A > 20.
       .
       .
       .
   300-ADD-RTN.
       ADD C TO B.
       ADD 1 TO A.

7.   PERFORM 600-TEST-IT 8 .TIMES.
       .
       .
       .
   600-TEST-IT.
       IF A = B GO TO 700-ADD-IT.
       ADD A TO B.
   700-ADD-IT.
       ADD 5 TO B.

8.   PERFORM 800-PROCESS-RTN
           UNTIL CTR = 8.
       .
       .
       .
   800-PROCESS-RTN.
       ADD A TO B.
       ADD 1 TO CTR.
       IF CTR = 8
           STOP RUN.

9. Using the TIMES option of the PERFORM statement, restate the following:

       MOVE 0 TO X1.
       PERFORM 700-LOOP UNTIL X1 = 10.
       .
       .
       .
   700-LOOP.
       .
       .
       ADD 1 TO X1.

10. Using the VARYING option of the PERFORM statement, write a routine to sum all even numbers from 2 through 100.

Solutions

1. the statement directly following the PERFORM
2. no (0)
3. an integer; 0
4. 9 times; 10 times; 10 times

5. (a)
```
        PERFORM 200-ADD-RTN 5 TIMES.
            :
    200-ADD-RTN.
        ADD A TO B.
```
   (b)
```
        MOVE 1 TO CTR.
        PERFORM 200-ADD-RTN UNTIL CTR = 6.
            :
    200-ADD-RTN.
        ADD A TO B.
        ADD 1 TO CTR.
```
   (c)
```
        PERFORM 200-ADD-RTN VARYING N FROM 1
            BY 1 UNTIL N > 5.
            :
    200-ADD-RTN.
        ADD A TO B.
```

6. A, the identifier in the PERFORM statement, should *not* be changed at 300-ADD-RTN. It is incremented automatically by the PERFORM ... VARYING statement.

7. 600-TEST-IT, a paragraph executed by a PERFORM statement, should not have a GO TO that transfers control outside its range. The following is valid:
```
        PERFORM 600-TEST-IT 8 TIMES.
            :
    600-TEST-IT.
        IF  A = B
            ADD 5 TO B
        ELSE
            ADD A TO B.
```

8. A PERFORM statement will automatically compare CTR to 8; thus the last conditional in 800-PROCESS-RTN is not only unnecessary, it is incorrect.

9. PERFORM 700-LOOP 10 TIMES.

10.
```
        PERFORM 900-SUM-RTN
            VARYING X FROM 2 BY 2 UNTIL X IS GREATER THAN 100.
            :
    900-SUM-RTN.
        ADD X TO EVEN-SUM.
```

PRACTICE PROGRAM

The problem definition for this program appears in Figure 10.3.

Given the initial cost of an item, we wish to print a table indicating the item's anticipated cost over a 10-year span taking inflation into account. Assume the inflation rate for the first 5 years is projected at 8% and the inflation rate for the next 5 years is projected at 6%. Be sure to accumulate the effects of inflation. Figure 10.4 has the pseudocode and hierarchy chart. Figure 10.5 has the program.

```
ITEM-COST: $1.00
YEAR 1        1.08     (1 X 1.08)
YEAR 2        1.08²    (1.08 X 1.08)
   :
YEAR 5        1.08⁵
YEAR 6        1.08⁵  X 1.06
   :
YEAR 10       1.08⁵  X 1.06⁵
```

Note: To begin printing on a new page, code WRITE ... AFTER ADVANCING PAGE. To double-space, code WRITE ... AFTER ADVANCING 2 LINES. We discuss the ADVANCING option in more detail in the next chapter.

Figure 10.3
Problem definition for Practice
Program.

Systems Flowchart

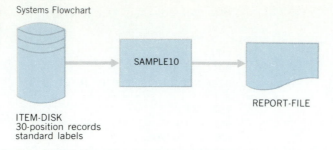

ITEM-DISK
30-position records
standard labels

REPORT-FILE

ITEM-DISK Record Layout

REPORT-FILE Printer Spacing Chart

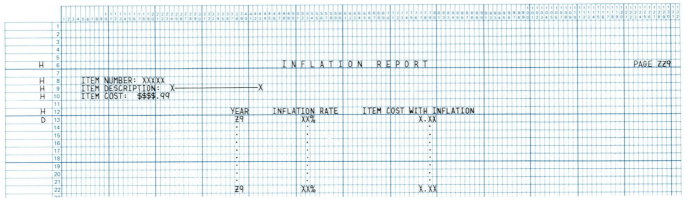

SAMPLE INPUT DATA

```
11111TEST            00100
12345RAKE            01245
```

Figure 10.3 SAMPLE OUTPUT
(continued)

```
                                         I N F L A T I O N   R E P O R T

          ITEM NUMBER: 11111
          ITEM DESCRIPTION:   TEST
          ITEM COST:     $1.00

                           YEAR      INFLATION RATE     ITEM COST WITH INFLATION
                            1            08%                     1.08
                            2            08%                     1.16
                            3            08%                     1.25
                            4            08%                     1.35
                            5            08%                     1.45
                            6            06%                     1.53
                            7            06%                     1.62
                            8            06%                     1.71
                            9            06%                     1.81
                           10            06%                     1.91

          ITEM NUMBER: 12345
          ITEM DESCRIPTION:   RAKE
          ITEM COST:     $12.45

                           YEAR      INFLATION RATE     ITEM COST WITH INFLATION
                            1            08%                    13.44
                            2            08%                    14.51
                            3            08%                    15.67
                            4            08%                    16.92
                            5            08%                    18.27
                            6            06%                    19.36
                            7            06%                    20.52
                            8            06%                    21.75
                            9            06%                    23.05
                           10            06%                    24.43
```

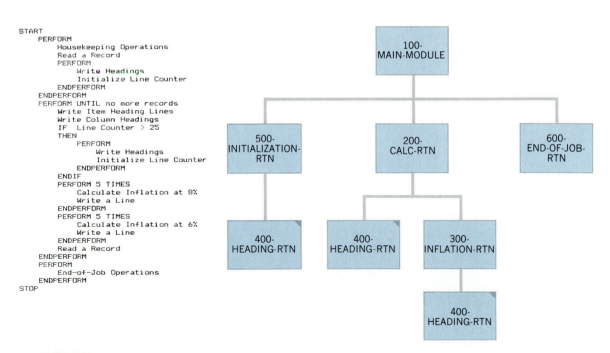

```
START
    PERFORM
        Housekeeping Operations
        Read a Record
        PERFORM
            Write Headings
            Initialize Line Counter
        ENDPERFORM
    ENDPERFORM
    PERFORM UNTIL no more records
        Write Item Heading Lines
        Write Column Headings
        IF  Line Counter > 25
        THEN
            PERFORM
                Write Headings
                Initialize Line Counter
            ENDPERFORM
        ENDIF
        PERFORM 5 TIMES
            Calculate Inflation at 8%
            Write a Line
        ENDPERFORM
        PERFORM 5 TIMES
            Calculate Inflation at 6%
            Write a Line
        ENDPERFORM
        Read a Record
    ENDPERFORM
    PERFORM
        End-of-Job Operations
    ENDPERFORM
STOP
```

Figure 10.4
Pseudocode and hierarchy
chart for Practice Program.

Figure 10.5
Solution to Practice Program.

```
IDENTIFICATION DIVISION.
PROGRAM-ID. SAMPLE.
AUTHOR. NANCY STERN.
**********************************************************
*   CREATES A REPORT TO DETERMINE PRICE OF AN ITEM  *
*   WITH INFLATION OVER THE NEXT TEN YEARS          *
**********************************************************
ENVIRONMENT DIVISION.
INPUT-OUTPUT SECTION.
FILE-CONTROL.
     SELECT ITEM-DISK-IN    ASSIGN TO DATA107.
     SELECT REPORT-FILE-OUT ASSIGN TO SYS$OUTPUT.
*
DATA DIVISION.
FILE SECTION.
FD  ITEM-DISK-IN
    LABEL RECORDS ARE STANDARD.
01  ITEM-REC-IN.
    05  ITEM-NO-IN                  PIC 9(5).
    05  ITEM-DESCRIPTION-IN         PIC X(20).
    05  ITEM-COST-IN                PIC 9(3)V99.
FD  REPORT-FILE-OUT
    LABEL RECORDS ARE OMITTED.
01  REPORT-REC-OUT                  PIC X(133).
WORKING-STORAGE SECTION.
01  WS-WORK-AREAS.
    05  ARE-THERE-MORE-RECORDS      PIC X(3)        VALUE 'YES'.
        88  MORE-RECORDS                            VALUE 'YES'.
        88  NO-MORE-RECORDS                         VALUE 'NO '.
    05  WS-INFLATION-RATE           PIC 9V99        VALUE ZERO.
    05  WS-INFLATION-RATE-1         PIC 9V99        VALUE 0.08.
    05  WS-INFLATION-RATE-2         PIC 9V99        VALUE 0.06.
    05  WS-CTR                      PIC 99          VALUE ZEROS.
    05  WS-LINE-CTR                 PIC 99          VALUE ZEROS.
    05  WS-YEAR-CTR                 PIC 99          VALUE ZEROS.
    05  WS-PAGE-CTR                 PIC 9(3)        VALUE ZEROS.
01  HL-HEADER1.
    05  FILLER                      PIC X(48)       VALUE SPACES.
    05  FILLER                      PIC X(35)
        VALUE 'I N F L A T I O N   R E P O R T '.
    05  FILLER                      PIC X(40)       VALUE SPACES.
    05  FILLER                      PIC X(5)
        VALUE 'PAGE '.
    05  HL-PAGE                     PIC ZZ9.
    05  FILLER                      PIC XX          VALUE SPACES.
01  HL-HEADER2.
    05  FILLER                      PIC X(5)        VALUE SPACES.
    05  FILLER                      PIC X(13)
        VALUE 'ITEM NUMBER: '.
    05  HL-ITEM-NO                  PIC 9(5).
    05  FILLER                      PIC X(110)      VALUE SPACES.
01  HL-HEADER3.
    05  FILLER                      PIC X(5)        VALUE SPACES.
    05  FILLER                      PIC X(19)
        VALUE 'ITEM DESCRIPTION: '.
    05  HL-ITEM-DESCRIPTION         PIC X(20).
    05  FILLER                      PIC X(89)       VALUE SPACES.
01  HL-HEADER4.
    05  FILLER                      PIC X(5)        VALUE SPACES.
    05  FILLER                      PIC X(12)
        VALUE 'ITEM COST: '.
    05  HL-ITEM-COST                PIC $$$$.99.
    05  FILLER                      PIC X(112)      VALUE SPACES.
01  HL-HEADER5.
    05  FILLER                      PIC X(37)       VALUE SPACES.
    05  FILLER                      PIC X(4)
        VALUE 'YEAR'.
    05  FILLER                      PIC X(5)        VALUE SPACES.
    05  FILLER                      PIC X(14)
        VALUE 'INFLATION RATE'.
    05  FILLER                      PIC X(5)        VALUE SPACES.
    05  FILLER                      PIC X(25)
        VALUE 'ITEM COST WITH INFLATION'.
    05  FILLER                      PIC X(38)       VALUE SPACES.
01  DL-DETAIL-LINE.
    05  FILLER                      PIC X(38)       VALUE SPACES.
    05  DL-YEAR                     PIC Z9.
    05  FILLER                      PIC X(12)       VALUE SPACES.
    05  DL-INFLATION-RATE           PIC V99.
    05  FILLER                      PIC X(20)
        VALUE '%'.
    05  DL-ITEM-COST-AFTER-INFLATION PIC ZZZZ.99.
    05  FILLER                      PIC X(47)       VALUE SPACES.
```

```
*
 PROCEDURE DIVISION.
 **********************************************
 *   CONTROLS DIRECTION OF PROGRAM LOGIC   *
 **********************************************
 100-MAIN-MODULE.
     PERFORM 500-INITIALIZATION-RTN.
     PERFORM 200-CALC-RTN
         UNTIL NO-MORE-RECORDS.
     PERFORM 600-END-OF-JOB-RTN.
 *****************************************************************
 *   PERFORMED FROM 100-MAIN-MODULE, PRINTS ITEM TITLES AND    *
 *   CONTROLS THE INFLATION RATE USED FOR ITEM CALCULATIONS.   *
 *****************************************************************
 200-CALC-RTN.
     MOVE ITEM-COST-IN TO HL-ITEM-COST.
     MOVE ITEM-NO-IN TO HL-ITEM-NO.
     MOVE ITEM-DESCRIPTION-IN TO HL-ITEM-DESCRIPTION.
     MOVE WS-INFLATION-RATE-1 TO WS-INFLATION-RATE DL-INFLATION-RATE.
     IF  WS-LINE-CTR > 25
         PERFORM 400-HEADING-RTN.
     WRITE REPORT-REC-OUT FROM HL-HEADER2 AFTER ADVANCING 2 LINES.
     WRITE REPORT-REC-OUT FROM HL-HEADER3 AFTER ADVANCING 1 LINES.
     WRITE REPORT-REC-OUT FROM HL-HEADER4 AFTER ADVANCING 1 LINES.
     WRITE REPORT-REC-OUT FROM HL-HEADER5 AFTER ADVANCING 2 LINES.
     ADD 3 TO WS-LINE-CTR.
     PERFORM 300-INFLATION-RTN
         VARYING WS-CTR FROM 1 BY 1
             UNTIL WS-CTR > 5.
     MOVE WS-INFLATION-RATE-2 TO WS-INFLATION-RATE DL-INFLATION-RATE.
     PERFORM 300-INFLATION-RTN
         VARYING WS-CTR FROM 1 BY 1
             UNTIL WS-CTR > 5.
     MOVE ZERO TO WS-YEAR-CTR.
     READ ITEM-DISK-IN
         AT END MOVE 'NO ' TO ARE-THERE-MORE-RECORDS.
 *****************************************************
 *   PERFORMED FROM 200-CALC-RTN,  COMPUTES ITEM    *
 *   COST AFTER INFLATION, PRINTS OUT INFORMATION   *
 *****************************************************
 300-INFLATION-RTN.
     ADD 1 TO WS-YEAR-CTR.
     COMPUTE ITEM-COST-IN = (ITEM-COST-IN * WS-INFLATION-RATE)
                           + ITEM-COST-IN.
     MOVE ITEM-COST-IN TO DL-ITEM-COST-AFTER-INFLATION.
     MOVE WS-YEAR-CTR TO DL-YEAR.
     IF  WS-LINE-CTR > 25
         PERFORM 400-HEADING-RTN.
     WRITE REPORT-REC-OUT FROM DL-DETAIL-LINE AFTER ADVANCING 1 LINES.
     ADD 1 TO WS-LINE-CTR.
 *********************************************************
 *   PERFORMED FROM 200-CALC-RTN, 300-INFLATION-RTN,    *
 *   500-INITIALIZATION-RTN.  INCREMENTS WS-PAGE-CTR    *
 *   PRINTS OUT HEADINGS AFTER ADVANCING A NEW PAGE     *
 *********************************************************
 400-HEADING-RTN.
     ADD 1 TO WS-PAGE-CTR.
     MOVE WS-PAGE-CTR TO HL-PAGE.
     WRITE REPORT-REC-OUT FROM HL-HEADER1 AFTER ADVANCING PAGE.
     MOVE ZEROS TO WS-LINE-CTR.
 *********************************************************
 *   PERFORMED FROM 100-MAIN-MODULE, OPENS FILES AND    *
 *                          PERFORMS INTIAL READ        *
 *********************************************************
 500-INITIALIZATION-RTN.
     OPEN INPUT  ITEM-DISK-IN
          OUTPUT REPORT-FILE-OUT.
     READ ITEM-DISK-IN
         AT END MOVE 'NO ' TO ARE-THERE-MORE-RECORDS.
     PERFORM 400-HEADING-RTN.
 *********************************************************
 *   PERFORMED FROM 100-MAIN-MODULE, CLOSES FILES AND   *
 *   RETURNS CONTROL TO OPERATING SYSTEM                *
 *********************************************************
 600-END-OF-JOB-RTN.
     CLOSE ITEM-DISK-IN
           REPORT-FILE-OUT.
     STOP RUN.
```

KEY TERMS

EXIT	Loop	PERFORM ... TIMES
GO TO	Module	PERFORM ... UNTIL
In-line PERFORM	Nested PERFORM	PERFORM ... VARYING
Infinite loop	PERFORM	Scope terminator
Iteration		

REVIEW QUESTIONS

T   F

I. True-False Questions

__ __ 1. A PERFORM statement permanently transfers control to some other section of a program.

__ __ 2. A GO TO must never be used in conjunction with a PERFORM statement.

__ __ 3. GO TO statements are generally avoided in structured programs.

__ __ 4. EXIT is a COBOL reserved word that performs no operation.

__ __ 5. Using a PERFORM ... UNTIL ... option, the condition is tested even before the paragraph is executed.

__ __ 6. PERFORM 400-LOOP-RTN N TIMES is only valid if N is defined as numeric.

__ __ 7. Using PERFORM 400-LOOP-RTN N TIMES, N should not be altered within 400-LOOP-RTN.

__ __ 8. It is valid to say PERFORM 400-LOOP-RTN N TIMES, where N = 0.

__ __ 9. The PERFORM and GO TO statements will cause identical branching.

__ __ 10. If several paragraphs are to be executed by a PERFORM statement, we may use the THRU option.

II. General Questions

1. Using a PERFORM statement with a TIMES option, write a routine to find N factorial, where N is the data item. You will recall that N factorial = $N \times (N - 1) \times (N - 2) \times \ldots \times 1$; that is, 5 factorial = $5 \times 4 \times 3 \times 2 \times 1 = 120$.

2. Rewrite the following routine using a PERFORM statement with a TIMES option:

```
MOVE ZEROS TO COUNTER.
READ SALES-FILE
    AT END MOVE 'NO ' TO ARE-THERE-MORE-RECORDS.
PERFORM 400-LOOP-RTN
    UNTIL COUNTER = 20.
    :
    :
400-LOOP-RTN.
    ADD QTY OF SALES-REC TO TOTAL.
    ADD 1 TO COUNTER.
    READ SALES-FILE
        AT END MOVE 'NO ' TO ARE-THERE-MORE-RECORDS.
```

3. Rewrite the solution to Question 2 using a PERFORM with a VARYING option.

4. Write two routines, one with a PERFORM ... TIMES and one with a PERFORM ... UNTIL to sum all odd-numbered integers from 1 to 1001.

5. In each case, indicate the number of times 300-PRINT-RTN is executed:
   (a) PERFORM 300-PRINT-RTN
           VARYING X FROM 1 BY 1 UNTIL X > 10.
   (b) PERFORM 300-PRINT-RTN
           VARYING X FROM 1 BY 1 UNTIL X = 10.
   (c) PERFORM 300-PRINT-RTN
           VARYING X FROM 0 BY 1 UNTIL X = 10.

```
(d) PERFORM 300-PRINT-RTN
        VARYING X FROM 10 BY -1 UNTIL X = 0.
(e) MOVE 0 TO X.
    PERFORM 300-PRINT-RTN X TIMES.
```

DEBUGGING EXERCISES

1. Consider the following coding:

```
PERFORM 400-ADD-RTN
    VARYING X FROM 1 BY 1 UNTIL X > 50.
    .
    .
400-ADD-RTN.
    ADD AMT TO TOTAL.
    ADD 1 TO X.
    READ AMT-FILE
        AT END MOVE 'NO ' TO ARE-THERE-MORE-RECORDS.
```

   (a) How many times is AMT added to TOTAL?
   (b) Is the logic in the program excerpt correct? Explain your answer.
   (c) What will happen if there are only 14 input records? Explain your answer.
   (d) Correct the coding so that it adds amounts from 50 input records and prints an error message if there are fewer than 50 records.

2. Consider the following coding:

```
PERFORM 100-RTN1 TO 200-RTN2.
    .
    .
100-RTN1.
    IF  A = B
        GO TO 200-RTN2
    ELSE
        ADD A TO TOTAL
        ADD 1 TO COUNTER.
200-RTN2.
    READ TRANS-FILE
        AT END MOVE 'NO ' TO ARE-THERE-MORE-RECORDS.
    EXIT.
```

   Two syntax errors result: one on the first line and one on the last line. Find and correct the errors.

3. Consider the following program excerpt:

```
    .
    .
    PERFORM 200-CALC-RTN
        UNTIL NO-MORE-RECORDS.
    .
    .
200-CALC-RTN.
    MOVE 0 TO COUNTER.
    PERFORM 300-LOOP-RTN
        UNTIL COUNTER = 5.
    MOVE TOTAL TO TOTAL-OUT.
    MOVE TOTAL-REC TO PRINT-REC.
    WRITE PRINT-REC.
    READ SALES-FILE
        AT END MOVE 'NO ' TO ARE-THERE-MORE-RECORDS.
300-LOOP-RTN.
    ADD AMT1 AMT2 GIVING AMT3.
    MULTIPLY 1.08 BY AMT3 GIVING GROSS.
```

```
SUBTRACT DISCOUNT FROM GROSS
        GIVING TOTAL.
```

(a) This coding will result in an abend condition. Indicate why. What changes should be made to correct the coding?

(b) Suppose COUNTER is initialized in WORKING-STORAGE with a VALUE of 0. Would it be correct to eliminate the MOVE 0 TO COUNTER instruction from 200-CALC-RTN? Explain your answer.

(c) Code the three arithmetic statements in 300-LOOP-RTN with a single COMPUTE statement.

PROGRAMMING ASSIGNMENTS

1. Write a program to prepare a chart indicating the weights on various planets that correspond to a series of weights on Earth. See the problem definition in Figure 10.6.

Notes

(a) Use the following table:

Planet	Percentage of Earth Weight
Mars	38
Venus	85
Jupiter	264
Saturn	116

(b) Note that no input is required.

(c) The chart should include Earth weights from 50 to 250 in increments of 50.

Systems Flowchart

WEIGHT-CHART

WEIGHT-CHART Printer Spacing Chart

		WEIGHT CHART			
	EARTH	MARS	VENUS	JUPITER	SATURN
D	50	XXX.X	XXX.X	XXX.X	XXX.X
D	100	XXX.X	XXX.X	XXX.X	XXX.X
D	150	XXX.X	XXX.X	XXX.X	XXX.X
D	200	XXX.X	XXX.X	XXX.X	XXX.X
D	250	XXX.X	XXX.X	XXX.X	XXX.X

Figure 10.6
Problem definition for
Programming Assignment 1.

2. Write a program to produce a bonus report. See the problem definition in Figure 10.7.

Notes

(a) The payroll records have been sorted into ascending sequence by office number within territory number. There are three territories and two offices within each territory. Thus, all employees within office 01 within territory 01 will appear before employee records for office 02 within territory 01, and so on.

(b) Only employees who were hired before 1980 are entitled to a 10% bonus.

(c) Print the names of all employees and their bonuses. Print a separate page for each office within each territory. Use a nested PERFORM to achieve page breaks for each office within each territory.

3. Write a program to print one line from X number of input records, where X is denoted in the first record of each group. The output is a printed report with each line consisting of salesperson name and the accumulated amount for X number of records. The problem definition is shown in Figure 10.8.

4. Write a program to print a temperature conversion table. Compute and print the Fahrenheit equivalents of all Celsius temperatures at 10-degree intervals from 0 to 150 degrees. The conversion formula is $C = 5/9 (F - 32)$.

Systems Flowchart

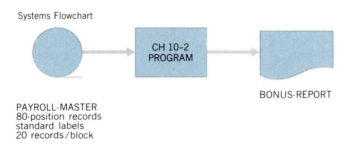

CH 10-2
PROGRAM

BONUS-REPORT

PAYROLL-MASTER
80-position records
standard labels
20 records/block

PAYROLL-MASTER Record Layout

EMPLOYEE NO.	EMPLOYEE NAME	TERRITORY NO.	OFFICE NO.	ANNUAL SALARY (in $)		DATE HIRED			
						MM	DD	YY	
1　　　5	6　　　25	26　　27	28　29	30　　35	36　　64	65　　　70	71　　　80		

BONUS-REPORT Printer Spacing Chart

Figure 10.7
Problem definition for
Programming Assignment 2.

Figure 10.8
Problem definition for
Programming Assignment 3.

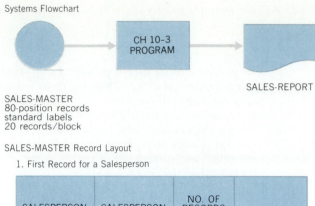

SALES-MASTER
80-position records
standard labels
20 records/block

SALES-MASTER Record Layout
1. First Record for a Salesperson

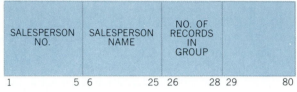

2. Subsequent Records for the Same Salesperson

SALES-REPORT Printer Spacing Chart

5. Write a program to compute class averages for an input disk file with the following format.

Record 1 for group:	1–5	Class number
	6–7	Number of students in class
	8–10	Not used
Remainder of records for group:	1–5	Class number
	6–8	Exam grade XXX
	9–10	Not used

Print: Class number and class average for each class. The average should be rounded to the nearest integer. The disk has standard labels and a blocking factor of 50.

6. Write a program to compute compound interest from disk records with the following format:

1–5   Account number
6–25 Depositor's name
26–30 Principal P_0

31–32 Interest rate (.XX)   r
33–34 Period of investment   n
35–80 Not used
(Block size is 20; standard labels)

For each record read, print the input data and the principal after n years of invest-ment. The principal after n years of investment is determined by the following formula:

$$P_n = P_0 (1 + r)^n$$

  r = interest rate expressed as a decimal number (e.g., 7% = .07)
  n = years of investment
  P_0 = initial principal amount
  P_n = principal compounded after n years of investment

7. Write a program to read in the payroll file described in Figure 10.7 for Programming Assignment 2. Perform the following for this file:
   (a) Find the total of all the salary fields.
   (b) Management is planning across-the-board salary increases for all its employees. They would like to see what the salary total would be if the increase is 5%, 6% ... 10%, in increments of 1%. Print a report as follows:

```
            SALARY INCREASE REPORT
            CURRENT TOTAL SALARY $X,XXX,XXX


    1.05 TIMES CURRENT SALARY = $X,XXX,XXX
    1.06 TIMES CURRENT SALARY = $X,XXX,XXX
    1.07 TIMES CURRENT SALARY = $X,XXX,XXX
    1.08 TIMES CURRENT SALARY = $X,XXX,XXX
    1.09 TIMES CURRENT SALARY = $X,XXX,XXX
    1.10 TIMES CURRENT SALARY = $X,XXX,XXX
```

11

Printing Well-Designed Reports

OBJECTIVES

To familiarize you with

1. The major characteristics of printed output.
2. Techniques for designing printed reports.
3. The types of editing performed to make printed output user-friendly.
4. Methods used to align and space forms.
5. The printing of headings.

I. How Printed Output Differs from Other Types of Output: A Systems Overview

A. Creating Output Files on Disk or Tape

There are two types of output most commonly produced by a computer. One type is for storing data so that it can be accessed by the computer at some later date. These data files are typically used for *maintaining information* needed by an organization. Such a file must be updated or revised on a regular basis so that it is current.

A master file, for example, would be created by computer and kept current with an update procedure. Such files are most commonly stored on disk or tape. They contain numerous records and, for each record, numerous fields of information. A payroll master file, for example, could consist of thousands of records, depending on the size of the company, and dozens of fields of information per record.

We will consider in detail how such master files are created and updated in Chapter 16. For now, keep in mind that files are created on disk or tape as efficiently as possible. The following are guidelines for designing files on disk or tape:

GUIDELINES FOR DESIGNING DISK AND TAPE FILES

1. The first field in each record should be a *key field*, which identifies the record. A key field, for example, might be Social Security number, transaction number, or customer number.

2. Records should be created as concisely as possible in order to save space on the disk or tape. For example, part numbers might be used in place of item descriptions in an inventory file because a part number field would require fewer characters.

3. Edit symbols such as commas and dollar signs waste space in a disk or tape file and should not be used.

4. Coded fields are used in place of descriptive fields (e.g., a code of 'M,' 'S,' or 'D' might be used to designate marital status in place of a descriptive entry such as 'Married,' 'Single,' or 'Divorced').

5. Care must be taken to minimize the possibility of creating erroneous output. (Chapter 13 focuses on the type of error control procedures frequently used.)

B. Features of Printed Output

Files that are maintained by computer must be printed or displayed in order to be accessed by users. *Output* that is *displayed* on a screen is useful for answering inquiries about the status of a file. *Printed reports*, on the other hand, are formal documents that provide users with the information they need to perform their jobs effectively. Because computer-produced displays and reports are to be read by people, they must be clear, neat, and easy to understand. Whereas conciseness and efficiency are the overriding considerations for designing disk and tape files, clarity is the primary concern when designing displayed output and printed reports.

Several characteristics, not applicable to disk or tape output, must be considered when designing and preparing reports. (Most of these apply to output displays as well.) We discuss these characteristics first and then illustrate techniques in COBOL that can be used to provide them.

1. Use of Edit Symbols

A disk or tape record may, for example, have two amount fields with the following data: 00450 and 3872658. Although these fields are acceptable in disk and tape files, the printed report should contain this information in *edited form* to make it more meaningful to the user. For example, $450.00 and $38,726.58 are better methods of presenting the data.

Editing is defined as the manipulation of fields of data to make them clearer, neater, and more useful. We have already seen, in Chapter 6, how we may use the dollar sign and decimal point for editing. In this chapter, we focus on types of editing that can be performed on both numeric and nonnumeric fields.

2. Spacing of Forms

The lines on printed output must be properly spaced for ease of reading. Some lines must be single-spaced, others double-spaced, and so on. Moreover, printed output must have margins at both the top and bottom of each page. This requires the computer to be programmed to sense the end of a page and then to transmit the next line of information to a new page.

3. Alignment of Information

Reports do not have fields of information adjacent to one another as is the practice with disk and tape. Printed output is more easily interpreted when fields are spaced evenly across the page. We have seen how the Printer Spacing Chart is used for planning the output design so that detail lines and heading lines are properly spaced for readability (see Figure 11.1).

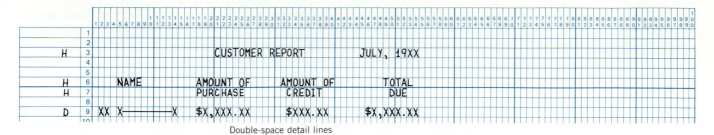

Figure 11.1
Sample Printer Spacing Chart.

4. Headings

Heading information, which supplies the report name, date, page number, and field designations, is essential for a clear and meaningful presentation of printed information.

Figure 11.2 provides a schematic of how data may actually be printed. The output would print according to the specifications provided in the Printer Spacing Chart in Figure 11.1. Because printed information has characteristics different from other output, we study the printed report as a separate topic.

5. Can Be of Different Types

Printed reports fall into three major categories.

    a. Detail or Transaction Reports.   These are reports that include specific output for *each* input record read. Customer bills generated from a master

Figure 11.2
Design features of printed
output.

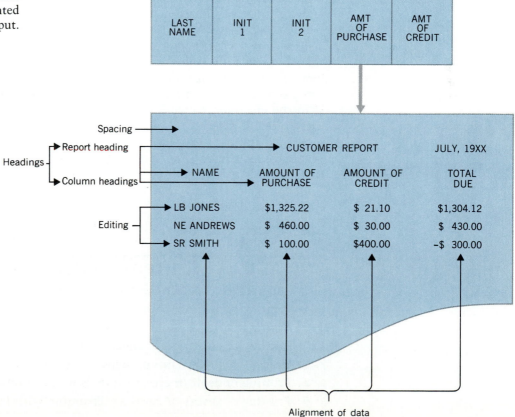

accounts receivable file would be an example of a *detail report*. Each input record results in one or more lines of output. Similarly, payroll checks generated from a master payroll file would be a detail report. Finally, a listing of each part number stocked by a company would be a detail report. Detail output is produced when individualized output such as bills or checks is needed or when itemizing is required.

Because detail reports generate output for each input record read, they can take a long time to produce. Printing 300,000 lines from a file of 300,000 records, for example, could take several hours.

b. Exception Reports.   Sometimes users ask for detail reports when, in fact, other types of output would be more appropriate. Suppose an insurance agent, for example, has requested a listing of all clients and their last payment date. When asked by a systems analyst why the detail report is necessary, she responds that she wants to contact all clients who have not made a payment within the last 90 days. An experienced computer professional would suggest an alternative type of output, one that lists *only* those clients who meet the criterion the insurance agent has set. A listing of only those clients who have not made a payment within 90 days would save the time and effort necessary to print out *all* clients, but more importantly it would make the insurance agent's job easier. Rather than having to sift through numerous pages of a listing, the agent would have a list of only those people to be contacted.

This type of output is called an *exception report*, which is a listing of individual records that meet (or fail to meet) certain criteria. Other examples of exception reports are a list of employees who are 65 or over and a list of part numbers in stock with a quantity on hand below some minimum value.

c. Summary Reports.   As the name suggests, a summary report summarizes rather than itemizes. If summaries or totals can provide a more comprehensive view for the user than a detail or exception report, then they should be suggested as alternatives.

As a rule, exception reports or summary reports should be generated rather than detail reports if they can serve the user's purpose. Detail reports take a long time to generate, they tend to be voluminous, and they often require some summarizing anyway before they are meaningful to users or managers.

In the chapters that follow, we will discuss the design and creation of all three types of reports.

II. The Editing Function

A. An Overview

The following editing functions will be discussed:

EDITING FUNCTIONS

1. Suppression of leading zeros.
2. Printing of decimal points where decimal alignment is implied.
3. Printing of dollar signs and commas.
4. Printing of asterisks for check protection.
5. Printing of plus or minus signs.
6. Printing of debit or credit symbols for accounting applications.
7. Printing of spaces or zeros as separators within fields.

The first six editing functions just described may only be performed on *numeric* fields, or fields with PICTURE clauses consisting of 9's. The last editing function, the printing of zeros or spaces as separators, may be performed on *any* data field.

All editing is accomplished by moving an elementary item to a **report-item.** An elementary item, you will recall, is a field with a PICTURE clause; that is, it is a data item that is not further subdivided. A *report-item* is an elementary item that has the appropriate PICTURE clause to perform editing functions. Note that it is the PICTURE clause of the receiving field, the report-item, that causes editing. The operation of editing is accomplished by moving a numeric sending field to a receiving field that has edit symbols in its PICTURE clause.

As in *all* MOVE operations, the sending field remains unchanged after the data has been transmitted to the report-item. The report-item itself may be defined as part of the output record or in a WORKING-STORAGE area that will be moved to the output area before writing. We have seen that it is best to define output records in WORKING-STORAGE.

It should be noted that the GIVING option of the arithmetic verbs (ADD, SUBTRACT, MULTIPLY, DIVIDE) permits the receiving field specified to be a report-item. Thus, in the following statement RESULT may be a report-item:

```
ADD  AMT1   AMT2   AMT3
     GIVING RESULT.
```

Similarly, the first identifier specified in a COMPUTE may be a report-item. That is, COMPUTE RESULT = AMT1 + AMT2 + AMT3 would produce an edited sum in the field called RESULT if RESULT were a report-item. In all instances, AMT1, AMT2, and AMT3 must be strictly numeric because they are part of the arithmetic operation. If RESULT is a report-item, it could not be used in any arithmetic operation other than as a receiving field.

Thus, we can accomplish editing by (1) moving a field to a report-item or (2) performing an arithmetic operation using the GIVING option or the COMPUTE statement where the result is a report-item.

B. Using Edit Characters

1. Printing Decimal Points

We have already considered the printing of decimal points in Chapter 6. The following discussion, then, will serve as a review.

As indicated in previous illustrations, a field such as TAX, with PICTURE 99V99 and contents of 12∧35, should print as 12.35 when edited. It is only through editing that the implied decimal point will be replaced with an actual decimal point. That is, printing TAX as is would result in output of 1235 since implied decimal points do not print.

The appropriate report-item that will print a decimal point will have a PICTURE of 99.99. The decimal point, which would not appear in the PICTURE clause of a numeric item, is part of a report-item. It instructs the computer to place an actual decimal point where it is implied in the sending field. If a sending field had a PICTURE of 999V999, its report-item would have a PICTURE clause of 999.999.

A sending field with PICTURE 99V99 takes *four* storage positions, since implied decimal points do not use storage, whereas the corresponding report-item takes *five* positions, since a real decimal point does, in fact, use one position. The number 12.35, when printed, uses five print positions.

2. Suppressing Leading Zeros

Nonsignificant or leading zeros are zeros appearing in the leftmost positions of a field and having no significant value. For example, 00387 has two leading zeros. Nonsignificant zeros should generally be omitted when printing. That is, 00387 should print as ƀƀ387, since the two numbers are numerically equivalent and the latter is easier to read. (The ƀ represents a blank). The operation to perform this type of editing is called **suppression of leading zeros.**

The number 10000 has *no* leading zeros. All zeros in the number 10000 have numeric significance because none appears in the leftmost position of the field. We would not want to suppress the printing of the zeros in 10000, since each adds value to the number.

The edit symbol $\boxed{Z}$ is used to suppress leading zeros and to replace them with blanks or spaces. WS-TOTAL, with a PICTURE of 999, might be edited by moving it to EDIT1, with a PICTURE of ZZZ, as shown here:

```
WORKING-STORAGE SECTION.
01   WORK-AREAS.
       .
       .
     05   WS-TOTAL    PIC 999.
01   PRINT-REC.
     05   FILLER      PIC X.
     05   EDIT1       PIC ZZZ.
       .
       .
     MOVE WS-TOTAL TO EDIT1.
```

Each Z represents one storage position that may accept data from a sending field. In addition, any nonsignificant zeros encountered in the sending field will be replaced with blanks. Thus, the following are examples of how WS-TOTAL will print depending on its initial value:

038 will print as ƀ38
003 will print as ƀƀ3
000 will print as ƀƀƀ

Any number that does not have leading zeros, such as 108, will print as is.

When suppressing leading zeros, the sending field must be defined as numeric. The receiving field should accept the *same number of integers* as the sending field. PICTURE ZZZ is a three-position storage area that may accept three integers and will suppress all leading zeros.

Often it is desirable to suppress only some leading zeros. Consider the case where the contents of four sending fields denoting Charitable Deductions are 0020, 4325, 0003, and 0000, respectively. The output may be as follows.

	SAMPLE OUTPUT	
NAME	SALARY	DEDUCTIONS FOR CHARITY
P. NEWMAN	13872	20
B. STREISAND	40873	4325
B. REYNOLDS	10287	3
T. SELLECK	25382	

All leading zeros for the Deductions field are suppressed. The PICTURE clause for the report-item is ZZZZ or Z(4).

As may be evident from this illustration, it is sometimes inadvisable to leave fields completely blank when a zero balance is implied. Users who question, at times, the accuracy of computer output, tend to regard blank fields suspiciously. Perhaps T. SELLECK did, in fact, make a contribution, but the computer, through machine malfunction, failed to indicate it. Or, the field may have been left blank and is to be supplied later.

For these reasons, it is sometimes good practice to print a *single* zero when a zero balance exists. In this way, the report will leave no doubt about the charitable inclinations of T. SELLECK.

Thus, if the four-position charity field has contents 0000, we want it to print as ƀƀƀ0. That is, we want only the three leftmost positions of the field to be zero suppressed and the rightmost position to print *without* suppressing the zero. The PICTURE clause of the report-item, then, would be ZZZ9. Z's indicate numeric characters to be zero suppressed, and 9's indicate numeric characters to be printed without zero suppression. Hence 0000 will print as ƀƀƀ0 if the report-item PICTURE clause is ZZZ9 or Z(3)9.

The combined use of Z's and 9's in a report-item requires that all Z's *precede* any 9's. Zeros may be suppressed only if they precede significant digits.

The following examples will clarify editing with zero suppression. We are assuming edited results are obtained by the operation: MOVE SENDING-FIELD TO REPORT-ITEM. Edited results may also be obtained by using the GIVING option of an arithmetic statement or by using the COMPUTE statement.

Examples of Zero Suppression			
Sending-Field		**Report-Item**	
PICTURE	*Contents*	PICTURE	*Edited Results*
1. 9(3)	109	ZZZ	109
2. 9(3)	007	Z(3)	ƀƀ7
3. 9(3)	000	ZZZ	ƀƀƀ
4. 9(3)	007	Z99	ƀ07
5. 9(4)	0082	Z999	ƀ082

We can combine the two editing functions thus far discussed so that we zero suppress *and* place decimal points in the edited field:

Examples of Decimal Point Insertion with Zero Suppression			
Sending-Field		**Report-Item**	
PICTURE	*Contents*	PICTURE	*Edited Results*
1. 99V99	02ᴧ38	ZZ.99	ƀ2.38
2. 99V99	00ᴧ03	ZZ.99	ƀƀ.03
3. 99V99	00ᴧ05	Z9.99	ƀ0.05

Since numeric positions to the right of a decimal point have significance even when they are zero, we will *not* perform zero suppression on these quantities. That is, .01 should *not* be edited to read .1, since the two numbers are not numerically equivalent. As a rule, then, we will *not* zero suppress characters to the right of a decimal point.

There is one exception to this rule. COBOL allows you to use a report-item with PICTURE ZZ.ZZ. This will suppress zeros to the right of the decimal point *only if the entire field is zero*, in which case all spaces will print. Thus 00∧03 prints as b̸b̸.03 but 00∧00 prints as five blanks. Because this PICTURE clause may be confusing, we will not, in general, use it.

Be Sure to Size the Report-Item Correctly

The number of Z's representing integers in the report-item should be equal to the number of integers or 9's in the sending field. Including too many Z's or two few Z's may produce either a syntax error or incorrect results, depending on the compiler being used.

If the sending field has decimal positions, however, we may truncate them if desired by including only integer Z's in the report-item. Similarly, an integer-only sending field may be made to print as a dollars and cents field by using .99 or .ZZ in the report-item. The following illustrates these points:

Examples of Decimal Point Insertion and Truncation of Decimal Digits			
Sending-Field		**Report-Item**	
PICTURE	*Contents*	PICTURE	*Contents*
1. 9(3)V99	008∧27	Z(3)	b̸b̸8
2. 9(3)	027	Z(3).99	b̸27.00
3. 9(3)	018	Z(3).ZZ	b̸18.00
4. 9(3)	000	Z(3).ZZ	b̸b̸b̸b̸b̸b̸

In all instances, the number of Z's to the left of the decimal point must equal the number of integer 9's in the sending field.

3. Printing Dollar Signs and Commas

Dollar signs and commas are editing symbols frequently used in conjunction with the suppression of leading zeros and the printing of decimal points, since many numeric quantities often appear on printed reports as dollars and cents figures. The dollar sign and comma are placed in the positions in which they are desired, as in the case with decimal points. If AMT-IN, with PICTURE 9999V99, is edited as a dollars and cents figure, the dollar sign is the first character, a digit from the sending field follows, then a comma, three more digits, a decimal point, and two decimal positions. Thus, the report-item has a PICTURE of $9,999.99. The following examples illustrate this point:

Examples of Dollar Sign and Comma Insertion

Sending-Field		**Report-Item**	
PICTURE	*Contents*	PICTURE	*Edited Results*
1. 9(4)V99	3812∧34	$9,999.99	$ 3 , 8 1 2 . 3 4
2. 99V99	05∧00	$ZZ.99	$ 5 . 0 0
3. 999V99	000∧05	$ZZZ.99	$. 0 5
4. 9(4)V99	0003∧82	$Z,ZZZ.99	$ 3 . 8 2
5. 9(7)V99	0038268∧45	$Z,ZZZ,ZZZ.99	$ 3 8 , 2 6 8 . 4 5

In example 1, the sending field uses six storage positions, whereas the receiving field uses nine. Dollar signs, commas, and decimal points each use one position of storage. When defining the print record in the DATA DIVISION, we must make sure that nine positions are included in the report-item for this example. Editing typically results in the use of more storage positions for a report-item to be printed than if the data were printed without editing.

Examples 2 through 5 illustrate zero suppression with dollar sign and comma insertion. In example 2, one leading zero is suppressed and replaced with a space. Thus, there is a single blank between the inserted dollar sign and the first significant digit. Example 4 indicates that the zero suppression character Z will also eliminate or suppress leading commas. Note that the result of the edit was *not* $, 3.82 , but $ 3.82 . The Z will *suppress both zeros and commas* until it encounters the first significant digit of a field. Thus, a comma will be appropriately suppressed if no significant digit precedes it. In example 4, *four* spaces will appear between the dollar sign and the first significant digit, three for the suppressed zeros and one for the suppressed comma.

Recall that the report-item must allow for the same number of integer positions as the sending field, but it can include *additional decimal positions* if desired. AMT-IN, with PICTURE 99 and contents 40, may be edited by moving it to AMT-OUT, with PICTURE $ZZ.99. In this case, the two decimal places are filled with zeros. The result, then, in AMT-OUT will be $40.00.

4. Printing Asterisks (*) for Check Protection

The suppression of zeros, with the use of Z, in conjunction with the printing of dollar signs may, at times, prove unwise.

Suppose we are using the computer to print checks. To print $ .05, as in example 3, may be inadvisable since the blanks between the dollar sign and the decimal point may easily be filled in by a dishonest person using a typewriter. It is therefore conceivable that someone could collect $999.05 on what should be a $.05 check.

To prevent such occurrences, a **check protection symbol,** the asterisk (*), is used in place of blanks when leading zeros are to be suppressed. Using the correct report-item, example 3 would print as $***.05. In this way, it would be more difficult to tamper with the intended figure.

To print an asterisk in place of a blank when zero suppression is to be performed, use an * instead of a Z in each position. Asterisks are zero-suppression characters that replace each nonsignificant zero and comma with * instead of a space.

Examples of Zero Suppression with Asterisk Insertion			
Sending-Field		**Report-Item**	
PICTURE	Contents	PICTURE	Edited Results
1. 9(3)V99	123ᴧ45	$***.99	$123.45
2. 9(3)V99	012ᴧ34	$***.99	$*12.34
3. 9(5)V99	00234ᴧ56	$**,***.99	$***234.56

The asterisk is used most often for the printing of checks or when there is some concern that resultant amount fields might be tampered with. Under other conditions, the use of Z's for normal zero suppression is sufficient.

5. Printing Plus or Minus Signs

a. Printing Minus Signs.
Unless the computer is instructed to do otherwise, numeric quantities will print without a sign. When reports are printed, we interpret the absence of a sign as an indication of a positive quantity.

If an amount is negative and no sign appears in the report-item, the amount will print without a sign, which will be interpreted as positive by the user. If we wish to print a minus sign when a number is negative, we must use an editing symbol. Note that the PICTURE clause of a numeric sending field must contain an S if it can have negative contents. Without the S, the field will be considered unsigned.

To print a minus sign for a negative sending field, we use the edit symbol −. This minus sign may be placed *either* to the right *or* to the left of the report-item. By placing the minus sign in one of these two positions, the computer is instructed to store it in the corresponding position *only if* the sending field is negative and to omit a sign when the sending field is signed positive or is unsigned.

In the examples that follow, the sign of a number in a sending field is indicated by placing it above the low-order or rightmost position of the number. The computer uses the rightmost position for storing the sign as well as the low-order digit. Consider the following:

Examples of Minus Sign Insertion			
Sending-Field		**Report-Item**	
PICTURE	*Contents*	PICTURE	*Edited Results*
1. S999	12$\bar{3}$	-999	− 123
2. S999	12$\bar{3}$	999-	123 −
3. 999	123	-999	ƀ123
4. S999	12$\overset{+}{3}$	-999	ƀ123
5. S99V99	02$_\wedge$3$\bar{4}$	ZZ.99-	ƀ2.34 −

Examples 1 and 2 illustrate that if the sending field is negative, the edited results print with the minus sign. Examples 1 and 2 also illustrate that the minus sign within a report-item may print to the right or the left of a field. Examples 3 and 4 illustrate that *no* sign will print if the sending field is signed positive or unsigned. Example 5 illustrates the use of the minus sign in conjunction with other editing symbols such as the Z.

b. Printing Either a Minus or Plus Sign.
There are occasions when a sign is required for *both* positive and negative quantities. That is, a + sign is required when the field is unsigned or signed positive, and a − sign is required when the field is signed negative. This will *not* be performed properly by using the edit symbol −, which only generates the minus sign if the quantity is negative and omits a sign for all other quantities.

To print either a plus sign *or* a minus sign for *all* values, the edit symbol + is used. To edit a sending field by moving it to a report-item with a + in its PICTURE clause will instruct the computer to always generate a sign. A + sign will be generated for positive or unsigned quantities, and a − sign will be generated for negative quantities. Once again, the sending field should have an S in its PIC clause for it to be interpreted as a signed number.

Like the minus sign, the plus sign may be made to appear either to the left or to the right of a field. Consider the following examples:

Examples of Plus or Minus Sign Insertion			
Sending-Field		**Report-Item**	
PICTURE	*Contents*	PICTURE	*Contents*
1. S999	12$\overset{+}{3}$	+999	+ 123
2. S999	12$\overset{+}{3}$	999+	123 +
3. S999	12$\overset{-}{3}$	+999	− 123
4. S9999V99	0387$_\wedge$2$\overset{-}{5}$	+Z,ZZZ.99	− ⊮⊮387.25

6. Printing Debit and Credit Symbols for Accounting Applications

For most applications, a plus or minus sign to indicate positive or negative quantities is sufficient. For accountants, however, a minus sign often indicates either a debit or a credit to a particular account.

For accounting functions, the edit symbols DB, for debit, or CR, for credit, may be used in place of the minus sign. If an amount is to be *debited* to an account *when it is negative,* DB will be used. If a quantity is to be *credited* to an account *when it is negative,* CR will be used. Once again, the sending field should have an S in its PIC clause for it to be interpreted as a signed number.

The DB and CR symbols must always be specified to the *right* of the report-item. Unlike the minus sign itself, these symbols may *not* be used to the left of a field. If the amount is negative and CR or DB is used, then either CR or DB will print, respectively. If the field is unsigned or signed positive, neither CR nor DB will print.

Whereas a minus sign uses *one* storage position, CR and DB each use *two* positions. The following examples illustrate the use of CR and DB:

Examples of CR or DB Insertion			
Sending-Field		**Report-Item**	
PICTURE	*Contents*	PICTURE	*Contents*
1. S999	12$\overset{-}{3}$.	999CR	123CR
2. S999	12$\overset{-}{3}$	999DB	123DB
3. S999	12$\overset{+}{3}$	999CR	123⊮⊮
4. S999	12$\overset{+}{3}$	999DB	123⊮⊮

7. Printing Spaces Or Zeros As Separators within Fields

Suppose the first nine positions of an input record contain a Social Security number. If the field is printed without editing, it might appear as: 080749263. For ease of reading, a better representation might be 080 74 9263. Spaces between the numbers would add clarity.

Any field, whether alphabetic, alphanumeric, or numeric, may be edited by placing blanks as separators within the field. The edit symbol B in a PICTURE clause of a report-item will cause a space to be inserted in the corresponding position.

Zeros may also be inserted into fields for editing purposes. The edit symbol ⓪ in the PICTURE clause of a report-item will cause a 0 to be inserted in the corresponding position of the receiving field without loss of characters from the sending field.

The following illustrates the use of spaces or zeros in report-item:

Examples of Blanks and Zeros As Separators				
	Sending-Field		**Report-Item**	
Identifier	PICTURE	*Contents*	PICTURE	*Edited Results*
SSNO	9(9)	089743456	999BB99BB9999	089 74 3456
NAME	X(10)	PASMITHƀƀƀ	XBXBX(8)	P A SMITH
DATE1	9(4)	0288	99BB99	02 88
QTY-IN-100S	999	153	99900	15300

Only this last category of edit operations, the use of blanks or zeros within a report-item, will accept data that is not numeric. For all other editing, the sending field must be numeric; that is, it must have a PICTURE clause of 9's, and may include an S and a V. Furthermore, only *elementary* numeric items may be used in edit operations. Recall that group items, even if they are subdivided into numeric fields, are treated as alphanumeric items by the computer. Thus, to obtain a valid numeric edit, only *elementary items* may be used.

Editing may be performed in three ways: (1) by *moving* a sending field to a report-item that has an appropriate PICTURE clause; (2) by using the GIVING option of an arithmetic statement where the resulting field is a report-item; or (3) by using a COMPUTE statement where the resulting field, to the left of the equal sign, is a report-item. It is the PICTURE clause itself that determines what type of editing is to be performed.

The following, however, results in an error if TOTAL-OUT is a report-item:

Invalid

```
ADD WS-TOTAL TO TOTAL-OUT.
```

The computer performs ADD instructions, and any other arithmetic operations, on numeric fields only. TOTAL-OUT, as a report-item, is *not* a numeric field. In this example, TOTAL-OUT is not simply the receiving field, it is part of the ADD itself.

Table 11.1 reviews edit operations.

**Table 11.1
Review of Edit Operations**

	Sending Field		**Report-Item**	
	PICTURE	**Contents**	**PICTURE**	**Edited Results**
1.	9(6)	123456	$ZZZ,ZZZ.99	$123,456.00
2.	9999V99	0012ˬ34	$Z,ZZZ.99	$ 12.34
3.	9(5)V99	00001ˬ23	$**,***.99	$*****1.23
4.	S9(6)	012345̄	+Z(6)	− 12345
5.	S9(6)	123456⁺	−Z(6)	123456
6.	S9999V99	1234ˬ56⁺	+Z(4).99	+1234.56
7.	S999	123̄	ZZZ−	123 −
8.	9(6)	123456	99BBBB9999	12 3456

9. S99	05̄	$ZZ.99DB	$ 5.00DB
10. 999	123	999000	123000
11. S99V99	12∧34̄	$ZZ.99CR	$12.34CR

De-editing

Using COBOL 85 you may move a report-item field, which contains edit symbols, to a strictly numeric field. This is called *de-editing*. The following, for example, is permitted:

```
01  REC-A.
    05  AMT-EDITED          PIC $ZZ,ZZZ.99
    :
01  REC-B.
    05  AMT-UNEDITED        PIC 9(5)V99.
    :
    MOVE AMT-EDITED TO AMT-UNEDITED.
```

Here, again, the receiving field must be large enough to accept the number of integers that are transmitted by the sending field.

Self-Test

1. All editing must be performed on _____ fields except editing using _____ .

2. To say MULTIPLY UNITS BY QTY GIVING TOTAL (is, is not) correct if TOTAL is a report-item.

3. A report-item is _____ .

4. How many storage positions must be allotted for a report-item with PICTURE $*,***.99?

5. How many integer positions should appear in the sending field to be moved to the report-item in Question 4?

6. Suppose NAME-FIELD with a PICTURE X(15) is part of an input record, where the first two positions of the field contain a first initial and a second initial. To edit this field so that a space appears between INITIAL1 and INITIAL2, and another space between INITIAL2 and LAST-NAME, the report-item will have the following PICTURE clause: _____ .

For Questions 7 through 20, fill in the edited results.

	Sending-Field PICTURE	Contents	Receiving-Field PICTURE	Edited Results
7.	9(6)	000123	ZZZ,999	
8.	9(6)	123456	ZZZ,999.99	
9.	9(4)V99	0000∧78	$Z,ZZ9.99	
10.	S9(4)V99	0000∧78̇⁺	$Z,ZZZ.99CR	
11.	S9(4)V99	0000∧78̄	$Z,ZZZ.99CR	
12.	S9(6)	123456̄	-999,999	
13.	9(6)	123456	-999,999	
14.	S999	123⁺	-999	
15.	999	123	+999	
16.	S999	123⁺	+999	
17.	S999	123̄	-999	
18.	9(6)	000092	Z(6)00	
19.	X(6)	123456	XXXBBXXX	
20.	9(4)V99	0012∧34	$*,***.99	

Solutions

1. numeric elementary; zeros or blanks as field separators
2. is
3. a field to be printed that contains the appropriate symbols to perform editing
4. Nine
5. Four
6. `XBXBX(13)`
7. ƀƀƀƀ123
8. 123,456.00
9. $ 0.78
10. $ .78
11. $ .78CR
12. − 123,456
13. ƀ123,456
14. ƀ123
15. + 123
16. + 123
17. − 123
18. ƀƀƀƀ9200
19. 123 456
20. $∗∗∗12.34

C. Floating Strings

Examine the following sample output:

```
    CUSTOMER NAME           QTY SOLD            AMT

    J. SMITH                   5,000            $38,725.67
    A. JONES                 -   2              $     3.00
```

Although the fields are properly edited, the format is striking in one respect. The dollar sign of AMT and the minus sign of QTY SOLD for A. JONES are separated from the actual numeric data by several spaces. This result is a necessary consequence of the type of editing that we have been discussing.

The report-item must contain enough positions to accommodate the entire sending field. If the sending field, however, has many nonsignificant zeros (e.g., 0000487), numerous blank positions will appear between the dollar sign and the first significant digit, or the sign and the first significant digit.

With the use of **floating strings,** a leading edit character such as a plus sign, minus sign, or dollar sign may appear in the position *directly preceding* the first significant digit. A dollar sign or a plus or a minus sign may be made to "float" with the field. That is, a floating string will cause suppression of leading zeros and, *at the same time,* force the respective floating character to appear in the position *adjacent to the first significant digit.*

With the proper use of floating strings in PICTURE clauses of report-items, the following sample output may be obtained:

	Sending-Field Contents	**Report-Item** Edited Results
1.	00123ᴧ87	$123.87
2.	00004ᴧ00	$4.00
3.	038̄7	− 387
4.	000005	+ 5

You will note that in this sample output the dollar sign, minus sign, or plus sign always appears in the position *directly preceding* the first significant digit. Only these three edit symbols may be made to float in this way.

To perform a floating-string edit operation, two steps are necessary:

1. Create the report-item PICTURE clause as in the previous section. Use the floating character of +, -, or $ in conjunction with Z's.
2. Then replace all Z's with the corresponding floating character.

Example 1   05 WS-TOTAL   PICTURE 9(4)V99.

Problem: Edit the field using a floating dollar sign. The report-item is called TOTAL-OUT.

In Step 1, the PICTURE clause of the report-item is created as usual: $Z,ZZZ.99.

In Step 2, all Z's are replaced with the floating character, a dollar sign: $$,$$$.99. This should be the PICTURE clause for TOTAL-OUT.

Note that there are *five* dollar signs in the report-item. The four rightmost dollar signs are zero suppression symbols. They cause suppression of leading zeros and commas and place the dollar sign in the position adjacent to the first significant digit. The leftmost dollar sign indicates to the computer that $ will be the first character to print. In total, there should be one more dollar sign than integer positions to be edited. *Four* integer positions are edited using *five* dollar signs. In general, *n* characters may be edited using a floating string of $n + 1$ characters. The extra floating character is needed in case the sending field has all significant positions; that is, the receiving field must have one additional position in which to place the floating character.

Example 2   05 WS-TAX   PICTURE S9(4).

Problem: Edit WS-TAX using a floating minus sign. The report-item is called TAX-OUT.

In Step 1, the PICTURE clause of the report-item is created according to the rules of the last section, using a minus sign and zero suppression: -ZZZZ.

In Step 2, all Z's are replaced with the appropriate floating character: -----.

Thus, TAX-OUT will have a PICTURE of ----- or -(5).

0032̄ will print as   -32
0487̄ will print as -487

Example 3   QTY-OUT has a PICTURE clause of +++99.

Problem: Find the PICTURE clause of the sending field, QTY-IN.

Note that the + will float but not completely. That is, the two rightmost digits always print even if they are nonsignificant zeros.

Three plus signs indicate a floating-string report-item that will accept *two* integers. The leftmost plus sign does *not* serve as a zero suppression character and is *never* replaced with integer data. Two characters of data will be accepted by three plus signs, and two characters of data will be accepted by two 9's. Thus, the sending field should have a PICTURE of S9(4). Consider the following examples of the editing that occurs with QTY-IN:

3826̇ will print as +3826
0382̄ will print as   -382
0002̇ will print as   +02

A floating-string character may be used in conjunction with other edit symbols such as 9's, decimal points, and commas, but it must be the leftmost character in the PICTURE clause of the report-item.

In addition, we may *not* use *two* floating-string characters in one report-item. If a dollar sign is to float, for example, then an operational sign may not be placed in the leftmost position of the field. You will recall, however, that signs may also appear in the rightmost position of a report-item. Thus, $$,$$$.99- is a valid PICTURE clause, but $$,---.99 or something similar is not valid. Only *one* character can float.

D. BLANK WHEN ZERO **Option**

It is often desirable to print spaces when a sending field consists entirely of zeros. With the use of complex editing, you may find, however, that $.00, −0, or a + or − sign by itself will print. This may detract from the clarity of a report. In such cases, the COBOL expression **BLANK WHEN ZERO** may be used *in conjunction with* the appropriate PICTURE clause.

Example   05   QTY-OUT   PICTURE +++.

This report-item will accept *two* characters of data, as in the following examples:

03̇ will print as   +3
7̄6 will print as   − 76
00 will print as   +

To eliminate the printing of + for a zero sending field as in the last case, the BLANK WHEN ZERO option may be added:

```
05   QTY-OUT    PICTURE +++ BLANK WHEN ZERO.
```

When using the BLANK WHEN ZERO option with a report-item, the normal rules of editing will be followed, depending on the edit symbols in the PICTURE clause. If the sending field is zero, however, spaces will print.

III. Printing Output

A. Using the WRITE ... FROM **Statement**

A MOVE operation, in which data is transmitted from WORKING-STORAGE to the output area, followed by a WRITE statement, may be replaced by a single WRITE ... FROM instruction. Thus, the following two excerpts are equivalent:

Method 1   MOVE DETAIL-LINE TO PRINT-REC.
WRITE PRINT-REC.

Method 2   WRITE PRINT-REC FROM DETAIL-LINE.

B. How to Space Forms

1. The ADVANCING Option
a. Advancing the Paper a Fixed Number of Lines.   When a file has been assigned to a printer, a simple WRITE statement will print *one line* of information. After the WRITE instruction, the paper will be advanced *one line* so that *single spacing* results.

Single spacing, however, is ordinarily not sufficient for most printing applications. Usually, programs require double or triple spacing between some lines.

We may obtain any number of blank lines between each line by using an **AFTER ADVANCING** or **BEFORE ADVANCING** option with WRITE instructions for a print file. The format for this WRITE statement is:

Format

$$
\texttt{WRITE}\ \ \text{record-name-1}\ \ [\underline{\texttt{FROM}}\ \ \text{identifier-1}]
$$

$$
\left[\left\{\begin{array}{l}\underline{\texttt{AFTER}}\\ \underline{\texttt{BEFORE}}\end{array}\right\}\ \texttt{ADVANCING}\ \left\{\begin{array}{l}\text{integer-1}\\ \text{identifier-2}\end{array}\right\}\ \left[\begin{array}{l}\texttt{LINE}\\ \texttt{LINES}\end{array}\right]\right]
$$

For ease of reading, code the WRITE ... FROM ... on one line and the ADVANCING option indented on the next. Or, code WRITE ... on one line, FROM ... on the second (indented), and BEFORE or AFTER ADVANCING on the third.

The integer, if used, must be any positive number; similarly, identifier-2, if used, may refer to an identifier containing any positive integer.

Typically, the paper can be spaced a maximum of 100 lines. Check your manual for the upper limit on this option for the compiler you are using.

If a line is to print *after* the paper is spaced, the AFTER ADVANCING option is used. WRITE PRINT-REC FROM DETAIL-REC AFTER ADVANCING 2 LINES will space two lines and *then* print. That is, after the paper advances two lines, printing will occur. If a line is to print *before* spacing occurs, the BEFORE ADVANCING option is used. WRITE PRINT-REC FROM HEADING-REC BEFORE ADVANCING 3 LINES will print and then advance the paper three lines.

The words ADVANCING, LINES, and LINE are not underlined in the instruction format, indicating that they are optional. Hence, the following two statements produce the same results:

1. WRITE PRINT-REC FROM DETAIL-REC
       AFTER ADVANCING 2 LINES.
2. WRITE PRINT-REC FROM DETAIL-REC
       AFTER 2.

In general, the first WRITE statement is preferred because it is clearer.

Overprinting

The BEFORE ADVANCING option should not be used in the same program as the AFTER ADVANCING option unless overprinting on the same line is desired. That is, consider the following:

```
WRITE PRINT-REC FROM HEADING-REC
    AFTER ADVANCING 2 LINES.
    .
    .
    .
WRITE PRINT-REC FROM REPORT-REC
    BEFORE ADVANCING 2 LINES.
```

The first WRITE statement causes two lines to be spaced and then the HEADING-REC to be printed. The subsequent WRITE instruction prints *first* and then spaces the form. This means that REPORT-REC will print *on the same line* as HEADING-REC. This overprinting would, in general, be incorrect unless you wished to use it for underlining a heading; that is, the first WRITE would print the heading and the second would print the underline. As a rule, to avoid any problems associated with printing two records on the same line, use *either* the BEFORE ADVANCING or the AFTER ADVANCING option in a particular program, but not both.

Note, also, that once the ADVANCING option is used for a print file, it should be specified for *all* WRITE statements for that file in the same program. Thus, if single spacing is sufficient for the entire report, you may use a simple WRITE statement. If single spacing is not sufficient, the ADVANCING option should be used with *all* WRITE statements for the print file.

SUMMARY

1. A WRITE statement without an ADVANCING option will result in single spacing.
2. If the ADVANCING option is used in a WRITE statement, every WRITE statement for records associated with the print file should contain an ADVANCING clause.
3. When the ADVANCING option is used, one extra character should be reserved for each record to be printed. The leftmost character is used by the system for forms control. Thus, for printers with 132 characters per line, each print record should be described as containing 133 characters and the leftmost position should not be accessed by the programmer.

In general, we will use the ADVANCING option when writing print records.

b. Advancing the Paper to a New Page.   Computer-generated reports are printed on **continuous forms.** Continuous forms have all pages connected, with perforations at the end of each page for separating the sheets. After a report is generated, these forms or pages must be separated into single sheets.

Unless the computer is instructed to do otherwise, it will write each line and advance the paper, printing from one sheet to another, ignoring the fact that each is really an individual page. At times, it may even print over the perforations, which is sloppy and makes reading difficult.

Although printing is performed from one page of the continuous form to another, the computer must be instructed to observe page delineations. Each page should generally begin with a heading. Data lines follow as the main component of the report, and when the end of a form is reached, we should skip to a new page and write the heading again.

We will consider several methods for advancing the paper to a new page. We recommend that you use the first one.

(1) The PAGE Option.   The word **PAGE** used after the word ADVANCING will cause the paper to skip to a new form. Thus, to advance the paper to the top of a new page and print a heading, we can code the following:

```
WRITE PRINT-REC FROM HEADING-REC
    AFTER ADVANCING PAGE.
```

HEADING-REC is a 133-position record described with appropriate VALUE clauses in the WORKING-STORAGE SECTION.

(2) Other Options.   Some computers allow the programmer to use the SPECIAL-NAMES paragraph of the ENVIRONMENT DIVISION to specify a "mnemonic name" for advancing the page.

CO1, which means Channel 01, is used to indicate the start of a new page on IBM and IBM-compatible systems. Channel 01 is set equal to a user-defined word that serves as a new page indicator in the SPECIAL-NAMES paragraph, which is part of the CONFIGURATION SECTION of the ENVIRONMENT DIVISION. Thus, the CONFIGURATION SECTION can be coded as follows:

```
CONFIGURATION SECTION.
SOURCE-COMPUTER.  computer-name.
OBJECT-COMPUTER.  computer-name.
SPECIAL-NAMES.  CO1 IS mnemonic-name.
```

That is, Channel 01 can be equated to any unique mnemonic-name that will be used for advancing the paper to a new page. (In CO1, the middle entry is the digit 0, not the letter O.)

Example

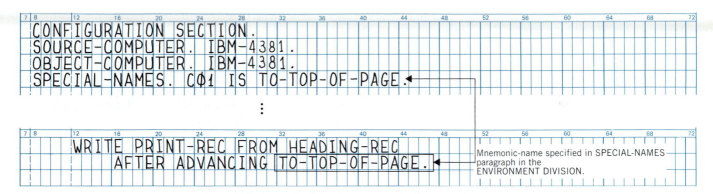

In this example, CO1 or Channel 01, which designates the top of a new form, is equated to the mnemonic-name TO-TOP-OF-PAGE. This name is then used in conjunction with the WRITE statement as shown.

The WRITE statement causes HEADING-REC data to print *on the top of a new form*, since TO-TOP-OF-PAGE is equated to Channel 01. The code CO1 is applicable to IBM and IBM-compatible computers, but it may be different for other computers.

The mnemonic-name following the COBOL reserved word ADVANCING must be the *same mnemonic-name* as the one equated to Channel 01 (CO1) in the SPECIAL-NAMES paragraph of the CONFIGURATION SECTION.

We can expand the instruction format of the WRITE statement to include *all* options of the ADVANCING clause thus far discussed:

Format—Expanded Version

$$
\text{WRITE} \quad \text{record-name-1} \quad [\text{FROM} \quad \text{identifier-1}]
$$

$$
\left\{ \begin{array}{l} \text{AFTER} \\ \text{BEFORE} \end{array} \right\} \quad \text{ADVANCING} \quad \left\{ \begin{array}{l} \underline{\text{PAGE}} \\ \text{identifier-2} \\ \text{integer-1} \\ \text{mnemonic-name-1} \end{array} \right\} \left[\begin{array}{l} \text{LINE} \\ \text{LINES} \end{array} \right]
$$

We recommend that you use the AFTER ADVANCING PAGE clause, if available, to skip to a new page.

2. End-of-Page Control—With the Use of a Programmed Line Counter

To ensure that information does not print over the perforations of a continuous form, an end-of-page control routine must be coded. The best method for testing if the end of a page has been reached is with a programmed **line counter.** Using a programmed line counter to achieve end-of-page control, we must do the following:

PROGRAMMED LINE COUNTER

1. Determine the number of lines to be printed.
2. Establish a WORKING-STORAGE line-counter field initialized at zero.
3. After each WRITE statement, increment the WORKING-STORAGE line-counter field by one. In this way, the number in the line-counter field will be equal to the number of lines actually printed.
4. After each WRITE statement, test the line-counter field to see if it equals the desired number of lines to be printed per page. If it does, print a heading on the top of a new page. If it does not, continue with the program.
5. If the line counter has reached the desired number, perform a heading routine. In that routine, reinitialize the line counter at zero.

The programmed line counter should be employed for all programs where the possibility exists that more than one page of printing will be required. Without such a procedure, the printer will simply print one line after another, paying no attention to page delineations or perforations.

We can use a programmed line counter that is incremented by one every time a line is written. When a specified number of lines have been written (e.g., 50), we can instruct the computer to print a heading on a new page:

Line Counting for Single-Spaced Reports

```
WRITE PRINT-REC FROM DETAIL-REC
    AFTER ADVANCING 1 LINE.
ADD 1 TO LINE-COUNT.
IF  LINE-COUNT = 50
    PERFORM 600-HEADING-RTN.
    :
    :
600-HEADING-RTN.
    WRITE PRINT-REC FROM HEADING-REC
        AFTER ADVANCING PAGE.
    MOVE ZEROS TO LINE-COUNT.
```

Note that LINE-COUNT must be a WORKING-STORAGE item that should be initialized at zero. The following routine, using the same method, allows for double spacing:

Line Counting for Double-Spaced Reports

```
WRITE PRINT-REC FROM DETAIL-REC
    AFTER ADVANCING 2 LINES.
ADD 1 TO LINE-COUNT.
IF  LINE-COUNT = 25
    PERFORM 600-HEADING-RTN.
    :
    :
600-HEADING-RTN.
    WRITE PRINT-REC FROM HEADING-REC
        AFTER ADVANCING PAGE.
    MOVE ZEROS TO LINE-COUNT.
```

Both routines assume that a page consists of 50 data lines. In the first case, we actually print 50 records, one per line. In the second, we print 25 double-

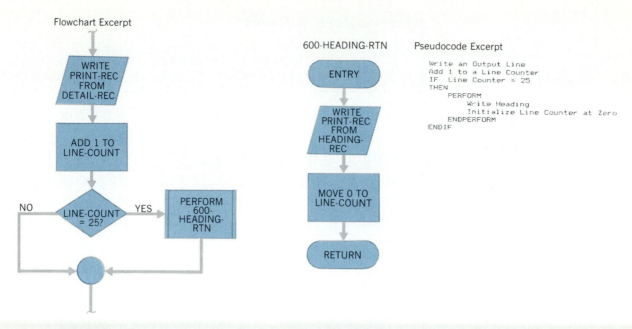

Figure 11.3
Flowchart and pseudocode for
line-counter routine.

spaced records. Thus, in the second routine, we have 25 print records and 25 blank lines. The flowchart and pseudocode for the latter procedure are illustrated in Figure 11.3.

With some computers, it is also possible to employ the SPECIAL-NAMES paragraph of the CONFIGURATION SECTION for sensing the end of a page as well as skipping to the top of a new page. See your manual for more details.

C. Spooling of Printed Output and the Use of Buffers

1. What is Spooling?

Because print operations are relatively slow, data to be printed is not always transmitted directly to the printer when a WRITE instruction is executed. Instead, the data is **spooled** onto some medium, such as a disk, in a high-speed operation. In this way, the relatively slow printing operation becomes a disk-to-print procedure that can be executed in an off-line mode. This frees the CPU to perform other functions while output is being printed.

2. Using Buffers as an Alternative to Spooling

When spooling is *not* performed, the computer generally establishes two storage areas or **buffers** for each print file. While data from one buffer is being printed (a relatively slow operation), the other buffer may be used for storing the next output line to be printed. Overlapped processing performed in this way increases the speed of the WRITE operation and may be used as an alternative to spooling.

If spooling is being performed, we do not need two buffers. The output operation onto disk is fast enough so that alternative I/O buffers for accumulating data are unnecessary. Thus, if your system spools printed data onto disk and then prints in a disk-to-print procedure, you might need to establish only one output area or buffer. This is performed with a **RESERVE** clause as follows:

When Spooling is Performed

```
SELECT  file-name-1  ASSIGN TO  implementor-name-1
        RESERVE 1 AREA.
```

Example

```
SELECT PRINT-FILE ASSIGN TO UR-S-1403
       RESERVE 1 AREA.
```

This RESERVE clause eliminates a second buffer so that spooling can be more easily achieved.

The following is a summary of entries used for skipping to a new page and for determining when the end of a page has been reached:

SUMMARY

1. To advance to a new page, code:

   AFTER ADVANCING PAGE

2. To print headings on each new page:
   a. Determine the number of lines to be printed per page.
   b. Use a line counter for counting the number of lines printed.
   c. Compare the line counter to the number of lines desired per page and advance to a new page when an equal condition is met.
   d. Remember to reset the line counter when an equal condition is met.

Self-Test

1. To space the paper two lines and then print a line, the WRITE statement would be coded as _____ .

2. Write a COBOL statement to print the record called TOTAL-LINE, which is part of the print file, and then advance the form two lines.

3. What, if anything, is wrong with the following statement?

   ```
   WRITE PRINT-REC
       AFTER ADVANCING TWO LINES.
   ```

4. To test for the last line of printing on a form, the programmer typically uses a _____ defined in WORKING-STORAGE.

5. Code a routine to write PRINT-REC from DETAIL-REC and space two lines; perform a HEADING-RTN if 30 lines have already been printed.

6. To skip to a new page, use the phrase AFTER ADVANCING _____ .

7. If the following is a statement in the PROCEDURE DIVISION, code the SPECIAL-NAMES paragraph:

   ```
   WRITE PRINT-REC FROM HEADING-REC
       AFTER ADVANCING ONE-PAGE.
   ```

8. The SPECIAL-NAMES paragraph is part of the _____ SECTION and follows the _____ paragraphs.

Solutions

1. WRITE ... AFTER ADVANCING 2 LINES.
2. WRITE PRINT-REC FROM TOTAL-LINE BEFORE ADVANCING 2 LINES.
3. Use the integer 2, unless TWO has been defined as a field with a value of 2.
4. line counter
5. WRITE PRINT-REC FROM DETAIL-REC
       BEFORE ADVANCING 2 LINES.
   ADD 1 TO LINE-CT.
   IF LINE-CT = 30
       PERFORM 500-HEADING-RTN.
6. PAGE
7. SPECIAL-NAMES. C01 IS ONE-PAGE.
8. CONFIGURATION; SOURCE-COMPUTER and OBJECT-COMPUTER

IV. Aligning Data and Printing Heading Information

A. An Overview

1. The Leftmost Position of a Record to be Printed is for Forms Control

You will recall that the print area must contain 133 characters when the ADVANCING option is used for writing records with 132 print characters per line. Regardless of the number of characters per print line, the first position of the area is used by the computer for proper spacing of forms and should *not* be accessed by the programmer. Thus, the second position denoted in the area is really the first *print* position. Positions 2 through 133 in the print area will be transmitted to the printer when a WRITE instruction is executed. We could set up our print area, then, as follows:

```
01  PRINT-REC.
    05  FILLER      PICTURE X.
    05  REAL-REC.
        10  FLDA    PICTURE X.
            :
            :
```

The first position is called FILLER to denote that it will not be accessed in the program. When a WRITE instruction is executed, whatever is in FLDA will appear in the *first print position*. The FILLER is used only for forms control.

Thus, in our example, 132 print positions are available. To produce clear and meaningful reports, information is ordinarily spaced on the line with margins on each side of the paper and fields evenly distributed across the line. In addition, headings are usually necessary to provide identifying information.

2. Types of Headings

Two types of headings generally appear on each page of a report:

1. *Report heading*—includes a title for the report, date, page number, etc.
2. *Column heading*—identifies the fields that will print on subsequent lines.

Figure 11.4 illustrates the two types of headings. The first heading (designated as H1) supplies information about the report; the second heading (designated as H2) describes the fields to be printed. Both types of headings are neatly spaced across the form, as noted in the Printer Spacing Chart.

All headings are printed on each page, since continuous forms are separated after they are generated.

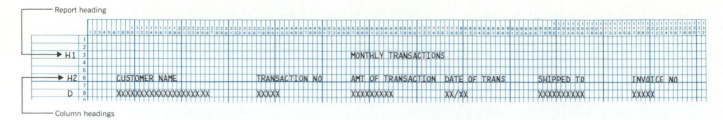

Figure 11.4
Printer Spacing Chart that
illustrates a report heading and
column headings.

B. The Printer Spacing Chart

A **Printer Spacing Chart,** sometimes called a Print Layout Sheet, is commonly used to assist the programmer in the preparation of reports. This chart is used for designing the report so that (1) headings appear properly spaced across the page and (2) fields are properly aligned under column headings and are evenly spaced across the page.

In our examples, the Printer Spacing Chart is subdivided into 132 print positions. The headings are spaced evenly across the page. From the numbered positions, the programmer can determine in which print positions he or she should place the literals and which positions should be left blank.

In our illustration in Figure 11.4 note that, for the first heading line, print positions 1–56 will be left blank as will print positions 77–132. The literal `'MONTHLY TRANSACTIONS'` will be placed in the area between. On the Printer Spacing Chart, X's indicate where the actual data will be placed. Twenty X's under the column heading CUSTOMER NAME denote that the field contains 20 characters. The H's in the left margin designate the lines as headings; the D designates the line as a detail or data line. If total lines were included, they would be designated with a T.

C. Defining Print Records in WORKING-STORAGE

1. A Review
If both heading and detail lines are required in the report, and they generally are, then several record formats must be specified.

As previously noted, we establish our print file FD with a 133-position PRINT-REC entry:

```
FD   PRINT-FILE
     LABEL RECORDS ARE OMITTED.
01   PRINT-REC   PIC X(133).
```

The actual heading records and the detail line records are best described in the WORKING-STORAGE SECTION. The main reason for describing these records in the WORKING-STORAGE SECTION is that values may be assigned to the various fields. Only WORKING-STORAGE entries may contain VALUE clauses for this purpose. This eliminates the necessity of moving spaces and specific literals to each field in the PROCEDURE DIVISION. Since VALUE clauses may *not* be assigned to fields in the FILE SECTION, the data to be printed should be stored in WORKING-STORAGE records. These records are then moved to the output area and written. We use a WRITE ... FROM statement to combine the move and write functions.

Thus, the FILE SECTION print area is defined as 133 positions. Data from the WORKING-STORAGE SECTION will be moved into this area. Fields need not be designated in the FILE SECTION, since an *entire* print record in WORKING-STORAGE will be moved to the print area.

The two heading records described in Figure 11.4 will be established in the WORKING-STORAGE SECTION as 01 entries:

```
WORKING-STORAGE SECTION.
01  HEADING-1.
    05  FILLER       PIC X     VALUE SPACE.
    05  FILLER       PIC X(56) VALUE SPACES.
    05  FILLER       PIC X(20) VALUE 'MONTHLY TRANSACTIONS'.
    05  FILLER       PIC X(56) VALUE SPACES.
01  HEADING-2.
    05  FILLER       PIC X     VALUE SPACE.
    05  FILLER       PIC X(6)  VALUE SPACES.
    05  FILLER       PIC X(13) VALUE 'CUSTOMER NAME'.
    05  FILLER       PIC X(17) VALUE SPACES.
    05  FILLER       PIC X(14) VALUE 'TRANSACTION NO'.
    05  FILLER       PIC X(6)  VALUE SPACES.
    05  FILLER       PIC X(18) VALUE 'AMT OF TRANSACTION'.
    05  FILLER       PIC XX    VALUE SPACES.
    05  FILLER       PIC X(13) VALUE 'DATE OF TRANS'.
    05  FILLER       PIC X(7)  VALUE SPACES.
    05  FILLER       PIC X(10) VALUE 'SHIPPED TO'.
    05  FILLER       PIC X(10) VALUE SPACES.
    05  FILLER       PIC X(10) VALUE 'INVOICE NO'.
    05  FILLER       PIC X(6)  VALUE SPACES.
```

Since none of the fields within HEADING-1 and HEADING-2 will be accessed in the PROCEDURE DIVISION, it is customary to call them all FILLER, even though some have nonnumeric literals as VALUE clauses. We will use this convention from this point on. The word FILLER itself may be omitted if you are using a COBOL 85 compiler.

Similarly, the DETAIL-LINE with FILLERs between significant fields will be defined in WORKING-STORAGE as follows:

```
01  DETAIL-LINE.
    05  FILLER            PICTURE X        VALUE SPACE.
    05  FILLER            PICTURE X(6)     VALUE SPACES.
    05  DL-NAME           PICTURE X(20).
    05  FILLER            PICTURE X(10)    VALUE SPACES.
    05  DL-TRANS-NO       PICTURE 9(5).
    05  FILLER            PICTURE X(15)    VALUE SPACES.
    05  DL-AMT-OF-TRANS   PICTURE $$,$$$.99.
    05  FILLER            PICTURE X(11)    VALUE SPACES.
    05  DL-DATE           PICTURE X(5).
    05  FILLER            PICTURE X(15)    VALUE SPACES.
    05  DL-DESTINATION    PICTURE X(10).
    05  FILLER            PICTURE X(10)    VALUE SPACES.
    05  DL-INV-NO         PICTURE 9(5).
    05  FILLER            PICTURE X(11)    VALUE SPACES.
```

Note that the DETAIL-LINE contains edit symbols in the field called DL-AMT-OF-TRANS. Input fields or work areas will be moved to the detail line. We use DL- as a prefix for all fields so that they are clearly designated as part of the detail line.

When using WORKING-STORAGE records to describe lines to be printed, all constants and blanks may be preassigned with VALUE clauses. Thus, data is stored in WORKING-STORAGE and then transmitted to the print area and printed with a WRITE ... FROM as follows:

```
500-HEADING-RTN.
    WRITE PRINT-REC FROM HEADING-1
        AFTER ADVANCING PAGE.
    WRITE PRINT-REC FROM HEADING-2
        AFTER ADVANCING 2 LINES.
    MOVE 0 TO LINE-CT.
```

It is unnecessary to clear PRINT-REC each time. The *entire* 133-position area called HEADING-1, which contains appropriate blank areas, is transmitted to the PRINT-REC area. Similarly, PRINT-REC need not be cleared before HEADING-2 is moved to it because HEADING-2 also contains the necessary blanks for the second heading line. LINE-CT, which counts the number of lines printed on a page, must be initialized at zero each time through the heading routine. The DETAIL-RTN requires a full series of moves, since data is to be moved to the various fields from the input area. The following is the coding in 300-DETAIL-RTN:

```
300-DETAIL-RTN.
    MOVE NAME-IN TO DL-NAME.
    MOVE TRANS-NO-IN TO DL-TRANS-NO.
    MOVE AMT-OF-TRANS-IN TO DL-AMT-OF-TRANS.
    MOVE DATE-IN TO DL-DATE.
    MOVE DESTINATION-IN TO DL-DESTINATION.
    MOVE INV-NO-IN TO DL-INV-NO.
    WRITE PRINT-REC FROM DETAIL-LINE
        AFTER ADVANCING 2 LINES.
    ADD 1 TO LINE-CT.
    IF  LINE-CT = 25
        PERFORM 500-HEADING-RTN.
    READ TRANS-FILE
        AT END MOVE 'NO ' TO ARE-THERE-MORE-RECORDS.
```

2. Combining Fields in Print Records

Several shortcuts may be used in the WORKING-STORAGE SECTION to enhance the efficiency of the program. HEADING-1, for example, was previously established as follows:

Example 1

```
01   HEADING-1.
     05   FILLER   PIC X        VALUE SPACE.
     05   FILLER   PIC X(56)    VALUE SPACES.
     05   FILLER   PIC X(20)    VALUE 'MONTHLY TRANSACTIONS'.
     05   FILLER   PIC X(56)    VALUE SPACES.
```

Notice that the term FILLER is used to describe each field within HEADING-1, even the field that contains 'MONTHLY TRANSACTIONS'. The term FILLER is used because only the record level entry, HEADING-1, is accessed in the PROCEDURE DIVISION.

This example could be coded more efficiently as:

```
01   HEADING-1.
     05   FILLER       PICTURE X(57) VALUE SPACES.
     05   FILLER       PICTURE X(20) VALUE 'MONTHLY TRANSACTIONS'.
     05   FILLER       PICTURE X(56) VALUE SPACES.
```

Note that the first two FILLERs have been combined into one. The first position of the record is typically used for forms control. It is unnecessary to set up *two* separate FILLER areas, one containing a single blank and one containing 56 blanks. One FILLER will serve just as well.

With COBOL 85, the preceding can be written without the word FILLER as follows:

```
01   HEADING-1.
     05   PIC X(57)   VALUE SPACES.
     05   PIC X(20)   VALUE 'MONTHLY TRANSACTIONS'.
     05   PIC X(56)   VALUE SPACES.
```

3. The JUSTIFIED RIGHT Clause

The preceding could be coded even more efficiently as follows:

```
01   HEADING-1.
     05   FILLER   PIC X(57)   VALUE SPACES.
     05   FILLER   PIC X(76)   VALUE 'MONTHLY TRANSACTIONS'.
```

Recall that nonnumeric literals are *left-justified* in a field. Thus, the literal 'MONTHLY TRANSACTIONS' will print in positions 57–76. The rest of the second FILLER area will be replaced with blanks. The VALUE clause has the same effect as moving 'MONTHLY TRANSACTIONS' to LITERAL1, where the second FILLER would be called LITERAL1.

Using the **JUSTIFIED RIGHT** clause, we may also code HEADING-1 as follows:

```
01   HEADING-1.
     05   FILLER       PICTURE X(77) VALUE
          'MONTHLY TRANSACTIONS' JUSTIFIED RIGHT.
     05   FILLER       PICTURE X(56) VALUE SPACES.
```

JUSTIFIED RIGHT alters the placement of data in *nonnumeric* fields. With the use of the JUSTIFIED RIGHT clause, 'MONTHLY TRANSACTIONS' will be placed in positions 58–77, instead of 1–20. Positions 58–77 in HEADING-1 correspond to *print positions* 57–76. The rest of the record will be blank.

4. Continuation of Nonnumeric Literals: A Review

HEADING-2 may also be coded more efficiently. We may use two literals, each containing the proper number of spaces, to specify the entire record. Figure 11.5 illustrates the necessary entries.

The continuation of a nonnumeric literal from one line to the next is illustrated in the coding of the first FILLER. Recall from Chapter 7 that the rules are as follows:

CONTINUATION OF NONNUMERIC LITERALS FROM ONE LINE TO THE NEXT

1. Begin the value or literal with a quote mark and continue to column 72.
2. Continue the literal on the next line with a hyphen in column 7 and a quote mark anywhere in Area B.
3. End the literal on the last line with a quote mark.

```
7 8    12    16    20    24    28    32    36    40    44    48    52    56    60    64    68    72
Ø1  HEADING-2.
    Ø5  FILLER            PICTURE X(75)            VALUE `            CUSTOMER NA
-   `ME                           TRANSACTION NO         AMT OF TRANSACTION'.
    Ø5  FILLER            PICTURE X(58)            VALUE `  DATE OF TRANS
-   `      SHIPPED TO            INVOICE NO          '.
```

Figure 11.5
Continuation of nonnumeric
literals.

D. Printing Page Numbers

Often, when printing headings, a page number is required as part of the first heading record. Consider the following WORKING-STORAGE record:

```
01   HEADING-LINE.
     05   FILLER     PIC X(61) VALUE SPACES.
     05   FILLER     PIC X(20) VALUE 'SALARY CHANGES'.
     05   FILLER     PIC X(8)  VALUE 'PAGE NO'.
     05   HL-PAGE-CT PIC ZZZZ.
     05   FILLER     PIC X(40) VALUE SPACES.
```

The prefix HL- is used for fields within the *Heading Line*.

A WORKING-STORAGE numeric item defined as COUNT1 PICTURE 9999 VALUE 0001 is established for actually counting pages. The following 500-HEADING-RTN will print a page number on each page:

```
500-HEADING-RTN.
     MOVE COUNT1 TO HL-PAGE-CT.
     WRITE PRINT-REC FROM HEADING-LINE
         AFTER ADVANCING PAGE.
     ADD 1 TO COUNT1.
     MOVE ZEROS TO LINE-CT.
```

500-HEADING-RTN should be performed initially, after the files are opened in the main module. To execute 500-HEADING-RTN again after the end of a page has been reached, we code our 300-DETAIL-RTN as follows:

```
300-DETAIL-RTN.
     :
     WRITE PRINT-REC FROM DETAIL-REC
         AFTER ADVANCING 2 LINES.
     ADD 1 TO LINE-CT.
     IF  LINE-CT = 25
         PERFORM 500-HEADING-RTN.
     READ ...
```

Each time through the 500-HEADING-RTN, COUNT1, which is a page counter, is incremented by 1. Before each record is printed, COUNT1 is moved to the report-item HL-PAGE-CT. Thus, a correct page number will appear on each form with leading zeros suppressed. Note that the following is *not* correct:

Invalid

```
ADD 1 TO HL-PAGE-CT.
```

HL-PAGE-CT is a report-item containing edit symbols that cause zero suppression. Only *numeric* items may be used in arithmetic operations. HL-PAGE-CT, as a report-item, is not a numeric field and cannot be part of an ADD operation. Hence, a separate field, referred to in this case as COUNT1, *must* be established in WORKING-STORAGE as a numeric field. It is incremented to reflect the actual page number. To suppress leading zeros in the page number, we then move COUNT1 to the report-item HL-PAGE-CT, which is defined as part of HEADING-LINE.

E. Printing the Date of the Run

One way to print the date of the run is to read in as input the actual date, in the form desired. This date will then be moved to a heading.

This method for obtaining the date is, however, inefficient because it requires (1) additional input instructions for reading the date and (2) additional set-up by a computer operator to enter the date in the correct format.

Since the computer itself stores the current date, it may be accessed directly from the system. We will consider two basic methods for retrieving the date stored by the system: (1) the ANS COBOL standard and (2) the IBM enhancement to the standard.

1. Accepting DATE

The computer stores the current date in a field that can be accessed with the COBOL reserved word **DATE**. DATE stores the run date as a six-digit field consisting of the following elements in the order specified:

DATE
Two-digit year (e.g., 89 for 1989)
Two-digit month (e.g., 02 for February)
Two-digit day (e.g., 01–31)

Suppose, for example, that 890223 is stored in DATE. This represents February 23, 1989.

Suppose we establish a WORKING-STORAGE entry as follows:

```
01  WS-DATE        PIC 9(6).
```

To obtain the current date in WS-DATE, we code:

```
            ACCEPT WS-DATE FROM DATE.
```

With this **ACCEPT** statement, there is no need to enter a date as input. The ACCEPT statement will move the date in the format yymmdd into the field called WS-DATE. (yy = the two-digit year; mm = the month number, dd = the day of the month.)

The format for obtaining the date in a program, then, is as follows:

Format
```
            ACCEPT  identifier-1  FROM DATE
```

The identifier must be a six-position unsigned numeric elementary item.

After the ACCEPT statement is executed, the identifier will contain the run date as yymmdd (year, month, day). But this date format is not very user-friendly. We would normally want to print this in a more readable form.

To better represent the date of the run, we will need to access the three components of year, month, and day separately. The identifier specified with the ACCEPT must be *elementary*, which means that it cannot be subdivided.

We must therefore first move WS-DATE to a group item:

```
01   WS-DATE        PIC 9(6).
01   WS-DATE-X.
     05   YEAR       PIC 99.
     05   MONTH      PIC 99.
     05   DAY-X      PIC 99.
```

Printing the date as month/day/year could be accomplished with the following coding:

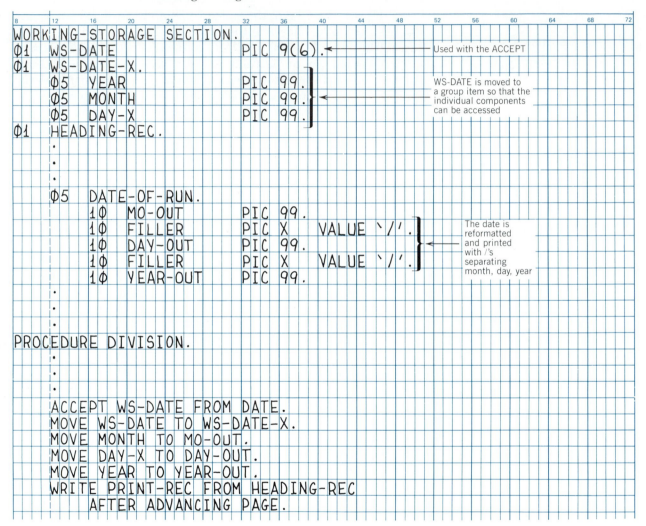

If DATE contained 890223, the heading would print with a run date of 02/23/89.

Note that it would *not* be valid to code the following:

```
ACCEPT WS-DATE-X FROM DATE.
```

With many compilers, the identifier following the word ACCEPT must be an *elementary numeric item with integer value.* WS-DATE-X is a group item. Some compilers, however, have an enhancement that allows the identifier to specify a group item.

2. The Use of the REDEFINES for Printing the Date of the Run

We could *redefine* WS-DATE so that the *same* six positions serve as both an elementary numeric item and a group item:

```
01   WS-DATE      PIC 9(6).
01   WS-DATE-X    REDEFINES WS-DATE.
     05   YEAR    PIC 99.
     05   MONTH   PIC 99.
     05   DAY-X   PIC 99.
```

The **REDEFINES** clause allows you to reformat the same storage area. Using the REDEFINES, only *one* six-position field is established. It is accessed as an elementary item for the ACCEPT and accessed as a group item with the MOVE.

Thus, only one six-position field needs to be defined. It is, however, specified in two different ways, as an elementary numeric item called WS-DATE and as a group item called WS-DATE-X.

Without a REDEFINES clause, we specified *two* separate six-position fields. To obtain the required date in WS-DATE-X, a MOVE WS-DATE TO WS-DATE-X was required. With a REDEFINES clause, the MOVE is not coded because both WS-DATE and WS-DATE-X define the *same* field.

3. The IBM Enhancement for Printing the Date of the Run

The preceding method for retrieving a date enables us to use the run date without the need to enter it as input. But it requires additional coding to convert a yymmdd date format to an mm/dd/yy format.

IBM and IBM-compatible computers use a special reserved word called **CURRENT-DATE**. CURRENT-DATE is an eight-position alphanumeric field that *already has* the date in an mm/dd/yy format, including the slashes for readability. This format simplifies the coding considerably. Note that a MOVE can be used in place of the ACCEPT:

```
01   HEADING-REC.
     .
     .
     05   DATE-OF-RUN      PIC X(8).
     .
     .
PROCEDURE DIVISION.
     .
     .
     MOVE CURRENT-DATE TO DATE-OF-RUN.
```

In addition to IBM, many other computer manufacturers offer this eight-character enhancement or option for the date of the run. Check your computer's specifications manual to see if you may use CURRENT-DATE or a similar field.

4. Accessing the Day of the Week Using COBOL 85

With COBOL 85, we can also obtain a numeric representation for the day of the week, where 1 represents Monday, 2 represents Tuesday, and so on. To obtain a digit 1 to 7, we code:

```
          ACCEPT identifier FROM DAY-OF-WEEK.
```

F. Printing Quotation Marks

As noted, nonnumeric literals are enclosed in quotation marks ("), or apostrophes ('), depending on the computer system. Thus, the quotation mark (or apostrophe) itself cannot actually be part of a nonnumeric literal.

To print a quotation mark, then, we would use the COBOL constant QUOTE. Suppose we wish to print a heading such as:

```
ITEM DESCRIPTION: 'SPECIAL'
```

This heading, which is to include quotation marks, is defined as:

```
01   HEADING-1.
     05   FILLER    PIC X(20)   VALUE SPACES.
     05   FILLER    PIC X(18)   VALUE 'ITEM DESCRIPTION: '.
     05   FILLER    PIC X       VALUE QUOTE.
     05   FILLER    PIC X(7)    VALUE 'SPECIAL'.
     05   FILLER    PIC X       VALUE QUOTE.
     05   FILLER    PIC X(86)   VALUE SPACES.
```

The word QUOTE can be used to print a quotation mark as shown here; it cannot, however, be used to surround a literal. Thus, MOVE QUOTE SPECIAL QUOTE... is not permissible.

CODING GUIDELINES FOR DESIGNING REPORTS

1. Include a heading that identifies the report.
2. Include the date and the page number in the heading.
3. Include column headings for identification.
4. Place the most significant fields where they are most visible.
5. Edit numeric fields for readability.
6. Include totals at the end of the report or at the end of a page.
7. Use *'s to identify the level of a total.

Example

```
DEPT TOTAL IS $33,266.25*
    .
    .
FINAL TOTAL IS $167,267.53**
```

CHAPTER SUMMARY

Table 11.2 reviews edit symbols used in a PICTURE clause. Table 11.3 illustrates the rules of editing when using floating strings and the BLANK WHEN ZERO option.

Table 11.2
Edit Symbols That May Be Used in a PICTURE Clause

	Symbol	Meaning
	X	Alphanumeric field
	9	Numeric field
	A	Alphabetic field
	V	Assumed decimal point; used only in numeric fields
	S	Operational sign; used only in numeric fields
Edit Symbols	Z	Zero suppression character
	.	Decimal point
	+	Plus sign

Table 11.2
(Continued)

Edit Symbols		
$-$	Minus sign	
$	Dollar sign	
,	Comma	
CR	Credit symbol	
DB	Debit symbol	
*	Check protection symbol	
B	Field separator—space insertion character	
0	Zero insertion character	

Table 11.3
Editing Using Floating
Strings and the BLANK
WHEN ZERO Option

	Sending-Field		Report-Item	
	PICTURE	Contents	**PICTURE**	**Edited Results**
1.	S999V99	012∧34⁺	$$$$.99−	$12.34 −
2.	S999	123	----	123
3.	S999	005⁻	----	−5
4.	99	37	+++	+37
5.	S99	05⁻	+++	−5
6.	S99	05⁺	+++	+5
7.	999	000	++++	+
8.	999V99	000∧00	$$$$.99	$.00
9.	999V99	000∧00	$$$$.99 BLANK WHEN ZERO	

1. The record length for a print record must be defined as one more than the number of characters per line. For example, specify 133 characters for printers with 132 print positions per line. The first position, which is used for forms control, should have a blank and should not be accessed in the program.
2. The AFTER or BEFORE ADVANCING option should be used with each WRITE instruction to indicate the spacing of the form. AFTER ADVANCING 1, 2, or 3 lines, for example, will cause zero, one, or two blank lines, respectively, to appear before the next record is written.
3. Records defining heading and detail lines should be established in WORKING-STORAGE so that VALUE clauses can be used. These records must be moved to the print area defined in the FILE SECTION. A WRITE ... FROM instruction may be used in place of a MOVE and a WRITE to print these lines.
4. Use a Printer Spacing Chart to assign the print positions to be used.
5. After each record is printed, a test for the end of a form should be performed so that the paper can be advanced to the top of a new page where headings will be printed.
6. The appropriate editing symbols should be specified in the PICTURE clauses of report-items within the detail record.
7. To skip to a new page code AFTER ADVANCING PAGE.

CHAPTER SELF-TEST

For Questions 1 through 10, fill in the missing column.

	Sending-Field		Report-Item	
	PICTURE	**Contents**	**PICTURE**	**Edited Results**
1.	999V99	000ᴧ05	$$$$.99	
2.	S999V99	000ᴧ05̄	$$$$.99−	
3.	9999V99	0026ᴧ54		ƀƀ26.54+
4.	S999	002̄	++++	
5.	S99		−−−	−4
6.	999V99	000ᴧ00	$$$$.99	
7.	999V99	000ᴧ00	$$$$.99 BLANK WHEN ZERO	
8.	9(3)	008	Z(3).99	
9.	9(5)	00123	$ZZ,ZZZ.ZZ	
10.	9(4)	0002	Z,Z99	

11. The two types of headings that may appear on a printed report are _____ and _____ .

12. (T or F) The leftmost character in a print record is used by the system for spacing the form.

13. Records to be printed are described in the WORKING-STORAGE SECTION because this section allows the use of _____ clauses.

14. Assume print records are described in the WORKING-STORAGE SECTION with appropriate VALUE clauses. Code a sample record description entry in the FILE SECTION for the print file.

15. Indicate how you might obtain underlining of headings by using the ADVANCING option.

16. The _____ is a tool used for aligning data to be printed.

17. To print a heading on a new page, we might code the following:

```
WRITE PRINT-REC FROM HEADING-REC
    AFTER ADVANCING _____ .
```

18. To obtain the date stored by the system, we may code ACCEPT DATE-IN FROM _____ .

19. In Question 18, DATE-IN is typically defined in the _____ SECTION as a(n) _____ field.

20. To override the normal rules of placing data in alphanumeric fields from left to right, we use the _____ clause along with the PICTURE specification.

Solutions

1. $.05
2. $.05 −
3. ZZZZ.99+
4. −2
5. 04̄
6. $.00
7. (7 blanks)
8. ƀƀ8.00
9. $ 123.00
10. ƀƀƀ02
11. report headings; column headings
12. T
13. VALUE

14. `01   PRINT-REC PICTURE X(133).` (No field descriptions are necessary.)
15. The following may be used as an example:

```
01   HDG1.
     05  FILLER      PIC X(57)      VALUE SPACES.
     05  FILLER      PIC X(76)      VALUE 'MONTHLY SALES REPORT'.
01   HDG2.
     05  FILLER      PIC X(57)      VALUE SPACES.
     05  FILLER      PIC X(76)      VALUE '_____'.
        .
        .
     WRITE PRINT-REC FROM HDG1 AFTER 2.
     WRITE PRINT-REC FROM HDG2 BEFORE 2.
```

16. Printer Spacing Chart
17. `PAGE` (or mnemonic-name used in conjunction with `SPECIAL-NAMES`)
18. `DATE`
19. `WORKING-STORAGE`; elementary numeric
20. `JUSTIFIED RIGHT`

PRACTICE PROGRAM

Consider the following problem definition:

Systems Flowchart

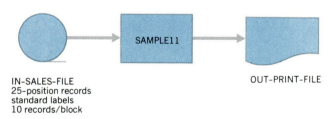

IN-SALES-FILE
25-position records
standard labels
10 records/block

OUT-PRINT-FILE

IN-SALES-FILE Record Layout

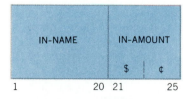

OUT-PRINT-FILE Printer Spacing Chart

SAMPLE INPUT DATA

```
PAUL  NEWMAN              12000
PAUL  NEWMAN              13000
PAUL  NEWMAN              10000
PAUL  NEWMAN              05000
PAUL  NEWMAN              02500
DIANA ROSS               01000
DIANA ROSS               02000
DIANA ROSS               03000
DIANA ROSS               04000
DIANA ROSS               05000
ROBERT REDFORD           10000
ROBERT REDFORD           20000
ROBERT REDFORD           30000
ROBERT REDFORD           40000
ROBERT REDFORD           50000
```

SAMPLE OUTPUT

```
          TOTAL OF GROUPS OF FIVE RECORDS      PAGE NO.      1

PAUL NEWMAN                      $***425.00  01/29/88

DIANA ROSS                      $***150.00  01/29/88

ROBERT REDFORD                  $*1,500.00  01/29/88
```

Write a program incorporating the following:

1. Printing of headings on each page.
2. Printing of page numbers on each page.
3. Double spacing between all detail lines.
4. Storing of output records in WORKING-STORAGE.
5. Printing the date of the run.

The program is to print the total of the amount fields of every group of five tape records.

Note: The name is the same for each group of five records. The number of tape records is a multiple of five.

Figure 11.6 illustrates the flowchart, pseudocode, and hierarchy charts. Figure 11.7 shows the solution.

KEY TERMS

ACCEPT

AFTER ADVANCING

BEFORE ADVANCING

BLANK WHEN ZERO
  option

Buffer

Check protection
  symbol (*)

Continuous forms

CURRENT-DATE

DATE

Editing

Floating string

JUSTIFIED RIGHT

Line counter

PAGE

Printer Spacing Chart

REDEFINES

Report-item

RESERVE

Spooling

Suppression of leading
  zeros

Figure 11.6
Flowchart, pseudocode, and hierarchy chart for the Practice Program.

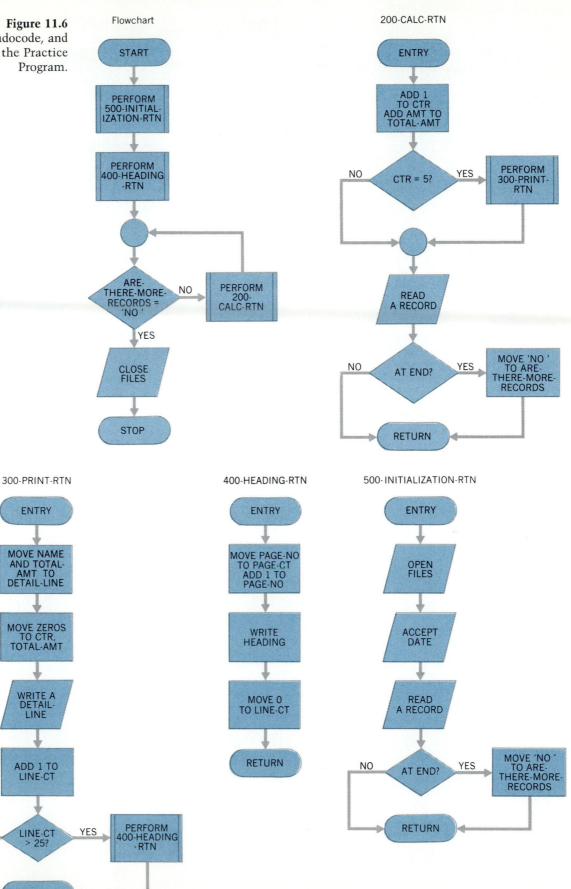

Pseudocode   Hierarchy Chart

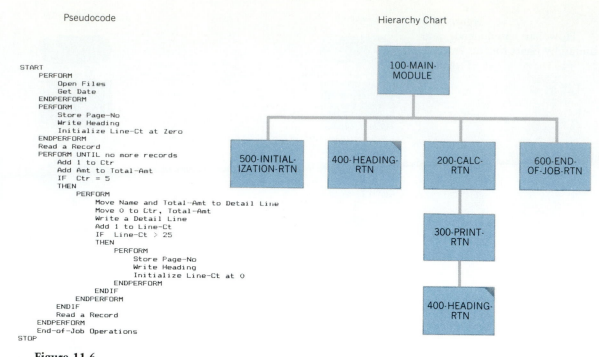

```
START
    PERFORM
        Open Files
        Get Date
    ENDPERFORM
    PERFORM
        Store Page-No
        Write Heading
        Initialize Line-Ct at Zero
    ENDPERFORM
    Read a Record
    PERFORM UNTIL no more records
        Add 1 to Ctr
        Add Amt to Total-Amt
        IF  Ctr = 5
        THEN
            PERFORM
                Move Name and Total-Amt to Detail Line
                Move 0 to Ctr, Total-Amt
                Write a Detail Line
                Add 1 to Line-Ct
                IF  Line-Ct > 25
                THEN
                    PERFORM
                        Store Page-No
                        Write Heading
                        Initialize Line-Ct at 0
                    ENDPERFORM
                ENDIF
            ENDPERFORM
        ENDIF
        Read a Record
    ENDPERFORM
    End-of-Job Operations
STOP
```

Figure 11.6
(continued)

Figure 11.7
Solution to the Practice
Program.

```
IDENTIFICATION DIVISION.
PROGRAM-ID. SAMPLE.
****************************************************************
*  SAMPLE    - CREATES A SALES REPORT PRINTING ONE OUTPUT  *
*               LINE FOR EACH GROUP OF 5 INPUT RECORDS      *
****************************************************************
ENVIRONMENT DIVISION.
CONFIGURATION SECTION.
SOURCE-COMPUTER. IBM-370.
OBJECT-COMPUTER. IBM-370.
INPUT-OUTPUT SECTION.
FILE-CONTROL.
    SELECT IN-SALES-FILE  ASSIGN TO DATA10.
    SELECT OUT-PRINT-FILE ASSIGN TO SYS$OUTPUT.
*
DATA DIVISION.
FILE SECTION.
FD  IN-SALES-FILE
    LABEL RECORDS ARE STANDARD.
01  IN-SALES-REC.
    05  IN-NAME               PIC X(20).
    05  IN-AMOUNT             PIC 9(3)V99.
FD  OUT-PRINT-FILE
    LABEL RECORDS ARE OMITTED.
01  OUT-PRINT-REC             PIC X(133).
WORKING-STORAGE SECTION.
01  WS-WORK-AREAS.
    05  ARE-THERE-MORE-RECORDS  PIC X(3)      VALUE 'YES'.
        88  MORE-RECORDS                      VALUE 'YES'.
        88  NO-MORE-RECORDS                   VALUE 'NO '.
    05  WS-TOTAL-AMOUNT         PIC 9(5)V99   VALUE ZEROS.
    05  WS-REC-CTR              PIC 9(3)      VALUE ZEROS.
    05  WS-PAGE-NO              PIC 9(3)      VALUE 1.
    05  WS-LINE-CT              PIC 99        VALUE ZEROS.
01  WS-DATE                     PIC 9(6).
01  WS-DATE-X REDEFINES WS-DATE.
    05  WS-YR-DATE              PIC 99.
    05  WS-MO-DATE              PIC 99.
    05  WS-DAY-DATE             PIC 99.
01  HL-HEADING-1.
    05  FILLER                  PIC X(16)     VALUE SPACES.
    05  FILLER                  PIC X(35)
        VALUE 'TOTAL OF GROUPS OF FIVE RECORDS'.
    05  FILLER                  PIC X(9)
        VALUE 'PAGE NO.'.
    05  HL-PAGE-CT-OUT          PIC ZZZ9.
    05  FILLER                  PIC X(69)     VALUE SPACES.
01  DL-DETAIL-LINE.
    05  FILLER                  PIC X(10)     VALUE SPACES.
    05  DL-NAME-OUT             PIC X(20).
    05  FILLER                  PIC X(10)     VALUE SPACES.
    05  DL-TOTAL-OUT            PIC $**,***.99.
    05  FILLER                  PIC XX        VALUE SPACES.
    05  DL-DATE-OUT.
        10  DL-MO-OUT           PIC 99.
        10  FILLER              PIC X         VALUE '/'.
        10  DL-DAY-OUT          PIC 99.
        10  FILLER              PIC X         VALUE '/'.
        10  DL-YR-OUT           PIC 99.
    05  FILLER                  PIC X(63)     VALUE SPACES.
```

Figure 11.7
(continued)

```
*
 PROCEDURE DIVISION.
*********************************************************
*  100-MAIN-MODULE - CONTROLS DIRECTION OF PROGRAM LOGIC   *
*********************************************************
 100-MAIN-MODULE.
     PERFORM 500-INITIALIZATION-RTN.
     PERFORM 400-HEADING-RTN.
     PERFORM 200-CALC-RTN
         UNTIL NO-MORE-RECORDS.
     PERFORM 600-END-OF-FILE-RTN.
*********************************************************
*  200-CALC-RTN - PERFORMED FROM 100-MAIN-MODULE   *
*                 INCREMENTS AND TESTS WS-REC-CTR  *
*                 ADDS IN-AMOUNT TO A TOTAL        *
*********************************************************
 200-CALC-RTN.
     ADD 1 TO WS-REC-CTR.
     ADD IN-AMOUNT TO WS-TOTAL-AMOUNT.
     IF  WS-REC-CTR = 5
         PERFORM 300-PRINT-RTN.
     READ IN-SALES-FILE
         AT END MOVE 'NO ' TO ARE-THERE-MORE-RECORDS.
*********************************************************
*  300-PRINT-RTN - PERFORMED FROM 200-CALC-RTN        *
*                  MOVES AND WRITES DATA FROM OUTPUT FIELDS  *
*                  INCREMENTS AND TESTS WS-LINE-CTR   *
*********************************************************
 300-PRINT-RTN.
     MOVE IN-NAME TO DL-NAME-OUT.
     MOVE WS-TOTAL-AMOUNT TO DL-TOTAL-OUT.
     MOVE ZEROS TO WS-REC-CTR.
     MOVE ZEROS TO WS-TOTAL-AMOUNT.
     WRITE OUT-PRINT-REC FROM DL-DETAIL-LINE
         AFTER ADVANCING 2 LINES.
     ADD 1 TO WS-LINE-CT.
     IF  WS-LINE-CT > 25
         PERFORM 400-HEADING-RTN.
*********************************************************
*  400-HEADING-RTN - PERFORMED FROM 100-MAIN-MODULE, 300-PRINT-RTN *
*                    WRITES HEADINGS AFTER ADVANCING TO NEW PAGE   *
*********************************************************
 400-HEADING-RTN.
     MOVE WS-PAGE-NO TO HL-PAGE-CT-OUT.
     ADD 1 TO WS-PAGE-NO.
     WRITE OUT-PRINT-REC FROM HL-HEADING-1
         AFTER ADVANCING PAGE.
     MOVE ZEROS TO WS-LINE-CT.
*********************************************************
*  500-INITIALIZATION-RTN  -  PERFORMED FROM 100-MAIN-MODULE  *
*                    CONTROLS OPENING OF FILES         *
*                    ACCEPTS DATE, PERFORMS INITIAL READ *
*********************************************************
 500-INITIALIZATION-RTN.
     OPEN INPUT  IN-SALES-FILE
          OUTPUT OUT-PRINT-FILE.
     ACCEPT WS-DATE FROM DATE.
     MOVE WS-MO-DATE TO DL-MO-OUT.
     MOVE WS-DAY-DATE TO DL-DAY-OUT.
     MOVE WS-YR-DATE TO DL-YR-OUT.
     READ IN-SALES-FILE
         AT END MOVE 'NO ' TO ARE-THERE-MORE-RECORDS.
*********************************************************
*  600-END-OF-FILE-RTN  -  PERFORMED FROM 100-MAIN-MODULE    *
*                    CONTROLS CLOSING OF FILES         *
*                    RETURNS CONTROL TO OPERATING SYSTEM *
*********************************************************
 600-END-OF-FILE-RTN.
     CLOSE IN-SALES-FILE
           OUT-PRINT-FILE.
     STOP RUN.
```

REVIEW QUESTIONS

I. True-False Questions

T F

__ __ 1. Editing is most often performed when output is to be printed.

__ __ 2. A report-item may be included in an arithmetic operation only if it follows the word GIVING or if it is used as a receiving field in a COMPUTE statement.

__ __ 3. If a sending field does not have an S in its PIC clause, it will never print as a negative amount, even if the report-item contains a minus sign.

__ __ 4. Without the use of an edit character, 11.55 might print as 1155.

__ __ 5. A plus or minus sign is most often transmitted to the computer along with the digit in the units position.

__ __ 6. AFTER ADVANCING PAGE is used for skipping to a new page when the end of the current page has been reached.

__ __ 7. The rightmost position of a print record is used for forms control.

—— —— 8. Once the ADVANCING option is used with a WRITE statement in a program, it should always be used for printing in that program.

—— —— 9. Print records are best described in WORKING-STORAGE and then moved to the output area defined in the FILE SECTION.

—— —— 10. ACCEPT DATE-IN FROM DATE requires DATE-IN to be a group item in WORKING-STORAGE.

II. General Questions

For Questions 1 through 15, fill in the missing entries.

	Sending-Field		Report-Item	
	PICTURE	Contents	PICTURE	Contents
1.	999	467	$ZZZ.99	
2.	S99V99	00∧9̄8	$ZZ.99+	
3.	S99V99	00∧8̟9	$ZZ.99-	
4.	S999	00̟5	$ZZZ.99CR	
5.	S999	00̟5	$ZZZ.99DB	
6.	S99V99	00∧05̟	$**.99-	
7.	9(4)	1357	$*,***.99	
8.	XXXX	CRDB	XXBBXX	
9.	999V99	135∧79	$$$$.99	
10.	999V99	000∧09	$$$$.99	
11.	S9(5)	0056̄7	++++++	
12.	S99	0̟0	+++	
13.	S99	0̟0	---	
14.	9999V99	0009∧88		$9.88
15.	9999V99	0009∧88		$ 9.88

16. What is spooling?

17. When is a RESERVE clause required in the ENVIRONMENT DIVISION?

18. Describe how CURRENT-DATE differs from DATE.

What, if anything is wrong with the following entries (19–20)?

19. WRITE PRINT-LINE FROM DATA-LINE AFTER ADVANCING 110 LINES.

20. ACCEPT DATE.

DEBUGGING EXERCISES

Consider the following DATA DIVISION entries:

```
01   IN-REC.
     05   AMT1        PIC 9(4)V99.
     05   AMT2        PIC 9(5)V99.
     05   AMT3        PIC 9(3)V99.
     05   AMT4        PIC 9(3).
     05   AMT5        PIC 9(3).
     :
     :
01   OUT-REC.
     05   FILLER      PIC X.
     05   AMT1-OUT    PIC $(4).99.
     05   FILLER      PIC X(10).
     05   AMT2-OUT    PIC ZZ,ZZZ.
     05   FILLER      PIC X(10).
```

```
05  AMT3-OUT        PIC ZZZZ.99
05  FILLER          PIC X(10).
05  AMT4-OUT        PIC Z(3).ZZ.
05  FILLER          PIC X(10).
05  AMT5-OUT        PIC -999.
05  FILLER          PIC X(10).
05  TOTAL1          PIC $(5).99
05  FILLER          PIC X(10).
05  TOTAL2          PIC Z(5).99.
05  FILLER          PIC X(26).
```

1. Before moving the amount fields of IN-REC to the corresponding amount fields of OUT-REC, is it necessary to MOVE SPACES TO OUT-REC? Explain your answer.

2. Should OUT-REC be defined within the FILE SECTION or the WORKING-STORAGE SECTION? Explain your answer.

3. Indicate which of the following would result in a syntax error and explain why.
   (a) MOVE AMT1 TO AMT1-OUT.
   (b) MOVE AMT2 TO AMT2-OUT.
   (c) MOVE AMT3 TO AMT3-OUT.
   (d) MOVE AMT4 TO AMT4-OUT.
   (e) MOVE AMT5 TO AMT5-OUT.
   (f) COMPUTE TOTAL1 = AMT1 + AMT2
   (g) ADD AMT2, AMT3 GIVING TOTAL2.

4. Suppose OUT-REC is defined in the WORKING-STORAGE SECTION and we add the following field:

```
05  AMT6      PIC $(5).99  VALUE ZERO.
```

Will this specification result in a syntax error? Explain your answer.

5. Consider the following:

```
WORKING-STORAGE SECTION.
01  HOLD-DATE       PIC X(6).
    05  YR          PIC 99.
    05  MO          PIC 99.
    05  DA          PIC 99.
        :
        :
    ACCEPT HOLD-DATE FROM DATE.
```

Two syntax errors will result. What are they and how could they be corrected?

6. Consider the following routine:

```
200-CALC-RTN.
    MOVE 1 TO PAGE-CT.
        :
        :
    WRITE PRINT-REC FROM DETAIL-REC.
    ADD 1 TO PAGE-CT.
    IF  PAGE-CT = 30
        PERFORM 300-HEADING-RTN.
    READ SALES-FILE
        AT END MOVE 'NO ' TO ARE-THERE-MORE-RECORDS.
```

300-HEADING-RTN never gets executed because there is a logic error in the program excerpt. Find the error and correct it.

7. Suppose you code the following:

```
ADD 1 TO LINE-COUNTER.
```

and you get an error message such as 'LINE-COUNTER INCORRECTLY USED'. Determine what caused the syntax error.

PROGRAMMING ASSIGNMENTS

Include the following in each Programming Assignment:

a. Print headings on each page.

b. Print the page number on each page as part of the report heading.

c. Print the date of the run on each page as part of the report heading.

d. Include an end-of-page routine to skip to the top of a new page and print appropriate heading information after 25 detail lines have printed.

e. Double space between all detail lines.

1. Write a program based on the problem definition shown in Figure 11.8.

Systems Flowchart

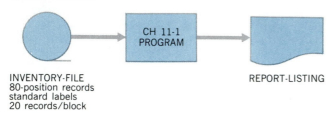

INVENTORY-FILE
80-position records
standard labels
20 records/block

REPORT-LISTING

INVENTORY-FILE Record Layout

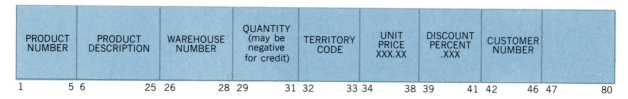

REPORT-LISTING Printer Spacing Chart

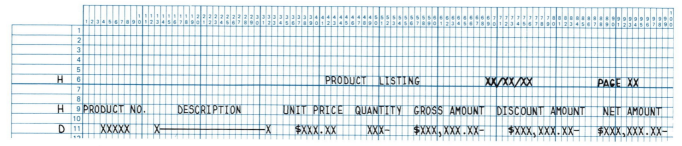

Figure 11.8
Problem definition for
Programming Assignment 1.

Notes

a. The following formulas apply to this problem:

Gross Amount = Quantity × Unit Price
Discount Amount = Gross Amount × Discount Percent
Net Amount = Gross Amount − Discount Amount

All result fields should be rounded to the nearest cent.

b. Zero suppress Unit Price, Quantity, Gross Amount, Discount Amount, and Net Amount.

c. Print a minus sign, where appropriate, for those fields indicated on the Printer Spacing Chart. A negative Quantity field in the input record indicates that the item has been returned for credit.

2. Write a program based on the problem definition shown in Figure 11.9.

Figure 11.9
Problem definition for
Programming Assignment 2.

Systems Flowchart

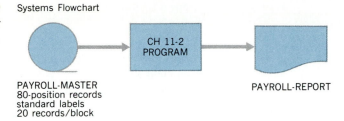

PAYROLL-MASTER
80-position records
standard labels
20 records/block

PAYROLL-REPORT

PAYROLL-MASTER Record Layout

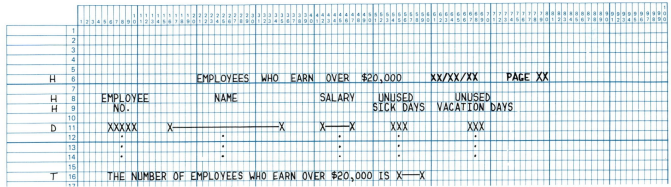

Notes

a. Use a floating dollar sign for the salary and print a comma, where appropriate.
b. Zero suppress unused sick days, unused vacation days, and the total that appears on the last line of the report.

3. Tape records with the following format will be entered as input. The tape has standard labels and a blocking factor of 20.

   1–2   TERR-NO
   3–20   EMPLOYEE-NAME
   21–25 ANNUAL-SALARY (in $)
   26–80 Unused

Write a program to accomplish the following:
a. Print each detail record.
b. At the end of each group of records for the same TERR-NO, print the total salaries paid for that TERR-NO. (Assume records have been entered in TERR-NO sequence.)
c. At the end of the run, print a final total of all salaries.

4. **Printing an Exception Report**

For each customer who subscribes to a popular computing magazine, a disk record is created. The input is as follows:

```
 1–20  Name
21–40  Address
   41  Country code (1 = U.S.; 2 = Canada)
42–45  Subscription charge (XX.XX)
   46  Subscription period (1 = 12 months; 2 = 24 months)
```

The following are valid subscription rates:

	12-month rate	**24-month rate**
US	$25.66	$22.00
Canada	$40.75	$38.00

Write a program to print an exception report consisting of the name, address, country, and subscription charge for each customer who was *not* charged the correct rate.

5. **Printing a Summary Report**

A toll road charges $1.75 for passenger cars, $2.00 for buses, $3.50 for trucks under 8000 pounds, and $5.00 for trucks 8000 pounds or more.

Write a program that reads as input a record for each vehicle that paid a toll. Each input record has a vehicle class field that contains either a p (for passenger car), b (for bus), or t (for truck). If the vehicle class is t (for truck), the weight field contains the vehicle's weight.

Print a summary report that indicates the total money collected by vehicle class:

```
                       SUMMARY REPORT


PASSENGER CAR TOTAL                          $XX,XXX.XX
BUS TOTAL                                    $XX,XXX.XX
TRUCKS < 8000 LBS TOTAL                      $XX,XXX.XX
TRUCKS >= 8000 LBS TOTAL                     $XX,XXX.XX


FINAL TOTAL COLLECTED                       $XXX,XXX.XX
```

6. Write a program that illustrates the effect of interest rates on monthly mortgage payments, total interest, and the total amount paid. Print the output in tabular form. The input is as follows:

```
1–6  Mortgage amount
7–8  Number of years
```

Print the monthly payments for interest rates that range from 10% to 17% (10%, 11%, . . . 17%). Prepare your own Printer Spacing Chart such that a single page is produced for each input record. The page should be identified as a Mortgage Interest Chart with Mortgage Amount and Years of Mortgage as part of the heading. Then print Monthly Payment, Total Interest, and Total Amount Paid for each interest rate from 10% to 17%. All output is to be in edited form.

UNIT III

WRITING HIGH-LEVEL COBOL PROGRAMS

12

Control Break Processing

OBJECTIVES

To familiarize you with

1. The main types of computer-generated reports.
2. The techniques used for efficient printing of group reports and control totals.
3. Control break processing and control break printing.

I. An Introduction to Control Break Processing

A. Types of Reports: A Systems Overview

As noted in the previous chapter, there are three general types of printed reports:

Detail Each input record generates one or more lines of output.
Summary or **Group** Data from groups of input records is summarized so that totals, rather than individual records, are printed.
Exception Only input records that fail to meet pre-established guidelines are printed.

Printing is a relatively slow input/output operation, as compared to processing operations such as addition and high-speed input/output functions such as reading from or writing onto a disk. Thus, any procedure that can minimize the amount of printing that is to be done and still satisfy users' needs should be recommended by the systems analyst and the programmer. In general, exception and summary reports are often suggested to users as alternatives to detail reports. These types of output take less time to produce and sometimes prove to be as useful, or even more useful, than detail reports. Often, analysts and programmers find that users who receive detail reports may also be manually preparing totals or looking for exceptions without realizing that they could have the computer perform these operations more efficiently. Thus, it is important for computer professionals to know *how output is being used*; this will help them to design the output more effectively.

You have learned the techniques necessary to print individual detail reports. Exception reports are produced by testing input records to see if they meet specified conditions. Some summary reports are produced by adding input data to total fields and simply printing those totals.

This chapter considers a type of summary procedure called **control break processing.** With this type of processing, control fields are used to indicate when totals are to print.

B. An Example of a Control Break Procedure

Consider the problem definition in Figure 12.1. A disk file consists of sales records, each with three input fields: a salesperson's department number, the salesperson's number, and the amount of sales accrued by that salesperson for the week. The input file is in sequence by the department number, so all records pertaining to salespeople in DEPT 01 are followed by all records pertaining to salespeople in DEPT 02, and so on.

There may be numerous salesperson records for DEPT 01, DEPT 02, and so on. That is, there may be several records with the same department number, depending on the actual number of salespeople within a given department. The output is a report that prints not only each salesperson's amount of sales but also *every department's total sales amount.*

For this problem, *detail printing* is required; that is, each input record containing a salesperson's total amount of sales is to be printed. Systems analysts and programmers would recommend such detail printing only if it were essential that the user see data from each input record. In addition to this detail printing, *summary lines* indicating *department totals* will also print. Thus, in this example, *group printing* is also required, where a total line is written for each department.

Thus, after all salesperson records for DEPT 01 have been read and printed, a total for DEPT 01 will print. Similarly, after all records for DEPT 02 have

Figure 12.1
Problem definition for sample control break procedure.

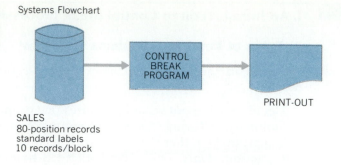

Systems Flowchart

SALES
80-position records
standard labels
10 records/block

CONTROL BREAK PROGRAM

PRINT-OUT

SALES Record Layout

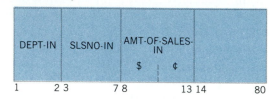

PRINT-OUT Printer Spacing Chart

been read and printed, a total for DEPT 02 will print, and so on. This type of processing requires all DEPT 01 records to be entered and processed first, followed by the next DEPT's records, and so on. That is, the file of input records *must be in sequence by department number.* All salesperson records for DEPT 01 must be entered first, followed by salesperson records for DEPT 02, and so on; otherwise it would not be possible to accumulate a total and print it at the end of a group. (Later on, we will see that files can always be *sorted* into the desired sequence.)

Detail lines print in the usual way, after each input record is read and processed. In addition to detail printing, after each input record is read, the amount of sales in that record is added to a DEPT total. This department total will be printed whenever a change in DEPT occurs. Since a change in DEPT triggers the printing of a department total, we call DEPT the **control field.**

Thus, all salesperson records for DEPT 01 will be read and printed, and a DEPT total will be accumulated. This processing continues until a salesperson record is read that contains a DEPT different from the previous one. When this record with a different DEPT is read, then the total for the previous department will be printed. Thus, the first input record pertaining to a salesperson in DEPT 02 will cause a total for DEPT 01 to print. Since totals are printed *after* a change occurs in DEPT, which is the control field, we call this type of group processing *control break processing.*

Figure 12.2
Flowchart and pseudocode for sample control break procedure.

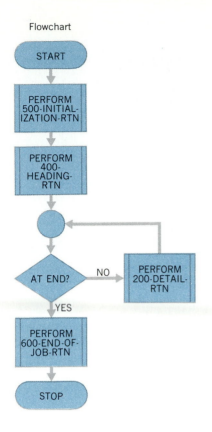

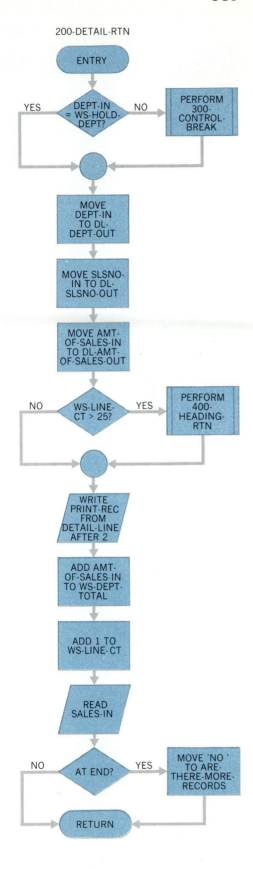

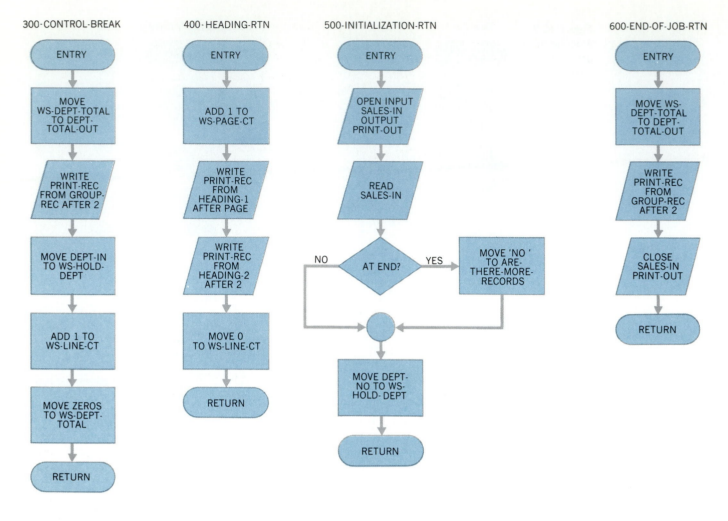

Pseudocode

```
PERFORM
    Open the Files
    Read a Record
    Store the Dept No
ENDPERFORM
PERFORM
    Write Headings
    Initialize Line Counter
ENDPERFORM
PERFORM UNTIL no more records
    IF  there is a change in Dept No
    THEN
        PERFORM
            Move Dept Total to Output
            Write Summary Line
            Store Dept No
            Add 1 to Line Counter
            Initialize Dept Total
        ENDPERFORM
    ENDIF
    Move Input Data to Detail Line
    Write a Record
    Add Amt to Dept Total
    Add 1 to Line Counter
    IF  Line Counter > 25
    THEN
        PERFORM
            Write Headings
            Initialize Line Counter
        ENDPERFORM
    ENDIF
    Read a Record
ENDPERFORM
PERFORM
    Write last Dept Total
    End-of-Job Operations
ENDPERFORM
```

Figure 12.2
(continued)

This section provides you with some definitions related to control break processing and with an actual illustration of the output produced by a control break procedure. In the next section, we focus on one way this procedure is actually coded. You may wish to examine Figure 12.2 for the planning tools used to prepare the program (we include both a pseudocode and a flowchart). The hierarchy chart will be discussed later. The program is designed at the planning stage with *either* a flowchart *or* pseudocode. Examine these carefully so that you understand the structure to be used in the programs. The program that will perform the above control break procedure is shown in Figure 12.3 and will be discussed in detail in the next section, along with the hierarchy chart in Figure 12.4.

II. Program Requirements for Control Break Processing

A. A Single-Level Control Break

For each input record read for the problem just outlined, we will perform two functions:

1. Print a detail line, with the salesperson's number, department number, and amount of sales.
2. Add `AMT-OF-SALES-IN` to a department total called `WS-DEPT-TOTAL`.

In addition, a total line (`"TOTAL FOR DEPT IS $XX,XXX.XX"`) will print only *after the first record with the next* `DEPT` *is read.* When this total prints, we reinitialize `WS-DEPT-TOTAL` by setting it back to zero and then process the new input record as in steps 1 and 2.

This is called a *single-level control break* because we have only one field, `DEPT-IN`, that triggers the printing of totals. To perform single-level control break processing, the following steps must be coded after the files have been opened:

> 1. Initialize a hold area with the contents of the first record's control field. This is performed in the main module after the initial read or in an initialization routine executed from the main module.

The first input record is read and its control field, in this case `DEPT-IN`, must be moved to a `WORKING-STORAGE` area in order to save it for comparison purposes. We will call the `WORKING-STORAGE` area `WS-HOLD-DEPT`. Thus, our main module would include:

Pseudocode Excerpt	Program Excerpt
| Open the Files | ```
100-MAIN-MODULE.
    OPEN INPUT  SALES-IN
         OUTPUT PRINT-OUT.
    READ SALES-IN
        AT END MOVE 'NO ' TO
            ARE-THERE-MORE-RECORDS.
    MOVE DEPT-IN TO WS-HOLD-DEPT.
    PERFORM 400-HEADING-RTN.
    PERFORM 200-DETAIL-RTN
        UNTIL NO-MORE-RECORDS.
``` |
Read a Record	
Store the Dept No	
PERFORM	
Write Headings	
ENDPERFORM	
PERFORM UNTIL no more records	
```

A More Modular, Top-Down `MAIN MODULE`

The preceding pseudocode and program excerpt are correct, but it is better form to *modularize* the program so that it can use a *top-down* approach. That is, the first set of instructions to be executed should be part of an *initialization routine* that is performed *from the main module:*

Pseudocode Excerpt	Program Excerpt
PERFORM	`100-MAIN-MODULE.`
Open the Files	`    PERFORM 500-INITIALIZATION-RTN.`
Read a Record	`    PERFORM 400-HEADING-RTN.`
Store the Dept No	`    PERFORM 200-DETAIL-RTN`
ENDPERFORM	`        UNTIL NO-MORE-RECORDS.`
PERFORM	
Write Headings	`500-INITIALIZATION-RTN.`
ENDPERFORM	`    OPEN INPUT  SALES-IN`
PERFORM	`             OUTPUT PRINT-OUT.`
UNTIL no more records	`    READ SALES-IN`
	`        AT END MOVE 'NO ' TO`
	`                 ARE-THERE-MORE-RECORDS.`
	`    MOVE DEPT-IN TO WS-HOLD-DEPT.`

This modularization makes a program easier to code and modify. The main module is subdivided into subordinate modules that perform initialization functions, heading functions, calculations, and end-of-job procedures. When coding the program, you would begin with the above three `PERFORM`s in the main module. Later, after the logic of the program has been mapped out, you could fill in the details in each of these subordinate routines. Such an approach will help you focus on the *design and structure* of a program, leaving minor details to the end. This top-down, modular style tends to produce programs that are better designed and easier to debug.

To code the required statements in the main module rather than in a separate paragraph is still correct, but we will focus on this more modular approach.

> 2. Process input records at `200-DETAIL-RTN`. Processing depends on whether or not the control field read in matches the one stored at `WS-HOLD-DEPT`.

We begin at `200-DETAIL-RTN` by comparing `DEPT-IN` to `WS-HOLD-DEPT`. The first time through, `WS-HOLD-DEPT` and `DEPT-IN` will be equal because we just moved `DEPT-IN` to `WS-HOLD-DEPT` in the main module. For all subsequent passes through `200-DETAIL-RTN`, `WS-HOLD-DEPT` will contain the `DEPT-IN` of the previous record read. When `WS-HOLD-DEPT` and `DEPT-IN` are equal, there is no control break and we perform three steps:

1. Move input data to a detail line and print:

Pseudocode Excerpt	Program Excerpt
PERFORM UNTIL no more records	
⋮	⋮
Move Input Data to Detail Line	`MOVE DEPT-IN TO DL-DEPT-OUT.`
Write a Record	`MOVE SLSNO-IN TO DL-SLSNO-OUT.`
	`MOVE AMT-OF-SALES-IN TO`
	`    DL-AMT-OF-SALES-OUT.`
	`WRITE PRINT-REC FROM DETAIL-LINE`
	`    AFTER ADVANCING 2 LINES.`

2. Accumulate a `WS-DEPT-TOTAL`:

Pseudocode Excerpt	Program Excerpt
Add Amt to Dept Total	`ADD AMT-OF-SALES-IN TO WS-DEPT-TOTAL.`

3. Read the next record:

Pseudocode Excerpt	Program Excerpt

Read a Record	`READ SALES-IN`
	`   AT END MOVE 'NO ' TO`
	`      ARE-THERE-MORE-RECORDS.`

Figure 12.2 also includes a line-counting routine; we will fill this in later.

We continue processing input records in this way until the `DEPT-IN` on an input record differs from the previous department number stored at `WS-HOLD-DEPT`. When they are different, a *control break* has occurred. Thus, each time `DEPT-IN` is not equal to `WS-HOLD-DEPT` we will perform the `300-CONTROL-BREAK` procedure, where we print the accumulated department total.

`300-CONTROL-BREAK` prints a total for the *previous* department. After the total is printed and then reinitialized at zero, we continue by processing the *current* record, which involves (1) printing a detail line and (2) adding `AMT-OF-SALES-IN` to `WS-DEPT-TOTAL`.

The full procedure at `200-DETAIL-RTN` (without the line counting routine) is as follows:

Pseudocode Excerpt	Program Excerpt

PERFORM UNTIL no more records
   IF there is a change in Dept No
   THEN
        PERFORM
     .   (Control break
     .   procedure is
     .   coded here)
        ENDPERFORM
   ENDIF
   Move Input Data to Detail Line
   Write a Record
   Add Amt to Dept Total
   Read a Record
ENDPERFORM
	`200-DETAIL-RTN.`
	   `IF  DEPT-IN NOT = TO WS-HOLD-DEPT`
	      `PERFORM 300-CONTROL-BREAK.`
	   `MOVE DEPT-IN TO DL-DEPT-OUT.`
	   `MOVE SLSNO-IN TO DL-SLSNO-OUT.`
	   `MOVE AMT-OF-SALES-IN TO`
	      `DL-AMT-OF-SALES-OUT.`
	   `WRITE PRINT-REC FROM DETAIL-LINE`
	      `AFTER ADVANCING 2 LINES.`
	   `ADD AMT-OF-SALES-IN TO`
	      `WS-DEPT-TOTAL.`
	   `READ SALES-IN`
	      `AT END MOVE 'NO ' TO`
	        `ARE-THERE-MORE-RECORDS.`

If there is a change in `DEPT-IN`, then `300-CONTROL-BREAK` is performed. In any case, the current record is printed and its amount is added to `WS-DEPT-TOTAL` before a new record is read. The full program in Figure 12.3 also checks for page overflow with a line-count procedure at `200-DETAIL-RTN`. When a field called `WS-LINE-CT` exceeds 25, we print headings on a new page and reinitialize `WS-LINE-CT` at zero.

> 3. Print a summary line in the `300-CONTROL-BREAK` module after a record is read that has a different department number than the one stored at `WS-HOLD-DEPT`.

300-CONTROL-BREAK is performed when an input record's DEPT-IN, the control field, differs from the one stored at WS-HOLD-DEPT. As we have seen, WS-HOLD-DEPT contains the previous DEPT-IN. When there is a change in DEPT-IN, we must:

1. Print a line with the department total accumulated in WS-DEPT-TOTAL.
2. Reinitialize WS-DEPT-TOTAL, the control total, so that the next department's total begins at zero before any amounts are accumulated.
3. Move the current DEPT-IN to WS-HOLD-DEPT so that we can compare succeeding input records to this new DEPT-IN control field.
4. Return to 200-DETAIL-RTN and process the current record by printing a detail line and adding the amount to the control total.

Consider the following 300-CONTROL-BREAK routine:

Pseudocode Excerpt	**Program Excerpt**

PERFORM UNTIL no more records
  IF there is a change in Dept No
THEN
    PERFORM
      Move Dept Total to Output
      Write Summary Line
      Initialize Dept Total
      Store Dept No
  ENDPERFORM
ENDIF
	300-CONTROL-BREAK.
	  MOVE WS-DEPT-TOTAL TO
	    DEPT-TOTAL-OUT.
	  WRITE PRINT-REC FROM GROUP-REC
	    AFTER ADVANCING 2 LINES.
	  MOVE ZEROS TO WS-DEPT-TOTAL.
	  MOVE DEPT-IN TO WS-HOLD-DEPT.

Since 300-CONTROL-BREAK is performed from 200-DETAIL-RTN, processing continues with the next instruction at 200-DETAIL-RTN. The detail line is then printed and the current amount added to the new total, which has been reset to 0. In Figure 12.3, 1 is also added to WS-LINE-CT as part of the line-counting routine, which will be discussed later.

> 4. Process the last department total when ARE-THERE-MORE-RECORDS = 'NO '. This condition is equivalent to the condition-name NO-MORE-RECORDS.

Thus far we have seen how 200-DETAIL-RTN is executed. When a record is read with the same DEPT-IN as the previous one, we print it and add AMT-OF-SALES-IN to WS-DEPT-TOTAL.

When a change in DEPT-IN occurs, DEPT-IN and WS-HOLD-DEPT will be different and 300-CONTROL-BREAK will be executed. At 300-CONTROL-BREAK, we print a total line, reinitialize WS-DEPT-TOTAL at zero, and store the current DEPT-IN at WS-HOLD-DEPT. We then return to 200-DETAIL-RTN, where we print the current input record and add its amount to a new WS-DEPT-TOTAL. What remains is the processing of the *very last control total* when an end-of-file condition is reached.

Forcing a Control Break When There Are No More Records

Control break printing of totals occurs when a record with a *new* control field is read. The total for the last group of records, then, will have been accumulated when ARE-THERE-MORE-RECORDS is equal to 'NO ', but a control total will not have been printed since there is no subsequent record to trigger a change. Consider the following:

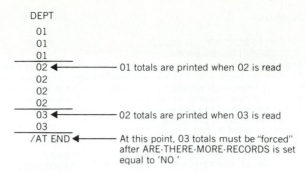

There must be a procedure to print the 03 totals. In the main module, after `200-DETAIL-RTN` has been executed and `ARE-THERE-MORE-RECORDS` is equal to `'NO '`, we must force a printing of this final total:

Pseudocode Excerpt	Program Excerpt
PERFORM	`PROCEDURE DIVISION.`
Open the Files	`100-MAIN-MODULE.`
Read a Record	`PERFORM 500-INITIALIZATION-RTN.`
Store the Dept No	`PERFORM 400-HEADING-RTN.`
ENDPERFORM	`PERFORM 200-DETAIL-RTN`
PERFORM	`UNTIL NO-MORE-RECORDS.`
Write Headings	`PERFORM 600-END-OF-JOB-RTN.`
ENDPERFORM	`STOP RUN.`
PERFORM UNTIL no more records	⋮
⋮	`600-END-OF-JOB-RTN.`
ENDPERFORM	`MOVE WS-DEPT-TOTAL TO`
PERFORM	`DEPT-TOTAL-OUT.`
Write last Dept Total	`WRITE PRINT-REC FROM GROUP-REC`
End-of-Job Operations	`AFTER ADVANCING 2 LINES.`
ENDPERFORM	`CLOSE SALES-IN`
	`PRINT-OUT.`

The full program for a single-level control break procedure with detail printing appears in Figure 12.3. Included in the program is a line-counting procedure that ensures that a maximum of 26 detail lines will print on any given page. After 26 detail lines have printed, `400-HEADING-RTN` is performed. Twenty-six detail lines print per page because (1) `WS-LINE-CT` is initialized at *zero* and (2) a test is made to determine if `WS-LINE-CT` is *greater than* 25 after a line is printed and 1 is added to `WS-LINE-CT`.

The program for this procedure is illustrated in Figure 12.3. The hierarchy chart is shown in Figure 12.4. Notice that in the hierarchy chart `400-HEADING-RTN` has a corner cut, indicating that it is executed from more than one point in the program.

Thus, the main module is now subdivided into individual modules, each with a specific function. With this organization, the overall structure of the program can be outlined in the main module with all the details left for subordinate modules. This is called *top-down programming*.

B. Refinements to Improve the Quality of a Control Break Report

The refinements discussed in this section are illustrated in Figure 12.5, a single-level control break program that incorporates the techniques discussed previously.

Figure 12.3
Program for sample control
break procedure.

Program

```
IDENTIFICATION DIVISION.
PROGRAM-ID. SAMPLE.
*********************************************************************
*  the program creates a departmental sales report using a control  *
*     break procedure.  comments are printed in lower case to set   *
*     them apart from the program instructions.                     *
*********************************************************************
ENVIRONMENT DIVISION.
INPUT-OUTPUT SECTION.
FILE-CONTROL.
    SELECT SALES-IN  ASSIGN TO DATA143.
    SELECT PRINT-OUT ASSIGN TO SYS$OUTPUT.
*
DATA DIVISION.
FILE SECTION.
FD  SALES-IN
    LABEL RECORDS ARE OMITTED.
01  SALES-REC-IN.
    05  DEPT-IN                 PIC 99.
    05  SLSNO-IN                PIC 9(5).
    05  AMT-OF-SALES-IN         PIC 9(4)V99.
    05  FILLER                  PIC X(67).
FD  PRINT-OUT
    LABEL RECORDS ARE OMITTED.
01  PRINT-REC                   PIC X(133).
WORKING-STORAGE SECTION.
01  WORK-AREAS.
    05  ARE-THERE-MORE-RECORDS  PIC X(3)        VALUE 'YES'.
        88  MORE-RECORDS                        VALUE 'YES'.
        88  NO-MORE-RECORDS                     VALUE 'NO'.
    05  WS-HOLD-DEPT            PIC 99          VALUE ZEROS.
    05  WS-DEPT-TOTAL          PIC 9(5)V99     VALUE ZEROS.
    05  WS-LINE-CT             PIC 99          VALUE ZEROS.
    05  WS-PAGE-CT            PIC 99          VALUE ZEROS.
01  HEADING-1.
    05  FILLER                 PIC X(50)       VALUE SPACES.
    05  FILLER                 PIC X(21)
        VALUE 'MONTHLY STATUS REPORT'.
    05  FILLER                 PIC X(9)        VALUE SPACES.
    05  FILLER                 PIC X(5)
        VALUE 'PAGE'.
    05  HL-PAGE-NO-OUT         PIC 99.
    05  FILLER                 PIC X(46)       VALUE SPACES.
01  HEADING-2.
    05  FILLER                 PIC X(11)       VALUE SPACES.
    05  FILLER                 PIC X(10)
        VALUE 'DEPT'.
    05  FILLER                 PIC X(20)
        VALUE 'SALESPERSON NO'.
    05  FILLER                 PIC X(12)
        VALUE 'AMT OF SALES'.
    05  FILLER                 PIC X(80)       VALUE SPACES.
01  DETAIL-LINE.
    05  FILLER                 PIC X(12)       VALUE SPACES.
    05  DL-DEPT-OUT            PIC 99.
    05  FILLER                 PIC X(9)        VALUE SPACES.
    05  DL-SLSNO-OUT           PIC 9(5).
    05  FILLER                 PIC X(14)       VALUE SPACES.
    05  DL-AMT-OF-SALES-OUT    PIC $$,$$$.99.
    05  FILLER                 PIC X(82)       VALUE SPACES.
01  GROUP-REC.
    05  FILLER                 PIC X(61)       VALUE SPACES.
    05  FILLER                 PIC X(18)
        VALUE 'TOTAL FOR DEPT IS '.
    05  DEPT-TOTAL-OUT         PIC $$$,$$$.99.
    05  FILLER                 PIC X(44)       VALUE SPACES.
*
PROCEDURE DIVISION.
*********************************************
*  controls direction of program logic.  *
*********************************************
100-MAIN-MODULE.
    PERFORM 500-INITIALIZATION-RTN.
    PERFORM 400-HEADING-RTN.
    PERFORM 200-DETAIL-RTN
        UNTIL NO-MORE-RECORDS.
    PERFORM 600-END-OF-JOB-RTN.
```

Figure 12.3
(continued)

```
          STOP RUN.
*****************************************************************
* performed from 100-main-module-rtn. controls department  *
* break, pagination, and reads the next record.            *
*****************************************************************
  200-DETAIL-RTN.
      IF   DEPT-IN NOT = WS-HOLD-DEPT
           PERFORM 300-CONTROL-BREAK.
      MOVE DEPT-IN TO DL-DEPT-OUT.
      MOVE SLSNO-IN TO DL-SLSNO-OUT.
      MOVE AMT-OF-SALES-IN TO DL-AMT-OF-SALES-OUT.
      IF WS-LINE-CT > 25
           PERFORM 400-HEADING-RTN.
      WRITE PRINT-REC FROM DETAIL-LINE
           AFTER ADVANCING 2 LINES.
      ADD AMT-OF-SALES-IN TO WS-DEPT-TOTAL.
      ADD 1 TO WS-LINE-CT.
      READ SALES-IN
           AT END MOVE 'NO ' TO ARE-THERE-MORE-RECORDS.
*****************************************************************
* performed from 200-detail-rtn, prints                    *
* department totals, resets control fields & totals.       *
*****************************************************************
  300-CONTROL-BREAK.
      MOVE WS-DEPT-TOTAL TO DEPT-TOTAL-OUT.
      WRITE PRINT-REC FROM GROUP-REC
           AFTER ADVANCING 2 LINES.
      MOVE ZEROS TO WS-DEPT-TOTAL.
      MOVE DEPT-IN TO WS-HOLD-DEPT.
      ADD 1 TO WS-LINE-CT.
*****************************************************************
* performed from 100-main-module 200-detail-rtn 300-control-break *
* prints out headings resets line counter.                 *
*****************************************************************
  400-HEADING-RTN.
      ADD 1 TO WS-PAGE-CT.
      MOVE WS-PAGE-CT TO HL-PAGE-NO-OUT.
      WRITE PRINT-REC FROM HEADING-1
           AFTER ADVANCING PAGE.
      WRITE PRINT-REC FROM HEADING-2
           AFTER ADVANCING 2 LINES.
      MOVE ZEROS TO WS-LINE-CT.
*****************************************************************
* performed from 100-main-module, opens files, performs the initial *
* read &  initializes dept-hold                            *
*****************************************************************
  500-INITIALIZATION-RTN.
      OPEN INPUT  SALES-IN
           OUTPUT PRINT-OUT.
      READ SALES-IN
           AT END MOVE 'NO ' TO ARE-THERE-MORE-RECORDS.
      MOVE DEPT-IN TO WS-HOLD-DEPT.
*****************************************************************
* performed from 100-main-module, performs end of job functions *
* closes files and returns control to operating system     *
*****************************************************************
  600-END-OF-JOB-RTN.
*****************************************************************
* the following 2 instructions force the printing of       *
* the last control totals after an at end has occurred     *
*****************************************************************
      MOVE WS-DEPT-TOTAL TO DEPT-TOTAL-OUT.
      WRITE PRINT-REC FROM GROUP-REC
           AFTER ADVANCING 2 LINES.
      CLOSE SALES-IN
           PRINT-OUT.
```

Sample Input Data

```
0112345098855
0112346353700
0112347003499
0212222987700
0212234008777
0315645098000
0312321198700
0412999134330
0416732177900
0416437493909
0409878056499
```

Figure 12.3   Sample Output
(continued)

```
                                           MONTHLY STATUS REPORT         PAGE 01

        DEPT      SALESPERSON NO      AMT OF SALES

        01        12345                 $988.55

        01        12346               $3,537.00

        01        12347                  $34.99

                                                         TOTAL FOR DEPT IS  $4,560.54

        02        12222               $9,877.00

        02        12234                  $87.77

                                                         TOTAL FOR DEPT IS  $9,964.77

        03        15645                 $980.00

        03        12321               $1,987.00

                                                         TOTAL FOR DEPT IS  $2,967.00

        04        12999               $1,343.30

        04        16732               $1,779.00

        04        16437               $4,939.09

        04        09878                 $564.99

                                                         TOTAL FOR DEPT IS  $8,626.38
```

Figure 12.4
Hierarchy chart for sample
control break procedure.

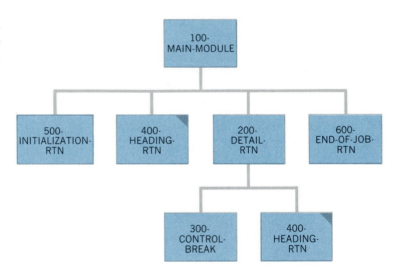

1. Printing a Final Total

Sometimes, control break processing also requires the printing of a *summary line* containing a final total. This would be printed *after* the last control total is written.

Method 1   The final total, which we will call WS-FINAL-TOTAL, may be accumulated by adding AMT-OF-SALES-IN for each record. This may be accomplished by changing the ADD instruction in the 200-DETAIL-RTN of Figure 12.3 to:

```
ADD  AMT-OF-SALES-IN TO WS-DEPT-TOTAL
                        WS-FINAL-TOTAL.
```

Method 2   The WS-FINAL-TOTAL may be accumulated, instead, by adding each WS-DEPT-TOTAL to it in 300-CONTROL-BREAK. This means that WS-FINAL-TOTAL would be accumulated, *not* for each detail record, but only when a control break has occurred. This would be accomplished by coding the following before we reinitialize WS-DEPT-TOTAL:

```
300-CONTROL-BREAK.
     :
     ADD WS-DEPT-TOTAL TO WS-FINAL-TOTAL.
     MOVE ZEROS TO WS-DEPT-TOTAL.
     :
```

Note that the second method is more efficient than the first. Suppose we have 10,000 input records but only 20 department control breaks. If we added AMT-OF-SALES-IN to WS-FINAL-TOTAL for each input record, we would be performing 10,000 additions. If, instead, we added the WS-DEPT-TOTAL to WS-FINAL-TOTAL when each control break occurred, we would be performing the addition only 20 times. Thus, to add WS-DEPT-TOTAL to WS-FINAL-TOTAL would result in far fewer additions than adding AMT-OF-SALES-IN for each record to WS-FINAL-TOTAL.

2. Starting A New Page After Each Control Break

It is likely that a control break report will be distributed to different users. For example, the listing pertaining to DEPT 01 in the preceding illustration might be transmitted to users in DEPT 01; the listing for DEPT 02 might go to that department, and so on. In this case, it is useful to have *each department's* data begin on a new page. Thus, a control break module would also include a statement to PERFORM the heading routine so that the paper is advanced to a new page when a control break occurs. We would add a PERFORM statement to the 300-CONTROL-BREAK module for printing headings on a new page each time that module is executed.

In this instance, it would be redundant to print the Department Number on each detail line. Rather, it would be better to print it *once* at the beginning of each page:

```
                    MONTHLY STATUS REPORT      PAGE xx

        DEPT-xx
                    SALESPERSON NO.              AMT OF SALES

                    12345                        $7,326.45
                    18724                        $9,264.55

                         TOTAL FOR DEPT IS   $16,591.00
```

3. Sequence-Checking or Sorting: To Ensure That Input Data was Entered in the Correct Sequence

For accurate control break processing, records must be in sequence by the control field. Consider the following sequence error:

```
DEPT
  01
  01
  02   ◄── Sequence error—DEPT 02 out of sequence
  01
  01
   :
   :
```

Because it is sometimes possible for input sequence errors to occur, it might be useful to check to make certain, after each control break, that the current DEPT-IN is greater than the previous one in WS-HOLD-DEPT. If a current DEPT-IN is less than WS-HOLD-DEPT, then a sequence error has occurred and an error message should be printed. We may also wish to terminate processing in such a case. The systems analyst typically provides the programmer with the actions to be taken in case of a sequence error.

One method to ensure that an input file is in the correct sequence is to *sort* it by computer. Computer-sorted files will always be in the correct sequence so that any processing with such files does not require a separate sequence-checking routine. The basic format for the sort procedure is as follows:

Format

```
SORT   (work-file-name)

ON   { ASCENDING  }   KEY (key field of work record)
     { DESCENDING }

USING  (unsorted file-name)
GIVING (sorted file-name)
```

The work file is an intermediate file to which unsorted records are moved and sorted.

The sort procedure that could be used as part of the control break program in Figure 12.3 is as follows:

```
      SELECT UNSORTED-SALES ...
      SELECT WORK-FILE ...
      SELECT SORTED-SALES ...
        .
        .
        .
  FD  UNSORTED-SALES
      LABEL RECORDS ARE STANDARD.
  01  UNSORTED-REC        PIC X(100).
 *
  SD  WORK-FILE.   ◄——— WORK-FILE gets SD, not FD; no LABEL RECORDS clause for SD
  01  WORK-REC.
      05  W-DEPT-NO       PIC 9(5). ◄——— This is the key field in the SD entry
      05  FILLER          PIC X(95).        (Only the key fields need be defined)
 *
  FD  SORTED-SALES
      LABEL RECORDS ARE STANDARD.
  01  SORTED-REC.
      05  DEPT-IN         PIC 9(5).      ⎫
      05  SLSNO-IN        PIC 9(5).      ⎬ These would be the same fields as used
      05  AMT-OF-SALES-IN PIC 9(3)V99.   ⎭ in any input file
      05  FILLER          PIC X(85).
        .                              ———(from low to high)
        .
      SORT WORK-FILE ON ASCENDING KEY W-DEPT-NO
          USING UNSORTED-SALES.
          GIVING SORTED-SALES.
      OPEN INPUT  SORTED-SALES
          OUTPUT PRINT-OUT.
        .   ⎫ The rest of the program is exactly the same as in Figure 12.3
        .   ⎭
        .
```

This illustration is meant as a brief exposure to sorting files. We discuss all elements of SORT procedures in their entirety in Chapter 17.

Once a file has been sorted, you can be certain that the records in the sorted file are in the correct sequence. Thus, a sequence-checking procedure is only necessary for manually sorted input files (e.g., a file keyed directly onto disk by an operator who is responsible for sorting the file before entering the data).

4. Executing the CONTROL-BREAK Module from the Main Module After an End-of-File Condition Has Been Met

Consider 600-END-OF-JOB-RTN in Figure 12.3, where we move WS-DEPT-TOTAL TO DEPT-TOTAL-OUT and WRITE the last output line. This MOVE and

WRITE could be replaced with the following:

```
PERFORM 300-CONTROL-BREAK.
```

Since we wish to "force" a control break at the end of the job, it might seem logical to execute the sequence of steps at the control break routine rather than duplicate the instructions in the end-of-job module.

Consider, however, the last statements of the control break procedure, 300-CONTROL-BREAK:

```
MOVE ZEROS TO WS-DEPT-TOTAL.
ADD 1 TO WS-LINE-CT.
MOVE DEPT-IN TO WS-HOLD-DEPT.
```

Once the last record has been read and processed and an AT END condition has been reached, these instructions are really not necessary. To avoid performing them on an AT END condition, we could code the last sentence of the 300-CONTROL-BREAK module as:

```
IF   MORE-RECORDS
     MOVE ZEROS TO WS-DEPT-TOTAL
     ADD 1 TO WS-LINE-CT
     MOVE DEPT-IN TO WS-HOLD-DEPT.
```

In this example, the condition-name MORE-RECORDS is equivalent to testing the condition IF ARE-THERE-MORE-RECORDS = 'YES'. WS-DEPT-TOTAL is initialized at 0, WS-LINE-CT is incremented by one, and the new DEPT-IN is stored *only if* an AT END condition has not been reached. Thus, our main module may be coded with the following:

```
        PERFORM 200-DETAIL-RTN
            UNTIL NO-MORE-RECORDS.
        PERFORM 600-END-OF-JOB-RTN.
            ⋮
600-END-OF-JOB-RTN.
        PERFORM 300-CONTROL-BREAK.
            ⋮
```

Another reason for testing for MORE-RECORDS is to print new headings in a control break program only if an AT END condition has not occurred. Otherwise, the last page of the report would just contain a heading and this would be incorrect.

The full single-level control break program that includes all the preceding refinements is illustrated in Figure 12.5.

C. Summary of a Single-Level Control Break Procedure

**SUMMARY OF STEPS INVOLVED IN A
SINGLE-LEVEL CONTROL BREAK PROBLEM**

1. Read the initial record.
2. Move the control field to a hold area in WORKING-STORAGE.
3. As long as the control field is equal to the hold area, execute the detail routine for the input record. This means: Add the appropriate amount to a control total, print the detail record (if desired), and read the next record.
4. If the control field is not equal to the hold area:

   Print the control total.
   Initialize the control total field to zero.

Reinitialize the hold field with the new control field value if ARE-THERE-MORE-RECORDS is not equal to 'NO '.

Process the detail record as in step 3.

Print headings on a new page if each control total is to appear on a separate page.

5. After all records have been processed, perform a control break to print the last control total.

Figure 12.5
Control break program with refinements.

```
IDENTIFICATION DIVISION.
PROGRAM-ID. SAMPLE.
***************************************************************************
*  This program uses lower case letters for comments to distinguish   *
*       them from program logic. Program creates                      *
*       a departmental sales report by use of a control break.        *
***************************************************************************
ENVIRONMENT DIVISION.
INPUT-OUTPUT SECTION.
FILE-CONTROL.
     SELECT SALES-IN  ASSIGN TO DATA146.
     SELECT PRINT-OUT ASSIGN TO SYS$OUTPUT.
*
DATA DIVISION.
FILE SECTION.
FD  SALES-IN
    LABEL RECORDS ARE OMITTED.
01  SALES-REC-IN.
    05  DEPT-IN                 PIC 99.
    05  SLSNO-IN                PIC 9(5).
    05  AMT-OF-SALES-IN         PIC 9(4)V99.
    05  FILLER                  PIC X(67).
FD  PRINT-OUT
    LABEL RECORDS ARE OMITTED.
01  PRINT-REC                   PIC X(133).
WORKING-STORAGE SECTION.
01  WORK-AREAS.
    05  ARE-THERE-MORE-RECORDS  PIC X(3)        VALUE 'YES'.
        88  MORE-RECORDS                        VALUE 'YES'.
        88  NO-MORE-RECORDS                     VALUE 'NO'.
    05  WS-HOLD-DEPT            PIC 99           VALUE ZEROS.
    05  WS-DEPT-TOTAL          PIC 9(5)V99      VALUE ZEROS.
    05  WS-FINAL-TOTAL         PIC 9(6)V99      VALUE ZEROS.
    05  WS-LINE-CT             PIC 99           VALUE ZEROS.
    05  WS-PAGE-CT             PIC 99           VALUE ZEROS.
01  HEADING-1.
    05  FILLER                 PIC X(50)        VALUE SPACES.
    05  FILLER                 PIC X(21)
        VALUE 'MONTHLY STATUS REPORT'.
    05  FILLER                 PIC X(9)         VALUE SPACES.
    05  FILLER                 PIC X(5)
        VALUE 'PAGE'.
    05  HL-PAGE-NO-OUT         PIC 99.
    05  FILLER                 PIC X(46)        VALUE SPACES.
01  HEADING-2.
    05  FILLER                 PIC X(11)        VALUE SPACES.
    05  FILLER                 PIC X(5)
        VALUE 'DEPT-'.
    05  HL-DEPT-OUT            PIC 99.
    05  FILLER                 PIC X(114)       VALUE SPACES.
01  HEADING-3.
    05  FILLER                 PIC X(18)        VALUE SPACES.
    05  FILLER                 PIC X(14)
        VALUE 'SALESPERSON NO'.
    05  FILLER                 PIC X(9)         VALUE SPACES.
    05  FILLER                 PIC X(12)
        VALUE 'AMT OF SALES'.
    05  FILLER                 PIC X(80)        VALUE SPACES.
01  DETAIL-LINE.
    05  FILLER                 PIC X(23)        VALUE SPACES.
    05  DL-SLSNO-OUT           PIC 9(5).
    05  FILLER                 PIC X(14)        VALUE SPACES.
```

Figure 12.5
(continued)

```
        05  DL-AMT-OF-SALES-OUT       PIC $$,$$$.99.
        05  FILLER                    PIC X(82)        VALUE SPACES.
    01  DEPT-TOTAL-REC.
        05  FILLER                    PIC X(61)        VALUE SPACES.
        05  FILLER                    PIC X(18)
            VALUE 'TOTAL FOR DEPT IS '.
        05  DEPT-TOTAL-OUT            PIC $$$,$$$.99.
        05  FILLER                    PIC X(44)        VALUE SPACES.
    01  FINAL-TOTAL-REC.
        05  FILLER                    PIC X(40)        VALUE SPACES.
        05  FILLER                    PIC X(25)
            VALUE 'THE FINAL TOTAL SALES IS '.
        05  FINAL-TOTAL-OUT           PIC $$$$,$$$.99.
        05  FILLER                    PIC XX
            VALUE '**'.
        05  FILLER                    PIC X(66)        VALUE SPACES.
    01  ERROR-REC.
        05  FILLER                    PIC X(40)        VALUE SPACES.
        05  FILLER                    PIC X(39)
            VALUE 'RECORDS OUT OF SEQUENCE--JOB TERMINATED'.
        05  FILLER                    PIC X(54)        VALUE SPACES.
 *
     PROCEDURE DIVISION.
 ********************************************
 *  controls direction of program logic.  *
 ********************************************
     100-MAIN-MODULE.
         PERFORM 500-INITIALIZATION-RTN.
         PERFORM 400-HEADING-RTN.
         PERFORM 200-DETAIL-RTN
             UNTIL NO-MORE-RECORDS.
         PERFORM 600-END-OF-JOB-RTN.
         STOP RUN.
 *********************************************************************
 *  performed from 100-main-module-rtn. controls department        *
 *  break, pagination, and reads next record.                      *
 *********************************************************************
     200-DETAIL-RTN.
         IF  DEPT-IN NOT = WS-HOLD-DEPT
             PERFORM 300-CONTROL-BREAK.
         MOVE SLSNO-IN TO DL-SLSNO-OUT.
         MOVE AMT-OF-SALES-IN TO DL-AMT-OF-SALES-OUT.
         IF  WS-LINE-CT > 25
             PERFORM 400-HEADING-RTN.
         WRITE PRINT-REC FROM DETAIL-LINE
             AFTER ADVANCING 2 LINES.
         ADD AMT-OF-SALES-IN TO WS-DEPT-TOTAL.
         ADD 1 TO WS-LINE-CT.
         READ SALES-IN
             AT END MOVE 'NO ' TO ARE-THERE-MORE-RECORDS.
 *********************************************************************
 *  performed from 200-detail-rtn, 600-end-of-job-rtn. prints      *
 *  department totals, checks for sequence error, and zeros ctr.   *
 *********************************************************************
     300-CONTROL-BREAK.
         MOVE WS-DEPT-TOTAL TO DEPT-TOTAL-OUT.
         WRITE PRINT-REC FROM DEPT-TOTAL-REC
             AFTER ADVANCING 2 LINES.
         IF  DEPT-IN < WS-HOLD-DEPT
             WRITE PRINT-REC FROM ERROR-REC
                 AFTER ADVANCING 2 LINES
             CLOSE SALES-IN PRINT-OUT
             STOP RUN.
         ADD WS-DEPT-TOTAL TO WS-FINAL-TOTAL.
         MOVE ZEROS TO WS-DEPT-TOTAL.
         IF  MORE-RECORDS
             MOVE DEPT-IN TO WS-HOLD-DEPT
             PERFORM 400-HEADING-RTN.
 *********************************************************************
 *  performed from 100-main-module, 200-detail-rtn, 300-control-break *
 *  prints out headings after advancing new page, resets line ctr. *
 *********************************************************************
     400-HEADING-RTN.
         MOVE DEPT-IN TO HL-DEPT-OUT.
         ADD 1 TO WS-PAGE-CT.
         MOVE WS-PAGE-CT TO HL-PAGE-NO-OUT.
         MOVE DEPT-IN TO HL-DEPT-OUT.
```

Figure 12.5
(continued)

```
        WRITE PRINT-REC FROM HEADING-1
            AFTER ADVANCING PAGE.
        WRITE PRINT-REC FROM HEADING-2
            AFTER ADVANCING 2 LINES.
        WRITE PRINT-REC FROM HEADING-3
            AFTER ADVANCING 1 LINES.
        MOVE ZEROS TO WS-LINE-CT.
*****************************************************************
*performed from 100-main-module opens files and performs initial read *
*****************************************************************
 500-INITIALIZATION-RTN.
        OPEN INPUT  SALES-IN
            OUTPUT PRINT-OUT.
        READ SALES-IN
            AT END MOVE 'NO ' TO ARE-THERE-MORE-RECORDS.
        MOVE DEPT-IN TO WS-HOLD-DEPT.
*****************************************************************
* performed from 100-main-module, processes last       *
* control break, prints final totals and closes files *
*****************************************************************
 600-END-OF-JOB-RTN.
        PERFORM 300-CONTROL-BREAK.
        MOVE WS-DEPT-TOTAL TO FINAL-TOTAL-OUT.
        WRITE PRINT-REC FROM FINAL-TOTAL-REC
            AFTER ADVANCING 2 LINES.
        CLOSE SALES-IN
            PRINT-OUT.
```

Sample Input Data

```
0112345098855
0112346353700
0112347003499
0212222987700
0212234008777
0315645098000
0212446200890
0312321198700
0412999134330
0416732177900
0416437493909
0409878056499
```

Sample Output

```
                                MONTHLY STATUS REPORT        PAGE 01

DEPT-01
        SALESPERSON NO        AMT OF SALES

            12345               $988.55

            12346             $3,537.00

            12347                $34.99

                                            TOTAL FOR DEPT IS  $4,560.54


                                MONTHLY STATUS REPORT        PAGE 02

DEPT-02
        SALESPERSON NO        AMT OF SALES
            12222             $9,877.00

            12234                $87.77

                                            TOTAL FOR DEPT IS  $9,964.77


                                MONTHLY STATUS REPORT        PAGE 03

DEPT-03
        SALESPERSON NO        AMT OF SALES
            15645               $980.00

                                            TOTAL FOR DEPT IS    $980.00

        RECORDS OUT OF SEQUENCE--JOB TERMINATED
```

Self-Test

1. When printing of totals is dependent on a change in a specific input field, we call this _____ .

2. In Question 1, the field that is used to determine when printing occurs is called the _____ .

3. For processing to be correct in Question 1, records must be in sequence by the _____ .

4. In control break processing, we typically MOVE the control field to _____ after reading the first record.

5. In control break processing, we typically compare _____ as the first instruction in the detail module (labeled in our control break programs as 200-DETAIL-RTN).

6. If an input control field is equal to the control field stored in the hold area, we _____ .

7. If an input control field is not equal to the control field stored in the hold area, we _____ .

8. After all records have been processed, we must _____ .

9. If each control group is to begin on a separate page, we would perform a heading routine at the _____ module.

10. If a final total is required, it is most efficient to accumulate the final total in the _____ module.

11. At the control break module, we must print _____ , initialize _____ at zero, and move _____ .

12. When each individual input record results in the printing of an output line, we call this _____ .

Consider the following output in answering Questions 13–15:

The input consists of 10-position disk records (blocked 5), each with a warehouse field (2 positions), part number (3 positions), and quantity on hand (5 positions). The first three divisions of a COBOL program to meet these requirements appear in Figure 12.6.

13. Code the main module for the preceding problem definition.

14. Code the 200-DETAIL-RTN for the problem definition.

15. Code the 300-CONTROL-MODULE for the problem definition.

Solutions

1. control break processing
2. control field
3. control field
4. a hold or WORKING-STORAGE area
5. the current input record's control field to the hold area
6. add to a control total and print, if detail printing is required
7. perform a control break procedure
8. force a control break to print the last total
9. control break

Figure 12.6
First three divisions of
program for Questions 13–15.

```
     IDENTIFICATION DIVISION.
     PROGRAM-ID. FIG12-6.
*
 ENVIRONMENT DIVISION.
 INPUT-OUTPUT SECTION.
 FILE-CONTROL.
     SELECT INVENTORY-IN ASSIGN TO DISK.
     SELECT REPORT-OUT ASSIGN TO PRINTER.
*
 DATA DIVISION.
 FILE SECTION.
 FD  INVENTORY-IN
     LABEL RECORDS ARE STANDARD
     BLOCK CONTAINS 5 RECORDS.
 01  INV-REC.
     05  WAREHOUSE-IN              PIC 99.
     05  PART-NO-IN                PIC 999.
     05  QTY-ON-HAND-IN            PIC 9(5).
 FD  REPORT-OUT
     LABEL RECORDS ARE OMITTED.
 01  REPORT-REC                    PIC X(133).
 WORKING-STORAGE SECTION.
 01  WS-AREAS.
     05  ARE-THERE-MORE-RECORDS    PIC X(3)    VALUE 'YES'.
         88  THERE-ARE-NO-MORE-RECORDS        VALUE 'NO '.
     05  WS-WH-HOLD                PIC 99      VALUE ZEROS.
     05  WS-PART-TOTAL             PIC 9(4)    VALUE ZEROS.
     05  WS-LINE-CT                PIC 99      VALUE ZEROS.
     05  WS-PAGE-CT                PIC 999     VALUE ZEROS.
 01  HEADING-1.
     05  FILLER                    PIC X(38)   VALUE SPACES.
     05  FILLER                    PIC X(21)
             VALUE 'ACME INVENTORY REPORT'.
     05  FILLER                    PIC X(11)   VALUE SPACES.
     05  FILLER                    PIC X(5)    VALUE 'PAGE '.
     05  HL-PAGE-OUT               PIC ZZZ.
     05  FILLER                    PIC X(55)   VALUE SPACES.
 01  HEADING-2.
     05  FILLER                    PIC X(10)   VALUE SPACES.
     05  FILLER                    PIC X(12)   VALUE 'WAREHOUSE-'.
     05  HL-WH-OUT                 PIC Z9.
     05  FILLER                    PIC X(109)  VALUE SPACES.
 01  HEADING-3.
     05  FILLER                    PIC X(20)   VALUE SPACES.
     05  FILLER                    PIC X(20)   VALUE 'PART NO'.
     05  FILLER                    PIC X(83)
             VALUE 'QUANTITY ON HAND'.
 01  DETAIL-LINE.
     05  FILLER                    PIC X(22)   VALUE SPACES.
     05  DL-PART-OUT               PIC 999.
     05  FILLER                    PIC X(18)   VALUE SPACES.
     05  DL-QTY-OUT                PIC Z(5).
     05  FILLER                    PIC X(85)   VALUE SPACES.
 01  TOTAL-LINE.
     05  FILLER                    PIC X(30)   VALUE SPACES.
     05  FILLER                    PIC X(44)
             VALUE 'TOTAL NUMBER OF ITEMS STORED IN WAREHOUSE - '.
     05  TL-TOTAL-PARTS-OUT        PIC Z(4).
     05  FILLER                    PIC X(55)   VALUE SPACES.
```

10. control break

11. the control total; the control total; the input control field to the hold area

12. detail printing

13.
```
PROCEDURE DIVISION.
100-MAIN-MODULE.
    OPEN INPUT INVENTORY-IN
         OUTPUT REPORT-OUT.
    READ INVENTORY-IN                                         }  This could be coded in
        AT END MOVE 'NO ' TO ARE-THERE-MORE-RECORDS.          }  an initialization routine
    MOVE WAREHOUSE-IN TO WS-WH-HOLD.
    PERFORM 400-HEADING-ROUTINE.
    PERFORM 200-DETAIL-RTN
        UNTIL THERE-ARE-NO-MORE-RECORDS.
    PERFORM 300-CONTROL-MODULE.                               }  This could be coded in
    CLOSE INVENTORY-IN                                        }  an end-of-job routine
          REPORT-OUT.
    STOP RUN.
```

14.
```
200-DETAIL-RTN.
        IF  WAREHOUSE-IN IS NOT EQUAL TO WS-WH-HOLD
            PERFORM 300-CONTROL-MODULE.
        MOVE PART-NO-IN TO DL-PART-OUT.
        MOVE QTY-ON-HAND-IN TO DL-QTY-OUT.
        WRITE REPORT-REC FROM DETAIL-LINE
            AFTER ADVANCING 2 LINES.
        ADD 1 TO WS-PART-TOTAL.
        ADD 1 TO WS-LINE-CT.
        IF  WS-LINE-CT > 25
            PERFORM 400-HEADING-ROUTINE.
        READ INVENTORY-IN
            AT END MOVE 'NO ' TO ARE-THERE-MORE-RECORDS.
```

```
15. 300-CONTROL-MODULE.
        MOVE WS-PART-TOTAL TO TL-TOTAL-PARTS-OUT.
        WRITE REPORT-REC FROM TOTAL-LINE
            AFTER ADVANCING 4 LINES.
        IF  ARE-THERE-MORE-RECORDS IS NOT EQUAL TO 'NO '
            MOVE WAREHOUSE-IN TO WS-WH-HOLD
            MOVE 0 TO WS-PART-TOTAL
            PERFORM 400-HEADING-ROUTINE.
```

III. Multiple-Level Control Breaks

You will recall that a file must be in sequence by the control field to perform control break processing. Suppose we require *two* fields as control fields. Consider the following transaction or detail input file:

TRANS-FILE

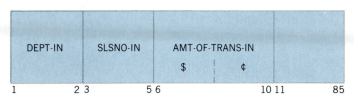

Each time a salesperson makes a sale, a record is created that indicates the department (DEPT-IN), salesperson number (SLSNO-IN), and the amount of the transaction (AMT-OF-TRANS-IN). In this instance, unlike the previous illustration, if a given salesperson has made numerous sales in a given period, there will be *more than one record for that salesperson.* That is, if salesperson 1 in DEPT 01 made three sales, there would be three input records for that salesperson; if salesperson 2 in DEPT 02 made four sales, there would be four records for that salesperson, and so on.

The difference between this input and the input used in the previous example is that in this instance each salesperson is assigned to a specific department and may have numerous records, one for each sale. The input file is sorted so that all salesperson records for DEPT 01 appear first, followed by all salesperson records for DEPT 02, and so on. In addition, all records for the first SLSNO-IN within each DEPT-IN appear *first,* followed by all records for the second SLSNO-IN in that DEPT-IN, and so on. Thus, the following input is a sample of what you might expect:

DEPT-IN	SLSNO-IN		AMT-OF-TRANS-IN
01	004		127.23
01	004	In	100.14
01	006	sequence	027.45
01	006	within	052.23
01	006	DEPT 01	126.27
01	008		223.28
02	003	In	111.14
02	003	sequence	027.23
02	003	within	119.26
02	005	DEPT 02	600.45
02	018		427.33
03	014		100.26
.	.		.
.	.		.
.	.		.

We have, then, *two control fields:*

SLSNO-IN—the minor control field
DEPT-IN—the major control field

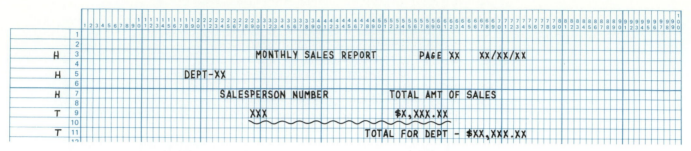

Figure 12.7
Printer Spacing Chart for
double-level control break
procedure.

Records are in sequence by SLSNO-IN within DEPT-IN. Note that for a given SLSNO-IN within a DEPT-IN, there may be numerous transaction records.

Suppose we wish to print a department report as indicated in the Printer Spacing Chart in Figure 12.7.

We accumulate the total amount of sales for each salesperson before printing a line. Thus, if SLSNO-IN 1 in DEPT-IN 01 has made three sales entered in three separate input records, we would print *one* line after all three records have been read and totaled.

No detail printing is required here; rather, the program results in *group printing* of salesperson totals and department totals. The printing of a SLSNO-IN total line is performed after all records for a given SLSNO-IN have been processed. Moreover, printing of a DEPT-IN total and headings for the next DEPT-IN are printed when a DEPT-IN break has occurred.

In our main module, we begin by performing an initialization routine that will open the files, accept a date, read the first record, and store the control fields. Then we perform a heading routine. Since the second heading line includes a literal 'DEPT' with the actual DEPT number, we *must* print headings *after* the initial read. In the first control break procedure in Figure 12.2, we could have printed a heading *before* the READ, since we did not need the first record's DEPT-IN to print as part of the heading.

First examine the planning tools used to prepare this program. The pseudocode is in Figure 12.8, and the hierarchy chart is in Figure 12.9. For this program we would use a *double-level control break* procedure. We need *two* hold areas for comparison purposes, one for DEPT-IN and one for SLSNO-IN.

Pseudocode Excerpt	Program Excerpt
PERFORM	100-MAIN-MODULE.
Open the Files	PERFORM 600-INITIALIZATION-RTN.
Accept a Date	PERFORM 500-HEADING-RTN.
Read a Record	PERFORM 200-DETAIL-RTN
Store Control Fields	UNTIL NO-MORE-RECORDS.
ENDPERFORM	⋮
PERFORM	600-INITIALIZATION-RTN.
Write the Headings	OPEN INPUT TRANS-FILE-IN
ENDPERFORM	OUTPUT REPORT-FILE-OUT.
PERFORM UNTIL there are no	ACCEPT WS-DATE FROM DATE.
more records	READ TRANS-FILE-IN
.	AT END MOVE 'NO ' TO
.	ARE-THERE-MORE-RECORDS.
.	MOVE SLSNO-IN TO WS-HOLD-SLSNO.
	MOVE DEPT-IN TO WS-HOLD-DEPT.

Figure 12.8
Pseudocode for double-level
control break procedure.

```
PERFORM
    Open the Files
    Accept a Date
    Read a Record
    Store Control Fields
ENDPERFORM
PERFORM
    Write the Headings
ENDPERFORM
PERFORM UNTIL there are no more records
    IF  there is a Dept-No change
    THEN
        PERFORM
            PERFORM
                Move Slsno-In Total to Output Area
                Write a Record
                Add Slsno-In Total to Dept-No Total
                Initialize Slsno-In Total
                Store Slsno-In
            ENDPERFORM
            Move Dept-No Total to Output Area
            Write a Record
            Initialize Dept-No Total
            Store Dept-No
            PERFORM
                Write Headings
            ENDPERFORM
        ENDPERFORM
    ENDIF
    IF  there is a Slsno-In change
    THEN
        PERFORM
            Move Slsno-In Total to Output Area
            Write a Record
            Add Slsno-In Total to Dept-No Total
            Initialize Slsno-In Total
            Store Slsno-In
        ENDPERFORM
    ENDIF
    Add Amt to a Total
    Read a Record
ENDPERFORM
PERFORM
    Dept break processing
ENDPERFORM
PERFORM
    End-of-Job Operations
ENDPERFORM
```

At 200-DETAIL-RTN we compare the two control fields to their respective hold areas. Given that there is no change in either DEPT-IN or SLSNO-IN, we simply add the AMT-OF-TRANS-IN to a WS-SLS-TOTAL and read the next record. Since there is no detail printing required in this program, there is no WRITE in 200-DETAIL-RTN.

Pseudocode Excerpt	Program Excerpt
IF there is a Dept-No change	`200-DETAIL-RTN.`
THEN	`    IF  DEPT-IN NOT EQUAL`
PERFORM	`            WS-HOLD-DEPT`
. (Major-level control	`        PERFORM 400-DEPT-BREAK.`
. break processing here)	`    IF  SLSNO-IN NOT EQUAL`
.	`            WS-HOLD-SLSNO`
ENDPERFORM	`        PERFORM 300-SLS-BREAK.`
ENDIF	`    ADD AMT-OF-TRANS-IN TO`
IF there is a Slsno-In change	`            WS-SLS-TOTAL.`
THEN	`    READ TRANS-FILE-IN`
PERFORM	`        AT END MOVE 'NO ' TO`
. (Minor-level control	`            ARE-THERE-MORE-RECORDS.`
. break processing here)	
.	

ENDPERFORM
ENDIF
Add Amt to a Total
Read a Record

We will fill in the major-level (or department change) procedure and the minor-level (or salesperson-number change) procedure *after* the main structure is defined. Top-down programs begin by developing the overall logic and leave the details until later on.

Similarly, in top-down fashion we code the 400-DEPT-BREAK before the 300-SLS-BREAK since DEPT-IN is the major control field.

A major control break routine should begin by forcing a minor control break. That is, the first thing we do when there is a change in DEPT-IN is to process the *last salesperson's total for the previous department*. The assumption here is that each salesperson works for only one department. Thus, the first instruction at 400-DEPT-BREAK would be to PERFORM 300-SLS-BREAK. This not only prints the previous salesperson's total, but it adds that salesperson's total to the department total, initializes WS-SLS-TOTAL at zero, and moves the new SLSNO-IN to WS-HOLD-SLSNO.

After executing 300-SLS-BREAK from 400-DEPT-BREAK, we need to perform the following steps:

1. Print the WS-DEPT-TOTAL.
2. Reinitialize the WS-DEPT-TOTAL at 0.
3. Move DEPT-IN to WS-HOLD-DEPT.
4. Print a heading on a new page.

Figure 12.9
Hierarchy chart for double-level control break procedure.

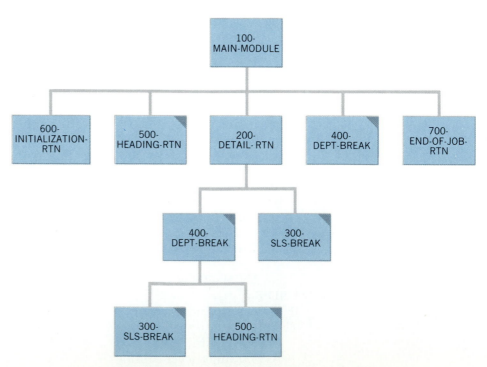

Note: A corner cut is made in the 300-SLS-BREAK, 400-DEPT-BREAK, and 500-HEADING-RTN procedures because they are each performed from two different modules.

Thus, `400-DEPT-BREAK` would be coded as follows:

Pseudocode Excerpt	**Program Excerpt**

```
IF there is a Dept-No change
THEN
    PERFORM
    .   (Sales-No break is
    .   to be filled in later)
    .
    ENDPERFORM
    Move Dept-No Total to Output
        Area
    Write a Record
    Initialize Dept-No Total
    Store Dept-No
    PERFORM
        .  (Heading routine is to
        .  be filled in later)
        .
    ENDPERFORM
ENDIF
```

```
400-DEPT-BREAK.
    PERFORM 300-SLS-BREAK.
    MOVE WS-DEPT-TOTAL TO
        DL-DEPT-TOTAL.
    WRITE REPORT-REC-OUT FROM
        DL-DEPT-LINE AFTER
            ADVANCING 2 LINES.
    MOVE ZEROS TO WS-DEPT-TOTAL.
    IF  MORE-RECORDS
        MOVE DEPT-IN TO
            WS-HOLD-DEPT
        PERFORM 500-HEADING-RTN.
```

When there is a change in `DEPT-IN`, this is considered a *major control break*. Note that we test for a major control break in `200-DETAIL-RTN` *before* we test for a minor control break. As a result, the major-level control routine will begin by forcing a minor-level control-break.

Recall that the last statement in `400-DEPT-BREAK` ensures that we store the new `DEPT-IN` and print a heading in all instances *except* after an `AT END` condition. This is required because `400-DEPT-BREAK` will be executed (1) from `200-DETAIL-RTN` and (2) after all records have been processed, when we must force a break.

Keep in mind that in top-down programs, major procedures are coded before minor ones. The hierarchy chart in Figure 12.9 shows the relationships among these modules.

When a change in `SLSNO-IN` occurs even *without* a change in `DEPT-IN`, this would force a *minor control break* called `300-SLS-BREAK`. Thus, when `SLSNO-IN` is not equal to `WS-HOLD-SLSNO` or when a department break has occurred, we do the following:

1. Print the total for the previous `SLSNO-IN`.
2. Add that total to a `WS-DEPT-TOTAL`.
3. Initialize the `WS-SLS-TOTAL` field at zero.
4. Move the new `SLSNO-IN` to `WS-HOLD-SLSNO`.

This would be performed as follows:

Pseudocode Excerpt	**Program Excerpt**

```
IF there is a Slsno-In change
THEN
    PERFORM
        Move Slsno-In Total to
            Output Area
        Write a Record
        Add Slsno-In Total to
            Dept-No Total
        Initialize Slsno-In Total
        Store Slsno-In
    ENDPERFORM
ENDIF
```

```
300-SLS-BREAK.
    MOVE WS-SLS-TOTAL TO
        DL-SLS-TOTAL.
    MOVE WS-HOLD-SLSNO TO DL-SLSNO.
    WRITE REPORT-REC-OUT FROM
        DL-SLS-LINE AFTER
            ADVANCING 2 LINES.
    ADD WS-SLS-TOTAL TO WS-DEPT-TOTAL.
    MOVE ZERO TO WS-SLS-TOTAL.
    IF  MORE-RECORDS
        MOVE SLSNO-IN TO
            WS-HOLD-SLSNO.
```

Here, too, we test for MORE-RECORDS in 300-SLS-BREAK because we want to avoid moving SLSNO-IN after an AT END.

After all records have been read and processed and an AT END condition occurs, control returns to the main module, where an end-of-job routine is executed. As with single-level control break processing, we must *force a break* at this point so that we print the last SLSNO-IN total *and* the last DEPT-IN total. To accomplish this, we perform 400-DEPT-BREAK from the main module after all records have been processed.

In 400-DEPT-BREAK and 300-SLS-BREAK, there are instructions that are to be executed under normal conditions but not on an AT END condition. These instructions are preceded with an IF MORE-RECORDS clause to ensure that they are not executed when an AT END condition occurs:

```
300-SLS-BREAK.
     .
     .
     IF  MORE-RECORDS
         MOVE SLSNO-IN TO WS-HOLD-SLSNO.
400-DEPT-BREAK.
     .
     .
     IF  MORE-RECORDS
         MOVE DEPT-IN TO WS-HOLD-DEPT
         PERFORM 500-HEADING-RTN.
```

The full pseudocode and hierarchy chart for this double-level control break procedure are illustrated in Figures 12.8 and 12.9, respectively. The complete program is shown in Figure 12.10.

Note that a program may have any number of control fields. The processing is essentially the same, with major-level control breaks forcing minor-level control breaks.

Figure 12.10
Double-level control break program.

Program

```
IDENTIFICATION DIVISION.
PROGRAM-ID. SAMPLE.
****************************************************
*   THIS PROGRAM CREATES A MONTHLY SALES REPORT   *
*   BY USING A DOUBLE-LEVEL CONTROL BREAK          *
****************************************************
ENVIRONMENT DIVISION.
INPUT-OUTPUT SECTION.
FILE-CONTROL.
    SELECT TRANS-FILE-IN    ASSIGN TO DATA1110.
    SELECT REPORT-FILE-OUT ASSIGN TO SYS$OUTPUT.
*
DATA DIVISION.
FILE SECTION.
FD  TRANS-FILE-IN
    LABEL RECORDS ARE STANDARD.
01  TRANS-REC-IN.
    05  DEPT-IN                 PIC 99.
    05  SLSNO-IN                PIC 9(3).
    05  AMT-OF-TRANS-IN         PIC 9(3)V99.
FD  REPORT-FILE-OUT.
01  REPORT-REC-OUT             PIC X(133).
WORKING-STORAGE SECTION.
01  WS-WORK-AREAS.
    05  WS-HOLD-DEPT            PIC 99           VALUE ZEROS.
    05  WS-HOLD-SLSNO           PIC 9(3)         VALUE ZEROS.
    05  ARE-THERE-MORE-RECORDS  PIC X(3)         VALUE 'YES'.
        88  MORE-RECORDS                         VALUE 'YES'.
        88  NO-MORE-RECORDS                      VALUE 'NO '.
    05  WS-SLS-TOTAL            PIC 9(4)V99      VALUE ZEROS.
    05  WS-DEPT-TOTAL           PIC 9(5)V99      VALUE ZEROS.
    05  WS-PAGE-CTR             PIC 99           VALUE ZEROS.
```

Figure 12.10
(continued)

```
01   WS-DATE.
     05   WS-YR                        PIC 99.
     05   WS-MO                        PIC 99.
     05   WS-DAY                       PIC 99.
01   HL-HEADING1.
     05   FILLER                       PIC X(30)       VALUE SPACES.
     05   FILLER                       PIC X(20)
          VALUE 'MONTHLY SALES REPORT'.
     05   FILLER                       PIC X(7)        VALUE SPACES.
     05   FILLER                       PIC X(5)
          VALUE 'PAGE '.
     05   HL-PAGE                      PIC Z9.
     05   FILLER                       PIC X(3)        VALUE SPACES.
     05   HL-DATE.
          10   HL-MO                   PIC 99.
          10   FILLER                  PIC X           VALUE '/'.
          10   HL-DAY                  PIC 99.
          10   FILLER                  PIC X           VALUE '/'.
          10   HL-YR                   PIC 99.
     05   FILLER                       PIC X(58)       VALUE SPACES.
01   HL-HEADING2.
     05   FILLER                       PIC X(18)       VALUE SPACES.
     05   FILLER                       PIC X(5)
          VALUE 'DEPT-'.
     05   HL-DEPT                      PIC 99.
     05   FILLER                       PIC X(108)      VALUE SPACES.
01   HL-HEADING3.
     05   FILLER                       PIC X(13)       VALUE SPACES.
     05   FILLER                       PIC X(19)
          VALUE 'SALESPERSON NUMBER '.
     05   FILLER                       PIC X(10)       VALUE SPACES.
     05   FILLER                       PIC X(18)
          VALUE 'TOTAL AMT OF SALES'.
     05   FILLER                       PIC X(63)       VALUE SPACES.
01   DL-SLS-LINE.
     05   FILLER                       PIC X(29)       VALUE SPACES.
     05   DL-SLSNO                     PIC 9(3).
     05   FILLER                       PIC X(21)       VALUE SPACES.
     05   DL-SLS-TOTAL                 PIC $$,$$$.99.
     05   FILLER                       PIC X(71)       VALUE SPACES.
01   DL-DEPT-LINE.
     05   FILLER                       PIC X(48)       VALUE SPACES.
     05   FILLER                       PIC X(17)
          VALUE 'TOTAL FOR DEPT - '.
     05   DL-DEPT-TOTAL                PIC $$$,$$$.99.
     05   FILLER                       PIC X(58)       VALUE SPACES.
*
 PROCEDURE DIVISION.
*****************************************
*   CONTROLS DIRECTION OF PROGRAM LOGIC   *
*****************************************
 100-MAIN-MODULE.
     PERFORM 600-INITIALIZATION-RTN.
     PERFORM 500-HEADING-RTN.
     PERFORM 200-DETAIL-RTN
         UNTIL NO-MORE-RECORDS.
     PERFORM 400-DEPT-BREAK.
     PERFORM 700-END-OF-JOB-RTN.
     STOP RUN.
*****************************************************************
*   PERFORMED FROM 100-MAIN-MODULE, TESTS FOR DEPT AND SLSNO BREAKS.   *
*   ADDS TRANSACTION AMOUNT TO WS-SLS-TOTAL, AND READS NEXT TRANS REC. *
*****************************************************************
 200-DETAIL-RTN.
     IF   DEPT-IN NOT EQUAL WS-HOLD-DEPT
          PERFORM 400-DEPT-BREAK.
     IF   SLSNO-IN NOT EQUAL WS-HOLD-SLSNO
          PERFORM 300-SLS-BREAK.
     ADD AMT-OF-TRANS-IN TO WS-SLS-TOTAL.
     READ TRANS-FILE-IN
          AT END MOVE 'NO' TO ARE-THERE-MORE-RECORDS.
*****************************************************
*   PERFORMED FROM 200-DETAIL-RTN AND 400-DEPT-BREAK   *
*   PERFORMS SLSNO BREAK                               *
*****************************************************
 300-SLS-BREAK.
     MOVE WS-SLS-TOTAL TO DL-SLS-TOTAL.
```

Figure 12.10
(continued)

```
      MOVE WS-HOLD-SLSNO TO DL-SLSNO.
      WRITE REPORT-REC-OUT FROM DL-SLS-LINE AFTER ADVANCING 2 LINES.
      ADD  WS-SLS-TOTAL TO WS-DEPT-TOTAL.
      MOVE ZERO TO WS-SLS-TOTAL.
      IF  MORE-RECORDS
          MOVE SLSNO-IN TO WS-HOLD-SLSNO.
 ****************************************************************
 *  PERFORMED FROM 100-MAIN-MODULE AND 200-DETAIL-RTN*
 *  PERFORMS DEPARTMENT BREAK.                        *
 ****************************************************************
  400-DEPT-BREAK.
      PERFORM 300-SLS-BREAK.
      MOVE WS-DEPT-TOTAL TO DL-DEPT-TOTAL.
      WRITE REPORT-REC-OUT FROM DL-DEPT-LINE AFTER ADVANCING 2 LINES.
      MOVE ZEROS TO WS-DEPT-TOTAL.
      IF  MORE-RECORDS
          MOVE DEPT-IN TO WS-HOLD-DEPT
          PERFORM 500-HEADING-RTN.
 ****************************************************************
 *  PERFORMED FROM 100-MAIN-MODULE AND 400-DEPT-BREAK.    *
 *  PRINTS OUT REPORT HEADINGS AFTER ADVANCING NEW PAGE   *
 ****************************************************************
  500-HEADING-RTN.
      ADD 1 TO WS-PAGE-CTR.
      MOVE WS-PAGE-CTR TO HL-PAGE.
      MOVE WS-HOLD-DEPT TO HL-DEPT.
      MOVE WS-YR TO HL-YR.
      MOVE WS-MO TO HL-MO.
      MOVE WS-DAY TO HL-DAY.
      WRITE REPORT-REC-OUT FROM HL-HEADING1 AFTER ADVANCING PAGE.
      WRITE REPORT-REC-OUT FROM HL-HEADING2 AFTER ADVANCING 2 LINES.
 ****************************************************************
 *  PERFORMED FROM 100-MAIN-MODULE. OPENS THE FILES     *
 *  GETS THE CURRENT DATE FROM THE OPERATING SYSTEM,    *
 *  PERFORMS INITIAL READ, AND INITIALIZES THE HOLD     *
 *  FIELDS IN WORKING-STORAGE                           *
 ****************************************************************
  600-INITIALIZATION-RTN.
      OPEN INPUT   TRANS-FILE-IN
           OUTPUT REPORT-FILE-OUT.
      ACCEPT WS-DATE FROM DATE.
      READ TRANS-FILE-IN
          AT END MOVE 'NO ' TO ARE-THERE-MORE-RECORDS.
      MOVE SLSNO-IN TO WS-HOLD-SLSNO.
      MOVE DEPT-IN TO WS-HOLD-DEPT.
 ****************************************************************
 *  PERFORMED FROM 100-MAIN-MODULE.  CLOSES FILES  *
 *                                                 *
 ****************************************************************
  700-END-OF-JOB-RTN.
      CLOSE TRANS-FILE-IN
            REPORT-FILE-OUT.
```

Sample Input Data

```
0100134555
0100154434
0100265544
0100376353
0200109377
0200192838
0200209374
0200209383
```

Figure 12.10 **Sample Output**
(continued)

```
                        MONTHLY SALES REPORT          PAGE  1    01/29/88


          DEPT-01


SALESPERSON NUMBER                TOTAL AMT OF SALES


               001                        $889.89


               002                        $655.44


               003                        $763.53


                                 TOTAL FOR DEPT -  $2,308.86


                        MONTHLY SALES REPORT          PAGE  2    01/29/88


          DEPT-02


SALESPERSON NUMBER                TOTAL AMT OF SALES


               001                       $1,022.15


               002                        $187.57


                                 TOTAL FOR DEPT -  $1,209.72
```

CHAPTER SUMMARY

The following is a PROCEDURE DIVISION shell that indicates the processing to be performed for any number of control breaks within a program:

```
100-MAIN-MODULE.
    OPEN INPUT INFILE                                 ◄── Can be performed in an
         OUTPUT OUTFILE.                                  initialization routine
    READ INFILE
        AT END MOVE 'NO ' TO ARE-THERE-MORE-RECORDS.
    PERFORM 600-HEADING-RTN.
    MOVE (all control fields to hold areas).
    PERFORM 200-DETAIL-RTN
        UNTIL THERE-ARE-NO-MORE-RECORDS.
    PERFORM (major control break, which forces all other  ◄── Can be performed in
              breaks).                                         an end-of-job
    [PERFORM final total routine, if needed.]                  routine
    CLOSE INFILE
          OUTFILE.
    STOP RUN.
200-DETAIL-RTN.
    IF (major control field) IS NOT EQUAL TO (major control
              field hold)
        PERFORM (major control break).
    IF (intermediate control field) IS NOT EQUAL TO
              (intermediate hold)
        PERFORM (intermediate control break).
         .
         .
         .
    IF (minor control field) IS NOT EQUAL TO (minor hold)
        PERFORM (minor control break).
        ADD (to minor total).
        [MOVE and WRITE, if detail printing is required.]
    READ INFILE
        AT END MOVE 'NO ' TO ARE-THERE-MORE-RECORDS.
300-MAJOR-BREAK.
    PERFORM 400-INTERMEDIATE-BREAK.
    MOVE and WRITE (major total line).
    [ADD major total to final total, if final total needed.]
    MOVE 0 TO (major total).
    IF  THERE-ARE-MORE-RECORDS
        MOVE (major control field to major hold)
        PERFORM 600-HEADING-RTN.
```

```
400-INTERMEDIATE-BREAK.
    PERFORM 500-MINOR-BREAK.
    WRITE (intermediate total line).
    ADD (intermediate total to major total).
    MOVE 0 TO (intermediate total).
    IF  THERE-ARE-MORE-RECORDS
        MOVE (intermediate control field to intermediate
                    hold area).
600-HEADING-RTN.
        .
        .
        .
```

In a control break program, all input records must be in sequence by minor control fields within intermediate control fields within major control fields. If the records are not already in this order, then the file must be *sorted* into the required sequence before it can be processed.

CHAPTER SELF-TEST

Consider the following problem definition. Each input record includes (1) a warehouse number where the item is stocked and (2) the value of that item's stock on hand.

INVENTORY-FILE Record Layout

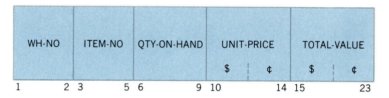

Note: The total number of items stored is equal to the sum of records or items (not quantities) for each warehouse

1. If the output report consists of each warehouse's total value of inventory, we would call this a _____ report.
2. To print warehouse totals using the format described in this chapter, input data must be in sequence by _____ .
3. Write the main module for this problem.
4. Assuming that you have called the detail module `200-DETAIL-RTN`, code that module.
5. Assuming that you have called the control break module `300-CONTROL-BREAK`, code that module.
6. Suppose you have the following sentence in the control break module:

```
300-CONTROL-BREAK.
    :
    IF  THERE-ARE-MORE-RECORDS
        MOVE WH-NO TO WS-WH-HOLD.
```

THERE-ARE-MORE-RECORDS is a condition-name equivalent to the condition IF ARE-THERE-MORE-RECORDS = 'YES'. Why must we check this condition before we move WH-NO to WS-WH-HOLD?

7. Suppose a control break procedure also requires printing of a final total inventory value. We could code the following in 200-DETAIL-RTN:

```
200-DETAIL-RTN.
    :
    :
    ADD TOTAL-VALUE TO WS-WH-TOT, WS-FINAL-TOT.
```

Indicate a more efficient way to obtain a final total and explain why it is more efficient.

8. If multiple control breaks are used in a program, the routine for producing the major-level control break would always begin by performing _____ .

9. (T or F) When a double-level control break is used, input data must be in sequence by major fields within minor fields.

10. (T or F) In a single-level control break program, when an AT END condition occurs the only processing that is required is to close the files.

Solutions

1. control break, group, or summary

2. warehouse number

3.
```
100-MAIN-MODULE.
    PERFORM 500-INITIALIZATION-RTN.
    MOVE WH-NO TO WS-WH-HOLD.
    PERFORM 200-DETAIL-RTN
        UNTIL THERE-ARE-NO-MORE-RECORDS.
    PERFORM 600-END-OF-JOB-RTN.
    :
    :
500-INITIALIZATION-RTN.
    OPEN INPUT  INVENTORY-FILE
         OUTPUT SUMMARY-LISTING.
    PERFORM 400-HEADING-RTN.
    READ INVENTORY-FILE
        AT END MOVE 'NO ' TO ARE-THERE-MORE-RECORDS.
    :
    :
600-END-OF-JOB-RTN.
    PERFORM 300-CONTROL-BREAK.
    CLOSE INVENTORY-FILE
          SUMMARY-LISTING.
    STOP RUN.
```

4.
```
200-DETAIL-RTN.
    IF  WH-NO IS NOT EQUAL TO WS-WH-HOLD
        PERFORM 300-CONTROL-BREAK.
    ADD 1 TO WS-TOTAL-ITEMS.
    ADD TOTAL-VALUE TO WS-WH-TOTAL.
    READ INVENTORY-FILE
        AT END MOVE 'NO ' TO ARE-THERE-MORE-RECORDS.
```

5.
```
300-CONTROL-BREAK.
    MOVE WS-WH-HOLD TO WH-OUT.
    MOVE WS-WH-TOTAL TO TOTAL-OUT.
    MOVE WS-TOTAL-ITEMS TO ITEMS-OUT.
    WRITE PRINT-REC FROM WH-REC
        AFTER ADVANCING 2 LINES.
    MOVE 0 TO WS-WH-TOTAL, WS-TOTAL-ITEMS.
    IF  THERE-ARE-MORE-RECORDS
        MOVE WH-NO TO WS-WH-HOLD.
```

6. At the end of the job, when THERE-ARE-NO-MORE-RECORDS (ARE-THERE-MORE-RECORDS = 'NO '), the input record and its fields are no longer available for processing. If we perform 300-CONTROL-BREAK from 600-END-OF-JOB-RTN after THERE-ARE-NO-MORE-RECORDS, the MOVE WH-NO TO WS-WH-HOLD instruction is unnecessary and might even cause an abnormal end to the program.

7. In `300-CONTROL-BREAK`, start with the following instruction:

```
300-CONTROL-BREAK.
    ADD WS-WH-TOTAL TO WS-FINAL-TOT.
```

Suppose there are 10000 input records but only 20 warehouses. Adding `TOTAL-VALUE` to `WS-FINAL-TOT` in `200-DETAIL-RTN` will perform 10000 additions, but adding `WS-WH-TOT` and `WS-FINAL-TOT` at `300-CONTROL-BREAK` will perform only 20 additions. This could save considerable computer time.

8. a minor-level control break

9. F—Sorting is by minor fields within major fields.

10. F—It is necessary to perform a control break to force the printing of the last control total.

PRACTICE PROGRAM

Consider the following problem definition:

Systems Flowchart

EMPLOYEE-FILE
32-position records
standard labels

REPORT-FILE

EMPLOYEE-FILE Record Layout

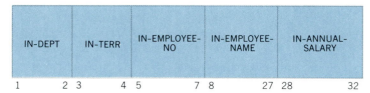

IN-DEPT	IN-TERR	IN-EMPLOYEE-NO	IN-EMPLOYEE-NAME	IN-ANNUAL-SALARY
1 2	3 4	5 7	8 27	28 32

IN-DEPT is a major control field; IN-TERR is a minor control field

REPORT-FILE Printer Spacing Chart

```
H    ALPHA DEPARTMENT STORE   PAGE XXX
H         PAYROLL FOR THE WEEK OF XX/XX/XX
H    DEPARTMENT - XX
H    TERRITORY - XX
H      EMPLOYEE NUMBER      EMPLOYEE NAME      ANNUAL SALARY
D            XXX         X------------X   $$$,$$$.99
D            XXX         X------------X   $$$,$$$.99
T        TOTAL SALARY FOR TERRITORY IS $$$$,$$$.99
T            TOTAL SALARY FOR DEPARTMENT IS  $$,$$$,$$$.99
T              TOTAL OF ALL SALARIES IS $$$,$$$,$$$.99
     END OF REPORT
```

Sample Input Data

```
0101001PAUL NEWMAN        31000
0101005ROBERT REDFORD     42000
0102007DIANA ROSS         41000
0102009BILL SMITH         15000
0207023JOHN DOE           27000
0207036JOHN BROWNE        52000
0309054NANCY STERN        99999
```

Sample Output

```
      A L P H A   D E P A R T M E N T   S T O R E     PAGE   1

           PAYROLL FOR THE WEEK OF 01/29/88

DEPARTMENT-  01

TERRITORY-  01

     EMPLOYEE NUMBER        EMPLOYEE NAME          ANNUAL SALARY

          001             PAUL NEWMAN             $31,000.00

          005             ROBERT REDFORD          $42,000.00


          TOTAL SALARY FOR TERRITORY IS      $73,000.00



      A L P H A   D E P A R T M E N T   S T O R E     PAGE   2

           PAYROLL FOR THE WEEK OF 01/29/88

DEPARTMENT-  01

TERRITORY-  02

     EMPLOYEE NUMBER        EMPLOYEE NAME          ANNUAL SALARY

          007             DIANA ROSS              $41,000.00

          009             BILL SMITH              $15,000.00


          TOTAL SALARY FOR TERRITORY IS      $56,000.00


             TOTAL SALARY FOR DEPARTMENT IS    $129,000.00



      A L P H A   D E P A R T M E N T   S T O R E     PAGE   3

           PAYROLL FOR THE WEEK OF 01/29/88

DEPARTMENT-  02

TERRITORY-  07

     EMPLOYEE NUMBER        EMPLOYEE NAME          ANNUAL SALARY

          023             JOHN DOE                $27,000.00

          036             JOHN BROWNE             $52,000.00


          TOTAL SALARY FOR TERRITORY IS      $79,000.00


             TOTAL SALARY FOR DEPARTMENT IS     $79,000.00
```

```
         A L P H A   D E P A R T M E N T   S T O R E        PAGE  4

                    PAYROLL FOR THE WEEK OF 01/29/88

         DEPARTMENT-  03

         TERRITORY-  09

             EMPLOYEE NUMBER        EMPLOYEE NAME         ANNUAL SALARY
                   054             NANCY STERN            $99,999.00


                      TOTAL SALARY FOR TERRITORY IS     $99,999.00


                          TOTAL SALARY FOR DEPARTMENT IS    $99,999.00


                             TOTAL OF ALL SALARIES IS    $307,999.00

         END OF REPORT
```

Write a program to produce the double-level control break printing described above. Figure 12.11 illustrates the hierarchy chart and pseudocode, and Figure 12.12 shows the program.

Figure 12.11
Pseudocode and hierarchy chart for the Practice Program.

```
START
    PERFORM
        Open the Files
        Read a Record
        Move Control Fields to Hold Areas
    ENDPERFORM
    PERFORM
        Accept Date
    ENDPERFORM
    PERFORM
        Write Headings
        Initialize Line Counter
    ENDPERFORM
    PERFORM
        IF  Dept Break
        THEN
            PERFORM
                PERFORM
                    Terr Break Routine
                ENDPERFORM
                Write Dept Total
                Initialize Dept Hold Area, Dept Total
            ENDPERFORM
        ENDIF
        IF  Terr Break
        THEN
            PERFORM
                Print Terr Total
                Add Terr Total to Dept Total
                Initialize Terr Hold Area, Terr Total
            ENDPERFORM
        ENDIF
        IF  end of page
        THEN
            PERFORM
                Write Headings
            ENDPERFORM
        ENDIF
        Write Detail Record
        Add Amt to Terr Total
        Read a Record
    ENDPERFORM
    PERFORM
        Dept Break Routine
    ENDPERFORM
    PERFORM
        Write Final Total
    ENDPERFORM
    PERFORM
        End-of-Job Operations
    ENDPERFORM
STOP
```

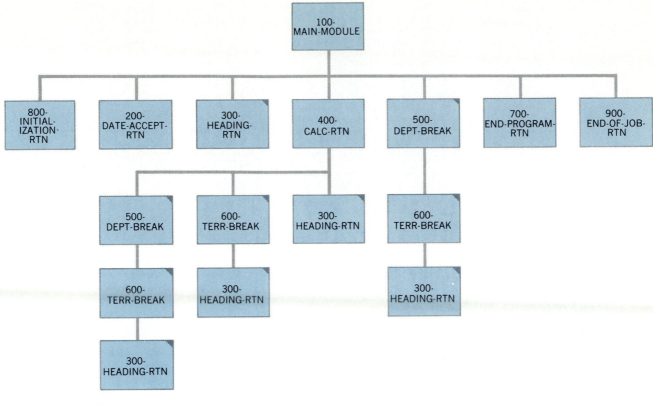

Figure 12.11
(continued)

Figure 12.12
Solution to the Practice
Program.

```
IDENTIFICATION DIVISION.
PROGRAM-ID. SAMPLE.
****************************************************************
*   SAMPLE          -   THIS IS AN EXAMPLE OF A DOUBLE LEVEL   *
*                       CONTROL BREAK. THE MAJOR FIELD IS      *
*                       DEPT AND THE MINOR FIELD IS TERR       *
****************************************************************
ENVIRONMENT DIVISION.
INPUT-OUTPUT SECTION.
FILE-CONTROL.
    SELECT IN-EMPLOYEE-FILE ASSIGN TO DATA11.
    SELECT OUT-REPORT-FILE  ASSIGN TO SYS$OUTPUT.
*
DATA DIVISION.
FILE SECTION.
FD  IN-EMPLOYEE-FILE
    LABEL RECORDS ARE STANDARD.
01  IN-EMPLOYEE-REC.
    05   IN-DEPT              PIC 99.
    05   IN-TERR              PIC 99.
    05   IN-EMPLOYEE-NO       PIC 9(3).
    05   IN-EMPLOYEE-NAME     PIC X(20).
    05   IN-ANNUAL-SALARY     PIC 9(5).
FD  OUT-REPORT-FILE
    LABEL RECORDS ARE OMITTED.
01  OUT-REPORT-REC           PIC X(133).
WORKING-STORAGE SECTION.
01  WS-WORK-AREAS.
    05   ARE-THERE-MORE-RECORDS   PIC X(3)     VALUE 'YES'.
        88   MORE-RECORDS                      VALUE 'YES'.
        88   NO-MORE-RECORDS                   VALUE 'NO '.
    05   WS-LINE-CTR          PIC 99          VALUE ZEROS.
    05   WS-PAGE-CTR          PIC 999         VALUE ZEROS.
```

Figure 12.12
(continued)

```
          05  WS-DEPT-SALARY              PIC 9(7)V99   VALUE ZEROS.
          05  WS-TERR-SALARY              PIC 9(6)V99   VALUE ZEROS.
          05  WS-DEPT-HOLD                PIC 99        VALUE ZEROS.
          05  WS-TERR-HOLD                PIC 99        VALUE ZEROS.
          05  WS-TOTAL-SALARY             PIC 9(8)V99   VALUE ZEROS.
          05  WS-T-DATE                   PIC 9(6).
          05  WS-T-DATE-X REDEFINES WS-T-DATE.
              10  WS-IN-YR                PIC XX.
              10  WS-IN-MO                PIC XX.
              10  WS-IN-DAY               PIC XX.
      01  HL-HEADING1.
          05  FILLER                      PIC X(24)     VALUE SPACES.
          05  FILLER                      PIC X(44)
              VALUE 'A L P H A   D E P A R T M E N T   S T O R E'.
          05  FILLER                      PIC X(10)
              VALUE '      PAGE '.
          05  HL-OUT-PAGE                 PIC ZZ9.
          05  FILLER                      PIC X(52)     VALUE SPACES.
      01  HL-HEADING2.
          05  FILLER                      PIC X(30)     VALUE SPACES.
          05  FILLER                      PIC X(24)
              VALUE 'PAYROLL FOR THE WEEK OF'.
          05  HL-TODAYS-DATE.
              10  HL-OUT-MO               PIC XX.
              10  FILLER                  PIC X         VALUE '/'.
              10  HL-OUT-DAY              PIC XX.
              10  FILLER                  PIC X         VALUE '/'.
              10  HL-OUT-YR               PIC XX.
      01  HL-HEADING3.
          05  FILLER                      PIC X(18)     VALUE SPACES.
          05  FILLER                      PIC X(15)
              VALUE 'EMPLOYEE NUMBER'.
          05  FILLER                      PIC X(9)      VALUE SPACES.
          05  FILLER                      PIC X(13)
              VALUE 'EMPLOYEE NAME'.
          05  FILLER                      PIC X(11)     VALUE SPACES.
          05  FILLER                      PIC X(13)
              VALUE 'ANNUAL SALARY'.
          05  FILLER                      PIC X(54)     VALUE SPACES.
      01  DL-SALARY-LINE.
          05  FILLER                      PIC X(29)     VALUE SPACES.
          05  DL-OUT-EMPLOYEE-NO          PIC 9(3).
          05  FILLER                      PIC X(10)     VALUE SPACES.
          05  DL-OUT-EMPLOYEE-NAME        PIC X(20).
          05  FILLER                      PIC XX        VALUE SPACES.
          05  DL-OUT-ANNUAL-SALARY        PIC $$$,$$$.99.
          05  FILLER                      PIC X(59)     VALUE SPACES.
      01  DL-TERRITORY-TOTAL-LINE.
          05  FILLER                      PIC X(29)     VALUE SPACES.
          05  FILLER                      PIC X(33)
              VALUE 'TOTAL SALARY FOR TERRITORY IS '.
          05  DL-OUT-TERR-SALARY          PIC $$$$,$$$.99.
          05  FILLER                      PIC X(60)     VALUE SPACES.
      01  DL-DEPARTMENT-TOTAL-LINE.
          05  FILLER                      PIC X(38)     VALUE SPACES.
          05  FILLER                      PIC X(31)
              VALUE 'TOTAL SALARY FOR DEPARTMENT IS '.
          05  DL-OUT-DEPT-SALARY          PIC $$,$$$,$$$.99.
          05  FILLER                      PIC X(47)     VALUE SPACES.
      01  DL-FINAL-TOTAL-LINE.
          05  FILLER                      PIC X(41)     VALUE SPACES.
          05  FILLER                      PIC X(25)
              VALUE 'TOTAL OF ALL SALARIES IS '.
          05  DL-OUT-TOT-ANN-SALARY       PIC $$$,$$$,$$$.99.
          05  FILLER                      PIC X(53) VALUE SPACES.
      01  DL-DEPT-HEADING.
          05  FILLER                      PIC X(15)     VALUE SPACES.
          05  FILLER                      PIC X(13)
              VALUE 'DEPARTMENT-'.
          05  DL-OUT-DEPT                 PIC 99.
          05  FILLER                      PIC X(103)    VALUE SPACES.
      01  DL-TERR-HEADING.
          05  FILLER                      PIC X(15)     VALUE SPACES.
          05  FILLER                      PIC X(12)
              VALUE 'TERRITORY-'.
          05  DL-OUT-TERR                 PIC 99.
          05  FILLER                      PIC X(104)    VALUE SPACES.
```

Figure 12.12
(continued)

```
01   HL-HEADING-FINAL.
     05  FILLER                         PIC X(10)      VALUE SPACE.
     05  FILLER                         PIC X(13)
         VALUE 'END OF REPORT'.
     05  FILLER                         PIC X(110)     VALUE SPACES.
*
 PROCEDURE DIVISION.
 ************************************************************
 *  100-MAIN-MODULE - CONTROLS DIRECTION OF PROGRAM LOGIC *
 ************************************************************
 100-MAIN-MODULE.
     PERFORM 800-INITIALIZATION-RTN.
     PERFORM 200-DATE-ACCEPT-RTN.
     PERFORM 300-HEADING-RTN.
     PERFORM 400-CALC-RTN
         UNTIL NO-MORE-RECORDS.
     PERFORM 500-DEPT-BREAK.
     PERFORM 700-END-PROGRAM-RTN.
     PERFORM 900-END-OF-JOB-RTN.
 ************************************************************
 *  200-DATE-ACCEPT-RTN - PERFORMED FROM 100-MAIN-MODULE. *
 *       GETS THE CURRENT DATE FROM THE OPERATING SYSTEM. *
 ************************************************************
 200-DATE-ACCEPT-RTN.
     ACCEPT WS-T-DATE FROM DATE.
     MOVE WS-IN-MO TO HL-OUT-MO.
     MOVE WS-IN-YR TO HL-OUT-YR.
     MOVE WS-IN-DAY TO HL-OUT-DAY.
 ****************************************************************
 *  300-HEADING-RTN - PERFORMED FROM 100-MAIN-MODULE, 400-CALC-RTN, *
 *            500-DEPT-BREAK AND 600-TERR-BREAK.             *
 *                PRINTS THE HEADINGS ON A NEW PAGE.        *
 ****************************************************************
 300-HEADING-RTN.
     ADD 1 TO WS-PAGE-CTR.
     MOVE WS-PAGE-CTR TO HL-OUT-PAGE.
     MOVE WS-TERR-HOLD TO DL-OUT-TERR.
     MOVE WS-DEPT-HOLD TO DL-OUT-DEPT.
     MOVE 0 TO WS-LINE-CTR.
     WRITE OUT-REPORT-REC FROM HL-HEADING1
         AFTER ADVANCING PAGE.
     WRITE OUT-REPORT-REC FROM HL-HEADING2
         AFTER ADVANCING 2 LINES.
     WRITE OUT-REPORT-REC FROM DL-DEPT-HEADING
         AFTER ADVANCING 2 LINES.
     WRITE OUT-REPORT-REC FROM DL-TERR-HEADING
         AFTER ADVANCING 2 LINES.
     WRITE OUT-REPORT-REC FROM HL-HEADING3
         AFTER ADVANCING 2 LINES.
 ****************************************************
 *  400-CALC-RTN - PERFORMED FROM 100-MAIN-MODULE  *
 *                 CONTROLS TERR AND DEPT BREAKS    *
 *                 PRINTS OUT EMPLOYEE INFORMATION  *
 ****************************************************
 400-CALC-RTN.
     IF   IN-DEPT NOT EQUAL TO WS-DEPT-HOLD
         PERFORM 500-DEPT-BREAK.
     IF   IN-TERR NOT EQUAL TO WS-TERR-HOLD
         PERFORM 600-TERR-BREAK.
     MOVE IN-EMPLOYEE-NO TO DL-OUT-EMPLOYEE-NO.
     MOVE IN-EMPLOYEE-NAME TO DL-OUT-EMPLOYEE-NAME.
     MOVE IN-ANNUAL-SALARY TO DL-OUT-ANNUAL-SALARY.
     ADD IN-ANNUAL-SALARY TO WS-TERR-SALARY.
     ADD 1 TO WS-LINE-CTR.
     IF   WS-LINE-CTR IS GREATER THAN 25
         PERFORM 300-HEADING-RTN.
     WRITE OUT-REPORT-REC FROM DL-SALARY-LINE
         AFTER ADVANCING 2 LINES.
     READ IN-EMPLOYEE-FILE
         AT END MOVE 'NO ' TO ARE-THERE-MORE-RECORDS.
 ****************************************************************
 *  500-DEPT-BREAK - PERFORMED FROM 100-MAIN-MODULE AND 400-CALC-RTN  *
 *                   FORCES A TERR BREAK THEN  PRINTS DEPT TOTALS     *
 ****************************************************************
 500-DEPT-BREAK.
     PERFORM 600-TERR-BREAK.
     ADD WS-DEPT-SALARY TO WS-TOTAL-SALARY.
```

Figure 12.12
(continued)

```
        MOVE WS-DEPT-SALARY TO DL-OUT-DEPT-SALARY.
        MOVE ZEROS TO WS-DEPT-SALARY.
        WRITE OUT-REPORT-REC FROM DL-DEPARTMENT-TOTAL-LINE
            AFTER ADVANCING 3 LINES.
        ADD 1 TO WS-LINE-CTR.
        IF  MORE-RECORDS
            MOVE IN-DEPT TO WS-DEPT-HOLD
            PERFORM 300-HEADING-RTN.
    **************************************************************************
    *  600-TERR-BREAK - PERFORMED FROM 400-CALC-RTN AND 500-DEPT-BREAK    *
    *              CONTROLS TERR BREAK AND PRINTS TERR TOTALS             *
    **************************************************************************
     600-TERR-BREAK.
        ADD WS-TERR-SALARY TO WS-DEPT-SALARY.
        MOVE WS-TERR-SALARY TO DL-OUT-TERR-SALARY.
        MOVE ZEROS TO WS-TERR-SALARY.
        WRITE OUT-REPORT-REC FROM DL-TERRITORY-TOTAL-LINE
            AFTER ADVANCING 3 LINES.
        ADD 1 TO WS-LINE-CTR.
        IF  MORE-RECORDS
            MOVE IN-TERR TO WS-TERR-HOLD.
        IF MORE-RECORDS AND IN-DEPT IS EQUAL TO WS-DEPT-HOLD
            PERFORM 300-HEADING-RTN.
    **************************************************************************
    *  700-END-PROGRAM-RTN - PERFORMED FROM 100-MAIN-MODULE           *
    *                     PRINTS OUT TOTAL EMPLOYEES SALARIES         *
    **************************************************************************
     700-END-PROGRAM-RTN.
        MOVE WS-TOTAL-SALARY TO DL-OUT-TOT-ANN-SALARY.
        WRITE OUT-REPORT-REC FROM DL-FINAL-TOTAL-LINE
            AFTER ADVANCING 3 LINES.
        WRITE OUT-REPORT-REC FROM HL-HEADING-FINAL
            AFTER ADVANCING 2 LINES.
    **************************************************************************
    *  800-INITIALIZATION-RTN - PERFORMED FROM 100-MAIN-MODULE    *
    *                        CONTROLS OPENING OF FILES           *
    *                        PERFORMS INITIAL READ              *
    **************************************************************************
     800-INITIALIZATION-RTN.
        OPEN INPUT  IN-EMPLOYEE-FILE
             OUTPUT OUT-REPORT-FILE.
        READ IN-EMPLOYEE-FILE
            AT END MOVE 'NO ' TO ARE-THERE-MORE-RECORDS.
        MOVE IN-DEPT TO WS-DEPT-HOLD.
        MOVE IN-TERR TO WS-TERR-HOLD.
    **************************************************************************
    *  900-END-OF-JOB-RTN  -  PERFORMED FROM 100-MAIN-MODULE     *
    *                         CLOSES THE FILES AND RETURNS       *
    *                         CONTROL TO THE OPERATING SYSTEM    *
    **************************************************************************
     900-END-OF-JOB-RTN.
        CLOSE IN-EMPLOYEE-FILE
              OUT-REPORT-FILE.
        STOP RUN.
```

KEY TERMS

Control break processing   Detail printing   Group printing
Control field   Exception printing   Summary printing

REVIEW QUESTIONS

T F

True-False Questions __ __   1. In order to execute a control break program, input data must be in sequence by the control fields.

__ __   2. In the main module of a control break program, we always perform a heading routine before reading the first record.

__ __   3. Before a detail or calculation routine is executed from the main module of a control break program, the control fields must be moved to hold areas in WORKING-STORAGE.

___ ___ 4. After ARE-THERE-MORE-RECORDS = 'NO ' and control is returned to the main module, the only other processing required is to print cumulative final totals, if desired. Then you may CLOSE and STOP RUN.

___ ___ 5. The detail module usually begins by testing for a minor-level control break, followed by tests for major-level control breaks.

___ ___ 6. The detail module of a control break program always has a WRITE statement.

___ ___ 7. One method for minimizing errors in a control break program is to perform a sequence-checking routine where you check that the control fields have been sorted properly.

___ ___ 8. The control break module must always clear the total fields to zero.

___ ___ 9. The control break module typically includes a WRITE statement.

___ ___ 10. A maximum of two levels of control breaks are permitted in a control break program.

DEBUGGING EXERCISES

Consider the following coding:

```
PROCEDURE DIVISION.
100-MAIN-MODULE.
    OPEN INPUT  TRANS-FILE
         OUTPUT PRINT-FILE.
    READ TRANS-FILE
        AT END MOVE 'NO ' TO ARE-THERE-MORE-RECORDS.
    MOVE ACCT-NO-IN TO WS-HOLD-ACCT.
    PERFORM 200-DETAIL-RTN
        UNTIL THERE-ARE-NO-MORE-RECORDS.
    CLOSE TRANS-FILE
          PRINT-FILE.
    STOP RUN.
200-DETAIL-RTN.
    PERFORM 300-ADD-IT-UP
        UNTIL ACCT-NO IS NOT EQUAL TO WS-HOLD-ACCT OR
            THERE-ARE-NO-MORE-RECORDS.
    MOVE WS-HOLD-ACCT TO ACCT-OUT.
    MOVE WS-TOTAL TO TOTAL-OUT.
    WRITE PRINT-REC FROM OUT-REC.
        :
        :
300-ADD-IT-UP.
    ADD AMT TO WS-TOTAL.
    READ TRANS-FILE
        AT END MOVE 'NO ' TO ARE-THERE-MORE-RECORDS.
```

1. This procedure for performing control break processing is different from the procedure used in the chapter. Is the overall logical structure correct?

2. After executing PERFORM 200-DETAIL-RTN UNTIL THERE-ARE-NO-MORE-RECORDS in the main module, should there be a PERFORM to print the last control group? Explain your answer.

3. There are two instructions missing from 200-DETAIL-RTN that will result in logic errors. Insert them.

4. Suppose 200-DETAIL-RTN had a READ as its last instruction. How would this affect processing?

5. Suppose we omitted the MOVE statement from the main module. Would this have any substantial effect on the processing? Explain your answer.

PROGRAMMING ASSIGNMENTS

1. Write a program to print a sales total from disk records for each of five transaction days. The problem definition is shown in Figure 12.13.

Figure 12.13
Problem definition for
Programming Assignment 1.

Systems Flowchart

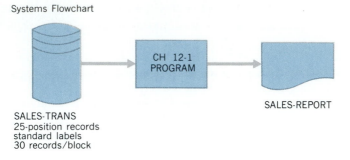

SALES-TRANS
25-position records
standard labels
30 records/block

SALES-REPORT

SALES-TRANS Record Layout

DAY NO.	SALESPERSON NO.	SALES AMOUNT $ ¢	
1 2	4 5	9 10	25

SALES-REPORT Printer Spacing Chart

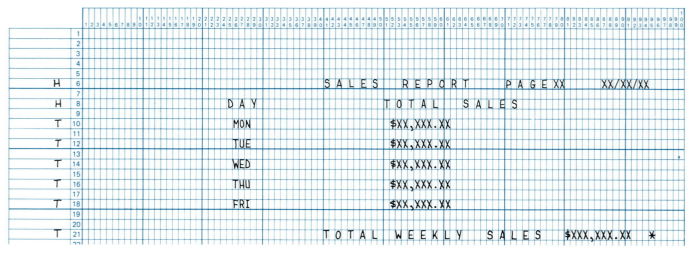

Notes

a. There is a disk record for each sale made by a salesperson; thus there are an undetermined number of input records.

b. Records are in sequence by day number, which ranges from 1 to 5 (Mon–Fri).

2. Write a program to list employees by territory number. The problem definition is shown in Figure 12.14.

Figure 12.14
Problem definition for
Programming Assignment 2.

Systems Flowchart

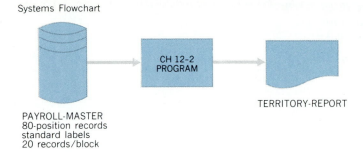

PAYROLL-MASTER
80-position records
standard labels
20 records/block

TERRITORY-REPORT

PAYROLL-MASTER Record Layout

EMPLOYEE NO.	EMPLOYEE NAME	TERRITORY NO.		ANNUAL SALARY (in $)	
1 5	6 25	26 27	28 29	30 35	36 80

TERRITORY-REPORT Printer Spacing Chart

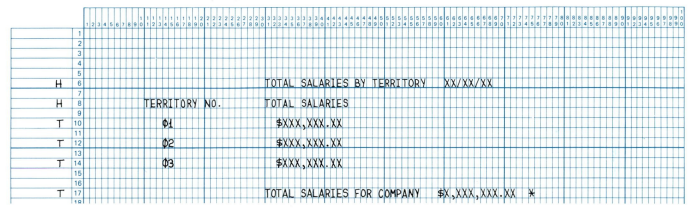

```
H  6              TOTAL SALARIES BY TERRITORY    XX/XX/XX
H  8    TERRITORY NO.      TOTAL SALARIES
T 10         01            $XXX,XXX.XX
T 12         02            $XXX,XXX.XX
T 14         03            $XXX,XXX.XX
T 17              TOTAL SALARIES FOR COMPANY  $X,XXX,XXX.XX  *
```

Notes

a. The input records are in sequence by territory number.
b. Print the total salaries for each territory. At the end of the report, print the total salaries for the entire company.
c. There are three territories: 01, 02, and 03.

3. Write a program to print a population total for each state. The problem definition is shown in Figure 12.15.

Figure 12.15
Problem definition for
Programming Assignment 3.

Systems Flowchart

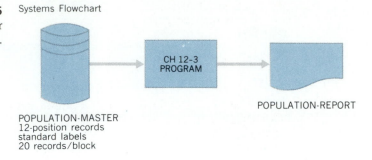

POPULATION-MASTER
12-position records
standard labels
20 records/block

POPULATION-REPORT

POPULATION-MASTER Record Layout

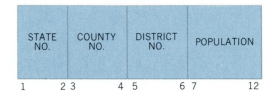

POPULATION-REPORT Printer Spacing Chart

```
                            POPULATION REPORT   XX/XX/XX  PAGE X

              STATE NO       TOTAL POPULATION
                 1           XX,XXX,XXX

                 2           XX,XXX,XXX

                 3           XX,XXX,XXX
                 .               .

                 .               .

                 .               .

                 .               .

                 .               .

                             TOTAL USA POPULATION  XXX,XXX,XXX
```

Note

Records are in sequence by county within state.

4. Write a program to tabulate the number of employees by territory within area within department. The input disk record has the following format:

1–2   Territory number
3–4   Area number
5–6   Department number
7–50 Not used

Labels are standard; blocking factor = 10.

Notes

a. There are three territories; there are three areas within each territory; there are 10 departments within each area.
b. Disk records are in sequence by department within area within territory.
c. Output is a report with the format shown in Figure 12.16.

Figure 12.16
Printer Spacing Chart for
Programming Assignment 4.

13

Debugging Programs and Validating Data

I. DETECTING PROGRAM ERRORS
  A. Syntax Errors
  B. Logic Errors
    1. Designing Test Data That Is Comprehensive and Realistic
    2. Checking for Logic Errors
II. AVOIDING LOGIC ERRORS BY VALIDATING INPUT
  A. Why Input to a Business System Must Be Validated
  B. Some Consequences of Invalid Input
    1. Inaccurate Output   2. Logic Errors Resulting from Input Errors
  C. Data Validation Techniques
    1. Testing Fields to Ensure a Correct Format
    2. Checking for Missing Data
    3. The INSPECT Statement: Tallying and Replacing Specific Characters With
       Other Characters to Minimize Errors
    Self-Test
    4. Testing for Reasonableness
    5. Condition-Names: Checking Coded Fields for Valid Contents
    6. Sequence Checking
  D. Using the EVALUATE Verb for Data Validation
  E. Other Methods for Validating Data
    1. Use of Control Listings for Manual Validation of Input
    2. Verification as a Means of Validating Input
III. WHAT TO DO IF INPUT ERRORS OCCUR
  A. Stop the Run
  B. Print an Error Record Containing the Key Field, the Contents of the Erroneous
     Field, and an Error Message
  C. Partially Process or Bypass Erroneous Records
  D. Stop the Run If the Number of Errors Exceeds a Predetermined Limit
  E. Use Switches
  F. Print Totals
    1. Print a Count of All Records and a Count of All Errors
    2. Print a Batch Total
IV. WHEN DATA SHOULD BE VALIDATED
END-OF-CHAPTER AIDS
    Chapter Summary   Review Questions
    Chapter Self-Test   Debugging Exercises
    Practice Program   Programming Assignments
    Key Terms

OBJECTIVES

To familiarize you with

1. The types of input errors that may occur.
2. The techniques used to validate input data.
3. The actions that can be taken when input errors are detected.

I. Detecting Program Errors

Everyone is aware of horror stories related to so-called computer errors. Newspapers provide almost daily accounts of people who erroneously receive computerized bills or checks for absurd amounts. Such errors almost always occur because of either *program errors* or *input errors.* In this section we focus on methods used to find program errors; in the next section we will focus on input errors.

A. Syntax Errors

After a program has been planned and coded, it must be keyed into a computer. The programmer should then check it for typographical errors. He or she should review the logic again in an effort to detect errors. After the program has been checked, it is ready to be compiled or translated into machine language. During this translation process, the compiler will list any violations in programming rules that may have occurred. These rule violations are called **syntax errors;** they must be corrected before the program can be executed. The list of these errors may appear (1) together at the end of the COBOL listing or (2) individually, preceding or following each erroneous statement. Note that logic errors are not detected during this phase; they can only be discovered during actual execution of the program.

The following are possible rule violations or syntax errors:

SAMPLE RULE VIOLATIONS

1. Attempting to add two operands using the verb AD instead of ADD.
2. Attempting to subtract from a nonnumeric field.
3. Using a field in the PROCEDURE DIVISION that has not been defined in the DATA DIVISION.

Such syntax errors are quite common even in programs written by experienced programmers.

Each compiler has its own set of **diagnostic** or error **messages.** Sometimes it takes practice to become accustomed to the succinct format of a diagnostic message. Consult your computer's specifications manual for a listing of common diagnostics. Note that although the messages illustrated in this section may not conform exactly to those for your compiler, the general format is the same. Thus, experience with diagnostics of one compiler will help you understand diagnostics of another compiler.

Most diagnostic messages have the following format:

Line No.   Error Code   Error Message

Line No. refers to the sequence number assigned to each line of a source program. This line number is assigned by the compiler and printed on the source program listing.

Error Code is a code number assigned to the specific message in the specifications manual. If you look up the Error Code in your manual, it will provide further clarification about the type of error that has occurred.

The printed Error Message is a concise description of the syntax error. After debugging a few programs, you will become familiar with these messages.

The following represents sample diagnostics:

Sample Diagnostics		
Line No.	**Error Code**	**Error Message**
18	1KF2041-C	NO OPEN CLAUSE FOUND FOR FILE
25	1KF0651-W	PERIOD MISSING IN PRECEDING STATEMENT
29	1KF5531-E	FIGURATIVE CONSTANT IS NOT ALLOWED AS RECEIVING FIELD
30	1KF4011-C	SYNTAX REQUIRES A DATA-NAME FOUND 'DATA'

It is simply not feasible to undertake a discussion of all possible diagnostics. Once you become familiar with the format of these messages, however, they will be easy to understand and very useful for correcting syntax errors.

Sometimes a single error results in several diagnostics. Similarly, the error detected by the compiler may have been triggered by a mistake several lines earlier. Thus, if the error is not readily found, examine the lines directly preceding the ones specified in the error message.

The Error Code accompanying all diagnostics contains, as the last character, usually a W, C, or E (or, correspondingly, a 0, 1, or 2). These letters or numbers indicate the *severity* of the error; the execution of the program may be terminated depending on the level of severity of errors.

a. W-Level or Level-0 Errors.

With minor-level errors, sometimes called warning, observation, W-level, or level-0 messages, the program can be executed after it has been compiled. The messages are merely warnings to the programmer. To attempt to place a five-position alphanumeric field into a three-position alphanumeric field, for example, may result in the following warning message:

```
DESTINATION FIELD DOES NOT ACCEPT THE WHOLE SENDING FIELD IN MOVE
```

To MOVE a larger field to a smaller one is *not* necessarily incorrect. The compiler is merely indicating that truncation will occur. If truncation occurs as a result of a programming oversight, it should be corrected. If, however, the programmer chooses to truncate a field, no changes are necessary. A program can still be executed with warning-level diagnostics.

b. C-Level or Level-1 Errors.

Intermediate-level errors are conditional errors, usually called C-level, where the compiler must make an assumption about what a coded statement means. The compiler then makes the necessary change so that the program is executable. This assumption is called a **default.** If the default is what the programmer wants, execution will proceed normally. Consider the following C-level diagnostic:

```
007020 C-QUALIFICATION-NAME REQUIRES MORE QUALIFICATION
       FIRST NAME DEFINED IS ASSUMED
```

which applies to the following statement 0072.

```
0072 MOVE NAME TO NAME OF REC-OUT.
```

Since NAME is an identifier that defines two different fields, the first NAME field in the statement was not properly qualified. That is, the first time NAME is specified it has no qualifier, so the compiler does not know which NAME you mean. It will *assume* you mean the first NAME field specified in the DATA DIVISION. If, in fact, the first NAME field designated in the DATA DIVISION is the required one, the statement need not be corrected for execution to continue properly. If, however, the NAME field required is *not* the first one, then the program must be corrected before execution can begin. In any case, all C-level diagnostics should eventually be corrected before the program is considered fully debugged.

c. E-Level or Level-2 Errors. Major-level errors, called execution errors or *fatal errors,* will prevent program execution. The compiler deems these errors of such magnitude that it aborts the run. The following are examples of major-level errors:

MAJOR-LEVEL ERRORS

```
FILE SECTION OUT OF SEQUENCE
ENVIRONMENT DIVISION MISSING
UNDEFINED IDENTIFIER
INVALID LITERAL: $100.00
INVALID IDENTIFIER: DISCOUNT-%
```

B. Logic Errors

Syntax errors are relatively easy to find and correct. Because the compiler lists these errors, it is difficult to overlook them. After a program has been compiled with no syntax errors occurring, it must be executed with test data to ensure that there are no logic errors. Recall that a logic error may result from a mistake in the sequencing of instructions as well as from an improperly coded instruction that does not accomplish what was desired.

Some logic errors result in a **program interrupt** or termination. These, of course, must be corrected before execution can continue. Other logic errors result in erroneous output. These will be detected if the test data is complete and the program is carefully checked by the programmer.

Sometimes logic errors that can result in erroneous output go undetected until after a program is operational. Correcting such errors after a program is being used on a regular basis is very difficult. The programmer may no longer be completely familiar with all aspects of the program and is likely to make changes that may compound the original problem or create other ones. Moreover, the company is now using the program as a scheduled run and the time it takes to correct errors will be costly and probably create backlogs.

In short, all logic errors should be found *before* a program becomes operational, which means that the program should be carefully debugged during the testing stage. We will focus on two methods for detecting logic errors.

1. Designing Test Data That Is Comprehensive and Realistic

Programs must be tested with input **test data** to ensure that they will run properly. Because debugging depends on complete and well-designed test data, the preparation of this test data is an important responsibility of the programmer. If the test data is not complete, the program will not be fully debugged and the possibility will exist that logic errors or erroneous output may occur later on during regular production runs.

Test data should be designed to include every condition the program tests for. At least one record for each given condition should be included. In addition, sufficient data should be supplied to ensure that routines designed to be executed more than once will, in fact, be properly performed each time. A procedure may be executed properly the first time, for example, but it may fail to reinitialize certain fields. This would mean that specific errors may only be detected the *second time* through the routine.

A program might contain a heading routine, for example, that is executed when 25 lines have been written:

```
IF  LINE-CT > 25
    PERFORM 700-HEADING-RTN.
```

If 700-HEADING-RTN fails to reinitialize LINE-CT at zero, this error would *not* be detected the first time through 700-HEADING-RTN, but only the second time through it.

Include test data that is invalid as well as data that is valid to make certain that the program detects the invalid data. (More on this in the next section.)

Be sure you use enough input records to create a significant amount of output. If, for example, your output would normally include numerous pages, be sure you produce at least two pages during a test to check for reinitialization of line counters, proper incrementing of page counters, and so on.

It is sometimes a good idea to use "real" or "live" input for test data or to have someone else prepare the test data. This is because a programmer who writes a program may fail to see some obvious omissions; if the program has omissions, it is likely the test data will have similar omissions. For example, if a programmer forgot to include an error procedure for a given condition, it is likely he or she would forget to include data that tested for that error. Using "real" or "live" input or having another person prepare test data will minimize this type of bias.

After the test data is prepared, perform a *structured walkthrough* to determine what results the computer *should produce* if the program is working properly. Then run the program with the test data and compare the computer-produced results with those of the walkthrough. If your structured walkthrough produced the same results as the computer, the program is correct and may be considered debugged. If not, you must find the source of the error, correct it, and re-run the program.

2. Checking for Logic Errors

In their eagerness to complete a program, programmers sometimes spend too little time testing their programs. If the output on page 1 of a test run looks perfect, some programmers are apt to assume that subsequent pages will similarly look perfect. If a specific type of test data is handled properly by a program, some programmers may assume that all types of test data will be processed properly. Such assumptions could, in the end, prove incorrect and costly.

There are debugging tools that can be used to check program logic and to help identify errors. Such tools are very helpful if an error occurs that is difficult to find. But just as importantly, these tools can be used for checking programs that *seem* to run properly; they may help in finding logic errors that might otherwise go undetected.

Two major instructions can be used as *part of* a COBOL program during the test phase for finding errors. These instructions are then removed once the program is fully debugged. The two debugging tools are:

DEBUGGING TOOLS

1. READY TRACE

2. DISPLAY

---

a. READY TRACE. A **READY TRACE** placed at the beginning of a program lists the actual sequence of paragraphs that the program executes during a specific run. This instruction is not part of the COBOL standard but is available with most compilers as an enhancement.

If, for example, you code READY TRACE as the first statement in 100-MAIN-MODULE, the computer may print the following before an abend occurs:

```
500-HEADING-RTN
300-CALC-RTN
400-LOOP-RTN
```

This means that the computer executed these three paragraphs, in the sequence specified. If this is all that prints, then you know there is a logic error within 400-LOOP-RTN, because that was the last paragraph executed.

Similarly, suppose you code READY TRACE as the first statement in 100-MAIN-MODULE for the following program:

```
PROCEDURE DIVISION.
100-MAIN-MODULE.
    READY TRACE.
    PERFORM 400-INITIALIZATION-RTN.
    PERFORM 200-CALC-RTN
        UNTIL THERE-ARE-NO-MORE-RECORDS.
    PERFORM 500-END-OF-JOB-RTN.
200-CALC-RTN.
    :
    :
    READ FILE-IN
        AT END MOVE 'NO ' TO ARE-THERE-MORE-RECORDS.
```

During execution, the following is displayed before an abend occurs:

```
400-INITIALIZATION-RTN
200-CALC-RTN
200-CALC-RTN
```

This means that the program was terminated during the *second time* through 200-CALC-RTN. Since the first pass through 200-CALC-RTN reads the second input record, you may assume that it was during the processing of the *second record* that an error occurred. Chances are the second record has incorrectly formatted data; for example, the program may be attempting to perform an arithmetic operation on an input field that is erroneously blank.

A READY TRACE is also used for following the path of a complex program. Suppose the following prints as a result of the READY TRACE entry:

```
200-CALC-RTN
300-UPDATE-RTN
700-ERROR-RTN
500-PRINT-RTN
```

You can then check to see if this was the logic path that should have been followed for the first record in your test data.

Some programmers always code READY TRACE when debugging a program so that they can follow the logic of a specific run. Other programmers only use READY TRACE after they have detected an error condition and cannot find the error during desk checking. If you wish to use a READY TRACE for just part of a procedure, you may code:

```
PROCEDURE DIVISION.
    :
    READY TRACE.
    :
    RESET TRACE.
```

When encountered, RESET TRACE will stop the printing of paragraph-names.

In summary, use a READY TRACE statement (if it is available with your compiler) during debugging to identify logic errors. Once all logic errors have been corrected, the READY TRACE and RESET TRACE statements must be removed from the source program. You would not want the regularly scheduled run of the program to print each paragraph-name as it is encountered.

b. DISPLAY Statement.   Programmers often find that their programs operate on all input data but that the calculated results are incorrect. While testing the program, then, it may help you to examine the contents of specific fields at key points in the logic flow to determine if calculations are being performed correctly.

To make debugging easier, it is possible to examine the contents of certain fields at various checkpoints in the program, usually after the fields have been altered. In this way, the programmer can easily spot a logic error by manually performing the necessary operations on the data and comparing the results with the computer-produced results that are displayed. When a discrepancy is found, the logic error must have occurred *after the previous checkpoint*.

The DISPLAY statement prints the contents of the specified fields on either the printer or a terminal, depending on the computer system. A simplified format of the DISPLAY statement is as follows:

Format

$$\underline{\text{DISPLAY}} \left\{ \begin{array}{l} \text{identifier-1} \\ \text{literal-1} \end{array} \right\} \dots$$

Example   Suppose your program accumulates a final total. When you check your program for logic errors, you find that the final total is incorrect. The following DISPLAYs will print *each input amount* and *the final total* as it is being accumulated:

```
200-CALC-RTN.
    :
    ADD AMT-IN TO WS-FIN-TOT.
    DISPLAY AMT-IN.
    DISPLAY WS-FIN-TOT.
```

In this way, you can check each addition to help isolate the error.

The DISPLAY statements should be placed at key locations in the program to test the outcome of specific arithmetic or logic instructions. During the run, the DISPLAY statements will print the contents of the named fields.

In the preceding example, you can check each addition by displaying the resulting field after each calculation. To ensure proper execution, you should step through the program manually, comparing your intermediate results with the displayed items.

The DISPLAY statement, then, can be used for debugging purposes to print intermediate results at crucial checkpoints in the program. If you are displaying a series of fields, it might be helpful to print the field name as a literal along with the data. A DISPLAY can print literals along with the contents of fields.

Examples

```
DISPLAY 'INPUT AMT = ', AMT-IN.
DISPLAY 'FINAL TOTAL = ', WS-FIN-TOT.
```

A DISPLAY statement is designed to output a *low volume* of data to some hardware device, most often a printer or CRT. It has two important uses in COBOL programs:

1. To provide output interactively.
   A request for a response to an inquiry made at a terminal might be provided with the use of a DISPLAY verb. We discuss this use of the DISPLAY in Chapter 19.
2. As a debugging aid.
   We have seen how a DISPLAY is used for printing fields in an effort to detect errors. In addition, a programmer frequently DISPLAYs records that are to be outputted to a disk or tape just to verify that they are correct. After the program has been fully debugged, this DISPLAY statement is then removed.

To say DISPLAY (identifier) will output the data to the computer center's standard display device, which is usually either a printer or a CRT.

Chapter 20 discusses more advanced methods for debugging a program.

II. Avoiding Logic Errors by Validating Input

A. Why Input to a Business System Must Be Validated

Programs written for business systems usually use input *defined and described by a systems analyst on an input layout form*. The programmer writes the program assuming that the actual input will conform to the format specified in this input layout form.

Most often the input itself is prepared by a data entry operator who keys it in from documents, such as sales slips and payroll forms; it is then stored on disk or some other machine-readable medium.

Most business systems have a large volume of input entered in this way. Because input to a business system tends to be voluminous, the risks of data entry or input errors are great. Steps must be taken by the systems analyst when designing the system to identify and correct these errors before they are processed by the computer. The programmer also should suggest *error control procedures* to be used in each program within the system to find input errors. We will consider the techniques used to validate data, that is, to determine if input fields have been entered properly. **Data validation** techniques are part of all well-designed programs.

All "real world" programs should include (1) routines that identify the various types of input errors that may occur and (2) error modules that print each specific error that has occurred.

B. Some Consequences of Invalid Input

1. Inaccurate Output

If a data entry operator enters a salary field for a payroll record as 43265 instead of 41265, the result will be inaccurate output. It would be extremely difficult for a program itself to find such an error. We must rely on the employees within the payroll department to double-check for such errors when records are created or updated.

Programs, then, cannot entirely eliminate some types of errors that will result in inaccurate output. They can, however, prevent many errors from being processed by making certain that the input is in the correct format and that it is *reasonable*. Thus, a salary field can be checked to make certain that it is numeric. It can also be checked to make certain that it falls within a normal range. For example, 15000 to 125000 may be reasonable limits for a given company's employee salaries and a program could check to make certain that each salary falls within that range. In this way, a salary entered as 257311 would be easily identified as an error.

Data validation procedures minimize the risk of an incorrectly entered field being processed. Finding these mistakes reduces the possibility of producing inaccurate output and improves the reliability of the program.

2. Logic Errors Resulting from Input Errors

One important component of data validation, then, is to detect input errors that will produce incorrect output. Sometimes, however, an input error can result in an *abend condition*, which means that the program cannot run at all with the given input.

Suppose an input field called NO-OF-COPIES-IN is used to determine the number of times we process a loop called 600-WRITE-A-MAILING-LABEL. In such a case we may code:

```
PERFORM 600-WRITE-A-MAILING-LABEL
    UNTIL WS-NO-OF-COPIES-PRODUCED = NO-OF-COPIES-IN.
    :
600-WRITE-A-MAILING-LABEL.
    :
    ADD 1 TO WS-NO-OF-COPIES-PRODUCED.
```

This program will work properly *only if* the input field called NO-OF-COPIES-IN contains valid data. This means it must contain either a 0 or a positive integer. If NO-OF-COPIES-IN is a negative number or has a nonnumeric value, then it will never equal WS-NO-OF-COPIES-PRODUCED. In such a case, the module 600-WRITE-A-MAILING-LABEL will be executed over and over again and the program will be in an *infinite loop*. The program will eventually abend when the operating system determines that the procedure is being executed endlessly. This type of input error, then, results in a logic error.

Well-designed programs should validate input to minimize the risk of such logic errors. Consider the following:

```
IF  NO-OF-COPIES-IN IS NOT NUMERIC
        OR IS < 0
    PERFORM 800-ERR-RTN
ELSE
    PERFORM 600-WRITE-A-MAILING-LABEL
        UNTIL WS-NO-OF-COPIES-PRODUCED = NO-OF-COPIES-IN.
```

The preceding example is just one illustration of the type of logic error that may occur if input is not valid.

Murphy's Law is one adage with which professional programmers are very familiar: if it is possible for something to go wrong, eventually it *will* go wrong. It is not unusual, for example, for programs that have been tested, debugged, and run regularly on a scheduled production basis to begin to produce errors. This situation will eventually arise if the programmer has not anticipated *every conceivable type of input error*; after a while, someone will enter input in an incorrect format and a program interrupt will occur.

Note that input errors are the cause of more programming problems than any other type of error. Validation procedures that can detect such errors will improve the overall reliability of computer-produced output.

C. Data Validation Techniques

In this section, we will focus on the programming methods that may be used to identify input errors.

1. Testing Fields to Ensure a Correct Format

a. The Class Test. Before actually processing input data, a program should first ensure that all input fields have the correct data format. If an input field is designated as numeric with a PIC of 9's, the programmer should make certain that the field is, in fact, numeric. Consider the following: ADD AMT-IN TO WS-TOTAL. If the AMT-IN field were erroneously entered as blanks or contained nonnumeric data, this could result in an abend condition or it could produce erroneous output.

The following program excerpt will minimize the risk of errors caused by fields that should contain numeric data but do not:

```
IF   AMT-IN IS NOT NUMERIC
     PERFORM 500-ERR-RTN
ELSE
     ADD AMT-IN TO WS-TOTAL.
```

It is good programming form, then, to test all fields to be used in arithmetic operations to make certain that they have numeric contents. This test should be made *before* performing the computations.

You will recall from Chapter 9 that the test for numeric data is called a **class test.** We review the instruction format for the class test here.

Format for Class Test

$$
\text{\underline{IF} identifier-1 \quad IS} \quad \begin{Bmatrix} \underline{\text{NUMERIC}} \\ \underline{\text{ALPHABETIC}} \end{Bmatrix} \quad \text{statement-1 \ldots}
$$

$$
[\underline{\text{ELSE}} \text{ statement-2 \ldots}]
$$

Use the NUMERIC class test to ensure that a field to be used in arithmetic has numeric value. If a field is to be alphabetic, you could similarly use the ALPHABETIC class test.

b. The Sign Test. If a numeric field is to have either positive or negative values, we may include a **sign test** to validate input data.

Format for Sign Test

$$
\text{\underline{IF} identifier-1 \quad IS} \quad \begin{Bmatrix} \underline{\text{POSITIVE}} \\ \underline{\text{NEGATIVE}} \\ \underline{\text{ZERO}} \end{Bmatrix} \quad \text{statement-1 \ldots}
$$

$$
[\underline{\text{ELSE}} \text{ statement-2 \ldots}]
$$

Use the class and sign tests to ensure that input data has the correct format. Note, however, that the identifier must have an S in its PIC clause when using the sign test. Without the S, the field will always be considered positive. An unsigned zero, however, is neither positive nor negative.

> Recall that we can say INITIALIZE REC-1, where REC-1 is a record subdivided into numeric and alphanumeric fields. The numeric fields will be set to zero and the alphanumeric fields will be set to spaces. This could minimize format errors later on.

2. Checking for Missing Data

One main source of error occurs when input fields are missing data. If a numeric field is to be used in either an arithmetic or a comparison operation, it *must contain numbers.* If it is blank, an abend will occur. In the following, each statement will result in an abend when executed, if AMT-IN is blank:

AMT-IN MUST BE NUMERIC

```
1. IF   AMT-IN < 65000
        PERFORM 100-OK-RTN.
2. ADD AMT-IN TO WS-TOTAL.
```

We should perform a validation routine prior to an arithmetic or comparison operation to avoid such abends:

```
IF   AMT-IN IS EQUAL TO SPACES
     PERFORM 900-ERR-RTN.
```

Another method for finding such errors is to use a class test. Testing an amount field for numeric data will avoid processing the field if it (1) has an invalid nonnumeric format or (2) is missing data.

3. The INSPECT Statement: Tallying and Replacing Specific Characters with Other Characters to Minimize Errors

The **INSPECT** statement may be used for replacing a specific character in a field with another character. It can also be used for counting the number of occurrences of a given character.

As noted, blanks in a numeric field will cause an abend condition if an arithmetic or a comparison operation is performed on the field. A common application of the INSPECT statement is to replace all blanks with zeros in numeric fields, or in an entire record. Because the INSPECT statement can substitute one character for another, it is an important part of validity checking routines.

An INSPECT statement also may be used for error control purposes. We may, for example, use the INSPECT to determine the number of erroneous characters that have been entered; we may wish to abort the run if the number of errors exceeds a predetermined value.

Although the INSPECT is commonly used for validity checking, it also has wider applicability. We will, therefore, consider this statement in its entirety. The two main functions of the INSPECT statement follow.

APPLICATIONS OF THE INSPECT STATEMENT

1. To count the number of occurrences of a given character in a field.
2. To replace specific occurrences of a given character with another character.

There are two basic formats of the INSPECT statement. Format 1 may be used to perform the first function just specified, that is, count the number of times a given character occurs.

Format 1

```
INSPECT identifier-1 TALLYING

    { identifier-2  FOR  { { ALL     }  { identifier-3 } }
    {                    { LEADING   }  { literal-1    } }
    {                    {           }                   }
    {                    { CHARACTERS }                  }

    [ { BEFORE }  INITIAL  { identifier-4 } ] } ...
    [ { AFTER  }           { literal-2    }   ]
```

Examples

```
     7 8   12    16    20    24    28    32    36    40    44    48    52    56    60    64    68    72
(1)      INSPECT ITEM-1 TALLYING CTR1 FOR ALL SPACES.
(2)      INSPECT ITEM-2 TALLYING CTR2 FOR CHARACTERS
         BEFORE INITIAL SPACE.
(3)      INSPECT ITEM-3 TALLYING CTR3 FOR LEADING ZEROS.
```

Items	Resulting Contents
ITEM-1 = ƀƀƀ67ƀ	CTR1 = 4
ITEM-2 = 01787ƀ	CTR2 = 5
ITEM-3 = 007800	CTR3 = 2

This format of the INSPECT statement will *always* count specified occurrences of identifier-3 or literal-1. Literal-1 must be a single character or a figurative constant. ZERO, SPACE, and 'X' are all valid entries for literal-1. The tallied count is placed in identifier-2, which is usually established as an elementary item in the WORKING-STORAGE SECTION. This count field is *not* automatically set to zero when the INSPECT is executed; thus the programmer must move 0 to the count field prior to each INSPECT instruction.

Example

```
MOVE 0 TO CTRA.
INSPECT ITEM-A TALLYING CTRA FOR ALL SPACES.
IF  CTRA > 0
    PERFORM 800-ERR-RTN.
```

An error routine is performed if *any* spaces exist in ITEM-A.

The BEFORE or AFTER INITIAL clause in Format 1 is an optional entry. If included, the count will be made according to the condition specified.

Statement	Meaning
INSPECT ITEM-B TALLYING CTRB FOR ALL '5' BEFORE INITIAL SPACE	Count the number of occurrences of the digit 5 until the first space is encountered.
INSPECT ITEM-C TALLYING CTRC FOR ALL '5' AFTER INITIAL SPACE	Count the number of occurrences of the digit 5 after the first space.

One of the following three clauses is required when using Format 1.

CLAUSES FOLLOWING FOR **IN THE** INSPECT **STATEMENT**
1. ALL $\begin{Bmatrix} \text{identifier-3} \\ \text{literal-1} \end{Bmatrix}$
2. LEADING $\begin{Bmatrix} \text{identifier-3} \\ \text{literal-1} \end{Bmatrix}$
3. CHARACTERS

1. If ALL is specified, *every* occurrence of the specified character in the field will be counted.

Examples

```
INSPECT ITEM-F TALLYING CTRF FOR ALL ZEROS.
INSPECT ITEM-F TALLYING CTRG FOR ALL ZEROS
     BEFORE INITIAL 2.
```

	ITEM-F		Resulting Value
	Before	*After*	
	102050	102050	CTRF = 3
	102050	102050	CTRG = 1

2. If LEADING is specified, all occurrences of the specified character *preceding any other character* will be tallied.

Examples

```
INSPECT ITEM-C TALLYING CTRH FOR LEADING 9.
INSPECT ITEM-C TALLYING CTRH FOR LEADING SPACE
     BEFORE INITIAL 2.
```

	ITEM-C		Resulting Value of CTRH
	Before	*After*	
	99129	99129	2
	ƀƀ12ƀ	ƀƀ12ƀ	2

3. If CHARACTERS is specified, *all characters* within the field will be tallied. This option may be used to determine the size of a field.

Examples

```
INSPECT ITEM-D TALLYING CTRQ FOR CHARACTERS.
INSPECT ITEM-D TALLYING CTRQ FOR CHARACTERS
     AFTER INITIAL 2.
```

	ITEM-D		Resulting Value of CTRQ
	Before	*After*	
	12300	12300	5
	12349	12349	3

Format 2 of the INSPECT statement will replace specified occurrences of a given character with another character. It will *not* tally the number of occurrences of any character.

Format 2

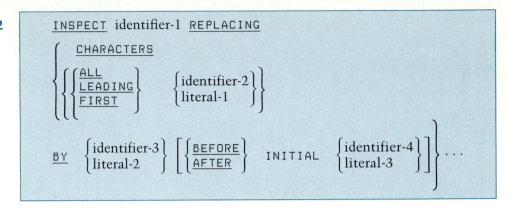

As in Format 1, literals must be single characters or figurative constants consistent with the type of field being inspected.

ALL, LEADING, and CHARACTERS have the same meaning as previously noted. If FIRST is specified in Format 2, then the first occurrence of literal-1 will be replaced by literal-2. That is, a single character replacement will occur if literal-1 is present in the field.

Examples

	ITEM-E	
	Before	*After*

```
7 8   12    16    20    24    28    32    36    40    44    48    52    56
    INSPECT ITEM-E REPLACING ALL 1 BY 2.
    INSPECT ITEM-E REPLACING LEADING '1' BY '2'.
    INSPECT ITEM-E REPLACING CHARACTERS BY '3'
        BEFORE INITIAL '2'.
    INSPECT ITEM-E REPLACING FIRST 'X' BY 'Y'.
```

Before	*After*
112111	222222
112111	222111
112111	332111
ABCXYZ	ABCYYZ

No counting operation is performed with Format 2. When using this format, rules for inserting characters in fields apply. Assume, for example, that we are inspecting a numeric field that has a PICTURE of 9's. We cannot replace a digit with an 'A' because 'A' is not a valid numeric character.

In summary, a primary use of the INSPECT statement is to replace blanks in a numeric field with zeros, but it has other uses as well. There are additional formats of the INSPECT that we will not discuss in this text.

Self-Test

1. The two major functions of the INSPECT statement are _____ and _____ .

2. (T or F) Literals in an INSPECT statement must be single characters or figurative constants.

For the following statements, fill in the missing columns, where applicable.

Statement	FLDX Before	After	Value of CTR1
3. INSPECT FLDX TALLYING CTR1 FOR ALL ZEROS.	10050		
4. INSPECT FLDX REPLACING ALL ZEROS BY SPACES.	10050		
5. INSPECT FLDX TALLYING CTR1 FOR LEADING ZEROS.	00057		

```
6.  INSPECT FLDX TALLYING              00579
    CTR1 FOR CHARACTERS
    BEFORE INITIAL '9'.
```

Solutions
1. to replace certain characters with other characters; to count the number of occurrences of a given character in a field
2. T

	FLDX	CTR1
3.	10050	3
4.	1ᵬᵬ5ᵬ	(Not used)
5.	00057	3
6.	00579	4

4. Testing for Reasonableness

As we have seen, it is usually not possible to determine definitively if input data is correct. This means that programmed routines can *minimize* the risk of errors going undetected, but they cannot be expected to detect *all* errors. Many of these routines include tests to determine if data is reasonable. Thus, although we may not be able to guarantee the validity of a salary field entered as 35000, for example, we can certainly flag as a probable error a salary field with a value of 998325. **Tests for reasonableness** include the following.

a. Range Tests.   One way to validate data is to make certain that fields pass a **range test**; that is, the value contained in a particular field should fall within pre-established guidelines. If an account number contains codes from 00001 to 85432 and also from 87001 to 89005, we may include a range test as part of our validity check:

```
IF (ACCOUNT-NO-IN > 00000 AND < 85433)
OR (ACCOUNT-NO-IN > 87000 AND < 89006)
    NEXT SENTENCE
ELSE
    PERFORM 600-ERR-RTN.
```

b. Limit Tests.   When a field is not to exceed a given limit we can perform a **limit test.** For example, a manager may establish a rule that the quantity on hand for any part must not exceed 980 units. The program should make certain that this limit is not exceeded:

```
IF  QTY-ON-HAND-IN > 980
    PERFORM 700-ERR-RTN.
```

Limit tests are important if a PERFORM statement is to be executed a fixed number of times depending on the contents of an input field. Suppose we wish to perform 600-WRITE-A-MAILING-LABEL a variable number of times depending on the contents of an input field called NO-OF-COPIES-IN, as noted previously. If NO-OF-COPIES-IN must be less than 7, for example, we should include a *limit test* before performing 600-WRITE-A-MAILING-LABEL:

```
        MOVE 0 TO WS-COUNTER.
        IF  NO-OF-COPIES-IN IS POSITIVE
                AND < 7
            PERFORM 600-WRITE-A-MAILING-LABEL
                UNTIL WS-COUNTER = NO-OF-COPIES-IN
        ELSE
            PERFORM 800-ERR-RTN.
          :
          :
    600-WRITE-A-MAILING-LABEL.
          :
          :
        ADD 1 TO WS-COUNTER.
```

With a range test, both ends of an identifier are compared, but with a limit test the comparison is in only one direction. To test that AMT1 is > 7 and < 25 is a *range test* but to test that AMT2 is > 250 is a *limit test*.

5. Condition-Names: Checking Coded Fields for Valid Contents

Coded fields are frequently used in input records to minimize keystrokes for data entry operators and to keep the input record format shorter and more manageable. Thus, a field used to indicate an individual's marital status is *not* likely to be keyed as "SINGLE," "MARRIED," "DIVORCED," and so on. Rather, MARITAL-STATUS is likely to be a one-position field that will be *coded* with a 1 to denote single, 2 for married, 3 for divorced, and so on. To make the coded field more easily understood, we may use instead 'M' for married, 'S' for single, and 'D' for divorced.

Programs should make certain that the contents of coded fields are valid. **Condition-names** are frequently used to facilitate the coding of error control procedures in a program.

We may use several condition-names along with one field:

```
05  GRADE                       PIC X.
    88  EXCELLENT               VALUE 'A'.
    88  GOOD                    VALUE 'B'.
    88  FAIR                    VALUE 'C'.
    88  POOR                    VALUE 'D'.
    88  FAILING                 VALUE 'F'.
```

Assuming that the above VALUEs are the only valid ones, a PROCEDURE DIVISION test may be as follows:

```
IF  EXCELLENT OR GOOD OR FAIR OR POOR OR FAILING
    NEXT SENTENCE
ELSE
    PERFORM 600-ERROR-RTN.
```

We may also say: IF NOT FAILING PERFORM 400-PASS-RTN, if we can be sure that the condition NOT FAILING guarantees an entry from A through D only. Or, we can code:

```
05  GRADE                       PIC X.
    88 CREDIT-GIVEN             VALUES 'A', 'B', 'C'.
    88 NO-CREDIT                VALUES 'D', 'F'.
        :
IF  CREDIT-GIVEN OR NO-CREDIT
    NEXT SENTENCE
ELSE
    PERFORM 600-ERROR-RTN.
```

A condition-name may contain a VALUE clause that specifies a range of values. The word THRU is used to indicate this range, as in the following:

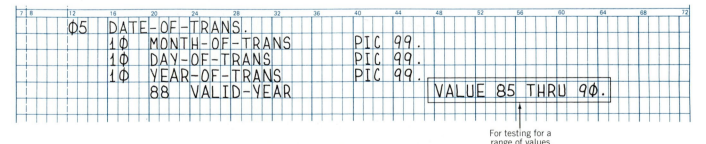

For testing for a range of values

The condition-name VALID-YEAR is "turned on" if YEAR-OF-TRANS, the field directly preceding it, has any value from 85 to 90 inclusive of the end points 85 and 90. Similarly, the statement IF NOT VALID-YEAR PERFORM

6OO-ERR-RTN will cause 6OO-ERR-RTN to be performed if YEAR-OF-TRANS is less than 85 or greater than 90.

In summary, condition-names are frequently used in the DATA DIVISION in conjunction with data validation routines.

6. Sequence Checking

Frequently, input records are entered in sequence by some control or **key field.** A Social Security number may be a key field for a payroll file, a customer number may be a key field for an accounts receivable file, and so on. A key field may also be a control field if it is used to signal a control break, as in the previous chapter.

If the keyed input data is intended to be in sequence, the actual order in which records are entered should be **sequenced checked.** Sometimes records are to be in **ascending,** or increasing, **sequence,** where the first record has a key field less than the next record, and so on; sometimes records are to be in **descending,** or decreasing, **sequence.**

For many types of procedures, such as control break processing, input records must be in sequence by the key or control field. Consider the following sequence error:

```
DEPT

 01
 01
 02   ◀──── Sequence error—DEPT 02 out of sequence
 01
 01
  .
  .
  .
```

If input is sequenced manually by a user or data entry operator, it would be useful to make certain, after each control break, that the current DEPT-IN is greater than or equal to the previous one stored in a hold area, WS-HOLD-DEPT, for example. If a current DEPT-IN is less than WS-HOLD-DEPT, then a *sequence error* has occurred and an error message should print. We may also wish to terminate processing in such a case.

Note that the systems analyst usually provides the programmer with the actions to be taken in case an input error occurs, such as a sequence error.

The following routine may be used for ensuring that an inventory file is in ascending PART-NO sequence, assuming that part numbers are numeric and that each input record has a unique part number (i.e., no two records have the same part number):

```
PROCEDURE DIVISION.
100-MAIN-MODULE.
    PERFORM 500-INITIALIZATION-RTN.
    READ INVENTORY-FILE
        AT END MOVE 'NO ' TO ARE-THERE-MORE-RECORDS.
    MOVE O TO WS-HOLD-PART.
    PERFORM 200-SEQUENCE-CHECK
        UNTIL THERE-ARE-NO-MORE-RECORDS.
        :
        :
    PERFORM 600-END-OF-JOB-RTN.
200-SEQUENCE-CHECK.
    IF  PART-NO > WS-HOLD-PART
        MOVE PART-NO TO WS-HOLD-PART
    ELSE
        PERFORM 500-ERR-RTN.
    READ INVENTORY-FILE
        AT END MOVE 'NO ' TO ARE-THERE-MORE-RECORDS.
```

TYPICAL VALIDITY CHECKS

1. Determine if numeric data fields do, in fact, contain numeric data. The *class test* is as follows:

```
IF identifier IS NUMERIC...
```

2. Determine if alphabetic data fields do, in fact, contain alphabetic data. The *class test* is as follows:

```
IF identifier IS ALPHABETIC...
```

3. Determine if data is missing. This can be accomplished with the following test:

```
IF identifier IS EQUAL TO SPACES...
```

4. Use the INSPECT statement to replace all blanks with zeros in numeric fields.

5. Determine if the value of a field falls within an established range; this is called a *range test*.

   Example: The value of a PART-NO field may be between 001 and 215, 287 and 336, or 415 and 555.

6. Determine if the value in a field does not exceed an established limit; this is called a *limit test*.

   Example: The value in a SALARY field is within the required limit if it is less than 95000, for example. That is, if $95000 is the highest salary paid, no salary should be greater than $95000.

7. Determine if specified fields contain valid codes or values. Use *condition-names* to help document such routines.

   Example

```
05   MODEL-CAR              PIC 9.
        88   COUPE           VALUE 1.
        88   SEDAN           VALUE 2.
        88   CONVERTIBLE     VALUE 3.
         :
IF   COUPE OR SEDAN OR CONVERTIBLE
     NEXT SENTENCE
ELSE
     PERFORM 800-ERROR-RTN.
```

   or

```
IF   NOT COUPE AND NOT SEDAN AND NOT CONVERTIBLE
     PERFORM 800-ERROR-RTN.
```

8. Determine, where applicable, if input records are in proper sequence, either ascending or descending, based on the control or key field.

D. Using the EVALUATE Verb for Data Validation

With COBOL 85 we use the **EVALUATE** verb to implement the **case structure,** which is a logical control construct described in Chapter 5. This verb can test for a series of conditions like those in data validation routines.

Suppose an input field called YEARS-IN-COLLEGE-IN is used to determine the type of processing to be performed. We could code:

```
IF  YEARS-IN-COLLEGE-IN = 1
    PERFORM 300-FRESHMAN-RTN.
IF  YEARS-IN-COLLEGE-IN = 2
    PERFORM 400-SOPHOMORE-RTN.
IF  YEARS-IN-COLLEGE-IN = 3
    PERFORM 500-JUNIOR-RTN.
IF  YEARS-IN-COLLEGE-IN = 4
    PERFORM 600-SENIOR-RTN.
```

To ensure correct processing, we must add a fifth condition to perform an error routine if the input field is invalid:

```
IF  YEARS-IN-COLLEGE-IN IS NOT = 1 AND NOT = 2
      AND NOT = 3 AND NOT = 4
    PERFORM 700-ERR-RTN.
```

The EVALUATE verb enables the series of cases to be coded more clearly and in a structured form:

```
EVALUATE YEARS-IN-COLLEGE-IN
    WHEN 1      PERFORM 300-FRESHMAN-RTN
    WHEN 2      PERFORM 400-SOPHOMORE-RTN
    WHEN 3      PERFORM 500-JUNIOR-RTN
    WHEN 4      PERFORM 600-SENIOR-RTN
    WHEN OTHER PERFORM 700-ERR-RTN.
```

The clause WHEN OTHER ... is executed when YEARS-IN-COLLEGE-IN is not 1, 2, 3, or 4. The flowchart for this case structure is in Figure 13.1.

The EVALUATE verb has the following instruction format:

Format

> EVALUATE $\begin{Bmatrix} \text{identifier-1} \\ \text{expression-1} \end{Bmatrix}$
>
>   WHEN condition-1   imperative-statement-1 ...
>
>   [WHEN OTHER   imperative-statement-2]
>
> [END-EVALUATE]

The full instruction format for the EVALUATE verb is more complex, but the format given here includes the basic elements. Note that condition-1 may be a value that identifier-1 can assume or a condition-name associated with identifier-1. We may also use a THRU clause with the EVALUATE. Suppose you wish to print class grades based on a student's average. The following is valid:

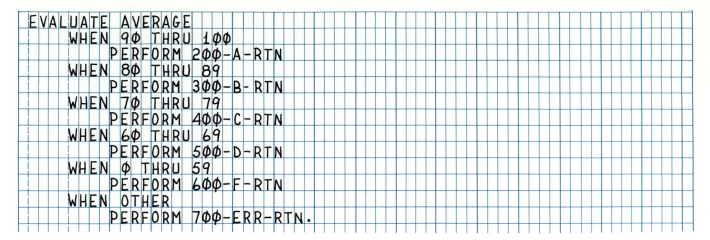

```
EVALUATE AVERAGE
    WHEN 90 THRU 100
        PERFORM 200-A-RTN
    WHEN 80 THRU 89
        PERFORM 300-B-RTN
    WHEN 70 THRU 79
        PERFORM 400-C-RTN
    WHEN 60 THRU 69
        PERFORM 500-D-RTN
    WHEN 0 THRU 59
        PERFORM 600-F-RTN
    WHEN OTHER
        PERFORM 700-ERR-RTN.
```

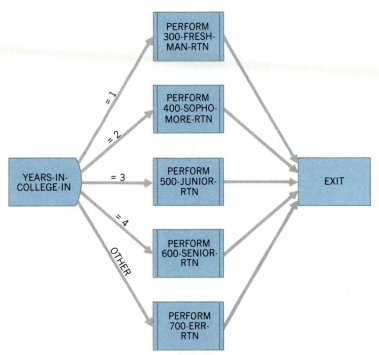

Figure 13.1
Flowchart for sample case structure.

We can also use the EVALUATE in conjunction with condition-names:

```
EVALUATE GRADE
    WHEN EXCELLENT PERFORM 500-A-RTN
    WHEN GOOD       PERFORM 600-B-RTN.
```

In this instance, GRADE would have condition-names associated with it as follows:

```
05  GRADE              PIC X.
    88  EXCELLENT       VALUE 'A'.
    88  GOOD            VALUE 'B'.
```

Expanding the Format

The EVALUATE statement can be coded in numerous ways. The following are the two most common:

1. EVALUATE identifier
       WHEN value(s) PERFORM ...

Example
```
EVALUATE AGE
     WHEN 0 THRU 19 PERFORM 400-MINOR-RTN
     WHEN 20 THRU 99 PERFORM 500-ADULT-RTN.
```

2. EVALUATE condition
```
     WHEN TRUE PERFORM ...
     WHEN FALSE PERFORM ...
```

TRUE and FALSE are COBOL reserved words that mean "if the condition is met" and "if the condition is not met," respectively.

Example
```
EVALUATE AGE <= 19
     WHEN TRUE PERFORM 400-MINOR-RTN
     WHEN FALSE PERFORM 500-ADULT-RTN.
```

Note, however, that the following is incorrect:

Invalid
```
EVALUATE AGE
     WHEN <= 19 PERFORM 400-MINOR-RTN.
```

When evaluating an *identifier*, the WHEN clause must specify precise values—for example, WHEN 1, WHEN 0 THRU 10, and so on.

In summary, the EVALUATE verb can be used to test the results of a series of conditions. It has numerous applications and is often used for validating data. That is, with the EVALUATE you test for all the valid entries in a field and then include a WHEN OTHER clause to determine if there is an invalid value in the field.

E. Other Methods for Validating Data

1. Use of Control Listings for Manual Validation of Input

Computer errors commonly result from erroneous input, but they can also result from an intentional attempt to sabotage or defraud the company.

One major method for minimizing the risk of any errors going undetected is to print a **control listing** that includes (1) the identifying data or key field in each input record, (2) any errors encountered, and (3) totals of amounts accumulated for groups of input records processed. Typically, an individual in the user organization is charged with the task of checking this control listing to make certain that the processing was performed correctly. Figure 13.2 illustrates a Printer Spacing Chart that describes a sample control listing. Most organizations require a control listing when output is to be produced on disk or tape, since these media are not visually readable.

2. Verification as a Means of Validating Input

Another way to minimize keying errors is to verify all data entered by using a rekeying or **verification procedure.** This verification procedure checks to see that the data originally keyed is the same as the data being keyed the second time. If it is not, then the operator who is verifying the data must find each error and correct it. Another way to verify data is to have an operator key it in, transmit it to the CPU, and have the computer "echo" it back to verify that what was transmitted is correct.

A verification procedure will detect approximately 90% of all data entry errors. Although this process minimizes mistakes, 10% of input errors still go

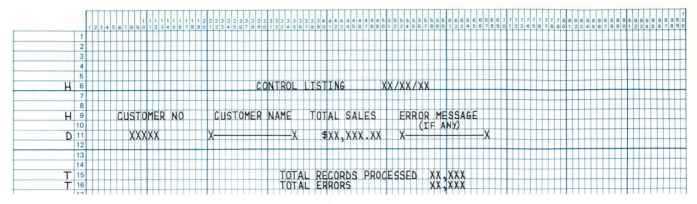

Figure 13.2
Printer Spacing Chart for a
sample control listing.

undetected. A combination of manual checking and programmed controls is
used to find most or all input errors.

III. What to Do If Input Errors Occur

Various types of procedures may be employed when input errors are detected.
The systems analyst, programmer, and user work closely together to establish
the most productive course of action to be followed when errors occur.

We consider several procedures, any one of which may be used in a program.

A. Stop the Run

If a major error occurs, it may be best simply to stop the run. This procedure
is followed when data integrity is the primary consideration and errors must
be kept to an absolute minimum. Usually, there is an employee in the user
department responsible for checking the data; he or she would need to correct
the error and arrange for the job to be restarted.

If your program is to terminate because of an error, remember to close all
files before stopping and to display or print a message explaining why the job
is being stopped.

B. Print an Error Record Containing the Key Field, the Contents of the Erroneous Field, and an Error Message

Errors should always be clearly displayed with an appropriate message. The
key field that identifies each erroneous record must also be included.

Example

Soc Sec No	Employee Name	Error
080-65-2113	BROWN JOSEPH	SALARY FIELD IS BLANK
092-11-7844	LOPEZ MARIA	MARITAL STATUS FIELD IS INVALID (= 'Q')

In addition, a count should be maintained of the number of occurrences of
each specific type of error. A user would be responsible for correcting all errors
that have occurred. This user can use the count field to determine if any major
programming or systems problem exists. That is, if the count of a specific
type of error is excessive, there may be a program error, or a data entry operator
may be making a particular mistake repeatedly.

C. Partially Process or Bypass Erroneous Records

Once an error is detected, the program could either (1) proceed to the next record, bypassing the erroneous record entirely, or (2) process some portion of the erroneous record. This, again, is a function of user needs.

Sometimes, for example, an erroneously entered numeric field is replaced with zeros; sometimes it is simply ignored.

D. Stop the Run If the Number of Errors Exceeds a Predetermined Limit

Sometimes we wish to continue processing even if errors occur, but if such errors become excessive, we stop the run. Consider the following error routine:

```
700-ERR-RTN.
    WRITE PRINT-REC FROM ERR-LINE.
    ADD 1 TO WS-SEQUENCE-ERRORS.
    IF  WS-SEQUENCE-ERRORS > 25
        MOVE ' JOB TERMINATED: SEQUENCE ERRORS EXCEED 25'
            TO PRINT-REC
        WRITE PRINT-REC
        CLOSE INFILE
              OUTFILE
        STOP RUN.
```

E. Use Switches

Suppose we perform multiple validity tests on each record and we wish to process valid records only, that is, records without any errors. We may use a **switch** for this purpose. We begin with a field called ERR-SWITCH initialized at 0. If any error occurs, we move 1 to ERR-SWITCH in each error routine.

After all validity tests, we test ERR-SWITCH. If it contains a 1, we know an error has occurred and we proceed accordingly. If ERR-SWITCH is a 0, then no error has occurred. Before processing each new record, be sure to reinitialize ERR-SWITCH at 0.

The field called ERR-SWITCH is actually a one-position field that will contain either a 0 or a 1. We may use condition-names to clarify this for documentation purposes:

```
01  ERR-SWITCH                  PIC 9.
    88  ERROR-HAS-OCCURRED      VALUE 1.
    88  NO-ERROR-HAS-OCCURRED   VALUE 0.
        :
        :
300-VALIDITY-TESTS.
    :
    :
    IF  ERROR-HAS-OCCURRED
        MOVE 0 TO ERR-SWITCH.
    ELSE
        PERFORM 500-OK-ROUTINE.
    READ ...
```

or

```
    IF  NO-ERROR-HAS-OCCURRED
        PERFORM 500-OK-ROUTINE
    ELSE
        MOVE 0 TO ERR-SWITCH.
    READ ...
```

F. Print Totals

1. Print a Count of All Records and a Count of All Errors

All programs should provide a count of records processed as well as a count of errors that have occurred. To determine the number of records processed, we simply ADD 1 TO WS-TOTAL-RECORDS each time we process a record and print the contents of WS-TOTAL-RECORDS at the end of the job. In most systems, a user is responsible for counting the number of records to be entered before processing begins. This person later compares the manually tabulated total to the total number of records processed and counted by the computer. The totals should match. If they do not match, records may have been misplaced or lost. The user must then find the discrepancy and correct the problem.

2. Print a Batch Total

If large groups of input records are processed during each run, a single count of all records may be insufficient to track down missing records. In this case, we might include **batch totals,** where we print a count of all records within specific groups or batches of records. Suppose we process transactions by TRANS-NO. We may include batch totals as follows:

```
        TOTAL RECORDS PROCESSED            1131
        RECORDS WITH TRANS-NO 001-082        48
        RECORDS WITH TRANS-NO 083-115        53
        RECORDS WITH TRANS-NO 116-246       387
        RECORDS WITH TRANS-NO 247-383       226
        RECORDS WITH TRANS-NO 384-452       417
```

Each individual total is called a *batch total.* A user manually determines the records to be processed in each batch before the data has been entered as input. The manual batch totals should match the computer-produced ones. If not, the user can track down the record or records that were not processed in the specific batch.

The program itself can be used to compare the manual batch totals to the computed ones. To do this, the manual batch totals are entered *along with the input.* Methods of entering manual batch totals include: (1) a control record, which may be the first record in the file containing batch total information, and (2) a separator record, which contains manual totals placed between groups or batches.

IV. When Data Should Be Validated

All programs to be run on a regularly scheduled basis should include data validation techniques designed to minimize errors. From this point on in the text, we will consider such techniques when discussing program excerpts. But Practice Programs at the end of each chapter will focus on illustrating the specific topics discussed in the chapter and, in the interest of brevity, will *not* focus on data validation techniques. The set of Review Questions at the end of each chapter, however, will ask you to modify the Practice Program to include the appropriate data validation routines.

CHAPTER SUMMARY

A. Types of Program Errors
1. Syntax errors—correct them before executing the program.
2. Logic errors—use a READY TRACE and/or DISPLAY to find these errors.

B. Validating Data to Minimize Errors
1. Error control procedures will minimize errors but will not eliminate them entirely.
2. Types of error control procedures
a. Range tests—to ensure that data falls within a pre-established range.
b. Limit tests—to ensure that data does not exceed a pre-established limit.
c. Format tests—to ensure, for example, that numeric fields do, in fact, contain numeric data.
d. Tests for missing data—to ensure that all critical fields contain nonzero or nonblank data.
e. Sequence checks—to ensure that data is in the correct sequence.
3. INSPECT
a. To replace invalid characters with valid ones.
b. To count the occurrences of invalid characters.
4. Use condition-names to specify given values that identifiers may assume.
5. Use EVALUATE verb to test for conditions if you are using COBOL 85.

C. Methods for Detecting Input Errors
1. Print control listings to be checked by the user department.
a. A control listing contains the key field and other identifying data for every record created, updated, or changed.
b. The control listing also indicates the total number of records processed and any errors encountered.
2. Verify input data.
a. Data keyed in may be rechecked through a rekeying or verification procedure.
b. If the rekeying produces different entries than the initial data entry, the reason for each discrepancy must be determined and corrective action taken.

D. How to Handle Input Errors
1. If critical errors occur, stop the run.
2. Always print error messages indicating all errors.
3. Fill erroneous fields with blanks or zeros.
4. Count the occurrences of errors and stop the run if the number of errors is considered excessive.

CHAPTER SELF-TEST

1. (T or F) If a program is written properly, all input errors will be detected.

2. A _____ is a printed report indicating records processed and errors found.

3. A _____ procedure is the process of rekeying input to ensure that it was entered correctly the first time.

4. The _____ statement is used to replace erroneous characters in an input field with other characters.

5. A _____ is the name assigned to a value of the field directly preceding it in the DATA DIVISION.

6. The sign test IF A IS NEGATIVE will produce correct results only if A has a(n) _____ in its PICTURE clause.

7. (T or F) A programmer should always stop a run if an input error is detected.

8. A count of all records within specific groups is referred to as a _____ total.

9. The _____ verb is used in COBOL 85 for the case structure.

10. (T or F) Condition-names can be used with WHEN clauses and the EVALUATE verb.

Solutions

1. F—One can only hope to minimize input errors, not eliminate them entirely.
2. control listing
3. verification
4. `INSPECT`
5. condition-name
6. `S`
7. F—Some errors can be handled by zeroing out erroneous fields, for example.
8. batch
9. `EVALUATE`
10. T

PRACTICE PROGRAM

Consider the following problem definition.

Systems Flowchart

TRANSACTION-FILE
100-position records
standard labels

CHAP13
SAMPLE
PROGRAM

ERROR-LISTING

TRANSACTION-FILE Record Layout

SS-NO	EMPL-NAME	EMPL-ADDR	TRANS CODE	ANNUAL SALARY	MARITAL STATUS	LEVEL	DEPT	
1 9	10 29	30 49	50	51 55	56	57	58 59	60 100
(NUMERIC)	(NON-BLANK)	(NON-BLANK)	(1-9)	(RANGE: 15000-87000)	(D, W, OR S)	(1-6)	(10,20, or 25)	

VALIDITY CHECKS:

ERROR-LISTING Printer Spacing Chart

```
H  6    LISTING OF TRANSACTION ERRORS        PAGE XX            XX/XX/XX
D  8  X                          X      X                    X       X                    X
      (NAME-OUT)                        (ERROR-MESSAGE)              (FIELD-IN-ERROR)
```

Sample Input Data

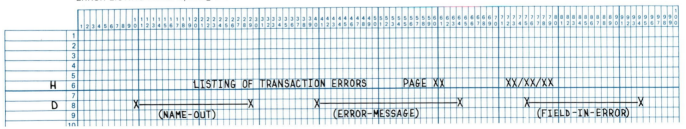

```
080243567PAUL NEWMAN          11 MAIN ST., NYC     118000D310
090263442LINDA GRAY           50 SPRING ST., NYC   021000D520
113547892ROBERT REDFORD       50 3RD AVE., NYC     612000S625
048239261JOAN COLLINS         20 SUTTER PL., NYC   886000Q510
070235826LARRY HAGMAN         40-21 3RD ST., NYC   943000R710
092487331JOHN SMITH           41 3RD AVE., NYC     943000S614
```

Sample Output

```
                 LISTING OF TRANSACTION ERRORS      PAGE   1            01/29/88
NAME                                ERROR MESSAGE                      VALUE IN ERROR FIELD

PAUL NEWMAN                         A-OK                               0

LINDA GRAY                          TRANS CODE IS INVALID              0

ROBERT REDFORD                      SALARY IS INVALID                  12000

JOAN COLLINS                        MARITAL STATUS IS INVALID          Q

LARRY HAGMAN                        MARITAL STATUS IS INVALID          R

LARRY HAGMAN                        LEVEL IS INVALID                   7

JOHN SMITH                          DEPT IS INVALID                    14
```

Figure 13.3 illustrates the pseudocode and hierarchy chart. Figure 13.4 shows a suggested solution.

Figure 13.3
Pseudocode and hierarchy chart for the Practice Program.

Pseudocode

```
PERFORM
    Open the Files
    Read and Store Date
ENDPERFORM
PERFORM
    Write Headings
    Initialize Line Counter
ENDPERFORM
Read a Record
PERFORM UNTIL no more data
    Move Name to Output Area
    IF Social Security Number is not numeric
    THEN
        PERFORM
            Write Error Record
            Increment Line Counter
            Increment Error Counter
        ENDPERFORM
    ENDIF
    IF  Name is blank
    THEN
        PERFORM
            Write Error Record
            Increment Line Counter
            Increment Error Counter
        ENDPERFORM
    ENDIF
    IF  Address is blank
    THEN
        PERFORM
            Write Error Record
            Increment Line Counter
            Increment Error Counter
        ENDPERFORM
    ENDIF
    IF  Code is erroneous
    THEN
        PERFORM
            Write Error Record
            Increment Line Counter
            Increment Error Counter
        ENDPERFORM
    ENDIF
    IF  Salary is not within required range
    THEN
        PERFORM
            Write Error Record
            Increment Line Counter
            Increment Error Counter
        ENDPERFORM
    ENDIF
    IF  Marital-status is erroneous
    THEN
        PERFORM
            Write Error Record
            Increment Line Counter
            Increment Error Counter
        ENDPERFORM
    ENDIF
    IF  Level is erroneous
    THEN
        PERFORM
            Write Error Record
            Increment Line Counter
            Increment Error Counter
        ENDPERFORM
    ENDIF
    IF  Dept is erroneous
    THEN
        PERFORM
            Write Error Record
            Increment Line Counter
            Increment Error Counter
        ENDPERFORM
```

Figure 13.3
(continued)

```
ENDIF
IF  no errors
THEN
        Write 'A-OK' line
ENDIF
IF  page overflow
THEN
        PERFORM
                Write Headings
                Reinitialize Line Counter
        ENDPERFORM
ENDIF
Read a Record
ENDPERFORM
PERFORM
        End-of-Job Operations
ENDPERFORM
```

Hierarchy Chart

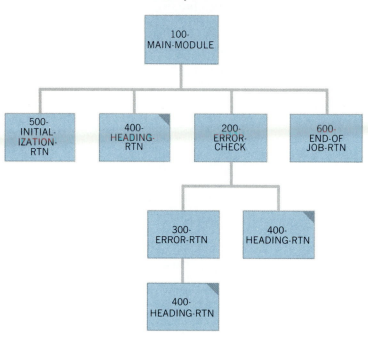

Figure 13.4
Solution to the Practice
Program.

```
IDENTIFICATION DIVISION.
PROGRAM-ID. SAMPLE.
***************************************************
*   VALIDATES TRANSACTION FILE AND PRINTS ERRORS   *
***************************************************
ENVIRONMENT DIVISION.
INPUT-OUTPUT SECTION.
FILE-CONTROL.
    SELECT TRANS-FILE-IN  ASSIGN TO INVALID1.
    SELECT ERROR-LIST-OUT ASSIGN TO SYS$OUTPUT.
*
DATA DIVISION.
FILE SECTION.
FD   TRANS-FILE-IN
     LABEL RECORDS ARE STANDARD.
01   TRANS-REC-IN.
     05   SS-NO-IN                      PIC 9(9).
     05   NAME-IN                       PIC X(20).
     05   EMPL-ADDR-IN                  PIC X(20).
     05   TRANS-CODE-IN                 PIC 9.
          88   VALID-CODE-IN                         VALUE 1 THRU 9.
     05   ANNUAL-SALARY-IN              PIC 9(5).
          88   ACCEPTABLE-SALARY-RANGE-IN            VALUE 15000 THRU 87000.

     05   MARITAL-STATUS-IN             PIC X.
          88   MARRIED                               VALUE 'M'.
          88   SINGLE                                VALUE 'S'.
          88   DIVORCED                              VALUE 'D'.
          88   WIDOWED                               VALUE 'W'.
```

Figure 13.4
(continued)

```
           05   LEVEL-IN                          PIC 9.
               88   ACCEPTABLE-LEVEL-IN                         VALUE 1 THRU 6.
           05   DEPT-IN                           PIC 99.
           05   FILLER                            PIC X(41).
       FD   ERROR-LIST-OUT
           LABEL RECORDS OMITTED.
       01   ERROR-REC-OUT                         PIC X(133).
       WORKING-STORAGE SECTION.
       01   WS-AREAS.
           05   ARE-THERE-MORE-RECORDS            PIC X(3)     VALUE 'YES'.
               88   MORE-RECORDS                                VALUE 'YES'.
               88   NO-MORE-RECORDS                             VALUE 'NO '.
           05   WS-LINE-CT                        PIC 99       VALUE ZEROS.
           05   WS-DATE                           PIC 9(6).
           05   WS-DATE-X REDEFINES WS-DATE.
               10   WS-YR                         PIC 99.
               10   WS-MO                         PIC 99.
               10   WS-DA                         PIC 99.
           05   WS-ERROR-CT                       PIC 9        VALUE ZERO.
           05   WS-PAGE-CT                        PIC 99       VALUE ZEROS.
       01   HL-HEADING-1.
           05   FILLER                            PIC X(20)    VALUE SPACES.
           05   FILLER                            PIC X(35)
               VALUE 'LISTING OF TRANSACTION ERRORS'.
           05   FILLER                            PIC X(5)
               VALUE 'PAGE '.
           05   HL-PAGE-NO                        PIC Z9.
           05   FILLER                            PIC X(10)    VALUE SPACES.
           05   HL-DATE.
               10   HL-MO                         PIC 99.
               10   FILLER                        PIC X        VALUE '/'.
               10   HL-DA                         PIC 99.
               10   FILLER                        PIC X        VALUE '/'.
               10   HL-YR                         PIC 99.
           05   FILLER                            PIC X(53)    VALUE SPACES.
       01   HL-HEADER-2.
           05   FILLER                            PIC X(10)    VALUE SPACES.
           05   FILLER                            PIC X(30)
               VALUE 'NAME'.
           05   FILLER                            PIC X(35)
               VALUE 'ERROR MESSAGE'.
           05   FILLER                            PIC X(58)
               VALUE 'VALUE IN ERROR FIELD'.
       01   DL-DETAIL-LINE.
           05   FILLER                            PIC X(10)    VALUE SPACES.
           05   DL-NAME                           PIC X(20).
           05   FILLER                            PIC X(10)    VALUE SPACES.
           05   DL-ERROR-MESSAGE                  PIC X(25).
           05   FILLER                            PIC X(10)    VALUE SPACES.
           05   DL-FIELD-IN-ERROR                 PIC X(20).
           05   FILLER                            PIC X(38)    VALUE SPACES.
       *
       PROCEDURE DIVISION.
       ***************************************
       *  CONTROLS DIRECTION OF PROGRAM LOGIC  *
       *  AND READS THE FIRST RECORD.          *
       ***************************************
       100-MAIN-MODULE.
           PERFORM 500-INITIALIZATION-RTN.
           PERFORM 400-HEADING-RTN.
           READ TRANS-FILE-IN
               AT END MOVE 'NO ' TO ARE-THERE-MORE-RECORDS.
           PERFORM 200-ERROR-CHECK
               UNTIL NO-MORE-RECORDS.
           PERFORM 600-END-OF-JOB-RTN.
       *************************************************************
       *  PERFORMED FROM 100-MAIN-MODULE TESTS INPUT DATA FOR ERRORS  *
       *  AND READS THE NEXT RECORD.                                  *
       *************************************************************
       200-ERROR-CHECK.
           MOVE NAME-IN TO DL-NAME.
           MOVE ZEROS TO WS-LINE-CT.
           IF  SS-NO-IN NOT NUMERIC
               MOVE SS-NO-IN TO DL-FIELD-IN-ERROR
               MOVE 'SS NO IS INVALID' TO DL-ERROR-MESSAGE
               PERFORM 300-ERROR-RTN.
           IF  NAME-IN = SPACES
               MOVE NAME-IN TO DL-FIELD-IN-ERROR
```

Figure 13.4
(continued)

```
                            MOVE 'NAME IS INVALID' TO DL-ERROR-MESSAGE
                            PERFORM 300-ERROR-RTN.
                   IF    EMPL-ADDR-IN = SPACES
                            MOVE EMPL-ADDR-IN TO DL-FIELD-IN-ERROR
                            MOVE 'ADDRESS IS INVALID' TO DL-ERROR-MESSAGE
                            PERFORM 300-ERROR-RTN.
                   IF    NOT VALID-CODE-IN
                            MOVE TRANS-CODE-IN TO DL-FIELD-IN-ERROR
                            MOVE 'TRANS CODE IS INVALID' TO DL-ERROR-MESSAGE
                            PERFORM 300-ERROR-RTN.
                   IF    NOT ACCEPTABLE-SALARY-RANGE-IN
                            MOVE ANNUAL-SALARY-IN TO DL-FIELD-IN-ERROR
                            MOVE 'SALARY IS INVALID' TO DL-ERROR-MESSAGE
                            PERFORM 300-ERROR-RTN.
                   IF    NOT MARRIED AND NOT SINGLE AND NOT DIVORCED AND NOT WIDOWED
                            MOVE MARITAL-STATUS-IN TO DL-FIELD-IN-ERROR
                            MOVE 'MARITAL STATUS IS INVALID' TO DL-ERROR-MESSAGE
                            PERFORM 300-ERROR-RTN.
                   IF    NOT ACCEPTABLE-LEVEL-IN
                            MOVE LEVEL-IN TO DL-FIELD-IN-ERROR
                            MOVE 'LEVEL IS INVALID' TO DL-ERROR-MESSAGE
                            PERFORM 300-ERROR-RTN.
                   IF    DEPT-IN NOT = 10 AND NOT = 20 AND NOT = 25
                            MOVE DEPT-IN TO DL-FIELD-IN-ERROR
                            MOVE 'DEPT IS INVALID' TO DL-ERROR-MESSAGE
                            PERFORM 300-ERROR-RTN.
                   IF    WS-ERROR-CT = ZERO
                            MOVE WS-ERROR-CT TO DL-FIELD-IN-ERROR
                            MOVE 'A-OK' TO DL-ERROR-MESSAGE
                            WRITE ERROR-REC-OUT FROM DL-DETAIL-LINE
                                   AFTER ADVANCING 2 LINES
                   ELSE
                            MOVE ZEROS TO WS-ERROR-CT.
                   IF    WS-LINE-CT > 25
                            PERFORM 400-HEADING-RTN.
                   READ TRANS-FILE-IN
                            AT END MOVE 'NO ' TO ARE-THERE-MORE-RECORDS.
           ***************************************************************
           *  PERFORMED FROM 200-ERROR-CHECK, PRINTS THE ERROR MESSAGES, *
           *                              WHEN ERRORS OCCUR.             *
           ***************************************************************
            300-ERROR-RTN.
                   WRITE ERROR-REC-OUT FROM DL-DETAIL-LINE
                            AFTER ADVANCING 2 LINES.
                   ADD 1 TO WS-LINE-CT.
                   IF    WS-LINE-CT > 25
                            PERFORM 400-HEADING-RTN.
                   ADD 1 TO WS-ERROR-CT.
           *****************************************************************
           *  PERFORMED FROM 100-MAIN-MODULE, 200-ERROR-CHECK, 300-ERROR-RTN *
           *  PRINTS OUT HEADINGS AFTER NEW PAGE, ZEROS OUT LINE CTR.      *
           *****************************************************************
            400-HEADING-RTN.
                   ADD 1 TO WS-PAGE-CT.
                   MOVE WS-PAGE-CT TO HL-PAGE-NO.
                   WRITE ERROR-REC-OUT FROM HL-HEADING-1
                            AFTER ADVANCING PAGE.
                   WRITE ERROR-REC-OUT FROM HL-HEADER-2
                            AFTER ADVANCING 1 LINES.
                   MOVE ZEROS TO WS-LINE-CT.
           ********************************************************
           *  PERFORMED FROM 100-MAIN-MODULE. OPENS THE FILES,  *
           *  READS IN THE CURRENT DATE & PERFORMS INITIAL READ *
           ********************************************************
            500-INITIALIZATION-RTN.
                   OPEN INPUT  TRANS-FILE-IN
                            OUTPUT ERROR-LIST-OUT.
                   ACCEPT WS-DATE FROM DATE.
                   MOVE WS-MO TO HL-MO.
                   MOVE WS-DA TO HL-DA.
                   MOVE WS-YR TO HL-YR.
           ****************************************************
           *  PERFORMED FROM 100-MAIN-MODULE, CLOSES FILES  *
           *  AND RETURNS CONTROL TO OPERATING SYSTEM       *
           ****************************************************
            600-END-OF-JOB-RTN.
                   CLOSE TRANS-FILE-IN
                            ERROR-LIST-OUT.
                   STOP RUN.
```

KEY TERMS

Ascending sequence	Descending sequence	`READY TRACE`
Batch total	Diagnostic message	Sequence checking
Case structure	`EVALUATE`	Sign test
Class test	`INSPECT`	Switch
Coded field	Key field	Syntax error
Condition-name	Limit test	Test data
Control listing	Murphy's Law	Test for reasonableness
Data validation	Program interrupt	Verification procedure
Default	Range test	

REVIEW QUESTIONS

T F

True-False Questions

__ __   1. Examples of batch totals are counts of records with transaction numbers 1–100, 101–200, and so on.

__ __   2. Control listings are considered optional and, in fact, are rarely produced by a program.

3. Consider the following:

```
05   FLDX        PIC 9.
     88  X-ON    VALUE 1.
```

__ __   The condition `FLDX = 1` may be referred to as `X-ON`.

__ __   4. In Question 3, we could code a `PROCEDURE DIVISION` entry as follows:

```
IF   X-ON = 1
     PERFORM 200-X-RTN.
```

__ __   5. An abend will cause the computer to terminate a run.

__ __   6. Data verification is rarely used to minimize errors, since it only eliminates a small percentage of data entry mistakes.

__ __   7. If a field `IS NOT ALPHABETIC`, then it must be `NUMERIC`.

__ __   8. If a field `IS NOT POSITIVE`, then it must be `NEGATIVE`.

__ __   9. An `INSPECT` statement can be used both to replace one character with another and to count the number of occurrences of a character.

__ __ 10. To reduce the number of characters in an input record, we frequently use coded fields.

DEBUGGING EXERCISES

Consider the following program excerpt:

```
01   REC-IN.
     05   ACCT-NO       PIC X(5).
     05   SALARY        PIC 9(4).
     05   AMT2          PIC 9(3).
     05   STATUS-CODE   PIC 9.
PROCEDURE DIVISION.
100-MAIN-MODULE.
     OPEN INPUT  TRANS-FILE
          OUTPUT PRINT-FILE.
```

```
        READ TRANS-FILE
            AT END MOVE 'NO ' TO ARE-THERE-MORE-RECORDS.
        PERFORM 200-EDIT-CHECK
            UNTIL THERE-ARE-NO-MORE-RECORDS.
        PERFORM 600-PRINT-TOTALS.
        CLOSE TRANS-FILE, PRINT-FILE.
        STOP RUN.
200-EDIT-CHECK.
        IF  SALARY IS NOT > 5000 OR < 98000
            PERFORM 300-SALARY-ERROR.
        IF  AMT2 IS NEGATIVE
            PERFORM 400-AMT2-ERROR.
        IF  STATUS-CODE > 5 AND SALARY NOT < 86000
            PERFORM 500-ERROR-IN-STATUS.
*******************************************************************
*          AN ERROR SWITCH IS SET AT EACH ERROR ROUTINE          *
*******************************************************************
        IF  ERR-SWITCH = 0
            WRITE PRINT-REC FROM OK-REC
        ELSE
            WRITE PRINT-REC FROM ERR-REC.
        READ TRANS-FILE
            AT END MOVE 'NO ' TO ARE-THERE-MORE-RECORDS.
        ADD 1 TO COUNT-OF-RECORDS.
```

1. A syntax error occurs on the line in which AMT2 is tested for a negative quantity. Find and correct the error.

2. Is ADD 1 TO COUNT-OF-RECORDS in the correct place? Explain your answer.

3. When the program is executed, 300-SALARY-ERROR is always performed even when the SALARY is within the correct range. Find and correct the error.

4. When an error occurs, all subsequent records are similarly printed as errors. Find and correct this error.

PROGRAMMING ASSIGNMENTS

1. Write a program to check if sales records are in ascending sequence by salesperson number. The problem definition is shown in Figure 13.5.

   Note

   For any record not in sequence, print the salesperson's number and name.

2. Write a program to validate payroll records for missing data. See the problem definition in Figure 13.6.

   Notes

   a. Perform a validity routine to ensure that:
      1. All fields except Employee Name are numeric.
      2. Employee Name is not missing.
      3. Annual Salary is not greater than $125,000.
   b. Include the date and page number in the heading.

3. Modify Programming Assignment 3 in Chapter 12 to abort the run if any input record has:
   a. Fields that are not numeric.
   b. A state code that is not between 1 and 50.

   If the run is aborted, print the message INVALID DATA IN RECORD followed by the unedited contents of the record.

4. Modify Programming Assignment 4 in Chapter 12 to perform the following validity checks on each input record:
   a. Territory number, area number, and department number should be numeric.
   b. Department number should be between 1 and 10, territory number between 1 and 3, and area number between 1 and 3.
   c. Do not process a record that has invalid data; however, keep count of how many invalid records are found.
   d. At the end of the report, print the message THE NUMBER OF RECORDS NOT PROCESSED WAS, followed by the number of invalid records found.

Figure 13.5
Problem definition for
Programming Assignment 1.

Systems Flowchart

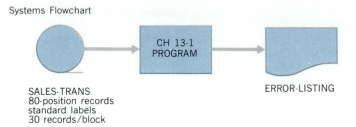

SALES-TRANS
80-position records
standard labels
30 records/block

ERROR-LISTING

SALES-TRANS Record Layout

ERROR-LISTING Printer Spacing Chart

Systems Flowchart

PAYROLL-MASTER
80-position records
standard labels
20 records/block

PAYROLL-LIST

PAYROLL-MASTER Record Layout

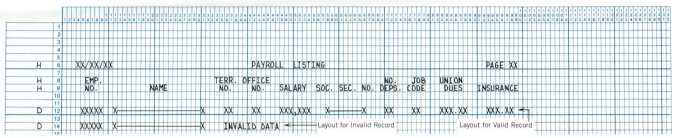

PAYROLL-LIST Printer Spacing Chart

Figure 13.6
Problem definition for
Programming Assignment 2.

UNIT IV

TABLE HANDLING AND ARRAY PROCESSING

14

Single-Level Arrays and Tables

OBJECTIVES

To familiarize you with

1. How to establish a series of items using an OCCURS clause.
2. How to access and manipulate data stored in an array or table.
3. The rules for using an OCCURS clause in the DATA DIVISION.
4. The use of a SEARCH or SEARCH ALL for a table look-up.

I. An Introduction to Single-Level OCCURS Clauses

A. Why OCCURS Clauses Are Used

We use an **OCCURS clause** in COBOL to indicate the repeated occurrence of fields with the same format. An OCCURS clause has the following uses:

USES OF OCCURS

1. For a series of input or output fields, each with the same format.
2. For a series of totals in WORKING-STORAGE to which amounts are added; after all data is accumulated, the totals can be printed.
3. For a table in WORKING-STORAGE to be accessed by each input record; with a **table,** we use the contents of some input field to "look up" the required data in the table.

---

1. Using an OCCURS to Define a Series of Input Fields Each with the Same Format
a. Defining Fields with an OCCURS Clause.

Example

Suppose we have one 72-character input record that consists of 24 hourly temperature fields. Each field is three positions long and indicates the temperature for the city of Los Angeles at a particular hour. Using traditional methods, coding the input record with 24 independent hourly fields would prove cumbersome:

```
01   TEMP-REC.
     05  ONE-AM          PIC 9(3).
     05  TWO-AM          PIC 9(3).    } 24 entries
     .                   .
     .                   .
     05  MIDNIGHT        PIC 9(3).
```

Moreover, to obtain an average daily temperature would also require a great deal of coding:

```
COMPUTE AVG-TEMP = (ONE-AM + TWO-AM + ... + MIDNIGHT) / 24
```

The dots (...) mean that the programmer would need to code all 24 entries.

The 24 temperature fields have exactly the same format, that is, three integer positions. Since the format or PIC clause for each of the 24 fields is identical, we could use an OCCURS clause to define the fields. We call the entire 72-position area an **array** and divide it into 24 three-position fields.

With an OCCURS clause, we specify the number of items being defined in the array and the PIC clause of each as follows:

```
01   TEMP-REC.
     05  TEMPERATURE    OCCURS 24 TIMES        PIC 9(3).
```

The OCCURS clause, then, defines 24 three-position numeric fields. Thus, TEMPERATURE is an array that refers to 72 positions or bytes of storage, or 24 three-byte fields. With one OCCURS clause, we define the 72 bytes as 24 fields each three positions long. See Figure 14.1 for a schematic.

b. Defining a Subscript.
Collectively, these 24 fields within the array are called TEMPERATURE, which is the identifier used to access them in the PROCEDURE DIVISION. We would use the identifier TEMPERATURE along with a

Figure 14.1
Schematic for storing 24 three-
position numeric fields in an
array.

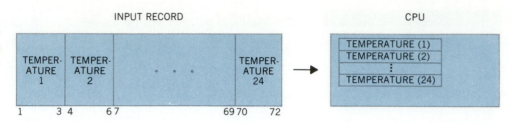

subscript that indicates which of the 24 fields we wish to access. To refer to an item defined by an OCCURS clause, we code the identifier, TEMPERATURE in our example, followed by the subscript, in parentheses. The subscript indicates the specific TEMPERATURE desired. Thus, to print the 2 A.M. temperature we code:

```
MOVE TEMPERATURE (2) TO TEMP-OUT.
WRITE PRINT-REC FROM OUT-REC.
```

Similarly, to print the 11 P.M. temperature we code:

```
MOVE TEMPERATURE (23) TO TEMP-OUT.
WRITE PRINT-REC FROM OUT-REC.
```

The relationship between OCCURS clauses and subscripts is as follows:

SUMMARY OF OCCURS AND SUBSCRIPTS

1. An **OCCURS clause** is defined in the DATA DIVISION to indicate the repeated occurrence of items with the same format within an array.
2. A **subscript** is used in the PROCEDURE DIVISION to indicate which specific item within the array we wish to access.

We use a subscript, along with the identifier that is defined with an OCCURS, to refer to an item within an array. In the preceding example, the subscript can have any value from 1 through 24. Any other value besides 1 through 24 would result in an error.

INVALID

```
MOVE TEMPERATURE (0) TO TEMP-OUT.
MOVE TEMPERATURE (25) TO TEMP-OUT.
```

Since there is no zero element or twenty-fifth element in the array, the subscript cannot take on the values 0 or 25; the subscript can take on only the integer values 1 through 24.

c. Coding Rules for Subscripts.   With many compilers, the coding of a subscript in the PROCEDURE DIVISION requires precise spacing. Usually, there must be at least one space between the identifier and the left parenthesis that precedes the subscript. Similarly, the subscript must be enclosed in parentheses *with no spaces within the parentheses.*

Example
```
ADD TEMPERATURE (22) TO TOTAL.
```

Depending on the compiler, the following might result in syntax errors:

Invalid Spacing	Reason
`ADD TEMPERATURE(22) TO TOTAL.`	One space is typically required between the word `TEMPERATURE` and the left parenthesis.
`ADD TEMPERATURE ( 22 ) TO TOTAL.`	No space is permitted after the left parenthesis and before the right parenthesis.

d. A Subscript May Be an Integer or an Identifier. Thus far, we have considered subscripts that are numeric literals. A subscript, however, may also be a data-name with a numeric `PICTURE` clause. Suppose `SUB` were defined in the `WORKING-STORAGE` section as follows:

```
01  WORK-AREAS.
    05  SUB PIC 99 VALUE 01.
```

We could move the first field of `TEMPERATURE` to `TEMP-OUT` as follows:

```
MOVE TEMPERATURE (SUB) TO TEMP-OUT.
```

Subscripts, then, identify items defined with `OCCURS` clauses and can be either integers or data-names. If a data-name is used as a subscript, it must have a numeric `PICTURE` clause and an integer value.

Using a data-name as a subscript enables us to vary the contents of the subscript so that we can process a series of items with a single routine.

Let us return to our initial `TEMPERATURE` array. To determine the average daily temperature, we can use numeric literals as subscripts, but to do so would not reduce the coding at all:

```
COMPUTE AVG-TEMP = (TEMPERATURE (1) + ... + TEMPERATURE (24)) / 24
```

It is far more efficient to write a routine that adds one temperature at a time to a total. We would vary the contents of a field called `SUB` from 1 to 24 so that all 24 temperatures are added. We define `SUB` as a `WORKING-STORAGE` entry with `PIC 99`.

The following is the pseudocode for this problem:

Pseudocode Excerpt
Initialize a Total-Temperature field
PERFORM UNTIL all Temperatures are added
    Add Temperatures to Total-Temperature
ENDPERFORM
Compute Average-Temperature = Total-Temperature / 24

The program excerpt that corresponds to this pseudocode is as follows:

Program Excerpt
```
    MOVE ZEROS TO TOTAL-TEMP.
    PERFORM 500-ADD-RTN
        VARYING SUB FROM 1 BY 1
            UNTIL SUB > 24.
    COMPUTE AVG-TEMP = TOTAL-TEMP / 24.
        .
        .
500-ADD-RTN.
    ADD TEMPERATURE (SUB) TO TOTAL-TEMP.
```

A subscript can be used as the field to be varied in a PERFORM statement. The PERFORM ... VARYING statement (1) initializes SUB at 1, (2) adds each TEMPERATURE within the array, and (3) increments SUB until it has processed all 24 temperatures.

The PERFORM ... VARYING is the most efficient instruction for processing all entries within an array. Note, however, that the PERFORM ... UNTIL could be used if desired, but that additional instructions would be necessary.

```
         MOVE 1 TO SUB.
         MOVE ZEROS TO TOTAL-TEMP.
         PERFORM 500-ADD-RTN
             UNTIL SUB > 24.
         COMPUTE AVG-TEMP = TOTAL-TEMP / 24.
             .
             .
     500-ADD-RTN.
         ADD TEMPERATURE (SUB) TO TOTAL-TEMP.
         ADD 1 TO SUB.
```

Similarly, the PERFORM ... TIMES could also be used if desired.

When using the UNTIL or TIMES option of the PERFORM, the subscript *must be initialized*; it must also be incremented within the routine to be performed.

We will use the PERFORM ... VARYING in most of our illustrations. It is the most suitable option for accessing subscripted entries since it initializes, increments, and tests the variable or subscript used in the procedure.

Relative Subscripting with COBOL 85

A subscript can be either (1) a data-name with numeric, integer value, or (2) a numeric literal with integer value. With COBOL 85, however, a subscript can also have a *relative* value, that is, a data-name or integer to which another data-name or integer is subtracted or added. Thus, the following is acceptable with COBOL 85:

Example

```
ADD TEMPERATURE (SUB - 12) TO TOTAL-AM-TEMP.
```

Self-Test   Consider the following for Questions 1 through 5.

```
01   IN-REC.
     05   AMT1        PIC 9(5).
     05   AMT2        PIC 9(5).
     05   AMT3        PIC 9(5).
     05   AMT4        PIC 9(5).
     05   AMT5        PIC 9(5).
```

1. An OCCURS clause could be used in place of defining each AMT field separately because _____ .

2. (T or F) Suppose AMT2 and AMT4 had PIC 9(3). An OCCURS clause could not be used to define all the AMT fields.

3. Recode the fields within IN-REC using an OCCURS clause.

4. To access any of the five items defined with the OCCURS clause, we must use a _____ in the PROCEDURE DIVISION.

5. Code a routine to determine the total of all five AMT fields.

Solutions   1. all AMTs have the same format or PIC clause
2. T

3.
```
01   IN-REC.
     05   AMT OCCURS 5 TIMES          PIC 9(5).
```
4. subscript
5.
```
WORKING-STORAGE SECTION.
01   STORED-AREAS.
     05   SUB PIC 9.
       :

     MOVE ZEROS TO TOTAL.
     PERFORM 500-TOTAL-RTN
          VARYING SUB FROM 1 BY 1
               UNTIL SUB > 5.
       :
   500-TOTAL-RTN.
     ADD AMT (SUB) TO TOTAL.
```

2. Using an OCCURS in WORKING-STORAGE for Storing Totals

Thus far, we have seen that an OCCURS clause may be used as part of an input record to indicate the repeated occurrence of incoming fields. Similarly, an OCCURS may be used as part of an output record in the same way. An OCCURS clause may also be used to define fields within WORKING-STORAGE.

Suppose, for example, that input consists of the following description for records transacted during the previous year:

```
01   IN-REC.
     05   TRANS-NO-IN               PIC 9(5).
     05   DATE-OF-TRANS-IN.
          10   MONTH-IN             PIC 99.
          10   DAY-NO-IN            PIC 99.
          10   YR-IN                PIC 99.
     05   AMT-IN                    PIC 9(3)V99.
```

Since there is no item that is repeated, we do not need to use the OCCURS clause within this input record. Suppose we wish to establish an array in WORKING-STORAGE that consists of 12 monthly transaction amount totals for the previous year:

```
WORKING-STORAGE SECTION.
01   TOTALS.
     05   MO-TOT OCCURS 12 TIMES     PIC 9(5)V99.
```

We would define 12 MO-TOT fields in WORKING-STORAGE to store the total transaction amounts for months 01–12 respectively. Each IN-REC read will include an AMT-IN and a MONTH-IN number. We will add the AMT-IN to a MO-TOT field determined by the contents of the MONTH-IN entered within DATE-OF-TRANS-IN. If MONTH-IN = 2, for example, we will add the AMT-IN to the second MO-TOT.

Note that we must initialize the MO-TOT fields to zero at the beginning of the program before any AMT-IN fields are added to them. As we will see, you cannot use a VALUE clause with an OCCURS. The best way to initialize the 12 MO-TOT fields is as follows:

```
     PERFORM 500-INIT-RTN
     VARYING SUB1 FROM 1 BY 1 UNTIL SUB1 > 12.
       :
   500-INIT-RTN.
     MOVE ZEROS TO MO-TOT (SUB1).
```

With most compilers we can also use the following to set all the MO-TOT fields to zero with one statement: MOVE ZEROS TO TOTALS.

> **Note:**   Code `MOVE ZEROS TO TOTALS`, *not* `MOVE 0 TO TOTALS`. The latter will clear only the leftmost position in the `TOTALS` array. This is because `TOTALS`, as a group item, is treated as an alphanumeric field. If a single character is moved to an alphanumeric field, that character is moved to the high-order position and remaining positions are filled with blanks.

The following pseudocode illustrates how we can accumulate the total transaction amounts for months 01–12:

Pseudocode

PERFORM
    Open the Files
    Initialize the Array
    Read a Record
ENDPERFORM
PERFORM UNTIL there is no more data
    Add the Input Amount to the corresponding Monthly Total
    Read a Record
ENDPERFORM
     ⋮

The corresponding program excerpt is as follows:

Program Excerpt

```
PROCEDURE DIVISION.
100-MAIN-MODULE.
    PERFORM 500-INITIALIZATION-RTN.
    PERFORM 200-CALC-RTN
        UNTIL THERE-ARE-NO-MORE-RECORDS.
        ⋮
200-CALC-RTN.
    ADD AMT-IN TO MO-TOT (MONTH-IN).
    READ INFILE
        AT END MOVE 'NO ' TO ARE-THERE-MORE-RECORDS.
        ⋮
500-INITIALIZATION-RTN.
    OPEN INPUT  INFILE
         OUTPUT PRINT-FILE.
    MOVE ZEROS TO TOTALS.
    READ INFILE
        AT END MOVE 'NO ' TO ARE-THERE-MORE-RECORDS.
```

A subscript called `MONTH-IN` determines the `MO-TOT` to which the inputted `AMT-IN` is to be added. In this case, this subscript is also an *input field*. Subscripts, then, can be data-names defined in either the `FILE SECTION` or the `WORKING-STORAGE SECTION`.

If `MONTH-IN` is 3, for example, we would add `AMT-IN` to the third `MO-TOT`. This is accomplished by coding: `ADD AMT-IN TO MO-TOT (MONTH-IN)`.

Performing an initialization routine from the main module results in a more modularized top-down program. In this way all the details such as opening files, setting fields to zero, and reading the first record, are left for a minor module.

Validating Input Data

You should use input fields as subscripts only if you are sure they have valid values; in this case, `MONTH-IN` should only vary from 1 to 12.

If MONTH-IN were erroneously entered with a value that was less than 01 or greater than 12, the program would not run properly. To minimize such errors, 200-CALC-RTN should include a validity check as follows:

Pseudocode Excerpt

PERFORM UNTIL there is no
    more data
    IF the Input Month field is Valid
    THEN
        Add the Input Amount to
        the corresponding
            Monthly Total
    ELSE
        Write an Error Message
    ENDIF
    Read a Record
ENDPERFORM

Program Excerpt

```
       :
       :
200-CALC-RTN.
    IF  MONTH-IN > 0 AND < 13
        ADD AMT-IN TO
            MO-TOT (MONTH-IN)
    ELSE
        PERFORM 400-ERR-RTN.
    READ INFILE
        AT END MOVE 'NO ' TO
            ARE-THERE-MORE-RECORDS.
```

From the pseudocode you can see that the module will read each record and, if it contains a valid MONTH-IN, will add the AMT-IN to the appropriate MO-TOT. After all the input has been processed, control will return to the main module where we will print out the monthly totals. The monthly totals are to print in sequence from 1 to 12. The pseudocode for this entire program is as follows:

Pseudocode

PERFORM
    Open the Files
    Initialize the Array
    Read a Record
ENDPERFORM
PERFORM UNTIL there is no more data
    IF the Input Month field is Valid
    THEN
        Add the Input Amount to the corresponding Monthly Total
    ELSE
        Write an Error Message
    ENDIF
    Read a Record
ENDPERFORM
PERFORM UNTIL the entire Array is printed
    Move Each Array Entry to the Output Area
    Write a Line
ENDPERFORM
PERFORM
    End-of-Job Operations
ENDPERFORM

We can use a PERFORM 300-PRINT-RTN VARYING ... statement, with a subscript varying from 1 to 12, to print the array:

```
    PROCEDURE DIVISION.
    ****************************************************************
    *  THIS MODULE CONTROLS READING OF INPUT AND PRINTING OF 12   *
    *  TOTAL LINES                                                *
    ****************************************************************
```

```
100-MAIN-MODULE.
    PERFORM 500-INITIALIZATION-RTN.
    PERFORM 200-CALC-RTN
        UNTIL THERE-ARE-NO-MORE-RECORDS.
    PERFORM 300-PRINT-RTN VARYING SUB FROM 1 BY 1
        UNTIL SUB > 12.
    PERFORM 600-END-OF-JOB-RTN.
*****************************************************************
* THIS MODULE PROCESSES INPUT BY ADDING THE INPUT AMOUNT     *
* TO THE CORRESPONDING MONTHLY TOTAL. IT IS PERFORMED        *
* FROM 100-MAIN-MODULE.                                      *
*****************************************************************
 200-CALC-RTN.
    IF  MONTH-IN > 0 AND < 13
        ADD AMT-IN TO MO-TOT (MONTH-IN)
    ELSE
        PERFORM 400-ERR-RTN.
    READ INFILE
        AT END MOVE 'NO ' TO ARE-THERE-MORE-RECORDS.
*****************************************************************
* THIS MODULE PRINTS THE 12 MONTHLY TOTALS IN ORDER. IT IS   *
* PERFORMED FROM 100-MAIN-MODULE.                            *
*****************************************************************
 300-PRINT-RTN.
    MOVE MO-TOT (SUB) TO MO-TOT-OUT.
    WRITE PR-REC FROM MO-TOT-LINE
        AFTER ADVANCING 2 LINES.
*****************************************************************
* THIS MODULE PRINTS AN ERROR IF THE INPUT MONTH IS NOT      *
* BETWEEN 01 AND 12. IT IS PERFORMED FROM 200-CALC-RTN.      *
*****************************************************************
 400-ERR-RTN.
    WRITE PR-REC FROM ERR-LINE
        AFTER ADVANCING 2 LINES.
*****************************************************************
* THIS MODULE OPENS THE FILES, INITIALIZES THE ARRAY, AND    *
* READS THE FIRST RECORD. IT IS PERFORMED FROM 100-MAIN-     *
* MODULE.                                                    *
*****************************************************************
 500-INITIALIZATION-RTN.
    OPEN INPUT  INFILE
         OUTPUT PRINT-FILE.
    MOVE ZEROS TO TOTALS.
    READ INFILE
        AT END MOVE 'NO ' TO ARE-THERE-MORE-RECORDS.
*****************************************************************
* THIS MODULE CLOSES THE FILES AND STOPS THE RUN. IT IS      *
* PERFORMED FROM 100-MAIN-MODULE.                            *
*****************************************************************
 600-END-OF-JOB-RTN.
    CLOSE INFILE
          PRINT-FILE.
    STOP RUN.
```

Thus, the WORKING-STORAGE array called MO-TOT is accessed in two ways:

1. For each record read, the input field called MONTH-IN indicates to which MO-TOT the AMT-IN is to be added. Data need not be entered in any specific sequence; the contents of MONTH-IN determines which MO-TOT is used in the addition.

2. After all input has been read and processed, a subscript called SUB is varied from 1 to 12 to print out the contents of all MO-TOTs in consecutive order.

B. Rules for Use of the OCCURS Clause

1. Levels 02—49

An OCCURS clause may be used on levels 02—49 only. That is, the OCCURS is not valid for 01, 77, and 88 levels.

Suppose we wish to read 15 input records with the same format. It is *not* valid to code the following:

INVALID

```
01  IN-REC OCCURS 15 TIMES.
```

To indicate 15 occurrences of IN-REC, we perform an initial read and execute a routine that reads records 15 times.

```
READ INFILE
    AT END MOVE 'NO ' TO ARE-THERE-MORE-RECORDS.
PERFORM 200-PROCESS-RTN 15 TIMES.
```

The PROCEDURE DIVISION, then, would include coding that reads 15 records. The DATA DIVISION would simply include the record format as in previous programs. OCCURS is used for repeated occurrences of fields, then, *not* records.

2. Defining an OCCURS Entry as Either an Elementary or Group Item

Thus far, we have focused on OCCURS clauses that define elementary items.

Example
```
WORKING-STORAGE SECTION.
01  TOTALS.
    05  MO-TOT OCCURS 12 TIMES  PIC 9(5)V99.
```

The 05-level item defined by an OCCURS has a PIC clause, making the 12 MO-TOT fields elementary items. Thus, TOTALS is an 84-byte array (12 × 7) consisting of 12 elementary items:

TOTALS

XXXXX.XX	XXXXX.XX	· · ·	XXXXX.XX
MO-TOT (1)	MO-TOT (2)		MO-TOT (12)

The identifier used with an OCCURS clause may be a group item as well:

```
01  TAX-TABLE.
    05  GROUP-X OCCURS 20 TIMES.
        10  CITY                PIC X(6).
        10  TAX-RATE            PIC V999.
```

In this instance, CITY and TAX-RATE each occurs 20 times within a group item called GROUP-X:

TAX-TABLE

GROUP-X (1)		GROUP-X (2)			GROUP-X (20)	
CITY (1)	TAX-RATE (1)	CITY (2)	TAX-RATE (2)	· · ·	CITY (20)	TAX-RATE (20)

Similarly, to print out 20 tax rates, we could have the following print record:

```
01  TAX-LINE.
    05  FILLER                    PIC X(13).
    :
    05  ENTRIES OCCURS 20 TIMES.
        10  TAX-RATE-OUT     PIC .999.
        10  FILLER          PIC X(2).
```

The FILLER that occurs 20 times will ensure that there are two spaces between each printed tax rate.

3. Accessing a WORKING-STORAGE Area Defined by an OCCURS Clause

Example 1   Consider again the array consisting of monthly totals that was defined previously:

```
WORKING-STORAGE SECTION.
01  TOTALS.
    05  MO-TOT OCCURS 12 TIMES  PIC 9(5)V99.
```

Suppose all the data has been read from the transaction records and added to the corresponding array entry. Now we wish to write a routine to find the yearly transaction total, that is, the sum of all monthly totals. The pseudocode for this procedure is as follows:

Pseudocode

```
PERFORM UNTIL all Array Elements have been added
    Add each Array Element to a Yearly Total
ENDPERFORM
Write a Record with the Yearly Total
```

The program excerpt for this procedure is as follows:

```
**********************************************************************
*    THIS PROCEDURE CALCULATES A YEARLY TOTAL FROM MONTHLY   *
*    TOTALS STORED IN AN ARRAY                               *
**********************************************************************
 200-YEARLY-TOTAL-RTN.
     MOVE ZEROS TO WS-YEARLY-TOTAL.
     PERFORM 300-ADD-RTN
         VARYING SUB FROM 1 BY 1 UNTIL SUB > 12.
     MOVE WS-YEARLY-TOTAL TO TOTAL-OUT.
     WRITE PRINT-REC FROM TOTAL-LINE
         AFTER ADVANCING 2 LINES.
 300-ADD-RTN.
     ADD MO-TOT (SUB) TO WS-YEARLY-TOTAL.
```

This procedure could be coded with a PERFORM ... UNTIL or a PERFORM ... TIMES as well.

Example 2   Using the same array, find the number of months in which the monthly total exceeded $10,000.

The pseudocode for this procedure is as follows:

```
Initialize a Counter
PERFORM UNTIL entire Array is processed
    IF a Monthly Total exceeds $10,000
    THEN
            Add 1 to the Counter
    ENDIF
ENDPERFORM
Print the value in the Counter
```

The program excerpt is as follows:

```
****************************************************************
* THIS PROCEDURE DETERMINES THE NUMBER OF MONTHS THAT HAD     *
* TOTALS IN EXCESS OF $10,000                                 *
****************************************************************
500-OVER-10000-RTN.
    MOVE ZEROS TO WS-CTR.
    PERFORM 600-TEST-RTN
        VARYING SUB FROM 1 BY 1 UNTIL SUB > 12.
    MOVE WS-CTR TO CTR-OUT.
    WRITE PRINT-REC FROM CTR-LINE
        AFTER ADVANCING 2 LINES.
600-TEST-RTN.
    IF  MO-TOT (SUB) > 10000
        ADD 1 TO WS-CTR.
```

II. Processing Data Stored in an Array

A. Using OCCURS with REDEFINES and VALUE Clauses

Note that once an entry has been defined by an OCCURS clause, it may *not* be redefined. Thus the following is invalid:

Invalid

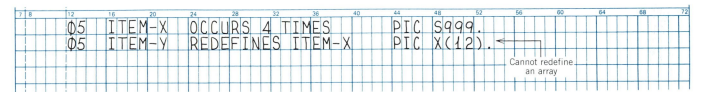

```
05  ITEM-X  OCCURS 4 TIMES        PIC S999.
05  ITEM-Y  REDEFINES ITEM-X      PIC X(12).
                                        Cannot redefine
                                        an array
```

> With COBOL 74, an entry defined with an OCCURS cannot have a VALUE clause. With COBOL 85, an entry defined with an OCCURS clause may also have a VALUE clause. This is true of an entry subordinate to an OCCURS item as well.
>
> The following is valid with COBOL 85:
>
> ```
> 05  AMTS OCCURS 50 TIMES  PIC 999   VALUE ZEROS.
> ```

Regardless of the compiler, you can always define an entry and *then redefine* it with an OCCURS clause. In addition, the first entry, which is defined without an OCCURS, may have a VALUE clause that is used to establish a constant, if it is in the WORKING-STORAGE SECTION.

The following example will illustrate how to define an entry with a VALUE and then redefine it with an OCCURS clause.

Example
```
01  MONTH-ARRAY.
    05  STRING-1              PIC X(36) VALUE
            'JANFEBMARAPRMAYJUNJULAUGSEPOCTNOVDEC'.
    05  MONTH REDEFINES STRING-1 OCCURS 12 TIMES PIC XXX.
```

The first 05 field, STRING-1, establishes a 36-position constant that contains a three-character abbreviation for each of the 12 months of the year. MONTH then redefines STRING-1 and allows each three-character abbreviation for months 1 through 12 to be accessed separately using a subscript. If we move MONTH (4), for example, to an output area, APR would print, which is an abbreviation for the fourth month. In this way, each abbreviation for a month can be accessed by using the corresponding subscript, as in the following:

JAN	FEB	MAR	APR	MAY	JUN	JUL	AUG	SEP	OCT	NOV	DEC
MONTH (1)	MONTH (2)	MONTH (3)	MONTH (4)	MONTH (5)	MONTH (6)	MONTH (7)	MONTH (8)	MONTH (9)	MONTH (10)	MONTH (11)	MONTH (12)

To print the appropriate three-character abbreviation for each month, we may use the following routine:

```
       :
       :
     PERFORM PRINT-TABLE
         VARYING SUB FROM 1 BY 1 UNTIL SUB  > 12.
       :
       :
   PRINT-TABLE.
       MOVE MONTH (SUB) TO MONTH-OUT.
       :
       :
       WRITE PRINT-REC FROM PRINT-OUT
           AFTER ADVANCING 2 LINES.
```

B. Printing Data Stored in an Array

At the beginning of this chapter, there was a problem that involved reading in 24 hourly temperatures for Los Angeles for a given day. The input record was defined as:

```
01  TEMP-REC.
    05  TEMPERATURE OCCURS 24 TIMES        PIC 9(3).
```

We could have several such records, each containing temperatures for a different day. Suppose that we want to print out on one line the 24 hourly temperature values in each input record.

Pseudocode Excerpt

Read a Record
PERFORM UNTIL there is no more data
    Clear the Output Area
    PERFORM UNTIL the entire Input Array has been processed
        Move Input Array Entry to Output Area
    ENDPERFORM
    Write an Output Record
    Read an Input Record
ENDPERFORM

We can also use the OCCURS clause in an output record, as illustrated in the following program excerpt.

```
    DATA DIVISION.
    FILE SECTION.
    FD  TEMP-FILE
        LABEL RECORDS ARE OMITTED.
    01  TEMP-REC.
        05  TEMPERATURE OCCURS 24 TIMES     PIC 9(3).
    FD  PRINT-FILE
        LABEL RECORDS ARE OMITTED.
```

```
01  OUT-RECORD.
    05  FILLER                          PIC X.
    05  AMT-OUT OCCURS 24 TIMES.
        10  TEMP-OUT                    PIC ZZ9.
        10  FILLER                      PIC X.
    05  FILLER                          PIC X(36).
WORKING-STORAGE.
01  WORK-AREAS.
    05  SUB                             PIC 99.
        .
        .
*
PROCEDURE DIVISION.
******************************************************************
*   THIS MODULE CONTROLS READING OF INPUT AND PRINTING  *
*   OF TEMPERATURES                                     *
******************************************************************
100-MAIN-MODULE.
    PERFORM 400-INITIALIZATION-RTN.
    PERFORM 200-PROCESS-RTN
        UNTIL THERE-ARE-NO-MORE-RECORDS.
    PERFORM 500-END-OF-JOB-RTN.
******************************************************************
*   THIS MODULE PROCESSES EACH INPUT RECORD. IT IS      *
*   PERFORMED FROM 100-MAIN-MODULE.                     *
******************************************************************
200-PROCESS-RTN.
    MOVE SPACES TO OUT-RECORD.
    PERFORM 300-MOVE-RTN
        VARYING SUB FROM 1 BY 1 UNTIL SUB > 24.
    WRITE OUT-RECORD
        AFTER ADVANCING 2 LINES.
    READ TEMP-FILE
        AT END MOVE 'NO ' TO ARE-THERE-MORE-RECORDS.
******************************************************************
*   THIS MODULE MOVES THE 24 TEMPERATURES FROM EACH     *
*   RECORD TO AN OUTPUT AREA. IT IS PERFORMED FROM      *
*   200-PROCESS-RTN.                                    *
******************************************************************
300-MOVE-RTN.
    MOVE TEMPERATURE (SUB) TO TEMP-OUT (SUB).
400-INITIALIZATION-RTN.
    OPEN INPUT   TEMP-FILE
         OUTPUT  OUT-FILE.
    READ TEMP-FILE
        AT END MOVE 'NO ' TO ARE-THERE-MORE-RECORDS.
500-END-OF-JOB-RTN.
    CLOSE TEMP-FILE
          OUT-FILE.
    STOP RUN.
```

AMT-OUT is a group item that consists of two elementary items: TEMP-OUT and a FILLER. The FILLER is necessary so that there is a single blank between each temperature for readability. The layout for the print positions of OUT-RECORD, then, is as follows:

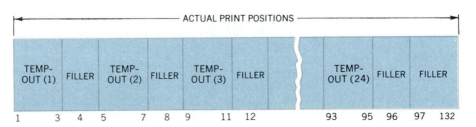

Self-Test

1. What, if anything, is wrong with the following?

```
01   TOTALS OCCURS 50 TIMES.
     05   SUB-TOT              PIC 9(5).
```

2. Indicate the difference between the following:

```
(a) 01   TOTAL1.
         05   STATE.
              10   STATE-NAME OCCURS 50 TIMES        PIC X(10).
              10   STATE-POP   OCCURS 50 TIMES        PIC 9(10).
(b) 01   TOTAL2.
         05   STATE OCCURS 50 TIMES.
              10   STATE-NAME        PIC X(10).
              10   STATE-POP         PIC 9(10).
```

3. Suppose the following area is stored in WORKING-STORAGE. It contains the combination of the numbers of the two horses that won the daily double each day for the last year. The data is stored in sequence from January 1 through December 31.

```
01   TOTALS.
     05   DAILY-DOUBLE OCCURS 365 TIMES        PIC 99.
```

Thus, if DAILY-DOUBLE (1) = 45, then horses 4 and 5 won the daily double on January 1. Print the combination of numbers that won the daily double on February 2.

4. For Question 3, indicate the number of times the winning combination was 25.

5. Consider the following total area in WORKING-STORAGE:

```
01   TOTALS.
     05   DOW-JONES OCCURS 365 TIMES        PIC 9(4)V9.
```

This total area lists the Dow-Jones industrial average from January 1 through December 31 of a given year. Print the number of days on which the Dow-Jones industrial average fell below 2200.

Solutions

1. Cannot use OCCURS on the 01 level.

2. The first total area, TOTAL1, defines *two* arrays:

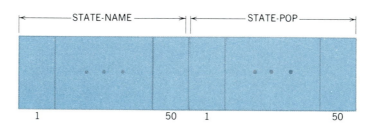

The second total area defines a *single* array with two elementary items:

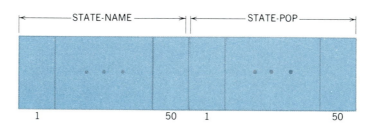

The first has a string of 50 state names followed by a string of 50 population figures. The second has each state name directly adjacent to its corresponding population figure.

3.
```
   MOVE DAILY-DOUBLE (33) TO NUM-OUT OF PRINT-REC.
   WRITE PRINT-REC
       AFTER ADVANCING 2 LINES.
```

Note: February 2 is the 33rd day of the year (31 days in January plus 2 in February).

4.
```
   **************************************************************
   *  THIS PROCEDURE PRINTS THE NUMBER OF TIMES THE COMBINATION *
   *  25 WAS FOUND IN THE ARRAY                                 *
   **************************************************************
       MOVE 0 TO WIN-25.
       PERFORM 500-CHECK-RTN
           VARYING SUB FROM 1 BY 1 UNTIL SUB > 365.
       MOVE WIN-25 TO NUM-OUT OF PRINT-REC.
       WRITE PRINT-REC
           AFTER ADVANCING 2 LINES.
         :
         :
   500-CHECK-RTN.
       IF  DAILY-DOUBLE (SUB) = 25
           ADD 1 TO WIN-25.
```

5.
```
   **************************************************************
   *  THIS PROCEDURE CALCULATES THE NUMBER OF DAYS WHEN THE     *
   *  DOW-JONES FELL BELOW 2200                                 *
   **************************************************************
       MOVE 0 TO UNDER-2200.
       PERFORM 600-LOW-DOW
           VARYING SUB FROM 1 BY 1 UNTIL SUB > 365.
       MOVE UNDER-2200 TO NUM-OUT OF PRINT-REC.
       WRITE PRINT-REC
           AFTER ADVANCING 2 LINES.
         :
         :
   600-LOW-DOW.
       IF  DOW-JONES < 2200
           ADD 1 TO UNDER-2200.
```

III. Using an OCCURS Clause for Table Handling

A. Defining a Table

Thus far, we have focused on the use of an OCCURS clause to:

1. Indicate the repeated occurrence of either input or output fields within the FILE SECTION.
2. Store arrays or total areas within WORKING-STORAGE.

In this section, we will focus on the use of an OCCURS clause to store table data. As we will see, tables and arrays are stored in exactly the same way; they are, however, used for different purposes.

A **table** is a list of stored fields that are looked up or referenced by the program. Tables are used in conjunction with table look-ups, where a **table look-up** is a procedure that finds a specific entry in the table.

Thus, an array stores data or totals to be outputted, whereas a table is used for looking up or referencing data.

Establishing the Need for a Table

Suppose that a mail-order company ships items to customers throughout the United States. A program is required that (1) reads customer input data containing billing information and (2) produces output in the form of bills. Since each county within the United States has a different local tax structure, a procedure must be established for calculating sales tax. Two techniques may be employed:

1. The actual sales tax rate may be entered as part of each input record.

    Entering the sales tax rate in each input record would be very inefficient. First, sales tax rates occasionally change; each time there is a change to a tax rate in a county, *all* input records pertaining to that county would need to be changed. Second, recording the sales tax rate for each input record means extra keying. That is, if 1000 input records all pertain to a single county, we would be entering the *same* sales tax rate 1000 times. This results in additional labor and added risk of input errors.

2. The sales tax rates may be entered as a *table* and referenced as needed.

    This is a far more efficient and effective method for storing tax rate data than the first method. Input to the program would consist of *two files*. The table file with sales tax rates corresponding to each county is entered as the first file and stored in WORKING-STORAGE. Then the input transaction file is read; for each input transaction record, we would use the table to "look up" the sales tax rate in the table that corresponds to the county specified in the input record.

Suppose there are 1000 tax rates and 10,000 customer records. To include a sales tax rate in each input record would require 10,000 additional fields to be entered as input. It is better to (1) enter the 1000 sales tax rates as a table and (2) look up the appropriate rate in the table for each input record.

B. Storing the Table in WORKING-STORAGE

Storing the sales tax data in a table rather than in each transaction record is more efficient, not only because it minimizes data entry operations, but also because the sales tax rates can be more easily maintained, or *updated*, in the table, as needed. That is, if there is a change to a specific tax rate we need only alter the single table entry pertaining to that rate. If the sales tax rate appeared in the input transaction customer file, we would need to revise all records affected by the sales tax change.

To store a table, we must associate a tax rate with each specific tax district. We may use the zip code to specify each tax district.

Assume that sales tax rate is stored using zip code. That is, corresponding to each zip code, we store a sales tax rate in the table:

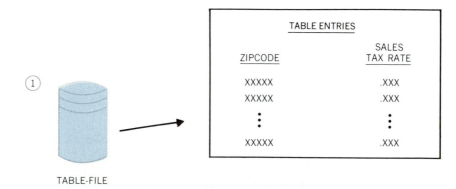

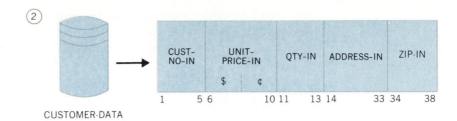

CUSTOMER-DATA

The table file is read first, with zip codes and tax rates stored in WORKING-STORAGE. Then the input customer file is read. The zip code from each customer record is compared to the zip code on the table until a match is found. The sales tax rate corresponding to a specific zip code is used to calculate a total price to be printed as follows:

The TABLE-FILE consists of table entries, where each table entry is a group item subdivided into a zip code field and its corresponding sales tax rate. The **table argument** is the table entry field that is used to locate the desired element. Here, the table argument is the table's zip code field. The element to be looked up is called the **table function.** In this case, the table function is the table's sales tax rate. The input field that is used for finding a match is called the **search argument.** We compare the search argument to the table argument to find the table function.

Example

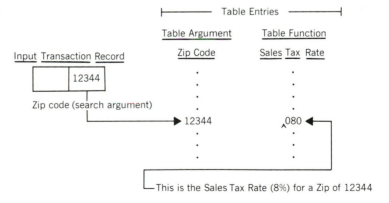

In this example, a zip code of 12344 is in the input transaction record. This is the search argument. We use this search argument to find the corresponding table argument, which is the zip code of 12344 in the table. The table function is the sales tax rate corresponding to that zip code, which is 8%.

After the table is stored, we enter input transaction records. For each transaction record, we search the table to find the table argument that matches the transaction record's zip code, or search argument. When a match is found between the input transaction zip code (the search argument), and the table's zip code (the table argument), we know the table function or sales tax rate is the corresponding table entry. That is, if the fifth table argument is a zip code of 12344, then the sales tax rate we want is also the fifth entry.

The COBOL program to produce the desired customer bills may be divided into two basic modules:

1. Reading and storing the table.
2. Processing each input record, which includes a *table look-up*.

Suppose this transaction file has customers from 1000 zip code locations. We would have, then, 1000 table entries with the following format:

TABLE-FILE
10-position records
20 records/block
1000 records

TABLE-FILE Record Layout

See Figure 14.2 for an overview of the hierarchy chart and the pseudocode for this problem.

The TABLE-FILE could be coded as follows:

```
FD   TABLE-FILE
     LABEL RECORDS ARE STANDARD.
01   TABLE-REC.
     05   T-ZIPCODE          PIC 9(5).
     05   T-TAX              PIC V999.
     05   FILLER             PIC XX.
```

Note that we do *not* indicate in the DATA DIVISION the number of table records that will be processed. Instead, in the PROCEDURE DIVISION we will perform the 200-TABLE-ENTRY module 1000 times.

Since table data must be stored before we begin processing the input customer file, we need a WORKING-STORAGE area to hold the 1000 table entries:

```
WORKING-STORAGE SECTION.
01   SALES-TAX-TABLE.
     05   TABLE-ENTRIES OCCURS 1000 TIMES.
          10   WS-ZIPCODE             PIC 9(5).
          10   WS-TAX                 PIC V999.
```

Because the word TABLE is a COBOL reserved word, it should not be used in a program as an identifier unless it has a prefix or suffix.

The WORKING-STORAGE table stores the 1000 entries as follows:

How the Table Data is Stored in WORKING-STORAGE

TABLE-ENTRIES (1)		TABLE-ENTRIES (2)		• • •	TABLE-ENTRIES (1000)	
WS-ZIPCODE (1)	WS-TAX (1)	WS-ZIPCODE (2)	WS-TAX (2)	• • •	WS-ZIPCODE (1000)	WS-TAX (1000)

Figure 14.2
Hierarchy chart and
pseudocode for sample table-
handling routine.

Hierarchy Chart

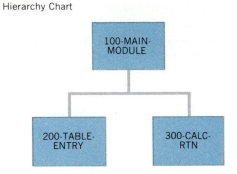

Pseudocode

```
START
    Open the Files
    PERFORM UNTIL Table is Loaded
        Read a Table Record
        Move Table Data to Storage
    ENDPERFORM
    Read a Transaction Record
    PERFORM UNTIL there is no more data
        Move Input Fields to Detail Line
        Search Table
            IF  a match is found
            THEN
                Compute Sales Tax using table function
                Compute Total
                Write Detail Line
            ELSE
                Move 0 to Sales Tax
            ENDIF
        Read a Transaction Record
    ENDPERFORM
    End-of-Job Operations
STOP
```

The main input file will contain customer billing or transaction data used to produce an output file of bills.

```
FD   CUST-FILE
     LABEL RECORDS ARE STANDARD.
01   CUST-REC.
     05   CUST-NO-IN            PIC 9(5).
     05   UNIT-PRICE-IN         PIC 9(3)V99.
     05   QTY-IN                PIC 9(3).
     05   ADDRESS-IN            PIC X(20).
     05   ZIP-IN                PIC 9(5).
FD   CUST-BILL
     LABEL RECORDS ARE OMITTED.
01   BILLING-REC               PIC X(133).
WORKING-STORAGE SECTION.
    :
    :
01   DETAIL-LINE.
     05   FILLER                PIC X(20)    VALUE SPACES.
     05   DL-CUST-NO-OUT        PIC 9(5).
     05   FILLER                PIC X(10)    VALUE SPACES.
     05   DL-UNIT-PRICE-OUT     PIC 999.99.
     05   FILLER                PIC X(10)    VALUE SPACES.
     05   DL-QTY-OUT            PIC ZZ9.
     05   FILLER                PIC X(10)    VALUE SPACES.
     05   DL-SALES-TAX          PIC Z(6).99.
     05   FILLER                PIC X(10)    VALUE SPACES.
     05   DL-TOTAL              PIC Z,ZZZ,ZZZ.99.
     05   FILLER                PIC X(38)    VALUE SPACES.
```

100-MAIN-MODULE would include references to both the 200-TABLE-ENTRY and 300-CALC-RTN modules.

Program Excerpt

```
PROCEDURE DIVISION.
***************************************************************
*   THIS MODULE CONTROLS READING AND STORING OF TABLE     *
*   RECORDS AND THEN READING AND PROCESSING OF            *
*   TRANSACTION RECORDS                                   *
***************************************************************
 100-MAIN-MODULE.
     OPEN INPUT   TABLE-FILE
                  CUST-FILE
          OUTPUT CUST-BILL.
     PERFORM 200-TABLE-ENTRY
         VARYING X1 FROM 1 BY 1
             UNTIL X1 > 1000.
     READ CUST-FILE
         AT END MOVE 'NO ' TO ARE-THERE-MORE-RECORDS.
     PERFORM 300-CALC-RTN
         UNTIL THERE-ARE-NO-MORE-RECORDS.
     CLOSE TABLE-FILE
           CUST-FILE
           CUST-BILL.
     STOP RUN.
```

Consider the PERFORM 200-TABLE-ENTRY statement. When X1 exceeds 1000, that is, when it is 1001, 200-TABLE-ENTRY has been performed 1000 times and control returns to the main module. Since X1 will vary from 1 to 1001, it must be defined as a *four-position numeric field.*

An initial READ is *not* necessary for processing the TABLE-FILE because we know precisely how many table records are to be read. Since 1000 table entries are to be read and stored, we execute the 200-TABLE-ENTRY routine 1000 times by varying the subscript from 1 to 1001. The 200-TABLE-ENTRY module could be coded as follows:

```
***************************************************************
*   THIS MODULE READS EACH TABLE RECORD AND STORES THE    *
*   TABLE DATA IN WORKING-STORAGE. IT IS PERFORMED        *
*   FROM 100-MAIN-MODULE.                                 *
***************************************************************
 200-TABLE-ENTRY.
     READ TABLE-FILE
         AT END DISPLAY 'NOT ENOUGH TABLE RECORDS'
         CLOSE TABLE-FILE, CUST-FILE, CUST-BILL
         STOP RUN.
     MOVE T-ZIPCODE TO WS-ZIPCODE (X1).
     MOVE T-TAX TO WS-TAX (X1).
```

We could also use an initial READ in the main module and code the READ within 200-TABLE-ENTRY as the last instruction rather than the first.

Subscripts must be used when referencing the table entries WS-ZIPCODE and WS-TAX in the PROCEDURE DIVISION. Recall that WS-ZIPCODE will be the table argument and WS-TAX the table function.

Validating Data

For this program, 1000 table records are to be read and stored. If an error has occurred and there are fewer than 1000 table records, the AT END is executed and the run terminates. If an error has occurred and there are more than 1000 table records, we would only process the first 1000. For validating purposes, we may want to ensure that there are precisely 1000 table records. We can code the following:

```
READ TABLE-FILE
    AT END MOVE 'NO ' TO MORE-TABLE-RECS.
```

```
PERFORM 200-TABLE-ENTRY
    VARYING X1 FROM 1 BY 1
        UNTIL X1 > 1000 OR MORE-TABLE-RECS = 'NO '.
IF  X1 NOT > 1000
    DISPLAY 'TOO FEW RECORDS IN THE FILE'.
IF  MORE-TABLE-RECS NOT = 'NO '
    DISPLAY 'TOO MANY RECORDS IN THE FILE'.
200-TABLE-ENTRY.
    MOVE T-ZIPCODE TO WS-ZIPCODE (X1).
    MOVE T-TAX TO WS-TAX (X1).
    READ TABLE-FILE
        AT END MOVE 'NO ' TO MORE-TABLE-RECS.
```

The DISPLAY verb is used, as shown here, to print brief messages on a terminal or printer.

C. Looking Up Data in a Table: Finding a Match

After the table entries have been stored in WORKING-STORAGE, we read customer billing data and produce bills. To find the sales tax rate or table function for each CUST-NO-IN, however, we must look up the zip code in the table (table argument) until it matches the zip code in the customer record (search argument). When a match is found between the table argument and the search argument, the corresponding sales tax rate (the table function) with the same subscript as the table's zip code will be used for calculating the sales tax.

Consider again the following pseudocode for this 200-CALC-RTN procedure:

Pseudocode
PERFORM UNTIL there is no more input
    Move Input Fields to Detail Line
    Search Table
        IF   a match is found
        THEN
                Compute Sales Tax using table function
                Compute Total
                Write Detail Line
        ELSE
            Move 0 to Sales Tax
        ENDIF
    Read a Transaction Record
ENDPERFORM

In the next section we discuss how a table is searched.

IV. Use of the SEARCH Statement for Table and Array Handling

A. Format of the SEARCH Statement

The best method for searching a table is with the use of a **SEARCH** statement. The format of the SEARCH is as follows:

Format

```
SEARCH identifier-1
    [AT END imperative-statement-1]

    WHEN condition-1 ⎰imperative-statement-2⎱ ...
                     ⎱NEXT SENTENCE         ⎰
```

Example
```
SEARCH TABLE-ENTRIES
    AT END MOVE 0 TO DL-SALES-TAX
    WHEN ZIP-IN = WS-ZIPCODE (X1)
        COMPUTE DL-SALES-TAX = WS-TAX (X1) *
            UNIT-PRICE-IN * QTY-IN
        COMPUTE DL-TOTAL = UNIT-PRICE-IN * QTY-IN + DL-SALES-TAX
        WRITE BILLING-REC FROM DETAIL-LINE
            AFTER ADVANCING 2 LINES.
```

The identifier used with the SEARCH verb is the table entry name specified on the OCCURS level, *not* on the 01 level.

The WHEN clause indicates what action is to be taken when the condition specified is actually met. This condition compares an input field or search argument (ZIP-IN in this example) with a table argument (WS-ZIPCODE (X1) in this example). Additional comparisons between search and table arguments can be made using other WHEN clauses. [Note the ellipses (. . .) in the instruction format.]

Using the SEARCH . . . AT END **for Data Validation**

With the SEARCH statement, the AT END clause specifies what should be done if the table has been completely searched and *no match is found.* That is, suppose the ZIP-IN field does not match any WS-ZIPCODE field in the table; such a condition will cause the AT END clause to be executed if it is specified. Since it is always possible for input errors to occur, we strongly recommend that you always use this optional clause. Without it, the "no match" condition would simply cause the program to continue with the next sentence. This could produce incorrect results or even cause an abend condition.

To use a SEARCH statement, two additional entries are required: the INDEXED BY clause and the SET statement.

B. The INDEXED BY **Clause and the** SEARCH **Statement**

When using a SEARCH statement, table entries must be specified with an **index** rather than a subscript. An index is used just like a subscript but it is defined along with the table entries as part of the OCCURS description:

```
01  SALES-TAX-TABLE.
    05  TABLE-ENTRIES OCCURS 1000 TIMES  INDEXED BY X1 .
        10  WS-ZIPCODE               PIC 9(5).
        10  WS-TAX                   PIC V999.
```

As noted, the index, X1 in this illustration, functions just like a subscript. Note, however, that unlike a subscript, an index is not defined separately in WORKING-STORAGE. It is defined with an **INDEXED BY** clause along with the OCCURS. The compiler *automatically* provides an appropriate PICTURE—in this case 9999, since there are 1000 entries in the table.

The SEARCH statement will perform a table look-up. TABLE-ENTRIES, the identifier used with the OCCURS and INDEXED BY clauses, is the item designated with the SEARCH as well. The 01-level entry, SALES-TAX-TABLE, could *not* be used with the SEARCH.

The table will be searched and the index *automatically* incremented until the condition specified in the WHEN clause is satisfied or until an AT END condition is met. The AT END indicates that the table has been completely searched without the condition being met; that is, no match has been found between an input field and a table entry. Frequently, we code the AT END as:
SEARCH ... AT END PERFORM 500-ERR-RTN WHEN ....

C. Modifying the Contents of an Index

1. The SET Statement

A *subscript* is a field defined in WORKING-STORAGE to access specific entries in an array. Its contents may be changed with the use of a PERFORM ... VARYING and with a MOVE, ADD, or SUBTRACT statement.

As we have seen, an index, however, is used in a table look-up and is defined with an INDEXED BY clause that follows a table's OCCURS clause. The index must be specified if a SEARCH is used to perform the table look-up. It can be modified with a PERFORM ... VARYING too. Thus, loading the table with a 200-TABLE-ENTRY routine as described previously is still correct.

Although a PERFORM ... VARYING may be used with an index, we may *not* modify the contents of an index with a MOVE, ADD, or SUBTRACT statement. Instead, we must use a **SET** statement to alter the contents of an index with *any instruction other than the* PERFORM ... VARYING.

Basic Format

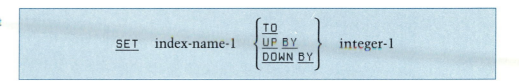

Examples

Statement	Meaning
1. SET X1 TO 1	Move 1 to the X1 index.
2. SET X1 UP BY 1	Add 1 to the X1 index.
3. SET X1 DOWN BY 1	Subtract 1 from the X1 index.

2. Initializing an Index Before Using the SEARCH

A SEARCH statement does not automatically initialize the index at 1. Initializing an index at 1 must be performed by a SET statement prior to the SEARCH to ensure that each table look-up begins with the first entry.

```
SET X1 TO 1.
SEARCH TABLE-ENTRIES
    AT END MOVE 0 TO DL-SALES-TAX
    WHEN ZIP-IN = WS-ZIPCODE (X1)
        COMPUTE DL-SALES-TAX = WS-TAX (X1) *
            UNIT-PRICE-IN * QTY-IN
        COMPUTE DL-TOTAL = UNIT-PRICE-IN * QTY-IN + DL-SALES-TAX
        WRITE BILLING-REC FROM DETAIL-LINE
            AFTER ADVANCING 2 LINES.
```

It would be more modular to code:

```
SEARCH ...
    WHEN ZIP-IN = WS-ZIPCODE (X1)
        PERFORM 400-CALC-AND-WRITE.
```

where the two COMPUTEs and the WRITE are part of 400-CALC-AND-WRITE.

Figure 14.3 illustrates a flowchart of the SEARCH procedure.

D. Avoiding Common Logic Errors

A word of advice: Avoid the use of the NEXT SENTENCE clause with the WHEN clause of the SEARCH when only one statement is to be executed. Consider the following coding, which could produce erroneous results:

Figure 14.3
Flowchart of the SEARCH procedure.

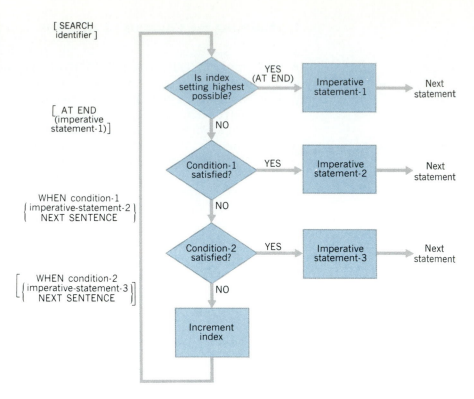

```
[ SEARCH
  identifier ]

[ AT END
  (imperative
  statement-1)]

        WHEN condition-1
     { imperative-statement-2 }
         NEXT SENTENCE

         WHEN condition-2
    [ { imperative-statement-3 } ]
          NEXT SENTENCE
```

```
                                INVALID

SET X1 TO 1.
SEARCH TABLE-ENTRIES
    AT END MOVE 0 TO DL-SALES-TAX
    WHEN ZIP-IN = WS-ZIPCODE (X1)
        NEXT SENTENCE.
COMPUTE DL-SALES-TAX = WS-TAX (X1) * UNIT-PRICE-IN * QTY-IN
 :
```

This procedure will function properly only if there is a match between each ZIP-IN and a WS-ZIPCODE (X1). If an AT END condition is reached because a particular ZIP-IN does not match any WS-ZIPCODE (X1), then 0 will be moved to DL-SALES-TAX and processing will continue with the *next sentence*. Thus, after an AT END is reached an effort will be made to multiply WS-TAX indexed by an undetermined X1 because the table has been exhausted. As a result, the computer may abort the run. To remedy this situation, simply code the COMPUTE as the imperative statement following the WHEN, as we illustrated at the beginning of this section. The NEXT SENTENCE clause is thus avoided.

Self-Test

1. Suppose an entire table has been searched using a SEARCH statement and the specific condition being tested has not been reached. What will happen?

2. If a SEARCH statement is used in the PROCEDURE DIVISION, then the OCCURS clause entry must also include a(n) _____ clause.

3. Suppose the following entry has been coded:

```
01   TABLE-X.
       05   CTRS OCCURS 100 TIMES INDEXED BY X1.
             10   FLD1    PIC 999.
             10   FLD2    PIC 9.
```

Write a statement to initialize the index at 1.

4. For Question 3, write a SEARCH statement to look up the table entries in CTRS until FLD1 = 123, at which time 300-PROCESS-TABLE-DATA is to be performed.

5. (T or F) The condition coded in a WHEN clause usually compares a table argument to a search argument.

Consider the following problem definition for Questions 6 through 9.

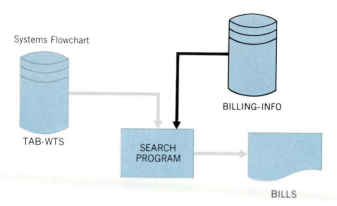

Systems Flowchart

TAB-WTS

BILLING-INFO

SEARCH PROGRAM

BILLS

TAB-WTS Record Layout (20 entries)

WEIGHT-MAX	DELIVERY-CHARGE
	$ ¢

1   5 6   10

BILLING-INFO Record Layout

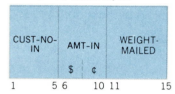

CUST-NO-IN	AMT-IN	WEIGHT-MAILED
	$ ¢	

1   5 6   10 11   15

BILLS Printer Spacing Chart

H 6	CUSTOMER NO	AMT OF SALES	DELIVERY CHARGE	TOTAL
D 8	XXXXX	$XXX.XX	$XXX.XX	$$,$$$.XX

Note:
The table contains the delivery charge for each weight category.
Entries are in sequence by WEIGHT-MAX.

Example

```
00500        100.25
  .
  .
  .
87320
99999        150.75
```

The first table entry indicates that the delivery charge for an item under 500 pounds is $100.25. The last table entry indicates that the delivery charge for an item that weighs between 87320 and 99999 is $150.75

6. Code the WORKING-STORAGE table area. Assume that a SEARCH will be used.

7. Code the 100-MAIN-MODULE for this program.

8. Code the 200-TABLE-ENTRY routine for this program.

9. Code the `300-CALC-RTN` using a `SEARCH` for the table look-up.

10. Indicate what, if anything, is wrong with the following.

```
01    TABLE-1.
      05   ENTRY-X OCCURS 20 TIMES  PIC 9(4)  INDEXED BY X1.
           ⋮
           ⋮
           SEARCH TABLE-1 ...
```

Solutions

1. The statement in the AT END clause will be executed if the clause has been included; if it has not, the next sentence will be executed. We recommend that you always use an AT END clause with the SEARCH statement.

2. INDEXED BY

3. SET X1 TO 1.

4.
```
SEARCH CTRS
     AT END PERFORM 500-ERR-RTN
     WHEN FLD1 (X1) = 123
     PERFORM 300-PROCESS-TABLE-DATA.
```

5. T

6.
```
WORKING-STORAGE SECTION.
01    WEIGHT-TABLE.
      05  STORED-ENTRIES OCCURS 20 TIMES INDEXED BY X1.
          10   T-WEIGHT-MAX          PIC 9(3)V99.
          10   T-DELIVERY-CHARGE     PIC 9(3)V99.
```

7.
```
PROCEDURE DIVISION.
100-MAIN-MODULE.
     PERFORM 400-INITIALIZATION-RTN.
     PERFORM 200-TABLE-ENTRY
         VARYING X1 FROM 1 BY 1 UNTIL X1 > 20.
     READ BILLING-INFO
         AT END MOVE 'NO ' TO ARE-THERE-MORE-RECORDS.
     PERFORM 300-CALC-RTN
         UNTIL THERE-ARE-NO-MORE-RECORDS.
     PERFORM 500-END-OF-JOB-RTN.
```

8.
```
200-TABLE-ENTRY.
     READ TAB-WTS AT END
             DISPLAY 'NOT ENOUGH TABLE RECORDS'
             CLOSE TAB-WTS
                     BILLING-INFO
                     BILLS
             STOP RUN.
     MOVE WEIGHT-MAX TO T-WEIGHT-MAX (X1).
     MOVE DELIVERY-CHARGE TO T-DELIVERY-CHARGE (X1).
```

9.
```
300-CALC-RTN.
     MOVE CUST-NO-IN TO CUST-NO-OUT.
     MOVE AMT-IN TO AMT-OF-SALES.
     SET X1 TO 1.
     SEARCH STORED-ENTRIES
         AT END MOVE 0 TO DELIVERY-CHARGE-OUT
             MOVE AMT-IN TO TOTAL
         WHEN WEIGHT-MAILED < T-WEIGHT-MAX (X1)
             MOVE T-DELIVERY-CHARGE (X1) TO DELIVERY-CHARGE-OUT
             COMPUTE TOTAL = AMT-IN + T-DELIVERY-CHARGE (X1).
     WRITE PRINT-REC FROM BILL-REC
         AFTER ADVANCING 2 LINES.
     READ BILLING-INFO
         AT END MOVE 'NO ' TO ARE-THERE-MORE-RECORDS.
```

10. SEARCH must be used in conjunction with the identifier ENTRY-X, *not* TABLE-1.

V. The SEARCH ALL Statement

A. Definition of a Serial Search

Thus far, we have discussed the method of table look-up called a **serial search.**

SERIAL SEARCH

1. The first entry in the table is searched.
2. If the condition is met, the table look-up is completed.
3. If the condition is not met, the index or subscript is incremented by one, and the next entry is searched.
4. This procedure is continued until a match is found or the table has been completely searched.

A sequential or serial search, as described here, is best used when either:

1. The entries in a table are *not* in either ascending or descending sequence; that is, they are arranged randomly; or,
2. Table entries are organized so that the first values are the ones encountered most frequently; in this way, access time is minimized because you are apt to end the search after the first few comparisons.

In many instances, however, the table entries are arranged in some numeric sequence. In a DISCOUNT-TABLE, for example, 50 customer numbers may be arranged within the table in ascending sequence:

	DISCOUNT-TABLE	
	T-CUSTOMER-NO	T-DISCOUNT-PCT
Ascending sequence	0100	2.0
	0200	1.0
	0400	5.0
	⋮	⋮

The table contains the discount percentage to which each customer is entitled. Note that although the customer numbers are in sequence, they are not necessarily consecutive.

We could code the table as follows:

```
01  TABLE-1.
    05  DISCOUNT-TABLE OCCURS 50 TIMES INDEXED BY X1.
        10  T-CUSTOMER-NO        PIC 9(4).
        10  T-DISCOUNT-PCT       PIC V999.
```

In this table, a discount of 2.0%, for example, is stored as $_\wedge$020.

In cases where the entries of a table are in sequence, a serial search may be inefficient. For example, it would be time-consuming to begin at the first table entry when searching for the T-DISCOUNT-PCT for customer number 9000. Since the table is in sequence, we know that customer number 9000 is somewhere near the end of the table; hence, beginning with the first entry and proceeding in sequence would waste time.

B. Definition of a Binary Search

When table entries are arranged in sequence by some table entry or table argument field, such as T-CUSTOMER-NO, the most efficient look-up performed is a **binary search.** The following is the way the computer performs a binary search:

ALTERNATIVE METHOD FOR TABLE LOOK-UP: BINARY SEARCH

1. Begin by comparing CUST-NO of the input customer record to the *middle table argument* for T-CUSTOMER-NO. In this instance, that would be the twenty-fifth entry in the table.

2. If CUST-NO-IN > T-CUSTOMER-NO (25) (which is the middle entry in our table), we have eliminated the need for searching the first half of the table.

   In such a case, we compare CUST-NO-IN to T-CUSTOMER-NO (37), the middle table argument of the second half of the table, and continue our comparison in this way.

3. If CUST-NO-IN < T-CUSTOMER-NO (25), we compare CUST-NO-IN to T-CUSTOMER-NO (12); that is, we divide the top half of the table into two segments and continue our comparison in this way.

4. The binary search is complete when a match has been made, that is, CUST-NO-IN = T-CUSTOMER-NO (X1), or the table has been completely searched.

On the average, a binary search takes fewer comparisons to find a match than does a serial search.

Example   Suppose CUST-NO-IN = 5000

DISCOUNT-TABLE

Table entry	T-CUSTOMER-NO (Table argument)	T-DISCOUNT-PCT (Table function)
1.	0100	2.0
2.	0200	1.0
3.	0400	5.0
4.	0500	3.1
⋮		

		Table entry	T-CUSTOMER-NO	T-DISCOUNT-PCT
1.	1st compare	25.	4300	4.3 (>)
3.	3rd compare	31.	4890	8.4 (>)
4.	4th compare	34.	5000	5.6 (=) *
2.	2nd compare	37.	5310	2.4 (<)
		50.	9940	7.1

A match of CUST-NO-IN with T-CUSTOMER-NO is found when the thirty-fourth entry of the table is compared. If a serial search were used, 34 comparisons would be required. Using the alternative binary search method, however, only four comparisons were required.

This alternative method is called a binary search because each comparison eliminates one half the entries under consideration; that is, each comparison reduces the entries to be considered by a factor of two.

A binary search is preferable to a serial search in the following instances:

USES OF A BINARY SEARCH

1. When table entries are arranged in some sequence—either ascending or descending.
2. When tables with a large number of sequential entries (e.g., 50 or more) are to be looked up or searched.

For small tables or those in which entries are *not* arranged in a sequence, the standard look-up method previously described is used. For large tables in which entries are arranged in a specific sequence, the binary search is most efficient. It is difficult to define a "large" table explicitly, but let us say that any table containing more than 50 entries that are in some sequence could benefit from the use of a binary search.

C. Format of the SEARCH ALL Statement

The **SEARCH ALL** statement is used to perform a binary search.

The format of the SEARCH ALL is very similar to that of the SEARCH.

Basic Format

```
SEARCH ALL identifier-1
     [AT END imperative-statement-1]
     WHEN  {data-name-1      {IS EQUAL TO}   {identifier-2
                             {IS =       }    literal-1
                                              arithmetic-expression-1}
            condition-name-1}

           [AND  {data-name-2      {IS EQUAL TO}   {identifier-3
                                   {IS =       }    literal-2
                                                    arithmetic-expression-2}
                  condition-name-2}
           . . .
           {imperative-statement-2}
           {NEXT SENTENCE        }
```

Note that the term data-name refers to an item that may not be subscripted, whereas an identifier may refer to a subscripted item.

A SET statement is *not* necessary with the SEARCH ALL, since the index is set to the appropriate point by the computer when a binary search is being performed.

Example

```
SEARCH ALL DISCOUNT-TABLE
     AT END PERFORM 500-ERR-RTN
     WHEN CUST-NO-IN = T-CUSTOMER-NO (X1)
          MULTIPLY AMT-OF-PURCHASE-IN BY T-DISCOUNT-PCT (X1)
               GIVING DISCOUNT-AMT-OUT.
```

Note the following limitations when using a SEARCH ALL.

LIMITATIONS OF THE SEARCH ALL

1. The condition following the word WHEN can only test for *equality*.

   Valid: WHEN CUST-NO-IN = T-CUSTOMER-NO (X1)
   Invalid: WHEN WEIGHT-MAILED $\boxed{<}$ T-WEIGHT-MAX (X1)

2. If the condition following the word WHEN is a compound conditional,
   a. Each part of the conditional can only consist of a relational test that involves an equal condition.
   b. The only compound condition permitted as condition-1 is a compound condition with ANDs, not ORs.

   Valid: WHEN AMT1 = S-AMT (X1) AND AMT2 = TAX-AMT (X1)
   Invalid: WHEN AMT3 = SALES-AMT (X1) $\boxed{OR}$ AMT4 = AMT5

3. Only one WHEN clause can be used with a SEARCH ALL.

D. ASCENDING or DESCENDING KEY with the SEARCH ALL Statement

To use the SEARCH ALL statement, we must indicate which table entry will serve as the *key field*. That is, we specify the table entry that will be in sequence so that the binary search can be used to compare against that field. We must indicate whether that KEY is ASCENDING or DESCENDING.

KEY FIELD

ASCENDING KEY   Entries are in sequence and increasing in value.
DESCENDING KEY   Entries are in sequence and decreasing in value.

The ASCENDING or DESCENDING KEY is specified along with the OCCURS and INDEXED BY clauses of a table entry when a SEARCH ALL is to be used, as shown in the following format:

Format

> (level-number 02–49)   identifier-1   <u>OCCURS</u> integer-1 TIMES
>
> $\begin{Bmatrix} \underline{ASCENDING} \\ \underline{DESCENDING} \end{Bmatrix}$ KEY IS identifier-2
>
> <u>INDEXED</u> BY index-name-1

Example

```
01   TABLE-1.
     05  DISCOUNT-TABLE OCCURS 50 TIMES
         ASCENDING KEY T-CUSTOMER-NO INDEXED BY X1.
         10  T-CUSTOMER-NO        PIC 9(4).
         10  T-DISCOUNT-PCT       PIC V999.
```

The identifier used in the ASCENDING KEY clause must be an entry within the table. If entries in the table decrease in value, then DESCENDING KEY would be used. In either case, the ASCENDING or DESCENDING KEY clause *must* be included and it must appear *before* the INDEXED BY clause.

In this example, T-CUSTOMER-NO increases in value as we move through the table; hence, T-CUSTOMER-NO is used with an ASCENDING KEY clause.

For best results, the KEY entries in the table should be unique; that is, no two fields (such as T-CUSTOMER-NO) should have the same value. If it happens, however, that two KEY entries in the table have identical values and one of them is to be accessed, it is difficult to predict which one the computer will use for the look up.

SUMMARY

Statement:	SEARCH ALL
Purpose:	To perform a binary search.
Limitations:	One of the table entries must be in sequence to use a binary search; there should be 50 or more table entries for a binary search to be beneficial.
Requirements:	ASCENDING or DESCENDING KEY must be used as part of the table entry specification. The specifications for the SEARCH are applicable to the SEARCH ALL as well, except that a SET index TO 1 is *not* required.

With COBOL 85 the END-SEARCH scope terminator may be used with either the SEARCH or SEARCH ALL statement.

CHAPTER SUMMARY

A. OCCURS clauses are used in the DATA DIVISION to specify the repeated occurrence of items with the same format.
1. OCCURS clauses may be written on any level except 01, 77, and 88.
2. An OCCURS clause may specify an elementary or group item.
B. Use an OCCURS clause to define arrays and tables.
1. Array: An area used for storing data or totals.
2. Table: A set of fields that are *referenced* as needed, usually with a table look-up.
C. Use of the SEARCH statement for table handling:
1. The identifier used with the SEARCH verb is the one specified on the OCCURS level.
2. The AT END clause specifies what is to be done if the table has been searched and the required condition has not been met.
3. The WHEN clause indicates the action to be taken when the condition is met.
4. Use of an index:
   a. When using a SEARCH statement, table entries are specified with the use of an index, rather than a subscript.
   b. The index is defined along with the OCCURS. For example,

```
01   UNIT-PRICE-TABLE.
     05 STORED-ENTRIES OCCURS 500 TIMES INDEXED BY X1.
```

   c. Unlike a subscript, an index is not defined separately in WORKING-STORAGE; it is part of the OCCURS definition itself.
   d. An index cannot be modified with a MOVE, ADD, or SUBTRACT statement. Use a SET statement when altering the contents of an index with any instruction other than the PERFORM ... VARYING.
   e. SET the index to 1 before using a SEARCH.
   f. Increment the index when loading a table defined with an index.
D. The SEARCH ALL statement—uses and limitations.
1. Used to perform a binary search.
2. Can only test an equal condition.
3. If using a compound condition,
   a. Each part can only test an equal condition.
   b. Only ANDs are permitted.
4. Only one WHEN clause can be used.
5. The ASCENDING or DESCENDING KEY is specified along with the OCCURS and INDEXED BY clauses of a table entry.

CHAPTER SELF-TEST

1. (T or F) The following are valid entries:

   ```
   FILE SECTION.
   FD  IN-FILE
       LABEL RECORDS ARE STANDARD.
   01  IN-REC OCCURS 50 TIMES.
   ```

2. (T or F) A subscript may be either a data-name or an integer.

3. If we store totals in WORKING-STORAGE, they must always be _____ before we add to them.

4. (T or F) An item defined by an OCCURS may be a group item that is further divided into elementary items.

Consider the following for Questions 5 and 6.

```
01  EX1.
    05  DAYS-TOGETHER            PIC X(21)
                    VALUE 'MONTUEWEDTHUFRISATSUN'.
    05  EACH-DAY REDEFINES DAYS-TOGETHER
            OCCURS 7 TIMES      PIC X(3).
```

5. (T or F) The entries are valid.

6. If we DISPLAY EACH-DAY (3), _____ will print.

7. (T or F) The identifier used with the SEARCH verb is the table-entry specified on the 01 level.

8. When using a SEARCH statement, table entries must be specified with the use of a(n) _____ , rather than a subscript.

9. (T or F) A SEARCH statement automatically initializes the index at 1.

10. The SEARCH ALL statement is used to perform a (binary/serial) search.

11. What, if anything, is wrong with the following SEARCH?

    ```
    SEARCH STORED-ENTRIES
        AT END DISPLAY 'NO ENTRY FOUND'
        WHEN ITEM-NO-IN = WS-ITEM-NO (X1)
            NEXT SENTENCE.
    COMPUTE PRICE = QTY * WS-UNIT-PR (X1).
    ```

12. A serial search of a table begins with the (first/middle/last) entry in the table whereas a binary search of a table begins with the (first/middle/last) entry.

13. (T or F) A SET statement is not necessary with the SEARCH ALL statement.

14. (T or F) The following is a valid SEARCH ALL statement.

    ```
    SEARCH ALL WEIGHT-TABLE
        AT END PERFORM 600-ERR-RTN
        WHEN WEIGHT-IN < WS-MAX-WEIGHT (X1)
            MULTIPLY WEIGHT-IN BY WS-RATE (X1)
                GIVING SHIPPING-COST.
    ```

15. The SEARCH ALL statement requires that a(n) _____ clause be specified along with the OCCURS and INDEXED BY clauses of a table entry.

Solutions

1. F—The OCCURS clause may not be used on the 01 level.
2. T
3. initialized (begin at zero)
4. T
5. T
6. WED

7. F—It is the name specified on the OCCURS level.

8. index

9. F—The index must be initialized with a SET statement prior to the SEARCH.

10. binary

11. This procedure will not function properly if an AT END condition is reached. In that case, an error message will be displayed and processing will continue with the next sentence—the COMPUTE. To remedy this situation, we could code the COMPUTE as the imperative statement specified with the WHEN clause.

12. first; middle

13. T—The index is automatically set at the appropriate point when a binary search is performed.

14. F—The SEARCH ALL can only test an equal condition.

15. ASCENDING or DESCENDING KEY

PRACTICE PROGRAM

Consider the problem definition in Figure 14.4.

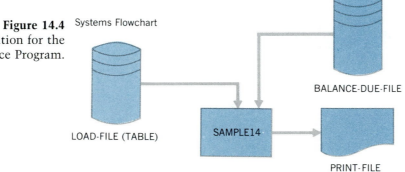

Figure 14.4
Problem definition for the Practice Program.

Systems Flowchart

LOAD-FILE (TABLE)

SAMPLE14

BALANCE-DUE-FILE

PRINT-FILE

LOAD-FILE Record Layout

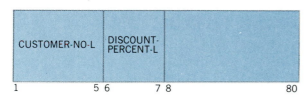

CUSTOMER-NO-L	DISCOUNT-PERCENT-L	
1 5	6 7	8 80

BALANCE-DUE-FILE Record Layout

CUSTOMER-NO-IN	CUSTOMER-NAME-IN	BAL-DUE-IN	
1 5	6 20	21 27	28 80

PRINT-FILE Printer Spacing Chart

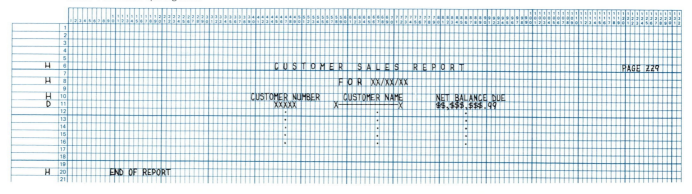

Figure 14.4
(continued)

SAMPLE INPUT DATA		SAMPLE TABLE DATA
00005JOHN WAYNE	0087625	0000510
00007BURT REYNOLDS	0787656	0000723
00100GEORGE BURNS	0088860	0010009
00111STEVE McQUEEN	0076890	0011107
00125SALLY FIELDS	8998800	0012506
00179MARK HAMILL	0985660	0017910
00182BILL DeWILLIAMS	0098900	0018211
00157CHRISTY FISHER	9999990	0015705
00155HARRISON FORD	0768800	0015510
00201HARPO MARX	0009778	0020109
00207BOB HOPE	0231400	0020704
00217DOROTHY LAMORE	0675500	0021720
00222BING CROSBY	0000450	0022209
00237BILL COSBY	0987998	0023711
00249BURT LANCASTER	0087650	0024902
00307DOUG FAIRBANKS	0857510	0030709
00515EDDIE MURPHY	0898800	0051521
00555NICK NOLTE	0566300	0055515
00565W.C. FIELDS	0005000	0056512
00600DON MEREDITH	0089750	0060018
00009BABE RUTH	0005700	0000908
00002HENERY AARON	6215200	0000205
00451ALAN ALDA	0036900	0045112
00499ALAN ARKIN	0927760	0049915
00404JOHN SMITH	0060000	0040417
00572JANE DOE	0876774	0057213
00231JACK KLUGMAN	0200910	0023117
00110TONY RANDALL	0089900	0011009
00313ART CARNEY	0977870	0031308
		0432312
		0987708
		0066709
		1112208
		0087702
		0888805
		0998801

Notes

1. Write a program that will read in 35 table records from a disk. These indicate the discount to which each of the 35 customers is entitled.
2. After the 35 table records have been read, read a master disk file called BALANCE-DUE-FILE that contains the balance due for each customer. These disk records are *not* in sequence.
3. For each master record read, find the corresponding discount from the table. Using the appropriate discount percent, print each customer's net balance due.
4. Use the SEARCH to find customer data in the table.
5. If there is no corresponding table entry for a particular customer, display the customer number, the message 'BAD DATA--RUN TERMINATED', and abort the run.

See Figure 14.5 for the hierarchy chart and pseudocode. See Figure 14.6 for a solution with sample output.

KEY TERMS

Array	SEARCH	Subscript
Binary search	SEARCH ALL	Table
Index	Search argument	Table argument
INDEXED BY	Serial search	Table function
OCCURS clause	SET	Table look-up
Relative subscript		

Figure 14.5
Pseudocode and hierarchy
chart for the Practice Program.

Pseudocode

```
START
    PERFORM
        Open the Files
        Initialize Table
        Read a Table Record
        Read a Transaction Record
        Accept Date
    ENDPERFORM
    PERFORM
        Write Headings
    ENDPERFORM
    PERFORM UNTIL Table is loaded
        Load the Table Entry
        Read a Table Record
    ENDPERFORM
    PERFORM UNTIL no more transaction data
        Search Table
            IF   a match is found
            THEN
                PERFORM
                    Compute Net Balance
                    Write an Output Line
                    IF   page overflow
                    THEN
                        PERFORM
                            Write Headings
                        ENDPERFORM
                    ENDIF
                ENDPERFORM
            ELSE
                PERFORM
                    Write Error Line
                ENDPERFORM
            ENDIF
        Read a Transaction Record
    ENDPERFORM
    PERFORM
        IF   page overflow
        THEN
            PERFORM
                Write Headings
            ENDPERFORM
        ENDIF
        Write Final Total
        End-of-Job Operations
    ENDPERFORM
STOP
```

Hierarchy Chart

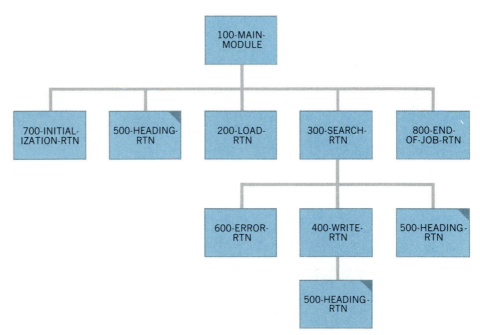

Figure 14.6
Solution to the Practice
Program.

```
IDENTIFICATION DIVISION.
PROGRAM-ID. SAMPLE.
AUTHOR. CHRISTOPHER HAMMEL.
******************************************************
*   THIS PROGRAM USES THE SEARCH INSTRUCTION TO     *
*   FIND CUSTOMER NUMBER AND USES CORRESPONDING      *
*   DISCOUNT PERCENTAGE TO DETERMINE BALANCE DUE     *
******************************************************
ENVIRONMENT DIVISION.
INPUT-OUTPUT SECTION.
FILE-CONTROL.
     SELECT BALANCE-DUE-IN   ASSIGN TO DATA136A.
     SELECT LOAD-FILE-IN     ASSIGN TO DATA136B.
     SELECT REPORT-FILE-OUT  ASSIGN TO SYS$OUTPUT.
*
DATA DIVISION.
FILE SECTION.
FD   BALANCE-DUE-IN
     LABEL RECORDS ARE OMITTED.
01   BALANCE-DUE-IN-REC.
     05   CUSTOMER-NO-IN           PIC 9(5).
     05   CUSTOMER-NAME-IN         PIC X(15).
     05   BAL-DUE-IN               PIC 9(5)V99.
FD   LOAD-FILE-IN
     LABEL RECORDS ARE OMITTED.
01   LOAD-REC-IN.
     05   CUSTOMER-LOAD-NO-IN      PIC 9(5).
     05   DISCOUNT-PCT-IN          PIC V99.
FD   REPORT-FILE-OUT
     LABEL RECORDS ARE OMITTED.
01   REPORT-REC-OUT               PIC X(133).
WORKING-STORAGE SECTION.
01   WS-WORK-AREAS.
     05   ARE-THERE-MORE-RECORDS PIC X(3)    VALUE 'YES'.
        88   MORE-RECORDS                    VALUE 'YES'.
        88   NO-MORE-RECORDS                 VALUE 'NO '.
     05   WS-CTR                  PIC 9(3)    VALUE ZEROS.
     05   WS-PAGE-CTR             PIC 9(3)    VALUE ZEROS.
     05   WS-LINE-CTR             PIC 9(3)    VALUE ZEROS.
     05   WS-T-DATE.
        10   WS-YR                PIC 99.
        10   WS-MO                PIC 99.
        10   WS-DA                PIC 99.
01   WS-BALANCE-TABLE.
     05   WS-TABLE-ENTRIES OCCURS 35 TIMES
             INDEXED BY SUB1.
        10   WS-CUST-NO-T         PIC 9(5).
        10   WS-DISCOUNT-PCT-T    PIC V99.
01   HL-HEADER1.
     05   FILLER                  PIC X(45)   VALUE SPACES.
     05   FILLER                  PIC X(42)
          VALUE 'C U S T O M E R   S A L E S     R E P O R T '.
     05   FILLER                  PIC X(33)   VALUE SPACES.
     05   FILLER                  PIC X(5)
          VALUE 'PAGE '.
     05   HL-PAGE-OUT             PIC ZZ9.
     05   FILLER                  PIC X(5)    VALUE SPACES.
01   HL-HEADER2.
     05   FILLER                  PIC X(59)   VALUE SPACES.
     05   FILLER                  PIC X(7)
          VALUE 'F O R '.
     05   HL-T-DATE.
        10   HL-MO                PIC 99.
        10   FILLER               PIC X       VALUE '/'.
        10   HL-DA                PIC 99.
        10   FILLER               PIC X       VALUE '/'.
        10   HL-YR                PIC 99.
     05   FILLER                  PIC X(59)   VALUE SPACES.
01   HL-HEADER3.
     05   FILLER                  PIC X(40)   VALUE SPACES.
     05   FILLER                  PIC X(15)
          VALUE 'CUSTOMER NUMBER'.
     05   FILLER                  PIC X(5)    VALUE SPACES.
     05   FILLER                  PIC X(15)
          VALUE 'CUSTOMER NAME   '.
```

Figure 14.6
(continued)

```
              05  FILLER                       PIC X(5)        VALUE SPACES.
              05  FILLER                       PIC X(15)
                  VALUE 'NET BALANCE DUE'.
              05  FILLER                       PIC X(38)       VALUE SPACES.
          01  HL-HEADER-FINAL.
              05  FILLER                       PIC X(10)       VALUE SPACES.
              05  FILLER                       PIC X(13)
                  VALUE 'END OF REPORT'.
              05  FILLER                       PIC X(110)      VALUE SPACES.
          01  DL-BALANCE-LINE.
              05  FILLER                       PIC X(45)       VALUE SPACES.
              05  DL-CUSTOMER-NO               PIC 9(5).
              05  FILLER                       PIC X(8)        VALUE SPACES.
              05  DL-CUSTOMER-NAME             PIC X(15).
              05  FILLER                       PIC X(7)        VALUE SPACES.
              05  DL-NET-BAL                   PIC $$,$$$,$$$.99.
              05  FILLER                       PIC X(40)       VALUE SPACES.
          01  DL-ERROR-REC.
              05  FILLER                       PIC X(20)       VALUE SPACES.
              05  DL-ERR-CUST-NO              PIC 9(5).
              05  FILLER                       PIC X(20)       VALUE SPACES.
              05  FILLER                       PIC X(24)
                  VALUE 'BAD DATA--RUN TERMINATED'.
              05  FILLER                       PIC X(64)       VALUE SPACES.
      *
          PROCEDURE DIVISION.
      ************************************************
      *   CONTROLS DIRECTION OF PROGRAM LOGIC   *
      ************************************************
          100-MAIN-MODULE.
              PERFORM 700-INITIALIZATION-RTN.
              PERFORM 500-HEADING-RTN.
              PERFORM 200-LOAD-RTN
                  VARYING WS-CTR FROM 1 BY 1
                      UNTIL WS-CTR > 35.
              PERFORM 300-SEARCH-RTN
                  UNTIL NO-MORE-RECORDS.
              PERFORM 800-END-OF-JOB-RTN.
      ********************************************************
      *   PERFORMED FROM 100-MAIN-MODULE                    *
      *   LOADS CUSTOMER FILE AND DISCOUNT PCT INTO ARRAY   *
      ********************************************************
          200-LOAD-RTN.
              MOVE CUSTOMER-LOAD-NO-IN TO WS-CUST-NO-T (WS-CTR).
              MOVE DISCOUNT-PCT-IN TO WS-DISCOUNT-PCT-T (WS-CTR).
              READ LOAD-FILE-IN
                  AT END DISPLAY 'ERROR - NOT ENOUGH TABLE RECORDS'
                  CLOSE BALANCE-DUE-IN
                          LOAD-FILE-IN
                          REPORT-FILE-OUT
                  STOP RUN.
      ************************************************************
      *   PERFORMED FROM 100-MAIN-MODULE -   SEARCH INSTRUCTION   *
      *   IS USED TO FIND A MATCH FOR INPUT RECORD.  IF NO MATCH  *
      *   IS FOUND, ERROR MESSAGE IS DISPLAYED AND RUN TERMINATED *
      ************************************************************
          300-SEARCH-RTN.
              SET SUB1 TO 1.
              SEARCH   WS-TABLE-ENTRIES
                          AT END PERFORM 600-ERROR-RTN
                      WHEN CUSTOMER-NO-IN = WS-CUST-NO-T (SUB1)
                          PERFORM 400-WRITE-RTN.
              READ BALANCE-DUE-IN
                  AT END MOVE 'NO ' TO ARE-THERE-MORE-RECORDS.
      ************************************************
      *   PERFORMED FROM 300-SEARCH-RTN -   COMPUTES   *
      *   CUSTOMERS NET BALANCE PRINTS OUT RECORD      *
      ************************************************
          400-WRITE-RTN.
              COMPUTE DL-NET-BAL =
                      BAL-DUE-IN - (WS-DISCOUNT-PCT-T (SUB1) * BAL-DUE-IN)
              MOVE WS-CUST-NO-T (SUB1) TO DL-CUSTOMER-NO.
              MOVE CUSTOMER-NAME-IN TO DL-CUSTOMER-NAME.
              IF  WS-LINE-CTR > 40
                  PERFORM 500-HEADING-RTN.
```

Figure 14.6
(continued)

```
        WRITE REPORT-REC-OUT FROM DL-BALANCE-LINE
            AFTER ADVANCING 1 LINES.
        ADD 1 TO WS-LINE-CTR.
****************************************************************
*  PERFORMED FROM 100-MAIN-MODULE, 400-WRITE-RTN   AND        *
*  800-END-OF-JOB-RTN - PRINTS OUT NEW PAGE WITH HEADINGS     *
****************************************************************
 500-HEADING-RTN.
        ADD 1 TO WS-PAGE-CTR.
        MOVE WS-PAGE-CTR TO HL-PAGE-OUT.
        MOVE 1 TO WS-LINE-CTR.
        WRITE REPORT-REC-OUT FROM HL-HEADER1
            AFTER ADVANCING PAGE.
        WRITE REPORT-REC-OUT FROM HL-HEADER2
            AFTER ADVANCING 2 LINES.
        WRITE REPORT-REC-OUT FROM HL-HEADER3
            AFTER ADVANCING 2 LINES.
****************************************************************
*  PERFORMED FROM 300-SEARCH-RTN  -  PRINTS  AN ERROR MESSAGE, *
*  CLOSES THE FILES, AND RETURNS CONTROL TO THE OPERATING SYSTEM*
*  IF THE SEARCH HAS FAILED.                                   *
****************************************************************
 600-ERROR-RTN.
        MOVE CUSTOMER-NO-IN TO DL-ERR-CUST-NO.
        WRITE REPORT-REC-OUT FROM DL-ERROR-REC
            AFTER ADVANCING 5 LINES.
        CLOSE BALANCE-DUE-IN
             LOAD-FILE-IN
             REPORT-FILE-OUT.
        STOP RUN.
****************************************************************
*  PERFORMED FROM 100-MAIN-MODULE -  OPEN FILES AND PERFORMS  *
*  INITIAL READS.   ACCEPTS TODAYS DATE FROM OPERATING SYSTEM *
*  AND ZEROS OUT FIELDS IN WORKING-STORAGE SECTION            *
****************************************************************
 700-INITIALIZATION-RTN.
        OPEN INPUT   BALANCE-DUE-IN
                     LOAD-FILE-IN
             OUTPUT REPORT-FILE-OUT.
        MOVE ZEROS TO WS-BALANCE-TABLE.
        READ LOAD-FILE-IN
            AT END DISPLAY 'ERROR - NOT ENOUGH TABLE RECORDS'
                    CLOSE BALANCE-DUE-IN
                          LOAD-FILE-IN
                          REPORT-FILE-OUT
                    STOP RUN.
        READ BALANCE-DUE-IN
            AT END MOVE 'NO ' TO ARE-THERE-MORE-RECORDS.
        ACCEPT WS-T-DATE FROM DATE.
        MOVE WS-MO TO HL-MO.
        MOVE WS-DA TO HL-DA.
        MOVE WS-YR TO HL-YR.
****************************************************************
*  PERFORMED FROM 100-MAIN-MODULE  -  PRINTS FINAL HEADER     *
*  CLOSES FILES AND RETURNS CONTROL TO OPERATING SYSTEM       *
****************************************************************
 800-END-OF-JOB-RTN.
        IF  WS-LINE-CTR > 40
            PERFORM 500-HEADING-RTN.
        WRITE REPORT-REC-OUT FROM HL-HEADER-FINAL
            AFTER ADVANCING 5 LINES.
        CLOSE BALANCE-DUE-IN
             LOAD-FILE-IN
             REPORT-FILE-OUT.
        STOP RUN.


             C U S T O M E R   S A L E S   R E P O R T

                     F O R  01/29/88

        CUSTOMER NUMBER      CUSTOMER NAME      NET BALANCE DUE
             00005           JOHN WAYNE              $788.62
             00007           BURT REYNOLDS         $6,064.95
             00100           GEORGE BURNS            $808.62
             00111           STEVE McQUEEN           $715.07
             00125           SALLY FIELDS        $84,588.72
```

Figure 14.6
(continued)

```
00179    MARK HAMILL        $8,870.94
00182    BILL DeWILLIAMS      $880.21
00157    CHRISTY FISHER    $94,999.90
00155    HARRISON FORD      $6,919.20
00201    HARPO MARX            $88.97
00207    BOB HOPE           $2,221.44
00217    DOROTHY LAMORE     $5,404.00
00222    BING CROSBY            $4.09
00237    BILL COSBY         $8,793.18
00249    BURT LANCASTER       $858.97
00307    DOUG FAIRBANKS     $7,803.34
00515    EDDIE MURPHY       $7,100.52
00555    NICK NOLTE         $4,813.55
00565    W.C. FIELDS           $44.00
00600    DON MEREDITH         $735.95
00009    BABE RUTH             $52.44
00002    HENERY AARON      $59,044.40
00451    ALAN ALDA            $324.72
00499    ALAN ARKIN         $7,885.96
00404    JOHN SMITH           $498.00
00572    JANE DOE           $7,627.93
00231    JACK KLUGMAN       $1,667.55
00110    TONY RANDALL         $818.09
00313    ART CARNEY         $8,996.40
```

REVIEW QUESTIONS

I. True-False Questions

T F

— — 1. If an input record contained 10 group items, each with a three-digit elementary item followed by a four-digit elementary item, then an OCCURS clause could be used to define the input fields.

— — 2. An input field may not be used as a subscript.

— — 3. An OCCURS clause may not be used on the 01 level.

— — 4. An OCCURS clause may only be used to define entries in the FILE SECTION.

— — 5. Data can be either moved or added to an array.

— — 6. After a WHEN condition has been met in a SEARCH, the index contains the number of the element that resulted in a match.

— — 7. When the SEARCH ALL statement is used, the table must be in either ASCENDING or DESCENDING sequence.

— — 8. SEARCH ALL is used for a binary search.

— — 9. An index used in a SEARCH may be initialized by a MOVE statement.

— — 10. An index, like a subscript, must be defined as an elementary entry in WORKING-STORAGE.

II. General Questions

1. An input record consists of 15 group items, each with a 3-digit PART-NO and associated 3-digit QUANTITY-ON-HAND. Use an OCCURS clause to define the input.

2. Assume a record has been read. Determine if the record contains the quantity on hand for PART-NO 126. If so, print the quantity.

3. Find the average quantity on hand for the 15 parts.

4. Assume there are 50 input records, each with fields described as in Question 1. Code the WORKING-STORAGE entry to store these part numbers and their corresponding quantities on hand.

5. Write a routine to load the 50 input records into the WORKING-STORAGE entry.

6. Assume that the array described in Question 5 has been stored. Write a routine to find the average quantity for all parts stored in WORKING-STORAGE.

7. Indicate the differences between a SEARCH and a SEARCH ALL.

8. Consider the following table in storage.

```
01    POPULATION-TABLE.
      05   STATE-POP OCCURS 50 TIMES  PIC 9(8).
```

Find both the largest and the smallest state population figures.

9. Using the table in Question 8, write a routine to print the total number of states that have populations smaller than 2,250,000.

10. Using the population table defined in Question 8, print the state number of each state with a population in excess of 2,250,000 people.

III. Validating Data

Modify the Practice Program so that it includes coding to (1) test for all errors and (2) print a control listing of totals (records processed, errors encountered, batch totals).

DEBUGGING EXERCISES

1. Consider the following:

```
WORKING-STORAGE SECTION.
01   STORED-AREAS.
     05   ARE-THERE-MORE-RECORDS   PIC X(3)        VALUE 'YES'.
          88   THERE-ARE-NO-MORE-RECORDS           VALUE 'NO '.
     05   SUB1                     PIC 9.
01   TABLE-IN.
     05   ENTRIES OCCURS 20 TIMES.
          10   CUST-NO             PIC 999.
          10   DISCT               PIC V99.
*
PROCEDURE DIVISION.
100-MAIN-MODULE.
     PERFORM 400-INITIALIZATION-RTN.
     READ TABLE-FILE
          AT END MOVE 'NO ' TO ARE-THERE-MORE-RECORDS.
     PERFORM 200-TABLE-ENTRY
          VARYING SUB1 FROM 1 BY 1 UNTIL SUB1 > 20.
     PERFORM 300-CALC-RTN
          UNTIL THERE-ARE-NO-MORE-RECORDS.
     PERFORM 500-END-OF-JOB-RTN.
200-TABLE-ENTRY.
     MOVE T-CUST-NO TO CUST-NO (SUB1).
     MOVE T-DISCT TO DISCT (SUB1).
     READ TABLE-FILE
          AT END MOVE 'NO ' TO ARE-THERE-MORE-RECORDS.
300-CALC-RTN.
          ⋮
```

There are two major logic errors in this program excerpt.

(a) After the table has been loaded, you find that 300-CALC-RTN is not performed. That is, the run is terminated after the table is loaded. Find the error and correct it.

(b) After receiving an obscure interrupt message you DISPLAY TABLE-IN entries and find that only the last nine have been loaded. Find the error and correct it.

Consider the following 700-CALC-RTN excerpt (not part of Exercise 1 above):

```
21      700-CALC-RTN.
22          SEARCH INV-ENTRIES
23              AT END MOVE 0 TO QTY-OUT
24              WHEN PART-NO-IN = T-PART-NO (X1)
25                  NEXT SENTENCE.
26          MOVE T-QTY-ON-HAND (X1) TO QTY-OUT.
27          MOVE PART-NO-IN TO PART-OUT.
28          WRITE PRINT-REC FROM DETAIL-REC.
29          READ INVENTORY-FILE
30              AT END MOVE 'NO ' TO ARE-THERE-MORE-RECORDS.
```

2. An abend condition will occur the first time through 700-CALC-RTN. Find and correct the error.

3. An abend condition will occur if there is no match between PART-NO-IN and T-PART-NO. Find and correct the error.

4. Suppose INV-ENTRIES is defined as follows:

```
01  INV-ENTRIES,
    05  TAB1 OCCURS 30 TIMES,
        10  T-PART-NO       PIC 9(3),
        10  T-QTY-ON-HAND   PIC 9(4),
```

This will cause two syntax errors on lines 22 and 24. Find and correct these errors.

PROGRAMMING ASSIGNMENTS

1. Write a program to print total sales for each salesperson. The problem definition is shown in Figure 14.7.

Figure 14.7
Problem definition for Programming Assignment 1.

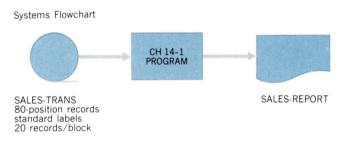

Systems Flowchart

SALES-TRANS
80-position records
standard labels
20 records/block

CH 14-1
PROGRAM

SALES-REPORT

SALES-TRANS Record Layout

SALESPERSON NO.	SALESPERSON NAME	AMOUNT OF SALES	
		$ ¢	
1 2	3 22	23 27	28 80

SALES-REPORT Printer Spacing Chart

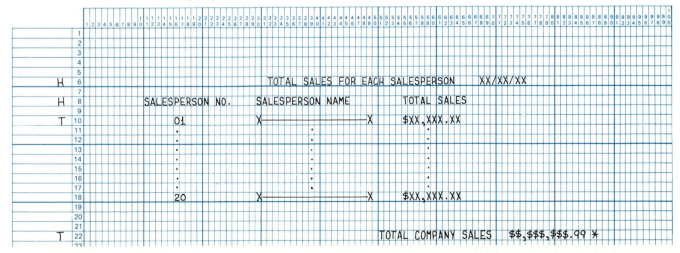

Notes

a. There are 20 salespeople, numbered 1 to 20.

b. Each sale that is made is used to create one input tape record; thus, there may be numerous input records for each salesperson if he or she made more than one sale.

c. Input records are not in sequence. (If they were, you could use a control break procedure.)

d. Print the total sales figure for each salesperson; thus, although the number of input records is variable, the output will consist of 20 totals.

e. All total fields should be edited.

2. Consider the problem definition in Figure 14.8.

Systems Flowchart

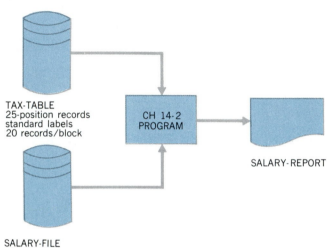

TAX-TABLE
25-position records
standard labels
20 records/block

CH 14-2
PROGRAM

SALARY-REPORT

SALARY-FILE
80-position records
standard labels
20 records/block

TAX-TABLE Record Layout

MAXIMUM TAXABLE INCOME	FEDERAL TAX .XXX	STATE TAX RATE .XXX	
1 6	7 9	10 12	13 25

SALARY-FILE Record Layout

EMPLOYEE NO.	EMPLOYEE NAME	ANNUAL SALARY (in $)		NO. OF DEPENDENTS	
1 5	6 25	26 29 30 35	36 44	45 46 47	8

SALARY-REPORT Printer Spacing Chart

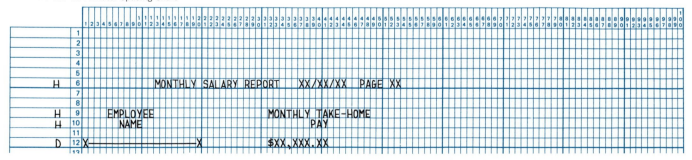

Figure 14.8
Problem definition for
Programming Assignment 2.

Notes

a. Monthly take-home pay is to be computed for each employee of Company ABC. A tax table must be read into main storage from 20 input disk records.

Example

Taxable Income	Federal Tax	State Tax
09800	.040	.010
12000	.080	.020

The state tax is 1% and the federal tax is 4% for taxable income less than or equal to 9800; for a taxable income between 9801 and 12000 (inclusive), the state tax is 2% and the federal tax is 8%, and so on.

b. After the table is read and stored, read a salary file. Monthly take-home pay is computed as follows.

(1) Standard deduction = 10% of the first $10,000 of annual salary

(2) Dependent deduction = 1080 × number of dependents

(3) FICA (Social Security tax) = 7.15% of the first $43,800 of annual salary

(4) Taxable income = Annual salary − standard deduction − dependent deduction

(5) Find the tax for the taxable income using the tax table.

(6) Annual take-home pay = Annual salary − (state tax % × taxable income) − (federal tax % × taxable income) − FICA

(7) Monthly take-home pay = Annual take-home pay / 12

(8) Print each employee's name and the corresponding monthly take-home pay (edited).

Figure 14.9
Problem definition for
Programming Assignment 3.

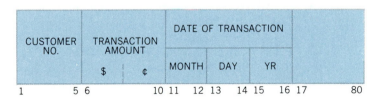

Systems Flowchart

CH 14-3 PROGRAM

TRANS-FILE
80-position records
standard labels
50 records/block

MONTH-REPORT

TRANS-FILE Record Layout

CUSTOMER NO.	TRANSACTION AMOUNT		DATE OF TRANSACTION			
	$	¢	MONTH	DAY	YR	
1	5 6	10	11 12	13 14	15 16	17 80

MONTH-REPORT Printer Spacing Chart

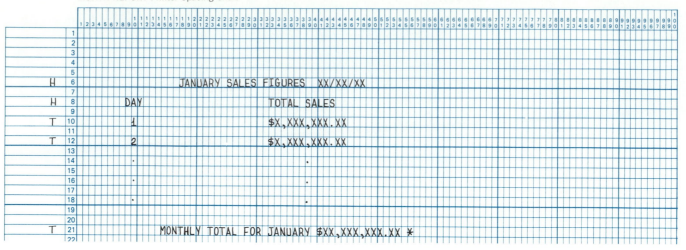

Figure 14.9
(continued)

3. Write a program to print a transaction report. The problem definition is shown in Figure 14.9.

Notes

a. The number of input records is variable. Print daily totals for each day of January and a monthly total for January as well.
b. Input records are not in sequence.
c. All numeric fields are to be edited.
d. Month in Date of Transaction varies from 1 to 12.

4. Write a program to print daily sales totals in sequence. The input consists of tape records with the following format.

    1–5   Amount of sales for Day X   (XXX.XX)
    6–10 Amount of sales for Day X + 1   (XXX.XX)
    11–80 Not used

Records are blocked 25; standard labels are used.

Notes

a. The first input record has amount of sales for days 29 and 30; the second for days 27 and 28, and so on. There are 15 input records.
b. Print the sales figures in proper sequence from Day 1 to Day 30. On each line, print the day number and the corresponding sales figure.
c. Include appropriate titles and the date on the output.

Figure 14.10
Problem definition for
Programming Assignment 5.

5. Consider the problem definition in Figure 14.10.

Systems Flowchart

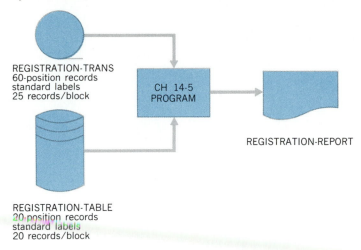

REGISTRATION-TRANS
60-position records
standard labels
25 records/block

CH 14-5
PROGRAM

REGISTRATION-REPORT

REGISTRATION-TABLE
20-position records
standard labels
20 records/block

REGISTRATION-TABLE Record Layout

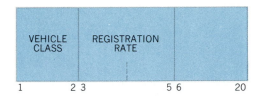

	VEHICLE CLASS	REGISTRATION RATE	
1	2 3	5 6	20

REGISTRATION-TRANS Record Layout

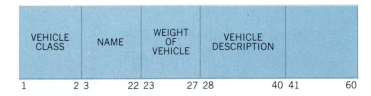

VEHICLE CLASS	NAME	WEIGHT OF VEHICLE	VEHICLE DESCRIPTION
1 2	3 22	23 27	28 40 41 60

REGISTRATION-REPORT Printer Spacing Chart

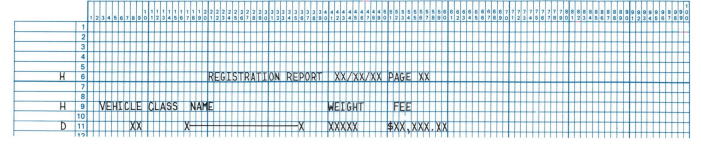

Notes

   a. There are 150 table entries (vehicle class is an alphanumeric field).

   b. After the table is read and stored, read in the transaction file.

   c. For each transaction record, the vehicle class must be found in the table to obtain the corresponding registration rate.

   d. Registration Fee = Vehicle Weight × Registration Rate (from the table).

Figure 14.11
Problem definition for
Programming Assignment 6.

6. Consider the problem definition in Figure 14.11.

Systems Flowchart

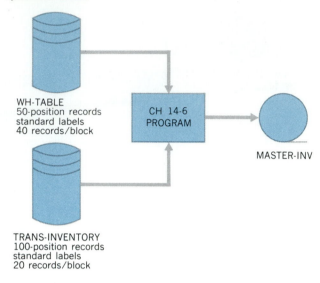

WH-TABLE
50-position records
standard labels
40 records/block

CH 14-6
PROGRAM

MASTER-INV

TRANS-INVENTORY
100-position records
standard labels
20 records/block

WH-TABLE Record Layout

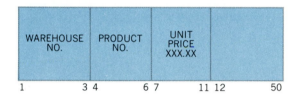

WAREHOUSE NO.	PRODUCT NO.	UNIT PRICE XXX.XX	
1 3	4 6	7 11	12 50

TRANS-INVENTORY Record Layout

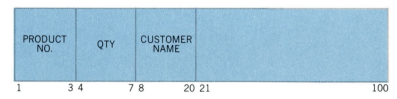

PRODUCT NO.	QTY	CUSTOMER NAME	
1 3	4 7	8 20	21 100

MASTER-INV Record Layout

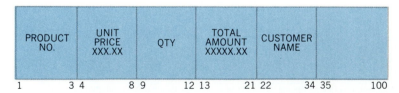

PRODUCT NO.	UNIT PRICE XXX.XX	QTY	TOTAL AMOUNT XXXXX.XX	CUSTOMER NAME	
1 3	4 8	9 12	13 21	22 34	35 100

Notes

a. Input table entries are entered first. There are 250 of these table entries.

b. Create an output tape containing product number, unit price, quantity, total amount, and customer name for each transaction inventory record. Total amount = Unit price × quantity.

c. For each transaction inventory record, the product number must be found in the table to obtain the corresponding unit price.

15

Multiple-Level Arrays and Tables

OBJECTIVES

To familiarize you with

1. How to establish a series of items using a double-level OCCURS clause.
2. How to store data in a double-level array.
3. How to look up data stored in a double-level table.
4. How to access and manipulate data defined with a triple-level (or more) OCCURS clause.

I. Double-Level OCCURS Clause

When describing an area of storage, more than one level of OCCURS may be used. Both double- and triple-level OCCURS are permitted with all COBOL compilers, but COBOL 85 permits up to seven levels.

Like a single-level OCCURS, multiple levels of OCCURS may be used for (1) accumulating totals in an *array* or (2) storing a *table* for "look-up" purposes.

We will look first at multiple-level arrays and then consider multiple-level tables.

A. Defining a Double-Level Array

Suppose we wish to establish in storage an array of hourly temperature readings for Los Angeles *during a given week*. Once the array is established, we will use it to determine various statistics.

The array consists of 7×24 temperature readings; that is, there are 24 hourly temperature readings for each of 7 days. The array is represented as follows:

TEMPERATURE-ARRAY-1

DAY 1 (SUN)				DAY 2 (MON)					DAY 7 (SAT)			
1-AM-TEMP	2-AM-TEMP	...	MIDNIGHT-TEMP	1-AM-TEMP	2-AM-TEMP	...	MIDNIGHT-TEMP	...	1-AM-TEMP	2-AM-TEMP	...	MIDNIGHT-TEMP

To define this array in WORKING-STORAGE with a *single*-level OCCURS would require the following coding:

```
01   TEMPERATURE-ARRAY-1.
     05   DAY-OF-WEEK OCCURS 7 TIMES.
          10   1-AM-TEMP            PIC 9(3).
          10   2-AM-TEMP            PIC 9(3).
            .
            .
          10   11-PM-TEMP           PIC 9(3).
          10   MIDNIGHT             PIC 9(3).
```

The dots (...) indicate that 24 elementary items must be coded, which would be rather cumbersome.

Instead, we could use a *double-level* OCCURS to define the array as follows:

```
01   TEMPERATURE-ARRAY.
     05   DAY-OF-WEEK OCCURS 7 TIMES.
          10   HOUR OCCURS 24 TIMES.
               15   MEAN-TEMP            PIC 9(3).
```

The following illustration shows how this array can be visualized in storage:

Hour / Day-of-Week	TEMPERATURE-ARRAY						
	1 A.M.	2 A.M.	3 A.M.	4 A.M.	...	11 P.M.	12 MID.
Day 1 (Sun)					...		
Day 2 (Mon)					...		
Day 3 (Tue)					...		
Day 4 (Wed)					...		
Day 5 (Thu)					...		
Day 6 (Fri)					...		
Day 7 (Sat)					...		

7 ROWS

24 COLUMNS

This array defines a storage area of 504 positions (7 × 24 × 3). For each DAY-OF-WEEK, we have 24 HOUR figures, each of which will consist of a MEAN-TEMP (average or mean temperature for that hour) that is three integers long.
The *two-dimensional array* is established as follows:

1. The array will have *7 rows* as indicated by the first OCCURS clause:

   ```
   05   DAY-OF-WEEK OCCURS 7 TIMES.
   ```

2. Within this array, each row will have 24 *columns*, as indicated by the second OCCURS clause:

   ```
   10   HOUR OCCURS 24 TIMES.
   ```

3. Each of the *elements* in this 7 × 24 array will be large enough to hold three integers, as indicated by the subordinate entry:

   ```
   15   MEAN-TEMP      PIC 9(3).
   ```

To access any of the temperature figures, we use the data-name on the *lowest* OCCURS *level* or any field subordinate to it. MEAN-TEMP could be used to access the fields, as well as HOUR. Because HOUR contains only one elementary item, MEAN-TEMP and HOUR refer to the same area of storage. Thus, the array could also have been defined as follows:

Alternative Coding

```
01   TEMPERATURE-ARRAY.
   05   DAY-OF-WEEK OCCURS 7 TIMES.
      10   HOUR     OCCURS 24 TIMES      PIC 9(3).
```

We have added the PIC clause to the second OCCURS level data-name, thereby eliminating the reference to the data-name MEAN-TEMP.

We will use the entry MEAN-TEMP throughout, however, since it is clearer. Note that we could *not* use DAY-OF-WEEK for accessing a single field in the array, since each DAY-OF-WEEK actually refers to 24 temperatures.

Using Subscripts with Double-Level OCCURS Entries

Since MEAN-TEMP is defined with two OCCURS, we must use *two* subscripts to access any mean temperature. The first subscript specified refers to the first or *major*-level OCCURS clause, which, in this example, defines the DAY-OF-WEEK. The second subscript refers to the second or *minor* OCCURS level, which, in this example, defines the HOUR. Thus, MEAN-TEMP (1, 6) refers to the average or mean temperature for Sunday (the first row) at 6 A.M. (the sixth column in the array). Assuming there is data in the array, we can display the mean temperature for Tuesday at noon with the following instruction:

```
DISPLAY 'MEAN TEMPERATURE FOR TUESDAY AT NOON IS ',
     MEAN-TEMP (3, 12).
```

Recall that a DISPLAY is used to print messages and will be discussed thoroughly in Chapter 19.

The first subscript, then, can vary from 1 to 7 since there are seven rows, one for each day. The second subscript varies from 1 to 24, since there are 24 columns, one for each hour of the day.

The following are *not* valid:

Invalid Subscripts

MEAN-TEMP (8, 4) The first subscript can vary from 1 through 7.
MEAN-TEMP (6, 25) The second subscript can vary from 1 through 24.

A pictorial representation of the table with its subscripts follows:

Temperature-Array

Hour Day-of-Week	1 A.M.	2 A.M.	3 A.M.	4 A.M.	. . .	11 P.M.	12 MID.
Day 1 (Sun)	(1,1)	(1,2)	(1,3)	(1,4)	. . .	(1,23)	(1,24)
Day 2 (Mon)	(2,1)	(2,2)	(2,3)	(2,4)	. . .	(2,23)	(2,24)
Day 3 (Tue)	(3,1)	(3,2)	(3,3)	(3,4)	. . .	(3,23)	(3,24)
Day 4 (Wed)	(4,1)	(4,2)	(4,3)	(4,4)	. . .	(4,23)	(4,24)
Day 5 (Thu)	(5,1)	(5,2)	(5,3)	(5,4)	. . .	(5,23)	(5,24)
Day 6 (Fri)	(6,1)	(6,2)	(6,3)	(6,4)		(6,23)	(6,24)
Day 7 (Sat)	(7,1)	(7,2)	(7,3)	(7,4)	. . .	(7,23)	(7,24)

The following are rules for using a double-level OCCURS:

RULES FOR USING A DOUBLE-LEVEL OCCURS

1. If an item is defined by a *double-level* OCCURS clause, it must be accessed by *two* subscripts.
2. The first subscript refers to the higher-level OCCURS; the second subscript refers to the lower-level OCCURS.
3. The subscripts must be enclosed in parentheses.
4. On most systems, the left parenthesis must be preceded by at least one space; similarly, the right parenthesis must be followed by a period, if it is the end of a sentence, or at least one space.
5. The first subscript within the parentheses is followed by a comma and a space.
6. Subscripts may consist of positive integers or data-names with positive integer contents.

Examples of Invalid Coding

Invalid Coding

REASON FOR INVALIDITY
(on some systems)

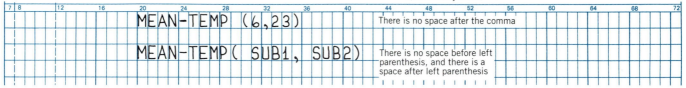

MEAN-TEMP (6,23)   There is no space after the comma

MEAN-TEMP(SUB1, SUB2)   There is no space before left parenthesis, and there is a space after left parenthesis

B. Accessing a Double-Level Array

Example 1   Suppose we wish to print an average temperature for the entire week. We need to add all the array entries to a total and divide by 168 (7 × 24). We can use *nested* PERFORMs for this purpose. The first PERFORM varies the major subscript, which we call DAY-SUB, and the second PERFORM varies the minor subscript, which we call HOUR-SUB.

```
600-AVERAGE-RTN.
    MOVE 0 TO TOTAL.
    PERFORM 700-MAJOR-LOOP
        VARYING DAY-SUB FROM 1 BY 1 UNTIL DAY-SUB > 7.
    COMPUTE WEEKLY-AVERAGE = TOTAL / 168.
    WRITE PRINT-REC FROM OUT-REC
        AFTER ADVANCING 2 LINES.
700-MAJOR-LOOP.
    PERFORM 800-MINOR-LOOP
        VARYING HOUR-SUB FROM 1 BY 1 UNTIL HOUR-SUB > 24.
800-MINOR-LOOP.
    ADD MEAN-TEMP (DAY-SUB, HOUR-SUB) TO TOTAL.
```

The PERFORM ... VARYING with the AFTER Option

The following expanded format for the PERFORM ... VARYING will result in nested PERFORMs *without the need for two separate* PERFORM ... VARYING *statements:*

Expanded Format

$$
\begin{aligned}
&\underline{\text{PERFORM}} \left[\text{procedure-name-1} \left[\left\{ \begin{array}{l} \underline{\text{THROUGH}} \\ \underline{\text{THRU}} \end{array} \right\} \text{procedure-name-2} \right] \right] \\[6pt]
&\quad \left[\underline{\text{WITH}}\ \underline{\text{TEST}} \left\{ \begin{array}{l} \underline{\text{BEFORE}} \\ \underline{\text{AFTER}} \end{array} \right\} \right] \\[6pt]
&\qquad \underline{\text{VARYING}} \left\{ \begin{array}{l} \text{identifier-2} \\ \text{index-name-1} \end{array} \right\} \underline{\text{FROM}} \left\{ \begin{array}{l} \text{identifier-3} \\ \text{index-name-2} \\ \text{literal-1} \end{array} \right\} \\[6pt]
&\qquad\quad \underline{\text{BY}} \left\{ \begin{array}{l} \text{identifier-4} \\ \text{literal-2} \end{array} \right\} \underline{\text{UNTIL}}\ \text{condition-1} \\[6pt]
&\qquad \left[\underline{\text{AFTER}} \left\{ \begin{array}{l} \text{identifier-5} \\ \text{index-name-3} \end{array} \right\} \underline{\text{FROM}} \left\{ \begin{array}{l} \text{identifier-6} \\ \text{index-name-4} \\ \text{literal-3} \end{array} \right\} \right. \\[6pt]
&\qquad\quad \left. \underline{\text{BY}} \left\{ \begin{array}{l} \text{identifier-7} \\ \text{literal-4} \end{array} \right\} \underline{\text{UNTIL}}\ \text{condition-2} \right] ... \\[6pt]
&\quad [\underline{\text{END-PERFORM}}]
\end{aligned}
$$

This format is particularly useful for processing multiple-level arrays and tables. The PERFORM ... VARYING varies the *major subscript* and the AFTER clause varies the *minor subscript*. Thus, we can simplify the preceding nested PERFORM as follows:

Alternative Coding

```
600-AVERAGE-RTN.
    MOVE 0 TO TOTAL.
    PERFORM 700-LOOP1
        VARYING DAY-SUB FROM 1 BY 1 UNTIL DAY-SUB > 7
            AFTER HOUR-SUB FROM 1 BY 1 UNTIL HOUR-SUB > 24.
    COMPUTE WEEKLY-AVERAGE = TOTAL / 168.
    WRITE PRINT-REC FROM OUT-REC
        AFTER ADVANCING 2 LINES.
700-LOOP1.
    ADD MEAN-TEMP (DAY-SUB, HOUR-SUB) TO TOTAL.
```

The sequence of values that these subscripts take on is (1, 1), (1, 2) . . . (1, 24), (2, 1), (2, 2) . . . (2, 24) . . . (7, 1) . . . (7, 24).

Consider the following double-level array and assume that data has been read into it:

```
01   POPULATION-ARRAY.
     05   STATE OCCURS 50 TIMES.
          10   COUNTY OCCURS 10 TIMES.
               15   POPULATION PIC 9(10).
```

This array defines 500 fields of data. Each of the 50 states is divided into 10 counties.
A pictorial representation of the array is as follows:

County State	County 1	County 2	POPULATION-ARRAY . . .	County 10
1 (Alabama)	(1,1)	(1,2)	. . .	(1,10)
2 (Alaska)	(2,1)	(2,2)	. . .	(2,10)
.	.	.	. . .	.
.	.	.	. . .	.
.	.	.	. . .	.
50 (Wyoming)	(50,1)	(50,2)	. . .	(50,10)

Note: The numbers in parentheses represent the subscripts for each entry.

Suppose we wish to accumulate a total United States population. We will add all 10 counties for each of 50 states. We access elements in the array by using the lowest level item, POPULATION. POPULATION must be accessed using *two* subscripts. The first defines the major level, STATE, and the second defines the minor level, COUNTY. POPULATION (5, 10) refers to the population for STATE 5, COUNTY 10. The first subscript varies from 1 to 50; the second varies from 1 to 10.

To perform the required addition, we will first accumulate all COUNTY figures for STATE 1. Thus, the second or minor subscript will vary from 1 to 10. After 10 additions for STATE 1 are performed, we will accumulate the 10 COUNTY figures for STATE 2. That is, we will increment the major subscript to 2 and then add COUNTY (2, 1), COUNTY (2, 2), ... COUNTY (2, 10) before we add the figures for STATE 3.

The required operations may be performed in two ways:

1. Nested PERFORMs

The minor loop will increment the minor subscript (COUNTY-SUB) from 1 to 10. The major loop will increment the major subscript (STATE-SUB) from 1 to 50:

```
    PERFORM 700-USA-TOT.
        :
        :
    700-USA-TOT.
        PERFORM 800-MAJOR-LOOP
            VARYING STATE-SUB FROM 1 BY 1 UNTIL STATE-SUB > 50.
        PERFORM 1000-PRINT-TOTAL.
    800-MAJOR-LOOP.
        PERFORM 900-MINOR-LOOP
            VARYING COUNTY-SUB FROM 1 BY 1 UNTIL COUNTY-SUB > 10.
    900-MINOR-LOOP.
        ADD POPULATION (STATE-SUB, COUNTY-SUB) TO TOTAL1.
            :
            :
```

2. PERFORM ... VARYING ... AFTER

Using the AFTER option of the PERFORM VARYING, we can simplify the coding as follows:

Alternative Coding

```
    PERFORM 700-USA-TOT.
        :
        :
    700-USA-TOT.
```

```
PERFORM 800-LOOP-IT
    VARYING STATE-SUB FROM 1 BY 1 UNTIL STATE-SUB > 50
    AFTER COUNTY-SUB FROM 1 BY 1 UNTIL COUNTY-SUB > 10.
PERFORM 1000-PRINT-TOTAL.
800-LOOP-IT.
    ADD POPULATION (STATE-SUB, COUNTY-SUB) TO TOTAL1.
```

Using either routine, we vary the minor subscript first, holding the major subscript constant. That is, when the major subscript is equal to 1, denoting STATE 1, all counties within that STATE are summed. Thus, we set STATE-SUB equal to 1 and vary COUNTY-SUB from 1 to 10. STATE-SUB is then set to 2, and we again vary COUNTY-SUB from 1 to 10, and so on.

The sequence of additions may also be performed as follows: POPULATION (1, 1), POPULATION (2, 1), ... POPULATION (50, 1); POPULATION (1, 2), POPULATION (2, 2), ... POPULATION (50, 2), ... POPULATION (50, 10). That is, we can add the population figures for COUNTY 1 in all 50 states, then COUNTY 2 in all 50 states, and so on. This means we vary the *major subscript first*, holding the minor subscript constant. We set COUNTY-SUB equal to 1 and vary STATE-SUB from 1 to 50; we then increment COUNTY-SUB to 2 and vary STATE-SUB from 1 to 50 again, and so on. The following coding illustrates how this procedure can be performed:

Alternative Coding

```
PERFORM 700-USA-TOT.
  ⋮
700-USA-TOT.
    PERFORM 800-MAJOR-LOOP
        VARYING COUNTY-SUB FROM 1 BY 1 UNTIL COUNTY-SUB > 10.
    PERFORM 1000-PRINT-TOTAL.
800-MAJOR-LOOP.
    PERFORM 900-MINOR-LOOP
        VARYING STATE-SUB FROM 1 BY 1 UNTIL STATE-SUB > 50.
900-MINOR-LOOP.
    ADD POPULATION (STATE-SUB, COUNTY-SUB) TO TOTAL1.
```

All the routines illustrated result in the same accumulated population figure.

Example 3   Let us establish an array that will contain 12 monthly figures for each of 25 salespersons in Company X. Each figure represents the monthly sales amount credited to a salesperson. Thus, the first element in the array will be January's sales amount for Salesperson 1, the second will be February's sales amount for Salesperson 1, and so on.

There are 25 salespeople, each having 12 monthly sales figures and the salespeople are numbered from 1 to 25 consecutively. The WORKING-STORAGE SECTION entry for this array is as follows:

```
01  COMPANY-SALES-ARRAY.
    05  SALESPERSON OCCURS 25 TIMES.
        10  MONTH-AMT OCCURS 12 TIMES  PIC 9(4).
```

The major-level OCCURS clause indicates that there are 25 salespeople represented in the array. *Each* of the 25 salespeople has *12* monthly figures. Thus the array has 300 fields, each four positions long.

Assume that data has already been stored in the array. We wish to print 12 lines of monthly totals. Each line will contain 25 figures, one for each salesperson. Line 1 will contain 25 sales figures for January. These include array elements (1, 1) ... (25, 1) or the January figures for salespersons 1 through 25, respectively. Line 2 will contain 25 sales figures for February, which would be (1, 2) ... (25, 2), and so on.

The format of each line to be printed is described in WORKING-STORAGE as follows:

```
WORKING-STORAGE SECTION.
01   SALES-LINE.
     05   FILLER                 PIC X.
     05   ITEMX OCCURS 25 TIMES.
          10   SALES-ITEM   PIC 9999.
          10   FILLER       PIC X.
     05   FILLER                 PIC X(7).
```

We use a *single-level* OCCURS *clause* to describe the 25 sales figures within SALES-LINE. Since each line will contain 25 figures, only one OCCURS clause is necessary. The fact that there will be 12 lines printed is *not* denoted by an OCCURS clause, but by repeating the print routine 12 times.

Note that ITEMX, which OCCURS 25 TIMES, consists of *two* fields, SALES-ITEM and a FILLER. This one-position FILLER will separate each of the 25 amount fields to make the entire line more readable. If all the sales items appeared next to one another, it would be difficult to read the line.

Using a nested PERFORM, the routine is as follows:

```
PERFORM 800-WRITE-RTN
    VARYING SUB2 FROM 1 BY 1 UNTIL SUB2 > 12.
    .
    .
    .
800-WRITE-RTN.
    MOVE SPACES TO SALES-LINE.
    PERFORM 900-MOVE-RTN
        VARYING SUB1 FROM 1 BY 1 UNTIL SUB1 > 25.
    WRITE PRINT-REC FROM SALES-LINE
        AFTER ADVANCING 2 LINES.
900-MOVE-RTN.
    MOVE MONTH-AMT (SUB1, SUB2) TO SALES-ITEM (SUB1).
```

What we have done is to take an array that consists of 25 rows and 12 columns and print it out in an order different from the one in which it is stored:

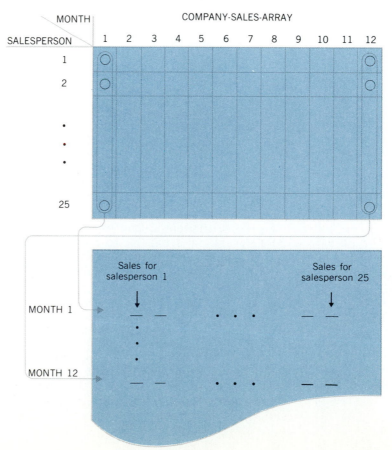

We use the *same subscript*, SUB1, to reference the number of the salesperson accessed in (1) COMPANY-SALES-ARRAY and in (2) the print line.

Self-Test   Using the TEMPERATURE-ARRAY defined in this chapter, code the solutions to the questions that follow:

```
01  TEMPERATURE-ARRAY.
    05  DAY-OF-WEEK OCCURS 7 TIMES.
        10  HOUR OCCURS 24 TIMES.
            15  MEAN-TEMP        PIC 9(3).
```

1. Find the average temperature for Sunday (Day 1).
2. Find the average weekly temperature for 2 A.M. (the second column).
3. Find the day of the week and the hour when the temperature was highest. Also indicate what the highest temperature was.
4. Find the number of days when the temperature fell below 32° at any hour. Could a PERFORM ... VARYING ... AFTER be used?
5. Print the mean temperatures for each day of the week.
6. Define a COMPANY-SALES-ARRAY that contains a name and 12 monthly amounts for each of 25 salespersons.

Solutions 1.
```
        MOVE 0 TO TOTAL.
        PERFORM 500-SUNDAY-AVERAGE
            VARYING X2 FROM 1 BY 1 UNTIL X2 > 24.
        COMPUTE AVERAGE = TOTAL / 24.
        DISPLAY 'AVERAGE TEMPERATURE FOR SUNDAY WAS ', AVERAGE.
           :
    500-SUNDAY-AVERAGE.
        ADD MEAN-TEMP (1, X2) TO TOTAL.
```

2.
```
        MOVE 0 TO TOTAL.
        PERFORM 2-AM-AVERAGE
            VARYING X1 FROM 1 BY 1 UNTIL X1 > 7.
        COMPUTE AVERAGE = TOTAL / 7.
        DISPLAY 'THE AVERAGE TEMPERATURE AT 2 AM WAS ', AVERAGE.
           :
    2-AM-AVERAGE.
        ADD MEAN-TEMP (X1, 2) TO TOTAL.
```

3.
```
        MOVE 0 TO HOLD-IT, STORE1, STORE2.
        PERFORM 200-MAJOR-LOOP
            VARYING X1 FROM 1 BY 1 UNTIL X1 > 7.
        DISPLAY 'HIGHEST TEMPERATURE WAS ', HOLD-IT.
        DISPLAY 'DAY OF WEEK OF HIGHEST TEMPERATURE WAS ', STORE1.
        IF  STORE2 < 12
            DISPLAY 'HOUR OF HIGHEST TEMPERATURE WAS ', STORE2, 'AM'
        ELSE IF STORE2 > 12 AND < 24
            SUBTRACT 12 FROM STORE2
            DISPLAY 'HOUR OF HIGHEST TEMPERATURE WAS ', STORE2, 'PM'
        ELSE IF STORE2 = 12
            DISPLAY 'HOUR OF HIGHEST TEMPERATURE WAS NOON'
        ELSE
            DISPLAY 'HOUR OF HIGHEST TEMPERATURE WAS MIDNIGHT'.
           :
    200-MAJOR-LOOP.
        PERFORM 300-MINOR-LOOP
            VARYING X2 FROM 1 BY 1 UNTIL X2 > 24.
    300-MINOR-LOOP.
```

```
IF   MEAN-TEMP (X1, X2) > HOLD-IT
    MOVE TEMP (X1, X2) TO HOLD-IT
    MOVE X1 TO STORE1
    MOVE X2 TO STORE2.
```

We could replace the first PERFORM with the following and eliminate 200-MAJOR-LOOP entirely:

```
PERFORM 300-MINOR-LOOP
    VARYING X1 FROM 1 BY 1 UNTIL X1 > 7
    AFTER X2 FROM 1 BY 1 UNTIL X2 > 24.
```

In WORKING-STORAGE, we could code:

```
01  DAYS.
    05  DAY-VALUE                           PIC X(21)
            VALUE 'SUNMONTUEWEDTHUFRISAT'.
    05  DAY-OF-THE-WEEK REDEFINES DAY-VALUE
            OCCURS 7 TIMES                  PIC X(3).
```

The second DISPLAY would then change as follows:

```
DISPLAY 'DAY OF WEEK OF HIGHEST TEMPERATURE WAS ',
    DAY-OF-THE-WEEK (STORE1).
```

4.
```
        MOVE 0 TO COUNTER.
        PERFORM 200-MAJOR-LOOP
            VARYING X1 FROM 1 BY 1 UNTIL X1 > 7.
        DISPLAY 'NUMBER OF DAYS WHEN TEMPERATURE < 32 WAS ',
            COUNTER.
        :
        :
    200-MAJOR-LOOP.
        MOVE 'NO ' TO FOUND.
        PERFORM 300-MINOR-LOOP
            VARYING X2 FROM 1 BY 1 UNTIL X2 > 24 OR
                FOUND = 'YES'.
    300-MINOR-LOOP.
        IF  TEMP (X1, X2) < 32
            ADD 1 TO COUNTER
            MOVE 'YES' TO FOUND.
```

We use a field called FOUND to terminate processing of 300-MINOR-LOOP when we find an hour in any day when the temperature falls below 32°. Because FOUND has one value ('NO ') when no match has been found, and another value ('YES') when a match occurs, we call this field a switch. Once we find a temperature lower than 32, we need not check the rest of the hours during that day.

A PERFORM ... VARYING ... AFTER could *not* be used because 200-MAJOR-LOOP has an operation to be performed *in addition to* varying the minor subscript.

5. **Note:** Use 01 DAYS established for Question 3 if an abbreviation for the day (SUN ... SAT) is to print rather than the day number.

```
        PERFORM 500-PRINT-RTN
            VARYING X1 FROM 1 BY 1 UNTIL X1 > 7.
        :
        :
    500-PRINT-RTN.
        MOVE 0 TO TOTAL.
        PERFORM 600-MINOR-LOOP
            VARYING X2 FROM 1 BY 1 UNTIL X2 > 24.
        MOVE DAY-OF-THE-WEEK (X1) TO DAY-OUT.
        COMPUTE AVERAGE-OUT = TOTAL / 24.
        WRITE PRINT-REC FROM OUT-REC
            AFTER ADVANCING 2 LINES.
    600-MINOR-LOOP.
        ADD MEAN-TEMP (X1, X2) TO TOTAL.
```

```
6.  01   COMPANY-SALES-ARRAY.
        05   SALESPERSON OCCURS 25 TIMES.
            10   NAME                        PIC X(20).
            10   MONTHLY-AMT OCCURS 12 TIMES  PIC 9(4).
```

C. Using a Double-Level Array for Accumulating Totals

Suppose a company has 10 departments and five salespeople (numbered 1–5) within each department. We wish to accumulate the total amount of sales for each salesperson within each department:

```
01   DEPT-TOTALS.
    05   DEPT OCCURS 10 TIMES.
        10   SALESPERSON OCCURS 5 TIMES.
            15   TOTAL-SALES          PIC 9(5)V99.
```

Before adding any data to a total area, we must ensure that the total area is initialized at zero. To initialize an entire array at zero, we could code the following on many computers:

```
MOVE ZEROS TO DEPT-TOTALS.
```

If your compiler permits you to reference DEPT-TOTALS in the PROCEDURE DIVISION, moving ZEROS to DEPT-TOTALS will replace all fields with 0; note, however, that MOVE 0 TO DEPT-TOTALS will only move a 0 to the leftmost position in the array. This is because DEPT-TOTALS, as a group item, is treated as an alphanumeric field; if you move a single 0 to an alphanumeric field, the 0 is placed in the leftmost position and all other positions are replaced with blanks.

On some computers, however, you may not reference the array entry itself. In such a case, you must code a full initializing routine prior to adding to TOTAL-SALES. We will use either nested PERFORMs or a PERFORM with the AFTER option in our illustrations:

```
PERFORM 700-INITIALIZE-RTN
    VARYING X1 FROM 1 BY 1 UNTIL X > 10
    AFTER X2 FROM 1 BY 1 UNTIL X2 > 5.
        :
700-INITIALIZE-RTN.
    MOVE 0 TO TOTAL-SALES (X1, X2).
```

This routine, which initializes each TOTAL-SALES field, will run on all computers; only some computers will allow you to code MOVE ZEROS TO DEPT-TOTALS.

Assume an input record has been created each time a salesperson makes a sale. Each input record contains a department number called DEPT-IN, a salesperson number called SALESPERSON-NO-IN, and an amount of sales called AMT-IN. There may be numerous input records for a salesperson if he or she made more than one sale. The coding to accumulate the totals after the array has been initialized at zero is as follows:

```
READ SALES-FILE
    AT END MOVE 'NO ' TO ARE-THERE-MORE-RECORDS.
PERFORM 200-ADD-RTN
    UNTIL ARE-THERE-MORE-RECORDS = 'NO '.
        :
200-ADD-RTN.
    ADD AMT-IN TO TOTAL-SALES (DEPT-IN, SALESPERSON-NO-IN).
    READ SALES-FILE
        AT END MOVE 'NO ' TO ARE-THERE-MORE-RECORDS.
```

As indicated previously, input fields may be used as subscripts. For correct processing, a validation procedure could be used to ensure that (1) `DEPT-IN` is an integer between 1 and 10 and (2) `SALESPERSON-NO-IN` is an integer between 1 and 5.

At the end of the job, we wish to print 10 pages of output. Each page will contain five lines, one for each salesperson in a given department. The full `PROCEDURE DIVISION` is as follows:

```
PROCEDURE DIVISION.
100-MAIN-MODULE.
    OPEN INPUT SALES-FILE
        OUTPUT PRINT-FILE.
    MOVE ZEROS TO DEPT-TOTALS.
    READ SALES-FILE
        AT END MOVE 'NO ' TO ARE-THERE-MORE-RECORDS.
    PERFORM 200-ADD-RTN
        UNTIL NO-MORE-RECORDS.
    PERFORM 300-PRINT-RTN
        VARYING X1 FROM 1 BY 1 UNTIL X1 > 10.
    CLOSE SALES-FILE
        PRINT-FILE.
    STOP RUN.
200-ADD-RTN.
    **********************************************************
    * NOTE: AMT-IN, DEPT-IN, SALESPERSON-NO-IN ARE INPUT FIELDS *
    **********************************************************
    ADD AMT-IN TO TOTAL-SALES (DEPT-IN, SALESPERSON-NO-IN).
    READ SALES-FILE
        AT END MOVE 'NO ' TO ARE-THERE-MORE-RECORDS.
300-PRINT-RTN.
    MOVE X1 TO DEPT-NO-ON-HDG-LINE.
    WRITE PRINT-REC FROM HDG-LINE
        AFTER ADVANCING PAGE.
    PERFORM 400-LINE-PRINT
        VARYING X2 FROM 1 BY 1 UNTIL X2 > 5.
400-LINE-PRINT.
    MOVE X2 TO SALESPERSON-NO-OUT.
    MOVE TOTAL-SALES (X1, X2) TO TOTAL-OUT.
    WRITE PRINT-REC FROM SALES-LINE-REC
        AFTER ADVANCING 2 LINES.
```

D. Loading Input Data Into a Double-Level Array

If an array is to be loaded with data such as temperatures or populations entered from an input file, we must use a `READ` statement and then move the data to the array.

Consider again our `TEMPERATURE-ARRAY` from the beginning of this chapter:

```
01  TEMPERATURE-ARRAY.
    05  DAY-OF-WEEK OCCURS 7 TIMES.
        10  HOUR OCCURS 24 TIMES.
            15  MEAN-TEMP        PIC 9(3).
```

Suppose we have seven input records, each with 24 three-position mean temperatures. The first input record to be loaded into the array is for Day 1 or Sunday, the second is for Day 2 or Monday, and so on:

```
FD  TEMP-FILE
    LABEL RECORDS ARE OMITTED.
01  IN-REC.
    05  HOURLY-TEMP OCCURS 24 TIMES    PIC 9(3).
```

The ARRAY-LOAD routine could be executed as follows. We use subscript names here that are more meaningful than X1 and X2.

```
READ TEMP-FILE
    AT END PERFORM 600-ERR-RTN,
PERFORM 200-ARRAY-LOAD
    VARYING DAY-SUB FROM 1 BY 1 UNTIL DAY-SUB > 7
                                  OR NO-MORE-RECORDS,
IF  ARE-THERE-MORE-RECORDS = 'YES' OR DAY-SUB NOT > 7
    PERFORM 600-ERR-RTN,
  :
200-ARRAY-LOAD,
    PERFORM 300-MINOR-LOAD
        VARYING HOUR-SUB FROM 1 BY 1 UNTIL HOUR-SUB > 24,
    READ TEMP-FILE
        MOVE 'NO ' TO ARE-THERE-MORE-RECORDS,
300-MINOR-LOAD,
    MOVE HOURLY-TEMP (HOUR-SUB) TO
        MEAN-TEMP (DAY-SUB, HOUR-SUB),
```

If there are not exactly seven records in TEMP-FILE, 600-ERR-RTN will be executed, which terminates the job.

E. Performing a Look-Up Using a Double-Level OCCURS

1. Performing a Full Table Look-Up

We will use a double-level OCCURS entry to define a table and then use a SEARCH to perform a table look-up.

Example   Assume that the following table has been loaded into storage:

```
01  INVENTORY-TABLE,
    05  WAREHOUSE OCCURS 50 TIMES,
        10  ITEM-X OCCURS 100 TIMES,
            15   PART-NO         PIC 9(4),
            15   UNIT-PRICE      PIC 999V99,
```

There are 50 warehouses, and each stores 100 items. Each warehouse stocks its own inventory, which is different from the inventory at other warehouses. This means that a specific PART-NO will appear *only once* in the table. There are 5000 table records, each with a warehouse number, part number, and unit price. The first table record refers to warehouse 1, part number 1; the next to warehouse 1, part number 2; the 101st to warehouse 2, part number 1, and so on.

Suppose that input transaction records have the following format:

```
1-4   PART-NO-IN
5-6   QTY-ORDERED
```

For each PART-NO-IN in a transaction record, we need to look up the corresponding PART-NO in the table and find its UNIT-PRICE. We store the unit price for each part in the table and *not* in the transaction record for the following reasons:

1. If each input transaction record contained a unit price, we would be keying unit price each time a part was ordered. This would increase keying costs and increase the risk of input errors.
2. Changes to unit prices can be more easily made to table entries than to a large number of input transaction records.

    We store prices in an **external table**, which is in a file and is loaded in, rather than in an **internal table**, which is established with VALUE clauses. External tables are used for this type of illustration because the table elements themselves are likely to change with some frequency. That is, because we anticipate that unit prices may change, we establish the INVENTORY-TABLE as an external table. If we defined it as an internal table with VALUE clauses, we would need to modify and recompile the program each time a change occurred.

The output from this program will be a printed transaction report. Each time a PART-NO is ordered, we will print the PART-NO and the TOTAL-AMT of the transaction, where TOTAL-AMT = QTY-ORDERED (from the transaction record) × UNIT-PRICE (from the table).

Since we will use a SEARCH, the table we have described must include the appropriate INDEXED BY clauses:

```
01   INVENTORY-TABLE.
        05   WAREHOUSE OCCURS 50 TIMES INDEXED BY X1.
              10   ITEM-X OCCURS 100 TIMES INDEXED BY X2.
                   15   PART-NO             PIC 9(4).
                   15   UNIT-PRICE          PIC 999V99.
```

The SEARCH is Used with the Lowest-Level OCCURS Entry

To SEARCH the table, we code SEARCH ITEM-X ... because ITEM-X is the *lowest-level* OCCURS *entry. Note that the* SEARCH *statement increments the lowest-level index only.* Hence if X1 is set to 1 initially, the SEARCH will perform a look-up on items in warehouse 1 only, that is (1, 1) through (1, 100). To search *all* warehouses, the SEARCH itself must be executed from a PERFORM ... VARYING that increments X1.

The routine would then appear as follows:

```
MOVE 'NO ' TO MATCH-FOUND.
PERFORM 500-SEARCH-IT
     VARYING X1 FROM 1 BY 1
          UNTIL X1 > 50 OR MATCH-FOUND = 'YES'.
IF  MATCH-FOUND = 'YES'
     WRITE OUT-REC FROM TRANS-REC-OUT
          AFTER ADVANCING 2 LINES
ELSE
     PERFORM 600-NO-MATCH-ERR.
   .
   .
   .
500-SEARCH-IT.
   SET X2 TO 1.
   SEARCH ITEM-X          ◄──── Use lowest-level OCCURS level here
        WHEN PART-NO-IN = PART-NO (X1, X2)
             MULTIPLY UNIT-PRICE (X1, X2) BY QTY-ORDERED
                  GIVING TOTAL-AMT
             MOVE 'YES' TO MATCH-FOUND. ◄──── Enables 500-SEARCH-IT to be
                                              terminated properly
```

MATCH-FOUND is a field that is initialized at 'NO ' and changed to 'YES' only when the corresponding PART-NO in the table is found. We terminate 500-SEARCH-IT when a match is found (MATCH-FOUND = 'YES') or the entire table has been searched (X1 > 50). 600-NO-MATCH-ERR would be executed only if no match existed between the PART-NO-IN and a table entry.

The full program for this example appears in Figure 15.1.

Figure 15.1
Program to search a
double-level table.

```
IDENTIFICATION DIVISION.
PROGRAM-ID. SEARCH.
*
ENVIRONMENT DIVISION.
INPUT-OUTPUT SECTION.
FILE-CONTROL.
     SELECT INVENTORY-TABLE-IN ASSIGN TO DISK1.
     SELECT TRANSACTION-FILE ASSIGN TO DISK2.
     SELECT REPORT-OUT ASSIGN TO SYSLST.
*
DATA DIVISION.
FILE SECTION.
FD   INVENTORY-TABLE-IN
     LABEL RECORDS ARE STANDARD.
01   INVENTORY-TABLE-REC.
     05   T-WAREHOUSE-NO          PIC 99.
     05   T-PART-NO               PIC 9999.
     05   T-UNIT-PRICE            PIC 999V99.
FD   TRANSACTION-FILE
     LABEL RECORDS ARE STANDARD.
01   TRANSACTION-REC.
     05   PART-NO-IN              PIC 9999.
     05   QTY-ORDERED             PIC 99.
     05   FILLER                  PIC X(14).
FD   REPORT-OUT
     LABEL RECORDS ARE OMITTED.
01   OUT-REC                      PIC X(133).
```

Figure 15.1
(continued)

```
WORKING-STORAGE SECTION.
01  WS-AREAS.
    05  ARE-THERE-MORE-RECORDS    PIC X(3)  VALUE 'YES'.
        88  NO-MORE-RECORDS                 VALUE 'NO '.
    05  MATCH-FOUND               PIC X(3)  VALUE 'NO '.
01  INVENTORY-TABLE.
    05  WAREHOUSE OCCURS 50 TIMES INDEXED BY X1.
        10  ITEM-X OCCURS 100 TIMES INDEXED BY X2.
            15  PART-NO           PIC 9(4).
            15  UNIT-PRICE        PIC 999V99.
01  TRANS-REC-OUT.
    05  FILLER                    PIC X(10) VALUE SPACES.
    05  PART-NO-OUT               PIC 9(4).
    05  FILLER                    PIC X(5)  VALUE SPACES.
    05  QTY-OUT                   PIC 999.
    05  FILLER                    PIC X(5)  VALUE SPACES.
    05  TOTAL-AMT                 PIC $ZZZ,ZZZ.99.
    05  FILLER                    PIC X(95) VALUE SPACES.
01  ERR-REC.
    05  FILLER                    PIC X(10) VALUE SPACES.
    05  ERR-PART                  PIC 9(4).
    05  FILLER                    PIC X(5)  VALUE SPACES.
    05  FILLER                    PIC X(114)
                    VALUE 'PART NUMBER IS NOT IN TABLE'.
01  HEADING-1.
    05  FILLER                    PIC X(13) VALUE SPACES.
    05  FILLER                    PIC X(120)
                    VALUE 'INVENTORY REPORT'.
01  HEADING-2.
    05  FILLER                    PIC X(19)
                    VALUE 'PART NO  ' JUSTIFIED RIGHT.
    05  FILLER                    PIC X(9)  VALUE 'QTY'.
    05  FILLER                    PIC X(105)
                    VALUE 'TOTAL AMT'.
*
PROCEDURE DIVISION.
100-MAIN-MODULE.
    PERFORM 700-INITIALIZATION-RTN.
    READ INVENTORY-TABLE-IN
        AT END MOVE 'NO ' TO ARE-THERE-MORE-RECORDS.
    PERFORM 200-TABLE-LOAD
        VARYING X1 FROM 1 BY 1 UNTIL X1 > 50.
    MOVE 'YES' TO ARE-THERE-MORE-RECORDS.
    READ TRANSACTION-FILE
        AT END MOVE 'NO ' TO ARE-THERE-MORE-RECORDS.
    PERFORM 400-CALC-RTN
        UNTIL NO-MORE-RECORDS.
    PERFORM 800-END-OF-JOB-RTN.
200-TABLE-LOAD.
    PERFORM 300-LOAD-IT
        VARYING X2 FROM 1 BY 1 UNTIL X2 > 100.
300-LOAD-IT.
    IF  T-WAREHOUSE-NO NOT EQUAL TO X1
        DISPLAY 'TABLE IS NOT IN SEQUENCE'
        CLOSE INVENTORY-TABLE-IN
              TRANSACTION-FILE
              REPORT-OUT
        STOP RUN.
    MOVE T-PART-NO TO PART-NO (X1, X2).
    MOVE T-UNIT-PRICE TO UNIT-PRICE (X1, X2).
    READ INVENTORY-TABLE-IN
        AT END MOVE 'NO ' TO ARE-THERE-MORE-RECORDS.
400-CALC-RTN.
    MOVE PART-NO-IN TO PART-NO-OUT.
    MOVE QTY-ORDERED TO QTY-OUT.
    MOVE 'NO ' TO MATCH-FOUND.
    PERFORM 500-SEARCH-IT
        VARYING X1 FROM 1 BY 1 UNTIL X1 > 50
                            OR MATCH-FOUND = 'YES'.
    IF MATCH-FOUND = 'YES'
        WRITE OUT-REC FROM TRANS-REC-OUT
            AFTER ADVANCING 2 LINES
    ELSE
        PERFORM 600-NO-MATCH-ERR.
    READ TRANSACTION-FILE
        AT END MOVE 'NO ' TO ARE-THERE-MORE-RECORDS.
500-SEARCH-IT.
    SET X2 TO 1.
    SEARCH ITEM-X
        WHEN PART-NO-IN = PART-NO (X1, X2)
            MULTIPLY UNIT-PRICE (X1, X2) BY QTY-ORDERED
                        GIVING TOTAL-AMT
            MOVE 'YES' TO MATCH-FOUND.
600-NO-MATCH-ERR.
    MOVE PART-NO-IN TO ERR-PART.
    WRITE OUT-REC FROM ERR-REC
        AFTER ADVANCING 2 LINES.
700-INITIALIZATION-RTN.
    OPEN INPUT INVENTORY-TABLE-IN
               TRANSACTION-FILE
         OUTPUT REPORT-OUT.
    WRITE OUT-REC FROM HEADING-1 AFTER PAGE.
    WRITE OUT-REC FROM HEADING-2 AFTER ADVANCING 2 LINES.
800-END-OF-JOB-RTN.
    CLOSE INVENTORY-TABLE-IN
          TRANSACTION-FILE
          REPORT-OUT.
    STOP RUN.
```

2. Searching Only Part of a Table

Suppose we wish to find the UNIT-PRICE for an input PART-NO-IN stored at WAREHOUSE 5. There is no need to search the entire table, just those entries within WAREHOUSE 5. Using the preceding INVENTORY-TABLE, we could code the SEARCH as follows:

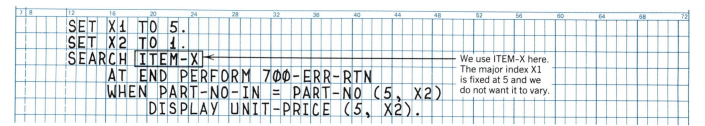

We always SEARCH ITEM-X, not WAREHOUSE, because we are looking for an item within a specific row, row 5 in this instance.

3. Searching Elements in an Array

A SEARCH can also be used with a multiple-level array for finding specific values in the array. Consider the following double-level array:

```
01   ARRAY1.
     05   STATE OCCURS 50 TIMES INDEXED BY X1.
          10   DISTRICT OCCURS 10 TIMES INDEXED BY X2.
               15 POPULATION          PIC 9(10).
```

We typically use the *lowest*-level OCCURS item with the SEARCH. Thus, to look up any element in the array, we would code SEARCH DISTRICT ...

Searching an Array until a Match is Found

In this example, there are 10 districts per state. Each state, then, has 10 districtwide population figures. Suppose there is *only one district* within the United States with a population of 123,000 and we want to print its state and district number. To do this, we must search the entire array until a match is found. When we find a match, we want to print the values of the indexes since X1 contains the state number and X2 the district number.

A PERFORM ... VARYING is coded to increment the major index. The paragraph that is performed will have a SEARCH that varies the minor index. That is, the statement SEARCH DISTRICT ... varies X2, the minor index, from 1 by 1 until a match is found or X2 exceeds 10. X1, *the major index, remains constant* in the SEARCH, at whatever value it was initially set to. The PERFORM ... VARYING will increment this major subscript. Thus, to SEARCH the array until a "hit" or match is found, we would have:

```
         MOVE 'NO ' TO MATCH-FOUND.
         PERFORM 500-SEARCH-RTN
             VARYING X1 FROM 1 BY 1
                 UNTIL X1 > 50 OR MATCH-FOUND = 'YES'.
         IF  MATCH-FOUND  NOT = 'YES'
             DISPLAY 'NO MATCH'.
     500-SEARCH-RTN.
         SET X2 TO 1.
         SEARCH DISTRICT
             WHEN POPULATION (X1, X2) = 123000
                 SET X1-OUT TO X1
                 SET X2-OUT TO X2
                 DISPLAY X1-OUT, X2-OUT
                 MOVE 'YES' TO MATCH-FOUND.
     *************************************************
     * Each SEARCH will test POPULATION (X1, 1) - POPULATION *
     * (X1, 10). The X1 index remains constant and is not   *
     * incremented by the SEARCH. It is incremented by the  *
     * PERFORM ... VARYING.                                  *
     *************************************************
```

SET is used in place of MOVE to transmit X1 and X2 to an output area

Each time through 500-SEARCH-RTN, X1 is set by the PERFORM, first to 1, then to 2, and so on. Then, in 500-SEARCH-RTN itself, X2 is set to 1 before the array is actually searched. Thus, the first execution of 500-SEARCH-RTN will search the entries (1,1), (1,2), ..., (1,10). If no match is found, the entries (2,1), (2,2), ..., (2,10) will be searched the second time through 500-SEARCH-RTN. This continues until a match occurs (i.e., a district population = 123000) or the array has been completely searched. If a match is found, we want to print the values of the indexes, since X1 will contain the state number and X2, the district number. To move an index to another field, we use the SET statement.

Searching an Entire Array for Multiple Matches

We can search the entire array for specific conditions *even after a match is found*. Suppose we wish to find the total number of districts within the United States that have populations in excess of 100,000. It is best to code the following routine, which does not use a SEARCH:

```
MOVE ZERO TO CTR.
PERFORM 200-COUNT-THEM
    VARYING X1 FROM 1 BY 1 UNTIL X1 > 50
    AFTER X2 FROM 1 BY 1 UNTIL X2 > 10.
DISPLAY CTR.
200-COUNT-THEM.
    IF  POPULATION (X1, X2) > 100000
        ADD 1 TO CTR.
```

Suppose we wish to find the total number of districts in STATE 3 with populations less than 50,000. In this case, we want to keep the STATE index, X1, constant at 3. To do this, we could code the following:

```
MOVE ZERO TO CTR2.
SET X1 TO 3.
PERFORM 300-SEARCH-RTN
    VARYING X2 FROM 1 BY 1 UNTIL X2 > 10.
DISPLAY CTR2.
300-SEARCH-RTN.
    IF  POPULATION (X1, X2) < 50000
        ADD 1 TO CTR2.
```

Guideline for Searching an Array or a Table

When an array or a table is to be searched for one specific entry or "hit," use the SEARCH verb. This is because the SEARCH instruction stops as soon as the WHEN clause is satisfied. When a table or an array is being searched where there may be more than one "hit" to be tabulated or counted, it is better to use PERFORMs or nested PERFORMs.

II. Triple-Level OCCURS Clause and More

We have seen that OCCURS clauses may be written on one or two levels. We may also use triple-level OCCURS clauses. A *maximum* of three levels of OCCURS clauses may be used with COBOL 74, but COBOL 85 permits up to seven levels.

Suppose we have a population table consisting of 50 state groups. Each state is further subdivided into 10 counties. Each county has precisely five district figures. The following array may be established in the WORKING-STORAGE SECTION:

```
01   POPULATION-TABLE,
     05   STATE OCCURS 50 TIMES,
          10   COUNTY OCCURS 10 TIMES,
               15   DISTRICT OCCURS 5 TIMES PIC 9(10),
```

In this way, we have defined 2500 fields (50 × 10 × 5) in storage, each 10 positions long. To access any field defined by several OCCURS clauses, we use the *lowest*-level data-name. In this illustration, the data-name DISTRICT must be used to access any of the 2500 fields of data.

Since DISTRICT is defined by a triple-level OCCURS clause, *three* subscripts are used to access the specific field desired. The *first* subscript refers to the *major*-level item, STATE. The *second* subscript refers to the *intermediate*-level item, COUNTY. The *third* subscript refers to the *minor*-level item, DISTRICT. Subscripts are always enclosed within parentheses. Each subscript is separated from the next by a comma and a space. Consider the following coding:

The DISTRICT specified refers to the population figure for:

```
STATE 5              COUNTY 4              DISTRICT 3
```

An item defined by a triple-level OCCURS clause is accessed with three subscripts.

Example   Write a routine to find the smallest population figure in the POPULATION-TABLE array. (We assume that data has already been placed in the array.) Store this smallest figure in HELD.

Using nested PERFORM ... VARYING statements to achieve this looping, we have:

```
MOVE DISTRICT (1, 1, 1) TO HELD,
PERFORM 200-RTN-1
     VARYING SUB1 FROM 1 BY 1 UNTIL SUB1 > 50,
PERFORM 500-NEXT-RTN,
PERFORM 600-EOJ-RTN,
200-RTN-1,
PERFORM 300-RTN-2
     VARYING SUB2 FROM 1 BY 1 UNTIL SUB2 > 10,
300-RTN-2,
PERFORM 400-RTN-3
     VARYING SUB3 FROM 1 BY 1 UNTIL SUB3 > 5,
400-RTN-3,
IF DISTRICT (SUB1, SUB2, SUB3) < HELD
     MOVE DISTRICT (SUB1, SUB2, SUB3) TO HELD,
```

Using a PERFORM ... VARYING ... AFTER in the first PERFORM, we can eliminate 200-RTN-1 and 300-RTN-2:

```
PERFORM  400-RTN-3
     VARYING SUB1 FROM 1 BY 1 UNTIL SUB1 > 50
     AFTER SUB2 FROM 1 BY 1 UNTIL SUB2 > 10
     AFTER SUB3 FROM 1 BY 1 UNTIL SUB3 > 5,
```

Note that more than one AFTER clause can be used in a PERFORM ... VARYING; with the last one being performed first. That is, the minor subscript is varied first.

Because seven levels of OCCURS are permitted with COBOL 85, a maximum of *six* AFTER clauses are therefore allowed with COBOL 85. The limit for the number of AFTER clauses with COBOL 74 is two.

CHAPTER SUMMARY

I. Multiple-level OCCURS
A. May be used for an array or a table.
B. The lowest-level OCCURS data-name or an item subordinate to it is used to access an entry in the array or the table.
C. If we use a SEARCH for accessing a multiple-level table, INDEXED BY must be used on all OCCURS levels.
D. The identifier used with the SEARCH statement should typically be the one on the lowest OCCURS level. Only the index on the same level as the OCCURS level will be incremented by the SEARCH. That is, SEARCH XXX, for example, will only vary the index specified with XXX. Consider the following:

```
05   XXX OCCURS 10 TIMES INDEXED BY X2.
```

X2 is the only index incremented in the search regardless of whether XXX is subordinate to an OCCURS or contains another level of OCCURS.

II. COBOL 74 permits three levels of OCCURS; COBOL 85 permits seven levels.

CHAPTER SELF-TEST

1. With MOVE ITEMX (SUB1, SUB2) TO HELD, SUB1 refers to the _____ -level OCCURS clause and SUB2 refers to the _____ -level OCCURS clause.

2. Consider the following DATA DIVISION entry:

```
01   ARRAY1.
     05   FIELDX OCCURS 20 TIMES.
          10   FIELDXX OCCURS 50 TIMES.
               15   ITEMX   PICTURE S99.
```

The number of storage positions reserved for this area is _____. The data-name that may be used to access a field in the PROCEDURE DIVISION is _____. If ITEMX (CTRA, CTRB) is used in the PROCEDURE DIVISION, then CTRA may vary from _____ to _____ and CTRB may vary from _____ to _____.

3. If three subscripts are used to access an item, the first refers to the _____ level, the second to the _____ level, and the third to the _____ level.

4. Each subscript within the parentheses is separated from the next by a _____ followed by a _____.

5. If a SEARCH is used for accessing a double-level table, a(n) _____ clause must be used on both OCCURS levels.

Solutions
1. major; minor
2. 2000 (20 × 50 × 2); ITEMX (or FIELDXX); 1 to 20; 1 to 50
3. major; intermediate; minor
4. comma; space
5. INDEXED BY

PRACTICE PROGRAM

Write a program to tabulate the number of employees by area within department. The problem definition appears in Figure 15.2.

Figure 15.2
Problem definition for the Practice Program.

Systems Flowchart

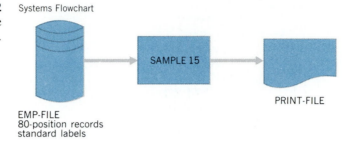

EMP-FILE
80-position records
standard labels

PRINT-FILE

EMP-FILE Record Layout

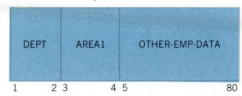

PRINT-FILE Printer Spacing Chart

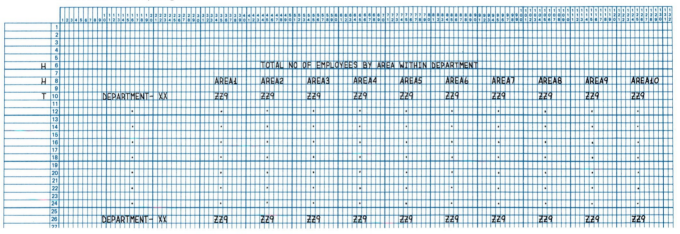

Notes:

(a) There are 10 areas within each department; there are 20 departments. Add 1 to a corresponding total for each employee record read.

(b) Records are not in sequence.

(c) All totals should be edited to suppress high-order zeros.

See Figure 15.3 for the hierarchy chart, pseudocode, and the program with sample output.

KEY TERMS

External table
Internal table

Figure 15.3
Hierarchy chart, pseudocode,
and solution for the
Practice Program.

a. Pseudocode

```
START
    Open the Files
    Move Zeros to the Array
    Move Spaces to the Print Area
    Read a Record
    PERFORM UNTIL no more input
        Add 1 to corresponding Array Element
        Read a Record
    ENDPERFORM
    PERFORM
        Write Headings
    ENDPERFORM
    PERFORM 20 times
        Add 1 to Dept-No
            PERFORM 10 times
                Move each Area to Print Line
            ENDPERFORM
        Write a Line
    ENDPERFORM
    End-of-Job Operations
STOP
```

b. Hierarchy Chart

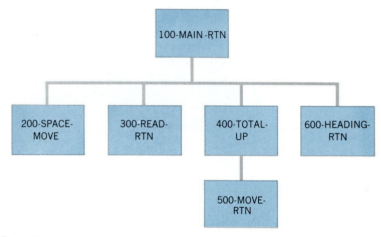

c. Program

```
IDENTIFICATION DIVISION.
PROGRAM-ID.     SAMPLE.
AUTHOR.         NANCY STERN.
*
ENVIRONMENT DIVISION.
CONFIGURATION SECTION.
SOURCE-COMPUTER.    IBM-4331.
OBJECT-COMPUTER.    IBM-4331.
INPUT-OUTPUT SECTION.
FILE-CONTROL.
    SELECT EMP-FILE ASSIGN TO DATA204.
    SELECT PRINT-FILE ASSIGN TO SYS$OUTPUT.
*
DATA DIVISION.
FILE SECTION.
FD  EMP-FILE
    LABEL RECORDS ARE STANDARD.
01  EMP-REC.
    05  DEPT                PIC 99.
    05  AREA1               PIC 99.
    05  OTHER-EMP-DATA      PIC X(76).
FD  PRINT-FILE
    LABEL RECORDS ARE OMITTED.
01  PRINT-REC               PIC X(133).
WORKING-STORAGE SECTION.
01  WORK-AREAS.
    05  ARE-THERE-MORE-RECORDS    PIC X(3) VALUE 'YES'.
        88  NO-MORE-RECORDS                VALUE 'NO '.
    05  CTR1                PIC 99   VALUE 1.
    05  CTR2                PIC 99   VALUE 1.
01  TOTALS.
    05  DEPTX OCCURS 20 TIMES.
        10  AREAX OCCURS 10 TIMES PIC 999.
01  HEADER1.
    05  FILLER             PIC X(44) VALUE SPACES.
    05  FILLER             PIC X(47)
```

Figure 15.3
(continued)

```
                         VALUE 'TOTAL NO OF EMPLOYEES BY AREA WITHIN DEPARTMENT'.
           05  FILLER                    PIC X(42) VALUE SPACES.
       01  HEADER2.
           05  FILLER                    PIC X(30) VALUE SPACES.
           05  FILLER                    PIC X(50)
               VALUE '      AREA1      AREA2      AREA3      AREA4      AREA5'.
           05  FILLER                    PIC X(50)
               VALUE '      AREA6      AREA7      AREA8      AREA9     AREA10'.
           05  FILLER                    PIC XXX   VALUE SPACES.
       01  DETAIL-LINE.
           05  FILLER                    PIC X(10) VALUE SPACES.
           05  FILLER                    PIC X(12) VALUE 'DEPARTMENT- '.
           05  DEPT-NO                   PIC 99.
           05  FILLER                    PIC X(8)  VALUE SPACES.
           05  ITEMX OCCURS 10 TIMES.
               10  FILLER                PIC XX.
               10  AREAY                 PIC ZZ9.
               10  FILLER                PIC X(5).
           05  FILLER                    PIC X     VALUE SPACES.
     *
       PROCEDURE DIVISION.
       100-MAIN-RTN.
           OPEN INPUT EMP-FILE
               OUTPUT PRINT-FILE.
           MOVE ZEROS TO TOTALS.
           PERFORM 200-SPACE-MOVE
               VARYING CTR1 FROM 1 BY 1
               UNTIL CTR1 IS GREATER THAN 10.
           READ EMP-FILE
               AT END MOVE 'NO ' TO ARE-THERE-MORE-RECORDS.
           PERFORM 300-READ-RTN
               UNTIL NO-MORE-RECORDS.
           PERFORM 600-HEADING-RTN.
           PERFORM 400-TOTAL-UP
               VARYING CTR1 FROM 1 BY 1
               UNTIL CTR1 IS GREATER THAN 20.
           CLOSE EMP-FILE
               PRINT-FILE.
           STOP RUN.
       200-SPACE-MOVE.
           MOVE SPACES TO ITEMX (CTR1).
       300-READ-RTN.
           ADD 1 TO AREAX (DEPT, AREA1).
           READ EMP-FILE
               AT END MOVE 'NO ' TO ARE-THERE-MORE-RECORDS.
       400-TOTAL-UP.
           ADD 1 TO DEPT-NO.
           PERFORM 500-MOVE-RTN
               VARYING CTR2 FROM 1 BY 1
               UNTIL CTR2 IS GREATER THAN 10.
           WRITE PRINT-REC FROM DETAIL-LINE
               AFTER ADVANCING 2 LINES.
       500-MOVE-RTN.
           MOVE AREAX (CTR1, CTR2) TO AREAY (CTR2).
       600-HEADING-RTN.
           WRITE PRINT-REC FROM HEADER1
               AFTER ADVANCING PAGE.
           WRITE PRINT-REC FROM HEADER2
               AFTER ADVANCING 2 LINES.
```

Sample Input Data

```
    0302
    0505
    0507
    0501
    0508
    0501
    1901
    2002
    1909
    2010
    1209
    0601
    0704
    0604
    0701
    2010
    1008
    1001
```

Figure 15.3
(continued)

```
1010
1608
1008
1310
1003
2004
0704
1008
1010
1009
0901
```

Sample Output

TOTAL NO OF EMPLOYEES BY AREA WITHIN DEPARTMENT

	AREA1	AREA2	AREA3	AREA4	AREA5	AREA6	AREA7	AREA8	AREA9	AREA10
DEPARTMENT- 01	0	0	0	0	0	0	0	0	0	0
DEPARTMENT- 02	0	0	0	0	0	0	0	0	0	0
DEPARTMENT- 03	0	1	0	0	0	0	0	0	0	0
DEPARTMENT- 04	0	0	0	0	0	0	0	0	0	0
DEPARTMENT- 05	2	0	0	0	1	0	1	1	0	0
DEPARTMENT- 06	1	0	0	1	0	0	0	0	0	0
DEPARTMENT- 07	1	0	0	2	0	0	0	0	0	0
DEPARTMENT- 08	0	0	0	0	0	0	0	0	0	0
DEPARTMENT- 09	1	0	0	0	0	0	0	0	0	0
DEPARTMENT- 10	1	0	1	0	0	0	0	3	1	2
DEPARTMENT- 11	0	0	0	0	0	0	0	0	0	0
DEPARTMENT- 12	0	0	0	0	0	0	0	0	1	0
DEPARTMENT- 13	0	0	0	0	0	0	0	0	0	1
DEPARTMENT- 14	0	0	0	0	0	0	0	0	0	0
DEPARTMENT- 15	0	0	0	0	0	0	0	0	0	0
DEPARTMENT- 16	0	0	0	0	0	0	0	1	0	0
DEPARTMENT- 17	0	0	0	0	0	0	0	0	0	0
DEPARTMENT- 18	0	0	0	0	0	0	0	0	0	0
DEPARTMENT- 19	1	0	0	0	0	0	0	0	1	0
DEPARTMENT- 20	0	1	0	1	0	0	0	0	0	2

REVIEW QUESTIONS

I. True-False Questions

____ 1. If an item is defined with a double-level OCCURS clause, the first subscript refers to the lower-level OCCURS.

____ 2. Triple-level subscripting is the maximum for COBOL 85.

____ 3. Subscripts and indexes must always be numeric.

____ 4. The following entries define 5000 positions of storage:

```
01  TABLE-1.
    05  ITEM-1 OCCURS 50 TIMES.
        10  ITEM-2 OCCURS 10 TIMES PIC S9(10).
```

____ 5. An entry in TABLE-1 in Question 4 can be referenced by using either ITEM-1 or ITEM-2 in the PROCEDURE DIVISION.

II. General Questions

1. There are 50 classes in College X. Each class has exactly 40 students. Each student has taken six exams. Write a *double*-level OCCURS clause to define an area of storage that will hold these scores.

2. Write a *triple*-level OCCURS clause for Question 1.

3. How many storage positions are reserved for the table in Question 1?

4. Write the file and record description entries for a file of input records that will contain students' test scores as described above. Each student record will contain six scores in the first 18 positions. The first record is for the first student in class 1, . . . the 40th record is for the 40th student in class 1, the 41st record is for the first student in class 2, and so on.

5. Using the solutions to Questions 2 and 4, write the PROCEDURE DIVISION routines to read the exam records and to accumulate the data in the array.

6. Write a routine to find the class with the highest class average.

7. Write a routine to find the student with the highest average.

8. If the following is a WORKING-STORAGE entry, write a routine to initialize the fields. Note that all areas to be used in arithmetic operations must first be cleared or set to zero. Assume that you cannot code MOVE ZEROS TO TOTALS.

```
01  TOTALS.
    05  MAJOR-TOTAL OCCURS 100 TIMES.
        10  INTERMEDIATE-TOTAL OCCURS 45 TIMES.
            15  MINOR-TOTAL OCCURS 25 TIMES  PICTURE S9(5).
```

Make necessary corrections to each of the following (Questions 9 and 10).

9.
```
01  ITEMX OCCURS 20 TIMES, VALUE ZEROS.
    05  MINOR-ITEM OCCURS 15 TIMES, PICTURE S9.
```

10.
```
01  TABLE-A.
    05  FIELDX OCCURS 10 TIMES, PICTURE S99.
    05  FIELDY REDEFINES FIELDX PICTURE X(20).
```

III. Validating Data Modify the Practice Program so that it includes coding to (1) test for all errors and (2) print a control listing of totals (records processed, errors encountered, batch totals).

DEBUGGING EXERCISES

Consider the following:

```
WORKING-STORAGE SECTION.
01  TABLE-1.
    05  WAREHOUSE OCCURS 5 TIMES.
        10  STOCK-ITEMS OCCURS 150 TIMES.
            15  ITEM-NO         PIC 9(3).
            15  PRICE           PIC 9(4).
*
PROCEDURE DIVISION.
100-MAIN-MODULE.
    OPEN INPUT TABLE-FILE
               TRANS-FILE
         OUTPUT PRINT-FILE.
    READ TABLE-FILE
        AT END MOVE 'NO ' TO MORE-TABLE-RECS.
    PERFORM 200-TABLE-ENTRY
        VARYING X1 FROM 1 BY 1 UNTIL X1 > 5.
    READ TRANS-FILE
        AT END MOVE 'NO ' TO MORE-TRANS-RECS.
    PERFORM 400-CALC-RTN UNTIL NO-MORE-TRANS-RECS.
    CLOSE TABLE-FILE
          TRANS-FILE
          PRINT-FILE.
    STOP RUN.
```

```
200-TABLE-ENTRY.
    PERFORM 300-ENTER-IT
        VARYING X2 FROM 1 BY 1 UNTIL X2 > 150.
300-ENTER-IT.
    MOVE T-ITEM-NO TO ITEM-NO (X2, X1).
    MOVE T-QTY-ON-HAND TO PRICE (X2, X1).
400-CALC-RTN.
    MOVE ACCT-NO TO ACCT-OUT.
    MOVE ACCT-NAME TO NAME-OUT.
    MOVE 0 TO FOUND-IT.
    PERFORM 500-SEARCH-TABLE
        VARYING X1 FROM 1 BY 1
            UNTIL X1 > 5 OR FOUND-IT = 1.
    WRITE PRINT-REC FROM DETAIL-REC
        AFTER ADVANCING 2 LINES.
    READ TRANS-FILE
        AT END MOVE 'NO ' TO MORE-TRANS-RECS.
500-SEARCH-TABLE.
    SET X2 TO 1.
    SEARCH STOCK-ITEMS
        WHEN ITEM-IN = ITEM-NO (X1, X2)
            MULTIPLY QTY-IN BY PRICE
                GIVING GROSS-OUT
            MOVE 1 TO FOUND-IT.
```

1. Two syntax errors occur on the lines associated with the SET and the SEARCH. Both errors are the result of an omission within TABLE-1. Find and correct the errors.

2. An abend condition occurs during execution of 300-ENTER-IT. Determine why and fix the error.

3. Suppose two warehouses have the same ITEM-NO (e.g., 127). How will this affect processing? Would this processing be correct? If not, explain how you would modify the program.

4. Suppose the company has decided to increase the price of each item by 10% but has not yet made the appropriate changes to the table entries. Make the necessary changes to 400-CALC-RTN so that GROSS-OUT is correct.

5. There is another way to make the 10% price increases. You can make them to the table entries as the table is entered. Recode the table-entry routine so that prices are increased by 10%. Which method is more efficient?

PROGRAMMING ASSIGNMENTS

1. Write a program to print two sales reports. The first report is a daily report giving seven daily figures, edited. The second report is a salesperson report giving 25 salesperson figures, edited. The problem definition is shown in Figure 15.4.

   Notes

   a. For the first report, each daily figure represents the sum of 25 salesperson figures for the corresponding day. For the second report, each salesperson figure represents the sum of seven daily figures for the corresponding salesperson.

   b. Records are not in sequence.

Figure 15.4
Problem definition for
Programming Assignment 1.

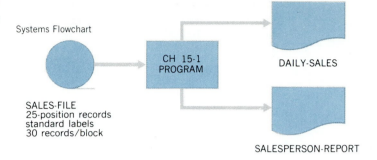

Systems Flowchart

SALES-FILE
25-position records
standard labels
30 records/block

CH 15-1
PROGRAM

DAILY-SALES

SALESPERSON-REPORT

SALES-FILE Record Layout

DAY NO.	SALESPERSON NO.	TRANSACTION AMOUNT $ ¢	

1   2 3   5 6   10 11   25

DAILY-SALES Printer Spacing Chart

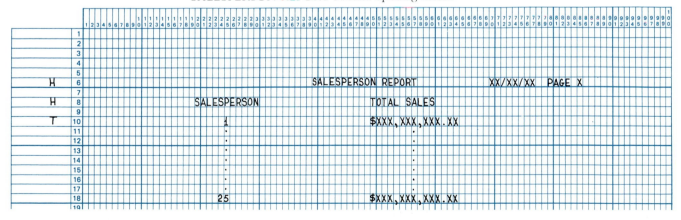

SALESPERSON-REPORT Printer Spacing Chart

2. Write a program to tabulate the number of employees by office within territory. The problem definition is shown in Figure 15.5. There is one input record for each employee.

Notes

a. There are two offices within each territory; there are three territories.

b. Records are not in sequence.

Figure 15.5
Problem definition for
Programming Assignment 2.

Systems Flowchart

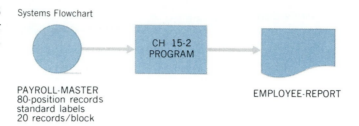

PAYROLL-MASTER
80-position records
standard labels
20 records/block

EMPLOYEE-REPORT

PAYROLL-MASTER Record Layout

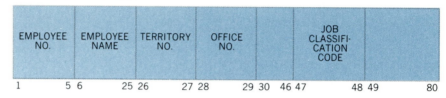

EMPLOYEE-REPORT Printer Spacing Chart

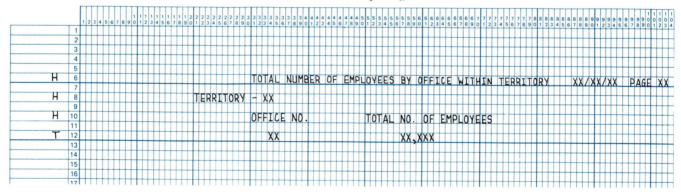

3. Redo Programming Assignment 2 to tabulate the number of employees by job classification within office within territory. Figure 15.6 shows the Printer Spacing Chart for this problem.

   Notes

   a. Job classification codes are 01, 02, and 03.
   b. Records are not in sequence.

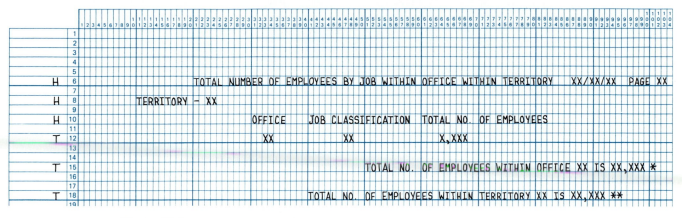

Figure 15.6
Printer Spacing Chart for
Programming Assignment 3.

4. Redo Programming Assignment 1 assuming the 25 salespeople have unique salesperson numbers that can be anything from 001 to 999.

UNIT V
FILE MAINTENANCE

16

Sequential File Processing

OBJECTIVES

To familiarize you with

1. Master file processing concepts.
2. Sequential update procedures using disk or tape as a master file.
3. How sequential disk files may be updated in place with a REWRITE statement.

I. Systems Overview of Sequential File Processing

A. Disk and Tape Master Files

This unit will focus on **master file** processing where a master file is the major collection of data pertaining to a specific application. Companies will have master files in application areas such as payroll, accounts receivable, accounts payable, production, sales, and inventory.

In most companies, a master file will be stored on either a magnetic disk or tape. The features of disk and tape that make them ideally suited for storing master file data include:

SUMMARY*

Common Features of Disk and Tape
1. Disks and tapes can store millions of characters of data.
2. Disk and tape drives can read and write data very quickly.
3. Disks and tapes can store records of any size.
4. Disks and tapes can be used as *either* input or output.

Whether a master file is stored on disk or tape depends on the needs of the company and on the ways in which the master file is to be accessed. Tape files *can only be accessed sequentially*, but disk files can be organized for either sequential *or* random access. Thus, if a master file is always processed sequentially, then it may be stored on either disk or tape. But if a file needs to be read or processed in some undetermined sequence, then it would be stored on *disk* and organized for *random access*. An airlines reservation system, for example, in which clerks check on flight availability for customers would need to access a master file randomly.

Distinctions Between Disk and Tape
1. Tapes *must* be processed sequentially.
2. Disks can be processed *either* sequentially or randomly.

Note that since disks have all the advantages of tape as well as many other advantages, many companies have begun to use disks exclusively for all their file processing needs.

In this chapter, we focus on **sequential file processing** procedures used for handling *master disk or tape files*. In Chapters 18 and 23 we discuss randomly accessible disk files.

B. Typical Master File Procedures: A Systems Overview

When a business system is computerized, the systems analyst decides whether the master file is to be organized for sequential processing or random processing. As noted, sequential organization is used for disk and tape files that are processed in some sequence; if a file needs to be accessed randomly, it *must be stored on disk* and have a method of organization that permits random access. In either case, the following are procedures that would need to be performed:

---

*See Appendix B for a summary of the physical features of disk and tape.

1. Creating a Master File

When a new system is implemented, or used for the first time, a master file must be initially *created*. This procedure can be performed by entering all master file data from a terminal or other data entry device. The data is then recorded on a disk or tape and becomes the new master file. Creating a master file is a one-time procedure. That is, once the master file is created, changes to it are made by a different procedure.

The primary objective of a program that creates a master file is ensuring *data integrity*. A master file is only useful if it contains valid and reliable data; hence, a creation program must be designed so that it minimizes input errors. Chapter 13 focused on some data validation techniques used to minimize the risk of errors when creating a master file.

When a master file is created, a *control listing* is also produced that prints the new master file data as well as whatever control totals are deemed necessary. This control listing should be checked or verified by the users.

2. Creating a Transaction File

After a master file is created, a procedure must be developed to make changes to it. Change records are stored in a separate file referred to as a **transaction file**. Changes to an accounts receivable master file, for example, may consist of sales records and credit records. Changes to a payroll master file may consist of name changes, salary changes, and so on. Such change records would be stored in a transaction file. The transaction file should also be validated to ensure data integrity. Just as with master file creation, validating transaction data will minimize the risk of errors.

3. Updating a Master File

The process of making a master file current is referred to as **updating**. The master file is updated or made current by incorporating the changes from the transaction records. This chapter emphasizes techniques used for performing *sequential updates* for master files stored on disk or tape. Sequential updates process transaction records that are stored *in sequence in a file*, rather than interactively. We call this **batch processing**. Chapters 18 and 23 illustrate techniques used for performing *random access updates* where the master file *must be on disk* and transaction records need not be in sequence.

4. Reporting from a Master File

The purpose of maintaining a master file is to store data that will provide users with meaningful output. Output in the form of reports are frequently *scheduled*, which means they are prepared on a regular basis. Sales reports, bills, and payroll checks are examples of output from master files that are prepared on a regularly scheduled basis.

Reports can also be prepared *on demand*. That is, they are requested whenever the need arises. If a manager or customer inquires about the status of a specific record, for example, we call the response *on demand output*.

The preparation of regularly scheduled reports using detail printing, exception printing, and group printing techniques have already been considered in Chapters 11 and 12. Chapter 19 will focus on *demand or interactive output*, which is often provided by files that are designed to be accessed randomly.

Using the data validation techniques discussed in Chapter 13, you should be able to write programs to create a master file and a transaction file from input data and to validate the data according to the system's specifications. Both master and transaction record formats should be designed by the analyst with the following in mind:

1. Key or identifying fields should appear first in the record. These might

be Social Security number and name for a payroll file, part number and part description for an inventory file, etc. Numeric key fields are best coded first.

2. All fields should be large enough to accommodate the largest value and to allow for growth where appropriate. If, for example, current salaries for a payroll file range from $15,000 to $96,000, the salary field should be *six integers* to allow for raises that might increase $96,000 to over $100,000 in the near future.

II. Sequential File Updating—Creating a New Master File

A. The Files Used

Both disk and tape master files can be updated by reading in the master file and a transaction file and creating a new master file. This means that the update procedure uses *three* files. Most often, a fourth print file that is used as a *control listing* (for printing all changes made, any errors found, and totals) is created as well.

Later in this chapter we will see that disks also can be updated using another method where the records to be updated on the master file are *rewritten in place*. This means that only two files would be needed—an input transaction file and a master file that is read from and written onto. For now, however, we focus on the traditional method of updating sequential files where there are two input and one output files.

1. Input Master File

The input master file is the master file that is current through the previous updating period. That is, if updates are performed weekly, the input master file is the file that was created as the master during the previous week. We call this file OLD-MASTER because it does not contain current changes.

2. Input Transaction File

The transaction file is the file that contains data to be used for updating the master file called OLD-MASTER. The input transaction file contains all changes that have occurred since OLD-MASTER was created. We call this file TRANS-FILE.

3. Output Master File

The output master file is the file that becomes the new master as a result of the updating procedure. The output master file will integrate data from the OLD-MASTER and the TRANS-FILE. We will call this file NEW-MASTER. Note that for the next week's update run, this NEW-MASTER will become OLD-MASTER.

In our illustration, we assume that all files—the input and output master and the transaction—are on disk, but they could have been stored on tape as well. The systems flowchart in Figure 16.1 summarizes the files used in an update procedure.

As noted, a print file or *control listing* is usually created during a sequential file update. This print file would list (1) changes made to the master file, (2) errors encountered during processing, and (3) totals to be used for control and checking purposes. Since you are already familiar with the techniques for creating print files, we will omit them from our sequential update illustrations for the sake of simplicity.

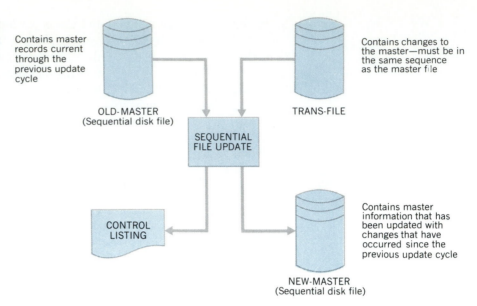

Figure 16.1
Systems flowchart of a
sequential update procedure.

Contains master records current through the previous update cycle

Contains changes to the master—must be in the same sequence as the master file

OLD-MASTER
(Sequential disk file)

TRANS-FILE

SEQUENTIAL
FILE UPDATE

CONTROL
LISTING

Contains master information that has been updated with changes that have occurred since the previous update cycle

NEW-MASTER
(Sequential disk file)

B. The Ordering of Records for Sequential Updates

OLD-MASTER contains master information that was complete and current through the previous updating cycle. The TRANS-FILE contains transactions or changes that have occurred since the previous updating cycle. These transactions or changes must be incorporated into the master file to make it current. The TRANS-FILE can be stored on any computer medium. The NEW-MASTER will include all OLD-MASTER data in addition to the changes stored on the TRANS-FILE that have occurred since the last update. The NEW-MASTER will typically be on the same medium as the OLD-MASTER, since the current NEW-MASTER becomes the OLD-MASTER for the next update cycle.

In a sequential master file, all records are in sequence by a **key field**, such as account number, social security number, or part number, depending on the type of master file. This key field uniquely identifies each master record. To update records in a sequential master file, the transaction file containing the change records must also be *in sequence by the same key field*. Thus, a transaction record will similarly be identified with a key field.

C. The Procedures Used For Sequential Updates

Let us consider the updating of a sequential master accounts receivable file. The key field used to identify records in the master file is account number, called M-ACCT-NO, for master account number. All records in the OLD-MASTER accounts receivable file are in sequence by M-ACCT-NO.

The transaction file contains all transactions to be posted to the master file that have occurred since the previous update. This transaction file also has an account number as a key field, called T-ACCT-NO for transaction account number. Records in the TRANS-FILE are in sequence by T-ACCT-NO.

The formats for the two input files are:

OLD-MASTER-REC

(in sequence by M-ACCT-NO)

```
1-5     M-ACCT-NO
6-11    AMOUNT-DUE XXXX.XX
12-100  FILLER
```

TRANS-REC

(in sequence by T-ACCT-NO)

```
1-5     T-ACCT-NO
6-11    AMT-TRANS-IN-CURRENT-PER   XXXX.XX
12-100  FILLER
```

Each transaction record contains the *total* amount transacted during the current period for a specific master record. Hence, there will be *one transaction record* for each master record to be updated.

NEW-MASTER becomes the current master accounts receivable file after the update procedure. It must have the same format as the OLD-MASTER. We will name the fields as follows:

NEW-MASTER-REC

```
1-5    ACCT-NO-OUT
6-11   AMOUNT-DUE-OUT
12-100 FILLER
```

The FILLERs may contain additional data used in other programs or for purposes not related to this update.

Keep in mind that records within OLD-MASTER are in sequence by M-ACCT-NO and that records within TRANS-FILE are in sequence by T-ACCT-NO. The NEW-MASTER file, then, will also be created in account number sequence.

Figure 16.2 is a flowchart of the procedures to be coded in this update program. We will consider each procedure in detail. Figure 16.3 shows the pseudocode for this program; Figure 16.4 is the hierarchy chart. Examine these charts carefully before looking at the program in Figure 16.5.

Figure 16.2
Flowchart of procedures to be used in a sample update program.

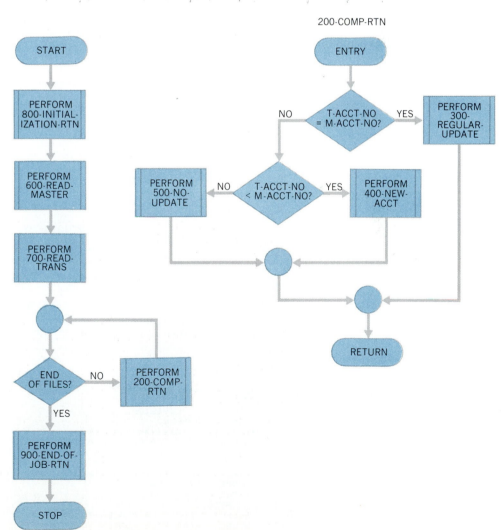

Figure 16.3
Pseudocode for sample
update program.

```
PERFORM
    Open the Files
ENDPERFORM
PERFORM
    Read Master Record
ENDPERFORM
PERFORM
    Read Transaction Record
ENDPERFORM
PERFORM UNTIL no more input
    IF  T-Acct-No = M-Acct-No
    THEN
        PERFORM
            Update the Master Record
            Read a Master Record
            Read a Transaction Record
        ENDPERFORM
    ELSE
        IF  T-Acct-No < M-Acct-No
        THEN
            PERFORM
                Write a New Master Record from Transaction Record
                Read a Transaction Record
            ENDPERFORM
        ELSE
            PERFORM
                Write a New Master from Old Master
                Read a Master Record
            ENDPERFORM
        ENDIF
    ENDIF
ENDPERFORM
PERFORM
    End-of-Job Operations
ENDPERFORM
```

Figure 16.4
Hierarchy chart for
sample update program.

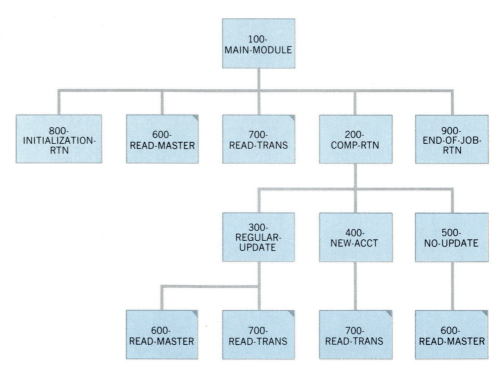

Figure 16.5
Sample update program.

a. Program

```
IDENTIFICATION DIVISION.
PROGRAM-ID. SAMPLE.
*****************************************************
*    SAMPLE      -  PROGRAM UPDATES THE OLD-MASTER  *
*                   FILE WITH A TRANSACTION FILE AND *
*                   AND CREATES A NEW-MASTER FILE.   *
*****************************************************
ENVIRONMENT DIVISION.
INPUT-OUTPUT SECTION.
FILE-CONTROL.
    SELECT OLD-MASTER ASSIGN TO DATA14O.
    SELECT TRANS-FILE ASSIGN TO DATA14T.
    SELECT NEW-MASTER ASSIGN TO DATA14N.
```

Figure 16.5
(continued)

```
*
DATA DIVISION.
FILE SECTION.
FD  OLD-MASTER
    LABEL RECORDS ARE STANDARD
    BLOCK CONTAINS 20 RECORDS.
01  OLD-MASTER-REC.
    05  M-ACCT-NO                    PIC X(5).
    05  AMOUNT-DUE                   PIC 9(4)V99.
    05  FILLER                       PIC X(89).
FD  TRANS-FILE
    LABEL RECORDS ARE STANDARD.
01  TRANS-REC.
    05  T-ACCT-NO                    PIC X(5).
    05  AMT-TRANS-IN-CURRENT-PER     PIC 9(4)V99.
    05  FILLER                       PIC X(89).
FD  NEW-MASTER
    LABEL RECORDS ARE STANDARD
    BLOCK CONTAINS 20 RECORDS.
01  NEW-MASTER-REC.
    05  ACCT-NO-OUT                  PIC X(5).
    05  AMOUNT-DUE-OUT               PIC 9(4)V99.
    05  FILLER                       PIC X(89).
*
PROCEDURE DIVISION.
**********************************************
*  CONTROLS DIRECTION OF PROGRAM LOGIC  *
**********************************************
100-MAIN-MODULE.
    PERFORM 800-INITIALIZATION-RTN.
    PERFORM 600-READ-MASTER.
    PERFORM 700-READ-TRANS.
    PERFORM 200-COMP-RTN
        UNTIL M-ACCT-NO = HIGH-VALUES
                    AND
              T-ACCT-NO = HIGH-VALUES.
    PERFORM 900-END-OF-JOB-RTN.
*****************************************************************
*  PERFORMED FROM 100-MAIN-MODULE.COMPARES THE   ACCOUNT   *
*  NUMBERS FROM BOTH FILES TO DETERMINE THE ACTION TO BE *
*  TAKEN.                                                 *
*****************************************************************
200-COMP-RTN.
    IF  T-ACCT-NO = M-ACCT-NO
        PERFORM 300-REGULAR-UPDATE
    ELSE
        IF  T-ACCT-NO < M-ACCT-NO
            PERFORM 400-NEW-ACCOUNT
        ELSE
            PERFORM 500-NO-UPDATE.
*****************************************************************
*  PERFORMED FROM 200-COMP-RTN, COMBINES OLD-MASTER AND   *
*  TRANSACTION FILE TO CREATE NEW-MASTER RECORDS          *
*****************************************************************
300-REGULAR-UPDATE.
    MOVE OLD-MASTER-REC TO NEW-MASTER-REC.
    COMPUTE AMOUNT-DUE-OUT = AMT-TRANS-IN-CURRENT-PER + AMOUNT-DUE.
    WRITE NEW-MASTER-REC.
    PERFORM 600-READ-MASTER.
    PERFORM 700-READ-TRANS.
*****************************************************************
*  PERFORMED FROM 200-COMP-RTN ADDS NEW ACCOUNT TO NEW-MASTER  *
*  FROM TRANSACTION FILE                                       *
*****************************************************************
400-NEW-ACCOUNT.
    MOVE SPACES TO NEW-MASTER-REC.
    MOVE AMT-TRANS-IN-CURRENT-PER TO AMOUNT-DUE-OUT.
    WRITE NEW-MASTER-REC.
    PERFORM 700-READ-TRANS.
*****************************************************************
*  PERFORMED FROM 200-COMP-RTN COPIES THE OLD-MASTER TO NEW-MASTER  *
*****************************************************************
500-NO-UPDATE.
    WRITE NEW-MASTER-REC FROM OLD-MASTER-REC.
    PERFORM 600-READ-MASTER.
*********************************************************
*  PERFORMED FROM 100-MAIN-MODULE 300-REGULAR-UPDATE  *
*  AND 500-NO-UPDATE, READS OLD-MASTER FILE           *
*********************************************************
600-READ-MASTER.
    READ OLD-MASTER
        AT END MOVE HIGH-VALUES TO M-ACCT-NO.
```

Figure 16.5
(continued)

```
****************************************************************
*   PERFORMED FROM 100-MAIN-MODULE 300-REGULAR-UPDATE   *
*   AND 400-NEW-ACCOUNT, READS TRANSACTION FILE         *
****************************************************************
 700-READ-TRANS.
     READ TRANS-FILE
         AT END MOVE HIGH-VALUES TO T-ACCT-NO.
****************************************************************
*   PERFORMED FROM 100-MAIN-MODULE, OPENS FILES   *
****************************************************************
 800-INITIALIZATION-RTN.
      OPEN INPUT  OLD-MASTER
                  TRANS-FILE
           OUTPUT NEW-MASTER.
****************************************************************
*   PERFORMED FROM 100-MAIN-MODULE, CLOSES FILES   *
*   AND RETURNS CONTROL TO OPERATING SYSTEM        *
****************************************************************
 900-END-OF-JOB-RTN.
      CLOSE OLD-MASTER
            TRANS-FILE
            NEW-MASTER.
      STOP RUN.
```

b. Sample OLD-MASTER Data	**c. Sample TRANS-FILE Data**
11111009967	11111009899
22222007666	22222087778
44444076566	33333092828
55555098988	44444092828
66666109899	66666083828
77777029282	77777092888
88888098272	88888020929
99999123456	

d. Sample NEW-MASTER Data

```
11111019866
22222095444
33333092828
44444169394
55555098988
66666193727
77777122170
88888119201
99999123456
```

1. The Main Module

The main module at 100-MAIN-MODULE performs an initialization routine that opens all files. Then a record is read from both the master and the transaction file. 200-COMP-RTN is performed until all records are processed. At that point, an end-of-job routine is executed from the main module; this routine closes the files and stops the run. The significance of the COBOL reserved word HIGH-VALUES in the PERFORM statement will be discussed later in this section.

2. How Input Transaction and Master Records Are Processed

Initially, a record is obtained from both the OLD-MASTER and the TRANS-FILE in read modules executed from the main module. 200-COMP-RTN then compares the account numbers, M-ACCT-NO of OLD-MASTER-REC and T-ACCT-NO of TRANS-REC. Since both files are in sequence by their respective account numbers, a comparison of M-ACCT-NO to T-ACCT-NO will determine the next module to be executed. Three possible conditions may be met when comparing M-ACCT-NO to T-ACCT-NO:

a. T-ACCT-NO IS EQUAL TO M-ACCT-NO. This means that a transaction record exists with the same account number that is on the master file. If this condition is met, we perform a procedure called 300-REGULAR-UPDATE where OLD-MASTER-REC is updated. That is, the transaction data is posted to the master record, which means that the NEW-MASTER-REC will contain the previous AMOUNT-DUE plus the AMT-TRANS-IN-CURRENT-PER of the transaction record. After a NEW-MASTER-REC is written, another record from both OLD-MASTER and TRANS-FILE must be read. Here, again, we are assuming that each master record can be updated by only *one* transaction record.

b. T-ACCT-NO IS GREATER THAN M-ACCT-NO. If T-ACCT-NO IS > M-ACCT-NO, then there is a master record with an account number *less than* the account number on the transaction file. This condition occurs in our program if the last ELSE is executed in 200-COMP-RTN. If T-ACCT-NO is not equal to M-ACCT-NO or T-ACCT-NO is not less than M-ACCT-NO, then T-ACCT-NO *must be* greater than M-ACCT-NO.

Since both files are in sequence by account number, this condition means that a master record exists for which there is *no corresponding transaction record*. That is, the master record has had no activity or changes occurring during the current update cycle and should be written onto the NEW-MASTER file *as is*. We call this procedure 500-NO-UPDATE. At 500-NO-UPDATE, we write the NEW-MASTER-REC from the OLD-MASTER-REC and read another record from OLD-MASTER. Since we have not yet processed the last transaction record that caused T-ACCT-NO to compare greater than the M-ACCT-NO of the OLD-MASTER, there is no need to read another transaction record at the 500-NO-UPDATE procedure. Consider the following example that illustrates the processing to be performed if M-ACCT-NO IS < T-ACCT-NO, which is the same as T-ACCT-NO > M-ACCT-NO:

```
M-ACCT-NO      T-ACCT-NO

00001          00001  ←——————  Update master record
00002          00003  ←——————  00002 is put in the NEW-MASTER as
                                is; the next master record is read;
                                T-ACCT-NO  00003 has not yet been
                                processed
```

c. T-ACCT-NO IS LESS THAN M-ACCT-NO. Since both files are in sequence by account number, this condition would mean that a transaction record exists for which there is no corresponding master record. Depending on the type of update procedure being performed, this could mean either (1) a new account is to be processed from the TRANS-FILE or (2) an error has occurred; that is, the T-ACCT-NO is wrong. In our illustration, we will assume that when a T-ACCT-NO is less than an M-ACCT-NO, this is a *new account*; but first let us consider the full range of procedures that could be executed if T-ACCT-NO is less than M-ACCT-NO:

(1) Create a New Account If T-ACCT-NO < M-ACCT-NO. As noted, for some applications a transaction record with no corresponding master record means a new account. We call this procedure 400-NEW-ACCOUNT in our program. In this instance, a new master record is created entirely from the transaction record. Then the next transaction record is read. We do *not* read another record from OLD-MASTER at this time, since we have not yet processed the master record that compared greater than T-ACCT-NO. The other possibility is to:

(2) Specify an Error Condition If `T-ACCT-NO < M-ACCT-NO`. For some applications, all account numbers on the transaction file *must* have corresponding master records with the same account numbers. For these applications, new accounts are handled by a different program and are *not* part of the update procedure.

Thus, if `T-ACCT-NO` is less than `M-ACCT-NO`, an error routine should be processed, which we could have labeled `400-ERROR-RTN`. The error routine would usually print out the transaction record that has a nonmatching account number and then read the next transaction record.

3. Illustrating the Update Procedure with Examples

In our program, a master and a transaction record are read from the main module. Then `200-COMP-RTN` is executed, where the account numbers are compared. Based on the comparison, `300-REGULAR-UPDATE`, `500-NO-UP-DATE`, or `400-NEW-ACCOUNT` will be executed. `200-COMP-RTN` is then repeated until there are no more records to process.

The following examples illustrate the routines to be performed depending on the account numbers read:

M-ACCT-NO	T-ACCT-NO	CONDITION	ACTION
00001	00001	`T-ACCT-NO = M-ACCT-NO`	`300-REGULAR-UPDATE`
00002	00004	`T-ACCT-NO > M-ACCT-NO`	`500-NO-UPDATE`
00003	00004	`T-ACCT-NO > M-ACCT-NO`	`500-NO-UPDATE`
00005	00004	`T-ACCT-NO < M-ACCT-NO`	`400-NEW-ACCOUNT`
00005	00005	`T-ACCT-NO = M-ACCT-NO`	`300-REGULAR-UPDATE`

Remember that this update procedure assumes that there is no more than a *single transaction record for each master record*. Later on we will consider the procedures used when there may be multiple transaction records with the same account number that are to update a single master record.

Review again the flowchart in Figure 16.2, the pseudocode in Figure 16.3, the hierarchy chart in Figure 16.4, and the program in Figure 16.5.

Two elements in the program require further clarification: (1) the nested conditional in `200-COMP-RTN`, and (2) the use of `HIGH-VALUES` in the master and transaction account number fields when an `AT END` condition is reached.

4. Additional Coding Techniques

a. Nested Conditional in `200-COMP-RTN`. A **nested conditional** with an `IF ... ELSE IF ...` format is particularly useful in an update procedure where we have three conditions to test. Nested conditionals function as follows:

Format

```
IF   condition-1
        statement-1
ELSE
        IF   condition-2
                statement-2
        ELSE
                IF   statement-3
                        ⋮
```

Meaning

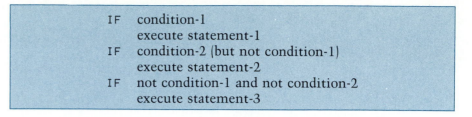

> IF   condition-1
>   execute statement-1
> IF   condition-2 (but not condition-1)
>   execute statement-2
> IF   not condition-1 and not condition-2
>   execute statement-3

In our program, the following was coded:

Condition	Result
`IF T-ACCT-NO = M-ACCT-NO`	`PERFORM 300-REGULAR-UPDATE`
`ELSE`	
`    IF T-ACCT-NO < M-ACCT-NO`	`PERFORM 400-NEW-ACCOUNT`
`    ELSE`	`PERFORM 500-NO-UPDATE`

The last `ELSE` is executed if `T-ACCT-NO` is greater than `M-ACCT-NO`.

Since we wish to execute `200-COMP-RTN` in its entirety for each master and transaction record to be processed, it is best to code it as a *single instruction* with this nested conditional structure.

b. The Use of `HIGH-VALUES` for End-of-File Conditions.

Because we have two input files, there are two possible end-of-file conditions that may occur. First, an `AT END` condition for the `TRANS-FILE` may occur *before* we have reached the end of the `OLD-MASTER` file. Or, we may run out of `OLD-MASTER` records before we reach the end of the `TRANS-FILE`. We must account for both possibilities in our program.

The COBOL reserved word **HIGH-VALUES** is used in the `600-READ-MASTER` and `700-READ-TRANS` procedures. Consider first `600-READ-MASTER`. When the `OLD-MASTER` file has reached the end, there may be additional transaction records to process. Hence, we would not want to automatically terminate all processing at an `OLD-MASTER` end-of-file condition; instead, we want to continue processing transaction records as new accounts. To accomplish this, we place `HIGH-VALUES` in `M-ACCT-NO` of `OLD-MASTER-REC` when an `AT END` condition occurs for that file. `HIGH-VALUES` refers to the largest value in the computer's collating sequence. This is a nonprintable character consisting of "all bits on" in a single storage position.

`HIGH-VALUES` in `M-ACCT-NO` ensures that subsequent attempts to compare the `T-ACCT-NO` of new transaction records to this `M-ACCT-NO` will always result in a "less than" condition. Thus, suppose we reach an `AT END` condition for `OLD-MASTER` first. The `400-NEW-ACCOUNT` routine would be executed until there are no more transaction records, because `M-ACCT-NO` has the highest possible value and will always compare "high" to `T-ACCT-NO`; that is, `T-ACCT-NO` is always < `M-ACCT-NO` if `M-ACCT-NO` has `HIGH-VALUES` in it.

Now consider `700-READ-TRANS`. We may reach an `AT END` condition for `TRANS-FILE` while there are still `OLD-MASTER` records left to process. In this case, we would continue processing `OLD-MASTER` records at `500-NO-UPDATE` until we have read the file in its entirety. Hence, at `700-READ-TRANS`, we move `HIGH-VALUES` to `T-ACCT-NO` on an `AT END` condition. `HIGH-VALUES` is a kind of "dummy" or "trailer" `T-ACCT-NO` that will always compare high, or greater than, `M-ACCT-NO`. In this way, `500-NO-UPDATE` will continue to be executed. Any remaining `OLD-MASTER` records will be read and processed using this `500-NO-UPDATE` sequence. This procedure will be repeated until an `AT END` condition at `OLD-MASTER` is reached.

Thus, we continue to process records at 200-COMP-RTN even if one of the two input files has reached an AT END condition. Only when *both* AT END *conditions* have been reached would control return to the main module where the program is terminated. To accomplish this, the main module executes 200-COMP-RTN with the following statement:

```
PERFORM 200-COMP-RTN UNTIL
    M-ACCT-NO = HIGH-VALUES
        AND
    T-ACCT-NO = HIGH-VALUES.
```

HIGH-VALUES may be used only with fields that are defined as *alphanumeric*. Thus M-ACCT-NO, T-ACCT-NO, and ACCT-NO-OUT must be defined with a PIC of Xs rather than 9s even though they typically contain numeric data. This does not affect the processing, since 9s are required only if a field is to be used in an arithmetic operation.

It may have occurred to you that moving 99999 to M-ACCT-NO or T-ACCT-NO on an end-of-file condition would produce the same results as moving HIGH-VALUES. That is, a trailer record of 9s in an account number field will always compare high. This use of 9s in the key field is only possible, however, if the key field could not, in reality, have a valid value of 9s. That is, if an account number of 99999 is a feasible entry, moving 99999 to an account number when an end-of-file condition is reached could produce erroneous results.

In summary, HIGH-VALUES means "all bits on," which is *not* a printable character. Using it on an end-of-file condition will ensure correct file handling regardless of the actual values that the account numbers can assume. This is because an incoming account number will always compare "less than" HIGH-VALUES.

DISPLAY **Output Records When Debugging Your Program**

When testing a program that creates a disk or tape as output, you should examine the output records to make sure that they are correct. You can do this by coding DISPLAY record-name just prior to writing the record. This will display the record on the screen or printer so you can see what it looks like. Most computer systems also have a *job control command* such as /PRINT file-name that will enable you to print the entire file that was created as output. Keep in mind that an update program is not fully debugged until all files have been checked to ensure that the updating was performed correctly.

Self-Test

1. A _____ is the major collection of data pertaining to a specific application.
2. (T or F) A disk file can be accessed either sequentially or randomly whereas tapes can only be accessed sequentially.
3. Changes to a master file are placed in a separate file called a _____ file.
4. In a sequential update procedure, three files may be used: they are _____, _____, and _____.
5. (T or F) In a sequential update procedure, all files must be in sequence by the same key field.
6. In a sequential update procedure, the key field in the transaction file is compared to the key field in the _____.
7. In Question 6, if the key fields are equal, a _____ procedure is performed. Describe this procedure.
8. In Question 6, if the transaction key field is greater than the master key field, a _____ procedure is performed. Describe this procedure.

9. In Question 6, if the transaction key field is less than the master key field, a _____ procedure is performed. Describe this procedure.

10. The statement READ TRANS-FILE AT END MOVE HIGH-VALUES TO T-ACCT-NO causes _____ if there are no more records in TRANS-FILE. T-ACCT-NO must be defined with a PIC of _____.

Solutions

1. master file
2. T
3. transaction
4. the old master file—current through the previous updating cycle; the transaction file; the new master file—which incorporates the old master data along with the transaction data
5. T
6. old master file
7. regular update; transaction data is added to the master data, a new master record is written, and records from the old master and the transaction file are read.
8. no update; a new master record is created directly from the old master record and a record from the old master file is read.
9. new account or error; if it is a new account, move transaction data to the new master and write; if it is an error, an error message is printed. In either case, a transaction record is then read.
10. all bits on in the T-ACCT-NO field. (Any subsequent comparison of T-ACCT-NO to an actual M-ACCT-NO will cause a ">" condition); Xs

III. Validity Checking in Update Procedures

Because updating results in changes to master files, data entry errors must be kept to an absolute minimum. For "real world" updates, therefore, numerous data validation techniques should be incorporated to minimize errors. Let us consider some common validity checking routines.

A. Checking for New Accounts

You will recall that there are two types of procedures commonly used if T-ACCT-NO is less than M-ACCT-NO, that is, if there is a transaction record for which there is no corresponding master record. For some applications, transaction records should always have corresponding master records; in this case, if T-ACCT-NO < M-ACCT-NO, we treat this as an error.

For other applications, if T-ACCT-NO < M-ACCT-NO, the transaction record could be a new account to be added to the NEW-MASTER file. To simply add this transaction record to the new master file, however, without any additional checking would be dangerous, since the possibility exists that T-ACCT-NO was coded incorrectly and that the transaction record is, in fact, *not* a new account.

To verify that a TRANS-REC is a new account, we usually include a *coded field* in the TRANS-REC itself. A more complete format for TRANS-REC would be as follows:

```
TRANS-REC
   1-5    T-ACCT-NO
   6-11   AMT-TRANS-IN-CURRENT-PER  XXXX.XX
   12-99  FILLER
  ┌─────────────────────────────────────┐
  │ 100    CODE-IN                       │
  │          1 = NEW-ACCT                │
  │          2 = REGULAR-UPDATE          │
  └─────────────────────────────────────┘
```

Thus, if T-ACCT-NO IS LESS THAN M-ACCT-NO, we would process the transaction record as a new account *only if* it also contains a 1 in CODE-IN. The procedure at 400-NEW-ACCOUNT in our sample update, then, could be modified to *validate* the data being entered:

Pseudocode Excerpt	Program Excerpt
IF new account	400-NEW-ACCOUNT.
THEN	IF CODE-IN = 1
Add a new record	MOVE SPACES TO NEW-MASTER-REC
ELSE	MOVE T-ACCT-NO TO ACCT-NO-OUT
PERFORM	MOVE AMT-TRANS-IN-CURRENT-PER
Write an error line	TO AMOUNT-DUE-OUT
ENDPERFORM	WRITE NEW-MASTER-REC
ENDIF	ELSE
PERFORM	PERFORM 800-ERROR-RTN.
Read a transaction record	PERFORM 700-READ-TRANS.
ENDPERFORM	

Similarly, CODE-IN may be used to validate transaction data processed at 300-REGULAR-UPDATE:

Pseudocode Excerpt	Program Excerpt
IF regular update	300-REGULAR-UPDATE.
THEN	IF CODE-IN = 2
Update the record	MOVE OLD-MASTER-REC
ELSE	TO NEW-MASTER-REC
PERFORM	COMPUTE AMOUNT-DUE-OUT =
Write an error line	AMT-TRANS-IN-CURRENT-PER
ENDPERFORM	+ AMOUNT-DUE
ENDIF	WRITE NEW-MASTER-REC
PERFORM	ELSE
Read a master record	PERFORM 800-ERROR-RTN.
ENDPERFORM	PERFORM 600-READ-MASTER.
PERFORM	PERFORM 700-READ-TRANS.
Read a transaction record	
ENDPERFORM	

It is better still to establish CODE-IN in the DATA DIVISION with condition-names as follows:

```
05  CODE-IN          PIC 9.
    88  NEW-ACCT              VALUE 1.
    88  UPDATE               VALUE 2.
```

Then, in 400-NEW-ACCOUNT, the conditional could be replaced by IF NEW-ACCT .... Similarly, in 300-REGULAR-UPDATE, the conditional could be replaced with IF UPDATE ....

The Practice Problem at the end of this chapter illustrates an update that uses coded transaction records.

B. Checking for Delete Codes and Deleting Records from a Sequential Master File

One type of update function not considered in our previous illustrations is that of *deleting master records*. Since accounts may need to be deactivated if customers give up their charge privileges or have not paid their bills, there must be some provision for eliminating specific records from the master file. We may use the technique of a coded transaction field as described earlier to accomplish this. We could add a code of '3' to indicate that a record is to be deleted:

TRANS-REC

```
  1-5    T-ACCT-NO
  6-11   AMT-TRANS-IN-CURRENT-PER XXXX.XX
 12-99   FILLER
100      CODE-IN
           1 = NEW-ACCT
           2 = UPDATE
           3 = DELETE-THE-RECORD
```

The procedure at 300-REGULAR-UPDATE might be revised as follows:

Pseudocode Excerpt	Program Excerpt
IF regular update	300-REGULAR-UPDATE.
THEN	IF UPDATE
Update the record	MOVE OLD-MASTER-REC
ELSE	TO NEW-MASTER-REC
IF delete code	COMPUTE AMOUNT-DUE-OUT =
THEN	AMT-TRANS-IN-CURRENT-PER
Continue	+ AMOUNT-DUE
ELSE	WRITE NEW-MASTER-REC
PERFORM	ELSE
Write an error line	IF DELETE-THE-RECORD
ENDPERFORM	NEXT SENTENCE
ENDIF	ELSE
ENDIF	PERFORM 800-ERROR-RTN.
PERFORM	PERFORM 600-READ-MASTER.
Read a master record	PERFORM 700-READ-TRANS.
ENDPERFORM	
PERFORM	
Read a transaction record	
ENDPERFORM	

Note that 300-REGULAR-UPDATE is performed only if T-ACCT-NO = M-ACCT-NO. Hence, at the end of 300-REGULAR-UPDATE, we read another record from each file. If CODE-IN = 3, the OLD-MASTER is *not* written onto the new file; it is, in effect, *deleted by not rewriting* the corresponding master record on to the new master file. To simply bypass records to be deleted, we code NEXT SENTENCE when that condition is met.

See the Practice Program in Figure 16.12 for a full illustration of how transaction codes are used.

The following is a summary of how transaction records with transaction codes can be processed:

SUMMARY
HOW TRANSACTION RECORDS ARE PROCESSED

A. T-KEY = M-KEY 1. Delete the master record if T-CODE indicates deletion.
  2. Change or update the master record if T-CODE indicates update.
  3. Process the transaction record as an error if T-CODE indicates new record.

B. T-KEY < M-KEY	1. Add transaction record to the master file if T-CODE indicates a new record.
	2. Process the transaction record as an error if T-CODE does not indicate a new record.
C. T-KEY > M-KEY	1. Rewrite the master record as is.

C. Checking for Sequence Errors

In an update program the sequence of the records in the transaction and master files is critical. If one or more records in the transaction or master file has been sequenced incorrectly, the entire production run could produce erroneous results.

If the possibility for a sequence error exists, it is advisable to include a sequence check in your program similar to the one described in Chapter 13.

Note, however, that both the TRANS-FILE and the OLD-MASTER can be sorted using a SORT statement, which is described in the next chapter. With a computerized SORT, you can be certain that a sorted disk or tape file is properly sequenced and you do not need to perform a sequence check.

IV. Update Procedures with Multiple Transaction Records for Each Master Record

We have thus far focused on an update procedure in which a *single transaction record* is used to alter the contents of a master record. For some applications, a single transaction record may be all that is required. For example, in a SALES file, we may use a single transaction record that indicates a salesperson's total sales for the current period to update his or her corresponding master record.

For other applications, there may be a need to process more than one change during each update cycle. For example, a master accounts receivable file may be updated with transaction records where a single transaction record is created for *each purchase or credit* charged to a customer. If a customer has purchased 12 items during the current updating cycle, then there will be 12 transaction records for that one master customer record. This requires a different type of updating from the one previously discussed.

The update procedure described in Figure 16.5 is suitable only if *one transaction per master* is permitted. If more than one transaction had the same account number as a master record, the second transaction would be handled incorrectly. Since an equal condition between the key fields in TRANS-REC and OLD-MASTER-REC causes a NEW-MASTER-REC to be written and a new TRANS-REC and MASTER-REC to be read, the processing would *not* function properly if multiple transaction records per master record were permissible.

The pseudocode for updating a file where multiple transactions per master record are permitted is in Figure 16.6, and the program is illustrated in Figure 16.7.

V. Sequential File Updating—Rewriting Records on a Disk

A. The REWRITE Statement for a Disk File Opened as I-O

As we have noted, both tape and disk can be organized sequentially and both can use a sequential update procedure like the one described in this chapter.

Figure 16.6
Pseudocode for sample update program where multiple transactions per master record are permitted.

```
PERFORM
    Open the files
    Read a master record
    Read a transaction record
ENDPERFORM
PERFORM UNTIL no more input
    IF   T-Acct-No = M-Acct-No
    THEN
        PERFORM
            PERFORM UNTIL T-Acct-No ≠ M-Acct-No
                Add transaction amount to master
                Read a transaction record
            ENDPERFORM
            Write a new master
            Read a master record
        ENDPERFORM
    ELSE
        IF   T-Acct-No < M-Acct-No
        THEN
            PERFORM
                Add a new record
                Read a transaction record
            ENDPERFORM
        ELSE
            PERFORM
                Write a new master from old master
                Read a master record
            ENDPERFORM
        ENDIF
    ENDIF
ENDPERFORM
PERFORM
    Close the files
    Stop run
ENDPERFORM
```

Figure 16.7
Sample update program where multiple transactions per master record are permitted.

a. Program

```
    IDENTIFICATION DIVISION.
    PROGRAM-ID. SAMPLE.
    **************************************************
    *    SAMPLE          - PROGRAM UPDATES AN OLD-MASTER*
    *                      FILE WITH A TRANSACTION FILE *
    *                      AND CREATES A NEW-MASTER FILE*
    *  MULTIPLE TRANSACTIONS PER MASTER ARE PERMITTED   *
    **************************************************
    ENVIRONMENT DIVISION.
    INPUT-OUTPUT SECTION.
    FILE-CONTROL.
        SELECT OLD-MASTER-IN  ASSIGN TO DATA140.
        SELECT TRANS-FILE-IN  ASSIGN TO DATA146T.
        SELECT NEW-MASTER-OUT ASSIGN TO DATA146N.
    *
    DATA DIVISION.
    FILE SECTION.
    FD  OLD-MASTER-IN
        LABEL RECORDS ARE STANDARD
        BLOCK CONTAINS 20 RECORDS.
    01  OLD-MASTER-REC-IN.
        05  M-ACCT-NO-IN          PIC X(5).
        05  AMOUNT-DUE-IN         PIC 9(4)V99.
        05  FILLER                PIC X(89).
    FD  TRANS-FILE-IN
        LABEL RECORDS ARE STANDARD.
    01  TRANS-REC-IN.
        05  T-ACCT-NO-IN          PIC X(5).
        05  AMT-TRANS-IN          PIC 9(4)V99.
        05  FILLER                PIC X(89).
    FD  NEW-MASTER-OUT
        LABEL RECORDS ARE STANDARD
        BLOCK CONTAINS 20 RECORDS.
    01  NEW-MASTER-REC-OUT.
        05  ACCT-NO-OUT           PIC X(5).
        05  AMOUNT-DUE-OUT        PIC 9(4)V99.
        05  FILLER                PIC X(89).
```

Figure 16.7
(continued)

```
*
  PROCEDURE DIVISION.
**************************************************
*   CONTROLS THE DIRECTION OF PROGRAM LOGIC   *
**************************************************
   100-MAIN-MODULE.
       PERFORM 800-INITIALIZATION-RTN.
       PERFORM 200-COMP-RTN
           UNTIL M-ACCT-NO-IN = HIGH-VALUES
                        AND
                    T-ACCT-NO-IN = HIGH-VALUES.
       PERFORM 900-END-OF-JOB-RTN.
************************************************************
*   PERFORMED FROM 100-MAIN-MODULE. COMPARES THE ACCOUNT NUMBERS *
*   TO DETERMINE THE APPROPRIATE PROCEDURE TO BE PERFORMED      *
************************************************************
   200-COMP-RTN.
       IF   T-ACCT-NO-IN = M-ACCT-NO-IN
           PERFORM 300-REGULAR-UPDATE
       ELSE
           IF   T-ACCT-NO-IN < M-ACCT-NO-IN
               PERFORM 400-NEW-ACCOUNT
           ELSE
               PERFORM 500-NO-UPDATE.
************************************************************
*   PERFORMED FROM 200-COMP-RTN. COMBINES THE OLD-MASTER AND *
*   TRANSACTION RECORDS TO CREATE THE NEW-MASTER RECORD.     *
************************************************************
   300-REGULAR-UPDATE.
       MOVE OLD-MASTER-REC-IN TO NEW-MASTER-REC-OUT.
       PERFORM 550-ADD-AND-READ-TRANS
           UNTIL T-ACCT-NO-IN NOT = M-ACCT-NO-IN.
       WRITE NEW-MASTER-REC-OUT.
       PERFORM 600-READ-MASTER.
************************************************************
*   PERFORMED FROM 200-COMP-RTN. ADDS A NEW ACCOUNT *
*   TO NEW-MASTER FROM THE TRANSACTION FILE.        *
************************************************************
   400-NEW-ACCOUNT.
       MOVE SPACES TO NEW-MASTER-REC-OUT.
       MOVE T-ACCT-NO-IN TO ACCT-NO-OUT.
       MOVE AMT-TRANS-IN TO AMOUNT-DUE-OUT.
       WRITE NEW-MASTER-REC-OUT.
       PERFORM 700-READ-TRANS.
************************************************************
*   PERFORMED FROM 200-COMP-RTN. COPIES THE OLD-MASTER RECORD *
*   TO THE NEW-MASTER FILE.                                   *
************************************************************
   500-NO-UPDATE.
       WRITE NEW-MASTER-REC-OUT FROM OLD-MASTER-REC-IN.
       PERFORM 600-READ-MASTER.
************************************************************
*   PERFORMED FROM 300-REGULAR-UPDATE. ADDS THE TRANSACTION AMOUNT *
*   TO THE AMOUNT DUE.                                            *
************************************************************
   550-ADD-AND-READ-TRANS.
       ADD AMT-TRANS-IN TO AMOUNT-DUE-OUT.
       PERFORM 700-READ-TRANS.
************************************************************
*   PERFORMED FROM 800-INITIALIZATION-RTN, 300-REGULAR-UPDATE *
*   AND 500-NO-UPDATE. READS THE OLD-MASTER FILE.            *
************************************************************
   600-READ-MASTER.
       READ OLD-MASTER-IN
           AT END MOVE HIGH-VALUES TO M-ACCT-NO-IN.
************************************************************
*   PERFORMED FROM 800-INITIALIZATION-RTN, 300-REGULAR-UPDATE, *
*   400-NEW-ACCOUNT, AND 550-ADD-AND-READ-TRANS. READS THE NEXT *
*   RECORD FROM THE TRANSACTION FILE.                          *
************************************************************
   700-READ-TRANS.
       READ TRANS-FILE-IN
           AT END MOVE HIGH-VALUES TO T-ACCT-NO-IN.
**************************************************
*   PERFORMED FROM 100-MAIN-MODULE.        *
*   OPENS FILES AND PERFORMS INITIAL READ *
**************************************************
   800-INITIALIZATION-RTN.
       OPEN INPUT  OLD-MASTER-IN
                   TRANS-FILE-IN
            OUTPUT NEW-MASTER-OUT.
```

Figure 16.7
(continued)

```
        PERFORM 600-READ-MASTER.
        PERFORM 700-READ-TRANS.
   ***************************************************
   *  PERFORMED FROM 100-MAIN-MODULE. CLOSES FILES  *
   *  AND RETURNS CONTROL TO THE OPERATING SYSTEM.  *
   ***************************************************
    900-END-OF-JOB-RTN.
        CLOSE OLD-MASTER-IN
              TRANS-FILE-IN
              NEW-MASTER-OUT.
        STOP RUN.
```

b. Sample OLD-MASTER-IN Data

```
11111009967
22222007666
44444076566
55555098988
66666109899
77777029282
88888098272
99999123456
```

c. Sample TRANS-FILE-IN Data

```
11111009899
11111007655
22222087778
33333092828
44444092828
44444098776
66666083828
77777092888
88888020929
```

d. Sample NEW-MASTER-OUT Data

```
11111027521
22222095444
33333092828
44444268170
55555098988
66666193727
77777122170
88888119201
99999123456
```

Disks, however, unlike tape, can serve as *both input and output during the same run.* Thus, it is possible to read a disk record, make changes *directly to the same record,* and rewrite it or update it in place. With this capability of disks, we need use only two files:

Open as	Name of File
I-O	MASTER-DISK
INPUT	TRANS-FILE

A disk file, then, can be opened as I-O, which means records from the disk will be accessed, read, changed, and rewritten.

We read each disk record in sequence; when a record is to be updated, we make the changes directly to the MASTER-DISK record and **REWRITE** it.

The program in Figure 16.8 provides an alternative method for updating sequential files, one that uses a master disk file as I-O and then REWRITEs records in place. This program assumes that transaction records with no corresponding master record are errors.

Note that the REWRITE statement replaces the disk record that was accessed by the preceding READ statement.

Updating Sequential Disks in Place Requires Creation of a Backup Disk As a Separate Procedure

Accessing a disk as I-O and rewriting records saves us the need for creating a new file, but some caution must be exercised when using this procedure. Since the master disk file is itself updated, there is no old master available for backup purposes. This means that if the master file gets lost, stolen, or damaged, there is no way of conveniently re-creating it.

Figure 16.8
Sample program to update a
sequential disk file.

a. Program

```
     IDENTIFICATION DIVISION.
     PROGRAM-ID.     SAMPLE.
**************************************************************
* SAMPLE - UPDATES A MASTER FILE WITH A TRANSACTION FILE. *
* THE TRANSACTION FILE MAY CONTAIN ONE RECORD PER MASTER  *
* RECORD.   MASTER RECORDS ARE REWRITTTEN IN PLACE        *
**************************************************************
     AUTHOR.         GLORIA FISHMAN.
     ENVIRONMENT DIVISION.
     INPUT-OUTPUT SECTION.
     FILE-CONTROL.
          SELECT TRANS-FILE ASSIGN TO DATA13A.
          SELECT MASTER-FILE ASSIGN TO DATA13B.
     DATA DIVISION.
     FILE SECTION.
     FD   TRANS-FILE
          LABEL RECORDS ARE STANDARD.
     01   TRANS-REC.
          05   T-CUST-NO              PIC X(5).
          05   T-AMT                  PIC 999V99.
          05   FILLER                 PIC X(90).
     FD   MASTER-FILE
          LABEL RECORDS ARE STANDARD.
     01   MASTER-REC.
          05   M-CUST-NO              PIC X(5).
          05   BAL-DUE                PIC 9(6)V99.
          05   FILLER                 PIC X(89).
     WORKING-STORAGE SECTION.
     01   WORK-AREA.
          05   ARE-THERE-MORE-RECORDS PIC X(3)    VALUE 'YES'.
               88  NO-MORE-RECORDS               VALUE 'NO '.
     PROCEDURE DIVISION.
**************************************************************
*   100-MAIN-RTN  - OPENS THE FILES, CONTROLS THE PROGRAM LOGIC, *
*                    AND CLOSES THE FILES.                       *
**************************************************************
     100-MAIN-RTN.
          OPEN INPUT TRANS-FILE
               I-O    MASTER-FILE.
          PERFORM 400-READ-TRANS.
          PERFORM 200-UPDATE-RTN
               UNTIL NO-MORE-RECORDS.
          CLOSE TRANS-FILE
               MASTER-FILE.
          STOP RUN.
**************************************************************
* 200-UPDATE-RTN   - COMPARES THE CUSTOMER NUMBER OF THE MASTER *
*                     FILE TO THAT OF THE TRANSACTION FILE AND  *
*                     PROCESSES THE RECORDS ACCORDINGLY         *
**************************************************************
     200-UPDATE-RTN.
          PERFORM 300-READ-MASTER
               UNTIL M-CUST-NO = T-CUST-NO
                         OR
                     M-CUST-NO > T-CUST-NO
                         OR
                     M-CUST-NO = HIGH-VALUES.
          IF M-CUST-NO = T-CUST-NO
             ADD T-AMT TO BAL-DUE
             DISPLAY T-CUST-NO, ' AMOUNT OF TRANSACTION ', T-AMT,
                      ' BALANCE DUE ', BAL-DUE
             REWRITE MASTER-REC
          ELSE
             IF M-CUST-NO > T-CUST-NO
                DISPLAY T-CUST-NO, ' NOT ON MASTER FILE'.
          PERFORM 400-READ-TRANS.
**************************************************************
* 300-READ-MASTER  -READS THE NEXT RECORD FROM THE MASTER FILE  *
*                    PERFORMED FROM 200-UPDATE-RTN             *
**************************************************************
     300-READ-MASTER.
          READ MASTER-FILE
               AT END MOVE HIGH-VALUES TO M-CUST-NO.
**************************************************************
* 400-READ-TRANS  -READS THE TRANSACTION FILE   *
*                   PERFORMED FROM 100-MAIN-RTN  *
*                   AND 200-UPDATE-RTN.          *
**************************************************************
     400-READ-TRANS.
          READ TRANS-FILE
               AT END MOVE 'NO ' TO ARE-THERE-MORE-RECORDS.
```

Figure 16.8 (continued)

b. Sample MASTER-FILE Data Before Updating

```
0000100045980
0000200047470
0000309847480
0000438383000
0000509363630
0000603736260
0000705454550
0000807773770
0000903783770
0001002833000
0001100034210
```

c. Sample TRANS-FILE Data

```
0000100245
0000102398
0000308989
0000409837
0000507864
0000604453
0000700800
0000863600
0000909878
0001009000
```

d. Sample MASTER-FILE Data After Updating

```
0000100048623
0000200047470
0000309856469
0000438392837
0000509371494
0000603740713
0000705455350
0000807837370
0000903793648
0001002842000
0001100034210
```

When performing a sequential update using an input old master that is separate from an output new master, we always have the old master as backup in case we cannot use the new master. However, since there is no backup when we *rewrite* a master disk, we must immediately create a duplicate copy of the master after the update procedure is performed. This duplicate is a *backup copy,* typically stored on tape. Backup copies should always be kept in a safe place in case something happens to the original.

Rewriting a Master Record with Multiple Transactions

The following update procedure with a REWRITE can be used if there are multiple transactions per master and both files are in sequence by the ACCT-NO key field. Assume that each transaction record should match a master record:

```
PERFORM 500-READ-TRANS.
PERFORM 200-UPDATE-RTN
    UNTIL NO-MORE-TRANS-RECORDS.
    :
    :
200-UPDATE-RTN.
    PERFORM 400-READ-MASTER
        UNTIL M-ACCT-NO = T-ACCT-NO
                OR
            M-ACCT-NO > T-ACCT-NO
                OR
            M-ACCT-NO = HIGH-VALUES.
    IF  M-ACCT-NO = T-ACCT-NO
        PERFORM 300-CHANGE-MASTER
            UNTIL T-ACCT-NO > M-ACCT-NO
        REWRITE MASTER-REC
    ELSE
        IF  M-ACCT-NO > T-ACCT-NO
            DISPLAY 'RECORD WITH ACCT-NO ',
                T-ACCT-NO, ' NOT ON MASTER'
            PERFORM 500-READ-TRANS.
300-CHANGE-MASTER.
    ADD T-AMT-OF-PUR TO M-BAL-DUE.
    PERFORM 500-READ-TRANS.
```

In summary, the primary advantage of using a REWRITE statement for a disk file opened as I-O is that records can be updated in place. A disadvantage of using a REWRITE is that a backup version of the updated master disk must be created in a separate procedure in case the master becomes unusable.

B. Using an Activity Status Field for Designating Records to be Deleted

When we created a NEW-MASTER file in an update procedure, we were able to delete master records by not writing them onto the new master. If a sequential disk file is to be updated by rewriting records directly on it, we need a *different procedure for deleting records*. One common technique is to begin each record with a one-character activity-status code that *precedes* the key field.

The activity-status code would have a specific value for active records, and the code would have a different value if a record is to be deleted. For example:

```
01  MASTER-REC.
    05  ACTIVITY-STATUS      PIC X.
        88  ACTIVE                      VALUE LOW-VALUES.
        88  INACTIVE                    VALUE HIGH-VALUES.
    05  M-CUST-NO            PIC X(5).
        :
        :
```

HIGH-VALUES represents the highest value in a collating sequence and LOW-VALUES represents the lowest value. We can use these figurative constants to distinguish active records from inactive ones, but, in fact, any two values could have been used (e.g., 1 for ACTIVE, 2 for INACTIVE).

When the master records are created, they are created with the ACTIVE value (LOW-VALUES in ACTIVITY-STATUS in our example). The only time an INACTIVE code of HIGH-VALUES would be moved to ACTIVITY-STATUS is if a transaction record indicated that the corresponding master record was to be deleted.

To report from a master file that has an activity-status field, we must include the following clause before printing a record:

```
IF  ACTIVITY-STATUS = LOW-VALUES
    PERFORM 500-PRINT-RTN.
```

or

```
IF  ACTIVE
    PERFORM 500-PRINT-RTN.
```

Thus, when a sequential disk file may have records that are to be deleted, we must use:

CODED FIELDS TO DESIGNATE RECORDS AS ACTIVE OR INACTIVE

1. Include an ACTIVITY-STATUS code as the first position in the record.
2. Set the ACTIVITY-STATUS code to a value designating the record as active.
3. Change the ACTIVITY-STATUS code to a value designating it as inactive only if the record is to be deleted.
4. Before printing, check first to see if the disk record is active.

Note that records that are inactive are *not physically deleted* from the file as they would be if an entirely new master file were created. This means that the record could easily be reactivated if the need arises or if the record were incorrectly deactivated—which would not be possible if they were physically deleted from the file. Moreover, a list of inactive records could easily be obtained:

```
200-LIST-INACTIVE-RECORDS.
    IF INACTIVE
        PERFORM 300-WRITE-RTN.
    READ ...
```

But having inactive records on the file could result in less efficient processing. When processing time becomes adversely affected by the number of inactive records on a file, it is time to perform a file "cleanup," where only the active records on a file are re-created onto a new file.

C. The EXTEND Option for Adding Records to the End of a Sequential File

In this section we have focused on how an I-O disk file can be updated with a transaction file (see Figure 16.8). This is an alternative to using an input master and an input transaction to create an entirely new master file, as in Figure 16.5.

Figure 16.8 illustrated how the update procedure with a REWRITE is performed on a disk opened as I-O. In this program, records were rewritten in place using the REWRITE verb. We also illustrated how records could be deactivated instead of deleted with the use of an ACTIVITY-STATUS code. Deactivating records serves the same purpose as deleting records, which was performed as part of the sequential update program in Figure 16.5.

But we have not considered in our REWRITE program the technique used to add records to a master file. In Figure 16.5, where an input master and an output master were used, if a transaction record existed for which there was no corresponding master, we were able to add it to the NEW-MASTER *in its proper sequence*. This is not, however, possible when rewriting onto a disk opened as I-O. Suppose the first two master disk records have CUST-NO 00001 and 00006. If a transaction record with a T-CUST-NO of 00003 is read and is a new account, there is *no physical space* to insert it in its proper place on the master disk. Thus, when a file is opened as I-O we can rewrite records and deactivate records but *we cannot add records* so that they are physically located in their correct place in sequence.

It is, however, possible to write a separate program or separate procedure to add records to the *end of a sequential disk (or tape) file* if you use the following OPEN statement:

OPEN EXTEND file-name

When the **OPEN EXTEND** statement is executed, the disk or tape is positioned at the *end* of the file, immediately after the last record. A WRITE statement, then, will add records to the *end of this file*. If the records that are added are not in sequence, the file must be sorted before it is processed again. Thus, if a T-CUST-NO of 00003 is added to the end of the file, the file will need to be sorted so that it is in proper sequence by CUST-NO.

In summary, to add records to the end of an existing file we must use a separate program or a separate procedure in which the file is opened in the EXTEND mode. The following illustrates how a *single* update program could use *two separate transaction files*—one with change records and one with new account records to be added to the file. Both transaction files could update an existing master disk in separate routines. Note that a transaction file of *change records* updates the master disk in I-O mode and a transaction file of *new records* updates the master disk in EXTEND mode:

```
100-MAIN-MODULE.
    OPEN INPUT TRANS-CHANGE
         I-O MASTER-DISK.
    READ TRANS-CHANGE
        AT END MOVE 'NO ' TO ARE-THERE-MORE-RECORDS.
    PERFORM 200-UPDATE-RTN
        UNTIL NO-MORE-RECORDS.
    CLOSE MASTER-DISK.
```

```
    OPEN INPUT TRANS-NEW
         EXTEND MASTER-DISK.
    MOVE 'YES' TO ARE-THERE-MORE-RECORDS.
    READ TRANS-NEW
        AT END MOVE 'NO ' TO ARE-THERE-MORE-RECORDS.
    PERFORM 300-ADD-RECORDS
        UNTIL NO-MORE-RECORDS.
    CLOSE TRANS-NEW
          MASTER-DISK.
    STOP RUN.
```

```
200-UPDATE-RTN.
*****************************************************
*      THIS ROUTINE IS THE SAME AS IN FIGURE 16.8.      *
*****************************************************
```

```
300-ADD-RECORDS.
    WRITE MASTER-REC FROM TRANS-REC.
    READ TRANS-NEW
        AT END MOVE 'NO ' TO ARE-THERE-MORE-RECORDS.
```

The boxed excerpts *without* 200-UPDATE-RTN could be an entirely *separate program* that just adds transaction records to the end of an existing sequential disk or tape file. If the key fields of these new records begin with a number greater than the last key on the master, the file will still be sequential. For example, if we add CUST-NO 775, 780, and 782 to a file that has CUST-NO 772 as its last entry, we still have a sequential file. But if the key fields of the new records contain numbers such as 026, 587, the master file will need to be sorted before it is processed again.

The following is a chart of permissible statements depending on how a file was opened:

	OPEN MODE			
Statement	INPUT	OUTPUT	I-O	EXTEND
READ	X		X	
WRITE		X		X
REWRITE			X	

SUMMARY: UPDATING A MASTER DISK IN PLACE

1. Open the file as I-O.
2. REWRITE records to be updated.
3. Instead of deleting records, establish each record with an activity code that indicates either an active record or a deactive record (e.g., 1 in CODE-X or 2 in CODE-X). All records are active (1 in CODE-X) unless the transaction record indicates that the master should be deactivated. To deactivate the record, change the activity code (MOVE 2 TO CODE-X).

To add records to the end of an existing sequential disk or tape in a separate program or procedure:

1. Open the file as EXTEND.
2. WRITE the new records to the end of the file.
3. The file will need to be sorted if the added records are not in sequence.
4. Adding records to an existing sequential disk or tape requires a *different procedure* than updating existing records because the file must be in EXTEND mode rather than I-O mode.

VI. Matching Files for Checking Purposes

It is sometimes necessary for checking purposes to *match* records from two or more files to ensure that (1) a match on key fields exists or that (2) a match on key fields does *not* exist. That is, for one application we may wish to have records on file 1 with the same key fields as on file 2; if a match does *not* exist, we print an error message. For other applications, we may want the two files to have unique keys with *no* matches.

Example 1: Matching Records
A company has two warehouses, each storing precisely the same inventory. The inventory file at each warehouse is in PART-NO sequence.

A monthly report is printed indicating the total quantity on hand for each part. This total is the sum of the QTY-ON-HAND field for each part from both warehouses.

If there is an erroneous PART-NO that appears in the file for warehouse 1 (WH-1) but not in the file for warehouse 2 (WH-2), the total for this part should *not* be included in the report. It should instead be displayed as an error. The same procedure should be followed if a PART-NO exists on the WH-2 file but does not exist on the WH-1 file.

The PROCEDURE DIVISION entries for this program appear in Figure 16.9.

Figure 16.9
PROCEDURE DIVISION
entries for matching record
program: Example 1.

```
*
 PROCEDURE DIVISION
 100-MAIN-MODULE.
     OPEN INPUT WH-1
               WH-2
          OUTPUT PRINT-REPORT-FILE.
     PERFORM 400-READ-WH-1-RTN.
     PERFORM 500-READ-WH-2-RTN.
     PERFORM 200-MATCH-IT UNTIL
         PART-NO OF WH-1-REC = HIGH-VALUES
             AND
         PART-NO OF WH-2-REC = HIGH-VALUES.
     CLOSE WH-1
           WH-2
           PRINT-REPORT-FILE.
     STOP RUN.
```

Figure 16.9
(continued)

```
200-MATCH-IT.
    IF  PART-NO OF WH-1-REC = PART-NO OF WH-2-REC
        PERFORM 300-REPORT-RTN
        PERFORM 400-READ-WH-1-RTN
        PERFORM 500-READ-WH-2-RTN
    ELSE
        IF  PART-NO OF WH-1-REC < PART-NO OF WH-2-REC
            DISPLAY WH-1-REC,
            'WAREHOUSE 1 RECORD -- NO MATCHING WAREHOUSE 2
-               'RECORD'
            PERFORM 400-READ-WH-1-RTN
        ELSE
            DISPLAY WH-2-REC
            'WAREHOUSE 2 RECORD -- NO MATCHING WAREHOUSE 1
-               'RECORD'
            PERFORM 500-READ-WH-2-RTN.
300-REPORT-RTN.
    ADD QTY-ON-HAND OF WH-1-REC
        QTY-ON-HAND OF WH-2-REC GIVING TOTAL.
    MOVE CORR WH-1-REC TO PRINT-REC.
    WRITE PRINT-REC
        AFTER ADVANCING 2 LINES.
400-READ-WH-1-RTN.
    READ WH-1
        AT END MOVE HIGH-VALUES TO PART-NO OF WH-1-REC.
500-READ-WH-2-RTN.
    READ WH-2
        AT END MOVE HIGH-VALUES TO PART-NO OF WH-2-REC.
```

Example 2: Matching Records—With a Variation

(a) MASTER-FILE is a master tape of all customers who have bank accounts with Bank ABC. This file is in sequence by ACCT-NO.

(b) TRANS-FILE is a transaction tape of all deposits and withdrawals made during the previous week. This file is also in sequence by ACCT-NO.

We wish to code an edit program to make certain that all records on the transaction tape, TRANS-FILE, refer to existing customers, that is, those with an ACCT-NO in MASTER-FILE. Thus:

1. Every ACCT-NO in TRANS-FILE *must* have a matching ACCT-NO in MASTER-FILE. If there is an ACCT-NO in TRANS-FILE with no matching ACCT-NO in MASTER-FILE, print the record from TRANS-FILE as an error.

2. There may be records in MASTER-FILE that have no corresponding records in TRANS-FILE. These would be customers who have not made any transactions—that is, deposits or withdrawals—during the previous week.

3. There may be *more than one* record in TRANS-FILE with the *same* ACCT-NO. This is because it is possible to make several transactions—deposits or withdrawals—in any given week.

The only output in this program is a listing of errors. See Figure 16.10 for the PROCEDURE DIVISION entries for this program.

Figure 16.10
PROCEDURE DIVISION entries for matching record program: Example 2.

```
*
PROCEDURE DIVISION.
100-MAIN-MODULE.
    OPEN INPUT   MASTER-FILE
                 TRANS-FILE
         OUTPUT PRINT-FILE.
    PERFORM 300-READ-MASTER-RTN.
    PERFORM 400-READ-TRANS-RTN.
    PERFORM 200-MATCH-CHECK UNTIL
        ACCT-NO OF MASTER-REC = HIGH-VALUES
            AND
        ACCT-NO OF TRANS-REC = HIGH-VALUES.
    CLOSE MASTER-FILE
          TRANS-FILE
          PRINT-FILE.
    STOP RUN.
```

Figure 16.10
(continued)

```
200-MATCH-CHECK.
    IF  ACCT-NO OF MASTER-REC < ACCT-NO OF TRANS-REC
        PERFORM 300-READ-MASTER-RTN
    ELSE
        IF  ACCT-NO OF MASTER-REC > ACCT-NO OF TRANS-REC
            MOVE 'NO MATCHING ACCT-NO FROM MASTER' TO
                ERR-MESSAGE
            MOVE ACCT-NO OF TRANS-REC TO ACCT-NO-OUT
            WRITE PRINT-REC FROM ERR-LINE
            PERFORM 400-READ-TRANS-RTN
        ELSE
            PERFORM 400-READ-TRANS-RTN UNTIL
                ACCT-NO OF TRANS-REC IS NOT EQUAL TO
                    ACCT-NO OF MASTER-REC
            PERFORM 300-READ-MASTER-RTN.
300-READ-MASTER-RTN.
    READ MASTER-FILE
        AT END MOVE HIGH-VALUES TO ACCT-NO OF MASTER-REC.
400-READ-TRANS-RTN.
    READ TRANS-FILE
        AT END MOVE HIGH-VALUES TO ACCT-NO OF TRANS-REC.
```

CHAPTER SUMMARY

I. Sequential updating by creating a new master.
    Use three files: an incoming master, a transaction file with change records, and a new output master that will incorporate all the changes. The techniques used are as follows:
    A. All files to be processed must be in sequence by the same key field.
    B. A record is read from each file and specified routines are performed depending on whether or not the key fields match.
    C. The transaction record could have a coded field to determine:
        1. What type of update is required.
        2. If the master record is to be deleted.
        3. If the transaction is a new account.
    D. The end-of-job test for each file must be processed individually. By moving HIGH-VALUES to the key field of the file that ends first, we can be assured that the other file will always compare low and hence will continue to be processed. The job is terminated only after both input files have been processed. HIGH-VALUES can only be moved to a key field that has been defined as alphanumeric.
II. Sequential updating by rewriting a disk.
    As an alternative to the preceding, records on a sequential disk can also be updated by *rewriting them* in place, if the disk file is opened as I-O. A backup disk file should be created in this case.
III. Records can be added to the end of a disk or tape file if we code OPEN EXTEND file-name.

CHAPTER SELF-TEST

1. The process of making a file of data current is called a(n) _____.
2. (T or F) A tape file may be processed sequentially or randomly.
3. (T or F) Files must be in sequence by key field to perform a sequential update.
4. The three files necessary to update a master tape file are _____, _____, and _____.
5. Suppose EMPLOYEE-NO is a field in a payroll record. Write a routine to make certain that the payroll file is in EMPLOYEE-NO sequence.
6. Assume the following statement is executed:

    ```
    MOVE HIGH-VALUES TO PART-NO OF TRANS-REC.
    ```

Suppose that the following is then executed:

```
IF  PART-NO OF MASTER-REC < PART-NO OF TRANS-REC
    PERFORM 500-MASTER-RTN
ELSE
    PERFORM 600-UPDATE.
```

Because PART-NO of TRANS-REC contains HIGH-VALUES, the IF statement causes the _____ routine to be executed.

7. If a disk file is opened as I-O, disk records to be updated can be changed directly on the file with the use of a _____ statement.

8. To add records to the end of a disk or tape file, open the file with the following statement: _____.

9. (T or F) In general, the same program can be used for updating a sequential file that permits (1) only one transaction per master and (2) multiple transactions per master.

10. (T or F) If a disk is opened in I-O mode, then we cannot add records to the end of it.

Solutions

1. update

2. F—Tapes may only be processed sequentially.

3. T

4. a transaction file; the old master file; the new master file

5.
```
    05  EMPLOYEE-NO-HOLD    PIC 9(5)  VALUE ZERO.
       .
       .
    READ PAYROLL-FILE
        AT END MOVE 'NO ' TO ARE-THERE-MORE-RECORDS.
    PERFORM 800-SEQ-CHECK
        UNTIL THERE-ARE-NO-MORE-RECORDS.
       .
       .
800-SEQ-CHECK.
    IF  EMPLOYEE-NO < EMPLOYEE-NO-HOLD
        PERFORM 900-ERR-RTN
    ELSE
        MOVE EMPLOYEE-NO TO EMPLOYEE-NO-HOLD.
    READ PAYROLL-FILE
        AT END MOVE 'NO ' TO ARE-THERE-MORE-RECORDS.
```

6. 500-MASTER-RTN—The comparison will always result in a 'less than' condition.

7. REWRITE

8. OPEN EXTEND file-name

9. F

10. T

PRACTICE PROGRAM

1. The problem definition for this practice problem is shown in Figure 16.11. Figure 16.12 illustrates the pseudocode, hierarchy chart, and program.

KEY TERMS

Batch processing	Nested conditional	Sequential file processing
HIGH-VALUES	OPEN EXTEND	Transaction file
Key field	REWRITE	Updating
Master file		

Figure 16.11
Problem definition for the
Practice Program.

Systems Flowchart

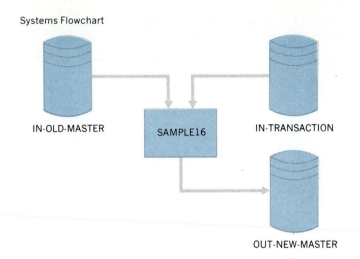

IN-OLD-MASTER   SAMPLE16   IN-TRANSACTION

OUT-NEW-MASTER

IN-OLD-MASTER Record Layout

IN-OLD-PART-NO	IN-OLD-QTY-ON-HAND [S9(5)]
1 5	6 10

IN-TRANSACTION Record Layout

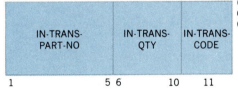

IN-TRANS-PART-NO	IN-TRANS-QTY	IN-TRANS-CODE
1 5	6 10	11

Code of 1 = Delete the master record
Code of 2 = Add a new master record
Code of 3 = Update the master record

OUT-NEW-MASTER Record Layout

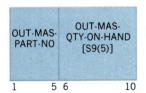

OUT-MAS-PART-NO	OUT-MAS-QTY-ON-HAND [S9(5)]
1 5	6 10

If OUT-MAS-QTY-ON-HAND falls below zero, display
a message indicating that OUT-MAS-PART-NO is to
be reordered

For example:

    DISPLAY 'REORDER, QUANTITY FELL BELOW ZERO'
    DISPLAY 'PART NUMBER', OUT-MAS-PART-NO.

Sample IN-TRANSACTION Data

```
00005001233
00007000001
00010009903
00014100002
00015000003
00020555553
00025600002
00030001003
00035001003
00036002202
00040000101
00050000103
```

Sample IN-OLD-MASTER Data

```
0000556452
0000776776
0001020000
0001530500
0002045667
0003065668
0003510000
0004030000
0005099999
```

Figure 16.11   **Sample Displayed Output**
(continued)   RE-ORDER, QUANTITY FELL BELOW ZERO
                     PART NUMBER   00020

                     0000556321
                     000101901{
                     000141000{
                     000153050{
                     0002009880
                     000256000{
                     000306556H
                     000350990{
                     000360022{
                     0005099981

Note: Letters and special symbols denote signed numbers (I = +9, { = +0, Q = −8, H = +8).

Figure 16.12   **a. Pseudocode**
Pseudocode, hierarchy chart,
and solution for the
Practice Program.

```
PERFORM
    Open the Files
    PERFORM
        Read a Master Record
    ENDPERFORM
    PERFORM
        Read a Transaction Record
    ENDPERFORM
ENDPERFORM
PERFORM UNTIL no more data
    IF  In-Old-Part-No = In-Trans-Part-No
    THEN
        PERFORM
            IF  delete code
            THEN
                Continue
            ELSE
                IF  add-a-record code
                THEN
                    PERFORM
                        Write an error line
                    ENDPERFORM
                ELSE
                    IF  update code
                    THEN
                        Update the record
                        IF  Qty-on-hand < 0
                        THEN
                            Print reorder message
                        ENDIF
                    ENDIF
                ENDIF
            ENDIF
            PERFORM
                Read a Master Record
            ENDPERFORM
            PERFORM
                Read a Transaction Record
            ENDPERFORM
        ENDPERFORM
    ELSE
        IF  In-Old-Part-No > In-Trans-Part-No
        THEN
            PERFORM
                IF  add-a-record code
                THEN
                    Write a Master Record from Transaction Record
                ELSE
                    Write an Error Line
                ENDIF
                PERFORM
                    Read a Transaction Record
                ENDPERFORM
            ENDPERFORM
```

Figure 16.12
(continued)

```
        ELSE
            PERFORM
                Write New Master from Old Master
                PERFORM
                    Read a Master Record
                ENDPERFORM
            ENDPERFORM
        ENDIF
    ENDIF
ENDPERFORM
PERFORM
    End-of-Job Operations
ENDPERFORM
```

b. Hierarchy Chart

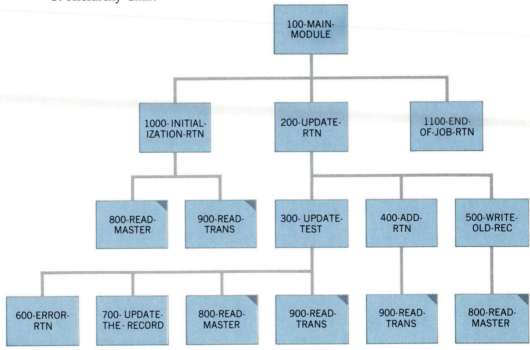

c. Program

```
IDENTIFICATION DIVISION.
PROGRAM-ID. SAMPLE.
AUTHOR. NANCY STERN.
******************************************************************
*  the program updates a master file with a coded transaction   *
*     file, comments are printed with lower case letters to      *
*     distinguish them from instructions                         *
******************************************************************
ENVIRONMENT DIVISION.
INPUT-OUTPUT SECTION.
FILE-CONTROL.
    SELECT IN-OLD-MASTER   ASSIGN TO DATA13O.
    SELECT IN-TRANSACTION  ASSIGN TO DATA13T.
    SELECT OUT-NEW-MASTER  ASSIGN TO DATA13N.
DATA DIVISION.
FILE SECTION.
FD  IN-OLD-MASTER
    LABEL RECORDS ARE STANDARD.
01  IN-OLD-REC.
    05  IN-OLD-PART-NO           PIC X(5).
    05  IN-OLD-QTY-ON-HAND        PIC S9(5).
FD  IN-TRANSACTION
    LABEL RECORDS ARE STANDARD.
01  IN-TRANS-REC.
    05  IN-TRANS-PART-NO          PIC X(5).
    05  IN-TRANS-QTY              PIC 9(5).
```

Figure 16.12
(continued)

```
         05  IN-TRANS-CODE              PIC 9.
             88   DELETE-THE-RECORD                     VALUE 1.
             88   ADD-THE-RECORD                        VALUE 2.
             88   UPDATE-THE-RECORD                     VALUE 3.
     FD  OUT-NEW-MASTER
         LABEL RECORDS ARE STANDARD.
     01  OUT-NEW-REC.
         05  OUT-MAS-PART-NO            PIC X(5).
         05  OUT-MAS-QTY-ON-HAND        PIC S9(5).
     *
     PROCEDURE DIVISION.
     ************************************************
     *  controls the direction of program logic.   *
     ************************************************
     100-MAIN-MODULE.
         PERFORM 1000-INITIALIZATION-RTN.
         PERFORM 200-UPDATE-RTN
             UNTIL IN-OLD-PART-NO = HIGH-VALUES
                 AND IN-TRANS-PART-NO = HIGH-VALUES.
         PERFORM 1100-END-OF-JOB-RTN.
     ****************************************************************
     *  performed from 100-main-module. determines input record  *
     *  processing path by comparing the master and transaction  *
     *  part numbers.                                             *
     ****************************************************************
     200-UPDATE-RTN.
         IF   IN-OLD-PART-NO IS EQUAL TO IN-TRANS-PART-NO
             PERFORM 300-UPDATE-TEST
         ELSE
             IF   IN-OLD-PART-NO IS GREATER THAN IN-TRANS-PART-NO
                 PERFORM 400-ADD-RTN
             ELSE
                 PERFORM 500-WRITE-OLD-REC.
     ****************************************************************
     *  performed from 200-update-rtn, determines transaction code  *
     *  and performs appropriate action.                            *
     ****************************************************************
     300-UPDATE-TEST.
         IF   DELETE-THE-RECORD
             NEXT SENTENCE
         ELSE
             IF   ADD-THE-RECORD
                 PERFORM 600-ERROR-RTN
             ELSE
                 PERFORM 700-UPDATE-THE-RECORD.
         PERFORM 800-READ-MASTER.
         PERFORM 900-READ-TRANS.
     ************************************************************
     *  performed from 200-update-rtn, adds new transaction to *
     *  master file, reads next transaction record.            *
     ************************************************************
     400-ADD-RTN.
         IF   ADD-THE-RECORD
             MOVE IN-TRANS-PART-NO TO OUT-MAS-PART-NO
             MOVE IN-TRANS-QTY TO OUT-MAS-QTY-ON-HAND
             WRITE OUT-NEW-REC
         ELSE
             DISPLAY 'ERROR IN DATA, SHOULD BE EQUAL TO 2 '
                 IN-TRANS-PART-NO.
         PERFORM 900-READ-TRANS.
     ********************************************************
     *  performed from 200-update-rtn and 300-update-test, *
     *  writes old master record to new master file.       *
     ********************************************************
     500-WRITE-OLD-REC.
         MOVE IN-OLD-PART-NO TO OUT-MAS-PART-NO.
         MOVE IN-OLD-QTY-ON-HAND TO OUT-MAS-QTY-ON-HAND.
         WRITE OUT-NEW-REC.
         PERFORM 800-READ-MASTER.
     ******************************************************
     *  performed from 300-update-test, displays error message  *
     ******************************************************
     600-ERROR-RTN.
         DISPLAY 'ERROR IN TRANSACTION TAPE, CODE SHOULD NOT EQUAL 2'.
     ****************************************************************
     *  performed from 300-update-test, updates transaction record with  *
     *  master record, displays a message if a quantity error occurs.    *
     ****************************************************************
     700-UPDATE-THE-RECORD.
         MOVE IN-TRANS-PART-NO TO OUT-MAS-PART-NO.
         COMPUTE OUT-MAS-QTY-ON-HAND = IN-OLD-QTY-ON-HAND - IN-TRANS-QTY.
```

Figure 16.12
(continued)

```
        WRITE OUT-NEW-REC.
        IF  OUT-MAS-QTY-ON-HAND IS LESS THAN ZERO
            DISPLAY 'RE-ORDER, QUANTITY FELL BELOW ZERO'
            DISPLAY 'PART NUMBER   ' OUT-MAS-PART-NO.
****************************************************************
*  performed from 300-update-test, 500-write-old-rec,  *
*  1000-initialization-rtn,    reads master file        *
****************************************************************
    800-READ-MASTER.
        READ IN-OLD-MASTER
            AT END MOVE HIGH-VALUES TO IN-OLD-PART-NO.
****************************************************************
*  performed from 300-update-test, 400-add-rtn,        *
*  1000-initialization-rtn, reads transaction file     *
****************************************************************
    900-READ-TRANS.
        READ IN-TRANSACTION
            AT END MOVE HIGH-VALUES TO IN-TRANS-PART-NO.
*************************************************************************
*  performed from 100-main-module, opens files performs initial reads *
*************************************************************************
    1000-INITIALIZATION-RTN.
        OPEN INPUT  IN-OLD-MASTER
                    IN-TRANSACTION
             OUTPUT OUT-NEW-MASTER.
        PERFORM 800-READ-MASTER.
        PERFORM 900-READ-TRANS.
****************************************************************
*  performed from 100-main-module, closes files and    *
*                returns control to operating system   *
****************************************************************
    1100-END-OF-JOB-RTN.
        CLOSE IN-OLD-MASTER
              IN-TRANSACTION
              OUT-NEW-MASTER.
        STOP RUN.
```

REVIEW QUESTIONS

T F

I. True-False Questions

__ __ 1. Updating is the process of making a file current.

__ __ 2. Exactly two files are required for updating a master tape.

__ __ 3. Records on a tape or disk can be any length.

__ __ 4. The nested conditional is used in a sequential update because it makes it possible to test three separate conditions in a single sentence.

__ __ 5. When the master file has been completely read and processed during an update procedure, the program should be terminated.

__ __ 6. A transaction record with no corresponding master record always means an error.

__ __ 7. A REWRITE statement may be used with a file that is opened as an OUTPUT file.

__ __ 8. A REWRITE statement may be used with a disk or tape master file.

__ __ 9. A file opened as I-O can be read from and written onto.

__ __ 10. If a file is opened as EXTEND, it is possible to add records to the end of it.

II. General Questions

1. In an update, describe three different ways that a transaction record might be processed if it is "less than" a master record.

Define the following (2–4):

2. "On demand" output.

3. Key field.

4. Sequential file processing.

III. Validating Data

Modify the Practice Program so that it includes coding to (1) test for all errors and (2) print a control listing of totals (records processed, errors encountered, batch totals).

DEBUGGING EXERCISES

Consider the following procedure in which there can be multiple transaction records
per master file. This procedure is somewhat different from the one coded in the chapter,
but that does not necessarily make it wrong.

```
100-MAIN-MODULE.
    OPEN INPUT TRANS-FILE
               MASTER-FILE
    OUTPUT MASTER-OUT
          PRINT-FILE.
    READ TRANS-FILE
        AT END MOVE 'NO ' TO RECORDS1.
    READ MASTER-FILE
        AT END MOVE 'NO ' TO RECORDS2.
    PERFORM 200-CALC-RTN
        UNTIL RECORDS1-OVER AND RECORDS2-OVER.
    CLOSE TRANS-FILE
          MASTER-FILE
          MASTER-OUT
          PRINT-FILE.
    STOP RUN.
200-CALC-RTN.
    IF ACCT-TRANS = ACCT-MASTER
        PERFORM 300-EQUAL-RTN.
    IF ACCT-TRANS < ACCT-MASTER
        PERFORM 400-TRANS-LESS-RTN.
    IF ACCT-TRANS > ACCT-MASTER
        PERFORM 500-TRANS-GREATER-RTN.
300-EQUAL-RTN.
    ADD TRANS-AMT TO MASTER-AMT.
    READ TRANS-FILE
        AT END MOVE 'NO ' TO RECORDS1.
400-TRANS-LESS-RTN.
    MOVE TRANS-NO TO TRANS-ERR.
    WRITE PRINT-REC FROM ERR-REC.
    READ TRANS-FILE
        AT END MOVE 'NO ' TO RECORDS1.
500-TRANS-GREATER-RTN.
    WRITE MASTER-REC-OUT FROM MASTER-REC-IN.
    READ MASTER-FILE
        AT END MOVE 'NO ' TO RECORDS2.
```

(1) Will this sequence of coding steps produce the correct results for a multiple
transaction update procedure? Explain your answer.

(2) How does the basic logic in this problem differ from the logic used for multiple
transaction updates in the chapter?

(3) This program does not use HIGH-VALUES. Will that cause a logic error? Explain
your answer.

(4) Could 300-EQUAL-RTN be eliminated entirely by coding 200-CALC-RTN as follows:

```
200-CALC-RTN.
    IF  ACCT-TRANS = ACCT-MASTER
        ADD TRANS-AMT TO MASTER-AMT
        READ TRANS-FILE AT END
            MOVE 'NO ' TO RECORDS1.
```

PROGRAMMING ASSIGNMENTS

1. Write a program to update a master sales file. The problem definition is shown in Figure 16.13.

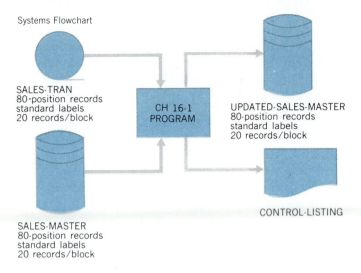

Systems Flowchart

SALES-TRAN
80-position records
standard labels
20 records/block

CH 16-1
PROGRAM

UPDATED-SALES-MASTER
80-position records
standard labels
20 records/block

CONTROL-LISTING

SALES-MASTER
80-position records
standard labels
20 records/block

Record Layout for SALES-MASTER and UPDATED-SALES-MASTER

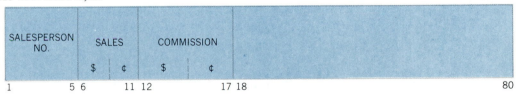

SALES-TRAN Record Layout

CONTROL-LISTING Printer Spacing Chart

Figure 16.13
Problem definition for
Programming Assignment 1.

Notes

a.   SALES-MASTER and UPDATED-SALES-MASTER are sequential disk files.

b.   For a transaction record that has a corresponding master record (match on salesperson number), add the transaction figures for sales and commission to the corresponding year-to-date figures and the current period figures.

c.   For a transaction record that has no corresponding master record, print the transaction record. Do not put the transaction record on the master file.

d.   Both files are in salesperson number sequence. Only one transaction per master may exist.

e.   Create a new SALES-MASTER file.

2. Write a program to update a payroll file using the problem definition in Figure 16.14.

Figure 16.14
Problem definition for
Programming Assignment 2.

Systems Flowchart

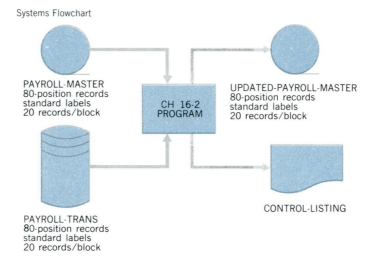

Record Layout for PAYROLL-MASTER and UPDATED-PAYROLL-MASTER

PAYROLL-TRANS Record Layout

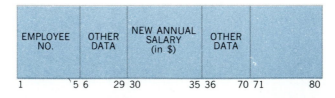

CONTROL-LISTING Printer Spacing Chart

```
                     CONTROL LISTING FOR PAYROLL UPDATE    XX/XX/XX     PAGE XX

   EMPLOYEE NO.    PREVIOUS ANNUAL SALARY    NEW ANNUAL SALARY     ACTION TAKEN

       XXXXX         $XXX,XXX.00             $XXX,XXX.00      {RECORD UPDATED
                                                             {NEW RECORD ADDED
```

Figure 16.14
(continued)

Notes

a. Assume both files are in employee number sequence.

b. For master tape records with no corresponding transaction records (no match on employee number), create an output record from the input tape record.

c. For transaction records with no corresponding tape records, create an output record from the input disk record.

d. For a master tape record with a corresponding transaction record, take the annual salary from the disk record and all other data from the tape record.

e. Print all updated records for control purposes.

3. Redo Problem 1 assuming that there may be numerous transactions per master.

4. Redo Problem 2 assuming that the PAYROLL-TRANS file has the following record description:

```
 1-5  EMPLOYEE-NO-IN
 6-25 EMPLOYEE-NAME-IN
26-27 TERRITORY-NO-IN
28-29 OFFICE-NO-IN
30-35 ANNUAL-SALARY-IN
   36 CODE-X-IN
       1 = Delete master
       2 = Add a new record
       3 = Change Name
       4 = Change Territory
       5 = Change Office
       6 = Change Salary
```

PAYROLL-MASTER has the same format for positions 1–35. Update the master assuming that numerous changes per master are possible.

5. There are two input tape files, one called MASTER-DEPOSITORS-FILE and the other called WEEKLY-TRANSACTION-FILE, each in sequence by account number and both with the same format:

```
FD  MASTER-DEPOSITORS-FILE
      .
      .
01  MASTER-REC.
      05  ACCT-NO1         PIC 9(5).
      05  OTHER-DATA1      PIC X(70).
FD  WEEKLY-TRANSACTION-FILE
      .
      .
01  TRANS-REC.
      05  ACCT-NO2         PIC 9(5).
      05  OTHER-DATA2      PIC X(70).
```

Each record from the WEEKLY-TRANSACTION-FILE must match a record on the MASTER-DEPOSITORS-FILE, although there may be MASTER-REC records with no corresponding TRANS-REC records. Moreover, there may be more than one TRANS-REC record for a given MASTER-REC record.

The output is a merged file that has records from both files in sequence by account number. For an account number with matching records from both files, the MASTER-REC record is followed by all TRANS-REC records with the same number.

Example

MASTER-REC	TRANS-REC
00120	00120
00124	00120
00125	00125
00127	00126

```
        MASTER-OUT-REC
        00120 M
        00120 T
        00120 T
        00124 M
        00125 M
        00125 T
        00127 M [00126 T is to be printed as an error]
M = MASTER-REC record
T = TRANS-REC record
```

Notes

a. All files have a blocking factor of 20 and standard labels.
b. Print all merged records for control purposes.

6. Redo Problem 1 by opening the master disk as I-O and rewriting records.

17

Sorting and Merging

OBJECTIVES

To familiarize you with

1. How files may be sorted within a COBOL program.
2. How to process a file during a SORT procedure before it is actually sorted.
3. How to process a file during a SORT procedure after it is sorted but before it is created as output.
4. How to use the MERGE verb for merging files.

I. The SORT Feature: An Overview

A. Format of the SORT Statement

When processing disk and tape files, we frequently wish to access them in a particular sequence. The SORT verb in COBOL can be used to sort a file as part of a program.

A simplified format for the **SORT** statement in COBOL is as follows:

Simplified Format

$$\text{SORT file-name-1}$$
$$\left\{ \text{ON} \left\{ \frac{\underline{\text{DESCENDING}}}{\underline{\text{ASCENDING}}} \right\} \text{KEY data-name-1} \right\} \ldots$$
$$\underline{\text{USING}} \text{ file-name-2}$$
$$\underline{\text{GIVING}} \text{ file-name-3}$$

B. ASCENDING or DESCENDING Key

The programmer must specify whether the key field is to be an ASCENDING KEY or a DESCENDING KEY, depending on which sequence is required:

(1) ASCENDING: From lowest to highest.

(2) DESCENDING: From highest to lowest.

Sorting a file into ascending CUST-NO sequence, for example, where CUST-NO is defined with PIC 9(3) would result in the following order: 001, 002, 003, and so on. The SORT can also be performed on non-consecutive key fields. That is, records 009, 006, 152 would be sorted into the proper sequence of 006, 009, 152 even though they are not consecutive. If several records had the same CUST-NO, *all* CUST-NO 01 records would precede records with CUST-NO 02, and so on, if ascending sequence were specified.

A file can also be sorted into descending sequence where a key field of 99, for example, precedes 98, and so on.

Records may be sorted using either numeric or nonnumeric key fields. Ascending sequence used with an alphabetic field will cause sorting into standard alphabetic order.

1. Collating Sequence

As indicated in Chapter 9, the two major codes used for representing data in a computer are **EBCDIC**, an abbreviation for Extended Binary Coded Decimal Interchange Code, and **ASCII**, an abbreviation for American Standard Code for Information Interchange.

The sequencing of characters from lowest to highest, which is referred to as the **collating sequence**, is slightly different in EBCDIC and ASCII:

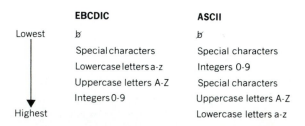

	EBCDIC	ASCII
Lowest	b	b
	Special characters	Special characters
	Lowercase letters a-z	Integers 0-9
	Uppercase letters A-Z	Special characters
	Integers 0-9	Uppercase letters A-Z
Highest		Lowercase letters a-z

We have not included the collating sequence for the individual special characters here because we rarely sort on special characters. See Appendix A for the collating sequence of all characters.

Basic numeric sorting and basic alphabetic sorting are performed similarly in EBCDIC and ASCII. These codes are, however, somewhat different when alphanumeric fields containing both letters and digits or special characters are sorted. Letters are considered "less than" numbers in EBCDIC, and letters are considered "greater than" numbers in ASCII. Moreover, lowercase letters are considered "less than" uppercase letters in EBCDIC and "greater than" uppercase letters in ASCII.

Thus, an ASCII computer could produce different sorting than an EBCDIC computer if an alphanumeric field is being sorted or if a combination of upper- and lowercase letters are used. "Box 891" will appear before "111 Main St." in an address field on EBCDIC computers, for example, but will appear *after* it on ASCII computers. Similarly, "abc" is less than "ABC" on EBCDIC computers whereas the reverse is true of ASCII computers.

2. Sequencing Records with More Than One SORT Key

The SORT verb may be used to sequence records *with more than one key field.* Suppose that we wish to sort a payroll file so that it is in ascending alphabetic sequence by name, within each level, for each office. That is:

Office number is the major sort field.
Level number is the intermediate sort field.
Name is the minor sort field.

Thus for Office 1, we want the following sequence:

```
OFFICE-NO    LEVEL-NO        NAME
    1           1         ADAMS, J. R.
    1           1         BROCK, P. T.
    1           1         LEE, S.
    1           2         ARTHUR, Q. C.
    1           2         SHAH, J.
    1           3         RAMIREZ, A. P.
    ⋮           ⋮            ⋮
```

For Office Number 1, Level 1, all entries are in alphabetic sequence. These are followed by Office Number 1, Level 2 entries, in alphabetic order, and so on.

We may use a *single* SORT procedure to perform this sequencing. The first KEY field indicated is the *major* field to be sorted, the next KEY fields represent *intermediate* sort fields, followed by *minor* sort fields.

The following is a SORT statement that sorts records into ascending alphabetic NAME sequence within LEVEL-NO within OFFICE-NO:

```
SORT SORT-FILE
    ON ASCENDING KEY OFFICE-NO
    ON ASCENDING KEY LEVEL-NO
    ON ASCENDING KEY NAME
    USING PAYROLL-FILE-IN
    GIVING SORTED-PAYROLL-FILE-OUT.
```

Because all key fields are independent, one key can be sorted in ASCENDING sequence and others in DESCENDING sequence. Note too that the words ON and KEY were *not* underlined in the instruction format, which indicates that they are optional words. If all keys are to be sorted in ascending sequence, as in the preceding, we can condense the coding by using ON ASCENDING KEY only once. For example:

```
SORT SORT-FILE
    ON ASCENDING KEY MAJOR-KEY
                     INTERMED-KEY
                     MINOR-KEY
    ⋮
```

With COBOL 74, if two or more records have the same value in the sort field (e.g., DEPT 01 on two or more records), you cannot predict which will appear first in the sorted file. With COBOL 85 you can request the computer to put such records into the sort file *in the same order* that they appeared on the original input file. We add the WITH DUPLICATES IN ORDER clause to accomplish this:

```
SORT ...
    ON ASCENDING KEY ...
    WITH DUPLICATES IN ORDER
    USING ...
    GIVING ...
```

This means that if the 106th record and the 428th record in the input file, for example, both had DEPT-NO 1 where DEPT-NO is the sort field, then record 106 will appear first in the sorted file. This is called the first in, first out (**FIFO**) principle.

C. Coding a Simple SORT Procedure with the USING and GIVING Options

There are three major files used in a sort:

FILES USED IN A SORT

1. Input file: File of unsorted input records.
2. Work or sort file: File used to store records temporarily during the sorting process.
3. Output file: File of sorted output records.

All these files would be defined in the ENVIRONMENT DIVISION using standard ASSIGN clauses, which are system dependent. Note, however, that a sort file is usually assigned to a special work device, indicated as SYSWORK in the following:

```
SELECT UNSORTED-MASTER-FILE ASSIGN TO DA-8433-S-SYS009.
SELECT SORT-FILE ASSIGN TO SYSWORK.
SELECT SORTED-MASTER-FILE ASSIGN TO DA-8433-S-SYS008.
```

Your system may use SYSWORK or some other special name in the ASSIGN clause for the work or sort file.

FDs are used in the DATA DIVISION to define and describe the input and output files in the usual way. The sort or work file is described with an SD entry (which is an abbreviation for *sort file description*). The only difference between SD and FD entries is that an SD must *not* have a LABEL RECORDS clause. Note, too, that the field(s) specified as the KEY field(s) for sorting purposes must be defined *as part of the sort record format*. In the following, the field to be sorted is S-DEPT-NO within the SD file called SORT-FILE:

```
DATA DIVISION.
FILE SECTION.
FD  UNSORTED-MASTER-FILE
    LABEL RECORDS ARE STANDARD.
01  UNSORTED-REC                        PIC X(80).
************************************************
SD  SORT-FILE.
01  SORT-REC.
    05  S-DEPT-NO                        PIC 99.
    05  FILLER                           PIC X(78).
************************************************
FD  SORTED-MASTER-FILE
    LABEL RECORDS ARE STANDARD.
01  SORTED-REC                           PIC X(80).
```

The SORT procedure would then be coded as follows:

```
SORT  SORT-FILE
      ON ASCENDING KEY  S-DEPT-NO  ◄————————Defined within the SD
      USING UNSORTED-MASTER-FILE
      GIVING SORTED-MASTER-FILE.
STOP RUN.
```

The only field descriptions required in the SORT record format are the ones used for sorting purposes; in this instance, only the S-DEPT-NO must be defined as part of the SD, since that is the only key field to be used for sorting.

In summary, the SORTED-MASTER-FILE would contain records with the same format as UNSORTED-MASTER-FILE, but the records would be placed on the file in department number sequence.

It is possible to sort any type of input file and place the sorted file on any type of output device, even a printer.

A SORT procedure can also *precede* an update or control break procedure *within the same program*. That is, where a file must be in a specific sequence, we can sort it first and then proceed with the required processing. In this case, the file defined in the GIVING clause would be opened as input, after it has been sorted:

```
PROCEDURE DIVISION.
100-MAIN-MODULE.
    SORT SORT-FILE
        ON ASCENDING KEY TERR
        USING UNSORTED-MASTER-FILE
        GIVING SORTED-MASTER-FILE.
    OPEN INPUT SORTED-MASTER-FILE
         OUTPUT CONTROL-REPORT.
    READ SORTED-MASTER-FILE
        AT END MOVE 'NO ' TO ARE-THERE-MORE-RECORDS.
        .
        .
        .
```
Standard processing {

Self-Test   1.   Suppose we want EMPLOYEE-FILE records in alphabetic order by NAME within DIS-TRICT within TERRITORY, all in ascending sequence. The output file is called SORTED-EMPLOYEE-FILE. Complete the following SORT statement:

   SORT WORK-FILE ...

2.   How many files are required in a SORT routine? Describe these files.

3.   The work or sort file is defined as an _____ in the DATA DIVISION.

4.   Suppose we have an FD called NET-FILE-IN, an SD called NET-FILE, and an FD called NET-FILE-OUT. We want NET-FILE-OUT sorted into ascending DEPT-NO sequence. Code the PROCEDURE DIVISION entry.

5.   In Question 4, DEPT-NO must be a field defined within the (SD/FD) file.

Solutions

1. ```
   ON ASCENDING KEY TERRITORY
   ON ASCENDING KEY DISTRICT
   ON ASCENDING KEY NAME
   USING EMPLOYEE-FILE
   GIVING SORTED-EMPLOYEE-FILE.
   ```
2. three; input—unsorted; work or sort file; output—sorted
3. SD
4. ```
   SORT  NET-FILE
         ON ASCENDING KEY DEPT-NO
         USING NET-FILE-IN
         GIVING NET-FILE-OUT.
   ```
5. SD

II. Processing Data before and/or after Sorting

Consider the following SORT statement:

```
SORT  SORT-FILE
      ON ASCENDING KEY TERR
      USING IN-FILE
      GIVING SORTED-MSTR.
```

This statement performs the following operations:

1. Opens IN-FILE and SORTED-MSTR.
2. Moves IN-FILE records to the SORT-FILE.
3. Sorts SORT-FILE into ascending sequence by TERR.
4. Moves the sorted SORT-FILE to the output file called SORTED-MSTR.
5. Closes IN-FILE and SORTED-MSTR after all records have been processed.

The SORT statement can, however, be used in conjunction with procedures that process records *before they are sorted* and/or process records *after they are sorted*.

A. INPUT PROCEDURE

In this section, we focus on the use of the SORT statement to perform a procedure *prior* to sorting the incoming records. This is accomplished with an **INPUT PROCEDURE** clause *in place of* the USING clause.

Expanded Format

$$\text{SORT file-name-1}$$
$$\left\{ \text{ON} \left\{ \begin{array}{l} \underline{\text{ASCENDING}} \\ \underline{\text{DESCENDING}} \end{array} \right\} \text{KEY data-name-1} \ldots \right\} \ldots$$
$$\left\{ \begin{array}{l} \underline{\text{INPUT}} \ \underline{\text{PROCEDURE}} \ \text{IS procedure-name-1} \left[\left\{ \begin{array}{l} \underline{\text{THRU}} \\ \underline{\text{THROUGH}} \end{array} \right\} \text{procedure-name-2} \right] \\ \underline{\text{USING}} \ \text{file-name-2} \ldots \end{array} \right\}$$
$$\underline{\text{GIVING}} \ \text{file-name-3}$$

The INPUT PROCEDURE processes data from the incoming file *prior* to sorting. We may wish to use an INPUT PROCEDURE, for example, to perform the following operations prior to sorting: (1) validate data in the input records, (2) eliminate records with blank fields, (3) count input records.

With COBOL 74, the procedure-name used with an INPUT PROCEDURE is called a section-name. A **section** is a series of PROCEDURE DIVISION paragraphs that is treated as a single entity or unit. Rules for forming section-names are the same as rules for forming paragraph-names. The word SECTION, however, follows a section-name (e.g., A000-ERROR SECTION). The end of a section is recognized when another section name is encountered, or when the end of the program is reached.

Example 1   We will code a SORT routine that eliminates records with a quantity field equal to zero *before sorting*. The test for zero quantity will be performed in an INPUT PROCEDURE. Consider the first three DIVISIONs of the COBOL program:

```
IDENTIFICATION DIVISION.
PROGRAM-ID. SORT-IT.
*
ENVIRONMENT DIVISION.
INPUT-OUTPUT SECTION.
FILE-CONTROL.
     SELECT IN-FILE ASSIGN TO DISK1.
     SELECT SORT-FILE ASSIGN TO WORK1.
     SELECT SORTED-MSTR ASSIGN TO DISK2.
*
DATA DIVISION.
FILE SECTION.
FD  IN-FILE
    LABEL RECORDS ARE STANDARD.
01  IN-REC.
    05  FILLER          PIC X(25).
    05  QTY             PIC 9(5).   ◄── Needed for INPUT PROCEDURE section
    05  FILLER          PIC X(70).
SD  SORT-FILE.
01  SORT-REC.
    05  TERR            PIC 9(5).   ◄── Needed for ASCENDING KEY clause
    05  FILLER          PIC X(95).
FD  SORTED-MSTR
    LABEL RECORDS ARE STANDARD.
01  SORTED-MSTR-REC PIC X(100).
```

The INPUT PROCEDURE identifies the section-name in which the test for zero will be performed:

```
                          SORT   SORT-FILE
                              ON ASCENDING KEY TERR
                                 INPUT PROCEDURE  A000-TEST-IT
                                 GIVING SORTED-MSTR.
                              STOP  RUN.
In this section we code the        A000-TEST-IT SECTION.
instructions that eliminate records   A100-PARA-1.
with a zero quantity field.             .
                                        .
                                        .
```

A section-name must conform to the rules for forming paragraph-names. The COBOL reserved word SECTION follows the actual section-name. In the preceding, A000-TEST-IT SECTION will be executed first, *before the input file is sorted*. Then the input file will be sorted in the main module, producing a sorted file called SORTED-MSTR. After the sorted records have been outputted, the STOP RUN is executed, terminating the program run.

More About Sections and Naming Conventions

A procedure may be a paragraph or section in the PROCEDURE DIVISION. In all programs thus far, we have used paragraphs as procedures. In this chapter we introduce the concept of a *section that can consist of one or more paragraphs.*

The PROCEDURE DIVISION, then, can be divided into individual paragraphs or into sections, where each section contains one or more paragraphs.

With COBOL 74, the clause INPUT PROCEDURE IS procedure-name-1 *must refer to a section*. With COBOL 85 this INPUT PROCEDURE may reference either a section or a paragraph. We will see that this feature in COBOL 85 results in less complex program structures.

Naming Procedures

When a program is subdivided into sections, we will use a more detailed numbering convention for prefixes of paragraphs. This convention will highlight the fact that given paragraphs are located within given sections. A SECTION named A000 or with a prefix of A000- will be followed by a paragraph with a prefix of A100-, A200-, and so on.

Example

```
PROCEDURE DIVISION.
A000 SECTION.
A100-PARA-1.
        .
        .
A200-PARA-2.
        .
        .
B000 SECTION.
B100-PARA-1.
        .
        .
B200-PARA-2.
        .
        .
```

The A000 SECTION has paragraphs with prefixes of A100, A200, and so on. Similarly, a section called A000-REARRANGE SECTION can be followed by a paragraph called A100-HSKPG-RTN, then a A200-PROCESS-RTN paragraph, and so on.

Another convention is to use four digits, with no letters, as a numeric prefix. Sections could have prefixes 0000-, 1000-, 2000-, and so on. Paragraphs within section 0000- would have a prefix of 0100-, 0200-, and so on. These are just two of the conventions you could adopt for prefixes of procedure names.

As noted, in our example we wish to sort only those input records that have a nonzero quantity. The coding required within the section specified by the INPUT PROCEDURE section-name includes the following instructions:

```
A000-TEST-IT SECTION.
A100-PARA-1.                           ⎡ On many systems, a paragraph-name must
    OPEN INPUT IN-FILE.                ⎣ follow a section-name
    READ IN-FILE
        AT END MOVE 'NO ' TO ARE-THERE-MORE-RECORDS.
    PERFORM A200-TEST-RTN
        UNTIL THERE-ARE-NO-MORE-RECORDS.
    CLOSE IN-FILE.
    GO TO A300-TEST-IT-EXIT.
A200-TEST-RTN.
    IF  QTY = ZEROS
        NEXT SENTENCE
    ELSE
        MOVE IN-REC TO SORT-REC
        RELEASE SORT-REC.          ─── Writes the record onto the sort file
    READ IN-FILE
        AT END MOVE 'NO ' TO ARE-THERE-MORE-RECORDS.
A300-TEST-IT-EXIT.                     ⎡ The last coded statement in the section must
    EXIT.                              ⎣ be the last statement executed
```

Let us consider each paragraph within A000-TEST-IT SECTION in depth.

A100-PARA-1

On most systems, each section-name must be followed by a paragraph-name. Thus, even though A100-PARA-1 is not referenced in the program, it is required as the *first* paragraph-name within the A000-TEST-IT section.

A100-PARA-1 is considered the *main module* within the A000-TEST-IT SECTION. Since this is part of the INPUT PROCEDURE, to be executed *prior* to sorting, this module must:

1. Open the input file.
2. Perform an initial read.
3. Perform some processing of input records at A200-TEST-RTN until there is no more data.

4. Close the input file.

5. Go to the last statement in the SECTION to indicate that the INPUT PROCEDURE has been completed. Control will not return to the sort procedure in the first section until the *last sentence* in the A000-TEST-IT SECTION is executed. More on this later.

A200-TEST-RTN

For all records with a nonzero QTY, the input fields are moved to the sort record. We do not WRITE records to be sorted; we **RELEASE** them for sorting purposes. We must release records to the sort file in an INPUT PROCEDURE. With a USING option, this is done for us automatically.

Note that the RELEASE verb is followed by a record-name, just like the WRITE statement. Note, too, that RELEASE SORT-REC FROM IN-REC can be substituted for:

```
MOVE IN-REC TO SORT-REC
RELEASE SORT-REC.
```

A300-TEST-IT-EXIT

The last statement coded in the A000-TEST-IT SECTION must be the last one executed before control can return to the SORT procedure. Thus, in A100-PARA-1 we must *branch* to a final paragraph within the SECTION, referred to here as A300-TEST-IT-EXIT. When the last statement in the A000-TEST-IT SECTION (the EXIT) has been executed, control will return to the SORT statement where the records that have been RELEASED are finally sorted. SORTED-MSTR is then produced as output. A paragraph in A000-TEST-IT SECTION that includes *only* an EXIT statement enables the program to "fall through" the entire section, so that control returns to the appropriate place, which in this case is the SORT procedure.

For many compilers, any time a section is used in the PROCEDURE DIVISION, *the entire* PROCEDURE DIVISION *must be subdivided into sections*, with each section-name followed by a paragraph-name.

Note that the use of GO TOs in an INPUT PROCEDURE is awkward and unstructured. With COBOL 85 we can eliminate this use of the GO TO and make the A000-TEST-IT procedure entirely structured as follows:

```
A000-TEST-IT SECTION.
A100-PARA-1.
    OPEN ...
    READ ...
    PERFORM B000-TEST-RTN
        UNTIL ARE-THERE-MORE-RECORDS = 'NO '.
    CLOSE IN-FILE.
B000-TEST-RTN  SECTION. ◄──────── Call this routine a section
    IF ...
        .
        .
    ELSE ...
    READ ...
```

By making B000-TEST-RTN a *section*, it becomes completely *independent* of the A000-TEST-IT section. When the computer executes A000-TEST-IT SECTION in its entirety, control returns to the SORT procedure. That is, after the input file is closed in A000-TEST-IT SECTION, the section has been completely executed and control returns to the SORT statement. Note that we have changed the prefix of TEST-RTN to B000 to highlight the fact that it is a separate section.

This type of coding is permitted only with COBOL 85, which is the first standard to permit execution of *sections* with a PERFORM statement that itself is in *another section*. With this added feature, SORT *procedures can be fully structured with no need for a* GO TO.

Note, too, that COBOL 85 permits the INPUT or OUTPUT PROCEDURE to specify a *paragraph* rather than a section. This means that the use of sections can be eliminated entirely.

If you have a COBOL 85 compiler, we recommend that you use paragraph names without sections, thereby eliminating the need for (1) a GO TO and (2) sections in the program.

INPUT PROCEDURE **SUMMARY**

1. Begin with the section-name defined in the INPUT PROCEDURE clause of the SORT statement. (You can use a paragraph-name with COBOL 85.)
2. A section-name is typically followed by a paragraph-name.
3. OPEN the input file.
4. READ input records and process them.
5. When an input record has been processed, MOVE it to the sort record area.
6. RELEASE sort records, which makes them available for sorting. The format of the RELEASE is the same as a WRITE:

$$\underline{\text{RELEASE}} \text{ sort-record-name-1}$$
$$[\underline{\text{FROM}} \text{ identifier-1}]$$

7. After all input records have been processed and released for sorting, CLOSE the input file.
8. GO TO the last paragraph in the section, which includes an EXIT statement. Control is then returned to the SORT instruction. (This EXIT paragraph is unnecessary with COBOL 85 if you use paragraph-names or section-names throughout.)

Self-Test Figure 17.1 illustrates the problem definition for a program that is to sort a disk file. Note that the sorted SORTED-FILE will have a *different format* from the incoming UNSORTED-FILE.

Consider the following FILE SECTION:

```
DATA DIVISION.
FILE SECTION.
FD  UNSORTED-FILE
    LABEL RECORDS ARE STANDARD.
01  REC-1.
    05  PART-NO-IN          PIC 9(5).
    05  QTY-IN              PIC 9(5).
    05  DEPT-IN             PIC 9(2).
SD  SORT-FILE.
01  SORT-REC.
    05  S-DEPT              PIC 9(2).
    05  S-PART-NO           PIC 9(5).
    05  S-QTY               PIC 9(5).
FD  SORTED-FILE
    LABEL RECORDS ARE STANDARD.
01  REC-2                   PIC 9(12).
```

Figure 17.1
Problem definition for
the Self-Test.

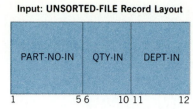

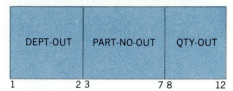

Notes
1. Sort into Department Number Sequence.
2. Sorted output will have a different format than input.

1. (T or F) It would be possible, although cumbersome, to (1) first sort the input and produce a sorted master, and (2) then code a separate module to read from the sorted master, moving the data in a rearranged format to a new sorted master.
2. (T or F) It would be more efficient to use an INPUT PROCEDURE for this problem.
3. Code the SORT statement.
4. Code the INPUT PROCEDURE SECTION assuming that you are using a COBOL 74 compiler.
5. Code the INPUT PROCEDURE SECTION assuming that you are using a COBOL 85 compiler.

Solutions

1. T
2. T
3.
```
SORT  SORT-FILE
    ON ASCENDING KEY S-DEPT
    INPUT PROCEDURE A000-REARRANGE
    GIVING SORTED-FILE.
    STOP RUN.
```
4.
```
A000-REARRANGE SECTION.
A100-PARA-1.
    OPEN INPUT UNSORTED-FILE.
    READ UNSORTED-FILE
        AT END MOVE 'NO ' TO ARE-THERE-MORE-RECORDS.
    PERFORM A200-CALC-RTN
        UNTIL NO-MORE-RECORDS.
    CLOSE UNSORTED-FILE.
    GO TO A300-REARRANGE-EXIT.
A200-CALC-RTN.
    MOVE PART-NO-IN TO S-PART-NO.
    MOVE QTY-IN TO S-QTY.
    MOVE DEPT-IN TO S-DEPT.
    RELEASE SORT-REC.
    READ UNSORTED-FILE
        AT-END MOVE 'NO ' TO ARE-THERE-MORE-RECORDS.
A300-REARRANGE-EXIT.
    EXIT.
```
5. Since the INPUT PROCEDURE can reference a paragraph, we can code INPUT PROCEDURE A100-PARA-1, omit the reference to A000-REARRANGE SEC-TION, omit the GO TO, and omit the entire A300-REARRANGE-EXIT paragraph:

```
    ⋮
    INPUT PROCEDURE A100-PARA-1
    ⋮
A100-PARA-1.
    OPEN INPUT UNSORTED-FILE.
    READ UNSORTED-FILE
        AT END MOVE 'NO ' TO ARE-THERE-MORE-RECORDS.
```

```
        PERFORM A200-CALC-RTN
            UNTIL NO-MORE-RECORDS.
        CLOSE UNSORTED-FILE.
    A200-CALC-RTN.
        MOVE PART-NO-IN TO S-PART-NO.
        MOVE QTY-IN TO S-QTY.
        MOVE DEPT-IN TO S-DEPT.
        RELEASE SORT-REC.
        READ UNSORTED-FILE
            AT END MOVE 'NO ' TO ARE-THERE-MORE-RECORDS.
```

B. OUTPUT PROCEDURE

After records have been sorted, they are placed in the sort file in the sequence required. If the GIVING option is used, then the sorted records are simply written onto the output file after they are sorted.

We may, however, wish to process the sorted records *prior* to, or perhaps even instead of, placing them in the output file. We would then use an OUTPUT PROCEDURE instead of the GIVING option. This OUTPUT PROCEDURE is very similar to the INPUT PROCEDURE. The full format for the SORT, including both INPUT and OUTPUT PROCEDURE options is as follows:

Full Format for Sort Statement

$$\underline{SORT}\ \text{file-name-1}\ \left\{ ON \left\{ \begin{array}{l} \underline{DESCENDING} \\ \underline{ASCENDING} \end{array} \right\} KEY\ \text{data-name-1} \dots \right\} \dots$$

$$\left\{ \begin{array}{l} \underline{INPUT\ PROCEDURE}\ IS\ \text{procedure-name-1} \left[\left\{ \begin{array}{l} \underline{THROUGH} \\ \underline{THRU} \end{array} \right\} \text{procedure-name-2} \right] \\ \underline{USING}\ \text{file-name-2} \dots \end{array} \right\}$$

$$\left\{ \begin{array}{l} \underline{OUTPUT\ PROCEDURE}\ IS\ \text{procedure-name-3} \left[\left\{ \begin{array}{l} \underline{THROUGH} \\ \underline{THRU} \end{array} \right\} \text{procedure-name-4} \right] \\ \underline{GIVING}\ \text{file-name-3} \end{array} \right\}$$

With COBOL 85 the word GIVING can be followed by more than one file-name, which means that we can create multiple copies of the sorted file.

As indicated, an INPUT PROCEDURE, if used, is processed prior to sorting. An **OUTPUT PROCEDURE** processes all sorted records *in the sort file* and handles the transfer of these records to the output file. This OUTPUT PROCEDURE must include the following:

OUTPUT PROCEDURE **SUMMARY**

1. Begin with the section-name defined in the OUTPUT PROCEDURE clause of the SORT statement. (You may use a paragraph-name instead with COBOL 85.)
2. A section-name is typically followed by a paragraph-name.
3. OPEN the output file.
4. Use a **RETURN** to read sorted records from the sort or work file as follows:

> RETURN sort-file-name-1
>   AT END imperative-statement-1.

The RETURN has the same format as a READ.

5. Perform a routine that processes the sorted records that are on the sort file, writes them onto the output file, and RETURNs or reads additional records from the sort file.

6. After all sorted records have been processed and written onto the output file, CLOSE the output file.

7. With COBOL 74, you must GO TO the last paragraph in the SECTION, which is coded with an EXIT statement. Control then returns to the statement following the SORT. The EXIT paragraph is unnecessary with COBOL 85 if the process routine in the OUTPUT PROCEDURE is given a section-name or all procedures are paragraph-names.

Example   After a file has been sorted but before it has been placed on the output file, MOVE .02 TO DISCOUNT for all records with AMT-OF-PURCHASE in excess of $500; otherwise there should be no DISCOUNT. The following indicates the correct coding:

```
IDENTIFICATION DIVISION.
PROGRAM-ID. SORT2.
*
ENVIRONMENT DIVISION.
INPUT-OUTPUT SECTION.
FILE-CONTROL.
    SELECT INPUT-FILE ASSIGN TO DA-S-SYS005.
    SELECT SORT-FILE ASSIGN TO WORK1.
    SELECT OUTPUT-FILE ASSIGN TO DA-S-SYS006.
*
DATA DIVISION.
FILE SECTION.
FD  INPUT-FILE
    LABEL RECORDS ARE STANDARD.
01  INPUT-REC                      PIC X(150).
SD  SORT-FILE.
01  SORT-REC.
    05  TRANS-NO                   PIC 9(5).
    05  AMT-OF-PURCHASE            PIC 9(5)V99.
    05  DISCOUNT                   PIC V99.
    05  FILLER                     PIC X(136).
FD  OUTPUT-FILE
    LABEL RECORDS ARE STANDARD.
01  OUT-REC                        PIC X(150).
*****************************************************
*  THIS SORT PROCEDURE USES SECTION-NAMES AND WILL  *
*  WORK WITH COBOL 74 OR 85                          *
*****************************************************
WORKING-STORAGE SECTION.
01  STORED-AREAS.
    05  ARE-THERE-MORE-RECORDS     PIC X(3)   VALUE 'YES'.
        88 THERE-ARE-NO-MORE-RECORDS          VALUE 'NO '.
PROCEDURE DIVISION.
A000 SECTION.
A100-MAIN-MODULE.
    SORT SORT-FILE
        ON ASCENDING KEY TRANS-NO
        USING INPUT-FILE
        OUTPUT PROCEDURE B000-CALC-DISCOUNT.
    STOP RUN.
B000-CALC-DISCOUNT SECTION.
B100-MAIN-PARAGRAPH.
    OPEN OUTPUT OUTPUT-FILE.
    RETURN SORT-FILE
        AT END MOVE 'NO ' TO ARE-THERE-MORE-RECORDS.
    PERFORM B200-DISC-RTN
        UNTIL THERE-ARE-NO-MORE-RECORDS.
    CLOSE OUTPUT-FILE.
    GO TO B300-CALC-DISCOUNT-EXIT.
B200-DISC-RTN.
    IF  AMT-OF-PURCHASE > 500
        MOVE .02 to DISCOUNT
    ELSE
        MOVE .00 TO DISCOUNT.
    WRITE OUT-REC FROM SORT-REC.
    RETURN SORT-FILE
        AT END MOVE 'NO ' TO ARE-THERE-MORE-RECORDS.
B300-CALC-DISCOUNT-EXIT.
    EXIT.
```

To access records from the sort file use a RETURN → RETURN SORT-FILE

Put sorted records from the sort file into the output file → WRITE OUT-REC FROM SORT-REC.

Functions like a READ → RETURN SORT-FILE

Consider the following alternative available to COBOL 85 users:

```
*****************************************************************
*         THIS PROCEDURE IS VALID ONLY WITH COBOL 85 COMPILERS      *
*****************************************************************
```

```
PROCEDURE DIVISION.
A100-MAIN-MODULE.
    SORT SORT-FILE
        ON ASCENDING KEY TRANS-NO
        USING INPUT-FILE
        OUTPUT PROCEDURE B000-CALC-DISCOUNT.
    STOP RUN.
B000-CALC-DISCOUNT.
    OPEN OUTPUT OUTPUT-FILE.
    RETURN SORT-FILE
        AT END MOVE 'NO ' TO ARE-THERE-MORE-RECORDS.
    PERFORM C000-DISC-RTN
        UNTIL THERE-ARE-NO-MORE-RECORDS.
    CLOSE OUTPUT-FILE.
C000-DISC-RTN.
    IF  AMT-OF-PURCHASE > 500
        MOVE .02 TO DISCOUNT
    ELSE
        MOVE .00 TO DISCOUNT.
    WRITE OUT-REC FROM SORT-REC.
    RETURN SORT-FILE
        AT END MOVE 'NO ' TO ARE-THERE-MORE-RECORDS.
```

With COBOL 85, you may use an END-RETURN scope terminator with the RETURN statement. Also, the RETURN statement may include a NOT AT END clause.

C. When To Use INPUT and/or OUTPUT PROCEDUREs

Sometimes it is more efficient to process data *before* it is sorted, whereas other times it is more efficient to process data *after* it is sorted.

For instance, suppose we wish to sort a large file into DEPT-NO sequence. Suppose, further, we wish to eliminate from our file all records with a blank PRICE or blank QTY field. We could eliminate the designated records *prior to* sorting in an INPUT PROCEDURE, or we could eliminate the records *after* sorting in an OUTPUT PROCEDURE.

If we expect only a few records to be eliminated during a run, then it really would not matter much whether we sort first and then eliminate those records we do not wish to put on the output file. If, however, there are many records that need to be eliminated, it is more efficient to remove them *before* sorting. In this way, we do not waste computer time sorting numerous records that will then be eliminated from the sorted file. Thus, in the case where a large number of records will be removed, an INPUT PROCEDURE should be used.

On the other hand, suppose we wish to eliminate records with a blank DEPT-NO, the key field. In this instance, it is far more efficient to eliminate records with a blank DEPT-NO *after* sorting, because we know that after sorting, all blank DEPT-NOs will be at the *beginning* of the file. (A blank is the lowest printable character in a collating sequence and thus will appear first in a sorted file.)

Both an INPUT PROCEDURE and an OUTPUT PROCEDURE can be used in a program by combining the preceding examples.

Keep in mind that you must use either an INPUT or an OUTPUT PROCEDURE if the unsorted and sorted files have different-sized fields or have fields in different order.

Figure 17.2
Options of the SORT feature.

SORT OPTIONS: A BRIEF OVERVIEW	
Format	**Result**
1. USING GIVING	File is sorted, no special handling.
2. INPUT PROCEDURE GIVING	Used for processing the unsorted input records before they are sorted. Write records to the sort file with a RELEASE verb.
3. USING OUTPUT PROCEDURE	Used for processing the sorted records before writing them on the output file. Access or read records from the sort file with a RETURN verb.
4. INPUT PROCEDURE OUTPUT PROCEDURE	Used for processing the data both before and after it is sorted.

Summary

Figure 17.2 provides a summary of the SORT feature and its options. The Practice Program at the end of the chapter illustrates a SORT with both an INPUT PROCEDURE and an OUTPUT PROCEDURE.

III. The MERGE Statement

COBOL has a MERGE statement that will combine two or more files into a single file. Its format is similar to that of the SORT:

Format

$$\underline{MERGE} \text{ file-name-1} \left\{ \text{ON} \left\{ \begin{array}{l} \underline{ASCENDING} \\ \underline{DESCENDING} \end{array} \right\} \text{KEY data-name-1} \dots \right\} \dots$$

$$\underline{USING} \text{ file-name-2 \{file-name-3\}} \dots$$

$$\left\{ \begin{array}{l} \underline{OUTPUT} \ \underline{PROCEDURE} \ \text{IS procedure-name-1} \left[\left\{ \begin{array}{l} \underline{THROUGH} \\ \underline{THRU} \end{array} \right\} \text{procedure-name-2} \right] \\ \underline{GIVING} \ \text{\{file-name-4\}} \end{array} \right\}$$

File-name-1 is a work file designated as an SD. The key field specified as data-name-1, and any subsequent key fields, are defined within the SD. The first key field indicated in the ASCENDING or DESCENDING KEY clause of the MERGE is the major one, followed by intermediate and minor key fields. Rules for ASCENDING/DESCENDING KEY, USING, GIVING, and OUTPUT PROCEDURE are the same as for the SORT.

With the USING clause, we indicate the files to be merged. At least two file-names must be included, but more than two are permitted. Unlike the SORT, however, an INPUT PROCEDURE may *not* be specified with a MERGE statement.

The **MERGE** statement automatically handles the opening, closing, and input/output (READ/WRITE functions) associated with the files. See Figure 17.3 for an illustration of a program with the MERGE instruction.

The files to be merged must each be in sequence by the key field. If

Figure 17.3
Illustration of the MERGE
instruction.

```
IDENTIFICATION DIVISION.
PROGRAM-ID. MERGE.
*
ENVIRONMENT DIVISION.
INPUT-OUTPUT SECTION.
FILE-CONTROL.
    SELECT INPUT-FILE-1 ASSIGN TO DA-S-SYS001.
    SELECT INPUT-FILE-2 ASSIGN TO DA-S-SYS002.
    SELECT MERGE-THEM ASSIGN TO WORK.
    SELECT OUTPUT-FILE ASSIGN TO DA-S-SYS003.
*
DATA DIVISION.
FD  INPUT-FILE-1
    LABEL RECORDS ARE STANDARD.
01  IN-REC-1              PIC X(100).
FD  INPUT-FILE-2
    LABEL RECORDS ARE STANDARD.
01  IN-REC-2              PIC X(100).
SD  MERGE-THEM.
01  MERGE-REC.
    05  KEY-FIELD         PIC 9(5).
    05  REST-OF-REC       PIC X(95).
FD  OUTPUT-FILE
    LABEL RECORDS ARE STANDARD.
01  OUT-REC              PIC X(100).
*
PROCEDURE DIVISION.
100-MAIN-MODULE.
    MERGE MERGE-THEM
        ON ASCENDING KEY KEY-FIELD
        USING INPUT-FILE-1, INPUT-FILE-2
        GIVING OUTPUT-FILE.
    STOP RUN.
```

ASCENDING KEY is specified, then the merged output file will have records in increasing order by key field, and if DESCENDING KEY is specified, the merged output file will have key fields from high to low.

An OUTPUT PROCEDURE for a MERGE may be used, for example, to:

1. Flag duplicate records as errors.
   If an UPSTATE-PAYROLL-FILE and a DOWNSTATE-PAYROLL-FILE are being merged to produce a MASTER PAYROLL-FILE in Social Security number sequence, we may use an OUTPUT PROCEDURE to ensure that no two records on the merged file have the same Social Security number.

2. Ensure duplicate records.
   If an UPSTATE-INVENTORY-FILE and a DOWNSTATE-INVENTORY-FILE store the same PART-NOs, we may MERGE them into a MASTER-INVENTORY-FILE and in an OUTPUT PROCEDURE check to see that there are two records for each PART-NO—an UPSTATE and a DOWNSTATE record.

IV. Using a Utility Program in Place of the SORT or MERGE Verb

A **utility program** is one designed to perform a specific task on any type of file. To use a utility program, the user provides specifications about the data files and how the task is to be performed. Most computer centers have separate *sort* or *sort/merge utility programs*. These are typically purchased from the computer vendor or from a software company. A sort or sort-merge utility would require the user to indicate the name of the input and output files and the characteristics of their records, the position and number of key fields, and whether ascending or descending sorting is required.

Note that sort/merge utility programs can usually sort or merge a file more quickly than the SORT or MERGE verb in COBOL. This is because the utility program uses more efficient procedures. The result is a sort or merge that not only takes less time but uses less disk space as well.

CHAPTER SUMMARY

I. The SORT is used for sorting records in either ascending or descending order. These records can be processed before sorting in an INPUT PROCEDURE and after sorting in an OUTPUT PROCEDURE.

 A. In an INPUT PROCEDURE, we OPEN the input file, READ records from the input file, process them, and then RELEASE the records to the sort file. When all the input has been processed, we CLOSE the input file and return to the SORT.
 B. In an OUTPUT PROCEDURE, we OPEN the output file, RETURN records from the sort file, process them, and WRITE them to the output file. When all records from the sort file have been processed, we CLOSE the output file and return to the statement following the SORT.

II. The MERGE statement can be used to merge two or more files. It has a USING and GIVING format; it can also have an OUTPUT PROCEDURE in place of the GIVING.

CHAPTER SELF-TEST

1. Code a simple SORT to read a file called IN-FILE, sort it into ascending name sequence, and create an output file called OUT-FILE.
2. It is possible to process records before they are sorted by using the _____ option in place of the _____ option.
3. A(n) (unsorted input, sorted output) file is opened in an INPUT PROCEDURE and a(n) (unsorted input, sorted output) file is opened in an OUTPUT PROCEDURE.
4. In place of a WRITE statement in an INPUT PROCEDURE, the _____ verb is used to write records onto the sort or work file.
5. In place of a READ statement in an OUTPUT PROCEDURE, the _____ verb is used to read records from the sort or work file.
6. (T or F) The RELEASE statement uses a file-name, as does the RETURN statement.
7. (T or F) If section-names are used in the PROCEDURE DIVISION, they must be followed by paragraph-names.
8. Code a simple SORT to read a file called IN-PAYROLL, sort it into ascending NAME sequence, and create an output file called OUT-PAYROLL.
9. Write the PROCEDURE DIVISION for a program to sort records into DEPT-NO sequence but, in an INPUT PROCEDURE, to eliminate blank DEPT-NOs before sorting. Use section-names and assume that you are using the COBOL 74 standard.
10. Recode the preceding, eliminating blanks *after sorting in an* OUTPUT PROCEDURE. Assume that you are using the COBOL 85 standard.

Solutions

```
1.  SORT   SORT-FILE ON ASCENDING KEY S-NAME
           USING IN-FILE
           GIVING OUT-FILE.
    (S-NAME is a field in the SORT-FILE.)
```

2. INPUT PROCEDURE; USING
3. unsorted input (FD); sorted output (FD)
4. RELEASE
5. RETURN
6. F—We RELEASE record-names and RETURN file-names.
7. T

```
8. SORT SORT-FILE ON ASCENDING KEY NAME
        USING IN-PAYROLL
        GIVING OUT-PAYROLL.
```

```
9.  PROCEDURE DIVISION.
    A000 SECTION.
    A100-MAIN-MODULE.
        SORT SORT-FILE
            ON ASCENDING KEY DEPT-NO
            INPUT PROCEDURE B000-TEST-DEPT
            GIVING SORTED-MSTR.
        STOP RUN.
    B000-TEST-DEPT SECTION.
    B100-PARA-1.
        OPEN INPUT UNSORTED-MSTR.
        READ UNSORTED-MSTR
            AT END MOVE 'NO ' TO ARE-THERE-ANY-UNSORTED-RECORDS.
        PERFORM B200-ELIM
            UNTIL THERE-ARE-NO-UNSORTED-RECORDS.
        CLOSE UNSORTED-MSTR.
        GO TO B300-PARA-3.
    B200-ELIM.
        IF  DEPT-NO-IN IS NOT EQUAL TO SPACES
            RELEASE SORT-REC FROM IN-REC.
        READ UNSORTED-MSTR
            AT END MOVE 'NO ' TO ARE-THERE-ANY-UNSORTED-RECORDS.
    B300-PARA-3.
        EXIT.
```

```
10.  PROCEDURE DIVISION.
     A100-MAIN-MODULE.
         SORT SORT-FILE
             ON ASCENDING KEY DEPT-NO
             USING INFILE
             OUTPUT PROCEDURE B100-PARA-1.
         STOP RUN.
    *
     B100-PARA-1.
         OPEN OUTPUT SORTED-MSTR.
         RETURN SORT-FILE
             AT END MOVE 'NO ' TO ARE-THERE-MORE-SORTED-RECORDS.
         PERFORM B200-ELIM-BLANK-RTN UNTIL
             DEPT-NO NOT = SPACES
             OR THERE-ARE-NO-MORE-SORTED-RECORDS.
         PERFORM B300-WRITE-RTN
             UNTIL THERE-ARE-NO-MORE-SORTED-RECORDS.
         CLOSE SORTED-MSTR.
     B200-ELIM-BLANK-RTN.
         RETURN SORT-FILE
             AT END MOVE 'NO ' TO ARE-THERE-MORE-SORTED-RECORDS.
     B300-WRITE-RTN.
         WRITE SORTED-MASTER-REC FROM SORT-REC.
         RETURN SORT-FILE
             AT END MOVE 'NO ' TO ARE-THERE-MORE-SORTED-RECORDS.
```

PRACTICE PROGRAM

The program definition appears in Figure 17.4.

Figure 17.4
Problem definition for the
Practice Program.

Systems Flowchart

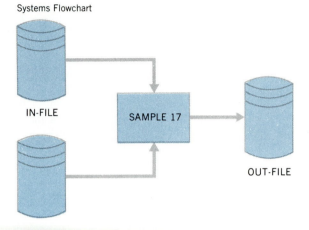

IN-FILE

SAMPLE 17

OUT-FILE

SORT-FILE
(*Note:* This is a work file)

IN-FILE Record Layout

TERR-IN	AREAX-IN	DEPT-IN	LAST-NAME-IN	FIRST-NAME-IN	
1 2	3 5	6 8	9 20	21 28	29 50

(*Note:* Field-names not really needed in this program)

SORT-FILE Record Layout

TERR	AREAX	DEPT	LAST-NAME	FIRST-NAME	
1 2	3 5	6 8	9 20	21 28	29 50

Sample Unsorted File

```
08432543STERN       NANCY
09484736STERN       ROBERT
02653727HAMMEL      CHRIS
08438438SMITH       JOHN
04745838PHILLIPS    TOM
09364737DOE         JOHN
01984848JONES       KATHY
07373626WASHINGTON  GEORGE
02934938JEFFERSON   TOMMY
03937474PETERSON    PETE
```

Sample File After Sort

```
01984848JONES       KATHY
02653727HAMMEL      CHRIS
02934938JEFFERSON   TOMMY
03937474PETERSON    PETE
04745838PHILLIPS    TOM
07373626WASHINGTON  GEORGE
08432543STERN       NANCY
08438438SMITH       JOHN
09364737DOE         JOHN
09484736STERN       ROBERT
```

1. Sort the records into DEPT sequence within AREAX within TERR.
2. In an INPUT PROCEDURE, count all input records processed. DISPLAY the value of the count field in the main module.
3. In an OUTPUT PROCEDURE, eliminate all records with a blank territory so that they are not included in the output file.

The pseudocode, hierarchy chart, and program for this problem appear in Figure 17.5. **Note:** The count field will be displayed on the screen as 10.

Figure 17.5
Pseudocode, hierarchy chart, and solution for the Practice Program.

a. Pseudocode

```
START
    Sort file into Terr, Area, Dept Sequence
    INPUT PROCEDURE - Before Sorting
        Open the input file
        Read a record
        PERFORM UNTIL no more input records
            Add 1 to counter
            Release input record for sorting
            Read a record
        ENDPERFORM
        Close the input file
    END INPUT PROCEDURE
    OUTPUT PROCEDURE - After Sorting
        Open the output file
        Read a record from the sort file
        PERFORM UNTIL no more sort file records
                 or Terr is not blank
            Read a record from the sort file
        ENDPERFORM
        PERFORM UNTIL no more sort file records
            Write an output record from the sort file
            Read a record from the sort file
        ENDPERFORM
    END OUTPUT PROCEDURE
    Display counter
STOP
```

b. Hierarchy Chart

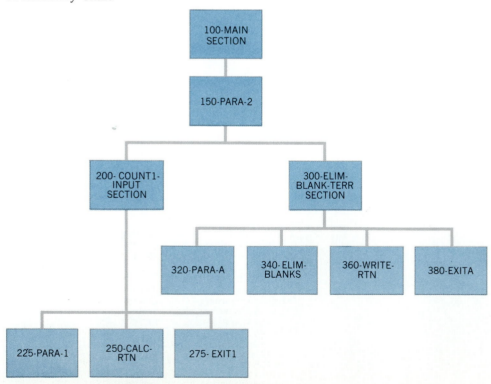

Figure 17.5
(continued)

c. Program

```
IDENTIFICATION DIVISION.
PROGRAM-ID.       SAMPLE.
AUTHOR.           NANCY STERN.
*******************************************************************
*    THIS PROGRAM SORTS A FILE INTO TERR AREA DEPT ORDER  *
*    AND ALSO INCLUDES AN INPUT AND OUTPUT PROCEDURE      *
*******************************************************************
ENVIRONMENT DIVISION.
CONFIGURATION SECTION.
SOURCE-COMPUTER.    VAX-11.
OBJECT-COMPUTER.    VAX-11.
INPUT-OUTPUT SECTION.
FILE-CONTROL.
     SELECT IN-FILE ASSIGN TO DAT167.
     SELECT SORT-FILE ASSIGN TO SORT1.
     SELECT OUT-FILE ASSIGN TO OUT167.
*
DATA DIVISION.
FILE SECTION.
FD  IN-FILE
    LABEL RECORDS ARE STANDARD.
01  IN-REC                       PIC X(50).
SD  SORT-FILE
    RECORD CONTAINS 50 CHARACTERS.
01  SORT-REC.
    05  TERR                     PIC XX.
    05  AREAX                    PIC XXX.
    05  DEPT                     PIC XXX.
    05  LAST-NAME                PIC X(12).
    05  FIRST-NAME               PIC X(8).
    05  FILLER                   PIC X(22).
FD  OUT-FILE
    LABEL RECORDS ARE OMITTED.
01  OUT-REC                      PIC X(50).
WORKING-STORAGE SECTION.
01  STORED-AREAS.
    05  ARE-THERE-MORE-RECORDS   PIC X(3) VALUE 'YES'.
        88  NO-MORE-RECORDS               VALUE 'NO '.
    05  COUNT1                   PIC 999  VALUE ZERO.
*
PROCEDURE DIVISION.
*******************************************************************
*    THIS IS THE CONTROLLING SECTION FOR THE PROGRAM    *
*******************************************************************
100-MAIN SECTION.
150-PARA-2.
    SORT SORT-FILE
        ASCENDING KEY TERR
            ASCENDING KEY AREAX
                ASCENDING KEY DEPT
        INPUT PROCEDURE IS 200-COUNT1-INPUT
        OUTPUT PROCEDURE IS 300-ELIM-BLANK-TERR.
    DISPLAY COUNT1.
    STOP RUN.
*******************************************************************
*    THIS IS THE INPUT PROCEDURE SECTION                *
*******************************************************************
200-COUNT1-INPUT SECTION.
*******************************************************************
*    OPENS THE INPUT FILE, READS RECORDS, COUNTS THEM   *
*        AND RELEASES THEM TO THE SORT FILE             *
*******************************************************************
225-PARA-1.
    OPEN INPUT IN-FILE.
    READ IN-FILE
        AT END MOVE 'NO ' TO ARE-THERE-MORE-RECORDS.
    PERFORM 250-CALC-RTN
        UNTIL NO-MORE-RECORDS.
    GO TO 275-EXIT1.
250-CALC-RTN.
    ADD 1 TO COUNT1.
    RELEASE SORT-REC FROM IN-REC.
    READ IN-FILE

        AT END MOVE 'NO ' TO ARE-THERE-MORE-RECORDS.
275-EXIT1.
    EXIT.
*******************************************************************
*    THIS IS THE OUTPUT PROCEDURE SECTION               *
*******************************************************************
```

Figure 17.5
(continued)

```
300-ELIM-BLANK-TERR SECTION.
************************************************************
*    OPENS THE OUTPUT FILE, RETURNS RECORDS FROM          *
*         THE SORT FILE, ELIMINATES BLANK RECORDS         *
*            AND WRITES RECORDS TO THE OUTPUT FILE         *
************************************************************
 320-PARA-A.
     OPEN OUTPUT OUT-FILE.
     MOVE 'YES' TO ARE-THERE-MORE-RECORDS.
     RETURN SORT-FILE
         AT END MOVE 'NO ' TO ARE-THERE-MORE-RECORDS.
     PERFORM 340-ELIM-BLANKS
         UNTIL TERR IS NOT EQUAL TO SPACES
                 OR NO-MORE-RECORDS.
     PERFORM 360-WRITE-RTN
         UNTIL NO-MORE-RECORDS.
     CLOSE OUT-FILE.
     GO TO 380-EXITA.
 340-ELIM-BLANKS.
     RETURN SORT-FILE
         AT END MOVE 'NO ' TO ARE-THERE-MORE-RECORDS.
 360-WRITE-RTN.
     WRITE OUT-REC FROM SORT-REC.
     RETURN SORT-FILE
         AT END MOVE 'NO ' TO ARE-THERE-MORE-RECORDS.
 380-EXITA.
     EXIT.
```

KEY TERMS

ASCII	INPUT PROCEDURE	RETURN
Collating sequence	MERGE	Section
EBCDIC	OUTPUT PROCEDURE	SORT
FIFO (first in, first out)	RELEASE	Utility program

REVIEW QUESTIONS

T   F

I. True-False Questions

— —   1. If the OUTPUT PROCEDURE is specified with the SORT verb, then the INPUT PROCEDURE is required.

— —   2. RELEASE must be used in an INPUT PROCEDURE.

— —   3. RETURN must be used in an OUTPUT PROCEDURE.

— —   4. The RELEASE statement is used in place of the WRITE statement in an INPUT PROCEDURE.

— —   5. A maximum of three SORT fields are permitted in a single SORT statement.

— —   6. The only method for sorting a disk file is with the use of the SORT statement in COBOL.

— —   7. Data may be sorted in either ascending or descending sequence.

— —   8. The EXIT statement is usually coded at the end of an INPUT PROCEDURE.

— —   9. If a file is described by an SD, it is not defined in a SELECT clause.

— —   10. In the EBCDIC collating sequence, a blank has the lowest value.

II. Validating Data

Modify the Practice Program so that it includes coding to (1) test for all errors and (2) print a control listing of totals (records processed, errors encountered, batch totals).

DEBUGGING EXERCISES

Consider the following:

```
PROCEDURE DIVISION.
100-MAIN-MODULE.
    SORT SORT-FILE
        ASCENDING KEY S-EMP-NO
        USING MASTER-FILE
        OUTPUT PROCEDURE A000-ADD-TAX.
    PERFORM A300-PRINT-RTN.
A000-ADD-TAX SECTION.
    OPEN OUTPUT SORTED-MASTER.
    RETURN SORT-FILE
        AT END MOVE 'NO ' TO ARE-THERE-MORE-RECORDS.
    PERFORM A100-RTN1 UNTIL NO-MORE-RECORDS.
    CLOSE SORTED-MASTER.
    GO TO A200-ADD-TAX-EXIT.
A100-RTN1.
    MOVE .10 TO TAX-OUT.
    WRITE SORTED-MASTER-REC FROM SORT-REC.
    RELEASE SORTED-MASTER-REC.
A200-ADD-TAX-EXIT.
    EXIT.
A300-PRINT-RTN.
    MOVE 'YES' TO ARE-THERE-MORE-RECORDS.
    OPEN INPUT SORTED-MASTER
              PRINT-FILE.
    READ SORTED-MASTER
        AT END MOVE 'NO ' TO ARE-THERE-MORE-RECORDS.
    PERFORM A400-PRINT-IT UNTIL NO-MORE-INPUT.
    CLOSE SORTED-MASTER
          PRINT-FILE.
A400-PRINT-IT.
    WRITE PRINT-REC FROM SORTED-MASTER-REC.
    READ SORTED-MASTER
        AT END MOVE 'NO ' TO ARE-THERE-MORE-RECORDS.
```

1. There is a line missing after A000-ADD-TAX SECTION. What is it?
2. There is an error associated with the RELEASE statement. Find and correct it.
3. Since A300-PRINT-RTN is not preceded by a section-name, what statement is executed after the A200-ADD-TAX-EXIT paragraph? Under what conditions would the failure to include a section-name prior to A300-PRINT-RTN cause errors?
4. Would you obtain a syntax error if you moved CLOSE SORTED-MASTER to A200-ADD-TAX-EXIT so that it replaced EXIT? Explain your answer.
5. Would you get an error if A200-ADD-TAX-EXIT with the EXIT statement were eliminated entirely? Explain your answer.
6. After all the preceding errors are corrected, you run the program and obtain all the appropriate results, but the program abends. You find that the program is attempting to continue execution even after all records have been processed. Find and correct the error.

PROGRAMMING ASSIGNMENTS

Use the specifications in Figure 17.6 for Programming Assignments 1 through 5.

Figure 17.6
Problem definition
for Programming
Assignments 1–5.

Systems Flowchart

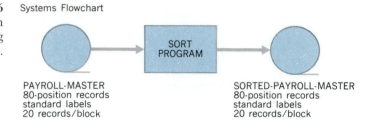

PAYROLL-MASTER
80-position records
standard labels
20 records/block

SORTED-PAYROLL-MASTER
80-position records
standard labels
20 records/block

Record Layout for PAYROLL-MASTER and SORTED-PAYROLL-MASTER

1. Sort the input tape file into ascending sequence by Territory Number, Office Number, and Social Security Number.
2. Sort the input tape file into descending sequence by Territory Number and Office Number, but eliminate all records that have a blank Territory Number, Office Number, or Social Security Number.
3. Sort the input tape file into ascending sequence by Territory Number, and add $1000 to the salaries of employees who earn less than $25,000. This may be performed either before or after sorting.
4. After sorting input tape records into ascending Office Number sequence but before creating the sorted output file, print the Social Security Number for all employees in Territory 14 who earn more than $75,000.
5. Sort the input tape file into ascending Territory Number sequence. Then write a control break program to print a report with the format shown in Figure 17.7.

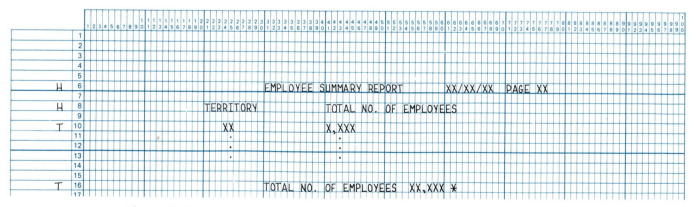

Figure 17.7
Printer Spacing Chart for
Programming Assignment 5.

6. A large corporation with two plants has discovered that some of its employees are on the payrolls of both of its plants. Each plant has a payroll file in Social Security number sequence. Write a program to merge the two files and to print the names of the double-dippers; that is, the employees who are on both files.

7. Merge an upstate transaction file with a downstate transaction file.

```
1-5    TRANS-NO
6-10   AMT-PURCHASED
```

The transaction numbers should be unique on each file, but it is permissible to have the same transaction number on both files (e.g., 00002 may be on both input files, but there should be at most one such record on each). Print the number of transaction numbers that appear on both input files.

18

Indexed File Processing

OBJECTIVES

To familiarize you with

1. Methods of disk file organization.
2. Random processing of disk files.
3. How to create and access indexed disk files.

I. Systems Considerations for Organizing Disk Files

Recall that the term *file* refers to a collection of records to be used for a given application. An accounts receivable file, for example, is the collection of all customer records. We now discuss the major ways in which files can be stored on a disk storage unit.

A. Sequential File Organization

The simplest type of disk file organization is *sequential*. Sequential files are processed in the same way regardless of whether they are stored on disk or tape. Typically, the records to be stored in a sequential file are first sorted into sequence by a key field such as customer number, part number, or employee number. It is then relatively easy to locate a given record. The record with employee number 00986, for example, would be physically located between records with employee numbers 00985 and 00987. To access that record, the computer must read past the first 985 records.

We have already seen in Chapter 16 how a master sequential file can be updated by either (1) creating a new master disk or tape file using the previous master and the transaction file of changes as input or (2) rewriting master disk records that have changes.

There are two methods of file organization that enable a disk file to be accessed randomly as well as sequentially. *Indexed files* and *relative files* can be processed both sequentially and randomly. In this chapter, we consider indexed file organization in depth. Chapter 23 considers relative files in depth.

B. Indexed File Organization

An **indexed file** is one that has an index for looking up locations of records on a disk. This index enables the user to access a disk file randomly. The **index**, or reference table, is created on the disk at the same time that the data is recorded on the disk. This index stores each record's key field and the corresponding disk address of that record.

When creating an indexed payroll file, for example, the programmer would indicate that the Social Security number of each record within the file is to be the key field. The computer then establishes the index on the disk, which will contain each record's Social Security number and its corresponding disk address.

To access a payroll record randomly, the Social Security number of the desired record is supplied by the user, and the computer "looks up" the address of the record in the index; it then moves the disk drive's access mechanism to the address where the employee record with that Social Security number is located. This is very useful for **interactive processing**, where a user communicates directly with the computer using a terminal and the key fields he or she is entering are not necessarily entered in sequence.

Once the address of the disk record is obtained from an index, the access mechanism can move directly to that address on the disk where the record is located. It is *not* necessary for the read/write heads to read sequentially past all the previous records in the file looking for the desired one.

The index on a disk is similar to a book's index, which has unique subjects (keys) and their corresponding page numbers (addresses). There would be two ways to find a topic in the book. You can read the book sequentially, from the beginning, until that topic is found, but this would be very time-consuming and inefficient. The best method would be to look up the topic in the index, find the page number, and go directly to that page. This is precisely how records can be accessed on a disk file that has an index.

With an indexed file we can access records *either* sequentially or randomly, depending on the user's needs. Keep in mind that the term **random access** implies that records are to be processed or accessed in some order other than the one in which they were physically written on the disk.

C. Relative File Organization

Other types of disk files, such as **relative files**, also permit random access. A relative file does not use an index to access records randomly. Rather, the key field of each record is used to calculate the record's relative location in the file. Relative files are discussed in Chapter 23.

II. Processing Indexed Disk Files

COBOL 85 is the first version of COBOL that has standardized the processing of indexed files. Hence, we focus primarily on COBOL 85 for this chapter. If you are using a COBOL 74 compiler, you may need to code entries that are slightly different from those discussed here. Most COBOL 74 compilers, however, provide enhancements that are close to or even identical with the features we present here. VSAM, which is IBM's implementation for the processing of indexed files, was one of the first indexed file implementations to incorporate the COBOL 85 features specified here.

A. Creating an Indexed File

Indexed files are created *in sequence*; that is, the indexed file is created by reading each record from an input file, in sequence by the key field, and writing the output indexed disk records *in the same sequence*.

Thus, creating the indexed file is performed in the same manner as creating a sequential disk or tape file, with some very minor differences. See Figure 18.1 for an illustration of a program that creates an indexed file sequentially. There are several new entries in this program that need a brief explanation. We will discuss each in detail.

Figure 18.1
Program that creates an indexed file sequentially.

```
IDENTIFICATION DIVISION.
PROGRAM-ID. SAMPLE.
********************************************************
*    THIS PROGRAM CREATES AN INDEXED                  *
*    DISK FROM AN INPUT TAPE FILE.                    *
********************************************************
ENVIRONMENT DIVISION.
INPUT-OUTPUT SECTION.
FILE-CONTROL.
    SELECT PAYROLL-FILE-IN ASSIGN TO DATA161.
    SELECT MASTER-FILE-OUT ASSIGN TO DATA161M
        ORGANIZATION IS INDEXED              ◄──  Establishes the file as
        ACCESS IS SEQUENTIAL          ◄──         indexed
        RECORD KEY IS INDEXED-SSNO-OUT.  ◄──      Indexed files are created
*                                                 in sequence
DATA DIVISION.
FILE SECTION.                                      Specifies the indexed
FD  PAYROLL-FILE-IN                                record's key field
    LABEL RECORDS ARE STANDARD.
01  PAYROLL-REC-IN.
    05   SSNO-IN                 PIC 9(9).
    05   NAME-IN                 PIC X(20).
    05   SALARY-IN               PIC 9(5).
    05   ADDTL-DATA-IN           PIC X(20).
FD  MASTER-FILE-OUT
    LABEL RECORDS ARE STANDARD.
```

Figure 18.1
(continued)

```
01   MASTER-REC-OUT.
       05   INDEXED-SSNO-OUT          PIC 9(9).
       05   INDEXED-NAME-OUT          PIC X(20).
       05   INDEXED-SALARY-OUT        PIC 9(5).
       05   INDEXED-DATA-OUT          PIC X(20).
WORKING-STORAGE SECTION.
01   WS-WORK-AREAS.
       05   ARE-THERE-MORE-RECORDS    PIC X(3)        VALUE 'YES'.
            88   MORE-RECORDS                          VALUE 'YES'.
            88   NO-MORE-RECORDS                       VALUE 'NO '.
*
PROCEDURE DIVISION.
*************************************************
*   CONTROLS DIRECTION OF PROGRAM LOGIC   *
*************************************************
100-MAIN-MODULE.
     PERFORM 300-INITIALIZATION-RTN.
     PERFORM 200-CREATE-RTN
         UNTIL NO-MORE-RECORDS.
     PERFORM 400-END-OF-JOB-RTN.
******************************************************************
*   PERFORMED FROM 200-CALC-RTN, CREATES NEW RECORDS IN    *
*   MASTER FILE FROM PAYROLL FILE                          *
******************************************************************
200-CREATE-RTN.
     MOVE PAYROLL-REC-IN TO MASTER-REC-OUT.
     WRITE MASTER-REC-OUT
         INVALID KEY DISPLAY 'INVALID RECORD ' PAYROLL-REC-IN.
     READ PAYROLL-FILE-IN
         AT END MOVE 'NO ' TO ARE-THERE-MORE-RECORDS.
***********************************************
*   PERFORMED FROM 100-MAIN-MODULE,          *
*   OPENS FILES AND PERFORMS INITIAL READ    *
***********************************************
300-INITIALIZATION-RTN.
     OPEN INPUT  PAYROLL-FILE-IN
          OUTPUT MASTER-FILE-OUT.
     READ PAYROLL-FILE-IN
         AT END MOVE 'NO ' TO ARE-THERE-MORE-RECORDS.
********************************************************
*   PERFORMED FROM 100-MAIN-MODULE, CLOSES FILES   *
*   AND RETURNS CONTROL TO OPERATING SYSTEM        *
********************************************************
400-END-OF-JOB-RTN.
     CLOSE PAYROLL-FILE-IN
           MASTER-FILE-OUT.
     STOP RUN.
```

◄— DISPLAY is executed if MASTER-REC-OUT's key field
1. is not in sequence
2. duplicates the key field of a record already on the disk
3. is blank (with some compilers)

1. The SELECT Statement

When an indexed file is being created, the full SELECT statement would be as follows:

> **CREATING AN INDEXED FILE: SELECT CLAUSE**
>
> SELECT file-name-1 ASSIGN TO implementor-name-1
>   [ORGANIZATION IS] INDEXED
>   [ACCESS MODE IS SEQUENTIAL]
>   RECORD KEY IS data-name-1

The implementor-name in the ASSIGN clause is *exactly* the same as for standard sequential disk files.

a. The ORGANIZATION Clause.

The clause ORGANIZATION IS INDEXED indicates that the file is to be created *with an index*. (For some versions of COBOL 74, an *I* may be used in the implementor-name of the ASSIGN clause in place of ORGANIZATION IS INDEXED.) Even though we are creating the file sequentially, we must instruct the computer to establish an index so that we can randomly access it later on.

   b. The ACCESS Clause.   Since indexed files may be accessed *either sequentially or randomly*, the ACCESS clause is used to denote which method will be used. If the ACCESS clause is omitted, the compiler will assume that the file is being processed in SEQUENTIAL mode. Indexed files are always created sequentially; that is, *the input records must be in sequence by key field.*

   c. The RECORD KEY Clause.   The RECORD KEY clause is used to name the *key field within the disk record* that will be used to form the index. This field must be in the same physical location in each indexed record. Usually, it is the first field. It must have a unique value for each record and it is usually numeric.

GUIDELINES FOR RECORD KEYs

1. COBOL 85 states that the RECORD KEY should be defined with a PIC of X's. Most compilers also allow a PIC of 9's as an enhancement. Regardless of whether the record key is defined with X's or 9's, it is best to use a RECORD KEY that contains numbers.
      Fields such as ACCT-NO in an accounts receivable record, SOC-SEC-NO in a payroll record, or PART-NO in an inventory record, for example, are commonly used key fields.
2. Key fields should be the first fields in a record. This is for ease of reference, but it is not required.

   Note that ACCESS IS SEQUENTIAL is the default, so that the ACCESS clause can be omitted entirely from the SELECT statement.
   Figure 18.1 illustrates these three additional clauses used in the SELECT statement for creating an indexed file. The only other difference between creating an indexed file as compared with a sequential file is in the use of the INVALID KEY clause with the WRITE statement.

2. The INVALID KEY Clause

Examine the WRITE statement in Figure 18.1. Note that it includes an **INVALID KEY** clause. The INVALID KEY clause is used with a WRITE instruction to test for two possibilities: to determine if the record to be written has a key that is erroneous because it is (1) not in sequence or (2) the same as one already on the indexed file (on many systems, a blank key field will also be considered an INVALID KEY). If any of these conditions exist, we call this an INVALID KEY *condition*. The computer checks for an INVALID KEY *prior to* writing the record.
   Thus, if you use an INVALID KEY clause with the WRITE statement and a record has an erroneous key, *the record is not written* and the statement(s) following INVALID KEY would be executed. Coding WRITE ... INVALID KEY, then, ensures that the key field of the record being written is acceptable, which means it is unique and sequential (and, for many systems, not blank). If, for example, two records have the same Social Security number, or the Social Security numbers are not entered in sequence, the index would not be able to associate the record or key field with a disk address.
   The INVALID KEY clause is required when writing records, unless a separate DECLARATIVE SECTION is coded for handling I/O errors. We will discuss this

section later on. For now, all our programs will include the `INVALID KEY` clause. It prevents erroneous keys from being written onto the disk.

The format for the `INVALID KEY` clause is:

Format

> `WRITE` record-name-1 `[FROM` identifier-1]
> `[INVALID KEY` imperative statement-1]

With COBOL 85, `NOT INVALID KEY` imperative-statement and `END-WRITE` are also options. Thus with COBOL 85 you may code:

```
WRITE     INDEXED-REC
          INVALID KEY PERFORM 500-ERROR-RTN
          NOT INVALID KEY PERFORM 400-OK-RTN
END-WRITE
```

In summary, creating an indexed file is not significantly different from creating a sequential file. The `SELECT` statement has an `ORGANIZATION IS INDEXED` clause, an `ACCESS IS SEQUENTIAL` clause (optional because `SEQUENTIAL` access is the default), and a `RECORD KEY` clause. In the `PROCEDURE DIVISION`, an `INVALID KEY` clause is used with the `WRITE` statement to ensure that only records with valid key fields are created on disk.

B. Updating an Indexed File Randomly

As we have seen, one main advantage of disk processing is that master records can be updated *directly* without having to create a new file. That is, a disk record can be read into storage where changes are made and the changed record can be rewritten back onto the disk in place.

Thus, when updating an indexed disk, only *two* files are needed—the transaction file and the master disk itself, which serves as *both* input and output.* Moreover, *since the indexed disk file may be accessed randomly, there is no need to sort the transaction file* before performing an update.

For accessing indexed files *randomly*, we may have either (1) a transaction file, which can be stored on any storage media (tape, disk, etc.) or (2) transaction data entered interactively as the change occurs; such changes are usually entered on a terminal. In either case, the transaction data will specify which disk records we want to read or access for updating purposes. We will assume, for now, that the changes are on a transaction file. In the next chapter we focus on interactive processing using a terminal.

Suppose we wish to update a record with `PART-NO 123` on an indexed inventory file that has `PART-NO` as its record key. We simply enter `123` in the `RECORD KEY` field of the disk record and instruct the computer to read from the indexed file. The computer will then randomly access the corresponding indexed record. In an update procedure, the transaction data consists of the `PART-NO`s of records to be changed or updated on the master file. To find each corresponding master record, we must perform the following:

1. Read the transaction record.
   (Each record contains a transaction part number called `T-PART-NO`.)
2. Move `T-PART-NO` to the `RECORD KEY` of the master file called `PART-NO`.
   (Move the transaction key field to the indexed record's key field, which is defined within the record description for the indexed file.)

---

*If disk records are updated in place, be sure you use a backup procedure to create another version of the master file in case something happens to the original.

3. When we READ from the indexed file, the computer will look up or access the disk record that has a key field equal to the value stored in PART-NO. If no such record is found, an error routine should be performed. This is accomplished by coding:

```
READ INDEXED-FILE
     INVALID KEY PERFORM 600-ERR-RTN.
```

The coding requirements for randomly updating an indexed file are:

1. The SELECT Statement
The SELECT statement for an indexed file that is to be *updated randomly* is as follows:

ACCESSING AN INDEXED FILE RANDOMLY

<u>SELECT</u> file-name-1 <u>ASSIGN</u> TO implementor-name-1
    [<u>ORGANIZATION</u> IS] <u>INDEXED</u>
    <u>ACCESS</u> MODE IS <u>RANDOM</u>
    <u>RECORD</u> KEY IS data-name-1

Example   An indexed file to be updated would have the following SELECT statement:

```
SELECT INDEXED-FILE ASSIGN TO DISK1
    ORGANIZATION IS INDEXED
    ACCESS MODE IS RANDOM
    RECORD KEY IS PART-NO.
```

2. OPEN I-O Indexed-File
When updating an indexed file, we open it as I-O because (1) it is used as input [I] for reading or accessing disk records, and (2) it is used as output [O] for rewriting or updating the records read.

3. The READ Statement
We read in the transaction record, which has the part number to be accessed from the disk. We move the transaction T-PART-NO to PART-NO, and then read the disk:

```
READ TRANS-FILE
    AT END MOVE 'NO ' TO ARE-THERE-MORE-RECORDS.
MOVE T-PART-NO TO PART-NO.
READ INDEXED-FILE
    INVALID KEY PERFORM 600-ERR-RTN.
```

The record read from INDEXED-FILE will have a RECORD KEY equal to T-PART-NO; if no such record is found, 600-ERR-RTN will be performed.

There Is No AT END Clause When Reading from a Disk Randomly

When reading a disk file randomly, we do not test for an AT END condition because we are not reading the file in sequence; instead, we include an INVALID KEY test. If there is no record in the INDEXED-FILE with a RECORD KEY equal to T-PART-NO, the INVALID KEY clause will be executed. Thus, the computer executes the INVALID KEY option only if the T-PART-NO does not match any of the master disk records.

4. REWRITE a Disk Record to Update It
Once a master indexed record has been accessed, transaction data is moved to the master record, and we code a REWRITE to change or overlay the indexed

master record on disk, so that it includes the additional data. Thus, for updating an indexed file, we have:

UPDATING AN INDEXED MASTER FILE

1. OPEN the indexed master file as I-O.
2. Read a transaction record.
   Move the key field of the transaction record to the RECORD KEY. When a READ (master) instruction is executed the computer will find the indexed record with that RECORD KEY and transmit it to the master record stored in the FILE SECTION.
3. After the READ, we have in storage both the transaction record and the corresponding master record that needs to be updated.
4. Make the changes to the master record directly by moving transaction data to the master I/O record area.
5. REWRITE the master record.

---

5. Illustrating a Simple Update Procedure for an Indexed File

Example   Assume that a master indexed disk file contains payroll data with Social Security number as its RECORD KEY. A tape file contains transaction or change records where each record is identified by a Social Security number and new payroll data for that employee. The tape's new payroll data is to be used to change the corresponding disk record. The following is an excerpt of the PROCEDURE DIVISION:

```
PROCEDURE DIVISION.
100-MAIN-MODULE.
    PERFORM 500-INITIALIZATION-RTN.
    PERFORM 200-CALC-RTN
        UNTIL THERE-ARE-NO-MORE-RECORDS.
    PERFORM 600-END-OF-JOB-RTN.
200-CALC-RTN.
    MOVE T-SOC-SEC-NO TO MASTER-SSNO.
    MOVE 0 TO WS-ERR-CODE.
    READ MASTER-FILE
        INVALID KEY PERFORM 400-ERROR-RTN.
    IF  WS-ERR-CODE = 0
        PERFORM 300-UPDATE-RTN.
    READ TRANS-IN
        AT END MOVE 'NO ' TO ARE-THERE-MORE-RECORDS.
300-UPDATE-RTN.
    MOVE T-PAYROLL-DATA TO MASTER-DATA.
    REWRITE MASTER-REC
        INVALID KEY DISPLAY 'REWRITE ERROR ', MASTER-SSNO.
400-ERROR-RTN.
    DISPLAY 'INVALID RECORD ', MASTER-SSNO.
    MOVE 1 TO WS-ERR-CODE.
500-INITIALIZATION-RTN.
    OPEN INPUT TRANS-IN
        I-O MASTER-FILE.
    READ TRANS-IN
        AT END MOVE 'NO ' TO ARE-THERE-MORE-RECORDS.
600-END-OF-JOB-RTN.
    CLOSE TRANS-IN
        MASTER-FILE.
    STOP RUN.
```

Handling Invalid Keys

If we attempt to read an indexed record at 200-CALC-RTN and get an INVALID KEY condition, 400-ERROR-RTN is performed, where an error message is displayed. This means that there is no record on the indexed file with a `RECORD KEY` equal to the transaction key field. If such an error occurs, `400-ERROR-RTN` is executed, but control then returns to `200-CALC-RTN`, where processing would continue *as if* there were an indexed record corresponding to the transaction record. To avoid such incorrect processing, we establish a one position `WS-ERR-CODE` in `WORKING-STORAGE` that will contain a 0 when there is no error and a 1 when an error occurs.

> With COBOL 85, we can use a `NOT INVALID KEY` clause with the `READ` statement to avoid the need for error codes as follows:
>
> ```
> READ    MASTER-FILE
>         INVALID KEY PERFORM 400-ERROR-RTN
>         NOT INVALID KEY PERFORM 300-UPDATE-RTN
> END-READ
> ```

6. Additional Features of an Update Procedure

The previous update procedure used transaction data to change a master record. We may use a coded field to designate different types of updating. Types of updating may include:

    a.   Making changes to existing records, as in the previous illustration. For example, promotions, salary increases, and transfers must be incorporated in existing payroll records. The `REWRITE` verb is used to alter existing records.

    b.   Creating new records. For example, new hires must be added to a payroll file. There is no need to look up a master disk record when a transaction record designates a new hire. Rather, the transaction data is moved to the master disk area and a simple `WRITE` instruction (*not* `REWRITE`) is used to create the new record.

    c.   Deleting some existing records. For example, the records of employees who have resigned must be deleted from a payroll file. If a transaction record indicates that a master record is to be deleted, we look up the corresponding indexed master record and code a **DELETE** statement. The format is as follows:

Format

> DELETE indexed-file-name-1 RECORD
>   [INVALID KEY imperative statement-1]

> With COBOL 85, `NOT INVALID KEY` is also an option with the `DELETE` verb. Also, `END-DELETE` may be used as a scope terminator.

We use the *file-name* with the `DELETE` verb, but the word `RECORD` can be specified as well. That is, the statements `DELETE INDEXED-FILE` and `DELETE INDEXED-FILE RECORD` are both permitted.

Example of a Full Update Procedure

Consider an update program where tape transaction records will be used to (1) change existing master records, (2) create new master records, or (3) delete some master records. Because an indexed master file can be accessed randomly, the transaction records need not be in the same sequence as the master records. The transaction tape record format is as follows:

1–9 Social Security number
10–29 Payroll data
30 Code (1-new employee, 2-update, 3-separation from company)

The master disk format is as follows:

1–9 Social Security number (RECORD KEY)
10–29 Payroll data

Figure 18.2 has the pseudocode and hierarchy chart. See Figure 18.3 for a suggested solution.

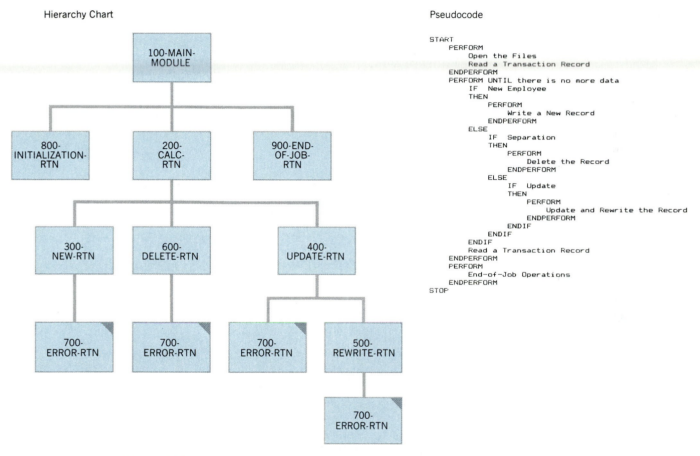

Hierarchy Chart

Pseudocode

```
START
    PERFORM
        Open the Files
        Read a Transaction Record
    ENDPERFORM
    PERFORM UNTIL there is no more data
        IF  New Employee
        THEN
            PERFORM
                Write a New Record
            ENDPERFORM
        ELSE
            IF  Separation
            THEN
                PERFORM
                    Delete the Record
                ENDPERFORM
            ELSE
                IF  Update
                THEN
                    PERFORM
                        Update and Rewrite the Record
                    ENDPERFORM
                ENDIF
            ENDIF
        ENDIF
        Read a Transaction Record
    ENDPERFORM
    PERFORM
        End-of-Job Operations
    ENDPERFORM
STOP
```

Figure 18.2
Pseudocode and hierarchy chart for updating an indexed file randomly.

Figure 18.3
Program to update an indexed
file randomly.

```
 IDENTIFICATION DIVISION.
 PROGRAM-ID. SAMPLE.
 **************************************************************
 *  THIS PROGRAM UPDATES A MASTER FILE WITH TAPE FILE TRANSACTIONS  *
 **************************************************************
 ENVIRONMENT DIVISION.
 INPUT-OUTPUT SECTION.
 FILE-CONTROL.
      SELECT TRANS-FILE-IN  ASSIGN TO DATA163.
      SELECT MASTER-FILE-IO ASSIGN TO DATA163M
          ORGANIZATION IS INDEXED
          ACCESS IS RANDOM
          RECORD KEY IS MASTER-SSNO-IO.
 *
 DATA DIVISION.
 FILE SECTION.
 FD  TRANS-FILE-IN
     LABEL RECORDS ARE STANDARD.
 01  TRANS-REC-IN.
     05  TRANS-SSNO-IN              PIC X(9).
     05  TRANS-PAYROLL-DATA-IN      PIC X(20).
     05  TRANS-CODE-IN              PIC X.
         88  NEW-EMPLOYEE                       VALUE '1'.
         88  UPDATE-EMPLOYEE                    VALUE '2'.
         88  SEPARATION                         VALUE '3'.
 FD  MASTER-FILE-IO
     LABEL RECORDS ARE STANDARD.
 01  MASTER-REC-IO.
     05  MASTER-SSNO-IO             PIC X(9).
     05  MASTER-DATA-IO             PIC X(20).
 WORKING-STORAGE SECTION.
 01  WORK-AREAS.
     05  ARE-THERE-MORE-RECORDS     PIC X(3)    VALUE 'YES'.
         88  MORE-RECORDS                       VALUE 'YES'.
         88  NO-MORE-RECORDS                    VALUE 'NO '.
     05  WS-ERROR-CODE              PIC 9       VALUE ZERO.
         88  NO-ERROR                           VALUE ZERO.
 *
 PROCEDURE DIVISION.
 ****************************************
 *  CONTROLS DIRECTION OF PROGRAM LOGIC  *
 ****************************************
 100-MAIN-MODULE.
      PERFORM 800-INITIALIZATION-RTN.
      PERFORM 200-CALC-RTN
          UNTIL NO-MORE-RECORDS.
      PERFORM 900-END-OF-JOB-RTN.
 ************************************************************
 *  PERFORMED FROM 100-MAIN-MODULE. DETERMINES THE  *
 *  TYPE OF ACTION REQUIRED BY THE TRANSACTION FILE.*
 ************************************************************
 200-CALC-RTN.
      MOVE ZERO TO WS-ERROR-CODE.
      IF  NEW-EMPLOYEE
          PERFORM 300-NEW-RTN
      ELSE
          IF  SEPARATION
              PERFORM 600-DELETE-RTN
          ELSE
              IF  UPDATE-EMPLOYEE
                  PERFORM 400-UPDATE-RTN.
      READ TRANS-FILE-IN
          AT END MOVE 'NO ' TO ARE-THERE-MORE-RECORDS.
 ************************************************************
 *  PERFORMED FROM 200-CALC-RTN. ADDS NEW RECORDS  *
 *  TO THE MASTER FILE                             *
 ************************************************************
 300-NEW-RTN.
      MOVE TRANS-SSNO-IN TO MASTER-SSNO-IO.
      MOVE TRANS-PAYROLL-DATA-IN TO MASTER-DATA-IO.
      WRITE MASTER-REC-IO
          INVALID KEY PERFORM 700-ERROR-RTN.
 ************************************************************
 *  PERFORMED FROM 200-CALC-RTN. READS A MASTER RECORD  *
 *  AND TESTS FOR ERRORS.                               *
 ************************************************************
 400-UPDATE-RTN.
      MOVE SPACES TO MASTER-REC-IO.
      MOVE TRANS-SSNO-IN TO MASTER-SSNO-IO.
      READ MASTER-FILE-IO
          INVALID KEY PERFORM 700-ERROR-RTN.
      IF  NO-ERROR
          PERFORM 500-REWRITE-RTN.
```

Accesses the disk record
that corresponds to the
Social Security number in
the transaction record

Figure 18.3
(continued)

```
*****************************************************************
*  PERFORMED FROM 400-UPDATE-RTN. UPDATES A RECORD ON THE  *
*  MASTER FILE WITH THE TRANSACTION DATA AND REWRITES THE  *
*  MASTER RECORD.                                          *
*****************************************************************
 500-REWRITE-RTN.
     MOVE TRANS-PAYROLL-DATA-IN TO MASTER-DATA-IO.
     REWRITE MASTER-REC-IO  ◄─────────────────── Updates the disk record
         INVALID KEY PERFORM 700-ERROR-RTN.        with the transaction data
*****************************************************************
*  PERFORMED FROM 200-CALC-RTN. DELETES A RECORD FROM  *
*  THE MASTER FILE.                                    *
*****************************************************************
 600-DELETE-RTN.
     MOVE TRANS-SSNO-IN TO MASTER-SSNO-IO.
     READ MASTER-FILE-IO
         INVALID KEY PERFORM 700-ERROR-RTN .
     IF  NO-ERROR
         DELETE MASTER-FILE-IO
             INVALID KEY PERFORM 700-ERROR-RTN.
*****************************************************************
*  PERFORMED FROM 300-NEW-RTN, 400-UPDATE-RTN,       *
*  500-REWRITE-RTN, AND 600-DELETE-RTN.  DISPLAYS    *
*  AN ERROR MESSAGE AND SETS THE ERROR-CODE TO 1.    *
*****************************************************************
 700-ERROR-RTN.
     DISPLAY 'ERROR ' TRANS-SSNO-IN.
     MOVE 1 TO WS-ERROR-CODE.
*****************************************************************
*  PERFORMED FROM 100-MAIN-MODULE. OPENS FILES AND    *
*  PERFORMS INITIAL READ FROM TRANSACTION FILE        *
*****************************************************************
 800-INITIALIZATION-RTN.
     OPEN INPUT TRANS-FILE-IN
         I-O   MASTER-FILE-IO.  ◄────────── When disks are updated
     READ TRANS-FILE-IN                       directly, they are opened
         AT END MOVE 'NO ' TO ARE-THERE-MORE-RECORDS.   as I-O
*****************************************************************
*  PERFORMED FROM 100-MAIN-MODULE. CLOSES FILES AND    *
*  RETURNS CONTROL TO THE OPERATING SYSTEM.            *
*****************************************************************
 900-END-OF-JOB-RTN.
     CLOSE TRANS-FILE-IN
           MASTER-FILE-IO.
     STOP RUN.
```

The IDENTIFICATION DIVISION of programs using disk is the same as previously described. The ENVIRONMENT DIVISION incorporates the clauses necessary for indexed disk files. Since the disk file is indexed and the records are *not accessed in sequence*, ORGANIZATION IS INDEXED and ACCESS MODE IS RANDOM. The RECORD KEY clause is a required entry for all indexed files.

The DATA DIVISION is basically the same as when describing sequential files. Note that disk records generally use standard labels. Typically, the first field within each disk record is the RECORD KEY.

In the PROCEDURE DIVISION, the transaction file's TRANS-SSNO-IN must be moved to the RECORD KEY field called MASTER-SSNO-IO before a disk record may be accessed randomly. The READ MASTER-FILE-IO instruction will read into storage a record with the *same* Social Security number as the one that appears in the TRANS-FILE-IN.

200-CALC-RTN re-initializes a WS-ERROR-CODE field to 0. We use this error code field at 400-UPDATE-RTN to indicate when an error has occurred so that we avoid processing records that could not be accessed properly. The condition name NO-ERROR means that WS-ERROR-CODE has a zero, that is, there is no error. Only if the condition-name NO-ERROR exists will processing of the corresponding indexed record continue; if WS-ERROR-CODE is not zero at 400-UPDATE-RTN, then it means we did not find a corresponding indexed record and we do not want to perform 500-REWRITE-RTN.

> With COBOL 85, use of an error code can be avoided entirely by coding:
>
> ```
> READ . . .
>     INVALID KEY PERFORM error-routine
>     NOT INVALID KEY PERFORM update-the-record-routine
> ```

C. Accessing or Reading from an Indexed File for Reporting Purposes

An indexed file may be read from, or accessed, either sequentially or randomly for reporting purposes.

Printing from an Indexed File Sequentially

Suppose we have an accounts receivable indexed master file that is in ACCT-NO sequence. Processing the ACCTS-RECVBLE file is *exactly the same* regardless of whether it is an indexed file accessed sequentially or a sequential file.

If we wished to print customer bills from the ACCTS-RECVBLE file in ascending alphabetic sequence by NAME, we could *still* use sequential processing even though the file is not initially in sequence by NAME. First, we would *sort* the file into alphabetic sequence by NAME and then print the bills:

```
SORT SORT-FILE
    ON ASCENDING KEY S-NAME
    USING ACCTS-RECVBLE
    GIVING AR-SORTED-BY-NAME.
OPEN INPUT AR-SORTED-BY-NAME
    OUTPUT PR-FILE.
READ AR-SORTED-BY-NAME
    AT END MOVE 'NO ' TO ARE-THERE-MORE-RECORDS.
PERFORM 200-PRINT-BILLS
    UNTIL THERE-ARE-NO-MORE-RECORDS.
CLOSE AR-SORTED-BY-NAME
        PR-FILE.
STOP RUN.
```

Even though we are not using the index of the ACCTS-RECVBLE file in this SORT procedure, the corresponding SELECT statement must have the clauses ORGANIZATION IS INDEXED and RECORD KEY IS ACCT-NO. In all other ways, however, the programs would be the same as if ACCTS-RECVBLE were a sequential file.

Figure 18.4 illustrates a program that accesses an indexed file sequentially.

Printing from an Indexed File Randomly When Inquiries Are Made

Indexed files may also be read randomly for printing purposes. That is, customers may call a store at any time to inquire about their current balance. Since these inquiries are random, we will need to access the indexed file randomly in order to print a reply to the inquiry. Figure 18.5 illustrates the PROCEDURE DIVISION for a program that makes random inquiries about the status of master disk records. The user enters a customer's account number and the computer accesses the corresponding disk record and prints the balance due for that customer.

Figure 18.4
Program that accesses an
indexed file sequentially.

```
       IDENTIFICATION DIVISION.
       PROGRAM-ID. SAMPLE.
      ****************************************************
      *    THIS PROGRAM ACCESSES AN INDEXED             *
      *    SEQUENTIAL FILE SEQUENTIALLY.                *
      *    DATA IS PRINTED FROM THE FILE IN THE         *
      *    SAME MANNER AS IF THE FILE WAS ON TAPE.      *
      ****************************************************
       ENVIRONMENT DIVISION.
       INPUT-OUTPUT SECTION.
       FILE-CONTROL.
           SELECT ACCTS-RECVBLE ASSIGN TO DA-I-SYS004
               ORGANIZATION IS INDEXED
               ACCESS IS SEQUENTIAL
               RECORD KEY IS M-CUST-NO-IN.
           SELECT PRINT-OUT ASSIGN TO UR-S-SYSOUT.
      *
       DATA DIVISION.
       FILE SECTION.
       FD  ACCTS-RECVBLE
           LABEL RECORDS ARE STANDARD
           BLOCK CONTAINS 20 RECORDS.
       01  MASTER-REC.
           05  M-CUST-NO-IN               PIC 9(9).
           05  M-NAME-IN                  PIC X(20).
           05  M-SALARY-IN                PIC 9(5).
           05  FILLER                     PIC X(66).
       FD  PRINT-OUT
           LABEL RECORDS ARE OMITTED.
       01  PRINT-REC                      PIC X(133).
       WORKING-STORAGE SECTION.
       01  WORK-AREAS.
           05  ARE-THERE-MORE-RECORDS     PIC X(3)   VALUE 'YES'.
               88  NO-MORE-RECORDS                   VALUE 'NO '.
           05  WS-LINE-CT                 PIC 99     VALUE ZEROS.
           05  WS-PAGE-CT                 PIC 999    VALUE ZEROS.
       01  HDG.
           05  FILLER                     PIC X(78)
                            VALUE 'PAYROLL SUMMARY REPORT'
                            JUSTIFIED RIGHT.
           05  FILLER                     PIC X(25) VALUE 'PAGE'
                            JUSTIFIED RIGHT.
           05  PAGE-OUT                   PIC ZZ9.
           05  FILLER                     PIC X(27) VALUE SPACES.
       01  DETAIL-REC.
           05  FILLER                     PIC X(10) VALUE SPACES.
           05  CUST-NO-OUT                PIC 9(9).
           05  FILLER                     PIC X(10) VALUE SPACES.
           05  NAME-OUT                   PIC X(20).
           05  FILLER                     PIC X(10) VALUE SPACES.
           05  SALARY-OUT                 PIC $ZZ,ZZZ.ZZ.
           05  FILLER                     PIC X(64) VALUE SPACES.
      *
       PROCEDURE DIVISION.
       100-MAIN-MODULE.
           OPEN INPUT ACCTS-RECVBLE
               OUTPUT PRINT-OUT.
           PERFORM 300-HDG-RTN.
           READ ACCTS-RECVBLE
               AT END MOVE 'NO ' TO ARE-THERE-MORE-RECORDS.
           PERFORM 200-CALC-RTN
               UNTIL NO-MORE-RECORDS.
           CLOSE ACCTS-RECVBLE
               PRINT-OUT.
           STOP RUN.
       200-CALC-RTN.
           MOVE M-CUST-NO-IN TO CUST-NO-OUT.
           MOVE M-NAME-IN TO NAME-OUT.
           MOVE M-SALARY-IN TO SALARY-OUT.
           WRITE PRINT-REC FROM DETAIL-REC
               AFTER ADVANCING 2 LINES.
           ADD 1 TO WS-LINE-CT.
           IF  WS-LINE-CT > 25
               PERFORM 300-HDG-RTN.
           READ ACCTS-RECVBLE
               AT END MOVE 'NO ' TO ARE-THERE-MORE-RECORDS.
       300-HDG-RTN.
           ADD 1 TO WS-PAGE-CT.
           MOVE WS-PAGE-CT TO PAGE-OUT.
           WRITE PRINT-REC FROM HDG
               AFTER ADVANCING PAGE.
           MOVE ZEROS TO WS-LINE-CT.
```

This is a typical SELECT
statement for an indexed
file that is to be accessed
sequentially

An AT END clause is used
with an indexed file when
is accessed sequentially

Figure 18.5
PROCEDURE DIVISION for a
program that makes random
inquiries about the status of
master disk records.

```
100-MAIN-MODULE.
    OPEN INPUT  QUERY-FILE
                ACCTS-RECVBLE
         OUTPUT PRINT-FILE.
    READ QUERY-FILE
        AT END MOVE 'NO ' TO ARE-THERE-MORE-RECORDS.
    PERFORM 200-CALC-RTN
        UNTIL THERE-ARE-NO-MORE-RECORDS.
    CLOSE QUERY-FILE
          ACCTS-RECVBLE
          PRINT-FILE.
    STOP RUN.
200-CALC-RTN.
    MOVE Q-ACCT-NO TO ACCT-NO.
    READ ACCTS-RECVBLE
         INVALID KEY
             DISPLAY 'ERROR ', ACCT-NO
             MOVE 1 TO WS-ERR-CODE.
    IF  NO-ERR
        MOVE BAL-DUE TO BAL-DUE-OUT
        MOVE ACCT-NO TO ACCT-OUT
        WRITE PRINT-REC
    ELSE
        MOVE O TO WS-ERR-CODE.
    READ QUERY-FILE
        AT END MOVE 'NO ' TO ARE-THERE-MORE-RECORDS.
```

D. Updating an Indexed File with Multiple Transaction Records for Each Master Record

In Chapter 16, we illustrated *two separate types* of updates for sequential master files: when (1) only one transaction per master is permitted or when (2) multiple transactions per master are permitted. With indexed master files, the *same procedure* can be used regardless of the number of transactions per master. That is, we can REWRITE the *same* master disk record each time a transaction record is read. Suppose 10 transaction records for a given master record are needed to add 10 amounts to the master's balance due. We simply retrieve the master record 10 times and each time add the corresponding transaction amount to the master record's balance due.

Thus, an indexed file update is exactly *the same* regardless of whether there is only one transaction record per master or there are multiple transactions per master.

Self-Test

1. (T or F) Records can be added directly to a disk file.
2. A field called a _____ within each record in an indexed file is used to locate records on the disk.
3. To access records in an indexed file randomly, we move the transaction record's key field to the _____.
4. When a record is to be deleted from an indexed file, we code _____.
5. The INVALID KEY option can be part of a _____ or _____ statement.
6. The INVALID KEY option tests the validity of the _____ KEY.
7. If READ FILE-X INVALID KEY PERFORM 800-ERROR-1 is executed, 800-ERROR-1 will be performed if _____.
8. (T or F) Indexed files are typically created sequentially.
9. If a record is to be added to a disk file, a (WRITE, REWRITE) statement is used.
10. Consider the following input transaction record:

1	Code (1-new account; 2-update account; 3-delete account)
2–5	Transaction number
6–80	Transaction data

   Consider the following indexed master disk record:

   | 1–4 | Transaction number |
   | 5–79 | Master data |

Write a PROCEDURE DIVISION routine to update the master file with input data. Stop execution if an INVALID KEY condition is encountered.

Solutions

1. T
2. RECORD KEY
3. RECORD KEY
4. DELETE file-name RECORD
5. READ; WRITE (REWRITE)
6. RECORD
7. a record with the indicated RECORD KEY cannot be found in FILE-X
8. T
9. WRITE
10.
```
PROCEDURE DIVISION.
100-MAIN-MODULE.
    OPEN INPUT TRANS
              I-O INDEXED-FILE.
    READ TRANS
        AT END MOVE 'NO ' TO ARE-THERE-MORE-RECORDS.
    PERFORM 200-CALC-RTN
        UNTIL THERE-ARE-NO-MORE-RECORDS.
    CLOSE TRANS
          INDEXED-FILE.
    STOP RUN.
200-CALC-RTN.
    MOVE TRANS-KEY TO MASTER-KEY.
    IF  CODE-X = 1
        PERFORM 300-NEW-ACCT
    ELSE
        IF  CODE-X = 2
            PERFORM 400-UPDATE-RTN
        ELSE
            PERFORM 500-DELETE-RTN.
    READ TRANS
        AT END MOVE 'NO ' TO ARE-THERE-MORE-RECORDS.
300-NEW-ACCT.
    MOVE TRANS-DATA TO MASTER-DATA.
    WRITE MASTER-REC
        INVALID KEY PERFORM 600-ERR-RTN.
400-UPDATE-RTN.
    READ INDEXED-FILE
        INVALID KEY PERFORM 600-ERR-RTN.
    MOVE TRANS-DATA TO MASTER-DATA.
    REWRITE MASTER-REC
        INVALID KEY PERFORM 600-ERR-RTN.
500-DELETE-RTN.
    READ INDEXED-FILE
        INVALID KEY PERFORM 600-ERR-RTN.
    DELETE INDEXED-FILE RECORD
        INVALID KEY DISPLAY 'ERROR ON DELETE'.
600-ERR-RTN.
    DISPLAY 'ERROR', TRANS-KEY.
    CLOSE TRANS
          INDEXED-FILE.
    STOP RUN.
```

III. Additional Options for Indexed File Processing

A. Using ALTERNATE RECORD KEYs

Indexed files may be created with, and accessed by, more than one identifying key field. To establish multiple key fields for indexing, we use an **ALTERNATE RECORD KEY** clause in the SELECT statement:

```
SELECT file-name-1
    ASSIGN TO implementor-name-1
    ORGANIZATION IS INDEXED
                      ⎧SEQUENTIAL⎫
    ACCESS MODE IS    ⎨RANDOM    ⎬
                      ⎩DYNAMIC   ⎭
    RECORD KEY IS data-name-1
    [ALTERNATE RECORD KEY IS data-name-2
            [WITH DUPLICATES]] . . .
```

1. More than one ALTERNATE record key can be used.
2. WITH DUPLICATES means that an ALTERNATE RECORD KEY need not be unique. Thus, fields like DEPT-NO or JOB-TITLE can be used as a key even though numerous records may have the same DEPT-NO or JOB-TITLE.
3. A record can be accessed by its RECORD KEY or any of its ALTERNATE RECORD KEYs.

Creating an Indexed File with Alternate Record Keys

Let us create an indexed file as in Figure 18.1, but we will add the ALTERNATE RECORD KEY clause to the SELECT statement:

```
SELECT   MASTER-FILE-OUT
         ASSIGN TO DISK1
         ORGANIZATION IS INDEXED
         ACCESS IS SEQUENTIAL
         RECORD KEY IS INDEXED-SSNO-OUT
         ALTERNATE RECORD KEY IS INDEXED-EMP-LAST-NAME-OUT
             WITH DUPLICATES.
```

If the ALTERNATE RECORD KEY is not unique, we use the clause WITH DUPLICATES. The key field(s) specified must be part of the indexed record. COBOL 85 indicates that keys should be alphanumeric, with a PIC of X's, but many compilers permit a PIC of 9's as well. If WITH DUPLICATES is not specified, the ALTERNATE RECORD KEY must be unique.

We typically use WITH DUPLICATES for a last name ALTERNATE RECORD KEY. Suppose an attempt is made to write a record with an ALTERNATE RECORD KEY of INDEXED-EMP-LAST-NAME-OUT and the name is 'BROWN' but WITH DUPLICATES was not specified. If a record already exists with the name 'BROWN', then the following statement will *not* write the record but will execute the INVALID KEY clause instead:

```
WRITE MASTER-REC-OUT
       INVALID KEY PERFORM 700-ERROR-RTN.
```

In summary, to create records on disk with last name as an ALTERNATE

RECORD KEY where two or more records might have the same last name, we must use the WITH DUPLICATES clause in the SELECT statement.

Accessing Records Randomly by Alternate Record Key

Consider a different program in which we wish to access a record that has SOC-SEC-NO as its RECORD KEY and EMP-LAST-NAME as its ALTERNATE RECORD KEY. We move the name we wish to access to EMP-LAST-NAME and code the READ as follows:

```
MOVE 'JONES' TO EMP-LAST-NAME.
READ INDEXED-PAYROLL-FILE
      KEY IS EMP-LAST-NAME
         INVALID KEY DISPLAY 'NO RECORD FOUND'.
```

The KEY clause is used with the READ statement when an indexed file has ALTERNATE RECORD KEYs that we want to use to randomly access a record. If the KEY clause is omitted, the RECORD KEY is assumed to be the KEY used for accessing the record. Include the KEY clause when you want one of the ALTERNATE RECORD KEYs to be used for look-up purposes.

Suppose ALTERNATE RECORD KEY WITH DUPLICATES was specified in the ENVIRONMENT DIVISION and there is more than one record with the same ALTERNATE RECORD KEY. The first one that was actually placed on the disk will be the one retrieved.

B. The START Statement

The **START** statement enables a program to begin processing an indexed file sequentially at a record location other than the first or next record in the file. Suppose an indexed file is in sequence by EMP-NAME. We may wish to print the file beginning with employees with a last name starting with 'M'.

The file to be processed this way must include an ORGANIZATION IS INDEXED and ACCESS IS SEQUENTIAL clause with the SELECT statement. Later on we will see that the ACCESS IS DYNAMIC clause could also be used. The format for the START is as follows:

Format

```
START file-name-1  ┌ KEY ┌ IS EQUAL TO            ┐              ┐
                   │     │ IS =                    │              │
                   │     │ IS GREATER THAN         │              │
                   │     │ IS >                    │  data-name-1 │
                   │     │ IS NOT LESS THAN        │              │
                   │     │ IS NOT <                │              │
                   │     │ IS GREATER THAN OR EQUAL TO*           │
                   └     └ IS >=*                  ┘              ┘
        [INVALID KEY imperative-statement-1]
        [NOT INVALID KEY imperative-statement-2]*
 [END-START]*
```

*Available with COBOL 85 only.

Let us begin with an illustration of how the START statement may be used without a KEY clause.

Consider the following input master file:

```
SELECT MASTER-PAY ASSIGN TO DISK1
    ORGANIZATION IS INDEXED
    ACCESS IS SEQUENTIAL
    RECORD KEY IS EMP-NO
    ALTERNATE RECORD KEY IS EMP-NAME
        WITH DUPLICATES.
    :
    :
01  MASTER-REC.
    05  EMP-NO
    05  EMP-NAME
    :
    :
```

Suppose the file is in EMP-NO sequence:

EMP-NO	EMP-NAME	EMP-NO	EMP-NAME	EMP-NO	EMP-NAME	EMP-NO	EMP-NAME
001	BROWN	006	SMITH	008	JONES	015	RICARDO
RECORD 1		RECORD 2		RECORD 3		RECORD 4	

To begin processing with an EMP-NO of 008 rather than with the first record, code the following:

```
MOVE 008 TO EMP-NO.
START MASTER-PAY
    INVALID KEY DISPLAY 'EMP-NO 008 DOES NOT EXIST'
                CLOSE MASTER-PAY
                STOP RUN.
READ MASTER-PAY
    AT END ...
```

When the record to be accessed has a key equal to the one placed in the RECORD KEY, the KEY clause in the START statement is not required.

In the above, a KEY option with the START statement is not needed; the computer will locate the record with 008 in EMP-NO, the RECORD KEY. That is, since 008 has been moved to the RECORD KEY, the START will locate the record with a RECORD KEY (EMP-NO in this case) of 008. The INVALID KEY clause is executed only if no such record is found.

Note that the START *locates* the desired record but it must be brought into storage with a READ statement. The READ follows the START and reads the record with EMP-NO equal to 008. When a READ is executed again, the next sequential record would be accessed. In our illustration, a second read would bring the record with EMP-NO 015 and EMP-NAME RICARDO into storage, since that is the next sequential record.

Suppose we wish to begin processing with an EMP-NO greater than 006. We would need to include a KEY clause with the START because we wish to position the file at a location *greater than* the value of a RECORD KEY:

```
MOVE 006 TO EMP-NO.
START MASTER-PAY
    KEY > EMP-NO
    INVALID KEY DISPLAY 'THERE IS NO EMP-NO > 006'
                CLOSE MASTER-PAY
                STOP RUN.
READ MASTER-PAY
    AT END MOVE 'NO ' TO ARE-THERE-MORE-RECORDS.
```

The READ will begin by reading the record with an EMP-NO of 008, which is the first one greater than 006 in our illustration. Note that a START locates the record; a READ is then required to actually access the record.

Thus, we must use the KEY clause with the START statement if the record to be accessed has a primary key either greater than or less than the one specified. In the next section we will see that the START is also used when an ALTERNATE RECORD KEY is needed for positioning the file. In that case, ACCESS IS DYNAMIC is required.

When using START, note the following:

RULES FOR USING THE START STATEMENT

1. The file must be accessed with ACCESS IS SEQUENTIAL (or ACCESS IS DYNAMIC as we will see in the next section).
2. The file must be opened as input or I-O.
3. If the KEY phrase is omitted, the relational operator 'IS EQUAL TO' is implied and the primary record key is the key of reference.
4. As we will see, we use KEY =, >, NOT < (or >= with COBOL 85) for accessing records by ALTERNATE RECORD KEY. We also use KEY >, NOT < (or >= with COBOL 85) for accessing records by a value that is correspondingly >, NOT < (or >=) the primary key.

C. Accessing an Indexed File Dynamically

1. The ACCESS IS DYNAMIC Clause

We have seen how indexed records can be accessed sequentially—when they are originally created and later on for reporting purposes. For this, we use the ACCESS IS SEQUENTIAL clause in the SELECT statement. Since ACCESS IS SEQUENTIAL is the default, we can omit this clause entirely when we wish to process indexed files in sequence. We have also seen how indexed records can be accessed randomly—for updating and inquiry purposes. For this, we use the ACCESS IS RANDOM clause in the SELECT statement.

Sometimes we wish to access an indexed file *both* randomly and sequentially in a single program. For this, we say that ACCESS IS DYNAMIC. Suppose we want to do a random update as in Figure 18.3, but before we end the job we wish to print a control listing of the entire indexed master file. This is a useful procedure because it enables the users in the payroll department to check the file.

2. The READ ... NEXT RECORD ... Instruction

To process records both randomly and sequentially in a single file, ACCESS IS DYNAMIC must be specified. To indicate that we wish to read records in sequence from a file accessed dynamically, we must use a **NEXT RECORD** clause:

```
SELECT INDEXED-PAY ASSIGN TO DISK1
       ORGANIZATION IS INDEXED
       ACCESS IS DYNAMIC
       RECORD KEY IS EMP-NO.
   :
MOVE 006 TO EMP-NO.
START INDEXED-PAY
    INVALID KEY DISPLAY 'EMP-NO 006 DOES NOT EXIST'
                CLOSE INDEXED-PAY
                STOP RUN.
READ INDEXED-PAY NEXT RECORD
    AT END MOVE 'NO ' TO ARE-THERE-MORE-RECORDS.
PERFORM 200-SEQ-PRINT
    UNTIL NO-MORE-DATA.
```

```
       ⋮
  200-SEQ-PRINT.
       ⋮

      READ INDEXED-PAY NEXT RECORD
          AT END MOVE 'NO ' TO ARE-THERE-MORE-RECORDS.
```

This NEXT RECORD clause is not necessary when ACCESS IS SEQUENTIAL has been coded and a standard sequential READ is used. It is used for sequentially reading from a file that has been accessed dynamically or for sequentially reading from a file using an ALTERNATE RECORD KEY.

Consider again the update procedure in Figure 18.3 that accesses a file randomly. Suppose we now want to access it sequentially. We must change the SELECT statement so that ACCESS IS DYNAMIC. Then at 900-END-OF-JOB we code:

```
900-END-OF-JOB.
    MOVE LOW-VALUES TO MASTER-SSNO-IO.
    START MASTER-FILE-IO
        KEY > MASTER-SSNO-IO                         ◄───── Positions the file at the first record.
        INVALID KEY PERFORM 1100-END-IT.
    READ MASTER-FILE-IO NEXT RECORD ◄
        AT END MOVE 'NO ' TO ARE-THERE-MORE-RECORDS.        The NEXT RECORD clause is used
    PERFORM 1000-CONTROL-LIST                               when reading sequentially from a
        UNTIL NO-MORE-RECORDS.                              file specified with an ACCESS IS
    PERFORM 1100-END-IT.                                    DYNAMIC clause.
1000-CONTROL-LIST.
    DISPLAY MASTER-REC-IO.
    READ MASTER-FILE-IO NEXT RECORD ◄
        AT END MOVE 'NO ' TO ARE-THERE-MORE-RECORDS.
1100-END-IT.
    CLOSE TRANS-FILE-IN
          MASTER-FILE-IO.
    STOP-RUN.
```

Moving LOW-VALUES to the RECORD KEY called MASTER-SSNO-IO and then starting the file at a RECORD KEY > MASTER-SSNO-IO ensures that the computer will begin *at the beginning of the file.*

If you omit the START in this procedure, the next record to be read will be the one directly following the last random access. Thus, if the last record updated had a Social Security number of 882073821, the next sequential Social Security number will be the one accessed. To begin a sequential access of an indexed file at the beginning of the file after the file has already been accessed randomly, use the START verb. We also use the START verb to begin sequential access of a file from some point other than where the file is currently positioned, as described below.

3. Sequential Access of Records with the Use of Alternate Record Keys

Suppose you wish to do an alphabetic printing of input records beginning with last names of 'J'. This can be accomplished if we have established EMP-LAST-NAME as an ALTERNATE RECORD KEY:

```
        MOVE 'J' TO EMP-LAST-NAME.
        START MASTER-PAY
            KEY NOT < EMP-LAST-NAME
            INVALID KEY DISPLAY 'ALL EMP-LAST-NAMES BEGIN WITH A-I'
                        CLOSE MASTER-PAY
                        STOP RUN.
        READ MASTER-PAY NEXT RECORD
            AT END MOVE 'NO ' TO ARE-THERE-MORE-RECORDS.
        PERFORM 200-PRINT-RTN
            UNTIL NO-MORE-RECORDS.
            ⋮
    200-PRINT-RTN.
        MOVE EMP-LAST-NAME TO LAST-NAME-OUT.
```

```
WRITE PRINT-REC FROM NAME-REC.
READ MASTER-PAY NEXT RECORD
        AT END MOVE 'NO ' TO ARE-THERE-MORE-RECORDS.
```

In this case EMP-LAST-NAME is the ALTERNATE RECORD KEY and a sequential read means reading records in sequence by that ALTERNATE KEY. Thus, the NEXT RECORD clause in the READ MASTER-PAY instruction is necessary when we wish to access the records sequentially by an ALTERNATE RECORD KEY.

The records in our file would print as follows:

```
JONES
RICARDO
SMITH
```

Note that these records print in order by last name even though the file is not in alphabetic order. This is because the ALTERNATE RECORD KEY index itself is stored in sequence. Hence, each READ can result in a sequential access by last name because the computer looks up the next sequential last name from the index.

4. A Review of INVALID KEY Clauses

A review of how the INVALID KEY clause is used with input-output verbs follows:

WHAT INVALID KEY **MEANS**

Operation	Meaning
READ	There is no existing record on the file with the specified key.
WRITE	The file already contains a record with the specified key. (It can also mean that the disk space allocated for the file has been exceeded.)
REWRITE DELETE START	No record with the specified key can be found on the file.

D. The FILE STATUS Clause

Consider the following coding:

```
WRITE INDEXED-PAY-REC
      INVALID KEY DISPLAY 'A WRITE ERROR HAS OCCURRED'.
```

If the INVALID KEY clause is executed, we know that a write error occurred, but we do not really know what specifically caused the error. It could be a duplicate key error, a sequence error, or some other error.

The **FILE STATUS** clause can be used with the SELECT statement to determine what type of error has occurred when either reading or writing a file.

The SELECT statement for an indexed file could include FILE STATUS as its last clause:

Format

```
                  SELECT ...
              [FILE STATUS is data-name]
```

where the data-name specified must appear in WORKING-STORAGE as a *two-position alphanumeric field*.

Example
```
SELECT INDEXED-PAY-FILE ...
    FILE STATUS IS WS-STATUS.
    :
    :
WORKING-STORAGE SECTION.
01  WS-STATUS          PIC X(2).
```

When an input or output operation is performed on the file, the operating system will place a value in WS-STATUS, which may be tested by the programmer. The following are possible values that may be placed in this field when an input or output operation is performed. FILE STATUS can be used with *any* type of file; we highlight those values relating to indexed file processing with an *.

Contents of the FILE STATUS **field after an input or output operation**	Meaning
Successful Completion	
* 00	Successful completion—no error occurred.
* 02	The record being processed has a duplicate alternate record key (*Note:* This is *not* an error when your program includes WITH DUPLICATES for the ALTERNATE RECORD KEY.)
04	A READ statement has been successfully completed, but the length of the record does not conform to the File Description specifications.
Unsuccessful Completion	
* 10	A sequential READ statement has been attempted, but there are no more input records.
* 21	A sequence error has occurred—keys are not in the correct order.
* 22	A duplicate primary key appeared during a WRITE.
* 23	The required record was not found during a read.
* 24	A boundary error has occurred—an attempt has been made to write beyond the pre-established boundaries of an indexed file.
* 30	A permanent data error has occurred (this is a hardware problem.)
34	A boundary error for a sequential file has occurred.
9x	Codes of 91–99 are specifically defined by the implementor—consult a manual.

As noted, the FILE STATUS clause can be used with *any* type of file, not only indexed files. The * entries, however, are those that apply specifically to indexed files.

Note that if the leftmost character is a 0, the I/O operation was successfully completed. If it is not zero, then the I/O operation resulted in an error.

Using the FILE STATUS field, we can display a more meaningful message if an input or output error occurs. Consider the following output routine:

```
WRITE INDEXED-PAY-REC
    INVALID KEY PERFORM 500-ERROR-RTN.
IF  WS-STATUS = '00'
    PERFORM 600-OK-RTN.
    :
    :
500-ERROR-RTN.
    IF  WS-STATUS = '21'
        DISPLAY 'KEY IS NOT IN SEQUENCE',
            EMP-NO-RECORD-KEY.
    IF  WS-STATUS = '22'
        DISPLAY 'DUPLICATE KEY',
            EMP-NO-RECORD-KEY.
    :
    :
```

Each time an input or output operation is performed on a file with a FILE STATUS clause, the specified data-name will be reset with a new value.

E. Exception Handling with the USE Statement

We have seen how an INVALID KEY clause can be used to indicate when an input or output error has occurred. The FILE STATUS positions defined in WORKING-STORAGE can be used to further clarify the type of error that has occurred.

The most comprehensive method for handling input/output errors is to establish a *separate section or sections* in a program. This technique is known as error or *exception handling* because it processes all 'exceptions to the rules.' The exception handling routines are placed in the DECLARATIVES segment of the PROCEDURE DIVISION, which itself consists of one or more sections. This segment always appears first. It must begin with a section-name. The USE statement is a coded in a section:

```
DECLARATIVES.
section-name SECTION.
    USE AFTER STANDARD  { EXCEPTION }  PROCEDURE
                        { ERROR     }
         ON file-name-1 ...
END DECLARATIVES.
```

The words ERROR and EXCEPTION mean the same thing and can be used interchangeably.

The following program excerpt will illustrate how exception handling is performed with the USE statement:

```
            SELECT INDEXED-FILE ...
                FILE STATUS IS TEST-IO.
                .
                .
                .
    01  TEST-IO.
        05  CHAR1            PIC X.
        05  CHAR2            PIC X.
                .
                .
                .
    PROCEDURE DIVISION.
    DECLARATIVES.
    A000-EXCEPTION-HANDLING SECTION.
        USE AFTER ERROR PROCEDURE
            ON INDEXED-FILE.
    A100-CHECK-IT.
        IF   TEST-IO = '23'
            DISPLAY 'REQUIRED RECORD NOT FOUND'
            .
            .
            .
    END DECLARATIVES.
    B000-REGULAR-PROCESSING SECTION.
            .
            .
            .
        READ INDEXED-FILE.
            .
            .
            .
        WRITE INDEXED-FILE.
```

Section header must follow DECLARATIVES

Will invoke the following paragraphs if any I/O error occurs with this file

Tests the value of the FILE STATUS field

Once a section header is used, as above, the rest of the PROCEDURE DIVISION must be divided into sections.

INVALID KEY is not specified because error handling is performed in the DECLARATIVES segment

The DECLARATIVES SECTION pertaining to the USE AFTER statement will automatically be executed by the computer whenever an input or output error has occurred. Thus there is no need for INVALID KEY clauses to display error messages.

Self-Test

1. To read an indexed file sequentially beginning at some point other than the first record in the file, you must use the _____ statement.

2. (T or F) The following is a valid use of the START verb if PART-NO is the RECORD KEY:

```
MOVE 123 TO PART-NO.
START INVENTORY-FILE
     INVALID KEY PERFORM 700-ERR-RTN.
```

3. (T or F) To begin a file at PART-NO 123 if PART-NO is an ALTERNATE RECORD KEY code:

```
MOVE 123 TO PART-NO.
START INVENTORY-FILE
     KEY = PART-NO
     INVALID KEY PERFORM 700-ERR-RTN.
```

4. (T or F) The START instruction actually reads a record into storage.

5. To read an indexed file both randomly and sequentially in the same program, you must specify ACCESS IS _____ in the SELECT statement.

6. (T or F) More than one ALTERNATE RECORD KEY may be established for a single indexed file.

7. Suppose ITEM-DESCRIPTION is an ALTERNATE RECORD KEY for an indexed file called INVENTORY. Code the program excerpt to read the record with an ITEM-DESCRIPTION of 'WIDGETS'.

8. Suppose the following clause is coded with the SELECT statement:

```
FILE STATUS IS WS-STATUS.
```

After a READ ... INVALID KEY ..., WS-STATUS will indicate _____.

9. (T or F) If you code a USE AFTER ERROR PROCEDURE ON file-name statement, you need not use an INVALID KEY with the READ or WRITE statement to display error messages.

10. (T or F) The USE statement is coded in the DECLARATIVES segment of a program.

Solutions

1. START
2. T—The record with a PART-NO of 123 will be brought into storage with the first READ.
3. T—The KEY = clause is required because we wish to access a record by its ALTERNATE KEY rather than its RECORD KEY.
4. F—It positions the index at the correct location, but a READ statement must be executed to input a record.
5. DYNAMIC
6. T
7.
```
MOVE 'WIDGETS' TO ITEM-DESCRIPTION.
READ INVENTORY
     KEY IS ITEM-DESCRIPTION
     INVALID KEY
          DISPLAY 'NO RECORD FOUND'.
```
8. whether or not the read was successfully completed; that is, WS-STATUS will contain a code to indicate whether or not an error has occurred.
9. T
10. T

IV. Using an Indexed Disk File as an External Table

Note that a table of data may be stored as an indexed disk file. With a table on an indexed file, it would *not* be necessary to read the entire table into storage using an OCCURS clause. Rather, we could randomly access each table entry from the disk as needed. We would use the key field in each input record to call into storage the corresponding table entry necessary for processing each input record. The indexed disk file would serve as *auxiliary storage*; an individual disk record would be called into primary storage as needed. This indexed disk file would be an external table but would differ from a standard table, which is read, in its entirety, into an area of primary storage that is defined with an OCCURS clause.

The main advantage of processing external tables in this way is to save primary storage space. Suppose we have table entries with the following format:

```
T-ZIP: PIC 9(5)          T-TAX: PIC V999
```

Assume the total number of zip codes is 40,000. Storing 40,000 zip codes and their corresponding tax rates would require 320,000 positions of storage (40,000 × 8). Many systems will not allot that much storage for an individual program and, even if they did, the program would not run very efficiently.

Since accessing disk records is fast (although not as fast as accessing data from primary storage), we could store the zip code table on disk and call into storage each zip code and its corresponding tax rate as needed. In this way, we would require only eight positions of storage for the disk area:

```
      SELECT INDEXED-TAX-TABLE ASSIGN TO DISK1
          ORGANIZATION IS INDEXED
          ACCESS IS RANDOM
          RECORD KEY IS T-ZIP.
      :
      :
FD   INDEX-TAX-TABLE
     LABEL RECORDS ARE STANDARD.
01   DISK-REC.
     05  T-ZIP          PIC 9(5).
     05  T-TAX          PIC V999.
```

To obtain the INDEXED-TAX-TABLE record desired, we would code:

```
400-CALC-RTN.
    :
    :
    MOVE ZIP OF IN-REC TO T-ZIP.
    READ INDEXED-TAX-TABLE
        INVALID KEY MOVE 1 TO ERROR-CODE.
    IF  ERROR-CODE = 0
        MOVE T-TAX TO TAX-OUT
    ELSE
        MOVE 0 TO ERROR-CODE
        DISPLAY 'NO MATCH FOUND'.
```

This is an *alternative* to traditional table handling as we learned it. Using the preceding, we do not need an OCCURS clause at all or a SEARCH statement. For each input record, we retrieve the corresponding indexed tax record from the disk by accessing the disk file randomly. Only one tax table entry is in storage at any given time. Although this saves storage, it means that a disk with the tax table information must be on-line during the processing of the program.

CHAPTER SUMMARY

I. Indexed File Processing
   A. ENVIRONMENT DIVISION—SELECT clause specifies:
      ORGANIZATION IS INDEXED
      ACCESS IS RANDOM—For nonsequential updates, inquiries, and so on.
               SEQUENTIAL—For reporting in sequence and updating
                       sequentially.
               DYNAMIC—For accessing both sequentially and randomly in
                       the same program.
      RECORD KEY—This is the key field in each disk record that is used for
      establishing an index and/or for accessing disk records.
         The SELECT clause can also specify ALTERNATE RECORD KEY(s) [WITH
      DUPLICATES] and FILE STATUS IS data-name for indicating whether an
      input or output operation was completed successfully.
   B. DATA DIVISION
      1. LABEL RECORDS are usually STANDARD.
      2. Records are usually blocked.
      3. Key field is usually the first field in the record.
   C. PROCEDURE DIVISION
      1. Creating an indexed file
         a. Indexed files are created with an ACCESS IS SEQUENTIAL clause in
            the ENVIRONMENT DIVISION.
         b. The WRITE statement should include the INVALID KEY clause. The
            statement following INVALID KEY is executed (1) if a record with
            the same key was already created, (2) if the record is out of sequence
            or, (3) on many systems, if the key is blank.
      2. Reading from an indexed file–in sequence
         a. Same as all sequential processing.
         b. Use READ ... AT END.
      3. Reading from an indexed file randomly
         a. ACCESS IS RANDOM (or DYNAMIC) in SELECT clause.
         b. If an indexed record is to be updated, use OPEN I-O.
         c. Transaction key is moved to the RECORD KEY and READ ... INVALID
            KEY is used.
         d. To write updated disk records back onto the disk, use REWRITE.
      4. Use START for positioning an indexed file at some point other than the
         beginning.

CHAPTER SELF-TEST

1. (T or F) Disks may not be processed sequentially.
2. (T or F) An indexed file is usually created in sequence by key field.
3. When writing a record onto disk, a(n) _____ clause should be used to test for a key that is not in sequence or is the same as one already in the indexed file.
4. To update an indexed file, the OPEN statement must have the following form: OPEN _____ file-name.
5. (T or F) An indexed file cannot be accessed both randomly and sequentially in the same program.
6. (T or F) The instruction START FILE-1 KEY > 008 will read a record into storage with a key greater than 008.
7. (T or F) The NEXT RECORD clause is always required to read from an indexed file sequentially.
8. (T or F) The FILE STATUS clause can be used with the SELECT statement to determine the specific type of error that has occurred when either reading or writing a file.
9. To delete a record from a master indexed file use a _____ statement.
10. To update an indexed record, use a _____ statement.

Solutions   1. F

2. T

3. INVALID KEY

4. I-O

5. F—Specify ACCESS IS DYNAMIC in the SELECT statement.

6. F—The START positions the file at the correct location but it does not read a record.

7. F—Only if the file has been accessed dynamically or an ALTERNATE RECORD KEY is being used for sequential access.

8. T

9. DELETE

10. REWRITE

PRACTICE PROGRAM

Write a program to update a master indexed disk file. The problem definition appears in Figure 18.6.

Notes

a. Tape records are to update amount fields in the disk file. If a tape record has the same transaction number as a disk record, process it; if not, display the tape record as an error.

b. Disk records are indexed; tape records are not in sequence by transaction number.

Figure 18.6
Problem definition for the
Practice Program.

Systems Flowchart

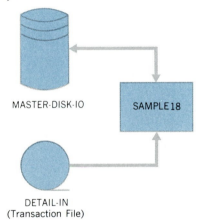

MASTER-DISK-IO   SAMPLE 18

DETAIL-IN
(Transaction File)

MASTER-DISK-IO Record Layout

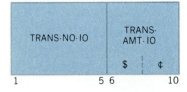

TRANS-NO-IO   TRANS-AMT-IO

$ ¢

1   5 6   10

DETAIL-IN Record Layout

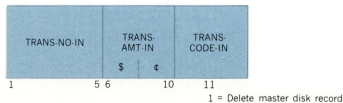

TRANS-NO-IN   TRANS-AMT-IN   TRANS-CODE-IN

$ ¢

1   5 6   10   11

1 = Delete master disk record

See Figure 18.7 for the pseudocode, hierarchy chart, and solution.

Figure 18.7
Pseudocode, hierarchy chart,
and solution for the
Practice Program.

a. Pseudocode

```
START
    PERFORM
        Open the files
        PERFORM
            Read a Transaction Record
        ENDPERFORM
    ENDPERFORM
    PERFORM UNTIL no more data
        Move Input Trans Data to Disk Area
        Read Corresponding Master Record
        IF  No Error
        THEN
            PERFORM
                IF  Delete Code
                THEN
                    PERFORM
                        Delete the Record
                    ENDPERFORM
                ELSE
                    Update the Record
                    Rewrite the Record
                ENDIF
            ENDPERFORM
        ELSE
            Reset error code
        ENDIF
        PERFORM
            Read a Transaction Record
        ENDPERFORM
    ENDPERFORM
    PERFORM
        End-of-Job Operations
    ENDPERFORM
STOP
```

b. Hierarchy Chart

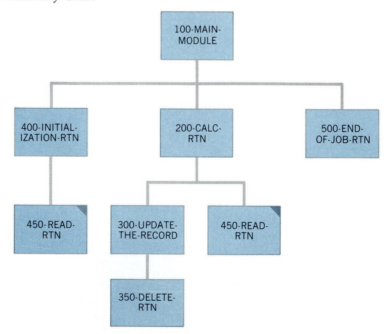

Figure 18.7
(continued)

c. Program

```
IDENTIFICATION DIVISION.
PROGRAM-ID. SAMPLE.
AUTHOR. NANCY STERN.
***********************************************
*    THIS PROGRAM UPDATES AN INDEXED FILE    *
***********************************************
ENVIRONMENT DIVISION.
INPUT-OUTPUT SECTION.
FILE-CONTROL.
     SELECT MASTER-DISK-IO ASSIGN TO DATA16
            ORGANIZATION IS INDEXED
            ACCESS IS RANDOM
            RECORD KEY TRANS-NO-IO.
     SELECT DETAIL-IN ASSIGN TO DATA16A.
*
DATA DIVISION.
FILE SECTION.
FD  MASTER-DISK-IO
    LABEL RECORDS ARE STANDARD.
01  MASTER-REC-IO.
    05   TRANS-NO-IO               PIC 9(5).
    05   TRANS-AMT-IO              PIC 9(3)V99.
FD  DETAIL-IN
    LABEL RECORDS ARE STANDARD.
01  DETAIL-REC-IN.
    05   TRANS-NO-IN               PIC 9(5).
    05   TRANS-AMT-IN              PIC 9(3)V99.
    05   TRANS-CODE-IN             PIC 9.
         88   DELETE-RECORD                       VALUE 1.
WORKING-STORAGE SECTION.
01  WS-WORK-AREAS.
    05   ARE-THERE-MORE-RECORDS  PIC X(3)      VALUE 'YES'.
         88   MORE-RECORDS                       VALUE 'YES'.
         88   NO-MORE-RECORDS                    VALUE 'NO '.
    05   ERROR-FOUND             PIC X(3)      VALUE 'NO '.
*
PROCEDURE DIVISION.
***********************************************
*   CONTROLS DIRECTION OF PROGRAM LOGIC   *
***********************************************
100-MAIN-MODULE.
    PERFORM 400-INITIALIZATION-RTN.
    PERFORM 200-CALC-RTN
        UNTIL NO-MORE-RECORDS.
    PERFORM 500-END-OF-JOB-RTN.
***************************************************
*   PERFORMED FROM 100-MAIN-MODULE. READS AND   *
*   UPDATES MASTER FILE.                         *
***************************************************
200-CALC-RTN.
    MOVE TRANS-NO-IN TO TRANS-NO-IO.
    READ MASTER-DISK-IO
        INVALID KEY DISPLAY 'INVALID TAPE RECORD ' DETAIL-REC-IN
        MOVE 'YES' TO ERROR-FOUND.
    IF ERROR-FOUND = 'NO '
        PERFORM 300-UPDATE-THE-RECORD
    ELSE
        MOVE 'NO ' TO ERROR-FOUND.
    PERFORM 450-READ-RTN.

300-UPDATE-THE-RECORD.
    IF  DELETE-RECORD
        PERFORM 350-DELETE-RTN
    ELSE
        ADD TRANS-AMT-IN TO TRANS-AMT-IO
        REWRITE MASTER-REC-IO
            INVALID KEY DISPLAY 'ERROR IN REWRITE'.
350-DELETE-RTN.
    DELETE-MASTER-DISK-IO
        INVALID KEY DISPLAY 'ERROR IN DELETE FILE'.

***********************************************
*   PERFORMED FROM 100-MAIN-MODULE.          *
*   OPENS FILES AND PERFORMS INITIAL READ    *
***********************************************
400-INITIALIZATION-RTN.
    OPEN INPUT DETAIL-IN
         I-O   MASTER-DISK-IO.
    PERFORM 450-READ-RTN.
```

Figure 18.7
(continued)

```
****************************************************************
*  PERFORMED FROM 200-CALC-RTN, 400-INITIALIZATION-RTN   *
*  READS NEXT TRANSACTION RECORD FROM DETAIL-IN           *
****************************************************************
 450-READ-RTN.
      READ DETAIL-IN
          AT END MOVE 'NO ' TO ARE-THERE-MORE-RECORDS.
****************************************************************
*  PERFORMED FROM 100-MAIN-MODULE, CLOSES FILES  *
*  RETURNS CONTROL TO OPERATING SYSTEM           *
****************************************************************
 500-END-OF-JOB-RTN.
      CLOSE DETAIL-IN
            MASTER-DISK-IO.
      STOP RUN.
```

d. Sample Master File Data Before Update

```
0000129694
0000250179
0000325389
0000554649
0000619359
0000728149
0000813532
0000908514
0001027222
```

e. Sample Detail File Data

```
00007093830
00009028380
00002233930
00001098980
00004094840
00005248830
00006064530
00003084630
00010000001
```

f. Sample Master File Data After Update

```
0000139592
0000273572
0000333852
0000579532
0000625812
0000737532
0000813532
0000911352
```

```
INVALID TAPE RECORD   00004094840
```

KEY TERMS

ALTERNATE RECORD KEY	Indexed file	Random access
DELETE	Interactive processing	Relative file
FILE STATUS	INVALID KEY	START
Index	NEXT RECORD	

REVIEW QUESTIONS

T   F

I. True-False Questions

— —   1. Indexed files can be processed interactively.

— —   2. An indexed file is usually created with ACCESS IS RANDOM but read with ACCESS IS SEQUENTIAL.

___ ___ 3. If the ACCESS IS SEQUENTIAL clause is included in the SELECT statement, then the file may later be accessed randomly if a KEY field is specified.

___ ___ 4. The procedures for updating an indexed file randomly are the same regardless of whether multiple transactions are permitted per master or only a single transaction per master is permitted.

___ ___ 5. The REWRITE clause may only be used with an I-O file.

___ ___ 6. The INVALID KEY clause may be used with READ or WRITE statements.

___ ___ 7. An indexed record can be deleted by coding DELETE (record-name).

___ ___ 8. The RECORD KEY entry must be a WORKING-STORAGE item.

___ ___ 9. The RECORD KEY entry is only used for indexed files.

___ ___ 10. Tape files cannot be accessed randomly.

II. General Questions

1. Write the ENVIRONMENT DIVISION entries for the creation of an indexed file called DISK-FILE.

2. Write the ENVIRONMENT DIVISION entries for an indexed file called IN-FILE that is in transaction number sequence but will be accessed by invoice number.

3. Explain the purpose of the REWRITE statement in a COBOL program.

4. Explain the use of the INVALID KEY option.

5. When is a file opened as I-O?

III. Validating Data

Modify the Practice Program so that it includes appropriate coding to (1) test for all errors and (2) print a control listing of totals (records processed, errors encountered, batch totals).

DEBUGGING EXERCISES

Consider the following coding:

```
PROCEDURE DIVISION.
100-MAIN-MODULE.
    OPEN INPUT TRANS-FILE
             I O INDEX-FILE.
    READ TRANS-FILE
        AT END MOVE 'NO ' TO ARE-THERE-MORE-DISK-RECORDS.
    PERFORM 200-CALC-RTN
        UNTIL THERE-ARE-NO-MORE-RECORDS.
    CLOSE TRANS-FILE
         INDEX-FILE.
    STOP RUN.
200-CALC-RTN.
    MOVE TRANS-NO TO DISK-TRANS-NO.
    READ INDEX-FILE
        AT END MOVE 'NO ' TO ARE-THERE-MORE-INDEXED-RECORDS.
    IF  TRANS-CODE = 'X'
        DELETE DISK-TRANS-REC
        REWRITE DISK-TRANS-REC.
    MOVE TRANS-AMT TO DISK-AMT.
    WRITE DISK-TRANS-REC
         INVALID KEY
             MOVE 'ERROR' TO MSSGE
             WRITE PRINT-REC FROM ERR-REC
    READ TRANS-FILE
        AT END MOVE 'NO ' TO ARE-THERE-MORE-DISK-RECORDS.
```

1. A syntax error occurs on the line associated with the OPEN statement. Find and correct the error.
2. A syntax error occurs on the lines associated with READ INDEX-FILE. Find and correct the error.
3. You find that the INVALID KEY clause associated with WRITE DISK-TRANS-REC is executed incorrectly. Find and correct the error. The DELETE and REWRITE also cause syntax errors. Find and correct them.
4. After execution of the program, you print INDEX-FILE for checking purposes. You find that records which were to be deleted were not, in fact, deleted. Find and correct the error.

PROGRAMMING ASSIGNMENTS

Code the following programs using an indexed file.

1. Write a program to update a master disk file that is indexed. The problem definition is shown in Figure 18.8.

Notes

a. Customer number is the key field for the disk file.
b. Do not create a disk record for any tape that does not have a corresponding master record. Display the contents of the tape record.
c. For all tape records with corresponding master records (these are master records to be updated), add the amount of purchase from the tape record to the amount owed in the disk record and update the date of last purchase.
d. There need not be a tape record for each master record.
e. Tape records are not in sequence.

Figure 18.8
Problem definition for
Programming Assignment 1.

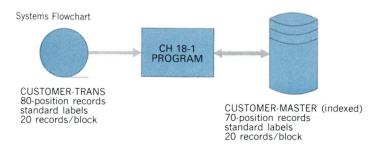

CUSTOMER-TRANS Record Layout

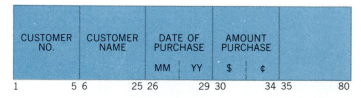

CUSTOMER-MASTER Record Layout

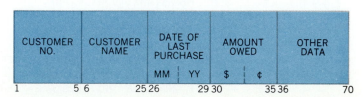

2. Write a program to create an indexed master payroll file from tape records. The problem definition is shown in Figure 18.9.

Notes

a. Employee number is the key field for the disk file.
b. Before placing a record on disk, add 5% to the employee's salary that is in the tape record.
c. Obtain a printout of the disk records.

Figure 18.9
Problem definition for
Programming Assignment 2.

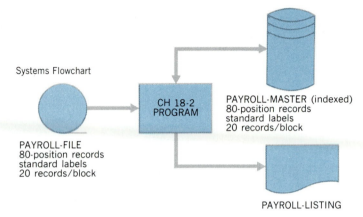

Systems Flowchart

PAYROLL-FILE
80-position records
standard labels
20 records/block

CH 18-2
PROGRAM

PAYROLL-MASTER (indexed)
80-position records
standard labels
20 records/block

PAYROLL-LISTING

Record Layout for PAYROLL-FILE and PAYROLL-MASTER

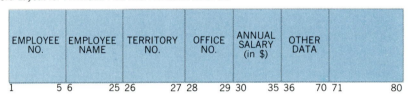

EMPLOYEE NO.	EMPLOYEE NAME	TERRITORY NO.	OFFICE NO.	ANNUAL SALARY (in $)	OTHER DATA	

1   5 6   25 26   27 28   29 30   35 36   70 71   80

PAYROLL-LISTING Printer Spacing Chart

3. Write a program to create an indexed master file from tape records. The problem definition is shown in Figure 18.10.

Notes

a. A table of product numbers and corresponding unit prices is to be created in storage from PRODUCT-MASTER. There are 50 product numbers.
b. Customer number is the key field for the CUSTOMER-MASTER file.
c. Amount owed = Quantity purchased × Unit price (from table).
d. Perform a table look-up using the product number from a PURCHASE-TRANS record to find the corresponding unit price in the table.

Figure 18.10
Problem definition for Programming Assignment 3.

Systems Flowchart

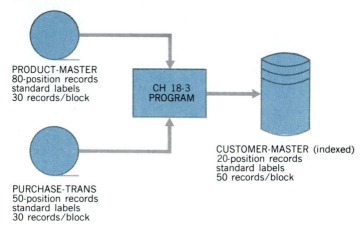

PRODUCT-MASTER Record Layout

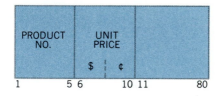

PURCHASE-TRANS Record Layout

CUSTOMER-MASTER Record Layout

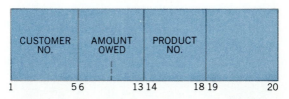

4. A disk file contains the following table records:

1–2   State number
3–4   County number
5–6   Tax rate .XXX
7–11   Not used

Labels are standard; the blocking factor is 100. State number is the key field.
  Write a program to create an indexed disk file from the following tape records:

1–5   Customer number
6–25   Customer name
26–28 Quantity
29–33 Price/unit XXX.XX
34–35 State number
36–37 County number
38   Not used

Labels are standard; the blocking factor is 50.
  The format for the output disk records is as follows:

1–37   (Same as tape positions 1-37)
38–45 Amount owed (XXXXXX.XX)
46   Not used

Labels are standard; the blocking factor is 75.

Amount owed = Quantity × Price / Unit + Tax rate × (Quantity × Price)

Tax rate is obtained from the table.

5. Three indexed disk files contain the following table records:

File 1   **File 2**
1–3   Employee number   1–3   Title number
4–20   Employee name   4–6   Job number
                                  7–20   Job name

File 3
1   Level number
2–8   Salary XXXXX.XX
9–20   Not used

Labels are standard; the blocking factor is 100 for each file. The first field of each
record represents the key field.
  Write a program to create an indexed disk file from IN-TRANS tape records with
the following format:

1–3   Employee number
4–6   Title number
7–9   Job number
10   Level number
11–80 Not used

The format for the output disk records is as follows:

1–3   Employee number
4–20   Employee name
21–23 Title number
24–26 Job number
27–40 Job name
41   Level number
42–48 Salary
49–50 Not used

Labels are standard; the blocking factor is 75.
  Employee name, Job name, and Salary are obtained from the three table files on
disk.
  (*Hint*: Define three input disk files. Use employee number in the IN-TRANS file
to look up employee name, and so on.)

19

Interactive Processing

OBJECTIVES

To familiarize you with

1. Methods of interacting with a computer at a terminal.
2. Use of ACCEPT and DISPLAY for handling input and output.
3. Text manipulation with the STRING and UNSTRING statements.

I. Processing Data Interactively

A. DISPLAY **Statement**

1. Format
One method for interacting with a computer is by using a terminal. A user keys or enters data, and the computer responds with a display on a screen. This is referred to as interactive processing.

The computer output to a screen is produced using a **DISPLAY** verb. The DISPLAY has the following format:

Format

$$
\underline{\text{DISPLAY}} \left\{ \begin{array}{l} \text{identifier-1} \\ \text{literal-1} \end{array} \right\} \cdots \\
[\underline{\text{UPON}} \{\text{mnemonic-name-1}\}]
$$

The identifier can be (1) an alphanumeric field, (2) an unsigned numeric field, or (3) a report item.

The UPON clause, which specifies the device or mnemonic-name, is optional. When omitted, data generally will be displayed on the CRT (cathode ray tube) or printer, depending on the standard or **default** established at a given installation. A DISPLAY is used for:

1. Displaying prompts on a screen when processing data interactively.

   Example: `DISPLAY 'ENTER ACCT NO:'`

2. Printing short messages to a computer operator on the operator's console or to data entry operators and users at their terminals.

   Example: `IF  AMT-IN NOT NUMERIC`
   `         DISPLAY 'INPUT IS NOT NUMERIC: ', AMT-IN`

3. Displaying output to the programmer for debugging purposes.

   Example: `DISPLAY 'THE SEARCH STATEMENT MATCH IS ',`
   `                UNIT-PRICE (SUB1),`

We use single quotes or apostrophes in this text for defining literals. Your system may use single quotes (') or double quotes (").

A DISPLAY verb may be used to print any data item, including an entire record. *No corresponding file* need be defined in the ENVIRONMENT DIVISION. Similarly, an OPEN or CLOSE statement would not be required. We may also say DISPLAY FIELDA, where FIELDA is *any* field defined in the DATA DIVISION, or we may say DISPLAY TOTAL-REC, where TOTAL-REC is described in WORKING-STORAGE. In fact, any field or record defined in the FILE or WORKING-STORAGE SECTION may be displayed. Similarly, we may say DISPLAY 'INVALID CODE', when the specific literal or message 'INVALID CODE' is to be printed.

Without an UPON clause the DISPLAY will write the output to a CRT or a printer, depending on the system's default. DISPLAY ... UPON (mnemonic-name) enables the user to display on any output device. A mnemonic-name is a device-name in this instance. If a mnemonic-name is used with the DISPLAY it must be defined in the **SPECIAL-NAMES** paragraph of the CONFIGURATION SECTION in the ENVIRONMENT DIVISION. The format is as follows:

```
SPECIAL-NAMES,
      implementor-name-1 IS mnemonic-name-1.
```

Example

```
ENVIRONMENT DIVISION.
CONFIGURATION SECTION.
     .
     .
     .
SPECIAL-NAMES.
     CONSOLE IS TYPEWRITER.    ←── Defined by implementor;
INPUT-OUTPUT SECTION.               device-dependent entry
     .
     .
PROCEDURE DIVISION.
     .
     .
     DISPLAY 'HELLO THERE' UPON TYPEWRITER.
```

CONSOLE is an implementor-name, which means that it is defined by the computer installation itself. Each computer has implementor-names for its own hardware. In the preceding example, CONSOLE refers to the terminal that is used by a computer operator for interacting with the computer. The word TYPEWRITER is a mnemonic-name assigned by the programmer to the implementor-name. The word TYPEWRITER (or any other user-defined term we want) can be used in the PROCEDURE DIVISION to indicate that output should be displayed on the system's CONSOLE.

2. Size of DISPLAY

When a field or literal is displayed on a terminal, console, or printer, the size of the data is restricted to the size of the display line. Most terminals have displays of 80 characters per line. Printers may be able to print 80, 100, 120, or more characters per line.

As noted in the instruction format, several fields or literals may be displayed with one statement.

Examples

```
(1)     DISPLAY FIELDA, FIELDB UPON CONSOLE.
(2)     DISPLAY 'THE MONTH OF ', MONTH.
```

Each DISPLAY statement prints one line of information. Thus, the following two routines will produce different results:

	Statements	Printed Results

(a) `DISPLAY 'INCORRECT TAX AMOUNT', TAX.` — INCORRECT TAX AMOUNT (contents of TAX)

(b) `DISPLAY 'INCORRECT TAX AMOUNT'.`
`DISPLAY TAX.` — INCORRECT TAX AMOUNT
(contents of TAX)

You should be careful about the use of the WRITE and DISPLAY verbs when the same device is employed. If a file is assigned to the printer in the ENVIRONMENT DIVISION, then displaying data on the printer may cause a problem. Depending on the system and the WRITE option used, the DISPLAY could cause *overprinting on the same line* that was already used for writing output. Hence, some systems do not even permit writing and displaying on the same device.

Format

With COBOL 85, the full format for the DISPLAY is as follows:

$$\underline{\text{DISPLAY}} \begin{Bmatrix} \text{identifier-1} \\ \text{literal-1} \end{Bmatrix} \dots$$

$$[\underline{\text{UPON}} \text{ mnemonic-name-1}]$$
$$[\text{WITH } \underline{\text{NO}} \text{ } \underline{\text{ADVANCING}}]$$

The clause WITH NO ADVANCING is most often used with CRT output if the display is prompting the user for a response. When the data is displayed, the CRT's cursor *will remain on the same line*.

Suppose we wish to prompt the user for an ACCT-NO. If we code:

```
DISPLAY 'ENTER ACCT-NO:' WITH NO ADVANCING
```

the user will be able to enter the ACCT-NO *on the same line as the prompt*:

ENTER ACCT-NO: ▲
└——— Cursor remains at this point

SUMMARY OF DISPLAY STATEMENT

1. A DISPLAY statement is used to produce a low volume of output. It is typically used for sending brief messages to a user or operator or for displaying fields during debugging.
2. DISPLAY statements can print output on the printer, computer operator's console, or any terminal.
3. Fields or records of data, defined in the DATA DIVISION, and literals may be DISPLAYed without the need for an OPEN statement.

B. ACCEPT Statement

The **ACCEPT** statement performs an *input* operation. It results in the *reading* of *fields* of data into some area of storage.

An ACCEPT statement is an input instruction that parallels the DISPLAY statement. As noted, the DISPLAY produces a low-volume of output data. The data displayed could be a literal, field, or record. Unlike the WRITE statement, the DISPLAY does not require a device assigned in the ENVIRONMENT DIVISION, an output area defined in the DATA DIVISION, or an OPEN statement in the PROCEDURE DIVISION.

Similarly, an ACCEPT statement reads a low volume of input data into the computer. Unlike the READ instruction, it does not require a device assigned in the ENVIRONMENT DIVISION, an input area defined in the DATA DIVISION, or an OPEN statement in the PROCEDURE DIVISION.

The format for an ACCEPT statement is:

Format

> ACCEPT   identifier-1
>   [FROM mnemonic-name-1]

The identifier may be any field or record defined in the DATA DIVISION. We may say ACCEPT CODE-X, where CODE-X is a work area in the WORKING-STORAGE SECTION or any item within an output record.

If the FROM option is not specified, data will be read from the system's logical input device, which is usually a terminal. To say ACCEPT CODE-X, where CODE-X is a four-position numeric field, will result in the storing of the first four keyed characters that are entered on a terminal.

We should not, in general, READ and ACCEPT from the same device.

The FROM option may be used with any device such as a typewriter. We may, for example, code ACCEPT data-name FROM TYPEWRITER if TYPEWRITER is assigned to a device in the SPECIAL-NAMES paragraph of the CONFIGURA-TION SECTION in the ENVIRONMENT DIVISION.

We have already seen, in Chapter 11, how the ACCEPT statement is used to read a date. Recall that ACCEPT data-name FROM DATE will read a YYMMDD entry into the data-name. If a date other than the current one is needed, such as date of last transaction, or end of fiscal year, then a date routine is required that also may use the ACCEPT.

Each use of the ACCEPT verb causes a temporary halt in the execution of the program. That is, after ACCEPT CODE-X is executed, the program pauses. The operator must enter input before the program will continue processing. This pause can make the ACCEPT verb inefficient or impractical for high-speed processing. Also, data is not transmitted from a terminal until the user hits the RETURN or ENTER key, which is similar to a carriage return on a type-writer.

The ACCEPT statement is an effective tool for transmitting a small amount of input data to the computer. It does not require the establishing of files and thus is easy to code. It should not be used, though, for large volumes of input since it is an instruction that can reduce computer efficiency. A READ state-ment transmits input data from an input device to the input area and contin-ues with the next instruction. An ACCEPT instruction causes a pause in exe-cution until the data is entered.

C. Combined Use of ACCEPT and DISPLAY for Interactive Processing

When the computer pauses after an ACCEPT statement is issued, the computer operator or user is expected to perform some function. Unless a prompt is displayed, *no* message is given, the computer indicates it is awaiting a response by displaying a question mark or a blinking cursor or a phrase such as 'AWAITING REPLY'.

It is not always feasible to expect the operator or user to be familiar with the program requirements and know what a halt in execution implies. For this reason, we generally DISPLAY a message *before* executing an ACCEPT statement. The message provides the necessary instructions.

Example 1   Consider the following coding:

```
DISPLAY 'ENTER DATE OF TRANSACTION -- MONTH IN 1-2, / IN 3,
    'YEAR IN 4-5'.
ACCEPT DATE1.
```

This literal prints a message to the user typically on a terminal. The ACCEPT statement follows, and the computer stops. The user reads the message, performs the required operations using the same terminal, and presses the RETURN key. The first five columns of the terminal line are then transmitted to the DATE1 field.

Example 2   ACCEPT or DISPLAY may also be used for an interactive query or updating of disk files.

Suppose a user at a terminal wishes to determine the BAL-DUE of several CUST-RECs stored in an indexed file. The PROCEDURE DIVISION could be coded as follows:

```
PROCEDURE DIVISION.
 100-MAIN-MODULE.
     OPEN INPUT INDEXED-CUST-FILE.
     DISPLAY 'ENTER CUSTOMER NUMBER OR 99999 WHEN DONE'.
     ACCEPT CUST-NO.
     PERFORM 200-CALC-RTN
         UNTIL CUST-NO = 99999.
**********************************************************
*  NOTE: 99999 IS A DUMMY ENTRY TO SIGNAL END OF DATA  *
**********************************************************
     CLOSE INDEXED-CUST-FILE.
     STOP RUN.
 200-CALC-RTN.
     MOVE CUST-NO TO CUST-KEY OF CUST-REC.
     READ INDEXED-CUST-FILE
         INVALID KEY DISPLAY 'NO SUCH CUSTOMER'
                     MOVE 1 TO ERR-SWITCH.
     IF  ERR-SWITCH = 0
         DISPLAY 'BALANCE DUE IS ', BAL-DUE
     ELSE
         MOVE 0 TO ERR-SWITCH.
     ACCEPT CUST-NO.
```

> These instructions will access the required record randomly from an indexed file.

This coding enables a user to enter a CUST-NO on a terminal and have the computer print the balance due owed by that customer.

> For COBOL 85 users, 200-CALC-RTN could be more appropriately coded as:
>
> ```
> 200-CALC-RTN.
>     MOVE CUST-NO TO CUST-KEY OF CUST-REC.
>     READ INDEXED-CUST-FILE
>         INVALID KEY DISPLAY 'NO SUCH CUSTOMER'
>         NOT INVALID KEY DISPLAY 'BALANCE DUE IS ', BAL-DUE.
>     ACCEPT CUST-NO.
> ```

We do not use an AT END with an ACCEPT statement, so we need some other method for indicating when there is no more terminal input. In this case, when the user is done, he or she types 99999 and the run is terminated. 99999 is referred to as a trailer value.

II. Text Manipulation with the STRING and UNSTRING Statements

When data is entered interactively, we sometimes need to convert it into a more concise form for processing purposes. Similarly, when data is to be displayed, we sometimes need to convert it from a concise form to a more readable form. We can use the STRING and UNSTRING for these purposes.

A. The STRING Statement

1. Basic Format

A **STRING** statement may be used to combine several fields to form one concise field. This process is called **concatenation**.

For example, we may have the following name field:

```
05  NAME,
    10  LAST-NAME      PIC X(10),
    10  FIRST-NAME     PIC X(10),
    10  MIDDLE-NAME    PIC X(6),
```

Suppose NAME had the following contents:

LAST-NAME	FIRST-NAME	MIDDLE-NAME
E D I S O N	T H O M A S	A L V A

1   10 11   20 21   26

We may wish to print the name in the usual way with only a single blank between each component as:

```
THOMAS ALVA EDISON
```

We can use the STRING statement to move, combine, and condense fields. We can also use the STRING to add literals such as 'WAS AN INVENTOR' to the name. The STRING, then, is a very useful instruction for text manipulation.

A simplified format of the STRING statement is:

Simplified Format

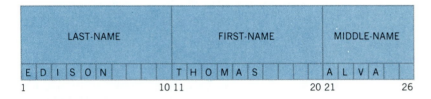

$$\text{STRING} \begin{Bmatrix} \text{identifier-1} \\ \text{literal-1} \end{Bmatrix}$$

$$\underline{\text{DELIMITED}} \text{ BY} \begin{Bmatrix} \text{identifier-2} \\ \text{literal-2} \\ \underline{\text{SIZE}} \end{Bmatrix}$$

$$\underline{\text{INTO}} \text{ identifier-3}$$

With this format of the STRING statement, we can instruct the computer to transmit only significant or nonblank characters in FIRST-NAME, MIDDLE-NAME, and LAST-NAME. Once a blank is reached, we stop transmitting that field:

```
STRING
    FIRST-NAME DELIMITED BY ' '
    MIDDLE-NAME DELIMITED BY ' '
    LAST-NAME DELIMITED BY ' '
    INTO NAME-OUT.
```

The delimiter itself would not be placed in the receiving field. Thus for our first example, THOMASALVAEDISON will appear in NAME-OUT using the preceding STRING statement.

Note, however, that we can use literals between clauses. Thus we would insert blanks between significant characters as follows:

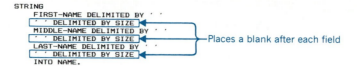

```
STRING
    FIRST-NAME DELIMITED BY ' '
    ' ' DELIMITED BY SIZE
    MIDDLE-NAME DELIMITED BY ' '
    ' ' DELIMITED BY SIZE
    LAST-NAME DELIMITED BY ' '
    ' ' DELIMITED BY SIZE
    INTO NAME.
```
Places a blank after each field

In this instance the NAME would be displayed as:

THOMAS ALVA EDISON

The delimiter SIZE means that the entire content of the specified literal is transmitted (it could have been a field as well). Each time ' ' DELIMITED BY SIZE is executed, a one-position blank is transmitted.

Consider the following record format:

CITY	STATE	ZIP	
N E W O R L E A N S	L A	1 1 3 2 6	
1	20 21 23	28	75

Suppose we wish to print the address. Simply to MOVE the three components and print them would result in:

NEW ORLEANS   LA11326

There would be nine spaces between the CITY and the STATE and no spaces between the STATE and ZIP.

Using a STRING verb, we can place the data in an ADDRESS-OUT field so that it will be more readable when displayed or printed:

```
STRING CITY DELIMITED BY ' '
    ', '   DELIMITED BY SIZE
    STATE  DELIMITED BY SIZE
    ' '    DELIMITED BY SIZE
    ZIP    DELIMITED BY SIZE
    INTO ADDRESS-OUT.
DISPLAY ADDRESS-OUT.
```

ADDRESS-OUT would then be displayed as:

NEW ORLEANS, LA 11326

As noted, the delimiter SIZE means that the entire content of the field (or literal) is transmitted. In the preceding, the delimiter for STATE and ZIP can also be SIZE because we will always print two characters for STATE and five characters for ZIP.

This STRING option may also be used for changing some of the contents of a field. You will recall that a MOVE operation always replaces the contents of a receiving field, either with significant characters or with spaces or zeros, depending on whether the field is alphanumeric or numeric. With a STRING statement, however, we can change specific characters. In this sense, the character manipulation features of a STRING statement are similar to an INSPECT.

Example
```
01   AGE-OUT          PIC X(12)    VALUE '21 YEARS OLD'.
       :
       :
     STRING '18' DELIMITED BY SIZE
        INTO AGE-OUT.
```

The result in `AGE-OUT` at the end of the `STRING` operation would be 18 YEARS OLD. In this way, we can make changes to a portion of a field, leaving the rest of the field intact.

There are numerous additional options available with the `STRING`, only some of which we will discuss.

2. OVERFLOW Option

```
STRING ...
     [ON OVERFLOW imperative-statement-1]
```

The `OVERFLOW` option specifies the operation(s) to be performed if the receiving field is not large enough to accommodate the result.

The clause `NOT ON OVERFLOW` is available with COBOL 85, as is an `END-STRING` scope terminator.

3. POINTER Option

We may also count the number of characters actually moved in a `STRING` statement:

```
STRING ...
     [WITH POINTER identifier-1]
     [ON OVERFLOW ...]
```

The identifier will specify the number of characters moved to the receiving field if it is initialized at *one*:

```
01   WS-COUNT   PIC 99.
```

Example
The following moves a `FIRST-NAME` field to a `NAME-OUT` field *and* determines the number of significant or nonblank characters in `FIRST-NAME`:

```
MOVE 1 TO WS-COUNT.
STRING FIRST-NAME DELIMITED BY ' '
     INTO NAME-OUT
     WITH POINTER WS-COUNT.
```

When the `STRING` is performed, `WS-COUNT` will be increased by one for every character actually moved into `NAME-OUT`. Thus, if `FIRST-NAME IS 'PAUL'`, for example, `WS-COUNT` will contain a *five* after the `STRING` operation. This means that it is ready to reference the fifth position in `NAME-OUT`. The following uses `WS-COUNT` to determine *the number of characters actually transmitted* in a `STRING`:

```
SUBTRACT 1 FROM WS-COUNT.
DISPLAY WS-COUNT.
```

Since `WS-COUNT` would contain a five after 'PAUL' is transmitted to `NAME-OUT`, we must subtract one from it to obtain the length of the move.

We may also use the `POINTER` option to move data to a receiving field *beginning at some point other than the first position.* If `WS-COUNT` in the preceding was initialized at 15, then `FIRST-NAME` would be moved to `NAME-OUT` beginning with the *fifteenth* position of `NAME-OUT`.

4. General Rules for Using the `STRING`

The following are rules governing the use of the `STRING` statement.

RULES FOR USING THE `STRING` STATEMENT

1. The `DELIMITED BY` clause is required. It can indicate:

   `SIZE`: The entire sending field is transmitted.

   Literal: The transfer of data is stopped when the specified literal is encountered; the literal itself is not moved.

   Identifier: The transfer of data is stopped when the contents of the identifier is encountered.

2. The receiving field must be an elementary data item with *no* editing symbols or `JUSTIFIED RIGHT` clause.

3. All literals must be described as nonnumeric.

4. The identifier specified with the `POINTER` clause must be an elementary numeric item.

5. The `STRING` statement moves data according to the rules for moving alphanumeric fields.

B. The `UNSTRING` Statement

1. The Basic Format

The **UNSTRING** statement may be used to convert terminal data to a form that is more appropriate for storing it on disk or tape.

For example, a program may include a statement that causes the following to print on a CRT or on a typewriter terminal:

```
ENTER NAME: LAST, FIRST, MIDDLE INITIAL
         : USE COMMAS TO SEPARATE ENTRIES
```

The message to the operator is fairly clear. When the name is entered, it will be stored in an alphanumeric field called `NAME-IN`. The routine may appear as follows:

```
WORKING-STORAGE SECTION.
01   NAME-IN          PIC X(36).
      :
      :
     DISPLAY 'ENTER NAME: LAST, FIRST, MIDDLE INITIAL'.
     DISPLAY '             : USE COMMAS TO SEPARATE ENTRIES'.
     ACCEPT NAME-IN.
```

Since each name has a variable number of characters, there is no way of knowing how large each individual last name and first name is.

Suppose we wish to actually store the name in an output disk record as follows:

```
01   PAYROLL-REC.
     05   NAME-OUT.
          10   LAST-NAME         PIC X(20).
          10   FIRST-NAME        PIC X(15).
          10   MIDDLE-INITIAL    PIC X.
```

With an UNSTRING statement, we can instruct the computer to separate the NAME-IN into its components and store them *without* the commas:

```
UNSTRING NAME-IN
    DELIMITED BY ','
        INTO LAST-NAME
            FIRST-NAME
            MIDDLE-INITIAL.
```

Suppose NAME-IN is entered as TAFT,WILLIAM,H. NAME-OUT will appear as follows after the UNSTRING:

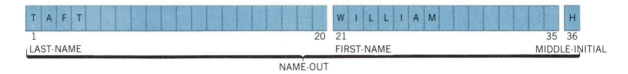

NAME-OUT

The format for the UNSTRING statement as we have used it is:

Format

$$
\begin{array}{l}
\underline{\text{UNSTRING}}\ \text{identifier-1} \\[4pt]
\left[\underline{\text{DELIMITED}}\ \text{BY}\ [\underline{\text{ALL}}] \left\{ \begin{array}{l} \text{identifier-2} \\ \text{literal-1} \end{array} \right\} \right. \\[10pt]
\qquad \left. \left[\ \underline{\text{OR}}\ [\underline{\text{ALL}}] \left\{ \begin{array}{l} \text{identifier-3} \\ \text{literal-2} \end{array} \right\} \right] \ldots \right] \\[10pt]
\underline{\text{INTO}}\ \text{identifier-4} \ldots
\end{array}
$$

We may use *any* literal, even a blank, as a delimiter. We may also ACCEPT a name from a terminal and UNSTRING it so that we can use just the last name for looking up a corresponding disk record with last name as a RECORD KEY or ALTERNATE RECORD KEY.

The UNSTRING also enables the programmer to use POINTER and ON OVERFLOW. With COBOL 85, NOT ON OVERFLOW and an END-UNSTRING scope terminator can also be used. END-STRING is also a valid scope terminator.

2. General Rules for Using the UNSTRING

SUMMARY
RULES FOR USING THE UNSTRING STATEMENT

1. The sending field must be nonnumeric. The receiving fields may be numeric or nonnumeric.
2. Each literal must be nonnumeric.
3. The [WITH POINTER identifier] and [ON OVERFLOW imperative-statement] clauses may be used in the same way as with the STRING.

Both the STRING and the UNSTRING have numerous options, many of which have not been considered here. Check Appendix A if you wish additional information on these verbs.

III. Designing Screen Layouts

A. Systems Considerations

As we have seen, data stored on a disk can be accessed randomly using a terminal. Most interactive terminals have a keyboard and a screen or CRT.

Consider an application in which a user wants to inquire about a record on an indexed file. The keyboard may be used for entering the key field. This input is also displayed on the screen. The program then ACCEPTs or reads the key as input. Next, the computer randomly accesses the corresponding record from a disk and DISPLAYs the record on the screen. Sometimes a STRING or UNSTRING is necessary to either store or display the data in a more appropriate format.

This type of interactive processing is used to find or display records for informational purposes. It is also used for enabling a clerk or user to change or update a displayed disk record. The program could ACCEPT certain changes and then REWRITE the disk record.

If a program includes an interactive dialogue between user and computer, the programmer or systems analyst must carefully design the elements of that exchange. Since users may not be familiar with computers, the exchange must be clear, concise, and as user-friendly as possible.

The following are systems concepts that should be considered when designing screen layouts:

1. The display should be informative but not cluttered. Most screens can display 24 lines of data with 80 characters per line:

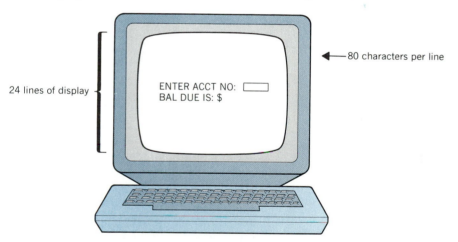

ENTER ACCT NO: ☐
BAL DUE IS: $

80 characters per line

24 lines of display

Include blank lines and wide margins to achieve an uncluttered look:

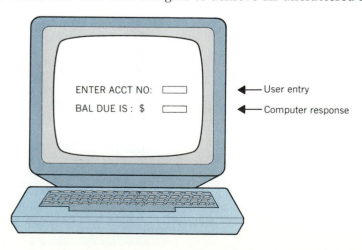

ENTER ACCT NO: ☐

BAL DUE IS : $ ☐

User entry

Computer response

2. Directions to the user, called **prompts**, should be clear and concise. To say "ENTER ACCT NO:" is a relatively clear and concise prompt. If you use the word "ENTER" in this exchange, be sure to use the same word in other prompts within the same program. That is, it could be confusing to change to a different type of prompt such as "KEY IN" or "TYPE IN." If terminology is standardized, there will be fewer misunderstandings. Depending on the experience of the user, you may want to add prompts such as "THEN PRESS RETURN". Such a prompt may be obvious to an experienced user but not to a novice.

   You may also want to add prompts such as "ENTER 99999 WHEN DONE" if 99999 is to signal an end of job.

3. Vertically align data for ease of reading, and position the cursor at appropriate places.

   With printed output, as opposed to displayed output, one line at a time in sequence is written. You cannot skip back to previous lines, for example. With a CRT, however, it may be possible to display a full screen of data and then direct the user to complete entries on previous lines. Consider the following:

   a. Display 1.

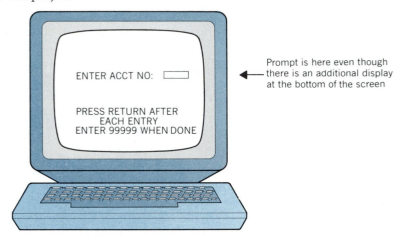

After this screen is displayed, the account number that the user enters will be displayed adjacent to the prompt "ENTER ACCT NO:". There will be a **cursor**, which is a blinking square or other highlighted symbol after "ENTER ACCT NO:" to remind the user that an entry is required. For the preceding, the cursor must be programmed to return to a previous line *after the full screen is displayed*.

   When the user responds, a new display can appear such as:

   b. Display 2.

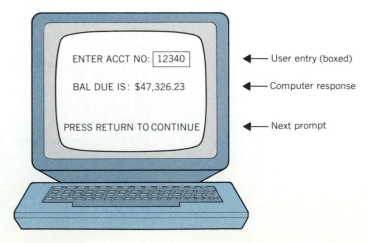

Screen displays such as this must be designed by the programmer or systems analyst to ensure a clear and concise exchange between user and computer. We use a Printer Spacing Chart for planning the format of a printed report; similarly, we can use a screen layout sheet (see Figure 19.1) for planning the displays and exchanges between user and computer.

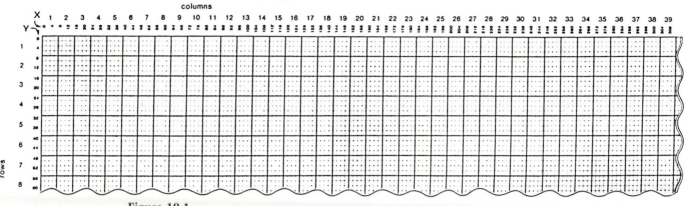

Figure 19.1
Screen layout sheet.

4. Where feasible, provide a **menu** of options available to the user from which he or she can select the desired operations to be performed:

```
DISPLAY 'TYPE 1 TO INQUIRE ABOUT A RECORD'.
DISPLAY 'TYPE 2 TO DELETE A RECORD'.
DISPLAY 'TYPE 3 TO UPDATE A RECORD'.
DISPLAY 'TYPE 4 TO ADD A RECORD'.
DISPLAY 'TYPE 5 WHEN DONE'.
ACCEPT CODE-IN.
```

The displays that would be printed represent a menu. The user selects a course of action by entering a digit from 1 to 5. The program would then EVALUATE CODE-IN and proceed to the appropriate routine.

5. Use screen features for highlighting.
Many screens can display certain data in color to highlight it. To distinguish user entries from computer responses, for example, you may want to use different colors. Or, if headings are required, you may want to display a company's name in color.
Other methods that can be used for highlighting entries on all screens, even monochrome ones, include:
a. Reverse video.
Most screens display data in a light color on a dark screen. This display can be programmed to be reversed for specific entries that are to be highlighted:

b. Blinking entries.
   An entry such as a direction to the user may be highlighted by having it continuously blink on the screen.
c. Dual intensity or boldface.
   An entry can be highlighted by displaying it in boldface.

Some screens can display graphics characters that enable the programmer to include boxes around certain entries or to include company logos or trademarks.

B. Nonstandard Entries for Displaying Screened Output

1. The Limitations of the DISPLAY and ACCEPT Verbs

Although the DISPLAY and ACCEPT can be used for interactive processing, they do have some limitations. With the use of simple ACCEPTs and DISPLAYs, vertical alignment and clear and concise terminology can be achieved; but advanced features such as color, highlighting, graphics, and positioning of the cursor require additional coding. Because each terminal is different and each computer interacts with its terminals differently, the more advanced coding used for screen displays are not part of the ANS standards and hence differ widely from compiler to compiler.

The DISPLAY and ACCEPT verbs have other limitations as well. An ACCEPT verb, for example, requires data to be entered in *fixed positions* and with a *precise format*. Consider the following:

```
05  AMT-IN          PIC 9(3).
```

In response to ACCEPT AMT-IN, an operator must key in the data as precisely three integers. If 0123 or 12.0 were keyed, the data would *not* be accepted properly. The ANS standards do *not* address these problems, leaving it to individual implementors to solve or ignore them.

Similarly, the DISPLAY statement displays a standard line of output. As we have seen, it is sometimes preferable to display output in boldface or with an underline or even in color. The COBOL standards do not set the rules for specifying these options either.

2. The SCREEN SECTION for Defining Screen Layouts

Some compilers have enhancements to the standard to improve interactive processing in COBOL. Because the need for interactive processing is greatest with microcomputers, micro-versions of COBOL tend to have the most advanced features. Micro-versions of COBOL usually have a SCREEN SECTION as the last one in the DATA DIVISION for defining screen layouts. They also have enhancements to the ACCEPT and DISPLAY verb that are very helpful for solving some of the problems we have described.

We will discuss some of the elements of the SCREEN SECTION that are common to many compilers. Keep in mind that because this section is not part of the standard, the available options will differ, depending on both the COBOL compiler and the hardware you are using. Most of the options presented here are available in one form or another. We have focused on the Microsoft version of COBOL for illustrating the SCREEN SECTION, because it is so popular.

The SCREEN SECTION of the DATA DIVISION describes the format of a screen so that (1) the DISPLAY statement can more dynamically display literals and data and (2) the ACCEPT statement can enter data in a more user-friendly way.

The following are some of the features that can be provided by a SCREEN SECTION:

Highlighted display—in boldface (dual intensity) or blinking.
Reverse video—the background and foreground colors are reversed.
Underlining.
Color display.
Sounding a bell to signal that input is to be entered.
Clearing the screen after each interaction.
Designating the specific positions in which data is to be entered on a screen.

The screen design is coded in the SCREEN SECTION of the DATA DIVISION, which follows the FILE and WORKING-STORAGE SECTIONs. The DISPLAY statement in the PROCEDURE DIVISION causes the screen to be displayed according to the specifications in the SCREEN SECTION; similarly, the ACCEPT statement enables users to enter input according to the same SCREEN SECTION specifications.

The SCREEN SECTION, like the other sections of the DATA DIVISION, consists of group items that themselves are subdivided into elementary items. Consider the following, in which the date is generated by the computer and a name is entered by the user:

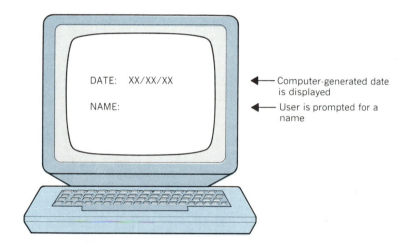

DATE: XX/XX/XX ← Computer-generated date is displayed

NAME: ← User is prompted for a name

The SCREEN SECTION elements that will enable the literals to print and the user to enter the date on the same line is as follows:

```
SCREEN SECTION.
01  SCREEN-1.
    05  BLANK SCREEN.
    05  FOREGROUND-COLOR 2.
    05  BACKGROUND-COLOR 9.
    05  LINE 1 COLUMN 1    VALUE 'DATE:'.
    05  COLUMN 8  PIC X(8)  FROM STORED-DATE.
    05  LINE 3 COLUMN 1    VALUE 'NAME:'.
    05  COLUMN 8  PIC X(20) TO NAME-IN.
```

STORED-DATE is a field already stored in the DATA DIVISION

The name is typed in columns 8-27. It will be transmitted to a NAME-IN field in the DATA DIVISION

To obtain the computer generated date and then to have the computer prompt for name, we code:

```
DISPLAY SCREEN-1.
ACCEPT  SCREEN-1.
```

Let us consider the SCREEN-1 entries in the SCREEN SECTION.

1. The first three entries within SCREEN-1 clear the screen and set the foreground and background colors.

2. The following two entries refer to LINE 1:

```
05   LINE 1 COLUMN 1     VALUE 'DATE:'.
05   COLUMN 8   PIC X(8)  FROM STORED-DATE.
```

Since the second line just has a column number, it is assumed by the computer that column 8 refers to LINE 1 specified in the previous entry.

STORED-DATE is a DATA DIVISION entry that must already have a value before we DISPLAY SCREEN-1. That is, we can read input with a date field that is moved to STORED-DATE or we can move a value into STORED-DATE before displaying SCREEN-1.

3. The next entry prompts the user for a name on LINE 3:

```
05   LINE 3 COLUMN 1   VALUE 'NAME:'.
```

4. The last entry will accept a 20-character field beginning in screen position 8 and move it to a predefined DATA DIVISION entry called NAME-IN:

```
05   COLUMN 8   PIC X(20) TO NAME-IN.
```

Since no line number appears here, the computer assumes that the data will be entered on LINE 3, as noted in the previous entry. NAME-IN is a field specified in either the FILE or WORKING-STORAGE SECTION.

In summary, we design screen formats using the SCREEN SECTION. Then we can display literals and any stored data with a DISPLAY statement. To enable a user to key in data, follow the DISPLAY screen-name statement with an ACCEPT screen-name statement. Thus, a single 01 screen item in the SCREEN SECTION can both DISPLAY and ACCEPT data.

The general form of a screen group item is as follows:

level-number   screen-name   [AUTO] [SECURE]   [REQUIRED]   [FULL].

1. Level-number ranges from 01–49.
2. Screen-name conforms to the rules for COBOL user-defined words.
3. AUTO—When an input field has been keyed, in its entirety, by a user, the AUTO clause enables the cursor to skip automatically to the next field to be inputted. Without the AUTO clause, the computer would wait for the user to hit the RETURN or ENTER key.

   Consider the following:

   ```
   ENTER ACCT NO:
   ENTER AMT OF PURCHASE:
   ```

   ```
   01   SCREEN1  AUTO.
        05   LINE 1 COLUMN 1        VALUE 'ENTER ACCT NO:'
        05   LINE 1 COLUMN 15   PIC 9(5)  TO ACCT-IN   AUTO.
        05   LINE 3 ...
             ⋮
   ```

   AUTO means that as soon as five integers are entered for ACCT NO, the cursor will *automatically* move to line 3. Without the AUTO clause, the cursor would not move until the user pressed the ENTER or RETURN key.

4. SECURE—With this clause, keyed data would *not be displayed*. This clause is used for security reasons. If a password or user identification is to be accepted, for example, the SECURE clause should be used.

   Typically asterisks (*) or pound signs (#) will appear in the data entry field in place of the actual data that is entered.

5. REQUIRED—This clause means that the corresponding entries to be accepted *must be keyed* before the cursor will move to the next field to be inputted. Pressing ENTER or RETURN without entering REQUIRED data will not bypass this entry; it must be keyed before the program can continue.

6. FULL—This clause means that the *entire* field must be filled. Pressing the ENTER or RETURN key will have no effect until the entry is complete. Thus, if the field has PIC 9(5), five digits must be entered; 123 would not be acceptable but 00123 would be okay.

When these options are specified, they apply to all elements in the group item. We will see that they can be specified on the elementary level instead, when they are applicable to some, but not all, screen entries.

The format for an elementary screen item is:

```
level-number   [screen-name]
     [BLANK SCREEN]
     [LINE NUMBER IS [PLUS]  integer-1]
     [COLUMN NUMBER IS [PLUS]  integer-2]
     [BLANK LINE]
     [BELL]
     [UNDERLINE]
     [REVERSE-VIDEO]
     [HIGHLIGHT]
     [BLINK]
     [FOREGROUND-COLOR  integer-3]
     [BACKGROUND-COLOR  integer-4]
     [VALUE IS  literal-1]
     [ {PICTURE}  IS  picture-string                      ]
     [ {PIC    }                                          ]
     [                                                    ]
     [      [ [FROM  {identifier-1}  ] ]                  ]
     [      [       {literal-2    }  ] ]                  ]
     [      [ [TO       identifier-2]                     ]
     [      [ [USING    identifier-3]                     ]
     [BLANK WHEN ZERO]
     [JUSTIFIED RIGHT]
     [AUTO]
     [SECURE]
     [REQUIRED]
     [FULL]
```

Level-number and *screen-name* are subject to the same rules as in the group screen description.

1. BLANK SCREEN will clear the screen, position the cursor at the home or first position, and return the screen to its usual color.

2. LINE and COLUMN specify the screen location of elements to be either displayed or accepted.

3. BELL causes a beep to sound when an ACCEPT is executed. This signals the user that data is to be entered.

   The next three options refer to *displayed data* only.

4. UNDERLINE underlines items that are displayed.

5. REVERSE-VIDEO causes items to be displayed with the foreground and background colors reversed.

6. BLINK causes a displayed item to blink.

7. FOREGROUND-COLOR numbers range from 0 to 15 and BACKGROUND-COLOR numbers range from 0 to 7. They could be specified if you are using a color monitor. The numbers refer to the following colors:

0 Black	8 Gray
1 Blue	9 Light blue
2 Green	10 Light green
3 Cyan	11 Light cyan
4 Red	12 Light red
5 Magenta	13 Light magenta
6 Brown	14 Yellow
7 White	15 High intensity white

8. VALUE is used for literals to be displayed.

9. PIC clauses are used for data fields to be displayed. We use the phrase FROM (data-name) with a PIC clause where the data-name indicates the DATA DIVISION field or record that contains the data to be displayed. PIC clauses are also used to accept data items. We use a PIC clause along with the phrase TO (data-name) to indicate where, in the DATA DIVISION, we wish to store the accepted entry.

10. BLANK WHEN ZERO displays a blank for a field that has a value of 0.

11. JUSTIFIED RIGHT—right justifies the item.

12. The last four entries (AUTO, SECURE, REQUIRED, and FULL) have the same meaning as specified with group items.

Example

```
SCREEN SECTION.
01   PASSWORD-SCREEN.
     05   BLANK SCREEN.
     05   LINE 5 COLUMN 18      PIC X(10) TO USER-PASSWORD
              SECURE BELL AUTO.
     05   LINE 10 COLUMN 10          VALUE
                                'ENTER PASSWORD ABOVE'.
     05   LINE 15 COLUMN 18     PIC X(25) TO USER-NAME.
     05   LINE 20 COLUMN 10          VALUE
                                'ENTER NAME ABOVE'.
PROCEDURE DIVISION.
100-SIGN-ON.
*GIVES THE PROMPTS
    DISPLAY PASSWORD-SCREEN.
*ACCEPTS PASSWORD AND NAME
    ACCEPT PASSWORD-SCREEN.
```

Another popular COBOL compiler for micros that is widely available is produced by the Ryan-McFarland Corporation and is called RM/COBOL-85. Although it does not include a SCREEN SECTION, it does have enhancements to the DISPLAY verb for displaying data on a screen:

$$\underline{\text{DISPLAY}} \begin{Bmatrix} \text{identifier-1} \\ \text{literal-1} \end{Bmatrix} \text{control-option-1} \ldots$$

Some of the control options are:

$$\left\{\begin{array}{l}\text{LOW}\\ \text{HIGH}\\ \text{REVERSED}\\ \text{BLINK}\end{array}\right.$$ Low intensity
Extra brightness
Dark characters on a light background
Displayed characters blink on and off $\left.\begin{array}{l}\\ \\ \\ \end{array}\right\}$

LINE   integer-1
POSITION   integer-2

$$\left\{\begin{array}{l}\text{ERASE}\\ \text{ERASE EOL}\\ \text{ERASE EOS}\end{array}\right.$$ Erases or clears entire screen
Erases or clears to the end of the line
Erases or clears to the end of the screen $\left.\begin{array}{l}\\ \\ \end{array}\right\}$

Example

```
DISPLAY 'This is it!' REVERSED LINE 2 POSITION 15 ERASE
EOS.
```

3. Enhancements to the COBOL Standard for the ACCEPT and DISPLAY Verbs

As noted, the SCREEN SECTION is a COBOL enhancement *not available with all compilers*. Similarly, there are enhancements to the ACCEPT and DISPLAY verbs available with some compilers that make interactive processing more user-friendly.

Consider the following options that may be available to you with the ACCEPT verb:

Format: Enhancement to the COBOL Standard

$$\underline{\text{ACCEPT}}\ \text{identifier-1}\ \underline{\text{WITH}}\ \left\{\begin{array}{l}\text{PROMPT}\\ \text{EMPTY-CHECK}\\ \text{AUTO-SKIP}\\ \text{BEEP}\\ \text{NO-ECHO}\end{array}\right\}$$

PROMPT—The prompt indicates the size and type of the field specified (0's are displayed for numeric fields, periods (.'s) for alphanumeric fields).

    Example: `ENTER CODE: 000`

The 0's indicate that a three-digit numeric field is to be entered.

EMPTY-CHECK means that at least one character must be keyed.

AUTO-SKIP means that the user need not hit the ENTER key when the full field has been entered. In the preceding example, if AUTO-SKIP were included with the ACCEPT statement, a user who entered 123 into a 3-position CODE field would not need to hit the ENTER key. The computer would automatically proceed to the next instruction after the data was entered.

BEEP means that the computer will beep or signal the user that an entry is required.

NO-ECHO is used so that data which is keyed will not be displayed. Instead, *'s appear on the screen. This option is used for passwords or sensitive data such as salaries that are not to be seen by everyone.

4. Customer Information Control System (CICS) as an Interface

Because the DISPLAY and ACCEPT verbs are rather limited, most mainframes use *utilities* for providing a more meaningful and user-friendly interaction between user and computer. A **utility** is a program or set of programs acquired by many different users to accomplish a relatively standard set of tasks. We discussed sort utilities in Chapter 17.

The most widely used utility for developing screen displays for interactive processing by mainframes is supplied by IBM and is called Customer Information Control System (CICS). **CICS** provides an interface between COBOL programs and the operating system. It can be used with programs written in other languages as well. In addition to generating meaningful screen displays, CICS also provides the interface for accepting input from numerous terminals in a multiuser environment. We will not consider the technical features of CICS in this text. Keep in mind, however, that COBOL programs used for interactive processing by mainframes usually interface with a utility such as CICS for generating displays and accepting data interactively.

CHAPTER SUMMARY

I. Both the DISPLAY and ACCEPT statements perform input/output functions on a low volume of data.

II. The DISPLAY statement may be used in conjunction with an ACCEPT statement for interactive processing. The DISPLAY prints an instruction to the operator, the operator enters the data, and the ACCEPT reads in the data.

III. No files need to be established nor records specified when DISPLAY and ACCEPT statements are used. You may ACCEPT or DISPLAY any field (or record) in WORKING-STORAGE or in the FILE SECTION.

IV. STRING

Purpose: To join or concatenate fields or portions of fields into one field.

V. UNSTRING

Purpose: To transmit or process a portion of a sending field rather than treating it as a total entity.

VI. There are various enhancements available with different COBOL compilers for designing screen layouts and making interactive processing more user-friendly.

CHAPTER SELF-TEST

1. In addition to the WRITE statement, a _____ verb may be used to produce output.

2. When displaying a data-name, it (must, need not) be part of an output record.

3. Besides the printer, data may be displayed upon the _____ or a _____.

4. If a device name is not specified in an ACCEPT statement, the _____ is generally assumed.

5. Joining two or more fields together is referred to as _____ and can be accomplished with the _____ statement.

6. Separating a field into different components can be accomplished with the _____ statement.

7. In a STRING statement, the field being moved may be delimited by _____, _____ or _____. In an UNSTRING statement, only _____ and _____ can be used as delimiters.

8. (T or F) In a STRING or UNSTRING statement, the delimiter specified must be alphanumeric.

9. Suppose a clause WITH POINTER CT is specified in a STRING statement, and CT has an initial value of 5. How will this affect processing?

10. (T or F) With an UNSTRING statement, the delimiter specified is itself transmitted.

Solutions

1. DISPLAY
2. need not
3. console; terminal

4. system logical input device—usually the console or a terminal

5. concatenation; `STRING`

6. `UNSTRING`

7. a literal; an identifier; the COBOL reserved word `SIZE`; literals; identifiers

8. T

9. The transfer of data will begin with the fifth position, not the first.

10. F—It delimits but is not transferred.

PRACTICE PROGRAM

Write a program to enter the account numbers of records to be deleted from a master indexed accounts receivable file. The account numbers are entered at a terminal. The master file has 100 character records and a `RECORD KEY` of `ACCT-NO` in the first five positions. Code the program with `ACCEPT`s and `DISPLAY`s so that the exchange between user and computer is clear and concise. Figure 19.2 illustrates the hierarchy chart, pseudocode, and program.

Figure 19.2
Pseudocode, hierarchy chart, and solution for the Practice Program.

a. Pseudocode

```
START
     Open the master file
     Display a prompt
     Accept Acct No
     PERFORM UNTIL Acct No = 99999
          Read the Record
          IF  not found
          THEN
               Display error message
          ENDIF
          IF  no error
          THEN
               Delete the Record
          ELSE
               Reset Error Switch
          ENDIF
          Accept Acct No
     ENDPERFORM
     Close master file
STOP
```

b. Hierarchy Chart

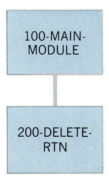

c. Program

```
IDENTIFICATION DIVISION.
PROGRAM-ID. SAMPLE.
ENVIRONMENT DIVISION.
INPUT-OUTPUT SECTION.
FILE-CONTROL.
     SELECT MASTER-AR-FILE ASSIGN TO DATA18A
          ORGANIZATION IS INDEXED
          ACCESS IS RANDOM
          RECORD KEY IS ACCT-NO.
```

Figure 9.2
(continued)

```
DATA DIVISION.
FILE SECTION.
FD  MASTER-AR-FILE
    LABEL RECORDS ARE STANDARD.
01  MASTER-REC.
    05  ACCT-NO             PIC 9(5).
    05  FILLER              PIC X(95).
WORKING-STORAGE SECTION.
01  STORED-AREAS.
    05  ERR-SWITCH          PIC 9        VALUE 0.
        88  ERR-SWITCH-OFF               VALUE 0.
        88  ERR-SWITCH-ON                VALUE 1.
PROCEDURE DIVISION.
100-MAIN-MODULE.
    OPEN I-O MASTER-AR-FILE.
    DISPLAY 'PROGRAM DELETES RECORDS - TYPE ACCT NO 99999 WHEN DONE'.
    DISPLAY 'ENTER ACCT NO OF RECORD TO BE DELETED'.
    ACCEPT ACCT-NO.
    PERFORM 200-DELETE-RTN
        UNTIL ACCT-NO = 99999.
    CLOSE MASTER-AR-FILE.
    STOP RUN.
200-DELETE-RTN.
    READ MASTER-AR-FILE
        INVALID KEY DISPLAY 'NO SUCH ACCT'
            MOVE 1 TO ERR-SWITCH.
    IF  ERR-SWITCH-OFF
        PERFORM 300-DELETE-THE-RECORD
    ELSE
        MOVE 0 TO ERR-SWITCH.
    ACCEPT ACCT-NO.
300-DELETE-THE-RECORD.
    DELETE MASTER-AR-FILE RECORD
        INVALID KEY DISPLAY 'ERROR ON DELETE'
*********************************************************************
*     For COBOL 85 users code 200-DELETE-RTN as follows:          *
*     200-DELETE-RTN.                                             *
*         READ MASTER-AR-FILE                                     *
*             INVALID KEY DISPLAY 'NO SUCH ACCT'                  *
*             NOT INVALID KEY                                     *
*                 PERFORM 300-DELETE-THE-RECORD.                  *
*         ACCEPT ACCT-NO.                                         *
*********************************************************************
```

KEY TERMS

ACCEPT	Default	SPECIAL-NAMES
CICS	DISPLAY	STRING
Concatenation	Menu	UNSTRING
Cursor	Prompt	Utility

REVIEW QUESTIONS

T   F

I. True-False Questions

__ __ 1. A DISPLAY statement may be used for printing fields, literals, or records.

__ __ 2. A WRITE statement, instead of a DISPLAY statement, is used to produce a low volume of output.

__ __ 3. A DISPLAY statement is often used to transmit messages to the computer operator.

__ __ 4. An ACCEPT statement may be used to read a field of data into WORKING-STORAGE.

__ __ 5. If a device is not specified in an ACCEPT statement, a disk drive is usually assumed.

__ __ 6. An ACCEPT statement causes a temporary pause in execution until the operator hits RETURN or restarts the program.

__ __ 7. Several data fields may be displayed with one DISPLAY statement.

—— 8. The POINTER is used with the STRING statement to count the number of sending fields.

—— 9. Several fields may be joined together to form one field using the STRING statement.

—— 10. The UNSTRING statement separates one field into several fields.

II. General Questions

1. Why are the ACCEPT and DISPLAY statements frequently used in place of the READ and WRITE statements?

2. A terminal is used for entering control data in a particular program. If the line begins with an X in column 1, then the MONTHLY-UPDATE routine is to be performed. If the line has a Y in column 1, then the WEEKLY-UPDATE routine is to be performed. Write the routine, with proper edit tests to accept and process this line.

3. When a particular error condition occurs, the program is to pause and print the message 'ERROR CONDITION X' on a terminal. If the operator types 'OK' in response, the program is to continue. If the operator types 'NO GO' in response, a STOP RUN instruction is to be executed. Write the routine necessary to perform these operations. Also, stop the run if NO rather than NO GO was typed.

   Consider the following for Questions 4 and 5:

```
01   STUDENT-REC              PIC X(40).
       :
01   STUDENT-PRINT.
     05   SSNO                 PIC X(9).
     05   FILLER               PIC X(10).
     05   FIRST-NAME           PIC X(10).
     05   MIDDLE-NAME          PIC X(10).
     05   LAST-NAME            PIC X(11).
     05   FILLER               PIC X(83).
```

4. Write a STRING statement that will condense the specified fields of STUDENT-PRINT into STUDENT-REC. The fields in STUDENT-PRINT are delimited by a space.

5. Assume there is data in STUDENT-REC. Write an UNSTRING statement to put the data into STUDENT-PRINT in the appropriate areas.

6. (T or F) We may use any literal, even a blank, as a delimiter in a STRING or UNSTRING statement.

7. Consider the following:

```
05   SSNO-IN    PIC X(11).
```

   SSNO-IN will have the following format: XXX-XX-XXXX. Transmit SSNO-IN to SSNO in condensed format by eliminating the dashes. SSNO has the following format:

```
05   SSNO    PIC X(9).
```

   Hint: SSNO-IN must be subdivided into three elementary fields.

8. (T or F) The OVERFLOW option of the STRING statement specifies the operations to be performed if the receiving field is not large enough to accommodate the result.

Consider the following for Questions 9 and 10, where MESSAGE-1 is a text:

```
05   MESSAGE-1   PIC X(500).
```

9. Remove all ANDs from the text and replace with commas.

10. Print the message with each line containing a *single sentence* from the field called MESSAGE-1.

III. Validating Data

Modify the Practice Problem so that it includes appropriate coding (1) to test for all errors and (2) to print a control listing of totals (records processed, errors encountered, batch totals).

DEBUGGING EXERCISES

Consider the following:

```
PROCEDURE DIVISION.
100-MAIN-MODULE.
    OPEN INPUT TRANS-FILE
         OUTPUT PRINT-FILE.
    ACCEPT TRANS-FILE
       AT END MOVE 'NO ' TO ARE-THERE-MORE-RECORDS.
    PERFORM 200-CALC-RTN
       UNTIL NO-MORE-RECORDS.
    CLOSE TRANS-FILE
          PRINT-FILE.
    STOP RUN.
200-CALC-RTN.
    MOVE IN-REC TO OUT-REC.
    IF  AMT < 0
       DISPLAY 'ERROR IN AMT'.
    WRITE PRINT-REC FROM OUT-REC
       BEFORE ADVANCING 2 LINES.
    ACCEPT TRANS-FILE
       AT END MOVE 'NO ' TO ARE-THERE-MORE-RECORDS.
```

1. The ACCEPT statements result in syntax errors. Correct the errors.
2. Is the ACCEPT statement used appropriately in this program? Explain your answer.
3. Is the DISPLAY statement used appropriately in this program? Explain your answer.
4. Would it have been better to DISPLAY an error message on a terminal or on the printer? Explain your answer.

PROGRAMMING ASSIGNMENTS

1. Print a table showing interest earned for each year of investment. ACCEPT the following from a terminal:

   1. Principal amount (up to six integers)
   2. Rate (.xxx)
   3. Number of years of investment (xx)

   Use a DISPLAY with an appropriate message to indicate what is to be entered on the terminal. (See page 337 for the formula to use.)

2. Read input records containing a series of valid passwords or codes. The codes are separated by slashes, and the last code ends with two slashes to designate it as the end of the record. Each code is numeric, and its maximum size is five digits; all codes are unsigned. A typical input record would appear as follows:

   ```
   /227/25/4/12773/2263//
   ```

   Write a program to retrieve each number from the input records and to display the valid passwords in list form.

3. Write a program using STRING statements to read a sentence entered in English and convert it to "Pig Latin." Words beginning with consonants are converted into Pig Latin as follows: TOY is OYTAY, ZOO is OOZAY, and so on. Words beginning with vowels are converted as follows: AUNT is AUNTAY, ACT is ACTAY.

4. Write a program to count the number of words and sentences in an input text entered on a terminal. Assume that every blank marks the end of a word and that a period marks the end of a sentence. Assume that the end of input is marked by a backslash (\).

5. Write an interactive program to accept a number between 1 and 100 in which the computer guesses the number in no more than seven tries. The only clues that the user will give to the computer are responses that indicate whether the guess is too high or too low.

UNIT VI
ADVANCED TOPICS

20

Using Advanced Debugging Aids and Improving Program Performance

OBJECTIVES

To familiarize you with

1. Methods used to debug COBOL programs.
2. Techniques used for finding errors.
3. Suggestions for improving the efficiency of COBOL programs.

I. Debugging Aids

A. Finding Errors in a Program

1. A Review of the READY TRACE and DISPLAY Statements

We have seen in Chapter 13 how debugging tools such as the READY TRACE or the DISPLAY can help to find logic errors. A READY TRACE, when executed (and if available), will list each module that the program performs. A DISPLAY is used to print or display fields or records that the programmer wishes to examine during the debugging phase. Three additional techniques can be used to further pinpoint logic errors.

2. The Debug Module

An additional method for debugging COBOL programs uses a **debug module,** which provides two types of debugging aids: (1) debugging lines and (2) debugging sections. Both debugging aids can be invoked by adding the WITH DEBUGGING MODE clause to the SOURCE-COMPUTER paragraph in the CONFIG-URATION SECTION of the ENVIRONMENT DIVISION.

Format

```
SOURCE-COMPUTER.
        [computer-name [WITH DEBUGGING MODE].]
```

a. Debugging Lines. When you specify the WITH DEBUGGING MODE clause, here, you may designate any source program line as a **debugging line** by keying a D *in column* 7. The D indicates that the designated line is for debugging purposes only. Such lines might DISPLAY intermediate fields or perform some intermediate calculations such as counting certain types of records processed.

The debugging lines with a D in column 7 will be compiled and executed whenever the WITH DEBUGGING MODE clause is used. Thus, during the testing of a program, you would include this clause.

When the program has been fully tested, the WITH DEBUGGING MODE clause can be removed from the SOURCE-COMPUTER paragraph. Then all debugging lines with a D in column 7 will be treated as comments and will no longer be compiled or executed. They remain useful, however, as documentation.

Any valid COBOL program statement beginning with the OBJECT-COMPUTER paragraph can be designated as a debugging line.

b. Debugging Sections. When the WITH DEBUGGING MODE clause is included with the SOURCE-COMPUTER, we can also perform error-checking operations whenever specified fields change. We do this by identifying these critical fields in a special section of the PROCEDURE DIVISION. Each time the specified field changes, we can print it out or perform any operation we wish. See Figure 20.1.

Figure 20.1
Program excerpt that illustrates the use of debugging sections in the PROCEDURE DIVISION.

```
PROCEDURE DIVISION.
DECLARATIVES.
Section-name SECTION.
Paragraph-name.
    USE FOR DEBUGGING ON BAL-DUE.
    .                      { Followed by paragraphs to be executed whenever
    .                        BAL-DUE is operated on in the main program
    .
Section-name SECTION.
Paragraph-name.
    USE FOR DEBUGGING ON TOTAL.
    .                      { Followed by paragraphs to be executed whenever
    .                        TOTAL is operated on in the main program
    .
END DECLARATIVES.
Section-name SECTION.

    .    { Main program goes here }
    .
    ADD AMT-IN TO BAL-DUE.◄── When this is performed the first section
                              within the DECLARATIVES will be executed
```

USE FOR DEBUGGING

The USE FOR DEBUGGING clause is coded in one or more sections within the DECLARATIVES segment of the program. These DECLARATIVES sections are separate from the main program and precede the sections or procedures that define the main program. The USE statement can monitor all references to an identifier, as illustrated in Figure 20.1. It can also be used whenever the following program elements are operated on or executed: (1) identifiers, (2) file-names, (3) procedure or section names, and (4) ALL PROCEDURES or sections. If USE FOR DEBUGGING ALL PROCEDURES is coded in a DECLARATIVES section, then each time any paragraph or section is executed in the main body of the program, the corresponding statements following the USE statement will be operated on.

Note that a DECLARATIVES segment can consist of one or more sections. The USE AFTER EXCEPTION PROCEDURE could be in one section, for example, and the USE FOR DEBUGGING in another section.

The full format for the USE FOR DEBUGGING statement is:

Format

$$
\text{USE FOR } \underline{\text{DEBUGGING}} \text{ ON } \left\{ \begin{array}{l} [\underline{\text{ALL}} \text{ REFERENCES OF}] \text{ identifier-1} \\ \text{file-name-1} \\ \text{procedure-name-1} \\ \underline{\text{ALL}} \text{ } \underline{\text{PROCEDURES}} \end{array} \right\} \dots
$$

The WITH DEBUGGING MODE, then, provides two debugging aids: (1) lines that can be executed when debugging a program but used as comments during normal execution, (2) the ability to interrupt a program at specified times to perform error-checking functions.

These debugging features have not been emphasized in this text because COBOL 85 has designated them as "obsolete," meaning that they will be deleted from the next standard. The American National Standards Committee has concluded that the use of extensive COBOL code to debug a program is somewhat complex and inefficient.

3. List the Actual Address of Each Instruction to Isolate the Statement That Caused a Program Interrupt

On many systems, job control commands can be used to provide a **PROCEDURE DIVISION map** that lists each instruction and *the actual storage location* where it is placed. If a program interrupt occurs, most computers will automatically indicate the storage location of the instruction that causes the abend, so that if you have a listing of a PROCEDURE DIVISION map, you can determine the specific instruction that was in error. This provides more information than the READY TRACE, which only lists the *paragraph* name that contained an error.

The job control command to obtain this PROCEDURE DIVISION map varies, but MAP=YES as part of the OPTION command is common.

The range of computer addresses that will be displayed in a map is also machine-dependent, as is the representation of an address. On some systems, an address such as AB9F is not uncommon. To actually determine the decimal equivalent of this address is beyond the scope of this text. For our purposes, it is sufficient to locate the COBOL instruction at that address without having to convert it to decimal form. Once you locate the specific instruction that caused an abend, it should be easier to debug the program. If you know which instruction caused an error but still cannot determine why, use a DISPLAY or obtain a memory dump (see next section) to determine the contents of fields used in the instruction.

4. Obtain a Memory or Storage Dump to Look at the Contents of Key Fields When a Program Interrupt has Occurred

Through job control, you can instruct the computer to print the entire contents of storage *if* an abend condition occurs. In this way, you can examine the contents of all data fields at the time of an error. This provides more information at the point when an error occurs than does a DISPLAY statement because *all* fields will be displayed on an abend condition.

A **storage dump** lists the contents of storage in both internal machine code format and in character format, for ease of reading. You need a DATA DIVISION map as well, which will indicate where in storage your fields are located. Typically, a job control command such as DUMP=YES is used with the OPTION command to get a storage dump.

Here, again, knowledge of machine-language representation is not necessary because most computers print the contents of storage in character form as well as in machine code format.

B. Understanding Program Interrupts

Each time an abend occurs, the computer prints a brief code that specifies the type of error that has occurred. The following is a list of common **program interrupts** and typical reasons why they occur.

COMMON PROGRAM INTERRUPTS	
Interrupt	**Cause**
DATA EXCEPTION	1. You may be performing an arithmetic operation on a field that contains blanks or other nonnumeric characters.
	2. You may be attempting to use a numeric field in a comparison and it contains blanks or other nonnumeric characters.
	3. You may have failed to initialize a subscript or index.
DIVIDE EXCEPTION	You may be attempting to divide by 0. (On some systems, an attempt to divide by 0 will *not* cause an interrupt but will produce unpredictable results.)
ADDRESSING ERROR	1. You may have placed (or left) an incorrect value in a subscript or index so that a table look-up exceeds the number of entries in the table.
	2. You may have coded nested PERFORMs or GO TOs improperly. This error will also occur if there is an improper exit from a paragraph being performed.
OPERATION ERROR	You may be attempting to access a file with a READ or WRITE before opening it.
SPECIFICATION ERROR	You may be attempting to access either an input area after an AT END condition or an output area directly after a WRITE.

II. Using Check Digits to Validate Data

In Chapter 13 we discussed validity checks commonly used to minimize the risk of errors. In this chapter, we will consider the use of a check digit, which can improve data validity for some types of programs.

A. Check Digit Defined

A key field such as Social Security number or account number is the most crucial field in a record because it uniquely identifies the record. If it is entered incorrectly, the record will not be easily accessible and the error will be difficult to find. Suppose we have a transaction file with an incorrect customer number that is being used to update an accounts receivable file. This type of error can result in the posting of a transaction to the wrong account.

Numeric fields such as key fields are more prone to being keyed incorrectly than are alphanumeric fields. An error in a name field, for example, is easier for the data entry operator to detect since vowels are expected in specific positions and names have recognizable contents. Suppose BROWN were to be entered as a name; BRXWN or BRIWN is likely to be spotted by either a data entry operator or a user as an error.

Names, however, are not generally useful as unique key fields since it is possible that two or more people might have the same name. Thus, numeric fields are most often used as keys. Note, however, that the problem of checking numeric fields during data entry is a more difficult one to resolve. Most often these numbers are initially entered by an operator as a series of unrelated integers. This means there is no visual procedure that the operator can use to check the field as it is being keyed.

One way to minimize keying errors is to *verify* all data entered by rekeying it or checking the inputted data against the source document *after it has been keyed.* This method of verification will detect 90% of all data entry errors. Although keying errors will be minimized by this verification technique, an error rate of 10% may still be unacceptable. To further reduce the chance of errors, many business applications use check digits as part of key fields.

A **check digit** is a computed integer added onto a key field such as Social Security number. The check digit becomes part of the key field and is used with it for identification purposes. Thus, a Social Security number will become a *10-digit field*—nine for the actual Social Security number and one for the check digit.

When a new record is added to a file, the check digit is computed using an arithmetic procedure. From then on, the key field will always include the check digit. Thus, if a nine digit Social Security number is to serve as a key field, a tenth digit called the check digit will be added and all 10 digits will serve as the overall key field.

Each time a transaction record or a query is entered to update or inquire about a master record, it will contain the full 10-digit code (Social Security and check digit). The computer will use the first nine digits entered to calculate a check digit; it will then determine if the tenth digit that was entered is, in fact, the same as the calculated check digit. If it is, the key was entered correctly and processing continues. If the tenth digit is not the same as the computed check digit, however, the program will assume that the nine-digit Social Security number was entered incorrectly. An error message will be displayed, and the record will not be processed.

B. Calculating Check Digits

Computations used to calculate a check digit are primarily designed to minimize the risk that **transposition errors** will go undetected. A transposition

As noted, PACKED-DECIMAL is only available for COBOL 85 users, but IBM and IBM-compatible computers permit a similar clause for all their compilers:

$$[\underline{\text{USAGE IS}}] \begin{Bmatrix} \underline{\text{COMPUTATIONAL-3}} \\ \underline{\text{COMP-3}} \end{Bmatrix}$$

We have not included all the options that can be used with a USAGE clause, only the most common ones. Appendix A has a complete list of options available.

Example The USAGE clause may be used with a group item or an elementary item. If it is used with a group item, then it refers to *all* elements within the group:

```
01   TABLE-X USAGE IS COMPUTATIONAL.
     05   ITEM-X OCCURS 40 TIMES   PIC S9(10).
     05   ITEM-Y OCCURS 40 TIMES   PIC S9(5).
```

B. USAGE IS DISPLAY

The USAGE IS DISPLAY clause means that the standard data format is used to represent a data item. That is, a single position of storage will be used to *store one character of data*. The clause USAGE IS DISPLAY stores *one character per storage position*, which is the default. Thus, unless the programmer specifies otherwise, data is always stored in DISPLAY mode.

C. USAGE IS PACKED-DECIMAL (COBOL 85) or COMPUTATIONAL-3 (COMP-3)(An IBM Enhancement)

PACKED-DECIMAL means that each digit is represented as compactly or concisely as is possible given the computer's configuration. Thus, each implementor determines the precise effect of the USAGE IS PACKED-DECIMAL clause. Typically, it is used to conserve storage space when defining numeric WORKING-STORAGE items because it enables numeric fields to be stored as compactly as possible.

On many computers, including IBM and IBM-compatibles, COMPUTATIONAL-3 or PACKED-DECIMAL (COBOL 85) enables the computer to store *two digits* in each storage position, except for the rightmost digit that holds the sign.

Suppose you move 1258738 into a WS-AMT field defined with PIC 9(7). This field will use *seven storage positions* in DISPLAY mode which is the default. If you define the field with PIC 9(7) USAGE IS PACKED-DECIMAL, it will, however, use only four positions:

12	58	73	8 +

We can save a significant amount of storage by using the USAGE IS PACKED-DECIMAL clause for numeric WORKING-STORAGE entries. It is also widely used for concisely storing numeric data on disk or tape.

Similarly, table entries are frequently defined as PACKED-DECIMAL fields:

Example
```
01   TABLE-1 USAGE IS PACKED-DECIMAL.
     05   ENTRIES OCCURS 1000 TIMES       PIC 9(5).
```

Each of the ENTRIES fields will use three storage positions instead of five. For example, 12345 can be stored as: | 1 | 2 | 3 | 4 | 5 + | rather than: | 1 | 2 | 3 | 4 | 5 |. Since there are 1000 ENTRIES, this USAGE clause can save thousands of storage positions.

The PACKED-DECIMAL (COBOL 85) or COMPUTATIONAL-3 (COMP-3) option should *not* be used for printing output because packed-decimal data is not readable. Since each storage position does *not* contain an actual character, printing it will produce unreadable output. To print packed data, it must first be *moved* to a numeric field in character (PIC 9 or PIC 9 USAGE IS DISPLAY) form or to a report-item.

Input disk or tape fields may also be defined using this PACKED-DECIMAL (or COMP-3) clause if the data was originally produced in packed-decimal form.

The computer automatically handles conversions from packed to unpacked form and vice versa. Thus, moving a packed numeric field to an unpacked numeric field will automatically unpack the sending field into the receiving field.

In summary, COMPUTATIONAL-3 or COMP-3 is not part of the standard but it is widely used, primarily with IBM and IBM-compatible computers that use the EBCDIC code. PACKED-DECIMAL is available with COBOL 85.

D. USAGE IS COMPUTATIONAL (COMP)

USAGE IS COMPUTATIONAL or COMP stores data in the form in which the computer actually does its computation. Usually this form is *binary*. Thus, defining WORKING-STORAGE entries in binary format is desirable when many repetitive arithmetic computations must be performed. Similarly, for some applications, it is more efficient to produce binary output, so that when the data is read in again at a later date, conversion to binary will not be necessary.

Subscripts and counters are typically generated in binary form on many computers. To avoid compiler-generated conversions of fields such as subscripts from binary to decimal, they should be defined with USAGE IS COMP or COMPUTATIONAL.

> COBOL 85 permits the USAGE IS BINARY clause as well to specifically represent data in binary form.

CHAPTER SUMMARY

I.   How to Find Errors in Programs
  A. READY TRACE—for listing the paragraphs actually executed. This is not part of the COBOL standards but is widely available.
  B. DISPLAY—for viewing fields during debugging.
  C. Code the WITH DEBUGGING MODE clause for:
    1. Establishing specified lines as executable only when the program is being debugged (D in column 7).
    2. Including a USE statement to interrupt processing when specified program elements are changed or encountered.
  D. Get a PROCEDURE DIVISION MAP to find the exact instruction that caused an abend.
  E. Get a storage dump that displays the entire contents of storage when an interrupt occurs.
II. Use Check Digits With Key Fields to Minimize Errors in Processing
III. USAGE Clause
  A. Specifies how data is to be stored internally.
  B. Options available:
    1. USAGE IS DISPLAY
      a. Data is stored in standard character form.
      b. If the clause is omitted, display mode is assumed.
      c. Used for printing output or reading in data in standard form.

2. USAGE IS $\begin{Bmatrix} \texttt{PACKED-DECIMAL} \\ \texttt{COMPUTATIONAL-3} \\ \texttt{COMP-3} \end{Bmatrix}$

    a. Stores numeric data in a concise format.

    b. Increases efficiency by reducing the number of positions needed ι store numbers.

    c. PACKED-DECIMAL is only available for COBOL 85 users an COMPUTATIONAL-3 or COMP-3 is widely available for COBOL 85 and 74 users.

3. USAGE IS COMPUTATIONAL

    a. Stores numeric data in the form in which the computer actually does its computation.

    b. Typically, this form is binary.

    c. Use for defining subscripts and counters.

CHAPTER SELF-TEST

1. A _____ may be used to list every paragraph encountered during program execution.

2. A _____ lists the entire contents of storage.

3. (T or F) Storage dumps are typically listed in machine code only.

4. A _____ is a condition that causes an abnormal end to a program.

5. Attempting to add a field that contains blanks to another field will cause a _____ error to occur.

6. (T or F) The error in Question 5 will result in an abend condition.

7. (T or F) A check digit is typically used only with key fields.

8. (T or F) A check digit is used for determining if arithmetic operations have been performed properly.

9. To store numeric fields in WORKING-STORAGE as concisely as possible, use the _____ USAGE clause.

10. Alphanumeric fields should always be stored in _____ mode.

Solutions

1. READY TRACE

2. storage dump

3. F—Storage dumps typically print data in character form as well as in machine form.

4. program interrupt (or abend)

5. data exception

6. T

7. T

8. F—It is used to validate key fields.

9. PACKED-DECIMAL (or COMP-3)

10. DISPLAY—This is the default, so it need not be specified except for documentation purposes.

KEY TERMS

Addressing error	Divide exception	Specification error
Check digit	Operation error	Storage dump
Data exception	PROCEDURE DIVISION	Transcription error
Debug module	map	Transposition error
Debugging line	Program interrupt	USAGE clause

REVIEW QUESTIONS

I. True-False Questions

T   F

___ ___   1. The only way to determine what is in storage when an abend condition occurs is by using a DISPLAY statement.

___ ___   2. Attempting to access an input area after an AT END condition has occurred will result in a specification error.

___ ___   3. As a general rule, always use check digits with all numeric fields.

___ ___   4. Verifying data by rekeying it will detect all data entry errors.

___ ___   5. The modulus-11 method of calculating check digits is used to detect transcription errors but not transposition errors.

___ ___   6. If the USAGE clause is omitted, data is assumed to be in DISPLAY mode.

___ ___   7. Packed decimal format is used only for numeric fields.

___ ___   8. The COBOL 74 standard itself does not include a clause for packing data.

___ ___   9. To store numeric data concisely using COBOL 85, we code USAGE IS PACKED-DECIMAL.

___ ___ 10. To represent data in binary form, we code USAGE IS COMPUTATIONAL.

II. General Questions

1. Using modulus-11 arithmetic, calculate the check digit for the Social Security number 087 37 0667.

2. Using modulus-11 arithmetic, calculate the check digit for a part number of 62513.

3. Indicate the difference between a transcription and a transposition error.

4. Suppose your friend's program abends and she cannot find the error. Describe what procedures you would recommend for trying to isolate the error.

5. Indicate how and why each of the following would be used in a COBOL program:
   a. USAGE IS DISPLAY.
   b. USAGE IS PACKED-DECIMAL.
   c. USAGE IS COMPUTATIONAL.

21

The COPY and CALL Statements

OBJECTIVES

To familiarize you with

1. The COPY statement for copying parts of a program that are stored in a library.
2. The CALL statement for executing called programs as subroutines.

I. COPY Statement

A. Introduction

A **COPY** statement is used to bring into a program a series of prewritten COBOL entries that have been stored in a **library**. Copying entries from a library, rather than coding them, has the following benefits:

1. It could save a programmer a considerable amount of coding and debugging time.
2. It promotes program standardization since all programs that copy entries from a library will be using common data-names.
3. It reduces the time it takes to make modifications. If a change needs to be made to a data entry, it can be made just once in the library without the need to alter individual programs.
4. Library entries need to be extensively annotated so that they are meaningful to all users; this annotation results in better-documented programs and systems.

Most often, the COPY statement is used to copy FD and 01 entries that define and describe files and records. In addition, standard *routines* to be used in the PROCEDURE DIVISION of several programs may also be stored in a library and copied as needed.

Organizations that have large data bases or files that are shared make frequent use of libraries from which entries are copied. Students may also find that file and record description entries for test data for programming assignments have been stored in a library, which may then be copied when needed.

Each computer has its own system-dependent job control statements for creating and accessing a library. You will need to check with your computer center for the required entries.

B. Entries that Can be Copied

With the COPY statement, you may include prewritten ENVIRONMENT, DATA, or PROCEDURE DIVISION entries in your source programs as follows:

ENVIRONMENT DIVISION

Option 1 (within the CONFIGURATION SECTION):

$$
\text{SOURCE-COMPUTER. } \underline{\text{COPY}} \text{ text-name } \left\{ \begin{matrix} \underline{\text{OF}} \\ \underline{\text{IN}} \end{matrix} \right\} \text{ library-name.}
$$

$$
\text{OBJECT-COMPUTER. } \underline{\text{COPY}} \text{ text-name } \left\{ \begin{matrix} \underline{\text{OF}} \\ \underline{\text{IN}} \end{matrix} \right\} \text{ library-name.}
$$

$$
\text{SPECIAL-NAMES. } \underline{\text{COPY}} \text{ text-name } \left\{ \begin{matrix} \underline{\text{OF}} \\ \underline{\text{IN}} \end{matrix} \right\} \text{ library-name.}
$$

Option 2 (within the INPUT-OUTPUT SECTION):

$$
\text{FILE-CONTROL. } \underline{\text{COPY}} \text{ text-name } \left\{ \begin{matrix} \underline{\text{OF}} \\ \underline{\text{IN}} \end{matrix} \right\} \text{ library-name.}
$$

$$
\text{I-O-CONTROL. } \underline{\text{COPY}} \text{ text-name } \left\{ \begin{matrix} \underline{\text{OF}} \\ \underline{\text{IN}} \end{matrix} \right\} \text{ library-name.}
$$

DATA DIVISION

Option 1 (within the FILE SECTION):

$$\text{FD file-name } \underline{\text{COPY}} \text{ text-name } \left\{ \begin{array}{c} \underline{\text{OF}} \\ \underline{\text{IN}} \end{array} \right\} \text{ library-name.}$$

Option 2 (within a File Description entry):

$$\text{01 data-name } \underline{\text{COPY}} \text{ text-name } \left\{ \begin{array}{c} \underline{\text{OF}} \\ \underline{\text{IN}} \end{array} \right\} \text{ library-name.}$$

PROCEDURE DIVISION

$$\text{paragraph-name. } \underline{\text{COPY}} \text{ text-name } \left\{ \begin{array}{c} \underline{\text{OF}} \\ \underline{\text{IN}} \end{array} \right\} \text{ library-name.}$$

The library-name is an external-name: 1 to 8 characters, letters and digits only.

C. An Example

Suppose we have created a library entry called CUSTOMER that contains the following:

```
01   CUSTOMER-REC.
     05   CUST-NO          PIC X(5).
     05   CUST-NAME        PIC X(20).
     05   CUST-ADDRESS     PIC X(30).
     05   CUST-BAL-DUE     PIC 9(4)V99.
```

To copy the entries in CUSTOMER into our source program, code the following at the point in the program where you want the entries to appear:

```
                            COPY CUSTOMER
```

The source listing would appear as follows (we use lowercase letters for the copied library entries to distinguish them from the source program coding):

The numbers are line or source statement numbers. The lines that include a C after the line number are the copied statements

```
 1   IDENTIFICATION DIVISION.
 2   PROGRAM-ID. CUST01.
 .   .
 .   .
 .   .
10   DATA DIVISION.
11   FD  CUSTFILE
12         LABEL RECORDS ARE STANDARD.
13   COPY CUSTOMER.
14C  01  customer-rec.
15C      05  cust-no          pic x(5).
16C      05  cust-name        pic x(20).
17C      05  cust-address     pic x(30).
18C      05  cust-bal-due     pic 9(4)v99.
```

The C following the source program line numbers indicates that these entries have been copied from a library. Some systems use an L (for library) or another letter to distinguish copied entries from programmer-supplied ones.

As noted, other prewritten program entries besides file and record descriptions can also be copied.

D. The Full Format for the COPY Statement

A COPY statement can also be used to copy prewritten entries and make certain changes to them in the source program. The full format for the COPY is:

Format

$$
\underline{\text{COPY}}\ \text{text-name-1}\ \left[\left\{\begin{array}{c}\underline{\text{OF}}\\\underline{\text{IN}}\end{array}\right\}\ \text{library-name-1}\right]
$$

$$
\left[\underline{\text{REPLACING}}\ \left\{\left\{\begin{array}{l}==\text{pseudo-text-1}==\\ \text{identifier-1}\\ \text{literal-1}\\ \text{word-1}\end{array}\right\}\ \underline{\text{BY}}\ \left\{\begin{array}{l}==\text{pseudo-text-2}==\\ \text{identifier-2}\\ \text{literal-2}\\ \text{word-2}\end{array}\right\}\right\}\ \ldots\right]
$$

If the REPLACING clause is omitted from the COPY statement, the library text is copied unchanged.

The REPLACING option allows virtually any library entry to be changed when it is being copied into the user's source program. This includes COBOL entries as well as comments or other elements that would appear as "pseudo-text." Literals and identifiers can also be changed as well as "words" that refer to COBOL reserved words.

Example   Using the library entry called CUSTOMER in the preceding example, suppose we code:

```
COPY CUSTOMER REPLACING CUST-NO BY
     CUST-NUMBER, ==X(5)== BY
               ==X(6)==,
```

This results in the following changes to the library entry when it is called into the source program:

```
14C  01  CUSTOMER-REC.
15C      05   CUST-NUMBER      PIC X(6).   ◄─── Data-name and PIC clause
16C      05   CUST-NAME        PIC X(20).       have been changed
17C      05   CUST-ADDRESS     PIC X(30).
18C      05   CUST-BAL-DUE     PIC 9(4)V99.
```

The REPLACING clause does *not* alter the prewritten entries in the library. That is, the changes are made *to the user's source program only*.

Self-Test
1. A single series of file or record description entries may be used in several different programs by placing it in a _____ and _____ it when needed.
2. With the _____ clause you can include prewritten entries in your program.
3. (T or F) The user program can copy library routines and make changes to the field names as they are specified in the user program.
4. (T or F) Using the REPLACING option of the COPY statement, it is possible to alter the field names stored in the library itself.
5. Two purposes of using library functions are to _____ and to _____.

Solutions
1. library; copying
2. COPY
3. T
4. F—This option only alters library functions *for the user program*.
5. make coding and debugging easier; increase standardization

II. CALL Statement

A. Why Use a CALL Statement?

You will recall that structured programs should consist of a series of independent modules that are executed from the main module.

When programs are properly structured:

1. Each module may be written, compiled, and perhaps even tested independently.
2. The modules may be written in different stages, in a top-down manner. They may even be coded by different programmers.
3. If a specific module needs to be modified, the entire logical flow should still function properly without the need for extensive revision to other parts of the program.

In a sense, modules within a program can be viewed as subroutines that are called or executed from the main module. But a program may also **CALL** or reference independent **subprograms** stored in a library that are *entirely separate* from the main program itself. The main program that references or calls a subprogram is referred to as the **calling program**. The subprogram that is linked and executed within the main program is referred to as the **called program**.

TERMS

Main (or user or source) program	Calling program
Subprogram	Called program

The called program would need to be compiled, debugged, and catalogued or stored in a library so that it may be called when needed. Typical subprograms that may be used by numerous calling programs include edit routines, error control checks, standard calculations, summary and total printing. Some programming languages use the term "external subroutines" to refer to these; the term "subprogram" is used in COBOL.

The technique of enabling a main program to call a subprogram has the following advantages:

ADVANTAGES OF CALLING SUBPROGRAMS

1. Avoids duplication of effort.
   When specific routines need to be included in more than one program, it is best to write them separately and call them into each program.
2. Improves programmer productivity.
   Programmers can "specialize" or code routines and modules that make use of their specific talents or skills.
3. Provides greater flexibility.
   Subprograms may be written in *any* programming language; they are typically written in a language best suited to the specific task required. Moreover, changes to the called program can be made without the need to modify the calling program.

Since a subprogram is really an independent module that is external to the main program, it may be called in just as one would use a PERFORM to execute an internal module.

Differences between CALL and COPY

The CALL statement is very different from the COPY statement. The COPY brings into a user program separate ENVIRONMENT, DATA, or PROCEDURE DIVISION segments *as is*. The copied entries are compiled and executed together with the source program. The CALL causes *an entire program*, which is already in machine language, to be executed. The two programs are separate, but data may be passed from the called program to the calling program *or* from the calling program to the called program. That is, a called program is stored in compiled form in a library. When the CALL is performed, data is passed from the calling to the called program (if appropriate). The entire called program is executed, data is passed from the called program back to the calling program, and control returns to the calling program.

Typically, we COPY ENVIRONMENT and DATA DIVISION entries into a source program and we CALL programs from a library rather than COPY them.

B. Format of the CALL Statement

Figure 21.1 illustrates the relationship between a calling and a called program.

Figure 21.1
The relationships between a calling and a called program.

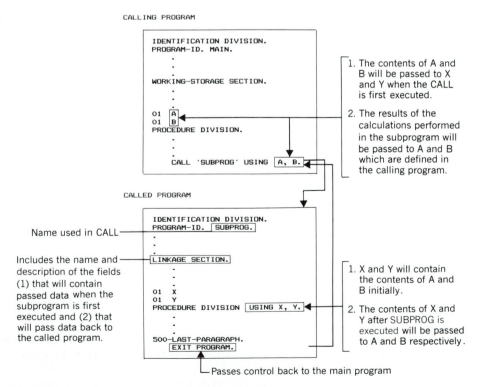

A subprogram is called into a main program with the CALL statement. The following is the basic format for the CALL statement:

Format

> CALL literal-1
>   [USING identifier-1 ...]

Literal-1 is the name of the called program as specified in its PROGRAM-ID statement. It must be a nonnumeric literal. Typically, it conforms to the rules for forming external-names: 1 to 8 characters, letters and digits only. Literal-1 must also be catalogued as the called or subprogram name. This is performed with job control commands that are system-dependent.

The USING clause of the CALL statement is required if the subprogram performs any operations that require results or data to be passed from one program to another. The CALL ... USING names items in the main or calling program that will be either passed to the called program before execution or passed back to the calling program after the called program has been executed. Since the purpose of calling a subprogram is to perform operations or calculations to produce results, we almost always employ the USING option.

Let us consider the coding requirements of the called program first and then consider the corresponding coding requirements of the calling program.

1. Called Program Requirements

a. PROGRAM-ID.   The literal used in the CALL statement of the main program to extract a subprogram or routine from a library and execute it must be identical to the called program's PROGRAM-ID:

CALLING PROGRAM
    CALL ⌐'literal-1'⌐ USING ...

CALLED PROGRAM
PROGRAM-ID. ⌐literal-1.⌐

b. LINKAGE SECTION.   A **LINKAGE SECTION** must be defined in the called program for identifying those items that (1) will be passed to the called program from the calling program and (2) passed back from the called program to the calling program. The LINKAGE SECTION *of the called program*, then, describes all items to be passed between the two programs.

The LINKAGE SECTION, if used, is coded after the FILE and WORKING-STORAGE SECTIONs of the called program. The format of entries in this section is similar to WORKING-STORAGE entries except that VALUE clauses for initializing fields are *not* permitted in the LINKAGE SECTION.

c. PROCEDURE DIVISION USING.   The identifiers specified in the USING clause in the PROCEDURE DIVISION entry include all fields defined in the LINKAGE SECTION; these identifiers will be passed from one program to the other. They are passed to and from corresponding identifiers in the CALL ... USING of the main program. See Figure 21.1 again.

d. EXIT PROGRAM.   The *last* executed statement in the *called program* must be the **EXIT PROGRAM**. It signals the computer to return control back to the calling program.

With COBOL 74, EXIT PROGRAM must be the *only* statement in the last paragraph. With COBOL 85, other statements can precede EXIT PROGRAM in the last paragraph.

2. Calling Program Requirements

We have seen that the called program will include the following PROCEDURE DIVISION entries:

```
                           CALLED PROGRAM
PROGRAM-ID. PROG1.
  :
  :
PROCEDURE DIVISION USING identifier-1A, identifier-2A, ...
```

Identifier-1A, identifier-2A, . . . must be defined in the LINKAGE SECTION of the *called program*.

To execute a subprogram stored in a library, the only statement required in the calling program is the CALL literal-1 USING . . . statement. The literal specified in the CALL statement of the main program should be identical to the PROGRAM-ID of the called program.

The calling program, then, will have the following entry:

```
          CALL 'PROG1' USING identifier-1, identifier-2, ...
```

Identifier-1, identifier-2, . . . must be defined in the calling program.

When the called program is executed, the contents of identifier-1 of the calling program will be passed to identifier-1A of the called program; the contents of identifier-2 of the calling program will be passed to identifier-2A of the called program, and so on. In this way, initial data may be passed from the calling program to the called program for execution. Then, after execution of the called program, identifier-1A of the called program is passed back to identifier-1 of the calling program, and so on. Thus, resultant data is passed from the called program back to the calling program for subsequent processing.

Data is passed in sequence so that the corresponding items in each statement are made equivalent (e.g., after the called program has been executed, identifier-1A is set equal to identifier-1). The PIC specifications for corresponding items must be the same. The names of data fields passed from a calling program to a called program may be the same or they may be different, as in our previous illustrations.

As noted, called programs must have a LINKAGE SECTION, the entry PROCEDURE DIVISION USING, and an EXIT PROGRAM at the end of the last module.

C. Examples

Example 1   Suppose that a called program is to determine the Social Security contribution for each employee. This field is commonly referred to as FICA (Federal Insurance Compensation Act) and is based on the employee's annual salary, which is read in by the calling program. The contents of ANN-SAL, a field in the calling program, must be passed to the called program before the calculation can be made.

Passing data from one program to another is performed with a USING clause. As indicated, the USING clause of both programs indicates fields to be transmitted. Thus,

USING defines data passed from calling to called *and* from called to calling. The following will clarify these points:

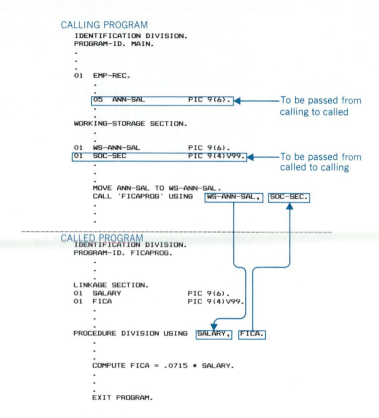

Note the following about the *called program*:

1. PROGRAM-ID. name.
   The PROGRAM-ID should be the same as the literal specified in the CALL statement of the calling program except that the literal is enclosed in quotes.

2. LINKAGE SECTION.
   All identifiers to be passed from called program to calling program *and* from calling program to called program must be defined here. The LINKAGE SECTION appears after the WORKING-STORAGE SECTION. Its format is similar to that of WORKING-STORAGE, but VALUE clauses are not permitted.

3. PROCEDURE DIVISION USING....
   Arguments or fields in the CALL are matched by position in the USING, not by location in the LINKAGE SECTION. The identifiers may be the same in both the called and calling programs, but we recommend you use different names.

4. EXIT PROGRAM.
   This must be the last entry in the called program. It must be in a paragraph by itself for COBOL 74.

With COBOL 74 you may pass 01- or 77-level items only. With COBOL 85 you can pass parameters *at any level* as long as they are elementary items.

Example 2   Consider the following:

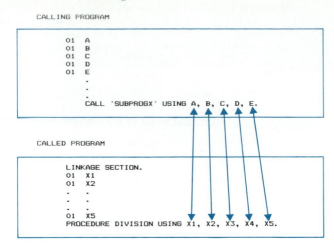

In the above, before X1, X2, X3, X4, and X5 are used in SUBPROGX, the contents of A, B, C, D, and E, respectively, in the calling program will be passed to them. That is, A will be transmitted to X1, B will be transmitted to X2, and so on. Correspondingly, after the called program has been executed, the contents of X1 will be passed to A, X2 to B, and so on. This occurs because of the *sequence* of the identifiers in the USING clause. It is *not* influenced by the sequence of the identifiers as they are defined in the DATA DIVISION. Thus, the following would produce the same results as the above:

```
CALL 'SUBPROGX' USING A, C, E, B, D.
```

```
PROCEDURE DIVISION  USING X1, X3, X5, X2, X4.
```

Note that the PIC clauses of corresponding fields must have the same specifications. That is, the PIC clauses of A and X1 must have the same number of characters as must B and X2, C and X3, D and X4, and E and X5. Moreover, the same names could have been used in both programs.

Passing Data from Called to Calling Only

In Example 2, data is passed in both directions—first, from calling to called and then, after the called program has been executed, the resultant data is passed back. Suppose we wish to do calculations in the calling program that are *not* affected by the initial values of A–E. Then we simply re-initialize X1–X5 in the called program before we perform any calculations.

Example 3   It is quite likely that a series of programs at a given computer center need to use a Julian date, which is the actual day of the year represented as YYDDD (YY = year, DDD = day of year). For example, the Julian date for January 1, 1988 is 88001; the Julian date for December 31, 1988 is 88366. Julian dates are very useful for determining the actual number of days between two dates. For example, suppose we want to determine whether the date of the last transaction is more than 90 days from today. If today's date is September 30, 1988, it converts to a Julian date of 88274. To determine if a date of transaction is more than 90 days from that date, convert it to a Julian date and see if it is greater than (88274 − 90) or 88184.

Typically, one programmer would write the full four divisions of a COBOL program that computes JULIAN-DATE. The program could be named SUBPROGR and may be called into *any main program* that needs it. After it has been called and executed, the computed result called JULIAN-DATE may be available to the calling program by using the same name, JULIAN-DATE, or a different name such as DATE-OF-RUN. The called program must be a full COBOL program beginning with an IDENTIFICATION DIVISION and a PROGRAM-ID, which is the name used to access it. Since JULIAN-DATE is calculated in SUBPROGR and then passed to the calling program, we code CALL 'SUBPROGR' USING DATE-OF-RUN in the calling program and code PROCEDURE DIVISION USING JULIAN-DATE in the called program.

The EXIT PROGRAM must be the *last statement* coded and executed in the called program; this ends the execution of the subprogram so that control can return to the calling program. The LINKAGE section in the called program includes all fields passed from it to the calling program.

Consider the following illustration:

Calling Program

```
        IDENTIFICATION DIVISION.
        PROGRAM-ID. MAIN.
             .
             .
             .
        01   DATE-OF-RUN            PIC X(5).
             .
             .
             .
        PROCEDURE DIVISION.
             .
             .
             .
           CALL 'SUBPROGR' USING DATE-OF-RUN.◄──── Will place result in
        *                                              DATE-OF-RUN
        * A JULIAN-DATE IS COMPUTED IN SUBPROGR
        * AND PASSED TO DATE-OF-RUN
```

Called Program

```
        IDENTIFICATION DIVISION.
        PROGRAM-ID. SUBPROGR.
       *THIS CALLED MODULE CALCULATES DAY OF YEAR   *
       *     FROM CURRENT MO/DA/YR                   *
       *DAY OF YEAR IS CALLED JULIAN DATE            *
        DATA DIVISION.
        WORKING-STORAGE SECTION.
        01   WS-DATE                PIC 9(6).
        01   WS-DATE-X.
             05   YR                PIC 99.
             05   MO                PIC 99.
             05   DA                PIC 99.
        LINKAGE SECTION.
        01   JULIAN-DATE            PIC 9(5).
        PROCEDURE DIVISION USING JULIAN-DATE.◄──── JULIAN-DATE will be
        100-MAIN-MODULE.                            passed to DATE-OF-RUN
           ACCEPT WS-DATE FROM DATE.                of calling program
        *
        * INCLUDES CALCULATIONS FOR CONVERTING
        * MO/DA/YR TO YYDDD FORMAT
        *
        500-RETURN-TO-MAIN.
           EXIT PROGRAM.
```

In this illustration, *no* data needs to be passed from the calling to the called program. The called program calculates a DATE-OF-RUN using DATE, which is accepted from the system in the called program. The initial content of DATE-OF-RUN in the called program is not used for calculation. If we wanted to use the *same* subprogram to calculate *both* the Julian date for today and the Julian date for date-of-last-transaction, we would need to code the following:

```
IDENTIFICATION DIVISION.
PROGRAM-ID. MAIN.
      .
      .
01   IN-REC.
      .
      .
     05   DATE-OF-LAST-TRANS              PIC X(6).
      .
      .
WORKING-STORAGE SECTION.
01   STORED-AREAS.
     05   WS-DATE                         PIC X(6).
     05   CALCULATED-JULIAN-DATE          PIC X(5).
     05   TODAYS-JULIAN-DATE              PIC X(5).
     05   JULIAN-DATE-OF-LAST-TRANS       PIC X(5).
      .
```

```
        ⋮
PROCEDURE DIVISION.
        ⋮
    ACCEPT WS-DATE FROM DATE.
    CALL 'SUBPROGR' USING WS-DATE, CALCULATED-JULIAN-DATE.
    MOVE CALCULATED-JULIAN-DATE TO TODAYS-JULIAN-DATE.
    READ IN-FILE
        AT END MOVE 'NO ' TO ARE-THERE-MORE-RECORDS.
    PERFORM 200-CALC-RTN
        UNTIL NO-MORE-RECORDS.
        ⋮
200-CALC-RTN.
    MOVE DATE-OF-LAST-TRANS TO WS-DATE.
    CALL 'SUBPROGR' USING WS-DATE, CALCULATED-JULIAN-DATE.
    MOVE CALCULATED-JULIAN-DATE TO JULIAN-DATE-OF-LAST-TRANS.
    PERFORM 300-TEST-FOR-90-DAYS.
        ⋮
```

Called program
```
IDENTIFICATION DIVISION.
PROGRAM-ID. SUBPROGR.
        .
        .
        .
LINKAGE SECTION.
01  DATE-ENTERED                          PIC X(6).
01  JULIAN-DATE                           PIC X(5).
        .
        .
        .
PROCEDURE DIVISION USING DATE-ENTERED, JULIAN-DATE.
*************************************************************
*   THE PROGRAM OPERATES ON DATE-ENTERED TO CALCULATE      *
*   JULIAN-DATE.                                           *
*************************************************************
200-SUBPROGR-END.
    EXIT PROGRAM.
```

With COBOL 85, the PROGRAM-ID paragraph in the IDENTIFICATION DIVISION of the called program may have the following INITIAL PROGRAM clause:

```
PROGRAM-ID. program-name [IS INITIAL PROGRAM].
```

If this clause is used, the called program will be restored to its initial state each time it is called. This means that all identifiers in WORKING-STORAGE will contain their original values as specified by their VALUE clauses before and after each call.

Data items passed *to* a subprogram may have their values protected from modification with the use of the BY CONTENT clause. Consider the following:

```
PROGRAM-ID. CALLING.
        ⋮
    CALL SUBPROG1
        USING BY CONTENT AMT-1 AMT-2.
        ⋮



PROGRAM-ID. SUBPROG1.
        ⋮
PROCEDURE DIVISION USING AMT-1 AMT-2.
```

Because the BY CONTENT clause is included, the called program *may not change* the value of AMT-1 or AMT-2.

CHAPTER SUMMARY

I. COPY statement
  A. To copy entries stored in a library into a user program.
  B. ENVIRONMENT, DATA, and PROCEDURE DIVISION entries may be copied.
  C. Most often used for copying standard file and record description entries or routines to be used in the PROCEDURE DIVISION.
  D. The entry coded is: <u>COPY</u> text-name $\left\{ \begin{array}{c} \underline{OF} \\ \underline{IN} \end{array} \right\}$ library-name.

II. CALL statement
  A. To call or reference *entire programs* stored in a library.
  B. The user program is referred to as the calling program; the program accessed from the library will serve as a subprogram and is referred to as the called program.
  C. Passing data from the called program to the calling program
    1. The CALL entry can include a USING clause that lists the names of the fields in the calling program that are passed to the called program and fields that will be passed back from the called program.
    2. The PROCEDURE DIVISION entry of the called program also includes a USING clause to indicate identifiers specified in this subprogram that will correspond to entries in the calling program.
    3. Identifiers in the called and calling program may be the same or they may be different.
    4. The called program must have a LINKAGE SECTION in which fields to be passed to and from the calling program are defined.
    5. The called program must end with an EXIT PROGRAM statement. This must be in a separate paragraph for COBOL 74.

CHAPTER SELF-TEST

1. The CALL statement is particularly useful in structured programs because _____.

2. When using a CALL statement, your program is referred to as the _____ program; the subprogram is referred to as the _____ program.

3. To CALL a program, you code _____.

4. In Question 3, the literal specified must be the same as _____.

5. If you include USING with the CALL statement in the calling program, the identifiers specified must be described in the (calling, called) program.

6. The program being called has a _____ SECTION in which data to be passed to the calling program is defined.

7. The PROCEDURE DIVISION entry for the called program includes a _____ clause.

8. The identifiers specified in the USING clause for Question 7 are defined in _____.

9. The last statement in the called program is _____.

10. (T or F) The identifiers specified in both the called and calling program must be the same.

Solutions
1. Subprograms being called can be coded and executed as independent programs
2. calling (or main or user); called
3. CALL literal-1
        USING identifier-1 . . .

4. the `PROGRAM-ID` entry in the called program; the literal is, however, enclosed in quotes.

5. calling

6. `LINKAGE`

7. `USING`; e.g., `PROCEDURE DIVISION USING` identifier ...

8. the `LINKAGE SECTION` of the called program

9. `EXIT PROGRAM`

10. F—They may be different.

PRACTICE PROGRAM

Consider the problem definition in Figure 21.2. The input consists of an address entered with street, city, state, and zip separated by /. The output requires this address component to be separated into individual fields using the `UNSTRING`. The `UNSTRING` routine is called in from a program called `UNSTR`. The program is illustrated in Figure 21.3.

Figure 21.2
Problem definition for the Practice Program.

Systems Flowchart

EMPLOYEE-FILE
standard labels

SAMPLE 21

REPORT-FILE

EMPLOYEE FILE Record Layout

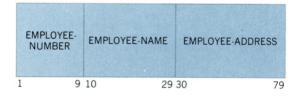

| EMPLOYEE-NUMBER | EMPLOYEE-NAME | EMPLOYEE-ADDRESS |

1   9 10   29 30   79

REPORT-FILE Printer Spacing Chart

Sample Input Data

```
345234231JOHN WAYNE              165 WEST ST/MIDDLETOWN/NY/10098/
986654543BURT REYNOLDS          56 EAST AVE/ANYTOWN/NJ/00876/
654898535GEORGE BURNS           100 NORTH ST/NEW YORK/NY/10000/
876567653STEVE McQUEEN          1452 WEST MAIN ST/WARYING/CA/90006/
567744544CHRISTOPHER PLUMMER    77 EAST 63 ST/NEW YORK/NY/00987/
611102388NICK NOLTE             432 CONCORD RD/HOLLYWOOD/CA/90078/
345443344ART CARNEY             98 WARD ST/WESTVILLAGE/VT/09898/
656554566HARRISON FORD          100 DELLWOOD RD/CENTERTOWN/ND/78776/
```

Figure 21.2
(continued)

Sample Output

E M P L O Y E E   A D D R E S S

EMPLOYEE NUMBER	EMPLOYEE NAME		EMPLOYEE ADDRESS		
345234231	JOHN WAYNE	165 WEST ST	MIDDLETOWN	NY	10098
986654543	BURT REYNOLDS	56 EAST AVE	ANYTOWN	NJ	00876
654898535	GEORGE BURNS	100 NORTH ST	NEW YORK	NY	10000
876567653	STEVE McQUEEN	1452 WEST MAIN	WARYING	CA	90006
567744544	CHRISTOPHER PLUMMER	77 EAST 63 ST	NEW YORK	NY	00987
611102388	NICK NOLTE	432 CONCORD RD	HOLLYWOOD	CA	90078
345443344	ART CARNEY	98 WARD ST	WESTVILLAGE	VT	09898
656554566	HARRISON FORD	100 DELLWOOD RD	CENTERTOWN	ND	78776

Figure 21.3
Solution to the Practice
Program.

```
IDENTIFICATION DIVISION.
PROGRAM-ID.  SAMPLE21.
AUTHOR. CHRISTOPHER HAMMEL.
ENVIRONMENT DIVISION.
INPUT-OUTPUT SECTION.
FILE-CONTROL.
    SELECT EMPLOYEE-FILE ASSIGN TO DISK15.
    SELECT REPORT-FILE    ASSIGN TO SYS$OUTPUT.
DATA DIVISION.
FILE SECTION.
FD  EMPLOYEE-FILE
    LABEL RECORDS ARE STANDARD.
01  EMPLOYEE-REC.
    05  EMPLOYEE-NUMBER          PIC 9(9).
    05  EMPLOYEE-NAME            PIC X(20).
    05  EMPLOYEE-ADDRESS         PIC X(50).
FD  REPORT-FILE
    LABEL RECORDS ARE OMITTED.
01  REPORT-REC                   PIC X(133).
WORKING-STORAGE SECTION.
01  WORK-AREAS.
    05  ARE-THERE-MORE-RECORDS   PIC X(3)       VALUE 'YES'.
        88  NO-MORE-RECORDS                     VALUE 'NO '.
01  DATA-TO-BE-SENT-TO-UNSTRING.
    05  EMPLOYEE-ADDRESS-STR     PIC X(50).
    05  DATA-UNSTRING.
        10  STREET-ADDRESS       PIC X(15).
        10  CITY                 PIC X(20).
        10  STATE                PIC XX.
        10  ZIP-CODE             PIC X(5).
01  HEADER1.
    05  FILLER                   PIC X(51)      VALUE SPACES.
    05  FILLER                   PIC X(32)
        VALUE 'E M P L O Y E E    A D D R E S S '.
    05  FILLER                   PIC X(50)      VALUE SPACES.
01  HEADER2.
    05  FILLER                   PIC X(20)      VALUE SPACES.
    05  FILLER                   PIC X(35)
        VALUE 'EMPLOYEE NUMBER     EMPLOYEE NAME'.
    05  FILLER                   PIC X(28)      VALUE SPACES.
    05  FILLER                   PIC X(16)
        VALUE 'EMPLOYEE ADDRESS'.
    05  FILLER                   PIC X(36)      VALUE SPACES.
01  DETAIL-LINE.
    05  FILLER                   PIC X(23)      VALUE SPACES.
    05  EMPLOYEE-NUMBER-OUT      PIC 9(9).
    05  FILLER                   PIC X(8)       VALUE SPACES.
    05  EMPLOYEE-NAME-OUT        PIC X(20).
    05  FILLER                   PIC X(5)       VALUE SPACES.
    05  STREET-ADDRESS-OUT       PIC X(15).
    05  FILLER                   PIC XX         VALUE SPACES.
    05  CITY-OUT                 PIC X(20).
    05  FILLER                   PIC XX         VALUE SPACES.
    05  STATE-OUT                PIC XX.
    05  FILLER                   PIC XX         VALUE SPACES.
    05  ZIP-CODE-OUT             PIC X(5).
    05  FILLER                   PIC X(20)      VALUE SPACES.
PROCEDURE DIVISION.
100-MAIN1.
    OPEN INPUT  EMPLOYEE-FILE
         OUTPUT REPORT-FILE.
    READ EMPLOYEE-FILE
        AT END MOVE 'NO ' TO ARE-THERE-MORE-RECORDS.
    PERFORM 300-HEADING-RTN.
    PERFORM 200-REPORT-RTN
        UNTIL NO-MORE-RECORDS.
    CLOSE EMPLOYEE-FILE
          REPORT-FILE.
    STOP RUN.
200-REPORT-RTN.
    MOVE EMPLOYEE-ADDRESS TO EMPLOYEE-ADDRESS-STR.
    CALL "UNSTR" USING DATA-TO-BE-SENT-TO-UNSTRING.
    MOVE EMPLOYEE-NUMBER TO EMPLOYEE-NUMBER-OUT.
    MOVE EMPLOYEE-NAME TO EMPLOYEE-NAME-OUT.
    MOVE STATE TO STATE-OUT.
    MOVE CITY TO CITY-OUT.
    MOVE ZIP-CODE TO ZIP-CODE-OUT.
    MOVE STREET-ADDRESS TO STREET-ADDRESS-OUT.
    WRITE REPORT-REC FROM DETAIL-LINE
        AFTER ADVANCING 2 LINES.
    READ EMPLOYEE-FILE
        AT END MOVE 'NO ' TO ARE-THERE-MORE-RECORDS.
```

Figure 21.3
(continued)

```
300-HEADING-RTN.
    WRITE REPORT-REC FROM HEADER1
        AFTER ADVANCING PAGE.
    WRITE REPORT-REC FROM HEADER2
        AFTER ADVANCING 4 LINES.


UNSTR Source Listing

IDENTIFICATION DIVISION.
PROGRAM-ID. UNSTR.
AUTHOR. CHRISTOPHER HAMMEL.
ENVIRONMENT DIVISION.
DATA DIVISION.
LINKAGE SECTION.
01   DATA-SENT-FROM-CALLING-PROG.
    05   EMPLOYEE-ADDR          PIC X(50).
    05   UNSTR-ADDR.
        10   STREET-ADDR        PIC X(15).
        10   CITY-ADDR          PIC X(20).
        10   STATE-ADDR         PIC XX.
        10   ZIP-CODEX          PIC X(5).
PROCEDURE DIVISION USING DATA-SENT-FROM-CALLING-PROG.
100-MAIN-PARA.
    UNSTRING EMPLOYEE-ADDR
            DELIMITED BY '/'
                INTO STREET-ADDR
                    CITY-ADDR
                    STATE-ADDR
                    ZIP-CODEX.
200-EXIT-PARA.
    EXIT PROGRAM.
```

KEY TERMS

CALL	COPY	LINKAGE SECTION
Called program	EXIT PROGRAM	Subprogram
Calling program	Library	

REVIEW QUESTIONS

                                    T   F

I. True-False Questions

— — 1. COPY and CALL statements may be used interchangeably in a COBOL program.

— — 2. In order to CALL or COPY an entry, it must be stored in a library.

— — 3. A COPY statement enables numerous users to call into their program standardized record description entries.

— — 4. A COPY statement may not be used for copying PROCEDURE DIVISION entries.

— — 5. When using a CALL statement, the data names specified must be identical in both the called and calling program.

— — 6. When using a CALL statement, the called program is typically referred to as the user program.

— — 7. A called program must have a LINKAGE SECTION.

— — 8. All calling programs must end with an EXIT PROGRAM entry.

— — 9. A called program is not altered when it is accessed by a calling program.

— — 10. Another term for a called program is a subprogram.

II. General Questions

1. Indicate the differences between the COPY and CALL statements.

2. Code a statement to COPY a record description called INVENTORY-REC from a library.

3. Code the shell of a calling program to access a subroutine called VALIDATE that will place the total number of errors found into a user-defined field called COUNT1.

4. For Question 3, assume that the called program stores the count of errors in a field called SUM-IT. Code the shell of the called program.

III. Validating Data Modify the Practice Program so that it includes appropriate coding to (1) test for all errors and (2) print a control listing of totals (records processed, errors encountered, batch totals).

DEBUGGING EXERCISES

1. Suppose SUBPROG is called with a CALL IS SUBPROGR USING X, Y. SUBPROG contains the following:

```
LINKAGE-SECTION.
    :
    :
    05   Q
    05   R
PROCEDURE DIVISION USING X, Y.
    :
    :            .
EXIT.
```

(a) The line containing LINKAGE SECTION results in a syntax error. Find the error and correct it.
(b) The PROCEDURE DIVISION entry results in a syntax error. Find and correct it.
(c) The last line results in a syntax error. Find and correct it.

PROGRAMMING ASSIGNMENTS

1. Write a subroutine called INFLTN to calculate the price of an item over a 10-year period taking inflation into account. You may modify the program illustrated in Figure 10.5 on page 330 so that it can be used as a subroutine. Write a second program to call in this subroutine and to pass to the calling program all the calculated variables.

2. A subroutine called BENEFITS is used to calculate certain benefits to which an employee is entitled, based on the employee's Job Classification Code. Write a program to call in this subroutine and to pass to the called program the following:

a. Number of vacation days.
b. Number of sick days.

The purpose of the program is to create an indexed master payroll file that adds vacation days and sick days to each employee's record. See the Problem Definition in Figure 21.4.

Figure 21.4
Problem definition for
Programming Assignment 2.

Systems Flowchart

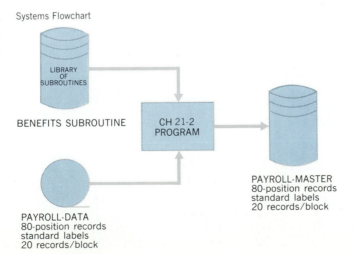

LIBRARY
OF
SUBROUTINES

BENEFITS SUBROUTINE

CH 21-2
PROGRAM

PAYROLL-MASTER
80-position records
standard labels
20 records/block

PAYROLL-DATA
80-position records
standard labels
20 records/block

Record Layouts
1. PAYROLL-DATA

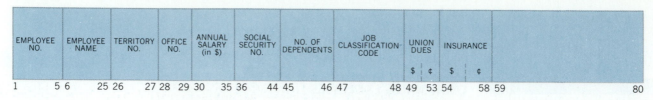

2. PAYROLL-MASTER

Figure 21.4
(continued)

22

The Report Writer Feature

OBJECTIVES

To familiarize you with

1. The Report Writer Feature.
2. The options available for printing reports.

I. Introduction

ANS COBOL has a Report Writer Feature that greatly facilitates print operations. By following basic rules for `DATA DIVISION` entries, the Report Writer Feature will automatically handle all:

1. Spacing of forms.
2. Skipping to a new page.
3. Testing for end of page.
4. Printing of report and page headings at the top of a page and report and page footings at the bottom of a page.
5. Accumulation of amount fields.
6. Testing for control breaks.
7. Detail and/or summary printing.
8. Printing of totals for control breaks.
9. Printing of a final total when there are no more input records.

The Report Writer Feature requires learning about many new `DATA DIVISION` clauses, but you will find that the amount of coding in the `PROCEDURE DIVISION` is significantly reduced.

II. The Benefits of the Report Writer Feature

A. For Detail and Summary Reporting

You will recall that many reports in businesses require:

1. **Detail printing**   The printing of one or more lines for each input record.
2. **Summary or group printing**   The printing of totals or other summary information for groups of records.

The Report Writer Feature can be easily used for both detail and/or summary reports.

B. For Control Break Processing

One type of summary or group printing uses a **control break** procedure as discussed in Chapter 12. We review control break procedures here.

Consider the output in Figure 22.1. This report has both detail and summary printing. That is, when input records with the same department number are read, the records are printed and the total amount of sales for each salesperson is accumulated. When a change or "break" in the department number occurs, the accumulated total of all amounts of sales is printed as a *control total line*. We call department number a *control field*. Summary printing is performed as a result of the control break that occurs when there is a change in the department number (see line 17 of Figure 22.1).

Note that department is not the only control field in this illustration. A change in *area* also results in a *control break* that produces a control total (see line 31). The area control field, however, is a *higher level control field* than department and is designated with two **'s rather than one. A change in area, therefore, forces a department or minor-level control break. Thus, while reading input records, when a change in the area occurs, the total amount of sales for the last department in the area is printed first; then the total amount of sales for the entire area is printed. For area 01, for example,

```
                                    MONTHLY SALES REPORT


    TERRITORY        AREA      DEPARTMENT          SALESPERSON   AMOUNT OF SALES

        1             1           01           A NEWMAN            417.45

        1             1           01           P PETERSON JR       628.14

        1             1           01           D SILVERS           404.55

                                                       TOTAL DEPARTMENT 01  $1450.14 *

        1             1           02           J ADAMS             379.23

        1             1           02           B JONES             298.16

                                                       TOTAL DEPARTMENT 02   $677.39 *

        1             1           03           A BYRNES            559.26

        1             1           03           F CARLETON          223.68

                                                       TOTAL DEPARTMENT 03   $782.94 *
                                                               TOTAL AREA 1        $2910.47 **

        1             2           04           A FRANKLIN          627.34

        1             2           04           D ROBERTS           572.26

        1             2           04           S STONE             426.32

                                                       TOTAL DEPARTMENT 04  $1625.92 *

        1             2           05           L DANTON            365.22

        1             2           05           R JACKSON           426.22

                                                       TOTAL DEPARTMENT 05   $791.44 *
                                                           TOTAL AREA 2          $2417.36 **
                                                           TOTAL TERRITORY 1        $ 5327.83 ***
```

Figure 22.1
Report with both detail and
summary printing.

we have three department totals and then an area total that is a higher-level total (see lines 29 and 31 of Figure 22.1).

Territory is the *major control field*. Area and department are control fields subordinate to territory. Thus, during the reading of input, when a change in territory occurs, first the corresponding department total is printed, then an area total is printed, and finally a major level territory total is printed. That is, a major territory break forces an intermediate area break, which forces a minor department break (see lines 45, 47, and 49).

The illustration in Figure 22.1 is intended as a review of the control break procedures that can be easily handled using the Report Writer Feature. The practice program at the end of this chapter illustrates how the Report Writer Feature can produce the report in Figure 22.1.

C. For Printing Headings and Footings

A Report Writer program can designate print lines of the following types:

REPORT HEADING (RH) Prints identifying information about the report *only once*, on the top of the first page of the report.

PAGE HEADING (PH) Prints identifying information on the top of each page. This may include page numbers, column headings, and so on.

CONTROL HEADING (CH) Prints a heading that typically contains new control values when a control break has occurred.

DETAIL (DE) Prints for each input record read.

CONTROL FOOTING (CF)   Prints control totals for the previous group of detail records just printed, after a control break has occurred.

PAGE FOOTING (PF)   Prints at the end of each page.

REPORT FOOTING (RF)   Prints only once, at the end of the report. This may include, for example, an 'End of Report' message.

The printing of each type of print line is controlled by the Report Writer Feature. That is, a line designated as a Report Heading is printed at the beginning of a report, a Page Heading line prints at the beginning of each page, and so on.

The Report Writer Feature makes it possible for the programmer to specify a report's format in the REPORT SECTION of the DATA DIVISION. The coding of PROCEDURE DIVISION statements is minimal; all required report features are specified in this REPORT SECTION.

III. The REPORT SECTION **in the** DATA DIVISION

The DATA DIVISION of a program using the Report Writer Feature can consist of three sections which must be coded in the order shown:

1. FILE SECTION
2. WORKING-STORAGE SECTION
3. REPORT SECTION

The REPORT SECTION is specified only when the Report Writer Feature is used. We can use this feature when complex summary or group printing is required, or it can be used for simple detail printing as well. Lines must be designated as heading, detail, and footing lines, and they will print as appropriate under the control of the Report Writer Feature.

Let us consider a sample program using the Report Writer Feature that produces a group report, as in Figure 22.2. This is also a control break procedure, but there is only one control field, Customer Number. Thus, this report is not quite as complex as in the previous illustration. A *Report Footing* indicating the Final Cost is printed at the end of the report.

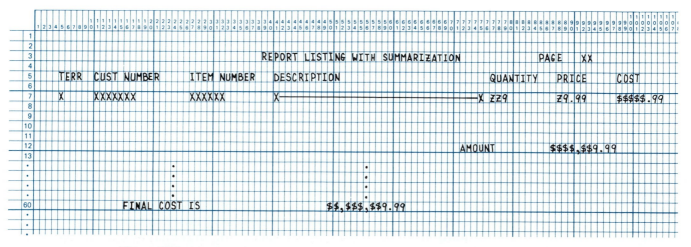

Figure 22.2
Printer Spacing Chart for sample program that uses the Report Writer feature.

The program listing, using the Report Writer Feature, appears in Figure 22.3. Note that although the DATA DIVISION tends to be more complex than in previous programs, the Report Writer results in a simplified PROCEDURE DIVISION.

The first part of the program is similar to other COBOL programs. That is, the first two divisions, the input File Description and the ARE-THERE-MORE-RECORDS field as specified in WORKING-STORAGE are all the same. The only change is in FD FILE-OUT, which contains a REPORT IS REPORT-LISTING clause in place of an 01 record description entry.

The FD for the print file in a program using the Report Writer Feature contains a LABEL RECORDS clause and may include a RECORD CONTAINS

Figure 22.3

Sample program that uses the Report Writer feature.

a. Program

```
IDENTIFICATION DIVISION.
PROGRAM-ID.      REPORT-WRITER2.
AUTHOR.          GLORIA FISHMAN.
****************************
*   THIS IS AN EXAMPLE OF  *
*   REPORT WRITER FEATURE  *
****************************
ENVIRONMENT DIVISION.
INPUT-OUTPUT SECTION.
FILE-CONTROL.
    SELECT FILE-IN ASSIGN TO DATA11.
    SELECT FILE-OUT ASSIGN TO SYS$OUTPUT.
*
DATA DIVISION.
FILE SECTION.
FD  FILE-IN
    LABEL RECORDS ARE STANDARD.
01  IN-REC.
    05  TERR                             PIC 9.
    05  CUST-NO                          PIC 9(7).
    05  ITEM-NO                          PIC 9(6).
    05  DESCRIPTION                      PIC X(35).
    05  QTY                              PIC 9(3).
    05  PRICE                            PIC 99V99.
    05  COST                             PIC 9(5)V99.
FD  FILE-OUT
    LABEL RECORDS ARE OMITTED
    REPORT IS REPORT-LISTING.
WORKING-STORAGE SECTION.
01  ARE-THERE-MORE-RECORDS               PIC X(3)   VALUE 'YES'.
    88  NO-MORE-RECORDS                             VALUE 'NO '.
REPORT SECTION.
RD  REPORT-LISTING
    CONTROLS ARE FINAL, CUST-NO
    PAGE LIMIT IS 60 LINES
    HEADING 3
    FIRST DETAIL 9.
01  TYPE IS REPORT HEADING.
    05  LINE NUMBER IS 3.
        10  COLUMN NUMBER IS 39          PIC X(33)
            VALUE 'REPORT LISTING WITH SUMMARIZATION'.
        10  COLUMN NUMBER IS 85          PIC X(4)
            VALUE 'PAGE'.
        10  COLUMN NUMBER IS 92          PIC 99
            SOURCE PAGE-COUNTER.
01  TYPE IS PAGE HEADING.
    05  LINE NUMBER IS 5.
        10  COLUMN NUMBER IS 5           PIC X(4)
            VALUE 'TERR'.
        10  COLUMN NUMBER IS 11          PIC X(11)
            VALUE 'CUST NUMBER'.
        10  COLUMN NUMBER IS 27          PIC X(11)
            VALUE 'ITEM NUMBER'.
        10  COLUMN NUMBER IS 41          PIC X(11)
            VALUE 'DESCRIPTION'.
        10  COLUMN NUMBER IS 77          PIC X(8)
            VALUE 'QUANTITY'.
        10  COLUMN NUMBER IS 88          PIC X(5)
            VALUE 'PRICE'.
        10  COLUMN NUMBER IS 98          PIC X(4)
            VALUE 'COST'.
```

Figure 22.3
(continued)

```
01   DETAIL-LINE TYPE IS DETAIL.
     05  LINE NUMBER IS PLUS 1.
         10   COLUMN NUMBER IS 5              PIC 9
              SOURCE IS TERR.
         10   COLUMN NUMBER IS 11 GROUP INDICATE PIC 9(7)
              SOURCE IS CUST-NO.
         10   COLUMN NUMBER IS 27            PIC 9(6)
              SOURCE IS ITEM-NO.
         10   COLUMN NUMBER IS 41            PIC X(35)
              SOURCE IS DESCRIPTION.
         10   COLUMN NUMBER IS 77            PIC ZZ9
              SOURCE IS QTY.
         10   COLUMN NUMBER IS 88            PIC Z9.99
              SOURCE IS PRICE.
         10   COLUMN NUMBER IS 98            PIC $(6).99
              SOURCE IS COST.
01   TYPE IS CONTROL FOOTING CUST-NO.
     05  LINE NUMBER IS PLUS 2.
         10   COLUMN NUMBER IS 72            PIC X(6)
              VALUE 'AMOUNT'.
         10   AMT COLUMN NUMBER IS 87        PIC $$$$,$$9.99
              SUM COST.
01   TYPE IS CONTROL FOOTING FINAL.
     05  LINE NUMBER IS 60.
         10   COLUMN NUMBER IS 16            PIC X(13)
              VALUE 'FINAL COST IS'.
         10   COLUMN NUMBER IS 50            PIC $$,$$$,$$9.99
              SUM AMT.
*
     PROCEDURE DIVISION.
     100-MAIN-MODULE.
         OPEN INPUT FILE-IN
              OUTPUT FILE-OUT.
         INITIATE REPORT-LISTING.
         READ FILE-IN
              AT END MOVE 'NO ' TO ARE-THERE-MORE-RECORDS.
         PERFORM 200-CALC-RTN
              UNTIL NO-MORE-RECORDS.
         TERMINATE REPORT-LISTING.
         CLOSE FILE-IN
              FILE-OUT.
         STOP RUN.
     200-CALC-RTN.
         GENERATE DETAIL-LINE.
         READ FILE-IN
              AT END MOVE 'NO ' TO ARE-THERE-MORE-RECORDS.
```

b. Sample Input Data

```
11234567123456SHOVEL                     01210000012000
31234567087600SNOW SHOVEL                01010000016950
31234567007601SMALL SNOW SHOVEL          00709990006993
22345678345678PICK                       10012500125000
42345678222222AX                         05017950089750
```

c. Sample Output

```
                              REPORT LISTING WITH SUMMARIZATION            PAGE   01

TERR  CUST NUMBER    ITEM NUMBER   DESCRIPTION                  QUANTITY   PRICE      COST


1     1234567        123456        SHOVEL                          12     10.00      $120.00
3                    087600        SNOW SHOVEL                     10     10.00      $169.50
3                    007601        SMALL SNOW SHOVEL                7      9.99       $69.93

                                                             AMOUNT            $359.43
2     2345678        345678        PICK                           100     12.50     $1250.00
4                    222222        AX                              50     17.95      $897.50

                                                             AMOUNT          $2,147.50


         FINAL COST IS                     $2,506.93
```

clause, but it *must not* include the DATA RECORDS clause, which is normally optional. Instead, a REPORT clause is coded as in the following:

Format

```
FD  print-file-name
    LABEL RECORDS ARE OMITTED
    [RECORD CONTAINS integer-1 CHARACTERS]
    ⎰REPORT IS  ⎱ report-name-1 . . .
    ⎱REPORTS ARE⎰
```

As noted, the RECORD CONTAINS clause is optional, but if used it should equal the number of characters per print line plus one for forms control.

The report-name must conform to the rules for forming data-names. In our program, the report-name is REPORT-LISTING.

Each report-name refers to a specific report, *not* just to a specific record format. That is, a report may (and usually does) contain several types of print records or report line formats. Most programs produce only *one report* in a program.

The use of the REPORT clause within the FD entry replaces the optional DATA RECORDS clause when the Report Writer Feature is employed. No 01 entry for a record description follows the FD for this file. Instead, each report-name listed in an FD entry must be further described by an RD entry with the same name, in the **REPORT SECTION** of the DATA DIVISION.

If a WORKING-STORAGE SECTION is required in a program, it follows the FILE SECTION, as illustrated in Figure 22.3. Note that since the Report Writer Feature handles all control breaks, page breaks, summations, and reset procedures, our program will use the WORKING-STORAGE SECTION only for the end-of-file indicator.

The REPORT SECTION, which follows, defines all aspects of the printed output. It specifies:

1. The line on which each record is to print. This can be specified as an actual line number (e.g., 3) or a relative line number that relates to a previous line (e.g., PLUS 2).
2. The report group type that describes each type of line (e.g., Page Heading, Detail).
3. The positions within each line where items or fields are to print. Each field can be given a VALUE or can have data passed to it from another field.
4. The control fields.
5. The fields to be used as summation fields.

With this information specified in the REPORT SECTION, the PROCEDURE DIVISION does not need to include coding for control break or summary operations.

A. RD **Entry**

The RD entry's name corresponds to the report name assigned in the FD for the output print file. Thus, in our program, we would have:

```
REPORT SECTION.
RD  REPORT-LISTING
```

Both the REPORT SECTION header and the RD entry are required.

The RD entry describes the report and, like its counterpart the FD entry in the FILE SECTION, it can have numerous subordinate clauses. The basic format for the *RD* or Report Description Entry is as follows:

Format

```
      REPORT SECTION.
      RD report-name-1

      [ {CONTROL IS    }  {{data-name-1} ...                } ]
      [ {CONTROLS ARE  }  {FINAL      [data-name-1] ...     } ]

      [      [LIMIT IS   ]              [LINE  ]   ]
      [ PAGE [LIMITS ARE ] integer-1   [LINES ]   ]

      [  [HEADING integer-2]           ]
      [  [FIRST DETAIL integer-3]      ]
      [  [LAST DETAIL integer-4]       ]
      [  [FOOTING integer-5]           ]
```

We will discuss the CONTROL and PAGE clauses in depth.

1. CONTROL Clause

The CONTROL clause specifies all fields to be used as control fields. These fields will be tested against their previous value to determine if a control break has occurred.

Major Control Fields Must be Specified before Minor Ones

The sequence in which the data-names are listed in the CONTROL clause indicates their level in the control hierarchy. Thus, in our illustration, the CONTROL clause must be specified as:

```
CONTROLS ARE FINAL, CUST-NO
```

This means that FINAL is at the highest level of control and CUST-NO is at a lower level of control. If there were several levels, they would be listed in sequence *with the first being the highest control level*. Thus for Figure 22.1, TERR, a field defined in the input record, is the major control item. AREA-IN is an intermediate control item, and DEPARTMENT is a minor control item. We would code, then, CONTROLS ARE TERR, AREA-IN, DEPARTMENT.

The Report Writer Feature automatically tests these control fields when input records are processed. We will see later on that this is accomplished with the GENERATE verb in the PROCEDURE DIVISION. The highest control level is tested first; if a control break occurs at this level, it automatically forces lower-level control breaks. Consider a date field that consists of MONTH and YEAR and is used for control breaks. A change in YEAR would force a break in MONTH, in this instance.

A FINAL control break occurs *after the last detail line is printed*.

How Lines Are Printed When a Control Break Occurs

The action to be taken when a control break occurs is specified by the programmer. To print a CONTROL FOOTING and/or a CONTROL HEADING after a control break occurs, we code both on the 01 level in the REPORT SECTION. CONTROL FOOTINGs (CF) print *followed by* CONTROL HEADINGs (CH). That is, CONTROL FOOTINGs typically contain accumulated control totals, so they should print first. Then, CONTROL HEADINGs, which relate to the *new control fields*, will print *before* any detail or summary lines for these new control fields.

If a major-level control break occurs, the Report Writer Feature prints minor-level CONTROL FOOTINGs first, followed sequentially by the next level CONTROL FOOTINGs until the major-level footings are printed. Then the major-level CONTROL HEADINGs, if any, are printed followed by any intermediate and minor level CONTROL HEADINGs. Thus, in the illustration in Figure 22.1, note that a DEPARTMENT control break first results in the printing of a TERR footing, followed by an AREA-IN footing, followed by a DEPARTMENT footing. We have not illustrated multiple-level control breaks in our first Report Writer program in Figure 22.3 because of their complexity.

2. PAGE LIMIT Clause

The PAGE LIMIT clause specifies the layout of a page of the report, indicating actual line numbers on which specific report group types are to print.
The PAGE LIMIT clause indicates:

1. The number of actual lines that should be used for printing (integer-1). Approximately 60 lines are usually allotted for a page; this would allow for adequate margins at both the top and bottom of the page.
2. The line on which the PAGE or first REPORT HEADING record may print (integer-2).
3. The line on which the FIRST DETAIL record may print (integer-3).
4. The line on which the LAST DETAIL record may print (integer-4).
5. The last line on which a CONTROL FOOTING record may print (integer-5). Only a PAGE FOOTING or REPORT FOOTING can print beyond integer-5.

Our illustration includes the following entries:

```
PAGE LIMIT IS 60 LINES
HEADING 3
FIRST DETAIL 9
```

The entire PAGE LIMIT clause is optional, but in order to use any of the subordinate clauses such as HEADING or FIRST DETAIL, PAGE LIMIT must be included. If the entire clause is omitted, the computer uses line numbering and page-length limits set by the implementor. If included, a PAGE-COUNTER field is maintained by the Report Writer Feature containing the number of pages generated, and a LINE-COUNTER field is maintained containing the number of lines generated on each page. These fields must *not* be defined in the DATA DIVISION; they are provided automatically by the Report Writer Feature. You can access the PAGE-COUNTER field in the report group description entries that follow to print a page number; similarly, you can access the LINE-COUNTER field to print the number of lines that actually appear on a page.

A period must follow the last clause of an RD or report description. The REPORT SECTION coding for our example, thus far, is as follows:

```
REPORT SECTION.
RD  REPORT-LISTING
        CONTROLS ARE FINAL, CUST-NO
        PAGE LIMIT IS 60 LINES
        HEADING 3
        FIRST DETAIL 9.
```

Self-Test   Consider the following input record:

DIV	DEPT	ITEM	AMT OF SALES	

Suppose we wish to print a report like the following:

```
                      SALES REPORT                   PAGE NO. XXXX
        DIV          DEPT       ITEM      AMT OF SALES
        XX           XX         XXX       $XXXX.XX
        XX           XX         XXX       $XXXX.XX
                          .
                          .
                          .
                          .
                     TOTAL ITEM AMT                  $XXXXX.XX*
        XX           XX         XXX       $XXXX.XX
        XX           XX         XXX       $XXXX.XX
                          .
                          .
                          .
                          .
                     TOTAL ITEM AMT                  $XXXXX.XX*
                     TOTAL DEPT AMT                  $XXXXX.XX**
        XX           XX         XXX       $XXXX.XX
        XX           XX         XXX       $XXXX.XX
                          .
                          .
                          .
                          .
                     TOTAL ITEM AMT                  $XXXXX.XX*
                   TOTAL DEPT AMT                    $XXXXX.XX**
                 TOTAL DIV AMT                       $XXXXX.XX***
                          .
                          .
                          .
              FINAL TOTAL                            $XXXXXX.XX****
```

1. DIV, DEPT, and ITEM are called _____ fields.
2. The first line printed is called a _____.
3. The printing of a line for each input record is called _____ printing.
4. The printing of total lines for DIV, DEPT, and ITEM is called _____ printing.
5. Each total line is referred to as a _____.
6. The major-level control item, as specified on the output, is _____.
7. The intermediate-level control item is _____, and the minor-level control item is _____.
8. A change in DEPT results in the printing of ___(no.)___ lines. That is, a DEPT control break also forces a(n) _____ control break.
9. A change in DIV results in the printing of ___(no.)___ lines. That is, a DIV control break causes a _____ line to print, followed by a _____ line and then a _____ line.
10. A _____ prints after all records and control totals, at the end of the job.
11. Assuming the Report Writer Feature will be used in this program, code the FD for the preceding output file.

12. (T or F) 01-level record description entries must not follow the above FD entries.
13. The REPORT SECTION must follow the _____ and _____ SECTIONs in the _____ DIVISION.
14. The name following the RD level-indicator is the same as the name following the _____ clause in the _____ SECTION for the output file.
15. Code the RD entry and its clauses for the preceding illustration.

Solutions

1. control
2. Page Heading (it is not a Report Heading, which would only appear on the first page of a report)
3. Detail
4. summary or group
5. CONTROL FOOTING
6. DIV (after FINAL)
7. DEPT; ITEM
8. two; ITEM
9. three; ITEM total or footing; DEPT total or footing; DIV total or footing
10. final total
11. A suggested solution is:

```
FD   OUTPUT-FILE
     LABEL RECORDS ARE OMITTED
     REPORT IS REPORT-OUT.
```

Note: The REPORT clause is required when using the Report Writer Feature.

12. T
13. FILE; WORKING-STORAGE; DATA
14. REPORT IS or REPORTS ARE; FILE
15. REPORT SECTION.

```
RD   REPORT-1
     CONTROLS ARE FINAL, DIV, DEPT, ITEM
     PAGE LIMIT IS 60 LINES
     HEADING 2
     FIRST DETAIL 5
     LAST DETAIL 58
     FOOTING 59.
```

Note: We are assuming that DIV, DEPT, ITEM are data-names used in the input record description.

B. Clauses Used at the Group Level within a Report Group Description

The first entry for a report group within the RD is called the *report group description entry*. It is coded on the 01 level.

The report groups within the REPORT SECTION are classified as headings, detail lines, and footings. The printing specifications and the format of each are defined in a series of *report group descriptions*.

AN OVERVIEW OF THE FORMAT FOR THE REPORT GROUP DESCRIPTION ENTRY

```
01   [data-name-1]
     TYPE Clause
     [LINE Clause]
     [NEXT GROUP Clause]
```

Data-name-1 is the name of the *report group*. It is a *required* entry *only* when the report group is specifically called for in the PROCEDURE DIVISION. We will see later that *detail report groups* are referenced in the PROCEDURE DIVISION with a GENERATE statement, but that headings and footings need not be identified with a data-name. This is because the Report Writer Feature will automatically print them at the appropriate time based on their TYPE.

Headings and footings, then, are given data-names only if a USE BEFORE REPORTING declarative will refer to them; we will *not* discuss this declarative here, but it is a method for interrupting the Report Writer sequence and performing procedures *prior to* printing certain lines of a report. With the Report Writer Feature, headings and footings automatically print at predetermined points, so that any record with a TYPE clause indicating a heading and footing need not have a data-name.

We discuss each clause in detail, beginning with the TYPE clause, which is the only required one. *Clauses may be coded in any sequence.* Note, however, that, as a convention, the TYPE clause is typically coded first in an 01-level entry.

1. TYPE Clause—Required

The TYPE clause specifies the category of the report group. The time at which each report group is printed within a report is dependent on its type. For example, a REPORT HEADING is printed before a PAGE HEADING, a CONTROL FOOTING is printed when a control break occurs, and so on. There are also established rules for the formation of each report group, which will be considered later on.

Format

```
01   [data-name-1]
       ⋮
                  ⎧ ⎧REPORT HEADING⎫                    ⎫
                  ⎪ ⎩RH            ⎭                    ⎪
                  ⎪                                     ⎪
                  ⎪ ⎧PAGE HEADING⎫                      ⎪
                  ⎪ ⎩PH          ⎭                      ⎪
                  ⎪                                     ⎪
                  ⎪ ⎧CONTROL HEADING⎫ ⎧data-name-2⎫     ⎪
                  ⎪ ⎩CH             ⎭ ⎩FINAL      ⎭     ⎪
                  ⎪                                     ⎪
     TYPE IS      ⎨ ⎧DETAIL⎫                            ⎬
                  ⎪ ⎩DE    ⎭                            ⎪
                  ⎪                                     ⎪
                  ⎪ ⎧CONTROL FOOTING⎫ ⎧data-name-3⎫     ⎪
                  ⎪ ⎩CF             ⎭ ⎩FINAL      ⎭     ⎪
                  ⎪                                     ⎪
                  ⎪ ⎧PAGE FOOTING⎫                      ⎪
                  ⎪ ⎩PF          ⎭                      ⎪
                  ⎪                                     ⎪
                  ⎪ ⎧REPORT FOOTING⎫                    ⎪
                  ⎩ ⎩RF            ⎭                    ⎭
```

Data-name-2 and data-name-3 in the format refer to control fields defined in the CONTROL clause of the RD entry.

Let us consider the report in Figure 22.4, which illustrates the various types of report groups.

Figure 22.4
Sample report that illustrates the various types of report groups.

Ⓐ ——————————— { ACME MANUFACTURING COMPANY
                  { QUARTERLY EXPENDITURES REPORT

JANUARY EXPENDITURES

	MONTH	DAY	DEPT	NO-PURCHASES	TYPE	COST	CUMULATIVE-COST
Ⓑ {							
Ⓒ {	JANUARY	01	A00	2	A	2.00	
			A02	1	A	1.00	
			A02	2	C	16.00	
Ⓓ —	PURCHASES AND COST FOR 1-01			5		$19.00	$19.00
	JANUARY	02	A01	2	B	2.00	
			A04	10	A	10.00	
			A04	10	C	80.00	
	PURCHASES AND COST FOR 1-02			22		$92.00	$111.00
	JANUARY	05	A01	2	B	2.00	
	PURCHASES AND COST FOR 1-05			2		$2.00	$113.00
	JANUARY	08	A01	10	A	10.00	
			A01	8	B	12.48	
			A01	20	C	38.40	
	PURCHASES AND COST FOR 1-08			38		$60.88	$173.88
	JANUARY	13	A00	4	B	6.24	
			A00	1	C	8.00	
	PURCHASES AND COST FOR 1-13			5		$14.24	$188.12
	JANUARY	15	A00	10	D	19.20	
			A02	1	C	8.00	
	PURCHASES AND COST FOR 1-15			11		$27.20	$215.32
	JANUARY	21	A03	10	E	30.00	
			A03	10	F	25.00	
			A03	10	G	50.00	
	PURCHASES AND COST FOR 1-21			30		$105.00	$320.32
	JANUARY	23	A00	5	A	5.00	
	PURCHASES AND COST FOR 1-23			5		$5.00	$325.32

Ⓔ ————————————————————————— REPORT-PAGE-01
Ⓕ ——————————— END OF REPORT

1. **A** represents the REPORT HEADING
   A REPORT HEADING, which can be abbreviated as RH, is the title of a report. It is the first item printed on each report. Note that there can be only one 01-level entry categorized as a REPORT HEADING. It appears once—at the top of the first page of the report.

2. **B** represents the PAGE HEADING
   A PAGE HEADING (or PH) indicates a report group that is produced at the beginning of each page. There can only be one 01-level entry categorized as a PAGE HEADING.

3. **C** represents the DETAIL line
   Each DETAIL (DE) record can be described with an 01-level entry. The first detail line of each group has the month and day indicated. We call these GROUP INDICATE fields. They only print when a control break has occurred.

4. **D** represents the CONTROL FOOTING
   The CONTROL FOOTING (or CF) report group is produced at the *end* of a control group for a given control item. The CONTROL FOOTING is printed when a control break occurs. It prints *prior to* any CONTROL HEADING, which would refer to the next control field's value. There is no CONTROL

HEADING in this report. There can be only one CONTROL FOOTING per control item. CONTROL FOOTING FINAL is used to print final totals at the end of a report.

5. **E** represents the PAGE FOOTING

The PAGE FOOTING (or PF) report group is printed at the end of each page. There can be only one 01-level entry designated as a PAGE FOOTING.

6. **F** represents the REPORT FOOTING

The REPORT FOOTING (or RF) report group is produced at the end of the report. There can be only one REPORT FOOTING.

We must designate the TYPE of a record or report group so that the Report Writer Feature can determine when it is to print. Remember that CONTROL FOOTINGs print before their corresponding CONTROL HEADINGs. This is because footings typically print control totals for the *previous group* and CONTROL HEADINGs print information relating to a new control group such as column headings and/or the *new control values*. Also, minor CONTROL FOOTINGs print before intermediate and then major CONTROL FOOTINGs. Note, too, that major CONTROL HEADINGs print before intermediate and minor CONTROL HEADINGs.

In the above, if we chose to print the date for each series of input records on a *separate line* rather than make it a GROUP INDICATE field, then it could be a control heading:

JANUARY 01

. . .

. . .

. . .

Control footing → PURCHASES AND COST FOR 1-01
Control heading → JANUARY 02

. . .

. . .

. . .

A CONTROL FOOTING need not print at the bottom of a page and that a CONTROL HEADING need not print on the top of a page. That is, a CONTROL HEADING can be programmed to print several lines after the previous CONTROL FOOTING totals by using relative line numbers (e.g., LINE NUMBER PLUS 3). This will be explained in the next section.

2. LINE Clause

The format of this clause is as follows:

Format

```
01    [data-name-1]
      ⋮

      ⎡                  ⎧ integer-1 [ON NEXT PAGE] ⎫ ⎤
      ⎢ LINE NUMBER IS   ⎨                          ⎬ ⎥
      ⎣                  ⎩ PLUS integer-2            ⎭ ⎦

      ⋮
```

This optional LINE clause specifies either:

1. An actual or absolute line number on which the corresponding report line is to be printed (e.g., LINE 3 or LINE 10).

or

> 2. A line number *relative to* the previous entry or to the previous page (e.g.,
> LINE PLUS 2).

The LINE NUMBER clause can appear on the 01 level or on a level subordinate to it. If *two detail lines* were to print, one on print line 5 and one on print line 7, a level number subordinate to 01 would be required for each.

Printing Two Detail Lines for Each Input Record

```
01   TYPE IS DETAIL.
     05  LINE NUMBER IS 5.
         10
          .
          .                        } Fields to print on line 5
          .
     05  LINE NUMBER IS 7.
         10
          .
          .                        } Fields to print on line 7
          .
```

Illustrations

> 1. Printing on actual Line Numbers.
>   Example:
>
> ```
> 01   TYPE IS REPORT HEADING.
>      05   LINE NUMBER IS 3.
> ```
>
> This could also be coded as 01 TYPE IS REPORT HEADING LINE NUMBER IS 3 if there is only one line generated for this report heading.
>
> 2. Relative Line Numbering.
>   Example:
>
> ```
> 01   DETAIL-LINE TYPE IS DETAIL.
>      05   LINE NUMBER IS PLUS 1.
> ```
>
> This means that detail lines will be single spaced.
>
> 3. The NEXT PAGE clause may also be used to print a line on the following page, as in:
>
> ```
> 01   TYPE IS REPORT HEADING.
>      05   LINE IS 10 ON NEXT PAGE.
> ```

We will use the convention of placing the LINE NUMBER clause *on a separate level* within the 01 although it sometimes can be coded along with the TYPE clause on the 01 level. If a specific report group has more than one line that is to print, it *must not have a LINE clause* in an 01-level entry. That is, if three lines are to print for an 01 level, they would all be coded on some subordinate level:

```
01    TYPE IS ...
      05   LINE 5.
       :
      05   LINE 7.
       :
      05   LINE 9.
       :
```

For consistency and ease of maintenance, then, *we code all LINE clauses on level 05 within the 01 level.* This is also a more structured way of coding.

The following is a brief review:

RULES

TYPE	NEXT PAGE	Absolute Line Number	Relative Line No.
REPORT HEADING	X[b]	OK[a]	Line number is relative to HEADING integer specified in RD (e.g., PLUS-1 prints at the HEADING integer-1 line)
PAGE HEADING	X	OK	Line number is relative to HEADING integer-1, or value of LINE-COUNTER, whichever is greater
CONTROL HEADING	OK	OK	OK*
DETAIL	OK	OK	OK*
CONTROL FOOTING	OK	OK	OK*
PAGE FOOTING	X	OK	Line number is relative to FOOTING integer
REPORT FOOTING	OK	OK	Line number is relative to FOOTING integer or LINE-COUNTER, whichever is greater

[a]OK—permitted.
[b]X—not permitted.

* The first relative line number on a page for a CONTROL HEADING, DETAIL line, or CONTROL FOOTING prints at the first detail line regardless of its PLUS integer-1 operand.

As noted, a `LINE-COUNTER` is established by the Report Writer Feature and used to control line numbering. The initial value of `LINE-COUNTER` will be the integer specified in the (`HEADING integer`) clause of the `RD`. Thus, if `HEADING 10` is specified, `LINE-COUNTER` begins with a 10.

3. `NEXT GROUP` Clause

This clause is most often used in a report group to indicate the line spacing (absolute or relative) to be performed when the last line of the control footing has been printed.

The format is as follows:

Format

```
01    [data-name-1]
      ⋮

    ⎡                    ⎧ integer-1      ⎫ ⎤
    ⎢ NEXT  GROUP  IS    ⎨ PLUS integer-2 ⎬ ⎥
    ⎣                    ⎩ NEXT PAGE      ⎭ ⎦
      ⋮
```

One main use of the `NEXT GROUP` clause is to provide some extra blank lines between the end of one control group and the start of the next. Another main use is to force a `REPORT HEADING` report group to print on a separate page before all other report groups. To accomplish this, the following is coded:

```
NEXT GROUP IS NEXT PAGE
```

Other Examples

1. To reinitialize `LINE-COUNTER` at a new line number after a report group is complete (line 6 for example), the following is coded:

```
NEXT GROUP IS LINE 6
```

2. To print a new group on a line that is a fixed number of lines from the previous group, the following is coded:

```
NEXT GROUP IS PLUS 3
```

Note that if a CONTROL FOOTING (NEXT GROUP integer-1) or (NEXT GROUP PLUS integer-2) causes a page change, the Report Writer Feature will advance the paper to a new page with proper formatting.

We have thus far considered all those items that can be designated on the 01 level. As in the other sections of the DATA DIVISION, we must specify the entries subordinate to the 01 report group description.

Self-Test

Consider the report in Figure 22.5.

Figure 22.5
Sample report for the Self-Test.

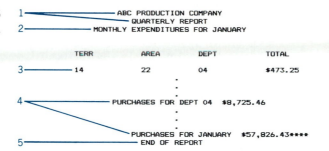

1. The lines indicated by 1 are considered TYPE _____; the line indicated by 2 is considered TYPE _____; the line indicated by 3 is considered TYPE _____; the lines indicated by 4 are considered TYPE _____; the line indicated by 5 is considered TYPE _____.
2. A CONTROL FOOTING or CONTROL HEADING prints when there is a _____.
3. Code the 01 level for the REPORT HEADING.
4. The NEXT GROUP clause (may, may not) be used with the REPORT HEADING.
5. Code the 01-level item for the PAGE HEADING.
6. Code the 01-level item for the DETAIL line, using double spacing.
7. Code the 01-level item for the CONTROL FOOTING that forces the next month's report groups onto the next page.
8. In the answer to Question 7, the word MONTH is necessary to _____.
9. (T or F) A minor-level CONTROL FOOTING prints before a major-level CONTROL FOOTING.
10. (T or F) A CONTROL FOOTING typically prints before a CONTROL HEADING.

Solutions

1. REPORT HEADING or RH if they are to print once, at the beginning. If they are to print on each page, they are PAGE HEADINGs.
   PAGE HEADING or PH—this heading changes when there is a new month—e.g., January to February, so it must be a PAGE HEADING.
   DETAIL LINE or DE
   CONTROL FOOTING or CF
   REPORT FOOTING or RF
2. change in a specific control item (TERRITORY, YEAR, CUSTNO, etc.). The control field is usually an input field.
3. A suggested solution is:

```
01  TYPE IS REPORT HEADING, LINE NUMBER 1,
```

   Note: We will not use a data-name after the 01 and before the TYPE unless it is a detail line to be referenced in the PROCEDURE DIVISION.

4. may not

5. `01 TYPE IS PAGE-HEADING, LINE NUMBER IS 5.`

6. `01 DETAIL-LINE TYPE IS DETAIL, LINE NUMBER IS PLUS 2.`

7. `01 TYPE IS CONTROL FOOTING MONTH, LINE PLUS 3`
           `NEXT GROUP IS NEXT PAGE.`

8. indicate the control item—a change in month (and a change in terr, area, and dept also cause control breaks)

9. T

10. T

C. Clauses Used at the Elementary Level within a Report Group Description

As in previous sections of the DATA DIVISION, we describe fields in entries subordinate to the 01 level. The format for fields within an 01 report group is:

Format

$$
\text{level-no [data-name-1]} \left\{ \begin{array}{l} \underline{\text{PICTURE}} \\ \underline{\text{PIC}} \end{array} \right\} \text{ IS character-string}
$$

$$
\left[\underline{\text{LINE}} \text{ NUMBER IS} \left\{ \begin{array}{l} \text{integer-1 [ON \underline{NEXT PAGE}]} \\ \underline{\text{PLUS}} \text{ integer-2} \end{array} \right\} \right]
$$

$$
[\underline{\text{COLUMN}} \text{ NUMBER IS integer-3}]
$$

$$
\left\{ \begin{array}{l} \underline{\text{SOURCE}} \text{ IS identifier-1} \\ \underline{\text{VALUE}} \text{ IS literal-1} \\ [\underline{\text{SUM}} \quad \{\text{identifier-2}\} \dots] \\ \left[\underline{\text{RESET}} \text{ ON} \left\{ \begin{array}{l} \text{data-name-2} \\ \underline{\text{FINAL}} \end{array} \right\} \right] \\ [\underline{\text{GROUP}} \text{ INDICATE}]. \end{array} \right\}
$$

For headings and footings that have VALUES, we need not indicate a field name or FILLER at all. We simply specify (1) the COLUMN in which the field is to print, (2) the field's PIC clause, and (3) its VALUE.

Data-names or identifiers are only required with detail, heading, and footing fields that are to be referenced elsewhere. For example, a data-name called AMT may be specified in the CUST-NO CONTROL FOOTING report group. This data-name may be needed because we will be summing or accumulating or "rolling forward" the AMT field to produce a CONTROL FOOTING.

The REPORT HEADING in Figure 22.3 has the following entries:

```
01  TYPE IS REPORT HEADING.
    05  LINE NUMBER IS 3.
        10  COLUMN NUMBER IS 39        PIC X(33)
                VALUE 'REPORT LISTING WITH SUMMARIZATION'.
        10  COLUMN NUMBER IS 85        PIC X(4)
                VALUE 'PAGE'.
        10  COLUMN NUMBER IS 92        PIC 99
                SOURCE PAGE-COUNTER.
```

PAGE-COUNTER is a COBOL special register that contains the number of the page to be printed.

The following clauses may be used to transmit the content in some named storage area to an individual field in a Heading, Footing, or Detail report group.

1. The SOURCE Clause

The SOURCE clause specifies that a data item is to be printed from a different field, usually defined in the input area or in WORKING-STORAGE. That is, the

SOURCE clause indicates a field that is used as a *source* for this report item. If an input field is designated as DEPT-IN, for example, we can indicate SOURCE IS DEPT-IN in any individual item within a report group. If SOURCE IS TERR for COLUMN 5 of a DETAIL line, then the input TERR field will print beginning in column 5 of that detail line.

2. The SUM Clause

The SUM clause is used for *automatic summation* of data. SUM is used only on a CONTROL FOOTING line. For example, 10 COLUMN NUMBER IS 50 ... SUM AMT in the CONTROL FOOTING FINAL report group in Figure 22.3 will print the sum of all AMT fields when that CONTROL FOOTING line prints.

Consider the following additional examples:

```
1. 05   COLUMN 14 PICTURE $ZZ,ZZZ.99 SOURCE IS COST.
2. 01   TYPE IS CONTROL FOOTING  LINE NUMBER IS PLUS 2.
       05   COLUMN 55 PICTURE $ZZ,ZZZ,ZZZ.99 SUM PRICE.
```

Example 1 indicates that beginning at Column 14 of the specified record, the contents of the field called COST should print. COST may be either a FILE or WORKING-STORAGE SECTION item, but usually it is an input field.

Example 2 is a CONTROL FOOTING group. In Column 55 of the CONTROL FOOTING report group, the sum of all accumulated PRICE fields will print. That is, PRICE is accumulated until the CONTROL FOOTING report group (of which Example 2 is a part) is to print; then the sum of all PRICE fields is printed, beginning in Column 55.

Thus, the use of SUM in an elementary item defines a summation counter. Each time a DETAIL report group is generated, the field specified (PRICE in the example) is summed.

3. The RESET Clause

The RESET clause may only be used in conjunction with a SUM clause. If the RESET clause is not included, a SUM counter will be reset immediately after it is printed. The RESET clause is used to *defer the resetting* of a SUM counter to zero until some higher-level control break occurs. Thus, the RESET clause permits a sum to serve as a running total for higher-level control breaks.

Examples

```
1. 05   COLUMN 65 PICTURE $$$$9.99 SUM COST
       RESET ON DEPT-NO.
2. 05   COLUMN 42 PICTURE $ZZZ.99 SUM AMT
       RESET ON MONTH.
3. 05   COLUMN 85 PICTURE $Z,ZZZ.99 SUM TOTAL
       RESET ON FINAL.
```

D. Review

In our program in Figure 22.3, we see that there are five report group types that are printed:

1. Report Heading

```
01   TYPE IS REPORT HEADING.
    05   LINE NUMBER IS 3.
        10   COLUMN NUMBER IS 39              PIC X(33)
            VALUE 'REPORT LISTING WITH SUMMARIZATION'.
        10   COLUMN NUMBER IS 85              PIC X(4)
            VALUE 'PAGE'.
        10   COLUMN NUMBER IS 92              PIC 99
            SOURCE PAGE-COUNTER.
```

a. Prints on line number 3.

b. The literal `'REPORT LISTING WITH SUMMARIZATION'` begins in column 39.

c. The literal `'PAGE'` begins in column 85.

d. The page number prints beginning in column 92. When the COBOL reserved word `PAGE-COUNTER`, which is a special register, is used as a `SOURCE`, the actual page number will automatically print.

2. Page Heading

```
01   TYPE IS PAGE HEADING.
    05  LINE NUMBER IS 5.
        10   COLUMN NUMBER IS 5              PIC X(4)
              VALUE 'TERR'.
        10   COLUMN NUMBER IS 11             PIC X(11)
              VALUE 'CUST NUMBER'.
        10   COLUMN NUMBER IS 27             PIC X(11)
              VALUE 'ITEM NUMBER'.
        10   COLUMN NUMBER IS 41             PIC X(11)
              VALUE 'DESCRIPTION'.
        10 COLUMN NUMBER IS 77               PIC X(8)
              VALUE 'QUANTITY'.
        10   COLUMN NUMBER IS 88             PIC X(5)
              VALUE 'PRICE'.
        10   COLUMN NUMBER IS 98             PIC X(4)
              VALUE 'COST'.
```

3. Detail Line

```
01   DETAIL-LINE TYPE IS DETAIL.
    05  LINE NUMBER IS PLUS 1.
        10   COLUMN NUMBER IS 5                        PIC 9
              SOURCE IS TERR.
        10   COLUMN NUMBER IS 11 GROUP INDICATE   PIC 9(7)
              SOURCE IS CUST-NO.
        10   COLUMN NUMBER IS 27                       PIC 9(6)
              SOURCE IS ITEM-NO.
        10   COLUMN NUMBER IS 41                       PIC X(35)
              SOURCE IS DESCRIPTION.
        10   COLUMN NUMBER IS 77                       PIC ZZ9
              SOURCE IS QTY.
        10   COLUMN NUMBER IS 88                       PIC Z9.99
              SOURCE IS PRICE.
        10   COLUMN NUMBER IS 98                       PIC $(6).99
              SOURCE IS COST.
```

a. Each detail line will print on the line following the previous detail line, which means that these lines will be single-spaced. Note that the *first* detail line on a page will print on the line specified by the `FIRST DETAIL` clause in the `RD` entry.

b. The input fields of `TERR`, `CUST-NO`, `ITEM-NO`, `DESCRIPTION`, `QTY`, `PRICE`, and `COST` will print in their specified columns.

c. The input field CUST-NO is a GROUP INDICATE field. This means that it prints when a change in the CUST-NO control field occurs (or after a page break). The source of a GROUP INDICATE field would typically be a control field.

d. QTY, PRICE, and COST are printed in edited form.

4. CONTROL FOOTING for Printing Control Totals

```
01   TYPE IS CONTROL FOOTING CUST-NO.
     05   LINE NUMBER IS PLUS 2.
          10   COLUMN NUMBER IS 72              PIC X(6)
               VALUE 'AMOUNT'.
          10   AMT COLUMN NUMBER IS 87          PIC $$$$,$$9.99
               SUM COST.
```

a. When there is a change in the CUST-NO control field, this footing will print.

b. LINE NUMBER PLUS 2 results in double-spacing.

c. The literal 'AMOUNT' and the sum of all input COST fields will print in the designated columns.

5. CONTROL FOOTING for Printing the Final Total

```
01   TYPE IS CONTROL FOOTING FINAL.
     05   LINE NUMBER IS 60.
          10   COLUMN NUMBER IS 16              PIC X(13)
               VALUE 'FINAL COST IS'.
          10   COLUMN NUMBER IS 50              PIC $$,$$$,$$9.99
               SUM AMT.
```

a. CONTROL FOOTING FINAL prints *after the last control break* at the end of the report. We will see later that this occurs when the TERMINATE statement is executed in the PROCEDURE DIVISION.

b. LINE NUMBER IS 60 in a report group, where a PAGE LIMIT of 60 has been designated in the RD, prints the footing on the bottom or last designated line of the page.

c. The literal 'FINAL COST IS' and the sum of all AMT fields will print. The sum of all AMTs, which themselves are SUMs, will print as a final total. AMT is a sum counter accumulated at the lower-level CONTROL FOOTING for CUST-NO.

IV. PROCEDURE DIVISION Statements

A. INITIATE Statement

The INITIATE statement begins the processing of a report. It is usually coded directly after the OPEN statement. It initiates the Report Writer Feature. Its format is:

Format

```
INITIATE report-name-1 . . .
```

The INITIATE statement sets all SUM and COUNTER fields to zero, including LINE-COUNTER and PAGE-COUNTER.

B. GENERATE **Statement**

The GENERATE statement is used to produce the report. It usually names a detail report group to be printed after an input record has been read. The format of this statement is:

Format

$$\underline{\text{GENERATE}} \quad \left\{ \begin{array}{l} \text{data-name-1} \\ \text{report-name-1} \end{array} \right\}$$

We may generate a DETAIL report group name (data-name-1 in this format) or an RD entry (report-name-1):

1. If the data-name is the DETAIL report group name, then the GENERATE statement performs all the functions of the Report Writer Feature, including control break processing, summary, and detail printing.
2. If the data-name identifies an RD entry, the GENERATE statement performs all functions of the Report Writer Feature *except detail printing*. In this way, only summary printing is achieved.

C. TERMINATE **Statement**

The TERMINATE statement completes the processing of a report after all records have been processed. Its format is:

Format

$$\underline{\text{TERMINATE}} \text{ report-name-1} \ldots$$

The TERMINATE causes the Report Writer Feature to produce all CONTROL FOOTING report groups beginning with the minor ones. That is, it forces all control totals to print for the last control group and also prints any final totals. It is usually coded just before the files are closed.

Note that the only report group format in Figure 22.3 that has a name is DETAIL-LINE. This is because DETAIL-LINE is the only report group accessed in the PROCEDURE DIVISION. Unless a USE BEFORE REPORTING declarative is coded, which we have not discussed here, only the report group with TYPE DETAIL needs to be given a data-name. We INITIATE and TERMINATE the report-name but GENERATE the detail line name (e.g., DETAIL-LINE) to achieve detail printing (as well as summary printing if the report contains CONTROL FOOTINGs).

Thus, the entire PROCEDURE DIVISION for our Report Writer program is:

```
PROCEDURE DIVISION.
100-MAIN-MODULE.
    OPEN INPUT  FILE-IN
         OUTPUT FILE-OUT.
    INITIATE REPORT-LISTING.
    READ FILE-IN
        AT END MOVE 'NO ' TO ARE-THERE-MORE-RECORDS.
    PERFORM 200-CALC-RTN
        UNTIL NO-MORE-RECORDS.
    TERMINATE REPORT-LISTING.
```

```
        CLOSE FILE-IN
              FILE-OUT.
        STOP RUN.
    200-CALC-RTN.
        GENERATE DETAIL-LINE.
        READ FILE-IN
             AT END MOVE 'NO ' TO ARE-THERE-MORE-RECORDS.
```

In summary, we can see that, although the Report Writer Feature requires a fairly complex REPORT SECTION of the DATA DIVISION, it results in simplified coding of the PROCEDURE DIVISION.

CHAPTER SUMMARY

I. DATA DIVISION Entries
  A. Code a REPORT SECTION following the WORKING-STORAGE SECTION.
  B. The FD for the output print file references the RD in the REPORT SECTION:

```
    FD  ...
           REPORT IS  [report-name-1.]
                ;
                ;
    REPORT SECTION.
    RD  [report-name-1.]  ◄
```

  C. RD clauses.
    1. Control fields are listed beginning with major controls as:

       CONTROLS ARE [FINAL,] major control field ...
                                minor control field.

    2. The PAGE LIMIT clause describes the number of print lines on each page; it can also include clauses that indicate what line a heading should print on and/or what line a first detail, last detail, and last CONTROL FOOTING should print on.
  D. 01 report group description entries can describe REPORT HEADING, PAGE HEADING, CONTROL HEADING, DETAIL line, CONTROL FOOTING, PAGE FOOTING, and REPORT FOOTING.
    1. A data-name is required on the 01 level only if the data-name is used in the PROCEDURE DIVISION (e.g., with TYPE DETAIL) or in a USE BEFORE REPORTING declarative, which has not been discussed here.
    2. A LINE NUMBER clause on the 05 level indicates what actual line or relative line the report group should print on.
    3. Specifying individual items within a report group:
      a. Each entry indicates the columns in which items are to print.
      b. Each entry can contain a (1) SOURCE—where the sending data is located, (2) VALUE, or (3) SUM if the item is the sum of some other field.
      c. A data-name is required after the entry's level number only if it is accessed elsewhere (e.g., in a CONTROL FOOTING's SUM clause).
    4. If a REPORT or PAGE HEADING or any detail printing requires more than one line, code each on an 05 level subordinate to the corresponding 01-level item.
II. PROCEDURE DIVISION Statements
  A. INITIATE report-name-1 after the files are opened.
  B. GENERATE detail-report-group-name after an input record has been read. The computer will print all headings, detail lines, control lines, and footings as well.
  C. Before closing the files, TERMINATE report-name-1.

CHAPTER SELF-TEST

1. Page numbers on each page of the report can be automatically generated by the computer if the _____ clause of the _____ SECTION is included in the program.

2. In order to print page numbers, the report group description entries defining the PAGE HEADING should reference a field called _____.

3. The CONTROL and PAGE-LIMIT clauses are defined in the _____ entry.

4. If a change in DISTRICT requires the printing of TOTAL-SALES, which is accumulated for each DISTRICT, then DISTRICT is called a _____ field.

5. The printing of TOTAL-SALES for each DISTRICT is called _____ printing, whereas the individual printing of each input record is called _____ printing.

6. The report-name referenced in the REPORT clause is defined in a(n) _____ entry of the _____ SECTION.

7. The three verbs required in the PROCEDURE DIVISION for using the Report Writer Feature are _____ , _____ , and _____ .

8. The identifier associated with the INITIATE verb is the _____ .

9. The identifier associated with the GENERATE statement is either the _____ for _____ printing or the _____ for _____ printing.

10. The TERMINATE statement has the same format as the _____ and is usually part of the _____ routine.

Solutions

1. PAGE LIMIT; REPORT
2. PAGE-COUNTER
3. RD
4. control
5. summary or group; detail
6. RD; REPORT
7. GENERATE; INITIATE; TERMINATE
8. report name (RD entry)
9. DETAIL report group name; detail; RD name; summary
10. INITIATE; end-of-job

PRACTICE PROGRAM

Write a program using the Report Writer Feature to generate the report in Figure 22.1. The solution is shown in Figure 22.6.

Figure 22.6
Practice Program that uses the Report Writer feature.

a. Program

```
IDENTIFICATION DIVISION.
PROGRAM-ID.     REPORT-WRITER2.
AUTHOR.         GLORIA FISHMAN.
**********************************************************
*   THIS IS AN EXAMPLE OF THE REPORT WRITER FEATURE   *
**********************************************************
ENVIRONMENT DIVISION.
INPUT-OUTPUT SECTION.
FILE-CONTROL.
     SELECT FILE-IN ASSIGN TO DATAH1.
     SELECT FILE-OUT ASSIGN TO SYS$OUTPUT.
*
DATA DIVISION.
FILE SECTION.
FD  FILE-IN
    LABEL RECORDS ARE STANDARD.
01  IN-REC.
    05  TERR                            PIC 9.
    05  AREA-IN                         PIC 9.
    05  DEPARTMENT                      PIC 99.
```

Figure 22.6
(continued)

```
          05  SALESPERSON                                    PIC X(20).
          05  SALES-AMOUNT                                   PIC 999V99.
      FD  FILE-OUT
          LABEL RECORDS ARE OMITTED
          REPORT IS REPORT-LISTING.
      WORKING-STORAGE SECTION.
      01  ARE-THERE-MORE-RECORDS                             PIC X(3)   VALUE 'YES'.
          88  NO-MORE-RECORDS                                           VALUE 'NO '.
      REPORT SECTION.
      RD  REPORT-LISTING
          CONTROLS ARE FINAL, TERR, AREA-IN, DEPARTMENT
          PAGE LIMIT IS 60 LINES
          HEADING 4
          FIRST DETAIL 10.
      01  TYPE IS REPORT HEADING.
          05  LINE NUMBER IS 4.
              10  COLUMN NUMBER IS 63                         PIC X(20)
                      VALUE 'MONTHLY SALES REPORT'.
              10  COLUMN NUMBER IS 85                         PIC X(4)
                      VALUE 'PAGE'.
              10  COLUMN NUMBER IS 92                         PIC 99
                      SOURCE PAGE-COUNTER.
      01  TYPE IS PAGE HEADING.
          05  LINE NUMBER IS 8.
              10  COLUMN NUMBER IS 6                          PIC X(9)
                      VALUE 'TERRITORY'.
              10  COLUMN NUMBER IS 19                         PIC X(4)
                      VALUE 'AREA'.
              10  COLUMN NUMBER IS 27                         PIC X(10)
                      VALUE 'DEPARTMENT'.
              10  COLUMN NUMBER IS 44                         PIC X(11)
                      VALUE 'SALESPERSON'.
              10  COLUMN NUMBER IS 57                         PIC X(15)
                      VALUE 'AMOUNT OF SALES'.
      01  DETAIL-LINE TYPE IS DETAIL.
          05  LINE NUMBER IS PLUS 1.
              10  COLUMN NUMBER IS 9 GROUP INDICATE  PIC 9
                      SOURCE IS TERR.
              10  COLUMN NUMBER IS 21                         PIC 9
                      SOURCE IS AREA-IN.
              10  COLUMN NUMBER IS 31                         PIC 99
                      SOURCE IS DEPARTMENT.
              10  COLUMN NUMBER IS 39                         PIC X(18)
                      SOURCE IS SALESPERSON.
              10  COLUMN NUMBER IS 60                         PIC ZZ9.99
                      SOURCE IS SALES-AMOUNT.
      01  TYPE IS CONTROL FOOTING DEPARTMENT.
          05  LINE NUMBER IS PLUS 3.
              10  COLUMN NUMBER IS 68                         PIC X(16)
                      VALUE 'TOTAL DEPARTMENT'.
              10  COLUMN NUMBER IS 85                         PIC 99
                      SOURCE IS DEPARTMENT.
              10  DEPT-TOT COLUMN NUMBER IS 89        PIC $$$$9.99
                      SUM SALES-AMOUNT RESET ON DEPARTMENT.
              10  COLUMN NUMBER IS 98                         PIC X
                      VALUE '*'.
      01  TYPE IS CONTROL FOOTING AREA-IN.
          05  LINE NUMBER IS PLUS 2.
              10  COLUMN NUMBER IS 79                         PIC X(10)
                      VALUE 'TOTAL AREA'.
              10  COLUMN NUMBER IS 90                         PIC 9
                      SOURCE IS AREA-IN.
              10  AREA-TOT COLUMN NUMBER IS 97        PIC $$$$$.99
                      SUM DEPT-TOT RESET ON AREA-IN.
              10  COLUMN NUMBER IS 107                        PIC XX
                      VALUE '**'.
      01  TYPE IS CONTROL FOOTING TERR NEXT GROUP IS NEXT PAGE.
          05  LINE NUMBER IS PLUS 2.
              10  COLUMN NUMBER IS 86                         PIC X(15)
                      VALUE 'TOTAL TERRITORY'.
              10  COLUMN NUMBER IS 102                        PIC 9
                      SOURCE IS TERR.
              10  TERR-TOT COLUMN NUMBER IS 111       PIC $$$$$9.99
                      SUM AREA-TOT.
              10  COLUMN NUMBER IS 121                        PIC XXX
                      VALUE '***'.
      01  TYPE IS CONTROL FOOTING FINAL.
          05  LINE NUMBER IS 60.
              10  COLUMN NUMBER IS 16                         PIC X(11)
                      VALUE 'TOTAL SALES'.
              10  COLUMN NUMBER IS 36                         PIC $$,$$$,$$9.99
                      SUM TERR-TOT.
```

Figure 22.6
(continued)

```
     *
      PROCEDURE DIVISION.
      100-MAIN-MODULE.
           OPEN INPUT FILE-IN
                OUTPUT FILE-OUT.
           INITIATE REPORT-LISTING.
           READ FILE-IN
                AT END MOVE 'NO ' TO ARE-THERE-MORE-RECORDS.
           PERFORM 200-CALC-RTN
                UNTIL NO-MORE-RECORDS.
           TERMINATE REPORT-LISTING.
           CLOSE FILE-IN
                FILE-OUT.
           STOP RUN.
      200-CALC-RTN.
           GENERATE DETAIL-LINE.
           READ FILE-IN
                AT END MOVE 'NO ' TO ARE-THERE-MORE-RECORDS.
```

b. Sample Input Data

```
1101A NEWMAN           41745
1101P PETERSON JR      62814
1101D SILVERS          40455
1102J ADAMS            37923
1102B JONES            29816
1103A BYRNES           55926
1103F CARLETON         22368
1204A FRANKLIN         62734
1204D ROBERTS          57226
1204S STONE            42632
1205L DANTON           36522
1205R JACKSON          42622
```

c. Sample Output

```
                              MONTHLY SALES REPORT   PAGE   01


TERRITORY    AREA    DEPARTMENT      SALESPERSON   AMOUNT OF SALES

    1          1        01        A NEWMAN           417.45
               1        01        P PETERSON JR      628.14
               1        01        D SILVERS          404.55


                                            TOTAL DEPARTMENT 01   $1450.14 *

    1          1        02        J ADAMS            379.23
               1        02        B JONES            298.16


                                            TOTAL DEPARTMENT 02    $677.39 *

    1          1        03        A BYRNES           559.26
               1        03        F CARLETON         223.68


                                            TOTAL DEPARTMENT 03    $782.94 *

                                                  TOTAL AREA 1      $2910.47  **

    1          2        04        A FRANKLIN         627.34
               2        04        D ROBERTS          572.26
               2        04        S STONE            426.32


                                            TOTAL DEPARTMENT 04  $1625.92 *

    1          2        05        L DANTON           365.22
               2        05        R JACKSON          426.22


                                            TOTAL DEPARTMENT 05    $791.44 *

                                                  TOTAL AREA 2      $2417.36  **

                                                        TOTAL TERRITORY 1      $5327.83 ***

            TOTAL SALES         $5,327.83
```

KEY TERMS

Control break	DETAIL	REPORT FOOTING
CONTROL FOOTING	PAGE FOOTING	REPORT HEADING
CONTROL HEADING	PAGE HEADING	REPORT SECTION

REVIEW QUESTIONS

1. What is the Report Writer Feature and when is it used?
2. Explain the meaning of the following terms:
   (a) CONTROL HEADING.
   (b) CONTROL FOOTING.
   (c) PAGE HEADING.
   (d) PAGE FOOTING.
3. Explain the differences between detail and group printing.
4. What is a control break and how is it used in group printing?
5. What section of the DATA DIVISION is required for writing reports using the Report Writer Feature?

DEBUGGING EXERCISES

Make necessary corrections to the following:

```
01   TYPE REPORT HEADING.
     05   LINE 1.
          10 COLUMN 44        PIC X(19)       VALUE 'COMPENSATION REPORT'.
*
01   TYPE PAGE HEADING.
     05   LINE 3.
          10 COLUMN 11        PIC X(16)       VALUE 'SALESPERSON NAME'.
          10 COLUMN 41        PIC X(12)       VALUE 'HOURS WORKED'.
          10 COLUMN 49        PIC X(11)       VALUE 'TOTAL SALES'.
          10 COLUMN 62        PIC X(10)       VALUE 'COMMISSION'.
          10 COLUMN 75        PIC X(05)       VALUE 'BONUS'.
          10 COLUMN 83        PIC X(10)       VALUE 'AMT. EARNED'.
*
01   DETAIL-LINE.
     TYPE DETAIL.
     LINE PLUS 1.
     05 COLUMN 11             PIC X(32)       SOURCE SALESPERSON-NAME-IN.
     05 COLUMN 43             PIC Z9          SOURCE YEARS-EMPLOYED-IN.
     05 COLUMN 49             PIC $ZZZ,ZZ9    SOURCE TOTAL-SALES-IN.
     05 COLUMN 63             PIC $ZZZ,ZZ9    SOURCE SALES-COMMISSION-IN.
     05 COLUMN 74             PIC $ZZ,ZZZ     SOURCE BONUS-IN.
     05 SUM AMT1 COLUMN 85 SOURCE BONUS-IN + SALES-COMMISSION-IN.
*
01   TYPE CONTROL FOOTING FINAL
     LINE PLUS 3.
     05 COLUMN 11             PIC X(18)       VALUE 'TOTAL COMPENSATION'.
     05 COLUMN 81 SUM AMT2    PIC $ZZZ,ZZZ,ZZ9.
```

PROGRAMMING ASSIGNMENTS

Code the programs at the end of Chapter 12 using the Report Writer Feature.

23

Relative File Processing

OBJECTIVES

To familiarize you with

1. How relative files are created, updated, and used for reporting.
2. Methods used for organizing relative files.

I. Processing Relative Disk Files

A. What Is a Relative File?

We have seen in Chapter 18 how disk files that are organized as INDEXED can be accessed and updated randomly. The relative method of file organization is another technique used when files are to be accessed randomly.

With indexed files, the key fields of records to be accessed are looked up in an index to find the address; with relative files, the key field is converted to an actual address. We begin with the simplest type of relative file where there is a direct one-to-one correlation between the value of the key and its disk location. That is, the key also serves as a relative record number.

Suppose, for example, that Accounts Receivable records are entered in sequence by ACCT-NO. If the ACCT-NOs vary from 0001 to 9999, then the record with ACCT-NO 0001 can be placed in the first disk location, the record with ACCT-NO 0002 can be placed in the next, and so on.

When a key does not have consecutive values, as in the case with many ACCT-NOs, we can still use the relative method of file organization by converting the key to a disk address using some type of algorithm or mathematical formula.

Relative file organization is best used where each record contains a kind of built-in relative record number. Since not all files lend themselves to this type of processing, relative files are not used as often as indexed files. One advantage of relative files, however, is that the random access of records is quite efficient because there is no need to look up the address of a record in an index; you simply convert the key to a disk address and access the record directly.

The field that supplies the key information, such as ACCT-NO above, also serves as a relative record number or **RELATIVE KEY**. The input-output instructions in the PROCEDURE DIVISION for random or sequential processing of relative files is very similar to that of indexed files.

The following is the SELECT statement used to create or access a relative file:

```
SELECT file-name-1 ASSIGN TO implementor-name-1
    [ORGANIZATION IS] RELATIVE
    [ ACCESS IS [ SEQUENTIAL  [RELATIVE KEY IS data-name-1] ]
                {RANDOM  }
                {DYNAMIC }   RELATIVE KEY IS data-name-1
    FILE STATUS IS data-name-2].
```

When ACCESS is SEQUENTIAL, as in the sequential reading of the file, the RELATIVE KEY clause is optional. When ACCESS is RANDOM or DYNAMIC, the RELATIVE KEY clause is required. A RELATIVE KEY must be unique and non-blank.

If ACCESS IS DYNAMIC is specified, you can use both sequential access and random access in the same program, using appropriate I/O statements. Suppose, for example, you wish to update a relative file randomly and, when the update procedure is completed, you wish to print the file in sequence. Use ACCESS IS DYNAMIC for this procedure, because it permits both sequential and random access. Here again, this is very similar to the processing of indexed files.

A `FILE STATUS` field may be defined in `WORKING-STORAGE` and used in exactly the same way as with indexed files, discussed in Chapter 18.

The `FD` that defines and describes the relative file is similar to indexed file `FD`s except that the `RELATIVE KEY` is *not* part of the record but is a `WORKING-STORAGE` entry:

```
FILE SECTION.
FD   file-name
     LABEL RECORDS ARE STANDARD.
01   record.
       :
WORKING-STORAGE SECTION.
       :
     05   (relative-key-field)      PIC ... .
```

Example
```
        SELECT REL-FILE
            ORGANIZATION IS RELATIVE
            ACCESS IS SEQUENTIAL
            RELATIVE KEY IS R-KEY.
               :
        FD   REL-FILE
               :
        WORKING-STORAGE SECTION.
        01   R-KEY                 PIC 9(3).
```

B. Creating Relative Files

Relative files are created sequentially, and either the computer or the user can supply the key. When a relative file's `SELECT` statement includes `ACCESS IS SEQUENTIAL`, the `RELATIVE KEY` clause can be omitted. If the `RELATIVE KEY` clause is omitted, the computer writes the records with keys designated as 1 to n. That is, the first record is placed in relative record number 1 (`RELATIVE KEY = 1`), the second in relative record number 2 (`RELATIVE KEY = 2`), and so on.

Suppose the programmer designates `CUST-NO` as the `RELATIVE KEY` when creating the file. The record with `CUST-NO 001` will be the first record on disk, the record with `CUST-NO 002` will be the second record, and so on. If there is no `CUST-NO 003`, then a blank record will automatically be inserted by the computer. Similarly, suppose a `CUST-NO` field that also serves as a `RELATIVE KEY` is entered in sequence as `10, 20, 30`, and so on; blank records would be inserted in disk locations 1 to 9, 11 to 19, 21 to 29, ... This allows records to be added later between the records originally created. That is, if a `CUST-NO` of `09` is inserted in the file later on, there is space available for it so that it will be in the correct sequence.

The following program excerpt writes 10 records with COBOL assigning `RELATIVE KEY`s 1 to 10 to the records:

```
            SELECT TRANS-FILE ASSIGN TO DISK2.
            SELECT REL-FILE ASSIGN TO DISK1
                ORGANIZATION IS RELATIVE
                ACCESS IS SEQUENTIAL.
                   :
            OPEN INPUT TRANS-FILE
                 OUTPUT REL-FILE.
            READ TRANS-FILE
                AT END MOVE 'NO ' TO ARE-THERE-MORE-RECORDS.
            PERFORM 200-WRITE 10 TIMES.
                :
```

```
200-WRITE.
    WRITE REL-REC FROM TRANS-REC
        INVALID KEY DISPLAY 'ERROR'.
******************************************************************
* The INVALID KEY clause is executed if there is                *
* insufficient space to store the record or if records          *
* are not in sequence.                                          *
******************************************************************
        READ TRANS-FILE
            AT END MOVE 'NO ' TO ARE-THERE-MORE-RECORDS.
```

In this case there is no need for a RELATIVE KEY clause in the SELECT statement because the computer will assign relative locations to each record.

The following example shows one way the programmer could supply the RELATIVE KEYs when creating a relative file:

```
        SELECT TRANS-FILE  ASSIGN TO DISK2.
        SELECT REL-FILE    ASSIGN TO DISK1
            ORGANIZATION IS RELATIVE
            ACCESS IS SEQUENTIAL
            RELATIVE KEY IS WS-ACCT-NO.
DATA DIVISION.
FILE SECTION.
FD  TRANS-FILE
    LABEL RECORDS ARE STANDARD.
01  TRANS-REC
    05  ACCT-NO                      PIC 9(5).
    05  REST-OF-REC                  PIC X(95).
FD  REL-FILE
    LABEL RECORDS ARE STANDARD.
01  REL-REC                          PIC X(100).
WORKING-STORAGE SECTION.
01  WORK-AREAS.
    05  ARE-THERE-MORE-RECORDS       PIC X(3)   VALUE 'YES'.
        88  NO-MORE-RECORDS                     VALUE 'NO '.
    05  WS-ACCT-NO                   PIC 9(5).
PROCEDURE DIVISION.
100-MAIN-MODULE.
    OPEN INPUT TRANS-FILE
         OUTPUT REL-FILE.
    READ TRANS-FILE
        AT END MOVE 'NO ' TO ARE-THERE-MORE-RECORDS.
    PERFORM 200-WRITE-RTN
        UNTIL NO-MORE-RECORDS.
    CLOSE TRANS-FILE
          REL-FILE.
    STOP RUN.
200-WRITE-RTN.
    MOVE ACCT-NO TO WS-ACCT-NO.
    MOVE TRANS-REC TO REL-REC.
    WRITE REL-REC.
        INVALID KEY DISPLAY 'WRITE ERROR'.
    READ TRANS-FILE
        AT END MOVE 'NO ' TO ARE-THERE-MORE-RECORDS.
```

In the preceding, the input ACCT-NO field also serves as a relative record number or RELATIVE KEY. Later on, we will see that if the ACCT-NO is not consecutive or is too long, we can *convert* it to a relative key using different types of procedures or algorithms.

C. Sequential Reading of Relative Files

The records in relative files may be read sequentially in the order that they were created. Because a relative file is created in sequence by RELATIVE KEY, a sequential READ reads the records in ascending relative key order.

There is no need to specify a RELATIVE KEY for reading from a relative file sequentially. Consider the following example:

```
SELECT REL-FILE  ASSIGN TO DISK1
    ORGANIZATION IS RELATIVE
    ACCESS IS SEQUENTIAL.
    :
OPEN INPUT REL-FILE
    OUTPUT PRINT-FILE.
READ REL-FILE
    AT END MOVE 'NO ' TO ARE-THERE-MORE-RECORDS.
PERFORM 200-CALC-RTN
    UNTIL NO-MORE-RECORDS.
CLOSE REL-FILE
    PRINT-FILE.
STOP RUN.
200-CALC-RTN.
    :      (process each record in sequence)
READ REL-FILE
    AT END MOVE 'NO ' TO ARE-THERE-MORE-RECORDS.
```

Note, then, that reading from a relative file sequentially is the same as sequentially reading from either an indexed file or a standard sequential file.

D. Random Reading of Relative Files

Suppose we wish to find the BAL-DUE for selected customer records on a relative file. An inquiry file includes the customer numbers of the specific records sought. Assume that the customer number was used as a relative record number or RELATIVE KEY.

```
SELECT REL-FILE  ASSIGN TO DISK1
    ORGANIZATION IS RELATIVE
    ACCESS IS RANDOM
    RELATIVE KEY IS WS-KEY.
SELECT QUERY-FILE  ASSIGN TO DISK2.
DATA DIVISION.
FILE SECTION.
FD  QUERY-FILE
    LABEL RECORDS ARE STANDARD.
01  QUERY-REC.
    05  Q-KEY                   PIC 9(5).
    05  FILLER                  PIC X(75).
FD  REL-FILE
    LABEL RECORDS ARE STANDARD.
01  REL-REC.
    05  CUST-NO                 PIC 9(5).
    05  CUST-NAME               PIC X(20).
    05  BAL-DUE                 PIC 9(5).
    05  FILLER                  PIC X(70).
WORKING-STORAGE SECTION.
01  STORED-AREAS.
    05  ARE-THERE-MORE-RECORDS  PIC X(3)  VALUE 'YES'.
        88  NO-MORE-RECORDS               VALUE 'NO '.
    05  WS-KEY                  PIC 9(5).
    05  ERR-SWITCH              PIC 9     VALUE 0.
        88 ERR-SWITCH-OFF                 VALUE 0.
PROCEDURE DIVISION.
100-MAIN-MODULE.
    OPEN INPUT QUERY-FILE
              REL-FILE.
    READ QUERY-FILE
        AT END MOVE 'NO ' TO ARE-THERE-MORE-RECORDS.
```

```
        PERFORM 200-CALC-RTN
            UNTIL NO-MORE-RECORDS.
        CLOSE QUERY-FILE
              REL-FILE.
        STOP RUN.
    200-CALC-RTN.
        MOVE Q-KEY TO WS-KEY.
        READ REL-FILE
            INVALID KEY
            DISPLAY 'ERROR = NO RECORD FOUND'
            MOVE 1 TO ERR-SWITCH.
        IF  ERR-SWITCH-OFF
            DISPLAY CUST-NAME BAL-DUE
        ELSE
            MOVE 0 TO ERR-SWITCH.
        READ QUERY-FILE
            AT END MOVE 'NO ' TO ARE-THERE-MORE-RECORDS.
```

The INVALID KEY phrase is executed if the *key* on the query file does not match a key on the relative file.

With COBOL 85, we could code 200-CALC-RTN without an error switch:

```
    200-CALC-RTN.
        MOVE Q-KEY TO WS-KEY.
        READ REL-FILE
            INVALID KEY DISPLAY 'ERROR - NO RECORD FOUND'
            NOT INVALID KEY DISPLAY CUST-NAME BAL-DUE.
        READ QUERY-FILE
            AT END MOVE 'NO ' TO ARE-THERE-MORE-RECORDS.
```

In the above, the computer assumes a direct conversion from the file's key field to its disk location. That is, the record with CUST-NO 942 is the 942nd record in the file. When the file is accessed randomly, the computer will directly access each record by the CUST-NO relative key.

We can also use a conversion procedure to convert a key field to a relative key, as we will discuss later.

E. Random Updating of Relative Files

When updating a disk file, you can access each record to be changed and REWRITE it directly. The relative file must be opened as I-O, the required record must be read, changed, and then rewritten for each update.

Suppose we wish to read a transaction file and add the corresponding transaction amounts to records in a relative master accounts receivable file:

```
SELECT TRANS-FILE  ASSIGN TO DISK2.
SELECT REL-FILE    ASSIGN TO DISK1
    ORGANIZATION IS RELATIVE
    ACCESS IS RANDOM
    RELATIVE KEY IS WS-KEY.
DATA DIVISION.
FILE SECTION.
FD  TRANS-FILE
    LABEL RECORDS ARE STANDARD.
01  TRANS-REC.
    05  T-KEY                   PIC 9(5).
    05  T-AMT                   PIC 999V99.
FD  REL-FILE
    LABEL RECORDS ARE STANDARD.
```

```
01  REL-REC.
    05  CUST-NO                    PIC 9(5).
    05  BAL-DUE                    PIC 9(5)V99.
WORKING-STORAGE SECTION.
01  STORED-AREAS.
    05  ARE-THERE-MORE-RECORDS PIC X(3)  VALUE 'YES'.
        88  NO-MORE-RECORDS                 VALUE 'NO '.
    05  WS-KEY                     PIC 9(5).
    05  ERR-SWITCH                 PIC 9     VALUE 0.
        88  ERR-SWITCH-OFF                   VALUE 0.
PROCEDURE DIVISION.
100-MAIN-MODULE.
    OPEN INPUT TRANS-FILE
              I-O REL-FILE.
    READ TRANS-FILE
        AT END MOVE 'NO ' TO ARE-THERE-MORE-RECORDS.
    PERFORM 200-CALC-RTN
        UNTIL NO-MORE-RECORDS.
    CLOSE TRANS-FILE
          REL-FILE.
    STOP RUN.
200-CALC-RTN.
    MOVE T-KEY TO WS-KEY.
    READ REL-FILE
        INVALID KEY DISPLAY 'ERROR ', WS-KEY
                    MOVE 1 TO ERR-SWITCH.
    IF  ERR-SWITCH-OFF
        PERFORM 300-UPDATE-RTN
    ELSE
        MOVE 0 TO ERR-SWITCH.
    READ TRANS-FILE
        AT END MOVE 'NO ' TO ARE-THERE-MORE-RECORDS.
300-UPDATE-RTN.
    ADD T-AMT TO BAL-DUE.
    REWRITE REL-REC
        INVALID KEY DISPLAY 'REWRITE ERROR'.
```

Using COBOL 85, we can replace 200-CALC-RTN with:

```
200-CALC-RTN.
    MOVE T-KEY TO WS-KEY.
    READ REL-FILE
        INVALID KEY DISPLAY 'ERROR ', WS-KEY
        NOT INVALID KEY PERFORM 300-UPDATE-RTN.
    READ TRANS-FILE
        AT END MOVE 'NO ' TO ARE-THERE-MORE-RECORDS.
```

The INVALID KEY clause of the READ statement is executed if the relative file's record corresponding to the one on the transaction file was not found.

The INVALID KEY clause of the REWRITE statement is executed if the key in WS-KEY is outside the file's range. The INVALID KEY clause is required when reading, writing, or rewriting records unless the USE AFTER EXCEPTION procedure is coded for performing I/O error functions. The FILE STATUS specification can also be used in the SELECT statement for determining which specific I/O error occurred when an INVALID KEY condition is met.

To delete relative records from a file, use the DELETE verb as we did with indexed files:

```
MOVE relative-record-number TO ws-key.
DELETE file-name RECORD
    INVALID KEY imperative-statement.
```

Once deleted, the record is logically removed from the file and cannot be read.

Self-Test
1. When creating a relative file, the ACCESS IS _____. When using a relative file as input, ACCESS IS either _____ or _____.
2. RELATIVE KEY is optional when reading or writing a relative file (<u>sequentially</u>, <u>randomly</u>).
3. (T or F) If ACCT-NO is used to calculate an address when writing records on a relative file, then ACCT-NO must be moved to a WORKING-STORAGE entry designated as the RELATIVE KEY before a WRITE is executed.
4. (T or F) To read the record with CUST-NO 125, move 125 to the record's CUST-NO and execute a READ.
5. (T or F) Relative file organization is the most popular method for organizing a disk file that may be accessed randomly.

Solutions
1. SEQUENTIAL; SEQUENTIAL; RANDOM (or DYNAMIC)
2. sequentially
3. T
4. F—125 must be moved to a WORKING-STORAGE *entry* specified in the RELATIVE KEY clause of the SELECT statement or converted to the WORKING-STORAGE RELATIVE KEY, as described in the next section.
5. F—Indexed files are still the most popular.

II. Converting a Key Field to a RELATIVE KEY

As noted, a key field such as CUST-NO or PART-NO can often serve as a relative record number or RELATIVE KEY. Sometimes, however, it is impractical to use a key field as a RELATIVE KEY.

Suppose a file has Social Security number as its key or identifying field for each record. It would not be feasible to also use this field as a relative record number or RELATIVE KEY. A record with a Social Security number of 977326322 could *not* easily be placed in relative record location 977,362,322. Most files do not have that much space allotted to them, and, even if they did, Social Security numbers as relative record locations would result in more blank areas than areas actually used for records.

Similarly, suppose we have a five-digit TRANS-NO that serves as a key field for records in a transaction file. Although TRANS-NO could vary from 00001 to 99999, suppose there are only approximately 1000 actual transaction numbers. To use TRANS-NO itself as a RELATIVE KEY would be wasteful since it would mean allocating 99999 record locations for a file with only 1000 records.

In such instances, the key field must be converted into a RELATIVE KEY. Methods used to convert or transform a key field into a relative record number are called **hashing**.

We could use the following hashing technique to compute a RELATIVE KEY for the preceding TRANS-NO example:

```
DIVIDE TRANS-NO BY 1009
    REMAINDER REL-KEY.
```

The REMAINDER from this division will be a number from 0 to 1008 that is a sufficiently large relative record number or RELATIVE KEY.

This is a rather simplified example, but such a direct conversion from key to address can be made. In this way, there is no need to establish an index, and records may be accessed directly, simply by including a formula for the conversion in the program.

The algorithm or conversion procedure, then, is coded:

1. When creating the relative file. Each record's key field is used to calculate the RELATIVE KEY.
2. When accessing the relative file randomly. Again, the inquiry or transaction record's key will need to be converted to a RELATIVE KEY before reading from the relative file.

This type of relative processing requires more programming than when processing indexed files because a conversion procedure is necessary and the hashing technique is sometimes complex. But the random access of relative files is faster than the random access of indexed files because there is no need to look up a record's address from an index.

When creating a relative file, then, it may be necessary to include a routine or algorithm for calculating the disk record's location or RELATIVE KEY. See Figure 23.1 for an illustration of a program that creates a relative file using a routine similar to the one described previously.

Collisions

A *collision* occurs when two or more relative keys are transformed by the randomizing algorithm into the same record address. The possibility of a col-

Figure 23.1
Program that creates a relative file.

```
          IDENTIFICATION DIVISION.
          PROGRAM-ID. CREATE.
          *******************************************************************
          *    THIS PROGRAM CREATES A RELATIVE FILE                         *
          *******************************************************************
          ENVIRONMENT DIVISION.
          INPUT-OUTPUT SECTION.
          FILE-CONTROL.
              SELECT TRANS-IN ASSIGN TO DISK1.
              SELECT RELATIVE-FILE ASSIGN TO DISK2
                  ORGANIZATION IS RELATIVE
                  ACCESS IS SEQUENTIAL
                  RELATIVE KEY IS RELATIVE-KEY-STORE.
          *
          DATA DIVISION.
          FILE SECTION.
          FD  TRANS-IN
              LABEL RECORDS ARE STANDARD.
          01  IN-REC.
              05  TRANS-NO                    PIC 9(5).
              05  QTY-ON-HAND                 PIC 9(4).
              05  TOTAL-PRICE                 PIC 9(5)V99.
              05  FILLER                      PIC X(64).
          FD  RELATIVE-FILE
              LABEL RECORDS ARE STANDARD.
          01  DISK-REC-OUT.
              05  DISK-REC-DATA.
                  10  D-PART-NO               PIC 9(5).
                  10  D-QTY-ON-HAND           PIC 9(4).
                  10  D-TOTAL-PRICE           PIC 9(5)V99.
                  10  FILLER                  PIC X(65).
          WORKING-STORAGE SECTION.
          01  WORK-AREAS.
              05  ARE-THERE-MORE-RECORDS      PIC X(3)   VALUE 'YES'.
                  88  NO-MORE-RECORDS                    VALUE 'NO '.
              05  STORE1                      PIC S9(8).
          01  RELATIVE-KEY-STORE              PIC 9(5).
          *
          PROCEDURE DIVISION.
          100-MAIN-MODULE.
              OPEN INPUT TRANS-IN
                   OUTPUT RELATIVE-FILE.
              READ TRANS-IN
                  AT END MOVE 'NO ' TO ARE-THERE-MORE-RECORDS.
              PERFORM 200-WRITE-RTN
                  UNTIL NO-MORE-RECORDS.
              CLOSE TRANS-IN
                    RELATIVE-FILE.
              STOP RUN.
          200-WRITE-RTN.
              MOVE IN-REC TO DISK-REC-DATA.
              DIVIDE TRANS-NO BY 1009 GIVING STORE1
                  REMAINDER RELATIVE-KEY-STORE.
          *******************************************************************
          ***   THE ABOVE INSTRUCTION IS ONE METHOD FOR CALCULATING ***
          ***   A RELATIVE RECORD NO.                               ***
          *******************************************************************
              WRITE DISK-REC-OUT
                  INVALID KEY DISPLAY 'WRITE-ERROR', IN-REC.
              READ TRANS-IN
                  AT END MOVE 'NO ' TO ARE-THERE-MORE-RECORDS.
```

lision always exists when creating or accessing relative files in which the key field needs to be converted into a relative record number or RELATIVE KEY.

In Figure 23.1, TRANS-NOs of 2019 and 4037 would both produce relative keys of 1. In fact, the only way a collision would be avoided entirely in this program is if the TRANS-NOs were consecutive (e.g., 4037–5036, 5045–6044, etc.: 4037/1009 has a remainder of 1, 4038/1009 has a remainder of 2, etc.).

One solution to the collision problem is to create a file where colliding records are placed in an *overflow area*. This overflow area would be in a part of the file beyond the highest possible address for records placed using the randomizing algorithm. This overflow area must be large enough to handle the anticipated number of collisions and would use a second algorithm for storing colliding records. This second algorithm would be executed if an IN-VALID KEY condition were met.

Accessing a relative file can be performed either sequentially or randomly. Sequential access of a relative file means that the records are read and processed in order by key field as with sequential disk and tape files that are sorted into key field sequence. This is rarely done with relative files because records with sequential key fields do not necessarily follow one another. When we randomly access a relative file, another input file (typically a transaction or query file) will indicate which disk records are to be accessed. Thus ACCESS IS RANDOM is the usual method for reading and updating relative files.

Suppose that a master payroll file has been created with Social Security number used to calculate the RELATIVE KEY. To access any payroll record on this file, we read in a transaction field called IN-SSNO, perform the calculations necessary for converting IN-SSNO to a disk address, and store that address in a WORKING-STORAGE field called SSNO-CONVERTED. Note that the RELATIVE KEY would also be defined as SSNO-CONVERTED. When the appropriate value has been moved to SSNO-CONVERTED, we can then execute the following: READ RELATIVE-FILE INVALID KEY .... The READ instruction will move into storage the record with a relative record number specified in SSNO-CONVERTED.

Many of the input-output instructions that apply to indexed files apply to all relative files, even those in which the RELATIVE KEY must be converted to a disk location.

CLAUSES USED TO UPDATE RANDOM-ACCESS FILES

OPEN I-O	Used when a relative file is being updated.
REWRITE	Writes back onto a relative file (you can only use REWRITE when the file is opened as I-O and a record has already been read from it).
INVALID KEY	Must be used with READ, WRITE, DELETE and REWRITE unless a USE AFTER STANDARD EXCEPTION declarative has been specified. The computer will perform the statements following the INVALID KEY if the record cannot be found or if the RELATIVE KEY is blank or not numeric. A NOT INVALID KEY clause may also be used with COBOL 85.
DELETE	Eliminates records from the file.
START	For logically positioning the file at some point other than the beginning; for subsequent sequential retrieval of records.

A FILE STATUS clause can be used in the SELECT statement with all relative files as well as with indexed files. Note, however, that *only one key* may be used with relative files; there is no provision for ALTERNATE RECORD KEYs as with indexed files.

Other algorithms for calculating relative file disk addresses are as follows:

RANDOMIZING OR HASHING ALGORITHMS

For transforming a numeric key field to a relative record number:

Algorithm	Explanation	Examples

Folding	Split the key into two or more parts, add the parts, truncate if there are more digits than needed (depending on file size)	1. An ACCT NO key= 0125
		    a. Split and add: 01 + 25 = RELATIVE KEY of 26.
		    b. The record would be placed in the 26th disk location.
		2. An ACCT NO key= 2341
		    Split and add: 23 + 41= RELATIVE KEY of 64.

Digit Extraction	Extract a digit in a fixed digit position—try to analyze digit distribution before selecting the digit position	1. An ACCT NO key =0125; we may make the RELATIVE KEY 15 if we assume that the second and fourth numbers are the most evenly distributed. 2. A RELATIVE KEY of 31 may be extracted from an ACCT NO of 2341.

Square value truncation	Square the key value and truncate to the number of digits needed	1. An ACCT NO key = 0125
		    a. Square the key giving a value of 15625.
		    b. Truncate to three positions; 625 becomes the RELATIVE KEY.

Here, again, if a collision occurs, the INVALID KEY clause of a READ or WRITE would be executed. Separate routines would then be necessary to handle these collisions.

In summary, one main difference between a relative file and an indexed file is that relative files may require a calculation for computing the actual address of the disk record. That is, relative files do not use an index for looking up addresses of disk records.

In general, it is *not efficient* to process relative files sequentially when a RELATIVE KEY is computed using a randomizing algorithm. This is because the records that are physically adjacent to one another do not necessarily have key fields such as ACCT-NO or PART-NO that are in sequence. Hence, relative file organization is primarily used for random access only. Note, too, that algorithms for transforming key fields into relative record numbers sometimes place records on a disk in a more-or-less haphazard way so that the disk space used is considerable. Thus, although relative files can be processed rapidly, they do not usually make efficient use of disk space.

CHAPTER SUMMARY

I. What is a Relative File?

    A. Relative files, like indexed files, are files that can be accessed randomly.

    B. With a relative file, there is no index. Instead, a record's key field such as `ACCT-NO` is converted to a relative record number or `RELATIVE KEY`. The conversion can be one-to-one (`RELATIVE KEY` = record key) or a randomizing algorithm may be used for calculating a relative record number from a record's key field.

    C. The random accessing of a relative file is very fast because there is no need to look up a disk address from an index.

    D. Sequential access of a relative file may be slow because records adjacent to one another in the file do not necessarily have key fields in sequence.

II. Processing Relative Files

    A. `SELECT` statement.

        1. Code `ORGANIZATION IS RELATIVE`

        2. `RELATIVE KEY` clause

            a. Uses

                (1) For randomly accessing the file.

                (2) For sequential reads and writes if a conversion is necessary from a record's key field to a `RELATIVE KEY`.

                (3) The data-name used as the relative record number or `RELATIVE KEY` is defined in `WORKING-STORAGE`.

        3. `ACCESS` can be `SEQUENTIAL`, `RANDOM`, or `DYNAMIC`. Use `DYNAMIC` when the file is accessed both randomly and sequentially in the same program.

    B. Processing routines.

        1. Creating a relative file:

            a. `ACCESS IS SEQUENTIAL` in the `SELECT` statement.

            b. Move the input record's key field to the `RELATIVE KEY`, which is in `WORKING-STORAGE` (or convert) and `WRITE ... INVALID KEY ....`

        2. Accessing a relative file randomly:

            a. `ACCESS IS RANDOM` in the `SELECT` statement.

            b. Move the transaction record's key field to the `RELATIVE KEY`, which is in `WORKING-STORAGE` (or convert) and `READ ... INVALID KEY ....`

        3. When updating a relative file, open it as `I-O`, `ACCESS IS RANDOM`, and use `READ`, `WRITE`, `REWRITE`, or `DELETE` with `INVALID KEY` clauses.

CHAPTER SELF-TEST

1. Suppose `PART-NO` in an inventory file is to be used as the `RELATIVE KEY`. Write the `SELECT` statement for the relative file. Include a `RELATIVE KEY` clause.

2. If two input records have the same `PART-NO`, an error (<u>will, will not</u>) occur.

3. The field used to specify a `FILE STATUS` code could be used to print a message if two records have the same _____.

4. The field specified with the `RELATIVE KEY` clause must be defined in _____.

5. It is generally faster to access a relative file randomly than a sequential file because _____.

6. Write a procedure to accept an input `T-PART-NO` from a terminal and use it to look up the corresponding relative record and print its `QTY-ON-HAND`. Assume that `T-PART-NO` can be used as the `RELATIVE KEY`.

7. Modify the procedure in Question 6 to enable the operator at the terminal to change the `QTY-ON-HAND`.

8. Suppose we want to print the QTY-ON-HAND for records with PART-NO 100 through 300. We use the _____ verb to position the file at the correct point.

9. For Question 8, the file must be accessed as either _____ or _____.

10. A RELATIVE KEY clause is not required in a program that reads from a relative file if _____.

Solutions

1.
```
SELECT INV-FILE
       ORGANIZATION IS RELATIVE
       ACCESS IS SEQUENTIAL
       RELATIVE KEY IS WS-PART-NO.
```

2. will

3. RELATIVE key

4. WORKING-STORAGE

5. there is no need to look up the address of the record from an index

6.
```
ACCEPT T-PART-NO.
MOVE T-PART-NO TO WS-PART-NO.
READ INV-FILE
       INVALID KEY DISPLAY 'ERROR'
                   MOVE 'YES' TO ERR-CODE.
IF  ERR-CODE = 'NO '
       DISPLAY QTY-ON-HAND
ELSE
       MOVE 'NO ' TO ERR-CODE.
```

For COBOL 85, we could code:

```
ACCEPT T-PART-NO.
MOVE T-PART-NO TO WS-PART-NO.
READ INV-FILE
       INVALID KEY DISPLAY 'ERROR'
       NOT INVALID KEY DISPLAY QTY-ON-HAND.
```

7.
```
DISPLAY 'DO YOU WISH TO CHANGE QTY-ON-HAND (Y/N)?'.
ACCEPT ANS.
IF  ANS = 'Y'
       ACCEPT QTY-ON-HAND
       REWRITE INV-REC
          INVALID KEY DISPLAY 'ERROR'.
```

Note: Both Questions 6 and 7 will need to be put into the context of a structured program if the procedures are to be repeated.

8. START

9. SEQUENTIAL; DYNAMIC

10. the file is accessed sequentially and the first record is to be placed in the first relative record area, the second in the second relative record area, and so on.

PRACTICE PROGRAM

Consider the problem definition in Figure 23.2.

Notes:

a. The QUERY-FILE contains the ACCT-NOs of all records that are to print, with their corresponding BALANCE-DUE.

b. The RELATIVE KEY is a WORKING-STORAGE entry called WS-KEY. It is the same as the ACCT-NO in the relative file.

The program, hierarchy chart, and pseudocode are in Figure 23.3.

a. Systems Flowchart

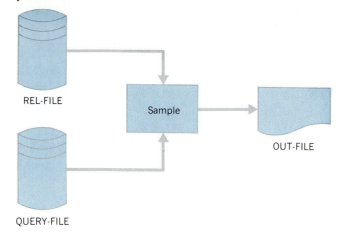

REL-FILE

Sample

OUT-FILE

QUERY-FILE

b. REL-FILE and QUERY-FILE Record Layouts

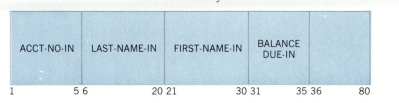

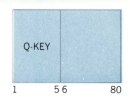

ACCT-NO-IN	LAST-NAME-IN	FIRST-NAME-IN	BALANCE DUE-IN	

1   5 6   20 21   30 31   35 36   80

Q-KEY

1   5 6   80

c. OUT-FILE Printer Spacing Chart

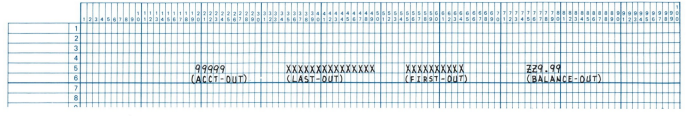

```
      99999              XXXXXXXXXXXXXXX     XXXXXXXXXX         ZZ9.99
     (ACCT-OUT)          (LAST-OUT)          (FIRST-OUT)       (BALANCE-OUT)
```

Figure 23.2
Problem definition for the
Practice Program.

Figure 23.3
Pseudocode, hierarchy chart,
and solution to the Practice
Program.

a. Pseudocode

```
START
    Open the Files
    Read a Record from the Query File
    PERFORM UNTIL no more Query Records
        Read a corresponding Relative Record
        IF   a match is found
        THEN
             Move Relative Data to Output Area
             Write Output Record
        ENDIF
        Read a Record from the Query File
    ENDPERFORM
    End-of-Job Operations
STOP
```

b. Hierarchy Chart

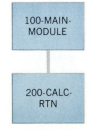

100-MAIN-
MODULE

200-CALC-
RTN

Figure 23.3
(continued)

c. Program

```
IDENTIFICATION DIVISION.
PROGRAM-ID.       SAMPLE.
AUTHOR.           GLORIA FISHMAN.
*****************************************************************
* THIS PROGRAM TAKES AN ACCOUNT NUMBER FROM THE QUERY FILE & READS THE*
* MASTER FILE FOR THAT ACCOUNT NUMBER. IF A MATCH IS FOUND THE ACCOUNT*
* NUMBER, NAME, AND BALANCE ARE PRINTED OUT.  IF NO MATCH IS FOUND THE*
* RECORD IS DISREGARDED & THE NEXT RECORD IS READ FROM THE QUERY FILE.*
*****************************************************************
ENVIRONMENT DIVISION.
INPUT-OUTPUT SECTION.
FILE-CONTROL.
    SELECT REL-FILE ASSIGN TO RELMDAT3
        ORGANIZATION IS RELATIVE
        ACCESS IS RANDOM
        RELATIVE KEY IS WS-KEY.
    SELECT QUERY-FILE ASSIGN TO RELQDAT3.
    SELECT OUT-FILE ASSIGN TO SYS$OUTPUT.
*
DATA DIVISION.
FILE SECTION.
FD  REL-FILE
    LABEL RECORDS ARE STANDARD.
01  REL-REC.
    05  ACCT-IN                       PIC 9(5).
    05  LAST-NAME                     PIC X(15).
    05  FIRST-NAME                    PIC X(10).
    05  BALANCE-DUE                   PIC 999V99.
    05  FILLER                        PIC X(45).
FD  QUERY-FILE
    LABEL RECORDS ARE STANDARD.
01  QUERY-REC.
    05  Q-KEY                         PIC 9(5).
    05  FILLER                        PIC X(75).
FD  OUT-FILE
    LABEL RECORDS ARE OMITTED.
01  OUT-REC                           PIC X(133).
WORKING-STORAGE SECTION.
01  WORK-AREAS.
    05  ARE-THERE-MORE-RECORDS        PIC X(3)  VALUE 'YES'.
        88  NO-MORE-RECORDS                     VALUE 'NO '.
    05  WS-KEY                        PIC 9(5).
    05  ERROR-CODE                    PIC 9     VALUE 0.
        88  ERROR-HAS-NOT-OCCURRED              VALUE 0.
01  DETAIL-LINE.
    05  FILLER                        PIC X(20) VALUE SPACES.
    05  ACCT-OUT                      PIC 9(5).
    05  FILLER                        PIC X(10) VALUE SPACES.
    05  LAST-OUT                      PIC X(15).
    05  FILLER                        PIC X(5)  VALUE SPACES.
    05  FIRST-OUT                     PIC X(10).
    05  FILLER                        PIC X(10) VALUE SPACES.
    05  BALANCE-OUT                   PIC ZZ9.99.
    05  FILLER                        PIC X(52) VALUE SPACES.
*
PROCEDURE DIVISION.
100-MAIN-MODULE.
    OPEN INPUT REL-FILE
         INPUT QUERY-FILE
         OUTPUT OUT-FILE.
    READ QUERY-FILE
        AT END MOVE 'NO' TO ARE-THERE-MORE-RECORDS.
    PERFORM 200-CALC-RTN
        UNTIL NO-MORE-RECORDS.
    CLOSE REL-FILE
          QUERY-FILE.
    STOP RUN.
200-CALC-RTN.
    MOVE Q-KEY TO WS-KEY.
    READ REL-FILE
        INVALID KEY MOVE 1 TO ERROR-CODE.
    IF ERROR-HAS-NOT-OCCURRED
        MOVE Q-KEY TO ACCT-OUT
        MOVE LAST-NAME TO LAST-OUT
        MOVE FIRST-NAME TO FIRST-OUT
        MOVE BALANCE-DUE TO BALANCE-OUT
        WRITE OUT-REC FROM DETAIL-LINE
            AFTER ADVANCING 2 LINES
    ELSE
        MOVE 0 TO ERROR-CODE.
    READ QUERY-FILE
        AT END MOVE 'NO ' TO ARE-THERE-MORE-RECORDS.
*****************************************************************
*   The following routine can be substituted for 200-CALC-RTN *
*      if you are using a COBOL 85 compiler                    *
*                                                             *
*200-CALC-RTN.                                                 *
*    MOVE Q-KEY TO WS-KEY.                                     *
*    READ REL-FILE                                             *
*        INVALID KEY NEXT SENTENCE                             *
*        NOT INVALID KEY                                       *
*                        MOVE Q-KEY TO ACCT-OUT               *
*                        MOVE LAST-NAME TO LAST-OUT           *
*                        MOVE FIRST-NAME TO FIRST-OUT         *
*                        MOVE BALANCE-DUE TO BALANCE-OUT      *
*                        WRITE OUT-REC FROM DETAIL-LINE       *
*                            AFTER ADVANCING 2 LINES.         *
*    READ QUERY-FILE                                           *
*        AT END MOVE 'NO ' TO ARE-THERE-MORE-RECORDS.         *
*****************************************************************
```

Figure 23.3
(continued)

Sample `REL-FILE` **Data**   **Sample** `QUERY-FILE` **Data**

```
00001FISHMAN      GLORIA   10000          00001
00002PRESLEY      ELVIS    20000          00009
00003SPRINGSTEEN  BRUCE    30000          00005
00004STERN        LORI     40000          00002
00005STERN        MELANIE  50000          00020
00006STERN        NANCY    60000          00006
00007STERN        ROBERT   70000
00008STEWART      JAMES    80000
```

Sample Output

```
00001          FISHMAN          GLORIA          100.00

00005          STERN            MELANIE         500.00

00002          PRESLEY          ELVIS           200.00

00006          STERN            NANCY           600.00
```

KEY TERMS

Digit extraction	Hashing	`RELATIVE KEY`
Folding	Randomizing algorithm	Square value truncation

REVIEW QUESTIONS

T   F

I. True-False Questions

__ __   1. A `RELATIVE KEY` clause is optional when reading from or writing to a relative file sequentially.

__ __   2. Relative keys must be unique.

__ __   3. The data-name specified with a `RELATIVE KEY` clause must be part of the relative file's record.

__ __   4. Relative keys must be entered sequentially when creating a relative file.

__ __   5. In general, accessing a relative file randomly is faster than accessing an indexed file randomly.

__ __   6. In general, accessing a relative file sequentially is faster than accessing an indexed file sequentially.

__ __   7. If an algorithm is used to convert an input record's key field to a `RELATIVE KEY` when creating a relative file, the same algorithm must be used when accessing that relative file.

__ __   8. An `INVALID KEY` clause is used with the `READ`, `WRITE`, `REWRITE`, and `DELETE` verbs for relative file processing. The clause is used in the same way as for indexed file processing.

__ __   9. If a disk file is to be accessed only sequentially, then the method of organization should be sequential, *not* relative or indexed.

__ __   10. A relative file can be accessed only randomly.

II. Validating Data   Modify the Practice Program so that it includes appropriate coding (1) to test for all errors and (2) to print a control listing of totals (records processed, errors encountered, batch totals).

DEBUGGING EXERCISES

Consider the following program excerpt:

```
        SELECT RELATIVE-FILE
            ASSIGN TO DISK1
            ORGANIZATION IS RELATIVE
            ACCESS IS RANDOM
            RELATIVE KEY IS R-ACCT-NO.
    DATA DIVISION.
    FILE SECTION
    FD  RELATIVE-FILE
        LABEL RECORDS ARE STANDARD.
    01  RELATIVE-REC.
        05  R-ACCT-NO              PIC 9(5).
        05  R-BAL-DUE              PIC 9(5)V99.
        05  FILLER                 PIC X(88).
    WORKING-STORAGE SECTION.
    01  ARE-THERE-MORE-RECORDS    PIC X(3)       VALUE 'YES'.
    PROCEDURE DIVISION.
    100-MAIN-MODULE.
        OPEN INPUT RELATIVE-FILE.
        DISPLAY 'ENTER ACCT NO:'.
        ACCEPT R-ACCT-NO.
        PERFORM 200-UPDATE-RTN
            UNTIL R-ACCT-NO = 99999.
        CLOSE RELATIVE-FILE.
        STOP RUN.
    200-UPDATE-RTN.
        READ RELATIVE-FILE
            AT END MOVE 'NO ' TO ARE-THERE-MORE-RECORDS.
        DISPLAY 'ENTER NEW BAL DUE:'.
        ACCEPT R-BAL-DUE.
        WRITE RELATIVE-RECORD.
        ACCEPT R-ACCT-NO.
```

1. Indicate what the program, in general, is intended to accomplish.
2. A syntax error occurs on each line where R-ACCT-NO is specified. Indicate why and make the necessary corrections.
3. The OPEN statement is incorrect. Indicate why and make the necessary corrections.
4. The READ statement produces a syntax error. Indicate why and make the necessary corrections.
5. The WRITE statement has *two* errors. Indicate what they are and make the necessary corrections.

PROGRAMMING ASSIGNMENTS

Redo Programming Assignments 1 through 3 in Chapter 18, assuming that the master file is relative instead of indexed.

APPENDIXES

Appendix A

COBOL Character Set, Reserved Words, and Instruction Formats

I. COBOL Characters

The following lists are in ascending order.

EBCDIC		ASCII	
	space		space
.	period, decimal point	"	quotation mark
<	less than	$	dollar sign
(	left parenthesis	'	single quotation mark
+	plus symbol	(	left parenthesis
$	dollar sign	)	right parenthesis
*	asterisk, multiplication	*	asterisk, multiplication
)	right parenthesis	+	plus symbol
;	semicolon	,	comma
-	hyphen, minus sign	-	hyphen, minus sign
/	slash, division	.	period, decimal point
,	comma	/	slash, division
>	greater than	0–9	digits
'	single quotation mark	;	semicolon
=	equal sign	<	less than
"	quotation mark	=	equal sign
a–z	lowercase letters	>	greater than
A–Z	uppercase letters	A–Z	uppercase letters
0–9	digits	a–z	lowercase letters

II. COBOL Reserved Words

Each COBOL compiler has a list of reserved words that

1. Includes most entries in the ANS COBOL standard.
2. Omits some ANS entries not used by the specific compiler.
3. Includes additional entries not part of the standard but that the specific compiler accepts. These are called enhancements.

Hence no list of COBOL reserved words will be complete. The following is based on the 1974 and 1985 American National Standard. You may find that your computer has additional reserved words. Diagnostic messages will print if you are using a reserved word incorrectly.

New reserved words that are not relevant for COBOL 74, but are only relevant for COBOL 85, are denoted with a single asterisk (∗). COBOL 74 reserved words that are *not* reserved in the new standard are denoted with a double asterisk (∗∗).

ACCEPT	CONTINUE *	END-PERFORM *
ACCESS	CONTROL	END-READ *
ADD	CONTROLS	END-RECEIVE *
ADVANCING	CONVERTING *	END-RETURN *
AFTER	COPY	END-REWRITE *
ALL	CORR	END-SEARCH *
ALPHABET *	CORRESPONDING	END-START *
ALPHABETIC	COUNT	END-STRING *
ALPHABETIC-LOWER *	CURRENCY	END-SUBTRACT *
ALPHABETIC-UPPER *		END-UNSTRING *
ALPHANUMERIC *	DATA	END-WRITE *
ALPHANUMERIC-EDITED *	DATE	ENTER **
ALSO	DATE-COMPILED	ENVIRONMENT
ALTER	DATE-WRITTEN	EOP
ALTERNATE	DAY	EQUAL
AND	DAY-OF-WEEK *	ERROR
ANY	DE	ESI
ARE	DEBUG-CONTENTS	EVALUATE *
AREA	DEBUG-ITEM	EVERY **
AREAS	DEBUG-LINE	EXCEPTION
ASCENDING	DEBUG-NAME	EXIT
ASSIGN	DEBUG-SUB-1	EXTEND
AT	DEBUG-SUB-2	EXTERNAL *
AUTHOR	DEBUG-SUB-3	
	DEBUGGING	FALSE *
BEFORE	DECIMAL-POINT	FD
BINARY *	DECLARATIVES	FILE
BLANK	DELETE	FILE-CONTROL
BLOCK	DELIMITED	FILLER
BOTTOM	DELIMITER	FINAL
BY	DEPENDING	FIRST
	DESCENDING	FOOTING
	DESTINATION	FOR
CALL	DETAIL	FROM
CANCEL	DISABLE	
CD	DISPLAY	GENERATE
CF	DIVIDE	GIVING
CH	DIVISION	GLOBAL *
CHARACTER	DOWN	GO
CHARACTERS	DUPLICATES	GREATER
CLASS *	DYNAMIC	GROUP
CLOCK-UNITS **		
CLOSE		
COBOL **	EGI	HEADING
CODE	ELSE	HIGH-VALUE
CODE-SET	EMI	HIGH-VALUES
COLLATING	ENABLE	
COLUMN	END	I-O
COMMA	END-ADD *	I-O-CONTROL
COMMON	END-CALL *	IDENTIFICATION
COMMUNICATION	END-COMPUTE *	IF
COMP	END-DELETE *	IN
COMPUTATIONAL	END-DIVIDE *	INDEX
COMPUTE	END-EVALUATE *	INDEXED
CONFIGURATION	END-IF *	INDICATE
CONTAINS	END-MULTIPLY *	INITIAL
CONTENT *	END-OF-PAGE	INITIALIZE *

INITIATE	PACKED-DECIMAL *	SELECT
INPUT	PADDING *	SEND
INPUT-OUTPUT	PAGE	SENTENCE
INSPECT	PAGE-COUNTER	SEPARATE
INSTALLATION	PERFORM	SEQUENCE
INTO	PF	SEQUENTIAL
INVALID	PH	SET
IS	PIC	SIGN
	PICTURE	SIZE
JUST	PLUS	SORT
JUSTIFIED	POINTER	SORT-MERGE
	POSITION	SOURCE
KEY	POSITIVE	SOURCE-COMPUTER
	PRINTING	SPACE
LABEL	PROCEDURE	SPACES
LAST	PROCEDURES	SPECIAL-NAMES
LEADING	PROCEED	STANDARD
LEFT	PROGRAM	STANDARD-1
LENGTH	PROGRAM-ID	STANDARD-2 *
LESS	PURGE *	START
LIMIT		STATUS
LIMITS	QUEUE	STOP
LINAGE	QUOTE	STRING
LINAGE-COUNTER	QUOTES	SUB-QUEUE-1
LINE		SUB-QUEUE-2
LINE-COUNTER	RANDOM	SUB-QUEUE-3
LINES	RD	SUBTRACT
LINKAGE	READ	SUM
LOCK	RECEIVE	SUPPRESS
LOW-VALUE	RECORD	SYMBOLIC
LOW-VALUES	RECORDS	SYNC
	REDEFINES	SYNCHRONIZED
	REEL	
MEMORY **	REFERENCE	TABLE
MERGE	REFERENCES *	TALLYING
MESSAGE	RELATIVE	TAPE
MODE	RELEASE	TERMINAL
MODULES **	REMAINDER	TERMINATE
MOVE	REMOVAL	TEST *
MULTIPLE	RENAMES	TEXT
MULTIPLY	REPLACE *	THAN
	REPLACING	THEN *
NATIVE	REPORT	THROUGH
NEGATIVE	REPORTING	THRU
NEXT	REPORTS	TIME
NO	RERUN **	TIMES
NOT	RESERVE	TO
NUMBER	RESET	TOP
NUMERIC	RETURN	TRAILING
NUMERIC-EDITED	REWIND	TRUE *
	REWRITE	TYPE
OBJECT-COMPUTER	RF	
OCCURS	RH	UNIT
OF	RIGHT	UNSTRING
OFF	ROUNDED	UNTIL
OMITTED	RUN	UP
ON		UPON
OPEN	SAME	USAGE
OPTIONAL	SD	USE
OR	SEARCH	USING
ORDER *	SECTION	
ORGANIZATION	SECURITY	VALUE
OTHER *	SEGMENT	VALUES
OUTPUT	SEGMENT-LIMIT	VARYING
OVERFLOW		

```
WHEN                          +
WITH                          -
WORDS **                      *
WORKING-STORAGE               /
WRITE                         **
                              >
ZERO                          <
ZEROES                        =
ZEROS                         >= *
                              <= *
```

III. Complete COBOL Language Formats

This appendix contains the composite language formats of the American National Standard COBOL. Shaded entries are those that are applicable to COBOL 85 only.

General Format for IDENTIFICATION DIVISION

```
IDENTIFICATION DIVISION.

PROGRAM-ID.    program-name  [ IS  { { COMMON  } }  PROGRAM ] .
                                   { { INITIAL } }

[AUTHOR.       [comment-entry] ... ]
[INSTALLATION. [comment-entry] ... ]
[DATE-WRITTEN. [comment-entry] ... ]
[DATE-COMPILED. [comment-entry] ... ]
[SECURITY.     [comment-entry] ... ]
```

General Format for ENVIRONMENT DIVISION*

```
[ENVIRONMENT DIVISION.
[CONFIGURATION SECTION.
[SOURCE-COMPUTER.  [computer-name  [WITH DEBUGGING MODE].]]
[OBJECT-COMPUTER.  [computer-name
    [PROGRAM COLLATING SEQUENCE IS alphabet-name-1]
    [SEGMENT-LIMIT IS segment-number].]]
[SPECIAL-NAMES.  [[implementor-name-1

    { IS mnemonic-name-1  [ON STATUS IS condition-name-1 [OFF STATUS IS condition-name-2]] }
    { IS mnemonic-name-2  [OFF STATUS IS condition-name-2 [ON STATUS IS condition-name-1]] } ...
    { ON STATUS IS condition-name-1 [OFF STATUS IS condition-name-2] }
    { OFF STATUS IS condition-name-2 [ON STATUS IS condition-name-1] }

    [ALPHABET alphabet-name-1 IS

    { STANDARD-1        }
    { STANDARD-2        }
    { NATIVE            } ...
    { implementor-name-2 }
    {                   }
    {          [ { THROUGH }        ] }
    { literal-1 [ { THRU    } literal-2 ] } ...
    {          [ {ALSO literal-3} ... ] }
```

---

*The ENVIRONMENT DIVISION, CONFIGURATION SECTION, and INPUT-OUTPUT SECTION entries are required for COBOL 74.

$$
\left[\underline{\text{SYMBOLIC}}\ \text{CHARACTERS}\left\{\left\{\{\text{symbolic-character-1}\}\ \dots\ \begin{Bmatrix}\text{IS}\\\text{ARE}\end{Bmatrix}\ \{\text{integer-1}\}\ \dots\ \right\}\ \dots\right.\right.
$$

$$
\left.\left.[\underline{\text{IN}}\ \text{alphabet-name-2}]\right\}\right]\ \dots
$$

$$
\left[\underline{\text{CLASS}}\ \text{class-name IS}\ \begin{Bmatrix}\text{literal-4}\ \left[\begin{Bmatrix}\underline{\text{THROUGH}}\\\underline{\text{THRU}}\end{Bmatrix}\ \text{literal-5}\right]\end{Bmatrix}\ \dots\ \right]\ \dots
$$

```
[CURRENCY SIGN IS literal-6]
[DECIMAL-POINT IS COMMA].]]]
[INPUT-OUTPUT SECTION.
FILE-CONTROL.
     {file-control-entry} . . .
[I-O-CONTROL.
```

$$
\left[\left[\underline{\text{SAME}}\ \begin{bmatrix}\underline{\text{RECORD}}\\\underline{\text{SORT}}\\\underline{\text{SORT-MERGE}}\end{bmatrix}\ \text{AREA FOR file-name-1}\ \{\text{file-name-2}\}\ \dots\ \right]\ \dots\right.
$$

```
[MULTIPLE FILE TAPE CONTAINS
     {file-name-3 [POSITION integer-1] } . . . ] . . . .]]]]
```

General Format for `FILE-CONTROL` **Entry**

SEQUENTIAL FILE

```
SELECT  [OPTIONAL]  file-name-1
```

$$
\underline{\text{ASSIGN}}\ \text{TO}\ \begin{Bmatrix}\text{implementor-name-1}\\\text{literal-1}\end{Bmatrix}\ \dots
$$

$$
\left[\underline{\text{RESERVE}}\ \text{integer-1}\ \begin{bmatrix}\text{AREA}\\\text{AREAS}\end{bmatrix}\right]
$$

```
[[ORGANIZATION IS]  SEQUENTIAL]
```

$$
\left[\underline{\text{PADDING}}\ \text{CHARACTER IS}\ \begin{Bmatrix}\text{data-name-1}\\\text{literal-2}\end{Bmatrix}\right]
$$

$$
\left[\underline{\text{RECORD}}\ \underline{\text{DELIMITER}}\ \text{IS}\ \begin{Bmatrix}\underline{\text{STANDARD-1}}\\\text{implementor-name-2}\end{Bmatrix}\right]
$$

```
[ACCESS MODE IS SEQUENTIAL]
[FILE STATUS IS data-name-2].
```

RELATIVE FILE

```
SELECT  [OPTIONAL]  file-name-1
```

$$
\underline{\text{ASSIGN}}\ \text{TO}\ \begin{Bmatrix}\text{implementor-name-1}\\\text{literal-1}\end{Bmatrix}\ \dots
$$

$$
\left[\underline{\text{RESERVE}}\ \text{integer-1}\ \begin{bmatrix}\text{AREA}\\\text{AREAS}\end{bmatrix}\right]
$$

```
[ORGANIZATION IS]  RELATIVE
```

$$
\left[\underline{\text{ACCESS}}\ \text{MODE IS}\ \begin{Bmatrix}\underline{\text{SEQUENTIAL}}\ [\underline{\text{RELATIVE}}\ \text{KEY IS data-name-1}]\\\begin{Bmatrix}\underline{\text{RANDOM}}\\\underline{\text{DYNAMIC}}\end{Bmatrix}\ \underline{\text{RELATIVE}}\ \text{KEY IS data-name-1}\end{Bmatrix}\right]
$$

```
[FILE STATUS IS data-name-2].
```

INDEXED FILE

SELECT [OPTIONAL] file-name-1

    ASSIGN TO $\left\{\begin{array}{l}\text{implementor-name-1}\\\text{literal-1}\end{array}\right\}$ ...

    $\left[\text{RESERVE integer-1}\left[\begin{array}{l}\text{AREA}\\\text{AREAS}\end{array}\right]\right]$

    [ORGANIZATION IS] INDEXED

    $\left[\text{ACCESS MODE IS}\left\{\begin{array}{l}\text{SEQUENTIAL}\\\text{RANDOM}\\\text{DYNAMIC}\end{array}\right\}\right]$

    RECORD KEY IS data-name-1
    [ALTERNATE RECORD KEY IS data-name-2 [WITH DUPLICATES]] ...
    [FILE STATUS IS data-name-3].

SORT OR MERGE FILE

SELECT file-name-1 ASSIGN TO $\left\{\begin{array}{l}\text{implementor-name-1}\\\text{literal-1}\end{array}\right\}$ ... .

REPORT FILE

SELECT [OPTIONAL] file-name-1

    ASSIGN TO $\left\{\begin{array}{l}\text{implementor-name-1}\\\text{literal-1}\end{array}\right\}$ ...

    $\left[\text{RESERVE integer-1}\left[\begin{array}{l}\text{AREA}\\\text{AREAS}\end{array}\right]\right]$

    [[ORGANIZATION IS] SEQUENTIAL]

    $\left[\text{PADDING CHARACTER IS}\left\{\begin{array}{l}\text{data-name-1}\\\text{literal-1}\end{array}\right\}\right]$

    $\left[\text{RECORD DELIMITER IS}\left\{\begin{array}{l}\text{STANDARD-1}\\\text{implementor-name-2}\end{array}\right\}\right]$

    [ACCESS MODE IS SEQUENTIAL]
    [FILE STATUS IS data-name-2].

General Format for DATA DIVISION

[DATA DIVISION.
[FILE SECTION.
[file-description-entry
{record-description-entry} ...] ...
[sort-merge-file-description-entry
{record-description-entry} ...] ...
[report-file-description-entry] ...]
[WORKING-STORAGE SECTION.

$\left[\begin{array}{l}\text{77-level-description-entry}\\\text{record-description-entry}\end{array}\right]$ ...

[LINKAGE SECTION.

$\left[\begin{array}{l}\text{77-level-description-entry}\\\text{record-description-entry}\end{array}\right]$ ...

[COMMUNICATION SECTION.

[communication-description-entry
[record-description-entry] ...] ...]
[REPORT SECTION.
[report-description-entry]
{report-group-description-entry} ...] ...]]

General Format for File Description Entry

SEQUENTIAL FILE

FD file-name-1
    [IS EXTERNAL]
    [IS GLOBAL]

$$\left[\text{BLOCK CONTAINS } [\text{integer-1 } \underline{TO}] \text{ integer-2} \left\{ \begin{array}{l} \text{RECORDS} \\ \text{CHARACTERS} \end{array} \right\} \right]$$

$$\left[\underline{RECORD} \left\{ \begin{array}{l} \text{CONTAINS integer-3 CHARACTERS} \\ \text{IS } \underline{VARYING} \text{ IN SIZE } [[\text{FROM integer-4}] \text{ } [\underline{TO} \text{ integer-5}] \text{ CHARACTERS}] \\ \qquad [\underline{DEPENDING} \text{ ON data-name-1}] \\ \text{CONTAINS integer-6 } \underline{TO} \text{ integer-7 CHARACTERS} \end{array} \right\} \right]$$

$$\left[\underline{LABEL} \left\{ \begin{array}{l} \underline{RECORD} \text{ IS} \\ \underline{RECORDS} \text{ ARE} \end{array} \right\} \left\{ \begin{array}{l} \underline{STANDARD} \\ \underline{OMITTED} \end{array} \right\} \right]$$

$$\left[\underline{VALUE} \text{ } \underline{OF} \left\{ \text{implementor-name-1 IS } \left\{ \begin{array}{l} \text{data-name-2} \\ \text{literal-1} \end{array} \right\} \right\} \dots \right]$$

$$\left[\underline{DATA} \left\{ \begin{array}{l} \underline{RECORD} \text{ IS} \\ \underline{RECORDS} \text{ ARE} \end{array} \right\} \{\text{data-name-3}\} \dots \right]$$

$$\left[\underline{LINAGE} \text{ IS } \left\{ \begin{array}{l} \text{data-name-4} \\ \text{integer-8} \end{array} \right\} \text{ LINES } \left[\text{WITH } \underline{FOOTING} \text{ AT } \left\{ \begin{array}{l} \text{data-name-5} \\ \text{integer-9} \end{array} \right\} \right] \right.$$

$$\left. \left[\text{LINES AT } \underline{TOP} \left\{ \begin{array}{l} \text{data-name-6} \\ \text{integer-10} \end{array} \right\} \right] \left[\text{LINES AT } \underline{BOTTOM} \left\{ \begin{array}{l} \text{data-name-7} \\ \text{integer-11} \end{array} \right\} \right] \right]$$

[CODE-SET IS alphabet-name-1].

RELATIVE FILE

FD file-name-1
    [IS EXTERNAL]
    [IS GLOBAL]

$$\left[\underline{BLOCK} \text{ CONTAINS } [\text{integer-1 } \underline{TO}] \text{ integer-2} \left\{ \begin{array}{l} \text{RECORDS} \\ \text{CHARACTERS} \end{array} \right\} \right]$$

$$\left[\underline{RECORD} \left\{ \begin{array}{l} \text{CONTAINS integer-3 CHARACTERS} \\ \text{IS } \underline{VARYING} \text{ IN SIZE } [[\text{FROM integer-4}] \text{ } [\underline{TO} \text{ integer-5}] \text{ CHARACTERS}] \\ \qquad [\underline{DEPENDING} \text{ ON data-name-1}] \\ \text{CONTAINS integer-6 } \underline{TO} \text{ integer-7 CHARACTERS} \end{array} \right\} \right]$$

$$\left[\underline{LABEL} \left\{ \begin{array}{l} \underline{RECORD} \text{ IS} \\ \underline{RECORDS} \text{ ARE} \end{array} \right\} \left\{ \begin{array}{l} \underline{STANDARD} \\ \underline{OMITTED} \end{array} \right\} \right]$$

$$\left[\underline{VALUE} \text{ } \underline{OF} \left\{ \text{implementor-name-1 IS } \left\{ \begin{array}{l} \text{data-name-2} \\ \text{literal-1} \end{array} \right\} \right\} \dots \right]$$

$$\left[\underline{DATA} \left\{ \begin{array}{l} \underline{RECORD} \text{ IS} \\ \underline{RECORDS} \text{ ARE} \end{array} \right\} \{\text{data-name-3}\} \dots \right].$$

INDEXED FILE

FD file-name-1
    [IS EXTERNAL]

[IS <u>GLOBAL</u>]

[<u>BLOCK</u> CONTAINS   [integer-1 <u>TO</u>]   integer-2   { <u>RECORDS</u> / <u>CHARACTERS</u> }]

[<u>RECORD</u>   { CONTAINS integer-3 CHARACTERS / IS <u>VARYING</u> IN SIZE [[FROM integer-4] [<u>TO</u> integer-5] CHARACTERS] / [<u>DEPENDING</u> ON data-name-1] / CONTAINS integer-6 <u>TO</u> integer-7 CHARACTERS }]

[<u>LABEL</u>   { <u>RECORD</u> IS / <u>RECORDS</u> ARE }   { <u>STANDARD</u> / <u>OMITTED</u> }]

[<u>VALUE OF</u>   { implementor-name-1   IS   { data-name-2 / literal-1 } } ...]

[<u>DATA</u>   { <u>RECORD</u> IS / <u>RECORDS</u> ARE }   {data-name-3} ...].

SORT-MERGE FILE

<u>SD</u>   file-name-1

[<u>RECORD</u>   { CONTAINS integer-1 CHARACTERS / IS <u>VARYING</u> IN SIZE [[FROM integer-2] [<u>TO</u> integer-3] CHARACTERS] / [<u>DEPENDING</u> ON data-name-1] / CONTAINS integer-4 <u>TO</u> integer-5 CHARACTERS }]

[<u>DATA</u>   { <u>RECORD</u> IS / <u>RECORDS</u> ARE }   {data-name-2} ...]

REPORT FILE

<u>FD</u>   file-name-1
[IS <u>EXTERNAL</u>]
[IS <u>GLOBAL</u>]

[<u>BLOCK</u> CONTAINS   [integer-1 <u>TO</u>]   integer-2   { <u>RECORDS</u> / <u>CHARACTERS</u> }]

[<u>RECORD</u>   { CONTAINS integer-3 CHARACTERS / IS <u>VARYING</u> IN SIZE [[FROM integer-4] [<u>TO</u> integer-5] CHARACTERS] / [<u>DEPENDING</u> ON data-name-1] / CONTAINS integer-6 <u>TO</u> integer-7 CHARACTERS }]

[<u>LABEL</u>   { <u>RECORD</u> IS / <u>RECORDS</u> ARE }   { <u>STANDARD</u> / <u>OMITTED</u> }]

[<u>VALUE OF</u>   { implementor-name-1 IS   { data-name-2 / literal-1 } } ...]

[<u>CODE-SET</u> IS alphabet-name-1]

{ <u>REPORT</u> IS / <u>REPORTS</u> ARE }   {report-name-1} ...

General Format for Data Description Entry

FORMAT 1

level-number   [data-name-1 / FILLER]

[<u>REDEFINES</u> data-name-2]
[IS <u>EXTERNAL</u>]
[IS <u>GLOBAL</u>]

$$\left[\begin{Bmatrix} \underline{\text{PICTURE}} \\ \underline{\text{PIC}} \end{Bmatrix} \text{ IS character-string}\right]$$

$$\left[\underline{[\text{USAGE}} \text{ IS}] \begin{Bmatrix} \underline{\text{BINARY}} \\ \underline{\text{COMPUTATIONAL}} \\ \underline{\text{COMP}} \\ \underline{\text{DISPLAY}} \\ \underline{\text{INDEX}} \\ \underline{\text{PACKED-DECIMAL}} \end{Bmatrix}\right]$$

$$\left[\underline{[\text{SIGN}} \text{ IS]} \begin{Bmatrix} \underline{\text{LEADING}} \\ \underline{\text{TRAILING}} \end{Bmatrix} [\underline{\text{SEPARATE}} \text{ CHARACTER}]\right]$$

$$\left[\begin{array}{l} \text{OCCURS integer-2 TIMES} \\ \quad \left[\begin{Bmatrix} \underline{\text{ASCENDING}} \\ \underline{\text{DESCENDING}} \end{Bmatrix} \text{ KEY IS } \{\text{data-name-3}\} \dots \right] \dots \\ \quad [\underline{\text{INDEXED}} \text{ BY } \{\text{index-name-1}\} \dots] \\ \underline{\text{OCCURS}} \text{ integer-1 } \underline{\text{TO}} \text{ integer-2 TIMES } \underline{\text{DEPENDING}} \text{ ON data-name-4} \\ \quad \left[\begin{Bmatrix} \underline{\text{ASCENDING}} \\ \underline{\text{DESCENDING}} \end{Bmatrix} \text{ KEY IS } \{\text{data-name-3}\} \dots \right] \dots \\ \quad [\underline{\text{INDEXED}} \text{ BY } \{\text{index-name-1}\} \dots] \end{array}\right]$$

$$\left[\begin{Bmatrix} \underline{\text{SYNCHRONIZED}} \\ \underline{\text{SYNC}} \end{Bmatrix} \left[\begin{matrix} \underline{\text{LEFT}} \\ \underline{\text{RIGHT}} \end{matrix}\right]\right]$$

$$\left[\begin{Bmatrix} \underline{\text{JUSTIFIED}} \\ \underline{\text{JUST}} \end{Bmatrix} \text{ RIGHT}\right]$$

$$[\underline{\text{BLANK}} \text{ WHEN } \underline{\text{ZERO}}]$$
$$[\underline{\text{VALUE}} \text{ IS literal-1}].$$

FORMAT 2

66   data-name-1 $\underline{\text{RENAMES}}$ data-name-2 $\left[\begin{Bmatrix} \underline{\text{THROUGH}} \\ \underline{\text{THRU}} \end{Bmatrix} \text{ data-name-3}\right].$

FORMAT 3

88   condition-name-1 $\begin{Bmatrix} \underline{\text{VALUE}} \text{ IS} \\ \underline{\text{VALUES}} \text{ ARE} \end{Bmatrix} \left\{\text{literal-1} \left[\begin{Bmatrix} \underline{\text{THROUGH}} \\ \underline{\text{THRU}} \end{Bmatrix} \text{ literal-2}\right]\right\} \dots .$

General Format for Communication Description Entry

FORMAT 1

$\underline{\text{CD}}$ cd-name-1

FOR   [$\underline{\text{INITIAL}}$] $\underline{\text{INPUT}}$ $\left[\begin{array}{l} [[\underline{\text{SYMBOLIC}} \text{ } \underline{\text{QUEUE}} \text{ IS data-name-1}] \\ [\underline{\text{SYMBOLIC}} \text{ } \underline{\text{SUB-QUEUE-1}} \text{ IS data-name-2}] \\ [\underline{\text{SYMBOLIC}} \text{ } \underline{\text{SUB-QUEUE-2}} \text{ IS data-name-3}] \\ [\underline{\text{SYMBOLIC}} \text{ } \underline{\text{SUB-QUEUE-3}} \text{ IS data-name-4}] \\ [\underline{\text{MESSAGE}} \text{ } \underline{\text{DATE}} \text{ IS data-name-5}] \\ [\underline{\text{MESSAGE}} \text{ } \underline{\text{TIME}} \text{ IS data-name-6}] \\ [\underline{\text{SYMBOLIC}} \text{ } \underline{\text{SOURCE}} \text{ IS data-name-7}] \\ [\underline{\text{TEXT}} \text{ } \underline{\text{LENGTH}} \text{ IS data-name-8}] \\ [\underline{\text{END}} \text{ } \underline{\text{KEY}} \text{ IS data-name-9}] \end{array}\right.$

```
                    [STATUS KEY IS data-name-10]
                    [MESSAGE COUNT IS data-name-11]]
           [data-name-1, data-name-2, data-name-3,
                 data-name-4, data-name-5, data-name-6,
                 data-name-7, data-name-8, data-name-9,
                 data-name-10, data-name-11]
```

FORMAT 2

```
CD   cd-name-1 FOR OUTPUT
     [DESTINATION COUNT IS data-name-1]
     [TEXT LENGTH IS data-name-2]
     [STATUS KEY IS data-name-3]
     [DESTINATION TABLE OCCURS integer-1 TIMES
           [INDEXED BY {index-name-1} ... ]]
     [ERROR KEY IS data-name-4]
     [SYMBOLIC DESTINATION IS data-name-5].
```

FORMAT 3

```
CD   cd-name-1

                    [[MESSAGE DATE IS data-name-1]
                     [MESSAGE TIME IS data-name-2]
                     [SYMBOLIC TERMINAL IS data-name-3]
     FOR [INITIAL] I-O [TEXT LENGTH IS data-name-4]
                     [END KEY IS data-name-5]
                     [STATUS KEY IS data-name-6]]
                    [data-name-1, data-name-2, data-name-3,
                          data-name-4, data-name-5, data-name-6]
```

General Format for Report Description Entry

```
RD   report-name-1
     [IS GLOBAL]
     [CODE literal-1]
     [ {CONTROL IS  }  {{data-name-1} ...        } ]
       {CONTROLS ARE}  {FINAL [data-name-1] ...  }

     [ PAGE [LIMIT IS  ] integer-1 [LINE ] [HEADING integer-2]
            [LIMITS ARE]           [LINES]

          [FIRST DETAIL integer-3]  [LAST DETAIL integer-4]

          [FOOTING integer-5] ] .
```

General Format for Report Group Description Entry

FORMAT 1

```
01   [data-name-1]
     [ LINE NUMBER IS  {integer-1 [ON NEXT PAGE]} ]
                       {PLUS integer-2            }

     [ NEXT GROUP IS  {integer-3      } ]
                      {PLUS integer-4 }
                      {NEXT PAGE      }
```

$$
\text{TYPE IS}
\left\{
\begin{array}{l}
\left\{ \begin{array}{l} \underline{\text{REPORT}}\ \underline{\text{HEADING}} \\ \underline{\text{RH}} \end{array} \right\} \\[4pt]
\left\{ \begin{array}{l} \underline{\text{PAGE}}\ \underline{\text{HEADING}} \\ \underline{\text{PH}} \end{array} \right\} \\[4pt]
\left\{ \begin{array}{l} \underline{\text{CONTROL}}\ \underline{\text{HEADING}} \\ \underline{\text{CH}} \end{array} \right\}
\left\{ \begin{array}{l} \text{data-name-2} \\ \underline{\text{FINAL}} \end{array} \right\} \\[4pt]
\left\{ \begin{array}{l} \underline{\text{DETAIL}} \\ \underline{\text{DE}} \end{array} \right\} \\[4pt]
\left\{ \begin{array}{l} \underline{\text{CONTROL}}\ \underline{\text{FOOTING}} \\ \underline{\text{CF}} \end{array} \right\}
\left\{ \begin{array}{l} \text{data-name-3} \\ \underline{\text{FINAL}} \end{array} \right\} \\[4pt]
\left\{ \begin{array}{l} \underline{\text{PAGE}}\ \underline{\text{FOOTING}} \\ \underline{\text{PF}} \end{array} \right\} \\[4pt]
\left\{ \begin{array}{l} \underline{\text{REPORT}}\ \underline{\text{FOOTING}} \\ \underline{\text{RF}} \end{array} \right\}
\end{array}
\right\}
$$

[[USAGE IS] DISPLAY].

FORMAT 2

level-number   [data-name-1]

$$
\left[\underline{\text{LINE}}\ \text{NUMBER IS}
\left\{ \begin{array}{l} \text{integer-1}\quad [\text{ON}\ \underline{\text{NEXT}}\ \underline{\text{PAGE}}] \\ \underline{\text{PLUS}}\ \text{integer-2} \end{array} \right\} \right]
$$

[[USAGE IS] DISPLAY].

FORMAT 3

level-number   [data-name-1]

$$
\left\{ \begin{array}{l} \underline{\text{PICTURE}} \\ \underline{\text{PIC}} \end{array} \right\}\ \text{IS character-string}
$$

[[USAGE IS] DISPLAY]

$$
\left[[\underline{\text{SIGN}}\ \text{IS}]\ \left\{ \begin{array}{l} \underline{\text{LEADING}} \\ \underline{\text{TRAILING}} \end{array} \right\}\ \underline{\text{SEPARATE}}\ \text{CHARACTER} \right]
$$

$$
\left[\left\{ \begin{array}{l} \underline{\text{JUSTIFIED}} \\ \underline{\text{JUST}} \end{array} \right\}\ \text{RIGHT} \right]
$$

[BLANK WHEN ZERO]

$$
\left[\underline{\text{LINE}}\ \text{NUMBER IS}
\left\{ \begin{array}{l} \text{integer-1}\quad [\text{ON}\ \underline{\text{NEXT}}\ \underline{\text{PAGE}}] \\ \underline{\text{PLUS}}\ \text{integer-2} \end{array} \right\} \right]
$$

[COLUMN NUMBER IS integer-3]

$$
\left\{ \begin{array}{l}
\underline{\text{SOURCE}}\ \text{IS identifier-1} \\
\underline{\text{VALUE}}\ \text{IS literal-1} \\
\{\underline{\text{SUM}}\ \{\text{identifier-2}\}\ \dots\ [\underline{\text{UPON}}\ \{\text{data-name-2}\}\ \dots\ ]\ \} \\
\qquad \left[\underline{\text{RESET}}\ \text{ON}\ \left\{ \begin{array}{l} \text{data-name-3} \\ \underline{\text{FINAL}} \end{array} \right\} \right]
\end{array} \right\} \dots
$$

[GROUP INDICATE].

General Format for PROCEDURE DIVISION

FORMAT 1

[PROCEDURE DIVISION   [USING   {data-name-1} ...].
[DECLARATIVES.

{section-name <u>SECTION</u> [segment-number].
   <u>USE</u> statement.
[paragraph-name.
   [sentence] ...] ... } ...
   <u>END</u> <u>DECLARATIVES</u>.]
{section-name <u>SECTION</u> [segment-number].
[paragraph-name.
   [sentence] ...] ... } ...]

FORMAT 2

[<u>PROCEDURE</u> <u>DIVISION</u> [<u>USING</u> {data-name-1} ...].
{paragraph-name.
   [sentence] ... } ...]

General Format for COBOL Verbs

<u>ACCEPT</u> identifier-1 [<u>FROM</u> mnemonic-name-1]

<u>ACCEPT</u> identifier-2 <u>FROM</u> $\begin{Bmatrix} \underline{DATE} \\ \underline{DAY} \\ \underline{DAY-OF-WEEK} \\ \underline{TIME} \end{Bmatrix}$

<u>ACCEPT</u> cd-name-1 <u>MESSAGE</u> <u>COUNT</u>

<u>ADD</u> $\begin{Bmatrix} \text{identifier-1} \\ \text{literal-1} \end{Bmatrix}$ ... <u>TO</u> {identifier-2 [<u>ROUNDED</u>]} ...

   [<u>ON</u> <u>SIZE</u> <u>ERROR</u> imperative-statement-1]
   [<u>NOT</u> <u>ON</u> <u>SIZE</u> <u>ERROR</u> imperative-statement-2]
   [<u>END-ADD</u>]

<u>ADD</u> $\begin{Bmatrix} \text{identifier-1} \\ \text{literal-1} \end{Bmatrix}$ ... <u>TO</u> $\begin{Bmatrix} \text{identifier-2} \\ \text{literal-2} \end{Bmatrix}$

   <u>GIVING</u> {identifier-3 [<u>ROUNDED</u>]} ...
   [<u>ON</u> <u>SIZE</u> <u>ERROR</u> imperative-statement-1]
   [<u>NOT</u> <u>ON</u> <u>SIZE</u> <u>ERROR</u> imperative-statement-2]
   [<u>END-ADD</u>]

<u>ADD</u> $\begin{Bmatrix} \underline{CORRESPONDING} \\ \underline{CORR} \end{Bmatrix}$ identifier-1 <u>TO</u> identifier-2 [<u>ROUNDED</u>]

   [<u>ON</u> <u>SIZE</u> <u>ERROR</u> imperative-statement-1]
   [<u>NOT</u> <u>ON</u> <u>SIZE</u> <u>ERROR</u> imperative-statement-2]
   [<u>END-ADD</u>]

<u>ALTER</u> {procedure-name-1 <u>TO</u> [<u>PROCEED</u> <u>TO</u>] procedure-name-2} ...

<u>CALL</u> $\begin{Bmatrix} \text{identifier-1} \\ \text{literal-1} \end{Bmatrix}$ $\begin{bmatrix} \underline{USING} \begin{Bmatrix} [\text{BY } \underline{REFERENCE}] \ \{\text{identifier-2}\} \ ... \\ \text{BY } \underline{CONTENT} \ \{\text{identifier-2}\} \ ... \end{Bmatrix} ... \end{bmatrix}$

   [<u>ON</u> <u>OVERFLOW</u> imperative-statement-1 [<u>END-CALL</u>]]

<u>CALL</u> $\begin{Bmatrix} \text{identifier-1} \\ \text{literal-1} \end{Bmatrix}$ $\begin{bmatrix} \underline{USING} \begin{Bmatrix} [\text{BY } \underline{REFERENCE}] \ \{\text{identifier-2}\} \ ... \\ \text{BY } \underline{CONTENT} \ \{\text{identifier-2}\} \ ... \end{Bmatrix} ... \end{bmatrix}$

   [<u>ON</u> <u>EXCEPTION</u> imperative-statement-1]
   [<u>NOT</u> <u>ON</u> <u>EXCEPTION</u> imperative-statement-2]
   [<u>END-CALL</u>]

<u>CANCEL</u> $\begin{Bmatrix} \text{identifier-1} \\ \text{literal-1} \end{Bmatrix}$ ...

$$
SW \;\underline{\text{CLOSE}} \; \left\{ \text{file-name-1} \; \left[\begin{Bmatrix} \underline{\text{REEL}} \\ \underline{\text{UNIT}} \end{Bmatrix} \; [\underline{\text{FOR}} \; \underline{\text{REMOVAL}}] \atop \underline{\text{WITH}} \; \begin{Bmatrix} \underline{\text{NO}} \; \underline{\text{REWIND}} \\ \underline{\text{LOCK}} \end{Bmatrix} \right] \right\} \; \ldots
$$

```
RI  CLOSE  {file-name-1  [WITH LOCK]} ...
    COMPUTE  {identifier-1 [ROUNDED]} ... = arithmetic-expression-1
        [ON SIZE ERROR imperative-statement-1]
        [NOT ON SIZE ERROR imperative-statement-2]
        [END-COMPUTE]
    CONTINUE
    DELETE file-name-1 RECORD
        [INVALID KEY imperative-statement-1]
        [NOT INVALID KEY imperative-statement-2]
        [END-DELETE]
```

$$
\underline{\text{DISABLE}} \; \begin{Bmatrix} \underline{\text{INPUT}} \; [\underline{\text{TERMINAL}}] \\ \underline{\text{I-O}} \; \underline{\text{TERMINAL}} \\ \underline{\text{OUTPUT}} \end{Bmatrix} \; \text{cd-name-1}
$$

$$
\underline{\text{DISPLAY}} \; \begin{Bmatrix} \text{identifier-1} \\ \text{literal-1} \end{Bmatrix} \; \ldots \; [\underline{\text{UPON}} \; \text{mnemonic-name-1}] \quad [\underline{\text{WITH}} \; \underline{\text{NO}} \; \underline{\text{ADVANCING}}]
$$

$$
\underline{\text{DIVIDE}} \; \begin{Bmatrix} \text{identifier-1} \\ \text{literal-1} \end{Bmatrix} \; \underline{\text{INTO}} \; \{\text{identifier-2} \; [\underline{\text{ROUNDED}}]\} \; \ldots
$$

```
        [ON SIZE ERROR imperative-statement-1]
        [NOT ON SIZE ERROR imperative-statement-2]
        [END-DIVIDE]
```

$$
\underline{\text{DIVIDE}} \; \begin{Bmatrix} \text{identifier-1} \\ \text{literal-1} \end{Bmatrix} \; \underline{\text{INTO}} \; \begin{Bmatrix} \text{identifier-2} \\ \text{literal-2} \end{Bmatrix}
$$

```
        GIVING  {identifier-3 [ROUNDED]} ...
        [ON SIZE ERROR imperative-statement-1]
        [NOT ON SIZE ERROR imperative-statement-2]
        [END-DIVIDE]
```

$$
\underline{\text{DIVIDE}} \; \begin{Bmatrix} \text{identifier-1} \\ \text{literal-1} \end{Bmatrix} \; \underline{\text{BY}} \; \begin{Bmatrix} \text{identifier-2} \\ \text{literal-2} \end{Bmatrix}
$$

```
        GIVING  {identifier-3 [ROUNDED]} ...
        [ON SIZE ERROR imperative-statement-1]
        [NOT ON SIZE ERROR imperative-statement-2]
        [END-DIVIDE]
```

$$
\underline{\text{DIVIDE}} \; \begin{Bmatrix} \text{identifier-1} \\ \text{literal-1} \end{Bmatrix} \; \underline{\text{INTO}} \; , \begin{Bmatrix} \text{identifier-2} \\ \text{literal-2} \end{Bmatrix} \; \underline{\text{GIVING}} \; \text{identifier-3} \; [\underline{\text{ROUNDED}}]
$$

```
        REMAINDER identifier-4
        [ON SIZE ERROR imperative-statement-1]
        [NOT ON SIZE ERROR imperative-statement-2]
        [END-DIVIDE]
```

$$
\underline{\text{DIVIDE}} \; \begin{Bmatrix} \text{identifier-1} \\ \text{literal-1} \end{Bmatrix} \; \underline{\text{BY}} \; \begin{Bmatrix} \text{identifier-2} \\ \text{literal-2} \end{Bmatrix} \; \underline{\text{GIVING}} \; \text{identifier-3} \; [\underline{\text{ROUNDED}}]
$$

```
        REMAINDER identifier-4
        [ON SIZE ERROR imperative-statement-1]
        [NOT ON SIZE ERROR imperative-statement-2]
        [END-DIVIDE]
```

$$\text{ENABLE} \quad \begin{Bmatrix} \underline{\text{INPUT}} \ [\underline{\text{TERMINAL}}] \\ \underline{\text{I-O}} \ \underline{\text{TERMINAL}} \\ \underline{\text{OUTPUT}} \end{Bmatrix} \quad \text{cd-name-1}$$

$$\underline{\text{EVALUATE}} \quad \begin{Bmatrix} \text{identifier-1} \\ \text{literal-1} \\ \text{expression-1} \\ \underline{\text{TRUE}} \\ \underline{\text{FALSE}} \end{Bmatrix} \quad \left[\underline{\text{ALSO}} \begin{Bmatrix} \text{identifier-2} \\ \text{literal-2} \\ \text{expression-2} \\ \underline{\text{TRUE}} \\ \underline{\text{FALSE}} \end{Bmatrix} \right] \ \dots$$

$$\left\{ \left\{ \underline{\text{WHEN}} \begin{Bmatrix} \underline{\text{ANY}} \\ \text{condition-1} \\ \underline{\text{TRUE}} \\ \underline{\text{FALSE}} \\ [\underline{\text{NOT}}] \begin{Bmatrix} \text{identifier-3} \\ \text{literal-3} \\ \text{arithmetic-expression-1} \end{Bmatrix} \left[\begin{Bmatrix} \underline{\text{THROUGH}} \\ \underline{\text{THRU}} \end{Bmatrix} \begin{Bmatrix} \text{identifier-4} \\ \text{literal-4} \\ \text{arithmetic-expression-2} \end{Bmatrix} \right] \end{Bmatrix} \right. \right.$$

$$\left[\underline{\text{ALSO}} \begin{Bmatrix} \underline{\text{ANY}} \\ \text{condition-2} \\ \underline{\text{TRUE}} \\ \underline{\text{FALSE}} \\ [\underline{\text{NOT}}] \begin{Bmatrix} \text{identifier-5} \\ \text{literal-5} \\ \text{arithmetic-expression-3} \end{Bmatrix} \left[\begin{Bmatrix} \underline{\text{THROUGH}} \\ \underline{\text{THRU}} \end{Bmatrix} \begin{Bmatrix} \text{identifier-6} \\ \text{literal-6} \\ \text{arithmetic-expression-4} \end{Bmatrix} \right] \end{Bmatrix} \right] \ \dots \left. \right\} \ \dots \left. \right\}$$

imperative-statement-1} . . .
[WHEN OTHER imperative-statement-2]
[END-EVALUATE]
EXIT
EXIT PROGRAM

$$\underline{\text{GENERATE}} \quad \begin{Bmatrix} \text{data-name-1} \\ \text{report-name-1} \end{Bmatrix}$$

$\underline{\text{GO}}$ TO [procedure-name-1]
$\underline{\text{GO}}$ TO {procedure-name-1} . . . $\underline{\text{DEPENDING}}$ ON identifier-1

$$\underline{\text{IF}} \ \text{condition-1} \ \text{THEN} \begin{Bmatrix} \{\text{statement-1}\} \dots \\ \underline{\text{NEXT}} \ \underline{\text{SENTENCE}} \end{Bmatrix} \begin{Bmatrix} \underline{\text{ELSE}} \ \{\text{statement-2}\} \dots [\underline{\text{END-IF}}] \\ \underline{\text{ELSE}} \ \underline{\text{NEXT}} \ \underline{\text{SENTENCE}} \\ \underline{\text{END-IF}} \end{Bmatrix}$$

$\underline{\text{INITIALIZE}}$ {identifier-1} . . .

$$\left[\underline{\text{REPLACING}} \begin{Bmatrix} \begin{Bmatrix} \underline{\text{ALPHABETIC}} \\ \underline{\text{ALPHANUMERIC}} \\ \underline{\text{NUMERIC}} \\ \underline{\text{ALPHANUMERIC-EDITED}} \\ \underline{\text{NUMERIC-EDITED}} \end{Bmatrix} \underline{\text{DATA}} \ \underline{\text{BY}} \begin{Bmatrix} \text{identifier-2} \\ \text{literal-1} \end{Bmatrix} \end{Bmatrix} \dots \right]$$

$\underline{\text{INITIATE}}$ {report-name-1} . . .
$\underline{\text{INSPECT}}$ identifier-1 $\underline{\text{TALLYING}}$

$$
\left\{
\text{identifier-2 } \underline{\text{FOR}}
\left\{
\begin{array}{l}
\underline{\text{CHARACTERS}} \left[\left\{ \begin{array}{l} \underline{\text{BEFORE}} \\ \underline{\text{AFTER}} \end{array} \right\} \text{INITIAL} \left\{ \begin{array}{l} \text{identifier-4} \\ \text{literal-2} \end{array} \right\} \right] \ldots \\[2em]
\left\{ \begin{array}{l} \underline{\text{ALL}} \\ \underline{\text{LEADING}} \end{array} \right\} \left\{ \left\{ \begin{array}{l} \text{identifier-3} \\ \text{literal-1} \end{array} \right\} \left[\left\{ \begin{array}{l} \underline{\text{BEFORE}} \\ \underline{\text{AFTER}} \end{array} \right\} \text{INITIAL} \left\{ \begin{array}{l} \text{identifier-4} \\ \text{literal-2} \end{array} \right\} \right] \ldots \right\} \ldots
\end{array}
\right\} \ldots
\right\} \ldots
$$

$\underline{\text{INSPECT}}$ identifier-1 $\underline{\text{REPLACING}}$

$$
\left\{
\begin{array}{l}
\underline{\text{CHARACTERS}} \ \underline{\text{BY}} \left\{ \begin{array}{l} \text{identifier-5} \\ \text{literal-3} \end{array} \right\} \left[\left\{ \begin{array}{l} \underline{\text{BEFORE}} \\ \underline{\text{AFTER}} \end{array} \right\} \text{INITIAL} \left\{ \begin{array}{l} \text{identifier-4} \\ \text{literal-2} \end{array} \right\} \right] \ldots \\[2em]
\left\{ \begin{array}{l} \underline{\text{ALL}} \\ \underline{\text{LEADING}} \\ \underline{\text{FIRST}} \end{array} \right\} \left\{ \left\{ \begin{array}{l} \text{identifier-3} \\ \text{literal-1} \end{array} \right\} \underline{\text{BY}} \left\{ \begin{array}{l} \text{identifier-5} \\ \text{literal-3} \end{array} \right\} \left[\left\{ \begin{array}{l} \underline{\text{BEFORE}} \\ \underline{\text{AFTER}} \end{array} \right\} \text{INITIAL} \left\{ \begin{array}{l} \text{identifier-4} \\ \text{literal-2} \end{array} \right\} \right] \ldots \right\} \ldots
\end{array}
\right\} \ldots
$$

$\underline{\text{INSPECT}}$ identifier-1 $\underline{\text{TALLYING}}$

$$
\left\{
\text{identifier-2 } \underline{\text{FOR}}
\left\{
\begin{array}{l}
\underline{\text{CHARACTERS}} \left[\left\{ \begin{array}{l} \underline{\text{BEFORE}} \\ \underline{\text{AFTER}} \end{array} \right\} \text{INITIAL} \left\{ \begin{array}{l} \text{identifier-4} \\ \text{literal-2} \end{array} \right\} \right] \ldots \\[2em]
\left\{ \begin{array}{l} \underline{\text{ALL}} \\ \underline{\text{LEADING}} \end{array} \right\} \left\{ \left\{ \begin{array}{l} \text{identifier-3} \\ \text{literal-1} \end{array} \right\} \left[\left\{ \begin{array}{l} \underline{\text{BEFORE}} \\ \underline{\text{AFTER}} \end{array} \right\} \text{INITIAL} \left\{ \begin{array}{l} \text{identifier-4} \\ \text{literal-2} \end{array} \right\} \right] \ldots \right\} \ldots
\end{array}
\right\} \ldots
\right\} \ldots
$$

$\underline{\text{REPLACING}}$

$$
\left\{
\begin{array}{l}
\underline{\text{CHARACTERS}} \ \underline{\text{BY}} \left\{ \begin{array}{l} \text{identifier-5} \\ \text{literal-3} \end{array} \right\} \left[\left\{ \begin{array}{l} \underline{\text{BEFORE}} \\ \underline{\text{AFTER}} \end{array} \right\} \text{INITIAL} \left\{ \begin{array}{l} \text{identifier-4} \\ \text{literal-2} \end{array} \right\} \right] \ldots \\[2em]
\left\{ \begin{array}{l} \underline{\text{ALL}} \\ \underline{\text{LEADING}} \\ \underline{\text{FIRST}} \end{array} \right\} \left\{ \left\{ \begin{array}{l} \text{identifier-3} \\ \text{literal-1} \end{array} \right\} \underline{\text{BY}} \left\{ \begin{array}{l} \text{identifier-5} \\ \text{literal-3} \end{array} \right\} \left[\left\{ \begin{array}{l} \underline{\text{BEFORE}} \\ \underline{\text{AFTER}} \end{array} \right\} \text{INITIAL} \left\{ \begin{array}{l} \text{identifier-4} \\ \text{literal-2} \end{array} \right\} \right] \ldots \right\} \ldots
\end{array}
\right\} \ldots
$$

$\underline{\text{INSPECT}}$ identifier-1 $\underline{\text{CONVERTING}}$ $\left\{ \begin{array}{l} \text{identifier-6} \\ \text{literal-4} \end{array} \right\}$ $\underline{\text{TO}}$ $\left\{ \begin{array}{l} \text{identifier-7} \\ \text{literal-5} \end{array} \right\}$

$\left[\left\{ \begin{array}{l} \underline{\text{BEFORE}} \\ \underline{\text{AFTER}} \end{array} \right\} \text{INITIAL} \left\{ \begin{array}{l} \text{identifier-4} \\ \text{literal-2} \end{array} \right\} \right] \ldots$

$\underline{\text{MERGE}}$ file-name-1 $\left\{ \text{ON} \left\{ \begin{array}{l} \underline{\text{ASCENDING}} \\ \underline{\text{DESCENDING}} \end{array} \right\} \text{KEY} \ \{\text{data-name-1}\} \ldots \right\} \ldots$

[$\underline{\text{COLLATING}}$ $\underline{\text{SEQUENCE}}$ IS alphabet-name-1]
$\underline{\text{USING}}$ file-name-2 {file-name-3} . . .

$$
\left\{
\begin{array}{l}
\underline{\text{OUTPUT}} \ \underline{\text{PROCEDURE}} \ \text{IS procedure-name-1} \left[\left\{ \begin{array}{l} \underline{\text{THROUGH}} \\ \underline{\text{THRU}} \end{array} \right\} \text{procedure-name-2} \right] \\[1.5em]
\underline{\text{GIVING}} \ \{\text{file-name-4}\} \ldots
\end{array}
\right\}
$$

$\underline{\text{MOVE}}$ $\left\{ \begin{array}{l} \text{identifier-1} \\ \text{literal-1} \end{array} \right\}$ $\underline{\text{TO}}$ {identifier-2} . . .

$\underline{\text{MOVE}}$ $\left\{ \begin{array}{l} \underline{\text{CORRESPONDING}} \\ \underline{\text{CORR}} \end{array} \right\}$ identifier-1 $\underline{\text{TO}}$ identifier-2

$\underline{\text{MULTIPLY}}$ $\left\{ \begin{array}{l} \text{identifier-1} \\ \text{literal-1} \end{array} \right\}$ $\underline{\text{BY}}$ {identifier-2 [$\underline{\text{ROUNDED}}$]} . . .

[ON $\underline{\text{SIZE}}$ $\underline{\text{ERROR}}$ imperative-statement-1]
[$\underline{\text{NOT}}$ ON $\underline{\text{SIZE}}$ $\underline{\text{ERROR}}$ imperative-statement-2]
[$\underline{\text{END-MULTIPLY}}$]

$$\text{\underline{MULTIPLY}} \quad \begin{Bmatrix} \text{identifier-1} \\ \text{literal-1} \end{Bmatrix} \quad \text{\underline{BY}} \quad \begin{Bmatrix} \text{identifier-2} \\ \text{literal-2} \end{Bmatrix}$$

\underline{GIVING} {identifier-3 [\underline{ROUNDED}]} ...
[ON \underline{SIZE} \underline{ERROR} imperative-statement-1]
[\underline{NOT} ON \underline{SIZE} \underline{ERROR} imperative-statement-2]
[END-MULTIPLY]

$$S \; \text{\underline{OPEN}} \quad \begin{Bmatrix} \text{\underline{INPUT}} \; \{\text{file-name-1} \;\; [\text{WITH } \underline{\text{NO}} \; \underline{\text{REWIND}}]\} \; ... \\ \text{\underline{OUTPUT}} \; \{\text{file-name-2} \;\; [\text{WITH } \underline{\text{NO}} \; \underline{\text{REWIND}}]\} \; ... \\ \text{\underline{I-O}} \; \{\text{file-name-3}\} \; ... \\ \text{\underline{EXTEND}} \; \{\text{file-name-4}\} \; ... \end{Bmatrix} \; ...$$

$$RI \; \text{\underline{OPEN}} \quad \begin{Bmatrix} \text{\underline{INPUT}} \; \{\text{file-name-1}\} \; ... \\ \text{\underline{OUTPUT}} \; \{\text{file-name-2}\} \; ... \\ \text{\underline{I-O}} \; \{\text{file-name-3}\} \; ... \\ \text{\underline{EXTEND}} \; \{\text{file-name-4}\} \; ... \end{Bmatrix} \; ...$$

$$W \; \text{\underline{OPEN}} \quad \begin{Bmatrix} \text{\underline{OUTPUT}} \; \{\text{file-name-1} \; [\text{WITH } \underline{\text{NO}} \; \underline{\text{REWIND}}]\} \; ... \\ \text{\underline{EXTEND}} \; \{\text{file-name-2}\} \; ... \end{Bmatrix} \; ...$$

$$\text{\underline{PERFORM}} \quad \left[\text{procedure-name-1} \; \left[\begin{Bmatrix} \text{\underline{THROUGH}} \\ \text{\underline{THRU}} \end{Bmatrix} \; \text{procedure-name-2} \right] \right]$$

[imperative-statement-1 \underline{END-PERFORM}]

$$\text{\underline{PERFORM}} \quad \left[\text{procedure-name-1} \; \left[\begin{Bmatrix} \text{\underline{THROUGH}} \\ \text{\underline{THRU}} \end{Bmatrix} \; \text{procedure-name-2} \right] \right]$$

$$\begin{Bmatrix} \text{identifier-1} \\ \text{integer-1} \end{Bmatrix} \quad \text{\underline{TIMES}} \quad [\text{imperative-statement-1} \; \text{\underline{END-PERFORM}}]$$

$$\text{\underline{PERFORM}} \quad \left[\text{procedure-name-1} \; \left[\begin{Bmatrix} \text{\underline{THROUGH}} \\ \text{\underline{THRU}} \end{Bmatrix} \; \text{procedure-name-2} \right] \right]$$

$$\left[\text{WITH } \underline{\text{TEST}} \; \begin{Bmatrix} \text{\underline{BEFORE}} \\ \text{\underline{AFTER}} \end{Bmatrix} \right] \; \text{\underline{UNTIL}} \; \text{condition-1}$$

[imperative-statement-1 \underline{END-PERFORM}]

$$\text{\underline{PERFORM}} \quad \left[\text{procedure-name-1} \; \left[\begin{Bmatrix} \text{\underline{THROUGH}} \\ \text{\underline{THRU}} \end{Bmatrix} \; \text{procedure-name-2} \right] \right]$$

$$\left[\text{WITH } \underline{\text{TEST}} \; \begin{Bmatrix} \text{\underline{BEFORE}} \\ \text{\underline{AFTER}} \end{Bmatrix} \right]$$

$$\text{\underline{VARYING}} \quad \begin{Bmatrix} \text{identifier-2} \\ \text{index-name-1} \end{Bmatrix} \quad \text{\underline{FROM}} \quad \begin{Bmatrix} \text{identifier-3} \\ \text{index-name-2} \\ \text{literal-1} \end{Bmatrix}$$

$$\text{\underline{BY}} \; \begin{Bmatrix} \text{identifier-4} \\ \text{literal-2} \end{Bmatrix} \quad \text{\underline{UNTIL}} \; \text{condition-1}$$

$$\left[\text{\underline{AFTER}} \quad \begin{Bmatrix} \text{identifier-5} \\ \text{index-name-3} \end{Bmatrix} \quad \text{\underline{FROM}} \quad \begin{Bmatrix} \text{identifier-6} \\ \text{index-name-4} \\ \text{literal-3} \end{Bmatrix} \right.$$

$$\left. \text{\underline{BY}} \; \begin{Bmatrix} \text{identifier-7} \\ \text{literal-4} \end{Bmatrix} \quad \text{\underline{UNTIL}} \; \text{condition-2} \right] \; ...$$

[imperative-statement-1 \underline{END-PERFORM}]

PURGE cd-name-1

SRI READ file-name-1 [NEXT] RECORD [INTO identifier-1]

  [AT END imperative-statement-1]

  [NOT AT END imperative-statement-2]

  [END-READ]

 R READ file-name-1 RECORD [INTO identifier-1]

  [INVALID KEY imperative-statement-3]

  [NOT INVALID KEY imperative-statement-4]

  [END-READ]

 I READ file-namc-1 RECORD [INTO identifier-1]

  [KEY IS data-name-1]

  [INVALID KEY imperative-statement-3]

  [NOT INVALID KEY imperative-statement-4]

  [END-READ]

RECEIVE cd-name-1 $\left\{ \begin{array}{l} \text{MESSAGE} \\ \text{SEGMENT} \end{array} \right\}$ INTO identifier-1

 [NO DATA imperative-statement-1]

 [WITH DATA imperative-statement-2]

 [END-RECEIVE]

RELEASE record-name-1 [FROM identifier-1]

RETURN file-name-1 RECORD [INTO identifier-1]

 AT END imperative-statement-1

 [NOT AT END imperative-statement-2]

 [END-RETURN]

S REWRITE record-name-1 [FROM identifier-1]

RI REWRITE record-name-1 [FROM identifier-1]

 [INVALID KEY imperative-statement-1]

 [NOT INVALID KEY imperative-statement-2]

 [END-REWRITE]

SEARCH identifier-1 $\left[\text{VARYING} \left\{ \begin{array}{l} \text{identifier-2} \\ \text{index-name-1} \end{array} \right\} \right]$

 [AT END imperative-statement-1]

 $\left\{ \text{WHEN condition-1} \left\{ \begin{array}{l} \text{imperative-statement-2} \\ \text{NEXT SENTENCE} \end{array} \right\} \right\}$ ...

 [END-SEARCH]

SEARCH ALL identifier-1 [AT END imperative-statement-1]

 WHEN $\left\{ \begin{array}{l} \text{data-name-1} \left\{ \begin{array}{l} \text{IS EQUAL TO} \\ \text{IS =} \end{array} \right\} \left\{ \begin{array}{l} \text{identifier-3} \\ \text{literal-1} \\ \text{arithmetic-expression-1} \end{array} \right\} \\ \text{condition-name-1} \end{array} \right\}$

 $\left[\underline{\text{AND}} \left\{ \begin{array}{l} \text{data-name-2} \left\{ \begin{array}{l} \text{IS EQUAL TO} \\ \text{IS =} \end{array} \right\} \left\{ \begin{array}{l} \text{identifier-4} \\ \text{literal-2} \\ \text{arithmetic-expression-2} \end{array} \right\} \\ \text{condition-name-2} \end{array} \right\} \right]$ ...

 $\left\{ \begin{array}{l} \text{imperative-statement-2} \\ \text{NEXT SENTENCE} \end{array} \right\}$

 [END-SEARCH]

SEND cd-name-1 FROM identifier-1

SEND cd-name-1 [FROM identifier-1] $\left\{ \begin{array}{l} \text{WITH identifier-2} \\ \text{WITH ESI} \\ \text{WITH EMI} \\ \text{WITH EGI} \end{array} \right\}$

$$\left[\begin{Bmatrix} \underline{BEFORE} \\ \underline{AFTER} \end{Bmatrix} \underline{ADVANCING} \begin{Bmatrix} \begin{Bmatrix} identifier\text{-}3 \\ integer\text{-}1 \end{Bmatrix} \begin{bmatrix} \underline{LINE} \\ \underline{LINES} \end{bmatrix} \\ \begin{Bmatrix} mnemonic\text{-}name\text{-}1 \\ \underline{PAGE} \end{Bmatrix} \end{Bmatrix} \right]$$

[REPLACING LINE]

$$\underline{SET} \quad \begin{Bmatrix} index\text{-}name\text{-}1 \\ identifier\text{-}1 \end{Bmatrix} \quad \ldots \quad \underline{TO} \begin{Bmatrix} index\text{-}name\text{-}2 \\ identifier\text{-}2 \\ integer\text{-}1 \end{Bmatrix}$$

$$\underline{SET} \quad \{index\text{-}name\text{-}3\} \quad \ldots \quad \begin{Bmatrix} \underline{UP}\ \underline{BY} \\ \underline{DOWN}\ \underline{BY} \end{Bmatrix} \begin{Bmatrix} identifier\text{-}3 \\ integer\text{-}2 \end{Bmatrix}$$

$$\underline{SET} \quad \left\{ \{mnemonic\text{-}name\text{-}1\} \quad \ldots \quad \underline{TO} \begin{Bmatrix} \underline{ON} \\ \underline{OFF} \end{Bmatrix} \right\} \ldots$$

$$\underline{SET} \quad \{condition\text{-}name\text{-}1\} \quad \ldots \quad \underline{TO}\ \underline{TRUE}$$

$$\underline{SORT}\ file\text{-}name\text{-}1 \quad \left\{ \underline{ON} \begin{Bmatrix} \underline{ASCENDING} \\ \underline{DESCENDING} \end{Bmatrix} KEY \quad \{data\text{-}name\text{-}1\} \ldots \right\} \ldots$$

[WITH DUPLICATES IN ORDER]
[COLLATING SEQUENCE IS alphabet-name-1]

$$\begin{Bmatrix} \underline{INPUT}\ \underline{PROCEDURE}\ IS\ procedure\text{-}name\text{-}1 \begin{bmatrix} \begin{Bmatrix} \underline{THROUGH} \\ \underline{THRU} \end{Bmatrix} procedure\text{-}name\text{-}2 \end{bmatrix} \\ \underline{USING}\ \{file\text{-}name\text{-}2\} \ldots \end{Bmatrix}$$

$$\begin{Bmatrix} \underline{OUTPUT}\ \underline{PROCEDURE}\ IS\ procedure\text{-}name\text{-}3 \begin{bmatrix} \begin{Bmatrix} \underline{THROUGH} \\ \underline{THRU} \end{Bmatrix} procedure\text{-}name\text{-}4 \end{bmatrix} \\ \underline{GIVING}\ \{file\text{-}name\text{-}3\} \ldots \end{Bmatrix}$$

$$\underline{START}\ file\text{-}name\text{-}1 \left[\underline{KEY} \begin{Bmatrix} IS\ \underline{EQUAL}\ TO \\ IS\ = \\ IS\ \underline{GREATER}\ THAN \\ IS\ > \\ IS\ \underline{NOT}\ \underline{LESS}\ THAN \\ IS\ \underline{NOT}\ < \\ IS\ \underline{GREATER}\ THAN\ OR\ \underline{EQUAL}\ TO \\ IS\ >= \end{Bmatrix} data\text{-}name\text{-}1 \right]$$

[INVALID KEY imperative-statement-1]
[NOT INVALID KEY imperative-statement-2]
[END-START]

$$\underline{STOP} \begin{Bmatrix} \underline{RUN} \\ literal\text{-}1 \end{Bmatrix}$$

$$\underline{STRING} \begin{Bmatrix} \begin{Bmatrix} identifier\text{-}1 \\ literal\text{-}1 \end{Bmatrix} \quad \ldots \quad \underline{DELIMITED}\ BY \begin{Bmatrix} identifier\text{-}2 \\ literal\text{-}2 \\ \underline{SIZE} \end{Bmatrix} \end{Bmatrix} \ldots$$

$\underline{INTO}$ identifier-3
[WITH $\underline{POINTER}$ identifier-4]
[ON $\underline{OVERFLOW}$ imperative-statement-1]
[$\underline{NOT}$ ON $\underline{OVERFLOW}$ imperative-statement-2]
[END-STRING]

$$\underline{SUBTRACT} \begin{Bmatrix} identifier\text{-}1 \\ literal\text{-}1 \end{Bmatrix} \quad \ldots \quad \underline{FROM}\ \{identifier\text{-}3\ [\underline{ROUNDED}]\} \ldots$$

[ON SIZE ERROR imperative-statement-1]

[NOT ON SIZE ERROR imperative-statement-2]

[END-SUBTRACT]

$$\underline{\text{SUBTRACT}} \left\{ \begin{array}{l} \text{identifier-1} \\ \text{literal-1} \end{array} \right\} \dots \underline{\text{FROM}} \left\{ \begin{array}{l} \text{identifier-2} \\ \text{literal-2} \end{array} \right\}$$

$\underline{\text{GIVING}}$ {identifier-3 [$\underline{\text{ROUNDED}}$]} . . .

[ON SIZE ERROR imperative-statement-1]

[NOT ON SIZE ERROR imperative-statement-2]

[END-SUBTRACT]

$$\underline{\text{SUBTRACT}} \left\{ \begin{array}{l} \underline{\text{CORRESPONDING}} \\ \underline{\text{CORR}} \end{array} \right\} \text{identifier-1} \underline{\text{FROM}} \text{identifier-2} [\underline{\text{ROUNDED}}]$$

[ON SIZE ERROR imperative-statement-1]

[NOT ON SIZE ERROR imperative-statement-2]

[END-SUBTRACT]

SUPPRESS PRINTING

TERMINATE {report-name-1} . . .

UNSTRING identifier-1

$$\left[\underline{\text{DELIMITED}} \text{ BY } [\underline{\text{ALL}}] \left\{ \begin{array}{l} \text{identifier-2} \\ \text{literal-1} \end{array} \right\} \left[\underline{\text{OR}} [\underline{\text{ALL}}] \left\{ \begin{array}{l} \text{identifier-3} \\ \text{literal-2} \end{array} \right\} \right] \dots \right]$$

INTO {identifier-4 [DELIMITER IN identifier-5] [COUNT IN identifier-6]} . . .

[WITH POINTER identifier-7]

[TALLYING IN identifier-8]

[ON OVERFLOW imperative-statement-1]

[NOT ON OVERFLOW imperative-statement-2]

[END-UNSTRING]

$$\underline{\text{USE}} [\underline{\text{GLOBAL}}] \text{ AFTER STANDARD } \left\{ \begin{array}{l} \underline{\text{EXCEPTION}} \\ \underline{\text{ERROR}} \end{array} \right\} \underline{\text{PROCEDURE}} \text{ ON } \left\{ \begin{array}{l} \{\text{file-name-1}\} \dots \\ \underline{\text{INPUT}} \\ \underline{\text{OUTPUT}} \\ \underline{\text{I-O}} \\ \underline{\text{EXTEND}} \end{array} \right\}$$

USE [GLOBAL] BEFORE REPORTING identifier-1

$$\underline{\text{USE}} \text{ FOR } \underline{\text{DEBUGGING}} \text{ ON } \left\{ \begin{array}{l} \text{cd-name-1} \\ [\underline{\text{ALL}} \text{ REFERENCES OF}] \text{ identifier-1} \\ \text{file-name-1} \\ \text{procedure-name-1} \\ \underline{\text{ALL}} \underline{\text{PROCEDURES}} \end{array} \right\} \dots$$

S WRITE record-name-1 [FROM identifier-1]

$$\left[\left\{ \begin{array}{l} \underline{\text{BEFORE}} \\ \underline{\text{AFTER}} \end{array} \right\} \text{ ADVANCING } \left\{ \begin{array}{l} \left\{ \begin{array}{l} \text{identifier-2} \\ \text{integer-1} \end{array} \right\} \left[\begin{array}{l} \text{LINE} \\ \text{LINES} \end{array} \right] \\ \left\{ \begin{array}{l} \text{mnemonic-name-1} \\ \underline{\text{PAGE}} \end{array} \right\} \end{array} \right\} \right]$$

$$\left[\underline{\text{AT}} \left\{ \begin{array}{l} \underline{\text{END-OF-PAGE}} \\ \underline{\text{EOP}} \end{array} \right\} \text{ imperative-statement-1} \right]$$

$$\left[\underline{\text{NOT}} \text{ AT } \left\{ \begin{array}{l} \underline{\text{END-OF-PAGE}} \\ \underline{\text{EOP}} \end{array} \right\} \text{ imperative-statement-2} \right]$$

[END-WRITE]

RI WRITE record-name-1 [FROM identifier-1]

[INVALID KEY imperative-statement-1]

[NOT INVALID KEY imperative-statement-2]

[END-WRITE]

	General Format for Copy and Replace Statements

COPY text-name-1 $\left[\left\{ \begin{array}{c} \underline{OF} \\ \underline{IN} \end{array} \right\} \text{library-name-1} \right]$

$\left[\underline{REPLACING} \left\{ \left\{ \begin{array}{l} \text{==pseudo-text-1==} \\ \text{identifier-1} \\ \text{literal-1} \\ \text{word-1} \end{array} \right\} \underline{BY} \left\{ \begin{array}{l} \text{==pseudo-text-2==} \\ \text{identifier-2} \\ \text{literal-2} \\ \text{word-2} \end{array} \right\} \right\} \dots \right]$

<u>REPLACE</u> {==pseudo-text-1== BY ==pseudo-text-2==} ...
<u>REPLACE</u> <u>OFF</u>

	General Format for Conditions

RELATION CONDITION

$\left\{ \begin{array}{l} \text{identifier-1} \\ \text{literal-1} \\ \text{arithmetic-expression-1} \\ \text{index-name-1} \end{array} \right\} \left\{ \begin{array}{l} \text{IS } [\underline{\text{NOT}}] \text{ } \underline{\text{GREATER}} \text{ } \underline{\text{THAN}} \\ \text{IS } [\underline{\text{NOT}}] \text{ } \underline{>} \\ \text{IS } [\underline{\text{NOT}}] \text{ } \underline{\text{LESS}} \text{ THAN} \\ \text{IS } [\underline{\text{NOT}}] \text{ } \underline{<} \\ \text{IS } [\underline{\text{NOT}}] \text{ } \underline{\text{EQUAL}} \text{ TO} \\ \text{IS } [\underline{\text{NOT}}] \text{ } \underline{=} \\ \text{IS } \underline{\text{GREATER}} \text{ THAN } \underline{\text{OR}} \text{ } \underline{\text{EQUAL}} \text{ TO} \\ \text{IS } \underline{>=} \\ \text{IS } \underline{\text{LESS}} \text{ THAN } \underline{\text{OR}} \text{ EQUAL TO} \\ \text{IS } \underline{<=} \end{array} \right\} \left\{ \begin{array}{l} \text{identifier-2} \\ \text{literal-2} \\ \text{arithmetic-expression-2} \\ \text{index-name-2} \end{array} \right\}$

CLASS CONDITION

identifier-1 IS [<u>NOT</u>] $\left\{ \begin{array}{l} \text{NUMERIC} \\ \text{ALPHABETIC} \\ \underline{\text{ALPHABETIC-LOWER}} \\ \underline{\text{ALPHABETIC-UPPER}} \\ \text{class-name} \end{array} \right\}$

CONDITION-NAME CONDITION
condition-name-1

SWITCH-STATUS CONDITION
condition-name-1

SIGN CONDITION

arithmetic-expression-1 IS [<u>NOT</u>] $\left\{ \begin{array}{l} \underline{\text{POSITIVE}} \\ \underline{\text{NEGATIVE}} \\ \underline{\text{ZERO}} \end{array} \right\}$

NEGATED CONDITION
<u>NOT</u> condition-1

COMBINED CONDITION

condition-1 $\left\{ \left\{ \begin{array}{c} \underline{\text{AND}} \\ \underline{\text{OR}} \end{array} \right\} \text{condition-2} \right\} \dots$

ABBREVIATED COMBINED RELATION CONDITION

relation-condition $\left\{ \left\{ \begin{array}{c} \underline{\text{AND}} \\ \underline{\text{OR}} \end{array} \right\} [\underline{\text{NOT}}] \text{ [relational-operator] object} \right\} \dots$

Qualification

FORMAT 1

$$\begin{Bmatrix} \text{data-name-1} \\ \text{condition-name} \end{Bmatrix} \quad \begin{Bmatrix} \left\{ \begin{Bmatrix} \underline{\text{IN}} \\ \underline{\text{OF}} \end{Bmatrix} \text{data-name-2} \right\} \dots \left[\begin{Bmatrix} \underline{\text{IN}} \\ \underline{\text{OF}} \end{Bmatrix} \begin{Bmatrix} \text{file-name} \\ \text{cd-name} \end{Bmatrix} \right] \\ \begin{Bmatrix} \underline{\text{IN}} \\ \underline{\text{OF}} \end{Bmatrix} \begin{Bmatrix} \text{file-name} \\ \text{cd-name} \end{Bmatrix} \end{Bmatrix}$$

FORMAT 2

$$\text{paragraph-name} \quad \begin{Bmatrix} \underline{\text{IN}} \\ \underline{\text{OF}} \end{Bmatrix} \quad \text{section-name}$$

FORMAT 3

$$\text{text-name} \quad \begin{Bmatrix} \underline{\text{IN}} \\ \underline{\text{OF}} \end{Bmatrix} \quad \text{library-name}$$

FORMAT 4

$$\underline{\text{LINAGE-COUNTER}} \quad \begin{Bmatrix} \underline{\text{IN}} \\ \underline{\text{OF}} \end{Bmatrix} \quad \text{report-name}$$

FORMAT 5

$$\begin{Bmatrix} \underline{\text{PAGE-COUNTER}} \\ \underline{\text{LINE-COUNTER}} \end{Bmatrix} \quad \begin{Bmatrix} \underline{\text{IN}} \\ \underline{\text{OF}} \end{Bmatrix} \quad \text{report-name}$$

FORMAT 6

$$\text{data-name-3} \quad \begin{Bmatrix} \left\{ \begin{Bmatrix} \underline{\text{IN}} \\ \underline{\text{OF}} \end{Bmatrix} \text{data-name-4} \left[\begin{Bmatrix} \underline{\text{IN}} \\ \underline{\text{OF}} \end{Bmatrix} \text{report-name} \right] \right\} \\ \begin{Bmatrix} \underline{\text{IN}} \\ \underline{\text{OF}} \end{Bmatrix} \text{report-name} \end{Bmatrix}$$

Miscellaneous Formats

SUBSCRIPTING

$$\begin{Bmatrix} \text{condition-name-1} \\ \text{data-name-1} \end{Bmatrix} \quad (\quad \begin{Bmatrix} \text{integer-1} \\ \text{data-name-2} [\{\pm\} \text{ integer-2}] \\ \text{index-name-1} [\{\pm\} \text{ integer-3}] \end{Bmatrix} \dots)$$

REFERENCE MODIFICATION

data-name-1 (leftmost-character-position: [length])

IDENTIFIER

$$\text{data-name-1} \quad \left[\begin{Bmatrix} \text{IN} \\ \text{OF} \end{Bmatrix} \text{data-name-2} \right] \quad \dots \quad \left[\begin{Bmatrix} \text{IN} \\ \text{OF} \end{Bmatrix} \begin{Bmatrix} \text{cd-name} \\ \text{file-name} \\ \text{report-name} \end{Bmatrix} \right]$$

[({subscript} . . .)]   [(leftmost-character-position: [length])]

General Format for Nested Source Programs

```
IDENTIFICATION DIVISION.
PROGRAM-ID.    program-name-1  [IS INITIAL PROGRAM].
[ENVIRONMENT DIVISION.   environment-division-content]
[DATA DIVISION.   data-division-content]
[PROCEDURE DIVISION.   procedure-division-content]
[[nested-source-program] . . .
END PROGRAM program-name-1.]
```

General Format for Nested-Source-Program

```
IDENTIFICATION DIVISION.
```

$$\text{PROGRAM-ID.} \quad \text{program-name-2} \quad \left[\text{IS} \left\{ \left| \begin{array}{c} \underline{\text{COMMON}} \\ \underline{\text{INITIAL}} \end{array} \right| \right\} \text{PROGRAM} \right].$$

```
[ENVIRONMENT DIVISION.   environment-division-content]
[DATA DIVISION.   data-division-content]
[PROCEDURE DIVISION.   procedure-division-content]
[nested-source-program] . . .
END PROGRAM program-name-2.
```

General Format for a Sequence of Source Programs

```
{IDENTIFICATION DIVISION.
PROGRAM-ID.    program-name-3  [IS INITIAL PROGRAM].
[ENVIRONMENT DIVISION.   environment-division-content]
[DATA DIVISION.   data-division-content]
[PROCEDURE DIVISION.   procedure-division-content]
[nested-source-program] . . .
END PROGRAM program-name-3.} . . .
IDENTIFICATION DIVISION.
PROGRAM-ID.    program-name-4  [IS INITIAL PROGRAM].
[ENVIRONMENT DIVISION.   environment-division-content]
[DATA DIVISION.   data-division-content]
[PROCEDURE DIVISION.   procedure-division-content]
[[nested-source-program] . . .
END PROGRAM program-name-4.]
```

Appendix B

Disk and Tape Concepts

OBJECTIVES

To familiarize you with

1. Physical features of magnetic disk and tape files and drives.
2. Characteristics of disk and tape processing.
3. Some methods of file organization on a disk and sequential file organization on a tape.

I. Disk and Tape for File Processing

Auxiliary or secondary storage is used for storing files and programs for future processing. Disk and tape are the primary auxiliary storage media for both mainframes and micros, with disk being far more prevalent.

The entire collection of data pertaining to any given application is called a **file.** The major collection of data used for storing critical information, answering inquiries, and producing output, such as bills and statements, is called a **master file.**

Master files are stored on media such as magnetic disk and magnetic tape that can be processed at high speeds. Disk and tape devices are not only fast, but they are capable of storing large volumes of data in a relatively small area.

Because of the following features of disks and tapes, they are ideal media for storing data bases consisting of master files, transaction files, or other high-volume data files:

FEATURES OF DISK AND TAPE PROCESSING

1. Disk and tape files can be created as output, then later read as input and changed as needed.
2. Disk drives and tape drives can read and write data at extremely fast rates.
3. Hundreds of thousands of records can be stored on one disk or one reel of magnetic tape.
4. Records can be of any size or format.

Tapes are best used for storing a master file if processing is performed in a *batch* mode, where records are typically processed in large quantities and *in sequence.* Disks can also be used for batch processing, but disks are best used if master file processing is performed *immediately* in an on-line environment, where records on a disk need to be accessed *randomly.*

Disks are the most popular media for storing files because disks can be accessed **randomly** as well as sequentially. This means that data can be retrieved very quickly from a disk regardless of its physical location on the disk. Tapes are not as widely used for storing files because tapes can only be accessed **sequentially.** This means that to find data in the tape, each record must be accessed in sequence, reading record 1 first, then record 2, and so on.

Because disks can be used for *either* batch or immediate processing, many computer centers use disks for *all* file processing and use tapes only for backup. Other computer centers have used tapes for batch processing for many years and continue to do so.

We will now consider the specific features of disks and tapes and their corresponding drives.

II. Magnetic Disk Files and Disk Drives

A. Features of Magnetic Disk

1. Physical Characteristics

Magnetic disk is a high-speed medium that can serve as either input to or output from a computer system, either a mainframe or a micro. The disk has an iron oxide coating that can store hundreds of millions of characters of data, or more. The magnetic disk drive (called a hard disk drive on the micro) is

Figure B.1
Example of magnetic disk
packs and disk drives.
(Courtesy of the Department
of the Air Force.)

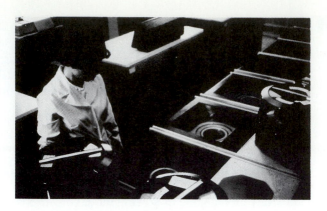

used both for recording information onto the disk and for reading information from it (see Figure B.1).

The standard magnetic disk for mainframes is really a **disk pack** consisting of a series of platters or disks, typically 14 inches in diameter, arranged in a vertical stack and connected by a central shaft. The concept is similar to a group of phonograph records stacked on a spindle. The actual number of disks in a pack varies with the unit, but many have 11 disks, as illustrated in Figure B.2.

Data may be recorded on *both* sides of each disk. There are, however, only 20 recording surfaces for an 11-disk pack unit, because the top surface of the first disk and the bottom surface of the last disk do not contain data; these two surfaces tend to collect dust and hence are not viable for storing data.

The **disk drive** used with an 11-disk pack (with 20 recording surfaces) would have 10 *access arms,* each with its own read/write head for reading and writing data. Figure B.3 also illustrates these read/write heads, each of which reads the bottom surface of one disk and the top surface of the next disk. One reason why access time for a disk is considerably shorter than for a tape is because disk drives have numerous read/write heads whereas a tape drive has only one read/write head.

Each disk surface records data as magnetized bits in concentric circles called **tracks** (see Figure B.4). The number of tracks varies with the disk pack, but 200 tracks per surface is common. Each track can store thousands of bytes of data. Although the surface area of tracks near the center is smaller than the surface area of outermost tracks, all tracks store precisely the same number of bytes. This is because data stored in the innermost tracks is stored more densely.

Figure B.2
Cross-sectional view of a
typical disk pack.

Figure B.3
How data is accessed from a disk pack. The read/write heads move in and out together as a function of the access mechanism.

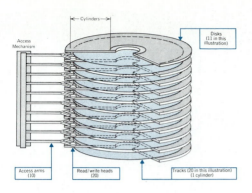

Figure B.4
Tracks on a disk surface.

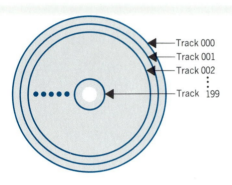

Disks vary widely in their storage capacity and their specifications. Individual records on most disks, however, can be addressed by:

ADDRESSING DISK RECORDS

1. Surface number.
2. Track number.
3. Sector number (for some disks).

A sector is a pie-shaped subdivision of a disk. See Figure B.5b.

Many disk packs also use the cylinder concept for addressing disk records. In Figure B.5a, for example, all tracks numbered 050 on all surfaces constitute a **cylinder** that is accessible by a read/write mechanism. If there are 200 tracks per surface, there would thus be 200 cylinders (numbered 000 to 199) for the disk pack.

2. Representation of Data on a Magnetic Disk

Data is represented on a disk using an 8- or a 9-bit code similar to the internal computer codes, ASCII or EBCDIC. Each byte or character is represented longitudinally along a disk track by an 8- or 9-bit configuration.

Figure B.5
(a) The cylinder concept on a magnetic disk. (b) The sector concept on a magnetic disk.

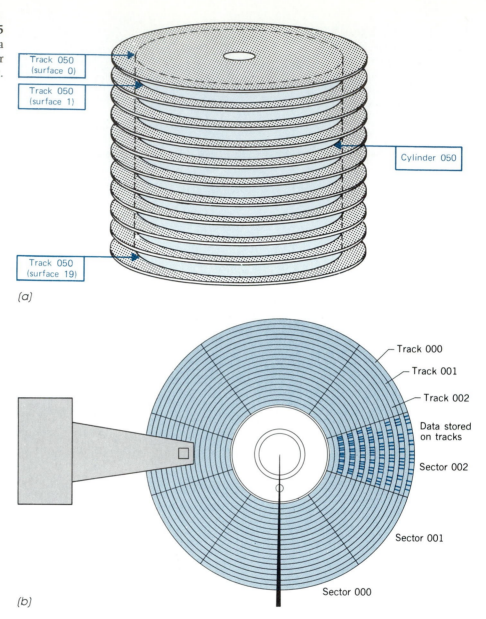

Track 050 (surface 0)

Track 050 (surface 1)

Cylinder 050

Track 050 (surface 19)

(a)

Track 000

Track 001

Track 002

Data stored on tracks

Sector 002

Sector 001

Sector 000

(b)

a. Using Fixed-Length or Variable-Length Records. A disk can have any record size; it is not restricted, like some printed or displayed lines entered on a CRT, to an 80-column format. Moreover, all disk records within a given file need not have the same length. That is, disks can store (1) **fixed-length records,** where all records are the same size, or (2) **variable-length records,** where the lengths differ. We focus on fixed-length records in this text because they are easier to process and are more common.

b. Blocking Records to Minimize Wasted Space and to Save Time. Between physical disk records the computer automatically reserves some blank space called an **interblock gap (IBG).** Thus when a disk is created as computer output, it is created as indicated in Figure B.6, with interblock gaps between physical records.

The IBG separates each physical disk record so that certain hardware functions can be performed. It permits, for example, proper timing for accessing records and activating read/write heads.

Figure B.6
Storing data on a disk track.

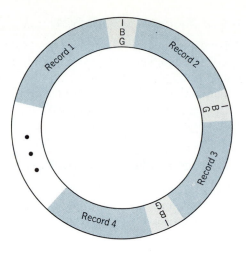

This interblock gap is usually a fraction of an inch, being as large as 0.6 of an inch for some disks. Thus if small record sizes are used, there will be a significant amount of unused or wasted disk space between each actual record. See Figure B.7 for an illustration of how interblock gaps can result in inefficient use of a disk.

To minimize wasted space and save access time, disk records are frequently blocked so that several actual or *logical* records are grouped together in a block or a *physical record* as in Figure B.8. **Blocking** of logical records maximizes the efficient use of the disk by decreasing wasted space and increasing the speed at which data is transferred to or from the CPU.

In COBOL, it is relatively simple to instruct the computer to block output records or to read in a block of input records. If there are, for example, 100-character logical records that are blocked 20, we say in the FD, RECORD CONTAINS 100 CHARACTERS, BLOCK CONTAINS 20 RECORDS. In that case, the computer will read in a block of 2000 characters (100 × 20), processing each logical record within the block in sequence. In short, blocking makes more efficient use of disk space and also increases processing speed; moreover, the handling of blocked files is relatively easy for the COBOL programmer.

Figure B.7
Representation of data showing unused disk space (IBGs).

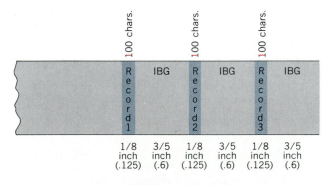

Figure B.8
Blocking of disk records.

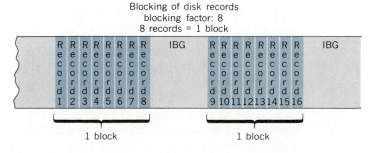

B. Features of Magnetic Disk Drives

Magnetic disk drives are direct-access devices designed to minimize the access time required to locate specific records. Each drive has a series of access arms that can locate records on different surfaces. For disk drives with 10 access arms as indicated in our illustration, the time it takes to locate specific records will be much less than that required by a tape drive, which has only one read/write mechanism.

C. Characteristics of Magnetic Disk Processing

1. Disks Are Used for High-Volume Files

Because magnetic disks can be processed very quickly and can store large amounts of data, they are frequently used for high-volume files.

2. Disks Are Used for Either Direct-Access or Sequential Processing

A main advantage of using a disk, as compared to tape, is its **direct-access feature**—the ability to access records randomly. Because a disk has numerous addressable recording surfaces and numerous read/write heads, records can be randomly accessed without the need to search the entire file. Chapters 18 and 23 describe two methods of organizing a disk file so that it can be accessed randomly.

3. Disk Files May be Easily Accessed and Modified as Needed

Disks have another major advantage over tapes. **Updates** or changes to existing records may be made on the *same* disk. In this way, a completely new disk need not be created to incorporate the current changes, as is required with tape processing. That is, the same disk may be used for *both* input and output. We can read a record from a disk and make changes to that record on the same disk; we can add records to the disk; we can delete records from the disk.

4. Maintaining Disk Files

Disks cannot be read manually; hence there is a need for appropriate controls to make certain that disk files are properly handled. The following controls are used for maintaining disks. As we will see, the same techniques are used for maintaining tapes as well, since data on tape is also not visible to the naked eye.

1. External labels are placed on disks for identification. See Figure B.9.
2. A programmed header label is created as the initial disk record, which is checked each time the disk is used to make certain that the correct one is being processed. This can be accomplished in COBOL by using a `LABEL RECORDS IS STANDARD` clause in the `FD`.
3. Hire a media librarian. Most medium- and large-sized companies have numerous disks that must be maintained and then released for reuse when no longer required. Such companies employ a librarian to maintain control of all files in the library. If he or she performs the job properly, there will be less misuse or misplacing of disks and tapes.

Disks, however, have an added control problem that does not affect tape processing. When changes are made directly to an existing disk, an update procedure will write over previous data; in such a case, there is no automatic backup file. To prevent the loss of master data resulting from erroneous processing or from sabotage or fire, disk files are usually copied onto a tape just for *backup* purposes. Thus a separate backup procedure is necessary after disks have been processed just in case something happens to them.

Figure B.9
External tape labels.

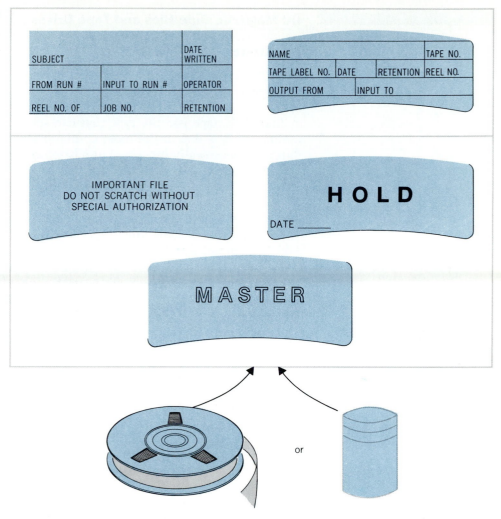

D. Other Types of Disks

Microcomputers can use hard disks and hard disk drives similar to the ones discussed here. They also use *floppy disk drives*, where a floppy disk is similar, in concept, to a single disk platter of a disk pack. See Figure B.10. It typically has two surfaces and a series of tracks and sectors that can be used to address each file or record.

Figure B.10
Floppy disk drive. (Courtesy of Mohawk Data Sciences.)

III. Magnetic Tape Files and Tape Drives

A. Features of Magnetic Tape

A magnetic tape drive is a high-speed device that is very similar to a home cassette or tape recorder. It can read (play) data from a magnetic tape and can also write (record) data onto a tape.

Like disk, tape is a file type that can serve as input to, or output from, a computer. It is one of the most common filc types for storing high-volume data that is typically processed in a batch mode. See Figure B.11 for an illustration of a magnetic tape and tape drive.

1. Physical Characteristics

A typical magnetic tape is generally 2400 to 3600 feet long, but both larger and smaller sizes exist. Most tapes are 1/2 inch wide. The tape is made of plastic with an iron oxide coating that can be magnetized to represent data. The magnetized spots or bits are extremely small and not visible to the human eye. One main advantage of tape (as well as disk) is that large volumes of data can be condensed into a relatively small area. Data that can be displayed on an 80-character line of a CRT, for example, can typically be stored in less than 1/10 inch of magnetic tape. The average tape, which costs approximately $20, can store more than 100 million characters. After tape files have been processed and are no longer needed, the tapes on which they are stored may be reused repeatedly to store other information by erasing and writing over the old files.

Specifying Tape Records

Like disks, tapes can have records of any size, can be fixed length or variable length, and can be blocked for efficiency.

2. Representation of Data on a Magnetic Tape

a. Nine-Track Representation. Data is represented on tape in a manner very similar to the CPU's internal code. For IBM and IBM-compatible mainframes that use the 9-bit EBCDIC code, a tape would have nine longitudinal tracks or recording surfaces, each capable of storing magnetized bits:

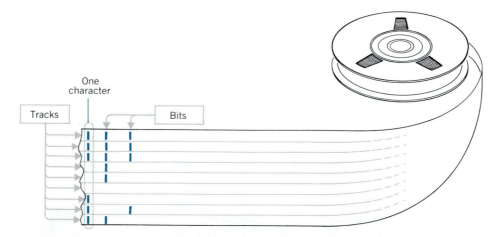

Because data is represented on tape as magnetized bits (1) Tapes can be written on, or read from, at high speeds and (2) Large volumes of data can be stored on a single tape.

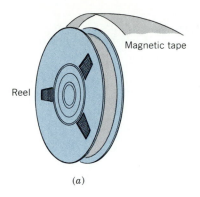

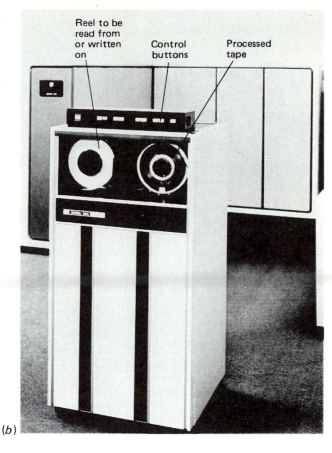

Figure B.11
(a) Magnetic tape reel. (b)
Magnetic tape drive. (Courtesy
of Control Data Corp.)

b. Tape Density.   Millions of characters can be recorded as magnetized bits on a single magnetic tape. This large storage capacity is possible because bits are exceedingly small so that hundreds of them can be placed on a very condensed area of tape. The actual number of characters that can be represented in an inch of tape is called the tape **density.** Since each character is represented by a series of bits in a specific position, tape densities are measured in **bits per inch (bpi).** The term bytes per inch would be more appropriate since the density indicates the number of characters per inch of tape, where each character may require numerous "on" bits. Despite the misnomer, the term bits per inch is still used. The most common tape densities are 800 bpi, 1600 bpi, and 3250 bpi, but some tapes have densities of 6250 or more characters per inch. Thus, even in the worst case, 800 to 1600 characters of data or the equivalent of 10 to 20 lines on a CRT can be represented in a single inch of tape. This high-storage capacity is a major reason why magnetic tapes are so frequently used at computer installations.

c. Recording Data on a Magnetic Tape.   Using a magnetic tape drive, a program can read data from some input device such as a terminal and produce, as output, a magnetic tape which is written onto by the read/write head of the tape drive (see Figure B.12). The **read/write head** can be programmed to either read data or write data, depending on the job requirements.

B. Characteristics of Magnetic Tape Drives

1. A Tape Drive Is Like a Tape or Cassette Recorder
A magnetic **tape drive** functions like a home recorder.

Figure B.12
(*a*) The read/write head on a tape drive. (*b*) A close-up of the read/write head.

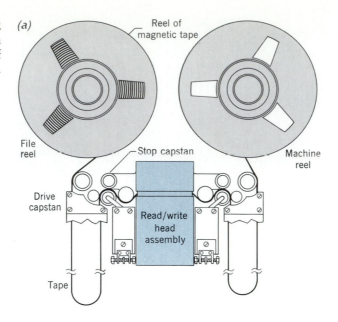

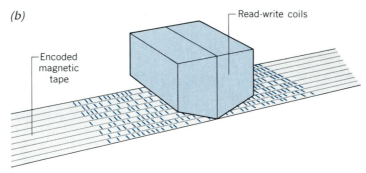

1. Data can be recorded or written onto a tape and stored for future processing.
2. Data can be read from the same tape at any time to produce output reports.
3. When data is written on a tape, all previous data is written over or destroyed. For this reason, precautions must be taken to prevent the accidental loss of important information.

2. Tape Drives Are High-Speed Devices

Tape drives process data at high speeds because (1) tape data is read electronically by sensing magnetized bits and (2) tape data is written electronically by actually magnetizing areas of tape. Data can be read or written at speeds of from 100,000 to 300,000 characters per second on the average, that is, approximately 200 inches per second.

C. Characteristics of Magnetic Tape Processing

1. Tapes Are Used for High-Volume Files

Because magnetic tapes can be processed very quickly and can store large amounts of data, they are frequently used for high-volume master files. The Internal Revenue Service, for example, stores some taxpayer information on tapes that can be accessed as needed to process tax returns.

2. Tapes Are Used for Sequential Processing

Processing records sequentially means that we begin with the first record, process it, then read the second one in sequence, process it, and so on.

Sequential processing of tapes makes them ideally suited for *batch processing*. That is, if a master file is to be updated or made current with input records that have been collected into another sequential file, batch processing is the best update technique to use.

Because tapes can only be processed sequentially, they are not generally used for immediate processing. When a master file is to be randomly accessed for immediate processing, it is unlikely that a tape drive would be fast enough to access the master file because the access time is too slow.

Similarly, if an inventory file is created on tape with 100,000 records and only a handful of these are required to be printed in an immediate mode, then tapes would once again not provide the best file type. Processing time and, thus, cost would be excessive, since most of the file must be read even to process only a small number of records. Sequential processing is beneficial, then, only when *most* records in a high-volume file are required for normal processing.

In short, tapes are well suited for batch processing but not for immediate processing. Since disks can be used for both batch and immediate processing, many organizations use disks for *all* their file processing.

3. It Is Not Practical to Rewrite or Alter Records on a Tape

If an input tape file is to be modified or altered so that it includes additional information, *two* tape files are required: one for the original file and one for the new file that will incorporate the changes. That is, the same tape cannot usually be read from and then written on, with additions or changes.

One advantage of an update procedure using tapes, however, is that an *automatic backup tape* always exists after updating. That is, the original tape that served as input can be used for re-creating a file in case the new tape is damaged, accidentally erased, misplaced, or stolen.

4. Maintaining Tape Files

Most medium- and large-sized organizations have hundreds or even thousands of magnetic tapes, each used for a specific application. These tapes are usually stored in a separate room called a tape library. See Figure B.13. There is a need for proper handling of tapes for control purposes. As with disks, labels are used, and librarians should see to it that tapes are properly maintained. Also, backup tapes should be stored in separate locations in case files are destroyed or lost.

Figure B.13
Tape library and librarian.
(Courtesy of Honeywell.)

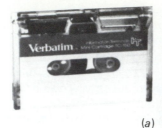

Figure B.14
(*a*) Tape cassette. (Courtesy of
Verbatim.) (*b*) Computer
system with tape cartridge
unit. (Courtesy of IBM.)

D. Other Types of Tapes

Microcomputer systems sometimes use tape cassettes or tape cartridges (see Figure B.14), which are miniature versions of the larger tapes. Originally, they were commonly used with micros, but they have been widely replaced with floppy disks and hard disks.

E. The Future of Tapes

Note that disks have all the advantages of tape plus some very useful additional features useful for immediate processing. Consequently, many companies have begun to phase out tapes altogether and are using disks exclusively. In organizations where data bases are available in an on-line environment and where inquiries into the status of records require immediate responses, tapes are simply not adequate.

Appendix C

Operating Systems and Text Editors: An Overview

I. The Operating System

All programs, whether written for a mainframe or micro, an IBM, Burroughs, or other computer, run under the control of an *operating system*. An operating system is itself a series of programs that monitor and control the overall operations of the computer.

Numerous operating systems are available for both mainframes and micros. OS, an abbreviation for full operating system is common for IBM computers, as is CMS, an abbreviation for Conversational Monitor System. VS or VMS is a virtual storage operating system that is also common on many computers. MUSIC, which is an abbreviation for McGill University System for Interactive Computing, is an operating system widely used in universities and colleges. Most micros use PC-DOS or MS-DOS for IBM and IBM-compatible personal computers or the newer OS/2; UNIX is also a common operating system for micros.

Before you can enter your program, which is usually keyed in on a terminal, you must learn how to *access the operating system.* You will be provided with a log-on (or log-in or user id) code and probably a password as well, which permits you to access the system. The operating system will then determine if you have proper authorization to use the computer.

You begin by turning on the terminal. Each terminal has its "on" switch in a different place. Then, most often, you hit the RETURN or ENTER key (sometimes marked ↵) to transmit your input. This is located where the carriage control is on a typewriter.

You will then be prompted for your log-on code. After each entry, you must hit the ENTER key to transmit the data.

If you have logged on successfully, you will then be prompted for your password, which as noted is also provided by your computer center.

Once you log on correctly, you must then communicate with the operating system in order to:

1. Enter a program and test data files.
   These files are created using a text editor (see next section).
2. Compile the program.
   Most often you type COMPILE (program name) or COBOL (program name).
3. Run the program.
   Most often you type RUN or EXEC (program name). Sometimes there are

779

intermediate instructions such as `LINK` that must be typed before you can `RUN`.

In addition, you may need to request certain options such as a hard-copy printout or a listing of error messages. Be sure you know your log-on codes, passwords, and the system command structure for compiling and running a COBOL program when you are ready to run a program.

The precise rules for communicating with an operating system are computer-dependent. You will need to check with your computer center for further instructions. The set of operating system commands used with a VAX or other DEC computer is called DCL (DEC Command Language). Most other computer manufacturers, including IBM, call this set of operating system commands JCL or Job Control Language.

The next section focuses on how to use two of the most common text editors for entering a program or a test data file.

To end a session on the computer, type `LOGOFF`.

II. General Facts about Text Editors

COBOL programs are usually entered using a keyboard for typing entries and a CRT or cathode ray tube for displaying each line that is entered.

Such programs are most often entered using a *text editor*. With a text editor, each line of a program can be easily keyed and also corrected. Every computer's text editor has different commands for entering the program and for correcting it. Less powerful text editors or *line editors* enable you to make corrections only one *line at a time*. The more powerful ones are *full screen editors* enabling you to correct any entries you wish that are displayed on a screen. Typically, you use the cursor arrows (↑ ↓ ← →) with a full screen editor to move around the screen so that changes can be easily made.

Regardless of the computer or text editor you use, you must first enter your log-on codes and any options required. Then you call in your text editor for entering the program. Most text editors have *help menus*, which provide you with assistance on a wide variety of topics.

Most text editors also make use of a terminal's *function keys*, which are usually labeled F1–F10 on the keyboard. The meaning of each function key is usually described by one of the help menus. Sometimes, the meaning of each function key is displayed on the bottom of the screen. One function key may be used for saving a file, another for editing a line, and so on. With some editors, you can program a function key so that when you press it, it performs any operation you have indicated.

In this appendix we focus on two of the most popular text editors, EDT used on DEC (Digital Equipment Corp.) equipment and XEDIT used with IBM systems.

A. Using EDT on a DEC VAX or PDP System

After logging on, type:

    EDIT (filename).COB

A file name is 1 to 9 characters, letters and digits only. If the file does not already exist, the computer will respond as follows:

    NEW FILE

To begin entering your COBOL source program, type I for insert. This edit command is used to insert, or enter, text rather than to change it.

You begin entering your COBOL program, line by line. Hit RETURN when you finish with a line. This transmits the entire line to the CPU.

If you detect a mistake before you hit RETURN, use the delete key to backspace to the error point. This deletes characters from right to left until the error is reached. The delete key is typically on the right of the keyboard and is marked as Del.

To delete an entire line *before* it has been transmitted, depress the Ctrl (control) key and, while it is depressed, hit the H key. This 'erases' an entire line. The Ctrl key is usually on the left of the keyboard. Hitting Ctrl and then H is typically specified as $_\wedge$H.

If you detect an error after a line has been entered, you can fix it by leaving the 'insert' or input mode and entering edit mode. You leave insert mode by typing $_\wedge$Z; that is, you press the Ctrl key along with the Z key and then hit RETURN. You are now in edit mode. One method for correcting a line is to substitute one value or set of characters for another.

You can substitute values as follows:

    S/(any existing value)/(any new value)

This command changes only the values within the slashes and *not* the entire line.

Suppose you have already transmitted the following line, that is, you have hit the RETURN key.

    FD   FILE 1

You realize that the space between FILE and 1 must be changed to a hyphen. You must enter *edit mode* and make the substitution as follows:

    $_\wedge$Z
    * S/FILE 1/FILE-1

The *, which precedes the edit command, is supplied by the computer and indicates that you are in edit mode.

The computer will then display the new line as:

    FD   FILE-1

All lines may be displayed in edit mode by typing:

    * TYPE WHOLE

Each line is printed without a line number. You can display parts of a program by typing:

    * T (beginning line number):(ending line number)

Example   T   100:125   (displays lines 100–125)

To delete a line in edit mode, type:

    * D (line number)

Example   D   20   (deletes line 20)

To insert a line between two existing lines, for example, lines 100 and 101, enter:

To save a file and leave the edit facility type:

```
* EXIT
```

This only works if you are in edit mode. If you are in insert mode, type $_\wedge Z$ before you exit. This will put you in edit mode.

A review of EDT entries is as follows (* preceding an entry means you must be in edit mode).

* I	To insert text
$_\wedge Z$	To leave insert mode and enter edit mode
* S/existing values/new values	Substitute new values for existing values
* TYPE WHOLE	Display the file
* Tn:n1	Type lines n to n1
* Dn	Delete line n
* C	Enables you to use the full screen editor with cursors to correct entries
* EXIT	Exit or leave the text editor; this will also save the file

The preceding entries use the editor in line edit mode. You can use EDT's keypad editor instead, which enables you to change as you are entering text. Type "C" for change command instead of I for insert. You may now use the cursor arrows to move around the screen and change any entry that is incorrect.

Remember to *save a file* after it has been created. You must first leave the editor, which returns you to command mode, and then type SAVE or simply type $_\wedge Z$, then EXIT.

B. IBM CMS XEDIT

CMS, an abbreviation for Conversational Monitor System, is an IBM operating system widely used on the 4300 series of computers. Its text editor is called XEDIT. Like DEC's text editor, XEDIT may be used as either a *line editor* with the ability to make in-line changes to a text or a *full-screen editor*, with the more advanced ability to make changes to an entire screen of a text. We will focus on XEDIT as a full-screen editor.

Entering and Editing a New File

You begin by keying:

```
XEDIT fn ft fm
```

where,

fn is a file name of eight characters or less
ft is a file type of eight characters or less (use COBOL for the file type of COBOL programs)
fm is an optional one-character file mode

Example   XEDIT TESTIT COBOL

The computer will respond with the following display:

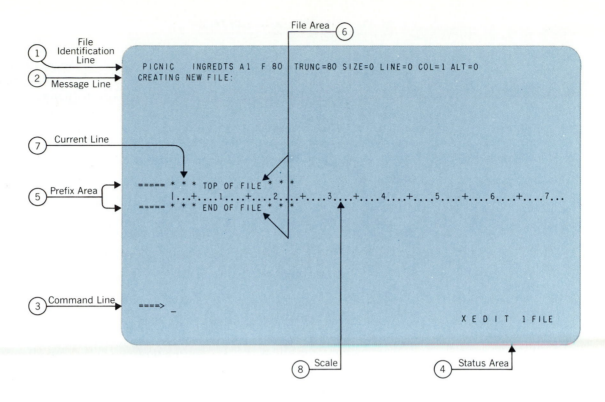

To begin entering your program, type insert or just I at the command line ===>.

You may now enter your program, line by line. At the end of each line, hit the RETURN key to transmit the line to the computer.

You may use the backspace key or the cursor arrows to correct errors in-line. To proceed to the next line, hit the ENTER or RETURN key.

Returning to Edit Mode

Before saving or correcting your file, you must leave insert or input mode and return to command mode. *Hitting the* ENTER *key twice returns you to edit mode.* You can make corrections or save your program at this point.

Saving a File and Ending a Run

To save a file, type SAVE at the ===> line.

To save the file you are editing *and* leave the editor, type FILE. To leave the editor entirely after you have saved a file, type QUIT. If you just type SAVE or FILE, the file will be saved under the originally defined name. The SAVE and FILE commands could also be followed by a *new* file-name (fn ft fm) if you wish to change the original name. Later, to access the file you have saved type XEDIT fn ft fm.

Listing All Files in Your Directory

When you are in command mode, you can list all files in your directory by typing filelist or just filel. Once the files are listed, you can use the ↑ and ↓ cursors to point to the file you want to work on. When you are on the line that designates the file you want to edit, hit the PF11 function key. This will call up your file and make it available for editing.

Making Corrections in Edit Mode

1. In edit mode, you can move the cursor to any line you wish. First position the cursor at the exact location you want to change, then you may write over wrong entries. The changes will replace the original entries. You may also use the delete key or insert key to delete or add characters, respectively.

   When you enter edit mode, you may wish to go to a specific line in your file. You can do this as follows:

Type	Meaning
TOP	Goes to the top of the file.
nnnn	Current line becomes line number nnnn (e.g., if you type 100, the 100th line becomes the current one).
DOWN n	Moves the display down n lines.
UP n	Moves the display up n lines.

2. You may change entries with the CHANGE command. It has the following format.

   CHANGE/oldstring/newstring/

   This will change characters at the current line only. That is, if you enter edit mode when you are on line 9 of your text, the change will be made to line 9. You can also achieve a *global change,* which means that *all* occurrences of a given string will be replaced. This is accomplished by keying:

   TOP
   CHANGE/oldstring/newstring/* *

   This positions the cursor at the *top* of the file and changes *every* occurrence of oldstring to newstring.

3. You may locate any entry within a file by typing:

   TOP
   LOCATE/entry

The locate command instructs the editor to search through the file until it finds the line containing the word specified after the /, in this case 'entry'. When it finds the first occurrence of this word, it makes the line that contains it the new current line.

Adding and Deleting Lines

You may delete lines using the prefix area when you are in edit mode. The prefix area appears as follows:

Prefix Area

```
00000       *** TOP OF FILE ***
00001           IDENTIFICATION DIVISION,
00002           PROGRAM-ID, TESTIT,
```

Type D anywhere in the prefix area of the line you wish to delete. When you press the ENTER key, the line will be deleted.

To add a line, you place an A in the prefix area of the line after which you want to make an insertion. To add a line after line 2, for example, put an A in the prefix area of line 2:

```
00000        *** TOP OF FILE ***
00001             IDENTIFICATION DIVISION.
A0002             PROGRAM-ID.  TESTIT.
```

When you hit the ENTER key, the editor will permit you to add a single line. To add 5 lines, type A5 in the prefix area of line 2.

The preceding discussions will provide you with enough information to get started with your text editor. As you become more familiar with your text editor, you can experiment with the multitude of other options available.

Appendix D

Microsoft COBOL*
and R/M COBOL†
for the IBM PC

In this Appendix we provide a brief overview of two popular PC versions of COBOL.

I. Microsoft COBOL

Elements Not Supported

Microsoft COBOL is a subset of COBOL 74. The following are differences between this version and the syntax discussed in this text:

NOT SUPPORTED BY MICROSOFT

1. INSPECT
2. Division remainders.
   For example, DIVIDE ... [REMAINDER (identifier)] is not permitted.
3. Multiple destinations for results of arithmetic statements.
   For example, ADD A TO B, C is not permitted.
4. MOVE, ADD, and SUBTRACT CORRESPONDING
5. Arithmetic expressions in conditionals.
   For example, IF A < B + 5 ... is not permitted.
6. The SORT statement

Distinctions

In addition, you should be aware of the following distinctions:

1. You may use *either* apostrophes or quotation marks to delimit a literal with Microsoft COBOL. If you use apostrophes, then you can use quotation marks in the literal. The following is a permissible literal.

   'THE WORD "DATA" IS RESERVED'

---

*Microsoft COBOL is a registered trademark of Microsoft.
†R/M COBOL and R/M COBOL-85 are registered trademarks of Ryan-McFarland.

786

2. If you use `DATE-COMPILED`, you must enter the date of the compilation yourself. It will not be supplied by the compiler.

3. The `CONFIGURATION SECTION` is optional. The `WORKING-STORAGE SECTION` is required.

4. `SELECT` statements may include the implementor-names of `PRINTER` and `DISK`. For example,

```
SELECT PAY-FILE  ASSIGN TO DISK.
SELECT PAYCHECKS ASSIGN TO PRINTER.
```

5. The program name used in the `PROGRAM-ID` paragraph must begin with a letter. It can be as long as you like, but the compiler will store only the first six characters of a program name used in the `PROGRAM-ID` paragraph.

Special Considerations for Data Files on Disk

1. For any input or output file assigned to a disk, the `FD` entry *must* include:

```
LABEL RECORDS ARE STANDARD
VALUE OF FILE-ID IS "(name of disk file)".
```

The `FILE-ID` entry in quotation marks is the name of the physical file on disk.

Example 1

```
         SELECT IN-PAY ASSIGN TO DISK.
           .
           .
FD   IN-PAY
         LABEL RECORDS ARE STANDARD
         VALUE OF FILE-ID IS "PAY.DAT".
```

The name of your input payroll file on the disk should be `PAY.DAT`. It should be on the same disk as your executable program. If it is on a different disk, you must use a device specifier as a prefix. That is, if your executable program is on drive A and your input data file is on B, `VALUE OF FILE-ID` should be `"B:PAY.DAT"`. Thus a device specifier such as `B:` must precede the file-name if the file is on a different disk drive.

2. Disk file-names are usually 1 to 8 characters beginning with a letter and followed by an optional 3-character extension. If you use the extension, it is separated from the file-name by a period.

Example 2

To create an output disk file you want stored as `PAY2.DAT` on drive `B:` you may code the following:

```
         SELECT IN-PAY ASSIGN TO DISK.
         SELECT OUT-PAY ASSIGN TO DISK.
           .
           .
FD   OUT-PAY
         LABEL RECORDS ARE STANDARD
         VALUE OF FILE-ID IS "B:PAY2.DAT".
```

Data Files Created by a Text Editor

Suppose you write a program that uses a disk file as input. If the disk file was created as output from some previous program, it is assumed to have a standard sequential organization.

If, however, you use a text editor to create the file, you would put each record on a single line and press the ENTER or RETURN key to end the record.

Consider the following series of 25-character records, where <ret> means the RETURN key has been pressed.

```
NEWMAN PAUL          45000 <ret>
EVANS LINDA          38000 <ret>
REAGAN RONALD        92000 <ret>
```

When you press the RETURN key at the end of a line, the text editor will insert a nonprintable character at the end of the line to designate a carriage return. Similarly, when you are done entering the file, it will insert a different nonprintable character to designate the end of the file. In order for the COBOL program to properly read this data file with these nonprintable carriage return and end-of-file designations, you must define the file with an ORGANIZATION IS LINE SEQUENTIAL clause in the SELECT statement.

In summary, ORGANIZATION IS LINE SEQUENTIAL is a required clause if an input disk file has been created by a text editor. If the input file was created as output from another program, this ORGANIZATION clause is not required.

An Overview of Procedures for Running a Microsoft Program

1. Create the source program as a file with a text editor. Give it any 8-character file-name. The file extension should be .COB. You may use any text editor for creating the source program.
2. Compile the source program.
3. Link the library modules, any subroutines you might have, and the object code file together to create an executable program file.
4. Run the executable program.

Compilation Steps

Put the Microsoft COBOL diskette in drive A. Then type:

```
A:COBOL
```

If you have a hard disk and the COBOL compiler is stored on it, you can type C:COBOL instead. (For hard-disk users, C: is most often used in place of A:.) You will be prompted for the name of your source file as follows:

```
Source filename [.COB]:
```

If the source program is on any drive but A, use the disk device as a prefix. You need not supply .COB unless your source file has a different extension. Your response might be:

```
Source filename [.COB]: B:PROG1
```

PROG1.COB is the name of your source program on drive B. The computer then prompts you for an object file-name.

```
Object filename [B:PROG1.OBJ]:
```

This will be the name of your translated file. If you just hit RETURN, the computer will save your object program as PROG1.OBJ on the B drive. If you wish to specify a different name, you may respond to the prompt with any other file-name.

The final prompt is:

```
Source listing [NUL.LST]:
```

Source listing is the name of the *disk file* that will contain your compiled source listing. If you just press the ENTER key, no listing will be provided.

This is because NUL stands for "nothing." If you do want a listing stored on disk, indicate the name.

Example

```
Source listing [NUL.LST]: B:PROG1.LST
```

PROG1.LST will be the full name of the source listing file on the B drive. You can display it at any time under DOS by typing TYPE B:PROG1.LST.

Note that you may *not* want a listing each time you compile. By pressing the Ctrl and PrtSc keys, or the Ctrl and Shift keys, you can get a listing of just the errors. This may prove more helpful if you need to compile your program numerous times.

After you respond to the three prompts, your program will be compiled and one of the following messages will print.

```
No Errors or Warnings
n Errors or Warnings
```

The letter n will indicate the actual number of errors if there are any. When the program has been compiled with no errors, you must *link* it before running. Insert the LIBRARY disk in A, leaving your program disk in B, and enter:

```
A:LINK
```

You will be prompted for the name of your object program as follows:

```
Object Modules [.OBJ]:
```

Enter the name of your object file. You need not include the extension if it is .OBJ.

Example

```
Object Modules [.OBJ]: B:PROG1
```

The next prompt is for the name to be assigned to your executable program.

```
Run File [B:PROG1.EXE]:
```

Enter the name you want to give to the file containing the executable program. If PROG1.EXE is acceptable, just hit RETURN. The name in brackets [ ] is the default, so that if you just press RETURN, whatever is in brackets is considered the entry you want. The next prompt is:

```
List File [NUL.MAP]:
```

This is a file that contains printed output about the linker program. If you hit RETURN, this map file will *not* be created. Normally you will not need it.

The next prompt is:

```
Libraries [.LIB]:
```

The names of the libraries are automatically supplied by the object file. The libraries must be in drive A. COBOL1.LIB and COBOL2.LIB are used during linking. Note that a library is necessary with certain verbs.

After linking, you will have an executable program, defined in our example as B:PROG1.EXE. To execute your program, just enter the name. The EXE extension is not required. Thus, to run the executable program PROG1, type:

```
B:PROG1
```

The library COBRUN must be in either the A or B drive to run a program.

The following are additional words that are reserved for Microsoft COBOL.

ASCII	EXHIBIT	READY
AUTO-SKIP	FILE-ID	RIGHT-JUSTIFY
BEEP	LEFT-JUSTIFY	SPACE-FILL
COL	LENGTH-CHECK	TRACE
COMP-3	LIN	TRAILING-SIGN
COMPUTATIONAL-3	NAMES	UPDATE
DISK	PRINTER	ZERO-FILL
ERASE	PROMPT	

Chapter 19 explains how the SCREEN SECTION can be used with Microsoft COBOL for displaying and accepting data interactively.

II. R/M COBOL and R/M COBOL-85

The following are features specific to Ryan-McFarland COBOL (R/M COBOL), which is another popular microcomputer version of the language. We also consider R/M COBOL-85, which is a PC version of COBOL that includes many features of COBOL 85.

1. The SPECIAL-NAMES paragraph of the CONFIGURATION SECTION is not used.
2. The SELECT statement has the following format.

$$\text{SELECT file-name ASSIGN TO} \left\{ \begin{array}{l} \begin{bmatrix} \text{DISK} \\ \text{INPUT} \quad \text{"disk-file-name"} \\ \text{OUTPUT} \quad \text{"disk-file-name"} \end{bmatrix} \\ \text{PRINT} \end{array} \right\}$$

DISK, INPUT, and OUTPUT all refer to disk files. The disk file-name is enclosed in quotes and conforms to the rules for forming file-names. It can be preceded by a disk drive identifier. Consider the following example.

```
SELECT IN-FILE ASSIGN TO INPUT "B:DATA1".
SELECT OUT-FILE ASSIGN TO OUTPUT "A:DATA2".
```

An ORGANIZATION IS LINE SEQUENTIAL may be used in the SELECT with R/M COBOL-85 as with Microsoft COBOL. No VALUE OF FILE-ID clause is, however, used in the FD.

To compile a program, type the following in response to the A prompt:

R/M COBOL: A> RSCOBOL prog-name options
R/M COBOL-85:   A> RMCOBOL prog-name options

One option that may be specified is L, which is used to obtain a listing. To run the compiled program with both compilers, type:

A> RUNCOBOL prog-name

Appendix E

Data Set for Programming Assignment 2 in Each Chapter

The following is a sample data set that can be used with Programming Assignment 2 of each chapter:

```
    1 00001ADAMSON      0101020000145503242010215000675000040010011576
    2 00002BAKER        0101050000195342502012755080005002500000332082
    3 00003CARTWELL     0101110000127831459050217050975250300032041080
    4 00004DORSEY       0101015000112805651020128000080050029027020275
    5 00005HAMMOND      0102150000085129750040219500900001000400500564
    6 00006NOLTE        0102002500012555832504021350090025022005062781
    7 00007REDFORD      0102018000122575983030229075850750180101110179
    8 00008JOHNKE       0201025000128532000002032200008002501001201584
    9 00009WHITE        0201019000018974437010235000675000050000062083
   10 00010MARSHALL     0201033000012580219602032702580005000803511298 0
   11 00011EISEN        0201050000135801277040132500900050045004093072
   12 00012SAGER        0202068000019553021902012900008002509504007 2569
   13 00013STERN        0202068000008856772404023207590000002001010 0183
   14 00014SUMMERS      0202017500003399552701013750060500025015020181
   15 00015JONES        0301140000011338772100321000995750170090505 0580
   16 00016JOHNSON      0301000000145881477020322525800075030012080177
   17 00017NOLAN        0301014750051873323020333250080025002007071585
   18 00018CANTWELL     0302018250181379550010225550675250870400630 70
   19 00019SMITH        0302125000011205030030301110008505005203902 1576
   20 00020HAMMEL       0302019100124986743020228000080000005002032085
```

Appendix F

Program Interrupts

COMMON PROGRAM INTERRUPTS

Interrupt	Cause
DATA EXCEPTION	1. You may be performing an arithmetic operation on a field that contains blanks or other nonnumeric characters. 2. You may be attempting to use a numeric field in a comparison and it contains blanks or other nonnumeric characters. 3. You may have failed to initialize a subscript or index.
DIVIDE EXCEPTION	This error will occur on some systems if you attempt to divide by 0; on other systems an attempt to divide by 0 will not cause an interrupt but will produce unpredictable results.
ADDRESSING ERROR	1. This usually means there is an incorrect value in a subscript or index so that a table look-up exceeds the number of entries in the table. 2. This error will also occur if there is an improper exit from a paragraph being performed. This may result if nested PERFORMs or GO TOs are used improperly.
OPERATION ERROR	You may be attempting to access a file with a READ or WRITE before opening it.
SPECIFICATION ERROR	You may be attempting to access an input area after an AT END condition or attempting to access an output area directly after a WRITE.

Appendix G

An Overview of Major Differences between COBOL 85 and COBOL 74

The following are some major additions to COBOL 85 that we have discussed in the text. This list does *not* include every change from COBOL 74, just the more significant ones.

1. **Scope Terminators**
   The use of the following terminators makes coding of conditionals more structured.

   ```
   END-ADD                    END-PERFORM
   END-COMPUTE                END-READ
   END-DIVIDE                 END-SEARCH
   END-EVALUATE               END-SUBTRACT
   END-IF                     END-WRITE
   END-MULTIPLY
   ```

   Examples

   ```
   1. IF   AMT1 = AMT2
           READ FILE-1
               AT END MOVE 'NO ' TO ARE-THERE-MORE-RECORDS
           END-READ.
   2. IF   AMT1 = AMT2
           ADD AMT1 TO TOTAL
               ON SIZE ERROR
               PERFORM 200-ERR-RTN
           END-ADD.
   ```

2. The reserved word THEN may be used in a conditional, which makes COBOL conform more specifically to an IF-THEN-ELSE structure.

   Example

   ```
   IF   AMT1 < 00
   THEN
        ADD 1 TO CTR1
   ELSE
        ADD 1 TO CTR2
   END-IF.
   ```

3. **INITIALIZE Verb**
   A series of elementary items contained within a group item can all be

793

initialized with this verb. Numeric items will be initialized at zero, and nonnumeric items will be initialized with blanks.

```
01   WS-REC-1.
     05   FILLER              PIC X(20).
     05   NAME                PIC X(20).
     05   FILLER              PIC X(15).
     05   AMT-1               PIC 9(5)V99.
     05   FILLER              PIC X(15).
     05   AMT-2               PIC 9(5)V99.
     05   FILLER              PIC X(15).
     05   TOTAL               PIC 9(6)V99.
     05   FILLER              PIC X(13).
       ·
       ·
     INITIALIZE WS-REC-1.
```

The above will set AMT-1, AMT-2, and TOTAL to zeros and will set all the other fields to spaces.

4. An in-line PERFORM is permitted, making COBOL more consistent with pseudocode.

Example

```
PERFORM
     ADD AMT1 TO TOTAL
     ADD 1 TO CTR1
END-PERFORM.
```

5. A TEST AFTER option may be used with the PERFORM ... UNTIL. This means that the test for the condition is made *after* the PERFORM is executed, rather than before, which ensures that the PERFORM is executed at least once.

Example

```
PERFORM 400-READ-RTN WITH TEST AFTER
     UNTIL NO-MORE-RECORDS.
```

6. **EVALUATE Verb**

The EVALUATE verb has been added. A programmer can now test a series of multiple conditions easily when each requires a different set of procedures to be performed. This, then, implements the case structure in COBOL.

Example

```
EVALUATE CODE-IN
     WHEN 0 THRU 30
          PERFORM NO-PROBLEM
     WHEN 31 THRU 40
          PERFORM WARNING
     WHEN 41 THRU 60
          PERFORM ASSIGNED-RISK
     WHEN OTHER
          PERFORM 400-ERR-RTN.
```

7. **OCCURS**
   a. Up to seven levels of OCCURS are permitted for COBOL 85 rather than three for COBOL 74.
   b. OCCURS items may contain initial contents with a VALUE clause. There is no need to REDEFINE the table or array.

8. **De-Editing: Moving Report Items to Numeric Fields**
   A report item such as one with a PIC $99,999.99 can be moved to a numeric item such as one with a PIC of 9(5)V99. This is called de-editing.

9. **DAY-OF-WEEK**

   DAY-OF-WEEK is a COBOL reserved word with a one-digit value. If the day of the run is Monday, DAY-OF-WEEK will contain a 1; if the day of the run is Tuesday, DAY-OF-WEEK will contain a 2; and so on.

10. **Relative MOVE**

   It is possible to reference a portion of an elementary item. Consider the following:

   ```
   MOVE CODE-IN (4:3) TO CODE-1.
   ```

   This moves positions 4–6 of CODE-IN to CODE-1. Suppose CODE-IN is an eight-character field with contents 87325879 and CODE-1 is three characters. The above MOVE will result in 258 being moved to CODE-1.

11. Nonnumeric literals may contain up to 160 characters. With COBOL 74, the upper limit is 120 characters.

12. EXIT need not be the only word in a named paragraph.

13. Procedure names, such as those used in SORT ... INPUT PROCEDURE and SORT ... OUTPUT PROCEDURE can reference paragraph-names as well as section-names, making coding more structured and easier to read.

14. The CONFIGURATION SECTION is optional. In fact, the entire ENVIRONMENT DIVISION is optional.

15. The BLOCK CONTAINS and RECORD CONTAINS clauses are optional.

16. The relational operators IS GREATER THAN OR EQUAL TO (>=) and IS LESS THAN OR EQUAL TO (<=) have been added.

17. The word TO in an ADD statement with a GIVING option is now optional.

Example

```
ADD AMT1 TO AMT2
    GIVING TOTAL.
```

18. NOT ON SIZE ERROR, NOT AT END, and NOT INVALID KEY clauses are now permitted.

19. The WITH NO ADVANCING clause has been added to the DISPLAY statement, which means that interaction between the user and the terminal can be made more user-friendly. For example, DISPLAY "ENTER ACCT NO." WITH NO ADVANCING means that the prompt for ACCT NO will remain on the same line as the displayed message.

20. Lowercase letters may be used in alphanumeric constants. They are considered alphabetic and will pass an ALPHABETIC class test.

Appendix H

Glossary

Abend condition. When a program is terminated or interrupted because of an error; abbreviation for *ab*normal *end*. See **program interrupt**.

ACCEPT. A statement used for reading in a low volume of input; unlike a READ, an ACCEPT does not require establishing of files, SELECT, or OPEN statements.

ADD. A statement used for performing an addition operation.

Addressing error. An error that occurs when an effort is made to access a table, array, or other data area incorrectly.

AFTER ADVANCING. An option with the WRITE statement that can cause the paper in a printer to space any number of lines *before* an output record is printed.

Alphanumeric literal. See **nonnumeric literal**.

ALTERNATE RECORD KEY. An option that allows an indexed file to be created with, and accessed by, more than one identifying key.

American National Standards Institute (ANSI). An organization of academic, business, and government users that develops standards in a wide variety of areas, including programming. There are several versions of American National Standard COBOL—1968, 1974, and 1985.

Area A. Columns 8–11 of a COBOL coding sheet or program; some COBOL entries must begin in Area A, that is, column 8.

Area B. Columns 12–72 of a COBOL coding sheet or program; most COBOL entries must begin in Area B, that is, anywhere from column 12 on.

Array. A storage area consisting of numerous fields, all with the same format; commonly used for storing totals.

Ascending sequence. The ordering of data so that a key field in the first record is less than the key field in the next, and so on.

ASCII code. A common computer code for representing data; an acronym for *Am*erican *S*tandard *C*ode for *I*nformation *I*nterchange.

AT END. A clause used with a sequential READ statement to indicate the operations to be performed when an end-of-file condition has been reached.

AUTHOR. A paragraph coded in the IDENTIFICATION DIVISION after the PROGRAM-ID. It is typically used for documentation purposes to identify the programmer.

Batch processing. A mode of processing where data is accumulated and processed as a group rather than immediately as the data is generated.

Batch total. A count of records within specific groups (e.g., departments, territories, and so on) used for control purposes to minimize the risk of records being misplaced or incorrectly transmitted.

BEFORE ADVANCING. An option with the WRITE statement that can cause the paper in a printer to space any number of lines *after* an output record is printed.

Binary search. An efficient method of searching a series of entries that are in sequence by some key field. Contrast with **serial search**.

Bits per inch (Bpi). See **bpi**.

BLANK WHEN ZERO. A clause used in the DATA DIVISION to ensure that a field consisting of all zeros will print as blanks.

BLOCK CONTAINS. A clause used in the DATA DIVISION to indicate the blocking factor of disk or tape files.

Blocking. Combining several logical records into one physical record to conserve space on a magnetic disk or tape.

Bpi (bits per inch). Tape and disk densities are measured in bits per inch (bpi), where a density of 1600 bpi, for example, is equivalent to 1600 characters per inch.

Buffer. An alternate input/output area designed to permit overlapped processing by the computer. Buffers may help to make programs run faster.

Business system. An organized set of procedures for accomplishing a set of business operations.

CALL. A COBOL statement for accessing a subprogram.

Called program. A subprogram or program called into a user program as needed.

Calling program. A program that calls a subprogram.

Case structure. A logical control structure used when there are numerous paths to be followed depending on the contents of a given field. The EVALUATE verb in COBOL is used for implementing the case structure.

Character. A single letter, digit, or special symbol. Fields such as NAME or SALARY are composed of individual characters.

Check digit. A computed integer added to a key field and used for minimizing the risk of transposition and transcription errors during the data entry process.

Check protection symbol (∗). A symbol used to minimize the risk of people tampering with a check amount; e.g., $ 1.25 would print as $∗∗∗∗∗1.25 using the asterisk (∗) as a check protection symbol.

CICS (Customer Information Control System). The most widely used utility for developing screen displays for interactive processing on mainframes. CICS is an interface between COBOL programs and an operating system that facilitates input/output processing particularly with terminals.

Class test. A data validation procedure used to ensure that input is entered in the appropriate data format, that is, numeric, alphabetic, or alphanumeric.

CLOSE. A statement that deactivates files and devices used in a program.

COBOL character set. The full set of characters that may be used in a COBOL program. These characters are listed in Appendix A.

Coded field. A type of field in which a code is used to designate data; for example, 'M' may be a code to designate 'Married' in a Marital Status field; keeps record formats shorter and more manageable.

Coding sheet. A form that contains the specific columns in which entries are required in a programming language.

Cohesion. A program exhibits cohesion when it has modules that perform only one self-contained set of operations leaving unrelated tasks to other modules.

Collating sequence. The specific order in which characters are represented by a computer; for example, A < B < . . . Z and 0 < 1, . . . < 9. The two common computer codes, ASCII and EBCDIC, have slightly different collating sequences with regard to special characters and lowercase letters.

Compile (Compilation). The process of translating a symbolic program into machine language before it can be executed.

Compiler. A special translator program used to convert source programs into object programs.

Compound conditional. An IF statement in which there are two or more conditions being tested; each condition is separated by the word OR or AND.

COMPUTE. A statement used for performing a series of arithmetic operations.

Concatenation. The process of joining several fields together to form one field; a method of linking records, fields, or characters into one entity.

Conditional statement. A COBOL statement that uses the word IF to test for the existence of a condition.

Condition-name. A name assigned to a specific value or a range of values that an identifier can assume; IF (condition-name) is the same as IF (identifier = value), where the value is assigned to the condition-name; used on the 88-level in the DATA DIVISION.

CONFIGURATION SECTION. A section of the ENVIRONMENT DIVISION that describes the overall specifications of the source and object computers and any SPECIAL-NAMES used.

Constant. A fixed value or literal that is used in a program.

Continuation position. Column 7 of a COBOL form can contain a hyphen (-) for continuing a nonnumeric literal from one line to the next.

Continuous form. A continuous sheet of paper separated only by perforations and typically used by a computer's printer for printed output.

Control break processing. The use of a control field for causing groups of records to be processed as one unit.

Control field. A key field used to indicate when totals are to print; used in control break processing.

CONTROL FOOTING. Produced by the Report Writer Feature, a control footing prints at the end of a control group for a given control item.

CONTROL HEADING. Produced by the Report Writer Feature, a control heading prints at the beginning of a control break for each new control group.

Control listing. A computer-produced report used for control or checking purposes; typically includes (1) identifying information about all input records processed by the computer, (2) any errors encountered, and (3) a total of records processed.

COPY. A statement for copying files, records, routines, and so on from a source statement library.

Counter field. A field used to sum the number of occurrences of a given condition.

CURRENT-DATE. A COBOL reserved word for IBM and IBM-compatible computers that represents an eight-position alphanumeric field with a mo/da/yr format, including the slashes. Contrast with **DATE**, which is in yymmdd format.

Cursor. A symbol, such as a blinking square or a question mark, that indicates where on a screen the next character will be entered.

Customer Information Control System. See **CICS**.

Cylinder. A series of vertical tracks on a magnetic disk pack that is used for storing data. Records on a disk are sometimes accessed by their cylinder number.

DATA DIVISION. One of the four major divisions of a COBOL program; it defines and describes all data to be used in a program.

Data exception error. A common logic error that occurs if data is designated in a PIC clause as numeric, but does not actually contain numeric data.

Data-name. The name assigned to each field, record, and file in a COBOL program. A data-name, unlike an identifier, may *not* be subscripted or qualified.

DATA RECORD(S). Used to name the record(s) within a file.

Data validation. Techniques used to minimize the risk of input errors by checking input, insofar as is possible, before processing it.

DATE. The COBOL reserved word used for obtaining the date of a program run in yymmdd format.

DATE-COMPILED. A paragraph in the IDENTIFICATION DIVISION for indicating the date when a program was compiled.

DATE-WRITTEN. A paragraph in the IDENTIFICATION DIVISION for indicating the date when a program was coded.

Debug module. A segment of a COBOL program that can be used to help in debugging programs.

Debugging. The process of testing a program to eliminate errors.

Debugging line. A line in a COBOL program that is only compiled and executed during the debugging phase; thereafter, it serves as documentation. It is useful for displaying the contents of fields during debugging.

Default. The computer system's normal options that are implemented unless the programmer specifically requests an alternative.

DELETE. A statement used to delete records from indexed files.

Density. The number of characters that can be represented in an inch of magnetic tape or on a disk track; often expressed as bpi (bits per inch).

Descending sequence. The ordering of data so that a key field in the first record is greater than the key field in the next and so on; that is, the first record has the highest key field.

Desk checking.   A method of debugging programs by manually checking for typographic, keying, and other errors prior to a compilation; this method of debugging reduces computer time.

DETAIL.   Produced by the Report Writer Feature, one or more detail lines are printed for each input record read.

Detail printing.   The printing of one or more lines for each input record read.

Diagnostic message.   An explanation of a syntax error.

Digit extraction.   One of numerous randomizing algorithms for converting a numeric key field to a disk address using the relative method of file organization.

Direct access.   See **random access**.

Disk drive.   A direct-access device designed to minimize the access time required to locate specific records; ideally suited for interactive processing.

Disk pack.   A storage medium that consists of a series of platters or disks arranged in a vertical stack and connected by a central shaft.

DISPLAY.   A statement used for printing or displaying a low volume of output; unlike a WRITE, a DISPLAY does not require establishing of files, or the use of SELECT and OPEN statements.

DIVIDE.   A statement used for performing a division operation.

Divide exception.   An error that occurs when you attempt to divide a field by zero.

DIVISION.   One of four major parts of a COBOL program.

Documentation.   The formal set of documents that describes a program or system and how to use it.

EBCDIC code.   A common computer code for representing data; an acronym for Extended Binary Coded Decimal Interchange Code.

Edit symbol.   A symbol such as $, −, and * used in a report-item to make printed or displayed output more readable.

Editing.   The process of converting data that is typically stored in a concise form into a more readable form; for example, $1,235.46 would be an edited version of 123546.

Elementary item.   A field that contains a PIC clause; a field that is not further subdivided.

End-of-file.   A condition that indicates when the last data record has been read and processed.

Enhancements.   Options that are provided by some COBOL compilers; these options are in addition to the standard requirements of an ANS compiler.

ENVIRONMENT DIVISION.   One of four major divisions of a COBOL program, it provides information on the equipment used with the program. This is the only division that may be machine-dependent.

EVALUATE.   A statement used to implement the case structure; it tests for a series of values.

Exception printing.   The printing of detail records that fall outside established guidelines, that is, records that are "exceptions" to a rule.

EXIT.   A COBOL reserved word that may be used to terminate a paragraph; for COBOL 74, it is used to indicate that "no operation" is required in the paragraph.

EXIT PROGRAM.   The last entry in a called program.

External table.   A table stored on disk or other auxiliary storage device that is loaded into the program as needed. Modifying or updating such tables does not require program modification. Contrast with **internal table**.

FD.   See **file description**.

Field.   A group of consecutive characters used to represent a unit of information; for example, a NAME field or an AMOUNT field.

FIFO (first in, first out).   The technique of storing records so that the first one entered is the first one available for outputting; analogous to a queue or waiting line where the first entry is the one handled first.

Figurative constant.   A COBOL reserved word, such as SPACES or ZEROS, where the word denotes the actual value; for example, MOVE ZEROS TO TOTAL will result in all 0's in the field called TOTAL.

File.   A major collection of data consisting of records.

FILE-CONTROL. A paragraph in the INPUT-OUTPUT SECTION of the ENVIRONMENT DIVISION where each file to be used in the program is assigned to a device.

File description (FD). Entries used to describe an input or output file.

FILE SECTION. The section of the DATA DIVISION in which input and output files are defined and described.

FILE STATUS. The FILE STATUS clause can be used with a SELECT statement for determining the result of an input/output operation. If an input or output error has occurred, the FILE STATUS field indicates the specific type of error.

FILLER. A COBOL reserved word used to designate a field that will not be accessed by the program.

Fixed-length records. Records within a file that are all the same length.

Flag. See **switch**.

Floating string. An edit symbol, such as a $, that will appear adjacent to the first significant digit.

Flowchart. A planning tool that provides a pictorial representation of the logic to be used in a program.

Folding. One of numerous randomizing algorithms used to convert a numeric key field to a disk address using the relative method of file organization.

GO TO. A branch instruction that transfers control from one paragraph to another; GO TO statements are to be avoided in structured COBOL programs; that is, PERFORM statements should be used in place of GO TOs where possible.

Group item. A field that is further subdivided into elementary fields with PICTURE clauses.

Group printing. The printing of one line of output for groups of input records; usually used to summarize data. Same as summary printing.

Hashing. A technique for transforming a record's key field into a relative record number.

Header label. The first record recorded on a disk or tape for identification purposes.

Hierarchy chart. A planning tool for specifying the relationships among modules in a program; another term for hierarchy chart is structure chart or visual table of contents (VTOC); a tool used to depict top-down logic.

High-order position. The leftmost, or most significant, character in a field.

HIGH-VALUES. A COBOL reserved word that represents the largest value in the computer's collating sequence; may only be used with fields defined as alphanumeric.

IBG. See **interblock gap**.

IDENTIFICATION DIVISION. The first division of a COBOL program; used for documentation purposes.

Identifier. The name assigned to fields and records in a COBOL program. An identifier, unlike a data-name, may be subscripted or qualified.

IF-THEN-ELSE. A logical control structure that executes a step or series of steps depending on the existence of a specific condition or conditions. Same as **selection**.

Imperative statement. A direct command to the computer; contrast with **conditional statement**.

Implementor-name. A system-dependent term that equates a user-defined entry with a specific device.

Implied decimal point. The place where a decimal point is assumed to be in a field; PIC 99V99, for example, has an implied decimal point between the second and third positions; for example, 1234 in a field with PIC 99V99 is assumed to have a value of 12.34 for arithmetic and comparison purposes.

Index (for an indexed file). A reference table that stores the key field and the corresponding disk address for each record that is in an indexed disk file.

Index (INDEXED BY with OCCURS). The indicator used to reference an item defined by an OCCURS clause or subordinate to an item defined by an OCCURS clause. An index functions just like a subscript; however, unlike a subscript, an index is not defined separately in WORKING-STORAGE.

Indexed file. A method of file organization in which each record's key field is assigned a disk address; used when the random accessing of disk records is required.

Infinite loop. An error condition in which a program would continue performing a module indefinitely or until time has run out for the program.

INITIALIZE. A COBOL 85 statement that will set numeric fields to zero and nonnumeric fields to spaces.

In-line PERFORM. A PERFORM statement without a paragraph-name, which is followed by all instructions to be executed at that point; it is delimited with an END-PERFORM. Available with COBOL 85.

Input. The data that is entered into a computer system.

INPUT-OUTPUT SECTION. That section of the ENVIRONMENT DIVISION that provides information on the input/output devices used in the program and the names assigned to the devices.

INPUT PROCEDURE. An option used with the SORT statement to process input records prior to sorting them.

INSPECT. A statement for counting the occurrence of specific characters in a field and for replacing one character with another.

INSTALLATION. A paragraph coded in the IDENTIFICATION DIVISION for documentation purposes; used to denote where the program is run.

Interactive processing. A mode of processing where data is operated on as soon as it is transacted or generated.

Interblock gap (IBG). An area of a disk or tape that separates physical records.

Intermediate result field. A field defined in WORKING-STORAGE that is necessary for performing calculations but is not part of either the input or the output areas.

Internal table. A table defined in a program with the use of VALUE clauses. Modifying or updating such tables requires program modification, which always increases the risk of errors. Contrast with **external table.**

INVALID KEY. A clause that can be used with READ, WRITE, and REWRITE statements for indexed files; checks that disk records have valid key fields.

I-O file. An indexed or relative file that is opened as both input and output when the file is to be updated.

Iteration. A logical control structure for indicating the repeated execution of a routine or routines.

JUSTIFIED RIGHT. A clause used in the DATA DIVISION with a nonnumeric field to store the data in the rightmost positions rather than the leftmost positions of the field.

Key field. A field that identifies a record; for example, ACCT-NO, EMPLOYEE-NO, or PART-NO.

LABEL RECORD(S). A clause in a File Description entry to designate whether header and trailer labels are standard or omitted.

Level number. A number from 01-49 to denote the hierarchy of data within records.

Library. A file of programs that can be called in by the operating system as needed.

Limit test. A data validation procedure used to ensure that a field does not exceed a specified limit.

Line counter. A field used for keeping track of the number of lines printed.

LINKAGE SECTION. A section used when calling subprograms to pass data from a called subprogram back to a calling program.

Logic error. A program error that can be caused by a mistake in the sequencing of instructions or from an improperly coded instruction that does not accomplish what was desired. Contrast with **syntax error.**

Logical control structures. The ways in which instructions in a program may be executed.

Loop. A programming technique for executing a series of steps a fixed number of times or until a specified condition is met.

Low-order position. The rightmost position in a field.

Machine language.   The only executable language; the language into which programs must be translated before execution.

Main module.   Usually the first module in a top-down program; all other modules are executed from the main module in a top-down program.

Master file.   The major collection of data pertaining to a specific application.

Menu.   A technique used for interactive processing; the user is offered various options from which to select the procedures or routines required.

MERGE.   A statement that combines two or more files into one main file. The statement has a format similar to the SORT and automatically handles the opening, closing, and input/output operations associated with the files to be merged.

Module.   A section, routine, procedure, or paragraph in a structured program.

MOVE.   A statement that transmits, or copies, data from a sending field to a receiving field.

MOVE CORRESPONDING.   A statement that transmits the contents of fields in the sending area to the same named fields in the receiving area.

MULTIPLY.   A statement used for multiplying one field by another.

Murphy's Law.   An adage that states that if it is possible for something to go wrong, eventually it will go wrong; should be kept in mind when you prepare test data so that you make sure you test for every conceivable condition.

Negated conditional.   An IF statement that tests for the absence of a condition; the word NOT is used in the statement; for example, IF A IS NOT EQUAL TO B ....

Nested conditional.   An IF within an IF; an alternative to writing a series of simple conditionals.

Nested PERFORM.   A PERFORM within a PERFORM.

NEXT RECORD.   A clause used for sequentially reading from an indexed or relative file that has been accessed dynamically.

Nonnumeric literal.   A constant or fixed value that may contain any character in the COBOL character set (except a quote); limited to 120 characters for COBOL 74 and 160 for COBOL 85; such literals are enclosed in quotes.

Numeric literal.   A constant that can contain only numbers, a decimal point, and a sign; typically used in arithmetic and comparison operations.

OBJECT-COMPUTER.   The paragraph of the ENVIRONMENT DIVISION that indicates the computer on which the program is executed or run.

Object program.   The machine-language equivalent of a source program.

OCCURS clause.   A clause used for indicating the repeated occurrence of items in the DATA DIVISION, all with the same format.

ON SIZE ERROR.   A clause used to indicate what operations are to be performed if a field is not large enough to hold the results of an arithmetic operation.

OPEN.   A statement used to designate which files are input and which are output, and to activate the appropriate devices.

OPEN EXTEND.   When a disk or tape file is opened in EXTEND mode, the disk or tape is positioned at the end of the file. This mode is used for adding records to the end of a file.

Operand.   A field or a literal that is specified in an instruction.

Operation error.   An error that occurs if a file is accessed before it is opened.

Output.   The information produced by a computer system.

OUTPUT PROCEDURE.   An option used with the SORT statement to process sorted records before they are outputted.

Overflow.   See truncation.

PAGE.   A reserved word used with the ADVANCING option of a WRITE statement so that the paper advances to a new page.

PAGE FOOTING.   Produced by the Report Writer Feature, a page footing prints whenever a page break occurs.

PAGE HEADING.   Produced by the Report Writer Feature, a page heading prints at the top of each new page.

Paragraph. A subdivision of a COBOL program consisting of statements or sentences.

PERFORM. A logical control statement used for executing a paragraph or series of paragraphs and then returning control to the original module.

PERFORM ... UNTIL. A statement that executes one or more paragraphs until the condition specified is met.

PICTURE (PIC). A clause that indicates the size and type of data to be entered in a field.

Printer Spacing Chart. A tool used to map out the proper spacing of output in a printed report.

PROCEDURE DIVISION. The division of a COBOL program that contains the instructions to be executed.

PROCEDURE DIVISION map. A list of the instructions and the storage locations where they are placed.

Program. A set of instructions that operates on input data and converts it to output.

PROGRAM-ID. The only paragraph required in the IDENTIFICATION DIVISION.

Program interrupt. An abnormal end (abend) condition that occurs if there is a major error in a program.

Program sheet. See **coding sheet**.

Program specifications. The precise instructions necessary for writing a program; consists of record layout forms for disk or tape input and output, and Printer Spacing Charts for printed output, along with notes specifying the logic required.

Programmer. The computer professional who writes the set of instructions to convert input to output.

Prompt. A request by the computer for user input. A prompt can be a blinking cursor, a ?, or a message.

Pseudocode. A program planning tool that uses English-like expressions rather than diagrams to depict the logic in a structured program.

Random access. The method of processing data independently of the actual location of that data. This method can be used with magnetic disk or floppy disk drives, which are classified as direct-access devices.

Randomizing algorithm. A method used for randomizing numbers or, with relative files, for determining disk addresses for each record on a random basis.

Range test. A data validation procedure to determine if a field has a value that falls within pre-established guidelines.

READ. The statement used to input a record from an input device.

READ ... INTO. A statement that reads a record from a file and stores it in a WORKING-STORAGE record area.

Read/write head. The mechanism in a magnetic disk or tape drive that enables the device to read data and to record data.

READY TRACE. A debugging aid that is used to print the sequence of paragraphs that a program executes during a specific run.

Receiving field. The field that accepts data from a sending field in a MOVE operation; in the statement MOVE AMT-IN TO AMT-OUT, AMT-OUT is the receiving field.

Record. A set of related fields treated as a unit. A payroll record on magnetic disk, for example, contains fields such as Social Security number, name, and salary.

RECORD CONTAINS. An optional clause within an FD for indicating the number of characters within a record.

Record description. Entries used to describe records within a file and within WORKING-STORAGE.

RECORD KEY. The key field within an indexed record used for establishing an index.

Record layout form. A form used in a problem definition to describe input and output formats on disk or tape.

REDEFINES. A clause used to describe a field of data in a different way.

Relative file. A randomly accessible file in which the key field converts to an actual disk address.

RELATIVE KEY. The key field in a relative file that is nonblank and uniquely identifies the record.

Relative subscripting. A subscript with a relative value (e.g., (SUB+12) would be a relative subscript).

RELEASE. A statement to write sorted records after they have been processed.

REMAINDER. A clause that may be used with the DIVIDE instruction for storing the remainder of a division operation.

REPORT FOOTING. Produced by the Report Writer Feature, a report footing prints once, at the end of the report.

REPORT HEADING. Produced by the Report Writer Feature, a report heading prints at the beginning of each report.

Report-item. A type of field used for storing edit symbols such as $, −, ∗ in addition to numeric data; report-items are typically used when data is to be printed or displayed in a readable form.

REPORT SECTION. This is a section in the DATA DIVISION that is used by the Report Writer Feature for defining print records.

RESERVE. A clause used for designating additional I/O buffer areas.

Reserved word. A word that has special significance to the COBOL compiler, such as ADD, MOVE, DATA.

RETURN. A statement to read records from a sorted work file after they have been processed.

REWRITE. A statement for altering existing disk records; used when disk records are to be updated.

ROUNDED. A clause used for rounding results to the specification of the receiving field.

Routine. A set of instructions used to perform a specific operation.

Scope terminator. A term that delimits the end of a logical control construct or the end of a statement with clauses. These include END-IF, END-PERFORM, END-EVALUATE, END-READ, etc.

SEARCH. A statement for looking up an item in a table; used to perform a serial search.

SEARCH ALL. A statement for looking up an item in a table using a more efficient method of searching that requires table entries to be in sequence; used to perform a binary search.

Search argument. The incoming field that is used for finding a match with a table entry.

Section. A series of paragraphs within a COBOL program.

SECURITY. A paragraph in the IDENTIFICATION DIVISION used to indicate the security classification for the program.

SELECT. A statement in the FILE-CONTROL paragraph of the ENVIRONMENT DIVISION that is used to assign an input or output file to a specific device.

Selection. A logical control structure that performs operations if a given condition is met and can perform other operations if the condition is not met. Same as IF-THEN-ELSE.

Sending field. The field that is to be transmitted, copied, or sent to another field as a result of a MOVE operation; in the statement MOVE AMT-IN TO AMT-OUT, AMT-IN is the sending field.

Sentence. A statement or series of statements treated as a unit in a COBOL program and ending with a period.

Sequence. A logical control structure in which a series of instructions are executed in the order in which they appear.

Sequence checking. A procedure that ensures that data entered is in the proper sequence, usually by a key field.

Sequential processing. The method of processing records in the order in which they are located in a file.

Serial search. A table look-up method in which each entry in the table is compared to an item; the entries are consecutively compared, beginning with the first. Contrast with **binary search**.

SET. The statement used to transmit data to an index or to increase or decrease the value of the index.

Sign test. A test performed to determine if a numeric field is positive or negative.

Simple condition. A test for the existence of one condition rather than many conditions. Contrast with **compound conditional**.

SORT. A statement used to order a file so that it is in a specified sequence.

SOURCE-COMPUTER. The paragraph of the ENVIRONMENT DIVISION that indicates the computer on which the program is compiled or translated.

Source program. A set of instructions that must be compiled into machine language before it can be executed.

SPECIAL-NAMES. The paragraph of the ENVIRONMENT DIVISION that assigns specific mnemonic-names to system-dependent implementor-names.

Specification error. An error that occurs if you attempt to access an input file after an AT END condition has been reached.

Spooling. The process of performing an input or output operation at high speeds using a disk or tape in an off-line operation; for example, output to be printed might be spooled onto disk in a high-speed operation and then transmitted to the printer off-line.

Square value truncation. One of numerous randomizing algorithms used to convert a numeric key field to a disk address using the relative method of file organization.

START. A statement that can be used to begin processing indexed records of an indexed file at any point, not necessarily at the beginning of the file.

Statement. An instruction.

Stepwise refinement. The process of continually breaking down a procedure into smaller segments; this is a top-down technique.

STOP RUN. A statement that tells the computer to terminate the program.

Storage dump. A list of the contents of storage during a particular run.

STRING. A statement used to join several fields together to form one field.

Structure chart. See **hierarchy chart**.

Structured programming. A technique that makes programs easier to read, debug, and modify; sometimes referred to as GO-TO-less programming; each section of a program is written as an independent module and executed using a PERFORM statement.

Structured walkthrough. See **walkthrough**.

Subprogram. A program or series of modules that can be called into a user program.

Subscript. An identifier used for accessing a specific field in an array or table.

SUBTRACT. A statement that subtracts fields or literals from another field or fields.

Summary printing. See **group printing**.

Suppression of leading zeros. The process of editing a field so that high-order zeros are replaced with blanks.

Switch. A type of field usually defined in WORKING-STORAGE for indicating the presence of a specific condition; the field is set equal to 1, for example, when a condition is met; at all other times, it remains at zero.

Symbolic programming language. A programming language that is relatively easy for a programmer to learn but that requires a translation process before the program can be run.

Syntax error. An error caused by a violation of a programming rule.

Table. A series of consecutive items, all with the same format, defined in the DATA DIVISION with an OCCURS clause; used for looking up or matching against an item read in or computed by the program.

Table argument. The table entry field that is used to locate the table function.

Table function. The element from the table that is being sought or "looked up."

Table look-up. A procedure where an item is matched against a table entry or argument for purposes of determining the value of some corresponding table entry or function.

Tape drive. Device used for storing files; tapes are used for sequential processing in batch mode.

Test data. Programmer-supplied data used to test the logic of a program.

Test for reasonableness. A data validation procedure to ensure that data entered as input is not obviously incorrect; for example, a year of transaction designated as 1998 (instead of 1989) would clearly be erroneous.

Top-down programming.   A programming technique in which main modules or procedures are coded before minor ones.

Trailer label.   An end-of-file label placed on disk or tape.

Transaction file.   A file that contains changes to be used for updating a master file.

Transcription error.   An error that occurs when data is keyed incorrectly.

Truncation.   When a receiving field is not large enough to accept a sending field, one or more significant digits may be truncated or lost.

UNSTRING.   A statement used to condense input into a more compact form.

Update procedure.   The process of making a master file current.

USAGE clause.   A clause that specifies the format in which data is stored.

User.   The individual who will actually use the output from a computer run.

User-friendly.   A technique for simplifying user interaction with a program.

Utility program.   A program acquired by many different users to accomplish a relatively standard set of tasks.

VALUE clause.   A literal or figurative constant to be placed in a `WORKING-STORAGE` field.

Variable data.   Data that changes during each run of a program; contrast with **constant**.

Variable-length records.   Records in a file that have different lengths. Contrast with **fixed-length records**.

Verification procedure.   A procedure used to determine if the data keyed into a computer matches the source document from which it was generated.

Visual Table of Contents (VTOC).   See **hierarchy chart**.

Walkthrough.   The process of checking a program to see if it will produce the results desired.

WORKING-STORAGE SECTION.   A section of the `DATA DIVISION` that contains data required for processing that is not part of input or output.

WRITE.   A statement used to produce output data.

WRITE ... FROM.   A statement that moves data to an output area and then produces it as output.

Index

COBOL Program Sheet

System		Punching Instructions		Sheet	of
Program		Graphic			Identification
Programmer	Date	Punch	Card # Form	73	80

Sequence		Cont.	A	B	COBOL Statement
(Page) 1 3	(Serial) 4 6	7	8	12 16 20 24 28 32 36 40 44 48 52 56 60 64 68 72	
	0 1				
	0 2				
	0 3				
	0 4				
	0 5				
	0 6				
	0 7				
	0 8				
	0 9				
	1 0				
	1 1				
	1 2				
	1 3				
	1 4				
	1 5				
	1 6				
	1 7				
	1 8				
	1 9				
	2 0				

COBOL Program Sheet

System				Punching Instructions										Sheet	of	
Program				Graphic								Card	#		Identification	
Programmer		Date		Punch								Form			73	80

Sequence		Cont.	A	B	COBOL Statement

Sequence (Page) 1 3 (Serial) 4 6 | 7 | 8 | 12 16 20 24 28 32 36 40 44 48 52 56 60 64 68 72

	0 1
	0 2
	0 3
	0 4
	0 5
	0 6
	0 7
	0 8
	0 9
	1 0
	1 1
	1 2
	1 3
	1 4
	1 5
	1 6
	1 7
	1 8
	1 9
	2 0

COBOL Program Sheet

System						Punching Instructions						Sheet		of	
Program					Graphic								Identification		
Programmer			Date		Punch					Card # Form		73]			[80

Sequence		Cont.	A	B	COBOL Statement
(Page)	(Serial)				

COBOL Program Sheet

System			Punching Instructions									Sheet	of	
Program			Graphic							Card #	Form	Identification		
Programmer		Date	Punch									73		80

Sequence		Cont.	A	B	COBOL Statement
(Page)	(Serial)				
1 3	4 6	7	8	12 16 20 24 28 32 36 40 44 48 52 56 60 64 68 72	
	0 1				
	0 2				
	0 3				
	0 4				
	0 5				
	0 6				
	0 7				
	0 8				
	0 9				
	1 0				
	1 1				
	1 2				
	1 3				
	1 4				
	1 5				
	1 6				
	1 7				
	1 8				
	1 9				
	2 0				

COBOL Program Sheet

System		Punching Instructions		Sheet	of
Program		Graphic		Identification	
Programmer	Date	Punch	Card Form #	73	80

Sequence		Cont.	A	B	COBOL Statement
(Page)	(Serial)				

1 3 4 6 7 8 12 16 20 24 28 32 36 40 44 48 52 56 60 64 68 72

0 1
0 2
0 3
0 4
0 5
0 6
0 7
0 8
0 9
1 0
1 1
1 2
1 3
1 4
1 5
1 6
1 7
1 8
1 9
2 0

COBOL Program Sheet

System				Punching Instructions										Sheet	of	
Program				Graphic							Card #			Identification		
Programmer		Date		Punch							Form			73		80

Sequence		Cont.	A	B	COBOL Statement

(Page) 1 3 (Serial) 4 6 7 8 12 16 20 24 28 32 36 40 44 48 52 56 60 64 68 72

0 1
0 2
0 3
0 4
0 5
0 6
0 7
0 8
0 9
1 0
1 1
1 2
1 3
1 4
1 5
1 6
1 7
1 8
1 9
2 0